The 1994 Good Weekend Guide

The 1994 Good Weekend Guide

Edited by Alisdair Aird

Deputy Editor: Fiona May

Associate Editors: Robert Unsworth, Milly Taylor, Karen Fick

Walks Consultant: Tim Locke

VERMILION
LONDON

This edition first published in 1993
by Vermilion, an imprint of Ebury Press
Random House, 20 Vauxhall Bridge Road
London SW1V 2SA

1 3 5 7 9 10 8 6 4 2

A catalogue record for this book may be found in the British Library.

ISBN 0 09 177785 2

Typeset from author's disk by
SX Composing Limited, Rayleigh, Essex
Printed and bound by Clays Ltd, St Ives plc

CONTENTS

Introduction

Almost every part of Great Britain has some special quality to enrich a short holiday. Even the most unlikely areas turn out to have surprising attractions. For this book, dividing the country into about a hundred areas, we have found that every single one has at least something to recommend it. It's true that a handful of areas are day visit territory rather than places that entice you to stay for longer: yet even these have unexpected riches. Whether you want to drift quietly through beautiful countryside, or would rather have plenty of lively things to see and do, a particularly good point is that, besides the famous places that attract all the other visitors, Britain is very rich in areas which have much the same virtues – and of course their own individuality – but which have escaped the crowds.

A special allure is that so much is going on in Britain: local festivals, customs, celebrations and other events can add a real depth of enjoyment to a short break somewhere. The trouble is that unless you're in the know you usually discover the year's special event was over a couple of days before you arrived. Tourism organisations reckon that they know of some 7,000 regular events of more than purely local interest each year, but admit to great difficulty in keeping tabs on them. We'd agree with that, having spent much of the spring and summer of 1993 on the phone trying to pin event organisers down to firm dates for 1994. In the end we have got dates for a remarkable range of events, some quite bizarre (of course, particularly with some of the smaller events, there must always be some risk of a change in plans). Our National Calendar at the back of the book picks out 500 or so of the most important and most interesting events of 1994, and each county chapter has its own more extensive calendar. Just to give an idea of the sort of things that will be going on in different places on any one day, we have picked two Saurdays at random, one in spring (23 April) and one in summer (9 July).

Our spring Saturday turns out to be St George's Day, with mummers and Morris dancers performing in Gloucester, while at the Guildhall in Lichfield (Staffs) there's a light-hearted version of the manorial court which has been held here on every St George's Day since records began. In Long Crendon (Bucks) they'll be rehearsing for one of the ancient traditional Mystery plays performed in the round at St Mary's Church that month. Down in Cornwall a gardens festival will now be in full swing, letting you into some of England's loveliest private gardens. In Sussex the great garden of Borde Hill, at its best in spring, will hold a gardening festival this weekend, and in Yorkshire the Harrogate Spring Show is one of the best and most lively in the gardening calendar. The miles of wild daffodils in Farndale up on the Yorkshire Moors should still be showing beautifully. But if nature appalls you, you'd probably prefer the Edinburgh Festival of Science and Technology, or perhaps the approaching climax of the world snooker championship at the Crucible Theatre in Sheffield (Yorks).

That Saturday several arts festivals, most lasting about a week, will be in full swing, including ones at Nailsworth (Glos), Bridlington (Yorks), Derby (outdoor and indoor music and dance), on the Isle of Skye and ('music for fun') on the Isle of Wight. Sutton Bonnington (Notts) has the National Folk Festival, and at Inverurie in Scotland there will be a fiddlers' rally. The Fordingbridge spring festival (Hants) will just be starting, with a pageant.

Stratford (Warwicks) will be busily celebrating Shakespeare's birthday. At a different point on the creative spectrum, the Newlyn Gallery in Cornwall will with equal pride be showing a large sculptural installation which should by then just have been completed for them by David Mach.

Sulgrave Manor (Midlands) will be in the middle of an ambitious historical re-creation, run exactly as it was in 1643, in the Civil War. All in full costume, there will be the Washington family (ironically, prominent royalists), other gentry, servants in a fully operational kitchen, and soldiers in their encampment. If you'd prefer your antiques more static, Hatfield House (Herts) will have an antiques fair. For transport enthusiasts there will be a railway weekend at the Tropical Bird Gardens, Rode (Somerset) and a veteran coach rally in Brighton (Sussex).

The number of things happening on Saturday 23 July is too wide to list individually here – our area calendars include over 70. Among many festivals, the range runs from quite modest ones to major events such as the Cheltenham, Exeter and City of London Festivals, the international Eisteddfod in Llangollen and the York early music festival. Some more bouncy affairs will include a Lake Windermere festival (Cumbria) with bungee jumping, Winchester's Hat festival (virtually non-stop street theatre), the Glasgow jazz festival, and Celtic and gaelic festivities at Llandysul and on the island of Barra. Spectacular period-costume affairs that day will include Newquay's continuing Victorian Week (Cornwall), period vehicles, craft fairs, entertainment and parades at Hawarden's Victorian festival (Cheshire) and a medieval fair at Tewkesbury (Glos).

A motley collection of sports that day runs from the world pea-shooting championships at Witcham (Cambs) and the Olympian Games at Much Wenlock (Shrops) through top-class horse trails and other country sports to Highland games in Dingwall (Scotland).

Besides the great Durham Miners Gala, there will be all sorts of other processions, fairs and carnivals (Norwich's is likely to be particularly spectacular this year, celebrating its 800th anniversary), with steam fairs at Bodiam (Sussex) and Wymeswold (Leics). There will be flower shows at Hampton Court Palace and Windsor Castle, the national organic food and wine fair at Ryton (Midlands), a mix of food, drink, music and dance in and around Grantham (Lincs), a beer festival in Hastings (Sussex) and an English wine festival at Cox Green (Berks). That July day will end with *The Marriage of Figaro* in the open air at Polesden Lacey (Surrey), *Richard III* at Hidcote gardens (Glos), a fireworks concert at Goodwood (Sussex), and music by moonlight at Fountains Abbey (Yorks).

This year places that charge admission are giving better value than in past years. A great many have assured us that they will not be putting their prices up, often holding them steady for the second year in succession. Moreover, lots of these have been putting in significant new attractions or improvements, but for once have refrained from making this an excuse for price rises: this has made even places that we previously saw as rather high-priced suddenly seem much better value (Madame Tussaud's in London springs to mind).

We have more appetite for visiting museums, galleries and similar places than people in any other country in the world. In the past, they just had to open their doors and let the queues in. Now, the spectre of falling attendance looms, and more seriously for many the threat or fact of a cut in grant support. This is paradoxically often turning out well for visitors. Many such places – small as well as large – are responding very positively by doing all they can to bring their displays to life, both to attract more visitors and to hold their attention better. This year we have seen the introduction of some splendid hi-tech interactive displays at the grander institutions, while places whose budgets are measured more in pennies than in millions of pounds have been livening up their approach entertainingly and interestingly, for example with staff or volunteers in appropriate period or trade costume, acting in character.

We have found that it is often these smaller less well-known places which turn out to be most rewarding, with a degree of individuality that can be lacking in the places that are household names. In the less familiar stately homes, castles and so forth, someone in the family is often around, full of a deep feeling for the place which you couldn't expect from a staff guide, and maybe a fund of entertaining anecdotes. The same sort of thing is true of the most specialised museums, if that's not too grand a word for places specialising in buttons, say, or lawnmowers, or household throwaways: here, we've found that the people in charge are often the people who have built up the collections from scratch, and have such an infectious enthusiasm for such unlikely prospects that they turn your visit into a surprisingly interesting and memorable occasion.

Among areas that are becoming increasingly attractive to visitors, with more and more to see and do (and local tourist organisations that are notable for the energy with which they are currently making the most of their areas' opportunities for visitors), we'd particularly pick out Derbyshire, Lancashire and Somerset, and above all that sleeping giant Northumbria where we have found a lot of interesting new things this year. Overall, our top recommendations for really enjoyable areas are Cumbria, Devon, the Yorkshire Dales, and the Cotswolds in Gloucestershire. Though all four are well known, all have parts where you can escape the crowds even at peak times, and some marvellous attractions that most people don't know about. But other areas abound in interest and beauty: particularly Shropshire, Herefordshire, west Dorset, the Isle of Wight; much of Cheshire, Cornwall, Northamptonshire and Sussex; parts of Norfolk, Suffolk and Wiltshire; most of Scotland and Wales. Once you know where to look, even the most unlikely areas tend to come up trumps: Surrey with its commuter-belt image is actually England's most wooded county; east Kent is excellent for family breaks; West Yorkshire stands out for its unusual sightseeing possibilities.

For a city break, York is superb, and other excellent cities for visitors are Edinburgh, Bath (Avon) and Chester. We'd also strongly recommend Cambridge, Oxford, Durham, Exeter (Devon) and Salisbury (Wiltshire), and perhaps Norwich, Lincoln and Shrewsbury. London of course is a special case, superb for shows, shopping, eating out and above all museums, galleries, cultural events and sightseeing.

Generally, the further north you go, the friendlier people are.

This year we have greatly expanded our choice of places to stay, in some areas nearly doubling the number. In line with readers' suggestions, we have found many more smaller places – not just small hotels, but country houses whose owners offer some very comfortable and individual accommodation, and farmhouses doing B & B in beautiful surroundings. As one of the lists at the back of the *Guide* shows, two or three hundred of the hotels and other places we recommend and describe are in such ideal positions that you can walk straight out of the door and into attractive countryside. If you'd rather your walking was confined to the short distance between your comfortable hotel and several interesting sightseeing attractions within an easy stroll, there are again plenty of places that can oblige (we pick out several dozen at the back of the book that are specially good for this).

Something we have been particularly pleased to find is the splendid choice of hotels where you can spend a very enjoyable couple of days without stirring into the outside world at all. Among the 150 or so that we pick out as specially good for this (again, at the back of the book), many have splendid grounds that you might not want to leave even in idyllic weather; many others are simply so hospitable that they make ideal indoor refuges in bad weather or at particularly unkind times of year.

Many of the nicest places to stay have held their prices down this year. Some have actually cut their published tariffs; many more have adopted a newly flexible approach to charging, so that now as never before it's well worth asking what sort of special deal they can offer. This is particularly good news for anyone deciding to take a few days off at short notice, or touring through the countryside without a fixed itinerary. Occupancy rates are unusually low at the moment (so there's no risk of finding yourself without a bed for the night), and you are much more likely to get a big discount on the usual room rate if you ring that day or even turn up on spec than if you are booking weeks in advance.

Future Guides

This is only the second edition of the *Guide*. It already draws greatly on the knowledge and experience of hundreds of readers, and we hope that future editions will gain more strength and of course new entries from readers' reports. The more people tell us about their own experiences and ideas, the better the book will become. So please write to us about hotels you've enjoyed for short or longer holiday stays, about restaurants, about cheaper places to stay or eat in, about interesting events, and about the things you've enjoyed doing and places you've enjoyed visiting. (And tell us about the bad times, too!) You can use the tear-out card in the middle of the book, report forms at the back of the book, or just write on ordinary paper. For letters posted in Britain you don't need a stamp: the address is *The Good Weekend Guide*, FREEPOST TN1569, WADHURST, E Sussex TN5 7BR.

Alisdair Aird

USING THE *GUIDE*

The Counties

England has been split alphabetically into county chapters. Occasionally, counties have been grouped together into a single chapter, and metropolitan areas have been included in the counties around them – for example, Merseyside in Lancashire. This follows the pattern which we have found works well in the companion *Good Pub Guide*, and allows people who have both books to cross-refer easily. If in doubt, check the Contents.

Scotland and Wales have been covered in single chapters, and London appears immediately before them at the end of England.

We have subdivided most chapters into smaller areas, each of which could form the basis of a weekend break or short holiday. So Devon, for instance, has five areas, while Yorkshire has seven.

Where to stay

In each section, hotels, inns and other places to stay such as farmhouses are listed in price order, starting with the most expensive.

The price we show is the total for two people sharing a double or twin-bedded room with its own bathroom, for one night in high season. It includes full English breakfast (unless only continental is available, in which case we say so), VAT and any automatic service charge that we know about. So the price is the total price for a room for two people. We say if dinner is included in this total price. It is included in some of the more remote places, especially in Scotland and Wales, and may also be in some other places where the quality of the food is a main attraction; in these cases, the establishment concerned does not normally offer B & B on its own. In some of the places we list, a few or occasionally even all the bedrooms share bathrooms; we say if this is the case.

An asterisk beside the price means that the establishment concerned assured us that that price would hold until the end of summer 1994. Many establishments were unable to give us this assurance; this last year, bedroom prices have been holding very steady, but to be on the safe side it might be prudent to allow for an increase of between 5% and 10% by then.

A few hotels will do a bargain break price at weekends even if you're staying for just one night. If so, that's the price we give, and we show this with a w beside the price. Many more hotels have very good value short break prices, especially out of season, if you stay a minimum of at least two nights; if you plan to stay in one area rather than tour around, it's well worth asking if there's a special price for short breaks when you book. In the present economic climate, many hotels also offer short-notice bargains which don't appear on their tariffs if they are underbooked on a particular night, in order to fill their rooms even at a discount. So, especially if you are not booking in advance, ask what price they can quote you for that particular night.

If there's a choice of rooms at different prices, we always give the cheapest, and if we know that maybe the back rooms are the quietest or the front ones have the best views or the ones in the new extension are more spacious then we say so. If you want a room with a sea view or whatever, you should always ask specifically for this, and check whether it costs extra.

If the hotel closes for any day or part of the year, we say so. But this last year we have found that in outlying areas some hotels which do close for the winter have closed earlier than the regular date, if their business is very slack; and there have been others which have have gone out of business. So don't head off into an area where there are no nearby alternatives without checking by telephone first.

Because of several unfortunate incidents involving our own contributors, we recommend that you confirm your booking in writing – and then to be doubly sure check by telephone that your booking has been received.

We always mention a restaurant if we know the inn or hotel has one. Note that we always commend food if we have information supporting a positive recommendation. So a bare mention that food is served shouldn't be taken to imply a recommendation of the food.

Where to eat

Restaurants are listed in rough price order, starting with the most expensive. The price in **bold type** is for one person having a typical three-course restaurant meal with half a bottle of wine, including any automatic service charge. So double it to get a meal for two. Prices in normal type are for more informal meals. The second price, before the |, is for a lunchtime sandwich or similar snack if the establishment offers one. The last price, after the |, is for a single-dish meal.

We list any scheduled closing dates. We have found quite a few instances of unscheduled closures in the last year or two, and recommend booking if your plans would be thrown into turmoil by finding a place unexpectedly closed. Moreover, many of the restaurants we list are very popular, and without a booking you may find there's no room for you.

If you want a good meal out in any area, look at the places to stay as well as the restaurants, especially in country areas. When we praise a hotel or inn for its food, that means it's well worth consideration as a place for a good meal out. In some parts of the country, it's in these hotel restaurants that you'll find the best food.

Children

We asked all hotels, restaurants and other places to stay in and eat at which have full entries in the *Guide* whether they allow children. If the entry doesn't mention children, that means the establishment has told us that it welcomes them, with no restrictions. If there are restrictions (either an age limit, or segregated early evening meals for them), we spell these out. We have found that very occasionally establishments turn out in practice to be more restrictive about children than they claim. And of course managements change, and so do their policies. If you are travelling with children, to avoid misunderstandings it's always worth checking ahead that there will be no problem. Please let us know if you find any difference from what we say. Obviously too you should bear in mind the character of the hotel or restaurant, as described, and in relation to your own children. While some children might fit perfectly into the atmosphere of a dignified and old-fashioned country house, others might be fractiously ill at ease there – no fun for you, or for the other guests.

Locations

As far as possible, we list places to see (and hotels and restaurants) under the name of the nearest village or town. We use **bold type** to name the locality, and SMALL CAPITAL LETTERS to name the establishment. If the village is so small that you probably wouldn't find it on a road map, we've listed it under the name of the nearest sizeable village or town instead.

The maps use the same locality name as the text. We always include places in their true geographical locations – so if a village is actually in Buckinghamshire that's where we list it, even if its postal address is via some town in Oxfordshire.

Map references

Most place names are given four-figure map references, looking like this: NT4892. The NT means it's in the square labelled NT on the map for that area. The first figure, 4, tells you to look along the grid at the top and bottom of the NT square for the figure 4. The third figure, 9, tells you to look down the grid at the side of the square to find the figure 9. Imaginary lines drawn down and across the square from these figures should intersect near the locality itself.

The second and fourth figures, the 8 and the 2, are for more precise pin-pointing, and are really for use with larger-scale maps such as road atlases or the Ordnance Survey 1:50,000 maps, which use exactly the same map reference system. On the relevant Ordnance Survey map, instead of finding the 4 marker on the top grid you'd find the 48 one; instead of the 9 on the side grid you'd look for the 92 marker. This makes it very easy to locate even the smallest village or place.

Prices and other factual details

Information about opening times and so forth is for 1994. In some cases establishments were uncertain about these when the *Guide* went to press during the summer of 1993; if so, we say in the text. (And of course there's always the risk of changed plans and unexpected closures.) When we say 'cl Nov-Mar' we mean closed from the beginning of November to the end of March, inclusive; however when we say 'cl Nov-Easter' we mean that the establishment reopens for Easter.

Where establishments were able to guarantee a price for 1994, we have marked this with an asterisk. In many cases establishments could not rule out an unscheduled price increase, and in these cases – ie, no asterisk against the price – it's probably prudent to allow for a 10% increase by the summer of 1994. If you find a significantly different price from that shown, *please let us know*.

National Trust

NT after price details means that the property is owned by the National Trust, and that for members of the Trust admission is free. There is a similar arrangement for properties owned by the National Trust for Scotlant (NTS); the two Trusts have a reciprocal arrangement, so that members of one may visit the properties of the other free. Membership is therefore well worth while if you are likely to visit more than a very few properties in the year – quite apart from its benefit to the Trusts' valuable work. Details from National Trust, PO Box 39, Bromley, Kent BR1 1NH (081-464 1111); or National Trust for Scotland, 5 Charlotte Sq, Edinburgh EH2 4DU (031-226 5922).

Disabled access

We always ask establishments if they can deal well with disabled people. We mention disabled access if a cautious view of their answers suggests that this is reasonable, though to be on the safe side anyone with a serious mobility problem would be well advised to ask ahead (many establishments made clear that this helped them to make any special arrangements needed). There are of course many places where we can't easily make this sort of assessment – particularly the less formal 'attractions' such as churches, bird reserves, waterside walks, viewpoints. In such cases (which should be obvious from the context) the absence of any statement about disabled access doesn't mean that a visit is out of the question, it simply means we have no information about that aspect. We're always grateful to hear of readers' own experiences.

Recommenders

At the end of each chapter we include the names of people who have given us help with that chapter for this new edition. Besides people who have written to us with information specifically for this book, some writing to us about the companion *Good Pub Guide*) have given us information which has proved useful for this book too. Where this has been a real help to the chapter concerned, we have in acknowledgement printed their names too.

Special interest lists

Lists at the back of the book pick out hotels and other places to stay which are by the waterside, which have good walks right on their doorstep, which are placed right by lots of other things to do, which have food that's good enough to count as a definite part of their appeal, which have under their roof or in their own grounds enough for you to be happy staying put for the day, and which are tucked away in really quiet spots.

Changes during the year – please tell us

Changes are inevitable during the course of the year. Managements change, and so do their policies. We very much hope that you will find everything just as we say. But if you find anything different, please let us know, using the report card in the middle of the book, the forms at the end of the book, or just a letter. For letters posted in Britain you don't need a stamp: the address is *The Good Weekend Guide*, FREEPOST TN1569, WADHURST, E Sussex TN5 7BR.

Reports

This *Guide* depends heavily on readers reporting back to it. In that sense it's very much a collaborative venture: and the more people that send us reports, the better the book will be. So please do help us by telling us about places you think should be added to the book, or removed from it, or even just confirming that places still deserve their entry. We try to answer all letters (though there may be a delay), and people who help us do get a special offer discount price on the next edition. There's a note on the sort of information we need at the back of the book, with report forms; and a tear-out report card in the middle of the book.

Symbols

We have used the same symbols in the text and on the maps to pick out all the main types of places to visit. Though you don't need to pay any attention to the symbols, you can if you like use them to scan the text or a map quickly, to see what castles, say, or gardens a particular area has. These are what we have used the symbols to denote:

★ Attractive village or town
Interesting house or building – anything from an intimate cottage to the stateliest of stately homes
Castle or romantic ruin
More or less archaeological site such as Roman remains, neolithic stone circles, early medieval mazes, Iron-Age hill forts
Church, cathedral, minster or abbey
Nature conservation, including wildlife reserves
Bird reserve, bird centre (including falconry)
Zoo, safari park, anywhere keeping exotic animals
Farm animals, farm park, country centre, farm museum, even vineyard
Anything to do with fish, including both fishing and aquariums
Garden, plant centre, arboretum, landscaped park
Wood, forest
Place or feature of great natural beauty
Viewpoints
Orchards, fruit farms, pick-your-own
Cave, cavern
Museum
Art gallery, sculpture park
Boat museum
Air museum
Motor museum
Open-air museum (including industrial museums)
Heritage centre such as the Jorvik Centre in York
Steam locomotives or railway
Boat trip
Amusement park, theme park, leisure park, permanent funfair
Craft centre or craft workshop: potters, glassblowers, weavers etc
Factory visit (including power station visits)
! Something exciting like hot-air balloon trips or somewhere with hands-on experiences

---

Some places embrace all sorts of different attractions in just the one locality. With these, instead of cluttering the maps with lots of different symbols, we show a ✪ on the map. Places to stay are indicated on the maps with a bed symbol, and places where you can eat with a knife and fork.

BERKSHIRE

The east part of the county has two exceptional attractions for a day's outing – Windsor, and a particularly fine stretch of the Thames, either for towpath sauntering or for boating. It has less to offer for a few days' stay.

In the west, rolling downland countryside, civilised small villages linked by pleasant minor roads, and comfortable and attractive places to stay combine to make it a good though not cheap prospect for a quiet weekend.

EAST BERKSHIRE

Though not a first choice for a short stay, this has the most beautiful stretch of the Thames; Windsor is exceptional for a day's sightseeing, and the area has some attractive gentle walks.

Strolls by the Thames or in Windsor Great Park can be very rewarding, and on a fine early summer or autumn day an afternoon's boating on the stretch of the Thames between Marlow and Henley can be almost magical (in holiday time the river gets very busy). There are several quietly attractive villages to explore. Windsor and, of course, the castle are an immensely powerful draw for visitors, with plenty to fill a day or more's sightseeing. A shortlist of other places of special appeal here would have to include the Savill Garden and Dorney Court, a fine ancient building with the deep charm of a proper family home.

Where to stay

Windsor SU9676 OAKLEY COURT SL4 5UR (0628) 74141 **£99w**; 94 rms. Splendid Victorian country-house hotel in 35 acres of grounds by the Thames with 9-hole golf course, croquet lawn, fishing and boating; beautifully restored, spacious lounges, lovely views, and two restaurants; disabled access.

Hurley SU8283 OLDE BELL Maidenhead SL6 5LX (0628) 825881 **£72**; 36 comfortable rms. Civilised and old-fashioned timbered inn with traces of its origins as a Norman monastic guesthouse, friendly service, peaceful garden.

Holyport SU9176 MOOR FARM Maidenhead SL6 2HY (0628) 33761 **£36**; 3 rms (no smoking). B & B in wing of timber-framed medieval house with beams, antiques, and flower-filled garden; no evening meals; also self-catering cottages; Suffolk sheep, horses, stabling, riding and tuition by arrangement.

We welcome reports from readers . . .

Readers who help us with reports for the GUIDE are offered a discount on the next edition: so please do help if you can!

To see and do

Windsor SU9676 Despite the disastrous Windsor Castle fire in 1992, this is still by far the greatest magnet for visitors in the east of the county; if you've never been, or not been for a long time, it's well worth an expedition. Besides the obvious tourist attractions, there's plenty to interest quieter tastes. The town is, of course, dominated by its famous castle, the largest inhabited one in the world. The little streets to the south of it have many pretty timber-framed or Georgian-fronted houses and shops. The High St, by contrast, is wide and busy. You can walk by the Thames (for example, from Home Park, beyond the station); or across to Eton – see below. There's also a good evening racecourse (and theatre).

! CASTLE Originally a wooden fort built by William the Conqueror, today this is still the official residence of the monarch, and part of its fascination is the way you can trace the substantial changes in its appearance and character over the centuries, as successive kings and queens have changed its function from a fortress to a palace. Henry II constructed the first stone buildings, inc the familiar Round Tower. From the top on a good day you can see 12 counties. A mass of towers, ramparts and pinnacles, it's an impressive place to wander round. You used to be able to stroll through the grounds free but unfortunately the enormous costs of restoration after the devastating fire in 1992 have put an end to that. It now costs £3, which also includes entrance to the magnificent ST GEORGE'S CHAPEL, a splendid example of Perpendicular architecture, with intricate carvings on the choir stalls, fine ironwork, an amazing fan-vaulted ceiling and the arms and pennants of every knight entered into the Order of the Knights of the Garter; shop, disabled access; chapel cl (1994) 10-14 Jun, 24-25 Dec and occasional other dates – check on (0753) 831118. Separate charges still apply for the

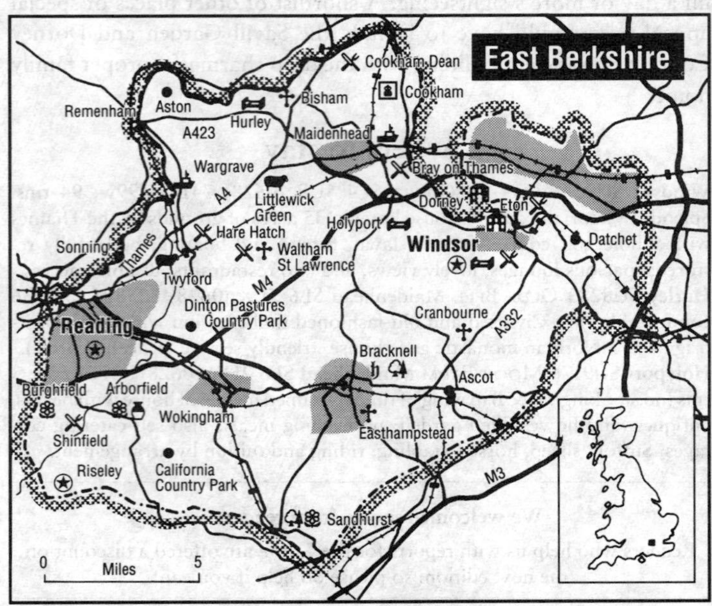

following three parts of the castle: STATE APARTMENTS This was where the fire did its worst, though only two of the 16 rooms were destroyed. They currently have Perspex covers letting you see the extent of the damage, and it's hoped that these will stay in place to show progress of the restoration work. Other rooms are decorated with carvings by Grinling Gibbons and ceilings by Verrio, and are full of superb paintings (which change from time to time) from the Royal Collection, inc notable Rembrandts and Van Dycks, porcelain, armour, and exceptionally fine furniture. Shop; cl Sun am and other dates when the Queen is in residence – best to check first (0753) 831118; £4. ROYAL CARRIAGES AND QUEEN'S PRESENTS A regularly changing display of gifts from foreign governments to the Queen, with some oddities, as well as the beautifully kept carriages – homely as well as stately. Hours as State Apartments; £1.50. QUEEN MARY'S DOLLS HOUSE An exquisite creation by Edwin Lutyens, built for Queen Mary in the 1920s, with perfectly scaled furniture and decoration. Hours as State Apartments; £1.50.

! ROYALTY & EMPIRE EXHIBITION (Thames St) A full-size recreation of Queen Victoria's Diamond Jubilee celebrations in 1897, with wax dummies by Tussaud's set in well-done period reconstructions. An unusual feature is a theatre show with moving and speaking models of eminent Victorians; good fun. The exhibition has been expanded to include a parallel celebration of the 40th anniversary of the coronation of their neighbour across the road, and comparing the two parts is an interesting way of looking at the changes over the last century; shops, Victorian stalls, snacks, good disabled access; cl 25 Dec; £3.95.

❀ SAVILL GARDEN 35 acres of colourful woodland with formal rose garden, rock plants, herbaceous borders and so forth; an outstanding place to visit – best in spring but good at any time of the year. Meals, snacks, shop, plant sales, disabled access; cl 25-28 Dec; £3.

❀ VALLEY GARDENS A lovely place for a relaxing stroll, with over 400 acres of woodland – 50 of which are devoted to rhododendrons, making this the largest planting of the species in the world. Also an outstanding collection of trees and shrubs, a heather garden, waterfowl lakes, and attractive landscaping. Both this and the previous garden are on the edge of Windsor Great Park; a £2 fee admits cars by a gate at Englefield Green.

FROGMORE HOUSE (Home Park) An impressive list of former tenants of this fine old house includes Queen Charlotte, Queen Victoria and Queen Mary; Henry VIII lived here in a predecessor of the current building, which went up in 1618. During the recent restoration a previously hidden mural was discovered on the staircase; a beautiful place, with 19 magnificent rooms to explore. They're switching the emphasis here to pre-booked guided tours, which take place Weds, Thurs and Fri from Aug-Oct, so it's now only open to individuals on weekends in Aug and early Sept; £3.20.

HOUSEHOLD CAVALRY MUSEUM (Combermere Barracks, St Leonards Rd) Fine and comprehensive display of weapons, armour, uniforms, and horse tack used from 1600 to present day. Shop, disabled access; cl 12.30-2, all day wknds and bank hols; from 1994 there will be a small charge, not decided as we went to press.

WINDSOR SAFARI PARK has now closed and the site is being redeveloped by its new Danish owners; among the new features will be a Legoland, which it's hoped will be open by Easter 1996.

Eton SU9678 has a restrained and decorous High St with a mix of interesting old shops and houses. Its glory is the COLLEGE, whose stately Tudor and later buildings in graceful precincts are marvellously calm during the school's holidays. The Museum of Eton Life includes modern videos of what actually goes on there today as well as more historical material, and the Brewhouse Gallery has some good watercolour drawings and Egyptian antiquities. Long or short tours; shop; cl am in term-time and Oct-Mar; from £2.20. The College runs residential courses in the summer with topics as diverse as rowing and choral singing: tel (0753) 671177.

! BRASS RUBBING CENTRE (St John the Baptist Church, Windsor High St) Replicas of 100 brasses. Snacks (Sat only), shop, disabled access; cl Sun, Good Fri, Nov-two weeks before Easter; rubbings from £1.60.

Other things to see and do

Boating on the Thames As well as rowing boats and motor launches, you can now hire very attractive (and silent) electric launches. This is a lovely stretch of the river, though busy in summer, flowing through lively towns and villages, past grand houses in imposing grounds to idyllic reaches by steep quiet woodland – with islets where you can picnic. A particularly pretty trip is from Wargrave to Henley to Medmenham Abbey to Hambleden, Hurley and Marlow Reach. A good shorter stretch is Cliveden Reach (the two miles between Cookham and Boulter's Lock). IPG Marine in Marlow (0628) 476800 have five centres; rowing boats £6, electric launches (6-8 people) £20 hour (or 8-hour day £100). Also Bray Boats, Maidenhead (0628) 37880: small boats/motor launches from £10 hour or £60 day.

Arborfield SU7567 HENRY STREET GARDEN CENTRE Specialist rose and bedding plant grower, with a well-stocked garden centre. From July-Sept you can wander through fragrant rose fields awash with colour from the massed blooms. Guided tours by appointment, snacks, shop.

Ascot SU9268 ROYAL ASCOT Queen Anne inaugurated the first meeting at this famous racecourse in 1711, and since then it's become synonymous with the English season and eccentric hats on Ladies' Day. To try for admission to the Royal Enclosure at Ascot, British citizens should apply to Ascot Races (Royal Enclosure and Members' Stand), St James's Palace, London SW1, foreign citizens to their Embassy. There are other races throughout the year, when ticket prices range from £3-£24 depending on which enclosure you head for (the Silver Ring is the cheapest). Meals, snacks, shop, disabled access; (0344) 22211 for dates.

✝ **Bisham** SU8485 The CHURCH is worth a look, and sitting on a seat in the churchyard by the Thames on a fine evening is rather special. The Bull is a decent pub here.

Bracknell SU8769 THE LOOK OUT A countryside and heritage centre in 2,600 acres of woodland, mainly conifer plantations but full of nature trails and wildlife; various exhibitions and displays in the visitor centre; meals, snacks, shop, disabled access; £1.50 for exhibitions.

Burghfield SU6668 OLD RECTORY Plantsman's garden inc oriental rarities and cottage-garden plants. Snacks, plant centre selling plants from other gardens in the area, some disabled access; open last Weds of month exc Nov-Jan; 50p.

Cookham SU8884 STANLEY SPENCER GALLERY (King's Hall) Former Methodist chapel devoted entirely to Spencer's work; includes 'Christ Preaching at Cookham Regatta' and 'The Last Supper'. Shop, disabled access; cl wkdys Nov-Easter, best to phone first other times (0628) 520890; 50p. The village, leading down to the Thames, is attractive, and has several decent pubs.

Dorney SU9278 DORNEY COURT Engaging partly 15th-c timber-framed manor house with pleasant gardens and some very fine furniture, as well as the Elizabethan Palmer Needlework tapestry and portraits representing the last 12 generations of the family who've owned the house for centuries. Shop, teas; open Easter and bank hols in May then pm Sun, Mon and Tues Jun-Sept; *£3.50.

Littlewick Green SU8379 COURAGE SHIRE HORSE CENTRE (A4, 2 miles W of Maidenhead) Follow the day-to-day life of working, prize-winning Shire horses, especially their important grooming, being plaited up and so forth – as show horses they have to look their best. You can go right up to the animals; also harness and rosettes display, free guided tours, audio-visual presentation, picnic area, and working forge. Meals, snacks, shop, disabled access; cl Nov-Feb (open half-term and part of Christmas school hols); £2.80.

! Reading SU7272 Now Berkshire's county town, Reading keeps its older parts well hidden, but you can still see the remains of the old ABBEY, where Henry I is buried, surrounded by pleasant parkland. MUSEUM OF ENGLISH RURAL LIFE (Univ of Reading, Whiteknights Park; 2m SE on A327, so you don't have to go into the busy centre). Interesting collection of farm tools, rural crafts, and other domestic exhibits representing life in the English countryside over the last 150 years; fine collection of waggons. Shop, disabled access; cl 1-2, Sun, Mon, 25 Dec-1 Jan; BLAKE'S LOCK MUSEUM (Gasworks Rd) Attractive Victorian building housing local history museum, with reconstructed bakery, barber's shop and printer's workshop; disabled access; cl am wknds and bank hols, Mon (exc bank hols). If you're feeling in an extravagant mood a BALLOON TRIP gives a very different view of Berkshire; lift off from town-centre parks every day in summer and wknds in winter, dawn and dusk – tel 081-840 0108 to check.

Riseley SU7263 WELLINGTON COUNTRY PARK AND NATIONAL DAIRY MUSEUM (off B3349 Reading-Basingstoke) A busy 550-acre country park, its meadows, woodland and lake surrounded by marked nature trails, a miniature steam railway, deer park, collection of small domestic animals, and adventure playground. Museum covers the history of the dairy industry with attractive copper, pewter and wooden tools, and milk delivery vehicles. You can fish, sail, windsurf or row on the lake, and there are one-day starter courses; booking essential (0734) 326505. Snacks, shop, disabled access; cl wkdys Nov-Feb; £2.80.

Sandhurst SU8361 TRILAKES COUNTRY PARK AND FISHERY Not just for fishermen, these attractive lakes and surrounding park and woodland have lots of animals and birds wandering round, some of which you can feed; Sun pm rides for small children on miniature horses £1.75.

Twyford SU7876 THAMES VALLEY VINEYARD (Stanlake Park) English wines made by a pioneering blend of tradition and technology. Pre-booked tours only inc tasting (0734) 340176; shop, limited disabled access; cl Sun am, 25 Dec-1 Jan; *£5 (or from £9.95 inc meal). The Lands End is useful for lunch.

† **Waltham St Lawrence** SU8276 Attractive quiet village with ancient centre, two decent pubs at either end; chiefly notable for magnificent 14th-c SHOTTESBROOKE CHURCH, in an attractive park just east.

Other churches at Cranbourne SU9372 and Easthampstead SU8667 are worth seeing if you pass, for their fine stained glass by William Morris, Edward

Burne-Jones and others.

For **children to let off steam,** CALIFORNIA COUNTRY PARK SU7864 (S of Wokingham on B3016, turning R at Wick Hill opp B3430) has woods to run around in, lots of sand, and a vast paddling place; very popular locally. DINTON PASTURES COUNTRY PARK SU7872 (off B3030 S of Hurst – which has decent pubs) has rather more for older children, inc windsurfing and canoeing.

★ **Other attractive villages,** worth looking at if you're near, and all with decent pubs, include Aston SU7884, Cookham SU8884, Datchet SU9876, Hurley SU8283, Sonning/Sonning Lock SU7575 (nice stroll through churchyard and along the Thames), Wargrave SU7878.

Walks

This is generally more an area for pleasant strolls rather than long hikes. In particular, the **Thames'** nostalgic qualities of boating and Edwardian England are seen to full effect from leisurely strolls along the towpath – easy going for even the most hesitant walker. A very fine stretch extends from **Maidenhead** SU8783 to **Henley** SU7882, sharing the river with Bucks and Oxon. There are lovely Thames walks from **Remenham** SU7683 in either direction. This reach is the course of the Henley Regatta; you can instead start from Henley itself (coming back over the bridge – see Oxon chapter) or **Aston** SU7884; the Flower Pots here is an engaging pub. Another good starting point for river walks is **Boulter's Lock** SU9082 (head upstream).

There are few bridges across, and much of the hinterland is developed, but opportunities for round walks abound at **Cookham** SU8884 and **Cookham Dean** SU8785, with the chalk escarpment of **Winter Hill** SU8786 giving a good vantage point. Paths in this area are very well kept, and it is hard to lose the way seriously, although woodland walking sometimes means you have to keep your eyes skinned for arrow markers painted on trees.

Windsor Great Park has miles of well-kept parkland, so well landscaped that it takes the occasional surprising find (statues, even a totem pole) to remind you that it's not natural. It's the only real prospect in this part of the county for walks that'll get you decidedly exercised. **Virginia Water** SU9768 is very beautiful, particularly in autumn; and the Long Walk gives glorious perspectives of the castle. Best access via Valley Gardens or Savill Garden car parks.

Finchampstead Ridges SU8063 is an altogether smaller steepish chunk of heather and pinewood, with good views and sheltered picnic spots. Not far off, the much broader stretches of pinewoods between **Crowthorne** SU8464 and **Bracknell** SU8769 offer much longer but less varied walks, with many tracks including some based on Roman ways; parking off A3095/B3430 – the best start is the well-organised and informative Look Out Point off B3430 at SU8766.

Maidenhead Thicket SU8581 (mixed old woodland and common) has easy access from A423 and A4.

Driving

This area is not really worth thinking about for pleasure driving. In the main, roads here are for traffic not scenery (though the B3348 W of Crowthorne takes you down a long wellingtonia avenue, still handsome despite storm losses, with good views before you turn back towards Wokingham on the B3016).

Where to eat

Bray on Thames SU9079 WATERSIDE (0628) 20691 Carefully and prettily refurbished restaurant with big windows overlooking the Thames, superb French cooking, fine French cheeses, lovely wines, and a smart but surprisingly relaxed atmosphere; small terrace, little electric launch for private hire; now does bedrooms; cl 26 Dec-29 Jan, bank hols, Mon, Tues am, Sun pm mid Oct-mid Apr; no children under 12; disabled access. **£40.**

Shinfield SU7368 L'ORTOLAN (0734) 883783 Luxurious and innovative French cooking in Victorian rectory with conservatory extensions; delicious puddings, fine cheeseboard, classic wine list inc French regional wines; disabled access; cl Sun evening, Mon, 2 wks end Aug, ditto Feb. **£37.50.**

Remenham SU7683 LITTLE ANGEL (0491) 574165 Intimate little restaurant with good seafood; also bar snacks. **£18|£2.75/£4.95.**

Waltham St Lawrence SU8276 PLOUGH (0734) 340015 Fine old country dining pub with good lunchtime food and Sun roasts and more elaborate evening meals with Thai chef doing specialities Fri pm and alternate Sat pm; happy atmosphere, quietly efficient service. **£20/£4.**

Places for decent light lunches include the Queen Victoria at Hare Hatch SU8077 (cheap and cheerful pub), Jolly Farmer at Cookham Dean SU8785 (rather smarter but relaxed), Eton Wine Bar in Eton High St (cosy; decent food and wines), and Royal Oak, Horse & Groom and Old Trout in Windsor itself (all reasonable pubs).

WEST BERKSHIRE

Civilised comfort, good food and bracing downland walks.

No single town or village here stands out as having everything you'd want to fill out a few days' stay. There is a fair amount to see, but scattered about so that you'd reckon on spending at least some time driving around to track things down; for the most part, roads are good and there are some attractive downland drives. This is also quite a good area for walking in attractive countryside, with a range of possibilities from gentle strolls to long hikes. Several hotels and inns give a good choice of comfortable and civilised places to stay, and there's no shortage of good food here. Particularly for families, the Beale Wildlife Gardens at Lower Basildon are very rewarding, and on a nice day a horse-drawn barge trip from Kintbury is tempting; our pick of places for older people to visit here would be Basildon Park.

Where to stay

Streatley SU5980 SWAN DIPLOMAT High St Reading RG8 9HR (0491) 873737 **£134**; 46 well-equipped, clean rms (many overlooking the water). Well-run and attractive riverside hotel, relaxed, airy lounges, waterside restaurant; restored Magdalen College Barge, popular leisure club, flower-filled garden; disabled access.

Newbury SU4666 HILTON NATIONAL Pinchington Lane RG14 7HL (0635) 529000 ***£95**; 109 rms. Unusually relaxed and friendly for a chain hotel, luxurious, spotless, buoyant atmosphere; attractive 2-level restaurant with good carvery, helpful service, swimming pool; disabled access.

Pangbourne SU6376 COPPER Church Rd Reading RG8 7AR (0734) 842244 **£92** (inc dinner); 22 rms, most overlooking gardens. Timbered and creeper-covered coaching inn with beamed bar, comfortable sitting room, smart lounge, charming restaurant; good, often unusual, food and some fine wines; disabled access.

Hungerford SU3368 BEAR Charnham St RG17 0EL (0488) 682512 **£65**; 41 comfortable, attractive rms with antiques and beams in older ones; civilised hotel bar with fresh flowers, open fires, and stuffed bear, restaurant; decent food, very good wines.

Kintbury SU3866 DUNDAS ARMS Newbury RG15 0UT (0488) 58263 **£65**; 5 rms in old stable block overlooking River Kennet. Old-fashioned pub by canal, lots of ducks and daffodils, good range of wines (esp clarets) and honest cooking using freshest ingredients in restaurant, decent bar food too, good breakfasts, pleasant service; cl Christmas-New Year; disabled access.

Hamstead Marshall SU4165 WHITE HART Newbury RG15 0HW (0488) 58201 **£50**; 6 beamed, comfortable rms in converted barn. Civilised Georgian country inn in quiet village, good food inc Italian dishes and popular puddings, friendly service, very pleasant walled garden; cl 25-26 Dec, 2 wks Aug.

Yattendon SU5574 ROYAL OAK The Square Newbury RG16 0UF (0635) 201325 **£50**; 5 rms, mostly with bath. Elegant and comfortable old inn in peaceful village, very good, sophisticated food, excellent wines, prettily decorated, panelled bar, good service, lovely garden; cl 25 Dec; disabled access in restaurant (not bedrooms).

Hungerford SU3368 MARSHGATE COTTAGE RG17 0QX (0488) 682307 ***£48.50**; 9 individually decorated rms, mostly with bath. Family-run little hotel backing on to Kennet & Avon Canal, seats overlooking water and marsh and in sheltered courtyard; mountain bikes for hire; cl Christmas; children over 5; disabled access.

East Ilsley SU4981 CROWN & HORNS Newbury RG16 0LH (0635) 281205 **£38**; 10 rms, some in converted stable block. Lively and friendly old pub in horse-training country with interesting beamed rooms, pretty paved stable yard, decent bar food, lots of whiskies.

To see and do

Basildon SU6078 BASILDON PARK Lovely Bath stone Palladian mansion with grand rooms full of fine pictures and furniture, and delicate plasterwork on ceilings and walls; old-fashioned roses, pretty terrace, grounds beyond. The classical frontage is particularly impressive; meals, snacks, shop, disabled access; cl am, all day Mon (exc bank hols), Tues, Good Fri, Weds after a bank hol, Nov-Mar; £3.50, £2.50 grounds only; NT. The Red Lion at Upper Basildon is useful for lunch.

Bucklebury SU5570 BUCKLEBURY FARM PARK Traditional farm animals and events such as lambing and shearing (and strawberry fields in summer), as well as a herd of red deer in the 60-acre park; trailer rides make sure you get a chance to see them. Snacks, shop; £2.

Kintbury HORSE-DRAWN BARGE TRIPS Round trip on restored Kennet & Avon Canal 1½ hrs (0635) 33154; cl

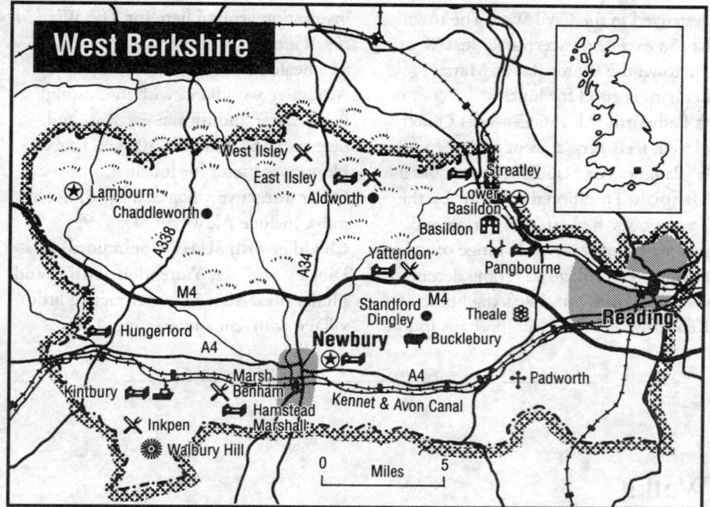

end Sept-Easter; £3.50. The Dundas Arms is useful for lunch.

Lambourn SU3278 Quiet streamside racehorse-training village below the downs. LAMBOURN TRAINERS' ASSOCIATION (Windsor House) Guided tours around racehorse training centre; you can watch the horses training up on the downland gallops, as well as see their stables and meet individual horses. Wear suitable shoes, and you must make an appointment, (0488) 71347; snacks; T-shirts for sale; disabled access; cl pm and bank hol Mon; £5 + VAT. Up on the downs (OS Sheet 174 SU329828) SEVEN BARROWS is a Bronze-Age cemetery with at least 32 barrows – a spectacle even for the uninitiated. CHURCH OF ST MICHAEL AND ALL ANGELS A fine parish church, originally Norman, with Perpendicular additions. The George is useful for lunch.

Lower Basildon SU6078 BEALE WILDLIFE GARDENS (Church Farm, Lower Basildon) Formerly the Beale Bird Park, now with a name that better describes its varied features: many kinds of game birds, waterfowl, owls and parrots (in conditions as near as possible to the wild), as well as Highland cattle, rare breeds of sheep, a deer park, pets' corner, tropical house and a good variety of plants and insects. There's a lot going on, and the surroundings well deserve their listing as an area of Outstanding Beauty; also Thames trips, narrow-gauge railway, the National Centre for Model Ships and Boats and children's playground. Lots of different events throughout the year. Meals, snacks, shop, disabled access; cl Jan-Feb; *£4.

Newbury SU4666 A busy shopping town, but there are some nice old parts, with interesting older buildings among the high-street shops. ST NICOLAS is a fine early 16th-c Perpendicular church with a magnificent pulpit. By here, West Mills (street) is the best evocation of the town's 18th-c prosperity, and leads to the attractively rejuvenated canal. BOAT TRIPS run some days from the old wharf, beyond the market square on the other side of the High St. There's a local MUSEUM here, with costumes and good displays on the area's history and archaeology. There are picturesque buildings in Argyll Rd and Newtown Rd, beyond the end of the High St S of the railway. Just N off B4494 is DONNINGTON CASTLE, a tall medieval ruined castle – actually the gatehouse of a much larger fortress destroyed in the Civil War. The town has an excellent racecourse. Just W of the town the Water Rat at Marsh Benham is good for lunch.

✝ **Padworth** SU6166 CHURCH Quietly placed, feels very ancient and peaceful.

Pangbourne SU6376 PANGBOURNE MEADOW Traditional meadow by the Thames, scythed after flowering and seeding to preserve wide range of wild flowers. The village has some decent shops and pubs, and was the home of Kenneth Grahame, who perhaps found inspiration around here for *The Wind in the Willows*.

Theale ENGLEFIELD HOUSE (A340) Attractive woodland with interesting trees, water and formal gardens, and deer park. Cl Mon; £1.50. The Fox & Hounds is useful for lunch.

Other attractive villages, all with decent pubs, include Aldworth SU5579, Chaddleworth SU4177, Standford Dingley SU5771, Yattendon SU1671 and Hungerford SU1612, an attractive little village with some interesting shops.

Walks

Around **Streatley** SU5980 there are walks along the Thames and contrasting paths up on the downs (the long-distance downs-top Ridgeway Path, one of the oldest tracks in England, follows surfaced farm roads in places hereabouts, but takes in some quiet countryside). More dramatic is the high escarpment of **Inkpen Beacon** SU3562 and **Walbury Hill** SU3761, reached from a minor road S of Inkpen SU3564 (where the Swan is good for lunch). The gibbet on top of the hill is a macabre relic from highwayman days. Immediately S lie some lovely rolling downlands laced with gentle and mostly well-marked tracks, field paths and woodland paths overlapping into Hants and Wilts. Other paths tap quickly into sections of the Ridgeway with good views from **Aldworth** SU5579 and **West Ilsley** SU4782 (both have good pubs).

Thatcham Moor SU5166 is said to be the largest area of inland freshwater reed-beds in England; lots of birds (some rare), moths, and marshland and aquatic plants. Car park S of A4.

The **Kennet & Avon Canal** has been well restored in the last few years, and is now very pleasant to stroll or cycle along, from Thatcham SU5167, Aldermaston Wharf SU6067, Hungerford SU3368, Kintbury SU3866, Marsh Benham SU4267 or Woolhampton SU5767 (the last four all have good civilised pubs).

Driving

The Lambourn Valley is one of the prettiest drives here – from Newbury out past Woodspeen through the pretty villages of Boxford, East Garston and Eastbury to Lambourn itself. The B4001 up over Lambourn Downs, into Oxon via Wantage, takes you back over the downs on the B4494 to Newbury. Other good quiet scenic routes include the B4009 Streatley-Newbury; and the back road Pangbourne-Upper Basildon-Aldworth, then L on B4009 and R towards Compton-the Ilsleys-Farnborough (lovely Georgian ex-rectory on right), then L on to B4494 towards Newbury.

For long-distance travel the A4 is quite a pleasant alternative to the M4.

Where to eat

Marsh Benham SU4267 WATER RAT (0635) 582017 Comfortable thatched restaurant with nice *Wind in the Willows* paintings around walls, some interesting dishes, also light meals in stylish bar; good service; disabled access. £19|£2.35/£4.95.

West Ilsley SU4782 HARROW (0635 28) 260 White-tiled village inn overlooking duck pond and green with friendly, lively atmosphere, good bar food inc country dishes like saddle of hare or local trout; no-smoking dining room at lunchtime, notable children's play area with lots of animals; disabled access. **£14**|£2/£5.50.

Inkpen SU3564 SWAN (048 84) 326 Rambling, beamed country inn with popular Singaporean food and a few western dishes at lunchtime; quiet village. £3.20/£5.50.

East Ilsley SU4981 SWAN (063 528) 238 Well-refurbished 17th-c coaching inn, good value bar food, pretty back terrace, sheltered lawn with play area. £1.50/£5.

Help this year from: *Ian Phillips, TBB, Frank Cummins, J A Collins, Paul and Janet Giles, Mayur Shah, J Steinert, P Thomas, Stephen and Julie Brown, Mark Shutler, Bill and Edee Miller, V Compton, A McGlynn, Werner Arend, Dr and Mrs R E S Tanner, Gladys Teall.*

BERKSHIRE CALENDAR

Some of these dates were provisional as we went to press.

JANUARY

1st **Savernake** Hot Air Ballooning Meet, *west of Newbury on A4 – Sun too*

APRIL

1st **Hungerford** Easter Eggstravaganza, *Littlecote House with hot air balloons and over 10,000 creme eggs; also* **Lambourn** Trainers Open Day

3rd **Riseley** Easter Fun & Crafts, *Wellington Country Park*

4th **Sandhurst** Trilakes Birds of Prey Display

30th **Chieveley** Steam Funtasia, *Newbury Showground*

MAY

2nd **Riseley** Animal Day, *Wellington Country Park, including terrier & ferret racing*

7th **Newbury** Spring Festival – *till Sat 21*

11th **Windsor** Royal Windsor Horse Show – *till Fri 15*

15th **Twyford** The Berkshire County Fayre, *The Straight Mile (B3018); also* **Yateley** Trilakes Sheep & Goat Shearing Demonstrations

28th **Newbury** Craft Fair, *Highclere House*; *also* **Riseley** Thames Valley Craft Fayre, *Stratfield Saye House – till Mon*

30th **Yateley** Trilakes Birds of Prey Display

May **Reading** Children's Festival

Berkshire Calendar

June

4th **Bagnor** Annual Summer Fair, *Watermill Theatre*

12th **Riseley** Sheepdog Demonstration, *Wellington Country Park*

14th **Ascot** Royal Ascot, *Ascot Racecourse – till Fri*

25th **Hurst** Horse Show & Country Fair, *Willowmead, School Rd; also* **Reading** Waterfest

26th **Yateley** Trilakes Birds of Prey Display

29th **Henley-on-Thames** Henley Royal Regatta – *till 3 July*

July

1st **Bracknell** Festival, South Hill Park – *till Sun*

6th **Henley-on-Thames** Henley Festival – *till Sat*

8th **Windsor** Royal Windsor Rose & Horticultural Show, *Windsor Castle Grounds – Sat too*

9th **Cox Green** London English Wine Festival, *Lillibrooke Manor – Sun too*

10th **Newbury** Carnival

15th **Reading** WOMAD International Music Festival

16th **Sonning Common** Country Fayre, *The Herb Farm – Sun too; also* **Woodcote** Steam Fair – *Sun too*

17th **Maidenhead** Dog Show, *Courage Shire Horse Centre*

21st **Reading** Jazz & Real Ale Festival, *Christchurch Meadow – till Sat*

31st **Riseley** Heckfield Horticultural Show, *Wellington Country Park*

August

5th **Hungerford** Wiltshire Balloon Festival, *Littlecote House*

12th **Warfield** Medieval Craft Fayre, *Moss End Farm – till Sun*

13th **Knowl Hill** Steam Fair – *Sun too*

14th **Riseley** Animal Day *at Wellington Country Park*

21st **Maidenhead** Vintage Day *at Courage Shire Horse Centre*

26th **Reading** Rock Festival, *Richfield Avenue – till Sun*

29th **Yateley** Trilakes Birds of Prey Display

September

3rd **Riseley** Shetland Pony Centre, *Wellington Country Park*

4th **Spencers Wood** Wokingham & Reading Agricultural Show, *White House Farm*

11th **Maidenhead** Owl, Hawk & Falconry Day, *Courage Shire Horse Centre*

17th **Newbury** & The Royal County of Berkshire Show, *Newbury Showground*

October

1st **Maidenhead** Heavy Horse Show, *Courage Shire Horse Centre – Sun too*

Buckinghamshire

The southern part of the county has some excellent places to stay, on or near what must rank as the finest stretch of the Thames, or among the beechwoods of the Chiltern Hills. It has quite a few beautifully placed villages, and plenty of good places for meals, from attractive old pubs to grand hotel restaurants. Though there are interesting places to visit here, it's the north and west of the county which have a remarkable collection of magnificent houses and estates open to the public. Yet these parts are off the usual tourist map, so their treasures tend not to be teeming with other visitors.

Thames and Chilterns

Fine places to stay in attractive surroundings, good eating out and the best walking near London.

There are some good well-run attractions here, including several to keep a young family happy, but the main appeal is the countryside – especially the wooded Chiltern Hills, with their charming quiet valleys, tucked-away villages, and endless possibilities for rewarding strolls and longer walks in lovely surroundings. Almost any season is good here, but spring and autumn through to November are particularly beautiful. There's a very good choice of relatively informal places to eat in, well suiting the area's character as good walking territory, though less choice for a spectacular evening out. The Thames here is best seen from a boat, but there are also a few good places to stroll along. A decent range of interesting places to stay includes Cliveden, one of England's grandest National Trust properties and now an extremely well-run hotel – very special if you can afford it. Our shortlist of top attractions here would include Cliveden's gardens, the Bekonscot Model Village in Beaconsfield, West Wycombe Park, the Chilterns Open Air Museum at Chalfont St Giles, and Chenies Manor House.

Where to stay

Taplow SU9082 Cliveden Maidenhead SL6 0JF (0628) 668561 £220; 31 luxurious, individual rms with maid unpacking service and a butler's tray. Superb Grade I listed stately home with gracious, comfortable public rooms, fresh flowers, a surprisingly unstuffy atmosphere; lovely views over the magnificent NT Thames-side parkland and formal gardens (open to the public); daily-changing, imaginative food in the two restaurants, very fine wines, friendly breakfasts around a huge table, and impeccable bright staff; pavilion with swimming pool and so forth, tennis, squash, croquet, riding, coarse fishing, boating; disabled access.

Marlow SU8586 COMPLEAT ANGLER Marlow Bridge SL7 1RG (0628) 484444 **£165**; 64 pretty, individually furnished rms overlooking garden or river. Famous Thames-side hotel with comfortable panelled lounge, balconied bar, spacious beamed restaurant with marvellous view, imaginative food, friendly, prompt service; tennis, croquet, coarse fishing; disabled access.

Aston Clinton SP8712 BELL London Rd Aylesbury HP22 5HP (0296) 630252 **£132**; 21 comfortable rms, some in main building with antiques, some (more modern but spacious) in converted stables around flower-filled courtyard; dogs by arrangement – will supply dog bowl/blanket. Early 17th-c coaching inn with elegant panelled drawing room, flagstoned smoking room, restaurant with pretty murals and excellent modern French cooking, formal but kind service; pretty, mature gardens; disabled access.

Cadmore End SU7892 BLUE FLAG High Wycombe HP14 3PS (0494) 881183 **£84**; 16 rms in little modern hotel by traditional pub. Several comfortable beamed areas with standing timbers and partitions, attractive small restaurant, wide choice of well-prepared food, efficient, uniformed staff; cl 25-26 Dec; no children.

Ibstone SU7593 FOX High Wycombe HP14 3GG (049 163) 289 **£58**; 9 rms. Really civilised, friendly 17th-c country inn with old-fashioned character, log fires, good food and wines, no-smoking dining area in bar, smart restaurant, pretty garden, and country views.

Fawley SU7586 WALNUT TREE Henley-on-Thames Oxon RG9 6JE (0491) 638360 **£50**; 2 rms with showers. Popular, attractive dining pub in lovely spot with Chilterns all around, imaginative food, decent wines, no-smoking conservatory.

Hambleden SU7886 STAG & HUNTSMAN Henley-on-Thames Oxon RG9 6RP (0491) 571227 **£48.50**; 3 good rms. Little country pub surrounded by Chilterns beechwoods with compact lounge, attractively simple public bar, good food, and pretty garden; cl 25 Dec pm; no children.

To see and do

! Beaconsfield SU9490 BEKONSCOT MODEL VILLAGE The oldest model village in the world, with churches, castles, a racecourse, zoo, villages and a gauge-1 railway, all set out to represent the mythical idyll of rural England. Snacks, shop, disabled access; cl Nov-Feb; *£2.80. The Old Hare is good for lunch.

✈ Booker SU8391 BOOKER AIRCRAFT CENTRE (Wycombe Air Park) There are a few old aircraft here inc a Vampire, but the main emphasis is on aircraft archaeology, with displays of wartime wrecks and the possessions found in them. They've taken trouble researching the history and background of the people on these flights, and it's this personal side of the exhibition which makes it so interesting; shop, disabled access; open weekends; *£1. There are lots of good pubs nearby for lunch, especially the Old Crown at Skirmett, Chequers at Fingest, Yew Tree at Frieth and Peacock at Bolter End.

Chalfont St Giles SU9993 CHILTERN OPEN AIR MUSEUM (Newland Park, Gorelands Lane) Traditional Chilterns buildings dismantled and rebuilt here, inc Iron-Age house, forge, barns, toll house, and cart sheds; also a nature trail through the parklands and adventure playground. Lots of events throughout the year. Snacks, shop, disabled access; cl until 2, Mon (exc bank hols), Tues, Nov-Mar; £2.50. MILTON'S COTTAGE (Deanway) This 16th-c timber-framed cottage is where the writer completed

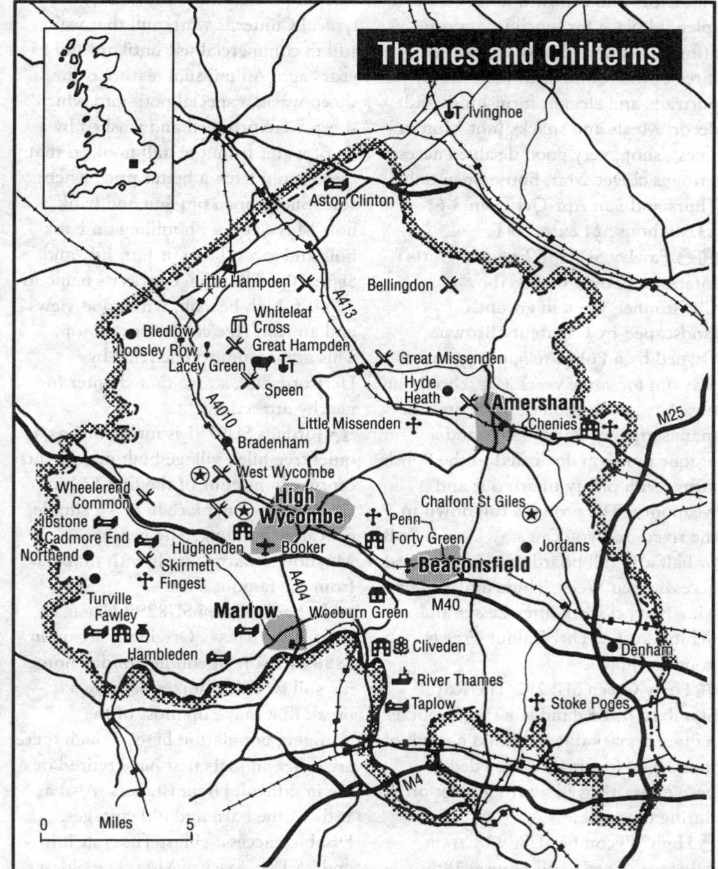

Paradise Lost and began *Paradise Regained*; first editions of these are among the rare books and memorabilia on display, and there's a charming garden. Shop, disabled access; cl 1-2, Sun am, all day Mon (exc bank hols), Nov-Feb; *£1.50. CHALFONT SHIRE CENTRE Home to several handsome horses, some of which they let children ride on, and there are also impressive collections of carriages and heavy harness; meals, snacks, shop, disabled access; cl Oct-mid-Mar; £2.50. The Pheasant is useful for lunch.

Chenies TQ0198 MANOR HOUSE 15th-c house with Tudor rooms, doll collection, tapestries, priests' hole and a 13th-c crypt; the gardens include a physic garden, herbs, and a maze. Snacks, shop; open pm Weds, Thurs and bank hols Apr-Oct; *£3.20 house and garden, *£1.60 garden only. ST MICHAEL'S CHURCH has the rich family monuments of the Bedfords (viewed through a glass panel), 15th-c brasses and a Norman font. The Red Lion is good for lunch.

Cliveden SU9185 CLIVEDEN GARDENS Nearly 400 acres of lovely formal gardens, woodland and parkland overlooking the Thames. The magnificent house used to belong to the Astors and is now a luxury hotel (a splendid place for lunch if you can afford it), although visitors can see three of the rooms with their family portraits and elegant furnishings and decor. Meals and snacks (not Mon or Tues), shop, very good disabled access; gardens cl Dec-Mar, house open only Thurs and Sun Apr-Oct from 3-6; £3.50, house £1 extra. NT.

Fawley SU7586 FAWLEY COURT Interesting house designed by Christopher Wren in grounds landscaped by Capability Brown. Owned by a Polish religious group, it was run for some years as a school, but now has a collection of portraits and manuscripts of Polish kings and a unique museum dedicated to the Polish army, with plenty of armour and weaponry. The grounds run down to the river, and you can stay here, B & B or half and full board; limited disabled access; open Weds, Thurs and Sun pm Mar-Nov, cl week after Easter and Whit Sun; £2. The Walnut Tree is good for lunch.

Forty Green SU9292 The Royal Standard of England PUB stands out as a quite remarkable old building, full of interesting furniture – crowded at weekends, it's well worth a quiet prowl during the week.

High Wycombe SU8593 CHAIR MUSEUM (Castle Hill House) 18th-c building with lots of local country furniture and objects of local interest. Shop, disabled access; cl 1-2 Sat, Sun, bank hols.

Hughenden SU8695 HUGHENDEN MANOR The home of Benjamin Disraeli until his death in 1881, this imposing old house still has many of the ex-Prime Minister's books and other possessions, as well as related memorabilia, portraits of friends and formal gardens. Shop, some disabled access; cl am, Mon, Tues, Nov-Mar; £3.30.

Ivinghoe SP9416 is a pleasant old village with the 18th-c FORD END WATERMILL, the only remaining working watermill in the county – a typical Chilterns watermill that was still in commercial use until around 15 years ago. An unusual feature is the sheep wash, a special pool into which sheep were dropped and washed by a jet of water from the mill pool, so that they would fetch a better price when sold. Shop; open pm Sun and bank hols May-Sept, with milling on bank hols and second Sun in Jun, July and Sept; 70p. The village gives its name to a 760-ft high beacon, with good views and an Iron-Age earthwork on top. This area is almost encircled by Hertfordshire, so see that chapter for nearby attractions.

★ **Jordans** SU9791 is interesting as a quiet tree-filled village built mainly this century in honour of the first 17th-c Quaker meeting place here – a simple, evocative building. The nearby Mayflower Barn is built with timbers from the famous ship.

Lacey Green SU8299 HOME OF REST FOR HORSES Originally set up in 1886 as a sort of equine holiday home, it's still working horses needing a break that make up most of the changing population here, though there are other animals that have retired or are in difficult circumstances. Also a 16th-c tithe barn and old cottages. Disabled access; cl last Thurs in July and 25 Dec. SMOCK MILL The oldest surviving smock mill in the country, and indeed the third oldest windmill of any type, built in 1650 at Chesham and moved here in 1821. It's been well restored after a period of neglect; open Sun pm Apr-Oct; 50p. Rupert Brooke's old favourite, the Pink & Lily, is good for lunch. Other well-restored windmills can be seen at nearby **Loosley Row** SP8100, **Pitstone** SP9415 (where there's also an interesting old church), and **Ibstone** SU7593, unusual for having 12 sides.

★ † **Little Missenden** SU9298 The CHURCH has some wall paintings from the 12th c and some pre-Norman traces, and the village itself has attractive old timbered and tiled houses. The Crown is useful for lunch.

West Wycombe SU8394 WEST WYCOMBE PARK 300 acres of beautifully laid-out parkland surround this 18th-c Palladian house, and inside there's a good collection of tapestries, furniture and paintings; the Italianate painted ceilings are particularly notable. Disabled access to grounds only; cl am, Fri, Sat, Sept-May; *£4, *£2.50 grounds only. HELL FIRE CAVES Sir Francis Dashwood who had these caves constructed was also the founder of the Hell Fire Club, and legend has it that the group used to meet in these tunnels to practise their black arts. You can well believe it judging by the spooky Gothic entrance. The tunnels extend for about a third of a mile underground, and are filled with colourful models and tableaux, inc the Great Hall of Statues; snacks, shop; cl am Mar and Apr and wknds Nov-Mar, wkdys Nov-Feb; £2.50. The CHURCH OF ST LAWRENCE is interesting, on the site of an Iron-Age fort, and again adapted by Dashwood. The view from the top of the tower is impressive. The George & Dragon in the middle of this attractive NT village is good for lunch.

Whiteleaf Cross SP8203 is a large ancient hill cross dug out of the chalk on the Chilterns escarpment, above which is a neolithic barrow. The Red Lion below is good for lunch.

Wooburn Green SU9188 GLASS CRAFT Glass-craft centre in 300-year-old converted barn, with demonstrations of glass-blowing and production of stained glass; they do one-day courses. Snacks, shop, limited disabled access; cl Mon, Christmas; *£2.

Boating on the Thames Marlow Reach is lively and attractive, and a good centre for trips in either direction (see East Berkshire chapter): IPG Marine here (0628) 476800 hires rowing boats £6, and silent electric launches (6-8 people) £20 hour (or 8-hour day £100). If you don't want to picnic on the boat, the Hare & Hounds a little way out towards Henley is now the best bet for lunch, though there are plenty of other decent pubs in Marlow.

This part of the county has a number of **attractive villages** with interesting things to see.

✝ Other **interesting churches** can be seen at **Fingest** SU7791 – famous for its huge Norman tower with a twin saddleback roof (the Chequers is nice for lunch); at **Stoke Poges** SU9983 where the churchyard inspired Thomas Gray's poem (he's buried here), and which has 17th-c stained heraldic glass in the 16th-c chapel; and at **Chalfont St Giles** SU9993 where there are retouched 14th-c wall paintings (the Greyhound is useful for lunch).

Bradenham SU8297 is a pretty village surrounded by ancient woodland.

★ **Other attractive villages**, with decent pubs, include Bledlow SP7702, Denham TQ0386, Great Missenden SP8901, Hambleden SU7886, Hyde Heath SU9399, Ibstone SU7593, Little Hampden SP8503, Marlow SU8586, Northend SU7392, Penn SU9193 (interesting church), Speen SU8399, Taplow SU9082, Turville SU7690 (lovely valley), and (despite the A40) West Wycombe SU8394.

Walks

Some would put this part of Buckinghamshire at the top of their personal list of favourite places for walks.

The well-wooded **Chilterns**, of which the finest tracts lie in Bucks, offer plenty of easy-going walks, with a good scattering of rural pubs and pretty villages, though sometimes you have to route walks carefully to avoid the numerous suburban developments. The escarpment where the hills drop sharply down to the plain gives some very distant views, for instance from above Bledlow SP7702 (good pub). The signposted Ridgeway takes in the most dramatic features, including **Coombe Hill** SP8506, the highest point in the Chilterns, with its Boer War Memorial on top (an excellent place for views – and for kite-flying). **Wendover Woods** with some well-marked nature trails are adjacent. The town of Wendover SP8607 gives nearby access, or you can follow paths from Ellesborough SP8306, and sneak views of Chequers, the Prime Minister's country retreat (emphatically private); an alternative path in is from Dunsmore SP8605 (decent pub).

Burnham Beeches SU9585 is a supreme example of a Chilterns beechwood, splendid in spring and autumn colours, and with maybe a glimpse of deer; maps are posted throughout the forest, but it is quite easy to lose one's bearings; the main starting-point is at East Burnham Common car park SU9584, opposite the W end of Beeches Rd at Farnham Common. Among several pubs dotted around the forest, one of the nicest for lunch is the Blackwood Arms on Littleworth Common SU9386.

A visit to the caves and village at **West Wycombe** SU8394 can be easily combined with a walk into the beechwoods just N; the pretty village of Bradenham SU8297 makes a good objective for longer circular walks.

Other places to start a Chilterns walk from (or finish at – all these have decent pubs) include Bolter End SU7992, Fawley SU7586, Fingest SU7791, Frieth SU7990, Hambleden SU7886, Hampden Common SP8401, Ibstone SU7593, Lower Cadsden SP8204, Northend SU7392, Skirmett SU7790, Wheelerend Common (SU8093; best for shortish potters) and Whiteleaf SP8104.

The **Chess Valley** TQ0098 shared with Herts is miniature and unspoilt, and accessible even without a car from Chalfont & Latimer station on the Metropolitan Underground line; Chenies, Latimer and, just over the Herts border, Sarratt are the villages to head for.

At Hedgerley SU9787 **Church Wood Nature Reserve** is managed by the RSPB, with over 80 species of birds in 34 acres. **Hodgemoor Woods** SU9693 W of Chalfont St Giles is an ancient woodland with three colour-coded nature trails. There's a good footpath along much of the **Thames** here (on either this bank or the opposite Berks one), and work is afoot to fill in the gaps. The footbridge over the weir at Hambleden SU7886 is attractive and the best starting point, and (besides Marlow itself) you can also get down to the river from Bourne End SU8985 and Taplow SU9082.

Driving

The byroads that take you through any of the villages mentioned above as attractive are worth while. The country lanes leading NW out of Chesham are all pretty. There are some good views from the B474 N of Beaconsfield (worth stopping in Penn for these). High Wycombe is best avoided.

Where to eat

For a special meal out, the three hotels heading the list of places to stay are (in order, and at a price) the first choice.

Amersham SU9597 HEDDON'S FRENCH CAFÉ (0494) 431491 Unlicensed restaurant with good atmosphere and food; cl 25 Dec. **£20**|£2.95/£6.

Skirmett SU7790 Old Crown (049 163) 435 Delightfully unspoilt village pub, imaginative food, popular restaurant, log fires, no-smoking tap room, pretty garden; cl Mon exc bank hols; no children under 10. **£20|£3.85/£9.**

Speen SU8399 Old Plow (0494) 488300 Wide choice of good food in bar and restaurant of this pretty country inn, decent wines, beamed rooms with cottagey decor, log fires; cl Sun pm, Mon; disabled access. **£20|£3.50/£5.95.**

Little Hampden SP8503 Rising Sun (0494) 488393 Imaginative food inc lovely home-made puddings in secluded upmarket dining pub, attractive terrace, good walking country; cl Sun pm, Mon Oct-Mar. **£19|£3.95/£8.**

Bellingdon SP9405 Bull (0494) 758163 Pretty old brick dining pub, innovative dishes, beams, fresh flowers, pretty garden; cl Sun pm, 25 Dec; disabled access. **£16.50/£5.50.**

Great Missenden SO8900 George (024 06) 2084 Attractive old place originally built as hospice for nearby abbey; beams, alcoves, big log fire, popular good value food, big secluded terrace; now has bedrooms; cl pm 25-26 Dec; disabled access. **£13.65|£1.25/£3.50.**

Wheelerend Common SU8093 Chequers (0494) 883070 Pleasant old pub with welcoming licensee, and wide range of bar food; cl Sun pm, Mon, pm 24-25 Dec; disabled access. **£12|£3.50/£6.**

Great Hampden SP8401 Hampden Arms (0494) 488255 Comfortable little two-room country pub by cricket green with good choice of well-presented food, friendly, efficient young licensees, good for walks; cl Sun pm, Oct-Feb; disabled access. **£10|£3.95/£5.25.**

West Wycombe SU8394 George & Dragon (0494) 464414 Striking partly Tudor inn in handsome NT village; lots of character, good bar food, big garden, bedrooms; near many places of interest. **£1.75/£5.50.**

North and West Buckinghamshire

Some splendid stately homes and landscape gardens, though countryside not special and there's little for younger people or families.

Off the main tourist track, this does have possibilities for a quiet and civilised break. The modest scenery is here and there punctuated by splendid landscaping around the several great houses which are the area's most striking attraction for visitors. These make this a rewarding area for people who enjoy stately homes; Ascott at Wing and Waddesdon Manor are both grand examples of the Rothschild family's remarkable combination of great taste with great wealth, and Stowe Landscape Gardens are among the world's finest. Chicheley Hall, and Claydon House at Middle Claydon, are also well worth visiting. There's a bit of walking – enough to keep strollers happy. The choice of places to eat out at and to stay in is reasonable though not outstanding.

Where to stay

Aylesbury SP8213 HARTWELL HOUSE Oxford Rd HP17 8NL (0296) 727444 ***£150.50**; 47 rms, some huge and well equipped, others with four-posters and fine panelling, and ten secluded suites in separate building with private garden and fine statues. Elegant, historic Grade I listed building with Jacobean and Georgian façades, wonderful decorative plasterwork and panelling, fine paintings and antiques, marvellous Gothic central staircase, and splendid morning room, library and dining room (excellent food); 80 acres of parkland with ruined church, lake and statues, and spa with indoor swimming pool, saunas, gym and so forth and informal restaurant; croquet, game fishing; children over 8; good disabled access.

Winslow SP7627 BELL Market Sq Buckingham MK18 3AB (0296) 714091 **£50**; 18 rms. Elegant black-and-white timbered inn with plush hotel bar, all-day coffee lounge, decent bar food, good restaurant food and wines, pleasant inner courtyard; disabled access.

Ashendon SP7014 RED LION Aylesbury HP18 0HB (0296) 651296 **£36**; 1 rm. Beautifully kept pub with good food, well-kept beers, garden; very handy for Waddesdon and Wotton House; cl Mon; no children.

To see and do

Aylesbury BUCKINGHAMSHIRE COUNTY MUSEUM These interesting old parish rooms are currently undergoing a massive refurbishment and many of the rooms will be closed until mid-1995. However, two of the bigger galleries are still open, one telling the story of life in Aylesbury since early times, and the other with various changing exhibitions. In the middle of 1994 they hope to be able to open their new Roald Dahl Children's Gallery. Shop, disabled access; cl 1.30-2, Sun, bank hols, 25 Dec, 1 Jan.

! **Boarstall** SP6214 DUCK DECOY Displays and working demonstrations of one of only three remaining 18th-c working duck decoys. Ducks today are lured into the pipes and ringed for migration info rather than eaten; also woodland walks and nature trail. Best to tel (0844) 237488 for opening times; NT. The Pheasant up at Brill (see below) is the nearest useful place we know of for lunch.

The windmill at **Brill** SP6513 is in a magnificent position right on the edge of the Chilterns, with distant views across Oxford (and places to picnic and a good pub nearby); there's been a mill on this site for over 700 years. The village itself is quietly attractive, too, and there's a decent walk along the ridge and down to Boarstall. As we've said, the Pheasant is good for lunch.

Buckingham SP6934 itself has quite a lot of attractive early 18th-c brick buildings, and much of the nostalgic charm of a once-important town that has been eclipsed by rivals (in this case Aylesbury and Milton Keynes), and has therefore been much less altered by development than would otherwise have been the case.

Chicheley SP9045 CHICHELEY HALL Particularly fine Georgian house with lovely plasterwork, panelling, and carving; also a naval museum (esp sea paintings), and gardens with 18th-c dovecot. Meals, snacks, shop, some disabled access; open pm Sun from Easter-end of May and in Aug; £3. The Swan at Astwood is a good nearby place for lunch.

★ **Long Crendon** SP6808 The cottages in the High St are very pretty, some little changed since the village was a rich wool centre in the 15th c. A particularly lovely timber-framed building is the early 15th-c

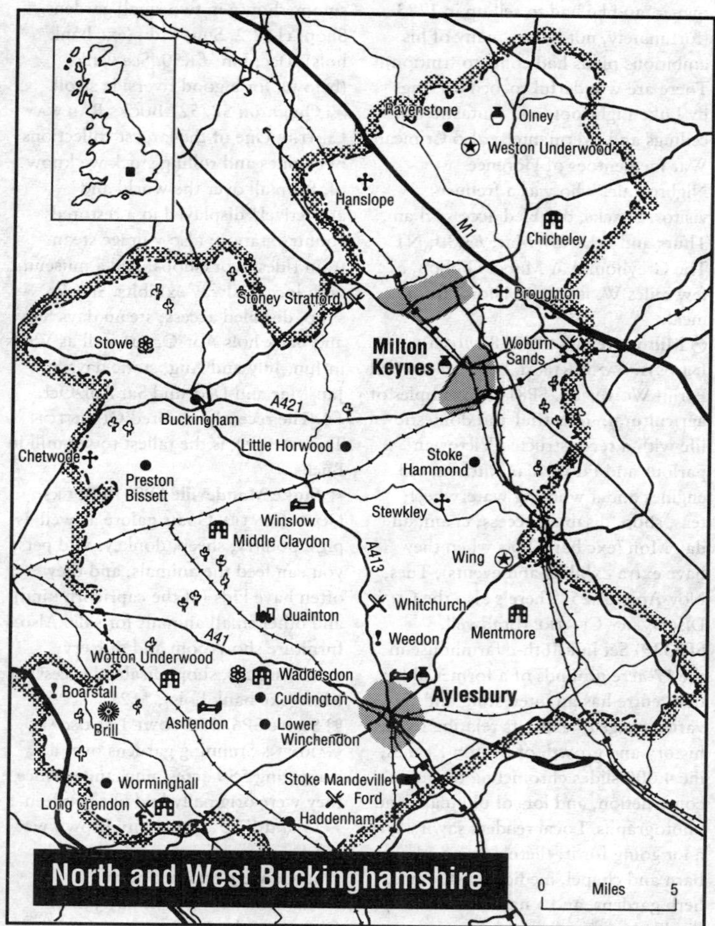

COURTHOUSE, probably built as a woolstore; open pm Weds, Sat, Sun and bank hols Apr-Sept; £1; NT. There are snacks in the nearby church house, and two decent (and pretty) pubs.

Mentmore SP9019 MENTMORE TOWERS An astonishingly grand mansion built in 1855 for Baron de Rothschild, its breathtaking grandeur giving a good idea of the family's wealth and power at the time. Designed by the architect of the Crystal Palace, the main rooms are assembled around the Grand Hall soaring up past the arcaded galleries to an elaborate cornice. Other rooms are similarly dramatic, with the sumptuous decor looking like a cross between an Italian palazzo and Versailles in France. In Sept there's a fireworks concert in the grounds; open only Sun 2.30-4.30; *£2. The Stag, built for the Rothschilds' estate, is a civilised place for lunch.

Middle Claydon SP7125 CLAYDON HOUSE The extravagant plans for the decor of this mainly 18th-c house eventually bankrupted the original owner, and he had to sell up in 1783 (fortunately, not before many of his ambitious plans had come to fruition). There are wonderful rococo carvings by Luke Lightfoot, and fantastic walls, ceilings and overmantels; also Crimean War mementoes of Florence Nightingale, who was a frequent visitor. Snacks, disabled access; cl am, Thurs and Fri, Nov-Mar; £3.30; NT. The Greyhound at Marsh Gibbon, a few miles W, is a good choice for a meal.

Milton Keynes SP8938 MUSEUM OF INDUSTRY AND RURAL LIFE (Stacey Hill Farm, Wolverton, SP8141) Examples of agricultural, industrial and domestic life with a reconstructed Victorian parlour and Edwardian kitchen, old engines and a working waterwheel; teas, shop, disabled access; cl am, all day Mon (exc bank hols when they have extra exhibits and events), Tues, Nov-Apr; £1.25. There's also the CITY DISCOVERY CENTRE (Bradwell, SP8339) Set in a 16th-c farmhouse in the 17-acre grounds of a former abbey, this centre has an interesting and varied range of exhibits relating to the history and growth of Milton Keynes, inc 4,000 slides chronicling the town's construction, and lots of old maps and photographs. Local readers say it's got a lot going for it; there's also a 14th-c barn and chapel, medieval fishponds, herb gardens, and a nature trail. Shop, disabled access; cl wknds (exc last Sun in month in summer), bank hols and Christmas-New Year – best to book yourself in on (0908) 227229 or (0908) 312332.

Olney SP8851 This pleasant stone-built extended village has the enthusiastically run COWPER MUSEUM, home from 1768-1786 of hymn-writer William Cowper, and now displaying various of his personal possessions, manuscripts and poems (and some belonging to his friend John Newton, curate of Olney and composer of *Amazing Grace*). Also fine lace exhibition, costume gallery, and summerhouse in two small gardens. Shop; cl 12-2, Sun, Mon (exc bank hols), Dec, Jan; £1.50. See walks (below), for a good riverside stroll.

Quainton SP7521 BUCKS RAILWAY CENTRE One of the largest collections of engines and rolling stock we know of, from all over the world and attractively displayed in a restored country station; also vintage steam-train rides, workshops, and a museum with local railway exhibits. Snacks, shop, disabled access; steam days Sun and bank hols Apr-Oct as well as Weds in Jun, July and Aug; static days Sun Jan-Mar and Dec, and Sat Apr-Oct; £4. The recently restored QUAINTON TOWER MILL is the tallest tower mill in Bucks.

Stoke Mandeville SP8310 BUCKS GOAT CENTRE Goats galore as well as pigs, poultry, sheep, donkeys and pets; you can feed the animals, and they often have kids (of the capricorn kind) and other small animals for sale. Also a furniture showroom and nursery; meals, snacks, shop, disabled access; cl Mon (exc bank hols); *£2.

Stowe SP6837 STOWE LANDSCAPE GARDENS Stunning gardens over a staggering 580 acres, unchanged since they were originally laid out between 1713 and 1775. Capability Brown was head gardener for ten years, and the grounds were adorned with monuments and temples by James Gibb, Sir John Vanbrugh and William Kent; the lovely mansion is now a public school. Snacks, shop, some disabled access. The opening hours are horrendously complicated, but roughly the grounds are open during school hols and also Mon, Weds and Fri throughout the year (exc Christmas). The house is open pm daily exc Sat during the Easter hols (exc Easter week) and summer hols (exc bank hol wknd); £3.50 grounds, £2 house. For confirmation of opening times, ring (0280) 813650. The Bull & Butcher at Akeley has a decent buffet lunch.

Waddesdon SP7417 WADDESDON

MANOR This late 19th-c Renaissance-style chateau built by Destailleur for Baron Ferdinand de Rothschild has been closed for restoration recently, so the parts that reopen at Easter 1994 should be at their finest. The ground floor and Bachelor's wing will be ready by then, with the rest of the house completed by the next year. The late Victorian formal gardens surrounding the house are quite splendid, and there's also a cast-iron rococo aviary (still in use). From this year too you should be able to go round the fabled wine cellars; snacks, shop, disabled access; open Mar-Oct, Weds-Sun and bank hols, though house cl Fri (exc in July and Aug), and Weds following a bank hol; *£3 grounds, with an extra *£3 for house (*£3.50 on Suns and bank hols) and *£1 for wine cellar. NT.

★ ! **Weedon** SP8118 Lovely little village with 17th- and 18th-c houses, including LILIES, a fine country house absolutely full of antiquarian books for sale – a must for bibliophiles; visits only for people intending to buy; cl Sun and bank hols; tel (0296) 641393. The White Swan in nearby Whitchurch is good for lunch.

Weston Underwood SP8650 FLAMINGO GARDENS AND ZOOLOGICAL PARK A lovely bird collection in fine surroundings, with unusual pink-backed pelicans, vultures, cockatoos, and toucans and mammals such as bison, llamas and white wallabies – as well as the flamingos. Shop, disabled access; cl am, Mon (exc bank hols), Tues and Fri (exc in July), Oct-Easter; £3.50.

† **Wing** SP8822 ASCOTT A lovely old house, again once the property of the Rothschilds, and filled with treasures such as Ming and K'ang Hsi porcelain, paintings by Hogarth, Rubens and Gainsborough, Dutch art by Hobbema, Cuyp and others, and French and Chippendale furniture. The 260-acre grounds have extensive gardens with many rare trees and shrubs. Some disabled access; house open pm mid-May-Sept exc Mon; gardens open Weds pm and last Sun of month Apr-Sept; *£5, *£3 garden only. NT. ALL SAINTS CHURCH has a fine monument to Sir Robert Dormer (died 1552), a 10th-c apse, crypt and nave, and 12th-c font. Mentmore is just to the south.

Wotton Underwood SP6815 WOTTON HOUSE Restored 18th-c house built to the same design as Buckingham Palace, with the park redesigned by Capability Brown. Small groups only, with guided tours at 2 and 3.15 on Weds in Aug and Sept only; *£2.

† **Interesting churches** include the one at STEWKLEY SP8525 which has good examples of late Norman work (two decent pubs here), BROUGHTON SP8940 for its retouched 14th-c and 15th-c wall paintings, CHETWODE SP6429 where there's some fine early glass and Early English windows, and at HANSLOPE SP8046 where the spire is higher than most in the county. A less traditional place of worship is KEACH'S MEETING HOUSE, WINSLOW SP7627, the oldest non-conformist chapel in the county.

For **children to let off steam** MOUNT FARM LANE has a lakeside children's play area, pitch and putt course, tennis courts, and wildfowl. WILLEN LAKESIDE PARK SP8241 (Brickhill St, Milton Keynes) actually has two lakes – one with water sports, hotel and restaurant, and the other for birdwatching. There's also a Japanese peace pagoda built by Buddhist monks, a turf maze, and nature trail.

You can book hour-long BALLOON TRIPS over the whole county from Stewkley SP8526; they cost £110 and only two people can go up at a time.

★ **Attractive villages** include Lower Winchendon SP7312, a secluded old place with carefully restored houses and a charming, simple church. The walk over the hill to Upper Winchendon gives interesting views.

Others, all with decent pubs, are: Cuddington SP7311, Haddenham SP7408, Little Horwood SP7930, Preston Bissett SP6529, Ravenstone SP8450, Stoke Hammond SP8829, Weston Underwood SP8650 and Worminghall SP6308.

Walks

Mildly undulating at best, this is not vintage walking territory, but there are pockets of minor interest for gentle strolling. Bucks County Council publish a series of circular walks (free from information centres, or from the County Hall, tel (0296) 382845). These include a 4½-mile route from **Thornborough Bridge** SP7233 on the A421, taking in a mill, the site of a medieval village, and the Buckingham Arm Canal.

Shabbington Wood SP6210 nr Oakley over on the W of the county has been designated a Site of Special Scientific Interest because of its rich butterfly habitats; a special butterfly trail has been created to help you spot some of the 40-odd species here.

There is reasonable scope for village-to-village walks such as those around Brill SP6513, Waddesdon SP7417 and Quainton SP7420. The last two are on the 30-mile **North Bucks Way** from Chequers Knap above Great Kimble SP8205 to Wolverton SP8140 in Milton Keynes; this includes the prominent viewpoint of **Quainton Hill** SP7521.

Milton Keynes SP8938 has several walks with local beauty spots and points of historical interest; leaflets available locally. There are good footpaths to nearby lakes from the Swan pub in the Old Village.

The **riverside** walk to Olney from the Robin Hood pub at Clifton Reynes SP9051 (or vice versa) is short but attractive, passing an old mill.

Several decent **canalside** walks include ones between Great Linford (SP8542; good family pub) and New Bradwell (SP8341; another pleasant pub); or at Marsworth, where there's an imposing flight of locks, and a family pub at Startops End SP9214; or near Stoke Hammond SP8829 (lockside pub).

The grounds of Stowe and Waddesdon Manor mentioned above are fine places for undemanding walks.

Driving

This part of the county has a fair variety of different landscapes, with modestly hilly country and some good views along the quiet country road NW from Aylesbury, through Quainton and Edgcott to Marsh Gibbon (where there's a good pub); and off the A41 just E of Waddesdon, turning S through Upper Winchendon to Long Crendon then right along the B4011, turning right off it to Brill and then back up to the A41 via Ludgershall. The B4033 S from Stony Stratford through Great Horwood to the pleasant small market town of Winslow is also a decent drive. Milton Keynes itself is beginning to mature, and as it's been so thoughtfully laid out with concern for its surrounding landscape is surprisingly pleasant to drive around – certainly not a place to avoid if your route looks like passing that way.

We welcome reports from readers . . .

Readers who help us with reports for the GUIDE are offered a discount on the next edition: so please do help if you can!

Where to eat

Stony Stratford SP7940 UMBRELLAS (0908) 567527 Pleasant, firmly run, very good fish restaurant. **£28**|£9.75; cl Sat lunch, all day Sun, bank hols; disabled access.
Woburn Sands SP9235 SPOONERS 61 High St (0908) 584385 Smart, pretty restaurant with good value French and English cooking, welcoming atmosphere; good value snacks downstairs; cl Sun/Mon, Christmas wknd, 1 week summer; disabled access. **£22.95**|£2.50/£5.75.
Ford SP7709 DINTON HERMIT (0296) 748379 Cosy, tucked away little stone pub, good home-made lunchtime bar food, more elaborate evening menu; no food Sun, Mon pm; disabled access. **£20**|£2/£5.
Long Crendon SP6908 ANGEL Bicester Rd (0844) 208268 Friendly dining pub with fresh, well-prepared food, esp fish; cheery young staff. **£20**/£4.25.
Whitchurch SO8020 WHITE SWAN (0296) 641228 Homely partly thatched old pub, very cheerful atmosphere and friendly service, good simple bar food; big garden. Fairly handy for both Waddesdon and Quainton. **£11.50**|£2.95/£5.

Help this year from: *Marjorie and David Lamb, B R Shiner, TBB, Mr and Mrs R J Fawthrop, David Surridge, Mr and Mrs A Noke, John Radford, Chris Cook, M J Hydes, Gwen and Peter Andrews, Mr and Mrs David Harvey, C D and M D Craigen, Howard Catiss, E G Parish, Jeff and Rhoda Collins, M and T Errington, Mr and Mrs T F Marshall, Dave Carter, Margater Drazin, Paul and Margaret Baker, P and J Roberts, Lyn and Bill Capper, Dr and Mrs Rackow, Pat and Derek Westcott.*

BUCKINGHAMSHIRE CALENDAR

Some of these dates were provisional as we went to press.

FEBRUARY

15th **Olney** Pancake Race, *the oldest in the country*

MARCH

Aylesbury Arts Festival – *phone Tourist Board for dates (0296 395000)*

APRIL

Long Crendon Mystery Plays

2nd **Great Kimble** Point-to-Point races

3rd **Chalfont St Giles** Chiltern Open Air Museum Spring Celebrations – *Mon too*

19th **Hughenden** Primrose Day, *on the anniversary of Disraeli's death (primroses being his favourite flower)*

MAY

1st **Lower Winchendon** May Day Ceremony; **Wycombe** Carnival

8th **Haddenham & Ford** Fraw Cup Sunday, *village festival including picking the last fritillaries, if any can be found*

14th **Wycombe** Arts Festival – *till 12 Jun*

15th **Chalfont St Giles** Chiltern Open Air Museum Transport Festival

29th **Chalfont St Giles** Music & Dance Through the Ages *at Chiltern Open Air Museum – Mon too*

Buckinghamshire Calendar

June

18th **Marlow** Regatta

23rd **Cliveden** Open Air Theatre Shakespearean Festival – *till early July*

24th **Newport Pagnell** Festival – *Sun too*

26th **Wendover** Carnival, *inc Horse Show & Gymkhana*

July

High Wycombe Swan Upping on the Thames – *phone Tourist Board for dates (0494) 421892*

9th **Aylesbury** Carnival

15th **Stoke Mandeville** Chiltern Show, *Chiltern Acres Showground, themed agricultural and horse show, only in its second year, inc music festival – till Sun*

16th **Newport Pagnell** Carnival – *Sun too*

17th **High Wycombe** Half Marathon

22nd **Stowe** Horse Trials, *Stowe Landscape Gardens – some 500 competitors at all levels, as well as a Dog Agility Challenge and other activities – till Fri*

25th **RAF Halton, nr Aylesbury** Air Show (*may be moved to the next weekend)*

29th **Stowe** Music & Fireworks *in the lovely landscaped gardens – till Sun*

August

28th **Chalfont St Giles** Museum Alive *at Chiltern Open Air Museum – Sun too*

29th **Winslow** Horticultural Show, *Public Hall*

September

1st **Weedon** Buckinghamshire County Show

3rd **High Wycombe** Show, *Wycombe Rye Meadows – Sun too*

October

16th **Buckingham** Charter Fair – *also on 23 Oct*

November

5th **Downley** Torchlight Procession and Bonfire, *procession starts at the War Memorial Hall*

11th **Fenny Stratford** Firing of the Fenny Poppers *at St Martin's*

December

3rd **Chalfont St Giles** Victorian Christmas Weekend *at Chiltern Open Air Museum – Sun too*

26th **Winslow** Boxing Day Hunt Meet, *Market Square*

CAMBRIDGESHIRE AND BEDFORDSHIRE

Apart from Woburn Abbey and Whipsnade, the area does not have an abundance of commercially exploited tourist attractions, and its scenery is generally too flat for great scenic interest. This does mean that, for the most part, it's not trampled by troupes of tourists, so many of the interesting places which it does have are not overrun with visitors.

There are several very pretty villages – and many more where a patient stroller with an eye for detail can pick out quite a lot of interest. The best of the countryside for walkers is up on the Dunstable Downs in Bedfordshire, though other parts are refreshing, such as the rolling farmland in parts of what used to be Huntingdonshire, and the swelling gallops towards Newmarket east of Cambridge. There's a melancholy open-sky grandeur about the dead level open fen country in the north of the area, especially in autumn or winter.

The city of Cambridge itself is the predominant reason for most people for coming here, and is a rewarding place for a short stay.

CAMBRIDGE AND THE SOUTH

Britain's most attractive ancient university city, with some good places for family excursions outside.

The city's pulse really quickens when the centre is filled with students during the university terms. There's altogether more peace for a leisurely look around in the (much longer) vacations. In the summer, when it is host to foreign students, its popularity with coach tours means that particular places can suddenly be flooded with herds of visitors, so perhaps the best time of all is spring or autumn.

Outside the city, the zoo at Lynton, the remarkable collection of aircraft and other fighting equipment at Duxford, and the stately Wimpole Hall are the pick of the area's attractions, and the M11 makes them good destinations for family outings from London. An older couple might well find plenty of other things to fill a quiet weekend.

Where to stay

Six Mile Bottom TL5757 SWYNFORD PADDOCKS Newmarket Suffolk CB8 0UE (063 870) 234 £107; 15 individually furnished rms with good bathrms. Gabled mansion in neat grounds with carefully furnished panelled rooms, log fire, relaxed atmosphere, and friendly service; tennis, putting, croquet.

Cambridge TL4658 CAMBRIDGE LODGE Huntingdon Rd CB3 0DQ (0223) 352833 **£65**; 11 rms. Edwardian house with comfortable rooms and good, freshly prepared food.
Eltisley TL2659 LEEDS ARMS The Green St Neots Huntingdon PE19 4TG (048 087) 283 **£42.50**; 9 rms, some in separate block behind. Tall white inn overlooking village green, attractive bars, big winter log fire, good value, popular food, and pleasant garden; disabled access.

To see and do

Cambridge Ancient and graceful university buildings dominate the centre, which is now largely pedestrianised (even the students' bicycles are banned from many areas during the day). More than any other town in England, it gives a real sense of centuries-spanning thought and learning. Though there's quite a bit of mostly hi-tech light industry towards the outskirts, the centre – unlike Oxford's – seems almost untouched by the outside world. It would be a shame not to see at least one of the colleges, and the Fitzwilliam Museum is very special. The Botanic Garden has a lot of unusual plants in fine surroundings.

COLLEGES The finest is Trinity, where the imposing Great Court is open to the public (the porters may intervene if you go into pretty Nevilles Court or New Court without looking as though you belong; the river's just beyond). Kings is probably the best known, with its magnificent chapel; pleasant to walk through and over the bridge. Gonville & Caius (pronounced 'keys') is small and snooty but very pretty. Peterhouse is the oldest; the buildings carry their years very gracefully and it has a park. St Johns has the very photographed Bridge of Sighs. Jesus, a bit off the main beat, is huge and grandly impressive, and Emmanuel has notable gardens. The Backs are the grounds behind many of the colleges, running down to the slow River Cam: very serene, shaded by tall trees. Some colleges may have a small charge for admission.

Almost any stroll through the central streets will give you numerous other things to look at. Between the colleges and university buildings are numerous less imposing but attractive old buildings, often grouped together quite picturesquely – a row of old-fashioned shops perhaps, or a cluster of very varied but harmonious houses. Quite a few shops are that bit different and worth popping into.

Don't try to drive around; there really is no parking, and apart from the pedestrianised centre there's a frustrating tangle of one-way streets. Head for one of the big NCPs. If you don't plan to take a car at all, it's worth noting that the bus station's a good deal more central than the train station. For a first-time visit, the TOUR BUS is good (about an hour), and does go along the Backs, too.

FITZWILLIAM MUSEUM (Trumpington St) This imposing building is one of Britain's oldest museums, and in its early days was open only to those members of the public considered properly dressed. These days it's rather more up-to-date, particularly in the way it displays its fine exhibits. These include Greek, Egyptian, and Roman antiquities, European ceramics, English glass, carvings, and armour; paintings include works by Titian, Canaletto and French Impressionists. Decent café, shop, disabled access (they prefer prior notice); cl Sun am, all day Mon, 24 Dec-1 Jan, Good Fri; wkdys lower gallery cl pm, upper gallery cl am.

UNIVERSITY BOTANIC GARDEN (Cory Lodge, Bateman St) The site has grown since the garden's foundation in 1762, and now covers 40 acres with some marvellous mature trees, a geographic rock garden, a scented garden, water and winter gardens, and many rare plants inc several National Collections. Rarely crowded, so it's pleasant to stroll through. Snacks, shop, disabled access; cl 25-26 Dec; glasshouses cl lunchtime; *£1.50.

Cambridge & County Folk Museum (2-3 Castle St) Former 17th-c inn now exploring the everyday life of people in the region over the last few centuries; lots of rooms display items from tools through toys to tea caddies. Regular craft days; shop, disabled access to ground floor only; cl Sun am, winter Mon, 24 Dec-2 Jan, Good Fri; *£1.

Kettle's Yard (Castle St) Set out as a private house with fascinating 20th-c paintings and sculptures, lovely 18th-c furniture and oriental carpets, and collections of shells and stones; there are interesting St Ives connections. Shop; cl am, Mon.

Museum of Classical Archaeology (Sidgwick Ave) One of the few surviving collections of casts of Greek and Roman sculpture; shop, disabled access; cl wknds, Easter, Christmas.

University Museum of Archaeology & Anthropology (Downing St) The story of man's development to the present day; world-wide coverage with emphasis on local and British archaeology. Shop, disabled access; cl am exc Sat, Sat pm, Sun, 24 Dec-2 Jan, Easter week, Aug bank hol.

Scott Polar Research Institute (Lensfield Rd) The international centre for Polar studies, with Arctic and Antarctic expedition displays (an emphasis on Captain Scott), Eskimo arts and crafts, and wildlife displays. Shop, disabled access; open 2.30-4 only, cl Sun, some bank hols, Fri before Christmas-2 Jan.

✝ Of the many lovely churches here, it's worth noting St Benet's, one of the city's oldest, the popular Holy Sepulchre or Round Church, and St Mary the Great's with its fine roof and good city views from the tower (another place with good views is Castle Mound, beyond Bridge Street, which has an indicator to pick out the sights).

There are lots of secondhand bookshops worth a look; Heffers children's bookshop is particularly good, and the general bookshops are as fine as you'd expect from this university town. On the first Sat of the month there's a Craft Fair on St Johns Green.

Attractive Snack Places include Clowns (King St, off Sidney St), a relaxed Italian café, with newspapers and posters of what's on; the Roof Garden (top floor of Arts Theatre – side entrance in St Edwards Passage opposite Kings), which is simple, with white conservatory and garden looking over the town; Boards, down a floor, for teas and enterprising snacks sharing big tables – it's licensed, with evening meals; the tiny Little Tea Room (All Saints Green), willow-pattern crockery, big fruit cakes; the Copper Kettle (Kings Parade – very central), roomier, with brown decor, teacherish cups and saucers, decent pastries; the Kings Pantry (Kings Par), rather cramped basement but well worth knowing for delicious interesting (often vegetarianish) food – snacks from breakfast on, more meals in the evening; Browns (Trumpington St) roomier than most, airy, ceiling-fan-colonial look, bustling short-skirted waitresses and burgers/pasta/steaks.

Decent Riverside Pubs include the Anchor (Silver St; specially useful as there's a good punt hire place just behind it, around £4 an hour; they will supply a boatered student to do the work for you; another place to hire punts is Scudamores), Boat House (Chesterton Rd), Fort St George (Midsummer Common), Pike & Eel (Water St, Chesterton) and Spade & Becket (Thompsons Lane). The best pub away from the river is the Free Press (Prospect Row), though the

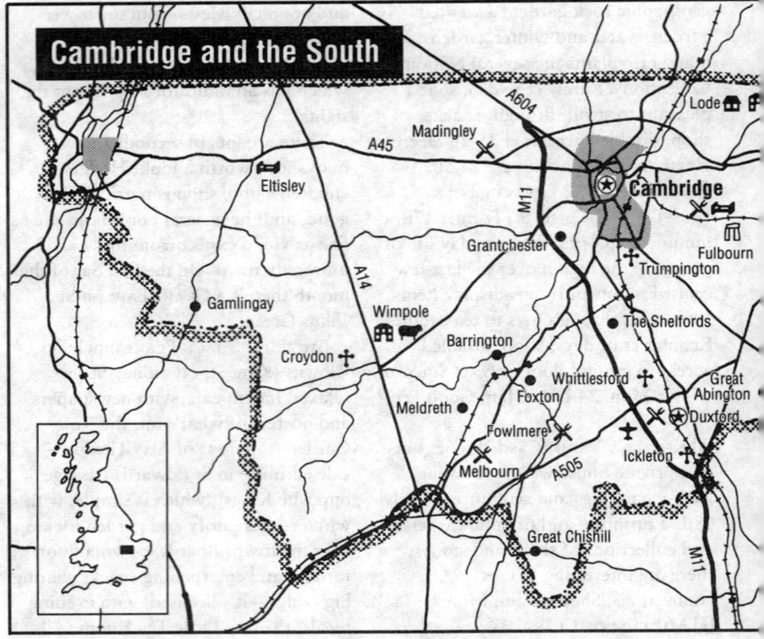

recently reopened Eagle (Bene't St) has a good deal of atmosphere.

Cyclists might like to know that the towpaths here are enjoyable to ride along, nettle-free, and safe if you have children with you.

Other things to see and do

Duxford TL4846 DUXFORD AIRFIELD Europe's best collection of military and civil aircraft, with tanks and other vehicles too, and an extremely hi-tech simulator (they prefer the more dramatic name of dynamic motion theatre). Other features inc the prototype Concorde, naval exhibits (plus a midget submarine), a summer narrow-gauge railway, pleasure flights, and an adventure playground. Lots to do, and don't worry about the weather – most exhibits are under cover. Outside they often fly historic aircraft. Meals, snacks, shop, disabled access; cl 24-26 Dec, 1 Jan; £5.80. The John Barleycorn is good for lunch.

Lode TL5362 ANGLESEY ABBEY The priory here was founded in 1135, though little survives from then except for a medieval undercroft. The later 17th-c house has a number of pictures and is surrounded by really lovely Georgian-style gardens, laid out by the first Lord Fairhaven. The grounds also have a WATERMILL, restored to working condition and once again milling flour. Meals, snacks, shop, disabled access; cl Mon and Tues, all Oct-mid-Mar; £2.50.

Linton TL5646 ZOOLOGICAL GARDENS (Hadstock Rd) Billed as Cambridgeshire's wildlife breeding centre, the emphasis here is on conservation, with the creatures

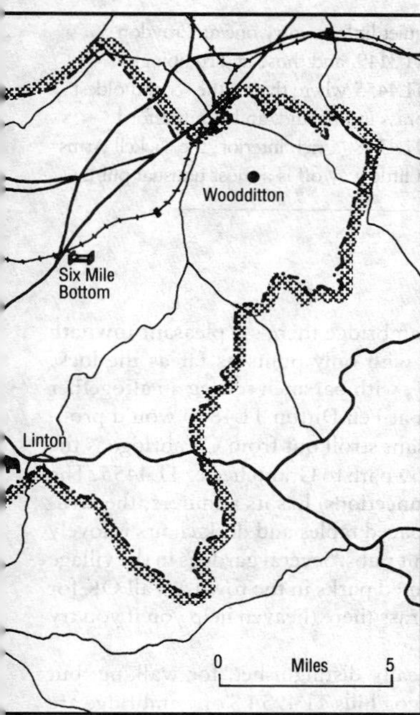

housed in enclosures as close to their natural habitats as possible. Unusual threatened species from around the world, with animals inc giant tortoises, snow leopards, Sumatran tigers, spiders, snakes and birds, all in acres of nicely landscaped grounds. Snacks, shop, disabled access; cl 25 Dec; £3.50.

Wimpole TL3351 Wimpole Hall Easily one of the most striking mansions in East Anglia, mainly 18th-c with imposing and harmonious Georgian façade, lovely *trompe l'oeil* chapel ceiling, and rooms by James Gibbs and Sir John Soane. Best of all are the 360 acres of parkland, designed by several different notable landscapers inc Capability Brown and Repton; the remains of a medieval village are under the pasture. Meals, snacks, shop, disabled access; cl am, Mon, Fri, Nov-Mar; £4.50. NT. Wimpole Home Farm Thatched and timbered buildings designed by Sir John Soane in 1794, when it was one of the most advanced agricultural sites in the country. Farm machinery and tools displayed in restored barn, rare farm animals, heavy horse wagon rides, children's corner and woodland play area. Meals, snacks, shop, disabled access; cl Mon, Fri; £3.50. NT.

★ **Villages** worth stopping at include Barrington TL3949, with its superb village green, attractive timbered houses, interesting church and a good pub, and nearby Foxton TL4148 is well worth a visit if you've brought *The Common Stream* by Rowland Parker as weekend reading (an intricate account of the village through the ages). Fulbourn TL5156 is an attractive largely thatched village, with a windmill on the Cambridge rd, and a pretty church; a path E takes you to the wooded line of the Fleam Dyke, a miles-long Dark-Age defence earthwork. Ickleton TL4943 has a fine church, with Roman columns as bases for its arches, and interestingly carved pews. The churchyard is lovely, and around the church and small green are several beautiful old houses – often a good deal older, in fact, than their Georgian refacing suggests. The Shelfords TL4652 will reward a slow stroll for those with an eye for architectural detail, and even a quick drive through will show up several delightful timbered houses. Other attractive villages include Linton TL5646, Meldreth TL3746, and (all

We welcome reports from readers . . .

Let us know what you think of places in the Guide, and any special tips you have. There are report forms at the back of the book, and a card in the middle.

with decent pubs) Eltisley TL2659, Gamlingay TL2452, Great Abington TL5348, Great Chishill TL4239 (well-restored windmill), and Woodditton TL6659.

✝ **Churches** worth visiting include the quiet little country one at Croydon TL3149, and those at Trumpington TL4455 where there's the second oldest brass in England, and Whittlesford TL4748 (a rich interior; the Tickell Arms a little way off is a most unusual pub).

Walks

From Magdalene Bridge in the city of Cambridge there's a pleasant **towpath walk** out into the meadows – tranquil, with only punts as far as the lock. Beyond that, you could walk as far as Ely, with oarsmen setting an altogether more vigorous tone – though the Plough at Fen Ditton TL4860 would probably weaken your resolve. Another pleasant stroll out from Cambridge is the walk from Mill Lane along the meadow towpath to **Grantchester** TL4455. The village (apart from its Rupert Brooke connections) has its admirers; the civilised Orchard Tea Gardens with widely spaced tables and deck chairs is lovely in summer, and there are a couple of decent pubs. Several gardens in the village open on 24 Jun. The various quaintly named parks in the town are all OK for strolling, and you can at least sit on the grass there (heaven help you if you try that in the colleges).

The surrounding countryside is not really distinguished for walking, but there are some possibilities. The **Gog Magog hills** TL4954 S of Cambridge are worth a passing visit; among tall trees you can trace the main rampart and ditch of Wandlebury Iron-Age fort, and there are good views of the city's distant towers and spires. Though it's not much of a topographical feature, and is crossed by one or two busy roads, the miles-long ancient embankment known as the **Devil's Ditch** E of the city lets you fuel a walk with thoughts of whether it was built to fight off the Romans, or some centuries later to protect the riches of East Anglia from Midlands warlords. A good start would be from the B1061 N of Dullingham TL6357 (where there's a good pub; there's another at nearby Woodditton TL6659).

Near Little Gransden TL2755 is **Hayley Wood** TL2952 which has a huge variety of wildlife; its hedges, trees and other plants have been little disturbed since the 13th c if not earlier.

Driving

The M11 and the A45 are generally fast and trouble-free. The A11 can have long queues and is not a pleasant road. On the whole the countryside here is too flat for interesting pleasure drives. There are one or two bright spots, such as the long-winded A14, an old coaching road on Roman foundations which carries little traffic now; and the A1304 towards Newmarket, passing handsome rolling gallops and the immaculate paddocks of top stud farms.

Where to eat

Cambridge TL4658 MIDSUMMER HOUSE (0223) 69299 Close to the river, with several small prettily furnished eating areas, imaginative French cooking, good wines; cl 1 Jan, Sat am, Mon am, Sun pm. £35.70|£13.60 (2-course lunch).

Also, see the places recommended above for snacks in Cambridge – many of these do decent meals too.

Melbourn TL3844 PINK GERANIUM Station Rd (0763) 260215 Pretty 16th-c thatched cottage with good sophisticated cooking, a homely, relaxed atmosphere, and cottagey garden; cookery courses too; cl Sun pm, Mon, 26 Dec; no children late evening. **£30|**2 courses £14.95.

Madingley TL3960 THREE HORSESHOES (0954) 210221 Smart, thatched dining pub, nicely decorated small dining area, attractive conservatory, good, well-presented food (popular summer buffet); pleasant village; cl evenings 27 Dec-3 Jan, restaurant cl Sun pm. **£25|**£2.50/£7.

Fowlmere TL4245 CHEQUERS (0763) 208369 Civilised old coaching inn with smartly dressed waiters, ambitious food in galleried restaurant, good puddings, excellent wines; log fire in bar, conservatory, attractive garden. **£22|**£3.50/£4.30.

Duxford TL4745 JOHN BARLEYCORN (0223) 832699 Pretty, early 17th-c thatched country pub, attractively furnished, quietly chatty bar, popular, good food, courteous service; fine hanging baskets and flower-filled back garden; no children. **£14.50|**£3.90/£7.

NORTH CAMBRIDGESHIRE

Civilised old hotels and inns, good food, some fine old buildings, but the countryside is generally very flat with little for young people.

A break in this part of the county might suit older people best, with some very civilised places to stay in, decent food, and cathedrals, churches and other fine buildings to look at. The fen country has a lot to offer bird watchers, who would also enjoy the waterfowl gardens at Peakirk. Otherwise, the flat silt fens and huge working fields reclaimed from the marshes can make much of the countryside rather monotonous – though some people love its misty bleakness in autumn, say. To the west, the land's drier and more rolling, with stonebuilt villages more reminiscent of Leicestershire. Ely with its graceful cathedral is the area's gem, though Wisbech also has much to repay a visit. The area can be very chill in winter.

Where to stay

Huntingdon TL2371 GEORGE George St PE18 6AB (0480) 432444 **£95.90**; 24 well-equipped rms. Fine galleried courtyard in old posting house, quietly elegant, comfortable lounge.

Huntingdon TL2371 OLD BRIDGE 1 High St PE18 6TQ (0480) 52681 **£95**; 26 excellent rms. Creeper-covered Georgian hotel, log fire in panelled bar, smart modern lounge; imaginative food, extensive wine list, quick, courteous service; riverside gardens.

Wansford TL0799 HAYCOCK Peterborough PE8 6JA (0780) 782223 **£89**; 51

attractively decorated rms. Old-fashioned, character-filled golden stone inn, relaxed, comfortable, carefully furnished lounges and pubby bar; pretty lunchtime café, smart restaurant with good food, excellent wines and efficient, friendly service; garden with boules, fishing and cricket. The little village it dominates is attractive, with a fine bridge over the Nene, and a good antique shop.
Ely TL5380 LAMB 2 Lynn Rd CB7 4EJ (0353) 663574 £75; 32 decent modern rms. Former coaching inn opposite cathedral, pleasant small lounge.
Needingworth TL3472 PIKE & EEL St Ives Huntingdon PE17 3TW (0480) 463336 £55; 6 rms. Very peaceful riverside spot with spacious lawns and marina, roomy, plush bar, big open fire and easy chairs in smaller room; glass-walled restaurant, good breakfasts, friendly staff.
Stilton High St TL1689 BELL Peterborough PE7 3RA (0733) 241066 **£45w**; 19 rms. Elegant, splendidly restored coaching inn combining authentic old-fashioned features with modern conveniences, attractive courtyard. Stilton cheese originates from here and is still on excellent menu; cl Christmas wk.

To see and do

Buckden TL1967 BUCKDEN TOWERS For centuries these grand old buildings were the palace of the Bishops of Lincoln, and a regular stopping point for other notable personages on their travels; perhaps the most famous (if least willing) guest was Henry VIII's first wife Catherine of Aragon, imprisoned here in 1533. The Civil War had a typically adverse effect on the site, and its later history has been rather chequered, but today it has returned to ecclesiastical hands and is being carefully restored. The 15th-c Great Tower and Gatehouse are particularly worth a look, as are the gardens, which are being reconstructed along 16th/17th-c lines. Shop, disabled access; cl Mon and Tues; donations appreciated. The rest of the village is attractive too.
Ely TL5380 is a busy little market town with good shops and some lovely old buildings – well worth a leisurely stroll around. After the Norman Conquest it was a centre of Anglo-Saxon resistance under Hereward the Wake. The main feature is the CATHEDRAL, one of England's most striking; its distinctive towers dominate the view from the surrounding countryside, esp coming in on the Soham rd. Completed by the late 12th c, it was restored in a surprisingly sympathetic manner mainly in the mid-19th c; features not to miss include the Lady Chapel, the lovely west front, Norman nave, fine stonework, and the Monks Door out to the medieval buildings. Most remarkable perhaps is the Octagonal Tower, over 400 tons suspended in space without any visible means of support; meals, snacks, shop, disabled access; £2.60. The unique STAINED GLASS MUSEUM is housed here to care for fine medieval and more modern stained glass rescued from redundant buildings and churches; various styles are displayed, and models show how the windows are made. Worth a visit – a bonus is the unusual views it gives of the cathedral; shop; cl Sun am, wkdys Nov-Feb exc some school hols; *£1.50. The good ELY MUSEUM in the High St has interesting displays on the history of the city and its people, inc an exhibition on Hereward the Wake, some vintage racing bicycles and a video with fascinating early footage; shop; cl 1-2.15, all day Mon, Christmas week; £1. The tourist information centre is in a fine old house that from 1636 belonged to Oliver Cromwell and his family, and several rooms are furnished in period style. There's also a video on the draining of the fens; cl winter Suns, 25-26 Dec, 1 Jan; £1.50 for exhibitions. They have details here of a route around the area

called the Cromwell Trail, taking in a number of other places in the county with Cromwell connections. The Cutter out at Annesdale off the A10 is an attractively placed riverside pub.

Hamerton TL1379 HAMERTON WILDLIFE CENTRE A recently opened centre, and already a favourite of several of our correspondents, providing sanctuary to over 120 different kinds of animal, with enclosures of meerkats, wallabies, marmosets, gibbons and many more unusual species, most of them in family groups. Among the weird and wonderful creatures they have the only breeding group of two-toed sloths in the country. Snacks, shop, disabled access; cl Christmas; £3.50.

Huntingdon TL2371 has grown considerably in recent years but one of its finer buildings is The George, a particularly handsome Georgian coaching inn. CROMWELL MUSEUM (Grammar School Walk) Commemorating the earlier of Huntingdon's two most famous MPs, this restored Norman building was where the future Lord Protector went to school (as did Pepys), and many of his possessions are on display. Shop, disabled access (though you'll need a hand getting inside); cl 1-2, all day Mon, 24-26 Dec.

Peakirk TF1606 PEAKIRK WATERFOWL GARDENS Perhaps best visited in spring when there are lots of baby birds, this water garden has over 100 different species of waterfowl inc rare and unusual breeds, all in a lovely setting; a good outing even if you're not exactly a twitcher, fascinating if you are. They sell corn in the gatehouse but if you have any spare bread, take that along to feed them – they seem to prefer it. Good snacks, shop, disabled access; cl 24-25 Dec; £2.50. The Ruddy Duck is good for lunch.

Peterborough TL1999 has preserved much of its long history and fine old buildings, though it expanded hugely in the mid-1970s and is now a thriving industrial town (with a good pedestrianised shopping centre). LONGTHORPE TOWER A 13th/14th-c fortified house with rare wall paintings; cl winter wkdys and 25-26 Dec, 1 Jan; £1.20. CITY MUSEUM AND ART GALLERY Detailed models made by Napoleonic prisoners of war held at Norman Cross prison camp, local history and archaeology displays, ceramics and glass; snacks, shop; cl Mon and some Sats. The CATHEDRAL has a marvellous west front and a very fine early 13th-c painted wooden nave; Cromwell is said to have looked on approvingly here as prayer books were torn up and the organ was smashed. ST MARGARET'S CHURCH in the suburb of Fletton has some exceptionally fine little Anglo-Saxon sculptures. FLAG FEN (2 miles E) is the site of a large Bronze-Age village – you can watch archaeologists painstakingly uncovering more of it (summer only). Displays of recent finds inc some ancient domestic animals, and there are several reconstructed buildings. Snacks, shop, disabled access; cl 25-26 Dec; £2.80.

Ramsey TL2885 ABBEY GATEHOUSE The ruins of an ornate Gothic gatehouse with buttresses and friezes, along with the 13th-c Lady Chapel (all that's left of the abbey itself); cl Nov-Mar. Some of the stone from the abbey is thought to have made up the RAMSEY MUSEUM, which has rural and agricultural exhibits and several reconstructed rooms and shops; snacks, shop, disabled access; open pm Thurs and Sun Apr-Sept, or by appointment, tel (0487) 813285.

Thornhaugh TF0600 SACREWELL FARM AND COUNTRY CENTRE A very busy place, based around an old working watermill, telling the story of farming and country life over the last few generations. Demonstrations and displays of rural crafts, tools and machinery, as well as gardens, maze and nature trails, lots of animals and pick-your-own fruit in season; snacks, shop, disabled access; £1.50.

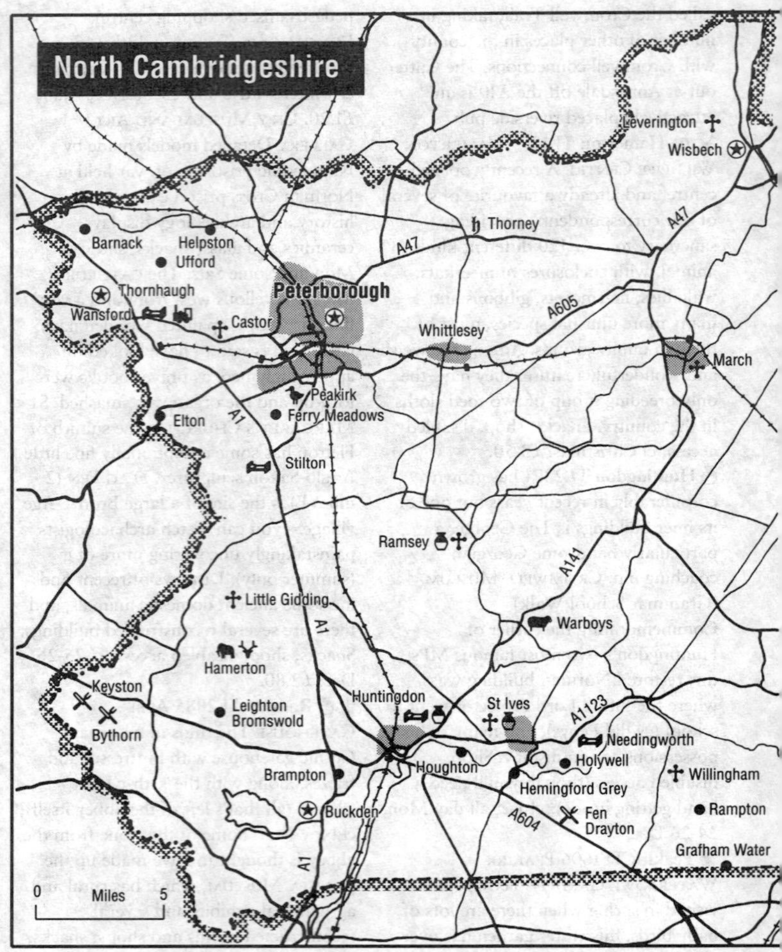

Thorney TF2804 rises from the flatlands like an island – which it was, when this was all half-submerged marsh. Much older than most villages in the area, it has a Norman-modified Saxon church on its green, and some interesting yellow-brick workers' houses put up by the Duke of Bedford. The HERITAGE CENTRE has good displays covering Thorney's long history, and organises tours of the village and abbey; shop, some disabled access; open pm wknds Apr-Oct and Weds pm Jun-Sept, or by appointment, tel (0733) 270006; the heritage centre is free, tours are £1.

Wansford TL0799 NENE VALLEY RAILWAY If this place looks uncannily familiar, it's because the site is a favourite with film makers – you may recognise it from the James Bond film *Octopussy*. Steam train rides through delightful countryside, fine collection of steam locomotives and rolling stock, small museum, and special events. Snacks, shop, disabled access; best to phone for train times (0780) 782854; £1 site admission, £5.50 for the train. The Haycock is particularly good for lunch.

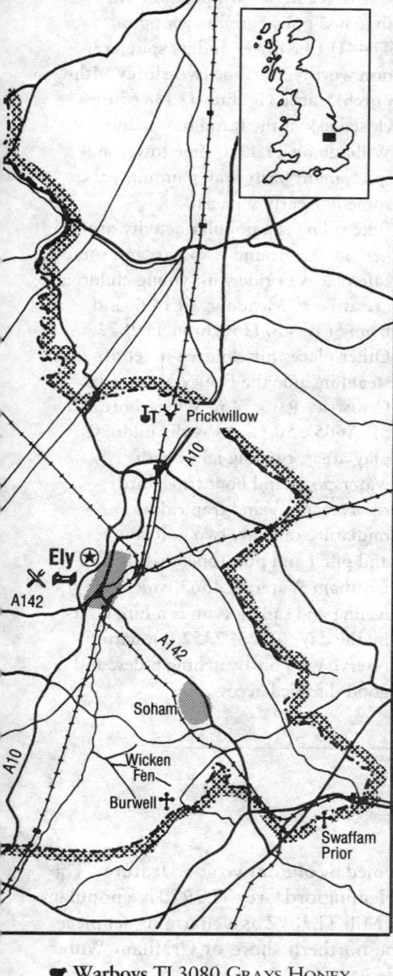

Warboys TL3080 GRAYS HONEY FARM (5 miles NE, off A141) A buzzing little place with exhibitions on the industrious little honey bee (inc an ingenious explanation of how bees communicate) and special hives to show her in action. Snacks, shop (with all kinds of honey-based products), disabled access; cl Sun, and Dec 24-Apr; *95p.

★ **Wisbech** TF4609 PECKOVER HOUSE Lovely early 18th-c house with rococo decoration, contemporary art exhibitions, and a two-acre Victorian garden with kitchen garden and greenhouses – where orange trees are still fruiting after 250 years. Afternoon tea; house open pm Weds, Sun and bank hols, garden open pm Sat-Weds, both cl Nov-Mar; £2.30, £1 garden only.

WISBECH & FENLAND MUSEUM Interesting displays covering local history and archaeology, geology and natural history, with good collection of ceramics, Parish Registers and lots of books inc early manuscripts. Interesting pictures inc old photographs of the local woad industry – which kept going till this century. Shop; cl Sun, Mon, Christmas. The North Brink along the River Nene has handsome Georgian houses (the Red Lion and the Rose are both decent pubs).

★ **Other attractive towns and villages** worth stopping at incl St Ives TL3171, a pleasant little town, with walks by the curving river (there's an unusual tiny chapel on the old bridge), graceful church, and small local museum. Hemingford Grey TL2970 is a charming village with a peaceful view of the church over the willow-bordered river (the odd church tower is the result of its spire being lopped off by an 18th-c storm); one stone house among the thatched brick ones is Norman and said to be England's oldest. Nearby Hemingford Abbots is also pretty. March TL4197 is pleasant, and a good base for exploring the Fens. The church with its wonderful angel roof was described by Betjeman as being 'worth cycling 40 miles in a headwind to see'. There's also a wonderful roof on the church at Isleham TL6474. Barnack TF0704 has interesting dotted-about clusters of stonebuilt houses, a windmill, a part-Saxon church, and a fine pub (the Millstone); for Burghley House see Leics chapter. There's also Brampton TL2170 (decent pub in converted watermill), Burwell TL5866, Helpston TF1205 (John Clare's village), Holywell TL3370, Leighton Bromswold TL1175 (decent pub too), Elton TL0893, Rampton TL4268, Swaffham Prior TL5764 (two churches sharing same churchyard;

decent pub), Ufford TF0904, and Whittlesey TL2797 (decent pubs).

This part of the country is particularly rich in **windmills** and **watermills**, and apart from the ones already mentioned fine examples can be found at Burwell TL5866, Houghton TL2871 (lovely building in pretty setting; the Jolly Butchers nearby is a decent family pub), and Soham TL5973, one of very few English villages where two mills still survive.

More industrial heritage at the PRICKWILLOW ENGINE TRUST MUSEUM at Prickwillow TL5892, with a collection of the equipment used to drain the fens; it's being redeveloped so details and prices for 1994 are provisional, but likely to be cl am, all day Mon and Oct-Mar. An example of what the fens looked like in their original undrained state can be seen at WICKEN FEN TL5670, the oldest nature reserve in the country; there's a windpump here too.

✝ Some interesting **churches** include those at Burwell TL5866 (handsome, airy building with fine oak roof), Castor TL1298 (two pleasant old thatched pubs here), Leverington TF4411 (the tower and its spire are noteworthy, as is the two-storey 14th-c porch), Little Gidding TL1382 (if closed ask at the farmhouse), and Willingham TL4070 (fine tower and spire, many early wall paintings, and some fine early screens).

Bike riding is a popular activity around here as the ground is so flat, and some safe places to ride with young children are at Ferry Meadows TL1497 and from St Ives to Houghton TL2872. Other places for **children to let off steam** include the FERRY MEADOWS COUNTRY PARK (4m W Peterborough off A605), 500 acres with children's play areas, two big lakes with watersports and boat trips, bird reserves, pony and trap rides, miniature railway, two golf courses and pitch and putt (open to all), and Grafham Water TL4363 which has fishing and sailing (you can hire boats by the day; (0223) 235235), nature reserve with birdwatching hides, and good disabled access.

Walks

The overall impression of flatness is redeemed by one or two good features. The **River Ouse** between St Ives TL3171 and Hemingford Grey TL2970 is a popular wknd stamping-ground, with Houghton Mill TL2872 as a charming set piece. An attractive waterside path follows the northern shore of **Grafham Water** TL1468, the huge reservoir NW of St Neots.

Wicken Fen TL5075 (NT) has a remarkable range of plants and insects, with good nature trails (one for wheelchairs); carefully preserved as an example of what the fens were like before they were drained – you can see what a punishing place it must have been, to scrape a living from. From near **Whittlesey** TL2799 you can walk along the Hereward Way (the Dog in a Doublet pub on B1040 is good).

Monks Wood at Wood Walton TL2180 has quite a variety of moths and butterflies. The ancient woods such as **Knapwell Wood** TL3367 and **Papworth Wood** TL3362 have lovely spring flowers (a decent pub at Elsworth is handy for both). For bird lovers the Wildfowl Trust Refuge at **Welney** TL5993 has a floodlit lagoon and observatory from which you can watch the thousands of wintering Bewick's swans and varied waterfowl, and there are conducted summer evening walks, tel (0353) 860711 for details.

Driving

Several former coaching villages such as Stilton and Buckden strung along beside the A1 make quietly interesting diversions from it now that they've been bypassed. From Buckden, the byroad to the Offords and then Papworth St Agnes is worth the short detour. The A1 itself carries a lot of traffic without many holdups, as does the A604. The B660 N of Kimbolton (starting with a passing look at Kimbolton and Stonely) is a very old coaching road taking you through gently rolling riding country and past some attractive ancient timbered and plastered buildings. It's pleasantly traffic-free, like many of the area's B roads. In the flat fens, distant villages make themselves known with a spire or church tower peeking up over a clump of trees on the horizon – there are often several in sight at a time. The straight but narrow byroads look temptingly fast on the map, but you do tend to find yourself trundling along behind tractors from time to time – and fenland roads have a nasty habit, very pronounced on rainy nights, of planting a sudden and unexpected right-angled bend in your tracks.

Where to eat

Bythorn TL0575 WHITE HART (080 14) 226 Relaxed, stylish inn with a variety of comfortable styles and furnishings, very friendly, good set menu in no-smoking restaurant. **£20.50** 4 courses, **£15.70** two lunchtime courses.

Ely TL5380 OLD FIRE ENGINE HOUSE (0353) 662582 Former fire engine station next to cathedral with good English cooking, nice puddings, interesting wine list, large walled garden; also, an art gallery; cl Sun pm, 2 wks after Christmas; disabled access. **£20**|£1.40/£10.80.

Keyston TL0475 PHEASANT (080 14) 241 Pretty thatched former smithy, full of character, rewarding, unusual food, good puddings and wines. **£19.50**|£5.95/£7.95.

Fen Drayton TL3368 THREE TUNS (0954) 30242 Friendly thatched inn on banks of stream in pretty village, full of Tudor beams and timbers, two inglenook fireplaces, good bar food; disabled access. **£14**|£1.25/£4.50.

BEDFORDSHIRE

Two outstanding family attractions – Woburn Abbey and Whipsnade.

Between them, these could fill a long, happy and exhausting family weekend. Woburn Abbey in particular has a remarkable variety of interest for people of any age, and enough space to absorb lots of visitors without getting overcrowded. There's quite a wide range of other things for visitors, most notably gorgeous Luton Hoo, and the interesting collection of veteran aircraft at Old Warden.

Dunstable Downs offer decent walking and remarkable views, though otherwise the county's scenery is generally not memorable.

The brickmaking which has so scarred the countryside south-west of Bedford has had its positive side – many towns and villages which might otherwise not be at all special have a sort of friendly glow from their warmly attractive masonry.

Where to stay

Flitwick TL0335 FLITWICK MANOR Church Rd Bedford MK45 1AE (0525) 712242 **£62.50**; 15 big, comfortable, thoughtfully decorated rms. 17th-c country house with log fire in entrance hall, comfortable lounge, library with drinks, smart restaurant overlooking gardens, delicious food; tennis, putting, croquet; disabled access.

Leighton Buzzard SP9225 SWAN High St LU7 7EA (0525) 372148 **£60**; 38 rms. Handsome coaching inn with pleasant lounge, relaxed bars, attractive restaurant with English cooking.

Woburn SP9433 BELL Milton Keynes Bucks MK17 9QD (0525) 290280 **£50w**; 27 rms, mostly with bath. Lovely old inn with beamed bar and restaurant on one side of the street, and attractively decorated bedrooms (some with antiques); lounge and bar in Georgian part opposite; cl 25 Dec.

To see and do

Bedford TL0449 itself has riverside gardens and a few nice buildings, but is really a straightforward modern town. CECIL HIGGINS ART GALLERY & MUSEUM Furnished Victorian house with room settings, and fine collection of watercolours, drawings, local lace, glass and ceramics in award-winning extension. Shop, disabled access; cl am, Mon (exc bank hols). BEDFORD MUSEUM has various displays of local history, geology and wildlife, as well as a reconstructed 19th-c farmhouse kitchen, labourer's sitting room, and dairy, some fine archaeological pieces, children's displays, and temporary exhibitions. Shop, disabled access; cl Mon, Sun am, 25 Dec, Good Fri.

Elstow TL0546 Perhaps the county's finest village, with a very attractive core of fine old timbered houses by the green, inc the MOOT HALL, an outstanding brick-and-timber medieval market house with a collection of John Bunyan's works (he was born nearby), a reconstruction of his writing room with fine 17th-c furniture and other items related to him; shop; disabled access; cl Sun am, Mon (exc bank hols); small charge. The attractive church with its unusual detached tower has a *Pilgrims Progress* window.

Leighton Buzzard SP9225 LEIGHTON BUZZARD RAILWAY Originally built to carry sand in 1919, and now operating rare steam and diesel engines on passenger trains through gently varied countryside. Snacks, shop, disabled access; open Sun and bank hols Easter-end Sept, also some summer wkdys and wknds up to Christmas – best to phone for details on (0525) 373888; £3.50.

Luton TL0921 is a big relatively modern industrial town; it's quite a surprise to find here, neatly between the M1 and Luton Airport, a magnificent country mansion in 1,500 acres of parkland – LUTON HOO, started by Robert Adam, and grandly remodelled early this century for Sir Julius Wernher. It still has his rich

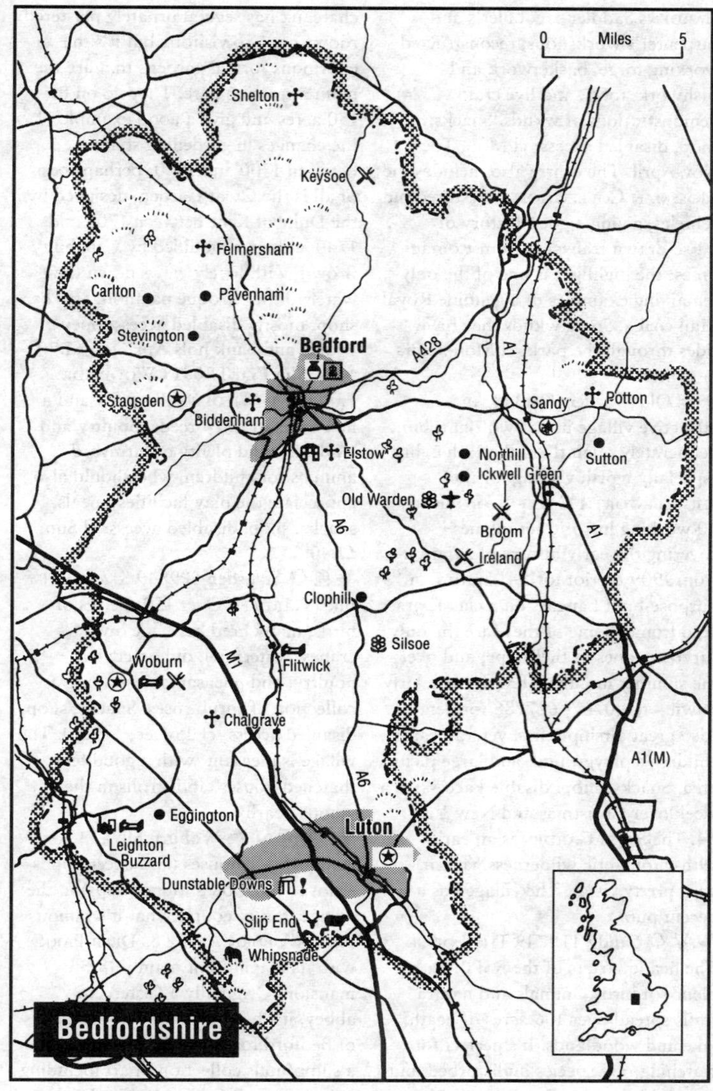

collection of furniture, Fabergé jewellery, tapestries, English porcelain, Russian royalty robes, and paintings. The grounds were landscaped by Capability Brown. Meals, snacks, shop, disabled access; cl Mon (exc bank hols); £4.50; garden only £2. You have to penetrate the town itself for LUTON MUSEUM & ART GALLERY (Wardown Park, Old Bedford Rd), a small Victorian mansion with local history and archaeology, lace-making, hat-making, a reconstructed street, children's gallery and a collection of the Bedfordshire & Hertfordshire Regiment. Snacks, shop, disabled access; cl 25-26 Dec, 1 Jan. STOCKWOOD CRAFT MUSEUM AND

GARDENS Saddler's, cobbler's and carpenter's workshops, reconstructed working forge, basketwork and rushwork, tools, and live craft demonstrations at wknds. Snacks, shop, disabled access; cl Mon, Tues, Nov-April. The centre also includes the MOSSMAN COLLECTION of restored old vehicles, giving a good history of horse-drawn transport from Roman times; the highlight is one of the only remaining examples of a genuine Royal Mail coach. Some wknds they have rides through the park; cl Mon-Thurs in winter.

Old Warden TL1343 An attractive village in its own right, built deliberately quaintly in the 19th c, but especially worth visiting for the SHUTTLEWORTH COLLECTION: nearly 40 working historic aeroplanes covering the early history of aviation from 1909 Bleriot to 1941 Spitfire in purpose-built hangars on a classic grass aerodrome. Some of these are the only surviving ones of their type, and over the summer months a few are regularly flown – tel (0767) 627288 for details. Also great airship relics, veteran cars, children's playground, and large picnic area. Snacks, shop, disabled access; cl a week over Christmas and New Year; £4. The SWISS GARDEN is an early 19th-c romantic wilderness garden, with pretty vistas. The village has a decent pub.

Sandy TL1749 THE LODGE The headquarters of the RSPB, with plenty of birds, animals and nature trails spread over 106 acres of heath, lake and woodlands. It's perfect for watching rare species undisturbed, but even if birdspotting's not your thing, this is a relaxing place to wander through, especially nice in spring when the woods are carpeted with bluebells. On Suns and bank hols there are pm guided tours; shop, some disabled access; cl Christmas-New Year; £2, free for RSPB members.

Silsoe TL0835 WREST PARK The 19th-c house inspired by French chateaux has several ornately plastered rooms open to visitors, but it's the enormous formal gardens that are the main attraction here. They go on for 150 acres and give a good example of the changes in gardening styles between 1700 and 1850; perhaps best of all is the Great Garden, designed by the Duke of Kent between 1706 and 1740 and later modified by Capability Brown, with lovely views down the water to the baroque pavilion. Snacks, shop, mostly disabled access; open wknds and bank hols Apr-Oct; £1.70.

Slip End TL0818 WOODSIDE FARM AND WILDLIFE PARK Six and a half acres of rare breeds, poultry and wildfowl, and plenty of farmyard animals for children, who should also appreciate the play facilities; meals, snacks, shop, disabled access; cl Sun; £1.40.

Stagsden SP9849 STAGSDEN BIRD GARDENS Over 150 species of birds, many bred here, inc owls, cranes, waterfowl, old breeds of poultry, and pheasants; also quite a collection of shrub roses. Snacks, shop, disabled access; cl 25 Dec; *£2.50. The village is pleasant, with a good few thatched houses, and strolls in the woods nearby.

★ **Woburn** SP9433 Some lovely 18th-c houses (and decent pubs – not to mention antique shops) in the village, but of course what it's famous for is WOBURN ABBEY & DEER PARK, with its magnificent mainly 18th-c mansion. Originally a Cistercian abbey, it's been the home of the Dukes of Bedford for over 350 years, and has a sumptuous collection of art including paintings by Rembrandt, Van Dyck and Gainsborough, lovely English and French 18th-c furniture and fine porcelain and ceramics. Outside, the 3,000 acres of parkland are populated by several varieties of deer, one of which was saved from extinction here; also a bird sanctuary, big antiques centre and mature trees. Meals, snacks, shop, disabled access (they prefer notice); cl Nov-Dec and wkdys Jan-Mar; *£6 (the antiques centre is 20p extra). WOBURN SAFARI PARK 300 acres of abbey parkland with the safari road travelling through an African plains area and tiger and lion enclosures, taking in along the way bears and monkeys, sealion, parrot and elephant shows, a pets corner, fairground attractions, cable railway and a boating lake. Meals, snacks, shop, disabled access; cl winter wkdys; £7.

Whipsnade TL0117 WHIPSNADE WILD ANIMAL PARK In a lovely downland setting, this enormous place has over 2,500 rare and endangered animals in big open paddocks, many of whom were born here. A steam railway can take you round (or you can take your own car), and as well as the usual animals there are daily demonstrations of birds from around the world and sealions and elephants at work; there's a very good children's zoo too. Meals, snacks, shop, disabled access; cl 25 Dec; £6.95. The Chequers and Old Hunters Lodge are the nearest decent pubs; the Red Lion at Studham is also quite close (with a common to stroll on).

★ ✝ **Interesting villages** include Shelton TL0368, where the pretty little cottages, Hall, and rectory are grouped around the quite delightful church, with 13th-c work inside, wall paintings, and a 14th-c font on seven legs. Felmersham SP9857 has a lovely church by a medieval tithe barn, and some other attractive old houses, with the river below. Nearby Pavenham SP9955 is also pretty, with a stroll down to the river. Sutton TL2247 is notable for its picturesque steeply humped packhorse bridge, looking more like a part of Devon or Derbys; ironically, cars have to use a more ancient crossing, the shallow ford beside it. A decent pub nearby is named after John o' Gaunt, the village's former owner. Other attractive villages include spacious Biddenham TL0249 (nice 12th-c church), Broom TL1743 and Northill TL1446 (all with good pubs), as well as Carlton SP9555, Clophill TL0837, Eggington SP9525 and Silsoe TL0835 (Wrest Park is a handsome chateau-style house with splendid landscaped gardens). Ickwell Green TL1545 nr Northill is well worth a look, too, with its colourful thatched houses around a broad green; Stevington SP9853 has a handsomely restored windmill, and a holy well opp the handsome church.

✝ Some other **churches** worth investigating include Chalgrave TL0027 and Potton TL2449 (it's the gravestones that are worth the visit).

! **Dunstable Downs** TL0019 let you watch GLIDERS being towed up by planes and returning on their own, at wknds or in summer; two car parks and lots of space to run around. And FIVE KNOLLS here is an important Bronze-Age burial mound, excavated by Agatha Christie's husband Sir Mortimer Wheeler and Gerald Dunning.

Walks

The **Dunstable Downs** TL0019 offer arguably the finest walk in Beds or Cambs, with great views from a spectacular escarpment path which can be linked in to a circuit incorporating Whipsnade village TL0018 and the nearby Tree Cathedral. Elsewhere the predominant interest for walkers is in the greensand country, with the long-distance **Greensand Ridge Walk** taking in Woburn Abbey SP9632 (a right of way crosses the park) and Ampthill Park TL0337 (surprisingly heathy but landscaped by Capability Brown, with lovely trees and a water-lily lake). The **Harrold-Odell Country Park** SP9657 also has a lake, with waterfowl (esp in winter), a nature reserve, and quite a few paths; decent pubs in both nearby villages. Summer is the best time to visit **Chicksands Wood** TL1439 for its butterflies, Chinese muntjac deer and varied flora. The ancient **Maulden Wood** TL0538 has a picnic site, marked walks, and more muntjac deer. **Sundon Country Park** TL0428 is sheep-cropped downland with good views and marked walks (some quite steep). Other after-lunchish walks are near **Eaton Bray** SP9620 (part of the Icknield Way Long Distance Footpath), near **Sharpenhoe** TL0630, and near **Shillington** (Aspley End) TL1232; all three places have decent pubs.

Driving

The road along Dunstable Downs and then through Totternhoe, Stanbridge and Egginton gives some fine views and is pretty, especially when the apple trees are out. The public roads through Woburn Park are very pleasant. Nowadays the A5 is a reasonably attractive alternative to the M1.

Where to eat

Woburn SP9433 PARIS HOUSE (0525) 290692 Half-timbered house in the Woburn estate (deer wandering about and lawns to enjoy aperitifs on); French cooking (good fish), decent wines, and relaxed, friendly atmosphere; cl Sun evening, Mon, Feb. **£20.50** lunch, **£34** evening|/£13.

Ireland TL1341 BLACK HORSE (0462) 811398 Busy, attractively refurbished beamed pub with interesting and generous food inc good fish dishes, nice restaurant; popular at wknds, so book; cl Mon, no food Sun evening; no children; disabled access. **£17**|£1.40/£4.75.

Keysoe TL0762 CHEQUERS (0234) 708678 Attractive pub with comfortably modernised beamed bars, consistently good food inc children's helpings, well-kept beer; cl Mon, 25-26 Dec. **£12.60**|£1.60/£6.30.

Broom TL1743 COCK (0767) 314411 Unspoilt 17th-c village inn with no bar counter and beers straight from the cask; decent lunchtime bar food esp good cheeses; some more elaborate evening dishes. £2.35/£6.30.

Help this year from: *Steve Goodchild, Frank Cummins, Gordon Theaker, Nigel Gibbs, Nigel and Sara Walker, Denise Plummer, Jim Froggatt, Barbara Hatfield, Wayne Brindle, Julian Holland, Michael Quine, M and J Back, Major and Mrs J A Gardner, Mrs M Lawrence, F J Robinson, Gwen and Peter Andrews, R C Wiles, Pauline and Martin Richardson, George Atkinson, Alan and Heather Jacques, Michael and Alison Sandy, Comus Elliott, Ron and Val Broom, Y Ou, Janet and Gary Amos, R F and M K Bishop, J Scotney, Roger Bellingham, Mary and Peter Clarke, M D Hare, Alan Burt, Stephen Brown.*

We welcome reports from readers . . .

Please send us your ideas for inclusion in the next edition: places to visit, eat at or stay in, attractive drives or walks, maybe even unusual interesting shops you know of. Use the card in the middle, the report forms at the end, or just write – no stamp needed: THE GOOD WEEKEND GUIDE, FREEPOST TN1569, Wadhurst, E Sussex TN5 7BR. Readers who help us with reports for the GUIDE are offered a discount on the next edition.

Cambridgeshire and Bedfordshire Calendar

Some of these dates were provisional as we went to press.

JANUARY

7th **Whittlesey** Straw Bear Festival

FEBRUARY

mid **Cambridge** University Lent Bumps – *similar races in Jun*

15th **Toddington** Shrove Tuesday Festival *on Conger Hill, village children gather to listen for the sound of the witch frying her pancakes as the clock strikes noon*

MARCH

19th **Peterborough** National Shire Horse Show, *at East of England Showground, with over 300 entries*

APRIL

1at **Riseley** Good Friday Cakes, *hot cross buns distributed by the vicar*

4th **Stockwood** Crafts Fair

MAY

1st **Ickwell** May Day Celebrations, *inc maypole dancing and stalls on the village green*

2nd **Stilton** Cheese Rolling; *also* Reach Fair, *an event held here for over 700 years*

9th **Leighton Buzzard** Beating the Bounds, *the choir marches from the Market Cross to the Almshouses, outside which a choirboy stands on his head while extracts from St Matthew's will are read*

14th **Bedford** Regatta, *on the River Great Ouse from 9.30 am – Sprint Regatta on Sun*

28th **Bedford** River Festival, *carnival weekend of watersports and activities – Sun too*

30th **Luton** Carnival Fair, *spectacular event with floats, stalls and live entertainment*

JUNE

4th **Cambridge** Strawberry Fair, *on Midsummer Common*

29th **Pavenham** Rush Ceremony *on the Feast of St Peter, recalling the annual renewal of rush floor coverings in the district*

JULY

3rd **Ely** Riverside Gala and Raft Race, *Willow Walk*

6th **Wisbech** Rose Fair, *East Anglia's main flower festival, based around St Peter's Church*

8th **Ely** Folk Weekend – *till Sun*

9th **Witcham** World Pea Shooting Championships

19th **Peterborough** East of England Show, *agricultural show at East of England Showground – till Thurs*

AUGUST

20th RAF **Alconbury** Air Display – till Sun

CAMBRIDGESHIRE AND BEDFORDSHIRE CALENDAR

AUGUST cont.

26th **Peterborough** Raft Race, *inc fancy-dressed entrants*

27th **Ely** Horticultural Show, *Newnham St – Sun too;* **Old Warden** Bedfordshire Festival, *Shuttleworth Estate, celebration of 1920s country life – till Mon;* **Quy** Fenland Country Fair – *Sun too*

SEPTEMBER

1st **Stamford** Burghley Horse Trials, *at Burghley House – till Sun*

4th **Dunstable Downs** Countryside Day

9th **Luton** British Craft Fayre, *at Luton Hoo – till Sun*

10th **Luton** Show, *at Stockwood Park – Sun too*

24th **Soham** Pumpkin Fair, *with fancy dress, clog dancing and car boot sale as well as the competition for the biggest pumpkin*

26th **Dunstable** 'Statty' Fair *at Vernon Place*

OCTOBER

9th **Ashton, nr Oundle** World Conker Championships *on green next to Chequered Skipper pub;* **Peterborough** Autumn Exhibition

11th **Shefford** Fair

NOVEMBER

5th **Cambridge** Bonfire and Fireworks *on Midsummer Common; more fireworks in* **Ely**, *in* **Luton**, *at Wardown Park, and in* **Springfields**

20th **Ely** Brass Band Championships of Cambridgeshire

DECEMBER

24th **Cambridge** Festival of Nine Lessons and Carols, *King's College Chapel*

We welcome reports from readers . . .

This GUIDE depends on readers' reports. Do help us if you can – in return, we offer a discount on the next edition to people who've helped us with reports for it. Tell us what you think about places already in it, and anything extra you think we should say about them. And send us your ideas for inclusion in the next edition: places to visit, eat at or stay in, attractive drives or walks, maybe even unusual interesting shops you know of. Use the card in the middle, the report forms at the end, or just write – no stamp needed: THE GOOD WEEKEND GUIDE, FREEPOST TN1569, Wadhurst, E Sussex TN5 7BR.

Cheshire

This is a rich county, and feels that way to visitors – its towns, villages and countryside leave a deep impression of well-looked-after, solid comfort. The scenery is attractively varied: a central plain of rich farmland, well broken up by woods, hedges and lakes, with splendid black-and-white timbered buildings; fine sandstone hills in the west; wilder steep moorland in the east. Chester itself is a glorious city to visit, full of interest, and on the whole the west of the county has most for visitors to enjoy, as well as the widest choice of good places to stay.

The east, though, does have a lot to discover. Former silk- and cotton-mill towns there such as Congleton, Macclesfield and Bollington have survived the shift of their industries to other countries without showing the stress and decay that's often marked such manufacturing changes elsewhere; all are pleasant places.

Throughout the county, an intricate network of canals takes in some of the most interesting scenery, with well-maintained towpaths. The modern industrial heartland is largely concentrated within a fairly self-contained and therefore easily avoidable area by the Mersey, with chemical works at Northwich and engineering around Crewe.

Chester and the West

Chester is a rewarding and richly preserved showpiece; attractive countryside studded with lovely villages, interesting places to visit, rather good walking, nice places to stay.

Chester itself is exceptional, with whole areas of beautifully restored and preserved timbered buildings within its partly Roman/medieval city wall – and yet plenty of up-to-date life. Its zoo is exemplary. Out in the country, narrow-boat canals and leafy lanes wind through pastures grazed by plump black-and-white cows or glossy-coated horses, villages have thatched black-and-white cottages, and romantic castles crown craggy wooded hills. Outside Chester, some of the most interesting places to visit include Britain's most spectacular garden centre at Bridgemere, the boat museum at Ellesmere Port, a vivid recreation of medieval monastic life in Runcorn, the botanic gardens at Neston, Arley Hall at Northwich, and romantic Peckforton Castle.

Where to stay

Chester SJ4166 Chester Grosvenor Eastgate St CH1 1LT (0244) 324024 **£196.15**; 86 well-equipped and individually furnished rms. Imposing half-timbered hotel with sumptuously furnished day rooms, relaxed cosy restaurant with imaginative food, and exemplary service; disabled access; cl 25-26 Dec.

Sandiway SJ6071 NUNSMERE HALL Tarporley Rd Northwich CW8 2ES (0606) 889100 **£120**; 32 attractive rms. Luxurious lakeside hotel on wooded peninsula with elegantly furnished lounges, wood-panelled cocktail bar, and a warm welcome; disabled access.

Nantwich SJ6552 ROOKERY HALL CW5 6DQ (0270) 610016 **£115**; 45 individually decorated rms. Fine early 19th-c hotel in lovely parkland with elegant lounges, log fires, intimate restaurant with enjoyable food, and friendly service; good disabled access.

Chester SJ4166 CRABWALL MANOR Parkgate Rd Mollington CH1 6NE (0244) 851666 **£100w**; 48 very comfortable, individually decorated rms. Partly castellated comfortable hotel in landscaped grounds with attractive lounge, very good, popular restaurant food, and friendly service; disabled access.

Sandbach SJ7661 OLD HALL Newcastle Rd CW11 0AL (0270) 761221 **£65**; 15 rms. 17th-c hotel with lots of panelling, friendly welcome, and popular restaurant; cl bank hol Mon.

Higher Burwardsley SJ5256 PHEASANT Chester CH3 9PF (0829) 70434 **£60**; 8 rms. Half-timbered old inn on top of Peckforton Hills, marvellous views, attractive old-fashioned bar, new conservatory, good food, lots of walks nearby.

Crewe SJ6755 CREWE ARMS Nantwich Rd CW1 1DW (0270) 213204 **£60**; 53 spacious rms. Sympathetically refurbished hotel with comfortable bar and lounge, spacious restaurant; close to station.

Weston SJ7352 WHITE LION Runcorn CW2 5NA (0270) 500303 **£57**; 17 comfortable rms. Relaxing 17th-c timbered inn, lots of exposed beams, friendly service, bowling green, wide range of popular food.

Cotebrook SJ5765 ALVANLEY ARMS Tarporley CW6 9DS (0829) 760200 **£50**; 2 rms. Handsome 16th-c creeper-covered farmhouse, garden with pond and geese, pleasant beamed bar, good food in vegetarian dishes.

Bickley Moss SJ5549 CHOLMONDELEY ARMS Malpas (0892) 720300 **£40**; 4 rms with showers. Airy converted Victorian schoolhouse close to castle and gardens, unusual atmosphere and furnishings, excellent imaginative bar inc choice of puddings and several vegetarian meals, interesting wines; disabled access.

Wettenhall SJ6261 BOOT & SLIPPER Winsford CW7 4DN (027 073) 238 **£40**; 5 rms with showers. 16th-c coaching inn with low beams, open fire, and relaxed atmosphere.

Higher Wych SJ4943 MILL HOUSE Malpas SY14 7JR (0948) 73362 **£30**; 2 rms. Very welcoming and friendly B & B in former farmhouse with relaxed atmosphere and good breakfasts – evening meals if requested; cl Christmas.

To see and do

Chester SJ4166 The city's old centre is ringed by a medieval TOWN WALL that's more complete than any other in the country and incorporates much of the original Roman one. You can walk the whole way round, enjoying marvellous views.

THE ROWS, which give the city's heart a magnificently Elizabethan look, are sets of ornamentally timbered two-storey shops – with open upper arcaded galleries – radiating from the central Cross. A particular charm of The Rows is that, besides being attractive to look at and charming to walk through, they include good shops (and a useful pub, the Boot, on Eastgate Row N). Some of Chester's most glorious timber-framed buildings are to be found in Watergate. There are more fine buildings jettied out over the pavement in Lower Bridge St (for instance, the late 17th-c Falcon, once a house used by the Duke of Westminster's ancestors but now a good pub), and in St Werbergh St off Eastgate (despite their Elizabethan look, built in the 1890s).

The beautifully vaulted CATHEDRAL has some marvellous medieval carving in and above the choir stalls. Unusually, at the Reformation its new dean (formerly the abbot of the Benedictine abbey which had been responsible for it) managed to preserve many of the former abbey buildings. So the precincts still include peaceful arcaded flagstoned cloisters, a medieval chapter house, and older Norman parts inc a refectory – fittingly brought back into use as a café. Meals, snacks, shop, disabled access. There are quiet cobbled Georgian lanes around Abbey Square, behind the cathedral a little way down Northgate.

ROMAN REMAINS include some broken Roman columns in a neat and peaceful garden running along the town wall by the gate at the bottom of Pepper St. Nearby is the excavated part of a very large Roman amphitheatre – probably big enough to seat nearly 10,000 people.

The GROSVENOR MUSEUM has an exceptionally well-displayed Roman collection inc an explanation of how the armies were organised and some ancient tombstones. There's also a Georgian house at the back with restored Georgian and Victorian rooms, as well as an art gallery, and displays of silver and furniture. Shop; cl Sun am, Good Fri, Dec 25-26.

The city's VISITOR CENTRE (Vicars Lane) has displays of the city's 2,000 years of history with videos and exhibitions, a recreated Victorian street, and a working pottery; tourist info desk and regular guided tours of the city. Meals, snacks, shop, disabled access to ground floor only.

Attractive VIEWPOINTS include the tree-shaded Groves looking out to the medieval bridge over the River Dee; and the bridge at the N end of Northgate, which gives a close view of the so-called Bridge of Sighs over the canal far below.

The CASTLE is now largely moated by car parks, but has some impressive buildings, both medieval and grand-manner late 18th-c.

CHESTER ZOO out on the city's N edge is the biggest in Britain, set in 110 acres of glorious gardens filled with rare animals in near-natural enclosures. Tropical house, chimpanzee island, penguin pool with underwater viewing panels, waterbus, a new overhead train zipping round the grounds, and children's farm. In summer there may be other attractions such as puppet shows and brass rubbings for children – a visit can easily last all day. Meals, snacks, shop, disabled access; cl 25 Dec; *£6.50.

Other things to see and do

! **Anderton** SJ6475 has a unique BOAT LIFT. Nearly 120 years old, this remarkable construction can simultaneously raise and lower two pairs of narrow boats in gigantic water tanks, bridging the 50ft drop between the Trent & Mersey Canal and the Weaver Navigation Canal.

Beeston SJ5459 BEESTON CASTLE A ruined 13th-c castle on a steep hill with wonderful views. Legend has it that Richard III left buried treasure here, and an exhibition tells of this and the rest of the castle's history. Shop; cl winter Mon, 25-26 Dec; £2. The pub of the same name is useful for lunch.

❀ **Bridgemere** SJ6352 BRIDGEMERE GARDEN CENTRE is a garden-lover's paradise – 25 acres of gardens (inc the WI cottage garden), plants, glasshouses, and garden furniture, with more plants in more varieties than anywhere else in Britain (indoor and outdoor), and professional help on hand for any sort of query. Best to visit in the morning before the coach parties arrive. Good meals and snacks, very good shop, disabled access; cl 25-26 Dec; free exc for garden kingdom, £1. Several contributors rate this as among the most worthwhile places to visit in the whole country. The BRIDGEMERE WILDLIFE PARK was closed as we went to press and is being redeveloped.

★ **Bunbury** SJ5758 WATERMILL Mid-19th-c mill that was worked until 1960; it was well restored in 1977 and now once again produces flour. Open pm wknds and bank hols Easter-Sept; £1. The village itself is attractive, with pretty cottages around the 14th-c church. There's another good watermill at **Stretton** SJ4553, with two ancient wheels turning the stones and exhibitions and displays on the milling process; cl am, all day Mon, wkdys in Mar and Oct and all Nov-Feb; £1. The Crewe Arms is useful for lunch.

Burwardsley SJ5156 CHESHIRE CANDLE WORKSHOPS You can watch individual hand-carved candles and glass figurines being made, and browse in the large craftshop; meals, snacks, shop, disabled access; cl Mon and Fri for around six weeks in the New Year. The Pheasant is good for lunch.

❀ **Cholmondeley** SJ5351 CHOLMONDELEY CASTLE GARDENS Pretty place with ornamental gardens, rare breeds of animals inc llamas, ancient private chapel, lakeside picnic area, and fine woodland and lakeside walks. Snacks, shop and plant centre, disabled access; open Sun and bank

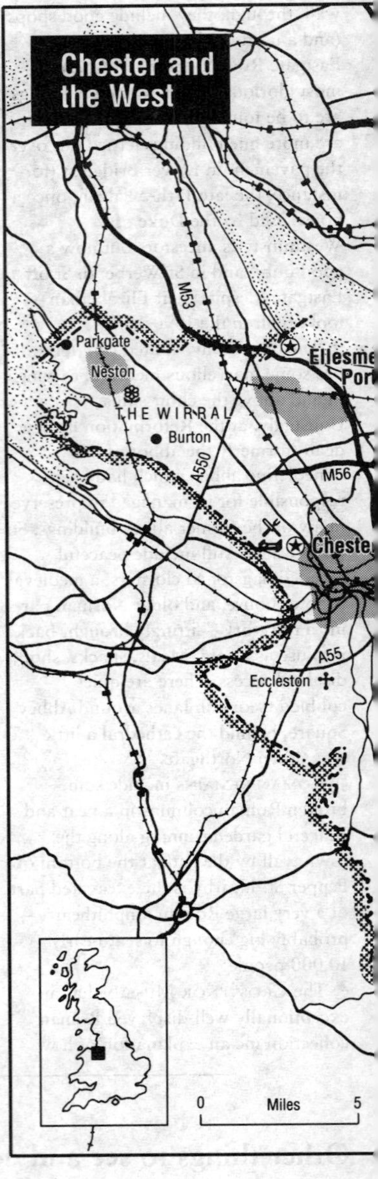

hols Apr-Sept; £2.50. The Cholmondeley Arms is excellent for lunch.

Crewe SJ7055 has changed a lot in the last decade or two, cleaned up and smarter, with bargains esp china in the

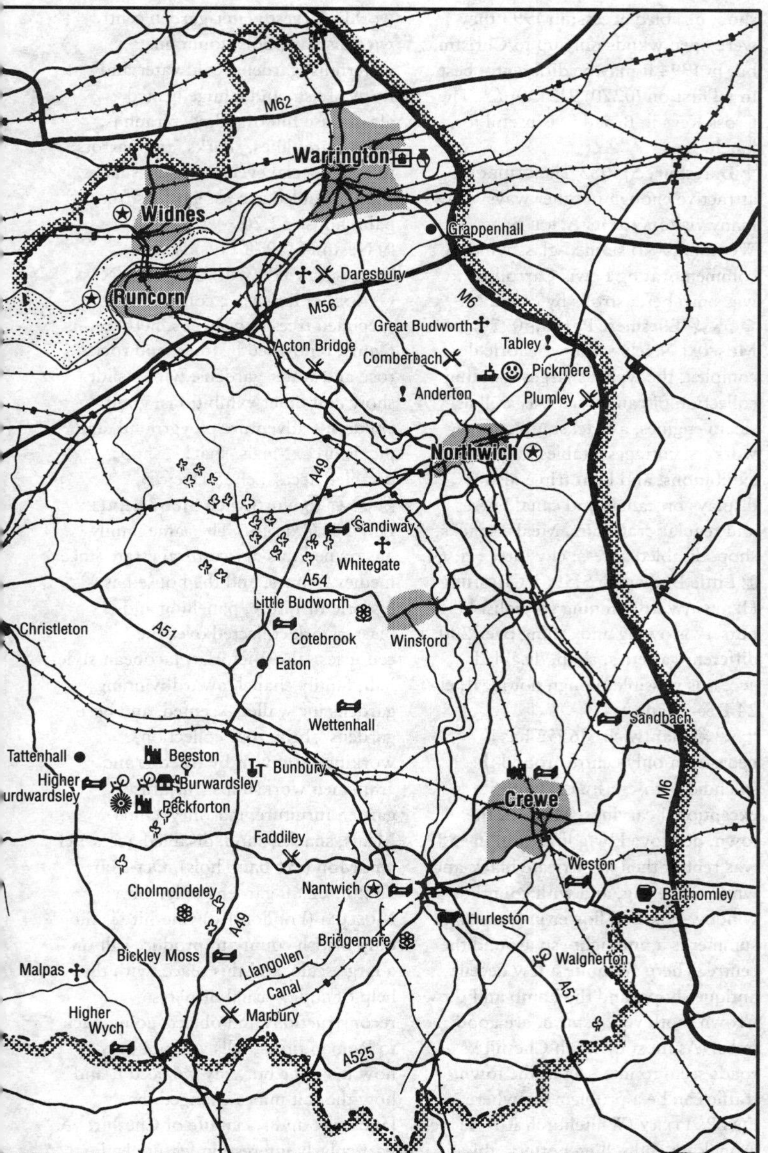

market, pedestrian centre, colourful Queens Park and useful foyer restaurant in Victorian theatre.

RAILWAY AGE (Vernon Way) Anyone who's ever travelled north by rail will be familiar with Crewe, and its long importance as a regional interchange is suitably commemorated at this developing exhibition, with displays, models, miniature and standard-gauge railways and restored diesel and, occasionally, steam engines. Snacks, shop, disabled access; in 1993 they were open wknds only up to Christmas but in 1994 it may be different – best to tel first on (0270) 212130; £2. The Cross Keys in Broad St is useful for lunch.

✝ **Daresbury** SJ5983 The CHURCH, attractive enough in other ways, draws many visitors for its ALICE IN WONDERLAND stained-glass window commemorating Lewis Carroll, who was born here; strolls by canal.

Ellesmere Port SJ4077 BOAT MUSEUM Nicely set in a historic dock complex, the world's largest floating collection of canal boats, as well as steam engines, a blacksmith's forge, workers' cottages, stables, big indoor exhibitions, and boat trips; also displays on canals and canal horses and regular craft fairs. Meals, snacks, shop, disabled access; cl winter Fri; £4.

Little Budworth SJ5965 CHESHIRE HERBS Award-winning specialist herb nursery growing and selling over 200 different varieties; shop, disabled access is possible though not ideal; cl 24 Dec-2 Jan.

✝ **Nantwich** SJ6552 has a pedestrian-only centre around the splendid 14th-c CHURCH, with its exceptional carvings. Much of the town, destroyed by a firestorm in 1583, was rebuilt then in intricate black-and-white timbering, and with countless window-boxes in flower in spring and summer is a fine sight esp around the centre. There are quite a few decent antique shops, and the Lamb and the Crown, both very central, are good pubs. (As most of south Cheshire's roads seem to intersect at the town, traffic can be a problem elsewhere.) FIRS POTTERY (Whitchurch Rd) As well as making and selling pottery, this friendly place also organises one-day workshops (half-days for children). Booking is essential, on (0270) 780345; £17 for a day course, inc lunch and tea and coffee. The Lamb is good for lunch. Off the A51 SE, STAPELEY WATER GARDENS is the world's largest water-garden centre with display pools, fountains, waterfalls, gardens, coldwater and tropical fish, and a huge heated glasshouse full of palms, piranhas, giant water lilies, sharks, and parrots; regular special events. Meals, snacks, shop, disabled access; gardens free, palm house £2.70.

Neston SJ2978 LIVERPOOL UNIVERSITY BOTANIC GARDENS (NESS GARDENS) Extensive collection of specimen trees and shrubs, herbaceous plants, renowned heather, and rock, rose and water gardens, with a slide show and other exhibitions; good children's adventure playground, and picnic area. Meals, snacks, shop, disabled access; cl 25 Dec; £3.

Northwich SJ6674 ARLEY HALL & GARDENS The same family has owned this agricultural estate since medieval times, and the house has historic furniture, panelling and plasterwork collected over the centuries; also Victorian Jacobean-style hall, family chapel, award-winning gardens inc walled, scented, and herb gardens, shrub rose collection, working-farm visit by tractor, and craftsmen workshops (furniture, garden furniture, masonry, china). Meals, snacks, shop, disabled access; cl am, Mon (exc bank hols), Oct-Mar; £3.20 , £2.60 gardens only. SALT MUSEUM (London Rd) Cheshire is the only British county to produce salt on a large scale, and this place, with the help of audio-visual displays, reconstructions and objects going back to Roman times, tells you not only how it's done but why we need it and how the salt mines changed the landscape and social life of Cheshire. A particularly interesting feature is the new gallery with microscopes allowing you to see the intricacy of each crystal; snacks, shop; cl am wknds, all day Mon (exc bank hols), 25-26 Dec, Good Fri; £1. Northwich was one of the main salt towns, and you can follow the Salt Heritage Trail around some of the other buildings.

Peckforton SJ5356 PECKFORTON CASTLE Built in 1840, using authentic medieval plans, by the architect Anthony Salvin, this is the only intact medieval-style castle in the country. It has only recently been opened to the public, and it's very interesting to see exactly what such castles looked like, with its forbidding gatehouse, ramparts, and broad battlements, fine chapel, stables, kitchens and servants' quarters; also attractive labourers' cottages, and fine views over the Cheshire plain; animatronic tour guides. Snacks, disabled access; cl mid-Sept-Easter; £2.50.

Pickmere SJ6877 has boat hire, lakeside funfair and plenty of open space.

Runcorn SJ5183 NORTON PRIORY MUSEUM & GARDENS A lovely 12th-c priory that developed into a Georgian stately home, with prize-winning exhibitions on medieval monastic life using a large amount of excavated materials, as well as demonstrations of tilemaking, carving and sculpture. Outside is an 18th-c walled garden with historic varieties of flowers and fruit, and beautiful woodland gardens. Snacks, shop, disabled access; cl am, 24-26 Dec, 1 Jan, walled gdn cl Nov-Feb; inclusive price £2.40, museum/grounds £1.70, garden 60p. More centrally, the Sunday-afternoon MINIATURE TRAIN RIDES in the Park on Stockham Lane are popular with children; there are views from the ruins of HALTON CASTLE SJ5382 up on its grassy hill.

Tabley SJ5779 TABLEY OLD SCHOOL CUCKOO CLOCK COLLECTION A unique collection of cuckoo clocks and other mechanical timepieces from all over the world. At the moment there are 400 rare and beautiful clocks, most of them working, but the number is constantly increasing, as the owners nip off to Europe to track down more. Because of this (and as it takes time to get them all going) the exhibition is open only by appointment (tel 0565 633039).

Walgherton SJ6949 DAGFIELDS CRAFT CENTRE All sorts of crafts and goods made and sold in picturesque country barns inc toys, model farms, oak garden furniture, dried flowers, leather woollens etc; animals, snacks, shop, some disabled access; free, but 50p for animals and pets' corner.

Warrington SJ6188 MUSEUM & ART GALLERY Enthusiastically done and right in the centre, interesting displays of wildlife, history and art, with a toy-packed nursery, fire engine and mummies among the highlights; shop, disabled access; cl Sun.

Widnes SJ5185 CATALYST Lively centre exploring the chemical industry and how it affects our lives. Don't worry if that doesn't immediately grab you, it's full of hands-on exhibits, computer games and fun demonstrations presented in a really enjoyable and entertaining way. Their novel approach won them the 1992 North West Museum and Visitor Attraction of the Year Award, and the views from the 10th floor are splendid. Snacks, shop, disabled access; cl Mon (exc bank hols), 24-26 Dec, 1 Jan; £2.

★ **The Wirral** (largely in Merseyside now) is much built up, with extensive dormitory villages as well as more industrial areas, but its Cheshire parts include the charming unspoilt village of Burton SJ3274 (strolls in wood of handsome old Scots pines just N), and nearby Parkgate SJ2878. This interesting village is the country's only inland seaside resort, the Dee estuary having retreated since its palmy days at the end of the 18th and early 19th c. Before that, it was a more important port than Liverpool, and there's an eerie charm in sitting in the Boathouse or the Red Lion on the 'Promenade', looking out over the marshes to the distant waters and the Welsh hills on the far side, and remembering those times of silk ships, and of long-gone kings and admirals and poets (and ev Handel) who took ship here.

Delightful villages are Barthomley SJ7752 (thatch, black-and-white timbering, up-and-down lanes, fine church); Christleton SJ4465 (village green, pond, almshouses, medieval packhorse bridges); Grappenhall SJ6386 (ancient grinning cat on church tower, canal strolls); Great Budworth SJ6778 (charming – imposing church and many pretty cottages); Malpas SJ4947 (extraordinarily uplifting ceiling in 14th-c hilltop church nr fragmentary castle ruin, pretty cottages and some grander buildings); and Tattenhall SJ4959. All these villages have the added attraction of a decent civilised pub that we can vouch for. Other charming villages include Eaton SJ5762 (unassuming picture-postcard combinations of thatch, stone and timbering); Eccleston SJ4163 (romantically eclectic 19th-c estate village built for the Duke of Westminster, with richly expansive sandstone church that's a culmination of Victorian ecclesiastical architecture); and Whitegate SJ6369 (thatch, village green, fragmentary remains of biggest English Cistercian monastery opp church, lakeside walk on nearby derelict railway).

Visits to working dairy farms that make their own **ice-creams** have become popular, especially Snugbury's (Park Farm) at Hurleston nr Nantwich SJ6552 and Cheshire Ice-cream Farm (Drumlan Hall Farm) nr Tattenhall SJ4858 – at both you can sample various flavours and see the cows being milked.

Walks

The 30-mile **Sandstone Trail** follows the romantically wooded sandstone ridges, crags and outcrops stretching right across this area from Overton SJ5276 in the N (the Ring o' Bells there is a most attractive pub, with Mersey views) to the Shropshire border S of Malpas (the ancient Bell o' the Hill pub nr Tushingham down there is a useful stop). The scenery is very varied, and this trail offers the best walking hereabouts. One particularly fine section is around the Peckforton Hills, with splendid views of real and real-looking romantic castles, and good pubs usefully placed at Bulkeley (SJ5052) and Higher Burwardsley (SJ5256). From the A534 nr Harthill SJ5055 the Trail ascends Raw Head, the most spectacular natural feature of the central Cheshire ridge, with sandstone cliffs weathered into bizarre shapes, and a cave to explore.

The Trail passes through another very popular area for walks, the **Delamere Forest.** Here, several square miles of mainly coniferous plantation, with some older oak and other woodland, inc plenty of open stretches and picnic places, and some small stretches of reedy water. There's good access from several places including Delamere SJ5669 and Hatchmere SJ5672, with decent prettily placed pubs in both villages.

The **Shropshire Union Canal** threads in various directions through the area, with interesting stretches for strolls, inc the flight of over a dozen locks near Audlem Wharf (SJ6543), the charming section through the richly wooded farming country below Beeston Castle at Wharton's Lock W of Tiverton SJ5360, and the pretty Llangollen branch, with good access from Marbury SJ5645 and Wrenbury SJ5948 (there are decent pubs in all these places, and the Dusty Miller at Wrenbury has an interesting lifting bridge by it).

Marbury Country Park has some quiet short walks, and gives on to the extensive Budworth Mere, with sailing, and herons, ducks, grebes and coots pottering around the rushes; good pubs nearby at Comberbach (pronounced Comberbatch) SJ6477 and Great Budworth SJ6778.

Little Budworth Country Park SJ5965 is a strong contrast to most of this area's richly manicured countryside: poor wild heath with young bogs and scrawny birch woods.

Several more or less isolated **pubs** make useful start or finish points for country walks: the Cock at Barton (SJ4554, nr the attractive village of Farndon – where you can get down to the River Dee); the Copper Mine at Fullers Moor (SJ4954), the Tigers Head at Norley SJ6772 (Pytchleys Hollow), and the Fiddle i' th' Bag up nr Penketh SJ5893 (Alder Lane off A49; an unexpectedly remote-feeling spot between the disused St Helens Canal and the broad River Mersey).

Driving

Any of the roads that link villages we've mentioned as attractive are worth taking, especially for instance the circular route linking Norbury, Marbury and Wrenbury in the S. Another interesting backroads drive is along the narrow lanes around Bickerton Hill, and then from Bulkeley on the A534 through Peckforton and Beeston, turning right there and going across to Bunbury. The B5152 from the A51 S of Tarporley up to Overton is a nice drive. Especially on a spring or summer evening, the A41, A49 and A51 can be surprisingly quick and pleasant. The A534 W of Nantwich is a good road with interesting views.

Where to eat

Chester SJ4166 FRANCS 14 Cuppin St (0244) 317952 Cheerful, timbered brasserie with French country food; cl 26 Dec, 1 Jan. **£21**|£3.10/£7.85.

Acton Bridge SJ5975 RHEINGOLD RIVERSIDE RESTAURANT (0606) 852310 A favourite of local contributors; cl Sun pm, Mon, 24 Dec, lunch 26 Dec; disabled access. **£16**|£2.25/£4.25.

Plumley SJ7175 SMOKER (0565) 722338 Popular thatched 16th-c pub, very handy for M6, relaxed atmosphere despite being very popular, interesting old prints, wide range of good food, decent wines, big garden; disabled access. **£14**|£1.85/£5.

Daresbury SJ5983 LORD DARESBURY HOTEL Chester Rd (0925) 267331 Bright, modern hotel with popular food in two restaurants; firmly tipped by local contributors; bedrooms; disabled access. **£12.50**|£2.50/£6.50.

Comberbach SJ6477 SPINNER & BERGAMOT (0606) 891307 Welcoming pebble-dashed pub with bowling green and lots of animals in garden, very cosy in winter, very good value bar lunches and good evening food, popular Sun lunches and vegetarian meals; cl 25 Dec pm; children over 12; disabled access. £1.80/£4.50.

Marbury SJ5645 SWAN (0948) 3715 Friendly pub in attractive village, good walks to Llangollen canal, good home cooking inc tasty puddings. £1.65/£4.70.

Faddiley SJ5953 TOLLEMACHE ARMS (0270) 74223 Friendly timbered 15th-c pub in unexpectedly quiet country setting, cosy cottagey feel, decent, good value bar lunches, good puddings, Wendy house in garden with toys for children; cl Mon; disabled access. £1.65/£4.50.

East Cheshire

Interestingly preserved mill towns and villages, Pennine-edge moorland, striking stately homes and other buildings, good walking.

The pick of the area's great houses include Tatton Park at Knutsford, Lyme Park near Disley, Little Moreton Hall at Scholar Green, and Gawsworth Hall. Macclesfield and Bollington have made the most of their mill-town past, with good walkways past interesting, very unsatanic buildings set into tortuously steep hillsides; the smaller Styal has been particularly well restored. The best of this area's scenery is in the east and north-east, with some terrific views and fine walks; small steep stone-walled pastures, shaggy sheep, deep twisty valleys, austere moorland. But even the flatter countryside of the Cheshire Plain is interestingly varied, with fine trees, rich parkland, leafy lanes and delightful hidden-away villages.

Where to stay

Macclesfield SJ9271 Sutton Hall Hotel SK11 0HE (0260) 253211 **£85**; 9 marvellous rms. Welcoming and secluded historic baronial hall, full of character, stylish rooms with suits of armour and so forth, friendly service, good food; can arrange clayshooting/golf/fishing.

Lymm SJ6787 Lymm Whitbarrow Rd WA13 9AQ (0925) 752233 **£60w**; 69 rms. Modernised hotel close to village centre; disabled access.

Lymm SJ6787 Dingle Rectory Lane WA13 0AH (0925) 752297 **£58**; 30 rms. Attractively situated above the sandstone ravine and close to village centre; cl 25 Dec-1 Jan.

Knutsford SJ7578 Long View 51-55 Manchester Rd WA16 0LX (0565) 632119 **£57.50**; 23 attractive rms. The former home of a Victorian merchant, it has period and reproduction furnishings, original fireplaces, very friendly service, good, well-presented food inc vegetarian dishes, and pleasant cellar bar; cl Christmas; disabled access.

Statham SJ6888 Statham Lodge Warrington Rd Lymm WA13 9BP (0925) 752204 **£54w**; 38 rms. Attractive country-house hotel; cl 25-26 Dec; disabled access.

Brereton Green SJ7864 Bears Head Sandbach CW11 9RS (0477) 535251 **£51w**; 24 comfortable rms in attached modern block, with others in an older part leading off a courtyard. Civilised timber-framed old pub, run by the same family for 50 years, with traditional beamed bars, good food in bar and candlelit restaurant, decent Italian wines, courteous Italian staff, summer barbecues; disabled access.

To see and do

Adlington ST9180 Adlington Hall Handel is reputed to have played the organ here in this imposing manor house, partly 16th-c timber-framed and

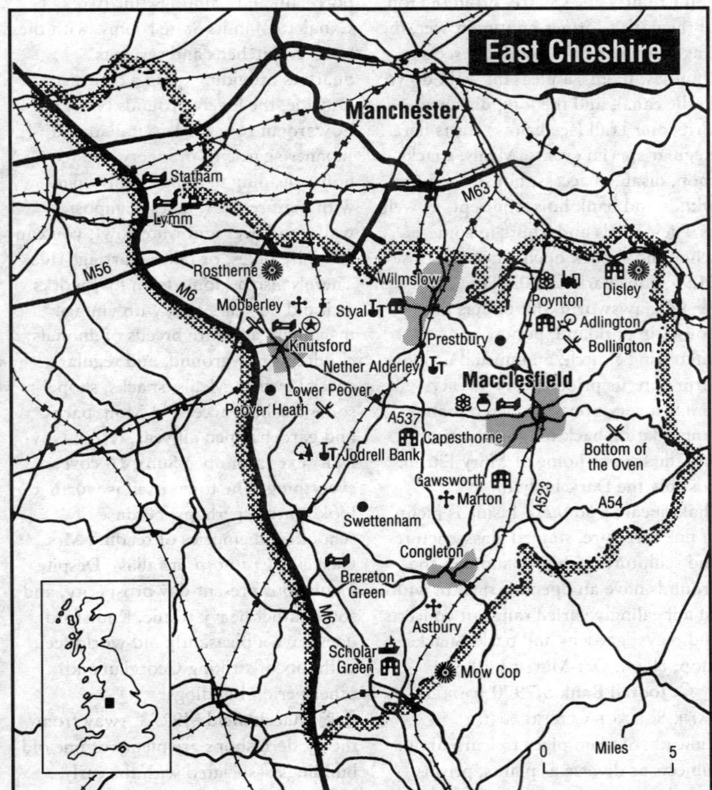

partly 18th-c red brick. It's built on the site of an 11th-c hunting lodge, and two oak trees that were part of the original building still have their roots in the ground and support the east end of the Great Hall. There's a fine yew walk and lime avenue in the landscaped gardens; antique/craft fairs held regularly. Snacks, shop, some disabled access; open pm Sun and bank hols from Good Fri-end Sept; house £2.70, gdn £1.

Capesthorne SJ8472 CAPESTHORNE HALL 18th-c family home of the Bromley-Davenports, with fine paintings, sculptures, furniture, and American-colonial furnishings; there's also a theatre, a lovely Georgian chapel, gardens, lakes, nature trail, and an arboretum. Meals, snacks, shop, disabled access; open pm, Apr Sun only, May & Aug-Sept Weds & Sun, Jun-July Tues-Thurs & Sun, bank hols; £2.

Disley SJ9784 Outside this pleasant hillside village is LYME PARK, a wonderful country estate, the Hall at its centre a magnificent blend of Elizabethan, Georgian and Regency architecture and styles. Tour guides in period costume show you round its treasures, which include intricate carvings, lovely tapestries, paintings and furniture, a particularly grand staircase, and a fine collection of English clocks. Around it are 17 acres of Victorian gardens with orangery, sunken Dutch garden and wilderness garden, and a sprawling ancient park with herds of red deer, nature trails, and Countryside Centre. From the top of the park's former hunting tower, the Cage, you can on a good day see six counties; there's a pleasant walk down to the canal, and the long-distance Gritstone Trail (see below) starts here. Regular special events. Meals, snacks, shop, disabled access; house open pm wknds and bank hols Apr-Sept, as well as Tues, Weds and Thurs in some school hols, park open all year; house £1.95, gdns/park £3.20. NT.

★ **Gawsworth** SJ8969 has fine houses in parkland, ponds, an interesting church, an unusual unspoilt farm pub; its pride is GAWSWORTH HALL, a very pretty timbered manor house dating back to Norman times and the former home of Mary Fitton, possibly the Dark Lady of Shakespeare's *Sonnets*. Inside is plenty of fine furniture, stained glass, pictures and sculptures, while in summer the grounds have an open-air theatre with an appealingly varied range of concerts and plays; gardens and park. Snacks, shop; cl am, Oct-Mar; £3.20.

Jodrell Bank SJ7970 JODRELL BANK SCIENCE CENTRE AND ARBORETUM Fun place to learn about subjects as diverse as plants, prisms and planets, with down-to-earth explanations of scientific facts, an arboretum with 2,500 types of tree, and the second-largest fully steerable radio telescope in the world, as big as the dome of St Paul's. Regular shows in the planetarium, interactive exhibits, nature trails, picnic spots, and Environmental Discovery Centre. Meals, snacks, shop, disabled access; cl Nov-Easter exc pm weekends and school hols; *£3.40.

The gem of **Knutsford** SJ7578 is TATTON PARK on its edge. The handsome neo-classical mansion at the centre of this busy estate is Georgian, but the more modest Old Hall hints at the long history of the site – they like to boast it has its roots in the Stone Age. The opulent mansion has a magnificent collection of furnishings, porcelain and paintings (inc two Canalettos) in its State rooms, with the restored kitchens and servants' quarters providing quite a contrast. Outside, the lovely grounds boast an Edwardian rose garden, Italian and Japanese gardens, orangery and fern house, leading to a big country park with mature trees, lakes, signposted walks and deer and waterfowl; you can fish, hire bikes, or take a carriage ride. There's also a Home farm that works as it did 60 years ago, with vintage machinery and rare breeds of animals; children's playground, and regular special events. Meals, snacks, shop, some disabled access; cl Mon, park and gardens open all year, rest cl Nov-Mar (exc farm open Sun); £6 covers everything. The town itself is worth a look (partly, perhaps, because of schoolday memories of reading Mrs Gaskell's *Cranford*, its alias). Despite its obvious present-day prosperity, and some rather heavy traffic, Knutsford does have a pleasantly old-world feel, with lots of striking Georgian and other period buildings.

Macclesfield SJ9273 Away from the modern shops are plenty of fine old buildings associated with the early industrial revolution and the silk industry, and a more ancient core with quaint little cobbled alleys. A good place to start is the SILK MUSEUM, which has an award-winning audio-visual programme covering the history of silk, and room settings, exhibitions, textiles and garments; meals, snacks, shop, disabled access; cl Mon (exc bank hols), Good Fri, 24-26 Dec, 1 Jan; £1.90. PARADISE MILL was a working mill until 1981 and now helpful guides (many of whom are former silk workers) demonstrate the silk production process on the restored handlooms; room settings give an impression of working conditions in the 1930s. Shop, good disabled access; cl am, Mon (exc bank hols), 24-26 Dec, 1 Jan, Good Fri; £1.90. WEST PARK MUSEUM Decent little museum with a wide range of decorative arts, some interesting Egyptian antiquities, 19th- and early 20th-c paintings inc fine bird and animal pictures, and local history items; shop, disabled access; cl am, Mon, 24-26 Dec, 1 Jan, Good Fri. HARE HILL Walled garden, pergola and fine spring flowers in lovely parkland. Open daily mid-May-June, then only Weds/Thurs/Sat/Sun until end Oct, cl winter; *£2. NT.

Mobberley SJ7879 HILLSIDE ORNAMENTAL FOWL Good private collection of wildfowl with rare species like magpie geese, white-headed stifftail and the Abyssinian black duck, as well as aviaries of softbills, flamingos and other exotic birds. Children should enjoy the penguin pool; meals, snacks, shop; open Weds, Sat, Sun and bank hols Easter-Oct; £2.50. The Bird in Hand is useful for lunch.

Mow Cop SJ8557 Right on the Staffs border is a shaggy steep hill with a castellated folly on top, and a rock pinnacle left by former quarrying; rich views over Cheshire (and the village just behind, which is in Staffs, somehow by contrast underlines the essential richness and grace of Cheshire itself). Worth a look if passing.

Nether Alderley SJ8476 NETHER ALDERLEY MILL Interesting 15th-c watermill with carefully preserved atmosphere, and restored working water wheels with Elizabethan timber work and Victorian machinery. They still grind flour for demonstration purposes; open pm Wed, Sun and bank hols from Apr-Oct, also Tues, Thurs, Fri and Sat Jun-Sept; £1.80. NT.

Poynton SJ9283 BROOKSIDE GARDEN CENTRE is worth visiting for its splendid miniature railway which travels through an authentically detailed circuit in a pretty garden setting. The replica West Country station is packed with railway memorabilia. Parking is not easy; open Weds and Sun Apr-Sept and Tues and Thurs too in July and Aug, Sun only in Oct and cl Nov-Apr.

★ **Rostherne** SJ7484 is a quiet little village worth a passing look. It has charming brick cottages along a cobbled pavement, and offers a lovely view over one of the county's broadest meres from the graveyard of the attractive timbered church.

Scholar Green SJ8356 LITTLE MORETON HALL is among the best preserved half-timbered buildings in Britain; an amazing-looking place, it was built in 1580 and is much the same now as it was then. Particularly special are the great hall, long gallery and chapel, and you can see the original gatehouse and moat. Regular open-air theatre and concert performances; meals, snacks, shop, some disabled access; cl am, all day Mon and Tues, Nov-Mar; £2.50 wkdys, £3.50 wknds, NT. Nearby HERITAGE NARROW BOATS at Kent Green have silent electric narrow boats to hire by the day (0782) 785700; cl lunch, Nov-Easter; £38 wkdys for 1-3 people, £48 wknds.

Styal SJ8383 QUARRY BANK MILL AND COUNTRY PARK One of the best and most extensive places in the country for visitors to get to grips with the Industrial Revolution, the 18th-c cotton mill that's the centrepiece here has been restored to working order and its three floors are once again producing cloth. There are demonstrations of spinning and weaving, and lively exhibitions on life for the millworkers and their bosses and conditions in the factory. The village was built by the mill owners for their workers, and has carefully preserved workers' cottages, chapels and shops, inc the house where the young pauper apprentices lived, while around it the lovely park has good woodland or riverside walks. You can buy cloth woven here, and there are lots of events throughout the year. Meals, snacks, shop, decent pub, disabled access; cl winter Mon; apprentice house only £2.50, mill only £3.30, mill and apprentice house

£4.25. The PEACOCK FARM SHOP nearby is a notable family-run business, very welcoming, too, thanks to the hundreds of colourful daffodils they've planted on the roadside; meat and greengrocery as well as the farm produce, and their pony and donkey are extremely family-friendly.

Churches of note include Astbury SJ8461 (graceful detached spire, spectacular roofing, rich carving; the village is very attractive, too), Marton SJ8568 (simple 14th-c shingle-roofed black-and-white timbering, in unpromising surroundings) and Mobberley SJ7879 (magnificently carved Tudor rood screen).

★ **Attractive villages**, all with nice pubs, include Lower Peover SJ7474 (many people's Cheshire favourite: cobbled lanes, glorious 14th-c black-and-white timbered church, quiet watermeadows); Lymm SJ6786 (pretty cottages in the Dingle, boat trips on Bridgewater Canal (092 575) 4900, strolls to the lake at Lymm Dam); Prestbury SJ9077 (very prosperous-feeling now, with good shops, Legh Arms and homelier Admiral Rodney; pleasant riverside walks to the S, along the Bollin); and Swettenham SJ8067 (rich paddocks with wrought-iron fences, daffodils in spring in a dell by an old mill).

Walks

The hilly eastern edge of the county forms part of the Peak District, and offers some grand views westwards towards N Wales. **Teggs Nose Country Park** SJ9573 has a useful summer information centre, and good walks with far views, punctuated by relics of the former quarrying here. By the turn off the A537 the Setter Dog is a good pub. From the park, a well-marked track heads off S into the **Macclesfield Forest**, with steep deep green pine plantations around neatly walled small reservoirs; on the far side of this the isolated Leathers Smithy E of Langley is a warmly welcoming moorside refuge.

This track is actually part of the long-distance **Gritstone Way**, which is well marked and offers a few days' walking of the highest quality. It runs along these western flanks of the Peak from Lyme Park SJ9682 (itself laced with gentle paths), to join the Staffordshire Way at Rushton Spencer SJ9462 (where the Crown is good for lunch). Further N the Way can be picked up to track across high stone-walled pastures at either Pott Shrigley SJ9478 (the Cheshire Hunt in Spurley Lane is a good pub here) or, with fine views, Rainow SJ9576 (the Highwayman, a mile above the village, is a distinctive old pub).

These hills and moors SE of Macclesfield have many other good walks. A particular delight is that so many can be based around good civilised country pubs with decent food: the Stanley Arms at Bottom of the Oven SJ9872, the Hanging Gate at Higher Sutton nr Langley SJ9569, the Ryles Arms near Sutton SJ9469, the Crag in its untypically leafy sheltered valley at Wildboarclough SJ9868, and the Ship at Danebridge, a particularly nice spot nr Wincle SJ9666.

The **Middlewood Way** is a sort of linear country park between Macclesfield and the N border, along a former railway; attractively bordered with wild flowers and trees, with tracks too for cyclists (bicycle hire at Lyme Park or Bollington) and horse rides (can also be hired by the hour, about £10); several decent pubs in Bollington SJ9377, one at Whiteley Green SJ9278. The pleasant stretches around the Poynton inclines SJ9283 are underrated. Bollington is itself certainly worth a stroll: handsome stone milltown buildings, grand viaducts, attractive perspectives of the surrounding villages; or the longer walk up to Rainow.

The **Macclesfield Canal** tracks through good high countryside from the N border near Disley to pass Bollington, Macclesfield and Congleton, with plenty of access points; S of the A54 just W of its junction with the A523, a staggering flight of ten locks leads down to a sturdily elegant iron aqueduct.

Alderley Edge SJ8677 (not to be confused with the straggling suburban settlement named after it, to the W) rises high out of the plain, with good walks through the woodland and fine views of the higher hills to the E. The local caving-club members are working towards opening some of the former copper mines which honeycomb the area.

The Cloud SJ9063 has a craggy summit and drops steeply to the plain, with grand views; the Coach & Horses at Timbersbrook SJ9063 is a useful nearby pub. **Kerridge Hill** SJ9475 above Bollington is topped by the curious folly known as White Nancy.

Driving

There are quite magnificent views from the A537 E of Macclesfield, and good ones from the A5002 NE. A quiet and pleasant country drive is that along the lanes through the rich parkland around Goostrey, Peover Heath and Over Peover N of Holmes Chapel. There are good hill drives around Macclesfield – for instance, through Sutton Lane Ends, Langley, the Macclesfield Forest and on up to the A537; or S from Sutton Lane Ends to Wincle and Danebridge. From off the A537 between Walker Barn and the Cat & Fiddle Inn (the 2nd-highest in England), an excellent moorland road heads N past the big reservoir, into fine empty countryside. Going across country, Congleton can be quite a bottleneck, and the A523 and A6 tend to be slow. In contrast the A50, made virtually redundant by the M6, is a good fast road.

Where to eat

Knutsford SJ7578 LA BELLE EPOQUE 60 King St (0565) 633060 Popular Art Nouveau restaurant with elaborate food and helpful, friendly staff; cl am, Sun, first wk Jan; children over 10. **£25**|£15.

Bollington SJ9377 MAURO's 88 Palmerston St (0625) 573898 Friendly Italian restaurant with excellent fresh fish and lovely puddings; cl Sat am, Sun, Mon, Easter, 3 wks in summer; disabled access. **£21**|£4.50.

Bottom of the Oven SJ9872 STANLEY ARMS (0260) 252414 Unspoilt isolated moorland pub close to Macclesfield Forest; very friendly, good, ambitious food inc memorable daily specials, excellent salads; cl 25 Dec; disabled access. **£17**|£1.85/£5.

Peover Heath SJ7973 DOG (0625) 861421 Busy pub in quiet lane with big helpings of interesting food, open fires, relaxing series of small enclaves around central bar. **£15.75**|£3.85/£6.30.

We welcome reports from readers . . .

This GUIDE depends on readers' reports. Please tell us what you think about places in it. And do recommend additions. Use the card in the middle, the report forms at the end, or just write – no stamp needed: THE GOOD WEEKEND GUIDE, FREEPOST TN1569, Wadhurst, E Sussex TN5 7BR.

Cheshire Calendar

Some of these dates were provisional as we went to press.

January

22nd **Nantwich** Holly Holy Day, *celebration of the Battle of Namptwyche, although as this year is the 350th anniversary of the battle Holly Holy Day, celebrations will be on a smaller scale, and the main events will take place in the grand August celebrations*

March

12th **Chester** North of England Head of River Race

April

2nd **Ellesmere Port** Boaters' Gathering, Maritime Festival – *till Mon 4*

17th **Sandbach** Transport through the Ages, *procession from the Common through the town centre*

May

1st **Knutsford** May Fair, *Tatton Park, inc maypole dancing – Mon too*

2nd **Northwich** Regatta, *on the River Weaver*; **Norton** Priory Mayday Celebrations, *inc drama and Morris men;* **Sandbach** Elizabethan Market, *costumed market with jugglers, jesters, fire-eaters*

7th **Knutsford** Royal May Day, *processions on pavements carpeted, after an ancient tradition, with sands of different colours in elaborate patterns;* **Marbury** Merry Days – *country fair*

14th **Chester** Lord Mayor's Show & Festival of Transport, *with procession through the city, Morris dancing and over 400 veteran cars*; **Reaseheath** Cheshire College of Agriculture Open Day, *with sheep-shearing, cheese-making, floristry, and welding demonstrations – till Sun (may be held the previous weekend instead)*

19th **Chester** Beating the Retreat – *colourful traditional military ceremony in the Castle Square*

28th **Knutsford** Country Crafts Festival, *Tatton Park – working demonstrations of skills such as thatching, beekeeping and chairbodging in tented craft village – till Mon*

June

2nd **Neston** Ladies Day – *traditional procession through the town, flower-bearing women and girls*

4th **Knutsford** Classic Car Spectacular, *inc auction, at Tatton Country Park – Sun too*

4th **Chester** Regatta and Flower Show

12th **Knutsford** Orchid Show, *Tatton Park*

mid-Jun **Warrington** Bawming the Thorn – *fete and traditional ceremony in which children dance round the Thorn tree*; **Winsford** Well Dressing *at St Chad's Church*

18th **Knutsford** Carriage Driving Trials and Country Fair, *Tatton Park – Sun too*

20th **Norton** Priory Midsummer Festival

Cheshire Calendar

June cont.

21st **Tabley, nr Knutsford,** Cheshire Agricultural Show, *with displays, showjumping, livestock competitions and other entertainments – Sun too*

24th **Middlewich** Boat Festival

25th **Willaston** 15th World Worm Charming Championships – *charming worms out of the soil is an ancient tradition and this event, held at the primary school, holds the world record for the greatest number ever charmed*

end Jun **Chester** Sports and Leisure Festival – *colourful carnival of sporting events and family entertainment*

July

1st **Warrington** Walking Day – *long processions wind round the town in a northern tradition originally supposed to draw people away from the sins of the Races at nearby Newton le Willows*

2nd **Northwich** Festival

9th **Hawarden** Festival – *Victorian festival with vintage machinery and vehicles, market and craft fair, parades and other Victorian entertainments – Sun too*

16th **Knutsford** Medieval Fair, *Tatton Park, with traditional crafts, music, archery and other entertainment – Sun too*; **Widnes** Halton Show, *Spike Island – Sun too*

22nd **Chester** Summer Music Festival, *inc Fringe Festival, which may start a little earlier – till Sat 30*

27th **Nantwich** & South Cheshire Agricultural Show, *Dorfold Park, inc the largest exhibition of cheese and dairy products in Europe*

August

Aug **Nantwich** celebration of 350th anniversary of Battle of Namptwyche

Aug **Macclesfield** Rushbearing Ceremony – *the tiny Macclesfield Forest Chapel, decorated with flowers and plaited rushes, becomes a place of pilgrimage*

21st **Macclesfield** West Park Family Fun Day

27th **Crewe** & Nantwich Carnival, *Queens Park – Sun too, with a spectacular firework display on Sat evening*; **Knutsford** Festival of Crafts, *Tatton Park, with working demonstrations – till Mon*; **Poynton** Show, *Poynton Park, South Park Drive*

September

9th **Nantwich** Crewe & Nantwich Folk Festival – *till Sun*

17th **Knutsford** Country Life Weekend, *Tatton Park – Sun too*; **Winsford** Vale Royal Show

18th **Norton** Priory Walled Garden Horticultural Show

October

19th **Knutsford** National Craft and Design Show – *till Sun 23*

Help this year from: *W C M Jones, Peter and Jenny Quine, R A Chesher, Pat Neate, David Heath, Mrs K A Ollerhead, R J and J C Moggridge, Neville Kenyon, Catherine and Andrew Brian, H Hazzard, Ian Sharp, Nick and Alison Dowson, John Evans, Jill and Peter Bickley, Mr and Mrs C J Frodsham, George Jonas, Gill and Maurice McMahon, E G Parish, J C Gould, C F Walling, Olive and Ray Hebson, Mr and Mrs Alex Williams, Andrew and Ruth Triggs, Nigel Pritchard, Jason Caulkin, C Roberts, Mrs J Oakes, Janet Naylor, Sue Holland, Dave Webster, Jennifer Sapp, Richard Dolphin, Roger Sherman, Dr S W Tham, Geoffrey and Brenda Wilson, Sue and Alan Gallagher, Hugh and Toni Saddington, Graham Bush, C Roberts, Paul and Gail Betteley, Gill and Mike Cross, Mrs D Craig, S Byron.*

Cornwall

Very good value for a short break, Cornwall offers attractive prices, lots to do, and lovely scenery. For most people, of course, getting there takes so long that this in itself is a big and perhaps overwhelming obstacle: from London, for example, even out of season you should allow about five hours' driving to get well into the county – and much longer in summer.

South-east Cornwall's chief charm is the relatively sheltered coast, with plenty of interesting villages and little coves. Mid Cornwall has much the same type of appeal, though with some more dramatic coast (and fewer fishing-village coves); it has the best choice of fine gardens to visit, and its bigger towns are more appealing to visitors. West Cornwall, again, has some charming little sheltered sea villages, but also a much wilder side. It's full of evocative prehistoric remains. Penzance is a nice town, and St Ives wears its popularity very well indeed – a lovely place. The Isles of Scilly are ideal for a really relaxing break, if you live anywhere within reach of Penzance, the quickest jumping-off point. North Cornwall's fishing villages are also attractive, though this region is better known for its more traditional old-fashioned beach resorts, which share its long coast with some unspoilt stretches of dramatic cliffs; inland, windswept Bodmin Moor is the county's most untouched area, and the best for inland walks. Generally, good places to eat are more easily found in the south than in the north and the west in particular.

Though there are plenty of attractions geared to visitors in each of the four mainland areas, the county's special charm for most people is its very relaxed pace of life, making it particularly good for a quiet break. A particular pleasure is to walk along stretches of the coast, from village to village; it's worth remembering that there are 500 miles of coastal walks in this area, with much of the land owned and beautifully preserved by the National Trust.

All four areas are within fairly quick reach of each other; so, staying in one, you can easily visit something that appeals to you in another. From the Devon border to Penzance takes around an hour and a half; the A30 has been greatly improved in recent years.

Late May and early June is an ideal time for a break here, when the days are long and bright, there are vivid wild flowers, remarkable shifting colours on the sea – and relatively few other visitors, so that you often get little coves, churchyards and other special places entirely to yourself. In the summer holidays the most popular places do get very busy indeed. September and October are the months when you've most chance of spotting the seal pups that are spending the first few days of their lives on the shore of some quiet cove; at other times you might see adults bobbing in the water offshore, or maybe basking together on an offshore rock.

SOUTH-EAST CORNWALL

The intricately varied coast is dotted with picturesque fishing villages and sheltered coves; there's a fine choice of places to stay, and good walking.

There are dramatic headlands and stretches of cliff for good bracing walks, but it's the abundance of sheltered little bays, creeks and pretty villages tucked between them which makes this area so picturesque, and so attractive to families. It's ideal for pottering about in boats. The area has Cornwall's most lovely house, Cotehele, near Calstock; Lanhydrock House, and Antony House, at Torpoint, are also well worth visiting, as are Trewithen Gardens near Probus and the Lost Gardens of Heligan near Mevagissey. Dobwalls Adventure Park is a family favourite.

There's an excellent choice of distinctive places to stay, with decent if not outstanding food, including plenty of genuinely fresh local fish.

Where to stay

Looe SX2652 TALLAND BAY Talland PL13 2JB (0503) 72667 **£130**; 24 rms with sea or country views. Country house in lovely gardens above the sea, comfortable lounges and bar with relaxed atmosphere, heated outdoor swimming pool, putting, croquet, snooker, sauna, solarium; cl Jan-mid-Feb; children over 6 in restaurant (high tea for younger ones); disabled access.

Calstock SX4368 DANESCOMBE VALLEY Lower Kelly PL18 9RY **£125**; 5 lovely rms. Most attractive small Georgian house with first-floor verandah and fine views over a wooded bend on Tamar River from most rooms; warmly friendly owners, quiet, relaxing atmosphere, open fires, flowers, books (no TV), and delicious food using fresh local produce; Cotehele House (NT) is just 15 mins walk; cl Nov-Mar; children over 12.

Carne Beach SW9038 NARE Par TR2 5PF (0872) 501279 **£108**; 36 lovely rms to suit all tastes (and pockets) – some stylish ones overlook garden and out to sea. Attractively decorated and furnished hotel with antiques and fresh flowers, magnificent clifftop position; very good food inc wonderful breakfasts, and run by staff who really care; very good for quiet family hols; cl 6 wks from 6 Jan; disabled access.

Liskeard SX2564 WELL HOUSE PL14 4RN (0579) 342001 **£105**; 7 good rms, fine views. Victorian country house, handy for inland Cornwall, big bay windows in dining room overlooking swimming pool; good food using seasonal local produce, fine wines, tennis, croquet; children over 8 at dinner (high tea available).

Gerrans Bay SW8937 PENDOWER BEACH HOUSE Portscatho, Truro TR2 5LW

(0872) 501241 **£100 inc dinner**; 12 rms, most with own bthrm. Carefully modernised 16th-c hotel in grounds on edge of lovely sandy beach, superb sea and coastal views, relaxed atmosphere; good fish dishes (cold lobster on the terrace is special), tennis court; cl Nov-mid-Mar; disabled access.

Portloe SW9339 LUGGER Truro TR2 5RD (0872) 501322 **£100**; 19 rms. Family-run, friendly smuggling inn right by sea, excellent views, smart, comfortable furnishings; good food at sensible prices, library, good nearby walks; cl 22 Nov-11 Feb; children over 12.

Golant SX1155 CORMORANT Fowey PL23 1LL (0726) 833426 **£92**; 10 rms, lovely views. Pretty riverside setting; lounge with log fire and big picture windows, candlelit dining rm with imaginative food inc fresh fish, home-made bread, cakes, pasta, marmalades/jams, heated swimming pool; children over 12.

Fowey SX1252 FOWEY HOTEL PL23 1HX (0726) 832551 **£80**; 32 rms, most with bthrm. Pleasant large hotel with informal atmosphere; good restaurant, and wonderful views from the bar; good disabled access.

Bodinnick SX1352 OLD FERRY Fowey PL23 1LX (0726) 870237 **£70**; 13 rms, mostly with bthrm. Ancient inn in lovely position on edge of Fowey estuary with splendid views; simple furnishings, tasty breakfasts, decent evening meals (not winter), games room hewn into the rock, good walks.

St Keyne SX2564 OLD RECTORY Liskeard PL14 4RL (0579) 342617 ***£60**; 8 comfortable rms. Friendly hotel in three acres of grounds; comfortably furnished lounge with open fire, help-yourself bar, and good homely atmosphere; cl week over Christmas; children over 12.

Fowey SX1252 MARINA PL23 1HY (0726) 833315 **£60**; 11 rms, several with lovely views (some with balcony). Elegant, homely hotel overlooking estuary; comfortable lounge, dining room and sheltered gardens share the fine view; helpful, friendly service, and good food (esp fish); cl Nov-Feb; children over 6 in restaurant.

Portscatho SW8735 ROSELAND HOUSE Truro TR2 5EW (0872) 580644 **£56**; 18 pleasant rms. Clean, well-kept and comfortably furnished hotel in isolated spot overlooking sea, with fine coastal views; welcoming, helpful staff, decent food (vegetarian dishes); good centre for exploring area.

Pelynt SX2055 JUBILEE Looe PL13 2JZ (0503) 220312 **£56**; 12 rms. Smart but relaxing pub with Queen Victoria theme, comfortable furnishings; good waitress-served bar food, well-equipped children's play area.

St Mawes SW8433 RISING SUN Truro TR2 5DJ (0326) 270233 **£55**; 12 rms, mostly with bthrm. Small hotel in popular, picturesque waterside village with harbourside views; quiet lounge and cocktail bar, lively locals' bar and airy conservatory.

Pillaton SX3664 WEARY FRIAR Saltash PL12 6QS (0579) 50238 **£45**; 13 rms. Pretty 12th-c inn by church in pleasantly remote village; lots of charm and character, attractive furnishings, good food.

Crafthole SX3654 FINNYGOOK Torpoint PL11 3BQ (0503) 30338 **£40**; 4 small but very warm and comfortable rms. Good sea views from residents' lounge; spacious modernised lounge bar, pleasant restaurant, good-value food, friendly service.

Looe SX2652 HARESCOMBE LODGE Watergate PL13 2NE (0503) 263158 **£40**; 4 rms. Carefully modernised 18th-c house with waterfalls and old stone bridges in quiet garden; no children.

Lanhydrock SX0763 TREFFRY FARM Bodmin PL30 5AF (0208) 74405 **£37**;

3 pretty rms. Friendly farmhouse with wood-panelled lounge, fine breakfasts, evening meals using home-grown veg and fruit, and calves to feed, cows to milk; Lanhydrock stately home (NT) is 300 yds away; cl Nov-Easter; children over 6.
Fowey SX1252 SHIP PL23 1AZ (0726) 832230 £35; 6 old-fashioned rms, one oak-panelled, mostly shared bthrm. Some nautical touches in comfortable bar, coal fire, family dining room with big stained-glass window, good mix of locals and visitors.

To see and do

Attractive seaside villages are the highlight of this area. Snuggled into the rocky coast, they are often really lovely, with friendly local people. Generally well sheltered, they're often pleasantly mild when other parts of the West Country are cold. In summer they manage to keep their charm, as the strolling crowds never override the natural local character.

Favourites include **Fowey** SX1252, lively and bustling, in an exceptional riverside position, with pretty views from up the hill on either side, some interesting shops, lots, from yachts to ocean-going ships, to look at in the harbour, car ferry to Bodinick SX1352 and foot ferry to Polruan (a very steep little harbourside hamlet, good pub), other boat trips; **Mevagissey** SX0145, a bustling picturesque fishing village with hillside cottages, narrow streets, a decent pub, gift shops, a busy working harbour; **Polperro** SX2051, with tiny streets around a very quaint sheltered fishing harbour, little cottages perched on rocks – once a busy smuggling place, now some quite decent craft shops tucked away, oddities like the shell-encrusted Shell House, and another good pub; **Portscatho** SW8735, very sheltered, with a picturesque little harbour, lovely clifftop walks, and some fine nearby beaches – excellent for families (decent pub); **St Mawes** SW8433, very pretty harbourside and estuary views, a long waterfront to stroll along, a foot-passenger ferry to Falmouth and other boat trips (full of yachtsmen and others in summer, lots of guesthouses). **Charlestown** SX0351 has an interesting working harbour, and may look familiar as it's been much used as a film/TV setting (e.g. for *Poldark*).

All these are sizeable villages with shops, teashops and decent pubs. Much smaller and quieter places, really just rocky coves tucked into the coast with maybe a few fishermen's cottages, but all with decent pubs, include Portloe SW9339 (good teashop/small restaurant, too), Porthallow SX2251 and Polkerris SX0952 (terrific view across St Austell bay).

🏛 ❀ ❄ **Calstock** SX4167 COTEHELE Gracefully aged 15th-c granite house, high above the Tamar; the inside has fine furniture, armour, tapestries and embroideries, while the grounds have lovely terraced GARDENS, a medieval dovecot, restored watermill in valley, NATIONAL MARITIME MUSEUM outstation, and lovely woods to walk in many directions. It is over-visited (indeed, the National Trust is doing all it can not to encourage further visits), so except out of season you might well decide not to swell the crowds yourself, despite its tremendous charm. Meals, snacks (tea room in pleasant riverside setting with good cream teas), shop; cl Fri and Nov-Apr, house cl am; £5. NT. There are pleasant walks along the Tamar from the village, where there's a decent pub.

❄ **Charlestown** SX0351 SHIPWRECK & HERITAGE MUSEUM Large collection of shipwreck items, along with photographs and stories of this unspoilt village. Diving exhibition, lifeboat and life-sized tableaux; meals, snacks, shop, disabled access; cl Dec-Feb; £2.95.

☺ **Dobwalls** SX2165 ADVENTURE PARK Particularly good theme park with steam and diesel train-rides along two-mile stretch of miniature American-theme railroads, adventureland with aerial cableways, remote-controlled model boats and American-style trucks, shooting gallery, and super slides. Meals, snacks, shop, disabled access; cl Nov-Easter; £6.50.

Lanhydrock SX0863 LANHYDROCK The highlight of this fine old house has to be the Long Gallery, with its magnificently illustrated Old Testament scenes. A disastrous fire in the 19th c resulted in major changes and refurbishments, though there are still a few 16th-c parts left; interesting kitchens, servants' quarters, larders and so forth, grand 'upstairs' rooms, pretty formal GARDENS. Good meals and snacks, shop, disabled access; house cl Mon (exc bank hols), all cl Nov-Mar; £5, £2.60 grounds only. NT.

Looe SX2756 is based on a working fishing village made up of East Looe and West Looe divided by the river, with narrow little back streets, a picturesque harbour, and good beach; it's also packed with tourist shops, teashops and pubs, but has a nice easy-going atmosphere even in high season. This is the main shark-fishing place. MONKEY SANCTUARY Protected breeding colony of rare Amazon woolly monkeys in wooded grounds – you can get right up to the monkeys; talks given. Meals, snacks, shop, limited disabled access; cl Fri, Sat, Oct-Easter; £3.50. LIVING FROM THE SEA An exploration of Cornwall's fishing history, from Tudor times to the present day, with a lobster and shellfish aquarium and an exhibition about sharks – in summer often displaying a locally caught shark in ice; shop, disabled access; cl 1-1.30 pm, Nov-Easter; £1.20. Summer BOAT TRIPS from here, inc out to nearby St Georges Island.

Mevagissey SX0145 LOST GARDENS OF HELIGAN Forgotten and neglected between 1914 and 1992, now experiencing an enormous restoration. Some very fine mature trees, Victorian walled gardens, lots of rhododendrons, lakes, and big collection of tree ferns, bamboos, palms and nursery. Meals, snacks, shop, partly disabled access; £2.50. WORLD OF RAILWAYS (Meadow St) Over 2,000 model trains trundling through a realistic little world that takes in Cornish china-clay pits, ski resorts, fairgrounds, towns and country; no parking. Shop, some disabled access; cl Oct-May exc Easter; £2.15. FOLK MUSEUM (East Quay) 18th-c boat-builder's shed with fishing equipment and china-clay industry displays. Small shop, disabled access ground floor only; cl Sun am and Oct-Easter; 30p.

! Polperro SX2051 LAND OF LEGEND & MODEL VILLAGE (The Old Forge) Replica of old Polperro in plant garden with animated tableaux of Cornish history and legend, photographs, model railway and commentary listening posts. Shop; cl Oct-Mar; *£2.

✝ **Probus** SW8947 TREWITHEN (A390 between Probus and Grampound) Early 18th-c country house with famous landscaped gardens, many rare trees and shrubs and nurseries. Snacks, rare plants for sale, disabled access; house open Mon and Tues pm Apr-July and Aug bank hol Mon, gardens open Mar-Sept, cl Sun; house £2.80, gardens £1.75 July-Sept, £2 Mar-Jun. The nearby COUNTY DEMONSTRATION GARDEN is quite interesting, on a much humbler scale: how to choose the right plants/layout for your individual garden, propagation displays, herb, vegetable and fruit trials, historical plant collection, some outside sculpture. Summer snacks, shop, disabled access; cl winter wknds, 25-26 Dec; *£2. The CHURCH has the tallest tower in

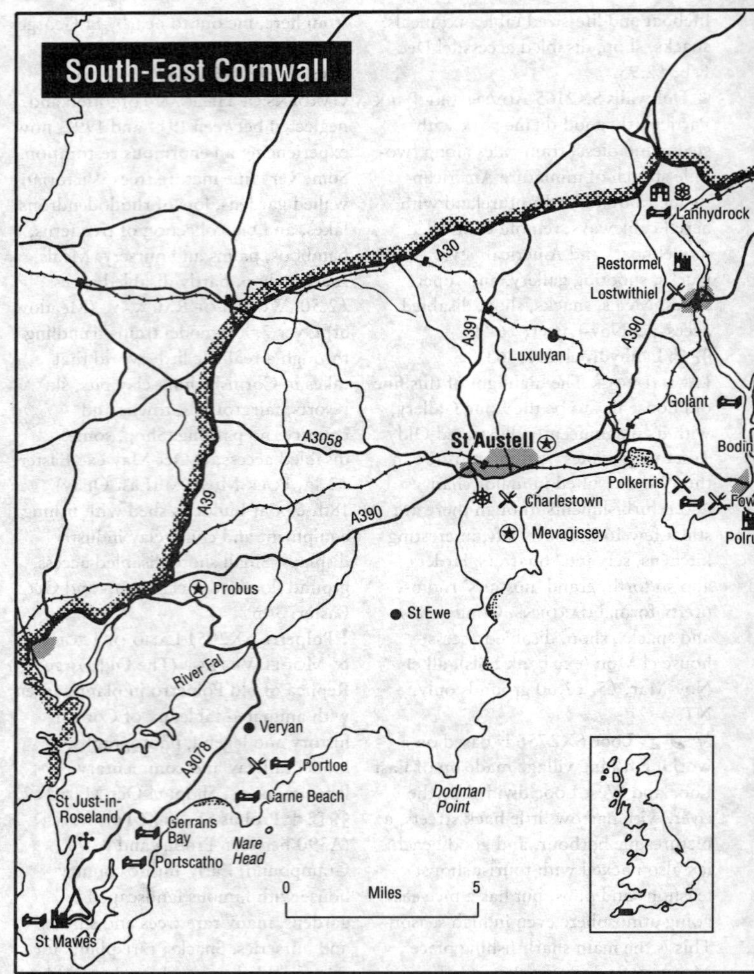

Cornwall but is not special inside.

✝ ⚱ 📷 **St Austell** SX0252 is the centre of the china-clay industry and a busy, modern shopping town, though its Holy Trinity CHURCH has a fine tower and interesting font. The area north of the town is a strange bleak moonscape of whitish spoil heaps with metallic blue lakes dotted amongst them. Up here off the A391 (so you don't have to go into the town) is the WHEAL MARTYN MUSEUM, an interestingly restored 19th-c clayworks showing the 200-year history of china-clay production; working waterwheels and other equipment, horse-drawn waggons, steam locomotives, working pottery, slide shows, nature trails, and children's adventure trail. Meals, snacks, shop; cl Nov-Mar; £3.80. AUTOMOBILIA (about 4 miles W of town) Over 50 cars, motorcycles and

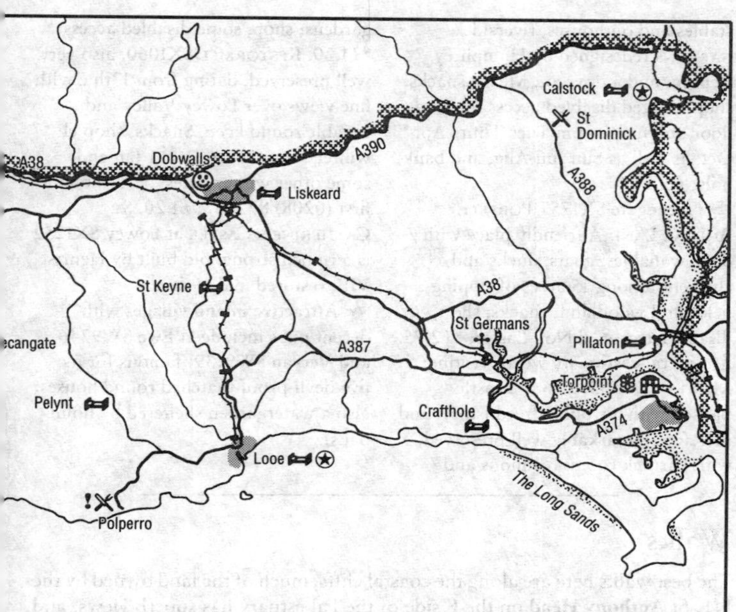

other vehicles from 1904 to the 1960s, inc a vintage Bentley, Rolls-Royce and Aston Martin and assorted memorabilia. There's also a permanent auto-jumble which vintage-car owners may find useful; snacks, shop, disabled access; cl Nov-Apr; *£2.80.

✝ **St Germans** SX3557 CHURCH has a wonderful Norman doorway and particularly fine east window; worth a look if you're passing.

✝ **St Just-in-Roseland** SW8435 CHURCH is in an idyllic creekside spot and its steep graveyard is like a lost subtropical garden – well worth a visit on a quiet sunny day, or in spring with the baby rooks blethering and the smell of wild garlic.

Torpoint SX4355 ANTONY HOUSE Little-changed early 18th-c mansion with family portraits and furniture in the panelled rooms, older stables and outhouses, riverside GARDENS redesigned by Humphrey Repton, and a dovecot. Meals, snacks, shop, limited disabled access (ground floor only); open pm Tues-Thurs Apr-Oct, as well as Sun Jun-Aug, and bank hols; £3.40. NT.

Trecangate SX1757 PORFELL ANIMAL LAND A friendly place with deer, wallabies, goats, ducks and chickens among 15 acres of sloping fields and woodland; snacks, shop, disabled access; cl Nov-Easter; *£2.75.

Several **castles** are worth visiting: ST MAWES SW8533, a 16th-c castle blessed with a trouble-free history, and therefore remarkably well preserved, with barrack rooms, cannons and gardens; shop, some disabled access; *£1.30. RESTORMEL SX1060, also very well preserved, dating from 13th c with fine views over Fowey Valley and notable round keep. Snacks, shop cl winter Mon, 24-26 Dec, 1 Jan and some other winter dates, best to phone first (0208) 872687; £1.20. ST CATHERINE'S CASTLE at Fowey SX1252 is a ruined stronghold built by Henry VIII, restored mid-19th c.

★ **Attractive inland villages** with decent pubs include St Ewe SW9746 and Veryan SW9139 (famous for its five devil-proof thatched round houses; also a watergarden sheltered by holm oaks).

Walks

The best walks here are along the coastal cliffs, much of the land owned by the NT. **St Anthony Head** on the E side of the Fal estuary has superb views, and easy walks along low, level cliffs; parking at the head itself, SW8431, or near Porth Farm on the way down). Virtually the whole of **Gerrans Bay** is good easy walking, from Portscatho SW8735 or Pendower Beach SW8938 (a good sandy stretch). The scenery is more rugged around **Portloe** SW9339, with stiffish climbs on to Nare Head. **Dodman Point** SX0039 (reached from Gorran Haven SX0141, or one of the closer car parks – for instance, at Hemmick Beach) lends itself to a round walk with three-quarters of the route being along cliff-tops.

From **Fowey** SX1251 a popular circular route is one where you go across on the Bodinnick car ferry, take the path through the steep creekside woods round to Polruan, and come back on the other foot ferry. **Talland Bay** SX2251 provides an easy one-mile walk along the coast to enter Polperro's harbour the best way – a sensible alternative to sweating out summer traffic jams in Polperro village itself. The Long Sands running down Whitsand Bay SX3952 are the longest beach walk in the area, but they do take the full force of any wind from the south-west. **Rame Head** SX4148 at the E end of Whitsand Bay juts far out and is capped by a primitive hermitage chapel – a worthwhile walk from the pretty village of Kingsand. Close by is the **Mount Edgecumbe Country Park** SX4552, with woodland and parkland walks and some striking waterside views of Plymouth.

Inland, from **Luxulyan** SX0558 (which has a pleasant church) you can walk along the lush wooded valley to the S, strewn with huge granite boulders and crossed by an impressive viaduct; if you feel adventurous you can climb up the valley to the top of the viaduct. Though the **Tamar Valley** is short on good circular walks, there are woodland paths close by Cothele SX4268.

We welcome reports from readers . . .

Readers who help us with reports for the GUIDE are offered a discount on the next edition: so please do help if you can!

Driving

In general, the roads in this area wind about so much that places where you can overtake safely are few and far between. In high summer, when there are a lot of drivers of varying speeds about (some with caravans), this means progress is very slow; and remember that, because the roads do twist about so much, what looks a short distance on the map works out much longer in practice. The unclassified roads are often single-track, though perfectly well surfaced, which slows things down even more, as you have to keep backing up to a passing place.

In spring and early summer, when the roads are much emptier, the roadside hedgerows are a particular pleasure. The Cornish 'hedge' is actually a built-up stone-and-earth bank with hedging on top, giving a virtual wall of wild flowers edging many byroads at this time of year. Wild orchids bloom among the violets, primroses, foxgloves and so forth. But this mass of vegetation does make good views uncommon, especially near the coast.

For long-distance work, the A30 is the fastest route from Exeter down to the far end of Cornwall, and very much improved over the last ten years. In this part of Cornwall, getting up on to the A30 is generally a quicker, even if longer, way of driving any distance than trying to wriggle about cross-country. The A390 is much slower.

An unusually good unclassified road in this area is the one running almost due S from off the A39 just SW of Indian Queens, down through Grampound Road, past the back entrance to Trewithen, and on to Tregony.

The King Harry chain-drawn car ferry on the B3269 N of St Mawes is a quaint way from this area through to Mid Cornwall – a favourite family crossing.

Where to eat

Several of the hotels and inns recommended as good places to stay are also good for diners eating out – see above.

Fowey SX1252 FOOD FOR THOUGHT Town Quay (072 683) 2221 Generous helpings of carefully presented food in quayside evening restaurant – fine fish and some simple as well as other elaborate dishes, and lovely puddings; cl Sun, Jan, Feb; children over 10. **£25**.

Polperro SX2051 KITCHEN The Coombes (0503) 72780 Cottagey evening restaurant with vegetarian and fish specialities; fresh lobster and crab are esp wonderful; cl wkdys Nov-Apr. **£21**|£9.50.

Portloe SW9339 TREGAIN TEA ROOMS Small restaurant serving interesting, well-cooked food and specialising in local seafood; 2 bedrooms; cl Sun pm, end Oct-1 Apr. **£18**|£1.80/£3.

Polperro SX2051 BLUE PETER The Quay (0503) 72743 Atmospheric old-fashioned inn well placed in picturesque harbour, strong fishing theme, good cheery bar food inc lots of fresh fish, vegetarian meals, children's menu, winter Sun roasts. **£15**|£2.50/£5.50.

Other places here worth knowing for reasonable food include the Royal Oak at Lostwithiel SX1059, Rashleigh at Polkerris SX0952, Crumplehorn Mill in Polperro SX2051, and Who'd Have Thought It at St Dominick SX3967.

Mid Cornwall

This region has a good mix of coastal scenery, comfortable places to stay, very enjoyable walks, great gardens and other interesting attractions; all other parts of the county are within easy reach.

The lush almost subtropical gardens at Trelissick and Mawnan Smith, spectacular in spring, are rewarding at any time, and Flambards leisure park near Helston is one of Britain's best family attractions. The Poldark Mine Centre at Wendron is well thought-out; Falmouth, with its huge harbour, and Truro are both sizeable towns with a good deal of appeal to visitors. The eastern part of the coastline is intricately cut into estuaries and hidden creeks, rich in bird life, with some beautifully placed pubs – good for leisurely exploration by car, better on foot, best of all for pottering about in a boat. Further west are some fine long sandy beaches. Walking can be very enjoyable, with some memorable highlights.

There's a good choice of places to stay on or near the south coast.

Where to stay

Mullion SW6719 POLURRIAN Helston TR12 7EN (0326) 240421 **£150**; 40 rms, some with memorable sea view. Civilised modern comfort, indoor and outdoor pool, path down the high cliff to sheltered private cove, squash, gym, mini golf, tennis; good with children; disabled access; cl Nov-Mar.

Mawnan Smith SW7728 NANSIDWELL COUNTRY HOUSE Falmouth TR11 5HU (0326) 250340 **£150 inc dinner**; 12 rms. Comfortable granite house in wonderful woodland garden with sea views and direct access to good beach; fine food inc home-grown veg and home-made jams, log fires, fresh flowers; popular with older people; excellent restaurant; several gardens to visit nearby; cl Jan; disabled access.

Mawnan Smith SW7728 MEUDON Falmouth TR11 5HT (0326) 250541 **£120**; 32 well-equipped, comfortable rms in separate wing. Old stone mansion with newer wing in beautiful subtropical garden laid out by Capability Brown; fine views from dining room, carefully refurbished lounge with log fire, helpful, friendly service; free golf at Falmouth (those on weekend breaks pay £12 per round); cl Dec-Feb; children over 5; dogs welcome (not in public rooms).

Truro SW8244 ALVERTON MANOR TR1 1XQ (0872) 76633 **£95**; 25 attractive rms. Thoughtfully converted convent with elegant lounge, welcoming staff, and decent food; disabled access.

St Agnes SW7250 ROSE-IN-VALE COUNTRY HOUSE Mithian TR5 0QD (0872) 552202 **£61**; 17 rms. Quietly set Georgian house, comfortably updated; outdoor swimming pool; good with children; disabled access.

Gillan SW6527 TREGILDRY Helston TR12 6HG (032 623) 378 **£60**; 10 good rms with fine views over Falmouth Bay. Quiet and comfortable family-run hotel; decent food, helpful service; cl Nov-Feb.

Lizard SW7712 HOUSEL BAY Housel Cove, Helston TR12 7PG (0326) 290417 £58; 23 rms. Clifftop hotel with marvellous view; comfortable rooms and friendly owners; cl Jan-15 Feb.
Redruth SW6942 INN FOR ALL SEASONS Treleigh TR16 4AP (0209) 219511 £50; 12 rms. Spacious, stylishly modern inn with restful atmosphere, carefully chosen muted colours in comfortable lounge, good, interesting food, and helpful service.

To see and do

✝ **Carharrack** CHURCH SW7341 has an exhibition on Cornish Methodism and John Wesley, who preached at the chapel that used to stand here; open am Tues-Thurs July and Aug, or by appointment. Wesley preached more regularly at nearby **Gwennap** SW7440, where GWENNAP PIT, the amphitheatre he used, still has services, and there's a visitor centre with exhibitions; centre cl 12.30-2 pm, pm Sat, all Sun; the peaceful theatre itself is open all the time.

★ ♜ ❄ **Falmouth** SW8032 has a huge natural harbour full of sailing boats of every description, big sea-going ships, and passenger ferries (to St Mawes and Truro – great fun) and boat trips; it's also a busy but pleasant shopping centre with some nice old-fashioned streets, ships' chandlers and a good bustling atmosphere. The spiky-leaved dracaena trees away from the centre give it a quite foreign feel. PENDENNIS CASTLE One of Henry VIII's chain of coastal defences, with later 16th-c fortifications and superb views. Summer snacks, shop, disabled access to lower gun deck, shop and coffee shop; cl winter Mon, 25-26 Dec; *£2. MARITIME MUSEUM (Bells Court) Explores the area's nautical heritage with a big exhibition of packet ships, and a display to commemorate the 50th anniversary of the Normandy landings; shop; £1. The Seahorse on Maenporth Beach and the Quayside are good for lunch.

Godolphin Cross SW6031 GODOLPHIN HOUSE 15th-c house of Earls of Godolphin, well known for its colonnaded front, and painting of one of the three Arab stallion ancestors of all British bloodstock. In the stables is an exhibition of old maps and documents, as well as a number of old farm waggons; teas, shop (plants and herbs for sale), disabled access (ground floor and garden only); open pm Thurs May-Sept (all day in Aug) as well as pm Tues July-Sept and bank hols; *£3.

Gweek SW7027 SEAL SANCTUARY & MARINE RESCUE CENTRE The biggest seal sanctuary in Europe with 9 pools of injured or ill seals – you can watch them being fed twice a day; also penguins, donkeys and sheep, audio-visual displays, aquarium, nature trail and wildlife identification. Snacks, shop, disabled access; cl 25 Dec; £4.50. The Trengilly Wartha at Nancenoy is good for lunch.

☺ **Helston** SW6626 is world-famous for its Furry Dance (see our calendar). It has a popular Saturday market. The simple Blue Anchor pub has a 15th-c brewhouse which you can usually look around at lunchtime (and enjoy the reasonably priced beer). There's a little FOLK MUSEUM. But the main draw here is FLAMBARDS, an interesting and beautifully kept leisure park with three main attractions: a reconstructed Victorian village with shops and houses, lifesized 'Britain in the Blitz' street, and collection of aircraft. Also adventure playground, many rides and other amusements; lots of events throughout the year. Meals, snacks, shop, disabled access; cl Nov-Easter; £7.50.

❀ **Mawnan Smith** SW7727 TREBAH

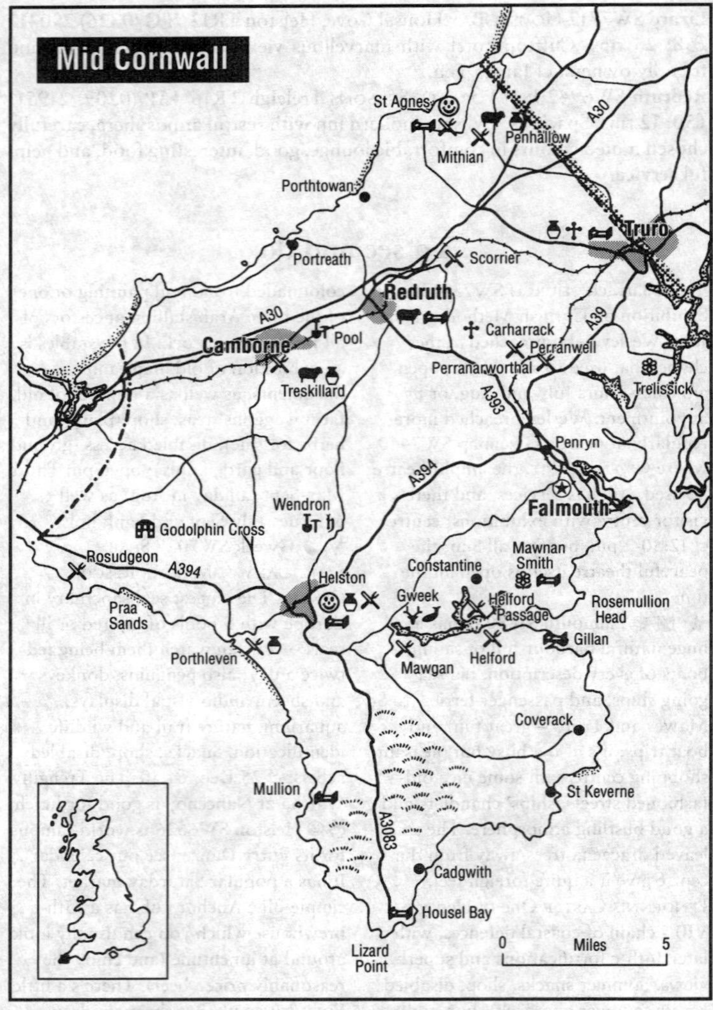

GARDEN This steeply wooded ravine garden, widely reckoned to be one of the finest in the world, falls from the 18th-c house down to a private beach on the Helford River; huge subtropical tree ferns and palms, giant gunnera, lots of blue and white hydrangeas, 100-year-old rhododendrons, some fine trees, and children's play area. Snacks, shop (plants for sale); *£2.50.

GLENDURGAN Lovely garden in valley above Helford River started by Alfred Fox in 1820; fine shrubs from all over the world, mature trees, walled garden. Cl Sun/Mon/Good Fri, cl Nov-Mar; *£2.50. NT.

Penhallow SW7651 CALLESTOCK CIDER FARM A traditional working cider farm producing scrumpy, country wines and jam, with demonstrations of each according to season, and friendly horses, rabbits, goats, pigs and donkeys. There's also a CIDER MUSEUM with old equipment such as ancient presses, a blacksmith's and cooper's workshops, and hives of the bees needed for pollination. Summer snacks, shop (with samples of everything they make), disabled access; cl Sun (exc shop 12-3 pm), Sat Nov-Dec, and all Jan-Easter; free, small charge for museum, which also incudes a tractor ride.

Pool SW6641 CORNISH ENGINES Two big beam engines originally used for pumping water from tin and copper mines, and also for lifting the men and ore from 1700 ft below ground. Shop; cl Nov-Apr; £1.80. NT.

Porthleven SW6225 SHIPWRECK CENTRE MUSEUM Appropriately situated on the rocks that brought so many sailors to their doom, the museum displays a good collection of various objects salvaged from wrecked ships, as well as a history of the harbour and the local lifeboat; shop; cl Jan and Feb, and part of Mar; *£1.30. The prettily placed Ship is good for lunch.

★ ☺ ! **St Agnes** SW7150 has some attractive steeply terraced cottages. ST AGNES LEISURE PARK Mature landscaped gardens with well-known Cornish buildings in miniature, dinosaur replicas, an animated circus and haunted house and fairyland; floodlit at night. Meals, snacks, shop, disabled access; cl Nov-Mar; £4.10. The Railway is an interesting pub for lunch.

Trelissick SW8339 TRELISSICK GARDEN Woodland park with beautifully kept gardens of camellias, magnolias and hydrangeas, also subtropical garden and other unusual plants; wonderful views of the King Harry Passage and over to Pendennis Castle. Meals, snacks, shop, disabled access; cl Sun am, garden cl Nov-Mar but park, shop, gallery, restaurant open until 22 Dec; £3. NT. The Punch Bowl & Ladle at Penelewey is good for lunch.

Treskillard SW6739 On Lower Gryllis Farm is the SHIRE HORSE FARM & CARRIAGE MUSEUM, where the horses actually do work the land; working blacksmith's and wheelwright's shops, good display of horse-drawn models, horse-drawn farm implements and carriages. Snacks, shop, disabled access; cl Sat and Nov-Easter; £2.75.

† **Truro** SW8244 is a busy town with good shops (market day Weds) and several decent pubs; Lemon Street is a particularly fine Georgian street, and Boscawen Street is cobbled. ROYAL CORNWALL MUSEUM (River St) Interesting county museum that always seems to be bigger on each visit; world-famous collection of minerals as well as pottery, fine ivories, paintings, toys and pewter, and good history displays. Meals, snacks, shop, disabled access; cl Sun, bank hols, 25-26 Dec, 1 Jan; *£1.20. The CATHEDRAL is in Early English style and finished in 1910; the twin spires of the west front are handsome. The Globe, William IV and Wig & Pen in Truro are all good for lunch.

Wendron SW6731 POLDARK MINE AND HERITAGE CENTRE Quite a jolly peculiarity at this old tin mine is its underground post box, the deepest in Britain and fun for children to send postcards from. More serious features include a tour of the mine, an 18th-c village, a film on the history of Cornish mining, old cottages, big collection of working beam engines and other antiquities, and children's amusements. Meals, snacks, shop; cl Nov-Easter; *£4.95.

★ **Attractive coastal villages** include Cadgwith SW7214 (fish stores and thatched cottages), Coverack SW7818 (good walks and view of The Manacle rocks), Mullion SW6719 (carved into fiercely craggy coast), Penryn SW7834 (pretty houses dropping down to the river), Porthtowan SW6948, Portreath SW6545, and St Keverne SW7821. Constantine SW7229 is an attractive inland village with a good pub.

Waterside pubs in delightful settings include the Pandora on Restronguet Creek past Mylor Bridge (SW8137; the best location of any Cornish pub), Shipwrights Arms at Helford SW7526 and Heron at Malpas SW8442.

Walks

The most southerly point in England, **Lizard Point** SW1177 (in itself not that special), is a good start for bracing cliff walks in either direction, with good views. Lizard village SW7012 (even less special) is well placed for longer walks encompassing Church Cove to the E and Kynance Cove to the W. Inland, the Lizard is largely flat and not really worth extended walks. Dramatic **Mullion Cove** SW6617 is best reached by a there-and-back walk along the cliff from Porth Mellin SW6618; the extension S to Kynance Cove is outstanding. A rewarding short stroll on the coast path from picturesque **Cadgwith** SW7114 leads S to Chynhalls Point past the aptly named Devil's Frying Pan, where the waves foam into a spectacular collapsed cavern. The NE part of the Lizard around **Helford** SW7526 and **Dennis Head** SW7825 is appreciably leafier, and has some intricate coves and an undemanding coast path.

Other rewarding stretches of coast path include **Rosemullion Head** SW7927 (from Mawnan SW7827, or Maenporth SW7929, where there's a sheltered sandy cove with decent modern pub/restaurant), the cliffs above **Mullion** SW6617, the walk down from Coverack SW7818 to **Black Head** SW7716 and maybe beyond, and **Lowland Point** SW8019 (reached from Coverack or St Keverne), for dramatic views of The Manacles. At **Rinsey** SW5927 the coast path passes two magnificently sited ruined tin and copper mine buildings, Wheal Prosper and Wheal Trewavas, both now maintained as landmarks by the NT; a few miles inland, **Tregonning Hill** SW6029, although it takes only a few minutes to climb, has an impressive view; here in 1746 William Cookworthy made the first discovery of china clay in England, and went on to make porcelain. A pleasant short walk with a good finish is the stroll round from **Mylor Bridge** SW8036 to the pub at Restronguet Passage.

Almost any stretch of the **coast path in the north** gives long bracing clifftop walks (a good base is Portreath SW6545, which has a decent pub); Wheale Coates is one of the most photogenic mine ruins on the Cornish coast, and the diversion up St Agnes Beacon SW7150 is well worth it for the commanding views.

The rock at **Roche** SW9860 has a 14th-c ruined ivy-covered chapel built into the rock and just off B3274 (decent pub nearby off past the station). Another inland viewpoint is **Carn Brea** SW6840, above the industrial towns of Redruth and Camborne.

A particularly fine beach is at **Kynance Cove** SW6813 on the Lizard peninsula; it's a long walk down from the car park but well worth it – strange rock formations and caves and sandy coves (lovely views from the cliff walk S). **Praa Sands** SW5727 is a popular summer family beach, and the long stretch of rocky beach S of Porthleven SW6225 (good pubs in the village) is a good walk if the surf's not beating in too fiercely.

Driving

The B3293 S from Helston and the A3083 down to the Lizard, and the byroad that runs between them across Goonhilly Downs, are unusual for the area in being relatively straight and high, giving quite distant views. Otherwise, roads near the coast tend to give few decent views – though in spring the massive banks and hedges that shut you in are delightfully colourful. In the north, there are some sea views from the B3301. The A39 between Falmouth and Truro can be tiresomely slow at almost any time of year.

Where to eat

Helford SW7526 RIVERSIDE (0326) 231443 Cosy creekside restaurant with carefully kept garden and terrace for aperitifs and meals, and daily changing, carefully cooked imaginative food with emphasis on fish and shellfish; cl end Nov-end Feb; children over 12 in restaurant; disabled access. **£26.25|£7.35.**
Mithian SW7450 MINERS ARMS (087 255) 2375 Secluded Tudor pub with lots of character, fine old furnishings, good reliable food and real ale; disabled access. **£12|**£2.50/£4.95.
St Agnes SW7150 TURKS HEAD The Quay (0720) 22434 Idyllically placed pub overlooking sweeping bay and with outstanding views, good food inc plenty of fresh fish, cream cakes/ices all afternoon, evening barbecues; can take food down to beach. £1.50/£4.25.
Besides places mentioned in passing in the text, others worth knowing here for reasonable food include the Old Shire in Camborne SW6440, Ferryboat at Helford Passage SW7627, Old Courthouse at Mawgan SW7323, Norway at Perranarworthal SW7839, Royal Oak at Perranwell SW7839, Coach & Horses at Rosudgeon SW5529, and Fox & Hounds at Scorrier SW7244.

WEST CORNWALL

This area is decidedly different and remote, with some wild coast, fine bracing walks and a good choice of places to stay.

West Cornwall's strongest appeal is to people who love the outdoors. Though in winter it's milder than most places, with violets out along the cliffs even in January, at any time of year the winds can be fierce. The landscape is appropriately austere: wild coastline with challenging clifftop walks and some magnificent scenery, small rather withdrawn-looking granite villages and farmsteads, wind-beaten pastures. Past the age of seven or so, children appreciate and enjoy the wildness, but there are fewer paid-for family outings here than in other parts of Cornwall: among them the fairy-tale castle on St Michael's Mount is well worth the visit from Marazion, and Paradise Park at Hayle is popular, while for quieter or older tastes Trengwainton Garden at Madron is excellent. No first-time visit to this part of Cornwall would be complete without a look at St Ives. There is an abundance of prehistoric remains, besides the remarkable prehistoric villages near Madron and Sancreed.

The area does have a noticeably separatist sense of its own identity, almost like the more nationalistic parts of Wales; but though visitors are clearly seen as outsiders, the locals are far from unfriendly.

Where to stay

Newlyn SW4628 HIGHER FAUGAN Penzance TR18 5NS (0736) 62076 **£88**; 12 rms. Country house in ten acres of quiet gardens and grounds; pleasantly old-

fashioned sitting room, helpful owners, good home-made food using local fish and veg, and outdoor swimming pool, tennis, putting green.
Lamorna Cove SW4524 LAMORNA COVE Penzance TR19 6XH (0736) 731411 **£75**; 15 well-furnished rms, most with cove views. Comfortable, beautifully situated hotel overlooking gardens to the sea; homely rooms, fresh local food, outdoor heated swimming pool; dogs by arrangement (not in public rms); marvellous walks.
Penzance SW4730 ABBEY HOTEL TR18 4AR (0736) 66906 **£75**; 7 rms. Relaxed 17th-c house close to harbour with marvellous views; comfortable homely rooms full of flowers, fine paintings and antiques; pretty garden, good food; cl 3 days over Christmas; no very small children.
St Ives SW5441 GARRACK TR26 3AA (0736) 796199 **£75**; 18 rms. Friendly hotel with wonderful sea views; cosy lounges, family room, restaurant with good food inc fresh shellfish; friendly staff, lovely garden, indoor leisure centre; disabled access.
Sennen SW3425 STATE HOUSE Penzance TR19 7AA (0736) 871844 **£75**; 34 cheerfully modern rms. Comfortable refurbished hotel with fine views (lots of glass to make the most of them); pretty restaurant, obliging staff, decent food.
Sennen SW3425 OLD SUCCESS Penzance TR19 7DG (0736) 871232 **£50**; 12 well-kept and attractive rms, mostly with bthrm. Friendly, 17th-c fisherman's inn with magnificent views; cottagey, comfortable lounge, lifeboat/shipwreck decorations, and good-value food inc fresh seafood.
Pendeen SW3834 TREWELLARD MANOR FARM Penzance TR19 7SU (0736) 788526 **£35**; 3 rms, 1 without bthrm. Victorian house in lovely coastal spot with log fire in lounge and fine walks all round; cl Christmas.
Buryas Bridge SW4429 ROSE FARM Penzance TR19 6AN (0736) 731808 **£34**; 2 delightfully furnished rms. Relaxed, informal, friendly farmhouse tucked away down remote country lane; excellent breakfasts around big wooden table; can see animals (working farm); children love it; cl 25-26 Dec.
Botallack SW3633 MANOR FARM St Just in Penwith Penzance TR19 7QG (0736) 788525 **£34**; 3 rms. Blissfully quiet and friendly 17th-c local granite farmhouse next to working farm, with medley of furnishings in comfortable lounge; good breakfasts with home-baked bread, and safe walled garden; no pets; marvellous walks along cliffs, lots of ruined mines, and small coves.

To see and do

Hayle SW5537 PARADISE PARK Exotic and endangered bird species from all over the world, from humming birds to eagles, with successful breeding too. The Victorian gardens also house the Cornish Otter Sanctuary, the World Parrot Trust, a lively falconry display, rare farm animals, miniature railway and amusement centre. A very busy and enjoyable centre. Meals, snacks (pub on site), shop, disabled access; £4.50.
Lamorna SW4424 LAMORNA POTTERY In school hols children can try their hands at the wheel here, and the rest of the time as well as the pottery there's a boutique selling locally made clothes and jewellery and a garden with acclaimed cream teas; meals, snacks, shop, disabled access; cl Nov-Feb. The Lamorna Wink is useful for lunch.
Land's End SW3425 The most westerly point of England, with wild and blustery walks along dramatic clifftops, and on a clear day VIEWS out as far even as the Scilly Isles. The 200-acre site has been extensively

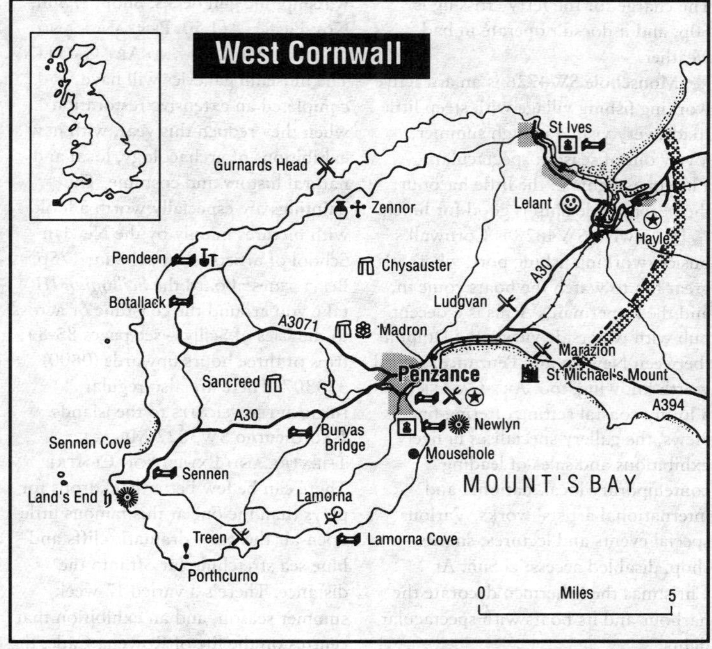

developed for visitors in the last few years, with interesting sound and light displays of Cornish sea life, and EXHIBITIONS tracing the history of the area. Children like the lifeboat they can clamber all over, and there are a couple of smugglers' coves to explore as well. Meals, snacks, neat shopping arcade, good disabled access; cl 25 Dec; *£4.95.

Lelant MERLINS MAGICLAND Adventure park with bumper boats, electric motor bikes, mini Ferrari Grand Prix rides, gun range, etc. Snacks; cl Nov-Easter; no entrance fee but pay for each ride.

Madron SW4532 TRENGWAINTON GARDEN Fine garden with magnolias, azaleas, rhododendrons, walled garden with plants that won't usually grow outside in England, lovely tree-fern grotto, and good views to Mounts Bay. Cl Mon, Tues, Sun, Nov-Feb; cream teas, disabled access, interesting plant sales; £2.20. NT.

nr Madron SW4734 CHYSAUSTER ANCIENT VILLAGE You can get a good impression of village life 2,000 years ago at this group of eight courtyard houses, with little terraced gardens, workshops and stables; the underground chamber here has unfortunately collapsed. Shop; cl Oct-Mar; £1.30.

Marazion SW5130 ST MICHAEL'S MOUNT There's something particularly awe-inspiring about this medieval castle, rising up majestically from the sea. In many ways it looks its best on gloomy or stormy days, when its picturesque silhouette seems even more dramatic. Still the home of the family which acquired it in 1660, the castle is reached by ferry or by foot along a causeway at low tide, and has fine Chippendale furniture, plaster reliefs, armour and pictures. Summer meals, snacks, shop; open Mon-Fri and most weekends Apr-Oct; for winter opening best to phone (0736) 710507; £3. NT.

The charge for the ferry crossing is 60p, and it doesn't operate in bad weather.

★ **Mousehole** SW4726 is an attractive working fishing village with steep little roads, very visited in high summer, lovely out of season; spectacular Christmas lights in the little harbour; the harbourside Ship is good for lunch.

Newlyn SW4628 is Cornwall's busiest working fishing port, where it's great fun to watch the boats come in, and the Fisherman's Arms is a decent pub with waterside views; the Dolphin (between Newlyn and Penzance) is well worth knowing, too. ART GALLERY In a lovely coastal setting offering fine views, the gallery specialises in lively exhibitions and sales of leading contemporary local, national and international artists' works. Various special events and lectures; snacks, shop, disabled access; cl Sun. At Christmas the fishermen decorate the harbour and its boats with spectacular lights.

Pendeen SW3834 LEVANT MINE An unusual mine beneath the sea, powered by the oldest steam engine in Cornwall. It stopped working in 1930, but is now operating again after a vigorous restoration campaign; shop, disabled access (but no facilities); open Sun-Fri July-Sept, and Fri Jan-Jun; £2. NT.

Penzance SW4730 is a nice, relaxed town by the sea, and a major shopping centre for the area – the Egyptian House is worth a look, and there are some good pubs. You can get a ferry to the Isles of Scilly from here. NATIONAL LIGHTHOUSE CENTRE (The Old Buoy Store, Wharf Rd) The finest collection of lighthouse equipment in the world, audio-visual displays showing the history of lighthouses, how they were built and how the lighthouse-keepers lived, with a reconstructed lighthouse room. Shop, disabled access; cl Nov-Apr; £2. MARITIME MUSEUM (19 Chapel St) Displays of treasures from wrecks and a full-scale section of an 18th-c warship, inc gun decks. Shop; cl Sun, Nov-Easter; *£1.50. PENZANCE AND DISTRICT MUSEUM AND ART GALLERY The museum galleries will have completed an extensive restoration when they reopen this year, with new exhibitions of archaeology, local and natural history and costume. The paintings are especially worth a look, with pictures mainly by the Newlyn School of artists; shop; cl Sun; *75p. BOAT TRIPS aboard the *Scillonian III* take you around the coastline or across to the Isles of Scilly – see pages 83-84; trips of three hours upwards (0800) 373307. There are also regular HELICOPTER FLIGHTS to the islands.

! **Porthcurno** SW3822 MINACK THEATRE AND EXHIBITION CENTRE There can be few better backdrops for plays than the one at this famous little open-air theatre – dramatic cliffs and blue sea stretching far off into the distance. There's a varied 17-week summer season, and an exhibition that centres on the life of Rowena Cade, the remarkable woman who built the theatre with her own hands; snacks, shop, disabled access; cl Nov-Mar, and exhibition cl during matinees; shows £5, exhibition £1.50.

★ **St Ives** SW5141 A pretty place, despite the summer crowds, with its attractive working harbour and narrow streets and alleys (the cobbled Fore Street is the prettiest). Its famous popularity with artists is best explored at the TATE GALLERY ST IVES, the recently opened gallery specialising in Cornish art. It's an impressive building, outside and in, that fully exploits its spectacular cliffside setting – views are best from the café. Works by the familiar St Ives-school names are regularly joined by new displays of 20th-c art with a Cornish connection, some of which were previously exhibited at the London Tate. Videos and other performances; meals, snacks, shop; cl Mon Sept-May; disabled access. The *£2.50 admission charge also covers entrance to the BARBARA

HEPWORTH MUSEUM & SCULPTURE GARDEN devoted to her work and life, with sculptures in the house, studio and subtropical garden, as well as photographs and letters.

Sancreed SW4229 CARN EUNY ANCIENT VILLAGE Dating from the 1st c, a little village of stone courtyard houses, and a 66-ft underground passage leading to a circular chamber, used as a hiding place by the locals.

✝ **Zennor** SW4538 WAYSIDE MUSEUM Sited next to a restored old watermill, this good local-history museum covers the last 5,000 years, with items such as a Bronze-Age axe hammer head, early cooking implements, and agricultural and mining tools. Teas, shop; cl Nov-Easter; £1.75. The CHURCH is best seen in its granite landscape from the hills above.

ISLES OF SCILLY

As well as for day trips by helicopter from Penzance, the islands are a great place for a really relaxing short stay if you're close enough for the travelling not to be a serious obstacle.

A charmingly unspoilt collection of low islands 28 miles W of Land's End, the Scillies enjoy beautiful scenery, a variety of shorelines, and an almost subtropical climate. They offer scope for excellent coastal walks; the largest, St Mary's, which is just six square miles, can be comfortably circuited in a day. Four thousand years ago they formed one landmass, but over the centuries subsidence and the relentless pounding of the waves have created over 100 islands and islets. St Mary's, Tresco and St Agnes are the main populated ones, while some of the rest are simply strange-shaped rocks jutting out of the sea, their only visitors seals, dolphins and puffins.

You can get to the islands from Penzance by ferry (£30 each way) or more spectacularly by helicopter, a 20-minute ride with really beautiful views of the Cornish coast and the approach to the islands (return fares start at £50). The islands also have their own little airline Skybus which leaves from Land's End, Newquay or Exeter several times a day. The trip from Land's End is the quickest and cheapest, and there may be cheaper standby flights available on the day (no flights Sun). They also do packages in conjunction with Intercity – (0736) 787017 for full details.

Where to stay

Tresco SV8914 ISLAND Tresco Isles of Scilly TR24 0PU (0720) 22883 **£170 inc dinner**; 40 rms, many with balconies and terrace overlooking gardens or sea. Tiny private island, renowned for its wonderful subtropical Abbey Gardens and reached by helicopter or boat – hotel tractor-drawn bus (no cars allowed; bike hire available) takes you to spacious, very friendly modern hotel with colonial-style bar, library, fine food, panoramic views, swimming pool, private beach; cl Nov-Feb.

St Mary's TREGARTHENS Hugh Town, St Mary's Isles of Scilly TR21 0PP (0720) 22540 **£110 inc dinner**; 29 rms, most with sea views. First opened in 1848 by Captain Tregarthen, owner of the locally famous steam packet LITTLE WESTERN, this modernised and extended hotel has magnificent views over the harbour and outer islands of Samson, Bryher and Tresco; good food and pleasant service; cl mid-Oct-mid-Mar.

Pelistry Bay CARNWETHERS St Mary's Isles of Scilly TR21 0NX (0720) 22415 **£84 inc dinner**; 10 rms. Well-run country guesthouse near very fine beach with lots of coastal walks all round; an acre of lovely gardens, heated swimming pool, croquet, games room with pool table and table tennis, and sauna; lounge with helpful books about the islands, well-stocked bar, good, freshly cooked set 4-course dinner using local produce, and sound wine list; cl Nov-Mar; children over 7. All the above have good food.

To see and do

As each of the islands is so small, few apart from Tresco have many specific attractions – visitors mainly come in order to 'get away from it all'. The total population of the islands is just 2,000, so there really can be a refreshing feeling of complete isolation. By far the best activity on all the islands is walking – there are plenty of white sandy beaches to stroll along, or unusual plants and birds to track down. Hiring bikes is another good way of exploring and enjoying the scenery. Thanks to the climate, flowers come out early, and spring and autumn sunsets can be particularly beautiful. A good plan is to island-hop – there are regular ferries between the larger islands, though it can prove expensive. Every Fri evening and some Weds in summer you can watch the racing of the traditional six-oar gigs that used to dash out to shipwrecks.

★ **St Mary's** SV9010 The hub of Scilly Isles life, though its centre, Hugh Town, is little more than a village by mainland standards. Most ferries and planes arrive here, and you can get a number of PLEASURE CRUISES from the Old Quay out to the bird and seal colonies on the outer islets and islands; there are fishing trips from here too. The MUSEUM is a good introduction to the area's geology and natural history, with a collection of shipwrecked treasures. The LONGSTONE HERITAGE CENTRE concentrates on the maritime history of the islands, and also has interpretative displays on their ecology. Up in the north at Bants Carn there's a burial chamber and ancient village. Back down south, walk out to Peninnis head for good views of the Wolf and Bishop's Rock lighthouses. Just along the coast is STAR CASTLE.

Tresco SV8915 The highlight here is the amazing SUBTROPICAL GARDEN around the grounds of the Abbey, begun in 1834 and which, despite storms, contains a magnificent collection of exotic plants from the southern hemisphere. Also in these grounds is VALHALLA, a collection of carved figureheads from wrecked ships, many dating back to the 17th c. Helicopters from Penzance land just outside the garden gate, so it's possible (though not cheap) to come here for just a day. The southern parts of the island are mainly sandy but in the north it's more wild and rugged, with the remains of castles of both Charles I and Oliver Cromwell, and a cave known as Piper's Hole.

St Agnes SV8807 has the most south-westerly community in the British Isles, and is joined to a smaller island called Gugh by a sandbar, awash at high tide. The sheltered cove here is especially popular, with the Turks Head pub an added attraction. The views from here out to the rocks and islets are very atmospheric – especially when you remember more ships have been wrecked here than anywhere comparable in the world.

Bryher SV8715 is a tiny quiet place, even by Scilly standards. The south bay has lots of wild flowers.

St Martins SV9215 is a narrow rocky ridge with flowers stretching down to the main attraction – the extensive beaches, very popular for picnics.

Walks

Most of the coastline is marvellous for clifftop walks – a lot harder work than those along the rest of the south coast to the east, and bracing winds too. At **Treen** SW3923 you can walk from the Logan Rock pub (good food) to the Logan Rock peninsula SW3922 (extraordinarily balanced boulder), and away along the NT cliffs to the magical open-air Minack Theatre, cut into the steep cliffs. When there isn't a performance on, you can wander around it (and then clamber down to the wonderful silver-sand Porthcurno beach SW3822 – at low tide you can walk round to the other side, but watch you don't get cut off). **Lamorna Cove** SW4520 (where there's another decent pub, a bit up the lane) also has some splendid cliff walks in both directions.

From **Land's End** there are fine cliff walks in both directions – the one to Sennen SW3425 is lovely, and the cove there is worth looking around. On a wild day **Botallack** SW3632, with its ruined engine house right down by the sea, is very dramatic, and there are fine steep walks all around. Around **St Just** SW3631 (the Star pub is good) are more bracing walks too.

On the north side, the moors nearly reach the sea around **Morvah** SW4035, from where in a few miles you can take in the cliff path, the moors close to the ruin of Ding Dong Mine, the prehistoric stone hoop of Men an Tol and the Iron-Age hillfort of Chûn Castle (close by Chûn Quoit, a Bronze-Age burial chamber). You can walk for miles without seeing another soul around **Zennor** SW4538 (decent pub); near Treen SW4337 (not to be confused with the one on the S coast), **Gurnards Head** SW4338 juts dramatically into the Atlantic.

Beaches to walk along include the long one below the cliffs at Whitesand Bay SW3527, stretching away N of Sennen Cove SW3524 (very popular with surfers), and (out of season, when the caravan and camp sites are empty) the magnificent sands around St Ives Bay SW5440. There are lovely silver sands near Porthcurno SW3822.

An inland viewpoint worth heading for is **Carn Brea** SW3828, between Penzance and Land's End.

Driving

Even the smaller lanes here are less hedged-in than in many other parts of the county, so you do get quite a few striking views of the sea and of the granite-flecked pastures. But, as elsewhere in Cornwall, the byroads do wiggle about quite sharply and tend to be narrow.

Where to eat

Places worth knowing here for reasonable food include the Gurnards Head Hotel on Gurnards Head SW4338, White Hart at Ludgvan SW5033, Station at Marazion SW5231, Turks Head in Penzance SW4730 and Logan Rock at Treen SW3824.

We welcome reports from readers . . .

Readers who help us with reports for the GUIDE are offered a discount on the next edition: so please do help if you can!

North Cornwall

This area has a combination of majestic coastal scenery with lively family attractions and some fine places to stay.

This long coast shares with West Cornwall the county's best walks. Unlike that area, it has an unusually successful mix of secluded coves and villages with old-fashioned seaside resorts and camp sites – sometimes even in the same place, as at Padstow. Newquay is a good family centre, and a full bag of family attractions includes the intriguing World in Miniature at Goonhavern, the otter park at North Petherwin, other animal centres at Bolventor, Tredinnick and Launceston, and steam trains from Bodmin, Launceston and Newlyn East. For quieter tastes there are attractive houses to visit at Trerice, Bodmin and Padstow, and some interesting prehistoric remains especially at St Neot, Minions and St Cleer. Inland, the windswept, rather inhospitable Bodmin Moor, though not so good for walkers as Dartmoor, has its own bleak character, with strange tors, prehistoric traces, wind-bent trees, granite walls and lonely lakes.

Though there's a very good choice of places to stay, those for eating out are rather thinner on the ground.

Where to stay

Constantine Bay SW8574 Treglos Padstow PL28 8JH (0841) 520727 **£108**; 44 light rms, some with balcony. Seaside hotel close to good sandy beach and with comfortable traditional furnishings; log fires, friendly helpful staff, quiet relaxed atmosphere, sheltered garden, indoor swimming pool; lovely nearby walks; also, four self-catering apartments; discounts at eight local golf courses; cl Nov-mid-Mar; disabled access.

Port Isaac SX0080 Port Gaverne PL29 3SQ (0208) 8802441 **£86**; 19 comfortable rms (sound of the sea). Particularly lovely place to stay and an excellent base for area (dramatic coves, good clifftop walks, and lots of birds); big log fires in well-kept bars, relaxed lounges, decent bar food, very good restaurant food, and fine wines; also, restored 18th-c self-catering cottages; cl 8 Jan-19 Feb.

Padstow SW9175 Old Custom House South Quay PL28 8ED (0841) 532359 **£76**; 27 attractive rms. Attractively refurbished hotel overlooking harbour; conservatory and spacious bar; good restaurant with lots of fish dishes.

Crackington Haven SX1396 Manor Farm Bude EX23 0JW (08403) 304 **£76 inc dinner**; 5 pretty rms. Lovely, secluded Domesday-listed manor with house-party atmosphere; antiques in several lounges, log fire, games room, home cooking, pretty garden; no smoking; no children.

Treyarnon Bay SW8673 Waterbeach Padstow PL28 8JW (0841) 520292 **£68**; 20 rms. Useful for families, with comfortable modern decor in light airy rooms, fine view of beach and bay; also, self-catering cottages; cl Nov-Feb; disabled access.

Trelights SW9979 LONG CROSS Port Isaac PL29 3TF (0208) 880243 **£58**; 10 rms, some with sea view. Well-modernised Victorian house with interesting period 'garden of secrets', attractive plants in carefully restored interlocking hedged enclosures snugged down against the winds; winter Victorian banquets with free accommodation.

Camelford SX1083 KINGS ACRE PL32 9UR (0840) 213561 **£56**; 5 rms. Attractive Georgian manor house offering B & B with cheerful welcome.

Newquay SW8161 HOTEL LOWENVA 103 Mount Wise TR7 2BT (0637) 873569 **£52**; 18 light and airy, well-equipped rms. Warmly welcoming modern family-run hotel in town centre with sea views; spacious lounge and well-stocked bar, pleasant dining room, good food, outside swimming pool; children welcome.

Maxworthy SX2592 WHEATLEY FARM Launceston PL15 8LY (056 681) 232 **£36**; 4 rms. Comfortable, pretty furnishings, log fires, games room, animals to visit, pony rides, play area for children; cl Oct-Mar.

Quintrell Downs SW8560 MANUELS FARM Newquay TR8 4NY (0637) 873577 **£36**; 4 rms, shared bthrm. B & B in 17th-c farmhouse; log fires, candle-lit dinners, pretty garden; good for children – bottle-feed calves, collect eggs and so forth (free babysitting, too).

Tregadillett SX2983 ELIOT ARMS Launceston TL15 7EU (0566) 772051 **£36**; 2 rms, shared bthrm. Friendly, creeper-covered old house; lots to look at such as 66 antique clocks inc seven grandfathers; very good food with plenty of fish and interesting daily specials.

Tregaswith SW8963 TREGASWITH FARMHOUSE Newquay TR8 4HY (0637) 881181 **£36**; 4 pretty, homely rms. 18th-c house with beams and antiques on smallholding breeding horses (pony rides) and rare poultry; dogs welcome by arrangement.

Crackington Haven SX1396 TREWORGIE BARTON Bude EX23 0NL (08403) 233 **£32**; 5 attractive rms. Traditional 16th-c farmhouse in quiet rolling farmland; friendly owners who've been here 20 years; good food using local produce, open fires; cl Oct, Dec, Jan.

To see and do

Bodmin SX0360 PENCARROW Notable 18th-c house with fine paintings and furniture, a rococo ceiling in the music room, and 50 acres of lovely formal and woodland gardens with over 600 different rhododendrons and an acclaimed conifer collection. The grounds also have marked trails, a children's play area, pets' corner, CRAFT CENTRE, and an ancient British encampment. Meals, snacks, shop, disabled access; house cl Fri and Sat, mid-Oct-Easter, garden open all the time; *£3.50, garden only *£1.50.

BODMIN & WENFORD RAILWAY Restored steam locomotives take you back to the glory days of the Great Western railway when hordes of holidaymakers travelled this route to the sun; only 3½ miles of track, but lovely views, and you can stop off for pleasant woodland walks. BR trains connect with the railway at Bodmin Parkway station. Snacks, shop, disabled access; cl Jan-Mar and usually Nov – best to phone for train times (0208) 73666; £4.50.

! **Bolventor** SX1876 POTTER'S MUSEUM OF CURIOSITY Few places included in this book are quite so bizarre as this astonishing Victorian collection of stuffed animals. Mr Potter's love of taxidermy went far beyond simply displaying animals in glass cases – he painstakingly constructed elaborate tableaux around

North Cornwall

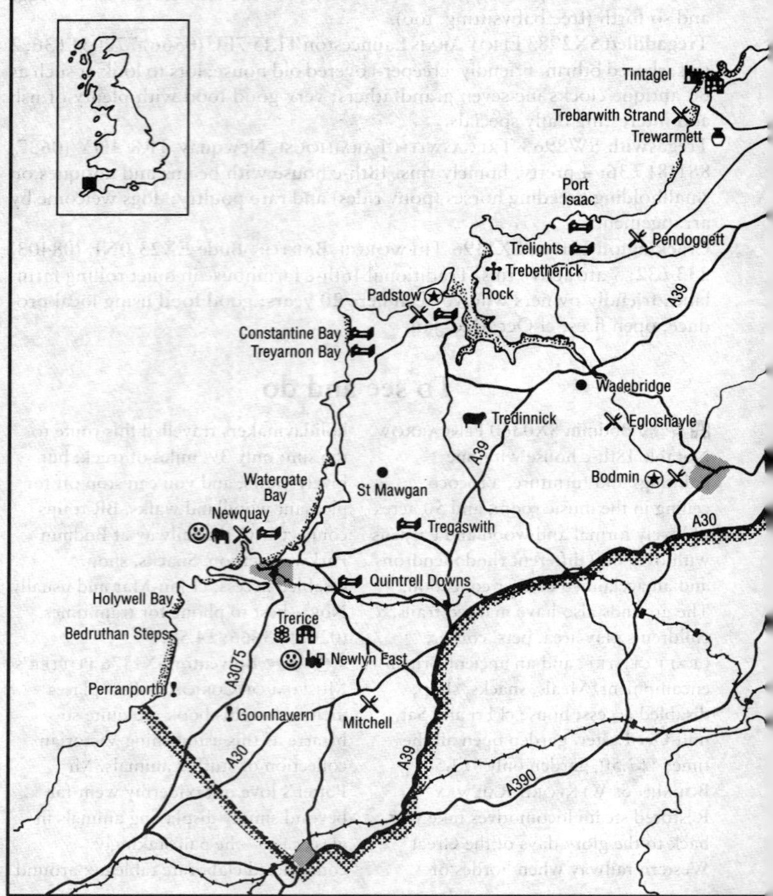

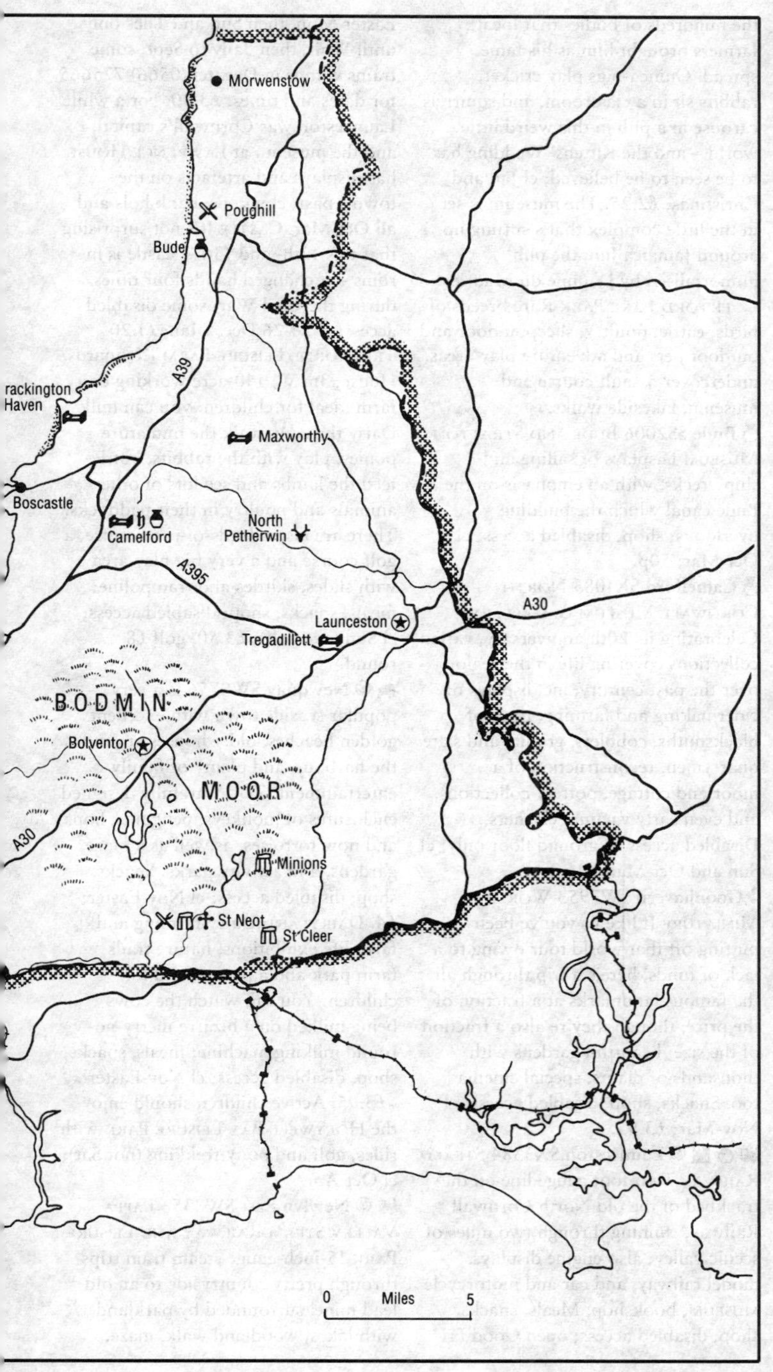
Morwenstow
Poughill
Bude
A39
rackington
Haven
Maxworthy
Boscastle
Camelford
North
Petherwin
A395
A30
Launceston
Tregadillett
BODMIN
Bolventor
MOOR
A30
Minions
St Neot
St Cleer
0
Miles
5

the hundreds of bodies that local farmers brought him as his fame spread. Guinea-pigs play cricket, rabbits sit in a classroom, and squirrels carouse in a pub in this weird little world – and the Kittens' Wedding has to be seen to be believed; cl Jan and Christmas; £2.25. The museum is set in the little complex that's sprung up around Jamaica Inn, the pub immortalised by Daphne du Maurier. COLLIFORD LAKE PARK Rare breeds of birds, cattle, poultry, sheep, indoor and outdoor pets and adventure play areas, undercover assault course and museum, lakeside walks.

Bude SS2006 BUDE AND STRATTON MUSEUM Displays of sailing and shipwrecks, with an emphasis on the Bude canal which the building overlooks; shop, disabled access; cl Oct-Mar; 50p.

Camelford SX1083 NORTH CORNWALL MUSEUM & GALLERY Celebrating its 20th anniversary, varied collections covering life in the region over the past century, inc displays of cidermaking and farming, tools of blacksmiths, cobblers, granite and slate quarrymen, reconstruction of a moorland cottage, pottery collections, and even early vacuum cleaners. Disabled access to ground floor only; cl Sun and Oct-Mar; £1.

! **Goonhavern** SW7953 WORLD IN MINIATURE If like us you've been putting off that world tour owing to a lack of funds, here's a trip through all the famous landmarks at a fraction of the price, though they're also a fraction of the size; beautiful gardens with thousands of plants, special cinema too. Snacks, shop, disabled access; cl Nov-Mar; £3.95.

☺ **Launceston** SX3384 STEAM RAILWAY Two-foot gauge line on the trackbed of the old North Cornwall Railway, running through two miles of scenic valley; also engine displays, model railway, and car and motorcycle MUSEUM, bookshop. Meals, snacks, shop, disabled access; open Good Fri-Easter Mon, then Sun and Tues only until Whit, then daily to Sept; some trains wknds in Dec, tel (0566) 775665 for dates and times; £3.30. For a while Launceston was Cornwall's capital, and the museum at LAWRENCE HOUSE has displays and artefacts on the town's past; cl wknds, bank hols and all Oct-Mar. CASTLE It's not surprising that this 12th- and 13th-c castle is in ruins – it changed hands four times during the Civil War; some disabled access; cl 24-26 Dec, 1 Jan; £1.20. TRETHORNE LEISURE FARM (Kennards House, 3m W) 140-acre working dairy farm ideal for children: you can milk Daisy the cow, walk the miniature ponies, play with the rabbits, bottle-feed the lambs and see lots of other animals and poultry in their paddocks. There are also a birds-of-prey centre, a golf course and a very big play area with slides, skittles and trampoline; meals, snacks, shop; disabled access; cl Sun (exc golf); £3.50, golf £8 round.

☺ **Newquay** SW8756 is a very popular seaside town with excellent golden beaches, older houses around the harbour, and plenty of family entertainment. ZOO Carefully designed enclosures of monkeys, penguins, lions and now tortoises, as well as a maze, gardens, and activity parks. Snacks, shop, disabled access; cl Nov-Easter; £4. DAIRYLAND Dairy-farming and farm-life exhibitions, nature trails, farm park and a playground for children. You can watch the cows being milked on a bizarre merry-go-round milking machine; meals, snacks, shop, disabled access; cl Nov-Easter; *£3.95. Active children should enjoy the HOLYWELL BAY LEISURE PARK with rides, golf and pony-trekking (not Sat); cl Oct-Apr.

☺ **Newlyn East** SW8356 LAPPA VALLEY STEAM RAILWAY AND LEISURE PARK 15-inch-gauge steam train trips through pretty countryside to an old lead mine, surrounded by parkland with lakes, woodland walk, maze, crazy golf and play areas. The grounds have wild flowers and shrubs and the Wheal Rose mine is being restored – there's a film on its history and the disaster that befell it in 1846; meals, snacks, shop, some disabled access; cl Nov-Apr; £3.95, covers fare and all attractions.

North Petherwin SX2889 TAMAR OTTER PARK Twenty acres of woodland where otters are bred for release. The attractive and playful Asian short-clawed otters are also bred here, and you can watch them playing. Three species of deer roam free, and there are waterfowl lakes, wallabies, and nature trails. Snacks, shop, disabled access; cl Nov-Mar; £3.

★ **Padstow** SW9175 has narrow streets, old buildings clustered around the working harbour, and attractive slate houses. PRIDEAUX PLACE The home of an ancient Cornish clan, this fine old house has been very well restored over the last few years. Not too much has changed since it was built in the late 16th c, but attention was needed in some of the 44 bedrooms left almost uninhabitable by American soldiers during the war. The rest of the well-furnished building is a good example of a lived-in family home, and there are concerts and special events in the grounds; snacks, shop; cl am, Fri and Sat, Oct-Easter; £3.50. SHIPWRECK MUSEUM Not far from the town's little habour, a collection of relics and tales of the plentiful shipwrecks along this coast; shop, disabled access; £1. The London Inn, Golden Lion and Old Custom House are useful for lunch.

! **Perranporth** SW7554 has GLIDER FLIGHTS under instruction from Trevellas Airfield (0726) 842798.

† **St Neot** SX1867 The village CHURCH is well known for its early stained glass.

★ **Tintagel** SX0588 TINTAGEL CASTLE Legends abound at these 12th- and 13th-c ruins, appropriately wild and windswept out of season but crowd-tamed in summer. Its famous links with King Arthur are probably fanciful (latest theories suggest he came from Shropshire), but there are plenty of more concrete historical connections. The dramatic ruins are good to wander through, have lovely views, and there's a small exhibition; lots of steep steps among the crags. Shop; cl 24-26 Dec, 1 Jan; £2. OLD POST OFFICE Small 14th-c manor house used in 19th c as a post office; shop; cl Nov-Apr; £1.90. NT. The Cornishman is useful for lunch.

† **Nr Trebetherick** SW9377 ST ENDOC'S CHURCH is tucked well away from the roads under a seaside hill, looking out to Padstow Bay; a nice stroll from the village.

Tredinnick SW9270 CORNISH SHIRE HORSE CENTRE This busy complex seems to offer more every year. The shire horses themselves are displayed in an indoor arena, and you can see them being groomed in their stables, where you'll also find rather less powerful Shetland ponies. There's an owl sanctuary where night-time flight is demonstrated, and lots more animals in a children's farm. As well as all this there's an exhibition of carts, waggons and rural equipment, a watermill, a photography display, working craftsmen and a big adventure playground. Though there's lots to see here for all ages, it's ideal for children; meals, snacks, shop, disabled access; cl Nov-Easter; *£3.95.

Trerice SW8457 TRERICE Pretty Elizabethan house with unusual gables and elaborate plasterwork ceilings in the magnificent Hall and Great Chamber. Fine furnishings from the 17th and 18th c, notable paintings inc several by John Opie, early embroideries, Oriental and English porcelain, and in the grounds a rather unusual collection of lawnmowers; lovely colourful GARDENS with Cornish fruit trees. Snacks, shop, very good disabled access; cl Tues and Nov-Apr; £3.60. NT.

Trewarmett SX0686 MUSEUM OF HISTORIC CYCLING The couple who run this comprehensive collection met through cycling, and really know their stuff. Housed in a former railway station are over 150 bicycles, from an original 1819 hobby horse through boneshakers and penny-farthings (properly called an ordinary) to the hi-tech bikes of today, with a reconstructed old repair shop and various assorted memorabilia. Outside is a sculpture made up of old bicycles; disabled access, shop; cl Fri and Sat and winter exc by appointment; *£2.

This part of Cornwall is full of interesting **prehistoric monuments**. The HURLERS STONE CIRCLES monument SX2571 nr Minions village is made up of three Bronze-Age circles – the central one still has 14 stones standing. Close by is the famous RILLATON BARROW SX2671 where the lovely Rillaton gold cup (now in the British Museum) was found, along with other interesting relics. At St Cleer is TRETHEVY QUOIT SX2568, the grandest megalithic tomb in Cornwall (very photogenic); the strange CHEESEWRING SX2676 on Bodmin Moor, another appealing camera subject, is made up of several improbably overhanging granite slabs. At St Neot SX1972 are the five **Brown Gelly Barrows** – the central one is 12 ft high and 60 ft in diameter – and some hut circles.

★ **Attractive coastal villages** include Boscastle SX0990 (pretty harbour with 16th-c pier, cottages converted from warehouses, gift shops, and decent pubs), and Port Isaac SW9980 (steep houses high over the harbour; good pub here, too).

★ **Attractive inland villages** with good pubs include Morwenstow SS2015 and St Mawgan SW8765.

Walks

Some particularly fine stretches of cliffs for walking are around **Port Isaac** SW9980 and **Tintagel** SX0588; a good start is from Rocky Valley E of Tintagel, a craggy valley leading from the B3263 to the sea. The **Bedruthan Steps** SW8469 off B3276 Newquay-Padstow are really special with their dramatic rock pinnacles, cliffs and lovely sandy coves, but otherwise the hinterland between Newquay and Padstow is generally too developed for pleasurable walking.

The **beach at Perranporth** SW7554 has magnificent surf backed and flanked by low cliffs and wind-battered pastures, and there are interesting natural rock arches. The **sand dunes** on the E side of the **Camel Estuary** SW9376 suddenly give way to a rocky headland, Rumps Point, which can be walked round in an hour or so. The rocky beach at **Trebarwith Strand** SX0585 is worth knowing, especially at low tide, particularly as there's such a good pub there. Other good spots for beach walks are at Holywell Bay SW7658, and the lovely long sandy stretches at Newquay Bay SW8262 and going north to Watergate Bay, Beacon Cove and Mawgan Porth. There are good popular family beaches both at Constantine Bay SW8675 and at Rock SW9475.

Along the **disused railway** from Wadebridge SW9872 to Padstow SW9275 – a level six miles along the edge of the Camel Estuary, with banks of wild flowers, birds, and lovely views between cuttings – you can walk or cycle (bike hire at either end), or picnic on the small beaches at low tide. Those with less energy could park at Wadebridge, walk to Padstow, have lunch and get the bus back (2.30 pm from the old station). You might then walk on through scenic countryside beyond Bodmin (worth stopping at Helland pottery, just by the path at Helland Bridge).

Bodmin Moor is not as richly endowed as Dartmoor for walking, and much is boggy and rough. For a taster of its bleak grandeur start at Darite SX2569 and explore the Hurlers stone circles SX2571 and the Cheesewring SX2572; you can follow a clear track between them. Brown Willy, the highest point in Cornwall, can be seen from the summit of Rough (pronounced Roe) Tor SX1480, itself reached from the car park off the A39 nr Camelford. The track from Sharptor SX2573 to Kilmar Tor SX2574 affords fine views, as does **Kit Hill** nr Callington SX3669, where there's a huge chimney stack and mine shafts. There are 20 miles of the Camel Trail from Bodmin to Wadebridge, Padstow and Wenford Bridge, and you can hire bikes from companies in Wadebridge. **Riding** is popular on the moor, and quite a few stables on or around it cater for all standards of riding ability.

Driving

The best views of Bodmin Moor are from the A30 rather than its minor roads, which tend to hug its valleys. The B3276 from Newquay to Padstow has some good sea views, and the B3254, an old coach road from Launceston up to Kilkhampton, gives good views of the contrasting north Cornish farming country. The B3266 S from Boscastle down towards Bodmin is a good road, fast by Cornish standards, and though the A39 is slow in summer it's an excellent road at other times.

Where to eat

Padstow SW9175 Seafood (0841) 532485 Wonderfully fresh seafood straight from the boats in busy, airy quayside restaurant, good puddings, and long, interesting and fairly priced wine list; conservatory for aperitifs; bedrooms. **£20 lunch, £33 dinner**|£5.50/£13; cl Sun, 1 May, late Dec/Jan.

Padstow SW9175 Taste Bud and Rafters (0841) 532565 Two eating places under one roof. Taste Bud is a charming friendly little restaurant, **£22**|£9, and Rafters is a bistro offering lighter meals, **£12.70**|£4.50; both places are served by the same kitchen; cl Mon (except during peak season) and Nov-Mar.

Other places worth knowing here for reasonable food include the Borough Arms nr Bodmin (A389 NW; SX0467), Earl of St Vincent at Egloshayle SX0172, Plume of Feathers at Mitchell SW8654, Cavalier in Newquay SW8161, Golden Lion in Padstow SW9175, Cornish Arms at Pendoggett SX0279, Preston Gate at Poughill SS2207, London Inn at St Neot SX1867, and Port William at Trebarwith Strand SX0585.

Help this year from: *J C Brittain-Long, Peter Neate, David Heath, David and Ann Stranack, Miss R M Tudor, David Brokensha, Mike Hallewell, Peter and Lynn Brueton, Miss R M Tudor, P and M Rudlin, Peter and Rose Flower, Bill Sharpe, H A P Russell, S Howe, Stephen Harvey, D P Pascoe, Alec and Marie Lewery, Stephen and Jean Curtis, E A George, LM, F Tomlin, Mark Walker, P and K Lloyd, K Harvey, David Mead, E M Hughes, Mark Walker, Mr and Mrs V Edmunds, Les King, Stephen Oxley, Anna Cwajna, Margaret and Roy Randle, Ian Phillips, Geoffrey Thompson, R and S Bentley, Norma Constable, Bjanka Kadic, Rita Horridge, Roy and Bettie Derbyshire, Ken Moreman, Phil and Heidi Cook.*

Cornwall Calendar

Some of these dates were provisional as we went to press.

February

7th **St Ives** Feast Monday, *with hurling and throwing of the silver ball*

19th **Truro** Spring Beer Festival *at the City Hall*

March

5th **Truro** Cornwall Brass Band Assoc Annual Contest, *at City Hall*

7th **Truro** County Music Festival, *St Mary Clement Methodist Church and Wesley Hall – till Sat 12*

9th **Liskeard** Annual Exhibition and Sale of Art and Craft, *at Public Hall*

April

1st **Cornwall** Gardens Festival *open thoughout the county – till 31 May*

2nd **Land's End** End-to-End Car Rally *sets off for John O'Groats*

3rd **St Endellion** Music Festival *– till Sun 10*

4th **Launceston** Trigg Morris Men's Easter Monday County Tour – *starts at Town Sq and ends at Jamaica Inn*, **Bolventor**

mid-April **Newlyn** David Mach Exhibition, *at Newlyn Art Gallery – large sculptural installation created for the gallery*

29th **Boscastle** Beer Festival and Charity Fun Day *– till 2 May; also* **Newquay** Great Cornwall Balloon Meet, *hot-air balloon festival on the sea front – till 2 May*

30th **Camborne** Trevithick Day, *steam-engine rally, street events, concerts*

May

1st **Bude** Fayre, *West Country festival of food & drink – till 25 Jun*; **Land's End** Cornish Festival of sport *inc Duchy marathon, fun run and traditional sports – till Mon 1*; **Padstow** 'Obby 'Oss Celebrations, *traditional May-Day custom celebrating the coming of spring*

7th **Helston** Furry Dance, *spring festival to celebrate the passing of winter*

14th **Stratton** Re-enactment of the Civil War Battle of Stamford Hill – *till Sun 15*

15th **St Germans** St Germans Church Bach Festival: *also Sun 21 May*

16th **St Ives** Mayor Choosing Ceremony

mid-May **Newlyn** Art Gallery New(live)lyn Art, *festival of live art with talks and lectures*

21st **Tintagel** Festival of Music and Arts *– till Sun 29*

23rd **Porthcurno** Minack Theatre Summer Festival, *plays and musicals at clifftop open-air theatre – till 17 Sept*

29th **Launceston** Steam Fair, *with crafts – till Mon 30*

30th **Polperro** Carnival

June

3rd **Bude** Folk Arts & Cider Festival *– till Sun 5*

9th **Wadebridge** Royal Cornwall Show, *major agricultural show, over 200 years old – till Sat 11*

CORNWALL CALENDAR

JUNE cont.

13th **Falmouth** D-Day Commemoration, *starts week of celebrations with an American theme, ends with a service on Sunday*

18th **Land's End** Steam Rally – *till Sun 19*

23rd **Callington** Midsummer Eve Celebrations, *Kit Hill*

29th **Truro** Three Spires Festival, *celebration of the arts in Cornwall – till 9 July*

JULY

2nd **Bodmin** Riding & Heritage Day

3rd **Tregony** Sheepdog Trials

3rd **Falmouth** Transatlantic Sailing Challenge, *amid celebrations continuing the American theme*

3rd **Newquay** 1900 Victorian Week *culminating with carnival, torchlight procession and fireworks – till Sun 10*

9th **St Austell** White Gold Festival – *till Sun 17*

17th **Bodmin** Pencarrow Sheepdog Trials

20th **Perranporth** Carnival – *till Weds 27*

21st **Launceston** Agricultural Show

23rd **Lostwithiel** Silver Band Carnival

AUGUST

2nd **St Endellion** Music Festival – *till Sat 13*

3rd **Land's End** Air Day *with Red Arrows and Falcon display*

3rd **St Mawgan** International Air Day

5th **Truro** Summer Beer Festival – *at City Hall till Sat*

7th **Falmouth** Week, *sailing events and entertainments*

14th **Fowey** Regatta Week *with carnival and floral dancing*

16th **Wadebridge** Cornwall Folk Festival, *with ceilidhs, singarounds, street events and real ale – till Mon 29*

27th **Bude** Jazz Festival – *till 3 Sept*

27th **Blisland** Sheepdog Trials

28th **Wadebridge**, Royal Cornwall Showground, *sheepdog trials*

29th **Commonmoor**, nr Liskeard, Sheepdog Trials

SEPTEMBER

6th **Newquay** Festival *ending with a Chinese Dragon Dance – till Sat 10*

6th **Newquay** World Life-saving Championships – *at Fistral beach, till Sun 11*

OCTOBER

5th **Callington** Honey Fair

12th **Perranporth** Lowender Perran, *festival of Celtic culture inc concerts and workshops*

30th **Lostwithiel** Cornwall Old Toy and Doll Fair

DECEMBER

13th **Looe** Torchlight Procession

CUMBRIA

England's most beautiful area, embracing a great wealth of picturesque landscapes from intimate and romantic lakeside scenes to sweeping felltop vistas. It's the best county for walks, whether you fancy a lazy waterside stroll or a taxing day on the high ridges. There are lots of interesting places to visit, particularly in the South Lakes, though fewer in the west and the Pennines. There's an excellent choice of places to stay, many of which serve really good food. For lunch, there are plenty of decent civilised pubs (allowing children) in town and country alike, and most tourist attractions and all the main centres have refreshments.

Out of season, we'd suggest that the areas to consider first are the Northern and Southern Lakes. But in the summer holidays and at other holiday peak times these parts do attract so many people that traffic jams the steep narrow lanes to some favourite spots. Though the pressure of visitors puts some strain on the more accessible of even the wilder places at these times, in high summer you've more chance of finding real peace in the west, and, particularly, over in the Pennines east of the M6. Though this part of the world does have a relatively high average rainfall, it's worth remembering that in a typical year three out of four Cumbrian weekends are dry and sunny.

For a weekend visit to central Lakeland, May (sheets of wild flowers on the hills) and June are ideal: more sun, far less crowded. People who know Cumbria really well say that the views are at their peak in October and November. Walkers benefit then from crisp air and (usually) dry ground, though the afternoons are quite short.

For all but the hardiest expert outdoorsmen, winter up here is too bleak for pleasure – except for a fireside armchair break, with just the stern sweep of the snow-topped fells out of the window reminding you of how cosseted you are.

Public transport in the Lakes, formal and informal, is good and useful for round-trip long walks; information service (0228) 812812. Local information leaflets offer plenty of choice of well-guided walks; information too from National Park visitor services (053 94) 46601, and from the flourishing Cumbria Wildlife Trust (053 94) 32476, which controls many reserves. Bicycles can be hired by the day in the main towns (considering the scenic grandeur, you can cycle for a surprisingly long way, at least in the central area, without having to struggle up steep hills). Many places offer riding: around £10 an hour for adults, £8 for children.

The National Trust controls over 25 per cent of the entire area of the Lake District National Park. Besides many of the area's most interesting houses and gardens, it owns or controls most of the high central fell country, the whole of Loweswater, Crummock Water, Buttermere and Wastwater and their shores, much of Windermere, Derwent Water, Ennerdale Water, Grasmere Lake and Rydal Water. This means two things. The main one is that preservation of and access to the countryside here is outstanding. The other point is that this is an area where membership of the Trust does particularly pay off: you can get into the NT buildings and gardens without charge and are able to use the Trust's countryside car parks without paying the usual small fee that non-members are charged.

SOUTHERN LAKES

Here there are exceptional riches of scenery and of places to stay as well as a great many interesting things to see and do; this area is best visited out of season.

This region concentrates more scenic beauty into a smaller central area than any other part of the Lakes. As a consequence, its heart around Ambleside and Windermere is very busy indeed in summer. The places we recommend to stay in do in themselves give considerable insulation against the summer crowds, but the area comes into its own at quieter times of year – and you really do need a degree of peace and quiet to enjoy the beauty of its quite exceptional central area between Grasmere and Windermere.

The choice of places to stay here is very good indeed, with a splendid range of styles and prices (the cheaper places are naturally a good deal humbler than the most expensive ones). The Langdales, particularly Great Langdale, are outstanding for a quiet break with plenty of walking on your doorstep.

The area has lots to see and do, apart from walking and enjoying the scenery; it offers more than any other part of Cumbria. Ambleside and Windermere are both quite intensively developed for visitors; Kendal, a genuine country town, has a good deal of interest. We'd recommend, too, a look at Hawkshead, Troutbeck and Cartmel, and among the many other places of interest the great houses and impressive gardens of Holker Hall at Cark-in-Cartmel, Levens Hall and Sizergh Castle probably take the pick. The Wordsworth trail at Grasmere and Rydal is heavily trodden in summer, but very rewarding at quieter times. Walking in this area is exceptionally good.

Where to stay

Grasmere NY3406 MICHAEL'S NOOK Ambleside LA22 9RP (053 94) 35496 **£152 inc dinner**; 12 lovely rms, 2 suites. Beautifully furnished hotel with fine antiques, paintings and rugs (the owner is also an antique dealer), lovely flowers, comfortable sofas by open fires in cosy bar or elegant drawing room, fine food, and good walks; also, a Great Dane, exotic cats and a parrot; free use of indoor pool and health facilities at nearby Wordsworth Hotel (under the same ownership, and listed below); children by arrangement.

Grasmere NY3406 WHITE MOSS HOUSE Rydal Water, Ambleside LA22 9SE (053 94) 35295 ***£150 inc dinner**; 5 individual rms in main house, 2 more in cottage. Attractive stripped-stone small country house in charming mature grounds overlooking lake; fine no-choice meals inc interesting local produce in no-smoking dining room; free use of hotel rowing boat, free fishing and free use of local leisure club; no toddlers – though babies and well-behaved older children welcome; cl Dec-Feb.

Windermere SD4109 MILLER HOWE Rayrigg Rd LA23 1EY (053 94) 42536 ***£150 inc dinner**; 13 rms, many fine views. Peaceful and very comfortable individual hotel high over the lake with splendid views from day rooms, conservatory and sloping garden; there's an expectant theatricality about the excellent evening meals which adds to the special-event feel of eating here; remarkably wide-ranging New World wine list with helpful tasting notes; no-smoking dining room; also, light lunches; children over 12; cl 7 Dec-11 Mar exc Christmas.

Grasmere NY3406 SWAN Ambleside LA22 9RF (053 94) 35551 **£148 inc dinner**; 36 comfortable well-equipped rms. Old-fashioned up-market Forte hotel with beams and inglenooks; elegant no-smoking dining room, attractive garden, beautiful fell-foot surroundings. Lovely walks.

Langdale NY2807 LANGDALE Ambleside LA22 0PN (053 94) 37302 ***£130**; 65 very comfortable rms in various blocks and cottages spread through woodland along with time-share cottages (best bedrooms in Edwardian house £30 extra); extensive central facilities inc heated pool. Great walks nearby.

Ambleside NY3804 WATEREDGE Borrans Rd LA22 0EP (053 94) 32332 ***£122 inc dinner**; 23 good comfortable rms. Welcoming hotel beautifully placed with garden running down to Windermere; good meals in no-smoking dining room, excellent service; children over 7; cl mid-Dec-early Feb.

Windermere SD4199 HOLBECK GHYLL COUNTRY HOUSE Holbeck Lane LA23 1LU (053 94) 32375 ***£120 inc dinner**; 14 individual rms, many with fine views. Charming and warmly friendly country house in mature landscaped gardens overlooking Lake Windermere, with comfortable lounges, billiard room, and very good food in oak-panelled restaurant; children over 8 in restaurant.

Grasmere NY3406 WORDSWORTH Ambleside LA22 9SW (053 94) 35592 **£118**; 37 rms. Well-run comfortable hotel, right in village, with stylish public rooms, friendly service, good garden and conservatory, heated indoor pool, tennis etc; good disabled access.

Windermere SD4199 LANGDALE CHASE LA23 1LW (053 94) 32201 **£110**; 31 rms, many with marvellous lake view. Welcoming family-run hotel in lovely position on the edge of Lake Windermere with water-skiing and bathing from the hotel jetty; tennis, croquet, putting and rowing, afternoon tea on the terraces, gracious oak-panelled rooms with antiques, paintings, fresh flowers, open fires, very good food inc huge breakfasts, and friendly service; disabled access.

Ambleside NY3804 ROTHAY MANOR Rothay Bridge (Coniston Rd) LA22 0EH (053 94) 33605 ***£108**; 18 attractive rms, many overlooking garden. Balconied country house in mature grounds; quietly civilised and deeply comfortable day rooms, good English food in no-smoking dining room; windsurfing/waterskiing etc close by and free use of nearby leisure club; good disabled access; cl 2 Jan-12 Feb.

Crook SD4695 WILD BOAR Windermere LA23 3NF (053 94) 45225 **£100**; 36 rms. Comfortable well-run extended hotel; period furnishings and log fires in its ancient core, no-smoking dining room.

Cartmel SD3879 UPLANDS Flaggs Lane Grange-over-Sands LA11 6HD (053 95) 36248 ***£80**; 5 rms. Comfortable Edwardian house, sea views, spacious garden, helpful service; main draw undoubtedly the richly imaginative food in the no-smoking dining room; children over 8; cl 1 Jan-24 Feb

Crook SD4695 GILPIN LODGE Windermere LA23 3NE (053 94) 88818 ***£80**; 9 individual and attractive rms. Country house with open fires in charming lounges, unobtrusive attention, good food, croquet lawn, and 20-acre grounds; rewarding walk to Masons Arms on Cartmel Fell; children over 9.

Bowness SD4097 BURN HOW GARDEN HOUSE Windermere LA23 3HH (053 94) 46226 **£76**; 26 rms of great character and style. Extended Victorian house or chalets set in beautiful grounds; good food in no-smoking restaurant; free use of nearby leisure club; good disabled access; cl Jan.

Spark Bridge SD3185 BRIDGEFIELD HOUSE Ulverston LA12 8DA (0229) 885239 ***£70**; 5 rms. Small, quiet Victorian country house in unspoilt countryside, with good, imaginative food in no-smoking dining room and friendly, helpful service; good with children; well-disciplined dogs welcome.

Rydal NY3706 GLEN ROTHAY Ambleside LA22 9LR (053 94) 32524 ***£68**; 11 comfortable individual rms. Friendly small hotel at foot of steep slope near Rydal Water; armchairs by log fire in beamed rooms, bar meals; cl 1st 2 wks Jan.

Grizedale SD3494 GRIZEDALE LODGE Ambleside LA22 0QL (053 94) 36532 ***£68**; 9 no-smoking rms. Friendly and comfortable hotel tucked quietly into the woods and hills; imaginative fresh food and good walks; cl Jan; good disabled access.

Hawkshead SD3598 DRUNKEN DUCK Barngates Ambleside LA22 0NG (053 94) 36347 **£65**; 9 rms. Very well-run happy inn alone in 60 hillside acres; good, interesting food inc fine puddings, several cosy rooms, good fires, views of Lake Windermere in distance; fishing in private tarn.

Grasmere NY3406 OAK BANK Broadgate LA22 9TA (053 94) 35217 **£64**; 14 comfortable rms. Sedately comfortable small hotel, family-run for last 20 years; modern furnishings, good food in dining room and adjoining carpeted conservatory, and secluded garden with River Rothay running along the bottom; cl Jan.

Little Langdale NY3204 THREE SHIRES Ambleside LA22 9NZ (096 67) 215 ***£64**; 11 rms, mostly with own bthrm. Stone-built country inn with beautiful views, comfortably old-fashioned residents' part; pretty gardens, separate walkers' bar; cl Jan.

Elterwater NY3305 BRITANNIA INN Ambleside LA22 9HP (053 94) 37210 ***£62**; 9 rms, mostly with shower. Simple, charmingly traditional pub, fine surroundings opp village green, very welcoming; hearty home-cooking, good walks; cl Christmas.

Coniston SD3098 YEWDALE Yewdale Rd LA21 8LU (053 94) 41280 ***£60**; 10 comfortable rms in smartly kept unpretentious and welcoming inn; cl 25 Dec.

Langdale NY2906 OLD DUNGEON GHYLL Tebay Penrith LA22 9JY (096 67) 272 **£59**; 14 rms, some with shared bthrm. Friendly, simple and cosy walkers' and climbers' inn dramatically surrounded by fells, wonderful views and terrific walks; popular food – best to book for dinner if not a resident.

Witherslack SD4384 OLD VICARAGE Grange-over-Sands LA11 6RS (053 95) 52381 **£58**; 15 rms. Very friendly comfortable hotel well away from the tourist bustle, with good walks nearby and excellent dinner.

Torver SD2894 OLD RECTORY Coniston LA21 8AX (053 94) 41353 **£56**; 8 well-equipped rms. Quiet tastefully furnished family-run hotel in NT farmland; elegant lounge and superb views from dining room (imaginatively served food); fine walks on doorstep, packed lunches; disabled access.

Hawkshead SD3598 HIGHFIELD HOUSE Hawkshead Hill Ambleside LA22 0PN (053 94) 36344 **£56**; 11 good rms. Welcoming Victorian country house, spacious woodland garden, peaceful countryside and views, generous food; cl 23-25 Dec.

Hawkshead SD3598 KINGS ARMS Ambleside LA22 0NZ (053 94) 36372 ***£52**; 9 rms, some with own bthrm. Picturesque old inn right in village, friendly and traditional; cl 25 Dec.

Far Sawrey SD3893 SAWREY Ambleside LA22 0LQ (053 94) 43425 ***£51**; 18 rms, most with bthrm. Friendly hotel well placed at the foot of Claife Heights; generous straightforward food and seats on pleasant lawn; kind to children; dogs allowed; cl mid-Dec-30 Dec.

Windermere SD4199 FIR TREES Lake Rd LA23 2EQ (053 94) 42272 ***£49**; 7 attractive spotless rms inc 2 big family ones. Well-run comfortable Victorian house with informal, relaxed atmosphere; attractive lounge, fine staircase, warmly helpful service (detailed suggestions of what to do), and hearty breakfast.

Bowland Bridge SD4289 HARE & HOUNDS Grange-over-Sands LA11 6NN (053 95) 68333 ***£46**; 16 simple but comfortable modern rms, mostly with own bthrm. Friendly extended village inn below fells with welcoming landlord who used to play football for Liverpool and England.

Hawkshead SD3598 SUMMER HILL COUNTRY HOUSE Hawkshead Hill, Ambleside LA22 0PP (053 94) 36311 ***£42**; 5 immaculate tasteful rms. Tranquil no-smoking B & B with friendly discreet owners, lovely setting overlooking village and mountains; good breakfast inc home-made bread and scones, tables in garden for afternoon tea; children over 7; cl end Oct-end Feb.

Torver SD2894 CHURCH HOUSE Coniston LA21 8AZ (053 94) 41282 **£40**; 5 spacious airy rms. Tidy inn with splendid views over surrounding hills; big fires, decent food, sizeable garden; good walks abound; cl 25 Dec, 1 Jan.

To see and do

Ambleside Just N of the lake NY3804, this has a busy holiday-oriented shopping centre strung along its central one-way system, with probably the quaintest information centre in the Lakes – the little National Trust shop in the tiny stone Bridge House over Stock Ghyll by the main car park. In the side lanes above here are one or two attractive older buildings. Traditional GLASS BLOWING at Adrian Sankey, Rydal Rd; good demonstrations and shop, but no pressure to buy. HAYES GARDEN WORLD (Lake Rd) is a big garden centre in landscaped gardens; café, disabled access. The Unicorn and the Churchill Hotel are useful for snacks.

STAGSHAW (just S, Waterhead) is a hillside woodland garden with lovely lake views, mature camellias, rhododendrons, magnolias and heathers; best in spring; cl July-Mar; £1. There's little left of the ROMAN FORT in nearby Borrans Park NY3703.
BROCKHOLE (A591 S, or launch from town pier) Exemplary National Park information centre in country house with well-landscaped gardens and attractive lakeshore grounds; also popular changing lectures/shows, and adventure play area. Meals, snacks, shop, disabled access; visitor centre cl Nov-Mar, gardens and grounds open all year; no charge but £2 for parking.

Kendal SD5293 is a real town as opposed to a tourist centre – and an interesting one at that, with lots of small closes leading off the main street, some of them attractively restored to give a feel of what the place was like in the 18th-c heyday of the wool-weaving industry. K Shoes have a big factory shop at Netherfield; café; cl Sun. Lakeland Canoes (Hollins Lane, Burneside) hire them by the day, and will take them to and fro for you. Webbs Garden Centre (Burneside Rd) is big, with lots of plants – where that Wonderful lettuce came from; decent café, disabled access. The Riverside is the town's best bet for lunch, and the Olde Fleece is useful for food too.

ABBOT HALL (Kirkland) Fine beautifully restored Georgian house with period furniture, silver, china and glass. The impressive art collection reflects Kendal's importance in the 18th c as the centre of an artists' school. The leading member of the group was George Romney, many of whose works are on display here, as are paintings by Ruskin, Turner and Constable, with many lovely landscapes and an enjoyable collection of modern art. Good craft shop, disabled access; cl am Sun and am Sat Nov-Apr, and possibly most days in Jan and Feb – best to tel (0539) 722464 to check; £3. The entrance cost now includes admission to the Museum of Lakeland Life & Industry.
MUSEUM OF LAKELAND LIFE & INDUSTRY behind Abbot Hall; convincingly and lovingly recreated period rooms, shops, workshops and any number of items on every aspect of life in the area – an almost palpable feel of the past. Rooms and displays on subjects as diverse as shoemaking, Arthur Ransome and Postman Pat; some disabled access; open as above, £1.50.
The KENDAL MUSEUM (Station Rd) specialises in Lakeland natural history and archaeology, with lots of realistically mounted stuffed animals, Roman antiquities and local geology and natural history, as well as a gallery devoted to the work of Alfred Wainwright; disabled access, open as above, £1.50. Ticket to all three above museums £3.
The ruined CASTLE on a small hill on the E edge was the birthplace of Henry VIII's wife Katherine Parr. There's little more now than parts of the outer wall with some towers – but children enjoy it, and there are fine views. A humble building associated with it is the CASTLE DAIRY (Wildman St), an unspoiled Tudor house with some period furniture; Weds pm only, Apr-Oct; one of the best-value old houses in the book at just *5p.
BREWERY ARTS CENTRE (Highgate; cl Sun) has changing events, exhibitions, café, bar in handsomely restored imposing stone building, landscaped garden; it's best to check in advance what's on currently (0539) 725133.
! On Saturdays in summer you can enjoy HARNESS RACING, inc some evenings, on County Showfield; £3.50.

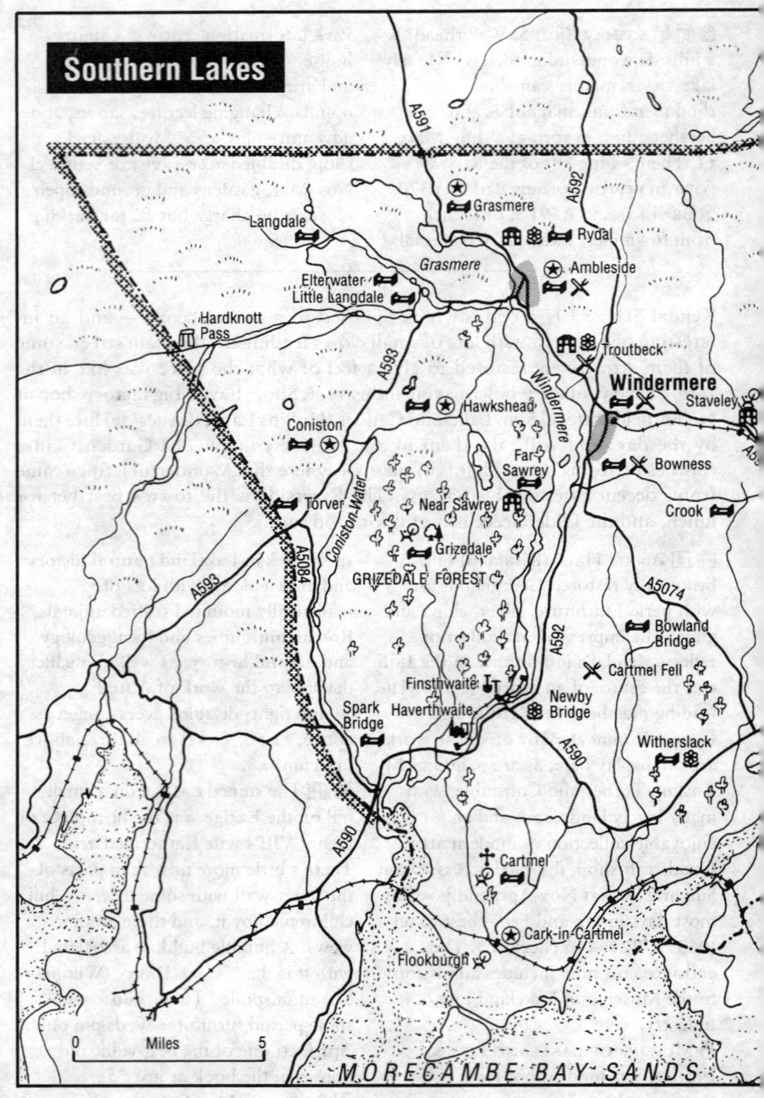

Windermere/Bowness An extensive largely Victorian development of guesthouses and small hotels spreads up between the older village of Bowness SD4097 and the hillside station. It has a touristy feel right through the year, especially around the main street down to the steamer piers.

In Bowness itself there is an inner core of narrower much older streets and buildings – one of the most ancient is the engaging Hole in t' Wall pub.

❀ Steamboat Museum (Rayrigg Rd) Nearly three dozen gleamingly restored graceful antique steamboats, inc the 1850 *S.L. Dolly*, the oldest

mechanically powered steamboat in the world and the famous record-breaker *Miss Windermere IV* ; also other vintage boats, a model pool, steam-launch trips (weather permitting), and an exhibition on transport across the lake. Various special events such as vintage-boat rallies and model-boat regattas; snacks, shop, disabled access; cl Nov-Easter; £2.80.

! WORLD OF BEATRIX POTTER (Old Laundry, Crag Brow, Bowness) Very popular with little girls: intriguingly detailed walk-in sets peopled by the story-book characters, big-screen video of Miss Potter's life etc. The latest feature is a Magic Tree, with models among its branches revealing the story of Peter Rabbit. Disabled access, teas, shop; £2.50.

RIDING, short or long, can be arranged from Wynlass Beck Stables (bottom of Patterdale rd). The Birdcage, College Rd, is a good ANTIQUE SHOP – mostly small things, esp lamps; cl Thurs, Sun.

Other things to see and do

★ **Beetham** SD5079 HERON CORNMILL AND MUSEUM OF PAPERMAKING A working 18th-c riverside watermill beside a big paperworks, with paper-making displays and a growing exhibition; shop, disabled access; cl Mon exc bank hols, all Nov-Easter; £1.25. Beetham itself is attractive, with a decent pub.

Brigsteer SD4889 The LOW PLAIN FARM PARK has animals and poultry, ponies and donkeys, antique machinery, nature trails, and a play area; craft shop, café, disabled access (but no facilities); cl Nov-Easter; *£2.

Cark-in-Cartmel SD3776 HOLKER HALL Opulently built and furnished mainly Victorian mansion with appealingly unstuffy and unregimented feel despite the beauty; glorious 25-acre formal and woodland GARDENS with spectacular water features, rose garden, rhododendron and azalea arboretum and rare plants and shrubs. Also deer park, kitchen museum, entertaining MOTOR MUSEUM, adventure playground; snacks, shop, disabled access; cl Sat, Nov-Mar; £2.90 gardens, grounds and exhibitions; Hall and motor museum extra.

★ ✝ ⚘ **Cartmel** SD3879 Picturesque little alleys lead off the delightfully harmonious central square – esp the one out through the former PRIORY GATEHOUSE. The PRIORY CHURCH, which towers massively over the village, is an interesting mix of architectural grandeur from 12th to 16th c, inc fine carving. Lots of arts and crafts in the village. CRAFT WORKSHOPS at Broughton Lodge Farm (N towards A590) inc demonstrations; a vegetarianish café, with home-baking; cl Mon/Tues exc bank hols, cl all Nov-mid-Apr. The Cavendish Arms is good for lunch.

Coniston SD3195 is an unpretentious village at the foot of its mountain, the Old Man. BRANTWOOD on the opposite shore of the lake has attractive and very extensive informal hillside woodland gardens (best in late May/Jun) surrounding Ruskin's rambling Victorian house, which has lots of his furniture, books and paintings. Good hour's walk on nature trail, mouth-watering views of lake and fells; book/craft shop, teas; disabled access (grounds steep in places); cl Mon/Tues mid-Nov-mid-Mar; £2.50. BOAT TRIPS on Coniston Water are a quiet joy in the opulent Victorian steam yacht which sails daily end Mar-Oct, from Coniston Pier, Brantwood and Park-a-Moor; (053 94) 41288 for times. Or hire rowing or other boats from the boating centre run by the National Parks, 15 mins walk from the village; rowing boats from £2.40 per hr, supplement £1.50 per extra person; motorboats from £10.30, electric boats £13. PONY TREKKING on the fells above, short or long rides, from Spoon Hall; cl Nov-Easter. Decent lunches in the Sun, Black Bull and Yewdale Hotel.

⚘ **Elterwater** NY3305 is a favourite village, with lake views, an excellent pub, and the BARNHOWE CRAFT CENTRE, a restored old barn with interesting yarns, weaving and spinning equipment, demonstrations and lessons; cl Sun and Dec-Easter. The Britannia is very popular for lunch.

Finsthwaite SD3788 STOTT PARK BOBBIN MILL Set in coppiced woodland, this former water-and-steam mill made wooden cotton reels etc from 1835-1971; demonstrations with the lethal-looking belt-drive lathes, good guides, and shop; cl Nov-Mar; £1.75.

⚘ **Flookburgh** SD3676 has excellent potted local shrimps; also decent craft shop.

★ **Grasmere** NY3406 The pretty village does swarm with visitors in summer, most of them here to see DOVE COTTAGE – still much as Wordsworth had it in his most creative years from 1799-1808 (he completed *The Prelude* here), with sister Dorothy's Journals and his extensive cottage garden. Gets quite crowded (though guided tours cope well), but in early morning (opens 9.30) out of season you may get some space to yourself. Good adjoining WORDSWORTH MUSEUM with pictures, manuscripts, explanatory displays, reconstructed lakeland kitchen, changing exhibitions on his friends. Meals, snacks, shop; cl 24-26 Dec, mid-Jan-mid-Feb; £3.70 both. The HEATON COOPER STUDIO has Lakeland watercolours and prints on display and for sale; cl Sun am. Decent bar lunches in the Wordsworth Hotel, Red Lion and (outside, N) Travellers Rest.

⚘ **Grizedale** SD3494 FOREST PARK Woodland trails from short strolls to half-day walks, punctuated by often hard-to-spot timber and rock sculptures. Lots of other activities too, with a CRAFT CENTRE, good information centre (cl winter), bookable deer observation hides, (0229) 860373, orienteering, adventure play area, and even a theatre/ concert arena – (0229) 860291 for programme. In all, six or seven square miles of mainly coniferous hillside timber to get lost in; some disabled access; parking £1.

Hardknott Pass NY2101 HARDKNOTT ROMAN FORT is quite

well preserved and very interestingly restored, but most notable for its staggering lonely position high in the mountains; magnificent views to sea. The drive here is daunting (see Driving, below), and the site can be hazardous in winter.

Haverthwaite SD3484 LAKESIDE & HAVERTHWAITE RAILWAY Short steam trip connecting with cruise boats, and a small collection of steam and diesel locomotives; restaurant, disabled access; (053 95) 31594 for times; no trains Nov-spring; £2.90 return.

★ **Hawkshead** SD3598 is a must to visit; a virtually unchanged Lakeland village with sturdy outside walls, and sheltered flower-filled inner courtyards. Though it is very popular with summer visitors, even at its busiest it has a pleasantly foreign 'different' feel, and the fact that cars are kept out helps a lot. The BEATRIX POTTER GALLERY, in the former offices of the author's husband, has a generous changing selection of the original illustrations of Peter Rabbit, Jemima Puddleduck and other favourites, as well as rather different more acutely (almost acidly) observed drawings. Get there early, as a timed ticket system operates to keep it uncrowded, so during peak holiday periods you may have to wait to get in; shop; cl wknds, Nov-Mar; £2.40. NT. The 15th-c COURT HOUSE is worth poking your nose into (unless it's being used as a village hall); key from National Trust Shop, cl Nov-Mar. The best pubs for lunch in the village are the Queens Head and Kings Arms, though on the outskirts the Outgate Inn and the beautifully placed Drunken Duck are well worth a visit. Trout FISHING and BOAT HIRE is available on nearby Esthwaite Water, the largest stocked lake in the region.

Holme (the one SE of Milnthorpe, off B6384; SD5278) The Dales of Bank House Farm, Holme Mills, make unusual CHESS SETS and nursery furniture; cl wknds.

Levens SD4985 LEVENS HALL is an impressive Elizabethan mansion based on older core, with fine carved oak chimney-pieces, ceiling plasterwork, Spanish leather panelling, and period furnishings. The magnificent topiary GARDENS in their original layout of 1692 are perhaps the highlight of a visit; also model and other STEAM ENGINES (pm only; in steam bank hol Mons, some summer Suns – maybe children's rides), play area, grand beech trees, and deer park; disabled access to grounds, teas, plant sales/shop; cl Fri and Sat, all Oct-Easter; £3.80, £2.50 grounds only. The Hare & Hounds is good for lunch.

Milnthorpe SD4981 LAKELAND WILDLIFE OASIS A6 S Lively jungle house with action models and interactive displays to explain evolution, as well as brightly coloured and unusual birds and animals, sea aquarium, and tropical butterflies; snacks, shop, disabled access; cl Christmas; £2.50.

Near Sawrey SD3796 HILL TOP Beatrix Potter's small, remote 17th-c farmhouse, kept exactly as she had it; no longer included in Tourist Board leaflets as NT (great beneficiaries of her generosity) feel too many people come already, and to reduce the pressure you may decide not to join the queuing crowds yourself; shop; cl Thurs and Fri (exc Good Fri); £3.20. NT. The old-fashioned NT-owned Tower Bank Arms is a good pub with nicely furnished bedrooms.

Newby Bridge SD3786 GRAYTHWAITE HALL GARDENS Well-kept late Victorian garden, strong on rhododendrons and late-spring-flowering shrubs; cl July-Mar; *£2.

Rydal NY3706 RYDAL MOUNT Where Wordsworth came after Grasmere, and lived for most of his adult life; it's a lovely setting overlooking mountains and lakes, near decent camp sites. The modest house has family portraits and period furniture, while the good-sized garden is still much as the poet laid it out – interesting, and consciously picturesque, with original ideas that people are still rediscovering today. Shop; cl Tues in winter; £2.

Sizergh SD4987 CASTLE Originally just a tall and sturdy 14th-c tower, this lovely lakeside house has been harmoniously extended over the centuries by the family who have lived here for generations. There's fine Tudor and Elizabethan carving, panelling and furniture, Jacobite relics, and terraced gardens surrounding a grand flight of steps to water. Lots to interest a gardener, inc an enormous rock garden, Japanese maples, water garden, wild flowers, and daffodils in the crab-apple orchard; teas, shop; cl am, all day Fri/Sat and Nov-Mar; £3.30, £1.70 garden. NT. THE BARN SHOP (Low Sizergh Farm) Recommended by several of our correspondents, plenty of fresh farm foods such as cheese, meat, ice-cream, sausage and bread, and other local produce such as Morecambe Bay shrimps, with a craft shop and pick-your-own strawberries in season. Teas (overlooking the milking parlour), disabled access. The Strickland Arms is quite useful for lunch.

Staveley (the one N of Kendal, SD4798) Peter Hall is a CABINET-MAKER, and at his shop you can see furniture being made or restored, and woodturners at work; shop, disabled access; cl Sun, and Sat and bank hols exc showroom and shop.

Troutbeck NY3926 is a delightful settlement of ancient farms strung along a steep valley below high fells. TOWNEND here in some ways sums up the Lake District: the perfectly preserved home of the same comfortably off, very traditional farming family for 300 years till 1940s, showing little change over all that time. Solid simple unshowy comfort, and a sensible, down-to-earth and entirely self-sufficient layout; cl am, all day Mon (exc bank hols) and Sat, Nov-Mar; £2.40. The beautifully placed hillside village has several more such 'statesmen's' farms. HOLEHIRD (off A592 S) is the Lakeland Horticultural Society's hillside garden, covering five acres with wide variety of well-growing plants inc the National Collections of hydrangeas and some other families; lovely views; disabled access. The quaint Queens Head is good for lunch.

Witherslack SD4384 HALECAT GARDEN Good example of modern landscaping with fine views from the mainly herbaceous garden; plants for sale (esp hydrangeas); cl Sun am and Sat.

Boating on Windermere

The silent steam launch *Osprey* does a stately 45-min tour of the lake, and if it's running – phone (053 94) 45565 – is the pick of the sightseeing boat trips. Lots of other launches, of all sorts of shapes and sizes, run cruises of varying lengths from Bowness Bay, Ambleside, Waterhead and (not Nov-Mar) Newby Bridge; at least one is equipped to take disabled people – ring (053 94) 43360 to check.

Rowing boats can be hired from the Bowness Bay Rowing Company; from £4 per hour or £14 for half a day, £20 for a full one. They also have motorboats, or try Lake Holidays Afloat; £6.50-£10. A pleasant place to hire rowing boats (not Nov-Easter) is Fell Foot Park nr Newby Bridge, with plenty of room for lakeside picnics; café, shop, adventure playground; parking £2.

Lakeland Sailing at Ferry Nab, Bowness, do day, weekend or longer cruises and courses on large sailing yachts; from £50 a day. Windsurfing or waterskiing can be arranged at Low Wood Water Sports Centre, Windermere; windsurfing, canoeing or dinghy sailing Mar-Oct at Windermere Sailing Centre,

Leigh Groves Building, Rayrigg Rd, Windermere.

The chain ferry linking the ferry road below Bowness with the Hawkshead road below Far Sawrey is a utilitarian way of taking to the water; but though it runs every 20 mins and saves miles of driving, queues mean that it saves time only out of season.

Walks

Many of the recommended places to stay here have grand walks right from their doorsteps. The area has a tremendous choice of other walks, short and long: the following suggestions would keep anyone busy for quite a long stay, but really only scratch this magnificent surface.

Grasmere Water, Rydal Water and **Elter Water** are famous for their lovely settings, and there are pleasant walks all around; you can even link all three together in a long afternoon's walk filled with glorious views. The walk up the good track to **Easedale Tarn** from Grasmere quickly gets you away from the crowds, into a fine valley; the lake itself is romantically set below rocks.

From Windermere (opp stn) the short steep walk (half-hour each way) up to **Orrest Head** SD4199 gives spectacular views over the lake and the Pennines; lovely at sunset. **Gummers How** SD3988 further S from Windermere is another hill, an easy 20-min climb from the road, for a fine view. There are also fine views over the lake from the walk up wooded **Claife Heights** SD3797 above the ferry at Far Sawrey; or more undemandingly from the track along the shore N from there. Windermere is surprisingly short on lakeside paths – there are short ones at Bowness SD4096 (to Biskey Howe) and along parts of the wooded western shore.

From Ambleside, a path leads up to **Wansfell Pike** NY3904, toylike in size compared with the bigger fells, but the view is as good as many. An even smaller protuberance is **Latterbarrow** SD3699 near Hawkshead, but it is elevated enough above a relatively low-lying area to give views over Windermere and Langdale. **Tarn Hows** SD3299, an easy hour's walk from Hawkshead, is a gorgeously photogenic small lake; particularly beautiful on a still clear autumn day. The sculpture trail in **Grizedale Forest** SD3494 (see To see and do, above) enlivens the forest plantations, making a good rainy-day activity; the sculptures are set in various spots throughout the forest. The visitor centre issues a map showing where to find them.

Coniston Water has a lovely path on its W side, S of Coniston; you can combine this walk with one on a higher-level route along the Walna Scar 'road' (an ancient hard track closed to through traffic) beneath the **Old Man of Coniston** SD2797, the outstanding viewpoint of the vicinity. Climb the Old Man from Coniston, go up past the remains of copper mines, and return down the Walna Scar Road.

The **Duddon Valley** is a favourite starting point for rather more demanding walks, either by the river or up into the heights, with the Newfield Inn at Seathwaite SD2396 a good base.

Great Langdale NY2906, dominated by the awesome Langdale Pikes, is the area's main centre for more serious fell-walking in grand scenery. One very popular shorter walk here is up the good track to Stickle Tarn, from the car park by the Stickle Barn (useful for refreshments). Wainwrights, in the not specially graceful settlement of Chapel Stile off the B5343, another useful refreshment place, is particularly popular with many of our contributors as a base for walks along here.

The sedately old-fashioned resort of Grange-over-Sands SD4077 is the start for summer guided walks over **Morecambe Bay Sands**, oddly other-worldly; glistening tidal flats, quick-stepping patrols of wading birds, distant hills, grisly tales of people and horses sucked under; phone (053 95) 34026 for times, which depend on tides. From here there's also a pleasant walk up through the woods to **Hampsfield Fell** SD3979 for terrific views over the Bay. Further stunning views of the bay are from **Humphrey Head Point** SD3973, a ¾-mile-long headland protruding into the sea, and from **Arnside Knott** SD4577, near Arnside, which looks across to the southern Lakeland fells.

Driving

In summer this area is decidedly not a place for the impatient driver, as its more beautiful parts tend to choke with slow queues of scenery-watchers.

The B5343 into Great Langdale is the least taxing road into this area's mountain scenery, an austere valley surrounded by awesome hills; you can keep on a poorer steeper road to go up and over, passing near pretty Blea Tarn, and coming back down through the gentler Little Langdale.

From Little Langdale the very steeply twisting back road up over Wrynose Pass gives exhilarating views; you can then either fork left down the glorious Duddon Valley past Seathwaite and Ulpha, or keep on over the breathlessly steep Hardknott Pass. Stop for Hardknott Fort (see above) over the summit.

The road along the Winster Valley turning off the A5074 S of Bowness at Winster and running down through Bowland Bridge and Cartmel Fell to Lindale is very pretty (and passes near the Masons Arms on Cartmel Fell, an outstanding pub).

The back roads through Grizedale Forest S of Hawkshead are usually quiet; we've seen deer on them on autumn and winter evenings.

The B5282 from Milnthorpe has quiet views across the Kent estuary, with good refreshment stops at Sandside (the Ship) and Arnside (the Albion, on the prom).

It's worth knowing that the M6 (and its now much less heavily trafficked elder sister the A6) has splendid distant fell and Pennine views. Incidentally, heading N from junction 38 the Tebay service area, locally owned and run, is unusually pleasant – much more personal-seeming than most; and heading S from junction 37 the Killington Lake service area does have a gorgeous lakeside setting.

Where to eat

Ambleside NY3804 SHEILA'S COTTAGE (053 94) 33079 Firmly recommended by local correspondents; cl Sun & all Jan; **£27**|£5.50.

Bowness SD4097 PORTHOLE 3 Ash St (053 94) 44793 Long-established bustling bistro with consistently good evening meals, some Italian and some very English dishes; genuine personal touch to service and olde-worlde surroundings; decent wine; a reliably enjoyable evening out; cl Tues, mid-Dec-mid-Feb. **£24**|£8.50.

Windermere SD4199 ROGERS 4 High St (053 94) 44954 Beautifully presented and individualistic French-based cooking in intimate evening restaurant, lovely and cosy; helpful service; cl Sun, 25-26 Dec. **£17**|£11.50.

Cartmel Fell SD4288 MASONS ARMS (053 95) 68486. Old-fashioned building

in unrivalled setting with wonderful views. Many different beers inc real German beer on draught; food is 50 per cent vegetarian and very popular, esp puddings. **£16.30**|£2.30/£6.60.
Troutbeck NY4103 QUEENS HEAD (053 94) 32174 Gabled 17th-c inn with rambling bar, some fine antique carving, and very good, imaginative bar food; bedrooms. **£14**|£2.60/£5.20.

NORTHERN LAKES

This area closely rivals the Southern Lakes for beauty; it is less crowded in summer and has fine gardens and excellent places to stay.

Ullswater and Derwent Water both have great beauty: Ullswater has some of the best (if most expensive) places to stay right by the lake shore; Derwent Water, with its islands and its handier proportions, is perhaps even more pleasant for idle boating. Borrowdale is splendid for a quiet break (perhaps at Seatoller House – if you can get in), with an almost endless variety of interesting walks from the simplest to the most challenging. Virtually all the other places we recommend to stay in are also well placed for walkers.

Keswick, the area's holiday heart, has lots going on for all ages. Penrith is more of a genuine market town, with a good deal of genuine local interest. Outside, Dalemain House at Dacre, Lingholm Gardens at Portinscale, Mirehouse near Bassenthwaite, Hutton-in-the-Forest at Skelton and perhaps the small town of Cockermouth are the pick of the places to visit, and there are quite a few very attractive little villages. Lowther Leisure Park at Hackthorpe has a lot to keep families occupied.

Where to stay

Pooley Bridge NY4724 SHARROW BAY Penrith CA10 2LZ (076 84) 86301 ***£245 inc dinner**; 28 individually furnished rms, mostly with bthrm. Country-house hotel in quiet idyllic spot by Ullswater; lovely views of lake and mountains and legendary for the years of loving care the owners have put into the distinctive style, furnishings and decor; perfect, unobtrusively attentive service, particularly good richly worked-out English cooking – vast choice (and two contrasting dining rooms, with a third for breakfast, all with great character); children over 13; good disabled access; cl early Dec-late Feb.
Watermillock NY4522 LEEMING HOUSE Penrith CA11 0JJ (076 84) 86622 **£149**; 40 cosseting rms, many with beautiful views. Well-run extended Forte hotel with quiet and spacious lakeside grounds, armchairs by log fires, warm conservatory, good generous food in lovely no-smoking restaurant; boating; good provision for disabled.
Lorton NY1525 NEW HOUSE FARM Cockermouth CA13 9UU (0900) 85404 ***£100 inc dinner**; 3 rms with wonderful hillside views. 17th-c house (not a

working farm) with very good food inc game and fish caught by owner and home-made scones and preserves; beams, flagstones and open fires, two residents' lounges, and lots of walks; no smoking; cl winter; children over 12.

Mungrisdale NY3731 MILL HOTEL Penrith CA11 0XR (076 87) 79659 ***£95 inc dinner**; 9 rms. Very friendly small streamside hotel beautifully placed in lovely valley hamlet hidden away below Blencathra; good food inc interesting vegetarian dishes and home-baking; cl Nov-Feb.

Bassenthwaite Lake NY1930 PHEASANT Cockermouth CA13 9YE (07687) 76234 ***£88**; 20 rms. Civilised old-fashioned hotel with delightfully old-fashioned pubby bar, other day rooms more spacious but more orthodox, and interesting gardens merging into surrounding fellside woodlands; cl 24-25 Dec; disabled access.

Derwentwater NY2618 LODORE SWISS Keswick CA12 5UX (076 87) 77285 **£80**; 70 rms. Long-standing but well-updated big holiday hotel; lots of facilities inc swimming, tennis and other games; particularly good with children (nursery with NNEB nannies, babysitting, baby-listening service).

Thirlmere NY3116 DALE HEAD HALL Keswick CA12 4TN (076 87) 72478 ***£70 inc dinner**; 9 pretty rms, most with lake views. Peaceful, partly 16th-c country house in lovely lakeside grounds; comfortable lounges, log fire, friendly owners, and home-cooked food using produce grown in own walled garden; children over 10.

Brackenthwaite NY1622 PICKETT HOWE Buttermere Valley, Wigton CA13 9UY (0900) 85444 ***£68**; 4 rms. At the end of its own track and surrounded by stunning mountain scenery stands this 17th-c longhouse; friendly, relaxed atmosphere, lovely antiques, log fires, beams and slate floors; fine food in candlelit dining room, fairly short but very sound wine list, and wonderful breakfasts inc home-made oatcakes, jam, marmalade and so forth; no smoking.

Ireby NY2439 OVERWATER HALL Carlisle CA5 1HH (076 87) 76566 ***£72**; 13 rms. Relaxed and friendly family-run hotel in 18 acres of gardens and woodland; elegant, comfortable drawing room, good, imaginative food, and lots of walks; children over 7 in restaurant (high tea 5 pm); well-behaved dogs welcome.

Braithwaite NY2324 IVY HOUSE Keswick CA12 5SY (076 87) 78338 **£62**; 12 comfortable individual rms in village house; beams and log fires, generous food, friendly staff.

Watermillock NY4522 OLD CHURCH Penrith CA11 0JN (076 84) 86204 **£60**; 10 rms, some with lovely Ullswater view. Attractive 18th-c Lakeland house peacefully situated in waterside gardens; rowing/windsurfing boats, attractive and civilised day rooms with log fires and individual furnishings, kind service, excellent English dinners at 8 pm in no-smoking dining room; cl Nov-Mar.

Brandlingill NY1626 LOW HALL Cockermouth CA11 0RE (0900) 826654 **£50**; 6 pleasant rms. Beautifully sited partly 17th-c farmhouse below Whinlatter Pass and close to Cockermouth; good home-cooking; cl Nov-Feb; children over 10.

Mungrisdale NY3731 MILL INN Penrith CA11 0XR (076 87) 79632 **£49**; 6 simple but clean, warm and pleasant rms. Unspoilt pub in lovely quiet surroundings; friendly staff, decent food; can arrange salmon and sea-trout fishing on River Eden; cl 25 Dec.

Seatoller NY2413 SEATOLLER HOUSE Keswick CA12 5XN (076 87) 77218 ***£45**; 9 rms. Guesthouse for over 100 yrs, still has holiday diary written by R Vaughan Williams, G M Trevelyan, G Moore and others when they were here as undergraduates; at foot of Honister Pass, perfect for walkers; friendly house-party atmosphere in comfortable lounges with self-service drinks, Scrabble etc. Good no-choice fixed-time hearty dinner (not Tues), sit together at big tables; packed lunches. Many walks from doorstep; children over 5; disabled access; book well ahead; cl Nov-Mar.

Dockray NY3921 ROYAL Ullswater CA11 0JV (076 84) 82356 **£45**; 10 rms. Homely, comfortable and friendly hotel; open fires in spacious bars, good-value hearty meals; fine spot between hills and lake, walks from doorstep; disabled access; cheap walkers' bunkhouse by 1994.

Keswick NY2624 GEORGE St John's St CA12 5AZ (076 87) 72076 **£40**; 17 unpretentiously comfortable rms. Beams and flagstones downstairs, little panelled bar with Wordsworth associations, trout fishing.

Cockermouth NY1231 HIGH STANGER FARM CA13 9TS (0900) 8223875 ***£29**; 2 rms, shared bthrm. 17th-c farmhouse in quiet spot with wonderful views; log fire in comfortable lounge, friendly owners.

To see and do

Keswick NY2624 is the tourist centre of the northern Lakes, with lots of Victorian villas (many of them now guesthouses and small hotels) outside quite a traditional centre, with small cobbled closes running off the main streets. It's full of breeches, boots and knapsacks in high season, and is a routine stop on coach tours. The lively Dog & Gun is probably the best value for lunch, with the Four in Hand also a useful food stop. The Wild Strawberry is a quaint tea-room with an upstairs gallery; cl Tues/Weds. Lakeside Tea Gardens (Lake Rd) have home-baking, lots for children, pleasant modern furniture and crockery inside and in garden with trees and chaffinches; cl about 5 pm. George Fisher (Borrowdale Rd) is a good big outdoors shop.

! CARS OF THE STARS (Standish St) An unusual collection of cars from film and television dating back to Laurel & Hardy's Model T Ford, taking in Chitty Chitty Bang Bang, the Batmobile and cars belonging to James Bond and Noddy along the way; snacks, shop, disabled access; cl Jan and Feb; *£2.50.

The PENCIL MUSEUM (Southey Works) is surprisingly interesting, with a good audio-visual presentation, and some unexpected exhibits; shop, disabled access; cl 25-26 Dec, 1 Jan; *£2.

BEATRIX POTTER'S LAKE DISTRICT (Packhorse Court) The main feature here is a 16-min multi-media show on the later life of Beatrix Potter, and the farms, land and scenery that she used so much of her money to preserve. Also a display on the work of the National Trust; shop, disabled access; *£2.50. NT.

The town also has a thoroughly traditional local MUSEUM (Fitzpark, Station Rd); some odd exhibits; cl lunchtime, Sun, Nov-Mar.

From the boat pier, a short stroll takes you up to Friars Crag for a fine lake view; the car park on the B5289 just S gives access to another great lake viewpoint, Castle Head.

The Castlerigg neolithic STONE CIRCLE NY2923 just E is well preserved and gives photogenic perspectives of the mountains (the best times for pictures are morning and evening); take a map to identify the peaks it aligns with. The site is owned by the National Trust, and there's a brief explanation of the stones' history.

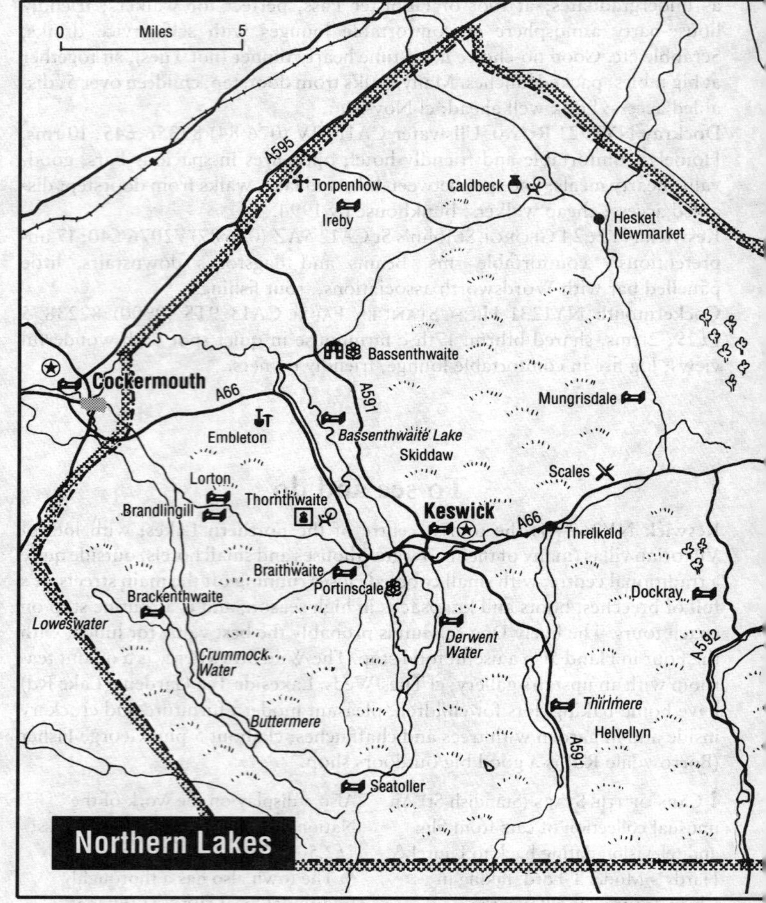

Penrith NY5130 is a real locals' rather than tourists' town, and the biggest in Lakeland. It is very much a northern country town, with solid stone streets, an unreconstructed traffic problem, farmers from far and wide descending on its Skirsgill agricultural market (Tues, sometimes Fri too in late summer/autumn), and genuinely traditional Lakeland/Pennine shops selling real fudge and toffee, rich cakes (Birketts), local cheeses (Grahams), prize Cumberland sausages (Cranstons), local antiquarian books, and cheap and sturdy country clothes. John Norris (21 Victoria Rd) is the outstanding fishing/outdoor wear shop, with something for everyone; good prices. The George, Gloucester Arms and Lowther Arms all have decent-value food inc lunchtime snacks.

CASTLE This was built in the 14th c as a defence against Scottish raids. Warwick the Kingmaker lived here, as did Richard III when he was Duke of Gloucester; it's now in ruins and is surrounded by a park.

The STEAM MUSEUM (Castlegate) is an exuberant and intriguing medley of working smithy, full-sized engines esp

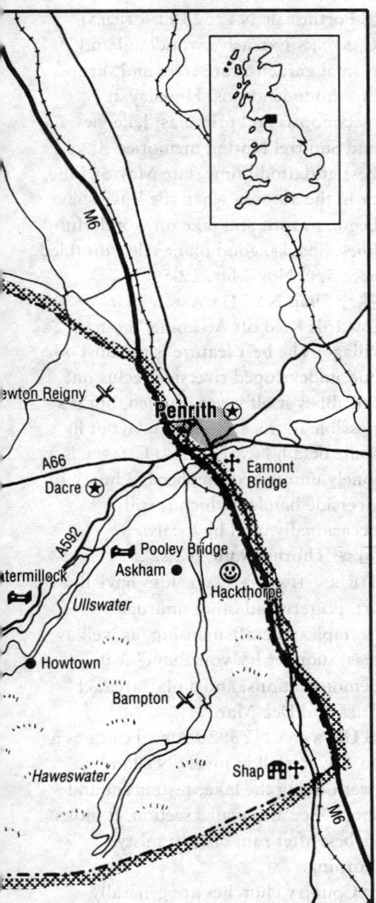

agricultural ones, a steam organ, and reconstructed Victorian settings; shop, disabled access; cl wknds exc bank hols, all Oct-Easter; *£2.

BROUGHAM CASTLE NY5329 (off A6 S) is a sturdy Norman ruin on steep lawns above riverside sheep pastures; you can trace the Roman remains too; shop; cl Nov-Mar; £1.10. BROUGHAM HALL CRAFT CENTRE nearby has many crafts inc wood-turning, silver and metal work, stonemasonry and handmade clothes and shoes in attractive stone courtyard of 15th-c castle (currently being restored); snacks, shop, disabled access.

WETHERIGGS POTTERY (Clifton Dykes NY5326, signed off A6 further S) Interesting working pottery – one of the oldest in the country – with 19th-c steam engine and equipment and smallish museum; children can try their hands at the wheel. Meals and snacks, shop, disabled access; cl 2 wks over Christmas and New Year; *£2.

MUSEUM A useful introduction to Penrith and the surrounding area; cl Sun exc pm in summer.

Other things to see and do

Bassenthwaite NY2228 MIREHOUSE (off A591 S) Happily lived-in 17th-c Lakeland family home with literary connections; fine rooms, interesting garden (bee/butterfly plants), lakeshore grounds, peaceful lakeside church, and woods with good adventure play areas. Good home-cooking in ex-mill tea room, shop, disabled access; house open pm Sun, Weds and bank hols Apr-Oct, also Fri in Aug; grounds open daily; £2.80. There's escorted RIDING through woodland from Armathwaite Hall Equestrian Centre, Coalbeck Farm. The Sun in the village and Pheasant on the other side of the lake are good for lunch.

Caldbeck NY3240 Riverside restaurant, craft shops and small mining MUSEUM in a restored watermill; cl Mon exc bank hols, Tues and Weds Oct-Nov, and all Dec-mid-Mar. John Peel's grave is in the nearby churchyard, and there's decent food at the Parkend Hotel, B5299 towards Aspatria.

★ **Cockermouth** NY1231 Quietly attractive riverside town. WORDSWORTH HOUSE The poet's happy childhood home, this is a handsome restored 18th-c town house. Fine furniture, pictures by friends and contemporaries, good original panelling, plasterwork and walled garden above river. Well worth a visit in its own right as well as for its Wordsworth associations. Snacks, shop; cl Sat exc on bank hol wknds, or in July and Aug, Sun and Nov-Mar; *£2.40. NT. The Norham limited disabled access; cl Dec-Jan; *£1.60. JENNINGS BREWERY Tours of traditional Castle Brewery, at 10.30 am and 2 pm – booking advisable, (0900) 823214; shop; cl wknds and Dec-Apr; *£2. Paintings and crafts for sale at CASTLEGATE HOUSE (Castlegate), lived-in Georgian house opp castle; cl Thurs, Sun, and all Jan, cl Feb exc Fri/Sat. The Trout is good for lunch.

Dacre NY4626 DALEMAIN HOUSE A fine Georgian and Elizabethan house, with a Norman pele tower (now a regimental museum); full of charm and splendid period furnishings and paintings. The same family have lived here for centuries, overseeing many of the changes and additions ranging from the medieval great hall, the Tudor parts and the 18th-c Chinese room to the Victorian nursery. The courtyard has rural bygones in the barn, and there's also an adventure playground, and deer in the carefully landscaped PARK with lake and mountain views; atmospheric restaurant, shop, disabled access; cl Fri and Sat and Oct-early Apr; £3.80, £2.80 grounds. The village CHURCH has pre-Norman sculpture, and quaint medieval stone bears in the graveyard.

Embleton NY1731 WYTHOP MILL Small watermill powering vintage woodworking machinery, with well-displayed joinery hand tools; meals, snacks; cl Mon (exc bank hols), wkdys Nov-Dec, Feb-Mar, all Jan; *£1.70.

Hackthorpe NY5423 LOWTHER LEISURE PARK (signed off A6 S of Penrith) Lots for families to do, funfair, safe boating, miniature train rides, challenging play areas, putting, kiosks, circus, and lots of events such as jousting, all in attractive parkland; disabled access; £4.95.

Portinscale NY2523 LINGHOLM GARDENS Extensive woodland and formal gardens, rare trees and shrubs esp rhododendrons, Himalayan meconopsis and primulas; lake views and Squirrel Nutkin memories. Best at daffodil time, late May or June, or in the autumn when the leaves have begun to turn and take on wonderful hues. Snacks, good plant sales, disabled access; cl Nov-Mar; £2.50.

Shap NY5415 ABBEY (left towards Keld off A6 going N out of village) The best feature is the unspoilt and undeveloped riverside seclusion; the abbey itself is very ruined, but it's possible to trace the 13th-c layout in some detail. Nearby KELD CHAPEL is a lonely untouched shepherds' church in riverside hamlet, which is still occasionally used by locals.

Thornthwaite NY2225 THORNTHWAITE GALLERIES have fine art, pottery and other unusual examples of craftsmanship, as well as teas, summer try-your-hand-at-it demonstrations, and a play area; cl Tues and Dec-Mar.

Ullswater NY3920 AIRA FORCE is a 65 ft waterfall in lovely NT land overlooking the lake; restaurant and shop – see also walks section. It looks its best after rain or on a misty morning.

Country **churches** are generally simple here, though candlelit ST WILFREDS (B6262 E of Eamont Bridge) NY5328 is an exception for its magnificent furnishings inc Continental treasures; others worth stopping at inc Watermillock NY4522 for its evocative photographs of all its 1930s parishioners; and Torpenhow NY2039 (formidably Norman, inc some Roman masonry).

★ **Other attractive villages** in fine scenery inc Askham NY5123 (two greens – each with a good pub), Dockray NY3921 (Royal Hotel has decent food), Hesket Newmarket NY3438 (interesting old inn brews its own beer) and Threlkeld NY3325.

Boating

On Ullswater, elegant Victorian steamers converted to diesel run between Pooley Bridge, Howtown and Glenridding; disabled access, cl Dec-Mar. Sailing dinghies can be hired by competent sailors from Ullswater Marina at Watermillock or the sailing school at Glenridding (cl winter). Rowing and other boats can be hired from Tindals in Glenridding; rowing boats from £1.50 per hr, motorboats from £11.

Regular Derwent Water launches run all year from Keswick to half a dozen points around the lake. Rowing boats and launches can be hired in Keswick.

You can also hire rowing boats on Buttermere and Crummock Water.

Walks

Head in practically any direction here and you can walk for minutes or hours. All the out-of-town places to stay that we list can recommend fine walks straight from their door.

Ullswater's eastern shore is outstanding; there are very many and different views, with a rewarding combination of waterside stretches and higher ground – from which to see more sweeping vistas. On the best and most popular stretch, Howtown-Patterdale-Glenridding, you will meet quite a few other people in summer (when it can be combined with the steamer for a round trip; best to take the steamer on the way out in case the service is cancelled). The Howtown Hotel is a good break, and Hallin Fell NY4319 nearby gives an aerial view of the lake. The main road runs along the western side, but over here there's a pleasant if more populated stroll from the car park on the A592 just NE of the A5091 junction through lakeshore woods to the **Aira Force** waterfalls NY3920 and the Gothick folly of Lyulphs Tower, with Wordsworth's daffodils a bonus in spring; above here, Gowbarrow Park NY4021 has the best lake views on this side.

Derwent Water too has gorgeous lakeside scenery, romantic little islets, ancient woodland where you're sure to see red squirrels, a variety of mountain backdrops. A boat service connects several points on the lake. From Keswick, the walk S to Friar's Crag NY2622 and up to Castlehead Wood gains exquisite views. Walla Crag above Great Wood NY2721 (often teeming with red squirrels) gains loftier heights, though the view is not that different; a moorland path heads to the photogenic Ashness Bridge NY2719, from where a rewarding return walk is one down to the shore and back again. Walks along the W shore, best reached from car parks off the back road between Grange NY2517 and Swinside NY2421, can be combined with the more demanding walk up Cat Bells NY2419 for the best views of the lake.

Buttermere lake shore is a splendid varied flat walk, with glorious views, plenty of safe opportunities for children aged 6 or more to let off steam, and even a tunnel; weather has to be really savage to spoil it. Parking at Gatescarth NY1915 £2. The Bridge pub in the little village is good for lunch. The walk from this village up Low Bank to Rannerdale Knotts NY1618 above nearby Crummock Water gives good views, and another rather more challenging but rewarding walk is up Hay Stacks NY1913 and Fleetwith Pike NY2014. You can walk round **Crummock Water** itself, best from the car park by Lanthwaite Wood NY1520 off the B5289 towards Loweswater at the N end; the scenery is less rewarding than around Buttermere, but there's a pretty view from the hill above the wood.

Borrowdale is many people's favourite Lakeland base for walks, with good paths along or just above the River Derwent, especially from Grange NY2517. Other prized walks all giving or leading to fine views include mossy Johnny Wood (from Rosthwaite NY2514 or Seatoller NY2413), the two famous waterfalls, both best after rain, Taylorgill Force NY2210 (above Seathwaite) and Lodore Falls NY2618 (behind Swiss Lodore Hotel), and a walk up to the lovely 'lost village' of Watendlath NY2716 (for instance, from Rosthwaite). More challenging walks with grand views include the path winding up the back of impregnable-looking Castle Crag NY2415 (terrific lake views) from Grange. From the summit of Honister Pass NY2213 you can tackle Brandreth NY2111, and perhaps head on via Windy Gap for the least taxing ascent of Great Gable NY2110. Determined fellwalkers enjoy the unspoilt packhorse track from Seathwaite over Styhead Pass NY2210 down into Wasdale, and the summit of the pass is a start point for a fiercely dramatic route up Scafell Pike NY2107.

Walks through the **Thornthwaite Forest**, the first-ever Forestry Commission plantation, and up to the fells above it (with lake and mountain views) are best started with a visit to the Whinlatter Visitor Centre NY1924 (B5292 above Braithwaite); good explanatory forestry displays, shop, forest maps, teas.

There's a pleasant walk up Hayeswater Gill to the isolated **Hayeswater** tarn NY4312, ringed by grand fells, from the well-restored picturesque hamlet of Hartsop NY4103, S of Patterdale.

Dodd Wood NY2427 (off A591 N of Keswick) has marked walks through the woods, or on open hillside, with Bassenthwaite views.

The northern part of the area is less interesting for walkers, though there's a pleasant stroll from Caldbeck NY3239 to a peaceful spot with a waterfall called the Howk NY3139. Binsey NY2235, a pathless lump of a hill, has splendid views by virtue of its geographical isolation.

The area's **great fell walks** include High Street NY4411 (a Roman ridge road), reached best from Haweswater; Blencathra NY3227; Skiddaw NY2629 (quite an easy haul up from Applethwaite, for far views); the walk up Martindale to Dalehead NY4316 from Howtown, then up over the fells to Bedafell Knott NY4216 and down into Patterdale (gorgeous views, Herdwick sheep, buzzards, ring ouzels); Fairfield NY3511, climbed by a horseshoe layout of ridges from Rydal. The green slatey fells N of Buttermere offer superlative routes along high ridges: Whiteless Pike NY1818, Causey Pike NY2120, Crag Hill NY1920 and Grasmoor NY1720 are among the most exciting points. Helvellyn NY3415 is most easily tackled from Thirlmere NY3116, but much more exciting when reached from Glenridding NY3817 and Striding Edge NY3415, where the path follows a narrow rocky edge (mild scrambling needed – best ascended rather than descended) above a great post-glacial corrie; it's a day's severe walking, for perhaps the grandest and certainly the most popular of all Lakeland panoramas, with dramatic ridges leading off for miles.

Driving

Even in high summer the area N of the A66 is much less heavily trafficked than the central Lakes area. Up here, the Mungrisdale-Hesket Newmarket-Caldbeck road signed off the A66 a mile W of the A5091 Windermere turn-off takes you through lovely quiet scenery.

The A66 itself is a good road for covering a lot of ground quickly at any time of year; all other A roads here can be tiresomely slow.

The B5289 along Derwent Water then up Borrowdale and over the Honister Pass has a fairly steady stream of traffic in summer – it's understandably popular for the enchanting lake views, the picturesquely wooded crags of riverside Borrowdale itself, and then the more austere high pass and the forbidding screes beyond; one or two craft shops, and tea breaks at Grange, Stonethwaite (signed off to the left) and Seatoller (inc a National Park base in a converted barn; cl Oct-Easter). On this road a stop by the river above Grange Bridge gives a romantic view of Maiden Moor; and on a clear autumn day the Ashness Bridge just up the Watendlath single-track turn-off is memorably photogenic. The full detour to Watendlath itself is recommended only for the most serenely patient summer driver, but is well worth while out of season; the little hamlet is very photogenic, and does have a café.

Other good scenic roads include the Keswick-Grange road, including a detour through the richly leafy lanes below Swinside, and then in clear weather on up the gauntly formidable Keskadale Pass; the Swindale road (gated), signed off Bampton-Shap road nr Rosgill; the B5322 Threlkeld-Thirlmere (there's a very photogenic view of Clough Head from the Brigham/Keswick side road turning off just past Yew Tree Farm; one of the prettiest views of Thirlmere itself is back down on the A591, from the lakeside car park).

Where to eat

Scales NY3427 WHITE HORSE (076 87) 79241 Dramatic setting under Blencathra, cosy and isolated farmhouse inn – perfect haven after walks; advisable to book as generously served food, using fresh local produce, very popular; cl Mon-Thurs pm March-Nov. **£15.50**|£1.75/£3.95.

Newton Reigny NY4832 SUN (0768) 67055 Small welcoming village pub with good original food, using fresh ingredients, and well-kept real ales; bedrooms; disabled access. **£12**|£5/£1.95.

Bampton NY5118 ST PATRICKS WELL (0931) 713244. Imaginative food in unpretentious surroundings (also simple good-value bedrooms); no children later in eve; cl winter Mon lunch; **£10**|£4.45/£1.25.

We welcome reports from readers . . .

This GUIDE depends on readers' reports. Do help us if you can – in return, we offer a discount on the next edition to people who've helped us with reports for it. Tell us what you think about places already in it, and anything extra you think we should say about them. And send us your ideas for inclusion in the next edition: places to visit, eat at or stay in, attractive drives or walks, maybe even unusual interesting shops you know of. Use the card in the middle, the report forms at the end, or just write – no stamp needed: THE GOOD WEEKEND GUIDE, FREEPOST TN1569, Wadhurst, E Sussex TN5 7BR.

Cumbrian Coast and West Lakes

Some grand austere scenery and unfrequented beaches are to be found here; there's much less to do than in central Lakeland and a much narrower choice of places to stay.

This area has some of the most impressive scenery and walking in the county, though it doesn't have anything to equal the mouth-watering loveliness of the famous lakes. Its coast is untouristy, with miles of unfrequented beaches. So it is altogether quieter than the central Lake District, and largely separated from it by high ridges with tortuous roads over the few passes. The choice of places to stay and things to do is very much more restricted. Ravenglass has a fine steam railway and a most enjoyable stately home; Furness Abbey at Barrow is attractive, and Maryport and Ulverston both have things worth seeing. Surprisingly, Sellafield at Seascale has an excellent visitor centre.

If you've never been to any other part of the Lakes, this is not the best place to start an acquaintance with them. But if you have – or are looking for somewhere really rather out of the usual run – then this area has a lot to recommend it.

Where to stay

Silloth NY1153 Skinburness Carlisle CA5 4QY (069 73) 32332 **£60**; 25 comfortable rms. Well-equipped Victorian seaside holiday hotel away from town, overlooking sea and Scotland; good provision for disabled.

Eskdale Green NY1400 Bower House Holmbrook CA19 1TD (0946) 723244 **£53.50**; 24 comfortable rms, some in annex. Relaxed and pleasantly isolated hotel with nicely tended sheltered garden; popular good-value food inc wonderful puddings.

Wasdale Head NY1808 Wasdale Head Seascale CA20 1EX (094 67) 26229 **£50**; 6 simple but warmly comfortable pine-clad rms. Old flagstoned and gabled walkers' and climbers' inn in magnificent setting surrounded by steep fells; popular home-cooking for 7.30 pm dinner, huge breakfasts, civilised day rooms, cheerfully busy public bar.

Greendale NY1406 Old Furnace Farm ST10 3AP (0538) 702442 ***£40**; 3 rms. B & B in modernised farmhouse (lovely surrounding countryside) with homely, relaxed atmosphere; big comfortable bedrooms with TV and good bthrms, large tasty breakfasts, very friendly, efficient service.

To see and do

✝ **Abbey Town** NY1750 Holme Cultram (B5302 Wigtown-Silloth) is the remains of formidably rich Cistercian abbey – extraordinarily grand for this quiet village.

✝ ⛫ **Barrow** SD2069 Furness Abbey (off A590 N) Impressive warm sandstone Norman remains of the one-

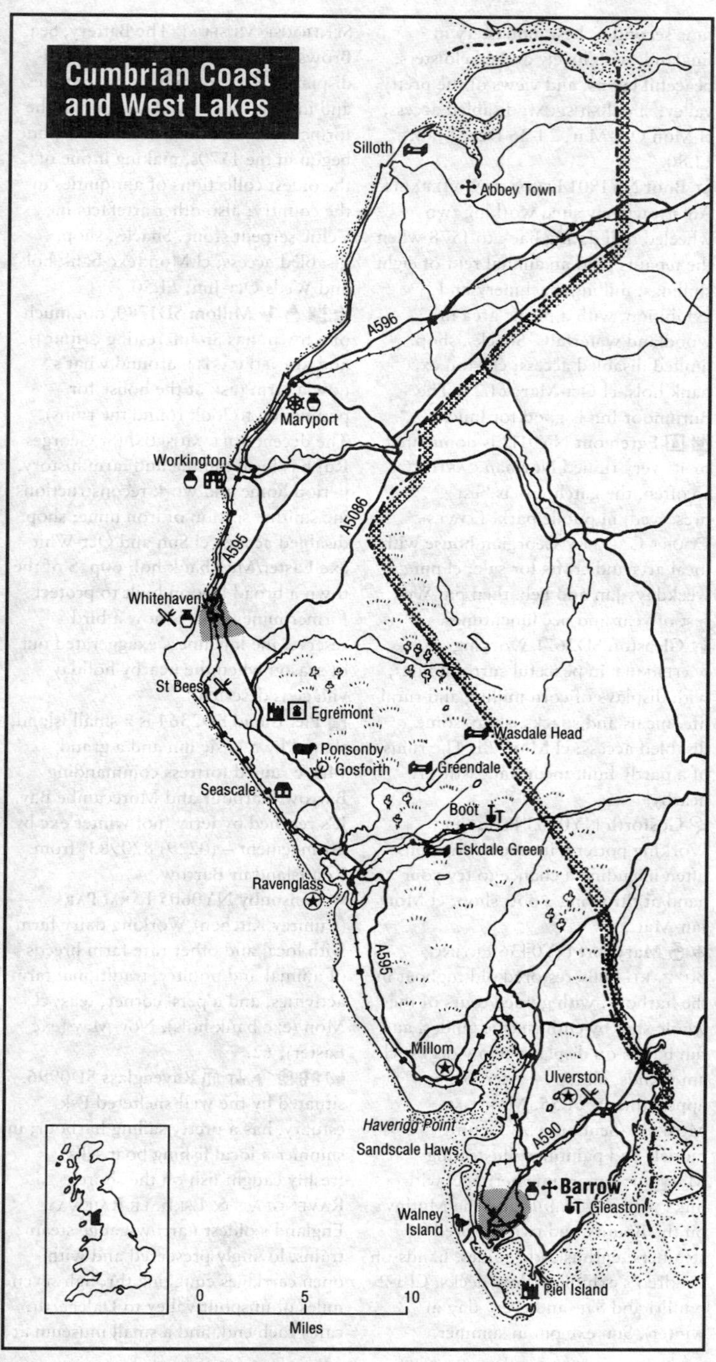

Cumbrian Coast and West Lakes
Silloth
Abbey Town
A596
Maryport
Workington
A5086
A595
Whitehaven
St Bees
Egremont
Wasdale Head
Ponsonby
Gosforth
Greendale
Seascale
Boot
Eskdale Green
Ravenglass
A595
Millom
Ulverston
Haverigg Point
Sandscale Haws
A590
Barrow
Gleaston
Walney Island
Piel Island
0
5
10
Miles

time second-richest monastery in England, with lovely arched cloisters, peaceful lawns, and views of the pretty valley; small MUSEUM; disabled access, cl Mon Oct-Mar, 24-26 Dec, 1 Jan; £1.80.

Boot NY1801 ESKDALE WATERMILL An attractively sited working two-wheeled mill dating back to 1578 when the tenants paid an annual rent of eight shillings; milling machinery and exhibition, with a picnic area nr woodland waterfalls. Snacks, shop, limited disabled access; cl Mon exc bank hols, cl Oct-Mar; £1.25. The Burnmoor Inn is good for lunch.

Egremont NY0111 is dominated by its very ruined Norman CASTLE (as so often, the gatehouse is best preserved) in public park. LOWES COURT GALLERY Georgian house with local arts and crafts for sale; cl pm weekdays Jan and Feb, then pm Wed rest of year and occ lunchtimes.

Gleaston SD2671 Working WATERMILL in peaceful surroundings, with displays of corn milling and rural life; meals and snacks, shop, some disabled access; cl Mon; £1. The ruins of a partly built medieval castle are nearby.

Gosforth NY0703 POTTERY Working pottery, its demonstrations often including a chance to try your hand at throwing a pot; shop; cl Mon Jan-Mar.

Maryport NY0436 FLYING BUZZARD Fully restored old tugboat in the harbour, with guided tours of the whole ship by enthusiastic guides, and fun hands-on displays below decks; cl am wknds, all Nov-Easter exc by appointment; £1.55. MARITIME MUSEUM (Senhouse St) Pictures, models and paintings illustrating Maryport's maritime heritage, with links with the *Titanic* and the Mutiny on the Bounty and two restored steamers; enthusiastic guides, hands-on children's exhibits below decks. Cl 1-2 pm Fri and Sat (and every day in winter), Sun exc pm in summer. SENHOUSE MUSEUM (The Battery, Sea Brows) Impressive collection of well-displayed Roman military altar stones and inscriptions, mainly dug up in the former fort next door in the 18th c but begun in the 1570s, making it one of the oldest collections of antiquities in the country; also other artefacts inc Celtic serpent stone. Snacks, shop, disabled access; cl Mon (exc bank hols) and Weds Oct-Jun; £1.50.

Millom SD1780, not much of a town, has an interesting CHURCH and RUINED CASTLE around what's now a farm (ask at the house for permission to look round the ruins). The decent FOLK MUSEUM (St Georges Rd) has local mining and farm history, period home and work reconstructions inc smithy, section of iron mine; shop, disabled access; cl Sun and Oct-Whit exc Easter/May bank hol; 60p. S of the town a broad lagoon built to protect former mineworks is now a bird reserve, the loneliness exaggerated out of season when the nearby holiday village is deserted.

Piel Island SD2364 is a small island, shared by a basic inn and a grand 14th-c ruined fortress commanding Barrow Harbour and Morecambe Bay. It's reached by ferry (not winter exc by arrangement – (0229) 820983) from Roa Island nr Barrow.

Ponsonby NY0605 FARM PARK (Cumrey Kitchen) Working dairy farm with local and other rare farm breeds of animal and poultry, traditional farm activities, and a pets' corner; teas; cl Mon (exc bank hols), Nov-May (exc Easter); £2.

Ravenglass SD0996, situated by the well-sheltered Esk estuary, has a pretty sailing harbour; in summer a local fishing boat sells freshly caught fish on the shore. RAVENGLASS & ESKDALE RAILWAY England's oldest narrow-gauge steam trains, lovingly preserved and with open carriages chugging through seven miles of unspoilt valley to Dalegarth; cafés each end, and a small museum at

Ravenglass. Meals, snacks, disabled access (advisable to arrange ahead); best to phone for train times and dates (0229) 717171; £5.40 return. Good 3-hr summer walk back from Boot (walks booklets from stations). MUNCASTER CASTLE, GARDENS & OWL CENTRE The same family have lived in this grand old house since King John granted them the land in 1208. It's been extended over the centuries (esp 19th) from its original tower, and its elegant rooms have rich furnishings and decor, inc fine Elizabethan furniture and embroidery; glorious Esk and mountain views from the terrace. The lovely 77-acre grounds are particularly rich in species rhododendrons, also unusual trees, nature trail, adventure play area and lots of owls and other rescued birds of prey (you can adopt one to help this rehabilitation work). Closed-circuit TV of nesting owls, along with talks and displays every afternoon at 2.30 – the birds fly, weather permitting. Meals, snacks, shop and plant centre, disabled access; house cl am, cl Mon exc bank hols, cl Nov-Mar; garden and owl centre open all year; £4.50, garden and owl centre £2.80. A well-restored working WATERMILL A595 NE, has Victorian machinery, a pets' corner, and flour for sale; disabled access; £1. The so-called WALLS CASTLE just outside the village is actually a Roman bath house, but its walls stand taller than any other building of its age so far north.

Seascale NY0401 SELLAFIELD Lots of time and money have been spent on the exhibition here, designed to make us more comfortable with nuclear power and using impressively up-to-date display techniques; also tours of the plant. Good disabled access; very popular with school parties. Seascale itself has a pleasant beach, and a singularly scenic golf course, where every hole offers views of the sea or the mountains; the third tee ironically puts Sellafield into the same scene as a ring of prehistoric stones.

Ulverston SD2978 SWARTHMOOR HALL A590 SW Lovingly restored Elizabethan manor with period furnishings, the birthplace of Quakerism after George Fox was sheltered here in 1652; it has his portable four-poster among other mementos. Guided tours twice a day, at 10 am and 2 pm; shop; cl Thurs and Sun (exc by appointment), Fri, mid-Oct-mid-Mar; donations appreciated (run by the Society of Friends). You can visit the factory of CUMBRIA CRYSTAL, and on weekdays watch the craftsmen blowing, cutting and (Mon-Thurs) engraving; 90p. The factory shop (cl Sun Oct-May) is good value, inc cheap seconds. LAUREL & HARDY MUSEUM (Upper Brook St) The only exhibition of its kind, fittingly in Stan Laurel's home town, with mementos and all-day films; the owner (a former mayor) really knows his subject; shop, disabled access; £2. The PORK PIE SHOP at the N end of Mkt Pl is perhaps England's best. The Dolls House Man (Furness Galleries, Theatre St) makes DOLL'S HOUSES, farms, wooden animals etc; open Thurs-Sat Jan-May, then daily exc Weds and Sun.

Walney Island SD1868 over the bridge from Barrow has some long roads of low houses but is mostly a windswept sweep of duney grass, very offshore-feeling; excellent bird watching at both ends – both are nature reserves, with interesting plants too. On the way out the gigantic folding gates of the shipyard in Barrow are a remarkable sight.

Whitehaven NX9718 Interesting, planned as 18th-c industrial town and major port, now being restored after decline. Harbour attractive at high tide (dirty at low tide). The local small MUSEUM (Civic Hall, Lowther St; cl Sun, bank hols) sets the context well. Michael Moon BOOKSHOP has vast and rewarding secondhand stock, the best in the Lakes; cl Sun, bank hols; some other interesting shops in side streets.

Workington NX9928 HELENA THOMPSON MUSEUM (Park End Rd) has some antique and Georgian costumes, as well as pottery, silver, furniture and local history, in period surroundings; cl Sun. WORKINGTON HALL (Curwen Pk, N) Substantial ruin of grandiose mansion around Norman tower, in public park – quite intriguing. A famous letter by Mary, Queen of Scots to her cousin Elizabeth I was written here; shop; cl 1-2 pm, Mon (exc bank hols), Nov-Easter; 65p. The Alamin Indian restaurant (Jane St) is good.

Walks

Eskdale is excellent for walks, especially around Boot NY1801, to the Stanley Ghyll Force waterfall SD1799 or up towards the open fells (the landlord of the Burnmoor Inn is helpful with route suggestions); or for good views up Muncaster Fell, above the Castle and the Mill. There is a nature trail in the grounds of Muncaster Castle. You can use the Ravenglass & Eskdale railway as part of a round trip.

Wasdale is unquestionably the most austerely imposing valley here, with awesome towering screes plunging dauntingly into deep Wast Water, and high peaks above including Scafell. Apart from around the interesting churchyard, the valley is not so good for easier walks, and parking at Wasdale Head NY1808 can be a problem in summer or at holiday times. But this is the start for many serious fell walks, including the ascents of Great Gable NY2110 and Scafell Pike NY2207; one less taxing walk is straight up the head of the valley to the summit of Black Sail Pass NY1811 and back. Besides the Wasdale Head Hotel, the Strands lower down is a useful stop for food.

The **coast** has one particular lure for walkers and birdwatchers: the section between Whitehaven NX9718 and St Bees NX9512 has a cliff path along its length, and each town has a railway station. From the beach car park NW of St Bees an easy walk takes you up the nature-reserve sandstone headland, famous for its bird life, and with magnificent sea and hill views.

There are lots of **long beaches**, deserted except in high season, from Ravenglass down to Hodbarrow Point SD1878, good for breezy seaside walks; one of the nicest spots on this entire coast is the huge stretch of impressive dunes on Haverigg Point SD1378, nr Millom, and the dunes at Sandscale Haws SD2075, nr Barrow, are protected as a nature reserve.

We've mentioned the **Duddon Valley** under the Southern Lakes – see above.

Driving

The daunting Hardknott Pass and the back road up the Duddon Valley from Ulpha which joins it both give magnificent mountain views – best in good weather out of season. For coastal views, the A5087 long way round between Ulverston and Barrow has fine views across Morecambe Bay and carries little traffic; up in the north, the B5300 coast road N of Maryport looking across the sea to Scotland is virtually deserted except in high summer. Traffic is generally relatively light throughout this area, though don't reckon on quick journey times along the A595 – which does have views of both hills and sea on many stretches.

Where to eat

Ulverston SD2978 Bay Horse (0229) 53972 Beautifully presented and very innovative food inc interesting vegetarian choices and emphasis on fresh fish dishes in nicely placed inn overlooking Morecambe Bay; bedrooms; cl Mon am; children over 12. **£25**|£1.35/£6.

St Bees NX9712 Seacote Hotel Beach Rd (0946) 822777 Lovely views and headland walks, with decent food in pleasant, roomy bar or restaurant; welcoming to children. **£16**|£3.50/£1.15.

Whitehaven NY9718 Brunos 10 Church St (0946) 65270 Candlelit Italian bistro in small tasteful rooms of Georgian house; bedrooms. **£15.50**.

Cumbrian Pennines and the North

Unspoilt even in summer, this area has quiet river valleys below desolate moors; attractive prices.

This part of Cumbria is one of England's least-known areas. Yet, though there are few set-piece tourist attractions here, there are a good many points of interest worth tracking down. Alston, Kirkby Lonsdale and Appleby are distinctive small towns of considerable character. Talkin Tarn, the Acorn Bank Garden at Temple Sowerby, and Birdoswald Roman fort near Gilsland are all worth visiting, and Brampton has an interesting priory and castle. Even the city of Carlisle has some unexpected treasures.

For most people, the chief attraction is the appealing mixture of quiet river valleys with more awesome open country and high moors. Much of the high country is too bleak and boggy for most walkers, but drivers have the joy of fine views from roads that see relatively little traffic. The railway crossing the moors between Carlisle and Settle is perhaps the best way of all of seeing this unusual part of England.

The Lakes themselves are of course within easy reach.

Where to stay

Brampton NY5361 Farlam Hall Hallbankgate (A689 S) CA8 2NG (069 77) 46234 ***£165 inc dinner**; 13 comfortable rms. Charmingly Victorian very civilised country house (the building's actually much older); log fires, excellent attentive service, and peaceful spacious grounds with croquet lawn and small pretty lake; children over 5; dogs welcome; cl Christmas-New Year.

Crosby on Eden NY4559 Crosby Lodge High Crosby Carlisle CA6 4QZ (0228) 573618 ***£88**; 9 spacious rms with 2 more in stable conversion. Imposing country house, comfortable, genuine and friendly inside, with appealing individual furnishings; attractive mature grounds, interesting food, nice countryside; cl 24 Dec, 1st 3 wks Jan.

Alston NY7246 Lovelady Shield Nenthead Rd CA9 3LF (0434) 381203 ***£78**; 12 rms. Wonderfully located country house with River Nene running along bottom of garden; tranquil atmosphere, courteous staff, log fires in comfortable rooms, very good food inc fine breakfasts; cl 4 Jan-15 Feb; children over 10 in restaurant (high tea).

Faugh NY5155 String of Horses Carlisle (0228) 70297 **£65**; 14 rms. Attractive and friendly 17th-c coaching inn in pleasant surroundings; interesting carved furniture in cosy communicating rooms, popular food, pleasant service, outdoor heated swimming pool and indoor leisure centre; cl 24-25 Dec; disabled access; dogs by arrangement.

Barbon SD6383 Barbon Inn Carnforth (052 42) 76233 **£55**; 10 simple but comfortable rms, some with bthrm. Small very friendly village inn in quiet spot below fells with relaxing bar, armchair lounge, good meals in candlelit dining room, decent bar food and good breakfasts.

Casterton SD6379 Pheasant LA6 2RX (052 42) 71230 **£55**; 10 rms. Small civilised inn with pleasant atmosphere; decent food in no-smoking dining room, garden lounge, small but sound wine list; cl 1 wk Jan; disabled access.

Ravenstonedale NY7204 Fat Lamb Cross Bank Kirkby Stephen CA17 4LL (053 96) 23242 **£54**; 12 comfortable rms. Remote, welcoming moorland inn with cheery log fire in bar and own 5-acre nature reserve; disabled access.

Lupton SD5581 Lupton Tower Kirkby Lonsdale LA6 2PR (053 95) 67400 ***£52**; 6 rms, most with bthrm. Stylish and idiosyncratic 18th-c country house with a hint of country chic, notable for only vegetarian food – outstanding quality; very good service; cl 24-26 Dec.

Sedbergh SD6692 Dalesman LA10 5BN (053 96) 21183 ***£50**; 6 comfortable and cheerful rms, most with bthrm. Nicely modernised old village pub with wide choice of popular food.

Kirkby Lonsdale SD6278 Snooty Fox Carnforth (052 42) 71308 **£46**; 3 cheerful well-furnished rms, most with bthrm – the ones overlooking the street are specially nice. Friendly, rambling pub with interesting things to look at in the several public rooms, and popular, interesting food inc good breakfasts.

Brampton NY5361 Kirby Moor Longtown Rd CA8 2AB (069 77) 3893 ***£44**; 5 comfortable rms. Beautifully furnished Victorian country house with open fires; conservatory, good home-cooked fresh food, fine views, attractive countryside; cl 25-26 Dec.

Hadrian's Wall NY6967 Holmhead Greenhead, Carlisle CA6 7HY (069 77) 47402 ***£43**; 4 rms. Friendly old house in sheltered valley, comfortably if simply furnished; plenty of games for children and decent freshly prepared food using local produce and served around big candlelit oak table; no smoking; also, separate cottage with good disabled facilities; cl 25 Dec, 1 Jan.

Talkin NY5557 Hullerbank Brampton CA8 2DX (069 77) 46668 ***£36**; 3 rms. Comfortable Georgian farmhouse in unspoilt countryside with lounge, dining room and good food using home-grown and local produce inc home-produced lamb; no smoking; cl 25 Dec, 1 Jan; children over 10.

Alston NY7246 Middle Bayles Farm CA9 3BS (0434) 381383 ***£34**; 2 cosy rms. Traditional 17th-c stone farmhouse in lovely spot with fine views and walks, cattle and Swaledale sheep; good home-made food, and open fires; no smoking; cl Christmas, April (lambing time).

Dent SD7187 Sportsmans Cowgill, Sedbergh LA10 5RG (0539) 625282 **£34w**; 6 rms with shared bthrm. Unassuming, comfortable pub notable for its wonderful position in Dentdale by the River Dee with the viaduct of the old Settle-Carlisle railway close by, and walks in all directions; open log fires and good-value home-made food; cl 25 Dec.

Winton NY7810 Bay Horse Kirkby Stephen CA17 4HS (076 83) 71451 **£30**; 3 rms. Well-kept unpretentious moorland pub with good generous home-cooking; children over 5.

Garrigill NY7441 George & Dragon Alston CA9 3DS (0434) 381293 **£30**; 4 small rms, shared bthrm but clean and comfortable. Friendly 17th-c pub on dead-end road in beautiful countryside, with decent food inc duck and game, and good service; children over 12.

See also Appleby, under Where to eat.

To see and do

Alston NY7246 Interesting little Pennine town with surprising number of pubs up and down its very steep cobbled main st, also craft shop with locally produced foods too, and home-baked teas, fresh coffee (cl Jan-mid-Feb). The chief attraction here is the South Tynedale Railway, with steam or diesel vintage narrow-gauge train trips of 40 mins along a lovely winding valley; shop, teas; cl Mon and Fri Jun, Sept, runs only certain days Oct-late May – phone (0434) 381696 for times; £1.60 return. Hartside Nursery (A686 W) is a beautifully situated alpine nursery with small streamside garden and rare plants for sale; cl wknds Nov-Feb. Gossipgate Gallery specialises in local art and crafts, with various changing exhibitions and a good big shop; snacks, disabled access; cl Jan-mid-Feb. The Angel is useful for lunch.

★ **Appleby** NY6921 is an attractive riverside town; the main street, rising from the harmonious 12th-c church to the castle, is still a grand sight despite the cars, with a good few attractive buildings inc a lovely courtyard of almshouses; there are pleasant strolls by the Eden. Appleby Castle Conservation Centre The castle itself is in remarkable shape for a partly 11th-c building, with one of the best-preserved keeps in the country; there are terrific views from the ramparts at the top. The Clifford family lived here for nearly 700 years, though they moved later to the grander house, the Great Hall of which has antiques, paintings and Chinese porcelain on display. The main feature of the attractive grounds is the collection of birds, waterfowl and rare farm animals in a lovely setting above the river. Snacks, shop; cl Oct-mid-Apr; £3.50. The Royal Oak is good for lunch, and recently we've had good reports on the Globe too.

★ **Barbon** SD6383 is an unpretentious village given appeal by its fine setting, just below the fells. The Barbon Inn is good.

Brampton NY5361 Lanercost Priory Impressive and extensive remains of Norman priory, built with stone recycled from Hadrian's Wall. A lovely riverside setting, with the entrance arch picturesquely framing the nave, restored in the 18th c as a red sandstone church with stained glass by William Morris and Burne-Jones, and Sun services by candlelight; disabled access; cl exc services Oct-Mar; 75p. Naworth Castle has an evocative Great Hall with huge tapestries, as well as medieval dungeons, a grand picture gallery, pre-Raphaelite library, and attractive wooded grounds; some disabled access, shop, teas; open pm Sat, Sun, Weds and bank hols Easter-Sept, plus Thurs and Fri in Aug; £2.50.

Brough NY7915 Castle Classic ruined Norman fortress, in a romantic setting on the moors above the village, with great views; cl Mon and Tues Oct-Mar, 24-26 Dec, 1 Jan; 75p. Coffee shop with home-baking (not Nov-Easter) in Clifford House craft

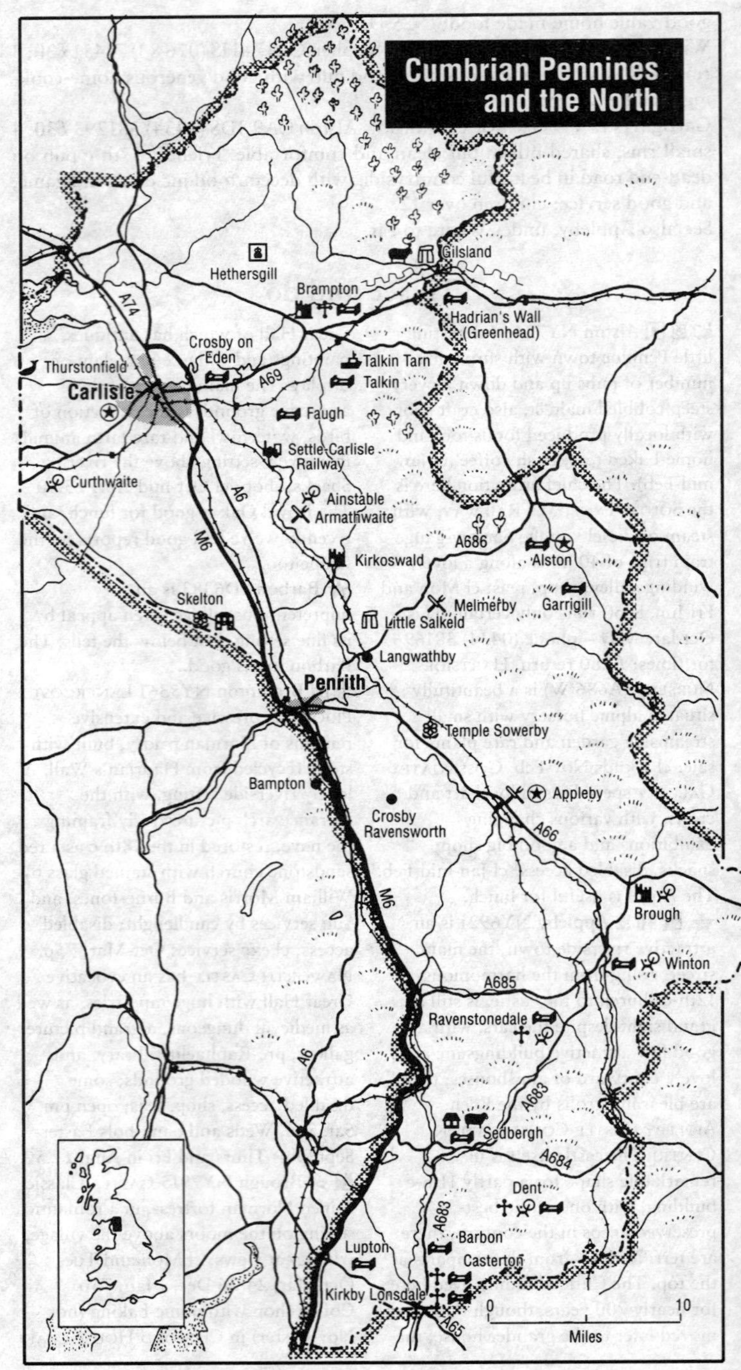
Cumbrian Pennines and the North
Gilsland
Hethersgill
Brampton
Hadrian's Wall (Greenhead)
A74
Crosby on Eden
Talkin Tarn
Thurstonfield
A69
Talkin
Carlisle
Faugh
Settle-Carlisle Railway
Curthwaite
A6
Ainstable
Armathwaite
M6
A686
Alston
Kirkoswald
Garrigill
Skelton
Melmerby
Little Salkeld
Langwathby
Penrith
Temple Sowerby
Bampton
Appleby
Crosby Ravensworth
A66
M6
Brough
Winton
A685
Ravenstonedale
A6
A683
Sedbergh
A684
Dent
A683
Barbon
Lupton
Casterton
Kirkby Lonsdale
A65
0
10
Miles

shop (esp handmade jewellery), in village.

Carlisle NY4056 is a sizeable town, not an obvious weekend destination, but does have plenty to interest the visitor, with several quietly attractive old buildings (and a very helpful visitor centre in one of them, the Old Town Hall). TULLIE HOUSE (Castle St) Exemplary new attention-holding displays of Border history, life and nature, inc evocative feel-hear-and-see 'experiences'; also more conventional free ground-floor art gallery/museum. Disabled access; cl Sun am, 25 Dec; £3.10. The unpretentious CATHEDRAL, founded in 1122, has fine examples of stained glass among its many treasures; try to go on a bright morning when the sunlight comes streaming colourfully through the east window. Also medieval carvings inc the Brougham Triptych, painted panels and stonework and crypt treasury; meals, snacks, shop, disabled access. The CASTLE is an extensive well-kept rather gaunt fortress militarily redeveloped several times since 12th c; dungeon, portcullised gatehouse, medieval furnished rooms, etc, also display of its history, and good regimental museum (cl Sun am winter) with battle models, weapons and videos; cl Mon Oct-Mar, 24-26 Dec, 1 Jan; £1.80. The GUILDHALL in Greenmarket is a handsomely restored medieval timbered hall; worth a look inside if passing – some displays; 50p. ST CUTHBERTS CHURCH is remarkable for its mobile pulpit. The RACECOURSE attractively placed out at Durdar has meetings every month exc Aug; (0228) 22973 for dates. Marys Chambers is good for lunch.

Casterton SD6379 has the CASTERTON SCHOOL of Brontë fame, and the CHURCH has some attractive pre-Raphaelite stained glass and paintings. The Pheasant is good.

★ **Dent** SD7187 has some modern outskirts but centrally is a delightful steep cobbled village, a rewarding end to an attractive drive; the Sun, an attractive and welcoming inn, brews its own beer, and the CHURCH is well worth a look. E of the village, towards Denthead, Colin Gardner (Stone House, Cowgill; also gun cabinets; cl weekends) and Little Oak Furniture (Bridge End, Denthead) both make TRADITIONAL FURNITURE.

Gilsland NY6166 BIRDOSWALD ROMAN FORT (off B6318 W) Big fortress, still being excavated, on well-preserved stretch of Hadrian's Wall in fine countryside above River Irthing; commanding views and good new display centre; snacks, shop; centre cl Nov-late Mar; £1.50. The GOAT FARM at Holme View nearby sells prize-winning traditional cheeses.

Hethersgill NY4867 SARK GALLERY A former village chapel with contemporary art studio and exhibitions, modern embroidery and pottery; great views; cl am, all day Mon, Jan-Mar.

★ **Kirkby Lonsdale** SD6278 is a small and usually quiet town of considerable character with interesting old yards and ginnels, good country shops, enjoyable pubs, and a fine CHURCH. It's lively on Thurs country-market day. Just below the town there's a pretty stretch of the River Lune, good for walking or just lazing about – or even swimming if it's hot. The Lune Valley is appealing countryside, little visited by tourists.

★ **Kirkoswald** NY5641 Ruins of 13th-c CASTLE, with the remains of three towers and a gatehouse and fine views towards the Pennines. The village is attractive, and has a decent pub.

Little Salkeld NY5736 gives access off the lane N to the quaintly named STONE CIRCLE Long Meg and her Daughters NY5737.

Ravenstonedale NY7203 The village is notable more for its pleasant riverside scenery than for its buildings – apart from the unspoilt CHURCH which escaped Victorian refitting; longitudinal pews, three-decker pulpit, steeply pitched gallery (steep stairs up), fine E window memorial to Fothergill family (one was last female Protestant martyr to be burned at the stake); choose a bright day for best light. Decent nearby pubs; Beckside Gallery makes hardwood TRADITIONAL FURNITURE. The Black Swan is useful for lunch.

Sedbergh SD6692 has a helpful Yorkshire Dales National Park Centre on Main St (cl Dec-Easter), concentrating on this area. PENNINE TWEEDS (Farfield Mill) is a factory shop for riverside Victorian mill using 1930s looms; cl Sun Nov-Mar. HOLME FARM 2 pm tours of traditional hill farm, with plenty of young animals and nature trail; cl Oct-mid-Mar; £2. The Dalesman and Red Lion are both good for lunch.

Skelton NY4435 HUTTON-IN-THE-FOREST Legend has it that this formidable mansion was the castle of the Green Knight of Arthurian legend; true or not, it's certainly had a distinguished history. It was grandly extended in the 17th c from its 14th-c pele tower core, then castellated more recently; it's crowded with interesting period furniture, tapestries and antiques, with a magnificent panelled gallery. Outside, a terraced garden runs down to the lake, and there's an 18th-c walled formal garden, a more romantic Victorian garden with grand trees, 17th-c dovecot and woodland nature walk; snacks, shop; house cl am and Sat, Mon (exc bank hols)-Weds and Oct-Easter; gdn open every day exc Sat; *£3, £1.50 garden only.

The **Settle-Carlisle** railway, up Ribbledale and into the Cumbrian Pennines, stopping at Dent Station, Garsdale Head, Kirkby Stephen, Appleby, Langwathby and other Eden Valley villages, is a memorable 70 miles of grand scenery; (0228) 44711 for times and fares.

Talkin Tarn NY5458 Lovely lake with partly wooded shores, peaceful mountain views, plenty of space for strolling, nature trail; rowing boat and mountain-bike hire, disabled access, teas.

Temple Sowerby NY6127 ACORN BANK Richly planted terraced and walled garden with 250 varieties of medicinal and culinary herbs, clematis, unusual old fruit trees, and herbaceous borders; the steep wild garden drops down to the stream; cl Nov-Mar; £1.50. NT.

Thurstonfield NY3257 TROUT-FISHING on well-stocked sizeable lake set in peaceful woodland at Lough Fishery; tackle and boat hire, inc one for disabled anglers; cl Oct-mid-Mar.

We've already mentioned a good few local craftsmen. Others can be found at **Curthwaite** NY3249, where Ian Laval of Meadow Bank Farm is a very traditional CABINET-MAKER, felling and drying his own hardwoods (cl wknds), and Michael King at Oakleigh, Todd Cl, nearby makes silver and gold JEWELLERY (cl Sun, Mon); and at **Ainstable** NY5346, where Jim Malone has a traditional WORKING POTTERY. Another good pottery at **Winton** NY7810 is the long-established LANGRIGG POTTERY; may close some days at quiet times – (076 83) 71542 to check; the Bay Horse here is useful for lunch.

Other attractive villages, all with decent pubs, include Bampton NY5118, Crosby Ravensworth NY6215 (Maulds Meaburn is also pretty) and Langwathby NY5734.

We welcome reports from readers . . .

Readers who help us with reports for the GUIDE are offered a discount on the next edition: so please do help if you can!

Walks

There are decent walks close to or even right from the door of all the places we suggest to stay in.

The **high Pennines** have few walking routes over them and are extremely bleak: this is the reserve of the dedicated peat-bog enthusiast. But High Cup Nick NY7426, a great scoop in the ridge, is one of the most dramatic features in the whole of the Pennine range. An easy way to get an idea of the remoteness of these hills is to walk from Dufton NY6825 along paths encircling Dufton Pike. The hill roads mentioned under Driving below give access to several worthwhile tracks. The back road from Langwathby NY5733 on the A686 through Skirwith to Kirkland leads to an old Roman track which plunges northwards into the Pennines. There are other walks from the clusters of sheep farms along the foot of the Pennines between here and Appleby.

Surviving traces of **Hadrian's Wall** can be reached on well-signed paths from the lanes between the A69 and B6318 N of Brampton NY5361.

The Nunnery Walks at Staffield NY5443 are private paths through old woodland inc lovely **Eden Valley** river gorge with waterfalls and quiet pools; teas; 50p. There are other good free walks in this delightfully wooded sheltered valley, for instance from Armathwaite NY5146 and Wetheral NY4654. The valley has the reputation of staying dry when it's pouring over in Lakeland.

Driving

Many roads here are very rewarding for country drives. The A683 Kirkby Lonsdale-Sedbergh-Kirkby Stephen passes through fine countryside, and the B6260 to Appleby has good views. The back road through the Lyent valley N of Orton takes you through very unspoilt quiet farmland and villages. N of Temple Sowerby, the B6412 to Lazenby and then the back road through the Eden valley to Armathwaite and on up to Wetheral affords delicious quiet views. The B6413 Lazonby-Brampton takes in some commanding high ground, and the A689 Brampton-Alston has very varied views. The road up Barbondale from Barbon and then on past Dent to Dent Head and the splendid railway viaduct, or perhaps round into Deepdale, reaches deep into the hills.

On the trunk roads, queues can build up on the A65 heading down into Yorkshire, and on parts of the A66 (though it's being improved). The A686 carries far less traffic but is more twisting. All three roads have fine views.

Where to eat

Appleby NY6921 Royal Oak (07683) 51463 Partly 14th-c, warmly welcoming coaching inn with deservedly popular, fresh, home-made bar food inc gigantic breakfasts and enterprising vegetarian meals; comfortable bedrooms. **£18.90**|£2.20/£8.40.

Melmerby NY6237 Shepherds (0768) 881 217 Friendly place in unspoilt sandstone village with popular home-made food inc delicious puddings and huge choice of over 25 cheeses; lots of daily specials using only local produce; quick, friendly table service; cl 25 Dec. **£16**|£1.25/£6.70.

Armathwaite NY5146 Dukes Head (069 92) 226. Comfortable and friendly pub/restaurant in attractive village with good home-cooking, decent wines; bedrooms. **£15.75**|£3.10/£1.90.

CUMBRIA CALENDAR

Some of these dates were provisional as we went to press.

At Rushbearing Festivals, costumed children carry colourful loads of flower-decorated rushes to the church, escorted by the town or village band.

JANUARY

1st **Carlisle** Potters of Cumbria 'Shaping the Earth', *at Tullie House*; **Winton Fell** Nine Standards Fell Race

FEBRUARY

6th **Grasmere** Wordsworth Winter School *at Dove Cottage – till Fri 11*

25th **Grasmere** Book Collectors Weekend *at Dove Cottage – till Sun 27*

APRIL

2nd **Whittington** Races, *point-to-point*

8th **Casterton** Folk-dance Weekend *– till Sun 10*

29th **Carlisle** and Borders Spring Horticultural Show *– till 1 May*

MAY

20th **Workington** Keswick Jazz Festival *- till Sun 22*

28th **Coniston** Water Festival; *sailing, skydiving, clog dancing – till 5 Jun*; **Ravenglass** Railway Family Day; *children with teddies or pets travel free*

29th **Calder Bridge** Country Field Day: *traditional outdoor pursuits inc wrestling, sheep-clipping, pillow-fighting, terrier-racing and sheep-penning*

30th **Kendal** Medieval Market, *procession and music*

JUNE

2nd **Appleby** Horse Fair; *gypsies gather from all over Europe on Fair Hill for this 300-year-old event; fortune-telling, camp fires, culminating in spectacular horse, carriage and van sales – till Weds 8*

19th **Kirkby Lonsdale** Brass Band Contest

26th **Endmoor** Country Fayre 'New Life from Old Coal'

29th **Warcop** Rushbearing

JULY

2nd **Ambleside** Rushbearing; **Lake Windermere** Festival *inc boat parades and bungee jumping – till Sun 10*; **Musgrave** Rushbearing

9th **Appleby** Town Carnival *– till Sun 10*

17th **Gosforth** Agricultural Show

18th **Grasmere** Sports *– mainly traditional inc Lakeland wrestling (unchanged for centuries, a trial show of strength)*

30th **Ambleside** Lake District Summer Music Festival *– till 13 Aug*; **Barbon** Sprint Hill Climb *– motorcycles and sidecars*; **Grasmere** Wordsworth Summer Conference *at Dove Cottage*; **Lake District** Summer Music Festival *– till 13 Aug*

AUGUST

3rd **Cartmel** Show

4th **Ings** Lake District Sheepdog Trials

CUMBRIA CALENDAR

AUGUST cont.

5th **Penrith** Lowther Horse Driving Trials and Country Fair – *till Sun 7*

6th **Windermere** Steamboat Museum: *viewing with demonstrations, the classic motor boat rally taking place on the lake*

9th **Kirkby Lonsdale** Lonesdale Agricultural Show

28th **Grange-over-Sands** Holker Hall MG Rally; **Kendal** Folk Festival, *at Brewery Arts Centre*

29th **Silloth** Carnival

SEPTEMBER

3rd **Hesket Newmarket** Agriculture Show; **Kirkby Lonsdale** Victorian Fair – *till Sun 4*

17th **Egremont** Crab Fair *inc world gurning (pulling a face) championships*

25th **Urswick** Rushbearing

OCTOBER

15th **Buttermere** Show

17th **Windermere** Power Boat Record Attempts – *till Fri 21*

NOVEMBER

4th **Kendal** Festival of Jazz and Blues

17th **Wasdale** Biggest Liar in the World Competition – *an evening event in a village that has the deepest lake, the highest mountain, the smallest church and the biggest liar*

DECEMBER

3rd **Kirkby Lonsdale** Christmas Fair – *lights-on celebration*

4th **Keswick** Victorian Fayre

Help this year from: *Mrs J D Hardman, Jim and Maggie Cowell, Dr P G McGrath, John Evans, Steve and Julie Cocking, David Heath, Roger and Jillian Shaw, Anne and Chris Norman, John Allsopp, Meredith Devereaux, Denis and Margaret Kilner, Alan Wilcock, Christine Davidson, M Hitchman, Phil and Heidi Cook, Philip Orbell, Andrew McKeand, David Wallington, K H and P C Richards, Gill and Maurice McMahon, George Dundas, Malcolm Taylor, A T Langton, David Cooke, Linda White, Jason Macniven, Dr Sherriff, W H and E Thomas, G and M Stewart, Dave and Jules Tuckett, Barry and Anne, Lorrie and Mick Marchington, Jacquie and Jon Payne, Peter and Pat Frogley, Ann and Bob Westbrook, C Roberts, Mike Muston, D J Underwood, Tim Gilroy, Paul and Gail Betteley, Martin and Jane Bailey, Richard Holloway, Gwen and Peter Andrews, Dick Brown, H K Dyson, Anthony and Elizabeth Watts, Brian Jones, Richard Waller, Mike and Jo, Greg Parston, J Dearn, Jane Thompson, Peter Barnsley, David Varney, Robert Neill, Bob Hurling, John Norris, Stephen Savill, TBB, C Roberts, John Crowe, Andrew Hazeldine, Michael Butler, E G Parish, Keith Croxton, John and Sherry Moate, Dave Webster, Sue Holland, Neil and Jenny Spink, Mr and Mrs J Denham-Vaughan, Walter Reid, Tony Bland, Barry and Diane Powderhill, John Oddey.*

Derbyshire and Staffordshire

Mid Derbyshire has a most appealing mix of beautiful scenery with interesting places to visit. It has the best choice of places to stay in the area, and is very good walking country. There is enjoyable walking in other parts of the county, too – particularly in the bleaker north, though Dove Dale, shared between the south of the county and Staffordshire, is a honeypot for walkers. The south of Derbyshire also has some very rewarding places to visit, from stately homes to restored survivals of early industry. Staffordshire, though not an obvious choice for a weekend break, has some surprising delights and is well worth considering – especially if you've already spent some time in Derbyshire.

Mid Derbyshire

This region has magnificent houses and other interesting buildings, delightful dales scenery; very civilised.

The beautiful dales country, which spreads into the southern area and the fringes of Staffordshire, is very rewarding both for walkers and for drivers (gentle pace), and is punctuated by charming villages. In summer the most lovely dales do have almost a crocodile of walkers snaking along them, though even then you can find quiet areas; as with other particularly popular areas, this is perhaps ideally suited to short breaks out of season – autumn and particularly late spring are good times. Our short list of outstanding places to visit in the area would start with Chatsworth, Hardwick Hall and Haddon Hall at Over Haddon, with Matlock/Matlock Bath being well worth a visit (the Riber Castle wildlife park is good), Lea Gardens gorgeous in late spring, and Bolsover Castle and Eyam Hall very attractive too. There's a very good choice of places to stay; eating out is rather good, too.

Where to stay

Baslow SK2572 Cavendish Bakewell DE4 1SP (0246) 582311 **£106**; 23 spotlessly kept, comfortable and individually furnished rms (varying in size) with fine views. Charming hotel on the edge of Chatsworth Park with most attractive, well-furnished day rooms (some furnishings come from Chatsworth House), open fires, fine food in two restaurants, and very courteous staff.
Baslow SK2572 Fischer's Baslow Hall Bakewell DE4 1RR (0246) 583259 **£95**; 6 comfortable, individual rms. Handsome building with lots of antiques and paintings, bold fabrics; open fires, fresh flowers, beautifully presented food

in airy dining room or in lunchtime Café Max; cl 25-26 Dec.

Bakewell SK2272 HASSOP HALL DE5 1NS (0629) 640488 **£93**; 13 spacious rms. Mentioned in the Domesday Book and in lovely parklands surrounded by fine scenery, this handsome hotel has oak-panelled bar, elegant lounge, friendly service, tennis; cl 24-26 Dec; disabled access.

Matlock SK3060 RIBER HALL DE4 5JU (0629) 582 795 **£92**; 11 rms with antiques, chocolates, baskets of fruit. Partly 15th-c manor house with thick stone walls and heavy beams, period furniture in the public rooms; popular elegant restaurant with ambitious food and fine wines, extensive grounds with tennis; children over 10.

Rowsley SK2566 PEACOCK Matlock DE4 2EB (0629) 733518 **£86.50**; 14 comfortable rms. 17th-c hotel with antiques, and good, very popular restaurant; private fishing in season.

Ashford in the Water SK1969 RIVERSIDE COUNTRY HOUSE Fennel St DE4 1QF (0629) 814275 **£80**; 15 individually decorated rms. Creeper-covered Georgian house in delightful village with pretty, river-fronted gardens; quiet, relaxed atmosphere, antiques and log fires in cosy day rooms, imaginative food (served all day), and good service; disabled access.

Ashford in the Water SK1969 ASHFORD HOTEL DE4 1QB (0629) 812 725 ***£65**; 7 decent rms. Small, traditional hotel with oak beams, open fires, bar, residents' lounge overlooking garden, and good food in country restaurant.

Monsal Head SK1871 MONSAL HEAD HOTEL Bakewell DE4 1NL (062 9640) 250 **£50***; 8 very good rms. Comfortable and enjoyable small hotel in marvellous setting high above River Wye; horsey theme in bar (converted from old stables), Victorian-style restaurant, well-prepared decent food, and good service; cl 25 Dec.

Grindleford SK2478 MAYNARD ARMS Sheffield S30 1HP (043 36) 30321 **£49.50**; 13 rms with sherry, fruit and chocolate provided. Pleasant first-floor lounge with good views over the Peak National Park, smart, welcoming hotel bar, good choice of food, and particularly attentive service.

Biggin-by-Hartington SK0673 BIGGIN HALL Buxton SK17 0DH (0298) 84451 ***£45**; 15 spacious rms with antiques. Lovely, carefully renovated 17th-c house in quiet grounds; two comfortable sitting rooms, log fires, and imaginative food using free-range produce and seasonal veg; children over 12; also, self-catering in recently converted 18th-c stone building and in bothy.

Buxton SK0673 WESTMINSTER HOTEL S17 6JR (0298) 23929 ***£42**; 12 rms. Modest, friendly hotel overlooking Pavilion Gardens; pleasant dining room (they do an early supper for opera/concert goers), lounge and bar, excellent breakfasts, and prompt, courteous service; cl Jan.

Rowland SK2072 HOLLY COTTAGE Bakewell DE4 1NR (0629) 640624 ***£36**; 2 rms, shared bthrm; 200-year-old cottage on a quiet lane and surrounded by peaceful rolling countryside; large lounge with open fire, attractive dining room, excellent breakfasts with home-made rolls and bread, and lovely gardens; cl Nov-Dec.

Great Longstone SK2071 BARN (0629) 640335 ***£32**; 2 warm, very comfortable and spotlessly clean ground-floor rms, shared bthrm. Converted barn on main street of attractive village; upstairs open-plan lounge and dining room; no smoking; cl Christmas wk; children over 10.

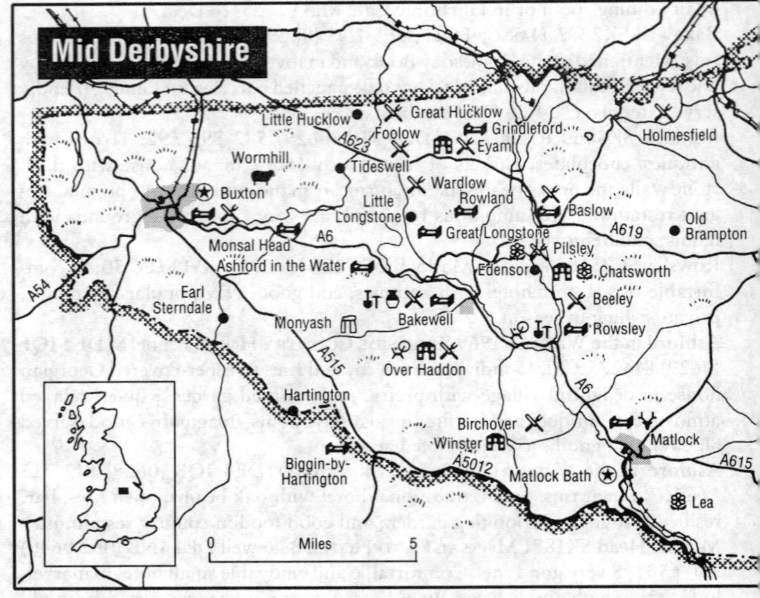

To see and do

Bakewell SK2168 is a civilised small town – and, yes, you can get those raspberry tarts here, from the Bakewell Pudding Shop in the main square where they were first made in 1860. OLD HOUSE MUSEUM 16th-c house with original wattle-and-daub interior walls and open-timbered chambers, and folk museum displaying 19th-c costumes on models, children's toys, lacework, craftsman's tools and farm implements. Cl am, Nov-Mar; £1. MAGPIE MINE Last worked in 1958 and stabilised in 1970s, these surface remains give a good idea of a 19th-c lead mine. The Castle Hotel, Red Lion and Sitch's Wine Bar are good for lunch.

Bolsover SK4770 The original CASTLE on this site dates back to the 12th c, but it was rebuilt in 1613 as a mock castle – about 200 years ahead of this fashion. Battlements and turrets adorn the outside, while inside are allegorical frescoes, fine panelling and ornate fireplaces; also 350-year-old indoor riding school used for riding by the disabled. Snacks, shop, disabled access to grounds and riding school only; cl winter Mon, 24-26 Dec, 1 Jan; £2.

! **Buxton** SK0673 has changed a lot over the years but does have some handsome buildings dating from its days as a flourishing spa resort, with Georgian terraces and a restored Edwardian opera house. Its annual festival puts a good deal of life back into those grand buildings and is very good indeed. MICRARIUM Exhibition of the wonders of nature magnified – the first museum of its kind, in the former Victorian pump room of the spa; shop, disabled access; cl Oct-Mar; £2.50. POOLE'S CAVERN (Buxton Country Park) is a natural limestone cavern in 100 acres of woodland, with well-lit stalactites and stalagmites, a video show and Roman exhibition and another exhibition of cave and

woodland; shop, disabled access into cavern; cl Oct-Easter; £3. GRIN LOW WOODS just S of the town are well landscaped with mature woodland and the Victorian folly of Solomons Temple; there's a useful information centre. The Railway, Devonshire Arms and Duke of York are useful for lunch.

Chatsworth SK2669
CHATSWORTH Famously splendid home of the Duke and Duchess of Devonshire on the banks of the River Derwent. Richly furnished and decorated, it's one of the grandest country houses in England, with a superb collection of fine and decorative arts. The lovely gardens cover over 100 acres and are full of surprises, while the surrounding park was landscaped by Capability Brown; also farmyard and adventure playground. Meals and snacks, shops inc perhaps the best farm shop in the country, garden centre, disabled access to garden only; house and garden cl Nov-Mar, farmyard and adventure playground Oct-Mar; house and garden £5, garden only £3, adventure playground and farmyard £1.90. Around Chatsworth are a couple of most attractive small estate villages, both with good pubs handy for lunch: Baslow SK2572 and Beeley SK2667.

† **Chesterfield** SK3871 is not a tourist town, but its largely 14th-c CHURCH has a really striking leaning spire, and is a rich building inside; its Victorian market hall has flourishing markets every day exc Tues and Sun (junk on Thurs, street entertainment on summer Sats). Nearby GRASSMOOR COUNTRY PARK is a pleasant place to stroll through, and an example of reclaimed land put to good use. The Derby Tup is an enjoyable ale house with good-value simple food.

Clay Cross SK3963
COUNTRYSIDE CENTRE Changing exhibitions of art and photography with a country-related theme, and plenty of details and advice for walks and nature trails; shop, disabled access; open Thurs-Sat, cl 1-2 pm – they hope to be open more days soon.

Creswell SK5274 CRESWELL CRAGS VISITOR CENTRE The caves and rock shelters in this limestone gorge are billed as the home of Stone-Age man, and though he's sadly moved away you can still see where he lived and hunted. You can't go in all the caves, but it's still a very interesting prehistoric site, with a good visitor centre explaining the period, reconstructions of family life in the Ice Age, and other displays and activities. Snacks, shop, disabled access; cl Nov-Jan exc Sun; best to check for dates of cave tours on (0909) 720378. Take along a torch.

Eyam SK2176 EYAM HALL
Handsome 17th-c manor house, recently opened by the Wright family who have lived here for generations; full of fine furniture, portraits and tapestries, fine Jacobean staircase and impressive stone-flagged hall. Please note no stiletto heels. Snacks, shop,

disabled access to ground floor only; open Weds, Thurs, Sun and bank hols Easter-Oct; £2.95. The Miners Arms is very good for lunch.

Hardwick Hall SK4463
HARDWICK HALL Built by Bess Hardwick at the age of 70 after the death of her fourth husband, with towers topped by her monogram ES and an amazing expanse of glass (some say to help her failing sight). The house and contents have remained largely unchanged, with fine tapestries and needlework inc some by Mary, Queen of Scots. Large park and gardens laid out in walled courtyard. Meals, snacks, shop, limited disabled access; house cl am, Mon, Tues and Fri Apr-Oct, every day Nov-Mar, garden cl Nov-Mar; house and garden £5, garden only £2. NT. The Hardwick Inn at the end of the park, also owned by NT, is useful for lunch, and much of the park is open free at all times – attractive for walks.

Lea SK3257 LEA GARDENS Beautiful woodland gardens with rhododendrons inc rare species and cultivars, azaleas and rock plants; snacks (home baking), shop and garden centre, some disabled access; cl Aug-20 Mar; £2.

Matlock SK3060 RIBER CASTLE WILDLIFE PARK Specialising in rare breeds and endangered species of birds and animals, the 25-acre park is set high up on Riber Hill in the grounds of ruined Riber Castle, with excellent views; snacks, shop, disabled facilities; cl 25 Dec; £3.80. The Three Stags is useful for lunch.

Matlock Bath SK2958 has a spectacular wooded cliff looking across the lower roadside town to pastures by the Derwent; up the side of the gorge, quiet lanes climb steeply with some 18th- and 19th-c villas. A pleasantly busy place, with lots to do. HEIGHTS OF ABRAHAM Cable cars provide a spectacular ride from Derwent Valley to the summit of this 60-acre country park, and perhaps just as thrilling are the two show caverns, one telling the story of 17th-c lead miners, the other introduced by a multi-vision programme. Also nature trail, play area and picnic sites; meals, snacks, shop, disabled access; cl wkdys in Nov and mid-Feb-mid-Mar, all Dec and Jan; £4.95. PEAK DISTRICT MINING MUSEUM Static and moving exhibits and an audio-visual display explaining the history of the lead industry from Roman times; also early 19th-c water-pressure pumping engine – unique in Britain. Shop, disabled access; cl 25 Dec; £1.20. TEMPLE MINE Self-guided tours around these old lead and fluorspar workings, currently being restored to what they were like in the 1920s and 1930s, and with a dressing plant where you can pan for minerals; shop; tours at 12 pm and 3 pm; £1.20. A joint ticket for these last two attractions is £1.20. AQUARIUM AND HOLOGRAM GALLERY Around 70 different species of tropical fish, including a mini-shark, several giant catfish, lots of terrapins and koi carp in a big tank that used to be a swimming pool; also an exhibition of holograms. Disabled access; open till 10 pm in summer; *£1.20. MODEL RAILWAY MUSEUM The main feature here is a scale working model of Mellorsdale as it was in 1906, and there's also a small display of railway memorabilia; it's attached to a model shop. Shop, disabled access; cl Mon, winter wknds, 25 Dec-2 Jan. GULLIVER'S KINGDOM AND ROYAL CAVE Growing family theme park with hectic rides and chair lift, cave tour, cowboy town and ghost town; also animated shows and play areas. Meals, snacks, shops; cl wkdys mid-Sept-end of Oct, all Nov-Mar; £4.25.

Monyash SK1566 has some mysterious ancient monuments, the ARBOR LOW STONE CIRCLE and the GIB HILL BARROW.

Old Whittington SK3874
REVOLUTION HOUSE 300 years ago this innocuous-looking old thatched cottage was an alehouse where three

noblemen took shelter from the rain and began to plot what came to be known as the Glorious Revolution. The whole story is told on an audio-visual display and there are period rooms and furniture; shop, disabled access to ground floor only; cl wkdys Nov-Easter exc 17-24 Dec and 27 Dec-2 Jan.

Over Haddon SK2066 HADDON HALL Perhaps the most perfectly preserved example of a medieval manor house in England, still with its 12th-c painted chapel and 14th-c kitchen and banqueting hall with minstrels' gallery. The rest of it has barely changed in 400 years, and as well as the beautiful long gallery there are long terraced rose gardens; meals, snacks; shop; cl Mon Apr-Sept, Sun July-Aug, all Oct-Mar; £3.50. LATHKILL DALE CRAFT CENTRE (Manor Farm) Plenty of crafts and demonstrations, inc stained glass, bookbinding, furniture, and barometer and clock workshops among others. Meals, snacks, shops, disabled access; cl 25 Dec. The Lathkil Hotel is good for lunch.

Pilsley SK2471 THE HERB GARDEN Big main garden with lots of herbs and old English roses and smaller gardens specialising in rare medicinal herbs, pot pourri or lavender; teas, shop, limited disabled access; cl Oct-Mar exc by arrangement. Pilsley itself is nice, and the Devonshire Arms is useful for lunch.

Rowsley SK2566 CAUDWELL'S MILL AND CRAFT CENTRE 19th-c working flour mill, powered by water turbines, with craft shop, glass-blowing workshop, wood-turning, antique restoration, and ceramic studio and country parlour. Meals, snacks, shop, disabled access; mill cl wkdys Nov-Feb; *£1.50. Rowsley also has an interesting STONE CIRCLE called the Nine Ladies. The Peacock is a very civilised place for lunch.

Winster SK2460, once a bustling market town, has just the MARKET HOUSE as a reminder of those days; thought to have been built in the 17th c, and one of the earliest to be acquired by the National Trust, for whom it's now an information centre; cl winter weekdays.

Wormhill SK1274 DONKEY VILLAGE Farm and picnic area surrounded by friendly donkeys. It's run by a trust which rescues donkeys and gives handicapped or disabled children a day out with them; no charge, but donations (and sponsors) very welcome – you can also book children's birthday parties, with rides etc.

Attractive villages with decent pubs include Ashford in the Water SK1969, Earl Sterndale SK0967, Hartington SK1360 (good cheese shop inc local stilton), Little Hucklow SK1678, Little Longstone SK1971 (Great Longstone nearby is charming, too), Old Brampton SK3372 (count the minutes between one and two o'clock on its church clock), Over Haddon SK2066, Pilsley SK2471, Tideswell SK1575 and Winster SK2460. Edensor SK2469 is a marvellous mix of styles, with fine views from the lane leading up out of it.

Walks

The White Peak area has high, flat pastures with small fields of rich grassland enclosed by silvery stone walls, clusters of often very photogenic farm buildings, small old-fashioned villages, and cutting through the limestone the intricate channels of the dales. It gives an abundance of generally gentle walking.

The winding **Monsal Dale** is the outstanding valley in this central area, its pastoral quality emphasised by the disused limestone cotton mills along the way. It's especially lovely in May and June with wild flowers enriching the pastures along the broader stretches. Don't expect to have it to yourself. There's good access from the A6 a couple of miles towards Buxton from Ashford in the Water SK1969; and from Monsal Head SK1452, where the hotel has good refreshment facilities and where a disused railway viaduct adds to the interest. This viaduct forms part of the Monsal Trail – see below.

The B6049 N off the A6 SE of Buxton gives access to **Millers Dale** SK1573, just past the little village of that name (where the Anglers Rest is a decent pub); upstream of Monsal Dale, this is rather less visited but also lovely – as is its continuation Chee Dale SK1273.

Lathkill Dale SK1865 has a charming combination of woods, steep pastures and more well-weathered signs of old mines; its short tributary Bradford Dale is also very attractive.

There are pleasant walks along stretches of the **River Derwent,** which Izaak Walton fished, either upstream from Rowsley SK2566, or from the B6012 N of there at the Calton Lees car park SK2568 – there's open access to Chatsworth Park on this W side of the river, which is particularly lovely.

The well-wooded **Goyt Valley** SK0177 with its three miles of reservoirs is a man-made landscape, but nonetheless charming, and very peaceful even though popular on fine weekends; reached off the A54 W of Buxton. Shining Tor SK1454 is a breezy but undemanding moorland walk from the summit of a minor road.

The E edges of the **Dark Peak** include the abrupt ramparts of Curbar Edge SK2575 and Froggatt Edge SK2476, popular with rock-climbers and easily accessible from the road. For walkers here, Birchen Edge SK2772 and Wellington's Monument SK2673 are obvious objectives from the Robin Hood's Inn at Curbar SK2574.

A particular virtue of the area is the large number of decent country pubs that seem as though they have been perfectly positioned for walkers. These include the Miners Arms at Milltown, Ashover SK3561 (despite quarrying), the Robin Hood at Baslow SK2572 (handy for the ridge of Baslow Edge), the Druid at Birchover SK2462 (handy for Stanton Moor, and the odd little Row Tor just behind the pub), the Barrel on the ridge at Bretton SK2077, the Lazy Landlord at Foolow SK1976, the Chequers just below Froggatt Edge SK2476, the Robin Hood at Lydgate nr Holmesfield SK3177 (for the Cordwell Valley), the Bull at Monyash SK1566, the unfashionably basic New Napoleon by Ogston Reservoir SK3761, the Lathkil at Over Haddon SK2066 (for Lathkill Dale), and the Bulls Head at Wardlow SK1874 (for well-wooded Cressbrook Dale).

The trails

The **Monsal Trail** outshines the other railway track walks in the Peak District and runs from Wye Dale SK1072 E of Buxton to Coombs Road viaduct SK2274 S of Bakewell. W of Millers Dale Station SK1573, the trail leaves the old railway (proposed to be reopened, but the trail will survive), and takes a stepping-stone route along the river beneath the towering cliffs of Chee Tor SK1273 before rejoining the railway track.

The **Tissington Trail** follows another disused railway track from Ashbourne SK1846 up to Parsley Hay SK1463 on the A515, where it joins the similar **High Peak Trail** from Buxton SK0673 to near Cromford SK2956. This has a particularly interesting finale from Middleton Top engine house to High Peak Junction, dipping down a great incline past old engine houses to reach the Cromford Canal, along which it's a short walk to Cromford (see South Derbyshire). Earlier, branching off at Roystone Grange is an archaeological trail.

These gently graded trails pass through some of the area's most attractive scenery, with occasional villages and quarries, and as the banks have been colonised by rabbits, foxes and so forth, as well as wild plants, there's plenty to see.

Though you can walk them, these trails, more exposed than the dales themselves, are best regarded as traffic-free long-distance cycleways. You can hire bicycles by the half-day or day from Ashbourne Cycle Hire, Mapleton Lane, Ashbourne SK1476; Parsley Hay Cycle Hire, Parsley Hay SK1463; and Middleton Top near Cromford SK2765. Charges are around £6 a day for an ordinary bicycle to £12 for a mountain bike.

Driving

Roads here give plenty of attractive views, though not usually very distant ones. Any route off the main roads W of a line drawn straight down through Chatsworth is likely to be enjoyable, with particular favourites including the B6012 past Chatsworth itself (busy in summer), the high roads above Lathkill Dale, the back road from Baslow through Hassop, the Longstones, Cressbrook and Litton to Tideswell, and the B6049 from Tideswell across Millers Dale.

Where to eat

Ridgeway SK4081 OLD VICARAGE Ridgeway Moor (0742) 475814 Country-house restaurant in neat gardens overlooking open fields; nicely decorated dining room and conservatory, excellent food (inc quite a few game dishes and lovely puddings and cheeses) served by staff in Victorian-style dress, and fine wines. **£25.70**|/£10.50.

Eyam SK2276 MINERS ARMS Water Lane (0433) 630853 Good dining pub in small village, with lovely food and decent wines; now run by ex-Savoy chef; bedrooms; cl Sun pm, Mon. **£18**|£1.75/£4.

Over Haddon SK2066 LATHKIL (0629) 812501 Very popular indeed – combining an outstanding setting with friendly, welcoming atmosphere and good food; no children pm; bedrooms. **£17.50**|£2/£4.50.

Birchover SK2462 DRUID (0629) 650302 Pleasantly remote creeper-covered house with huge choice of very popular, often unusual food and good, friendly service; cl 25 Dec. **£17**|£3.80/£8.

Foolow SK1976 LAZY LANDLORD (0433) 630873 Simply furnished moorland pub in pretty village close to village green and pub with interesting daily specials and good home-made puddings; cl Mon, 25 Dec. **£17**|£2/£7.

Holmesfield SK3277 ROBIN HOOD (0742) 890360 Rambling ex-farmhouse with consistently good food inc interesting daily specials; open all day Sun for food. **£15**|£2.95/£4.95.

Wardlow SK1874 THREE STAGS HEADS (0298) 872268 Popular dining pub with good home-made food. **£13.10**/£8.40.

Buxton SK0673 DANDELION DAYS 5 Bridge St (0298) 22843 Very good, generous helpings of vegetarian food in restaurant above a health-food shop; pleasant prompt service. **£6.80**|55p/£2; cl Mon.

Some other places to eat in this area include the Devonshire Arms at Baslow SK2572, the Devonshire Arms in Beeley SK2667, the Railway in Buxton (Bridge St) SK0673, the Miners Arms at Eyam SK2276, the Queen Anne at Great Hucklow SK1878, and the Devonshire Arms in Pilsley SK2471.

SOUTH DERBYSHIRE

This region includes Dove Dale, which is a landscape gem, great houses and interesting well-restored industrial remains.

The tramway museum at Crich is one of Britain's most unexpectedly interesting places to visit, and Sudbury Hall, Calke Abbey and Kedleston Hall are all splendid. Cromford is beautifully preserved as a survivor of the earliest days of the Industrial Revolution. The dales country in the northern part of the area has the best of the scenery, especially Dove Dale. The countryside there is particularly appealing, with man-made intrusions on nature definitely adding to the attraction – the stone buildings and network of pale stone walls across the pastures and hillsides somehow underline the beauty.

Where to stay

This area is of course within easy reach of the places we list under Mid Derbyshire, and some of those in Staffordshire.

Ashbourne SK1846 CALLOW HALL Mappleton Rd DE6 2AA (0335) 343403 **£90**; 12 lovely, well-furnished rms and excellent bthrms. Friendly and informal 19th-c country-house hotel up long drive through grounds with fine trees; very good food in the popular restaurant (they have their own patisserie, and the meat is hung and butchered on the premises) inc breakfasts with home-made sausages and freshly squeezed orange juice; good service; private fishing, disabled access; cl 25-26 Dec, one wk Feb.

Dove Dale SK1452 PEVERIL OF THE PEAK Ashbourne DE6 2AW (033 529) 333 **£85**; 47 rms with sherry and chocolates provided. Relaxing hotel in pretty village; comfortable sofas and log fire in lounge, modern bar overlooking garden where there's tennis; wonderful walking nearby.

Shottle SK3149 DANNAH FARM Bowmans Lane DE56 3DR (0773) 550273 ***£54**; 7 rms with old pine and antiques. Pretty Georgian farmhouse, carefully restored, with popular, imaginative cooking inc home-made bread, two comfortable sitting rooms; calves, ducks, hens, lambs in spring, Vietnamese pot-bellied pigs and farm dogs and cats.

Shirley SK2141 SHIRLEY HALL FARM Ashbourne DE6 3AS (0335) 60346 **£36**; 2 rms. Peaceful old farmhouse with oak-panelled sitting room, beams, and good breakfasts; guests are welcome to look at the animals and watch cows being milked; also self-catering.

Kirk Ireton SK2650 BARLEY MOW Ashbourne DE6 3JP (0335) 370306 **£35.75**; 5 rms. 17th-c building with lots of woodwork in straightforward series of interconnecting bar rooms; cl Christmas wk.

To see and do

Alkmonton SK1838 BENTLEY FIELDS OPEN FARM You can see every aspect of life and work on the farm at this unspoilt traditional place; they have large herds of cows and flocks of sheep, so in spring if you're lucky you may see calving or lambing – or chicks pecking their way out of their eggs;

South Derbyshire

teas, shop, some disabled access; open Easter wk, early May bank hol wknd, all late May bank hol wk and Sun in July and Aug; *£1.20.

✝ 🏠 **Ashbourne** SK1846 has a good few interesting Georgian buildings in the streets off the hillside market place, esp in the street to its elegantly proportioned CHURCH. DERWENT CRYSTAL CENTRE (Shaw Croft) Quality glassworks and engravers, with demonstrations and factory shop; disabled access; cl Sun, Christmas and New Year. Smiths is useful for lunch.

🏛 ❀ **Calke** SK3722 CALKE ABBEY Very popular early 18th-c baroque mansion, richly decorated with various displays and treasures inc an extensive natural history collection, Chinese silk State bed, and carriages in the stable block. Also extensive wooded parkland and walled gardens. Meals, snacks, shop, disabled access; cl Thurs and Fri, Nov-Mar, house cl am; £4.20, garden only £1.90. NT. The house has a timed ticket entry system. The Chequers in Ticknall SK3423 is quite handy.

🚋 **Crich** SK3554 NATIONAL TRAMWAY MUSEUM A favourite of many correspondents: lovingly restored vintage trams from all over the British Isles, many of them in working order and running along a one-mile period street overlooking the Derwent Valley. The price includes unlimited rides on the vehicles, as well as entry to very good museums, exhibitions and displays. Meals, snacks, shop, disabled access; cl Fri in May and Sept, wkdys during first fortnight in Oct, Nov-Mar exc Santa specials; £4.20. The Yew Tree at Holloway SK3357 is handy for lunch. The village is pronounced 'Cry', not 'Critch'.

Cromford SK2956 is a good example of an 18th-c cotton-milling village, little developed after its original building, and rewarding to stroll through. CROMFORD MILL Richard Arkwright established the world's first successful water-powered cotton-mill here in 1771, giving it a strong claim to be one of the birthplaces of the Industrial Revolution; it's being restored by the Arkwright Society. Meals, snacks, shop, disabled access; cl 25 Dec; £1.50 for guided tour. The nearby restored CANAL is a quiet and attractive early Industrial-Revolution setting with a restored steam-powered pumping house and a fine aqueduct over the river; pleasant walks along here.

Derby SK3536 is a big busy city, but not too daunting for a visitor to penetrate, and has several things worth visiting; it's got far more open spaces than you'd expect. The 16th-c tower of the CATHEDRAL is the second-highest in the country, though the rest of the building was replaced in the 18th c by the current design by James Gibbs. Bess of Hardwick is buried in the vaults beneath the elaborate monument she ordered to be constructed for herself. DERBY MUSEUM AND ART GALLERY (The Strand) Important collections of porcelain and paintings by local artist Joseph Wright, as well as other antiquities, natural history, militaria, and new geology gallery. Shop, disabled access; cl am Sun and bank hols, 25-26 Dec. INDUSTRIAL MUSEUM (Full St) Restored early 18th-c silk mill and adjacent flour mill, inc display of Rolls-Royce engines from 1915, exhibitions about local industries inc railways; shop, disabled access; cl 25-26 Dec; *30p, free on Sun. PICKFORDS HOUSE MUSEUM (Friargate) Built in 1770 as a combined workplace and family home, the house is now Derby's biggest museum showing domestic life in the 18th and 19th c. Other galleries devoted to temporary exhibitions, and Georgian garden; shop, disabled facilities; cl 25-27 Dec, 3 Jan; 30p, free Sun. ROYAL CROWN DERBY (Osmaston Rd) Displays and tours of bone-china factory, with museum tracing industry's development from 1748; tours by arrangement; snacks, shop; cl 12.30-2 pm, wknds, 25 Dec; tour £2.50 – no children under 10.

Donington Park SK4427 DONINGTON COLLECTION Largest private collection of single-seater racing cars in the world; also Speedway Hall of Fame. Meals and snacks, shop, disabled access but no facilities; cl Christmas wk; £4.

Elvaston SK4132 ELVASTON CASTLE COUNTRY PARK 200 acres of lovely 19th-c landscaped parkland, with formal and Old English gardens, wooded walks, and wildfowl on the ornamental lake. Also restored estate workshops with exhibitions of blacksmithing, saddlery and further traditional crafts, nature trails and further exhibitions and displays; snacks, shop, disabled access; museum cl am, Mon and Tues, Nov-Mar, visitor centre cl wkdys Nov-Mar; gardens and grounds free (though there is a car-parking charge); museum £1.20.

Heanor SK4346 SHIPLEY COUNTRY PARK Medieval estate developed and landscaped in the 18th c, now with 600 acres of woodland, lakes and fields. A pleasant place to wander, with the former railway lines transformed into leafy walkways; you can hire bikes (daily Easter and Jun-early Sept, wknds only rest of year, £2.25 for two hours) and decent cycle routes are available from visitor centre; snacks, shop, disabled access; visitor centre cl am winter wkdys.

☺ **Ilkeston** SK4642 AMERICAN ADVENTURE THEME PARK Fully themed park over 200 acres, with hugely varied rides involving many of the different facets of that continent. Meals and snacks, shop, disabled facilities; cl Mon and Tues May-early Jun exc bank hols, Nov-wk before Easter; £8.99.

Kedleston SK3041 KEDLESTON HALL Home of the Curzon family since the 12th c, the current Palladian mansion was built in the 18th c and is thought by many to be the finest example of Robert Adam's work in the country – it's certainly the least altered. Interesting *objets d'art*, original furnishings and good collection of paintings; Indian museum of items collected by Lord Curzon when Viceroy of India; and, outside, extensive formal gardens with marvellous rhododendrons and long woodland walks. Adam also designed a charming boathouse and bridge in the park; meals, snacks, shop, some disabled access (best to phone in advance on (0332) 842191); house and shop cl am, Thurs and Fri, Nov-Mar; grounds open daily in season, then cl wkdys Nov-Christmas wk, then cl till Apr; £3.95. NT.

Melbourne SK3825 is a pleasant small town, with a good relaxed feel and villagey lanes; the Railway Hotel and White Swan are good for lunch. MELBOURNE HALL Behind its 18th-c façade, this grandly extended house dates back in part to the 13th c, and during its illustrious history it has twice been the home of British prime ministers; fine pictures and furnishings inside. Glorious formal gardens with fountains, pools, and famous yew tunnel; interesting craft centre. Meals, snacks, shop, disabled access; gardens open pm Weds, Sat, Sun & bank hols Apr-Sept, house open pm Aug only; £3, £2 for house or garden only.

Middleton by Wirksworth SK2756 MIDDLETON TOP ENGINE HOUSE This beam engine built in 1829 used to haul waggons up the Middleton incline on the Cromford and High Peak Railway, by cable from this engine house. The visitor centre tells the story of the historic railway; shop, disabled facilities by prior arrangement (0629) 823204; open every Sun Easter-Oct (engine static), and first wknd each month (engine in motion); static engine *35p, in motion *60p.

Ripley SK3950 MIDLAND RAILWAY CENTRE Regular steam-train passenger service and also an industrial museum displaying aspects of the golden days of the Midland Railway. Meals and snacks, shop, disabled access; cl 25 Dec; best to ring for train timetable (0773) 747 674; Sun and bank hols £4.95, other days £4.50.

DENBY POTTERY VISITORS CENTRE Knowledgeable guided factory tours (not Fri pm) showing intricate skills of potters and craftsmen. Also museum, large factory shop and children's play area; snacks, shop, disabled access; craftroom cl wkdys; tours *£2.95, craftroom *£2.

Sudbury SK1632 SUDBURY HALL Superbly imposing Stuart mansion with elaborate carving, frescoes, murals and plasterwork inside the splendidly elegant rooms; also very good MUSEUM of childhood. Snacks, shop, limited disabled access; cl am, Mon (exc bank hols), Tues, Good Fri, Nov-Mar; £4, house only £3, museum only £2. NT. The Vernon Arms, built to match, is handy for lunch.

Wirksworth SK2854 NATIONAL STONE CENTRE The main features of the site are the tropical lagoons and limestone fossil reefs – 330 million years old; there's also an exhibition called the Story of Stone, looking at the formation and uses of stone from prehistoric pick-axes to hi-tech factories. Snacks, shop, some disabled access; *£1.80. WIRKSWORTH HERITAGE CENTRE Old silk and velvet mill, with displays of the town's past history as a centre of the lead-mining industry, computer games and workshops showing the skills of local crafts, and explanations of local customs such as well dressing. Meals, snacks, shop; cl Sun am, Mon (exc bank hols and Mon Aug-mid-Sept), Tues (exc Tues Aug-mid-Sept), Christmas-end Jan; *85p.

A special attraction of this area is that lots of its villages, many of which have interesting buildings and surroundings, are very pleasant places to stroll through. **Particularly appealing villages** include Bradbourne SK2152 (with an ancient Saxon cross outside its Norman church), Brassington SK2354 (the Olde Gate here is a lovely old pub), Dale Abbey SK4338 (the Carpenters Arms at Ilkeston is handy, and it's sited nr the Hermits Cave and remarkable All Saints Church, part of which was formerly the village inn), Duffield SK3443, Idridgehay SK2849, Lullington SK2513 (the Colvile Arms is a nice unspoilt pub), Osmaston SK1944 (pleasant path through lakeside park), Parwich SK1854, Repton SK3026, and Tissington SK1752 (the grey stone gardener's cottage is familiar from many calendars – and one of our contributors' aunts lives there; craft centre, garden centre, decent homely café).

The RIVER TRENT impresses with its silent power; Ingleby SK3426 is one good access point – for example, from the big garden of the John Thompson pub, which brews its own beer. The **Shardlow** SK4330 CANAL BASIN is attractive, with some handsome former wharf buildings – one now an antiques warehouse, another a pub/restaurant.

Walks

Dove Dale, shared with Staffordshire (the River Dove marks the boundary), is the most popular of all the dales. Partly wooded, it has a beautifully varied mixture of water, trees and pastures, and is lined with crags and curiously shaped outcrops of rock. To see fewer people, head for the upstream sections: the barer pastures and steep hillsides of Milldale SK1354, the wooded peace of Beresford Dale SK1259, or Wolfscote Dale SK1357, with its dramatic rocky gorge and still trout pools (best reached from Hartington SK1260, where the Jug & Glass up on the main road is useful for lunch). Other handy nearby refreshment places (to be found on the Staffordshire side) are the Izaak Walton Hotel nr Ilam (cosier inside than it looks from out), Watts Russell Arms at Hopedale and George at Alstonefield.

See Mid Derbyshire for the Tissington and High Peak Trails.

Driving

Many of the minor roads W of the A6 wind attractively through silver-walled pastures and past quiet farming hamlets. Of the main roads, the B5056 N of Ashbourne up towards Bakewell, B5053 Ashbourne-Wirksworth and A5012 Cromford-Grangemill give a good feel of the character of the dales.

Where to eat

Melbourne SK3825 BAY TREE 4 Potter St (0332) 863358 Small, family-run cottagey restaurant with beams and simple furnishings; carefully presented, popular food (Sun lunch is booked up weeks ahead), and thoughtful, relaxed service. £30|£3.10/£10; cl Sun pm, Mon, all Jan.

Church Broughton SK2034 HOLLY BUSH Main St (0283) 585345 Refurbished homely and friendly pub with good home-made food like mother used to make – very cheap too; popular Sun lunches. **£13.65**|£1/£6.30.

Kings Newton SK3826 HARDINGE ARMS (0332) 813808 Good quickly served roasts, fish, salads and other food in comfortable, interesting, beamed and timbered 17th-c inn; disabled access. £1.50/£6.

Some other places worth knowing about here for decent food include the Olde Gate at Brassington SK2354, the Green Man at Clifton Campville SK2510 (see Staffs), the Bluebell in Farnah Green SK3346, the Railway and the White Swan in Melbourne SK3825, the Old Crown and the Malt Shovel at Shardlow SK4330, and the Staff of Life in Ticknall SK3423.

NORTH DERBYSHIRE: THE HIGH PEAK

This territory is more austere than other parts of the county; it perhaps holds most appeal for serious walkers.

Castleton has most of the area's relatively few visitor attractions clustered around it, chiefly the various underground show caverns. It also has the most varied walks in the area; the further north you head into the High Peak, the bleaker it becomes – territory for the really serious long-distance walker. The whole area can be forbidding in winter, and at any time of year has a more austere appeal than the rest of the county, lacking its luscious landscapes and picturesque villages.

Where to stay

Hathersage SK2381 GEORGE S30 1BB (043 36) 650436 **£77**; 18 pretty rms (the back ones are quietest). Substantial comfortably modernised attractive old inn with popular food, neat flagstoned back terrace by rose garden; a comfortable base for walks; children under 16 free if sharing room with parents.

Castleton SK1582 CASTLE S30 2WG (0433) 620 578 **£59**; 9 well-equipped rms. Handsome flagstones, beams and stripped stonework in plush hotel bars; decent bar and restaurant food, open fires; cl 25 Dec.

Castleton SK1582 OLDE NAGS HEAD S30 2WH (0433) 620248 **£52**; 8 warm, comfortable rms. Village hotel renovated to preserve character; open fire, antique furniture, small bar, well-presented traditional bar food, and decent restaurant.

Hope SK1783 POACHERS ARMS S30 2RD (04336) 20380 **£52**; 6 rms. Village pub with welcoming bar, good decor, efficient service; generous helpings of interesting and varied well-cooked food inc adventurous vegetarian dishes.

Hathersage SK2381 HIGHLOW HALL S30 1AX (04336) 50393 **£46**; 6 quiet, well-equipped rms, 3 with own bthrm. B & B in big 16th-c farmhouse in lovely countryside; excellent breakfasts (evening meals by arrangement); can walk into village.

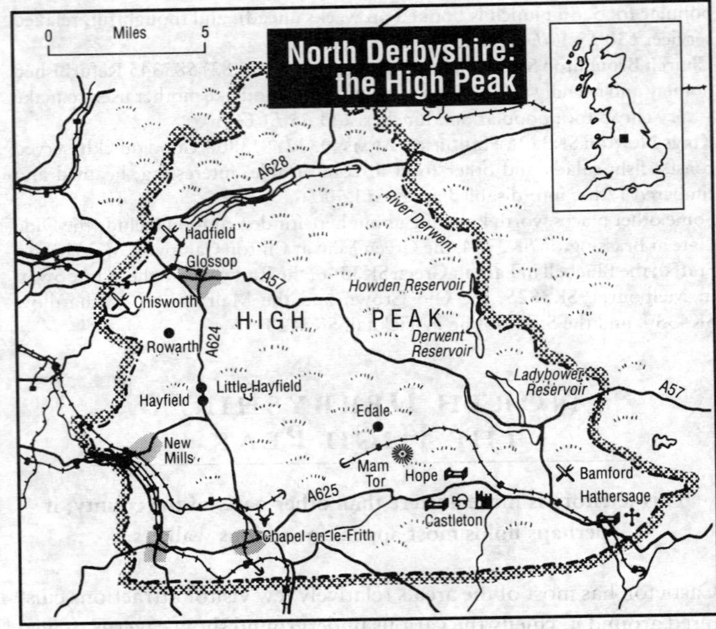

To see and do

Castleton SK1582 is very much a visitors' village now, full of breeches and boots (and caving equipment) in summer, with cafés, and shops selling polished pieces of the Blue John fluorspar that's found only in the nearby mine workings. It does have attractive dark stone buildings (one of the most impressive now a youth hostel), and is dominated by the ruins of PEVERIL CASTLE, built in the 12th c for Henry II, high above the village and with magnificent views; shop; cl 24-26 Dec, 1 Jan and Mon Oct-Mar; £1.20. BLUE JOHN CAVERN AND MINE Containing eight of the 14 known veins of Blue John, this has been the main source of the mineral for nearly 300 years. It's an impressive example of a water-worn cave, over a third of a mile long, with chambers 200 ft high; snacks, shop; cl 25-26 Dec, 1 Jan; £4. SPEEDWELL CAVERN by contrast was a lead mine, until 1790. It's very atmospheric, with a long flight of steps down to a half-mile underground boat trip along floodlit passages, finishing up in a cathedral of a cavern with impressive 'bottomless pit'; snacks, shop; cl 25-26 Dec; £4. TREAK CLIFF CAVERN Blue John mine working since 1750, with amazing stalactites and stalagmites and veins of the mineral, and good informative tours. The entrance is very narrow, and it's quite steep; snacks, shop; cl 25 Dec, winter opening weather permitting; *£3.50. PEAK CAVERN Marvellous limestone cave with a half-mile-long electrically lit subterranean walk; snacks, shop, some disabled access; cl Nov-Easter; £2.60.

Chapel-en-le-Frith SK0580 CHESTNUT CENTRE Conservation park, otter haven and owl sanctuary; snacks, shop; cl wkdys Jan and Feb; £3.

† **Hathersage** SK2381 HATHERSAGE CHURCH is the legendary site of Little

John's grave, and the village also has connections with Charlotte Brontë, who wrote *Jane Eyre* here.

At **Hayfield** SK0387 you can hire bikes to take along the Sett Valley Trail, about which there's also an information centre here.

Walks

Castleton SK1583 and **Hope** SK1783 have the most varied walks in the High Peak. The great walk here is to take in Castleton, the Lose Hill/Mam Tor ridge SK1383, the caves and Winnats Pass SK1382; Mam Tor is so shaly that it's been called the Shivering Mountain. Cave Dale is an optional side trip from the back of Castleton. Quarrying has had an unfortunate effect on the local landscape in the area, and limits walks further afield, though there are some pleasant walks to be had in the gentler high pastures of the limestone country to the south. The Poachers Arms in Hope has good food, and there are several pubs and cafés in Castleton (which is a good deal busier).

Edale SK1285, famous as the start of the Pennine Way into Scotland, has a good information centre and a couple of hikers' pubs. It tends to be packed with expectant long-distant walkers on Sunday mornings. For a taste of the Dark Peak proper, this can be the start for half-day walks that quite quickly take you up through the stone-walled pastures of the valley on to the edge of the dark plateau above. The track signposted as the alternative Pennine Way route up Jacob's Ladder is easier to find, and has more to see, than the official Pennine Way plod across a huge blanket bog.

The lane up past **Ladybower Reservoir** to the car park by the Derwent Reservoir (with a summer minibus service beyond to Howden Reservoir) gives plenty of easy waterside-forest walking on the relatively sheltered stone-walled slopes of the upper parts of Derwent Dale, with access to the higher moors for better views – for example, up on to Win Hill, or on a kind day on to the formidable Derwent Moors to the E. The Ladybower pub down on the main road is useful.

The dark moors of the real High Peak in the north of the area are one of England's great wildernesses. But they have few easy circular routes, are largely very bleak indeed, and often consist of private grouse moor with no rights of public access. The car park at the top of Snake Pass (A57 Glossop-Hathersage) is near the centre of the biggest of the National Trust's moorland holdings here, giving free access to the miles of misnamed **Hope Woodlands** SK1091 (there aren't many trees on these high moors).

The moorland village of **Hayfield** SK0387 and its attractive nearby smaller sister Little Hayfield have good walks around them, both up towards Kinder Scout SK0888 and to the Lantern Pike viewpoint SK0288 in the opposite direction. There's also a popular walk along a hillside former railway to New Mills SK0085, looking down on the mill buildings by the River Sett. The George and Pack Horse in Hayfield are good.

There are good walks in the countryside around **Hathersage** SK2381 – for example, in the attractive moorland, pastures and woodland making up Longshaw SK2678, near the Fox House Inn up on the Sheffield road; or, closer and gentler, down along the River Derwent towards Grindleford SK2478.

The deep gorge below New Mills has been protected as the **Torrs Riverside Park** SJ9985, and is a good place for people who enjoy pottering among the ivy-covered remains of former mills and other industrial relics; the new Goyt Way between here and Marple, partly following the Peak Forest Canal, is a pretty walk.

Though it has to be approached from outside this area (off the A626 Glossop-Marple), the Little Mill at **Rowarth** SK0185 is well placed in off-the-beaten-track walking country, with a good walk up to Lantern Pike SK0288.

Driving

The High Peak is very rewarding for drivers – a car may be an easy way out, but is certainly the quickest and least strenuous way of getting a good visual impression of the magnificent scenery. An advantage is that there's rarely the traffic congestion which mars other such areas. The A6024, A628 (rather slow), A57, A624 and A625 all have some outstanding views. Particularly rewarding back roads include the circuit through Edale from Hope; the B6061 from the A625 to Sparrowpit; and the B6001 S of Hathersage.

Where to eat

Hadfield SK0296 OLD HOUSE Woodhead Rd (0457) 854009 Old farmhouse with stone walls and views of reservoir in the valley with friendly, prompt staff and good food from a constantly changing menu; vegetarian dishes, and decent puddings and wines; cl Mon; **£14**|£2.25/£6.

Besides those already mentioned in the text, some places to eat in this area include the Derwent Hotel in Bamford SK2083 and Hunters in Chisworth SJ9992. The A624 moors road between Glossop and Chapel-en-le-Frith runs past several locally popular eating places.

STAFFORDSHIRE

A county with unexpected pleasures, it has some good scenery, and an interesting industrial past.

Sharing Dove Dale with Derbyshire, and with its own fine Manifold Valley and Churnet Valley, Staffordshire has some good walking and handsome drives, especially in its north-east corner. The Potteries, and to a less extent Burton-upon-Trent, have some engaging industrial museums, though many weekend visitors might prefer the more rustic surroundings of Shugborough Hall or the garden of Biddulph Grange. The canal network has some particularly attractive stretches, and the county has a good many charming villages, and quite a few other places worth visiting. Prices here are on the low side, so Staffordshire is good value for a weekend with a difference.

We welcome reports from readers . . .

Readers who help us with reports for the GUIDE are offered a discount on the next edition: so please do help if you can!

Where to stay

Butterton SK0756 Black Lion Leek ST13 7SP (0538) 304 232 **£47**; 3 rms. Unspoilt 18th-c stone inn in lovely countryside, not far from interesting places to visit/opportunities to enjoy lots of country sports; good food and a parakeet called Sergeant Bilko.

Alrewas SK1715 Claymar Hotel 118A Main St Burton-upon-Trent DE13 7AE (0283) 791281 **£45**; 21 rms. Spotlessly clean and comfortable hotel with good food inc excellent Sunday lunch served on Wedgwood china, and very good cheerful service; disabled access.

Betley SJ7549 Adderley Green Farm Heighley Castle Lane Crewe CW3 9BA (0270) 820203 ***£36**; 3 rms, 1 with bthrm. Georgian farmhouse on big dairy farm with large garden; fishing; cl Christmas, New Year; children over 5.

Warslow SK0858 Greyhound Buxton SK17 0JN (0298) 84249 ***£34**; 4 clean and comfortable rms. Warm, welcoming atmosphere in plain-slated stone building; generous helpings of home-made food inc hearty breakfasts; handy for many of the Peak District features.

To see and do

☺ ❀ **Alton** SK0742 Alton Towers Britain's leading theme park, in the stunning former estate of the Earls of Shrewsbury, and around the ruins of their once-grand house. Expanding all the time, it currently has more than 125 rides, live shows and attractions, as well as lovely extensive gardens and a new less-daredevil section for younger children. Meals, snacks, shops, disabled access (for most rides too); cl early Nov-mid-March; *£13. There are also free public footpaths through the Capability Brown parkland.

❀ **Biddulph** SJ8858 Biddulph Grange Garden Extensively restored high Victorian garden, divided by its founder into a number of smaller themed gardens to house specimens from all over world. Snacks, shop; cl am wkdys, Mon, Tues, Nov-Mar; £3.70.

Burton-upon-Trent SK2423 This town is dominated by its connections with the brewing industry, and has a fine museum devoted to it at the Bass Museum, Visitor Centre and Shire Horse Stables, amply demonstrating the history of the industry from earliest times to the present day. Outside are larger exhibits such as a Daimler van in the shape of a bottle of IPA; also stables with shire horses (the horses can take you on a tour of the town), special events throughout summer and a brass-band concert every fourth Sun lunchtime. Meals, snacks, shop, disabled access; *£3.45. The nearby Coopers Tavern – selling the beer of a different brewer – is a fine example of what pubs were like 50 years or more ago, and in the same town down by the river the little Burton Bridge Brewery shows brewing at the very opposite end of the scale. The Queens Hotel is a comfortable place for lunch.

! **Cauldon** SK0749 is notable for its pub, the Yew Tree; a very unpretentious place packed with an extraordinary and delightfully higgledy-piggledy collection of remarkable bygones, esp more or less musical ones such as polyphons and grandfather clocks.

Chartley Castle SK0128 (just over 6 miles W of Uttoxeter) is a fine old ruin, with good views.

Cheddleton SJ9752 Flint Mill 17th- and 18th-c fully preserved water mills, with a little museum specialising in the history and preparation of the raw materials used in the pottery industry; disabled access; closed am

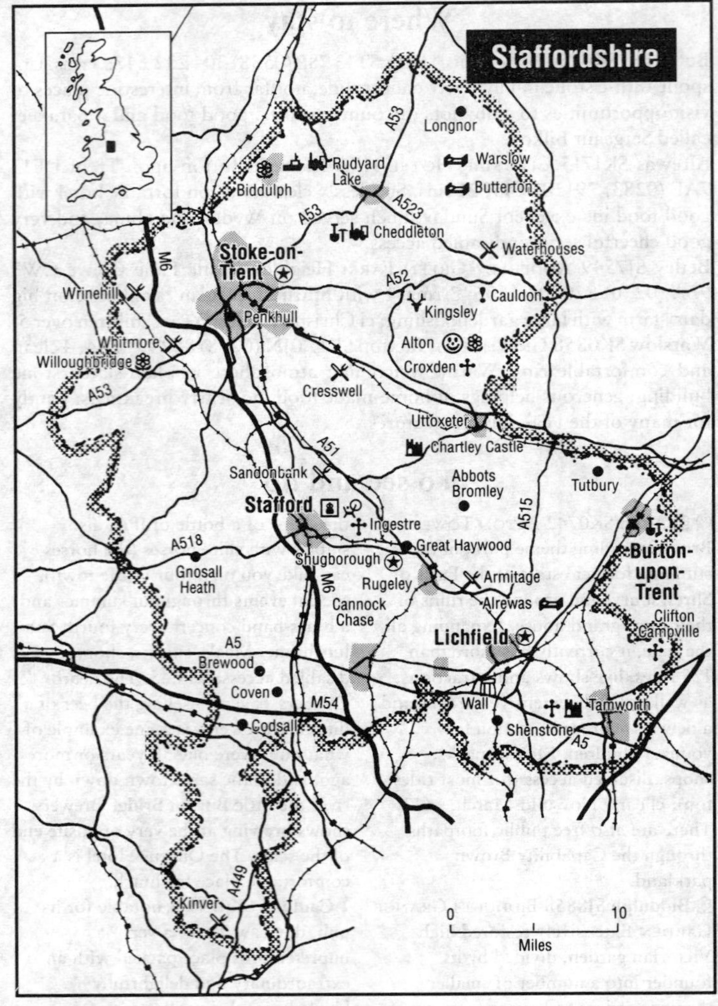

wknds. The Railway Centre is a small steam locomotive museum housed in the Victorian station building and has occasional short steam runs in summer. The Boat down by the canal is useful for lunch.

✝ **Clifton Campville** SK2510 church is lovely – practically perfect, and the Green Man nearby is a useful lunch stop.

✝ **Croxden** SK0639 Abbey ruins in quiet surroundings, with some towering arches surviving.

✝ **Ingestre** SJ9724 church was designed by Christopher Wren and is reckoned by some to be the finest smaller 17th-c church outside London.

Kingsley SK0147 Falconry, Otter and Wildlife Sanctuary Otters, birds of prey and other unusual animals can be viewed at close quarters. Guided tours are at 11 am and 2.30 pm only; snacks, shop; cl 25 Dec; £2.

★ **Lichfield** has an attractive centre, largely pedestrianised, with many 18th-c and older buildings among the more modern shops (and antique shops), inc the house where DR JOHNSON was born on Breadmarket St (now furnished in period, with many mementos of him). The CATHEDRAL, with its three graceful spires and close with lovely buildings around it, is magnificent inside, and its west front, alive with statues, is memorable. HERITAGE EXHIBITION AND TREASURY Sympathetically restored old chapel site with an audio-visual exhibition on Lichfield's history and a display of ceremonial silver and old documents; £1. By prior arrangement you can go up to the viewing platform in the spire, from where there are splendid views of the surrounding countryside. HANCH HALL (4 miles NW) is an interesting little mansion with an unusual mixture of architectural styles, and collections of needlework, old dolls and costumes and a rare Regency bed used by Shelley; good views from the observation tower, and the partly landscaped grounds are fun, with peacocks and pheasants wandering about. Snacks, shop, some disabled access; cl am, Oct-Apr; £3. The George IV and Kings Head are useful for lunch. Out at Whittington SK1508 is the STAFFORDSHIRE REGIMENT'S MUSEUM, by the barracks; shop, disabled access; cl bank hols, 25 Dec-1 Jan.

The Potteries (Stoke-on-Trent SJ8745 and the five towns around it) These linked towns cling to small steep hills, giving some memorable urban landscapes. Pride in their past (and present) has focused museum attention well on the Staffordshire pottery industry, and you can visit several factories, ancient and modern – there's still a great deal of hand work in china production, inc modelling and painting. GLADSTONE POTTERY MUSEUM (Uttoxeter Rd, Longton) Currently being redeveloped, this is a pottery in a restored 'potbank', complete with old warehouses, workshops and four huge bottle kilns; daily demonstrations. Improvements should be finished by late spring 1994. Meals, snacks, shop, disabled access; cl Sun and Mon Nov-Feb, part of Christmas and New Year; £2.75. MINTON MUSEUM (London Rd, Stoke) Displays of factory's production from 1800 to present day; teas, shop; closed factory holidays – usually around end of Jun, tel (0782) 744766 to check; *£2.50. SIR HENRY DOULTON GALLERY (Nile St, Burslem) Displays of pottery treasures from the famous company covering 150 years, along with archive material; tours of factory available. Meals, snacks, shop, disabled access to shop only; cl wknds and factory and bank hols – tel (0782) 575454 to check; museum free, tours *£2.50. SPODE (Church St, Stoke) Oldest manufacturing ceramic factory here – prior booking essential, tel (0782) 744011. Meals, snacks, shop; cl Fri pm, wknds (the shop is open Sat) and factory holidays; *£2.25/£6. WEDGWOOD VISITOR CENTRE (Barlaston) The story of that favourite item on wedding lists; art gallery, museum and reconstruction of Wedgwood's original 18th-c Etruria workshops, with demonstrations of how the china is produced. Snacks, shop, disabled access; cl Sun Oct-Easter, 25 Dec, 1 Jan; £2.50. CITY MUSEUM AND ART GALLERY (Bethesda St, Hanley) Interesting displays giving full picture of the potteries – not just the magnificent collection of pottery and porcelain, but also social and natural history, and archaeology; meals, snacks, shop, disabled access; cl Sun am, 25 Dec-1 Jan. The New Inn in Derby St is useful for lunch. The CHATTERLEY WHITFIELD MINING MUSEUM, in a former mine in Tunstall, is fascinating, with coal-face underground visits, pit ponies, working mining equipment, and vivid tours conducted by ex-miners. Sadly, it is in receivership as we go to press, so its future must therefore be in doubt. Meals and snacks (served in 1930s pit canteen), shop, disabled access; cl winter Mon, 25-26 Dec; £4.15. The Gardeners Rest at Brindley Ford is a useful lunch stop.

Rudyard Lake SJ9558 is reckoned by some of our readers to be one of the most beautiful sights in Staffordshire; you can hire a boat, there's a miniature railway (Mar-Oct) and the muddy marshland provides a haven for wading birds; the meadows and forested slopes above are pleasant for walks and picnics.

Shugborough SHUGBOROUGH HALL AND COUNTY MUSEUM Imposing ancestral home of the Earls of Lichfield, begun in the late 17th c and enlarged in the 18th c; magnificent state rooms featuring fine glass and silverware and art, and restored working kitchens, laundry, pantry and brewhouse. The museum also has interesting marionettes transferred from the former Puppet Theatre Museum at Abbots Bromley. The Park has a variety of unusual neo-classical monuments, working rare-breeds farm, agricultural museum and restored corn mill. Meals, snacks, shop, disabled access; cl Oct-Mar; entry to estate £1, museum £3, house £3, farm £3, combined ticket £7.50. NT.

Stafford SJ9223 ART GALLERY Temporary exhibitions of contemporary art, craft and photography, with a shop selling contemporary British crafts; cl Mon, Sun.

Tamworth SK2004 TAMWORTH CASTLE Glorious mixture of architectural styles from the original Norman motte and bailey walls through the Elizabethan timbered hall to the fine Jacobean state apartments. Also interesting CHAPEL, haunted bedroom, dungeon, Victorian nursery and Norman exhibition; pleasure grounds and adventure playground. Shop; cl am Sun; £2.75.

Wall SK0906 ROMAN SITE Known to its former inhabitants as Letocetum, this Roman fort was an important military base from around AD 50; excavations began in the 19th c and revealed one of the most complete Roman bath houses in this country. Also furnace room, exercise hall and various finds from this site and others nearby; cl 1-2 pm, 24-26 Dec, 1 Jan and Mon Oct-Mar; *£1.20.

Willoughbridge SJ7540 DOROTHY CLIVE GARDEN Woodland gardens created by the late Cl Harry Clive in memory of his wife; at their best perhaps in spring and early summer, but lovely all year. Rhododendrons, azaleas, old roses, water garden, rock garden; snacks, disabled access; cl Nov-Mar; £2.

Quietly **attractive villages,** all with decent pubs, include Abbots Bromley SK07240, Butterton SK0756, Coven SJ9006, Kinver SO8483 (the one right over in the W; some of Britain's only rock houses nearby, still lived in 30 years ago; there are good views from the Iron-Age fort on top of the ridge), Penkhull SJ8644 (somehow undisturbed by the development of the Potteries around it), Rugeley SK0418 (with a beautiful 12th-c church), Shenstone SK1004, Tutbury SK2028 (the Norman church has a notable West doorway and elaborate carvings and there's also an attractive ruined castle with good views), and Waterhouses SK0851. Longnor SK0965 is more of a small town, but despite its grand church has a pleasantly villagey feel (and a good craft centre). Brewood SJ8808 is another small charming town, with many attractive Georgian and older buildings. Codsall SJ8602 is notable in summer for its profusion of lupins (Moors Farm has a good farm shop and small country restaurant). MOSELEY OLD HALL is listed in the Midlands chapter.

Walks

Dove Dale, perhaps the finest of all the Dales, is shared with South Derbyshire (and described in the Walks section of that county).

There are many good walks too in the **Manifold Valley**, with fewer of the sensational rock features that abound in Dove Dale, but plenty of charm – more or less steep riverside pastures, ancient woodland in the narrower steeper gorges, waterside caves; there's good access to the hills above it, such as Wetton Hill SK1056, which have attractive views. The best viewpoint of all, not to be missed, is Thor's Cave SK0954, high above the dale. Wooded **Ilam Park** SK1351 shows the Manifold Valley at its most sheltered. The branch off up **Hamps Dale** SK0654 is also extremely pretty. There are good pubs nearby at Warslow, Wetton and Hulme End.

The **Churnet Valley** gives very pretty walks from Alton SK0742 or Oakamoor SK0544; the best goes through Hawksmoor and Greendale to pass the broad fishponds in wooded Dimmings Dale and comes back down to the river past an old smelting mill – and a good café called the Ramblers Retreat (cl Mon). Hawksmoor Wood SK0344 is itself an attractive nature reserve, and the Talbot in Alton is useful for lunch.

There are **moorland** walks from the side roads off the A53 N of Leek, and up here The Roaches SK0062 form an impressive western barrier at the edge of the Dark Peak; there are exhilarating walks atop, and said to be wallabies in the area (though none of our correspondents reports seeing any recently).

Cannock Chase SK0017 is the breathing space for the county's more industrial area: miles of forest and rolling heath, with fallow deer often seen. The large Castle Ring hill fort SJ0412 has fine views over the woods to the Trent Valley, and there are good views west towards the Welsh borders from the heights N of Broadhurst Green SJ9815. The German war cemeteries near here are rather moving.

The county is liberally laced with **canals**, and their towpaths give many miles of good interesting walks. The Caldon Canal and the Staffordshire & Worcester Canal have the best scenery. There's usually something happening at the Froghall Wharf SK0247 canal terminus (maybe including horse-drawn barge trips – (0538) 266486), with an interesting walk along the canal to Consallforge SK0049 (unusual remote pub here). The nearby Nature Park continues this strange lost-valley scenery. There's also good canal access at Gnosall Heath SJ8220 and Great Haywood SJ9922 (nr the longest packhorse bridge in the country), and from the decent pubs at Amington SK2304 (the Gate), Armitage SK0816, Cheddleton SJ9651, High Offley SJ7826 (Bridge 42 on the Shrops Union – a very unusual pub), Denford nr Leek SJ9553 and Filiance Bridge in Penkridge SJ9214. The Trent & Mersey Canal has little towpath here, but Fradley Junction SK1414, with a good waterside pub, is an attractive place for a stroll, with lots happening on the water.

Driving

The NE corner has the county's most interesting roads. The A53 high moorland road N of Leek has good views, and again up in this part of the county the B5054 gives an excellent impression of the dales country. The B5417 and B5032 E of Cheadle are both pretty roads. You can drive through Cannock Chase on quiet side roads, and the countryside around Abbots Bromley is quietly attractive.

Where to eat

Waterhouses SK0850 OLD BEAMS Main Rd (0538) 308254 Very pretty cottage surrounded with flowers and creepers; oak beams, antique furniture, a cosy, friendly atmosphere, excellent food and good service; bedrooms; disabled access. **£26.45**|/2-course meal £10.50; cl Sat am, Sun pm, Mon, 3 wks Jan.
Armitage SK0816 OLD FARMHOUSE (0543) 490353 Pleasant restaurant with good, very popular food, and friendly service; cl Sun pm, Mon, Sat am, 1st wk Jan, last 2 wks Aug; disabled access. **£24**|/£7.95.
Cresswell SJ9739 IZAAK WALTON (0782) 392265 Very neatly kept, upmarket dining pub with good, impressive food and pretty, country furnishings; cl 25-26 Dec. **£14**|£1.95/£4.95.
Other places worth knowing in this area for decent food include the Whittington at Kinver SO8483, the Seven Stars in Sandonbank SJ9428, Mainwaring Arms at Whitmore SJ8141, and the Crown at Wrinehill SJ7547.

Help this year from: *B M Eldridge, Tim Britton, E P Jobling, Paul Dunaway, Jane Owen, Chris and Chris Vallely, John Voos, J Morris, Lorrie and Mick Marchington, Trevor Scott, Sean Bathe, Colin Steer, N Clack, V Ogden, R Rayner, Ian Sharp, Doug Kennedy, Joan and Michel Hooper-Immins, Derek and Sylvia Stephenson, Andrew Stephenson, Helen Crookston, Roger Taylor, Anthony John, Richard and Maria Gillespie, Pauline Crossland, Dave Cawley, Russell Edwards, Jane Owen, Alan Wright, L S Manning, T G Thomas, DC, Mark and Mary Fairman, Dr and Mrs Richard Neville, Mrs C Heaps, Caroline Midmore, E N and I J Wilkinson, Tim Gilroy, CW, JW, Mrs C McAleese, George Atkinson, M A Cameron, C Roberts, Mike and Shelagh Watson, M Back, Janet Brown, C J Westmorland, Harry and Irene Fisher, D W Taylor, Dr K Bloomfield, Anne Wren, Jim Farmer, A W Dickinson, Peter and Lynn Brueton, Barry and Anne, Mr and Mrs A E McCully, Graham Bassett, A Preston, Trevor Scott, Jonathan and Nicky Teare, Malcolm and Penny Locker.*

We welcome reports from readers . . .

Please send us your ideas for inclusion in the next edition: places to visit, eat at or stay in, attractive drives or walks, maybe even unusual interesting shops you know of. Use the card in the middle, the report forms at the end, or just write – no stamp needed: THE GOOD WEEKEND GUIDE, FREEPOST TN1569, Wadhurst, E Sussex TN5 7BR. Readers who help us with reports for the GUIDE are offered a discount on the next edition.

Derbyshire and Staffordshire Calendar

Some of these dates were provisional as we went to press.

During the summer, many Derbyshire villages decorate their wells and springs with flowers and flower-petal pictures in their annual festive Well Dressings. *Originally a pagan water-worshipping ceremony, this is now part of the Christian calendar. A procession, led by the clergy, and a blessing of the wells usually initiate a week of village celebrations. Some of the main ones are included here. To avoid the crowds go a day or two after the actual ceremony – you'll be able to get a good close view of the elaborate flower 'pictures' which should stay fresh for almost a week.*

February

15th *(Shrove Tuesday)* **Ashbourne** Shrovetide Football Game, *between the Up'ards and Down'ards (from above and below Henmore Brook), who compete to get their team and the ball to one of the mills 3 miles apart along the brook;* **Winster** Pancake Races

April

4th **Chesterfield** Easter Market

5th **Flagg** Moor Point-to-Point, Steeplechase & Drag Hunt

10th **Burton-upon-Trent** Tulip Festival, *stalls horticultural and general, live bands and entertainments in Stapenhill Gardens*

16th **Derby** Festival, *outdoor and indoor music and dance events – till 1 May;* **Milford** Game Keepers' Fair *at Shugborough – till Sun 17*

23rd **Lichfield** St George's Day Court

May

2nd **Newborough** Well Dressing

12th **Tissington** Well Dressing, *perhaps the best known, around Ascension Day every year since 1349*

15th **Stafford** Staffordshire International Tattoo, *Wolseley Garden Park*

25th **Weston** Staffordshire County Show, *County Showground – till Thurs 26*

28th **Ashford-in-the-Water** Flower Festival and Well Dressing, *sheep washed in the River Wye at Sheepwash Bridge – till 4 Jun;* **Endon** 150th Well Dressing Festival – *till Mon 30;* **Hartington** Derbyshire Steam Fair – *till Mon 30;* **Milford** Shugborough Craft and County Show – *till Mon 30*

29th *(Oak Apple Day)* **Castleton** Garland Ceremony – *the Garland King (Charles II on the anniversary of his restoration in 1660) and his consort, on horseback and garlanded with flowers, lead a procession of bands and dancers, inc the Castleton Silver Band, through the village to the church, where the garland is hauled up to the top of the tower*

30th **Bamford** Sheepdog Trials; **Borrowash** Derbyshire County Show, *Elvaston Castle*

June

4th **Derby** City Motor Show – *new and vintage – till Sun 5*

5th **Uttoxeter** Midland Counties Show

11th **Ilkeston** Carnival; **Yoxall** Woodlane Fete

Derbyshire and Staffordshire Calendar

June cont.

12th **Alfreton** Rhododendron Sunday *at Alfreton Hall*; **Milford** Victorian Street Market *at Shugborough*

17th **Lichfield** Folk Festival – *till Sun 19*

18th **Long Eton** Carnival; **Tutbury** Midsummer Music Festival, *Tutbury Castle – till Sun 19*

25th **Rowsley** Flower Festival *inc Well Dressing – till 2 July*

26th **Bakewell** Well Dressing and Carnival – *till 2 July*

July

July **Buxton** International Arts Festival

2nd **Borrowash** Elvaston Castle Festival of Steam and Transport – *till Sun 3*; **Uttoxeter** Festival

3rd **Alport** Lovefeast *at Alport Barn, 1 mile W of Woodlands Chapel up Snake Pass; the feast (fruit cake and mugs of spring water) dates back to the 18th-c religious revival, when secret meetings were held in remote parts of the country*

8th **Lichfield** Festival and Fringe – *till Sun 17*

9th **Burton** Regatta – *till Sun 10*; **Stafford** Festival – *till around Sun 17*

10th **Milford** Shugborough Teddy Bear Festival; **Ticknall** Village Gardens Open Day

13th **Derby** CAMRA Beer Festival – *till Sun 17*

mid-July **Burton-upon-Trent** Summer Festival of Music and Art – *till mid-Aug*

17th **Ashbourne** Highland Gathering *inc pipe band contest and Highland dancing*

23rd **Bolsover Castle** Outdoor Opera – *till Sun 24*; **Milford** Shugborough Firework and Laser Symphony Concert

30th **Bradwell** Carnival

August

3rd **Bakewell** Show, *Coombs Road showground – till Thurs 4*

6th **Bradwell** Well Dressings – *till Sat 13*

7th **Derby** Military Tattoo, *Moorways Stadium*; **Stafford** Staffordshire Highland Gathering *in Wolseley Garden Park hosts the All England Pipe Band Championships this year, and may begin on Sat 6*

8th **Derby** Summer Extravaganza – *evening events in the week leading up to the weekend which incl the Royal Navy, band competitions, shire horses and parade – till Sun 14*

10th **Ashover** Show

17th **Ilam** Dovedale Sheepdog Trials

20th **Saddleworth** Rush Bearing Ceremony

27th **Crich** Transport Extravaganza *at the Tramway Museum – till Mon 29*; **Eyam** Well Dressing – *till 3 Sept*; **Matlock Bath** Illuminations Grand Switch-on, *events inc parading of illuminated*

Derbyshire and Staffordshire Calendar

August cont.

boats every weekend evening, concerts, Victorian fair and clifftop fireworks – till end Oct; **Milford** Shugborough Summer Craft Festival – *till Mon 29*

29th **Burton-upon-Trent** Carnival; **Chesterfield** Market and Fun Fair, *music and fireworks*; **Froggatt** Show, *Stoke Lane*; **Hope** Show and Sheepdog Trial

September

2nd **Glossop** Victorian Weekend; *many dress in period costume, with barrel organs, vintage cars, horse-drawn drays and market stalls – till Sun 4*

3rd **Chatsworth** Country Fair – *till Sun 4*

4th **Derby** Darley Park Concert *with synchronised fireworks*; **Mayfield** Gala Day/Produce Show

5th **Abbots Bromley** Ancient Annual Horn Dance *in the village streets – dancers inc Robin Hood and hobby horse, Maid Marian and others wearing reindeer antlers*

10th **Lichfield** Sheriff's Ride, *after meeting in the market square at 10 am, the Sheriff and over 100 entrants ride the 20-mile city boundary, stopping off for lunchtime races in the grounds of Freeford Manor*; **Weston** Staffordshire Great Autumn Show, *County Showground – till Sun 11*

24th **Dronfield** North-east Derbyshire Brass-band Festival

October

3rd **Burton-upon-Trent** Statutes Fair – *till Tues 4*

15th **Milford** Shugborough Craft Show – *till Sun 16*; **Stoke-on-Trent** Beer Festival, *Kings Hall*

30th **Bolsover** Castle Fireworks and Laser Spectacular

November

5th **Alton** Firework Display, *Alton Towers Theme Park – till Sun 6*; **Derby** Firework Display *in Markeaton Park*

December

6th **Milford** Christmas at Shugborough – *till Fri 9*

DEVON

One of Britain's finest areas for a short holiday, this county is best visited in spring, early summer and autumn, when it has a sense of space and peace not attainable in the busier peak summer period: no hold-ups on the roads, even richer colours in the countryside. There's a tremendous variety of scenery, a relaxed pace of life, and plenty of interesting things to see and do.

The sheltered seaside villages of the south coast have a lot going on and a delightful hinterland: they might be the first choice for a relaxing weekend, and stay relatively mild even in winter – when other parts of the county can be very bleak. For more energetic tastes, Dartmoor and its surroundings probably have more to offer the first-time visitor than Exmoor. Exeter is a charming small city, and good roads allow fast access from there both to the coast and to Dartmoor.

The county has a lot to please everyone – including children. There are lovely gardens, delightful thatched villages clustered around ancient church and equally ancient pub, glorious vistas of coast and moor, some decidedly unstuffy museums, all sorts of rustic pursuits, and vintage steam trains puffing through gorgeous river valleys. There is a splendid range of places to stay, and some very good food.

EXETER AND EAST DEVON

This is an area of contrasting seaside resorts and interesting places to visit; Exeter is a very good weekend base.

The prettiest place on the coast here is Branscombe, which comprises a series of largely unspoilt thatched hamlets strung along a lovely seaside valley. Devon's east coast is very popular for family summer holidays, and there are four old-fashioned resorts. Exmouth is the liveliest and biggest, a family beach resort doubling as a working port. Seaton, quieter, is a more typical family resort, with much less of a beach. Budleigh Salterton, the quietest, is rather retiring and genteel. Sidmouth is slightly busier, with a good deal of character as well as plenty for families – for most people, it's the most attractive of the four for a short break.

Inland, coastal downs give a gently varied landscape of charming wooded valleys with views and high pastures between, and several attractive villages. North of the A30/A35 is more self-contained farmland, mainly well-hedged traditional stock and dairy farms.

Exeter itself is a good choice for a short break. With the M5 so close and with fast trains, it's easy to reach from a long way away. A quietly attractive city in its own right, it has a lot to see. There are interesting places to visit close by, and good roads which bring the other parts of Devon within comfortable reach for a day out. Very quiet at weekends, during the week it's active without being crowded or noisy.

Elsewhere, some of the most enjoyable places to visit include Killerton, the working-mill museum at Uffculme, Bicton Park gardens, Farway countryside park and the village of Ottery St Mary.

There is much better walking in other parts of the county.

Where to stay

Hawkchurch ST3400 FAIRWATER HEAD COUNTRY HOUSE Axminster EX13 5TX (0297) 678 349 **£120**; 21 rms (the garden wing ones are best). Family-run country house overlooking picturesque Axe valley; log fire, pleasantly old-fashioned rooms; good, traditional home-made food using fresh local produce; friendly, helpful staff, and lovely garden; cl Jan/Feb.

Gittisham SY1398 COMBE HOUSE Honiton EX14 0AD (0404) 42756 ***£97**; 15 individually decorated rms. Peaceful Elizabethan country hotel in gardens with lawns and shrubbery; elegant day rooms furnished with antiques, family portraits, and fresh flowers; a happy, relaxed atmosphere, good food using some home-grown produce, and fine wines; cl Mon in Jan/Feb; disabled access.

Whimple SY0497 WOODHAYES Exeter EX5 2TD (0404) 822237 **£80**; 8 lovely spacious rms; big Georgian country house with comfortable, quietly decorated lounges, small library, open fires, flagstoned bar and pretty dining room; fine food, excellent breakfasts, neat grounds, children over 12.

Branscombe SY1988 LOOK OUT Seaton EX12 3DP (029 780) 262 **£79**; 5 pretty rms. Early 19th-c very atttactively converted coastguards' cottages with lots of beams, antiques, flagstones; good food using local produce; secluded cottage garden and marvellous views; fine walks along beach or cliffs; cl 1 wk Christmas; children over 6.

Higher Bulstone SY1988 BULSTONE Seaton EX12 3BL (029 780) 446 ***£69**; 12 rms, 6 with shared bthrm. Set in over 3 acres and surrounded by fields, this is a super place for family holidays – with both parents' and children's needs catered for; lots of facilities and warm, friendly, personal staff; children under 5 free; cl Dec/Jan.

Rousdon SY2990 DOWER HOUSE Lyme Regis DT7 3RB (0297) 21047 ***£66**; 9 rms. Family-run hotel with log fires in the hall and lounge; good bar and restaurant food (especially fish dishes), big breakfasts, efficient but unobtrusive service, indoor swimming pool; disabled access; cl Nov.

Exeter SX9292 WHITE HART South St EX1 1EE (0392) 79897 **£44w**; 62 decent rms. Rather splendid, well-run 14th-c inn with lots of different eating areas (wine-bar-type as well as a proper restaurant); marvellous atmospheric bar, open fires, beams, antiques, excellent range of wines, and friendly service.

Chardstock ST3004 GEORGE Axminster EX13 7BX (0460) 20241 **£42.50**; 4 rms. Neatly thatched old village inn with character furnishings, beams and old gas lamps; a quietly chatty feel, good food in bar and restaurant, and close to good walks.

Tipton St John SY0991 GOLDEN LION Sidmouth EX10 0AA (0404) 812881 **£41.12**; 2 rms. Bustling village local with lots of fresh flowers in softly lit bar, small no-smoking restaurant, good food, and decent wines; several golf courses nearby; cl 25-26 Dec; children over 7.

Sidford SY1390 Blue Ball Sidmouth EX10 9QL (0395) 514062 **£36**; 3 rms with nice touches like free papers, fruit and fresh flowers; shared bthrm. Welcoming, thatched 14th-c inn run by the same family since 1912; very friendly service, decent food inc hearty breakfasts.

Cullompton ST0107 Oburnford Farm EX15 1LZ (0884) 32292 **£34**; 6 rms. Working farm with Channel Island dairy cows (lovely clotted cream), beef cattle and some cereal (guests can help feed calves); attractive lounge and dining room, log fires, and good food using home-grown produce.

Sidmouth SY1287 Higher Weston Farm EX10 0PH (0395) 513741 **£33**; 3 rms. Secluded family farmhouse with good breakfasts; croquet lawn, badminton, and stabling for children's ponies; lots of footpaths; cl Oct-Mar; children over 9.

Stockland ST2404 Kings Arms Honiton EX14 9BS (0404) 881361 **£30**; 3 rms. Cream-faced thatched pub with elegant rooms, very good bar lunches and evening restaurant food (esp fish), very good wine list; skittle alley, keep-fit classes and live music Sun pm; cl 25 Dec pm; well-behaved children only.

Newton Poppleford SY0889 Southern Cross Sidmouth EX10 0DU (0395) 68439 **£29**; 8 rms. To enjoy the good food here, you have to stay in this old low-beamed farm cottage which has pleasant gardens and gift shop; good cream teas; cl 25-26 Dec.

Axminster SY2998 Goodmans House Furley Membury EX13 7TU (0404) 88690 **£22**; 8 rms. Friendly early 19th-c house in 12 acres; good food and small, decent wine list in attractive candlelit dining room, and verandah/conservatory; cl Jan.

Colaton Raleigh SY0787 Drupe Farm EX10 0LE (0395) 68838; phone for details and prices. Attractively decorated self-catering holiday cottages in converted old farmhouse and outbuildings grouped around landscaped courtyard; lots of space, games room, barbecue; short lets available.

To see and do

Exeter This ancient city has a good relaxed atmosphere, buoyed up by the thriving university. From the old mainly pedestrianised High Street, picturesque partly Tudor narrow lanes lead into the serene tree-shaded cathedral close, with one or two Tudor buildings among gracious Georgian ones. In the centre, modern shops are integrated into the old layout very discreetly indeed. With many smaller churches, decent book and other shops, pubs and so forth nearby, this is a very pleasant part for browsing around. Particularly attractive streets include Southernhay at the end of the close, and Stepcote Hill, a picturesque detour from Fore Street.

The Quay, beyond the streams of fast traffic on the ring road (there are quiet underpasses), has become lively and entertaining. It has handsomely restored buildings, resurgent pubs and cafés, and a growing number of craft shops and the like. There are boat trips down the ship canal to Exminster; or you can walk down, passing the Double Locks (a favourite pub) and ending at the Turf Hotel looking out over the estuary.

✝ The cathedral is well worth visiting: England's finest example of decorated Gothic architecture, with its magnificent nave soaring to the fan-vaulted roof, and intricately carved choir stalls. It also boasts the longest gothic vault in Europe; meals, snacks, shop, disabled access; voluntary donations.

❅ The Maritime Museum (The

Haven), at the heart of the quay area, has an extraordinary collection of over 130 boats from all over the world – gondolas to steam dredgers to African dug-out canoes, some under cover, others out on the water, inc a fully rigged play ship for children. There's no nonsense about keeping your hands off the exhibits, quite the opposite; snacks, shop, limited disabled access; cl Oct-Apr; *£3.80. Part of the fun is the historic wire-drawn ferry which can take you across to the second part of the collection.

The medieval GUILDHALL (High St) with its ornately colonnaded Elizabethan façade is one of the oldest municipal buildings still in use; the roof timbers rest on bosses of bears holding staves, and there are paintings and civic silver and regalia; shop; cl pm Sat, all Sun and bank hols, and during civic functions.

! A rather more unusual medieval attraction is the network of UNDERGROUND PASSAGES (entrance via Boots Arcade in High St), built in the 13th c to bring water into the city; introductory exhibition and video. Flat shoes are recommended. They've just started new tours on Sat for those who want to go into the more creepy and constricted parts – great fun, and very atmospheric, but be prepared to get muddy. Shop; cl Sun, Mon, am winter wkdys; *£1.95.

Earlier remains can be seen at ST NICHOLAS' PRIORY (Mint Lane), an 11th-c Benedictine monastery housing an unusual Norman undercroft, Tudor room and 15th-c kitchen. Occasional historical days with costumed characters; disabled access to ground floor only; cl Sun, Mon, Oct-Easter; 50p.

The ROUGEMONT HOUSE MUSEUM, an elegant Regency building in the grounds of the city's former Norman castle, is now called the CONNECTIONS DISCOVERY CENTRE and is mainly open only to schools, though there are selected days and wknds when anyone can have a go on the lively hands-on exhibits and games – best to tel (0392) 265858 to see when. Part of the castle's formidable very early gateway still survives.

ROYAL ALBERT MEMORIAL MUSEUM (Queen St) Regional silver, archaeology, paintings and natural history; also African wood-carvings. Meals, snacks, shop, disabled access; cl Sun, Mon.

Apart from the White Hart, decent pubs in fine buildings near the cathedral are the Ship (Martins Lane) and Well House (The Close); down on the Quay the Prospect is good. The Cowick Barton out on Cowick Lane is worth knowing, too.

Other things to see and do

Beer ST2389 This is a steep fishing village of stone and flint cottages, with its boats pulled up on the shingle beach. PECORAMA PLEASURE GARDENS Fun for railway lovers, with the house containing models and train collections; there's also a miniature steam and diesel passenger line with stunning views of the bay. Other features include a putting green, aviary, and children's play area with maze and assault course; meals, snacks, shop, disabled access; cl Sat pm, Sun (exc Jun-Sept), outdoor features cl Oct-Easter (except half-term); £2.75. The village was famous from Roman times for its cavernous whitestone quarries, which can be visited. The waterside Anchor has good fresh local fish.

Bicton SY0684 BICTON PARK GARDENS Over 50 acres of gardens, shrubs, woodlands and lakes, fuschia, geranium and orchid houses, restored palm house with tropical and sub-tropical areas; also bird garden, woodland railway, crazy golf and adventure playground. Meals, snacks, shop and plant centre, disabled access; cl Nov-Feb; £4.90. Nearby, the entirely separate gardens of BICTON COLLEGE OF AGRICULTURE are of great if more specialised appeal; long monkey-puzzle avenue through parkland, rich collection of magnolias, camellias and flowering cherries, national pittosporum and agapanthus collection, many other plants, and 17-acre arboretum with woodland garden. Snacks, garden and plant centre; cl bank hols and wknds; £1.50.

† **Broadclyst** SX9897 is a pretty thatch-and-cob village, with a fine photogenic church – interesting inside, too. The New Inn and Red Lion are decent pubs.

☺ **Clyst St Mary** SX9790 CREALY COUNTRY Ideal for children, a bustling complex with acres of activities such as go-karts, archery, a farm where you can milk the cows, slides and boats, pony rides, adventure playgrounds, lakeside walks and special events each Sun in season from car rallies to conker championships; meals, snacks, shop, disabled access; cl wkdys Nov and Dec and all Jan-early Mar; £3.75.

❀ **Dalwood** SY2499 BURROW FARM GARDENS Part of this 5-acre site has been created from an ancient Roman clay pit, and there are spacious lawns, borders and unusual shrubs and trees as well as a woodland garden, pergola walk with old-fashioned roses, and super views; cream teas Sun, Weds and bank hols, nursery; cl am, all Oct-Mar; £1.50. The Tuckers Arms is good for lunch.

† **East Budleigh** ST0684, an attractive and quietly placed cob and thatch village, has a pleasant CHURCH with fascinating Jacobean carved pew ends – some grotesque, some hilarious, some frankly rude.

! **Exmouth** SY0080 More of a family seaside holiday place than somewhere for a short break, this is still worth a visit for its lively working docks area, its long sandy beach and its stately church; summer boat trips. WONDERFUL WORLD OF MINIATURE Home of the world's biggest OO model railway, 7,500 ft of track indoors with another 1,800 outside, a varied landscape that took 14 years to assemble. Some of the detail is amazing, right down to the birds in the trees; shop, disabled access; cl Nov-Easter; £1.80. WORLD OF COUNTRY LIFE 40 acres of good family-based activities, with friendly animals in the Pets' Corner, an adventure playground

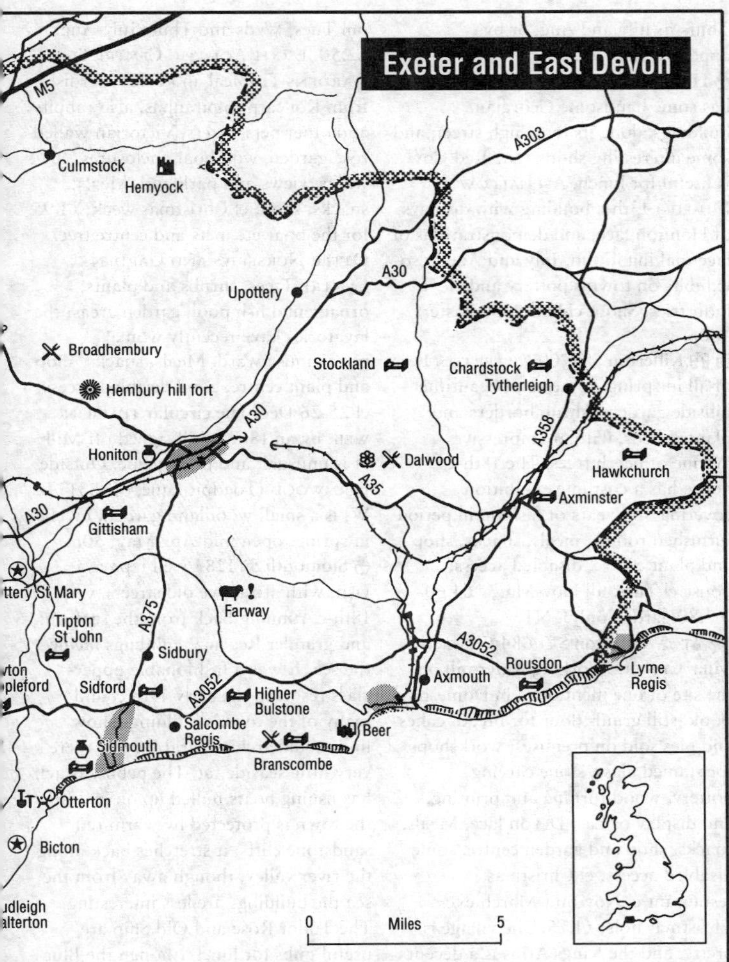

and safari rides through the paddocks of deer and llamas; also reconstructed Victorian street, classic motorcycle collection, crafts, and steam engines. Meals, snacks, shop, disabled access; cl Nov-Mar; £3.50. The Deer Leap is useful for lunch.

! Farway SY1895 Farway Countryside Park Traditional and modern breeds of farm animals over 108 acres of beautiful countryside, tropical butterfly house, pony and donkey-cart rides and trekking, and nature trails. Meals, snacks, shop, disabled access; cl Oct-Easter; £1.50.

Hemyock ST1313 Castle A friendly low-key castle where the family that run it really take care with the guided tours. It was used as a Civil War prison for Royalists, and the site's 700-year history is illustrated by life-size tableaux in the visitor centre; they've recently re-erected the castle's old cider press and apple mill. Shop, disabled access; open pm Suns and bank hols Easter-Sept as well as pm Tues and

Thurs in July and Aug, or by appointment; *£1.

Honiton ST1500 This country town has some handsome Georgian buildings along its long high street, and some interesting shops. The Red Cow is useful for lunch. ALLHALLOWS MUSEUM 13th-c building with displays of Honiton lace, and demonstrations of lace-making in Jun, July and Aug; also exhibits on town's pottery and clock industries. Shop; cl Sun, Nov-Easter; *60p.

Killerton SS9700 KILLERTON Best of all in spring, 15 acres of beautiful hillside gardens, shrub borders and planted beds, with an impressive avenue of beech trees. The 18th-c house has a costume exhibition covering 300 years of fashion in period furnished rooms; meals, snacks, shop and plant centre, disabled access; house cl Tues, all Nov-Mar; *£4.60 (£2.80 garden only). NT.

★ **Otterton** SY0684 OTTERTON MILL CENTRE Working watermill on the site of one mentioned in Domesday Book, still grinds flour for bread, cakes and pies sold on premises; workshops for stained glass, stone carving, pottery, wood-turning and printing, and display of East Devon lace. Meals, snacks, shop and garden centre, some disabled access; cl Christmas, restaurant cl Nov-mid-March exc Christmas hols; £1.75. The village is pretty, and the Kings Arms is a decent pub.

Ottery St Mary SY0995 is a restrained small town – or extended village – with some attractive old buildings around its twin-towered church. There are a couple of decent pubs. CADHAY Beautiful Tudor and Georgian manor house, its Great Hall has a fine timbered 15th-c roof, and there's an unusual Court of Sovereigns – a courtyard with statues of various monarchs; the house may be familiar to viewers of TV's *Miss Marple*. Disabled access to garden and downstairs; open Whit bank hol then pm Tues, Weds and Thurs July-Aug; £2.50. ESCOT AQUATIC CENTRE & GARDENS Tropical and coldwater fish from Koi carp to piranhas, also rabbits and other pets, otters, Victorian walled rose garden, wild boar enclosures, walks, views and parkland. Meals, snacks, shop; cl Christmas week; £1.95 for the boar etc, pets and centre free. OTTER NURSERIES AND GARDEN CENTRE Trees, shrubs and plants, ornamental fish pool, garden areas; the lavatories have recently won a prestigious award. Meals, snacks, shop and plant centre, good disabled access; cl 25-26 Dec. The circular TUMBLING WEIR by an 18th-c mill signed off Mill St is unusual, and photogenic. Outside FERNWOOD (Toadpit Lane, off B3174 W) is a small woodland garden, lovely in spring; open mid-Apr-May; 50p.

Sidmouth SY1287 well repays a visit, with attractive old streets, very 18th-c, running back from the seafront, and grander Regency buildings facing the sea. It was a fashionable upper-class resort in the early 19th c, and many of the town's buildings show undoubted architectural verve – there's very little seaside tat. The pebbly beach has fishing boats pulled up on it, and the town is protected by warm red sandstone cliffs; it stretches back along the river valley, though away from the sea the buildings are less interesting. The Tudor Rose and Old Ship are useful pubs for lunch (though the Blue Ball up at Sidford is best of all here). VINTAGE TOY & TRAIN MUSEUM Toys, games and children's books from 1925-1975, inc the first and last Dinky toy, Hornby trains, military figures and several temporary exhibitions. Snacks, shop; cl Sun, bank hols, Nov-Easter; *£1.50. SIDMOUTH MUSEUM Fine Regency house with prints, lace and other local history, geology and archaeology; shop; cl 12.30-2 for lunch, am Sun and Mon, Nov-Mar; 50p. They also organise walking tours round the town, Tues and Thurs at 10.15 am. DONKEY SANCTUARY 5,500 distressed donkeys have passed through this centre over the last 20 years; it's a really dedicated place, and you can see the care and effort put into making their guests' stay comfortable. Snacks, shop, disabled access.

★ ❄ **Topsham** SX9687 is an old-world seaside village, its buildings (and large number of good pubs and inns – the Passage is currently the best for food) showing its past importance as a port. Well worth a quiet potter. There's a small local maritime museum. Just outside, the Bridge Inn on the Clyst St George rd has hardly changed in style since the 16th c.

♣T ✝ **Uffculme** ST0612 is a big but pleasant village above the Culm River, where the COLDHARBOUR MILL WORKING MUSEUM shows every stage in the production of wool, on two working levels; also weaver's cottage, carpenters' workshops, restoration of steam engine and other displays. Meals, snacks, shop, disabled access; cl winter wknds; £2.95. The attractive CHURCH has a magnificent carved screen.

✝ Interesting **churches** at Cullompton ST0107 (remarkable painted screen; a busy little town), Culmstock ST1014, Sidbury SY1391 (a pretty village, with a very good pub nearby at Sidford) and Silverton SS9502 (another attractive village).

★ **Attractive villages**, all with decent pubs, include seaside Axmouth SY2591 and Branscombe SY1988, Broadhembury ST1004, Butterleigh SS9708, Otterton SY0684, Salcombe Regis SY1488, Tytherleigh ST3103, Upottery ST2007 and Woodbury SY0187.

Walks

The best walks here are along the **coastal cliffs**, for example the walk to the broken white cliffs of Beer Head SY2287 from Beer itself or from Branscombe; the Hooken undercliff here is a tremendous chalk jumble of collapsed cliff-lands. There's a long stretch of red sandstone cliffs between Sidmouth and Branscombe, reached from either place (or, steeply but very prettily, from Salcombe Regis). The steeply tumbled brambly wooded wilderness of Dowlands Cliffs E of Axmouth is interesting, with a lot of small birds. The High Land of Orcombe SY0279, reached by the shore road E out of Exmouth and protected against camp-site encroachment by its National Trust ownership, is useful for a shorter stroll with sea views.

Off the B3180 E of Woodbury are miles of **heath** with some pinewoods, a place to get away from people even in high summer (red flags warn if there's firing on one section which is a shooting range). From the highest points, near the road, there are far views along the coast and to Dartmoor. The wooded hill fort right by the road is worth a look, and it's a bit eerie tracing the ramparts through the beech trees.

Off the A373 NW of Honiton you can walk up into **Hembury hill fort** ST1103; not spectacular, but worth a look if you're passing; it does have views.

Driving

Some fine views are to be had from the A375 S of Honiton, as you come over the heath of Gittisham Hill; on the left you can pick out one or two of the Bronze-Age burial mounds which dot this area, with many more by the B3174 towards Beer. There are more good views from the B3180 over Woodbury

Common, which cuts through a wooded Iron-Age hill fort.

The back road forking S of the A30 just SW of its junction with the A303 near Upottery is a good ridge road, giving fine views of the surrounding farmland. The remains of the hill fort on the left a mile or so short of the transmission mast is worth the short detour.

A quiet and pretty valley drive is the B3397 through Uffculme to Culmstock, and then the back road to Hemyock (which has the ruined remains of a medieval castle, over a stream from the church).

Of the more long-distance roads, the A3052 is good, with attractive scenery virtually all the way along to the Dorset border. Except at busy times it's also quite quick. From it, the detour down through Branscombe is thoroughly worth while. The A30 can be rather tedious E of Exeter.

For getting into Exeter, much the quickest way from either the M5 or the A38 is to keep on round to the westbound A30 and go into the city from the Alphington roundabout.

Where to eat

Lympstone SX9984 RIVER HOUSE (0395) 265147 Marvellous river views from big picture windows in lounge, interesting food (inc fresh fish) in first-floor restaurant using some home-grown produce and kind, friendly service; cl Sun/Mon pm, Christmas; children over 6; disabled access. **£41**|£5.25.

Topsham SY9688 AMADEUS (0392) 873759 Small, popular restaurant with cosy, relaxed atmosphere and four little rooms (one is a lounge); generous helpings of good honest food using local produce; friendly courteous service; children must be well behaved. **£19.50**|2-course lunch £9, 2-course dinner £13.50.

Dalwood ST2400 TUCKERS ARMS (040 488) 342 Delightful thatched medieval longhouse with well-prepared, enterprising bar food and lots of colourful hanging baskets; bedrooms. **£18**|£2.65/£7.

Branscombe SY1988 FOUNTAIN HEAD 14th-c inn in lovely sheltered village with lots of beams, panelling, and log fires; good-value bar food, own-brew beers, quick service, and friendly dog; disabled access. **£13**|£1.40/£4; the self-catering flat and cottage is recommended by contributors.

Broadhembury ST1004 DREWE ARMS (0404) 84267 Friendly 15th-c pub with old-fashioned feel and excellent, perfectly cooked, very fresh fish dishes; good wines, restaurant, pleasant garden. £5.20/£8.50.

Budleigh Salterton SY0682 SALTERTON ARMS (0395) 445048 Tucked-away but busy little pub with wide choice of food inc enormous salads, lots of fresh fish, and several vegetarian dishes. £2.60/£6.30.

Exeter SX9292 DOUBLE LOCKS Canal Banks, Alphington (0392) 56947 Friendly lockside pub with good, simple bar food (available all day exc Sun afternoon), summer barbecues, up to 10 real ales on handpump, and relaxed atmosphere; disabled access. £1.70/£3.30.

We welcome reports from readers . . .

Please send us your ideas for inclusion in the next edition: places to visit, eat at or stay in, attractive drives or walks, maybe even unusual interesting shops you know of. Use the card in the middle, the report forms at the end, or just write – no stamp needed: THE GOOD WEEKEND GUIDE, FREEPOST TN1569, Wadhurst, E Sussex TN5 7BR.

Dartmoor

The county's finest scenery, varied and intricate, is to be found here; there are very interesting places to visit and excellent places to stay.

The moor itself is a magnificent brooding wilderness, with excellent walking. All sorts of points of interest, especially perhaps its prehistoric remains, make it far from monotonous. Around its edges are many lovely valleys and villages, delightful to explore. Among many other attractions for visitors, front-runners include Morwellham Quay, Castle Drogo at Drewsteignton, Lydford Gorge, Buckland Abbey and the Garden House at Buckland Monachorum, Canonteign Falls and the rare breeds farm at Bovey Tracey. The steam railway from Buckfastleigh to Totnes (described in the South Devon section) is a delightful outing.

Where to stay

Chagford SX7087 GIDLEIGH PARK Newton Abbot TQ13 8HH (0647) 432367 **£275 inc dinner**; 15 opulent and individual rms with fruit and flowers provided. Luxurious Dartmoor-edge mock Tudor hotel with very comfortable drawing room, conservatory overlooking the fine grounds (of which there are 40 acres, with walks straight up on to the moor), log fires, particularly fine cooking and exceptional wine list; caring staff.

Lewdown SX4486 LEWTRENCHARD MANOR Okehampton EX20 4PN (056 683) 256 **£130**; 8 well-equipped rms with fresh flowers and period furniture. Lovely 17th-c manor house with dark panelling, ornate ceilings, antiques, fresh flowers, log fires and comfortable seating; friendly welcome and relaxed atmosphere, and candlelit restaurant with very good food; garden with shooting, fishing and croquet; children over 8 (unless by arrangement).

Haytor SX7677 BEL ALP HOUSE Newton Abbot TQ13 9XX (0364) 661217 **£126**; 9 spacious rms. Handsome Edwardian country house with elegant, airy rooms, comfortable furniture, log fires, friendly atmosphere, and fine, careful cooking in pretty restaurant; wonderful views and pretty garden; cl Dec-Feb; disabled access.

Chagford Sandy Park SX7087 MILL END Newton Abbot TQ13 8JN (0647) 432 282 ***£90**; 17 neat rms. Former flour mill with waterwheel in neatly kept grounds below Dartmoor; comfortable lounges, interesting food, good service; cl 10-20 Dec, 10-20 Jan; disabled access.

Lifton SX3885 ARUNDELL ARMS PL16 0AA (0566) 784 666 **£77**; 29 well-equipped rms. Carefully renovated old coaching inn with 20 miles of its own waters – fishing is the main thing; comfortable lounge, log fires, very good food in smart restaurant, decent wines and kind service; cl 2 days over Christmas.

Moretonhampstead SX7585 WHITE HART Newton Abbot TQ13 8NF (0647) 40406 **£63**; 20 rms. Former Georgian posting house, well run and comfortable, with interesting furnishings in civilised lounge bar and hall; lively back bar, good bar food and no-smoking restaurant; children over 10.

Doddiscombsleigh SX8586 NOBODY Exeter EX6 7PS (0647) 52394 **£53**; 7 rms, some in Georgian manor house 150 yds down rd, and most with own bthrm. Friendly, atmospheric thatched 16th-c pub with attractively furnished, two-roomed lounge bar, beams, heavy wooden furniture, inglenook fireplace; outstanding cellar running to 700 wines, 250 malts, decent food in bar and restaurant inc 40 Devon cheeses, and good views from garden; local church worth visiting for its fine stained glass; no children.

South Zeal SX6593 OXENHAM ARMS Okehampton EX20 2JT (0837) 840244 **£50**; 8 rms. Grandly atmospheric old inn dating back to 12th c and first licensed 1477 (neolithic standing stone still forms part of the wall in the TV room); elegant beamed and panelled bar with chatty, relaxed atmosphere and open fire, decent food and wines, charming ex-monastery small garden.

Lydford SX5184 CASTLE Okehampton EX20 4BH (082 282) 242 **£47.50**; 8 rms, most with own bthrm. Friendly old inn in ancient village with lots of interesting antiques and furnishings; decent food, nice garden with new covered terrace, and animals; next to castle and near attractive gorge.

Holne SX7069 CHURCH HOUSE Newton Abbot TQ13 7SJ (036 43) 208 **£45**; 6 rms. Medieval Dartmoor-edge inn with comfortable, atmospheric pine-panelled lounge bar, freshly prepared food using local produce, restaurant, decent wine list, pleasant service, and lots of good walks close by.

Moretonhampstead SX7586 GREAT SLONCOMBE FARM TQ13 8QF (0647) 40595 **£34**; 3 rms – the big double is the favourite. Peaceful B & B in lovely 13th-c farmhouse on a working farm; carefully polished old-fashioned furniture, decent food, friendly owners, log fires, and good walking and birdwatching nearby.

Gulworthy SX4472 RUBBYTOWN FARM Tavistock PL19 8PA (0822) 832493 **£34**; 3 rms, 1 with shared bthrm. Comfortably and prettily furnished 17th-c farmhouse in the Tamar Valley; cl over Christmas; children over 5.

Haytor Vale SX7677 ROCK Newton Abbot TQ13 9XP (0364) 661305 **£31.50**; 9 rms. Civilised old inn in Dartmoor village with good food (inc fresh fish); a good mix of visitors and locals in the two rooms of the panelled bar, open fires, no-smoking restaurant, courteous service, and big garden; walking, fishing, riding and golf nearby.

To see and do

Dartmoor itself is classic moorland, where distant vistas of changing greens and browns fade into the austere grey-blues of far shoulders and edges. The moor is punctuated with all sorts of interesting focal points and features: numerous easily traceable prehistoric remains; strange wind-sculpted, eroded granite tors which crown many of the slopes; the little streams that thread over boulders; tamed water-courses where leats or miniature canals (dating back to the 16th-c one cut by Drake to supply Plymouth) curl carefully around the contours; sheltered valleys cut into the moors, where white houses crouch among sycamores and oaks; occasional higher miniature forests of much more stunted oaks clustered around the rocks; abandoned tin-mine workings with ruined wheelhouses; the shaggy ponies hoping for a hand-out.

The **villages** around it are well worth exploring. Typically they are composed of thatched white-plastered stone cottages clustered around an interesting and ancient if not showy stone church, often with a church-house inn beside it as old as the church itself. One rated by many contributors as the most attractive in the whole of England is Lustleigh SX7881, with charming riverside walks in utterly unspoilt woodland around it, or up to Hunters Tor on Dartmoor. Primrose Cottage is hotly tipped for cream teas, and the Cleave Inn is good. Other particularly noteworthy ones include Bridestowe SX5189, Holne SX7069, Manaton SX7581 (the Becky Falls private riverside woodland on the B3344 to Bovey Tracey is very pretty for family walks; restaurant, shop; cl Dec-Easter; £2.50 per car), Meavy SX5467 (where the parish still owns the pub), Moretonhampstead SX7585 (less secluded than the others, but more to see), North Bovey SX7483, Peter Tavy SX5177, South Zeal SX6593, and Throwleigh SX6690. All these have good pubs.

Bickington SX7972 GORSE BLOSSOM MINIATURE RAILWAY AND WOODLAND PARK Unlimited rides on 7¼-inch-gauge steam railway through 35 acres of woodland; also toytown village and nature trails. Meals, shop, some disabled access; cl Oct-Easter; £3.50.

★ **Bovey Tracey** SX8078 PARKE RARE BREEDS FARM (B3344 W) Lots of animals inc rare cattle, sheep and pigs in fields and stalls, and remarkable poultry and waterfowl in walled garden with pond; also fine walks through extensive parkland by wooded river. Dartmoor National Park information centre. Snacks, shop; cl Nov-Mar or Easter, whichever is earlier; £3.50. The CRAFT CENTRE at Bovey Tracey Mill is in a former watermill, with a wide range of good-value handicrafts from the humble to the special, and regularly changing exhibitions; meals, snacks, shop, some disabled access; cl Christmas; £1 for exhibitions. There's a glass factory specialising in making marbles at TEIGN VALLEY GLASS & HOUSE OF MARBLES in Pottery Rd, where there's also other decorative glass, and a little museum devoted to the tiny round things that too many people seem to lose; meals, snacks, shop, disabled access; cl Sun Oct-Easter. The LOWERDOWN POTTERY (off B3344) does fine decorated pottery; cl Sat exc summer. The Dolphin and Riverside in the little town (attractive without being a special attraction) are useful for lunch.

† **Brentor** SX4780 CHURCH (above back rd Lydford-Tavistock, just S of North Brentor), 12th-c, is one of England's smallest and notable for its lonely position on a hill with remarkable views of coast and Dartmoor.

† **Buckfastleigh** SX7367 BUCKFAST ABBEY Originally founded in 1018 but left abandoned after Dissolution of the monasteries until refounded in 1882. It was reconstructed on the same site by four remarkable monks who did most of the work themselves over a period of 32 years; much of their splendid craftsmanship is on display, and there's also an exhibition on the abbey's first thousand years. Meals, snacks, shop, disabled access. BUTTERFLY PARK AND DARTMOOR OTTER SANCTUARY You can watch the otters swimming and playing from the underwater viewing tunnel here, or see them in the other four big landscaped enclosures, and there's a specially designed undercover tropical garden with free-flying butterflies and moths from all over the world. The otters are fed four times a day in summer; meals, snacks, shop, disabled access; cl Dec-Mar; £3.50. Just out of town the PENNYWELL FARM CENTRE is a very friendly place, with 400 animals in 80 acres, lovely scenery, wildlife viewing hides, and falconry demonstrations. Children can feed some of the animals, and every half-hour there are different events from milking to ferret racing, so there's always something going on – a very good place for families. Snacks, shop, disabled access; cl Nov-mid-Mar; £3.95. The BUCKFAST STEAM RAILWAY to Totnes is described in the South

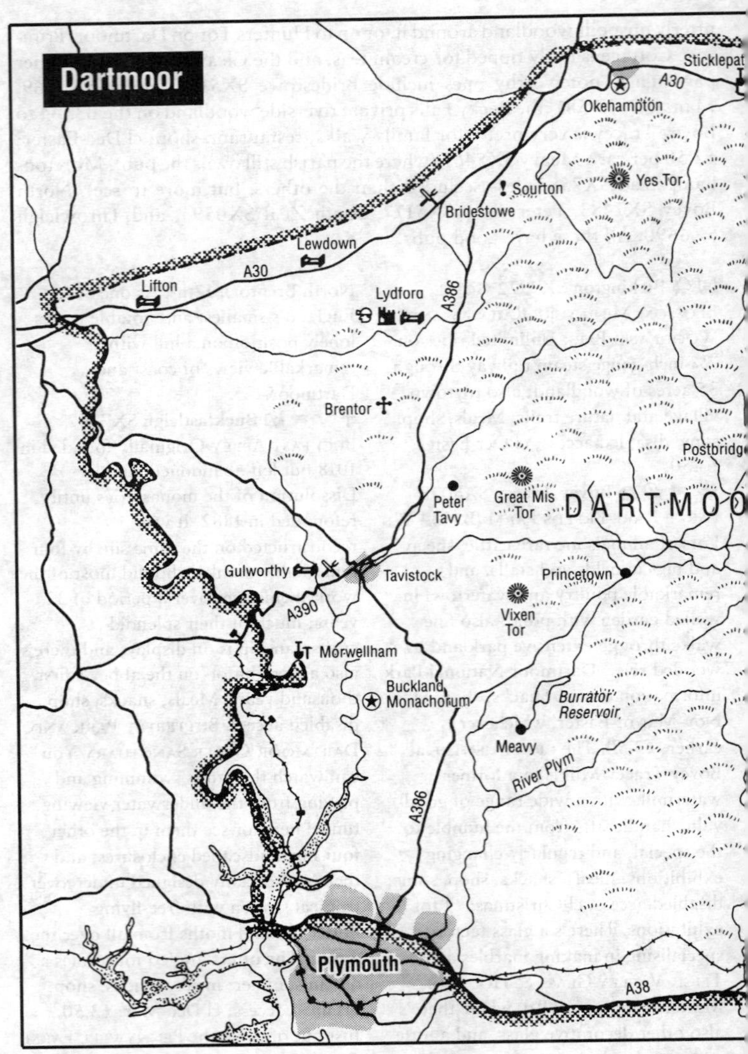

Devon section. The Dartbridge is useful for lunch.

Buckland Monachorum

SX4868 BUCKLAND ABBEY Originally a Cistercian abbey, this was the home of Sir Francis Drake until his death in 1596, and of his family until 1946. History of the abbey and of Drake, with the famous drum said to sound whenever England is in danger; also craft workshops and good walks. Meals, snacks, shop, disabled access, but tricky in places; cl Thurs, winter wkdys and wknd am; £4 grounds and abbey. GARDEN HOUSE Profusion of unusual plants beautifully laid out in warm garden sheltered by picturesque partly ruined walls of former abbey buildings, rare trees and shrubs outside; interesting plant sales, snacks

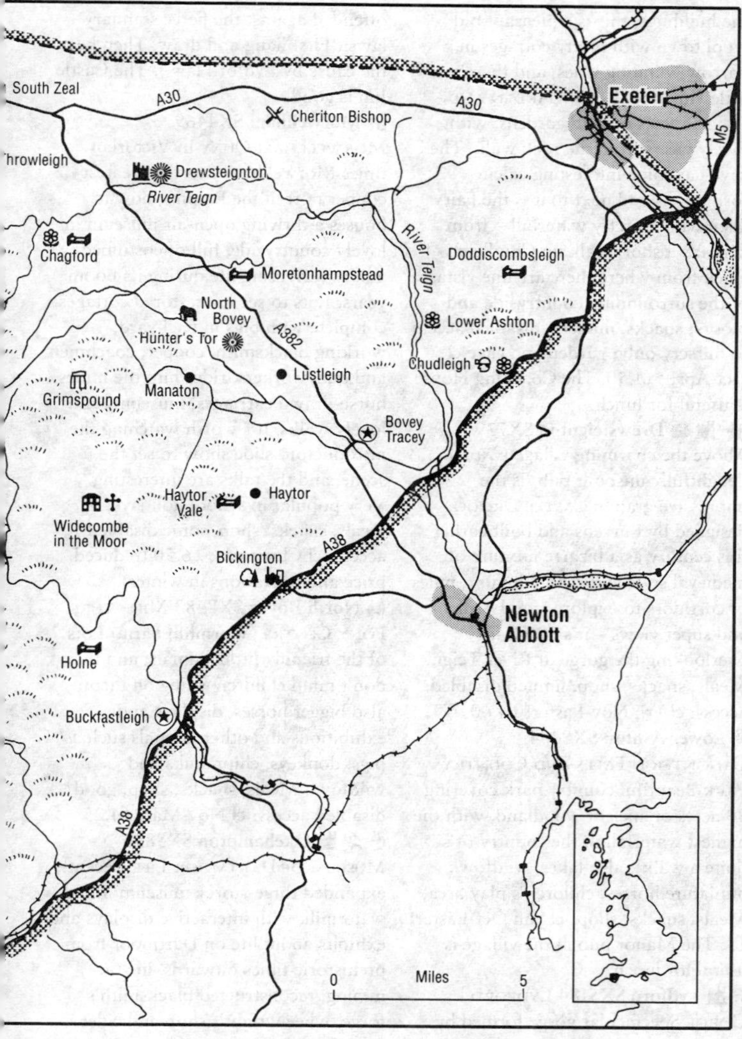

and teas Apr-Sept; cl Dec-Feb; £2.50. The Drakes Manor is good for lunch.

❀ Nr **Chagford** SX7087 Gidleigh Park Lovely grounds of luxury country-house hotel (see Where to stay) with colourful woodland walks and water garden using the natural Dartmoor streams and rocks, as well as immaculate more formal gardens; excellent lunches, cream teas; cl bank hols and wknds; 50p. Chagford itself is an attractive quite busy village; even the bank is thatched, and the two old-fashioned general stores are fun. The Ring o' Bells is good for lunch, and the Bullers Arms, Globe and Three Crowns Hotel (said to be based on a 13th-c monks' hospice) are useful too.

★ ❀ ⛨ **Chudleigh** SX8679 Despite the 1807 fire which destroyed lots of the buildings, this is a pleasant old wool town with pretty cottages in narrow, winding lanes, and there's a little vineyard. ROCK GARDEN AND CAVE 3 acres of wild gardens, with lovely views from the rock walk. The cave has some interesting calcite formations and next to it is the Fairy Glen with a pretty waterfall – from here it's a short walk up Chudleigh Rock from where there are fine vistas of the surrounding countryside and moors; snacks, nursery, disabled access to nursery only; garden and cave cl Oct-Apr; *£1.50. The Coaching House is useful for lunch.

Drewsteignton SX7390
Above the charming village (with a delightfully unspoilt pub) is the impressive granite CASTLE DROGO, designed by Lutyens and built earlier this century as a bizarre mixture of medieval style and 20th-c luxury; miles of corridors to explore, good walks and super views – it's 900 ft up overlooking the gorge of River Teign. Meals, snacks, shop, limited disabled access; cl Fri, Nov-Easter; £4.60. NT.

Lower Ashton SX8484
CANONTEIGN FALLS AND COUNTRY PARK Beautiful country park covering 80 acres of ancient woodland, with the highest waterfall in the country (it's quite a walk); also lakes, wildfowl, miniature horses, children's play area. Meals, snacks, shop; cl Sun Oct-Easter; £3. The Manor pub in the village is useful for lunch.

Lydford SX5184 LYDFORD GORGE Spectacular gorge formed by the River Lyd cutting into the rock, causing boulders to scoop out potholes in the bed of the stream. Dramatic sights such as Devil's Cauldron and White Lady Waterfall; children like it but need to be watched carefully; snacks, shop; most parts cl Nov-Apr; £2.80. NT. The forbidding CASTLE has a daunting stone keep dating from 1195; the upper floor was used originally as a tin-mine law court, the second as prison for those who offended against the fierce stannary laws ('First hang and draw, Then hear the cause by Lydford law'). The Castle Inn is good.

Morwellham SX4469
MORWELLHAM QUAY In Victorian times Morwellham was the greatest copper port in the Empire; now it houses a thriving open-air museum in lovely countryside, full of costumed guides recreating life during its boom years. Lots to see inc restored cottages complete with pigs in backyard, working blacksmith, cooper, coachmen and quayworkers, rides into the mines, horse-drawn carriages, museums and lovely walks. It's worth watching the introductory slide show to set the scene, and the talks are interesting. Very popular in school holidays; meals, snacks, shop, some disabled access; cl Christmas; £6.50 (reduced price and operations in winter).

North Bovey SX7483 MINIATURE PONY CENTRE (Wormhill Farm) Lots of the friendly little animals, and they don't mind children riding on them; also bigger horses, displays and exhibitions and other animals such as pigs, donkeys, chipmunks and wildfowl. Meals, snacks, shop, good disabled access; cl Nov-Mar; £4.25.

Okehampton SX5895
MUSEUM OF DARTMOOR LIFE Recently expanded three-storey museum in old watermill, with interactive displays and exhibits about life on Dartmoor from prehistoric times onwards, inc tin-mining, reconstructed blacksmith's forge, wheelwright's shop and cider press. Dartmoor Tourist Information Centre and working craft studios are next door; meals, snacks, shop, some disabled access; cl Nov-Easter, Sun Apr, May, Oct; £1.50. The CASTLE tower on a steep grassy mound above the river is remarkable above all for the way it stays standing – a balancing act of ruined masonry zigzagging up into the sky. It's the biggest medieval castle in Devon, with sections dating from 11th to 14th c; good woodland walks.

Snacks, shop; cl 1-2 pm, Mon Oct-Mar, 24-26 Dec, 1 Jan; £1.70.

Roadford Lake SX4291 is a new reservoir, carefully landscaped and recently opened – a peaceful place populated only by brown trout; cl Nov-Mar; £12.50 for a day's permit.

! **Sourton** SX5390 The HIGHWAYMAN is an extraordinary pub, one bar recalling a galleon, the other a sort of fairy-tale fantasy, and the garden demonstrates yet more exuberant imagination – all meticulously done by the owners, not some brewery theme pub; you'll love it or hate it.

Sticklepath SX6494 MUSEUM OF WATERPOWER AND FINCH FOUNDRY No longer producing the sickles, shovels and tools for which it was known in the 19th c, but still has all the waterwheels and machinery working; also display of tools, gallery devoted to water power, occasional craft days. Snacks, shop, limited disabled access; cl Sun exc Jun-Sept, mid-Nov-Mar; £1.80. The thatched Devonshire Inn in the village is 16th-c.

★ † **Widecombe in the Moor** SX7176 is one of the most interesting (and most visited) little villages in the area, immortalised by the trip of Uncle Tom Cobbleigh and all to Widecombe Fair. The granite-carved village sign shows them all crowded on to their old grey mare. The CHURCH is known as the Cathedral of the Moors, and has a distinctive and disproportionately high tower. The adjoining 16th-c CHURCH HOUSE AND SEXTON'S COTTAGE are worth a visit. Church House open Tues and Thurs pm Jun-mid-Sept; adjacent Sexton's Cottage is National Trust and Dartmoor National Park information centre and gift shop, cl 24 Dec-mid-Feb. As well as the little shops there are several places doing nice cream teas, and clotted-cream ice-cream; the reconstructed Olde Inne in the village is very popular with tourists, but for more of a Tom Cobbleigh flavour, try the Rugglestone Inn just outside.

Walks

Dartmoor is outstanding for walking, but you should be aware that mist can come down very suddenly, and if you venture on to the open moor you must carry a compass. A lot of the moor is a long way from the road, hence rather inaccessible. There are more paths for walkers than the right-of-way network suggests, but don't assume a right of way marked on the OS map will be visible on the ground (the black dashed lines on these maps are generally more reliable). Old mineral railways and cart tracks make for some good walkers' routes.

Among the finest paths is **Dr Blackall's Drive** (not named on the OS map), from Bel Tor Corner to New Bridge: this specially created carriage drive gives splendid views of the Dart Valley. Elsewhere, walks are particularly appealing because it's so easy to include something that gives you a destination or a sense of purpose – most strikingly, perhaps, one of the tors (beware: the rounded rocks of the tors themselves can be a good deal more slippery than they look). Among these, one of the most popular (partly because it's easily accessible) is the fortress-like collection of **Haytor Rocks** SX7577, near which is an abandoned quarry that has an unusual 19th-c tramway with grooved-granite rails. In this same general area the majestically monumental **Hound Tor** SX7478 is usually quieter, with an interesting excavated abandoned medieval village nearby. **Honeybag Tor** SX7278 close by has marvellous views over Widecombe (though not shown on the OS map, there's a path to it along the spine of the ridge). A bit further N is the quaint **Bowerman's Nose** SX7480 looking snootily out over a patchwork of pastures. In the west, the **Vixen Tor** SX5474 towering up from the bracken looks unclimbable, but is quite easily reached from behind; this area of the Walkham Valley is relatively lush and green, with old railway tracks from mineral lines which once served local quarries. Near Lustleigh, a ridge path to **Hunter's Tor** SX7682 gives panoramic views of Lustleigh Cleave and the Bovey Valley. Up in the lonelier northern part of the moor, **Yes Tor** SX5890 and **Great Mis Tor** SX5676 have great views over the moor, though as throughout this northern area access is often barred by army firing practice.

The bridges and particularly the stone-slab ancient packhorse clapper bridges also serve as nuclei for strolls and walks. Two attractive and popular ones are those by the roads at **Postbridge** SX6478 and **Dartmeet** SX6773. There are others more isolated if less imposing, such as the one at the head of the Teign river at SX6587, W of Chagford; or the one at SX6277, off the B3212 a couple of miles NE of Two Bridges. A path along the gently graded Devonport Leat (a watercourse first engineered 200 years ago to give Devonport a water supply) in the western moors takes in some remote scenery and makes getting lost quite difficult; it's easily reached off the B3212 NE of Yelverton.

Hundreds of ancient sites exist, but the large majority shown on the OS maps are invisible to all but the most astute archaeologist. The most impressive is by a stream at **Grimspound** SX7080, with a fine old lichened granite cross nearby to mark the way for later medieval travellers. There are numerous hut circles, stone rows and cairns around the upper valley of the **Plym river** SX5866.

Hardened moor walkers use the **Dartmoor letter boxes** as way stations. Another approach to walking here is to use a pub or hotel as a start or finishing point. The Peter Tavy Inn SX5177, Elephants Rest at Horndon SX5280, Forest Hotel at Hexworthy SX6572, East Dart Hotel at Postbridge SX6579, Warren House SX6780 E of there, Plume of Feathers in Princetown SX5873, Dartmoor Inn at Merrivale SX5475 and Two Bridges Hotel at Two Bridges SX6175 are all situated right on the moor, and the Church House at Holne SX7069, Devonshire Inn at Sticklepath SX6494, Highwayman at Sourton SX5390 and Oxenham Arms Hotel at South Zeal SX6593 are close by. Elsewhere, the Anglers Rest at Fingle Bridge SX7499 is outstandingly placed on a particularly lovely wooded stretch of the Dart and has a splendid round-trip walk to Castle Drogo, the Artichoke at Christow SX8383 is quite well placed for the Canonteign waterfalls and country park, and the Church House at Meavy SX5467 and Skylark at Clearbrook SX5265 are both near the wooded River Meavy.

The **Burrator Reservoir** SX5567 gives a five-mile walk in beautiful woodland and moorland surroundings (Sheepstor church on the way has interesting memorials to the Brookes family, former rajahs of Sarawak). **Yarner Wood** SX7778 near Bovey Tracey is a National Nature Reserve and has a nature trail.

Driving

A good road right across the moor is the B3212 (though very slow going once off the moor to the E, where it becomes virtually impossible to overtake crawlers). The B3357 also gives a good visual impression of the moor, and passes a well-defined Bronze-Age site just E of Merrivale. The back road off the B3344 just NW of Manaton southwards towards Ashburton is good.

Where to eat

Gulworthy SX4472 Horn of Plenty A390 just W of Tavistock (0822) 832528 Relaxed restaurant in 17th-c house overlooking the Tamar Valley, with excellent, carefully cooked food inc fresh fish and local meat, lovely puddings and cheeses, good wine list, friendly service, and vine-covered terrace for aperitifs; good bedrooms; children over 13 (though younger are welcome for Sun lunch); disabled access. £23.50|2 courses £14.50; cl Mon am, 25-26 Dec.

Cheriton Bishop SX7793 Old Thatch (0647) 24204 Welcoming 16th-c inn with good bar food from big menu inc interesting puddings; cl 1st 2 wks Nov; no children. £1.85/£4.25.

Bridestowe SX5189 White Hart Friendly 17th-c village inn with consistently good food in pleasant restaurant, good bar food too; bedrooms; fishing nearby; no children in bar (allowed in restaurant). £20|£2/£3.95.

South Devon

South Devon offers intimate coastal scenery, attractive seaside towns of considerable character, interesting places to visit – not to mention Torbay.

Dartmouth has particular charm as a place for a weekend break or short stay at any time of year, and many parts of the coast and countryside here share its intimate, relaxed and unshowy appeal, as does Totnes. By contrast, there are the promenades, low cliffs, bright gardens and palm trees of Torbay and its English Riviera. And at the opposite end of this stretch of coast busy Plymouth has some interesting and unusual rainy-day attractions.

Inland, the countryside is typified by well-hedged hilly pastures, small combes and steeply wooded valleys, and occasional vividly deep-red earth fields. The coast has an intricate mixture of small coves, stretches of cliff, and sheltered creeks and estuaries cut deeply into the coastal hills – very popular in summer with sailors.

Among a good choice of things to do and places to visit, highlights are the steam railway between Buckfastleigh and Totnes (perhaps combined with a river trip), magnificent Saltram near Plympton, Coleton Fishacre garden at Kingswear, Powderham Castle, Paignton Zoo, Overbecks garden near Salcombe, and the shire-horse centre at Dunstone. There are some beautifully situated places to stay.

We welcome reports from readers . . .

Let us know what you think of places in the Guide, and any special tips you have. There are report forms at the back of the book, and a card in the middle.

Where to stay

Burgh Island SX6443 BURGH ISLAND Bigbury-on-Sea TQ7 4AU (0548) 810514 **£156 inc dinner**; 14 Art Deco seaview suites, most with balconies. Cut-off small island – access by hotel Land-Rover (or foot) at low tide, seagoing summer tractor-on-stilts at high tide, 300-yd crossing from Bigbury. Lovingly extravagant 1930s restoration: domed palm court, sun lounge, classic cocktail bar. Tennis, mini gym, snooker, walks, and sea fishing. Island has romantic 14th-c pub – and summer crowds. No dogs; cl Mon-Thurs Jan/Feb.
Torquay SX9264 IMPERIAL Park Hill Rd TQ1 2DG (0803) 294301 **£140**; 167 rms. Modern-looking Forte resort hotel in commanding spot just above sea; fitness centre etc, heated indoor and outdoor pools, lots to do, good programme of event wknds.
Malborough (2m S) SX7037 SOAR MILL COVE Salcombe TQ7 3DS (0548) 561566 ***£120**; 16 comfortable rms. Idyllic spot in peaceful and very beautiful cove on NT coast (excellent walks); single-storey building with lovely views, extensive private grounds, tennis/putting, very warm indoor pool; outstanding service, log fires, very good food inc local produce esp fish, good wines; thoughtful early-evening children's meal; cl Nov-Jan; disabled access.
Salcombe SX7337 TIDES REACH South Sands TQ8 8LJ (0548) 843466 **£104**; 38 rms, many with estuary views. Unusually individual resort hotel run by long-standing owners and set in pretty wooded cove by the sea; airy luxury day rooms, restaurant strong on fresh fish, friendly, efficient service; squash, snooker, leisure complex, health area, and big heated pool; windsurfing etc, beach over lane, coast walks; cl Nov-Mar; children over 8.
Goveton (just E) SX7546 BUCKLAND-TOUT-SAINTS Kingsbridge TQ7 2DS (0548) 853055 **£100**; 12 luxuriously period rms. Handsome Queen Anne mansion in well-kept grounds with croquet/putting; antiques, panelling, fine plasterwork; imaginative food using good local produce in no-smoking restaurant, notable wines, excellent personal service; children and dogs by arrangement.
Galmpton SX8754 LOST & FOUND Maypool Churston TQ5 0ET (0803) 842442 **£71**; 16 rms. Down tree-lined quiet lane, overlooking Dart estuary – steam train runs below. A mile from ferries to Dittisham or Dartmouth. Peaceful and clean; cheerful friendly service, decent food in several dining rooms or out on attractive terrace, good bar.
Dartmouth SX8751 ROYAL CASTLE 11 The Quay TQ6 9PS (0803) 8330333 ***£70w**; 25 rms. Well-restored Georgian hotel overlooking the inner harbour – great views from most rooms – with 16th-c core; all-day lively and interesting public bar, quiet library/lounge, winter spit-roasts in lounge bar, elegant upstairs seafood restaurant, decent bar food, friendly staff; live music Weds, Thurs, Sun.
Ermington SX6353 ERMEWOOD HOUSE Totnes Rd Modbury PL21 9NS (0548) 830741 ***£60**; 12 decent rms, front with view but some traffic noise, back quiet. Ex-rectory with fine log fire in lounge, drinks terrace over garden, pleasant dining room, decent wines, and amiable service; cl Christmas and New Year; children over 12.
Plymouth SX4775 MAYFLOWER POST HOUSE Cliff Rd The Hoe PL1 3DL (0752) 662828 **£55.40w**; 106 comfortable rms, most with great views of the Sound – as have day rooms. Big Forte hotel, but friendly atmosphere, good parking (at a premium here), heated indoor pool etc.
Ashprington SX8157 WATERMANS ARMS Tuckenhay Rd Bow Bridge Totnes TQ9 7EG (0803) 732214 **£57**; 10 comfortable rms. Nice old inn with upstairs

residents' lounge, beamed and flagstoned bar, decent bar food, evening restaurant, caring staff, and riverside tables; over quiet lane from tidal creek; pets welcome.

Dartington SX7762 COTT Totnes TQ9 6HE (0803) 863777 **£50**; 6 character rms, some cheaper share bthrm. Ancient inn with fine thatched roof (the longest in S England); heavy-beamed communicating rooms with open fires, good food and wines (lots by the glass), no-smoking restaurant, and good nearby walks.

Totnes SX8060 OLD FORGE Seymour Pl TQ9 5AY (0803) 862174) **£50**; 10 rms, 2 with shared bthrm. Carefully restored 600-year-old building, still a working forge, with lounge, good breakfasts, and big walled garden; good disabled access.

Blackawton SX8050 NORMANDY ARMS Totnes TQ9 7BN (080 421) 316 **£48**; 4 pretty rms. Quaint, friendly pub in quiet village, with decent generous food in bar and restaurant; cl 24-26 Dec.

Staverton SX7964 SEA TROUT Totnes TQ9 6PA (0803) 762274 **£48**; 10 newly decorated cottagey rms. Comfortable pub in quiet hamlet near River Dart, with decent bar food, and new dining conservatory and terraced garden with fountains and waterfalls; cl Christmas; children over 7.

Aveton Gifford SX6947 COURT BARTON FARMHOUSE Kingsbridge TQ7 4LE (0548) 550312 **£42**; 7 rms, 1 with shared bthrm. Pretty creeper-clad 16th-c farmhouse on 300 acres of arable land, with log fire, cosy lounge, and warm welcome; cl Christmas.

Frogmore SX7742 GLOBE Kingsbridge TQ7 2NR (0548) 531351 **£40**; 6 rms, most with own bthrm. 18th-c inn with pleasant atmosphere, friendly owners, bar snacks, evening meals and summer-afternoon teas.

Ermington SX6353 CROOKED SPIRE Ivybridge PL21 9LP (0548) 830202 **£35**; 3 decent rms, shared bthrm. Friendly village pub with generous fresh food and good service.

Slapton SX6643 TOWER Kingsbridge TQ7 2PN (0548) 580216 **£34**; 3 simple rms, shared bthrm. Ancient pub under ivy-covered ruined tower in steep village near Slapton Sands and Ley, with informal, young atmosphere (many real ales) and some simple Italian food (Italian part-owner) in bar and small restaurant; decent garden.

Topsham Bridge SX7351 YEO FARM Kingsbridge TQ7 4DR (0548) 550586 **£31**; 3 rms. Friendly, relaxed farmhouse B & B, right by Avon (with one mile of salmon fishing), plump friendly labradors, peaceful sheep-farm surroundings, and good walks; small touring-caravan site too; cl Christmas.

Hazlewood SX7148 CRANNACOMBE FARM Loddiswell Kingsbridge TQ7 4DX (0548) 550256 **£31**; 2 rms. Quietly set Georgian farmhouse on working farm with prize-winning cider, hearty food, and fine views; cl Christmas.

To see and do

Dartmouth SX8751 Charming waterside small town with many exceptional buildings, especially around the inner harbour. Though so popular, it's kept its own strong character, and stays very much alive through the winter. Cobbled Bayards Cove, with old fort and steep wooded hills behind, is particularly photogenic, as is pedestrianised Foss St. Markets Tues, Fri: Old Market is picturesque. The Royal Naval College is a striking building. Interesting shops, plenty of waterside seats, lots of action on the river. Parking in summer can be trying; best to use good park-and-ride on B3207 Halwell Rd.

RIVER TRIPS up to Totnes pass some of Devon's prettiest scenery that is impossible to walk or drive by; can combine with steam trains (see above) or connecting bus back – which saves hearing the commentary a second time; tel (0803) 832109 for details; cl Nov-Easter; £5 return. Also quaint car and pedestrian ferries to Kingswear and A379 (can be 2-hr car wait at peak summer times).

MUSEUM (The Butterwalk, Duke St) Well-restored 17th-c timbered house with rich panelling and plasterwork, largely nautical local displays, lots of ship models; shop, some disabled access; 70p.

CASTLE Classic late 15th-c battlemented fortress, cannon and later gun batteries, port for raising harbourmouth blockade chain. Shop; cl 1-2 pm and Mon from Oct-Easter; £1.70.

ST SAVIOUR'S Lots of charming detail, well worth a close look, inc altar, pulpit, painted rood screen, brasses on chancel floor, elaborate 14th-c hinges on S door.

NEWCOMEN ENGINE HOUSE (Royal Ave Gdns) Huge steam-powered atmospheric beam-engine pump, perhaps the world's oldest, worked 1720-1913; shop, disabled access; cl winter 1-2 pm and Suns in summer 12.30-1 pm for lunch, all day Sun in winter, 24-26 Dec; *50p.

HENLEY MUSEUM (Anzac St) has a collection of local history and botany, worth a look if passing; cl Oct-May; *25p.

Paignton SX8960 Down by the sea this is a typical resort, with long promenade between good sandy beach and green; but the little harbour is pretty, with working fishing boats as well as yachts. The original inland core has an attractive red sandstone church with some interesting buildings nearby, esp KIRKHAM HOUSE, a handsome sandstone Tudor merchant's

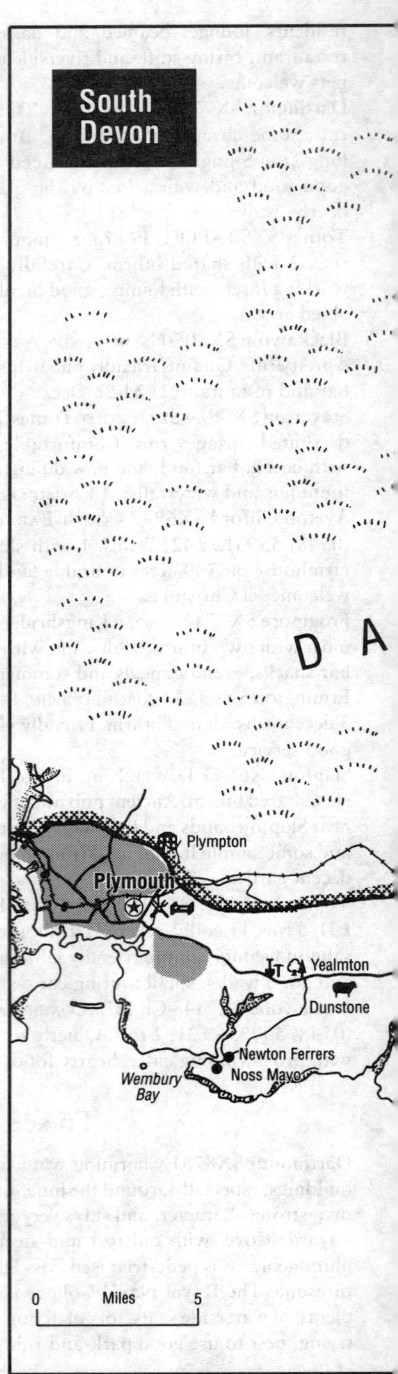

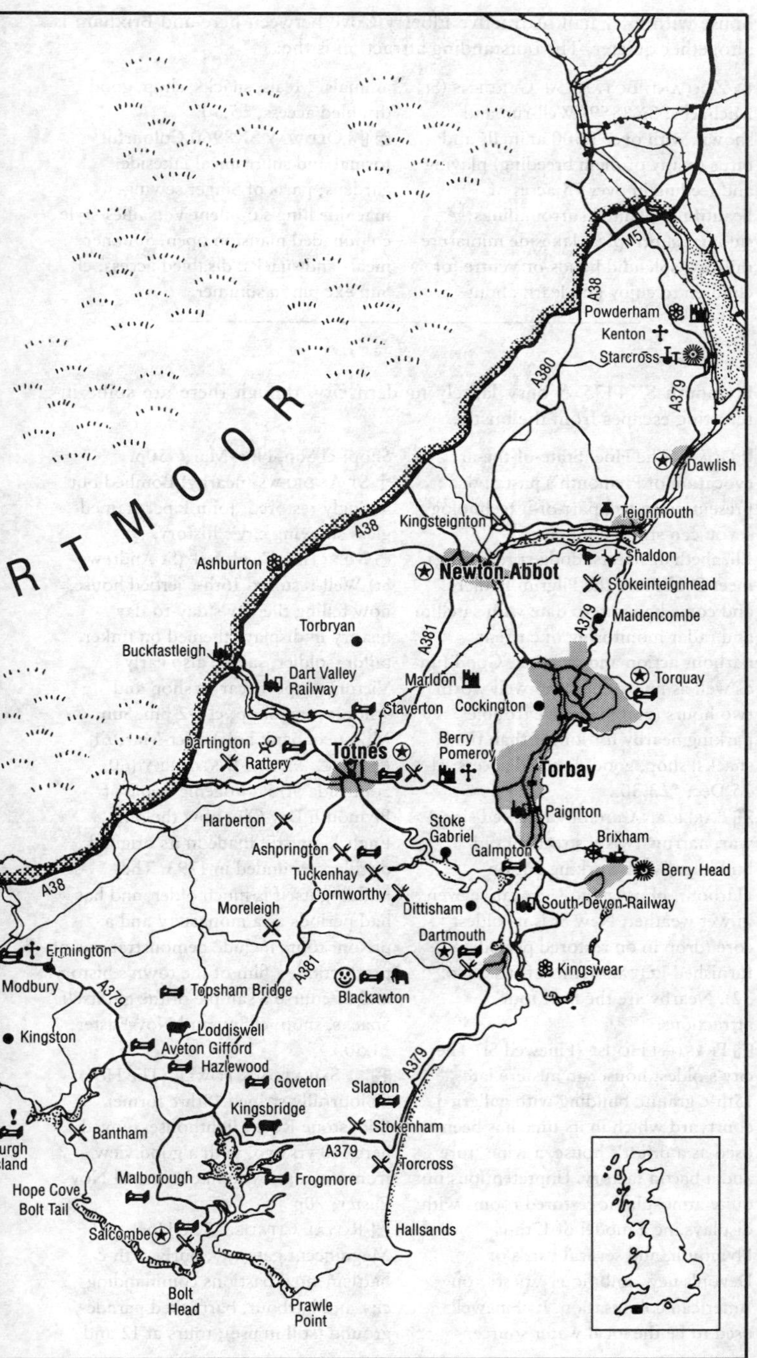
DARTMOOR
A38
M5
A380
A379
A381
Powderham
Kenton
Starcross
Dawlish
Teignmouth
Kingsteignton
Shaldon
Newton Abbot
Stokeinteignhead
Ashburton
Maidencombe
Torbryan
Buckfastleigh
Dart Valley Railway
Marldon
Torquay
Staverton
Cockington
Dartington
Rattery
Totnes
Berry Pomeroy
Torbay
Paignton
Harberton
Stoke Gabriel
Brixham
Ashprington
Galmpton
Berry Head
Tuckenhay
Cornworthy
Moreleigh
Dittisham
South Devon Railway
Dartmouth
Ermington
Kingswear
Modbury
Topsham Bridge
Blackawton
Kingston
Loddiswell
Aveton Gifford
Hazlewood
Goveton
Slapton
Kingsbridge
Stokenham
Bantham
Burgh Island
Torcross
Malborough
Frogmore
Hope Cove
Bolt Tail
Hallsands
Salcombe
Bolt Head
Prawle Point

house with lofty hall. Attractive Elberry Cove between here and Brixham is altogether quieter. The outstanding attraction is the:

ZOO AND BOTANICAL GARDENS (St Michael's; SX8859) Well-run and shown, with over 1,300 animals and birds (many of them breeding) playing and feeding in over 75 acres of beautifully planted surroundings; summer subtropical lakeside miniature railway, splendid hands-on centre for children to enjoy and learn about animals. Meals, snacks, shop, good disabled access; £5.50.

OLDWAY SX8960 Colourful formal and subtropical lakeside gardens; parts of Singer sewing-machine king's opulent Versailles-style colonnaded mansion open. Summer meals and snacks, disabled access; cl Sun exc pm in summer.

Plymouth SX4475 A busy largely modern city, though there are some interesting escapes from the bustle.

DOME (The Hoe) State-of-the-art evocation of Plymouth's past and present using feel-part-of-it technology – you can stroll along lively Elizabethan streets, dodge press gangs, meet Drake and the Pilgrim Fathers, and come bang up to date with satellite and radar monitoring of current harbour action and weather. Good fun as well as interesting, and well worth two hours (you may have trouble parking nearby for longer than that); snacks, shop, good disabled access; cl 25 Dec; *£3.30.

BARBICAN Carefully restored since war, narrow twisty streets of old buildings W of working Sutton Harbour, photogenic – evocative even in wet weather. New St is its oldest core (drop in on restored period-furnished ELIZABETHAN HOUSE, No. 32). Nearby are the next four attractions:

PRYSTEN HOUSE (Finewell St) The city's oldest house, an austere late 15th-c granite building with galleried courtyard which in its time has been used as a priest's house, a wine store and a bacon factory. Unpretentious but quite atmospheric restored rooms with displays inc a model of 17th-c Plymouth, and several yards of Devon's new ambitious tapestry on American colonisation. Its Finewell used to be the local water source. Shop; cl Sun, Nov-Mar; *50p.

ST ANDREWS (nearby) Bombed but lovingly restored, John Piper stained glass showing city's history.

MERCHANT'S HOUSE (St Andrews St) Well-restored 16th-c jettied house, now telling the city's day-to-day history in displays themed on tinker, tailor, soldier, sailor; also early Victorian apothecary's shop and schoolroom. Shop; cl 1-2 pm, Sun, Mon (exc bank hols), Oct-Mar; £1.

BLACK FRIARS DISTILLERY (60 Southside St) Photogenic home of Plymouth Dry Gin, now the only English gin still made in its original distillery, founded in 1793. The building itself is much older, and has had periods as a monastery and a prison; tours include demonstrations of production, a film of the town's history and of course a sample of the gin itself. Snacks, shop; cl Sun and Nov-Easter; £1.50.

SMEATON'S TOWER (The Hoe) Colourfully striped 18th-c former Eddystone Rocks lighthouse, moved here 110 yrs ago, with a good view from the top if you like steps. Cl Nov-Easter; 70p.

ROYAL CITADEL (The Hoe) Magnificent gateway, burly 17th-c battlemented bastions commanding city and harbour, barracked parade-ground (still in use); tours at 12 and

2 pm May-Sept; £2.50.

AQUARIUM (just outside Citadel) Comprehensive collection of sea fish, crustaceans etc, run by scientific institution; shop, disabled access; cl 25-26 Dec; £2.

TAMAR CRUISES (Mayflower Steps, off Madeira Rd, Barbican) 1-hr commented boat trips of the naval fortifications, warships etc. £2.50.

CITY MUSEUM (Drake Circus) Well-shown collections of prints, drawings, archaeological displays and natural history, esp West Country interest; changing art shows. Snacks, shop, disabled access; cl Sun am, Mon (exc bank hols).

Totnes SX8060 Picturesque Elizabethan area known as THE NARROWS, esp High St down to arch at top of Fore St, with quaint pillared arcades. Bustling on Tues May-Sept, when many traders wear Elizabethan costume. There may be horse-drawn omnibus rides down at Steamer Quay in summer; fun for children. See above for excellent Dartmouth river trips; working harbour too. You can walk some way downstream on either side of the River Dart.

CASTLE Part Norman, part 14th-c, these classic circular remains were lucky enough to avoid any battles, so the keep is pretty much intact. There's a tree-shaded inner lawn, and lovely views of the town and down to the river. Shop; cl 1-2 pm, Mon Oct-Easter; *£1.30.

BOWDEN HOUSE (Ashprington Rd, S; SX8059) Costumed guides for handsomely restored grand Tudor and baroque rooms with weaponry, and separate PHOTOGRAPHY MUSEUM with still and moving pictures (inc cartoons) in attractive grounds. Snacks, disabled access to museum only; open Mar-Oct Tues-Thurs, and bank hol Sun and Mon Apr-Sept, cl Sun but is car boot-sale then; £2.50 for museum or house only, £4 combined.

MUSEUM (70 Fore St) Stately Elizabethan merchant's house with galleried courtyard, herb garden, local costumes, bygones and oddities, Victorian toys and shop, inventions of local Charles Babbage inc ancestral computer. Shop; cl lunchtime (except July, Aug), Sat (except July, Aug), Sun, Nov-mid-Mar; 60p.

MOTOR MUSEUM (Steamer Quay) Mainly vintage and racing cars and motorcycles, all good runners, even an amphibious Amphicar; shop, disabled access to ground floor only; cl Nov-Easter; £2.80.

DEVONSHIRE COLLECTION OF PERIOD COSTUME (43 High St) Good collection of period costumes and accessories from the 18th c to the present day, ranging from high fashion to ordinary work clothes, with changing annual exhibitions, and useful background explanations; shop; cl Sat am, Sun, Oct-May; *£1.

Torquay SX9264 Palm trees and rocks, promenades, colourful gardens, decorous guesthouses and huge hotels, broad Victorian streets, apparently recession-proof smooth shops, sheltered red beaches; summer bustle around attractive harbour with lots of shops, boat trips, aquarium.

! MODEL VILLAGE (Hampton Ave, Babbacombe; SX9265) Town and village scenes with extensive model railway, sound effects, summer-night lighting; hundreds of buildings in 4 acres of miniaturised landscape, very touristy but beautifully done. Shop, good disabled access; £3.40 + parking.

KENTS CAVERN (Wellswood; SX9264) Striking well-lit caves, with colourful stalagmites and stalactites, and its highly important archaeological past dramatised by well-guided tours; summer snacks, shop, disabled access (with prior notice); cl 25 Dec; £3.

TORRE ABBEY (Kings Dr; SX9063) Some of the earlier parts of the abbey remain, inc the medieval sandstone gatehouse, ruined Norman tower, and tithe barn, but have been eclipsed by the later house with its 17th-, 18th- and 19th-c period rooms. There's an art gallery, showy garden and palm house and the Agatha Christie room full of possessions of the author, who was born in Torquay. Snacks, shop; cl Nov-Mar exc by appointment; £2.

BYGONES (Fore St, St Marychurch; SX9166) Reconstructed life-sized Victorian street, with period shops and rooms and upstairs a big model railway and fantasyland. Café, shop; *£2.50.

MUSEUM (529 Babbacombe Rd) Impressive archaeological and natural-history displays inc fascinating finds from Ice Age and older Devon caves, as well as local bygones and pictures; shop; cl Sat exc Easter-Oct, Sun exc pm July, Aug, Sept; *£1.75.

★ COCKINGTON SX8963 Winding lanes of olde-worlde thatched cottages and bric-a-brac/craft shops in sheltered village with millpond etc, well preserved by Torbay Council. The matching pub was actually designed by Lutyens in 1934. Frightfully pretty, very touristy in summer, with open horse-drawn carriages.

! CLIFF RAILWAY SX9265 Dizzy swoop from Oddicombe Beach to high wooded clifftop; disabled access; cl Oct-Easter; 40p each way.

Other things to see and do

Ashburton SX7569 RIVER DART COUNTRY PARK is pleasant for walking or fishing, with adventure playgrounds for children (cl Oct-Mar; £3.55).

Berry Head SX9456 has tremendous coast, sea and shipping views from ex-quarry country park; squat lighthouse, formidable Napoleonic War battlements with cannon (and guardhouse café), nature trail takes in kittiwakes and guillemots on cliffs, uncommon plants.

✝ **Berry Pomeroy** (off A385 just E of Totnes; keep on past village) SX8362 CASTLE Massive Norman gatehouse and wall around imposing ruined Tudor mansion, hidden away on crag over quiet wooded valley. Very haunted, and with an interesting 15th-c fresco inside. Snacks, shop, disabled access; cl Oct-Mar; *£1.70. The red sandstone 15th-c village CHURCH is worth a look on the way; odd monument in Seymour Chapel.

☺ **Blackawton** SX8050 WOODLAND LEISURE PARK Parkland with extensive play areas from toddlers' village to scary mega slides; also a little zoo with wallabies, llamas and foreign birds. Meals, snacks, shop, disabled access; £3.50.

Brixham SX9256 Busy fishing port, lots of activity (and summer seaside shops and cafés) in harbour, some pretty, narrow streets on hill above. Summer boats around Torbay. MUSEUM (Bolton Cross) Local history museum with good trawler, boatbuilding and coastguard displays inc models and reconstructions, as well as costumes, lace and other antiquities, with an old fisherman's cottage; shop, mostly disabled access; cl Sun, Nov-Easter; £1.20.

Buckfastleigh SOUTH DEVON RAILWAY GWR steam train along wooded River Dart – lovely unspoilt scenery. Stops at Staverton (and at interesting restored Victorian Littlehempston, but no exit/access here yet), and you can combine it with river trip Dartmouth-Totnes and bus link Totnes-Buckfastleigh. Usually every 1½ hrs summer, less often other times; cl Nov-Mar, some days Apr, May, Oct, Santa trains Dec – (0364) 42338 for times; £5.20.

! **Burgh Island** SX6443 Across the broad tidal sands from Bigbury-on-Sea, a true island and quite remote-seeming when the tide's in – in summer an odd giant tractor-on-stilts wades back and forth with passengers.

Dartington SX8062 CIDER PRESS CRAFT CENTRE A cluster of 16th- and 17th-c buildings with craft shops, farm foods, herbs and such, and restaurants, inc a good vegetarian one; the surroundings add a lot to the attraction, with nearby medieval great hall on photogenic lawned courtyard, sculpture gardens, and streamside nature trail. Cl Sun and 25-26 Dec.

Dawlish SX9879 DAWLISH WARREN Sandy grassy spit (with golf course) largely blocking in Exe estuary, glistening tidal flats full of wading birds, dunes with some rare plants. In summer get well out to the point, to avoid the seaside tat, crowds and caravan parks at the station end; in winter it's splendidly wild and blowy, with thousands of ducks, brent-geese and waders (even avocets) congregating at high tide to wait till the mudflats show again; spring/autumn migrants. (0626) 8863980 for guided summer nature walks; £1. The TOWN just S (SX9676) is an old-fashioned small resort with modern developments and camps outside; red sandstone cliffs, good beach, waterside parks with black swans, prom, pier; the mainline railway cut through the cliffs right by the water is striking. MUSEUM (Knowle House, Barton Terr) Victorian room reconstructions, local pictures, costumes, toys, railway and military memorabilia; disabled access to ground floor only; cl Sun am and Oct-Apr; *70p.

Dunstone SX5951 NATIONAL SHIRE HORSE CENTRE A good fine-weather family outing, with shire horses and foals, waggon rides, smithy and saddlery, butterfly house, adventure playground and pets' corner – you can get right up to the animals. Ranks of benching to watch caparisoned horses parading 11.30 am, 2.30 pm, 4.15 pm, falconry displays at 1.00 pm and 3.30 pm. Meals, snacks, shop and craft centre, disabled access; cl 24-26 Dec; *£5.50, reduced rates in winter as less displays.

★ **Kingsbridge** SX7344 Small town of character, pretty cobbled lanes diving off steep Fore St, arcaded shops, pillared market house (market day Weds), interesting monuments in church, boats on tidal estuary (and ferry to Salcombe), decent pubs – esp waterfront Crabshell. COOKWORTHY MUSEUM (Fore St) Lively local-history museum in 17th-c grammar school, with Victorian rooms and Edwardian pharmacy reconstructions, farm, cider-making and other local bygones. Shop; cl Sun, Oct wknds, Nov-Mar; *£1.40.

Kingswear (2m E, off Lower Ferry Rd at Tollhouse) SX9050 COLETON FISHACRE D'Oyly Carte's romantic and lush subtropical garden, with 20 colourful acres dropping down to a pretty cove; formal terraces, walled garden with stream-fed ponds, unusual trees and shrubs, grassy woodland paths. Snacks, some disabled access; cl Mon, Tues, Sat, Nov-Mar (exc Sun pm Mar); *£2.60. NT. More ambitious marked paths beyond the gardens take you along the cliffs, showing how wild this part was before the garden was planted.

Loddiswell (Lilwell) SX7148 VINEYARD 10 acres, part under polythene, producing award-winning medium wines; tastings and wine-making videos. Snacks, shop with herbs and vines for sale (also open Fri), disabled access; cl am, Sat, Sun (exc July and Aug and bank hol wknds), guided tours at 2.15 pm and 4 pm; tours *£2.50, walkabouts *£1.50.

Marldon (1m N, off A3022; or off A381 at Ipplepen turnoff) SX8664 COMPTON CASTLE Formidably fortified and rather picturesque 14th- and 16th-c manor around courtyard with portcullised entrance, particularly interesting for its completeness; galleried great hall, ancient kitchen, chapel and rose garden. Snacks, shop, some disabled access; cl 12.15-2 pm, Tues, Fri-Sun, Nov-Mar; £2.60. NT.

★ **Modbury** SX6551 has attractive buildings esp in steep Church St, with quite photogenic church at top and pretty Exeter Inn (good pub) at bottom. Brownston St quite interesting too, esp ornate water conduit at top.

Newton Abbot SX8671 PLANT WORLD (St Marychurch Rd) Quite a wacky little garden, built and planted as a giant map of the world, with all the countries containing their correct native plants, trees and flowers – many of them quite rare in this country, but flourishing in the mild Devon climate. Children can climb up Mount Everest while parents perhaps take more pleasure in seeing what grows there. Also a good plant centre (with seeds of some of the rarest plants), old-fashioned English garden and fine views; disabled access to plant centre only; 50p for garden. TUCKERS MALTINGS (Teign Rd) One of the few remaining working malthouses in the country, and the only one open to the public – every year they produce enough malt for 15 million pints of beer. The tours show all aspects of malting (you can touch the grain and taste the malt) and there's a reconstructed old street; meals, snacks, shop; cl Sat, Nov-Easter; *£3.25. BRADLEY MANOR (off A381 S) Peaceful 15th-c house nr stream through extensive wood-fringed grounds, quiet walks. Open Wed pm Apr-Sept; *£2.60. NT.

★ **Newton Ferrers/Noss Mayo** SX5447 Picturesque twin villages on very sheltered rocky wooded creek of Yealm estuary; besides modern development some attractive whitewashed cottages; lots of yachting in summer, fine setting.

Paignton/Kingswear SX8960/SX8851 DART VALLEY RAILWAY GWR steam train runs right by sea along Torbay (halts at Goodrington Beach, which has closer parking, and Churston), then along Dart estuary to Kingswear. The front Pullman coach is less crowded, and there's a model railway at the Paignton end. Can combine with boat Dartmouth-Totnes, bus Totnes-Paignton. Every 45 mins high summer, less often other times; buffet, disabled access; cl Nov-Mar exc some of Dec, and maybe other days out of season, (0803) 555872 for times; £5.20.

★ **Plympton** (2m W, off A38/A379 at Marsh Mills roundabout) SX5255 SALTRAM Magnificent George II furnishings, decoration and paintings (strong on Reynolds) in NT mansion, interesting period kitchen, stately garden with orangery, parkland by wooded Plym estuary. Restaurant, gift shop, local-art/crafts gallery, disabled access; cl Nov-Mar; £5, garden only £2.20, parking may be extra. NT. The OLD TOWN around St Maurice Church is worth a look if you're here: attractive partly arcaded streets, very ruined motte and bailey castle.

Powderham SX9683 CASTLE The ancestral home of the Earls of Devon, badly damaged in the Civil War but grandly restored in the 18th and 19th c, with rich decorations and furnishings. Spectacular rose garden, broad deer park with good views over Exe estuary; meals, snacks, shop, some disabled access; cl Sat, Oct-Easter; £3.95.

★ **Salcombe** SX7337 Steep narrow-streets fishing village, full of enjoyable holiday bustle in summer, with lots of souvenirs, bric-a-brac, boating shops, teashops and pubs overlooking sea, nearby beaches and coves. BOAT trips and boat hire. OVERBECKS SX7237 (South Sands; also signed from Malborough) Luscious terraced plantings among woodland, many rarities inc subtropical, lushly framing glorious estuary views. Also colourful statue garden, picnic belvedere and toys, odd devices and taxidermy in quaint museum; outstanding late May-June for the magnolias, but worth a trip any time of year. Snacks, shop; cl Sat and Nov-Mar; £3.40. NT.

★ **Shaldon** SX9372 Interesting and colourful mix of seaside houses spanning 200 years of architectural fancy, some lovely corners esp down by water away from the centre, also much older cottages in Crown Sq. High grassy sandstone Ness overlooks sea and Teignmouth, tunnel cut by 19th-c landowner to sheltered beach. WILDLIFE TRUST (Ness Dr) Breeding collection of rare and endangered foreign birds, and small mammals inc monkeys; cl 25 Dec; *£2.30.

Starcross SX9781 ATMOSPHERIC RAILWAY Enthusiastically displayed relics and working model of experimental 1845 vacuum-powered railway; tower views. Cl wkdys Oct-Easter; £2.

★ **Stoke Gabriel** SX8457 is a steep village above a sheltered side-pool of the Dart estuary, with 14th-c church (with ancient yew) and associated pub perched prettily on a high cobbled terrace.

Teignmouth (French St) SX9473 MUSEUM Shipwreck salvage and pictures, local bygones; £1. The resort town, with some handsome 19th-c streets and active docks, is very popular for family holidays, with good beaches, windsurfing etc.

Yealmpton SX5751 KITLEY CAVES Tours of stunning illuminated caves; 50 acres of pretty woodland and riverside walks; lots of varieties of plants, shrubs and trees, displays and exhibitions and the story of the creator of Old Mother Hubbard and her canine companion. Snacks, shop; cl Nov-Good Fri; £2.90.

✝ Good CHURCHES at **Ermington** SX6353, where there's a crooked 14th-c stone spire above tower (Victorian rebuilding kept the tilt), and **Kenton** SX9583, its harmonious medieval sandstone masonry photographing well against blue sky; fine carving inside.

Other attractive villages, all worth looking at if you're near, and all with decent pubs, include Dittisham (SX8654), Harberton (SX7758), Maidencombe (SX9268), Rattery (SX7461), Slapton (SX8244), Stokeinteignhead (SX9170, Stokenham (SX8042) and Torbryan SX8266.

Walks

The coast path is the main attraction for walkers. The finest part of Devon's southern seaboard is between Plymouth and Brixham – much of it quite unspoilt. In summer ferries cross the Rivers (except the River Erme S of Ermington, which you have to cross at low tide). **Bolt Head/Bolt Tail** is 6 miles of one of the best coast-path sections, with remote exposed clifftops, glorious coves, far views; all NT. Well-preserved earth ramparts of Iron-Age fort on Bolt Tail. Best access via Overbecks SX7237, Soar Mill Cove SX7037 or Hope Cove SX6739. **Prawle Point** SX7735 further E also has impressive scenery; wind-blasted gorse, grass and thrift above low but fierce cliffs, lending itself to a round walk, with a useful network of green lanes leading inland to the village of East Prawle SX7836 (where the Pigs Nose is a useful stop). **Dartmouth Castle** and **Compass Cove** SX8849 make an enjoyable excursion on foot, though the immediate hinterland is unremarkable.

Slapton Sands are 6 miles of almost straight shingle N of the lighthouse at

Start Point SX8337, backed by hills in the S and by road, shingle bank, lake (Slapton Ley nature reserve, marked nature trail) and marsh, then low cliffs, in the N. Good for out-of-season desolation, sheltered from W winds. Storm-ruined village at Hallsands SX8138, salvaged tank memorial to US Normandy landings practice at Torcross SX8242. Take-away picnics from Green Dragon at Stoke Fleming (A379 N).

There are attractive walks by the wooded **Yealm estuary** from Noss Mayo SX5447, then beyond to Gara Point SX5246 and exposed cliff; largely NT. Can be reached in sections via coastal ridge rd Noss Mayo-Holbeton.

Bantham sands allow a gentle walk through the dunes from Bantham SX6643 to the broad stretch of rivermouth sand facing Burgh Island. You can go on above the rocks S, for views of Bolt Tail and the coves between. **Wembury Bay** is also a walk with good views, from Wembury SX5248 past church at start of NT clifftops; woods and pastures on opposite shore, Plymouth shipping in the distance.

Other good places for walks include Lannacombe beach (SX8837; hillside tracks above turbulent rocky shore); Loddiswell (SX7248; cross river by lane towards Woodsleigh, then quiet walk upstream by riverside pastures and woods towards Topsham Bridge); Tuckenhay (SX8156; a pretty mile E along wooded Bow Creek from Maltsters Arms); Kingston (SX6347; several walks down to unspoilt beach).

Driving

Pretty or interesting stretches of road include parts of the A384 Buckfastleigh-Totnes; A379 Shaldon-Maidencombe (sea views), and Stoke Fleming-Stokenham; B3210 Totnes-Ermington; B3210 off A38 S of South Brent, continuing from Avonwick on back road Diptford-Moreleigh (can link with next suggestion); back road to Slapton signposted off A381 a mile or so S of Halwell; coast road along Kingsbridge estuary, S of South Pool; Ashburton-Woolston Green-Littlehempston-Berry Pomeroy-Stoke Gabriel; coast ridge road Holbeton-Noss Mayo. If you want to do much driving here, come out of season: in summer, negotiating the narrow lanes can be very slow and frustrating.

The A38 is the backbone of getting around here, fast except at the worst summer peaks: it's a pleasant road, too, with good views. The A380 is fairly fast out of season. On other main roads, be prepared for slowish traffic at almost any time of year, and reckon to go really slowly on most back roads (though the milk tankers seem to use them as race tracks). As an example, allow 50 mins to an hour to get to Dartmouth from the end of the M5 – longer at peak holiday times. From most places here you can get well into Dartmoor by car in about an hour or less.

Where to eat

Dartmouth SX8751 CARVED ANGEL South Embankment (0803) 832465 Subtly tuned yet unpretentious combinations of unexpected flavours with carefully chosen fresh ingredients make for memorable meals in outstanding restaurant, smart yet friendly, with a view of the kitchen on one side and the water on the other; fine wines at every price range; cl Sun pm, Mon, Christmas, 6 wks from early Jan. **£34.50 lunch, £49.50 dinner.**

Tuckenhay SX8156 MALTSTERS ARMS (0803) 732350 Known also as FLOYD'S INN, this airy, popular restaurant – overlooking a picturesque creek – offers enterprising cooking using first-class ingredients; the old-fashioned back bar serves good bar food. **£35**|£7.50.

Plymouth SX4755 Chez Nous 13 Frankfort Gate (0752) 266793 Proper French bistro with careful cooking of fresh local produce, esp fresh fish and fine puddings, some distinguished wines, and friendly atmosphere; cl Sun/Mon, 3 wks Feb, 2 wks Sept; children over 8. **£26**|£17.

Plymouth SX4755 China House Sutton Harbour via Sutton Rd off A374 (0752) 260930 Well-converted 17th-c waterside warehouse above marina, very lofty and spacious, with beams, log fire, flagstones and bare slate, nautical decorations, and first-floor dining area which becomes evening restaurant; good disabled access. **£18**|£2.50/£4.90.

Cornworthy SX8255 Hunters Lodge (0803) 732204 Unpretentious country local, with cottagey log-fire restaurant and tables on big lawn, serving remarkable range of interestingly cooked generous food. **£18**|£1.90/£4.25.

Dartmouth SX8751 Cherub Higher St (080 43) 2571 Interesting seafood specialities in one of Dartmouth's most ancient and picturesque buildings. Children in upstairs restaurant only. **£18**|£1.95/£4.25.

Stokeinteignhead SX9170 Church House (0803) 865555 Wide choice of good-value food from simple snacks to lobster inc children's menu in picturesque 13th-c thatched inn's beamed bar and restaurant; nice back garden. **£16.80**|£2.10/£5.25.

Ashprington SX8156 Durant Arms (0803) 732 240 Friendly gable-ended cottage with good, pubby atmosphere and decent food. **£16**|£1.50/£3.50.

Salcombe SX7338 Spinnakers (0548) 843408 Relaxed waterside restaurant with good, popular food inc fresh local fish and nice puddings. **£15.75**|£6.30.

Bantham SX6643 Sloop (0548) 560489 Characterful 16th-c nautical village inn with wide choice of good home cooking esp seafood in bar and restaurant; a stroll over dunes from sea; they have holiday cottages. **£14**|£2/£5.

Totnes SX8060 Kingsbridge Leechwell St (0803) 863324 Several unexpected dishes among more usual bar food in plushly refurbished but interesting pub, town's oldest building; cl 25 Dec. **£11.75**|£1.75/£4.95.

Rattery SX7461 Church House (0364) 42220 Decent bar food in one of Britain's oldest pubs, friendly atmosphere, and beamed, newly refurbished dining room with open fires. **£10.50**|£2.50/£4.95.

Torcross SX8241 Start Bay (0548) 580553 Notable fresh seafood generously served in busy thatched 14th-c pub overlooking 3-mile pebble beach; live cider; family room. **£10**|£2/£3.70.

Kingsteignton SX8773 Old Rydon (0626) 54626 Cosy old pub with constantly changing menu of imaginative bar food inc good puddings, and big garden. £2.60/£6.30.

Harberton SX7758 Church House (0803) 863707 Careful home-cooking inc some of their own produce in interestingly furnished ancient pub; decent wines. Children in family room only. £2.10/£6.30.

Kingsteignton SX8773 Old Rydon (0626) 54626 Imaginative, popular food using fresh ingredients in small cosy bar with upper gallery (children to keep to this) and prettily planted dining conservatory; nice biggish sheltered garden. £2.25/£5.45.

Stokenham SX8042 Church House (0548) 580253 Wide range of well-presented food esp local fish and seafood in friendly rambling pub; nice garden. £2/£5.

Moreleigh SX7752 New Inn (0548) 82326 Wholesome and generous home-cooking inc fresh wild salmon in country local's chatty inglenook bar; decent wines; exceptional value. £2.10/£4.70.

North Devon

This area has attractive places to visit and some charming civilised places to stay; it's relatively untouristy away from the few traditional resorts.

Ilfracombe, the main resort, stays active all year; it's a pleasant and distinctive place that has family attractions but doesn't become too trippery in summer. The lower-key beach resorts such as Woolacombe and Westward Ho! go into mothballs when the season's over – without the summer sun-seekers their marvellous beaches are good for lonely walks, and elsewhere there are fine bracing cliff walks. Outside the few resorts and the legendarily pretty Clovelly and Combe Martin, this part of Devon is largely untouched by tourism, and there are long stretches of coast which are empty even in summer. Major attractions include Bickleigh (for its castle and Devonshire's Centre), Arlington Court, the woodland gardens at Rosemoor near Great Torrington and at Knighthayes Court at Bolham, and Hartland Quay.

Where to stay

South Molton SS7125 Whitechapel Manor EX36 3EG (0769) 573377 ***£98**; 10 pretty rms. Carefully restored, Grade I listed Elizabethan manor with magnificent Jacobean carved oak screen in the entrance hall, fine panelling, beams and log fires; relaxed atmosphere in cosy bar and comfortable lounge, excellent, thoughtful service, fine, modern cooking, carefully chosen wines, large grounds, handy also for Exmoor.

Chittlehamholt SS6420 Highbullen Umberleigh EX37 3EG (0769) 540561 **£95 inc dinner**; 37 comfortable, often spacious rms in main building and various annexes. Victorian gothic mansion set in huge wooded parkland and gardens with 9-hole golf course, indoor tennis court and swimming pool, table tennis, and squash court; food consistently good, intimate restaurant overlooking the valley, busy little bar, reasonable library, relaxed, informal service (no reception, you ring a bell and wait); children over 8.

Bishops Tawton SS5630 Halmpstone Barnstaple EX32 0EA (0271) 830321 ***£80**; 5 pretty rms. Small country hotel with relaxed atmosphere, and enjoyable food in the panelled dining room, good breakfasts, and caring service; pretty garden, nice views; cl Jan/Feb; no children.

Morchard Bishop SS7707 Wigham Crediton EX17 6RJ (036 37) 350 **£80 inc dinner**; 5 rms. Picturesque thatched longhouse in 30-acre farm with house-party atmosphere, two sitting rooms, big log fires, snooker room, dining room with honesty bar and set dinner using home-grown fruit, veg and dairy produce; no smoking and no pets (they have their own); outdoor heated swimming pool; children over 8.

Hatherleigh SS5404 Tally Ho Okehampton EX20 3JN (0837) 810306 ***£68**; 3 rms. Friendly old inn with genuinely old-fashioned fittings, welcoming Italian licensees, lots of Italian food, no-smoking restaurant, and interesting own-brew beers; landlord will arrange fishing; children over 8.

Clawton SX3599 Court Barn Holsworthy EX22 6PS (040 927) 219 **£60**; 8 rms. Charming country house in 5 acres of pretty grounds with croquet, 9-hole putting green, small chip-and-putt course, tennis and badminton courts; comfortable lounges, log fires, library/tv room, good service and food, and quiet, relaxed atmosphere; cl 1-7 Jan.

East Buckland SS6731 Lower Pitt Barnstaple EX32 0TD (0598) 760 243 **£60**; 3 comfortable rms. Quiet, pretty stone farmhouse with log fire in cosy lounge, good, well-presented food using herbs and veg from own garden and fresh local produce in simply furnished dining room and conservatory, and friendly service; cl 24-26 Dec; children over 12.

Sheepwash SS4806 Half Moon Beaworthy EX21 5NE (040 923) 376 **£60**; 15 rms. Civilised heart-of-Devon hideaway in colourful village square; neatly kept, friendly bar, big log fire, good wines, evening restaurant, lots of lunchtime bar snacks, and solid old furnishings.

Knowstone SS8223 Masons Arms South Molton EX36 4RY (039 84) 231 **£55**; 4 rms, 2 with bthrm. Delightfully unspoilt 13th-c thatched pub with very individual character and relaxed, friendly service; good homely bar food, Thurs curry night, restaurant, decent wines and nice garden; good walks nearby.

Croyde SS4439 Whiteleaf Braunton EX33 1PN (0271) 890266 **£54**; 3 rms. Attractively furnished and thoughtfully run comfortable guesthouse with concentration on really notable food (menu changes each night), and decent wines; close to village and beach; dogs welcome; cl 2 wks Jan/Apr/July/Oct.

West Buckland SS6531 Huxtable Farm Barnstaple EX32 0SR (0598) 760254 ***£44**; 6 rms. 16th-c farmhouse surrounded by carefully converted listed stone buildings, open fields, fine views, sheep, chickens, rabbits and Squeak the Shetland pony; candlelit dinner with wholesome home-made food using home-grown produce, home-made wine and bread, and relaxing sitting room; cl Christmas.

Buckland Brewer SS4220 Coach & Horses Bideford EX39 5LU (0237) 451395 **£40**; 2 rms above bar. Welcoming, well-preserved 13th-c thatched village pub with cosy beamed bar, log fires in inglenook fireplaces, truly home-made enjoyable food, dining room, and pleasant garden.

Oakford SS9121 Newhouse Farm Tiverton EX16 9JE (039 85) 347 **£35**; 3 rms. 17th-c longhouse on edge of Exmoor National Park and part of working farm with beef suckler cows and small flock of friendly sheep; cottage sitting room, inglenook fireplace, beams, and country dining room serving home-made food inc good bread, patés and puddings; cl Christmas; children over 10.

Great Torrington SS4919 Black Horse High St EX38 8HB (0805) 22121 **£28**; 3 rms. Pretty twin-gabled inn – reputedly the headquarters of General Fairfax in the Civil War – with good-value bar and restaurant food; handy for RHS Rosemoor garden and Dartington crystal.

Ilfracombe SS5147 Altro Fore Street EX34 9DN (0271) 862096 **£70 per week**; 42 comfortable, homely rms. Good-value family-run hotel overlooking seafront with comfortable bar, TV lounge, first-floor smaller lounge, dining room, decent food, and good service; resident organist, disabled access, cl Jan.

We welcome reports from readers . . .

Readers who help us with reports for the Guide are offered a discount on the next edition: so please do help if you can!

To see and do

★ ⛽ ❄ **Appledore** ST0614 has a pretty centre of narrow cottagey streets off the quayside road which looks out over the Taw estuary, and ship- and boat-building in the yard just upstream. NORTH DEVON MARITIME MUSEUM Each room shows a different aspect of Devon's maritime history; also includes steam, motor coasters and reconstructed turn-of-century kitchen. Shop; cl Nov-Easter, am Easter-May bank hol and Oct; *£1.

Arlington SS6140 ARLINGTON COURT Fascinating early 19th-c house in attractive landscaped gardens, home to Shetland ponies and sheep; house has lots of models, costumes, shells, furnishings and other period pieces. Also Victorian garden and conservatory, nature trails by lake and through woods, interesting and unusual collection of carriages and other horse-drawn vehicles with rides available. Meals, snacks, shop, disabled access; cl Sat, Nov-Easter; £4.60, garden only £2.40. NT.

★ **Barnstaple** SS5533 This busy town is the main shopping centre for the area; as big new stores have opened outside the centre and as there's now a bypass, the old part has got its second wind. It has a good deal of unforced charm, with many interesting buildings including an imposing 18th-c colonnaded arcade on the Great Quay, a lofty Victorian market hall (market days are Tues and Fri), almshouses behind the church, more off the square by the long old stone bridge, and some interesting shops. It's still a working port, though in a very small way now. The best nearby pub is the Chichester Arms up in Bishops Tawton. MARWOOD HILL GARDENS (Marwood; off A361 towards Braunton) 18 acres inc rare trees and shrubs, small lakes, extensive bog garden, collections of clematis, camellias, alpines and eucalyptus, and the national collections of astilbes and tulbachia; shop and plant centre, some disabled access; cl 25 Dec; *£2. MUSEUM OF NORTH DEVON Rapidly expanding centre becoming more interactive all the time, with a new Tarka exhibition concentrating on the local environment; shop, disabled access to ground floor only; cl Sun and Mon; £1. They also have an exhibition at St Anne's Chapel nearby, which recreates the 17th-c school that was here; cl 1-2 pm, Sun and Mon, Oct-Mar; 50p. LYNTON & BARNSTAPLE RAILWAY MUSEUM Next to the current town station, an exhibition of memorabilia of the old railway, which closed in 1935, with interesting old photos and maps. They hope to have a couple of miles of the line running again before too long; cl Sun, mid-Oct-Easter. BRANNAMS (Roundswell Industrial Estate) Guided tours of big pottery (their terracotta pots are indispensable to many gardeners) with chance to throw your own pot and a small museum of world pottery; meals, snacks, shop, disabled access; no tours most wknds, but shop open then (exc winter Suns); £2.50.

Bickleigh SS9407 BICKLEIGH CASTLE Over nine centuries of history on view at this fascinating moated and fortified manor house (still a family home) – the 11th-c chapel is said to be Devon's oldest complete building; also medieval hall, armoury and guard room, Tudor bedroom, 17th-c farmhouse, moated garden, museum of 19th-c domestic objects and toys, and exhibitions on maritime history, wartime spy equipment and the Civil War. Snacks, shop, some disabled access; open every pm end May-early Oct, Weds, Sun and bank hols from Easter-end May; £2.90. DEVONSHIRE'S CENTRE Something here to occupy most people, with a restored working watermill, unusual breeds, shire horses, bird area with flamingos and penguins, agricultural and motor museums, railway, farm and craft shops and a notable 'craft' grocer's shop; meals, snacks, shops, some disabled access; cl winter wkdys; *£3.50. The pretty riverside village has two good pubs.

★ **Bideford** SS4526 Quiet hillside town now bypassed, with notable medieval bridge and some pleasant old streets, partly pedestrianised, behind the Quay. One of the oldest streets is Bridgeland St, and up towards the top of Bridge St there are quite a few antique or antiqueish shops. Hand-painted wooden JIGSAW PUZZLES are made by Mrs Bix at 36 Lower Gunstone (cl 12.30-2.30 pm, cl wknds). The day-trip boat for LUNDY sails from here year round, though not every day, and only rarely in March – a good long day. THE BIG SHEEP (2m W on A39) Exuberant sheep centre which, as well as the things you might expect such as lambing and shearing, has rather more eccentric events such as sheep-racing and miniature sheep-dog trials – with ducks; also exhibitions and displays on everything related to sheep, nature trails. Meals, snacks, shop, disabled access; £3.25.

Bolham SS9514 KNIGHTSHAYES COURT This lovely woodland garden has acres of unusual even unique plants, especially lovely in spring but a glory at any time of year; attractive walks, good Exe Valley views, alpine and more formal gardens too, ancient yew topiary. The house itself is extravagantly ornate Victorian Gothic, with elaborate painted ceilings and decor. Melas, snacks, shop and plant centre, disabled access; cl Dec-Mar, house cl am and all day Fri exc Good Fri; £4.80, garden only £2.80.

Bratton Fleming SS6437 EXMOOR STEAM RAILWAY (Cape of Good Hope Farm) Enthusiastically run family-owned narrow-gauge railway with half-sized steam trains winding through a mile of countryside, and a small display of traction engines; open Sun all year, plus pm Sat Feb-Apr, then daily to the end of Sept; £1.75. The White Hart is useful for lunch.

Chittlehampton SS6325 COBBATON COMBAT COLLECTION Growing private collection of over 50 British and Canadian WWII vehicles, quite tightly packed under cover but looking ready for action; also mock-ups of wartime scenes, weaponry, all sorts of other wartime memorabilia, and play area with Sherman tank; snacks, shop, some disabled access; cl winter weekends; £3.

★ **Clovelly** SS3124 has one of Devon's most famous views, down the very steep old street to the harbour (you have to park up at the top, outside the village). It's a delightful little village, best appreciated out of season. The parkland gardens of CLOVELLY COURT have tranquil sea views, and a fine walled garden; some disabled access; open only Thurs pm Apr-Sept; *£1. THE MILKY WAY Lots to see and do at this lively place, one of the biggest undercover attractions in the South West. Visitors can try milking one of the 160 dairy cows or feeding some of the other baby animals, and there's also the North Devon Bird of Prey Centre, with twice-daily falconry displays, a working pottery centre, laser clay-pigeon shooting, a farmhouse exhibition and adventure playground. Meals, snacks, shop, disabled access; cl Nov-Mar; £4. The nearby beachside hamlet of BUCKS MILLS is well worth a visit.

! **Combe Martin** SS5847 is a string of former smallholdings and cottages scattered down a lovely sheltered valley, and an odd pub, the Pack of Cards, built to celebrate a cards win – four floors, 13 doors, 52 windows. There's a little fishing harbour in the shingly cove between the cliffs. BODSTONE BARTON FARMWORLD Busy 17th-c working farm with lots of animals, displays of old and new agricultural methods, pretty nature trails with plenty of

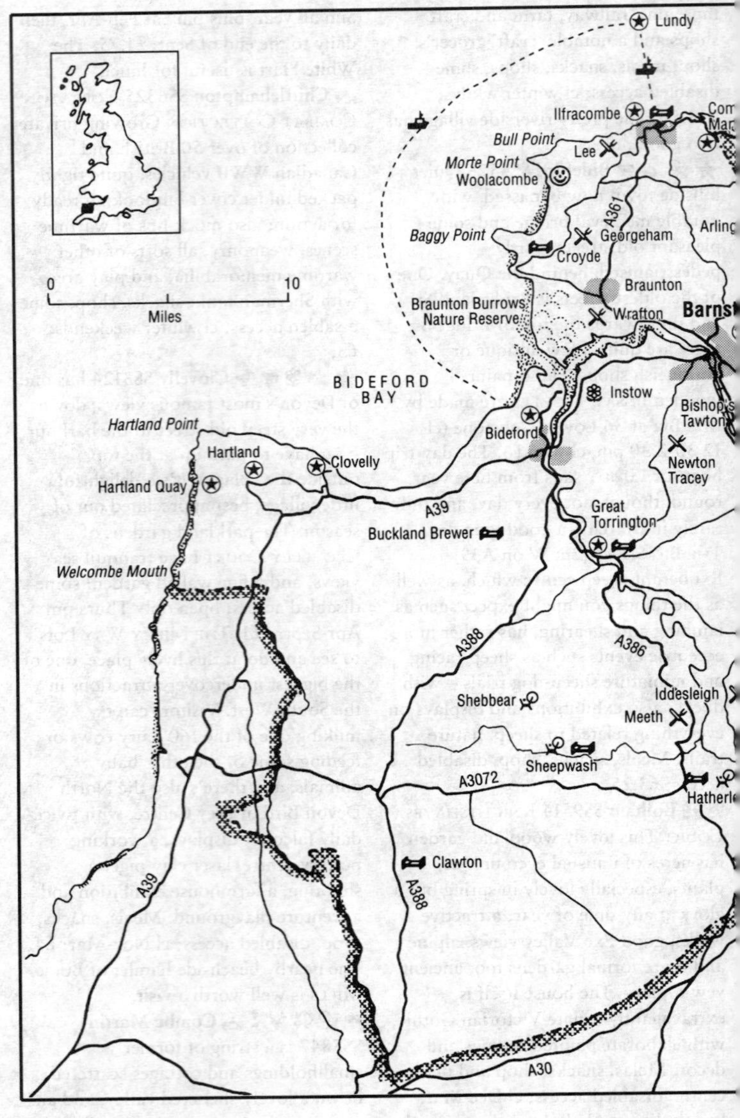

wildlife, huge adventure playground, tractor and trailer rides, craft displays such as spinning and pottery, and regular special events. Meals, snacks, shop, disabled access; cl Nov-Feb; *£2.99. COMBE MARTIN WILDLIFE AND DINOSAUR PARK Twenty acres of woodland with lots of animals and birds; the otters in the stream are especially popular, as are the generously housed meerkats; also gardens, rare plants, tropical plants and animated life-sized dinosaurs; meals, snacks, shop; cl second week Nov-Mar; *£4.50. COMBE MARTIN MOTORCYCLE COLLECTION Growing

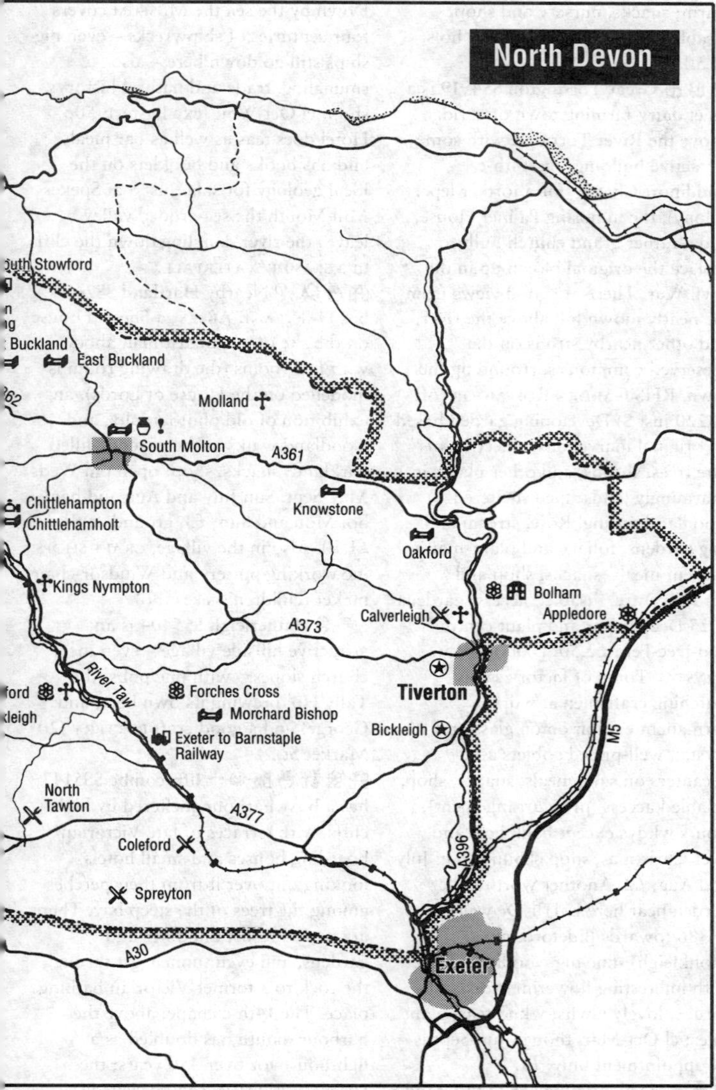

collection of British bikes displayed against old petrol pumps, signs and garage equipment; shop, disabled access; cl Oct-May exc Easter; £1.50.

✝ ❀ **Eggesford** SS6811 is a quiet Taw Valley village with a 14th-c CHURCH and a GARDEN CENTRE prettily set in the walled garden of a ruined house; refreshments on a terrace with lovely views.

❀ **Forches Cross** SS7309 ORCHID PARADISE Colourful indoor orchid displays, with lots of rare and endangered species in elaborate reconstructions of their natural habitats. Good in winter – it's always warm; snacks, nursery and shop, disabled access; cl winter bank hols; £1.50.

Great Torrington SS4919 is a quiet dairy-farming town on a ridge above the River Torridge, with some attractive buildings inc 14th-c Taddiport Chapel (for a former leper colony), the imposing Palmer House, and a rather grand church built to replace the original blown up in the Civil War. There are good views from the neatly mown hill above the river, and other nearby strolls on the preserved commons surrounding the town. RHS GARDEN ROSEMOOR (off B3220 just S) Developing garden based on original marvellous collection of rare trees, shrubs, and other plants in charmingly landscaped sheltered woodland setting. Rose, stream and bog gardens, foliage and plantsman's garden; meals, snacks, shop and garden centre, disabled access; gardens cl 25 Dec, visitor and plant centre cl mid-Dec-Feb; £2.50. DARTINGTON CRYSTAL Tours of factory safely watching craftsmen at work, permanent exhibition on glass and crystal, well-priced goblets and decanters on sale; meals, snacks, shop, disabled access (prior arrangement). Tours wkdys except bank hols and over Christmas, shop cl Sun exc in July and Aug; £2. Another worthwhile garden near here is THE DOWNES (A386 towards Bideford, nr Monkleigh): fine big woodland garden with interesting flowering trees and shrubs, lovely lawns; wknd teas, plant sales; cl Oct-Mar, though Jun-Sept is by appointment only; £1.

Hartland Quay SS2224 Grand isolated spot at foot of toll road, on jagged coast which looks a dramatic cross between illustrations for geology textbooks and ones for a shipwreckers' manual. On way down, detour to DOCTON MILL, an interestingly planted, largely naturalised, extensive, sheltered streamside garden by ancient restored watermill; cl Oct-Feb; £1.50. Down by the sea the MUSEUM covers four centuries of shipwrecks – even big ships still go down here – also smuggling, trade and natural history; shop; cl Oct-Whit (exc Easter); 50p. Hotel does teas as well as bar meals, and has books and booklets on the local geology for sale. Just S at Spekes Mill Mouth the sea-eroded valley leaves the river dangling down the cliff in a SEASIDE WATERFALL.

Nearby **Hartland** SS2624 has HARTLAND ABBEY, a fine old house on the site of an Augustinian abbey, with fine rooms (the drawing room is modelled on the House of Lords), an exhibition of old photography, and woodland walks in the peacock-filled parkland; snacks, shop; open pm Weds May-Sept, Sun July and Aug and bank hol Mon and Sun; £3, grounds only £1.50. Also in the village, CRAFT SHOPS inc working pottery and Windsor-chair maker (children's sizes too).

★ **Hatherleigh** SS5404 is an attractive hillside village – even the church slopes – with fine pubs (the Tally Ho, brewing its own beer, and George) and a good craft POTTERY (20 Market St).

Ilfracombe SS5147 has a busy harbour sheltered by high cliffs, with terraces of late Victorian boarding houses and small hotels looking out over it from their perches among the trees of the steep bay. There are period resort buildings and gardens, and even tunnels cut through the rock to a former Victorian bathing place. The 14th-c chapel above the harbour mouth has doubled as a lighthouse for over 450 years; the LIFEBOAT STATION can be visited (donation requested). The Royal Britannia by the harbour is useful for lunch. There are day trips to Lundy in summer. CHAMBERCOMBE MANOR, in a lovely secluded valley just SE, is one of the country's oldest houses, dating from 1066, with eight rooms (one haunted) furnished in period from Elizabethan to Victorian. Grisly stories on the guided tour, 11th-c private chapel, gardens and wildfowl ponds and new natural-history museum; snacks; cl Sat, Oct-Easter; *£3. HELE MILL Early 16th-c mill still producing wheatflakes and four grades of wholemeal flour; many pieces of machinery on view; shop; cl Sat, am Sun and Nov-Easter; £1.60. Not far away Bicclescombe Park has a restored 18th-c CORNMILL. ILFRACOMBE MUSEUM Local history, geology and archaeology with costumes, china and brass-rubbings; shop, disabled access; 60p. WATERMOUTH CASTLE (A339 E), billed as 'Devon's Happy Castle', is a fine 19th-c castle overlooking the bay; it's ideal for families, having lots of vivid attractions such as a musical water show, slides, carousels, Dungeon Labyrinth and Gnomeland. Meals, snacks, shop, disabled access; cl Sat, Nov-week before Easter, am out of season; £4.50. Ilfracombe also has the ROLLING FALLS MODEL VILLAGE (cl Sat, all Oct-Mar; *£1.80), and HOLY TRINITY CHURCH (Church St) is worth a look for its richly carved 15th-c waggon-roof, one of the most striking in the area.

Instow SS4730 at the mouth of the Torridge estuary has an expanse of tidal sands, with dozens of moored boats stranded on them at low tide. TAPELEY PARK Italianate garden with rococo features, walled kitchen garden, pets' corner, play area, and woodland walk – there may be jousting some days; teas and snacks in period dairy, shop, disabled access; cl Sat, Oct-Easter; prices vary but start at £1. The Quay in the village is a useful waterside pub.

Shebbear SS4409 is a quiet village notable if you're passing for its odd Devil's Stone by the green; also working wood-fired POTTERY.

★ **Sheepwash** SS4806 is another nice village with cob-and-thatch houses around green, good pub; a mile N is Duckpool Cottage traditional wood-fired POTTERY.

! **South Molton** SS7125 This country town has an attractive central square and imposing church, and its farming roots show in the Thursday cattle market. The Old Coaching Inn is a comfortable place for lunch. The MUSEUM in the 18th-c Guildhall specialises in local history, very well displayed, with charters, fire engines and giant cider press; monthly art-and-craft shows. Shop, disabled access; cl Mon and Dec-Feb. QUINCE HONEY FARM The biggest wild-bee farm in the world, with specially designed tunnels between observatories to avoid disturbing them, and observation hives looking right into the centre of colonies; snacks, shop with lots of honey; cl Nov-Easter; *£2.75.

South Stowford SS6541 (off B3226 N of Bratton Fleming – where there's a good pub) EXMOOR BIRD GARDENS Largest collection of tropical birds in the area, and monkeys, lots of other wildlife, and landscaped gardens, good views, and an assault course for children; snacks, disabled access; *£3.50.

Tiverton SS9512 CASTLE Built in 1106 as a Royal fortress dominating the River Exe, this still has a Norman tower and gatehouse, as well as an interesting clock collection and one of the best collections of Civil War armour and arms; snacks, shop, disabled access; cl Fri, Sat, Sun, Oct-Easter, open winter am by arrangement; £2.75. The nearby ST PETER'S CHURCH is magnificently decorated with rich carving, and there are other grand buildings (inc the Jacobean council offices) in this formerly prosperous wool town. Well worth walking around. Local history MUSEUM in former 19th-c school with lacemaking and agricultural displays, lacemaking machinery, complete smithy, two waterwheels and excellent railway gallery; shop, mostly disabled access; cl Sun, Christmas-Jan; *£1. TIVERTON CRAFT CENTRE Four showrooms with the work of over 170 local craftsmen – inc pottery, jewellery, glass, paintings, prints and spinning; shop, limited disabled access; cl Sun. HIGHFIELD VINEYARDS (Longdrag Hill) Tours of working vineyard with free tastings; shop; cl Sun, 25 Dec-Feb. In summer there are HORSE-DRAWN BOAT TRIPS along the attractively restored canal from the wharf; snacks, shop, disabled access (with prior notice); cl Oct-Easter, booking advisable (0884) 253345; £5.65. They do motor-boat trips too.

☺ **Woolacombe** SS4543 ONCE UPON A TIME Run by the same people as Watermouth Castle at Ilfracombe, this is a super place for children, with lots of rides and other activities; the newest feature is a children's driving school which even offers tests. Meals, snacks, shop, disabled access; cl Sat, Nov-Mar; *£2.25. The beach at Woolacombe is particularly nice, and its Atlantic breakers have begun to attract a number of surfers.

The ordinary British Rail **Exeter-Barnstaple** line, mostly tracking along closer to the River Taw than the road does, is one of the finest of all for scenery.

Other attractive small villages with decent pubs include Buckland Brewer SS4220, Calverleigh SS9214 (good church), Kings Nympton SS6819 (another fine church), Molland SS8028 (yet another), Knowstone SS8223, Lee SS4846 and Winkleigh SS6308.

The day trip to **Lundy** by boat from Bideford or, in summer, Ilfracombe is difficult to fit into a short stay in Devon, but is well worth considering if you're there for any longer. There are of course the spring and autumn migrant birds for which the island is famous; the remoteness and loneliness could also be a powerful draw. It has lovely walks along its seven miles of formidably high cliffs, windswept rough pastures, small church, castle, store-cum-pub, two lighthouses, freely wandering goats, small Soay sheep and ponies, the chance of seeing seals (especially in autumn), the introduced small sika deer – and, of course, puffins. Accommodation can be arranged through the Landmark Trust (0628) 825925. The return boat trip (about 2¼ hours each way) is about £20; (0237) 423365 for sailing times.

Walks

Good spots for **wild coast** walks include the cliff walks around Welcombe Mouth SS2117 (the Old Smithy in Welcombe is a good stop); those around Hartland Quay SS2224 and on both sides of Hartland Point SS2326 (toll gates to both); the woods, cliffs and clifftop farmland W of Clovelly, reached from the village or from the NT's isolated farmhouses at The Brownshams SS2826; the cliffs between Ilfracombe and Lee Bay (the Grampus up the sheltered wooded valley in the pretty village of Lee SS4846 is a useful stop); and Bull Point SS4646 and Morte Point SS4545 (the Ship Aground by the church in Mortehoe is a good start). Baggy Point SS4240 reached from Croyde (where the Thatched Barn is a good family pub) has a path good enough for wheelchairs.

Other fine coastal walks include the vast expanse of great swelling dunes at the **Braunton Burrows** Nature Reserve SS4535 reached from the B3231 W of Braunton (red flags will warn if there's shooting on the range here; the Mariners Arms in South St in Braunton itself is a useful pleasantly untouristy pub); the dunes, sand slacks and meres behind the pebble ridge at Northam Burrows SS4430 W, with the Atlantic rollers swinging in along the rock-strewn tidal sands beyond; the long stretch of broad tidal beach at **Saunton Sands**

SS4437, deserted out of season (but popular with families in summer); and the great surfy beach at **Woolacombe** SS4543, a fine place out of season when the resort has shut down.

The **Tarka Trail** (see Exmoor) includes sections on disused railways from Barnstaple and Bideford, which can be walked or cycled (local bicycle hire £5 a day, more for mountain bikes). The best section is the one from Barnstaple through Instow and Bideford up to Great Torrington. In autumn and winter particularly it gives close views of the wading birds massed on the tidal sands of the estuary, and year-round the section up to Great Torrington is very attractive.

The **Old Railway** above Ilfracombe is another popular disused railway trail, with a tunnel, interesting plants, attractive scenery inc the lakes of Slade Reservoirs SS5045. For a one-way walk it's best to do it in reverse, for better views – and it's downhill all the way; Red Bus 31 or Filers 303 up from the town to Lee Bridge or Lee Cross (or to the Fortescue Hotel for a preliminary bracer).

Eggesford SS6811 is a good base for inland walks (and a stop on the Barnstaple-Exeter rail line): in Flashdown Wood, up wooded Hayne Valley to Wembworthy (the Odd Wheel is a decent family pub), or through Heywood Wood, where the mound of the former castle gives good views (and there are picnic-table sets).

Bradworthy SS3214 is another good jumping-off point, with some quiet local strolls on the common, or over by the Tamar Lake a couple of miles SW.

Driving

The A361 North Devon Link Road from the M5 makes getting into this area much more tolerable than it used to be. Moreover, it has taken enough pressure off several other roads here to make them enjoyable as routes for pleasure drives (eg the old B3221, see below).

The A377 along the Taw Valley has pretty views of this twisty wooded valley, but is not a quick road. The B3217 southwards off it through High Bickington, Dolton and Monkokehampton is a good rolling old coach road. Another of these is the B3220 from Great Torrington through Beaford and Winkleigh. Yet another is the former B3221, now declassified, from South Molton through Ash Mill, Rackenford (with Devon's oldest pub, and a craftsman cabinet-maker at Woodpeckers) and Calverleigh to Tiverton. From all these, the views are of rather reserved rolling farmland. For something wilder, try the moorland road NW from Stibb Cross on the A388 to Woolfardisworthy and on towards Clovelly.

There are impressive sea views from the B3231 looping through Croyde W of Braunton and more scenically from the back road between Woolacombe and Mortehoe; the A399 has good views out to sea E of Ilfracombe. The best coast drive is the Hobby Drive, a toll-road track through the Clovelly woods below the A39.

Where to eat

Coleford SS7701 New Inn (0363) 84242 Comfortable thatched inn, six centuries old, with good and often unusual food, good wines, and attractive garden with stream; recently refurbished bedrooms; cl 25-26 Dec. £10|£1.55/£4.75.

Iddesleigh SS5708 DUKE OF YORK (0837) 810253 Thatched mainly 14th-c pub with homely country furnishings and good food. £1.25/£4.30.

Some of the best food here is to be found at most of the hotels and inns we've recommended as places to stay. Some other decent places to eat here include the White Hart at Bratton Fleming SS6437, Rose & Crown at Calverleigh SS9214, Rock at Georgeham SS4639, Bull & Dragon at Meeth SS5408, Hunters at Newton Tracey SS5226, Grampus in Lee SS4846, Copper Key in North Tawton SS6601, Tom Cobbley at Spreyton SX6996, Kings Arms in Winkleigh SS6308 and Williams Arms in Wrafton SS4935.

EXMOOR

Exmoor is acclaimed for its outstanding scenery, particularly on the coast.

The moor and especially its steep and interesting coast has excellent walking – by no means a second-best to Dartmoor in that respect, and with the virtue of having fewer people around in summer. Where it drops away sharply to the sea, fast streams and rivers cut deeply into wooded valleys which can be of outstanding beauty. The moor itself has in some places been more tamed than Dartmoor, in that it's been drained and resown with richer-growing grasses for better pasture. But it's still a wild place, with hawthorns and low oak trees bent and gnarled by the winds, and (unlike Dartmoor) wild deer.

It is above all the scenery which is the lure here: among the handful of places to visit, Selworthy, Lynmouth and Allerford (with its farm park) are probably the pick.

Though part of Exmoor lies in Somerset, we've covered the whole area in this chapter.

Where to stay

Dulverton SS9127 ASHWICK HOUSE TA22 9QD (0398) 23868 **£112 inc dinner**; 6 rms. Very warmly recommended by contributors though unfortunately we have no other details; children over 8 only.

Countisbury SS7449 EXMOOR SANDPIPER Lynton EX35 6NE (05987) 263 **£86**; 16 comfortable rms. Nice spot opposite moorland church; low-beamed, dimly lit rooms set out for eating, decent food, friendly service, and good nearby walks.

Exford SS8538 WHITE HORSE TA24 7PY (064 383) 229 **£86**; 19 comfortable rms. Three-storey Exmoor village inn with country-kitchen furnishings in open-plan bar; log fire, good-value bar food, real ales, and friendly and efficient staff; disabled access.

Lynmouth SS7249 RISING SUN Mars Hill EX35 6EQ (0598) 53223 **£79**; 16 rms. Historic thatched 14th-c inn with lovely views from little harbour out to sea, decent food and good wines, charming garden and good nearby walks; children over 5.

Dulverton SS9127 Ashwick Country House TA22 9QD (0398) 23868 **£78**; 6 quiet and thoughtfully decorated rms. Small Edwardian country house in six peaceful acres of sweeping lawns, water gardens, and mature trees; galleried entrance hall warmed by a log fire, comfortable lounge, good careful cooking using fresh local produce, and excellent service; children over 8.

Lynton SS7149 Hewitt's The Hoe North Walk EX35 6HJ (0598) 52293 **£78**; 10 rms. You can walk for miles through this friendly hotel's wooded 27 acres and on down to the sea, and the formal terraced gardens are being gradually restored; comfortable rooms with fine oak panelling and stained glass, antiques, log fires, and good food in no-smoking candlelit restaurant; children by arrangement.

Dulverton SS9127 Tarr Steps TA22 9PY (0643) 85293 ***£76**; 14 rms, 11 with own bthrm. Set in 500 acres of land with rough shooting and trout-filled river, riding, free clay-pigeon shoot on Sun mornings; relaxed atmosphere and decent food; cl Feb, 1st two wks Mar; disabled access.

Lynton SS7149 Lynton Cottage EX35 6ED (0598) 52342 **£74**; 17 well-equipped, comfortable rms, many with sea view. Relaxed and homely family-run hotel with fine views over the sea and countryside; friendly small bar, comfortable lounge with big windows, good food; cl Jan.

Exebridge SS9244 Anchor Dulverton TA22 9AZ (0398) 23433 ***£64**; 6 rms. Peaceful place with river running past inn's sheltered lawn; companionable bar with individually chosen pieces of furniture, and warm woodburning stove, good simple bar food inc vegetarian dishes, and decent children's menu.

Withypool SS8435 Westerclose Country House Minehead TA24 7QR (064 383) 302 ***£56**; 10 rms. 1920s hunting lodge in 9 acres of gardens and paddocks, with moorland views, comfortable lounges and good food using local produce.

Porlock SS8846 West Porlock House Minehead Somerset TA24 8NX (0643) 862880 **£45**; 4 rms. Nicely proportioned former manor house in its own gardens and grounds with very good food (evening meals only served at wknds), carefully furnished rooms and kind personal service; cl Dec.

Dulverton SS9127 Highercombe TA22 9PT (0398) 23451 **£39**; 3 rms. Imposing country house in 8 acres of fine mature gardens and close to open moorland; big lounge, open fire, and fine views; may do evening meals; self-catering also.

Porlock SS8846 Ship Minehead TA24 8QT (0643) 862507 **£39**; 11 rms. 13th-c village inn with characterful low-beamed front bar, traditional old benches on tiled and flagstoned floor, simple, popular food and close to sea and moor; disabled access.

Bossington SS8947 Orchard Guest House (0643) 862 336 ***£34**; 10 rms. Small, family-run and very friendly B & B with cream teas and evening meals too; lots of good nearby walks, horse-riding.

To see and do

There are rather fewer places to visit in this area – the main attraction is the scenery, and there are some lovely little towns and villages worth a look.

★ 🐄 ⛾ ⚲ **Allerford** SS9047 is a pretty stonebuilt village with a lovely packhorse bridge. Somerset Farm Park Traditional farm buildings including the Saxon manor house with its large exhibition of horse-drawn trade vehicles, rare breeds of farm animals, heavy horses in use, baby

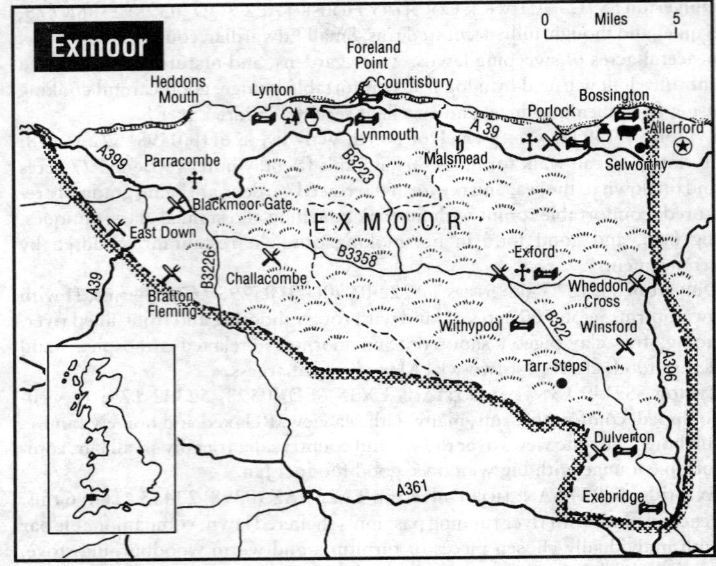

animals; snacks, small shop, disabled access; cl Sat and Oct-Easter; £3 (this includes admission to Bossington Manor). In the village, the former village SCHOOLROOM is set out as it would have been a hundred years ago, in an enthusiastically run local museum with other room re-creations and summer craft demonstrations; cl Sun, cl mid-Oct-Easter. The Victory is useful for lunch.

Lynton SS7149 and its harbourside extension, Lynmouth, down at the bottom of the cliff railway track, is a delightfully situated steep village tucked into the wooded seaside gorge where the East and West Lyn tumble down to the sea. Lynton itself, the main settlement, clearly shows its origins as a Victorian resort in what was then known as Little Switzerland, with hillside villas now quiet boarding houses, photogenic corners and some older cottages. There are pretty cottages down by the little tidal harbour itself, also craft shops and so forth. In the old part of the upper village the LYN AND EXMOOR MUSEUM is in an 18th-c cottage with its kitchen restored to authenticity, displays on traditional Exmoor farming and crafts, and other local-interest displays such as lifeboat models and a scale model of the former Lynton-Barnstaple narrow-gauge railway (you can still walk much of its track bed); shop; cl 12.30-2 pm, Sat, Nov-Easter; 70p. GLEN LYN GORGE has been well restored after the Lynmouth flood of 1952, and as well as fine walks and wildlife there's a new exhibition on water power; exhibition cl Oct-Easter; £2. WATERSMEET HOUSE (1½m E) The 19th-c fishing lodge itself is not particularly remarkable except for its interesting local wildlife displays, but the estate that surrounds it really is attractive – a perfectly relaxing wooded valley, with the house at the meeting point of the rivers. Some of the walks can be steep; teas, disabled access by appointment; cl Nov-Mar. NT. The Royal Castle and Olde Cottage Hotel are useful for lunch, and the Rising Sun down by the harbour is good.

ђ **Malsmead** SS7947 The NATURAL

Centre is enthusiastically run by the Exmoor Natural History Society and has displays, maps and games about Exmoor and its wildlife. On Wednesdays at 2 pm in summer they organise walks through the striking local scenery, which is much as it must have been when Jan Ridd brought his bride Lorna here in *Lorna Doone*; disabled access; open pm Weds and Thurs May-Sept plus Tues mid-July-Aug.

Dulverton SS9127, the main town for Exmoor, is a civilised place with a handsome old stone market house and a fine bridge over the river which has cut this steeply wooded valley. The Caernarvon Arms is useful for lunch.

☩ **Porlock** SS8846 has a lot of traffic, but some attractive cottages with distinctive lighthouse-like chimneys and thatched roofs (one is the Ship, good pub); nearby the much quieter harbour of **Porlock Weir** is tucked below the wooded cliffs – long walks along the coast, or through the woods up to the tiny and quite isolated CULBONE CHURCH.

★ **Selworthy** SS9246 is a glorious unspoilt village, rated by a number of our contributors as the most attractive they've ever seen, with groups of white thatched cottages around a prettily planted hillside green looking out over Exmoor, and trees behind.

★ ☩ **Exford** SS8538 is prettily set in a sheltered valley by a small streamside green; the CHURCH up the hill a bit is well worth a look, and there are no less than eight bridges. The White Horse is good for lunch, and the staghound kennels are here.

★ ☩ **Parracombe** SS6644 is a lovely little village worth visiting in its own right, but particularly interesting is ST PETROC'S CHURCH, one of the few churches to have a completely unspoilt medieval fabric with Georgian interior; cl Nov-Easter but key available from custodian. There's a scale model of the old Lynton-Barnstaple railway (see above).

Walks

The coast is an enticing mix of upland, plunging wooded river valleys and wild clifftops – ideal for super-varied walks. The cream of it is around **Lynton** SS7149 and **Lynmouth** SS7249. To the east, paths run along the Lyn River to **Watersmeet** SS7448, where the Farley Waters tumble down to meet the East Lyn in a series of rocky cascades among steeply picturesque oak woods (there's a discreet NT refreshment pavilion here). There's another scenic path high above the same valley along its S side, and riverside paths head on further upstream, to the good Rockford Inn SS7547 and beyond. Just N of Watersmeet, the **Foreland Cliffs** SS7551 are the highest in the country – a good walk with dramatic views.

West from Lynton, the **Valley of the Rocks** SS7049 is a great valley bowl with steep crags and pinnacles of rock dividing it from the sea (and a dreadful unscreened car park smack in the middle). It's reached by an easy coast path, or by paths over **Hollerday Hill** SS7149 (wooded, but opens out dramatically on top). Further W are some rugged moorland hills by the sea, with secretive wooded combes: **Heddons Mouth Cleave** SS6549 (there's a good walk down from the Hunters Inn SS6548 W of Martinhoe), and the terraced walkway known as the **Ladies Mile** SS6448 which runs along a charming valley near Trentishoe. Heading W from **Porlock Weir** SS8647 along the shore at the foot of the wooded cliffs, even the most avid pebble-hunter would find all he wanted.

The peaceful countryside of inland Exmoor is perhaps best appreciated from along paths by the rivers. A notable stretch is to be found along the **River Exe** between Exford SS8538 and Winsford SS9034. The **River Barle**'s most famous feature is the **Tarr Steps** SS8632, the finest of all the stone-and-slab clapper bridges for packhorses; the path along the river, which runs between Simonsbath SS7739 and Dulverton SS9127, is uneven and surprisingly slow-going in places. **Badgworthy Water** SS7944 can be taken in by a path from Malmsmead SS7947, getting into the heart of the Lorna Doone country – it gets wilder and more remote with every step southwards (the surrounding moors provide a handful of return routes). Note that some of Exmoor's moorland paths have a disconcerting habit of fizzling out without warning.

Exmoor's great ridge walk is **Dunkery Hill**, with Dunkery Beacon SS8941 as its high point surveying a huge chunk of south-west England and south Wales. It is easily walked from the nearby road; a splendid place to leave the car is Webbers Post SS9043 (which is also good for local pottering). It can also be incorporated into longer walks from Horner Woods SS8944 or Luccombe SS9144. Less well known but also recommended is **Grabbist Hill** SS9844, which can be climbed from nearby Dunster SS9943. Above Selworthy, there are walks with excellent views on **Selworthy Beacon** SS9148.

The **Tarka Trail**, not yet complete, will eventually run to nearly 200 miles linking Exmoor, Dartmoor and the N Devon coast, following the route of Henry Williamson's *Tarka the Otter* – and is most enjoyable with a copy of the book. One beautiful section in this area is the route around Pinkworthy Pond SS7242 and The Chains SS7342, reached from the car park a couple of miles along the B3358 E of Challacombe (where the Black Venus is good). Others are around Watersmeet and along the coast path westwards – see above.

Driving

The B roads and the minor roads up over Exmoor (for instance, the one running due N from Exford, or the Yarde Down road out of Simonsbath) all have good views, and except at peak holiday times are usually pretty empty. Some smaller roads particularly worth exploring include the toll roads W of Lynton; the narrow back road on the Exmoor bank of the East Lyn, through Brendon, Malmsmead and Oare; and the road from Wheddon Cross N to Luccombe, over Dunkery Hill (this route is not so good in reverse). Even the main A39 has some outstanding views (and some very steep hills).

Where to eat

Dulverton SS9225 Carnarvon Arms Brushford (0398) 23302 Good bar and restaurant food and friendly staff in comfortable sporting hotel with its own stabling, fishing and shooting; bedrooms; disabled access. **£23.50**|£1.20/£3.50.

East Down SS5941 Pyne Arms (0271) 850207 Popular pub near Arlington Court with interesting old rooms, very good bar food and decent wines; cl 25 Dec; no children; disabled access. **£16**|£1.70/£4.95.

Wheddon Cross SS9238 Rest & Be Thankful Helpful staff and varied bar food in comfortably modern three-room bar with two log fires and aquarium; restaurant, children's room (though, if staying, must be over 11); disabled access; cl 25 Dec; **£15**|£2.50/£4.98.

Porlock SS8846 LAPSEWOOD High St (0643) 862288 Well-prepared and consistently good food – monthly 5-course gourmet meals are not to be missed, and very good value; cl Weds, one wk over Christmas. **£10.80**|£3.95.
Porlock SS8846 LAPSEWOOD (0643) 862288 Very good, well-presented and reasonably priced food; cl Weds, Jan/Feb. **£9.25**|£2.25/£4.25.
Winsford SS9034 ROYAL OAK (064 385) 455 Prettily placed thatched inn with cosy bars, log fire, and wide choice of often very good bar and restaurant food; bedrooms. £3/£8.
Other places providing decent food in this area include the Station House at Blackmoor Gate SS6443, the White Hart at Bratton Fleming SS6437, the Black Venus at Challacombe SS6941 and the Crown in Exford SS8538.

Help this year from: B M Eldridge, Tom Evans, P and J Shapley, Chris and Debra, J Harris, Tony Evans, Chris and Chris Vallely, Jan Thompson, John and Beryl Knight, Peter Neate, E G Parish, John Horsthuis, David and Ann Stranack, WHBM, Ian Sharp, Mr and Mrs B H Robinson, E V M Whiteway, Carol and Mike Muston, David Watson, Christian Farmer, R Shelton, John and Marianne Cooper, Mrs L Powys-Smith, Alison Trace, Peter Adcock, Steven Tait, Susie Lorie, JM, PM, Werner Arend, Nigel Gibbs, David Gittins, Mrs K Jeal, Dr P D Putwain, Robert Crail, K Harris, Howard and Margaret Buchanan, C A Hall, C J Westmoreland, M Veldhuyzen, Paul and Heather Bettesworth, George Jonas, Dick Brown, Dr and Mrs Paveley, BHP, Jim and Maggie Cowell, Peter Churchill, Martyn John, Dorothee and Dennis Glover, Mr and Mrs D V Morris, Gethin Lewis, Mrs M C Barrett, Robin and Janice Dewhurst, Mrs S Burrows-Smith, Brian and Gill Hopkins, Derek Clarke, Michael and Alison Sandy, David Shillitoe, Joan and Tony Walker, Dave and Louise Clark, Graeme Jameson, David Wallington, Lawrence Pearse, Owen Davies, Fiona Monroe, Peter Richards, Chris and Eleri Richards, John Knighton, Dave Braisted, Reg Nelson, David and Celia Burke, T G Saul, Mrs C Heaps, Phil and Sally Gorton, John Barker, Mr and Mrs J D Marsh, Marian Greenwood, Jo Rees, John Fazakerley, Jane Pendock, J B and F M Merritt, N P Cox, Mike and Terri Richards, C A Blake, John Evans, P Bell.

We welcome reports from readers . . .

This GUIDE depends on readers' reports. Do help us if you can – in return, we offer a discount on the next edition to people who've helped us with reports for it. Tell us what you think about places already in it, and anything extra you think we should say about them. And send us your ideas for inclusion in the next edition: places to visit, eat at or stay in, attractive drives or walks, maybe even unusual interesting shops you know of. Use the card in the middle, the report forms at the end, or just write – no stamp needed: THE GOOD WEEKEND GUIDE, FREEPOST TN1569, Wadhurst, E Sussex TN5 7BR.

Devon Calendar

Some of these dates were provisional as we went to press.

March

27th **Lynton** Jazz Festival – *till Tues 29*

April

22nd **Newton Abbot** Tuckers Maltings Real Ale Festival – *over 80 ales to sample in Britain's only traditional working malt house*

30th **East Budleigh** Bicton Horse Trials *at Bicton Arena – till 2 May*

May

2nd **Blackawton** International Worm-charming; *teams of three compete to catch the most worms – any means except digging are acceptable inc dancing*; **Uffculme** Sheep Show and Trials, *Coldharbour Mill Working Wool Museum*

5th **Torrington** May Fair, *celebrates the charter granted in 1554*

19th **Clyst St Mary** Devon County Show, *Westpoint Showground – till Sat 21*

21st **Plymouth** Lord Mayor's Day Parade

28th **Budleigh Salterton** Gala Week – *till 4 Jun*; **Torquay** Dance Festival: *national competition inc ballroom and Latin American with many well-known dancers – till 11 Jun*

30th **Bickleigh** Street Market; **Combe Martin** Hunting of the Earl of Rone Ceremony; **Kingsteignton** Ram Roasting Fayre

June

beg. June **Beer** Pecorama, *clowns, magicians, Punch & Judy, children's entertainers – till end Aug*

4th **South Molton** Vintage Car Rally – *till Sun 5*

11th **Ilfracombe** Victorian Week, *procession, music halls, barn dances, nautical events, bathing belles and gala ball*; **Plymouth** D-Day Anniversary Ceremony, *Plymouth Hoe, with march-past on Sun 12*; **South Molton** Old English Fayre Week, *possibly with town criers competition, ends with carnival Sun 19*

17th **Kenton** Devon and Exeter Motor Show *at Powderham Castle*

18th Port of **Brixham** International Trawler Race (*around Torbay*) and Quay Festival

19th **Ilfracombe** Victorian Week – till Sun 26

23rd **Axminster** Festival, *orchestral concert, chamber music, drama and guest speakers – till 3 July*

25th **Ottery St Mary** Pixie Day – *commemorates the legendary events that led to the overthrow of the wicked pixies that held control of the village. When the monks carried a new church bell from Exeter the pixies tried to divert the bell and send it over the cliff and into the sea; one of the monks, tripping, swore 'God bless my soul, St Mary' and the spell was broken*

30th **Exeter** Festival – *till 17 July*

July

1st **Exeter** Festival, *2-week celebration of live events till Sun 17*

DEVON CALENDAR

JULY cont.

2nd **Teignmouth** Golf Festival, *Teignmouth golf club: competitions every day for visitors and members – till Fri 8*; **Torquay** to Brixham, *the Torbay swim*

3rd **Hatherleigh** Week *begins*

16th **Tavistock** Carnival Procession, *at the end of Carnival Week*; **Ashburton** Ancient Ceremony of Ale-tasting and Bread-weighing – *procession by local councillors around the public houses and bakeries followed by a medieval fair with bread auction (this date is provisional)*; **Yealmpton** National Shire Horse Centre, *cowboys and Indians re-enactment – till Sun 17*

17th **Salcombe** Merlin Rocket Week, *racing in the estuary, open to the public – till Fri 22*

19th **Honiton** Hot Pennies Ceremony *in the High St (fair starts the next day)*

22nd **Yelverton** Jazz *in the barn, pre-concert jazz suppers and picnics with music; licensed bar*

23rd **Halberton** Mid-Devon Town and Country Show, *Hartnoll Farm*

25th **Clovelly** Woolsery and District Agricultural Show

27th **Barnstaple** Royal Air Force Chivenor Air Day

29th **Sidmouth** International Festival of Folk Arts *in arena and other venues, till 5 Aug*

31st **Bovey Tracey** Carnival Week – *till 7 Aug*

AUGUST

1st **Combe Martin** Carnival Week *begins*

4th **Honiton** Show, *the largest one-day agricultural event in this part of the country*

5th **South Zeal** Dartmoor Folk Festival, *dances, music hall, ceilidh, workshops, Dartmoor step-dance and broom-dance championships, folk service, pub music sessions – till Sun 7*

6th **Paignton** Regatta *(fireworks on Tues 9) – till Sun 14*

7th **East Budleigh** Clowns International Charity Day

13th **Manaton** Show and Fayre *inc 5-mile Bowerman's nose race and classic cars*; **Yealmpton** Steam and Vintage Rally *at the National Shire Horse Centre – till Sun 14*

18th **Chagford** Agricultural and Flower Show

22nd **Ilfracombe** Boat and Shore Open-fishing Festival, *fishing contest under-16 section – till Mon 29*

24th **South Molton** Sheep Fair

25th Port of **Dartmouth** 150th Royal Regatta, *inc rowing and sailing, classic craft and steamboat rally, Kon-Tiki raft races, barrel-rolling and other events – till Sat 27*

26th **Hope Cove** Weekend – *till Mon*

27th **Yealmpton** Medieval Combat *at National Shire Horse Centre, with knights, squires, yeomen, pikemen, Celts, Saxons and archers, ancient combat skills*

DEVON CALENDAR

AUGUST cont.

29th **Chagford** Carnival Week, *ends with a procession evening 3 Sept*; **Dartington** Literature Festival, *Dartington Hall*

SEPTEMBER

3rd **Ashburton** Ilsington Sheepdog Trials, *West of England & Devon County sheepdog championships at Halshanger Manor*; **Kingsbridge** Agricultural Show

4th **Barnstaple** Fair; **Colyton** Carnival Week – *till Sun 11*; **Thorverton** River Exe Struggle, *raft race along a 9-mile stretch of the river from Tiverton to Thorverton*; **Yealmpton** Classic Car and Bike Show *at the National Shire Horse Centre*

10th **South Hams** Vintage Machinery Show

13th **Widecombe-in-the-Moor** Fair and Agricultural Show

14th **Barnstaple** Ancient Chartered Fair, *traditional West Country fair opened by a fair proclamation ceremony held at the Guildhall – till Sat 17*

17th **Tiverton** Carnival

24th **South Molton** Carnival

OCTOBER

2nd **Totnes** River Dart Raft Race

8th **Exeter** Carnival – *grand illuminated procession, the largest carnival procession in the West Country*

12th **Tavistock** Traditional Goosey Fair

15th **Lynton** Jazz Festival

31st **Newton Abbot** Halloween Hauntings *at Tuckers Maltings (ghost is said to be very friendly)*

NOVEMBER

5th **Ottery St Mary** Tar-barrel Rolling and Carnival

6th **Yealmpton** Duck Race – *buy a plastic duck and throw it in the river; also craft stalls*

Dorset

West Dorset has a very wide appeal, its largely quiet coast backed by a varied hinterland, with secluded valleys, narrow lanes threading through peaceful farmland and tucked-away villages, and some splendid high viewpoints. There are plenty of interesting places to visit in this area, and a good choice of attractive places to stay. Bournemouth is a thoroughly civilised, sedate resort.

Bournemouth and East Dorset

Well-kept resort area which has miles of sandy beaches.

The Bournemouth complex, stretching for miles along good beaches, dominates the area, with a lot to do and look at – particularly in and around Poole. Away from Poole's busy waterfront, the conurbation is comfortable – civilised and spacious rather than lively. There is an enormous choice of places to stay, from big resort hotels to quiet guesthouses tucked away in the extensive leafy suburbs (we include a very selective shortlist).

Inland, Wimborne Minster has the most interesting places to visit, and there are several other worthwhile attractions in the vicinity – enough, certainly, to fill a weekend. This part of Dorset does not have the county's best scenery, and though there are some pleasant places for a stroll there is little to satisfy the keen walker. We have been surprised to find such a scarcity of really recommendable places to eat at here.

Where to stay

Poole SZ0190 Mansion House BH15 1JN (0202) 685 666 **£85**; 28 cosy rms. Civilised, old merchant's townhouse close to waterfront; good food in bar and restaurant, courteous, old-fashioned service.

Bournemouth SZ0991 Langtry Manor BH1 3QB (0202) 553887 **£79**; 27 rms, some in the manor, some in the lodge. Built by Edward VII for Lillie Langtry; Edwardian dinner every Sat evening; disabled access.

Horton SU0307 Northill House Wimborne BH21 7HL (0258) 840407 **£63**; 9 comfortable rms. Family-run, 19th-c former farmhouse with small bar, lounge with log fire, good food in attractive conservatory, prompt, courteous service; good nearby walking; cl 20 Dec-15 Feb; children over 8 only; good disabled access.

Winkton SZ1696 Fishermans Haunt Salisbury Rd Christchurch BH23 7AS (0202) 477283 **£59**; 20 comfortable rms, most with own bthrm. Much extended and modernised former fishing inn with decent restaurant as well as food in spacious series of interestingly furnished bar rooms; cl 25 Dec; disabled access.

Farnham ST9515 MUSEUM Blandford Forum DT11 8DE (0725) 516261 **£50**; 4 rms in converted stables. Traditional, civilised, Cromwellian country inn in attractive thatch and stone village, with inglenook fireplace and classical music in lounge bar, conservatory; decent food, excellent breakfasts; sheltered terrace and garden.

Poole SZ0590 INN IN THE PARK Pinewood Rd Branksome Chine BH13 6JS (0202) 761 318 **£45**; 5 comfortable rms. Small hotel with lots of pine in residents' area, attractive dining room, decent small bar, good-value bar food; tables on small, sunny terrace, nice steep walks down to sea.

Cranborne SU0513 FLEUR-DE-LYS Wimborne BH21 5PP (0725) 517282 ***£42**; 8 rms, 1 without bthrm. Nicely placed, old creeper-clad pub in *Tess of the d'Urbervilles* country, close to New Forest, with attractively modernised oak-panelled lounge bar, simply furnished beamed public bar, and decent bar food; cl 24-26 Dec.

To see and do

Bournemouth SZ0991 Neatly kept streamside gardens in the centre, a pier that's one of the few to look as fresh as when it was built, long promenades below the low cliff, miles of sandy beach; things like a good local orchestra raise the tone well above the usual seaside resort average.

All this, with the mild climate, has made the town expansively popular both as a civilised place to retire to and as a centre for regular development. So behind the resort area is a big, busy town surrounded by suburbs, with tall modern buildings and monumental traffic schemes. But down by the sea you're well insulated from all of that. And the western residential suburbs of Westbourne and particularly Branksome Park (the Inn in the Park, Pinewood Rd, is a good stop here) are quiet, with pinetree valleys winding down to the sea.

! DINOSAUR SAFARI is a family favourite, full of computerised displays, fossils and bones comparing the prehistoric beasts to more familiar mammals, with a daunting-sounding section devoted to building your own dinosaur; shop; cl 24-26 Dec; £2.95. MUMMIES AND MAGIC nearby has the same mix of fun and education on the subject of mummification.

RUSSELL-COTES ART GALLERY AND MUSEUM Collections of 17th-c to 20th-c paintings, ceramics and furnishings; snacks, shop, disabled access; cl Mon, 25-26 Dec; *£1 wkdys, wknds free.

SHELLEY ROOMS Small museum devoted to the life and work of the poet, with displays of other romantic literature; cl am, all day Mon, 25-26 Dec, Good Fri.

DC-3 DAKOTA NOSTALGIA FLIGHTS planned in summer 1994; (0202) 593939 for details.

Poole SZ0190 merges indistinguishably into Bournemouth on the edges, but in its centre is wholly distinct, with a more lively feel, especially around The Quay. The broad natural harbour is still busy with the comings and goings of boats and small ships (several decent pubs to watch them from); there are also launch ferries around the harbour, and to Brownsea Island. The Custom House is a fine sight, and there are a good many other interesting old buildings along here; the streets behind, some pedestrianised, are well worth strolling through. The harbour view changed dramatically in 1993, when the twin towers of Hamworthy power station were demolished.

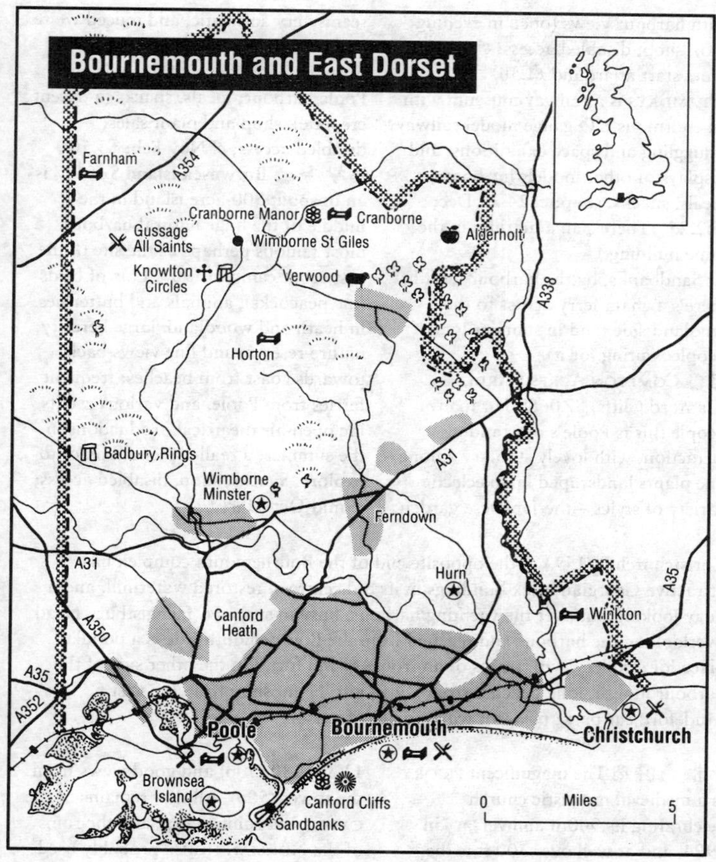

GUILDHALL (Market St) Fine Georgian building, now a modest local museum; the nearby pub named after it has good local fish. WATERFRONT MUSEUM (High St) Unusually housed in the medieval town cellars as well as a later 18th-c mill; tells the story of Poole's seafaring past, with sections on Romans, smuggling and sailing; reconstructed Victorian street and tableaux of subjects like the first scout camp. Summer snacks, shop, disabled access; cl wkdys Nov-Feb, 25-26 Dec, 1 Jan, Good Fri; £1.95 inc the next-door SCAPLEN'S COURT, a well-restored medieval merchant's home showing domestic life through the ages. Also Georgian furnishings, children's toys, walled garden and a Victorian kitchen; shop; cl as above; although the price is inc in the cost of a ticket to the Waterfront Museum (nice to see a museum *reducing* its prices this year), you can just visit here for 75p. POOLE POTTERY (Quay) has been producing its distinctive china here since 1873, and this last year has seen a real upgrading of its facilities for visitors. Tours of the factory (complete with walkman commentary), museum and a film; and you can have a go at throwing and decorating your own pot – or, if it all gets too much for you, smash up a few plates; new restaurant with harbour views (open in evening too), shop, disabled access; cl 25 Dec; tours start at around £1.50.

STEAMDAYS is a railway museum with an enormous OO gauge model railway, smuggling and space exhibitions, and displays of other models inc boats; meals, snacks, shop; cl 24-25 Dec; *£2.25. (There's an aquarium in the same building.)

At Sandbanks, by the harbour mouth, there's a chain ferry across to the Studland side (and in summer lots of people waiting for it).

COMPTON ACRES GARDENS (Canford Cliffs) SZ0689 For many people this is Poole's outstanding attraction, with lovely statuary among fine plants landscaped in an eclectic variety of styles – the Japanese garden seems very authentic, and indeed we're told it's the only one of its type in Europe. Good views of the hills and Poole harbour; meals, snacks (a decent crêperie), shop and plant sales, disabled access; cl Nov-Feb; £3.50.

Brownsea Island SZ0187 is an unspoilt 500-acre island in the middle of the huge natural harbour, most famous perhaps as the site of the first scout camp in 1907. Lots of birds (inc peacocks), animals and butterflies in heath and woodland, large heronry, nature reserve, and fine views back towards coast from beaches; frequent ferries from Poole, and various events inc open-air theatrical productions in the summer; a really splendid place to explore. Snacks, shop, disabled access; cl mid-Oct-Mar; £2.

Christchurch SZ1593 at the opposite end of the Bournemouth complex has attractive Georgian brick buildings in its old centre, a restored watermill, and a quay looking out over the yachting harbour, busy in summer. Hengistbury Head overlooking the harbour and reached from the Bournemouth side is a popular place for strollers, with traces of an Iron-Age hill fort. On the other side of the harbour mouth, long beaches stretch way into Hampshire from the vast Mudeford car park; pleasant walking out of season.

The magnificent PRIORY is a medieval monastic church celebrating its 900th anniversary in 1994, and at well over 300 ft is the longest parish church in the country. It well repays a good look, interesting outside and very striking inside, with remarkable carving and the 'Miraculous Beam', which apparently received divine assistance in fitting the roof, so prompting the renaming of the borough to Christchurch in recognition of the miracle. Shop, disabled access; cl 25 Dec exc for services. The church has a little museum open in the summer (cl 12.30-2.30; 50p) and good views from the tower (50p). All that remains of the CASTLE is a ruined keep, and the ruins of the NORMAN HOUSE probably used by the castle constable; it's quite well preserved, with one of the earliest chimneys constructed in this country, and an ancient dung heap by a millstream. RED HOUSE MUSEUM & GARDENS Georgian house displaying local and natural history, Victoriana, dolls and costumes; herb garden and new archaeology and fishing galleries; shop, some disabled access; cl Sun am, Mon Oct-Mar, Christmas week; *£1.

We welcome reports from readers . . .

Let us know what you think of places in the GUIDE, and any special tips you have. There are report forms at the back of the book, and a card in the middle.

Other things to see and do

Alderholt SU1212 CRANBORNE FARM is good for pick-your-own fruit.

Badbury Rings ST9602 just off the B3082 NW of Wimborne are the ramparts of a formidable late hill fort, associated by some with King Arthur.

Cranborne SU0513 CRANBORNE MANOR 17th-c gardens originally laid out by Tradescant; Jacobean Mount garden, herb garden, lovely river garden and avenues of beech and lime; all particularly attractive in spring. Shop and garden centre, limited disabled access; gardens open Weds only Mar-Sept, garden centre daily exc Mon all year; *£2.50. The village is a peaceful place, with a good pub well known to Hardy and the subject of an entertaining poem by Rupert Brooke (framed inside).

! **Hurn** SZ1296 ALICE IN WONDERLAND MAZE Maze made up of 5,200 bushes cleverly cut into shape of Alice characters; also play areas, croquet lawns, herb gardens, farmyard, and pick-your-own fields with berries, beans, potatoes, courgettes and sweetcorn; snacks, shop; cl Nov-Easter; *£2.50. The Avon Causeway is useful for lunch.

Verwood SU0908 DORSET HEAVY HORSE CENTRE Six different breeds of huge heavy horse and miniature Shetland ponies at the other extreme; regular commentaries, and pets corner; one horse, Percy, stands over 19 hands and is a dedicated beer drinker. Snacks, shop, disabled access; cl Sat in winter and over Christmas; £2.95, half price out of season. The Albion is handy for lunch.

† **Wimborne Minster** SZ0199 has Georgian houses (and decent antique shops and auctions) in the narrow central streets around the MINSTER – a fine, well-preserved, largely Norman church with contrasting red and grey masonry, twin towers, and a rather jolly, brightly coloured jack striking the clock bell every quarter. Interesting things inside include the Norman crypt, a distinctive astronomical clock and the original chained library; shop, disabled access. Close by is the PRIEST'S HOUSE MUSEUM, an interesting historic townhouse with a good range of local history in carefully researched period rooms. Working period kitchen (with regular cooking displays), Victorian stationer's and parlour, walled garden. Teas, shop, some disabled access; cl 27 July, Sun exc pm bank hol wknds and all Jun-Sept, every day Nov-Mar; *£1.50. The Lost Keys, Rising Sun and Old Thatch are all worth knowing for civilised pub lunches. KINGSTON LACY HOUSE, GARDEN & PARK Impressive 17th-c mansion just W of town, with grand Italian marble staircase, superb Venetian ceiling, outstanding paintings such as the *Judgement of Solomon* by Sebastiano del Piamtino, as well as others by Titian, Rubens and van Dyck; enormous grounds with landscaped garden; meals, snacks, shop, disabled access to park and gardens; cl Thurs and Fri and Nov-Mar; *£5 (£2 grounds). KNOLL GARDENS Rare and exotic collection of plants in various colourfully themed gardens, with well over 4,000 different named species; meals, snacks, shop and garden centre, disabled access; cl Nov-Feb; *£2.95. STAPEHILL ABBEY 19th-c Cistercian abbey with craft workshops, agriculture exhibition and lessons in monastic life; acres of park and landscaped gardens with waterfalls and woodland walk; snacks, shop, some disabled access; cl winter Mon and Tues, and first week Jan; £3.95. WALFORD MILL Former 18th-c flour mill, now home of the Dorset Craft Guild, with various changing exhibitions, and lots of local hand-made crafts; meals, snacks, shop; cl 25-26 Dec, 1 Jan. MERLEY HOUSE &

Model Museum Fine 18th-c mansion with interesting plaster ceilings and excellent collection of some 5,000 toys inc model cars, ships and aeroplanes, and working model railways; snacks, shop, disabled access; cl Oct-Easter (except Sun and half-term in Oct); £1.50. Merley Bird Gardens Beautiful historic walled gardens with collection of exotic birds, shrubs and water gardens; snacks, shop, disabled access; cl Christmas; £3.

Some places to see **snowdrops**, usually at their best in Feb and the first week of Mar, inc Kingston Lacy ST9701 (see above, under Wimborne), Wimborne St Giles SU0312 (by fine church and almshouses; just off the B3078 S, and the prehistoric Knowlton Circles SU0209 with a ruined medieval church is a nice spot nearby – though sans snowdrops). Farnham ST9515 is an attractive village with a decent pub.

Walks

This is not generally a good area for the sort of walking that gets your appetite up. Bournemouth is, of course, just a very short drive from the New Forest – see Hampshire chapter. Closer, by far the best place for a stroll is **Hengistbury Head** SZ1790: not a long walk, but the feeling of space and views are outstanding. Apart from places we've already mentioned above, you can strike out northwards for miles along the track of the old Roman road from the hill fort of **Badbury Rings** ST9602. It may be worth noting that Bournemouth's two municipal golf courses, Queens Park and Meyrick Park, are open to walkers, both surprisingly picturesque and somewhat hilly. Although there are several tracks across **Canford Heath** SZ0395 on the edge of Poole, the casual visitor will have difficulty finding access (the south side, near Poole, is fenced).

Driving

In the hinterland, the B3078 up to Cranborne and crossing it the minor road from Three Legged Cross to the Gussages give a good taste of the countryside. Traffic in the Bournemouth conurbation is well managed, but as elsewhere in big urban areas strangers will find the flow a bit baffling and daunting at first. The foolproof way into the centre is the A338.

Where to eat

Besides the establishments recommended as places to stay, and others referred to in the text, the Drovers out at Gussage All Saints SU0010 can be relied on for a decent meal. Additional eating places on which we have had promising reports in the last few months inc Sophisticats, 43 Charminster Rd, Bournemouth; the Beehive, Sandbanks Rd, Lilliput, Poole; the Crab & Ale House, 165 Old Christchurch Rd, Bournemouth; and the Royalty in Christchurch.

We welcome reports from readers . . .

Let us know what you think of places in the Guide, and any special tips you have. There are report forms at the back of the book, and a card in the middle.

Dorset Coast

Grand scenery is complemented by a couple of elegant, old seaside towns, charming small villages, and good places to stay.

There are some very civilised places to stay here, serving good food, as well as good-value, simpler establishments. This area has the best walking in the county, chiefly along the coast, with some marvellous views; you have to go right down to Cornwall to find anything as good on England's south coast. Outside the traditional resorts which do have the sorts of attractions you'd expect of them (Weymouth has the most to offer for a short stay), the area doesn't abound in places to visit. We'd pick as its most rewarding the gardens and swannery at Abbotsbury, and Corfe Castle. There are plenty of pretty villages.

The most striking countryside is on the Isle of Purbeck, a mixture of rugged coast with quieter farmland, and attractive villages nestling into folds in the hills. North of the hills towards Poole Harbour and Studland Bay the heathland, partly planted with conifers, is a popular roaming ground for nature lovers. West of Weymouth, a pleasantly busy mix of port and resort, there's the tremendous sweep of the Chesil Beach, its pebbles and boulders immaculately graded by millennia of storms, and the long lagoon behind it. Lyme Regis is a civilised period resort, with high downs inland between here and Bridport.

The flatter heathland west of Wareham has been tank training ground for decades, and is generally not nearly so interesting.

Where to stay

Corfe Castle SY9383 Mortons House Wareham BH20 5EE (0929) 480988 *£80; 17 rms (the best are in the extension). Elizabethan manor house with comfortable, oak-panelled drawing room, winter log fire, and attractive restaurant with very good food and fine wines; pretty walled garden overlooking the thatched cottages of this lovely village.

Wareham SU9287 Priory BH20 4ND (0929) 551 666 £80; 19 very comfortable rms – the best being in the converted boathouse. Beautifully converted medieval buildings set in four acres of carefully kept riverside gardens; two elegant lounges furnished with antiques (pianist on Saturday evening), delicious English cooking served in the converted abbot's cellar, and genuinely welcoming service.

West Bexington SY5387 Manor Dorchester DT2 9DF (0308) 897616 *£75; 13 rms with sherry and decent tea; most with own bthrm. Handsome and civilised old stone hotel mentioned in Domesday Book and in pleasant, remote setting not far from beach; relaxed, informal atmosphere, comfortable lounge, popular pubby cellar bar, log fires, good bar food, excellent restaurant food, and friendly service.

Swanage SZ0278 PINES Burlington Rd BH19 1LT (0929) 425211 **£64**; 43 rms. Airy hotel notable for its terrific position overlooking the sea; popular food; disabled access.

Abbotsbury SY5785 ILCHESTER ARMS Weymouth DT3 4JR (0305) 871243 **£55**; 10 comfortable rms – the back ones have sea view. Handsome, old stone inn close to abbey with famous swannery; rambling beamed bar decorated with hundreds of swan pictures, log fire; popular food, breakfasts served in attractive no-smoking conservatory, restaurant, and pleasant staff; plenty of coastal and country walks.

Osmington Mills SY7381 SMUGGLERS Weymouth DT3 6HF (0305) 833125 **£50**; 6 rms. Best out of season, this much-extended, thatched stone pub – just above the sea – has cosy corners, log fires, appropriate woodwork and nautical decorations; good-value bar food, and partly no-smoking restaurant.

East Knighton SY8185 COUNTRYMAN Dorchester DT2 8LL (0305) 852666 **£42**; 6 rms. Attractively converted pair of old cottages with decent food in carvery restaurant and bar – open fires, sofas.

West Lulworth SY8280 CASTLE Wareham BH20 5RN (0929) 41311 **£41**; 14 comfortable rms, most with own bthrm. Bustling thatched pub, nr Lulworth Cove, with good food in bar and dining room, lively flagstoned bar and quieter, more modern lounge, and award-winning garden (Morris dancers in summer); good walking country.

Corfe Castle SY9681 KNITSON OLD FARMHOUSE Wareham BH20 5JB (0929) 422836 ***£32**; 3 rms. Big, ancient cottage on working farm with Jersey cows, sheep, large garden with hens, pigs and 3 horses, pleasant walks; good evening food (Fri-Mon pm only) using home-reared pork and lamb; no smoking; cl Dec-Jan.

Another decent place to stay recommended by contributors is Caythorpe House in Swanage SZ0278.

To see and do

Abbotsbury SY5785 is a delightful Dorset village with many interesting places to visit, the most famous being the unique SWANNERY, founded by monks 600 years ago and still home to the only sizeable colony of swans in the world that can be seen during nesting time; the swan families quite happily come right up to visitors. Also the country's oldest working duck decoy, children's activities and interesting reed-bed walks. Snacks, shop, good disabled access; cl Nov-Mar exc Sun pm; £2.90 (but only £2 in winter, so a good place for a Sunday afternoon trip – it then has myriad other waterfowl). Continuing the area's natural theme are the SUBTROPICAL GARDENS, 20 acres of beautiful woodland with very mild coastal climate allowing rare and record-breaking plants and trees to flourish; the central walled garden in spring is a mass of azaleas, camellias and rhododendrons. Also woodland trail, aviary and play area; snacks, shop and plant centre, some disabled access; cl 25-26 Dec; *£2.80 summer, £1 winter. TITHE BARN COUNTRY MUSEUM Fascinating exhibition of rural life in ancient, thatched tithe barn; craft fairs and dovecot; good disabled access. Cl winter except Sun pm; £1.50. The Ilchester Arms here is good for lunch.

Bovington Camp SY8388 TANK MUSEUM Over 260 armoured fighting vehicles from 23 countries, some of which you can go inside; tank simulators, costumes, medals, weapons, videos, and special displays, going right up to the Gulf War. There are a number of new World War II exhibits and in 1994 they celebrate the 50th anniversary of D-Day. Meals, snacks, shop, disabled access; cl 10 days at Christmas; £4. CLOUDS HILL Lawrence of Arabia's cottage while he was a private in the tank corps here; his sleeping bag, furniture and other memorabilia can be seen in three ascetic little rooms on display; cl am, Mon (exc bank hols), Tues, Sat, all Nov-Mar; £2.20.

Bridport SY4692 MUSEUM Fine Tudor building in historic town centre, with interesting collections and local history displays; shop, some disabled access; cl Sun am, Mon, Tues, Thurs and Fri Nov-Mar; 70p. The HARBOUR MUSEUM just S of town is also worth a look, with its rope and net-making displays (disabled access; cl Oct-Mar; 50p), as is the CHANTRY, Bridport's oldest secular building, a medieval priest's house with many original features; by arrangement with Museum. The George Hotel is a friendly place for lunch. Bridport is still the country's main producer of rope, and its old harbour is now the busy fishing port of nearby West Bay, a restrained small resort.

! **Corfe** SY9681 CORFE CASTLE is the most spectacular ruin in the area, with superb views from its dramatic hilltop position – and itself immeasurably enhancing the views from the surrounding countryside. Snacks, shop; cl winter except wknds 12-3.30; £2.80. If you then wonder what the Norman castle looked like before Parliament destroyed it in 1646, the CORFE CASTLE MODEL VILLAGE has a faithful reconstruction set in attractive gardens; cl Nov-Easter; *£1.50. CORFE CASTLE MUSEUM Tudor building with history of the area, local relics and dinosaur footprints; disabled access; cl wkdys Nov-Mar exc some school hols. Parking can be a problem in the town in summer. The Greyhound and Fox are both decent pubs; the Greyhound at Norden Heath (A351 towards Wareham), also good, may be quieter in summer.

✝ **East Fleet** SY6380 nr Chickerell is interesting, particularly for the former church which was wrecked by a legendary 1824 storm. Swans nest on the nearby Fleet lagoon and can be seen free, and there are pleasant walks in the vicinity. Specially interesting if you've read J M Faulkner's *Moonfleet*. The Elm Tree at nearby Langton Herring is good for refreshments.

Kimmeridge Bay SY9079 has intriguing rock strata, and is a lovely spot; kept quieter than it might be by the toll.

Littlebredy SY5889 Bridehead's LAKESIDE GROUNDS below the church (public path alongside) are lovely – like Stourhead in miniature.

★ **Lyme Regis** is an attractive old seaside town, with rather an elegant, steep main street and interesting side streets; the esplanade is pretty, there's a lively little fishing and yacht harbour, and there are some pleasant coast and valley walks. The Pilot Boat on the front is the best place for lunch; last year the Royal Standard pub had a splendid Guy Fawkes fireworks party, but we don't know whether they're planning one this year. DINOSAURLAND Quite why children are so fascinated by dinosaurs is a mystery, but they should find plenty to entertain and educate them here; there's an excellent collection of fossils (constantly changing as more are discovered), and they do fossil walks along the beach; snacks, shop, disabled access to ground floor only; cl winter wkdys exc school hols; £2.50, guided beach walks £2.90. MARINE AQUARIUM Small, family-run exhibition of local marine life found in the sea and on the shore, very well placed on the historic harbour wall (though this makes parking tricky); disabled access; cl Nov-Apr; £1.10. They also run scenic BOAT TRIPS around the coast; £3 an hour. The LYME REGIS EXPERIENCE gives a lively

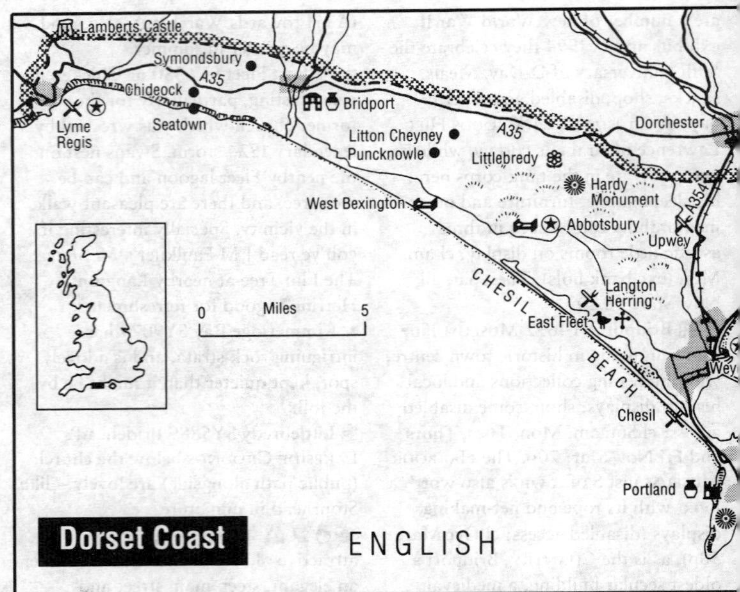

history of the town's development from port to resort, with a huge collection of fossils; cl Nov-Mar; £2.20.

Owermoigne SY7685 MILL HOUSE CIDER MUSEUM Displays of 18th-c and 19th-c cider-making equipment (during Oct-Dec harvest season), with a video demonstrating its application, and sales of the cider produced. They've also recently added a collection of clocks; cl 1-2 (exc Sun, when cider sales are restricted by licensing laws).

Portland SY6870 This odd, much-quarried promontory with its narrow neck and long naval connections gives tremendous views from its peak. Nearer at hand, the remarkable sea defences of Portland Harbour laid out below are a fine sight. The interesting CASTLE was built under Henry VIII to defend the south coast; there's a special D-Day exhibition May-July; snacks, shop; cl 1-2, all Oct-Mar; £1.70. PORTLAND MUSEUM Cottage used by Hardy in *The Well-Beloved*, now housing historical and maritime displays, also in 1994 Home Front displays to celebrate 50th anniversary of D-Day; shop, limited disabled access; cl 1-1.30, Mon Sept-Easter; £1.15. The Cove House just above the beginning of Chesil Beach is good for lunch.

Swanage SZ0278 is a quiet 19th-c resort. SWANAGE RAILWAY Exhibition of old railway memorabilia inc wartime troop and evacuee trains; six-mile steam train rides; snacks, shop, disabled access; cl winter wkdys except school hols, phone (0929) 425800 for train times; £4. DURLSTON COUNTRY PARK 260 acres of spectacular scenery and unspoilt countryside; good spots to watch seabirds, butterflies or deer, traditional farming – or pleasant for just walking. Snacks, shop, disabled access; information centre cl wkdys Nov-Mar. There wil be local D-DAY EXHIBITIONS Jun-Oct at the Tourist Information Centre; Town Hall (radar development); and Tithe Barn Museum.

★ **Tyneham** SY8880 This ABANDONED VILLAGE on the army's

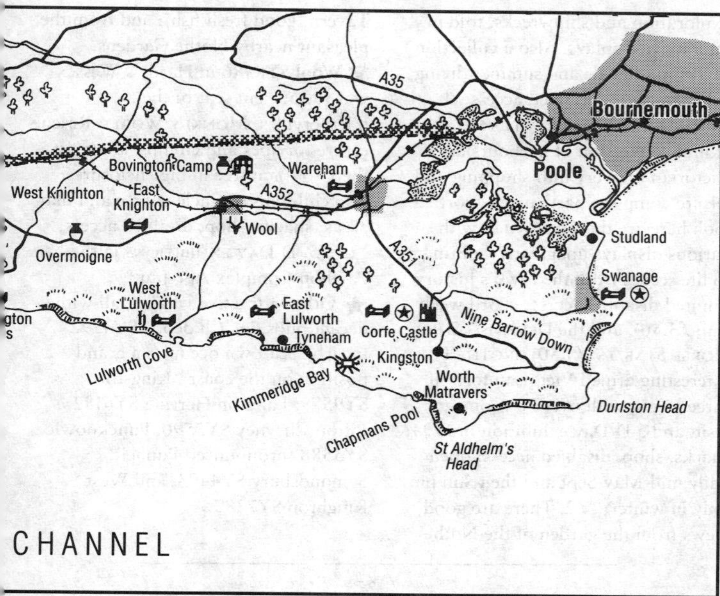

Purbeck firing ranges (open holidays and most wknds) is quite poignant; there's an explanatory exhibition in the former schoolroom.

☀ ⚘ ⚱ **Wareham** SY9287 BLUE POOL (3 miles S at Furzebrook) Peaceful beauty spot with curious colour changes whenever the weather alters, from light green to blue to suddenly a rich turquoise; it's bluest on an overcast day. Around it are 25 acres of heathland with lots of rare plants and animals, and there's a museum about the history of the site and the clay industry for which it was originally excavated. Snacks, shop; cl Oct-Mar; *£2.

West Lulworth SY8280 LULWORTH COVE HERITAGE CENTRE Interesting exhibitions and displays on smuggling, local wildlife and plants, and country wines amongst other topics; shop, disabled access. The museum will be cl until 1 Apr 1994 for rebuilding, but from then on should be open all year; *£1.50. A lovely spot, the cove itself is very beautiful, with extraordinary nearby rock formations; the thatched Castle Inn is useful for lunch.

★ ! ❀ ⚱ **Weymouth** SY6778 has elegant 18th- and 19th-c terraces along its curving esplanade, and some older buildings in the narrower streets behind. The harbour is lively, with big ferries leaving from the outer quay, and the town's inner ring road running one-way around the inner harbour. Overlooking the harbour, the Old Rooms and the Ship are both useful for lunch. On the far side of the harbour the narrow streets of the old town are worth exploring. The resort has a good beach, and lots of lively family attractions such as the SEA LIFE PARK, part of Lodsmoor Country Park; stunning marine life displays, observatories for close-up views of sharks, blue whale splash pool, children's adventureland, and lakeside picnic area; meals, snacks, shop; cl 25 Dec; £4.50. DEEP SEA ADVENTURE & TITANIC STORY There's something quite fascinating about the search for buried treasure, and this place brings it all vividly to life, with the full story of underwater exploration and shipwrecks, told in interactive displays. Also a collection of Titanic signals and summer diving displays; shop, disabled access; cl 24-26 Dec; £3.35. BREWERS QUAY Skilful conversion of harbourside Victorian brewery into shopping and leisure complex: particularly worth a look here are the TIMEWALK, with various displays imaginatively bringing to life scenes from the town's history (limited disabled access; cl 3rd week Jan; £3.50), and the DEVENISH SHIRE HORSE STABLES (£1.50). NOTHE FORT Interesting armed Victorian fort on three levels, with over 70 rooms to visit, and a D-Day exhibition in 1994; snacks, shop, disabled access; open daily mid-May-Sept and then Sun pm only in winter; *£2. There are good views from the garden of the Nothe Tavern (good fresh fish); and from the pleasant nearby Nothe Gardens.

♈ **Wool** SY8486 in Hardy's Wessex was the ancient seat of the d'Urbervilles. MONKEY WORLD Rescue centre for apes and chimps, allowing them to roam free in big enclosures; also childrens obstacle course and play areas; snacks, shop, disabled access; *£3.75. D-DAY EXHIBITIONS in the Pavilion Complex Apr-Jun.

★ Other **attractive villages**, all with decent pubs, inc Chideock SY4292 (nearby Seatown occupies a grand position on the coast), Kingston SY9579, Langton Herring SY6182, Litton Cheyney SY5590, Puncknowle SY5388 (pronounced Punnel), Symondsbury SY4493, and West Knighton SY7387.

Walks

This area has the county's best walking. The **Dorset Coast Path**, part of the 500-mile South West Peninsula Path, follows the entire coastline where practicable; sheer unfenced drops from the clifftops (particularly on Purbeck) are not to everyone's taste.

The most remarkably varied short walk in the county is from **Studland** SZ0382. In a couple of hours you can take in Ballard Down (huge views over Poole Harbour), Old Harry Rocks (tooth-like chalk pinnacles detached from the cliff) and the Agglestone (a rock standing solitary on Dorset's largest surviving heath). **Nine Barrow Down** SZ0081, the main Purbeck ridge, has far-ranging two-way views and makes a good goal for walks from Corfe Castle.

Westwards from Lyme Regis SY3492, a path snakes through an intriguing nature-reserve undercliff, still subject to landfalls, a celebrated area for fossils and flora. **Golden Cap**, the highest point on the county's coast, can be reached from Chideock SY4292 or Seatown SY4291 (useful pubs in both places), a stiff but rewarding haul either way. Abbotsbury SY5785 (again, a good pub here) is the start for strolls around **Chapel Hill** SY5784 and on to the massive shingle bank of **Chesil Beach** (exhausting to walk any distance along). Paths leading north from the village get lovely views from the chalk downs. From a tiny ruined church at **East Fleet** SY6380 you can get close up to the great lagoon enclosed by Chesil Beach, which was used for trying out the 'dam-busting' bouncing bomb during the Second World War; it is a peaceful spot with a diverse bird population.

At **Lulworth Cove** SY8280 (the Castle up the lane is a good pub), the classic mini-walk is westwards along the cliffs to Durdle Door, a natural arch eroded by the sea; inland is prairie-like monotony, and it is best to return the same way. East of Lulworth Cove is army training land, which means high-security fences and dire warning notices, but you are allowed in most wknds and daily in Aug and during Easter (keep to the paths).

The excellent coast walk between **Lulworth Cove** and **Kimmeridge Bay** SY9078 heads past the surreal 'fossil forest' (formed of petrified algae that once clung to tree-trunks) to Mupe Bay SY8479. Another path ascends **Bindon Hill** SY8380, looking down over the semi-circular cove. Be warned that this fine stretch of coast may be closed for army firing practice; information boards by road junctions off the A351 and A352 nr Wareham give warning. Or ring (0929) 462721 ext 4824 and ask for the Guardroom.

At Kingston SY9579 (where the Scott Arms is a good family pub) an easy level path goes to **Hounstout Cliff** SY9577. Turn left at the end and you are into Dorset fossil country, presided over by the primitive hermitage chapel on **St Aldhelm's Head** SY9675; the path here is of the switchback sort, and the chalk mud can make it tough going. Swanage SZ0278 has on its edge **Durlston Head Country Park** SZ0377, with the headland and the Great Globe, a 40-ton global representation in Purbeck marble, in close reach.

The Square & Compass at **Worth Matravers** SY9777 is another good base for coast walks. Near here, the rock pool at Dancing Ledge SY9976 is said to have been cut by a local schoolmaster.

Just E of Charmouth a steep narrow road leads up to **Stonebarrow Hill** SY3893; good easy walking, fine sea and inland views, disabled WC, NT shop in season.

The memorably hideous Hardy Monument (commemorating the admiral) dominates the high heathland above **Portesham** SY6085, but the compensation is a view which covers the entire sweep of the West Dorset coast. A track south-east from the summit, along Bronkham Hill, has an evocatively ancient feel about it, with ancient burial mounds flanking the way. Lamberts Castle SY3799 is an unspoiled hill fort, charming for strolls (esp late summer when the heather is out).

Driving

The B3157 coast road is very attractive, with fine views W of Abbotsbury. Most of the small back roads burrow into quietly interesting countryside, for the most part very unspoilt. There are toll gates in Purbeck on some of the lanes leading down to the prettiest coves, and the attractive route between Purbeck and East Lulworth over the West Creech Hills may sometimes be closed for army firing practice.

The A35 running right across this area gives a good feel of the changing scenery, with some excellent views particularly between Chideock and Lyme Regis; there can be queues of traffic in summer.

Where to eat

Chesil SY6973 Cove House (0305) 820895 Excellent sea views from simple old pub virtually on the beach; separate seafood menu as well as bar food and à la carte. **£16.80**|£2.60/£7.80.
Lyme Regis SY3492 Pilot Boat (02974) 43157 Welcoming old smugglers inn not far from beaches; lots of seafood in bar and restaurant, children's menu, decent wines. **£15**|£1.75/£5.50.
Langton Herring SY6182 Elm Tree (0305) 871257 Busy pub in pretty thatched village with good range of interesting, home-cooked bar food, children's menu; close to coastal path. £2/£6.10.
In the last few months we've had extremely promising reports on the food at the Old Ship at Upwey SY6684.

North and Central Dorset

An area that has interesting places to visit, charming country towns, good places to stay, and includes Hardy country.

This part of the county has more places to visit than the coastal area. Among them, Forde Abbey at Thorncombe is outstanding, and Athelhampton House is still very well worth visiting despite the 1992 fire. Dorchester, Sherborne, Beaminster, Shaftesbury and Blandford Forum are all interesting towns with much to explore, and have a good few craft and antique shops without being overtly touristy. Of many charming villages here, Milton Abbas takes the crown. Though the area's main attractions are mostly of an adult nature, there's plenty to keep children amused, too: the butterflies at Over Compton and the rare farm breeds at Gillingham are particularly well displayed.

This is, of course, Thomas Hardy country, and many people get extra pleasure from the many direct memories of his books which particular villages and tracts of countryside conjure up. It has a fine mix of scenery from the chalk uplands and intricate valleys of the central area to the quiet seclusion of the more intimate farming country in the west. There is pleasant walking, though sometimes the longer paths can be difficult to follow.

There is also a good choice of places to stay in and to eat at, and the area is a good deal quieter in summer than the coast.

Where to stay

Sherborne ST6316 Eastbury Long St DT9 3BY (0935) 813131 ***£98**; 15 pretty rms. Elegant Georgian townhouse with comfortable lounge, library, good food, relaxing atmosphere, and garden; close to abbey and castles.

Chedington ST4805 Chedington Court Beaminster DT8 3HY (0935) 891265 ***£95**; 10 rms. Handsome Jacobean-style hotel in fine hillside setting with lovely views, an elegant lounge, pretty conservatory, library, billiard room, and a tranquil atmosphere; very good dinners in civilised restaurant, and a fine wine list; 10 acres of gardens with croquet and a par 74 nine-hole golf course; cl 1 Jan-4 Feb.

Gillingham ST8026 Stock Hill SP8 5NR (0747) 823 626 **£110**; 9 lovely, very comfortable rms. Marvellously relaxing, carefully run Victorian manor house in 10 acres of parkland, with antiques and paintings in opulent day rooms; particularly welcoming service, and excellent food in the no-smoking restaurant using home-grown herbs and veg, local meat and fish; all-weather tennis court, croquet; children over 7 only.

Evershot ST5403 Summer Lodge DT2 0JR (0935) 83424 ***£100**; 17 big, individually decorated rms. The Earl of Ilchester's former dower house is a beautifully kept, peaceful hotel with really lovely flower displays in the comfortable and elegantly furnished day rooms; very attractive restaurant with fine views of the pretty garden, excellent food using the best local produce, fine breakfasts, and personal, caring service; outdoor swimming pool, tennis and croquet; children over 8 only; disabled access; dogs allowed.

Dorchester KINGS ARMS High St East DT1 1HF (0305) 265353 **£79**; 33 rms – the Lawrence of Arabia and the Tutenkhamun suites are extraordinary. Smart, thriving coaching inn made famous by Hardy's *Mayor of Casterbridge*; different menus in restaurant, coffee shop and bar, old-fashioned public bar with real ales, live music twice a week; children under 12 sharing parents' room are only charged for food.

Evershot ST5704 ACORN Dorchester DT2 0JW (0935) 83228 **£60**; 8 comfortable rms. Comfortable L-shaped lounge bar, pretty furnishings and fine old fireplaces; good food, decent wines and real ales, very good breakfasts, friendly service, no-smoking restaurant; surrounded by attractive Hardy walking country.

Halstock ST5407 HALSTOCK MILL Yeovil BA22 9SJ (0935) 891278 ***£50**; 4 rms. Attractive 17th-c house quietly set in 10 acres with lots of surrounding walks; log fire in cosy lounge, pleasant little dining room, and good food using home-grown fruit and veg, local fish and cheese; stabling; cl Christmas; children over 5 only.

Milton Abbas ST8001 HAMBRO ARMS Blandford Forum DT11 0BP (0258) 880233 **£50**; 2 rms. Pretty and popular old inn in beautiful 1770s landscaped village; with beamed front lounge, log fire, decent food, and prompt friendly service; children over 10 only.

Powerstock SY5196 THREE HORSESHOES Bridport DT6 3TF (0308) 85328 **£45**; 4 rms. Busy stone and thatch pub in lovely setting, ideal for fishing nearby; imaginative food and around 10 fresh fish dishes.

Lydlinch ST7413 HOLEBROOK FARM Sturminster Newton DT10 2JB (0258) 817348 ***£44**; 2 rms in farmhouse, with 3 (usually self-catering) in comfortable converted stables; also 4 self-catering cottages in converted byre – all very flexible. 18th-c house on family-run, grassland farm in very peaceful setting, small swimming pool, games room and clay pigeon shooting.

Cerne Abbas ST6601 NEW Long St Dorchester DT2 7JF (03003) 41274 **£40**; 4 comfortable rms, some with four-poster. Pretty 15th-c inn with beamed L-shaped lounge bar, warm atmosphere; carefully cooked food inc marvellous breakfasts, good, interesting wine list (around a dozen by the glass too), considerate service, and sheltered back lawn.

Child Okeford ST8313 SAXON Gold Hill Blandford Forum DT11 8HD (0258) 860310 **£32**; 2 simple rms. Notably friendly little village pub in converted farmhouse, lots of animals.

To see and do

Dorchester SY6890 The county town was laid out by the Romans, and the main streets still follow their plan; the tree-lined Walks follow part of the line of their walls, and other traces of their time include the amphitheatre on Weymouth Ave, not far from ELDRIDGE POPE'S VICTORIAN BREWERY (which can be visited by arrangement).

Dorchester is a thriving country town, with busy shopping streets (and several worthwhile antique and print shops). Though most of the more attractive Georgian buildings are just out of the bustle, there are distinguished buildings on the main streets, including the timbered building of JUDGE JEFFREYS' LODGINGS in High West St – this was where he stayed during his notorious Bloody Assizes.

In the same street the COUNTY MUSEUM provides a good clear introduction both to the town and to the whole area, running from dinosaur remains through displays on prehistoric villages and farms to rural life and crafts, and with the reconstructed study of Thomas Hardy, who used the town as the centre of events in *The Mayor of Casterbridge*; shop; cl Sun, 25-26 Dec, Good Fri; £2. Along in High East St the Kings Arms Hotel, full of Hardy associations, is a good place for lunch (other places to consider include the Bakers Arms in Monmouth Rd and the Stationmasters House down by the South Station).

More dinosaurs at the lively DINOSAUR MUSEUM (Icen Way), the largest such single-minded display in the country, with skeletons, fossils, reconstructions and interactive displays. Children are encouraged to touch and feel things; shop, disabled access; cl 24-26 Dec; £2.95.

A similar approach is found at the TUTANKHAMUN EXHIBITION (High West St), recreating the discovery of ancient treasures using a mix of sights, sounds and smells; details as Dinosaur Museum (see above).

The DORSET MILITARY MUSEUM is in a splendid building, the Keep (Bridport Rd); a landmark here ever since it was built as the Victorian gatehouse of the regimental barracks. Now it houses exhibits from all the county's regiments and there are 1994 D-Day displays; shop; cl Sun; £1.

MAIDEN CASTLE a mile or so SW is one of best examples of an Iron-Age fort, covering 47 acres.

Just out of town, on the edge of Puddletown Heath ('Egdon Heath'), thatched HARDY'S COTTAGE hasn't changed much since the author was born here in 1840, though the heath's now largely forested (there is a stretch of open heathland much as he knew it just SE). The cottage is open mainly by appointment (0305) 262366, shop; cl 1-2, Thurs, Nov-Mar; *£2.30.

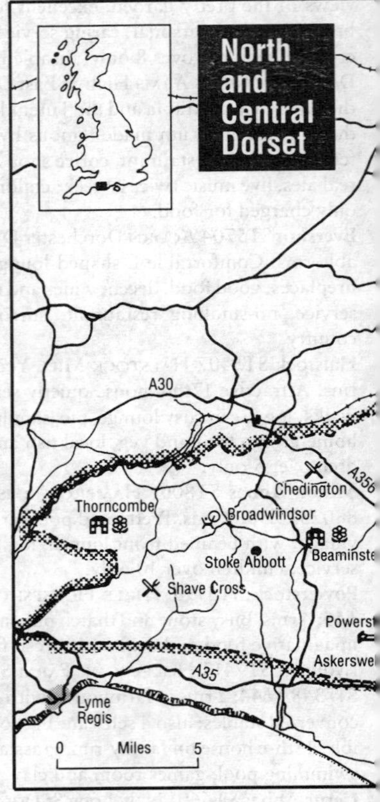

Other things to see and do

Athelhampton SY7794

ATHELHAMPTON HOUSE Magnificent 15th-c house with beautiful furnishings and hall, acres of formal and landscaped gardens with rare plants, topiary and fountain pools, antiques, occasional craft fairs. There was a bad fire here in Nov 1992, but fortunately most exhibits were saved; Perspex screens in front of the damaged rooms let you see restoration in progress. Meals, snacks, shop, disabled access; open pm Weds, Thurs, Sun and bank hols Easter-Oct, also Tues May-Sept and Mon and Fri in Aug; £3.80 house and gardens, £1.90 garden only. In **Puddletown** SY7594 nearby, ILSINGTON HOUSE is another

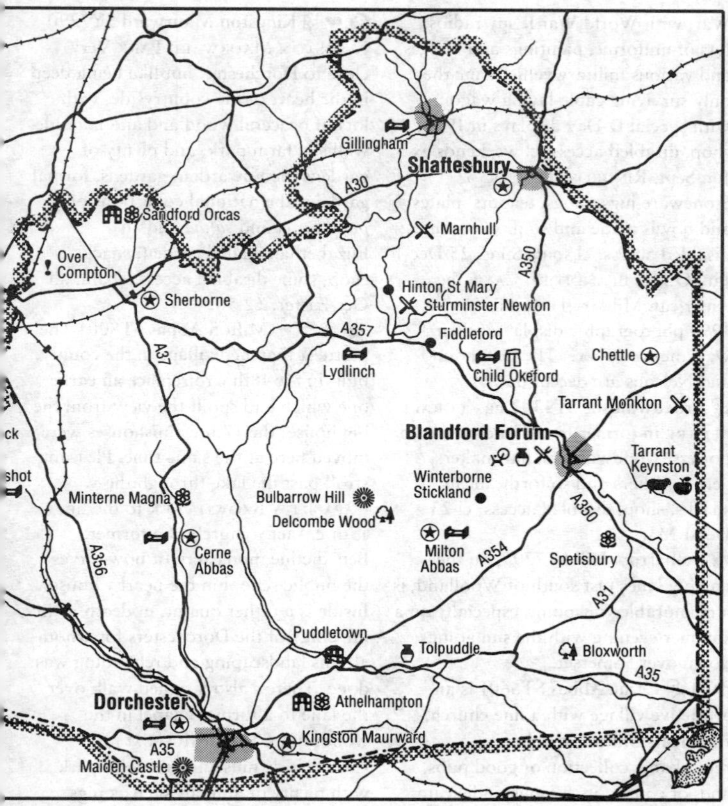

interesting old house, with some scandalous, ancient history, Royal connections; open pm Weds, Thurs, Sun and bank hols May-Sept.

Beaminster ST4701 PARNHAM (A3066 towards Bridport) Fine Tudor mansion, surrounded by 14 acres of lovely gardens, now famous as home of John Makepeace furniture-maker; workshop open, completed pieces shown around house, exhibitions by other designers and craftsmen. Snacks, shop, mostly disabled access; open Sun, Weds and bank hols, Apr-Oct; £3 (£2 for woods). MAPPERTON GARDENS (off B3163 E) Several acres of terraced hillside gardens in grounds of 16th-c manor house, specimen trees and shrubs, fountains, grottoes, fishponds, orangery, good walks and views. Shop, some disabled access; cl am, all Nov-Feb; *£2.50. HORN PARK (A3066 N) Unusual plants in series of gardens with bluebell woods, ponds, wild flowers and good views; open pm Tues, Thurs and 1st and 3rd Suns of each month; *£2. Pickwicks is good for lunch.

★ **Blandford Forum SY8806** Georgian market town, rebuilt in 1731 after older buildings destroyed by fire, very interesting to walk round. MUSEUM Good local history displays, with exhibition of local art and crafts; shop; disabled access to ground floor only; cl Sun, Nov-Mar; *30p. ROYAL SIGNALS MUSEUM The history of army communications from the Crimean

War, with World War II spy radios, lots of uniforms, paintings and badges, and various military vehicles inc the only surviving cable-laying wagon, with special D-Day displays in 1994; shop, disabled access; cl weekends exc Jun-Sept. RINGROSE POTTERY Stoneware jugs, mugs, teapots, plates and bowls made and sold on premises; disabled access; cl some Suns, 25 Dec-1 Jan. Out at BLANDFORD CAMP the American Military Hospitals have a 1994 photographic display of their wartime work here. The Greyhound and Nelsons are decent pubs.

Broadwindsor ST4302 has a CRAFT CENTRE in former farm buildings, with potters, woodworkers, hat-makers, gem-polishers and so forth; meals, snacks, shop, disabled access; cl 23 Dec-1 Mar.

Bulbarrow Hill ST7705, on the narrow lanes just south of Woolland, is a memorable viewpoint, especially on a summer evening with the sun going down over Somerset.

✝ **Cerne Abbas** ST6601 is an attractive village with a fine church, fragments of the old abbey, a remarkable collection of good pubs, and, of course, its famous, indelicate prehistoric giant cut into the chalk above – best seen from the main road north. There's a working POTTERY (cl Mon) on the way up to the giant.

Chettle ST9413 CHETTLE HOUSE Fine example of a baroque country house designed by Thomas Archer, with beautifully laid-out gardens, vineyard, gallery; various craft weekends and special events. Teas, no disabled access to house; cl Tues, Sat, 3rd Sun Oct-Easter; *£1.80.

Hambledon Hill ST8412 is a very imposing hill fort in a commanding position just above Child Okeford – where the Saxon Inn is a good lunch stop.

★ **Fiddleford** ST8013 is an attractive village, and the Fiddleford Inn is now one of the best places for eating out in the area.

Kingston Maurward SY7290 KINGSTON MAURWARD PARK Very close to Dorchester, but like being deep in the heart of the countryside, with lots of peaceful woodland and lakeside walks, a farm park, and plenty of gardens inc Edwardian gardens, formal gardens, the national collections of *penstemon* and *salvia* and an Elizabethan walled garden; snacks, shop, some disabled access; cl am, all Oct-Easter; £2.50.

★ ✝ **Milton Abbas** ST8001 The prettiest thatched village in the county, built in the 18th c to replace an earlier one which had spoilt the view from the big house; the 17th-c almshouses were moved here at the same time. Pleasant stroll past the lake through the CAPABILITY BROWN PARK to the fine 15th-c ABBEY church of a former Benedictine monastery (it now serves the public school in the nearby house). Inside is a rather quaint, in-death-as-in-life effigy of the Dorchesters for whom all this landscaping and rebuilding was done. There's also a signed walk over the lane to a former chapel in the wood. PARK FARM MUSEUM Countryside museum and farm park, with plenty of animals such as pigs, donkeys, rabbits and goats to touch and feed; snacks, shop; cl Nov-Mar; £2. RARE POULTRY, PIG AND PLANT CENTRE Ten breeds of pig and piglets, all sorts of unusual poultry inc hens laying eggs in dazzling blues and browns, baby chicks to touch, other animals, and local crafts; snacks, shop; cl Weds, mid-Oct-Easter; *£1.60. The village inn is good.

Minterne Magna ST6504 MINTERNE GARDENS Lovely landscaped gardens, with lakes, cascades, streams, rare trees and impressive spring shows of azaleas, rhododendrons and spring bulbs; cl Nov-Mar; *£2.

! **Over Compton** ST5817 WORLDWIDE BUTTERFLIES AND LULLINGSTONE SILK FARM Superb collection of butterflies from all over the world, flying free in reconstructions of their natural habitat inside Elizabethan Compton Hall; silk farm demonstrates production of English silk used for coronations and royal weddings. They also have a new exhibition on conservation; snacks, shop, some disabled access; cl Fri and Sat exc mid-July-Aug, all Nov-Mar; £4.25.

Sandford Orcas ST6220 MANOR HOUSE Interesting little Tudor manor house, largely unaltered since 16th c, with fine furnishings and family portraits, also pleasant gardens; open Easter Mon, Sun pm and all day Mon May-Sept; *£2.

★ **Shaftesbury** ST8622 This hilltop town has good views from Castle Hill and Park Walk, and attractive corners like St James below the hill to the south. ABBEY RUINS AND MUSEUM Part of a nunnery founded by Alfred the Great, the abbey was destroyed in the Reformation, but the foundations still exist, and the museum has plenty of remains found during excavations, as well as an Anglo-Saxon herb garden; shop, disabled access; cl Nov-Easter; 90p. The LOCAL HISTORY MUSEUM at the top of Gold Hill, the pretty steep hill used in the TV Hovis commercials, has interesting displays of old domestic items, toys, pottery and excavated remains; cl Oct-Easter, may open some winter weekends; 60p. The Grosvenor Hotel and, down Gold Hill, the Two Brewers are both good for lunch, and the Ship is a quaint old tavern. There are several craft shops and workshops.

★ **Sherborne** ST6316 is an attractive town to wander through, given a feeling of unchanging solidity by the handsome, stone medieval abbey buildings that mix in with later ones of the public school here, and by many other fine old buildings in the main street and off it. The ABBEY itself is a glorious golden stone building with a beautifully vaulted nave; at the Dissolution the townspeople raised the money to buy it, and it's remained the local parish church ever since. SHERBORNE CASTLE Built by Sir Walter Raleigh in 1594 and home of the Digby family since 1617, this is a fascinating fully furnished historic house, with interesting paintings and porcelain, gardens designed by Capability Brown, and beautiful parklands with an enormous lake. Snacks, shop; open pm Thurs, Sat, Sun, and bank hols Easter-Oct; £3.60 house and gardens, £1.50 grounds only. SHERBORNE OLD CASTLE The original 12th-c castle, destroyed by Cromwell in the Civil War, but still plenty of interesting ruins; shop, mostly disabled access; cl winter Mon; £1.20. SHERBORNE MUSEUM Interesting local history exhibits, reconstruction of original castle, Victorian dolls' house, ecclesiastical Roman remains; shop; cl Sun am, Mon, Nov-week before Easter; 50p. The Digby Tap is recommended for lunch. Several craft shops include a working saddlery in the main street.

Spetisbury ST9102 OLD MILL Pretty, medium-sized riverside water garden, with lots of plants for sale; open Weds pm Apr-Oct; £1.

Tarrant Keynston ST9204 KEYNSTON MILL FRUIT FARM Interesting vineyard and farm shop, with 21 different kinds of pick-your-own; meals, snacks, shop; restaurant cl winter Mon.

Thorncombe ST3504 FORDE ABBEY The extensive gardens here have just won an award for Garden of the Year, and they really are special, with glorious trees and shrubs, a fine collection of Asiatic primulas, many interesting plants, and sweeping lawns. The abbey buildings still retain some of the features of the original 12th-c Cistercian monastery, though it was modernised in 1500 by Abbot Chard and it is his Great Hall and Tower that remain. Cromwell's Attorney-General later turned the abbey into a house, and the interior has changed little since, with magnificently furnished rooms, unusual plaster ceilings and a set of Raphael tapestries; it's a very striking building. Meals and snacks (in 12th-c undercroft), shop, disabled access to gardens only; house open pm Weds, Sun and bank hols Apr-Oct, garden and nursery all year; £4.30, £3 garden only.

Tolpuddle SY7994 Famous for the agricultural workers who united to improve their working conditions and terms of employment. The MARTYRS' TREE under which they supposedly met still remains, and six cottages contain the TOLPUDDLE MUSEUM telling their story; shop; cl Sun, Christmas week. The Martyrs pub is useful for lunch.

★ Other **attractive villages** with decent pubs include Chedington ST4805, Evershot ST5704, Hinton St Mary ST7816 (superb manor house, medieval tithe barn), Powerstock SY5196, Tarrant Monkton ST9408, and Winterborne Stickland ST8304. You might also like to explore the bridleway from Stubhampton ST9114 along Ashmore Bottom to Ashmore (can be muddy in a wet spring).

Walks

Despite the ultra-English charm of much of inland Dorset – chalk downs, sleepy thatched villages, clumps of beechwoods and fine views – the area is surprisingly little walked, and careful map-reading is necessary as field routes are often not obvious. The best areas inc those where agricultural improvement has been limited: the vicinities of **Powerstock** SY5196 and **Stoke Abbott** ST4500, for example, have delectable downland and valley landscapes, with a reasonably good path network (and both have good pubs). In the attractive downland west of Melcombe Bingham ST7602, the dry ground of the **Dorsetshire Gap** ST7403 comes as a pleasant surprise on those days when you begin to think that all Dorset is turning to chalky mud.

The picturesque village of **Milton Abbas** ST8001 has attractive paths through the abbey estate and into Green Hill Down Nature Reserve; a longer walk continues north-west to **Bulbarrow Hill** ST7605, which looks far into Somerset and Wiltshire. **Maiden Castle** SY6890, near Dorchester, is so vast that the tour of its grassy ramparts almost qualifies as a fully fledged walk.

From the birthplace of Thomas Hardy at **High Bockhampton** SY7292 you can walk into nearby forest plantations and on to Black Heath and Duddle Heath, the 'untamed and untameable' Egdon Heath of Hardy's novels: further Hardyesque features abound locally, including the church at Stinsford ('Mellstock') SY7191, where Hardy's heart is buried beside his first wife – a path from the river at Lower Bockhampton SY7290 leads to the village.

Cranborne Chase ST9217, shared with Wiltshire, offers good walking with some fine views, especially around Ashmore ST8920.

There's a fine **bluebell wood** at Bere Wood SY8794 at the west end of Bloxworth; the track can be followed right through to Bere Regis. (There are even more bluebells at Delcombe Wood ST7805, but the only public track just skirts the west edge of the wood.)

Driving

The central downland has some interesting drives through largely unspoilt countryside. The valley road N from Winterborne Whitechurch through the Winterbornes up to Okeford Fitzpaine gives good changing views of the downland on either side, wooded and steeply chiselled as you approach Okeford.

The high road E from Holywell, on the A37 nr Evershot over Batcombe Hill, and Gore Hill to Minterne Magna offers memorable views. A pleasant circular drive is from Piddletrenthide through Plush and Mappowder to Hazelbury Bryan, then S along the ancient ridge road over Bulbarrow Hill, through Ansty and Melcombe Bingham, to turn right at Cheselbourne for Piddletrenthide again. There are some bracing views from the ridge road which forks off the A352 at Middlemarsh and runs along above Cerne all the way down to Dorchester. The zigzag road down to Shaftesbury from Ashmore has an almost alpine quality.

In the west of the county, the B3165 through Marshwood and then along the B3164 to Broadwindsor takes you through a little-known and quite unspoilt valley.

The east-west main roads across the county tend to be slow, with traffic queues building up quite readily.

Where to eat

Sturminster Newton ST7813 PLUMBER MANOR Hazelbury Bryan Rd (0258) 72507 Fine 17th-c manor that has always belonged to the same family; at its heart are three stylish, evening dining rooms (though they also do Sun lunch); imaginative cooking, good wine list and friendly service; bedrooms; cl Feb; children over 10; disabled access. **£24.**

Blandford Forum ST8806 LA BELLE ALLIANCE Whitecliff Mill St (0258) 452842 Attractive little country-style restaurant in Victorian house with pleasant, friendly staff, excellent food, carefully chosen wine list, and open fire in cosy lounge; bedrooms; cl Sun, Mon (exc bank hols), 1st 3 wks Jan; children by arrangement. **£20.**

Marnhull ST7718 BLACKMORE VALE (0258) 820701 Relaxed and friendly atmosphere in this pleasant old pub with wide choice of good-value, home-cooked food; your order can be brought to the garden where one of the tables is thatched. **£13.50**|£2/£5.

Chedington ST4805 WINYARDS GAP (0935) 891244 Comfortable pub with marvellous views and nearby walks; good bar food with some unusual dishes and lots of home-made puddings, separate vegetarian and children's menus; self-catering flats in converted barn; cl 25 Dec pm. £1.40/£5.

Tarrant Monkton ST9408 LANGTON ARMS (025 889) 225 Thatched 17th-c pub in pretty village, with comfortable bar, open fire, skittle alley, good, popular food and summer barbecues. £1.75/£4.75.

Askerswell SY5292 SPYWAY (0308) 85250 Former smugglers look-out with exceptional value, very popular bar food, lots of salads and cheesecakes; plenty of views and walks nearby. £2.90/£3.70.

Other places worth knowing about for decent food inc the Anchor at Chideock SY4292 and the Shave Cross at Shave Cross SY4198 (both in lovely positions too).

Help this year from: *WHBM, HNJ, PEJ, Denise Plummer, Jim Froggatt, Dr and Mrs D M Gunn, Dave Braisted, Paul McPherson, J Ferguson, M E A Horler, P and J Roberts, Nigel and Bridget Pullan, Tony and Val Marshall, R B Crail, Andy and Jill Kassube, Jane Pendock, Shirley Pielou, Peter Churchill, David Gray, Julian and Sarah Stanton, Mr and Mrs A R Hawkins, Alan Kilpatrick, Chris Woodward, Iris and Eddie Brixton, Dr G Buckton, Mr and Mrs Michael Howl, Mrs C A Blake, Stan Edwards, David Brown, CG, Romey Heaton, Mrs A E Sargent, Ian Phillips, Steve Huggins, W H and E Thomas, A Baron, A Campbell, Michael and Rachel Brookes, Marjorie and David Lamb, John and Christine Simpson, M and J Back, G Washington, Derek Patey.*

Dorset Calendar

Some of these dates were provisional as we went to press.

JANUARY

Dorchester Exhibition of the Botanical Drawings and Paintings of Mary Tarraway *at County Museum – till Tues 11*

FEBRUARY

27th **Kingston Maurward** Book Fair *at Dorset College of Agriculture and Horticulture, with thousands of antiquarian, secondhand books, maps and prints for sale*

APRIL

1st **Athelhampton** Craft Fair *– till Mon 4*

MAY

10th **Weymouth** Water Festival

25th **Isle of Portland** WWII and D-Day Military Vehicle Display and Parade

28th **Weymouth** Oyster Festival *– till Sun 29*

30th **Blandford** South of England Town Crier Competition; **Weymouth** International Beach Kite Festival; *also* Trawler Race

31st **Bovington** Military Vehicle Rally *at the Tank Museum – till 5 Jun*

JUNE

2nd **Weymouth** D-Day Military and Veteran Parade *inc military bands, WWII military vehicles and an outdoor service; also* Royal Navy Warship Exercises *inc veteran coastal patrol vessel, armed forces display teams, searchlight display and 40s dancing band*

3rd **Poole** WWII Commemorative Events and Services *inc parade of standards and military parade*

4th **Bournemouth** International Festival *– till Sun 19*

5th **Bovington** Military Parade *(similar) at Tank Museum*; Weymouth Seafront Military Parade *with historic tanks and the latest British hardware, followed by an embarkation off the beach on to a landing craft assault ship (HMS Fearless)*

5th **Poole** Powerboat Race *in the bay*

8th **Weymouth** 'We'll Meet Again' Gala, *a music hall production, at Pavilion Theatre – till Thurs 9*

JULY

1st **Lyme Regis** Jazz Festival

9th **Charmouth** Challenge and Fun Run *over NT land along cliffs*; **Maiden Newton** Summer Event *– till Sun 10*; **Puddletown** Carnival; **Yetminster** Chartered Village Fair *with the Yetties (1970s folk group) concert in the evening*

16th **Bradford Peverell** Village Fayre

17th **Tolpuddle** Martyrs Rally, *national march of unions parading traditional banners, with speakers, possibly from South Africa*; **Weymouth** Cutty Sark Tall Ships Race *with over 100 ships – till Weds 20 when the ships parade*

22nd **Cerne Abbas** Chamber Music Festival, *St Mary's church – till Sun 24*

DORSET CALENDAR

JULY cont.

23rd **Lyme Regis** Lifeboat Week – *till Sun 31*

24th **Poole** Camden Trophy Powerboat Race *in the bay*

27th **Athelhampton** Craft Fair

31st **Weymouth** Family Beach Kite Festival and Fun Day

AUGUST

6th **Shave Cross** Marathon; **South Perrott** Open Weekend – *gardens, cream teas, ferret racing and old working forge*

7th **Puddletown** County Arts and Crafts Show – *till Thurs 11*

14th **Bridport** Carnival Week *ending with torchlight procession – till Sun 21*; **Dorchester** Dorset Hunt Fair *at Came Park*; **Kingston Maurward** Book Fair *at Dorset College of Agriculture and Horticulture*

17th **Weymouth** Carnival, *inc air, sea and firework displays*

21st **Poole** The Needles International Power Boat Race *in the bay*

24th **Motcombe** Gillingham and Shaftesbury Agricultural Show

25th **Bridport** Melplash Show

31st **Tarrant Hinton** Great Dorset Steam Fair *at Showground, inc exhibits from abroad – till 4 Sept*

SEPTEMBER

3rd **Dorchester** Agricultural Show *with main ring attractions*

OCTOBER

17th **Westbury** Pack Monday Michaelmas Fair

NOVEMBER

5th **Weymouth** Guy Fawkes Night, *inc beach bonfire, fireworks, fair and barbecue*

13th **Kingston Maurward** Book Fair *at Dorset College of Agriculture and Horticulture*

We welcome reports from readers . . .

This GUIDE depends on readers' reports. Do help us if you can – in return, we offer a discount on the next edition to people who've helped us with reports for it. Tell us what you think about places already in it, and anything extra you think we should say about them. And send us your ideas for inclusion in the next edition: places to visit, eat at or stay in, attractive drives or walks, maybe even unusual interesting shops you know of. Use the card in the middle, the report forms at the end, or just write – no stamp needed: THE GOOD WEEKEND GUIDE, FREEPOST TN1569, Wadhurst, E Sussex TN5 7BR.

Essex

Both inland and along the coast of this county there are some interesting places – on the whole more appealing to adults than to children, though there are several good family attractions. While the countryside is far from spectacular and the coast is not the sort to fascinate most walkers, there is a quiet charm here which can bring visitors back again and again. The coastal areas have a wider choice of places to visit, but the inland villages and small towns tend to be more picturesque.

Inland Essex

Though Saffron Walden is a good place to stay and there are several other pleasant places, this area is not in the front rank of weekend destinations.

Saffron Walden, the county's most attractive small town, scores doubly by having magnificent Audley End nearby – and is only a short drive from Cambridge, just over the county border. Other places most worth visiting here include – at or near the top of the list – Castle Hedingham, Coggeshall, and the wildlife park at Widdington. Villages in this area often have attractive houses with distinctive colour-washed plasterwork, and churches that well repay a passing look.

Where to stay

Broxted TL5726 Whitehall Church End CM6 2BZ (0279) 850603 ***£105**; 25 pretty rms. Fine old manor house set in lovely walled gardens, with restful lounge, pleasant bar, ancient beams, big fireplaces, good food in pretty timbered restaurant, and friendly service; cl 25 Dec-31 Dec; disabled access.

Coggeshall TL8522 White Hart Colchester CO6 1NH (0376) 561654 ***£82**; 18 rms. 15th-c hotel with beamed lounge bar, log fires, friendly staff, and good food in bar and restaurant (which is cl Sun pm).

Thaxted TL6130 Swan Dunmow CM6 2PL (0371) 830321 **£65**; 21 comfortably modernised rms. Four-gabled, late 15th-c inn with pleasantly pubby refurbished circular bar, soft lighting, traditional furnishings, and good food.

Saffron Walden TL5438 Saffron High St CB10 1AY (0799) 522676 **£55**; 17 rms. Friendly 16th-c hotel with panelled bar, beams, and good bar restaurant food.

Rickling Green TL5029 Cricketers Arms CB11 3YG (0799) 543210 **£50**; 7 rms in modern block behind. Cheerful family-run pub by village green, cricketing mementoes, decent food in bar and restaurant.

Duddenhoe End TL4636 Duddenhoe End Farm Saffron Walden CB11 4UU (076 383) 8258 **£35**; 3 rms. 17th-c farmhouse with inglenook fireplaces and beams; no smoking; cl over Christmas; children over 10 only.

To see and do

Audley End House TL5438 Spectacularly grand Jacobean mansion and former Royal palace remodelled by Robert Adam, serenely surrounded by gardens landscaped by Capability Brown. It actually used to be much bigger, being described by James I as 'too large for a king': two-thirds were demolished during the 19th-c changes. Beautiful Great Hall, drawing room and lots of other rooms with fine furnishings and art. The gardens are splendid. Occasional special events; meals, snacks, shop, disabled access to gardens and ground floor; cl am, Mon (exc bank hols), Tue, Oct-Easter; *£4.90. A miniature railway is nearby, and the Queens Head at Littlebury has good food.

Braintree TL7622 WORKING SILK MUSEUM A rare opportunity to see the material made by hand, in a restored old mill building. The hand-looms they use are over 150 years old, and there's a display of fine silks and industrial machinery; shop, disabled access; cl 12.30-1.30, all day Sun and bank hols; *£2.75. The White Hart is useful for lunch; the Green Dragon, just outside at Youngs End, has good food.

Bures TM8835 PARADISE CENTRE (Lamarsh; so in fact just over the border in Essex) Fun for children, with miniature goats, bantams and play area, and fascinating for gardeners, with a very wide variety of unusual plants beautifully laid out and for sale, particularly woodland ones. Snacks; open wknds and bank hols Easter-Dec; *£1.50.

Castle Hedingham TL7835 has a good CHURCH with grand Norman masonry and interestingly carved choir seats, and some other attractive buildings. It's named for the Norman CASTLE which dominates it, its magnificent keep – one of the tallest in Europe – towering above the trees around the castle mound. The castle is exceptionally well preserved, its keep still with four floors and roof, and there's also a banqueting hall and minstrels' gallery; the wooded grounds are pleasant. Teas, shop; cl Nov-Easter; £2.50. COLNE VALLEY RAILWAY & MUSEUM Victorian railway buildings with collection of vintage engines and carriages, short steam-train trips every summer Sun, also Weds and Thurs in hols, check for timetable (0787) 61174; meals on Pullman coaches, snacks, shop; cl 23 Dec-1 Feb; £4, £2 when trains not running. There's a good working POTTERY in St James St, and the Bell is good for lunch.

Chappel TL8927 EAST ANGLIAN RAILWAY MUSEUM Comprehensive collection of railway memorabilia, in restored old station buildings, with a new miniature railway and steam days throughout the year; snacks, shop, disabled access; cl 25 Dec, steam days first Sun monthly as well as bank hols and Weds in Aug; £2, £3.50 steam days. The prettily sited Swan is good for lunch.

Chelmsford TL7006 CATHEDRAL was consecrated as such only in 1914; it's 15th-c with a real unity to its Perpendicular architecture; worth penetrating the town for if you are a church enthusiast.

★ **Coggeshall** TL8522 This attractive small town has a good few antique shops, and PAYCOCKE'S (NT), a fine, timber-framed, medieval merchant's home with unusual panelling and carvings, and a pretty garden behind; disabled access; open pm Tues, Thurs, Sun and bank hols mid-Mar-Sept; £1.40. The ancient Fleece next door is useful for lunch, and there's a working POTTERY further along the street. Another inn, the Woolpack out by the church, is a magnificent timbered building. There seem to be an inordinate amount of pubs for so small a place (another good one is the Chapel), and earlier in the

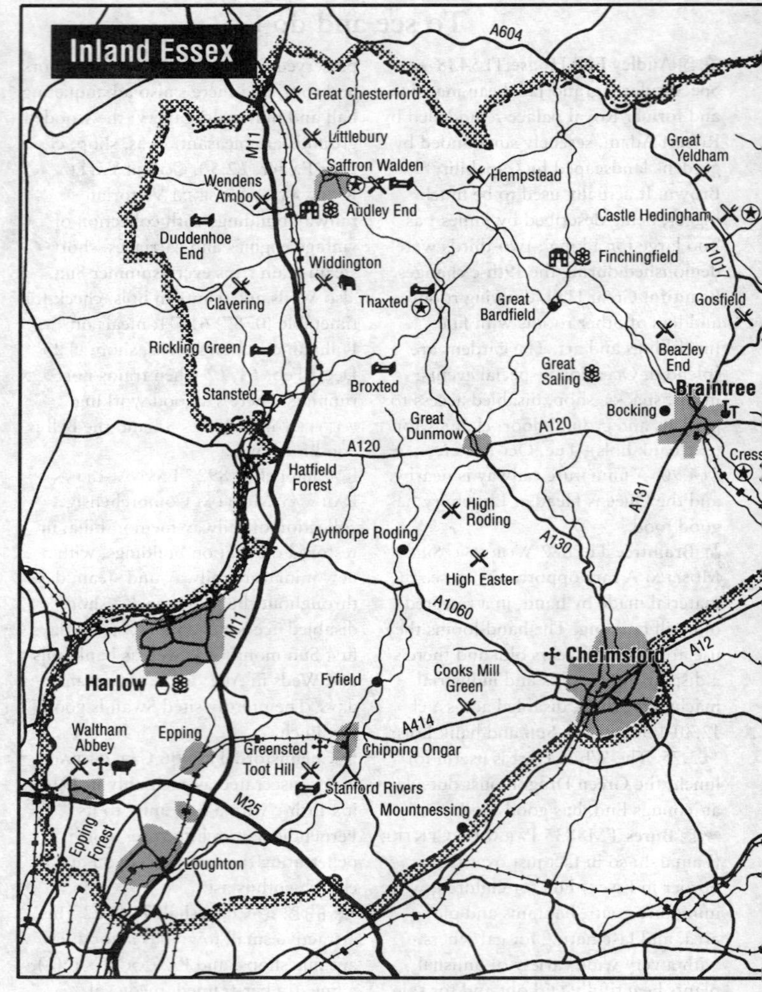

century there were around 10 of them in all. GRANGE BARN The oldest surviving timber-framed barn in Europe (now NT), dating from around 1140; it was originally part of the Cistercian monastery here; disabled access; hours as Paycocke's (see above); £1.10, or joint ticket with Paycocke's £2.

Cressing TL7920 CRESSING TEMPLE A working farm for over 800 years, its present appearance owes much to the Knights Templar in the 12th c – they commissioned the two splendid timber barns here. Also later buildings and walled garden, very varied events; snacks, shop, disabled access; cl Sat, Oct-Apr; £1 wkdys, £2 Sun.

Nr Feering TL8621 FEERINGBURY MANOR has a fine, big, riverside garden with ponds, streams, a little waterwheel, old-fashioned plants and bog gardens; disabled access; cl pm,

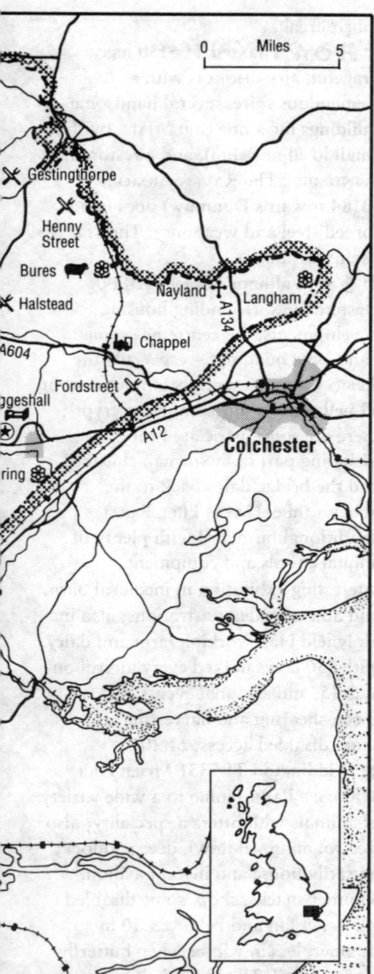

wknds and bank hols, Aug-Apr; *£1.50.

★ Finchingfield TL6832 is by general agreement the county's prettiest village, with charming houses in an exceptionally harmonious landscape – a neat bowl of a valley with a stream running through. SPAINS HALL is a fine old family home, part of which dates back to the 14th c; the 16th-c owner, who was responsible for most of the current building, kept silent for seven years after falsely accusing his wife of being unfaithful. Disabled access; gardens only £1. There's a small windmill, and the Fox (one of the most attractive buildings) and Red Lion are useful for lunch.

Great Saling TL7025 SALING HALL This big garden has a late 17th-c walled garden, water gardens and a growing collection of unusual trees in parkland; open Weds pm Apr-Aug; £1.50. The White Hart is a handsome old timbered inn.

✝ **Greensted** TL5303 ST ANDREWS The country's oldest wooden church, dating from the 9th century, also Tudor chancel.

Harlow TL4510 is not perhaps the most obvious spot for interesting things to do, but there's a surprising number of good museums such as the town MUSEUM in Third Ave, set in a Georgian building and telling the story of the area from prehistoric to modern times, with an important Roman collection. Snacks, shop, disabled access; cl Sun, Mon, 25-26 Dec; £1. Close by in Muskham Rd is the MARK HALL CYCLE MUSEUM AND GARDENS charting the history of bicycles from 1819 to the present day; there's also a Tudor herb garden and three walled gardens. Shop, disabled access; cl 1-2 Sun, Fri, Sat and bank hols.

Langham TM0233 THE FENS Friendly little cottage garden with pond, woodland and ditch, specialising in primulas; garden open under National Gardens Scheme 3 and 24 Apr, 4 Jun, 10 July, as well as daily in Apr and other times by arrangement; nursery Thurs and Sat, and again by arrangement – phone (0206) 272259; *£1. The Shepherd & Dog is handy for lunch.

✝ **Nayland** TL9734 well rewards a stroll – its fine CHURCH has an altar painting by Constable; the White Hart is a decent old inn.

★ ✝ ! **Saffron Walden** TL5438 is the finest small town in the region. Throughout there are fine examples of warmly colourwashed, decorative plasterwork – the pargeting that's an Essex and Suffolk speciality. Walking around to look at the buildings, you'll find it difficult to avoid being tempted into one of the many antique shops (or David Prue, the fine cabinet-maker in Radwinter Rd; cl wknds). The grand airy CHURCH has a magnificent spire, and the very ruined CASTLE up on a grassy mound is worth prowling around. The nearby MUSEUM has local history, archaeology, ceramics, toys and furniture; Shop, disabled access; cl am Sun and bank hols, Mon Nov-Mar, 24-25 Dec, Good Fri; £1. BRIDGE END GARDENS Very pleasant, early-Victorian gardens spread over 3½ acres, with rose garden, formal Dutch garden, Renaissance-style yew hedge maze, kitchen garden and an atmospheric wilderness leading to a little grotto; cl 25 Dec. The Eight Bells does good food.

Stansted TL5222 HOUSE ON THE HILL TOY MUSEUM Fully animated toy museum housing one of the most comprehensive toy collections in the country, along with a collector's shop – great fun, with moving battles, trains and Meccano; cl most winter wkdys exc school hols – check first, tel (0279) 813237; £3. Next door (and run by the same enterprising people) is the MOUNTFICHET CASTLE AND 1066 VILLAGE, a fully reconstructed Norman castle and village, complete with animals, houses and gruesome examples of torture and punishment; snacks, shop; cl mid-Nov-mid-Mar; £3.50. There's a well-preserved 18th-c WINDMILL, unusual in having much of its equipment original rather than rebuilt; shop; open pm first Sun of month, also bank hol Sun and Mon; cl Nov-Mar; 50p. The airport nearby is also well worth a look – quick to get in and out of – and the Cricketers Arms at nearby Rickling Green is good for a lunch break.

✝ **Thaxted** TL6130 has a graceful, airy CHURCH with a tremendous spire, several handsome buildings inc a fine GUILDHALL (with a small local museum), and a restored WINDMILL. The RAVEN ARMOURY (B184 towards Dunmow) does hand-forged steel and weaponry. The Star is useful for lunch.

✝ **Waltham Abbey** TL3800 Despite the surrounding housing developments, the centre has some handsome buildings – especially the ABBEY CHURCH with its famous peal of 13 bells (and a museum in the crypt); there are some associated ruins including part of a Norman cloister, and the bridge dates back to the abbey's time. HAYES HILL FARM Traditional farmyard with plenty of animals, tools and equipment, interesting exhibition in medieval barn, and Sun craft demonstrations; also inc Holyfield Hall working farm and dairy, with 150 cows milked every afternoon at 2.45, and seasonal events such as sheep-shearing and harvesting; snacks, shop, disabled access; £1.20.

Widdington TL5331 MOLE HILL WILDLIFE PARK Home to a wide variety of animals with otters a speciality; also free-roaming wildfowl, deer paddock, butterfly house and insect pavilion. Summer snacks, shop, some disabled access; cl Jan and Feb; *£3.50 in summer, less in winter when butterfly house closed. The Fleur de Lys is a good dining pub.

Windmills are quite a feature of this part of the county – given the relatively unhilly landscape, and they serve as attractive landmarks for miles around. Among them are Aythorpe Roding TL5815, Bocking TL7524 and Mountnessing TQ6297.

★ Other **attractive villages** with decent pubs are Great Chesterford TL5143 and Fyfield TL5606.

Walks

For walkers, inland Essex lacks defined physical features and has too many vast arable fields. In places, a shortage of paths confines you to the road. That said, the prettiness of the villages, particularly in the north, encourages walks wherever there are connecting paths.

Finchingfield TL6832 and Great Bardfield TL6730 both have windmills and charming cottages, with an easily followed path along the **Finchingfield Brook** leading from one to the other. A goodish network of tracks serves the area around Saffron Walden TL5438, into the parkland of nearby Audley End House. Longer rambles can take in Newport TL5234, where the houses display characteristic pargeted plaster walls, and Wendens Ambo TL5136.

Epping Forest TQ4197 is a magnificent survival, an expansive tract of ancient hornbeam coppice, mainly tucked between the M25 and outer London. There are miles of leafy walks (and rides – you can hire horses locally), with some rough grazing and occasional distant views. There are so many woodland paths that getting lost is part of the experience; the long-distance Forest Way is however well marked. On the W side there's a pleasant diversion to High Beach TQ4097, from where a few field paths lead SW.

Hatfield Forest TL5320 just S of Stansted Airport is more of the same, not on quite the same scale but still extensive enough, with a nature trail and boating lake.

Driving

The B184 from Chipping Ongar right up to Saffron Walden and the B1053 between there and Braintree are admirable for country drives – little traffic, pleasant scenery, quietly attractive villages and quite a few distinctively colour-washed, often timbered houses that are surprisingly close to the road. The B1058 through Castle Hedingham, then left on the minor road through Gestingthorpe (where the Pheasant's a good stop) and the Belchamps up to Clare (just over the Suffolk border) is another very pleasant run, as is the back road down the Stour valley from Sudbury through Henny Street, Lamarsh and Bures.

The area's trunk roads tend to be rather traffic-heavy, though the A12 is not usually clogged.

Where to eat

Clavering TL4731 CRICKETERS CB11 4QT (0799) 550442 Attractive and cosy L-shaped dining pub with low beams, two open fires, and a wide choice of imaginative, well-presented food in bar and restaurant; disabled access; **£24**|£1.60/£2.10.

Toot Hill TL5103 GREEN MAN (0992) 522255 Simple pub in attractive countryside, close to Greensted with the country's oldest wooden church; good, interesting food in bar and restaurant, plenty of fish and game, over 100 wines; children over 10. **£21**|£2.50/£5.

Saffron Walden TL5438 EIGHT BELLS Bridge St (0799) 522790 Handsome Tudor inn in good walking area, nr Audley End; plenty of fresh fish, children's menu, splendidly timbered weekend restaurant; disabled access. **£20**|£2/£6.25.

Great Yeldham TL7638 White Hart Poole St (0787) 237250 Striking Tudor inn with attractive garden, beams and oak-panelling, bar food and restaurant; cl Sun pm, Mon; disabled access. **£20**|£1.70/£5.

Littlebury TL5139 Queens Head on B1383 NW of Saffron Walden (0799) 522251 Friendly, connected beamed areas with real ale and good bar food that features some inventive dishes; cl 25-26 Dec; disabled access. **£14**|£1.50/£5.90.

Castle Hedingham TL7835 Bell St James's St (0797) 60350 Friendly restaurant with decent food in popular pub; lovely big walled garden behind. £3.15/£4.20.

Widdington TL5331 Fleur de Lys High St (0799) 40659 Wide choice of generous, reasonably priced bar food inc local game, and decent house wines in well kept, unpretentious village pub; good real ales, log fire, and beams. £2.10/£5.25.

Other places with decent food are the Cock at Beazley End TL7428, the Fox & Goose at Cooksmill Green TL6305, the Compasses in Pattiswick nr Coggeshall TL8224, the Three Ashes at Cressing TL7920, the Queens Head at Fordstreet TL9126, the Pheasant at Gestingthorpe TL8138, the Green Man at Gosfield TL7829, the Plough at Great Chesterford TL5143, the Swan at Henny Street TL8738, the Bull at Halstead TL8130, the Bluebell at Hempstead TL6337, the Cock & Bell at High Easter TL6214, the Black Lion at High Roding TL6017 and the Bell at Wendens Ambo TL5136.

Colchester and the Coast

Interesting quiet corners, especially on the coast and in Constable country, as well as a fair number of places to visit.

This part of Essex has all sorts of peaceful corners, and out of season some of the smaller places on the coast have a secluded charm. Constable country – around Dedham along the border with Suffolk – is the county's prettiest area. There is plenty to see in Colchester, and many of the area's main family attractions are around it – more a place to visit by the day than a base for a short stay, as it's very much a busy working town.

Elsewhere, among the most appealing places are Burnham-on-Crouch, Layer Marney Tower, Beth Chatto's gardens at Elmstead Market, and the Heybridge barge basin at Maldon.

Southend is very much as you'd expect of this favourite seaside escape from London – lots to do in summer, a bit desolate in winter.

Where to stay

Dedham TM0533 Maison Talbooth Colchester CO7 6HN (0206) 322367 **£102.50**; 10 carefully furnished rms. Victorian hotel in fine Constable country; with deeply comfortable seating in elegant lounge, fresh flowers, and very good imaginative food in lovely timber-framed restaurant (a stroll away) which overlooks the river and gardens.

Maldon TL8506 BLUE BOAR Silver St Maldon CM9 7QE (0621) 852681 **£86 inc dinner**; 29 comfortable rms. 14th-c coaching inn with cosy little beamed rooms, open fire, good food inc interesting breakfasts, and friendly staff.

West Mersea TM0112 BLACKWATER Colchester CO5 8QH (0206) 383338 **£68**; 7 pretty rms. Creeper-covered inn with neat little sitting room, fresh flowers, good French food in bistro-type restaurant, and big breakfasts; cl Jan.

Horndon-on-the-Hill TQ6683 HILL HOUSE High Rd Stanford Le Hope SS17 8LD (0375) 672451 ***£55**; 10 rms. Friendly and interestingly converted old house in pretty village, particularly colourful in last wknd of Jun when there is a craft fair and period costume festivities; disabled access.

Burnham-on-Crouch TQ9596 WHITE HART CM0 8AS (0621) 782106 **£50.60**; 19 rms, 8 with shared bthrm. Old-fashioned, 17th-c yachting inn overlooking anchorage, with high ceilings, oak tables, polished parquet, sea pictures, panelling, decent bar food, and restaurant; cl 25-26 Dec.

Dedham TM0533 MARLBOROUGH HEAD Colchester CO7 6DH (0206) 323250 **£50**; 3 rms. Old-fashioned, comfortable early 18th-c inn in heart of Constable's home town; interesting carved woodwork in central lounge, wide choice of interesting food (not 25-26 Dec); disabled access.

West Mersea TM0533 VICTORY Colchester CO5 8LS (0206) 382907 ***£37**; 3 rms. Decent pub, newly refurbished, in fine spot overlooking the entrance to Strood Channel; good fresh fish; disabled access.

Tillingham TL9903 CAP & FEATHERS CM0 7TH (0621) 779212 **£30**; 3 rms, shared bthrm. Quaint old pub nr village green, extremely friendly and welcoming, good bar food with meats from their own smokery.

To see and do

★ **Bradwell-on-Sea** TM0006 is worth the long drive for the sense of being right out on the edge of things – the timeless emptiness if anything exaggerated by distant views of vast industrial installations. The walk eastwards down the old Roman road across the marshes takes you to a little restored Saxon chapel right on the sea wall, the scene of an annual pilgrimage in July.

★ ♁ **Burnham-on-Crouch** TR9595 is an attractively old-fashioned yachting station, lively in summer, packed around the Aug bank hol for its regatta, nice in winter too with rigging clacking forlornly against the masts of those yachts left to ride at anchor off shore. There's a small museum, and the White Harte on the quay is good for lunch.

✺ **Clacton** TM1715 and the quieter nearby **Frinton** TM2319 are roomy family seaside resorts, with long stretches of gently shelving sandy beach and all the usual amusements. Beyond, the blowy open space of The Naze is pleasant for strolling, especially out of season when you're likely to have its 150 acres virtually to yourself, with good views out over the water.

Colchester TM0025 is Britain's oldest recorded town, the capital of Roman Britain. You can trace the Roman wall (the Hole in the Wall, Balkerne Gdns, is a decent pub built into the one surviving fragmentary gatehouse) – best armed first with a map-leaflet from the exemplary museum in COLCHESTER CASTLE. This has the remains of the splendid Roman Temple of Claudius, although they're now rather overshadowed by the castle itself, which has the largest Norman keep in Europe, and an excellent collection of Roman relics, esp relaid mosaics; snacks, shop, good disabled access; cl Sun am in summer, all day winter and 24-26 Dec; *£2.50. The well-established public park around the castle is very pleasant. An interesting collection of museums inc the NATURAL HISTORY MUSEUM and HOLLYTREES MUSEUM on the High St, the latter featuring lots of toys, costumes and curios from the last two centuries, and round the corner in Trinity St the SOCIAL HISTORY MUSEUM and TYMPERLEYS CLOCK MUSEUM, a particularly unusual selection housed in a fine 15th-c house. All cl Sun, Mon and 24-26 Dec, social history and clock museums also cl Nov-Mar. The High St has handsome buildings, some extravagantly timbered, and plenty more historical buildings inc ST BOTOLPHS, the oldest Augustinian priory in the country. Two miles out of town in 40 acres of parkland is COLCHESTER ZOO which has the widest variety of animals in the area, and is home to elephants, parrots, tigers, and sealions among others; demonstrations such as feeding, or snake-handling. Meals, snacks, shop, some disabled access; cl 25 Dec; £5.50. Children should like ROLLERWORLD, the only international-standard roller-skating rink in Britain; cl Mon eve; £3. BOURNE MILL (just off B1025 S) is a delightfully quaint restored watermill by a pretty millpond; always worth looking at from outside; open Sun and Mon of bank hol wknds, also pm Sun and Tues in July-Aug only; £1.50.

✝ **Copford** TL9222 CHURCH is a fine Norman building with well-restored 12th-century wall paintings.

✝ 🐑 **Dedham** TM0533 has several fine old buildings, esp the CHURCH, its pinnacled tower familiar from so many Constable paintings; there's also the school Constable went to; good walks

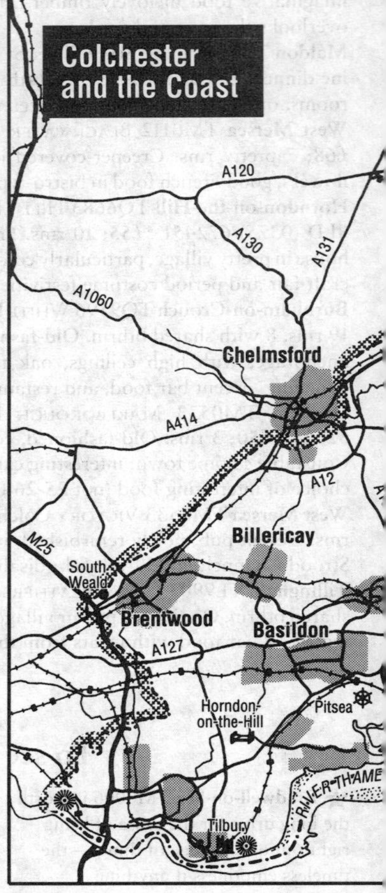

through the protected riverside meadows to his father's mill at Flatford (across the river lock, so in Suffolk). DEDHAM RARE BREEDS FARM Lots of cattle, sheep, goats, pigs, birds and waterfowl; two paddocks for children to walk through and stroke and touch the animals; shop, disabled access; cl 12 Jan-Feb; *£2.50. The handsome Marlborough Head has good food, and the Sun here is useful too.

❀ **Elmstead Market** TM0624 BETH CHATTO GARDENS These attractive gardens have been transformed from four acres of wasteland, and are a riot of colour in summer; lots of gardening

ideas, plant sales inc unusual varieties; cl Sun, bank hols and winter Sats; £1.50.

Harwich TM2632 The Redoubt Circular fort built in 1808 in case of invasion by Napoleon, with three small museums; snacks, shop; open Sun all year (cl 1-2 for lunch), Sat pm in Jun and Sept, every pm July and Aug; *£1. Harwich also has an interesting little Maritime Museum in a lighthouse by the harbour; shop; open Sun Easter-Sept; 50p. There are cruises around the harbour in summer. From the A120 W there's an unusual sight for this part of Essex – a tall narrow windmill (actually an interloper, as it was brought from Suffolk).

Hockley TQ8293 Volpaia (54 Woodlands Rd) Lily specialist's small but beautiful woodside garden, rare collected plants, species and own-bred hybrid lilies, shade-loving shrubs; interesting plant sales. Teas; open Thurs, Sun, cl early July-mid-Apr; 70p. There are good paths through the deciduous woods behind.

Hullbridge TQ8194 Jakapeni Farm Small rare breeds park, specialising in pigs and sheep, with other pets and wildlife; snacks, shop, disabled access;

open Easter, then all Sun and bank hols to Oct; £1.50.

Layer Marney TL9317 LAYER MARNEY TOWER The mansion here was never completed; its eight-storey Tudor gatehouse, the tallest of its kind in the country, is however most impressive. The mansion's west wing and gallery give some idea of how magnificent it would have been; also formal gardens, rare breeds farm, medieval barn, farm shop and deer park. Snacks, shop, disabled access to grounds and rare breeds farm; open Thurs and Sun pm Apr, May, Jun and Sept, every pm except Sat in July and Aug. *£3.

✝ **Maldon** TL8506 has a lively BOAT AND BARGE QUAY at Heybridge Basin just outside – the best chance to see one of the classic Thames barges with its ox-blood sails in action. You can tour the old MOOT HALL, where they have been displaying an ambitious tapestry commemorating the 1,000th anniversary of the Battle of Maldon, a crucial moment in English history. This may move to another site down the road in 1994; cl Sun; £1. The MILLENNIUM GARDENS are named for the same event, and recreate what a garden would have looked like at the time of the battle. Also a CHURCH with an unusual triangular tower, some decent shops, a couple of small museums, and a riverside stroll past the golf course to the pretty weir by Beeleigh Abbey.

Mersea Island TM0413, much of it a National Nature Reserve for its shore life, is linked to the mainland by a bridge. It does feel very much an island, and away from the extended village of West Mersea, popular for retirement homes, there are few people about out of season (in summer the caravan parks bring in lots of families).

Mistley TM1231 has an interesting CRAFT CENTRE by the old barge quay, with musical-instrument makers as well as potters and so forth; vegetarian restaurant.

Pitsea TQ7488 WAT TYLER COUNTRY PARK has a little motor boat museum.

★ ✝ **St Osyth** TM1215 is a pretty little village distinguished by the remarkable crenellated flint gateway of a ruined NORMAN PRIORY.

! ☺ **Southend-on-Sea** TQ8885 This traditional seaside resort recently celebrated its centenary, and has long been popular with East Londoners, with many of the attractions you'd hope to find in such a place. Most famous is the PIER, the longest in the world if somewhat battered by storms and ships, excellent for fishing, with a museum and restored train service. CENTRAL MUSEUM AND PLANETARIUM The only planetarium in the south-east outside London, with local history too; disabled access to ground floor only; cl Sun, Mon, bank hols and day after; £2. SEA LIFE CENTRE Great fun, a lively way of exploring underwater life, with special bubble-windows that make it seem you're in there with the sharks; there's a special shark exhibition, as well as a pedestrian tunnel through a reconstructed sea bed and other hi-tech displays. This is the latest (and probably the best) of what is becoming a thriving little chain. Meals, snacks, shop, disabled access; cl 25 Dec; £3.95. Less expected finds are the SOUTHCHURCH HALL MUSEUM, a medieval moated manor house in an attractive park, with various period room settings, and the PRITTLEWELL PRIORY MUSEUM, a 12th-c Cluniac priory with various displays and nice grounds; both cl Sun and Mon, priory also cl mornings in termtime. Children should enjoy NEVER NEVER LAND, a fantasy park where animation and illusion recreate familiar stories, from Snow White to Masters of the Universe (open wknds Easter-Nov and school hols; *£1.50), or the children's fairground PETER PAN'S PLAYGROUND (varying charges per ride). Like many such resorts, Southend in winter has a special appeal for people who wouldn't like it in summer – seafront shops by the endless promenade looking closed for ever, the sea itself a doleful grey. Summer BOAT TRIPS include occasional runs on a vintage paddle-steamer: phone (0634) 827648 for dates; £8.50. There are year-round ferries to Felixstowe; £3 return. Though attached, LEIGH-ON-SEA TQ8385 has a quite distinct character, more intimate, with shrimp boats in the working harbour; Ivy Osborne's shellfish stall here is justly famous, and the Crooked Billet is a good old-fashioned pub.

Tilbury TQ6476 TILBURY FORT Tudor riverside fort with double moat, very good views of the Thames estuary, its boats and container ships; shop, some disabled access; cl Mon Oct-Mar, 24-26 Dec; £1.80.

Upper Mayland TL9200 EWENNY FARM ALTERNATIVE ENVIRONMENT CENTRE (B1018 from Althorne to Southminster) All sorts of ways of saving energy and the environment; windmills, lots of organic gardens, solar heating etc – even the power for the video in the visitor centre comes from the wind; snacks, shop, disabled access; cl week after Christmas; £2.50.

★ Other **attractive villages**, all with decent pubs, inc Battlesbridge TQ7894 (also a popular antiques centre, walks to head of Crouch estuary), Paglesham TQ9293, Rowhedge TM0021 (nearby nature reserve among former gravel workings at Fingringhoe), South Weald TQ5793 and Wivenhoe TM0321 (particularly the Black Buoy). All these except South Weald are quite close to the waterside.

Down at **Purfleet** TQ5578 the Royal Hotel has good Thames views.

Don't be tempted by the map into the long drive to **Foulness Island**; it is indeed an island, and wonderfully remote-feeling considering how close it is to London. But with a big atomic weapons establishment it's almost entirely owned by the Ministry of Defence, and their checkpoint at Landwick TQ9687 will turn you back unless you've arranged a pass.

Walks

The county's low-lying, much indented coast does have opportunities for walking, though the immediate hinterland is generally too dull to make circular walks worthwhile. Vast skies, the boating scene and birdlife provide the main interest in the vicinity of the **Blackwater** estuary, where the pick of local walks include paths along the dykes from Tollesbury TL9510 and towards isolated St Peter's Chapel from Bradwell-on-Sea TM0006. More boats are on view at Burnham-on-Crouch TQ9596, along the Crouch itself. The Ferryboat down by the River Crouch at the end of the lane through North Fambridge TQ8597 is a good base for lonely waterside walks.

Mersea Island has a bracing coastal walk from East Mersea along the sea-dyke overlooking the Colne estuary.

We welcome reports from readers . . .

This GUIDE depends on readers' reports. Please tell us what you think about places in it. And do recommend additions. Use the card in the middle, the report forms at the end, or just write – no stamp needed: THE GOOD WEEKEND GUIDE, FREEPOST TN1569, Wadhurst, E Sussex TN5 7BR.

Driving

On the whole this is not an area for rewarding country drives, as it's mostly too flat to give worthwhile views. Also the back roads are generally slow, and in the flatter parts many have unexpected turns. The A12 is now a good road, and the A120 between Colchester and Harwich is usually fairly quick. The A127 and A13 always seem a little nerve-wracking, perhaps because of the way their regular users jostle for quick getaway positions at the traffic lights.

Where to eat

Burnham-on-Crouch TQ9596 CONTENTED SOLE 80 High St (0621) 782139 Though there's an obvious emphasis on fine seafood, meat dishes feature as well in this consistently good restaurant; disabled access; cl Sun pm, Mon, also last fortnight July and 4 wks around Christmas; £25.70|£3.10/£9.40.
West Mersea TM0112 WILLOW LODGE 108 Coast Rd (0206) 383568 Large, busy restaurant with a wide range of very good food inc lots of fresh fish as well as vegetarian dishes; disabled access; cl Sun pm, Mon; £19|£1.80/£4.
Dedham TM0533 MALLARD Riverside Cottage Mill Lane (0206) 322066 Unlicensed little riverside restaurant with homely, relaxed atmosphere, and good straightforward food; cl Mon, Tues, Thurs and Fri lunchtime, Sun pm, Jan; £14.80|£.50/£3.90.
Colchester TM0025 CLOWNS 61-62 High St (0206) 578631 Huge helpings of good, straightforward food in clean, spacious restaurant; disabled access; cl 25-26 Dec; £10|£3.35.
Other places with decent food are the Wooden Fender at Ardleigh TM0529, the Anchor at Danbury TL7905, the Cherry Tree at Great Stambridge TQ9091, the Old Crown at Messing TL8918, the Plough & Sail at Paglesham TQ9293, and the Anchor at Rowhedge TM0221.

Help this year from: *Derek and Sylvia Stephenson, Chris Dewhurst, John Baker, Mike Simpson, Mrs P R M Baker, Margaret Drazin, Bernard Phillips, Nigel Gibbs, Joanne Suter, Simon Ince, George Atkinson, Gwen and Peter Andrews, Wayne Brindle, Y Cotterill, David and Ruth Hollands, Brian Shiner, Ian Bourne, Ernest Hofer, C Bushby, Anthony Barker, Graham Bush.*

Essex Calendar

For details of forthcoming events Essex has a 24-hour 'leisure link' line on (0891) 345386.

Some of these dates were provisional as we went to press.

February

19th **Colchester** Primrose Festival *at Bypass Nurseries – till Sun 20*

April

2nd **Gosfield** Custom and American Car Show – *till Mon 4*

May

1st **Chelmsford** Motor Show *at Hylands Park*

14th **Chelmsford** Cathedral Festival and Fringe – *till Sat 21*; *also throughout* **Essex** Dance Festival – *till 26 Jun*

29th **Braintree** Country Fair and Festival *at Towerlands Centre*; **Southend-on-Sea** Air Show – *till Mon 30*

June

17th **Chelmsford** County Show *at the Showground – till Sun 19*; **Thaxted** Festival *every weekend – till 10 July*

25th **Colchester** Summer Show – *till Sun 26*

26th **Harwich** Festival – *till 2 July*; **Canvey Island** Castle Point Show *at Waterside Farm recreation ground*

July

22nd **Cressing Temple** Festival of Early Music and Drama – *till Sun 24, also on Fri 29 – till Sun 31*

August

6th **Clacton-on-Sea** Carnival; **Southend-on-Sea** Jazz Festival – *till Sun 7*

7th **Chappel** Beer Festival *at Railway Museum – till Sat 10*

26th **Chelmsford** Spectacular, *fireworks concert at Hylands park – till Mon 29*; **Clacton-on-Sea** Jazz Festival – *till Sun 28*

27th **Southend-on-Sea** Thames Sailing Barge Race

30th **Colchester** Carnival

September

3rd **Orsett** Show, *at The Showground*

24th **Billericay** Steam Rally and Craft Fair *at Barleylands Farm*

November

5th **Colchester** Fireworks; **Harwich** Guy Carnival; **Southend-on-Sea** Guy Fawkes Celebrations

Gloucestershire

The Cotswolds area is near ideal for a short break – among our readers, Britain's most popular destination for a weekend away. It has a succession of delightful villages and small towns with handsome buildings largely unchanged since the heyday of the wool trade several centuries ago, many interesting places to visit, charming countryside, civilised and individual places to stay in, and good food.

The north Cotswolds area is the best known, with more famously beautiful villages and towns than the south, rather more in the way of tourist attractions, and the widest choice of really good places to stay at. But the south has a richer variety of relatively undiscovered villages, and in summer is less swamped by visitors. Its countryside, although perhaps less classically Cotswoldy, has a great diversity of scenery, including the very up-and-down area around Stroud.

Of course, there's no reason to see the north and south Cotswolds as rivals or in any way mutually exclusive: you can quickly get from one area to the other, and there's no real division between them. But it would be utterly exhausting to try to cram the whole of the Cotswolds into one short stay, and we'd suggest that for a relaxing time it would be sensible to stay within either one area or the other.

The Forest of Dean – very different indeed – has possibilities for a quiet weekend break, especially at times of year when the Cotswolds are at their most popular. And it's within easy reach of Gloucester – a busy modern city, but with several things well worth seeing.

Though the county does have places that are a lot of fun for families, on the whole this wouldn't be first choice as an area to take young children to.

North Cotswolds

Idyllic villages and traditional small towns, lots of interesting places to visit, excellent places to stay.

Beautiful stone-built villages and small towns bulging with antique shops punctuate classic rolling countryside, traditional dry stone-walled fields with occasional beechwoods and meandering streams. A good many lovely places to visit include among their special highlights two glorious gardens near Mickleton, Stanway Manor, Snowshill Manor, the farm park at Guiting Power, Sudeley Castle near Winchcombe, and the Batsford Arboretum at Moreton-in-Marsh. It's worth noting that several of the finest gardens and parks are clustered around Moreton-in-Marsh and Chipping Campden. Cheltenham still has a considerable degree of Regency elegance, and makes a nice contrast to the older and more intimate style of the rest of the area.

There are good walks and though there are things for children to enjoy here, it's for adults that the area has real appeal. Springtime can be specially charming, with the daffodils in many of the villages seeming almost designed to match perfectly the lichened stone of the ancient cottages. In the summer the area does attract a lot of visitors, but even then you can find delightful villages that have escaped fame and the crowds.

An excellent choice of places to stay runs from small village inns and civilised B & Bs to some delightfully individual country hotels in former manor houses.

Where to stay

Buckland SP0836 BUCKLAND MANOR Faringdon WR12 7LY (0386) 852626 **£145**; 10 sumptuous rms. Really lovely 13th-c building in 10 acres of beautifully kept gardens, comfortable lounges with magnificent oak panelling, flowers and antiques, elegant restaurant; outdoor swimming pool, riding, tennis, croquet, putting; cl 3 Jan-5 Feb; children over 12 only.

Lower Slaughter SP1622 LOWER SLAUGHTER MANOR Cheltenham GL54 2HP (0451) 820456 ***£120**; 15 luxurious rms with thoughtful extras. Grand 17th-c manor house on the edge of a particularly pretty village; with very comfortable seating, antiques and paintings, log fires, lovely flower arrangements, fine plaster ceilings, excellent food in the elegant restaurant, and a very good wine list; 15th-c dovecot, croquet lawn and all-weather tennis court in the gardens and indoor heated swimming pool; cl 2 wks Jan; children over 10 only.

Upper Slaughter SP1523 LORDS OF THE MANOR Cheltenham GL54 2JD (0451) 820243 **£115**; 29 rms carefully furnished with antiques, Victorian sketches and paintings. Warmly friendly hotel with mid-17th-c heart (though it's been carefully extended many times); lovely views over eight acres of grounds from very comfortable library and drawing room, log fires, fresh flowers, fine modern English cooking in attractive candlelit restaurant (overlooking the original rectory gardens), good breakfasts, and kind service; the original cellars are lovely; disabled access.

Charingworth SP2039 CHARINGWORTH MANOR Cheltenham GL55 6NS (0386) 78555 **£110**; 24 lovely rms with thoughtful extras. Early 14th-c manor with Jacobean additions set in fine grounds; with mullioned windows, antiques, log fires and oak beams, good, modern cooking, excellent breakfasts, friendly staff; new leisure spa with indoor swimming pool, and all-weather tennis court; children over 10 only in evening restaurant.

Stow-on-the-Wold SP1925 GRAPEVINE Cheltenham GL54 1AU (0451) 830344 **£98**; 23 well-furnished rms. Warm, friendly and very well-run hotel with antiques, comfortable chairs and a relaxed atmosphere in the lounge; beamed bar, attractive restaurant and good food; cl 24 Dec-11 Jan; disabled access.

Chipping Campden SP1539 COTSWOLD HOUSE GL55 6AN (0386) 840330 **£90**; 15 charming rms (the ones at the back overlook the pretty garden). Elegant Regency building with comfortable seating, antiques, beautiful flowers, an impressive spiral staircase, open fires; all-day bar, formal restaurant (pianist

3 evenings a week), and cheerful staff; cl 25-27 Dec; children over 8 only.

Moreton-in-Marsh SP2032 Manor House GL56 0LJ (0608) 50501 **£83**; 39 rms – traditional or more modern. Lovely 16th-c manor house with quiet, thoughtfully planted gardens, log fires in the lounge, cosy bar, and good English cooking in bar and restaurant, excellent service; indoor swimming pool; disabled access.

Chipping Campden SP1539 Noel Arms GL55 6AT (0386) 840317 **£80**; 26 rms. Bustling 14th-c inn with old agricultural implements and open fire in the bar; comfortable, traditionally furnished small lounge areas, armour and antiques, conservatory, restaurant, and decent wines; disabled access.

Moreton-in-Marsh SP2032 White Hart Royal GL56 0BA (0608) 50731 ***£80**; 17 good rms. Comfortable, partly 15th-c inn with blazing inglenook fire in bar, and attractive courtyard.

Willersey SP1039 Old Rectory Broadway WR12 7PN (0386) 853729 **£75**; 8 rms. Friendly and homely B & B in pretty 17th-c house set opposite little village church; good breakfasts, walled gardens, and attractive village; no evening meals – though several places nearby; cl Christmas.

Stow-on-the-Wold SP1925 Old Stocks Cheltenham GL54 1AF (0451) 830666 **£66**; 19 good-value rms. Well-run, simple hotel with cosy, clean and welcoming small bar, good food, friendly staff, and sheltered garden; cl 21-29 Dec; disabled access.

Lower Swell SP1725 Old Farmhouse Cheltenham GL54 1LF (0451) 830232 **£64**; 14 rms, some in main building but most in various barns, stables and outbuildings. Peaceful and unpretentious 16th-c manor farm with log fire; good food using fresh local produce, friendly staff, and walled rose garden; cl 2 wks Jan.

Chipping Campden SP1539 Kings Arms GL55 4AW (0386) 840256 ***£60**; 14 rms. Civilised small hotel with comfortably old-fashioned bar, log fires, excellent service; generously served good food, intimate candlelit restaurant, and lots of wines; they're kind to children, and hope to have ground-floor rooms by mid-1994.

Laverton Meadows SP0937 Leasow House Broadway WR12 7NA (038 673) 526 **£56**; 8 spacious rms. Newly renovated, 17th-c stone house with lovely views, friendly owners, and comfortable library; good disabled access.

Bledington SP2422 Kings Head Chipping Norton OX7 6HD (0608) 658365 **£52**; 6 rms. Very nicely placed 15th-c Cotswold inn by duck-filled stream; atmospheric bar with cheery log fire, lounge overlooking garden, excellent food in bar and restaurant (partly no smoking, cl Sun pm), and friendly service; cl 25 Dec.

Moreton-in-Marsh SP2032 Redesdale Arms GL56 0AW (0608) 50308 **£51.95**; 17 individually decorated rms, some in an annexe. Lively early 18th-c inn with well-renovated and comfortable pub bar and buttery, restaurant, and good food served by helpful staff.

Oddington SP2225 Horse & Groom Kidlington GL56 0XH (0451) 30584 **£46**; 7 quaint and comfortable rms. Attractive, well-run inn in pretty Cotswold village; with handsome old furnishings, big log fire, candlelit dining room, and good garden with aviary and large play area.

Great Rissington SP1917 Lamb Cheltenham GL54 2LP (0451) 820388 ***£46**; 13 rms – one has a four-poster carved by the landlord – inc two new suites. Civilised 17th-c inn in pretty countryside with sheltered hillside garden; cosy two-roomed bar, log fire, indoor swimming pool, and good nearby walks; cl 25-26 Dec.

Greet SP0230 MANOR FARM Cheltenham GL54 5BJ (0242) 602423 £40; 3 rms. Mixed farm with carefully restored 16th-c manor house, fine views, big garden and croquet; self-catering also.
Bourton-on-the-Hill SP1732 HORSE & GROOM Moreton-in-Marsh GL56 9AQ (0386) 700413 £35; 3 rms. Quiet roadside pub with attractive, high-beamed little lounge bar, big log fire, locals' bar, decent food, restaurant, pretty hanging baskets.
Naunton SP1123 BLACK HORSE Cheltenham GL54 3AD (0451) 850378 *£30; 2 rms, shared bthrm. Small inn with a smartly stylish atmosphere, simply furnished beamed bar with big woodburning stove, and very good bar and restaurant food; cl 25-26 Dec; no children.
Contributors have warmly recommended the self-catering cottages at Lower Farm in Blockley SP1634 – you can book them for a few nights only, as well as for longer stays (0386) 700237.

To see and do

Cotswold villages The greatest attraction of the Cotswolds is the host of delightful stone-built villages, usually with handsome medieval churches. The cottages and houses don't hide away behind gardens and high walls, but tend to be right by the road. Up in this part, they are usually built in a warm golden-tinted stone, and roofed in picturesque slabs of heavy stone. Often, there's a strip of grass between pavement and road, and sometimes a little stream. Lower Slaughter SP1622, with its sister village Upper Slaughter, is the prettiest village in the whole of Britain – a perfect harmony of stone, water, grass and trees. It's not nearly as overwhelmed by summer visitors as its nearby rival Bourton-on-the-Water (see below), though it certainly gets its fair share.

Many lesser-known villages are almost as beautiful. We have picked out a short list which have the added attraction of a decent village pub: Bledington SP2422, Blockley SP1634, Broad Campden SP1637 (the Bakers Arms), Broadwell SP2027, Ebrington SP1840, Great Barrington SP2013, Lower Swell SP1725, Naunton SP1123 and Stanton SP0734 (an absolute charmer). Though there's no pub to recommend there, Saintbury SP1139 is a winner when the daffodils are out.

Other things to see and do

❀ 🏛 **Bourton-on-the-Hill** SP1732 SEZINCOTE Classic, early 19th-c water garden by onion-domed forerunner of Brighton Pavilion, also more recent Indian-style garden to match the building; garden open pm Thurs, Fri and bank hols (cl Dec), house Thurs and Fri pm May-Sept; £3.50, £2.50 garden only. Children are not allowed in the house. BOURTON HOUSE Unusual plants inc tender ones in attractive garden around fine old house (not open) with 16th-c tithe barn; teas in tithe barn, shop; open Thurs and Fri pm late May-Sept; *£2. The Horse & Groom is a civilised place for lunch.

★ 🐦 ! **Bourton-on-the-Water** SP1620 One of the best-known Cotswold villages, and disfigured by sprawly crowds in summer unless you get there very early in the morning – when it's enchanting. Full of tourist attractions: BIRDLAND Eight-acre garden on banks of River Windrush, with lots of penguins, parrots, cockatoos, macaws and other birds, and a new play area for children; snacks, shop, disabled access; cl 25 Dec; £3. VILLAGE LIFE EXHIBITION A complete Edwardian village shop,

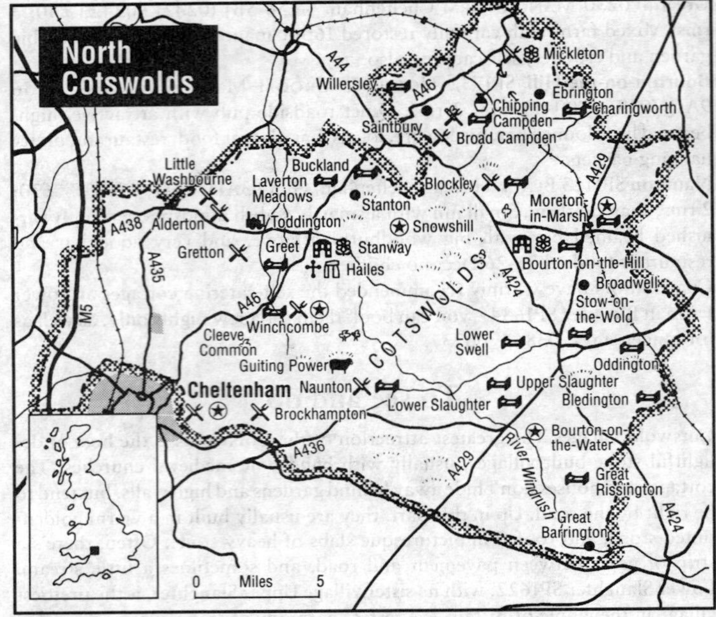

bathroom, kitchen, bedroom, blacksmith's forge, photographs and toys; shop; cl Dec-Feb, occ winter wkdys; 70p, or free if visiting the Cotswold Motor Museum Housed in an old watermill, cars and motorcycles from vintage years to 1950s, 800 advertising signs, 8,000 pieces of automobilia, and toy collection; home of Brum the children's television character. Shop, disabled access; cl Dec-Jan, occ winter wkdys; *£1.20. Model Village A quick way of exploring the area, this is a perfect replica of the village built from Cotswold stone to a scale of one-ninth, complete with working waterwheel, music in the church, shrubs, trees and plants, and a model of the model. Shop, limited disabled access; cl 25 Dec; £1.20. Folly Farm Waterfowl Lakes and pools with over 160 kinds of waterfowl, also friendly ducks, geese and poultry, and hand-reared animals; snacks, shop, disabled access; cl 25 Dec; £2.70. Perfumery Exhibition Aromatic displays and demonstrations covering scent extraction, a scented garden with plants chosen for their smells and a specially designed theatre with an audio-visual show on olfaction; shop, disabled access; cl 25-26 Dec; £1.30.

★ **Cheltenham** SO9422 Beautiful spa town useful for exploring Cotswolds, shopping or admiring the elegant Regency architecture of its tree-lined avenues. Pittville Pump Room and Museum Generally regarded as the city's finest building, 19th-c Greek Revival with a colonnaded façade and balconied hall; spa water available, super park and gardens. The museum has a history of Cheltenham, and an imaginative use of original costumes, from the city's Regency heyday to the Swinging Sixties; various other exhibitions. Summer snacks, shop; cl Oct-May, Mon exc summer bank hols; £1. Art Gallery and Museum Excellent collection of furniture and metalwork inspired by William Morris, local history, fine paintings inc 17th-c Dutch works, and rare porcelain and ceramics. Meals, snacks, shop, disabled access; cl Sun and bank hols. HOLST BIRTHPLACE MUSEUM Regency house where composer was born in 1874 and furnished in period style; drawing room, nursery, working kitchen, laundry and Holst's original piano. Shop; cl Sun, Mon. Taylors in Cambray Pl is a good wine bar, the Cotswold in Portland St is useful for lunch, and the well-run café in the beautiful Imperial Gardens is suitable for families.

★ **Chipping Campden** SP1539 An attractive town well worth exploring, with interesting old buildings and shops, and fine old inns. Many of our contributors would put it among the country's most delightful small towns, though until they get the cars out of the centre not all would agree. WOOLSTAPLERS HALL MUSEUM Eleven rooms of 14th-c wool hall packed with domestic items, medical equipment, typewriters, costumes and more; there are some particularly interesting children's chairs and unusual linen. Shop; cl Nov-Mar; *£2. The Eight Bells is useful for lunch.

★ **Guiting Power** SP0924 COTSWOLD FARM PARK Ideal for children, here is a comprehensive collection of rare breeds in a typical Cotswold farm setting, at various stages of the year filled with lambs, foals, piglets and fluffy chicks; adventure playground, nature trails, seasonal events such as lambing and shearing. The various temporary exhibitions inc such intriguing displays as honey bee keeping and foot trimming and shoeing of horses great and small. Meals, snacks, shop, disabled access; cl Oct-Mar; £3. The village itself is lovely, and the Olde Inne has good food.

✝ **Hailes** SP0228 HAILES ABBEY 13th-c Cistercian abbey founded by Henry III's brother after he narrowly escaped a shipwreck, now a simple but graceful ruin. The museum has lots of evidence of its former splendour and archaeological remains, inc fine sculptures and floor tiles. Shop, some disabled access; cl 1-2, Mon Oct-Mar, 25-26 Dec, 1 Jan; £1.80. Hailes Fruit Farm down the road is good for snacks.

Mickleton SP1643 HIDCOTE MANOR GARDEN Looking particularly trim this year, a delightful series of small gardens separated by walls and hedges of different species, with rare shrubs, trees and roses; very popular, even midweek. Meals, snacks, shop, limited disabled access; cl Tues, Fri, Nov-Mar; £4.40. The adjacent KIFTSGATE COURT GARDEN is renowned for its old-fashioned roses, inc the largest rose in England; other rare plants, shrubs and trees. Teas, rare plant sales; open pm Weds, Thurs, Sun and bank hols Apr-Sept, as well as Sat Jun and July; £2.50. The Kings Arms is very good value for lunch.

Moreton-in-Marsh SP2032 Attractively bustling old place, once an important linen weaving centre and coaching town, now with popular Tues market. COTSWOLD FALCONRY CENTRE Daily demonstrations of falconry, with eagles, hawks, falcons and owls bred and conserved, and in the breeding season close-circuit TVs giving literally a bird's-eye view of life in the nest; shop, disabled access; cl Nov-Mar exc wknds up to Christmas; *£2.50. BATSFORD ARBORETUM Ideal for a relaxing stroll, this is a private collection of trees with over 1,000 rare and beautiful species over 50 acres; hundreds of maples, 90 magnolias, flowering cherries, super views. Several features reveal the Japanese influence on the garden's original designer. Best in May and autumn, but good at any time. Snacks, shop; cl mid-Nov-Feb; £2. WELLINGTON AVIATION ART From paintings to tie pins, prints to propellers, a unique collection of WWII aircraft pictures, sculptures and other related material. Shop, disabled access; cl 12.30-2, Mon; *£1. The Black Bear, Farriers Arms and White Hart Royal are all useful for lunch.

Snowshill SP0933 SNOWSHILL

Manor This may look like an ordinary Cotswold manor house but it's actually far more unusual, housing an incredible collection of just about everything from clocks and toys to bicycles and musical instruments. Particularly interesting are the suits of Japanese Samurai armour, arranged to look like a group of warriors meeting in the gloom – very creepy. Shop; cl 1-2, Mon (exc bank hols), Tues, Nov-Mar; £4. The National Trust are so concerned about the number of visitors this already gets that they'd rather not encourage further visits, so you might prefer to go at a quiet time out of season, or midweek. The nearby Snowshill Arms is popular for lunch.

Stanway SP0632 Stanway Manor One of the most beautiful 16th-c manor houses in the country, with classic great hall and screens passage, typical squire's family portraits, unusual furnishings, interesting golden-stone gate house, medieval tithe barn, folly pyramid, waterworks, and ice house – all in early 18th-c pleasure grounds with fine trees. Open pm Tues and Thurs, cl Sept-May; *£2.50, garden only £1.50.

★ **Stow-on-the-Wold** SP1925 is an extremely handsome stone-built market town with fine buildings around its square and in the narrow lanes off, and a good few antique shops, book shops and so forth. It's something of an antidote to the more sweetly pretty Cotswold villages, on quite a high plateau and altogether more austere in style – not for nothing was it known as 'Stow-on-the-Wold, where the wind blows cold'. The Fosse Manor Hotel, Queens Head and Old Stocks Hotel are all good for lunch here.

Toddington SP0333 Gloucestershire-Warwickshire Railway Steam and diesel train trips through four miles of quiet countryside, departing from restored GWR stations either here or at Winchcombe; trains run every wknd Mar-Oct and every day in summer and some school holidays – for a timetable write to The Station, Toddington, Glos GL54 5DT, enclosing a stamped addressed envelope. Snacks, shop, disabled access; *£4.80. It stops near the Harvest Home at Greet, a good family pub, and Royal Oak at Gretton (see Where to eat).

★ **Winchcombe** SP0228 Very peaceful and photogenic – once the capital of Mercia, now worth a stop for a look at the church with its grotesque gargoyles, or just to soak up the tranquil atmosphere. Sudeley Castle and Gardens Catherine Parr, the luckiest of Henry VIII's wives, was perhaps the most famous resident of this delightful historic house. The original medieval castle was largely destroyed in the Civil War, but the remains were skilfully blended into the 19th-c reconstruction. Inside is a rich collection of furniture, porcelain and tapestries, as well as notable paintings by Turner, van Dyck and Rubens, while outside the eight splendid gardens are unmissable; various special events and regular craft workshops. Meals, snacks, shop and specialist plant centre, disabled access to garden; cl Nov-Mar; *£4.75. Railway Museum and Garden Behind an ordinary-looking door is a rather more unusual Victorian garden full of lovingly rescued railway memorabilia inc booking office, working signals and signal box; snacks, shop, disabled access; cl wkdys Oct-Easter; *£1.75. Folk and Police Museum Local history, and a collection of British and international police uniforms and equipment; shop; cl Sun, Nov-Mar; *50p. Good High St eating places are the Plaisterers Arms and Corner Cupboard, and there are interesting craft and other shops here.

Cotswold garden tours taking in some private gardens as well as the more famous ones are organised by Jane Roberts, usually four-day coach tours; phone (0242) 602822 for details.

Walks

The **Cotswold Way**, a 100-mile path from Chipping Campden SP1539 to Bath ST7464, carefully picks out some of the most choice bits of landscape – a worthwhile aid for those planning a shorter stroll, for instance between the timeless villages of Stanway SP0632, Stanton SP0734 and Buckland SP0836 (field paths and farm track let you detour to Snowshill SP0933).

Another attractive village-to-village stroll is the leisurely mile or so following the river between Lower Slaughter SP1622 and Upper Slaughter SP1523. To make a longer walk for a circuit of a couple of hours, you can follow the signposted **Warden's Way**. The best way back out of Bourton is the exit by the church, heading out W past the school and over the old railway line, then following the lanes and tracks S of Upper Slaughter to rejoin the River Windrush to Bourton-on-the-Water SP1620.

For views here, the steep grassy slopes of the W escarpment of the Cotswolds can't be bettered, and make for fine walking. **Cleeve Common** SO9925, the highest point of the Cotswolds, has breezy, unkempt grassland on its open expanses and can either be reached from the nearby village of Cleeve Hill SO9826 on the A46, or integrated into a circular walk to include Belas Knap long barrow SP0125 and Winchcombe SP0228. There's also a pleasant walk up to Belas Knap from the Craven Arms (a decent pub, with a nice garden) in Brockhampton SP0322.

Driving

The back roads through the villages we suggest visiting make for pleasant drives. The road along the sparkling River Windrush through Snowshill, Ford, Kineton and Naunton is a particular delight.

You can quickly get from this area to the south Cotswolds – from Chipping Campden down to Cirencester in under an hour, for instance.

Where to eat

Gretton SP0131 Royal Oak (0242) 602477 Enterprising and original food in a long series of flagstoned or bare-boarded rooms; beams, dim lighting from candles in bottles, entertaining medley of furnishings, and friendly young service; cl 25-26 Dec. £15|£2.75/£4.50.

Blockley SP1634 Crown (0386) 700245 Smart and civilised Elizabethan stone inn with very good food in bar or one of two restaurants (seafood specialities with up to 25 fresh fish main courses), lots of good wines; children allowed if well behaved. £2/£4.95.

Broad Campden SP1637 Bakers Arms (0386) 840515 Atmospheric ex-granary in tranquil village; very good-value bar food (inc children's menu), summer barbecues, pleasant garden, and regular events like beer festivals or ballooning meets; cl 1st Sat lunchtime after late May bank hol, 25 Dec, pm 26 Dec. £1.50/£3.50.

Cheltenham SO9422 Morans (0242) 581411 Highly recommended by contributors; cl Sun, bank hols. £2.95/£3.25.

Besides eating places mentioned in the text, others with decent food inc the Gardeners Arms in Alderton SP0033, Craven Arms at Brockhampton SP0322, Hobnails at Little Washbourne SO9833, and Foxhill at Naunton SP1123.

South Cotswolds

More variety both in scenery and in places to visit than the north Cotswolds; it is an excellent area for a short break.

Besides the classic Cotswold scenery, this area also includes the quiet watermeadows of the upper Thames, the Severn estuary, and the tortuous steep hills around Stroud. It has a splendid choice of picturesque villages, many of them little-visited by tourists. Cirencester, Northleach and Painswick are all handsome Cotswold towns with interesting sightseeing possibilities. Among other places, the wildfowl reserve at Slimbridge, Westonbirt Arboretum, the Chedworth Roman villa and the never-finished gothic mansion at Nympsfield are all outstanding in their different ways.

Like the north Cotswolds, this part has more things to do which are likely to appeal to adults – though there are attractions here which children enjoy.

There's no shortage of recommended places to stay (though the choice is not quite as wide as in the north Cotswolds).

Where to stay

Bibury SP1106 SWAN Cirencester GL7 5NW (0285) 740695 ***£128**; 18 individually decorated rms. Handsome creeper-covered hotel on the banks of the River Coln with pretty, formal gardens; cosy no-smoking parlour, carefully furnished, comfortable lounges, log fires, and very good food in opulent dining room; disabled access.

Cheltenham SO9422 GREENWAY GL51 5UG (0242) 862352 **£120**; 19 well-equipped, spacious and pretty rms. Very well-run, lovely 16th-c manor house with antiques, fresh flowers and comfortable seats in the attractive drawing room, cosy cocktail bar; very good modern British cooking, excellent wine list, good service, and neatly kept gardens; no lunch Sat, cl 5 days after 1 Jan; children over 7 only; disabled access.

Tetbury ST8893 CALCOT MANOR GL8 8YJ (0666) 890391 **£87**; 15 carefully and individually decorated rms. Exceptionally well-run manor house with deeply comfortable lounge and smaller drawing room with log fires, relaxed atmosphere, very good food, carefully chosen wines; outdoor swimming pool, croquet, clay-pigeon shooting; cl 1st week Jan, disabled access.

Tetbury ST8893 SNOOTY FOX GL8 8DD (0666) 502436 ***£80**; 12 good rms. Charming 16th-c inn with comfortable lounges (one is no smoking), open fire in the bar, and good food.

Tetbury ST8893 CLOSE GL8 8AQ (0666) 502272 **£75**; 15 individually furnished rms, some with garden views. Civilised 16th-c hotel with cosy little bar, a relaxing, dome-ceilinged lounge, very good food, excellent service; walled garden – floodlit at night; disabled access.

Westonbirt ST8589 HARE & HOUNDS Tetbury GL8 8QL (0666) 880233 ***£75**; 30 comfortable rms. Cotswold stone hotel with pleasant old-fashioned bar, relaxed lounges, open fires, decent food, friendly service; garden, tennis, squash, putting, croquet, snooker; disabled access.

Ewen SU0097 WILD DUCK Cirencester GL7 6BY (0285) 770310 ***£65**; 9 rms, 2 with four-poster. Attractive, old-fashioned 16th-c inn with handsome Elizabethan fireplace, decent bar food (fresh fish specialities), and prize-winning garden; children up to 10 can share parents' room.
Cirencester SP0201 FLEECE Cirencester GL7 2NZ (0285) 658507 **£56w**; 25 well-equipped rms. Tudor coaching inn with oak beams and log fires in the comfortable lounge, an attactive restaurant and bistro with very good food, pretty courtyard; children under 16 free if share parents' room; disabled access.
Fossebridge SP0811 FOSSEBRIDGE GL54 3JS (0285) 720721 ***£55**; 13 rms. Popular, partly Tudor inn by River Coln with two attractively furnished beamed bars, fine log fire, good restaurant, and helpful service; pretty lawns and terraces.
Winchcombe SP0228 SUDELEY HILL FARM Cheltenham GL54 5JB (0242) 602344 ***£40**; 3 no-smoking rms. Friendly 15th-c farmhouse on working mixed farm; with log fires, dining room, large garden, and barbecues; no dogs.
Painswick SO8609 DAMSELS FARM Stroud GL6 6UD (0452) 812148 **£35**; 3 rms. Quietly set farmhouse where children can feed animals; cl Nov-Feb.
North Nibley ST7496 NEW INN Waterley Bottom, Dursley GL11 6EF (0453) 543659 **£35**; 2 rms, shared bthrm. Simple inn with character landlady, wholesome home-made food, plentiful breakfasts, several interesting ales; neatly kept garden, small orchard, and good nearby walks; cl Christmas-New Year.
Contributors have warmly recommended the self-catering Owlpen Manor Cottages at Uley ST7898 (0453) 860261.

To see and do

★ **Cotswold villages** One of the most popular villages of all here is Bibury SP1106 on the River Coln. In summer it is so busy as to blunt its appeal, but nearby on the same stream there are other villages, off the main road and therefore bypassed by most visitors yet very appealing too, particularly Coln St Aldwyns SP1405 (excellent inn) and Quenington SP1404 (a decent village pub). On the far side of Bibury the back road tracking along the river passes through a string of pleasant little villages such as Coln Rogers, Coln St Dennis and (lovely at daffodil time) Yanworth SP0713, and eventually reaches the pretty village of Withington SP0315 (delightful pub right on the stream).

Other villages well worth tracking down, all with decent pubs and many well off the usual tourist routes, inc Bisley SO9005, Chedworth SP0511, the Duntisbournes SO9709 (the Five Mile House is a real step back in time), Eastleach SP1905 (a lovely ancient clapper bridge links the two Norman churches, very photogenic at daffodil time), Ewen SU0097, Frampton Mansell SO9102, North Cerney SP0208, Sapperton SO9403, Selsley SO8304, Sheepscombe SO8910, Slad SO8707, South Woodchester (at least for the views) SO8302, Southrop SP1903 (another village that really comes into its own when the daffodils are out) and (more small town than village) Wotton-under-Edge ST7593.

Many of these villages have most attractive churches, few of them as yet locked. A rewarding way of visiting Cotswold villages is to plan a circuit of neighbouring villages all with churches worth seeing. Cirencester is a good base for this. One such group, east of the town, consists of Ampney Crucis SP0602, Ampney St Peter SP0801, Ampney St Mary SP0802, Down Ampney SP1097 (Vaughan Williams was the vicar's son), Hampnett SP1015 and Northleach SP1114. Another group, north-west of Cirencester, is Elkstone SO9612, Duntisbourne Abbots SO9707, Duntisbourne Rouse SO9806, Daglingworth SO9905, Stratton SP0103, Baunton SP0204 and North Cerney SP0208.

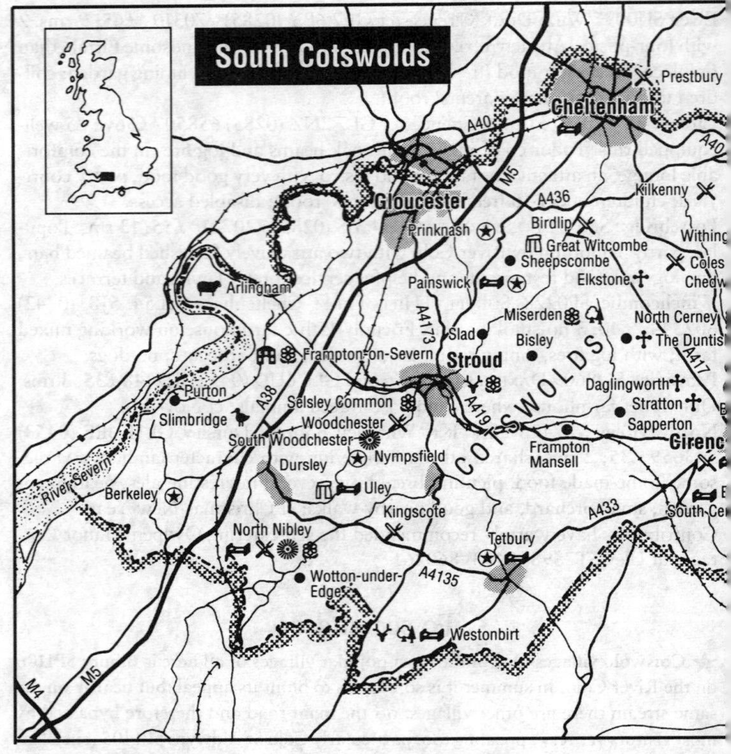

Other things to do and see

Arlingham SO7010 St Augustine's Working Farm You can take part in a typical day's activities on this friendly dairy farm, which, as well as cows and calves, has pigs, goats, hens, sheep and rabbits, all of which you can go right up to; also a display of old farming equipment. Snacks, shop, disabled access; cl Oct-Mar; £2.50. They expect to be moving to another site nearby early in 1994, best to ring (0452) 740277 to check.

Barnsley SP0705 Barnsley House Garden Lovely little herb, vegetable and knot gardens, fruit trees and decorative plants, laburnum and lime walks, 18th-c summerhouses, around Queen Anne manor house (not open); especially attractive spring blossom and autumn colours. Plant sales, disabled access; cl Tues, Fri, Sun; £2. The village pub is good.

Berkeley ST6899 Berkeley Castle The same family have lived in this excellently preserved castle for nearly 850 years, through its transition from Norman fortress to stately home; impressive paintings and furnishings, keep, hall, terraced gardens, park, extensive butterfly farm and the dungeon where Edward II was murdered in 1327. Snacks, shop, limited disabled access; cl am Sun and every day in Apr, Mon exc bank holidays, Oct exc Sun, Nov-Mar; £3.70, £1 gardens only, 50p butterfly farm. Jenner Museum Interesting and largely unchanged Georgian home of Edward Jenner, who discovered the vaccine against smallpox and also

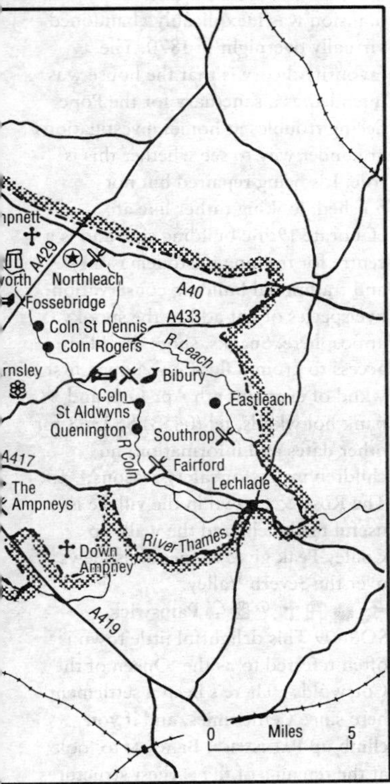

dabbled in hydrogen balloons and hibernating hedgehogs. It now houses a museum about his life, and the thatched hut where he vaccinated the poor free of charge can still be seen in the attractive grounds. Snacks, shop, disabled access; cl am, Mon exc bank hols, Oct exc Sun, Nov-Mar; £1.20. The Salmon at Wanswell Green is a useful nearby pub for lunch.

Bibury SP1106 TROUT FARM Well placed by one of the most beautiful and oft-photographed Cotswold villages, a working farm breeding rainbow trout in 20 ponds; visitors can feed the fish. Snacks, shop, disabled access; cl 25 Dec, possibly other dates, phone (0285) 740215 to check; £1.80. The Catherine Wheel is the best place here for lunch.

Cirencester SP0201 is a busy country town, particularly on its Mon and Fri market days, with a succession of fine Cotswold stone streets off the long market place. It has many attractive buildings, and interesting antique and other shops inc traditional country saddlers' etc. Though perhaps the most handsome of all the Cotswold towns, it is not too touristy. The CHURCH is very grand. CORINIUM MUSEUM (Park St) Cirencester was one of the most important cities in Roman Britain, and this museum has one of the finest collections of antiquities from the period, inc mosaic floors, sculptures and full-scale reconstructions of a dining room and kitchen complete with menus. Shop, excellent disabled access; cl Mon Nov-Mar; £1.25. BREWERY COURT 20 independent craft businesses and shops in former brewery building (cl Sun); also theatre, gallery, café. There are also a number of old, wool merchants' houses around the city worth looking at, besides the 12th-c remains of ST JOHN'S HOSPITAL and the NORMAN ARCH. Decent pubs include the Slug & Lettuce, Black Horse and (very local but good value for lunch) Golden Cross. Tatyans is a good Chinese restaurant.

Frampton-on-Severn SO7407 FRAMPTON COURT Interesting Georgian stately home, with original furniture, porcelain and paintings, and fascinating gardens. The 18th-c orangery has been well converted into self-catering holiday flats. Disabled access to garden only; open all year by appointment, phone (0452) 740698 or 740267; £3. The village green is immense, perhaps the largest in the country, with the orangery on one side, and a civilised Georgian pub on another; just outside the village the Gloucester & Sharpness Canal passes grand colonnaded lock keepers' houses by pretty swing bridges.

Great Witcombe SO9114 WITCOMBE ROMAN VILLA Remains of a big villa built around a courtyard, several mosaics and evidence of an underfloor heating system.

❀ ✺ ⚘ **Miserden** SO9308 MISERDEN PARK Fine views over the wooded Golden Valley from the handsome gardens of a 17th-c manor house (not open), some Lutyens topiary, mature shrubs and trees, colourful walled garden; nursery, some disabled access; cl Fri-Mon, Oct-Mar; £1.50. Also woodland trail down by the river.

❀ **North Cerney** SP0208 CERNEY HOUSE Expansive old garden behind 13th-c church, with old roses, trees, shrubs, walled and herb gardens; snacks, shop; open Weds and Sat pm, cl Nov-Feb; £1. The Bathurst Arms is good for lunch.

❀ ✺ **North Nibley** ST7495 HUNTS COURT Old roses, unusual shrubs and other plants inc heathers; fine views. Plant sales; cl Sun and Mon exc bank hols and some midsummer Suns, all Aug; £1. The nearby Black Horse is useful for lunch, and the walk up to the Tyndale Monument above the wooded slope gives even better views.

✝ 𝔥 ! **Northleach** SP1114 is a fine example of an unspoilt, small wool town, with a particularly interesting CHURCH. COTSWOLD COUNTRYSIDE COLLECTION Formerly the Northleach House of Correction, these buildings tell the story of rural Cotswold life, with particular emphasis on horse-drawn equipment, e.g. shepherds' and harvest wagons; also interesting agricultural displays, reconstructed dairy, kitchen, laundry and courtroom. Snacks, shop, disabled access; cl Sun am; *£1.25. KEITH HARDING'S WORLD OF MECHANICAL MUSIC Unusual collection of clocks, musical boxes and instruments in old wool merchant's house, displayed and played in period settings; shop, good disabled and blind access; cl 25-26 Dec; *£3.50. The Red Lion (see Where to eat) and Wheatsheaf are both pleasant for lunch.

⛫ ! ✺ **Nympsfield** SO8000 WOODCHESTER MANSION Tucked away in a wooded valley, the construction of this splendid Gothic mansion was inexplicably abandoned virtually overnight in 1870. The favourite theory is that the house was intended as a sanctuary for the Pope fleeing troubles at home; investigations are under way to see whether this is true. It's being repaired but not finished, looking rather like an elaborate 19th-c building site, and is a centre for training in stonemasonry and traditional building conservation; five species of bat add to the spooky atmosphere. Snacks, shop, disabled access to ground floor only; open first wknd of every month Apr-Oct, and bank hol wknds, tel (0453) 882368 for other dates and information; no children inside for safety reasons; *£3. The Rose & Crown in the village is useful for lunch, and the walk up Coaley Peak gives tremendous views over the Severn Valley.

★ ✺ ⛫ ✝ ⚲ ❀ ⚘ **Painswick** SO8609 This delightful little town is often referred to as the 'Queen of the Cotswolds'. There's been a settlement here since Celtic times, and if you climb up PAINSWICK BEACON to look at the remains of the earliest structures there are fine views towards the Malvern hills. There are plenty of old buildings to look at, such as the 15th-c POST OFFICE and the CHURCH OF ST MARY with its fine tombs and churchyard, also craft workshops and antique shops. PAINSWICK ROCOCO GARDEN (The Stables, Painswick House) Careful restoration of sizeable 18th-c garden to match 1748 painting of its rococo mix of precisely trimmed hedging, paths and shrubs with unrestrained trees and slightly zany garden buildings; pleasant vistas, woodland walks. Restaurant, shop, plant sales; cl Mon and Tues exc bank hols, cl mid-Dec-Jan; *£2.40. The Royal Oak is good for lunch, and the Kings Arms does food all day in summer.

✝ ⚲ ✺ 🐦 **Prinknash** SO8614 PRINKNASH ABBEY AND POTTERY Rather unusual 20th-c Benedictine monastery and earlier house, now home to the world-famous pottery; you can watch the hand-made crafts being produced from the viewing gallery. Meals, snacks, shop, disabled access; cl 25-26 Dec, Good Fri; only charge 75p for pottery viewing gallery. There are good views from the grounds. PRINKNASH BIRD PARK Very attractive parklands and grounds of abbey filled with exotic pheasants, peacocks and other birds; also deer, goats and waterfowl, monks' haunted fishpool, pets corner; lots of the birds are very friendly. Shop; cl Christmas; *£2.60.

Selsley Common SO8304 SELSLEY HERB FARM Sizeable herb gardens, also old-fashioned roses and butterfly plants, goats to feed. Shop, plant sales, cream teas summer Suns and bank hols, some disabled access; cl Sun am, Nov-Feb; *£1.

South Cerney SU0497 COTSWOLD WATER PARK 2,000 acres of lakes with facilities for angling, windsuring, sailing and other watersports, country parks and walks, bird-watching, nature reserves. Snacks, disabled access; car parking charge.

Slimbridge SO7703 WILDFOWL AND WETLANDS TRUST This enormous wildfowl reserve is the headquarters of the trust and where it was founded in 1946; hundreds of acres filled with probably the world's most comprehensive collection of geese, swans and ducks (you can adopt one if you like), as well as six flocks of flamingos, rare and wild birds, and a tropical house; excellent viewing and feeding facilities. Meals, snacks, shop; cl 24-25 Dec; *£4.50. The Tudor Arms by the swing bridge across the canal is a useful food stop.

Tetbury ST8993 has a splendid raised MARKET HOUSE and some interesting little lanes, with quite a few antique shops and craft workshops. CHAVENAGE Unspoilt 16th-c manor house which may be familiar from various TV programmes; tapestries, furniture, Cromwellian relics, Edwardian wing, big gardens. Disabled access to ground floor only; open Easter Sun and Mon pm, Thurs and Sun May-Sept; £2.50. The Hunters Lodge nearby is good for lunch, and the Crown in the town is useful.

Uley ST7898 ULEY TUMULUS Quite daunting 180 ft-long burial mound known as Hetty Pegler's Tump, with stone central passage and three burial chambers. The former weaving village has some attractive 18th-c or older stone houses, and the Kings Head is useful for lunch.

Westonbirt ST8589 WESTONBIRT ARBORETUM Over 18,000 numbered plants and shrubs fill the 17 miles of pathways at this magnificent collection, begun in 1829 and run as a family hobby for years until it was bought by the Forestry Commission. Outstanding in spring and autumn, but worth a stop any time; various events throughout the year. Meals, snacks, shop, disabled access; *£2.50. The Hare & Hounds is handy for food.

Yanworth SP0513 CHEDWORTH ROMAN VILLA This villa, excavated in 1864 and in pleasantly secluded woodland, is the best example of a 2nd-c Roman house in Britain; well-preserved mosaics, rooms and bath houses, with smaller remains in the museum. Shop, some disabled access; cl Sun am, Mon Nov-Mar, Good Fri, Feb exc by appointment, possibly other days in Nov and Dec; £2.50. The Mill at Withington and Seven Tuns in Upper Chedworth are both quite handy for lunch – and the walk is very attractive.

On the River Thames, a quiet reed-fringed stream along these upper reaches, Lechlade SU2199 is a graceful village with one or two decent antique shops, and access to the river. The Red Lion and (with good arrangements for wheelchairs) Crown here are both useful for lunch. Fairford SP1501 has pleasant riverside meadows; the Bull by the attractive 15th-c church is good for lunch. The source of the river, off the A433 nr Kemble ST9898, is unremarkable.

A good quiet spot to get down to the River Severn is from Purton SO6904, where the Berkeley Arms has a wonderful estuary view.

Walks

The **Cotswold Way** (see north Cotswolds) continues here, again with a good many worthwhile stretches from which to select walks. It takes in a series of excellent viewpoints: among them the Devil's Chimney SO9418, a rock pinnacle amid old quarries on Leckhampton Hill, perched above Cheltenham; and Painswick Beacon SO8612 and Haresfield Beacon SO8208, reached by short ascents from the road.

Elsewhere, the **Chedworth Woods** SP0513 provide scope for short walks if you want the satisfaction of reaching Chedworth Villa (see above) on foot. A field path from Chedworth SP0511 heading N through the woods is a little tricky to find; much easier is the level track along the N edge of the woods, which approaches the site from the E.

The rich, steeply sheltered valleys around Stroud make up a complicated landscape, seen to best advantage for example between Chalford SO8903 and Sapperton SO9403, where the derelict **Thames & Severn Canal** is atmospherically overgrown, although its towpath survives as a walkway.

Not far from Wotton-under-Edge ST7593, the valley of **Ozleworth Bottom** ST7992 has a nostalgically forgotten quality about it, providing a walk between Lasborough Manor and Ozleworth Park, with its unusual Norman church endowed with a hexagonal tower.

An appropriately quiet approach to Bibury SP1106 is along the path by the **River Coln** from the toll-house just south of Coln St Aldwyns. This route takes you in by the mill and bridge over the Coln itself.

Extended walks over the Cotswold plateau are not always rewarding, with unchanging views of arable fields often the rule.

Pubs that are good jumping-off points for walks here inc the Black Horse at Cranham SO8912 for Cranham Woods, the Crown at Frampton Mansell SO9102 or Daneway at Sapperton SO9403 for the derelict canal mentioned above, the Edgemoor at Edge SO8509, the Amberley Inn or Black Horse at Amberley SO8401, the Bell at Selsley SO8304, the Fleece at Hillesley ST7689 (very recently restored to Glos from Avon), and the Berkeley Arms by the Severn estuary at Purton SO6904.

Driving

An area much less visited than most yet with outstanding scenery is that between Wotton-under-Edge and Stroud, with the roads around there (B4066, B4058, the steep lanes up on to Minchinhampton Common nr Amberley, for example) all worthwhile. The main A46, which goes through this area, is not overly busy and gives some fine views.

The Cotswold plateau is intersected by Roman roads with far Cotswold views: of the modern roads following their course, the A429/A433 doesn't carry too much traffic and is a pleasant drive; the A435 is also quite enjoyable, but the A417 has too much traffic for leisurely driving. There are good views from the road off the A419 W of Cirencester, through Frampton Mansell and Sapperton.

Meandering along the back roads through and between any of the villages we've recommended is the best way of all of seeing the area; one of the nicest of these drives is along the Coln Valley – see Cotswold villages, above.

Where to eat

Birdlip SO9214 KINGSHEAD HOUSE (0452) 862299 Imaginative food using organic, locally grown produce in popular, welcoming restaurant; cl Sat am, Sun pm, Mon, 26-28 Dec, 1 Jan. **£27.30**|£4/£6.

Cirencester SP0201 TATYANS (0285) 653529 Very good Chinese food in prettily decorated restaurant; disabled access; cl Sun, 25-26 Dec. **£22**|£5.95.

Kilkenny SP0018 KILKENEY (0242) 820341 Spacious, modernised, old Cotswold country pub with attractive views; good, interesting food, decent little wine list; children lunchtimes only; cl Sun pm, 25-26 Dec, Jan-Mar. **£19**|£2.75/£7.50.

Kingscote ST8196 HUNTERS HALL (0453) 860393 Civilised, creeper-covered old inn with an elegant series of high-beamed connecting rooms, some fine old furniture, big log fires; good bar and restaurant food, children's menu, excellent breakfasts, quite a few wines by the glass; big garden with children's play area; bedrooms; disabled access. **£18.50**|£1.70/£5.25.

Northleach SP1114 RED LION Market Pl (0451) 860251 Good-value, well-presented simple food in comfortable and friendly pub, popular Sun roast, open fire; disabled access. **£14.20**|£2.10/£5.50.

Woodchester SO8302 RAM Bustling, cheerful pub with spectacular views of valley from terrace, decent bar food, prompt, friendly service, and lots of real ales. **£12.60**|£1.85/£4.95.

Southrop SP1903 SWAN (036 785) 205 Smart, old stone-tiled pub in pretty daffodil-filled village, decent bar and restaurant food, children's menu, and respectable wine list. £1.10/£5.25.

Besides places mentioned in the text, others with decent food inc the Crown of Crucis at Ampney Crucis SP0602, the Colesbourne Inn at Colesbourne SO9913, the Bull in Fairford SP1501, the Blackhorse in North Nibley ST7496 and the Plough at Prestbury SO9624.

GLOUCESTER AND THE FOREST OF DEAN

Unusual countryside characterises the Forest of Dean; Gloucester is interesting, but more for day visits than as a place to stay in.

Gloucester has three exceptional attractions – the cathedral, and two excellent and most enjoyable specialist museums. It's a big city and, though it has other attractions too, it is perhaps best seen as a place to visit by the day (preferably on a weekend, when it's quieter), rather than as a place to stay in. It's quickly reached from Cheltenham, incidentally, as well as from other places within this area. It would be a tiring city to inflict on a family with children: probably the best place for them in this part of the county would be Newent.

The Forest of Dean has a unique landscape: hilly woodland, much of it ancient, that shows many traces of the way it has provided a livelihood for the people living around it. And it's flanked by a spectacular stretch of the Wye Valley. Some people find the scenery of the forest a bit disappointing; it has most impact on those prepared to delve into its past a bit, perhaps at the heritage centre at Soudley. Given that, it's as attractive an area for walking as the Cotswolds. Its woodland colours are at their best in late May and autumn.

The quiet orchard and farming countryside around the Severn Valley and north of the Forest of Dean is well worth discovering. As the Severn itself is still a formidable barrier to travel here, with very few river crossings, there aren't that many people passing through, which has kept it very unspoilt. The little villages down by the west bank of the Severn have a timeless, unchanging feel.

There are not nearly so many places of interest to visit in this part of the county. Newent has a reasonable number of worthwhile attractions; elsewhere, the most notable are Littledean Hall, the steam railway at Lydney, the caverns at Clearwell, and, particularly in late May, the gardens of Lydney Park.

Prices over on this side of the Severn are rather lower than in the Cotswolds.

Where to stay

Corse Lawn SO8330 CORSE LAWN HOUSE Gloucester GL19 4LZ (0452) 780479 **£90**; 19 individually furnished rms. Magnificent Queen Anne building with attractive bar, lounge, distinguished restaurant, excellent wines, and a relaxed atmosphere; disabled access; dogs welcome.

Clearwell SO5708 CLEARWELL CASTLE Coleford GL16 8LG (0594) 832320 **£85**; 16 spacious rms mostly with four-posters or half-testers. Early 18th-c castle with huge halls and antiques, cosy bar, and there's a chapel in the basement; croquet in garden.

Clearwell SO5708 WYNDHAM ARMS GL16 8JT (0594) 833666 **£55**; 17 well-equipped rms. Smart old country inn near Wye Valley and Forest of Dean; comfortable beamed bar, open fire, big helpings of often unusual food, good service, neat gardens, and friendly dogs; cl Christmas; children free if sharing parents' room; disabled access.

Brookthorpe SO8312 GILBERTS Gilberts Lane, Gloucester GL4 0UH (0452) 812364 **£42**; 4 rms. 400-year-old house with woodburning stove in sitting room, organic produce from the surrounding smallholding used for breakfast, and relaxed atmosphere.

St Briavels SO5605 GEORGE Lydney GL15 6TA (0594) 530228 **£40**; 4 rms. Pleasant old pub in particularly interesting village, overlooking 12th-c castle; three rambling rooms with big stone fireplace, a Celtic coffin lid dating from 1070 (found in a fireplace here) is mounted next to the bar counter; decent food in no-smoking eating area; outdoor chessboard.

Viney Hill SO6506 LOWER VINEY COUNTRY GUEST HOUSE Lydney GL15 4LT

(0594) 516000 £38; 6 well-furnished, comfortable rms. Delightful old no-smoking farmhouse with half-acre garden, in lovely countryside; two lounges (one with TV), lots of books and local information, decent evening meal and good breakfast, friendly, efficient service; very good walking all around.

To see and do

Gloucester SO8318 This is a busy modern city, and though there are old buildings you have to search them out among the big modern shops (for instance the splendid timber-framed house tucked down a passageway off 26 Westgate St). If you do want to track down such treasures the efficient Tourist Office (itself in a fine ancient building, St Michaels Tower at the central Cross) will send you off well equipped for the hunt. The Linden Tree (Bristol Rd-A38 past docks), Tailors House (Westgate St) and York House (London Rd) are all useful for a quick lunch.

✝ The CATHEDRAL towers majestically over the city's more recent buildings; it has delicate fan-vaulted cloisters, the second largest medieval stained-glass window in the country, and a fine collection of church plate in the Treasury. Meals, snacks, shop, disabled access.

☸ Gloucester is the furthest inland harbour in England, and the NATIONAL WATERWAYS MUSEUM (The Docks) vividly recreates the story of Britain's inland waterways, especially the heyday of Gloucester Docks after the opening of the Gloucester & Berkeley Canal; recently judged one of the top seven museums in Europe, with working engines, boats, demonstrations, reconstructed maintenance yard, craft displays. Snacks, shop, disabled access; cl 25 Dec; *£4.25.

The revitalised museum also houses the fascinating ROBERT OPIE COLLECTION MUSEUM OF ADVERTISING AND PACKAGING, a real treat for nostalgia-lovers, with a massive assembly of packets, tins, bottles, posters, street signs and more from Victorian days onwards; continuous showing of vintage TV commercials. Snacks, shop, disabled access; cl winter Mon, 25-26 Dec; *£2.50.

CITY EAST GATE (Eastgate St) Some Roman and medieval gate towers and a moat remain in an underground exhibition chamber below the shopping centre; the adjacent walls may be open at times; cl Sun.

FOLK MUSEUM (Westgate St) Housed in a group of Tudor and Jacobean timber-framed houses, displays showing various aspects of local history, domestic life and rural crafts. Among the reconstructions is a turn-of-the-century schoolroom where children can take part in period lessons, but be warned – if they don't behave they could get a mock caning; also reconstructed dairy, shoemaker and wheelwright's shops, an original pin factory and forge, and events throughout the year. Shop, some disabled access; cl Sun exc Jul-Sept, 25-26 Dec, 1 Jan, Good Fri.

REGIMENTS OF GLOUCESTERSHIRE MUSEUM (The Docks) Unusually lively regimental museum with reconstructions and sound-effects showing the soldier's life over the last 300 years at home and abroad. Shop, disabled access; cl Mon (exc bank hols, July and Aug), Christmas; £2.50.

CITY MUSEUM AND ART GALLERY (Brunswick Rd) Furniture, archaeology, silver, local history and paintings by Gainsborough, Turner and others; cl Sun, 24-26 Dec, Good Fri.

! HOUSE OF THE TAILOR OF GLOUCESTER (College Ct) Inspiration

for Beatrix Potter's story, now with an exhibition and shop; disabled access downstairs; cl Sun and bank hols.

GLOUCESTER ANTIQUES CENTRE (The Docks) Four floors of restored riverside warehouse housing 68 shops with collections of all kinds, nicely arranged and displayed in Dickensian arcades; meals, snacks, disabled access; cl 25-27 Dec.

The Forest of Dean Still largely ancient oak woodland despite encroaching pine plantations, the forest rolls over many miles of hilly countryside, giving plenty of space – even in summer you can often have much of the woods to yourself. There are ponds, streams with stepping stones, cattle and maybe fallow deer (a good place to see these is the NAGSHEAD NATURE RESERVE SO6008), sudden distant views, the humps and gouges that mark ANCIENT IRON WORKINGS, the tracks of abandoned railways and tramways, and still one or two of the freeminers, who've been digging coal by hand from surface seams for hundreds of years. There are good paths throughout. The paving of a ROMAN ROAD can be tracked just off the B4431 at Blackpool Bridge SO6508. SYMONDS YAT ROCK SO5616 is perhaps the most spectacular part, where the River Wye rolls around a monumental wooded cliff barrier. There are tremendous views in all directions from the top, and at the bottom a ferry runs between two inns.

Around the edges of the forest the scenery changes to a patchwork of steep pastures – also very attractive.

To make the most of the forest it's well worth getting a forest map, either from the Dean Heritage Centre (see below) or direct from the Forestry Commission in Coleford (0594) 833057.

Other things to see and do

Clearwell SO5608 CLEARWELL CAVES Iron ore was extracted from these mines from Iron Age times until 1945; nine big caverns to be seen, with deeper trips for the more adventurous, and exhibitions of engine rooms and equipment. At Christmas they create lively themed displays in the caves. Meals, snacks, shop; cl Nov, Jan, Feb; £2.50. The Wyndham Arms is splendid for lunch.

! Coleford SO5710 GREAT WESTERN RAILWAY MUSEUM Converted Coleford GWR goods station housing several large-scale model steam locomotives, relics, photographs and a Victorian ticket office. Shop; cl am, Mon (exc bank hols), wkdys Nov-Easter; *£1. PUZZLE WOOD Just off B4228, wooded paths arranged in a puzzle, landscaped in 19th c; also remains of Roman iron mines. Snacks, shop; cl Mon (exc bank hols), Nov-Easter; £1.50.

✝ Deerhurst SO8729 has ancient remains including ODDA'S CHAPEL, a restored 11th-c chapel discovered as part of a farmhouse, and the mainly Saxon ST MARY'S PRIORY, which has a lovely atmosphere.

Littledean SO6713 LITTLEDEAN HALL Interesting house largely unchanged since the 19th c, but actually dating back to Norman times; especially worth a look are the displays and reconstruction of the Saxon hall, and the beautiful grounds with ancient trees, fishpools and the recently discovered Roman temple – the largest in Britain. Snacks, shop; cl Nov-Feb; £2.50.

Lydney SO6303 DEAN FOREST RAILWAY Lots of locomotives, wagons and equipment, steam days and other events; snacks, shop, disabled access; tel (0594) 843423 for train times and prices. LYDNEY PARK Extensive sheltered spring garden rich with flowering shrubs, rhododendrons, azaleas, magnolias; there are also lakes, a deer park, the remains of a Roman temple among the trees and a Roman museum. Snacks, shop, plant sales; open Sun, Weds and bank hols early Apr-early Jun, every day late May; £1.50 (£1 Weds).

Newent SO7226 is a small country town with some timbered buildings which have a bit of a Worcestershire or Herefordshire look. NATIONAL BIRDS OF PREY CENTRE Exceptional collection of birds of prey, displays of falcons and other trained birds, breeding aviaries; birds flown four times each day. Meals, snacks, shop, some disabled access; cl Dec-Jan; £3.75. SHAMBLES MUSEUM OF VICTORIAN LIFE A full recreation of Victorian life: cobbled square, shops and furnished tradesman's house. Meals, snacks, shop, some disabled access, though there are stairs in places; cl Mon (exc bank hols), Christmas-Mar; £2.45. The George opposite is handy for lunch. NEWENT BUTTERFLY AND NATURAL WORLD CENTRE Tropical butterflies flying free in exotic setting; also spiders, snakes, wildfowl, rabbits, peacocks and small birds. Shop, some disabled access; cl Oct-Mar; £2.95. THE GLASSBARN They don't have demonstrations of blowing don't have demonstrations of blowing and fashioning glass here any more, but there's still an interesting gallery of colourful designer glassware, including some rather unusually fashioned products. Shop; cl 12.30-1.30, Sat pm, Sun, Mon, Christmas and Easter. THREE CHOIRS VINEYARD (off B4215 towards Dymock) Tours of rapidly expanding vineyard, now one of the six largest in the country, free wine tastings. Meals, snacks, shop, disabled access; cl 24 Dec-mid-Mar exc wknds by arrangement. ST ANNES VINEYARD (Oxenhall, off B4221) 150 varieties of vine are grown here, and many are for sale. So too are the wines, of which there are free tastings; cl am exc summer.

Parkend SO6208 has a good co-operative CRAFT CENTRE (cl Christmas). The Woodman is good for lunch, and the Fountain here is useful too.

★ **St Briavels** SO5605 is an attractive small village focused on the ruins of its 13th-c castle (the inhabited part is a youth hostel), with a grassy former moat and views from the ramparts of the curtain wall. The George here is good for lunch.

Soudley SO6513 DEAN HERITAGE CENTRE The story of the Forest of Dean, set around an old watermill in pretty wooded valley; reconstructed cottage and coal mine, nature trails, craft workshops and displays, adventure playground. Meals, snacks, shop, disabled access; cl wkdys Nov-Jan exc for pre-booked groups and during Christmas week, also cl 24-26 Dec; £2.50.

★ **Taynton** SO0933 is an attractive village – particularly when the daffodils are out, and the TAYNTON FARM CENTRE is a friendly little working farm (cl Nov-Mar exc shop).

★ **Tewkesbury** SO8932 Important medieval town and site of the last battle in the Wars of the Roses in 1471, still full of attractive half-timbered buildings with a maze of small alleyways. Two of these old houses are home to the TOWN MUSEUM and the JOHN MOORE COUNTRYSIDE MUSEUM. Most impressive is the ABBEY, of which the massively confident Norman tower must be one of the finest in existence; there are regular concerts in the abbey; snacks, disabled access. The historic Bell Hotel is useful for lunch, with a Severn-side walk; the Gardeners Arms is also useful.

Twigworth SO8422 NATURE IN ART Growing collection of wildlife art of various types and origin; the only museum of its kind, located in a very attractive house. Regular events, displays and talks; meals, snacks, shop, disabled access; cl Mon, 24-26 Dec; £2.50.

Westbury-on-Severn SO7114 WESTBURY COURT (NT) Formal Dutch garden with canals, yew topiary, etc, restored to its 1700s layout using pre-1700 cultivars inc old fruit varieties; cl Mon (exc bank hols), Tues, Good Fri, Nov-Mar; *£2. The White House is good for lunch.

River Severn Good places to get down to the river, with riverside pubs, are Apperley SO8628, Norton via Wainlode Hill SO8523 and Twyning SO8936, though best of all is Ashleworth Quay SO8125, where the very traditional pub has been in the same family for centuries. There's a handsome 15th-c TITHE BARN in the village; cl Good Fri, Nov-Mar; 60p.

Walks

The **Forest of Dean** rises and rolls, and is well equipped with car parks, picnic sites and forest trails. A good start is at the Soudley Heritage Centre (see above). The **Sculpture Trail** takes a four-mile route passing nearly 20 specially commissioned sculptures hidden deep in the forest (from picnic site near Speech House Hotel SO6611). The **Kidnalls Forest Trail** is a good way of tracking down some early industrial sites. The **Foundry Wood Trail** passes Soudley fish ponds SO6212 and gains some fine views. The **Wench Ford Forest Walk** leads past a series of quite interesting rock outcrops. Signposted paths ensure easy route-finding up to the open summit of May Hill SO6921, where on a clear day you can see the Cotswolds, Malverns, Welsh Marches and Severn Estuary.

The lower **Wye Valley** on the west side of the Forest of Dean cuts through a gorge giving some very picturesque views. As there are few crossing points, and the scenery away from the gorge is relatively unspectacular, walks along it are generally of the there-and-back sort. On this Gloucestershire side the valley is tracked by the **Offa's Dyke Path** (the **Wye Valley Walk** takes in the western bank). Southern highlights include Wintour's Leap ST5496, a sheer cliff N of Chepstow with dizzy views downwards, and the Devil's Pulpit ST5499, where trees frame a perfect vista of Tintern Abbey far below on the opposite bank. Further N, the **Kymin** SO5212 can be climbed from May Hill just across the river border opposite Monmouth; at the summit is the Naval Temple, a quaint rustic conceit put up in 1800 to commemorate admirals of the Napoleonic Wars.

Useful pubs to start walks from inc the Rising Sun at Moseley Green SO6308, Woodman at Parkend SO6208, Dog & Muffler at Joyford SO5813 and White Horse at Staunton SO5412 (all Forest of Dean), Yew Tree at Cliffords Mesne SO6922 (for May Hill), Glasshouse Inn by Newent Woods SO7122, Brockweir Inn in Brockweir SO5401, the Boat over the river from Redbrook SO5309 and Ostrich in the charming village of Newland SO5509 (all three Wye Valley) and Wyndham Arms at Clearwell SO5708. There's a pleasant short stroll down to the Severn from the Red Hart at Awre SO7108.

The countryside around Gloucester is pancake-flat, unrewarding for walkers.

Driving

On the whole this is not a very good area for country drives. Though there are good roads through the heart of the Forest of Dean, the trees tend to cut off the views. The B4432 to Symonds Yat does give some good views, and the B4228 down past St Briavels is a pleasant country road. Don't try to navigate the confusing little lanes around the edges of the Forest of Dean without a large-scale map – but if you can find your way around them, they are very rewarding.

Where to eat

Newland SO5509 OSTRICH (0594) 833260 Particularly attractive 13th-c inn in pretty village; with big log fire, comfortable seating, attentive service, and freshly prepared, good food. £3.50/£5.

Other places with decent food inc the Red Hart at Blaisdon SO7016, the Yew Tree at Cliffords Mesne SO6922, the New County Hotel in Gloucester (Southgate St) SO8318, and the Boat at Redbrook SO5410.

Help this year from: *Pam Adsley, Joan Olivier, Neil and Anita Christopher, Jane and Ian Williams, John Bowdler, Barry and Anne, Richard Carpenter, Dr and Mrs Peter Simpson, Dorothee and Dennis Glover, P R Cowan, S J Isles, John Knighton, Gabrielle and John Clezy, D J Williams, Andrew and Ruth Triggs, Andy and Ali Sweetman, Chris and Chris Vallely, Maureen Hobbs, Simon Collett-Jones, Peter Lloyd, Michael Heald, Alastair Campbell, Mr and Mrs G J Rice, Alain and Rose Foote, Roger Taylor, John and Audrey Davidson, G W H Kerby, Helen Chalmers, Gwen and Peter Andrews, Leslie and Dorothy Pilson, A T Langton, T M Dobby, George Atkinson, Jane and Ian Williams, Adrian Zambardino, Paul Weedon, J Boylan, D H Buchanan, Peter and Jenny Quine, Klaus and Elizabeth Leist, Steve Goodchild, Ted George, David and Anne Smith, Mrs M C Barrett, Roger Huggins, Mr and Mrs P B Dowsett, M A and C R Starling, DC, Joan and Michel Hooper-Immins, R Smylie, Debbie Hawkins, J Deave, John and Barbara Gibson, Pauline Crossland, Dave Cawley, C F Walling, Lyn and Bill Capper.*

Gloucestershire Calendar

Some of these dates were provisional as we went to press.

April

23rd **Gloucester** St George's Day Celebrations *with mummers and Morris dancers*; **Nailsworth** Festival – *till May 2*

30th **Minchinhampton** Craft Fair *at Gatcombe Park – till 2 May*

May

1st **Lydney** Dean Forest Railway Steam Days – *every Sun and some weekdays till end Sept*; **Randwick** Cheese Rolling – *cheese is blessed, garlanded and rolled anti-clockwise around the church*

12th **Bisley** Ascension Day Well Blessing – *seven wells decorated with flowers*

14th **Randwick** Wap – *fair and procession with the cheese, the mayor is carried shoulder high and dipped in the pond*

22nd **St Briavels** Bread and Cheese Ceremony *in which they are thrown from a wall near the castle to be scrambled for in the lane below, a tradition practised since the reign of King John to affirm the villagers' rights to local woodland*

30th **Brockworth** Cheese Rolling *at Coopers Hill – in a 400-year-old ritual emphasising the right of the people to graze their sheep on the hill, cheeses are rolled down and competitors try to catch them*; **Tetbury** Woolsack Races and Medieval Fayre – *teams race with 60lb sacks of wool on their backs*

June

3rd **Chipping Campden** Dover's Games and Scuttlebrook Wake – *17th-c 'Olympicks' of rural sports such as cudgel and slingstick and shin kicking – till Sat 4*; **North Nibley** Tyndale Rally *at Nibley House – till Sun 5*

4th **Gloucester** Folk Festival *at The Docks – till Sun 5*

10th **Dursley** Festival – *till Sun 26*

24th **Cirencester** Festival – *till 9 July*; **Naunton** The Lindsay Quartet *at St Andrews church*

Gloucestershire Calendar

JULY

2nd **Cheltenham** 50th International Festival of Music *with very extensive fringe – till Sun 17*; **Tewkesbury** Carnival – *till Sun 3*

3rd **Cirencester** Carnival

5th **Chipping Campden** Summer Play *at Hidcote Manor Gardens: Richard III – till Sat 9*

9th **Tewkesbury** Medieval Fayre – *till Sun 10*

23rd **Gloucester** Carnival – *entertainment in the park till Sat 6 Aug and simultaneous with the Gloucester community arts festival*

AUGUST

11th **Northleach** National Sheepdog Trials – *till Sat 13*

22nd **Frampton** Deer Roast *on the village green*

27th **Frocester** Beer Festival – *till Mon 29*

29th **Bourton-on-the-Water** Football – *six-a-side football in the River Windrush*; **Berkeley** Hunt Agricultural Show

SEPTEMBER

1st **Tetbury** Blue Grass Festival *at Holford Arms*

3rd **Moreton-in-Marsh** Show

18th **Painswick** Clypping of the Church Ceremony – *the church is encircled by singing and dancing parishioners and flower-bearing children*

24th **Cirencester** Cotswold Country Fair – *till Sun 25*

OCTOBER

1st **Stroud** District Arts Festival – *till Sun 16*

7th **Cheltenham** Festival of Literature – *till Sun 16*

10th **Tewkesbury** and **Cirencester** Mop Fairs; *traditionally the time of year when domestic and agricultural labour was hired*

17th **Cirencester** Mop Fair

DECEMBER

26th **Gloucester** St Stephen's Day Morris Dance – *12 noon at Gloucester Cathedral and 1 pm at New Inn*

HAMPSHIRE

Quietly charming, gentle countryside in this county mixes rolling chalk downland, a patchwork of hedged fields and clumps of beechwood, the rich valleys of the clear chalk streams, the emptier heathland of the New Forest, and attractive small villages often of brick and flint. Down along the coast much – though not all – is built up, and up in the north-east the chalk downs give way to poorer heathy soils and fat fingers of urbanisation poking down the M3 and the trunk roads. So for visitors the prime areas tend to be from Andover, Stockbridge and Romsey along the Test Valley in the west, through Winchester and Alresford to Alton and Petersfield in the east; and the New Forest. There are a good many places of particular interest in the county, which can be enjoyable at any time of year – not too crowded in summer, not too bleak in winter.

CENTRAL HAMPSHIRE

A great many places for sightseeing, though the countryside does have its quiet charm too.

An excellent choice of things to do and see here is topped by the exemplary Marwell Zoo at Colden Common, the Watercress Railway Line from Alresford, Mottisfont Abbey and its lovely rose garden. Of the area's many great houses, Broadlands near Romsey, The Vyne near Sherborne St John, Hinton Ampner, Breamore and Stratfield Saye are all rewarding. The Hillier Gardens at Ampfield, the Sandham Memorial Chapel at Burghclere, the Hollycombe Steam Collection at Liphook and the Hawk Conservancy at Weyhill are much enjoyed even by people whose thoughts wouldn't normally turn in those directions. So the area's strongest appeal is perhaps for those who like to spend much of their time out and about visiting things.

Though the country areas don't have the obvious picturesque appeal of say the West Country, they do have their own rather retiring charm, with secluded valleys, quiet riverside villages, steep beechwoods and blowy downs. A good choice of places to stay, from comfortable cottages and simple inns to stylish country-house hotels, is complemented by an excellent choice of country pubs that serve good food, and are well placed for after-lunch strolls.

The two main towns to consider as candidates for a weekend break are Winchester and Portsmouth. Winchester has a charming old quarter around its cathedral and plenty of opportunities for strolls nearby, so is worth thinking about for rather a sedate urban break (a rival to Salisbury perhaps, though not to York). Portsmouth, larger and busier, has the very specific appeal of its well-preserved and displayed naval heritage – with a lot to amuse children.

Where to stay

Rotherwick SU7156 TYLNEY HALL Basingstoke RG27 9AJ (0256) 764881 **£147**; 91 comfortable, well-equipped rms. Grand Victorian mansion in 66 acres of gardens and parkland; with gracious day rooms, ornate plasterwork, oak panelling, log fires, interesting food in candlelit restaurant, and good, attentive service; tennis, golf, indoor and outdoor swimming pools.

Hurstbourne Tarrant SU3853 ESSEBORNE MANOR Andover SP11 0ER (0264) 76444 **£95**; 12 individually decorated rms. Small Victorian manor with calm, relaxed atmosphere, comfortable lounge, snug little bar, and good modern cooking; neat gardens with tennis, croquet and golf; cl 27-29 Dec; children over 12 only; disabled access.

Middle Wallop SU2838 FIFEHEAD MANOR Stockbridge SO20 8EG (0264) 781565 **£85**; 16 spacious rms. Friendly and comfortable old brick manor house in several acres of lovely gardens; with restful atmosphere, pleasant small lounge and bar, and good food in candlelit restaurant; croquet; cl 10 days over Christmas and New Year; disabled access.

Winchester SU4829 ROYAL SO22 8BS (0962) 840840 **£85**; 75 comfortable rms in original building or annexe. Well-kept, surprisingly peaceful hotel with pretty flowers, neat garden and terrace, comfortable lounge, and conservatory restaurant.

Winchester SU4829 WYKEHAM ARMS SO23 9PE (0962) 853834 **£72.50**; 7 rms. Very popular, smart, old town pub, close to cathedral, with excellent daily changing menu, fine wines (lots by the glass), and several no-smoking areas.

Hayling Island SU7201 COCKLE WARREN COTTAGE 36 Seafront PO11 9HL (0705) 464961 **£60**; 5 pretty, well-equipped rms. Carefully run and attractive traditional-style house on the seafront with friendly, courteous owners; log fire in the cosy lounge, very good food in the conservatory dining room, and heated swimming pool; children over 12 only (though they will accept those under 12 months).

Colden Common SU5021 MARWELL RESORT Winchester SO21 1JY (0962) 777681 **£60** inc dinner and entrance to zoo; 16 clean, modern rms. Colonial-style, modern hotel with lots of pine and bamboo cane, set in the grounds of Marwell Zoo; decent food in restaurant; health club with swimming pool; children free in parents' room; disabled access.

Crawley SU4234 FOX & HOUNDS SO21 2PR (0962) 776285 **£55**; 3 well-equipped rms. Striking almost Tyrolean pub with elegant timbering and oak parquet, lounge with log fire, good, interesting bar and restaurant food, and prompt, unobtrusive service.

Lee-on-the-Solent SU5600 BELLE VUE PO13 9BW (0705) 550258 **£51.50w**; 27 rms, some with sea view. Pleasant, quiet hotel on seafront with fine views across to the Isle of Wight; decent bar and restaurant food, helpful and friendly staff; nightly entertainment; cl 25-26 Dec; disabled access.

Droxford SU6018 WHITE HORSE Southampton SO3 1PB (0489) 877490 **£50**; 3 rms. Rambling 16th-c coaching inn with friendly atmosphere and particularly good food.

Portsmouth SU6501 SALLY PORT High St Old Town PO1 2LU (0705) 821293 £49; 10 rms. Beautifully kept 16th-c inn in a quiet position; good food, and very friendly, efficient service; said to have been a favourite of Nelson.
Cheriton SU5828 FLOWER POTS Alresford SO24 0QQ (0962) 771318 £40; 5 rms. Unspoilt and quietly comfortable village local run by very friendly family; extremely obliging service and decent bar food.
Eastleigh SU4518 PARK FARM SO5 3HS (0703) 612960 £35; 3 rms, 2 with shared bthrm. Lots of country walks around these converted coaching stables, coarse fishing in own lake; breakfast and evening meals by arrangement.

To see and do

Portsmouth SZ6399 and its residential/resort part Southsea is an island town, with just two roads and the motorway bridging it to the mainland – traffic can be very slow indeed on the main approaches. Its great claim on the imagination is its place at the heart of English naval history, and the two parts that are interesting to visitors are the Old Town and the Dockyard, on either side of the ferry berths and well away from the traffic. Overlooking the narrow harbour neck, Georgian buildings on an old-fashioned cobbled hard give a good feel of the old days, and the little inner Camber Harbour still has fishing boats. The town could keep a museum-lover happy for a week or more, but its naval displays in particular have very wide appeal. By the harbour neck, the Spice Island and Still & West are beautifully placed and useful for lunch, as is the Dolphin in the Old Town High St. The CATHEDRAL, dating from the 13th c to the present, is a delightful departure from the traditional layout.

❄ ⛽ HMS VICTORY, Lord Nelson's flagship, is in dry dock but still in commission, and manned by regular serving officers. Guided tours of the ship bring those days of two centuries ago very close – the smell of the sea, the creaking timbers, the towering rigging and ratlines, the sailors' quarters crowded among the heavy cannon, the red paint to mask the blood in the surgeon's quarters, and, of course, the spot where Nelson died. All the boats open to the public and the museum are on the same site, with snacks, shop and generally good disabled access to all of them. Each ship costs £4 to visit (the HMS *Victory* ticket also inc entry to the Royal Naval Museum), a ticket for two ships is £7.50, and there's a ticket for £10.50 that covers the cost of everything. HMS WARRIOR was in her day (launched 140 years ago) the most fearsome battleship in the world, and the first iron-clad dreadnought, with inches of armour-plating over her extraordinarily thick teak hull. She's been immaculately restored, with

We welcome reports from readers . . .

This GUIDE depends on readers' reports. Please tell us what you think about places in it. And do recommend additions. Use the card in the middle, the report forms at the end, or just write – no stamp needed: THE GOOD WEEKEND GUIDE, FREEPOST TN1569, Wadhurst, E Sussex TN5 7BR. Readers who help us with reports for the GUIDE are offered a discount on the next edition.

equipment just as it would have been, and is manned by a crew in period uniform – again, all very vivid. MARY ROSE The raising of the Mary Rose, preserved in the Solent silt for 437 years, provided a wealth of material and information about the Tudor period, and the discoveries are well shown in an airy hall, with a 12-minute audio-visual display on the raising and conservation of the ship. Many of the objects found inside the ship are shown in their contexts. The great oak hull itself is in a separate shed, sprayed almost constantly to prevent the timbers from drying out. ROYAL NAVY MUSEUM brings the naval past up to date, with large displays in handsome 18th-c dockside buildings showing the development and history of the navy up to and beyond the Falklands War (or as it's called here the South Atlantic Campaign), and this year a special D-Day display. Ships cl 25 Dec, museum 24 Dec-1 Jan.

Several other places here also concentrate attention on the town's fighting history. Through audio-visual shows, displays and military vehicles, the D-DAY MUSEUM (Clarence Esplanade, Southsea) vividly recalls and explains the Normandy landings from the point of view of both sides, and also has the remarkable 272 ft Overlord embroidery; there's a wider-ranging exhibition devoted to the war as a whole, particularly from Portsmouth's (devastated) point of view. Shop, disabled access; cl 24-26 Dec; £3. The ROYAL MARINES MUSEUM is as vigorous a museum as you'd hope from its subject – much more than the dreaded regimental displays of medals and maps. All sorts of things from vivid recreations of major amphibious actions to a junior commando assault course and a chilling display of conditions in the far North, with special D-Day displays this year. Meals, snacks, shop; cl few days over Christmas; £2.50. SOUTHSEA CASTLE AND MUSEUM Built in 1545 as part of Henry VIII's coastal defences, with displays showing the development of Portsmouth as a military fortress, aspects of naval history (inc some splendid fish-bone model ships made by Napoleonic prisoners-of-war here) and local archaeology. There's also a lively new exhibition featuring episodes from the history of the castle itself; snacks, shop; cl 24-26 Dec; £1. A good way to wind up an exploration of Portsmouth's naval past is the boat trip out to SPITBANK FORT, a mile out to sea. This granite, iron and brick fortress was built on the sea bed as part of the coastal defences against Napoleon III. It contains two floors linked by a maze of passages, a working Victorian cooking range and a 420 ft-deep well which still draws fresh water. The inner courtyard is now a sheltered terrace for summer refreshments from the café; cl Mon (exc bank hols), Oct-Easter; £4 inc boat trip.

The fortifications in defence of Portsmouth Harbour, here, around Gosport and up on Portsdown, give a remarkably complete picture of the development of defensive strategy from Tudor times to the fears of French invasion in the 1860s, though they have more appeal to people interested in warfare than to those who like the romantic idea of a regular 'castle'. Among the most formidable are the 19th-c FORT WIDLEY up on Portsdown Hill, and FORT BROCKHURST, Gosport (with a good overview exhibition of how the various series of forts were supposed to work). On the seaward side of Southsea there are sturdy Tudor and later towers, bastions and batteries, alongside the resort's gardens and entertainments; there are interesting sea views from here. Good guided walks around the Tudor fortifications and the best parts of the Old Town leave the Square Fort at 2.30 on Sun (not late Sept-mid Apr).

SEA LIFE CENTRE (Clarence Esplanade) Hi-tech displays and

observation bubbles letting you get close to all kinds of underwater creatures and feel as though you're walking on the sea bed; also a shark exhibition. Meals, snacks, shop, disabled access; cl 25 Dec; *£4.25, you can keep going in and out all day. CUMBERLAND HOUSE NATURAL SCIENCE MUSEUM AND BUTTERFLY HOUSE (Eastern Parade, Southsea) Interesting exploration of the natural history and geology of the area, with displays such as free-flying butterflies, a full-size reconstruction of a dinosaur and seasonal displays of woodland, downland and marshland ecology. Shop; cl 24-26 Dec; *£1. CITY MUSEUM (Museum Rd) A non-naval local museum, with reconstructed rooms from various points in the city's history and displays of decorative art and crafts. The old barracks the museum is housed in look amazing. Snacks, disabled access; cl 24-26 Dec; *£1. DICKENS' BIRTHPLACE (Old Commercial Rd, in the main town) Restored in early 19th c, modest middle-class style; exhibits inc various Dickens-related objects such as the couch on which he died. Occasional special events; shop; cl Nov-Feb; £1.

★ † ▣ ⌂ **Winchester** SU4829 The most attractive part of the city is the glorious and peaceful CATHEDRAL CLOSE, surrounded by a very harmonious and distinguished collection of buildings. The handsome old Eclipse Inn nr the north-eastern edge is a useful refreshment break. The CATHEDRAL itself is an awesome building, full of interest – one of Europe's finest, with the longest of all Gothic naves. The cathedral library has many rare books and manuscripts inc the famous 12th-c illuminated Bible, and the sculpture gallery has some of the best late-Gothic sculpture in Europe. There are good guided tours of various parts. Meals, snacks, shop, disabled access; cl during services. The best way out of the cloisters is through the medieval Kings Gate, which has

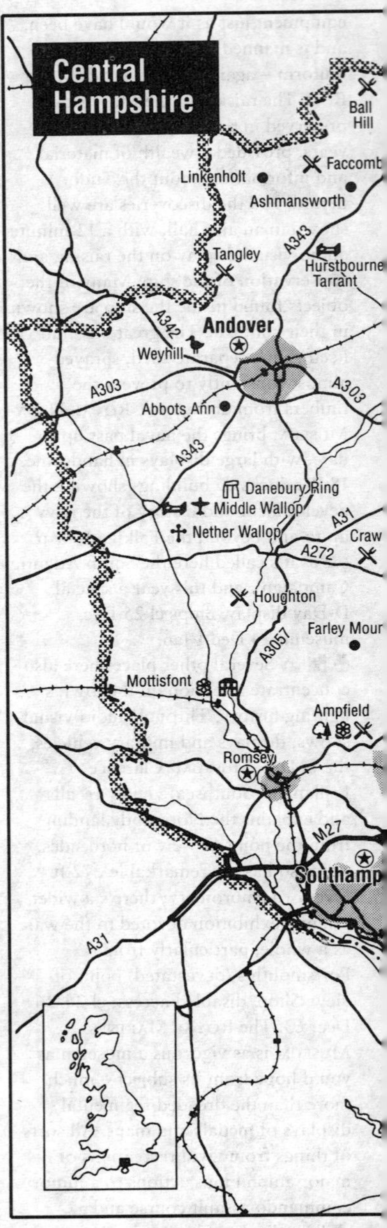

above it the church of St Swithin. This takes you into Kingsgate St, calm and old-fashioned (with an excellent pub, the Wykeham Arms). All along here

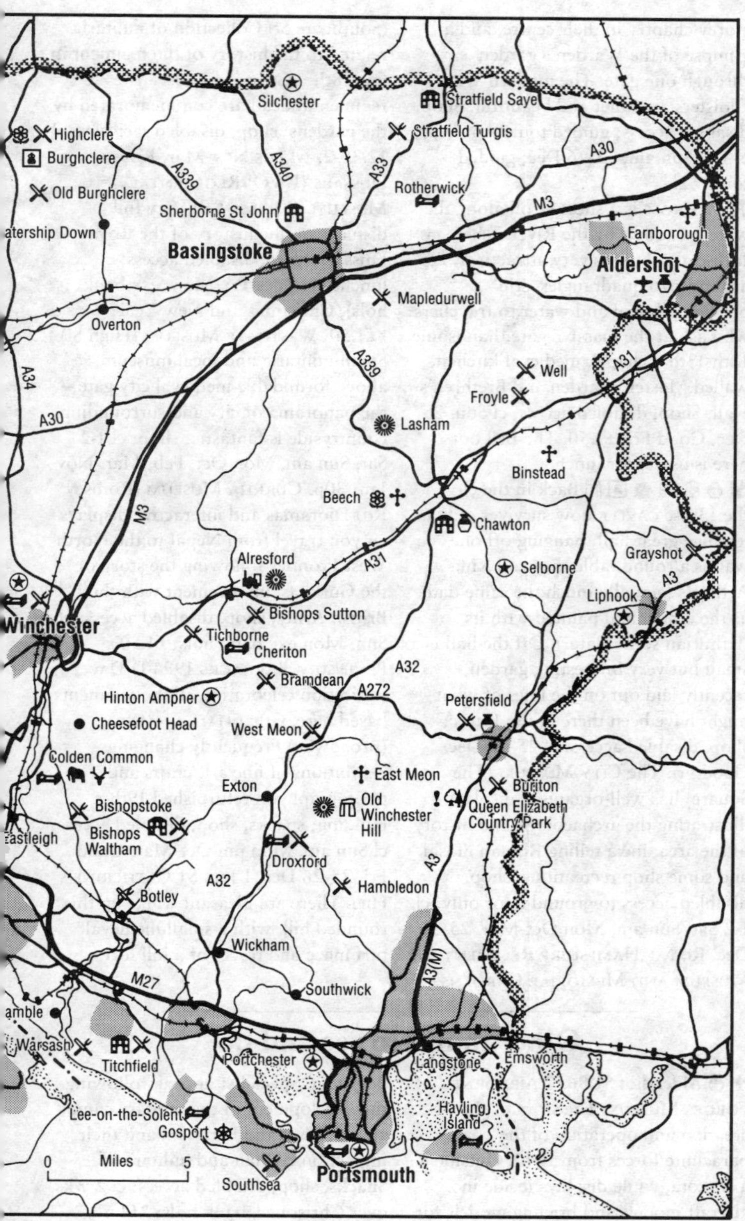

are buildings connected with WINCHESTER COLLEGE, the oldest school in the country. Although there has been great expansion on this site most of the original buildings of the college remain intact, especially around the grand 14th-c chapel and its calm, tilting cloisters with a delightful two-storey chantry in their centre, and a glimpse of the Warden's garden through one gate. The modern War Cloisters are quiet and beautiful. Shop, disabled access; guided tours Apr-Sept; cl 1-2, Sun am, 25-26 Dec; guided tours £2.

ST CROSS is a short stroll along the watermeadows by the River Itchen; 15th-c almshouses very attractively set around two quadrangles, still providing bread and water to travellers who ask at the massive gate; handsome 12th-13th-c chapel, medieval kitchen, walled Master's garden and Brethren's Hall. Shop, disabled access; cl Sun, 25 Dec, Good Fri; £1.50. The Bell out here is useful for lunch.

Back in the city, the 13th-c CASTLE now survives only in its huge great hall; hanging off one wall is a round table they call King Arthur's (actually much the same date as the castle, and painted with its Arthurian scenes later). Off the hall is a small but very interesting garden, recently laid out on the lines of what might have been there in the 13th c; shop, disabled access; cl 25-26 Dec, Good Fri. The CITY MUSEUM (The Square) has well-organised displays illustrating the archaeology and history of the area, inc a telling Roman mosaic and some shop recreations; shop, disabled access to ground floor only; cl 1-2 Sat, Sun am, Mon Oct-Mar, 25-26 Dec. ROYAL HAMPSHIRE REGIMENT MUSEUM AND MEMORIAL GARDENS (Southgate St) Collection of militaria related to the history of the regiment in fine 18th-c Georgian house. The regimental dead are commemorated by the gardens; shop, disabled facilities; cl 12.30-2, wknds Nov-Mar. ROYAL HUSSARS (PWO) REGIMENTAL MUSEUM (Romsey Rd) Very full displays on the history of the Royal Hussars; shop, disabled access; cl lunchtime Tues-Fri, Mon (exc bank hols), Christmas and New Year; *£1.50. WESTGATE MUSEUM (High St) Small militaria and local museum above formidable medieval city gate – the panorama of city and surrounding countryside is fantastic; shop; cl 1-2 Sat, Sun am, Mon Oct, Feb, Mar, Nov-Jan; 30p. GURKHA MUSEUM (Romsey Rd) Dioramas and interactive displays let you travel from Nepal to the North-West Frontier following the story of the Gurkhas' involvement with the British Army; shop, disabled access; cl Sun, Mon exc bank hols; £1.50. PENINSULA BARRACKS 1994 D-Day exhibition celebrating all the regiments based here. GUILDHALL GALLERY (Broadway) Frequently changing exhibitions of fine art, crafts and photography in refurbished 19th-c building; snacks, shop, disabled access; cl Sun am, Mon pm Oct-Mar, Good Fri, 25-26 Dec, 1 Jan. ST CATHERINE'S HILL There are pleasant walks up this rounded hill, with a small medieval turf maze and traces of a hill fort.

Other things to see and do

Aldershot SU8650 AIRBORNE FORCES MUSEUM The story of the creation and operation of the parachute forces from 1940. Outside is a Dakota, while displays inside inc aircraft models and briefing models for World War II operations, captured enemy arms, vehicles and other pieces of equipment. Shop, disabled access; cl Mon, 25 Dec and Easter; £1.25. MILITARY MUSEUM Very well done despite its specialist appeal, following the development of the military camps at Aldershot and Farnham and their impact on civilian and military life. Snacks, shop, disabled access; cl 2 wks over Christmas, bank hols; *£1.50. The Aldershot/Farnborough area has quite a lot of parks, and open spaces out in the surrounding pinewoods for children to let off steam, with boating lakes and so forth.

Alresford (Old and New) SU5931 WATERCRESS LINE The Mid-Hants railway along 10 or so miles of the old Winchester-Alton line between Alresford and Alton gives wonderful views of the countryside and its watercress beds – hence the unusual name. It aims to create the feel of pre-war BR, with stations en route decked out accordingly; there are connections to Waterloo. The steepness of some of the gradients led generations of railwaymen to describe it as 'going over the Alps'. Meals, snacks, shop, disabled access; phone for timetable (0962) 734866; £6.50. Alresford is a charming little town, from the Roman ponds in Old Alresford to the so-called New Alresford which was founded around 1200; good antiquarian bookshop here. The Horse & Groom is the best simple place for lunch here; the Old School House is a smart restaurant.

Ampfield SU4023 SIR HAROLD HILLIER GARDENS AND ARBORETUM 160 acres of beautiful landscape provide the setting for this impressive collection of trees and shrubs – the largest of its kind in the British Isles – which inc many rarities. Summer meals, snacks, shop, disabled access; cl Sat Dec-Feb, 25-28 Dec, 1 Jan; £2.50. The White Horse nearby is a comfortable lunch break.

! **Andover** SU3645 Nr the church at the top of the impressive High St of this very extended country town is the MUSEUM, in a fine Georgian building with displays of local history and natural history; cl Sun and Mon. The adjacent MUSEUM OF THE IRON AGE interprets the site of Danebury Hill Fort (see below) and the finds from that area, which after decades of painstaking archaeology have given a vivid impression of life for the pre-Roman Celts. Shop, limited facilities for disabled; cl Sun (exc summer pm), Mon; £1.20. The conference room of the borough council office houses the remarkable TEST VALLEY TAPESTRY, each of its many panels embroidered by a different village to show a scene of that village; disabled access; generally open for viewing Mon lunchtimes and one Thurs pm each month – best to phone (0264) 364144 first. FINKLEY DOWN FARM PARK (just NE of the town) There are some rare breeds among the wide range of farm animals and poultry here – and some tame animals that can be handled. Housed in a barn here is a countryside museum with Romany caravans and other rural artefacts and bygones; also an adventure playground and picnic site. Snacks, shop, disabled access; cl Oct-Apr; £3. Three or four miles down the Roman road, the Coronation Arms at St Mary Bourne is useful for lunch. There are well-stocked trout fishing lakes around Andover, for example at Rooksbury Mill.

✝ **Beech** SU6938 ALTON ABBEY The home of a community of Benedictine monks and set amid peaceful woodland, this is a relaxing place for a stroll; the grounds have a number of mature specimen trees and shrubs, esp rhododendrons and azaleas.

✝ **Binsted** SU7740 CHURCH where Field Marshal Montgomery is buried; after the war he lived a mile away at Islington Mill SU7742 – a pretty spot.

Bishops Waltham SU5517 PALACE The remains of the palace date from the 12th c and consist of state apartments round a cloister court, with great hall and tower – still impressive; shop, disabled access to the ground floor; cl 1-2, Mon in winter, 24-26 Dec, 1 Jan; £1.50.

Burghclere SU4761 SANDHAM MEMORIAL CHAPEL (NT)Built in memory of H W Sandham who was killed in the First World War, this is Stanley Spencer's moving masterpiece, with 19 frescoes showing the ordinary soldier's wartime life. Disabled access; cl Mon, Tues, wkdys Nov-Mar; £1.20. The Carpenters Arms opposite is useful for lunch.

Chawton SU7037 JANE AUSTEN'S HOUSE Restored to look as it did in the early 1800s when Jane Austen lived and wrote here. Shop, limited disabled facilities; cl Mon, Tues, Nov, Dec, Mar and other wkdys Jan, Feb, 25-26 Dec; £1.50.

Colden Common SU5021 (off A333 towards Bishops Waltham) MARWELL ZOO is a good one, in a spacious park giving plenty of room for the well-designed breeding enclosures for its 1,000 animals; from the first it's been devoted to the conservation and breeding of rare creatures, and some of the species which live here no longer exist in the wild. Many can be approached and stroked; there's also a children's farmyard and road trains. They've just installed a glass wall at one end of the tiger cage, so you can enjoy the terrifying, though completely safe, experience of one of the beasts jumping up at you. Meals, snacks, shop, disabled access; cl 25 Dec; £5.50. On the downs above, the Ship at Owslebury is useful for lunch.

Danebury Ring SU3237 is an Iron-Age hill fort rich in (excavated) remains, interestingly waymarked.

Farnborough SU8753 Though the town itself is scarcely a place for visitors, ST MICHAEL'S ABBEY is an interesting old church with the tombs of Emperor Napoleon III of France, his wife and son in the Imperial Crypt; it's still maintained by resident Benedictine monks. Guided tours 3.30 Sat, also July-Sept same time Weds and Sun; crypt £2.

Gosport SZ6199 ROYAL NAVY SUBMARINE MUSEUM The highlight here is the beached WWII submarine HMS *Alliance*, still in full working order, fascinating inside to small boys of any age; the more conventional part of the museum illustrates the development of submarines, with some attempt to give an international angle to the information, and this year a special D-Day display. Snacks, shop; cl 24 Dec-1 Jan; £3.

Hamble SU4806 in HOWARDS WAY country has interesting views of the yachts, and you can walk a long way up river or towards the Solent; there's a friendly little ferry from Warsash – about 10 people at a time (30p).

Highclere SU4360 HIGHCLERE CASTLE (best approached from A34 rather than Highclere itself) This magnificent pastiche of a medieval castle may look familiar because of its frequent appearance in films and television programmes – or because its architect used a similar style in his design for the Houses of Parliament. The interior is just as impressive, with sumptuous rooms filled with Old Masters, and a collection of Egyptian treasures. The grounds are lovely. Snacks, shop; open pm Weds-Sun July, Aug and Sept; £4. The closest pub for lunch is the Caernarvon Arms, but if you go a bit further the Yew Tree does excellent meals.

Hinton Ampner SU5927 HINTON AMPNER (NT)Good views from this Georgian house, sensitively restored after a terrible fire in 1960. Fine Regency furniture, pictures and porcelain, and outside the grounds are impressive, with tranquil 20th-c shrub gardens. Teas, disabled access; open Apr-Sept, house and garden pm Tues and Weds, garden only pm wknds (exc house open Aug wknds too); £3.50 house and garden, £2.20 garden only. The Fox at Bramdean nearby is good for lunch.

Langstone SU7105 has thatched cottages, an old tidal mill, and a couple of decent pubs looking out over the thousands of acres of silted-up harbour. Swans float up at high tide, with oystercatchers and droves of darting dunlins on the low-tide mud flats. Interesting walks along the old sea wall.

Lasham SU6742 is a pleasant place to watch gliders over the Downs.

Liphook SU8431 BOHUNT MANOR Owned by the Worldwide

Fund for Nature, lovely woodland gardens with water garden, roses and herbaceous borders, a lakeside walk, and filled with ornamental birds and unusual trees and shrubs; disabled access; *£1.50. HOLLYCOMBE STEAM COLLECTION Huge collection of steam-driven equipment, from paddle-steamers to fairground equipment, with demonstrations of threshing and steam rolling, traction engine rides and a steam locomotive running through a woodland setting; also gardens and miniature railway. Snacks, shop; open pm Sun, bank hols and some other days in July and Aug; phone (0428) 724900 to check; £4.

Middle Wallop SU2938 MUSEUM OF ARMY FLYING The story of flying from the 19th c is told using kites, balloons, vintage aircraft and WWII gliders, photographs and interactive displays; May-Sept this year sees re-creation of D-Day landings, with viewing from inside a German bunker. Some of the exhibits can even be seen flying at wknds. Meals, snacks, shop, facilities for disabled; cl week before Christmas; £3.75. The Five Bells tucked away in nearby Nether Wallop is a pleasantly modest place for lunch.

Mottisfont SU3226 MOTTISFONT ABBEY 12th-c priory salvaged from the Reformation as a delightful family house, in wonderful, peaceful surroundings. The gardens are an absolute delight, housing the National Collection of old roses (largely scented), and a couple of rooms inc one decorated richly by Rex Whistler can be visited if there aren't too many other people trying to get in (tour 50p extra, open pm Tues, Weds and Sun, Apr-Oct). Shop, good disabled access; cl am, all day Thurs and Fri, Oct-Mar (open till 8.30 in Jun); £2.50.

Old Winchester Hill SU6420 The HILL FORT here gives wide views of Hampshire, the Solent and Isle of Wight, with nature trails through natural downland that's never been ploughed and resown; fairly busy on fine wknds, wonderfully remote on a blustery spring or autumn weekday.

Petersfield SU7423 BEAR MUSEUM Teddies, dolls and toys displayed in a nursery, and a hospital for any sick furry friends you may have lying sadly at home. Children (or anyone else for that matter) can cuddle the exhibits. Shop, limited disabled access; cl most Suns exc Christmas. The Good Intent is good for lunch.

Portchester SU6105 PORTCHESTER CASTLE Visible remains on this site include the imposing high walls and towers of a 3rd-c Roman fort, a church built in 1133, and the great tower dating from 1367. Richard II converted the buildings in the inner courtyard and the remains of the kitchen, hall and great chamber can still be seen. Snacks, shop, disabled facilities; cl Mon, Oct-Mar, Mon, 25 Dec; £1.70.

! Queen Elizabeth Country Park SU7219 has woodland walks and rides (stables at the park), open downland, quite a lot going on almost all year from hang-gliding through to sheep-shearing demonstrations and conker championships; phone (0705) 595040 for current events information. Shop and café (which are cl wkdys Nov-Feb and Sat Jan-Feb); parking £1.50, 80p winter.

Romsey SU3521 BROADLANDS (just S) Elegant Palladian mansion on the banks of the River Test, surrounded by beautiful, landscaped grounds; fine furnishings and paintings, and the Mountbatten Exhibition, well illustrating the life and times of just one of the notable figures who've lived here over the years. Snacks, shop, disabled access; cl am, Fri exc Good Fri and during Aug, all Oct-Easter; £5. ROMSEY ABBEY Completed by the 13th c and bought by the townspeople for their parish church at the Dissolution, an interesting old abbey with some notable Saxon crosses and a 16th-c panel painting; Earl Mountbatten is buried here. The Dolphin (Cornmarket) is good for lunch.

Selborne SU7433 GILBERT WHITE'S HOUSE Naturalist Gilbert White lived in this impressive 18th-c house with extensive gardens. In separate galleries Captain Oates and Frank Oates are commemorated. Shop, disabled access to ground floor only; cl Mon (exc bank hols) in Apr and Oct, wkdys Nov and Dec, all Jan, Feb; *£2.50. There are good interesting walks tracing White's steps, and the Selborne Arms is useful for lunch.

Sherborne St John SU6255 THE VYNE (NT) Quite a lot here is unchanged since the house was built at the beginning of the 16th c, inc most of the exterior, plenty of panelling, and the stained glass in the chapel. Other interesting features from later periods inc the staircase, and the earliest classical portico on an English country house. Meals, snacks, shop, disabled access; cl am, Mon, Fri, Nov-Apr; £4, £2 grounds only.

Silchester SU6262 CALLEVA MUSEUM Small museum with maps, models and displays on the finds from the site of Calleva Atrebatum, a Roman town excavated nearby. The site itself has recently been restored, and has 1½ miles of city wall to walk along, and a 9,000-seat amphitheatre. There's a 12th-c church on the site of the Roman temples. The nearby Calleva Arms does cheap lunches, and also sells guides to the site.

Southampton SU4211 It's not generally realised that this huge bustling town has one of the three best-preserved medieval town walls in the country. The best stretch is along the western side of the old core, around from the magnificent partly Norman BARGATE (which inc a small local museum). There are also a lot of distinguished ancient buildings dotted around among the modern ones, though the effort of tracking them down among stretches of decidedly less appetising modern townscape means that someone with only a passing interest in fine old buildings would probably be best confining a brief visit to the area around St Michael's Sq, Bugle St and perhaps the old High St. The quayside nearest here has been cleaned up, with modern café-bars overlooking yachting berths. This general area has the pretty 15th-c timber-framed TUDOR HOUSE, with a re-created Tudor garden behind, and a collection of mainly Victorian artefacts exhibited within – inc some room setting, domestic items, dolls and mourning jewellery. Shop, some disabled access; cl 12-1, Sun am, Mon. There's also the MARITIME MUSEUM, a fine 14th-c warehouse with impressive timber ceiling, displaying models and other exhibits centring on the Victorian and modern days of the port; deals especially with the great liners. Shop; cl 1-2, Sun am, Mon; admission charge. GOD'S HOUSE TOWER (Town Quay) is an early 15th-c prototype gun battery, which now houses the city's Museum of Archaeology; shop; cl 1-2, Sun am, Mon. The nearby bowling green is said to be the oldest in the world. HALL OF AVIATION (Albert Rd S) Built around a huge Sandringham flying-boat which visitors can board, this museum examines the development of various aircraft of local interest – inc prototype helicopters and the Spitfire; also exhibits on aviation production and engineering in the south of England. Shop, disabled access; cl Mon exc bank hols, 25-26 Dec; £2.50. CITY ART GALLERY The biggest gallery in the South, with British and European paintings and sculptures from over six centuries, and a particular emphasis on 20th-century art. Meals, snacks, shop, disabled access; cl Sun am, Mon, 25-27 and 31 Dec. To celebrate D-Day a wartime double-decker will be running most spring and summer evenings and weekends, with people in 1940s dress on board; route/timetable from (0703) 553011. The Red Lion in the High St does food all day, and is chiefly notable for its genuine great medieval hall.

Stratfield Saye SU6861 STRATFIELD SAYE HOUSE 17th-c house given by the nation to the first Duke of Wellington in 1817 after Waterloo, full of fascinating objects relating to him inc his splendid funeral carriage. Meals, snacks, shop, disabled access; cl am, all day Fri, Oct-Apr; £4. The New Inn is useful enough for lunch, the Wellington Arms at nearby Stratfield Turgis rather more stylish. There are pleasant walks east of the park, on Heckfield Heath.

Titchfield SU5305 TITCHFIELD ABBEY Founded in 1232, the abbey was closed during the Dissolution, then its nave and gatehouse were incorporated into the fine Tudor mansion which the Earl of Southampton built on this site; disabled access.

Weyhill SU3146 HAWK CONSERVANCY You can watch birds of prey from all over the world in action here, and even handle some of them; very well thought out. You can also book a day's hawking under instruction. Meals, snacks, shop, disabled access; cl Nov-Feb; £3.50. The Star and Weyhill Fair are handy for lunch.

★ Among the county's many **attractive villages**, ones with decent pubs inc Abbots Ann SU3243, Cheriton SU5828, Crawley SU4234, East Meon SU6822 (splendid Norman church), Faccombe SU3858, Hamble SU4806 (the Olde Whyte Harte, near the water), Mapledurwell SU6851, Nether Wallop SU3036 (the Saxon church is well worth seeing), Overton SU5149 and Tichborne SU5630. Other good villages are Exton SU6121 (beautifully set by the river under the chalk hills), and Wickham SU5711, with its huge village square, and in the north, Ashmansworth SU4157 and Linkenholt SU3658 are high enough to give fine views from many of their lanes (best explored by car). This year Southwick SU6208 will no doubt see many visitors recalling its central role in the D-Day preparations: commemorative exhibition at the Brewhouse, and the Golden Lion, used as an unofficial mess by Eisenhower and Montgomery, is recalling those days.

Walks

In the east of the country there are some good scenic pockets around **Selborne** SU7433, the countryside recorded in such detail by naturalist Gilbert White; the zigzag path he created with his brother in 1753 still climbs Selborne Hanger. The hangers hereabouts are beechwoods which cling to the abrupt escarpments; **Noar Hill** close by has been designated a nature reserve for its chalkland flora.

Farley Mount SU4029 is an attractive area for walking, with plenty of space in downland and woodland, and good views.

Watership Down SU4957 just south of Kingsclere was the home of therabbits in the novel by Richard Adams – their final adventure was down at Freefolk SU4848, where the local pub fittingly has a batch of bunnies. Pleasant wooded walks through this area.

Cheesefoot Head SU5327 (locally pronounced Chesford) is good for walks; a natural amphitheatre where Eisenhower and Montgomery addressed the troops before the Normandy invasion.

Old Winchester Hill SU6420 (see To see and do, above) is a good place for breezy strolls.

Many of the woodlands in this part of Hampshire fill with snowdrops in

February (Warnford SU6223 is a good example); in May there are bluebells, for example at Froxfield SU7025, East Tisted SU7032 and Ropley SU6431.

Good pubs on which to base walks inc the Milburys at Beauworth SU5726, Bat & Ball on Broadhalfpenny Down SU6716, Five Bells at Buriton SU7420, Red Lion at Chalton SU7315, Mill Arms at Barley Hill, Dundridge SU3126, George at East Meon SU6822, Vine at Hannington SU5355, Hawkley Inn on Pococks Lane, Hawkley SU7429, Bush at Ovington SU5531, White Horse near Priors Dean above Petersfield SU7129 (our favourite country pub), Selborne Arms in Selborne SU7433, Coronation Arms at St May Bourne SU4250 (Test Way), Harrow at Steep SU7425 (the beechwood hangers) and George at Vernham Dean SU3456 (Fosbury hill fort).

Driving

Some of the nicest drives are through the valleys of the rivers and tributaries of the Test (B3048, B3400, back road through Longstock and Houghton to Mottisfont), Itchen (back road from Ovington to Easton) and Meon (the back road through Soberton is preferable to the A32 N of Wickham). The B3046 N of Alresford gives a good impression of downs farming country, and the A272 Winchester-Petersfield is another long-winded downland road. Even better than the A272 is the old high road it replaced, running from Winchester through Alresford, Ropley, Hedge Corner and Stoner Hill to Steep.

There's an attractive circular drive from Bishops Waltham N over Stephens Castle Down, past the Owslebury crossroads and over Lane End Down to the Milburys pub S of Beauworth, and on to Warnford, getting back to Bishops Waltham along the A32 to Corhampton and then the B3035. On this drive, the diversion to the viewpoint of Beacon Hill is well worth while – either from the Kilmeston crossroads between the Milburys and Warnford, or from Exton just off the A32.

In the N of the county relatively empty highlands overlapping with Wilts and Berks offer some fine views, though some of the lanes are narrow with sharp bends and steep hills. Hurstbourne Tarrant is a good centre for this largely unspoilt area, and attractive lanes include Hurstbourne Tarrant to Faccombe and Walbury or to Inkpen via the Netherton Valley, Faccombe to Walbury Hill, Walbury Hill to Inkpen Beacon, Faccombe to Linkenholt, and Vernham Dean to Oxenwood (via the Weyhill road up Conholt Hill, turning right on its summit).

Where to eat

Botley SU5112 Cobbetts 15 The Square (0489) 782068 Nicely presented, mainly French food in 16th-c cottage with relaxed atmosphere and friendly staff; cl Mon and Sat lunchtimes, Sun; disabled access. **£37.20**|£13.10 (2-course lunch).

Emsworth SU7406 36 On The Quay South St (0243) 375592 Very good French cooking in charming quayside restaurant, with helpful service and sound wine list; cl Tues, 2 wks Oct; children over 11. **£35 for 4 courses.**

Old Burghclere SU4758 Dew Pond (063 527) 408. Beautiful 16th-c country house with log fires and friendly atmosphere; good food using fresh local produce on a frequently changing small menu; no smoking; cl Sun, Mon, early Jan, mid-Aug; children over 12. **£27.50**|£16 (2 courses).

Highclere SU4360 YEW TREE (Andover Rd A343 S) (0635) 253360 Cheerfully decorated L-shaped bar with big log fire, enterprising food such as river trout or crispy duck, and good, unobtrusive waitress service; disabled access. **£21**|£2.50/£6.

Bishops Waltham SU5517 TONY'S BRASSERIE (0489) 8963252 The Old Granary, corner of Brook St and Bank St (0489) 896352 Cosy restaurant with friendly service, simple French and other international dishes, and decent wines; cl Sun pm, Mon; **£20**|£7.50 (2 courses).

Southsea SZ6498 A FISTFUL OF TACOS Albert Rd (0705) 293474 Evening restaurant with good Californian/Mexican food; cl Christmas and New Year; disabled access. **£18**.

Grayshot SU8735 WOODS PLACE Headley Rd (0428) 605555 Pretty restaurant in former butcher's shop with panelling and wall tiles; most enjoyable modern cooking, and friendly service; cl Sun, Mon, Christmas, 2 wks Aug; disabled access. **£16.90**|£7.

West Meon SU6424 THOMAS LORD (0730) 829244 Attractive village local with strong cricketing influence, welcoming atmosphere, generous helpings of good-value food, and helpful service; no children; disabled access. **£15.75**|£1.30/£5.25.

Droxford SU6018 HURDLES (0489) 877451 Pretty creeper-covered building, simple home cooking, and friendly staff; cl 25-26 Dec; no children; disabled access. **£12.50**|£2/£3.70.

Tichborne SU5630 TICHBORNE ARMS (0962) 733760 Attractive, thatched country pub in rolling countryside, with very good, imaginative bar food, and delicious puddings; big garden; no children; disabled access. **£12**|£1.20/£4.50.

Buriton SU7420 FIVE BELLS (0730) 263584 Popular, unpretentious country local with very good bar food. £3.10/£6.25.

Bramdean SU6128 FOX (0962) 771363 Welcoming 17th-c dining pub with famous fox masks on the wall, very appetising bar food (lots of fish), and obliging service. £2.60/£6.25.

Faccombe SU3858 JACK RUSSELL (0264) 87315 Pleasant little place with very good food, service and welcome; bedrooms. £2/£4.75.

Winchester SU4829 PAPPAGALLOS City Rd (0962) 841107 Good Italian dishes; cl Sun, bank hols; £4.

Well SU7646 CHEQUERS (0256) 862605 Neatly kept and rather smart country pub with relaxed atmosphere, snug rooms, beams, lots of 18th-c country-life prints, and very good, unusual bar food; disabled access. £2.50/£4.50.

Houghton SU3432 BOOT (0794) 388310 Flourishing dining pub with pleasant service and good restaurant food; disabled access. £2.50/£3.50.

Other decent places to eat inc the White Horse in Ampfield SU4023, the Furze Bush at Ball Hill SU4263, the Ship at Bishops Sutton SU6031, the River at Bishopstoke SU4619, the Fox & Hounds at Crawley SU4234, the Hen & Chicken in Froyle SU7542, the Bat & Ball at Hambledon SU6414, the Gamekeepers at Mapledurwell SU6851, the Good Intent in Petersfield (College St) SU7423, the Wine Vaults in Southsea SZ6498, the Wellington Arms Hotel in Stratfield Turgis SU6960, the Fox at Tangley SU3252, the Wheatsheaf at Titchfield TL5305, and the Jolly Farmer at Warsash (Locks Heath) SU5006.

New Forest

Beaulieu and Exbury Gardens have strong appeal; pleasant walks in the forest.

The forest, largely heathland rather than wood, has the particular appeal for walkers that you can head off in virtually any direction you want without worrying about trespassing. Children like it: apart from the ponies, there's plenty of space to let off steam and generally run riot without coming to grief.

Down on the coast there are sheltered yachting harbours, the pleasant waterside town of Lymington with warm Georgian buildings, and the area's two great visitor attractions, Beaulieu and the much less visited Exbury Gardens. There are not that many other paid-entry attractions in the area; foremost among them are perhaps the maritime museum in the pretty village of Bucklers Hard, the imaginative Spinners garden at Boldre and the butterfly farm at Ashurst; children enjoy Paultons Park at Ower.

Where to stay

New Milton SZ2495 Chewton Glen BH25 6QS (0425) 275341 **£196**; 58 really beautiful rms. Luxurious hotel in lovely grounds, with sumptuous day rooms, antiques, excellent modern French cooking, and very good service; gardens inc nine-hole golf course, swimming pool, tennis (two indoor courts as well) and croquet; also health club with indoor swimming pool, gym, saunas, treatment rooms; children over 7 only; disabled access.

Lymington SZ3295 Passford House Mount Pleasant Lane SO41 8LS (0590) 682398 ***£101**; 56 neatly kept airy rms, inc 8 more special ones. Attractive hotel on the edge of the New Forest, with comfortable day rooms, open fires, excellent service; garden with indoor and outdoor swimming pools, tennis, croquet, putting; disabled access.

Beaulieu SU3802 Montagu Arms Palace Lane SO42 7ZL (0590) 612324 **£95.90**; 24 individually decorated rms. Very pretty, creeper-clad hotel with lovely back garden, conservatory lounge, very good food, and attentive staff; they also run the village shop, post office and bakery.

Lymington SZ3295 Stanwell House High St SO41 9AA (0590) 677123 **£98**; 35 rms. Handsome townhouse with comfortable, attractively furnished rooms, good, imaginative food, and pretty walled back garden.

Lyndhurst SU2908 Parkhill Beaulieu Rd SO43 7FZ (0703) 282944 **£94**; 20 carefully furnished rms, some overlooking the lawns. 13th-c hunting lodge rebuilt by Duke of Clarence in mid-18th c and set in parkland with fine views; comfortable lounges, antiques, flowers, and a civilised atmosphere; good food in attractive dining room, and friendly, professional staff; disabled access.

Emery Down SU2808 New Forest Lyndhurst SO4 7DY (0703) 282329 ***£55**; 4 rms. Extremely popular old inn in one of the prettiest areas of New Forest; well-kept garden with a variety of animals, excellent food, very good service, and nice nearby walks; no accom 24-26 Dec; disabled access.

Rockbourne SU1118 SHEARINGS Fordingbridge SP6 3NA (072 53) 256 ***£44**; 3 rms. Warmly welcoming and pretty 16th-c thatched cottage beside a winter stream in charming village; with inglenook fireplaces, ancient beams (some nearly 1,000 years old), comfortable sitting room, and home-cooked food; candlelit dinner if requested; children over 12only; no dogs.
Copythorne SU3114 OLD WELL Southampton SO4 2PE (0703) 812321 **£40**; 6 rms. Well-kept, family-run restaurant with bedrooms, decent food, pleasant bar, and friendly service; evening meals Fri and Sat.
Lymington SZ3295 KINGS ARMS SO41 9NB (0590) 672594 ***£36**; 2 rms, shared bthrm. Small inn with two bars (one for eating), very friendly licensees, real ales, and decent food; busy Sat lunchtimes when local market is on; no accom 24-26 Dec; children over 5 only.
Also recommended by contributors is the Sandy Balls Holiday Centre at Godshill SU1715 – well organised and with nice nearby walks (0425) 53042.

To see and do

Ashurst SU3310 NEW FOREST BUTTERFLY FARM Indoor tropical jungle with free-flying butterflies and moths from all over the world; also insectarium, woodland walk, dragonfly ponds, adventure playground and wagon rides. Meals, snacks, shop, disabled access; cl Nov-Mar; £3.50.
Beaulieu SU3802 The NATIONAL MOTOR MUSEUM here is one of the largest in the world and features an automated trip through a spectacular display of 100 years of motoring; also a high-level monorail through the grounds, model railway and veteran bus rides. Meals, snacks, shops, disabled access; cl 25 Dec; *£7, which also covers entrance to BEAULIEU ABBEY. The house, properly called the Palace House, dates from the 16th c and is full of fine paintings and furnishings. It's based on the gatehouse of the huge abbey which stood here until the Reformation, and graceful ruins of other monastic buildings, inc a lovely row of arches, can be seen in the beautiful lakeside parkland and gardens. In the village facing the Palace House gates, the Wine Press is good for lunch, and a marked trail leads from it down to Bucklers Hard – see below.
Boldre SZ3198 SPINNERS Wonderful gardens created since the 1960s; the nursery is famed for its rare and less common trees (esp maples and magnolias), shrubs and plants, and attracts visitors from all over the world. Some disabled access; gardens cl Sept-late Apr, Mon and Tues July and Aug; nursery open all year exc Mon and Tues July-Apr, 25 Dec; £1. The Red Lion (no children) is good for lunch.
Breamore SU1517 BREAMORE HOUSE Good example of a late Elizabethan manor house, owned for the last two-and-a-half centuries by the descendants of Queen Anne's doctor. The grand rooms have furnishings, tapestries and paintings (mainly 17th- and 18th-c Dutch school), and there's an interesting countryside museum with reconstructed scenes of village life inc a farm worker's cottage, brewery, school and various shops. The stables have a fine collection of horse-drawn carriages and fire-fighting equipment. Snacks, shop, disabled facilities; open pm Tues, Weds and Sun Apr-Sept, plus Thurs and Sat May-Sept, every day in Aug and all holidays; *£4.
★ **Bucklers Hard** The waterside village is very pretty, with long red-roofed cottage rows flanking a wide, grassed waterside street. Its MARITIME MUSEUM tells the story of the local ship-building industry, right up to the voyages of Sir Francis Chichester. The village itself brings this history to life: ships were built here

from New Forest oak, and it's possible to view the 18th-c homes of a shipwright and labourer, and a typical inn scene has been created complete with costumed figures, smells and conversation. Meals, snacks, shop; cl 25 Dec; £2.50 (you have to pay – just to come to the village). There are summer boat trips. The Master Builders House is useful for lunch.

Calshot Castle SU4802, down past the oil refineries and power stations, is a Tudor fort at the end of the spit of land out over the tidal mudflats at the end of Southampton Water; splendid views of the shipping and the Isle of Wight.

★ **Damersham** ST1015 In spring, it's worth visiting the churchyard here to see the carpet of snowdrops.

Exbury SU4200 EXBURY GARDENS 200-acre landscaped woodland gardens on the east bank of the River Beaulieu, with splendid rock garden, heather garden and river walk, and above all the Rothschild collection of rhododendrons, azaleas, magnolias and camellias – one of the world's finest, and at its best in May and early Jun. In the woods the Japanese maples are a glory in autumn. Meals and snacks, shop, disabled access; cl 25 Oct-26 Feb; £3.50.

Hurst Castle SZ3189 Reached on foot or by boat from Keyhaven (there's a pleasant walk from the Gun pub), this fortress was built by Henry VIII to protect the coast, occupied during the Civil War and fortified again in the 19th c. Snacks, shop; cl wkdys Oct-Mar, 25-26 Dec; £1.50.

★ **Lymington** SZ3295 is a handsome and relaxed waterside town, very popular in summer with yachting people; it has quite a number of attractive Georgian buildings and some good shops. The Chequers down Ridgeway Lane, south of Pennington, is excellent for lunch.

Lyndhurst SU2907 is the tourist centre of the New Forest, as well as the main shopping town for people living

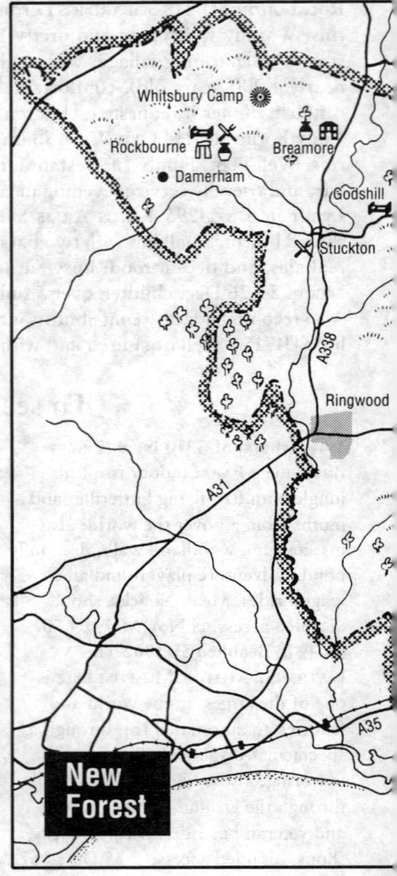

here – so has craft shops, antique shops etc. NEW FOREST MUSEUM All about the forest, with life-size models of forest characters, good audio-visual explanations of its history and wildlife, and the famous New Forest embroidery. Shop, disabled access; cl 25 Dec; £2.50. The Crown Hotel is useful for lunch.

Minstead SU2711 FURZEY GARDENS Eight peaceful acres surrounding a 16th-c cottage with a gallery displaying local arts and crafts; disabled access; cl 25-26 Dec; £2.50 summer, £1.50 winter. The village itself is pretty, with a decent pub.

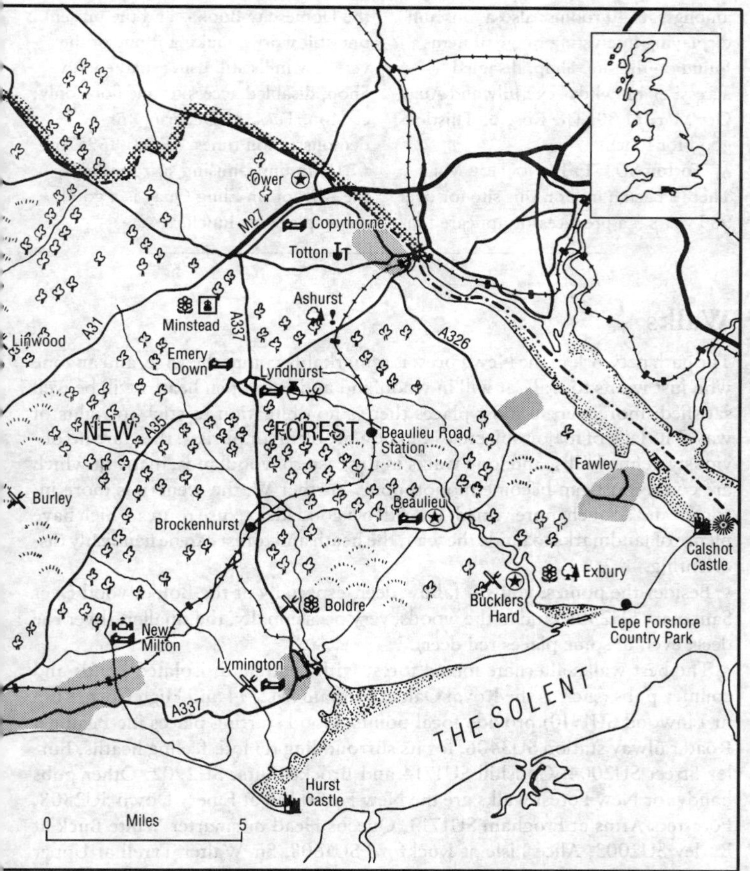

New Milton SZ2495 SAMMY MILLER MUSEUM Some people consider this changing collection of fully restored motorbikes to be the best in Europe; the machines date back to 1900, many are the only surviving examples in the world. Snacks, shop, disabled access; cl 25 Dec; *£3.

! Ower SU3216 PAULTONS PARK 140 acres with over 1,000 species of animals, birds and wildfowl, and hours of fun for children in the various theme areas, with 40 different attractions; there's also a 10-acre lake with working waterwheel and a miniature Rio Grande railway. During the summer hols there is live entertainment. Meals, snacks, shop, disabled access; cl Nov-Feb; £5.99, covers everything.

Ringwood SU1505 MOORS VALLEY COUNTRY PARK Nearly 400 hectares of forest, plenty of animals and nature trails, unusual treetop walkway giving a rather different view of the forest; meals, snacks, shop, disabled access; car parking charge. The riverside Fish is good for lunch.

Rockbourne SU1118 ROMAN VILLA Remains of largest known Roman villa in the area, with fine displays of mosaics and hypocaust amongst its 40 rooms; also a museum displaying interesting range of items found on the site. Shop, disabled access; cl am wkdys exc July and Aug, Oct-Mar; £1.30. The Rose & Thistle is good for lunch.

Totton SU3513 Eling Tide Mill There's been a mill on this site for over 900 years – a predecessor appeared in the Domesday Book – and the present one still works, making it one of the very few mills still using tidal energy. Shop, disabled access to one floor only; cl Mon, Tues, 25 Dec, ring for demonstration times, (0703) 869575; £1.15. In unpromising surroundings, the Anchor on Eling Quay is a good cheap place for lunch.

Walks

The path network in the **New Forest** is remarkably comprehensive, and anyone who just wants to walk at will in woodland and over open heaths will be well satisfied; moreover, in most places there's no obligation to stick to rights of way. The lack of major objectives can be a problem for purists: there are no obviously defined hills, and long walks in the eastern woodlands, many of which are coniferous, can become monotonous. Further W, the scenery is more intricate and a touch more varied. It is often a good idea to use routes which have plenty of landmarks to guide the way; the heath and forest can be fiendishly disorienting.

Besides the ponies, you see fallow deer, especially at the Bolderwood Deer Sanctuary SU2308 (and in the woods, very occasionally, the smaller, shyer roe deer; even in some places red deer).

The best walks alternate mixed forest with heathland; isolated ponds and country pubs (such as the Royal Oak at Fritham SU2314 and High Corner Inn nr Linwood SU1910) provide focal points. Good starting places inc Beaulieu Road railway station SU3406, for its surrounding remote-feeling heaths, Burley Street SU2004, Godshill SU1714 and Brockenhurst SU2902. Other pubs handy for New Forest walks are the New Forest Inn at Emery Down SU2808, Foresters Arms at Frogham SU1713, Queens Head or smarter White Buck at Burley SU2003, Alice Lisle at Rockford SU1608, Sir Walter Tyrell at Upper Canterton SU2613, and perhaps Turf Cutters Arms at East Boldre SU3700 and Filly at Setley SU3000.

Just out of the New Forest proper to the west is Breamore SU1518, a thatched village within walking distance of Breamore House (Elizabethan, open to the public) and the mysterious Mizmaze, cut in the turf. On the east side is **Lepe Forshore Country Park** SZ4598, for mild saunters along the coast. Up in the north of the area, a steep walk behind the Cartwheel at **Whitsbury** SU1219 takes you up to the hill fort of **Whitsbury Camp**, for good views.

Driving

The two best drives through the New Forest are the slow back road from Brockenhurst north through Bolderwood and then round past Linwood to Rockford, and the drive from Brockenhurst to Burley. Both have plenty of stopping places. Though the A31 does have some good views over the heathland, it's too fast and busy for you really to appreciate them – and beware that heading west down it there are no right turns into the forest between Cadnam and Ringwood.

The B3054 from Dibden Purlieu is a quick retreat from industrial expanses into another much quieter world; pretty all the way to Lymington.

Where to eat

Stuckton SU1613 THREE LIONS (0425) 652489 Warmly welcoming restaurant (in pub guise – but the food's of good restaurant quality), with fresh flowers, interesting, wholesome food (decent bar snacks too), reasonable wines, and good service. **£26.25**|£3.15/£8.40.

Rockbourne SU1118 ROSE & THISTLE (07253) 236 Very attractive, thatched 17th-c pub with a smartly civilised feel; wide menu with popular food, and extensive wine list. **£18**|£3.25/£7.50.

Boldre SZ3298 RED LION (0590) 673177 Very busy, friendly pub on edge of New Forest with very good bar food; worth getting there early; no children; disabled access. **£17.20**|£2.80/£5.50.

Other places with decent food inc the Master Builders House at Bucklers Hard SU4000, the Queens Head and the White Buck in Burley SU2003, the High Corner at Linwood SU1910, and the Toll House in Lymington SZ3295.

Help this year from: *HNJ, PEJ, Heather Carpenter, Gill and Brian Pacey, Stephen Brown, Gordon B Mott, Hugh Spottiswoode, Gethin Lewis, John and Joan Calvert, R Kelly, G Shannon, JW and S B McClenahan, Jo Rees, Mr and Mrs I Langrish, Dr and Mrs R E S Tanner, David Storey, R C Morgan, S C Harvey, Mr and Mrs B Salter, Ian Phillips, Brian Kneale, Hope Chenhalls, John and Joan Nash, Patrick Godfrey, P R Cobb, John Woodward, Jerry and Alison Oakes, D H T Dimock, P and R Wayth, R C Davis, M J D Inskip, Keith Stevens, Mr and Mrs Dara de Cogan, Mr and Mrs A R Hawkins.*

Hampshire Calendar

Some of these dates were provisional as we went to press.

January

1st **Winchester** Antiques Fair *at River Park Leisure Centre*

8th **Winchester** Book Collectors Fair *at Guildhall*

29th **Winchester** Jazz and Jive *at the Railway Inn, St Pauls Hill*

30th **Winchester** City Festival Choir *at Winchester College*

March

6th **Portsmouth** Collectors Fair *at Mountbatten Centre*

12th **Winchester** Book Collectors Fair *at Guildhall*

26th **Portsmouth** England v Wales Netball Match *at Mountbatten Centre*

April

1st **Gosport** Easter Festival – *till Mon 4*

3rd **Riseley** Easter Fun and Crafts – *till Mon 4*

23rd **Fordingbridge** Spring Festival *starts with pageant – till 14 May*

28th **Portsmouth** International Hockey Festival *at Mountbatten Centre – till Mon 30*

30th **Itchen Abbas** Craft and Gardens Fayre *at Avington Park – till 2 May*; **Portsmouth** British Baton-Twirling Championships *at Mountbatten Centre – till 2 May*

May

1st **Southsea** Heavy Horse Parade and Obstacle Driving Championships *at Castle Field Arena*

7th **Eastleigh** South Coast Custom Car Show *at Fleming Park leisure centre*; **Fordingbridge** D-Day Vehicle Rally (date not confirmed, may take place on Sat 14); **Newbury** Spring Festival: *music and visual arts – till Sat 21*; **Southwick** Pageant *where D-Day was planned – will take in local history from 12th c to D-Day – till Sun 8*

8th **Calshot Spit** Calshot Small Boat Show

14th **Middle Wallop** International Air Show, Fair and D-Day Air Display – *till Sun 15*; **Winchester** Book Collectors Fair *at Guildhall*

27th **Netley** International Veterans Parade *based on order of battle for Operation Overlord, service and review, at Royal Victoria Country Park – till Sat 28*

28th **Portsmouth** WWII Military Vehicle Rally – *over 1,000 vehicles from all over the world on Southsea Common*

29th **Rockbourne** Roman Weekend *inc legionary drilling, cooking, crafts and costume, at Roman Villa – till Mon 30*; **Romsey** Classic Car Show *at Broadlands Park – till Mon 30*

30th **Alton** Carnival

June

7th **Southampton** Winners of Round-the-World Yacht Race – *expected between now and mid-Jun*

Hampshire Calendar

June cont.

8th **Bishops Waltham** Agricultural Show

25th **Eastleigh** Dance Festival and Workshops – *till Sun 26*; **Portsmouth** D-Day Exhibition *of WWII artefacts at Mountbatten Gallery – till Wed 29*; **Sarisbury** Country Fair

July

2nd **Hedge End** Carnival and Gala Day; **Southampton** Balloon and Flower Festival *on the Common – till Sun 3*

7th **Portsmouth** Tour de France – *second stage begins and ends after tour of county*

9th **Southampton** Carnival; **Winchester** 20th Hat Festival, *a celebration of street theatre – till Sun 10*

16th **Fordingbridge** Show; **Winchester** Book Collectors Fair *at Guildhall*

17th **Alton** Agricultural Show

23rd **Romsey** Carnival – *till Sat 30*

26th **Brockenhurst** New Forest & Hampshire County Show *at New Park – till Thurs 28*

30th **Aldershot** Steam Rally – *till Sun 31*

August

5th **Portsmouth** Southsea Show – *till Sun 7*

13th **Popham** Vintage Fayre and D-Day Salute *on airfield*

16th **Eastleigh** Town and Country Show – *till Sun 17*

27th **Portsmouth** International Kite Festival – *till Sun 28*

29th **Catherington** Show – *till Mon 29*; *also* **Emsworth** Show

September

5th **Farnborough** International Aerospace Exhibition and Flying Display – *till Sun 11*

10th **Alresford** 'War on the line', *Mid-Hants railway – till Sun 11*; **Romsey** Show; **Winchester** Book Collectors Fair *at Guildhall*

October

7th **Itchen Abbas** Home Design and Interiors Exhibition *at Avington Park – till Sun 9*

November

5th **Aldershot** Fireworks; **Alton** Fireworks

12th **Winchester** Book Collectors Fair *at Guildhall*

Hereford and Worcester

For a first-time visit there's a lot to be said for basing yourself somewhere around Ledbury, which puts virtually any part of the three areas that we've divided this county into within reach. The east is more obviously geared to visitors; over in the west, the countryside becomes quieter and progressively more unspoilt (with increasingly good-value prices). For a really peaceful break Herefordshire has a great deal to recommend it, with attractive scenery, surprisingly good food, and plenty of interesting but uncrowded places to visit. The twin counties have a good few lovely gardens, especially in Herefordshire.

The orchards in Herefordshire and the Vale of Evesham make blossom time (usually April through early May) and harvest time (September) attractive. Asparagus fanatics have a bonus in May, when there is an abundance of fresh, local asparagus. In winter big log fires and generous central heating are the rule – people here really seem to appreciate their warmth.

The Vale of Evesham, Malvern Hills and Ledbury

Mainly for quiet, adult holidays – Ledbury is a good base, with stirring scenery in the Malvern Hills.

This area has some lovely villages, often little-changed over the ages, with an interesting variety of building – from warmly handsome stonework around Broadway to the classic black-and-white timbering of places like Bretforton. The Malvern Hills are scenically most alluring; the richer farmland and orchard country around the River Avon in the Vale of Evesham is less striking (except at blossom time), but still pleasant to drive around – and as well as the villages, the many farm shops punctuate it with points of passing interest.

Ledbury, Broadway, Great Malvern and Evesham are all attractive, with several appealing places to visit – generally quiet and adult, though many children enjoy the Domestic Wildfowl Trust at Evesham; there's a teddy bear museum and good country park at Broadway. Eastnor Castle is well worth a visit.

There are fine hotels and inns to choose from. Ledbury has a lot going for it as a base for exploration of this area; a charming town in its own right, and with good roads out. Broadway, of course, puts you on the doorstep of the Cotswolds, too.

Where to stay

Broadway SP0937 LYGON ARMS High St WR12 7DU (0386) 852255 ***£152.75**; 65 lovely rms, some with antiques and beams, some more modern. Strikingly handsome hotel with interesting old rooms, oak panelling, antiques, log fires; fine traditional food in the great hall with minstrels' gallery and heraldic frieze, excellent service, and charming garden; Oliver Cromwell and King Charles I are said to have stayed here; disabled access.

Broadway SP9037 DORMY HOUSE WR12 7LF (0386) 852711 **£110**; 49 rms. Overlooking the Vale of Evesham, this carefully converted 17th-c farmhouse has relaxed lounges with fresh flowers, beams, log fires and exposed stonework; interesting food in the conservatory restaurant; cl 24-28 Dec.

Ledbury SO7138 HOPE END COUNTRY HOUSE HR8 1JQ (0531) 3613 ***£99**; 9 rms. Once the home of Elizabeth Barrett Browning and a wonderfully peaceful place to stay, with huge organic walled garden where most of the veg, fruit and herbs are grown for the very good English cooking (roaming chickens provide the eggs); a fine Georgian landscaped garden, lots of books, woodburning stoves, comfortable seating, lovely breakfasts, and unobtrusive service; cl mid-Dec-early Feb; children over 12 only.

Malvern Wells SO7845 COTTAGE IN THE WOOD WR14 4LG (0684) 573487 ***£95**; 20 compact but pretty rms. Georgian dower house with splendid views across the Severn Valley, antiques, fresh flowers, and good food in attractive restaurant; neat lawns in the seven acres of grounds.

Evesham SP0344 EVESHAM Coopers Lane WR11 6DA (0386) 765566 ***£94**; 40 spacious rms. Comfortably modernised, family-run hotel dating back to 16th c; with friendly, relaxed atmosphere, very good food (esp the lunchtime buffet), indoor swimming pool, and croquet; well-behaved children welcome with games and teddy bears in the rooms; cl 25-26 Dec.

Broadway SP0937 COLLIN HOUSE WR12 7PB (0386) 858354 **£86**; 7 warm, comfortable and quiet rms. Golden-stone Cotswold house in 3 acres of gardens, orchards and meadowland; with restful public rooms, oak beams, log fires, very good English food in candlelit restaurant, and friendly service; cl 24 Dec for 5 days; disabled access.

Ledbury SO7138 FEATHERS HR8 1DS (0531) 5266 ***£78.50**; 11 carefully decorated rms making the most of the old beams and timbers. Striking, mainly 16th-c, black-and-white hotel with a relaxed and attractively decorated beamed and timbered bar, smart lounge; good food in bar and restaurant, and decent wine list.

Upton-upon-Severn SO8540 WHITE LION High St WR8 0HJ (0684) 592551 ***£74.50**; 10 rms. Comfortable lounge bar and restaurant, very good food, and pleasant service; cl 25-26 Dec.

Great Malvern SO7845 COTFORD 51 Graham Rd WR14 2HU (0684) 572427 **£55**; 16 rms. Family-run hotel with really friendly atmosphere, generous helpings of decent food, and personal service; disabled access (single rm only).

Ledbury SO7138 OLDE TALBOT New St HR8 2DX (0531) 632963 **£54**; 7 rms. Cosy, friendly bar in modernised ancient building, open fire, and good food that inc popular Sunday lunch in fine oak timbered dining room; cl 24-25 Dec.

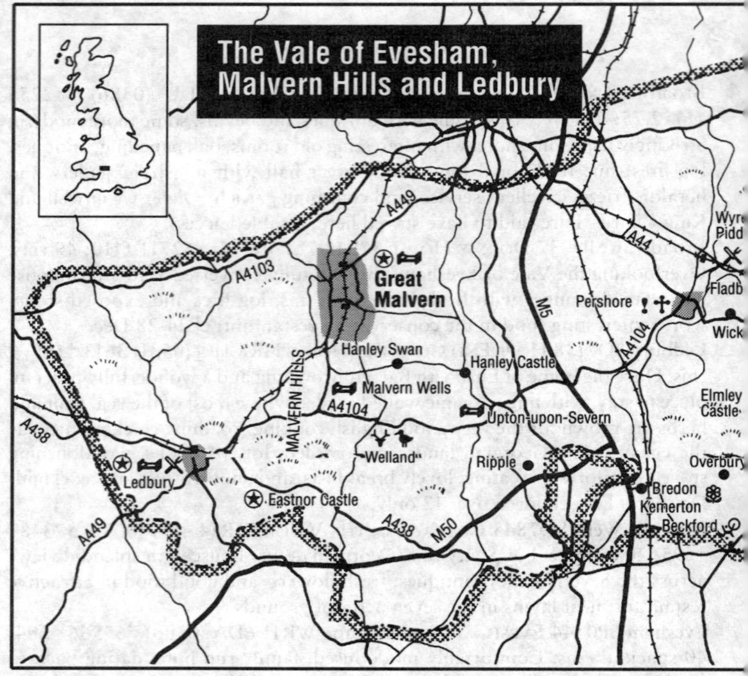

To see and do

Beckford SO9735 SILK SHOP prints, scarves and ties; processes demonstrated, shop with good-value seconds, café.

★ ✝ Bretforton SP0943, one of the prettiest black-and-white thatched villages, it has an interesting church and a splendid medieval pub, the Fleece, left to the National Trust after being in the same family for several centuries; a proper pub, it's kept just as it was, with a magnificent collection of Jacobean oak furniture and pewter.

★ ! Broadway SP0937 is an exceptionally harmonious, stone-built Cotswold village, with the golden stone and uneven stone-tiled roofs perfectly blending the grand houses and the humbler cottages together, in a long, grass-lined main street. It's on a main road and decidedly on the coach-tour trail, getting very busy indeed in summer. There are fine things for sale in extraordinarily expensive antique shops, and a very grand old inn, the Lygon Arms, with a useful side wine bar. A good escape from the tourists is the Crown & Trumpet in Church St, an archetypal Cotswold pub. Above the village the late 18th-c folly

We welcome reports from readers . . .

Do send us reports on places in the GUIDE, or ones you think should be in. Use the card in the middle, the report forms at the end, or just write – no stamp needed: THE GOOD WEEKEND GUIDE, FREEPOST TN1569, Wadhurst, E Sussex TN5 7BR.

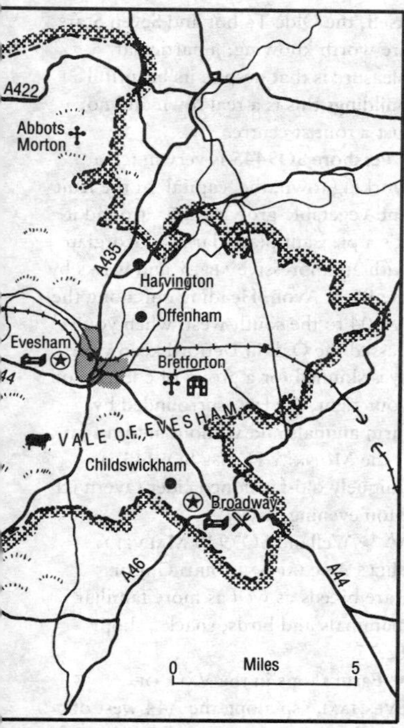

BROADWAY TOWER has marvellous views from its three levels, each with exhibitions. On an exceptionally clear day you can see 12 counties through the telescope here. The well-laid-out and cared for country park around it has farm animals and rare breeds, nature trails, an adventure playground and giant chess and draughts boards. Good-value meals and snacks, shops, some disabled access; cl Nov-Mar; £2.75. Back down in the village the COTSWOLD TEDDY BEAR MUSEUM has a big collection of old bears, dolls and toys; shop; *£1.50.

Eastnor Castle SO7336 (just E of Ledbury) Splendid neo-Gothic castle, with fine collections of armour, tapestries, furniture and paintings in the breathtaking, richly decorated rooms; attractive grounds have arboretum and 300-acre deer park. Meals, snacks, shop; open every Sun pm from Easter-Oct, bank hols, and wkdys in Aug; £3.50.

Evesham SP0344 has a pedestrianised market square with some fine buildings inc a 12th-c ABBEY GATEWAY; other handsome buildings elsewhere inc the striking, well-preserved 16th-c bell tower of the abbey, with some altogether more ruined remnants in the town park beyond it leading into riverside meadows. A good place to start is the tourist information centre in another attractive abbey building, the ALMONRY, a Tudor timbered house with craft shows and small local museum. The gardens are very nice. The Queens Head is useful for lunch. The interesting DOMESTIC FOWL TRUST, a non-profit charity, has rare breeds of hens, ducks, geese and turkeys, some of them quite extraordinary, over 10 acres of well-labelled breeding paddocks; young chicks, children's farm, adventure playground. Snacks, tearoom, shop, disabled access; cl Fri, 25-26 Dec; *£3. TWYFORD COUNTRY CENTRE (just N on A435) A busy little complex, with farm and craft shops, adventure playground, conservatory, and wildlife and falconry centre – there may also be miniature train rides at wknds. Meals, snacks, shop, disabled access; free exc falconry and wildlife, £2.50.

★ **Great Malvern** SO7746 Elegant hillside spa town with easy access to inspiring hill scenery. MALVERN MUSEUM Former Benedictine monastery buildings with displays on subjects as diverse as cars, radar, silicone chips and the life of Sir Edward Elgar, much of whose work was inspired by the splendid countryside around here. Shop; cl Weds in termtime, all Nov-Easter; *50p. A good few craft workshops include musical instrument-makers such as Hibernian Violins, Players Ave; cl lunch and wknds. On the east side of the hills BARNARDS GREEN HOUSE SO7945 has an attractive garden with a wide range of gardening ideas around a gracious, half-timbered 17th-c house (not open). The owner is an authority on dried flowers. Teas, plant sales, disabled access; open Thurs pm Apr-Sept, and first Sun May-Sept; *£1.50. The nearby Bluebell is useful for lunch. On the west side (Walwyn Rd, Colwall), PICTON GARDEN at Old Court Nurseries has a nicely laid out cottagey collection of hardy plants and shrubs, best in summer, with a national collection of asters (late summer/autumn) and rock garden. Plants sales, disabled access; cl 1-2.15, Mon, Tues, Nov-Mar; £1.50. The Chase Inn at Upper Colwall is quite handy for lunch.

† ★ ❀ **Kemerton** SO9437, below Bredon Hill, is an attractively leafy village with pretty stone-built houses among the trees. One of the most attractive is THE PRIORY, with a big garden richly planted with colourful borders; also cool streamside plantings, handsome trees and shrubs. Plant sales; open Thurs pm only, cl Oct-May; *£1.50. The Crown is useful for lunch.

Ledbury SO7138 has a spaciously leisured high street with some fine buildings – the old MARKET HOUSE, the FEATHERS HOTEL and LEDBURY PARK HOUSE are famous for their well-balanced timbering, but there are plenty of other 16th- and 17th-c timbered structures. From the Market House an exceptional alley of ancient jettied buildings leads to the partly Norman church of ST MICHAEL AND ALL ANGELS, with an unusual spire tower detached from the main building, and its carillon ringing out a well-known hymn every third hour. The OLD GRAMMAR SCHOOL has been restored as a heritage centre, cl winter wkdys, and the council offices must be the only ones in the country to have their walls decorated not with poll tax arrears charts but with MEDIEVAL WALL-PAINTINGS; cl am, Mon (exc bank hols), Thurs, Fri. There are craft workshops, antique shops and a decent book shop, and besides the Feathers itself, the Olde Talbot and Seven Stars are worth knowing; a particular pleasure is that despite its beautiful buildings this is a real town and not just a tourist centre.

! **Pershore** SO9445 is very much a working town, the 'capital' of the fruit- and vegetable-growing area around it. It's a pleasant place, largely Georgian, with an impressive ABBEY and walks by the River Avon. Heading out along the A4104 to the south-west, when you've passed the Oak in Defford keep your eyes skinned for a group of cottages on your right; the last, surrounded by farm animals and without an inn sign, is the MONKEY HOUSE SO9143, a uniquely old-fashioned cider tavern (cl Mon evening, Tues).

Welland SO7940 MALVERN HILLS ANIMAL AND BIRD GARDEN Rare breeds as well as more familiar mammals and birds; snacks, shop; £2.75.

Farm shops in the VALE OF EVESHAM, esp along the A44 west of Broadway, are good for all manner of local produce inc eggs, jams, pickles and trout as well as fruit and veg, but the highlights of the year are asparagus in May and apples and particularly plums in Sept. The Chapel Hill nursery about ½ mile west of Broadway has good-value plants for sale.

★ A tremendous wealth of **attractive villages** inc black-and-white Abbots Morton SP0353 (with a lovely church); Ashton-under-Hill SO9938 below Bredon Hill, with many charming black-and-white timbered houses, and a good Norman church; Bredon SO9236, with a magnificent medieval tithe barn (and a good pub, the Fox & Hounds); Childswickham SP0738 (streamside, timbered stone cottages); largely black-and-white Elmley Castle SO9841 under Bredon Hill (a lovely church, and an unusual rustic tavern – the Queen Elizabeth); Fladbury SO9946 by the Avon, with riverside walks, a 9th-c Saxon cross, and a handsome Georgian village green (the

Chequers, partly 14th-c, is good value for lunch); Hanley Castle SO8442, a rustic little place around a great cedar tree, with both its church and its unusually unspoilt pub looking like an attempt to glue two half-buildings in entirely different styles together to make one; Hanley Swan SO8142 (pleasant traditional pub by village green and duck pond); brilliantly black-and-white Harvington SP0548, one of the oldest in the area; Offenham SP0546, with an original, gaily striped maypole in its wide black-and-white main street; Overbury SO9537, an immaculate, stone-built estate village with older buildings and a fine church; Ripple SO8737, with finely carved choir seats in its imposing, largely 13th-c church; Wick SO9645, on the Avon, with a good church.

Walks

It is easy to understand Elgar's enthusiasm for the **Malvern Hills**. From the distance (and they form a splendid backdrop to the Vale of Evesham) they look a formidable mountain range, but seem to get milder and more welcoming as you approach. The gentle up-and-down path along their spine makes one of England's great ridge walks, with the Cotswolds and Midland plain on one side and wilder Wales on the other. The **Herefordshire Beacon** SO7640, capped by ramparts of an Iron-Age hill fort, is easily reached from the car park on the A449 near Little Malvern. For long circular walks based on the Malverns, Great Malvern is well placed for the Worcestershire Beacon SO7645, the highest point of the range (1,395 ft). The Chase Hotel at Upper Wyche SO7643 and Malvern Hills Hotel by the British Camp car park on Wynds Point SO7641 are also starting or finishing points for walkers. Ledbury SO7138 and Eastnor SO7337 are good bases for rambles into the attractive western slopes.

In the Vale of Evesham, the one notable feature for walkers is the rounded and on cloudy days rather ominous **Bredon Hill**, an outlier of the Cotswolds. It's easily reached from Overbury SO9537, but the best walk over it is from Bredons Norton SO9339 to Elmley Castle SO9841.

Driving

In and around the Malvern Hills, the B4232 from Upper Colwall to Wynds Point has some of the best high views, while the B4218 on the E side gives several good views of the hills themselves. There's nothing finer than to have Elgar playing on your car audio as you drive.

N of Ledbury, there's quite a dramatic drive on the rather narrow road heading N through Wellington Heath, to bear right along the wooded hillside for views out over the farmland.

The classic circular tour of the Vale of Evesham orchards is A435 N of Evesham to Harvington, left through Atch Lench and Church Lench, left opposite Church Lench church, then right at Handgate Farm to Badgers Hill, left at the Hill Furze T-junction to Fladbury Cross, then left on to the B4084 through Wood Norton and Chadbury, and back to Evesham. The Vale is at its best in Apr or early May when the orchards are full of blossom, first plum and then apple.

There's a fine panorama of the vale from the A44 dropping down out of Oxfordshire towards Broadway.

Other drives based on the villages we recommend will take you through quiet lanes and past individual black-and-white farmhouses and cottages.

Where to eat

Broadway SP9037 HUNTERS LODGE High St (0386) 853247 Pretty Cotswold house with lovely food cooked by Swiss owner, and friendly, helpful service; open pm Weds, Thurs, Fri, Sat, open am Sat and Sun only; cl 1st 3 wks Aug and 2 wks Feb; children welcome at lunch but over 8 only at dinner; disabled access. **£19.40.**

Wyre Piddle SO9647 ANCHOR (0386) 552799 Relaxing pub with excellent views from the lawn over the river; comfortable bar, popular bar food with interesting puddings; restaurant cl Sun pm; disabled access. **£15|£2.35/£6.**

Ledbury SO7138 MARKET PLACE (0531) 634250 Decent restaurant open all day for morning coffee, lunch and afternoon tea with home-made cakes, flans and puddings; cl pm, Sun, Jan. **£9.80|£1.70/£3.75.**

HEREFORDSHIRE

Unspoilt and quintessentially English, this area makes a very good choice for a quiet break.

Virtually the whole of this very English county preserves the landscape at its unspoilt best. Its chief appeal is as an escape into the sort of peaceful world that elsewhere tends to survive only in people's memories. Where old villages have been extended, their appearance has rarely suffered. There's very little real urbanisation, and as the county is outside the main motorway area its character hasn't been damaged or diluted by commuters and country-cottagers. There aren't that many tourists about, even at the height of summer. People who have been lured here have brought values thoroughly in tune with the county's appeal – so art galleries and bookshops crop up in the most unlikely places (Hay-on-Wye, that town-sized bookshop, is just over the border in Wales), and ostensibly quite humble inns and pubs turn out to have cooks far better than you'd expect.

Of the towns, Hereford itself is engaging and relaxing, with plenty of varied attractions – well worth a day out. Kington and Ross-on-Wye are also both good to visit. Elsewhere, the black-and-white villages are a particular delight, and Berrington Hall at Ashton, Goodrich Castle and the nearby farm park, Lower Brockhampton House at Brockhampton, Croft Castle and Dinmore Manor all make pleasant outings. There are several fine gardens to look at, and no stay here would be complete without a visit to a cider farm. The area's not strong on conventional visitor attractions, and it might be difficult to keep young children amused here.

Where to stay

Eyton SO4861 MARSH just NW of Leominster Leominster HR6 0AG (0568) 613952 ***£110**; 5 comfortable rms with garden views. Carefully restored, 14th-c timbered country hotel with quietly relaxing atmosphere in prettily furnished beamed rooms; good food using home-grown herbs, and colourful big garden.

Ullingswick SO5950 THE STEPPES Hereford HR1 3JG (0432) 820424 **£70**; 6 large, well-furnished rms in recently restored timber-framed barn and stable set around central courtyard. 17th-c, beautifully restored building with low beams, inglenook fireplaces and lots of antiques; cellar bar, cosy, atmospheric dining room, good food using local produce and home-grown herbs; decent wine list, attentive, friendly service, and big breakfasts; pleasant garden; cl 2 wks before Christmas, re-open 24 Dec, cl 3 Jan for 2 wks; children over 12 only.

Brimfield SO5368 ROEBUCK Ludlow S18 4NE (0584) 711230 ***£65**. Very civilised restaurant with a few rooms; excellent food in elegant, modern, no-smoking restaurant, unusual bar food, good wines; cl Sun pm, Mon, 1 wk Oct, 2 wks Feb.

Ross-on-Wye SO6024 KINGS HEAD 8 High St HR9 5HL (0989) 763174 ***£60**; 25 rms. Comfortable 14th-c coaching inn with good atmosphere, and decent food in bar and small restaurant; cl 25 Dec; disabled access.

Whitney-on-Wye SO2647 RHYDSPENCE Hereford HR3 6EU (0497) 831262 ***£60**; 5 pretty rms. Delightful timbered pub right on Welsh border with fine views of the Wye Valley and beyond; rambling beamed rooms and good food; cl 25 Dec.

Trumpet SO6539 VERZONS COUNTRY HOUSE Ledbury HR8 2PZ (0531) 670381 **£60**; 10 rms. Popular hotel, warmly recommended by contributors; cl 25 Dec.

Symonds Yat SO5616 WOODLEA Ross-on-Wye HR9 6BL (0600) 890206 ***£55**; 9 rms, most with own bthrm. Family-run guesthouse in fine position overlooking Wye Rapids, with comfortable lounges and good food; cl part of Jan and Feb.

Weobley SO4052 OLDE SALUTATION Hereford HR4 8SJ (0544) 318443 ***£54**; 5 rms. Friendly, 500-year-old inn looking down on attractive half-timbered village, with decent food in bar and no-smoking restaurant; cl 25 Dec; no children except babies.

Pontrilas SO4027 HOWTON COURT Hereford HR2 0BG (0981) 240249 **£50**; 2 rms. In the same family for four generations, this friendly stone and timber-frame house has panoramic views across a secluded garden to the nearby Welsh mountains; good local and home-produced food in oak-panelled, flagstoned dining room, log fire in family drawing room; pleasant walks, fishing, horse riding and shooting (by arrangment); high tea for children on request.

Ruckhall Common SO4539 ANCIENT CAMP Hereford HR2 9QX (0981) 250449 ***£48**; 5 rms. Smart country inn in pleasantly remote spot with good views of River Wye and beyond from terrace; beamed and flagstoned bar, good bar and restaurant food (not Sun pm or Mon); children over 8.

Fownhope SO5834 Green Man Hereford HR1 4PE (0432) 860243 **£48**; 19 rms. Attractive and atmospheric Tudor inn close to River Wye, with impressive oak-beamed lounge and good-value bar food.

Carey SO5631 Cottage of Content Hereford HR2 6NG (0432) 840242 **£45**; 4 rms. Very pretty, isolated 500-year-old country pub with attractive bars, lots of wines and decent breakfast; quiet village setting.

Symonds Yat SO5616 Saracens Head Ross-on-Wye HR9 6JL (0600) 890435 **£45**; 10 rms, 3 with shared bthrm. This former cider mill is now a small, comfortable hotel on the banks of the River Wye, with excellent restaurant food, decent wine list, and friendly staff; good base for fishing and canoeing.

Vowchurch SO3636 Croft Country House Hereford HR2 0QE (0981) 550226 ***£44**; 8 well-furnished rms. Well-run small hotel in 7 acres with attractive gardens, orchard, paddocks and tennis court; good food and lovely views; children over 10; no pets.

Leysters SO4959 Hills Farm Leominster HR6 9HP (056 887) 205 ***£40**; 3 rms. Traditional stone-and-brick, 15th-c farmhouse in 120 arable acres; with rambling beamed rooms, pretty sitting room, good fresh food, and fine views; no smoking; cl family hols, Christmas; children by arrangement.

Woolhope SO6136 Butchers Arms Hereford HR1 4RF (0432) 860281 **£39**; 3 neat, attractive rms with fruit and chocolates. An exceptionally nice, family-run place with very friendly staff, lots of flowers, and decent food (good breakfasts); lovely surrounding walks; children under 10 only £10.

Stretton Grandison SO6344 Moor Court Farm Ledbury HR8 2TR (0531) 670408 **£32**; 3 rms. Hop and livestock farm with B & B in fine 15th-c timber-framed farmhouse, beamed rooms, and adjoining oast houses; no children.

Kinnersley SO3449 Upper Newton Farmhouse Hereford HR3 6QB (0544) 327727 **£30**; 3 pretty rms, shared bthrm. 17th-c farmhouse in middle of working farm, with open fires, beams, sloping floors, and good food (inc vegetarian) using fresh farm veg; no smoking or pets; self-catering cottage.

To see and do

★ **Hereford** SO5140 The city's importance came largely from its role as a regional market centre, and every Weds there's still a busy livestock and general market. For the rest of the week the city feels very quiet-paced and old-fashioned, its streets (some pedestrianised now) lined with handsome Georgian and other buildings (Church St is almost wholly medieval). The many antique shops are by no means over-priced. The best place to start is the CATHEDRAL, nicely placed on the bank of the Wye and perhaps most famous as the home of the Mappa Mundi, the largest complete example of a 13th-c world map, though this fine Norman building with its lovely 13th- and 15th-c chapel has many other treasures – inc the country's biggest chained library (the second biggest is at All Saints church, at the opposite end of the main st). CIDER MUSEUM (Pomana Pl) The story of cider-making through the ages, with enormous old presses inc a 17th-c French one, original cellars, 1920s bottling line and a working cider-brandy distillery – the first licensed for over 250 years. Shop, disabled access to ground floor only; cl Sun Nov-Easter, 25-26 Dec and 1 Jan; *£1.95. The enormous modern BULMER'S CIDER MILL (Plough Lane) has tours and tastings; cl Jan, Feb, tours by appointment, tel (0432) 352000; £2.95. ST JOHN AND CONINGSBY MUSEUM (Widemarsh St) 13th-c hospice telling the story of the Ancient Order of St John and its role in the Crusades, with costumed displays and tales of other local characters, inc Nell Gwynne and a mysterious 15th-c skeleton; cl am, Mon, Fri, Oct-Easter; *50p. THE OLD HOUSE (High Town) Glorious Jacobean house with period furnishings, paintings and style throughout its three floors. Has been closed for most of 1993 for essential repairs. Shop; cl 1-2, Mon pm, Sat pm in winter; 80p. You can also buy a joint ticket for the CHURCHILL GARDENS MUSEUM (Venns Lane, northern outskirts), a Regency house in fine grounds, with good displays of 18th- and 19th-c furniture, costumes and paintings, nursery, laundry, kitchen and parlour; the gallery showcases work of local artist Brian Hatton killed in WWI. Shop, some disabled access; cl am, Sun exc summer, Mon exc bank hols. WATERWORKS MUSEUM (Broomy Hill) Restored Victorian pumping station housing the giant Broomy Hill steam pumping engines, with interesting displays and boilers illustrating the development of the waterworks, and a new vintage diesel engine; lots of the pumps can be operated by visitors. Snacks, shop, disabled access; open mainly summer Suns only, best to check on (0432) 870411 or 273635; £1.50. BULMER RAILWAY CENTRE (Whitecross Rd) Houses a collection of mainly industrial locomotive and rolling stock inc ex-LMS 6201 Princess Elizabeth; open wknds only, phone (0432) 358892 for details and dates of steam days. CITY MUSEUM AND ART GALLERY (Broad St) Natural history and archaeology of the area from prehistoric times, inc interesting beekeeping display and changing exhibitions of paintings. Snacks, shop, disabled access; cl Mon exc bank hols, 25-26 Dec, Good Fri. Wye-side walks give a pleasing view of the city, its spires and towers. Saxtys and the Bunch of Carrots are both useful for lunch.

Other things to see and do

❀ ✺ **Abbey Dore** SO3830 ABBEY DORE COURT GARDEN Attractive riverside lawns, gardens, and good views across to the nearby surviving fragments of the former 12th- and 13th-c Cistercian abbey; unusual plant sales and gift shop, teddy bear collection, café in 17th-c stables. Meals, snacks, shop, disabled access; cl Weds, mid-Oct-mid-Mar, but shop open till Christmas; £1.50.

⌂ ❀ **Ashton** SO5164 BERRINGTON HALL (NT) Elegant, late 18th-c neo-Classical house, very elaborate inside with beautiful furnishings and decor, the Digby collection, charming nursery and interesting examples of 'downstairs' life in Georgian dairy and laundry; the grounds were landscaped by Capability Brown. Meals, snacks, shop, some disabled access; cl am, Mon exc bank hols, Tues, Nov-Mar; £3.20.

♣ ✿ ✺ **Bodenham** SO5450 QUEENSWOOD COUNTRY PARK AND ARBORETUM 170 acres of woodland and arboretum with over 500 varieties of tree; also wildlife displays, nature trails, good views and events. Meals, snacks, shop and info centre, disabled access; shop and café cl 25-26 Dec.

❀ ✺ ▣ **Brobury** SO3444 BROBURY HOUSE GALLERY Seven acres of semi-formal gardens with fine views; also watercolours and prints for sale. Shop, some disabled access; cl Sun, 25 Dec, 1 Jan; gardens £1.50 summer, £1 winter – the gallery is free.

⌂ ✝ **Brockhampton** SO5931 LOWER BROCKHAMPTON (NT) Idyllic timber-framed and moated 14th-c manor house in attractive secluded countryside; particularly interesting are the 15th-c gatehouse, a rare example of this kind of building, and the ruins of a 12th-c chapel. Shop, some disabled access; cl 1-2, Mon exc bank hols, Tues, and Nov-Mar; £1.50.

🐄 **Bromyard** SD6554 SHORTWOOD DAIRY FARM Working farm ideal for children, with afternoon activities like watching the milking and feeding the calves. Snacks, shop, disabled access; cl Sat, Oct-Easter exc for last week Oct when open for cider-making; *£2.75. The Crown & Sceptre is useful for lunch.

Burford SO5868 BURFORD HOUSE GARDENS Charmingly designed landscaped gardens around 18th-c house (not open). The nursery has hundreds of clematis cultivars for sale; meals, snacks, disabled access; cl Sun am, 25-26 Dec; *£1.95.

Croft SO4764 CROFT CASTLE The walls and turrets date from the 14th and 15th c, while the inside is mostly 18th c, with an interesting staircase and plastered ceilings. The attractive parklands have an avenue of 350-year-old chestnuts, and there's a footpath to CROFT AMBREY, an Iron-Age fort. Disabled access; open pm Weds-Sun and bank hols May-Sept, also wknds Apr and Oct; £2.80.

Dinmore SO4950 DINMORE MANOR Spectacular views of the surrounding countryside from this manor house's hilltop position. Closely linked to the Knights Hospitaller of St John, the house has architecture ranging from the 14th c to the present, with notable chapel, cloisters and hall, and a good stained-glass collection; the grounds have a collection of farm animals. Summer snacks, shop, plant centre, disabled access; cl 25 Dec; *£2. Nearby Green Acres has organically grown PICK-YOUR-OWN fruit and veg; DINMORE FRUIT FARM has a very wide choice of apple varieties, as well as more conventional pick-your-own.

★ **Eardisland** SO4258 This gorgeous, riverside black-and-white village inc BURTON COURT, an interesting old house with 14th-c great hall and collections of ship models, European and Oriental costumes, natural history specimens, working model fairground and, in the grounds, pick-your-own berries. Teas, shop, disabled access; cl am, Mon, Tues, Fri, winter; *£2. The nearby White Swan is useful for lunch.

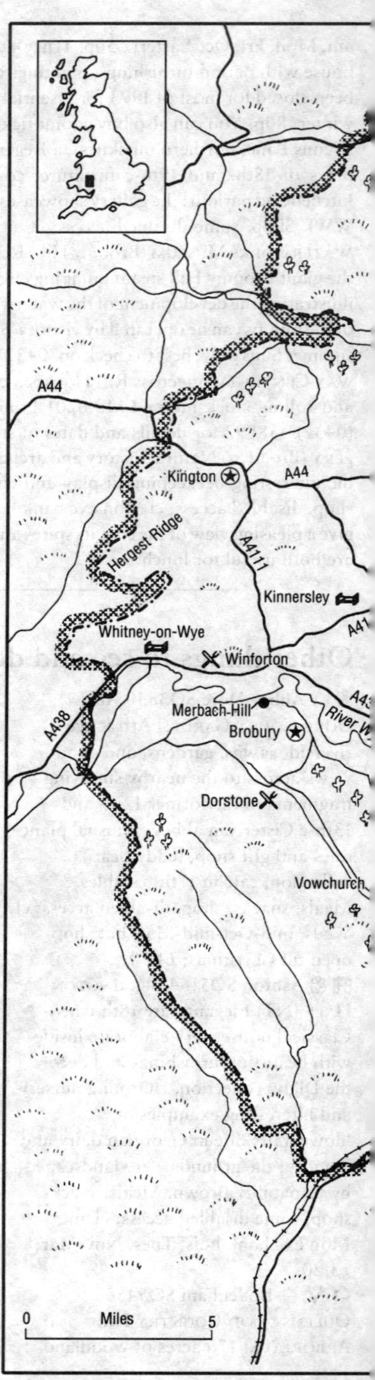

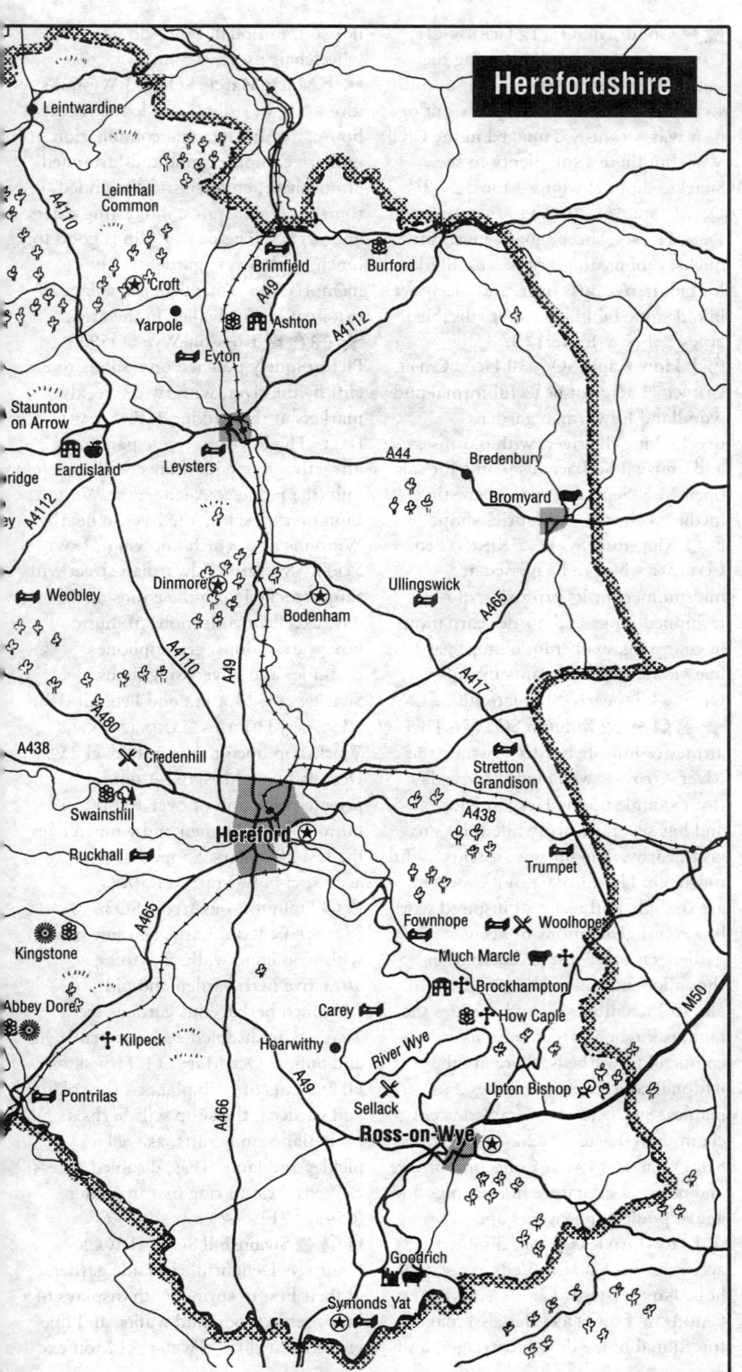
Herefordshire
Leintwardine
A4110
Leinthall
Common
Brimfield
Burford
Croft
Yarpole
A49
Ashton
A4112
Eyton
Staunton
on Arrow
Eardisland
Leysters
A44
Bredenbury
Bromyard
ridge
A4112
Dinmore
Weobley
Bodenham
Ullingswick
A465
A4110
A49
A417
A480
A438
Credenhill
Stretton
Grandison
Swainshill
A438
Hereford
Ruckhall
Trumpet
A465
Fownhope
Woolhope
Kingstone
Much Marcle
Brockhampton
M50
Abbey Dore
How Caple
Carey
Kilpeck
Hoarwithy
River Wye
A49
Upton Bishop
Pontrilas
A466
Sellack
Ross-on-Wye
Goodrich
Symonds Yat

Goodrich SO5719 GOODRICH CASTLE 12th-c castle built using the same red sandstone rock it stands on, so that it seems almost to grow out of it; it was seriously damaged in the Civil War, but there's still plenty to see. Snacks, shop; cl winter Mons, 24-26 Dec, 1 Jan; *£1.70. WYE VALLEY FARM PARK Horses, sheep, goats, pigs, cattle, ducks, rabbits and rare breeds all ideal for children to fuss over, and nicely set in old stone buildings. Shop, disabled access; cl Nov-Easter; £3.

† **How Caple** SO6030 HOW CAPLE COURT 11 acres of peaceful formal and woodland Edwardian gardens overlooking the river, with old roses and unusual herbaceous plants for sale; open May-Sept; £2. Also interesting medieval church and fabrics shop.

Kingstone SO4235 KINGSTONE COTTAGES Not to be missed at midsummer for its profusion of old-fashioned pinks and border carnations in charming, exuberant cottage garden; fine views, unusual plants for sale. Open wkdys early May-late Jun; £1.

★ **Kington** SO2956 This attractive hillside border town by the River Arrow is well placed for walks (for example up the Hergest Ridge), and has several worthwhile things to visit nearby. The Burton Hotel is useful for lunch. HERGEST CROFT GARDENS are the splendid result of inspired work by several generations of keen gardeners; some of the centenarian rhodododendrons in the woods are of almost incredible size and, besides the famous kitchen garden with its colourful flowerbeds, there are the national collections of birches and maples. Snacks, shop, disabled access; cl am, Nov-Easter; *£2.20. OAKLANDS SMALL BREEDS FARM Collection of rare and unusual miniature horses, pigs and goats, poultry, pheasants and waterfowl; snacks, shop, disabled access; cl am Sat and Weds exc school hols, Nov-Easter; *£2.50. MONTFORD CARRIAGE BUILDERS (Hergest) make traditional horse-drawn carriages, and not so traditional – they do one for wheelchair users; cl Sun.

† **Much Marcle** SO6633 Weston's CIDER FARM, still alongside the family house, has an engaging combination of modern equipment and old-fashioned atmosphere; enthusiastically guided tours, liberal tastings, interesting ciders and perries. The nearby Slip is good for lunch (with lovely gardens). The memorial monuments in the village CHURCH are unrivalled in the area.

★ **Ross-on-Wye** SO5923 Picturesquely perched on a sandstone cliff by the river, with twice-weekly markets at the striking 17th-c MARKET HALL. The lower riverside part has attractive waterside walks, and a useful pub (the Hope & Anchor; the White Lion prettily set by the river in nearby Wilton is also worth knowing). LOST STREET MUSEUM Edwardian street with shops stocked with the goods of the day, excellent collections of music boxes, toys, dolls, gramophones, costumes and advertising items. Snacks; cl wkdys Jan and Feb, all Dec; £2. C & J HUGHES CANDLEMAKERS Workshop open to the public; cl 25-26 Dec. BUTTON MUSEUM A unique private collection of over 10,000 buttons worn by men and women over the last 200 years. Shop, disabled access; cl Nov-Mar; *£1.50.

Staunton-on-Arrow SO3660 STAUNTON PARK Large lakeside garden with woodland walk, fine trees, attractive herb garden and old-fashioned herbaceous gardens etc. Teas, shop, disabled access; open Weds and Sun, cl Oct-Mar; *£1. HORSEWAY HERBS Lots of herb plants, other plants and gardens; the shop sells herbs as both plants and crafts, as well as pickles and jams. Teas, disabled access; cl Weds, best to ring first in winter, (05447) 212.

Swainshill SO4541 WEIR GARDENS Delightful riverside gardens at their best in spring, with displays of bulbs set in woodland walks, and fine views from clifftop walks; cl Mon exc bank hols, Tues, Nov-mid-Feb; £1.50.

Symonds Yat SO5616 (shared with Glos on the other side of the river) is a spectacular bend of the River Wye through a steep, wooded rock gorge, where peregrine falcons nest (the RSPB have a demonstration area); splendid Wye views, nature trails; two inns on either side of the river are linked by a hand-pulled ferry, and there's ample (walkers would say over-generous) parking. Among other things to amuse visitors here (it is a popular tourist destination) is the JUBILEE PARK, home to the Jubilee Maze built for the Queen's Silver Jubilee, the lively MUSEUM OF MAZES telling the history of similar labyrinthine creations, unusual shops and the WORLD OF BUTTERFLIES, where hundreds of butterflies fly free in a big tropical indoor garden. Meals, snacks, shop, disabled access; World of Butterflies cl Nov-Mar, other attractions cl Mon and Fri Nov-Mar; *£2.50, butterflies another £2.25.

Upton Bishop SO6527 Wobage Farm CRAFT WORKSHOPS have several potters, a furniture-maker, wood-carver and jeweller; cl wkdys exc by appointment, phone (098985) 495.

★ The many **black-and-white villages** are a particular characteristic of the country. Besides Eardisland (see above), best of all is probably Pembridge SO3958, full of fine timbered buildings – one of the most ancient is the New Inn, well worth knowing. Dunkerton's small CIDER FARM (nearby at Luntley SO3956) uses ancient, traditional, local cider-apple and pear cultivars, for distinctive ciders and perries; free tastings; cl Sun. Another of the finest villages is Weobley SO4052, with its long sloping green, and stroll out past the bowling green to the church; the Olde Salutation is good for lunch. Other favourite villages in the county, all with decent pubs, inc Carey SO5631, Bredenbury SO6156 (despite the main road), Dorstone SO3141, Hoarwithy SO5429, the riverside Leintwardine SO4174 (its church is much bigger than usual for this county), and streamside Yarpole SO4765 (with a free-standing medieval bell tower). One of the most charming churches in the area is the small but beautifully preserved Norman one at Kilpeck SO4530, itself a delightful little hamlet.

Walks

Herefordshire's most satisfying walks are around its edges, in the Wye Valley on the southern fringes, around Woolhope and the western part of the Malverns on its eastern margins, and up the Golden Valley and the hills of the Welsh Marches to the west and north-west. The centre is for the most part an undulating plain, with a dozy agricultural charm and some very pretty villages.

The Herefordshire part of the Wye Valley includes **Symonds Yat** SO5616, something of a motorists' viewpoint over a tight meander of the Wye (there's a prominent car park), but with potential for more ambitious walks into the gorge, where an old railway line follows the river; south-westwards an entertainingly rickety, wire-mesh suspension bridge gives access to the west bank. Meanwhile to the north, the formidable ruins of **Goodrich Castle** SO5719 are a feasible objective or start point for gorge walks. In the more open stretches of the valley, Ross-on-Wye SO5923 has pleasant woodland walks in **Penyard Park** south-east of the town. The elevated country around **Woolhope** SO6136 has good variety, with the views from Ridge Hill east of the village and the more densely wooded hills nr Mordiford SO5737 among the highlights.

In western Herefordshire, **Merbach Hill** SO3044 can be reached by driving up from Bredwardine SO3344, where Rev Francis Kilvert's grave can be seen in the churchyard, and then walking from the top of the lane; there's a view right over the Black Mountains, Herefordshire and Radnorshire, and a short stroll along the lane south-east brings you to Arthur's Stone, a prehistoric burial chamber. **Hergest Ridge** SO2556, reached via a cul-de-sac from Kington, is north-west Herefordshire's answer to the Malvern Hills – and like them inspired Elgar, in this case to write his *Introduction and Allegro for Strings* (more recently, Mike Oldfield has dedicated an album to the ridge). It's another of those ridges for those who can't decide whether they prefer the gentle lowland textures of England or the more rugged offerings of Wales. The walk gets better with every step, as the wide ridge tapers into horseback width at the far end, above Gladestry in Powys. **Leinthall Common** SO4467, a brackeny expanse scattered with cottages, is a quiet corner of Herefordshire where you can walk around the estate of Croft Castle and scale the modest heights of Croft Ambrey, an Iron-Age hill fort with a view into Shropshire.

Other walks can start or finish at country pubs, such as the Penny Farthing at Aston Crews SO6723, Tally Ho! at Broad Heath SO6665, Crown at Howle Hill SO6020, Three Crowns at Ullingswick SO5949 or Carpenters at Walterstone SO3425.

Driving

For driving on relatively quiet roads in countryside studded by black-and-white farmsteads and villages, the best area is between Kingsland, Pembridge and Weobley, where there is a Black-and-White Villages Trail.

The B4347 and B4348 up the Golden Valley is a very pretty drive. If you keep on to Hay and loop back by the B4350, you can cross the old toll bridge over the Wye for the short stretch past Whitney-on-Wye, with distant lush views; the road becomes much less interesting as you approach Hereford, though.

A short stretch of back country road that gives an excellent taste of the quieter parts of the county is the one off the B4224 S of Fownhope at Crossway, through How Caple and Penalt to Hoarwithy; but many other country roads give a fine sense of time slowing right down.

Another approach to tracing your way through the area's lovely villages and country lanes is to take a group fairly close together each of which has an attractive church – such as Bredwardine, Moccas, Tyberton and Eaton Bishop, strung along the upper Wye Valley; or rather more tortuously Fownhope, Brockhampton, Hoarwithy, Kings Caple and Foy, again nr the Wye.

Where to eat

Credenhill SO4544 JASMINE HOUSE (0432) 760945 Very good Chinese food, decent wine; also take-aways; disabled access. **£16.80**|£6.30.
Sellack SO5627 LOUGHPOOL (098 987) 236 Attractive timbered cottage surrounded by lovely countryside, with lots of nice touches, good bar food and restaurant dishes; well-behaved children in snug only; disabled access. **£14**|£6.
Woolhope SO6135 CROWN (0432) 860468 Very popular pub, generous helpings of reasonably priced food, good real ales, decent wines, and pleasant service; cl 25 Dec for food, children over 5. **£12.60**|£2.85/£4.70.
Dorstone SO3141 PANDY (0981) 550273 Friendly 12th-c inn, good bar food; cl Mon am, Tues from 1 Nov-Easter. **£10**|£1.40/£4.95.
Winforton SO2947 SUN (0544) 327677 Attractive beamed pub with very good, daily changing bar food and lots of home-made puddings. £2.75/£8.40.

Worcestershire

Some attractive places; perhaps best for people who already know and like other parts of this twin county and want to explore more of it.

Worcester is a busy city: not a place for quiet relaxation, but with a good deal of interest at least for adults to track down. For younger people, a better bet would be Bewdley: the terminus for Britain's most lively steam railway, as well as other things to do. Elsewhere, highlights include Great Witley with its extraordinary ruin and splendid church, Britain's best garden centre at Wychbold, Hanbury Hall (with several other places to visit nearby), and the buildings' museum at Bromsgrove. There are a good few attractive villages, and some interesting patches of countryside for walkers – though on the whole those parts of the county already discussed are more beautiful, and, being further from Birmingham, less busy.

There's a reasonable choice of places to stay.

The Vale of Evesham is described separately, in the first section of this chapter.

Where to stay

Bromsgrove SO9570 GRAFTON MANOR B61 7HA (0527) 579007 ***£105**; 9 individually decorated rms. Impressive early 18th-c mansion with an Elizabethan core, and lovely grounds; splendid restaurant with very good modern British cooking using home-grown herbs, comfortable lounge, good service; croquet and riding.

Abberley SO7667 ELMS Stockton Rd WR6 6AT (0299) 896666 **£97**; 25 comfortable rms. Lovely Queen Anne mansion with fine views from the well-kept grounds; elegant, restful drawing room with antiques, log fires and flowers; very good food, and friendly, efficient staff.

Chaddesley Corbett SO8973 BROCKENCOTE HALL Kidderminster DY10 4PY (0562) 777876 ***£90**; 17 individually decorated rms. Grand country-house hotel in 70 acres of grounds with half-timbered dovecot and lake; large, airy and attractively furnished rooms, conservatory-style restaurant with good, modern French and English cooking, and very good service; children under 12 free if share parents' room; disabled access.

Worcester SO8555 FOWNES RESORT City Wall Rd WR1 2AP (0905) 613151 **£72w**; 61 comfortable, well-equipped rms. Close to the centre and cleverly converted from a famous glove factory, this is a smart hotel with restful public rooms, cosy library, restaurant, and canalside walk; disabled access.

Knightwick SO7355 TALBOT Knightsford Bridge Worcester WR6 5PH (0886) 21235 **£52.50**; 10 rms. Rambling 14th-c inn with heavy beams, interesting prints, decent food and lots of puddings.

Ombersley SO8463 CROWN & SANDYS ARMS Droitwich WR9 0EW (0905) 620252 ***£42**; 7 no-smoking rms. Pretty Dutch-gabled pub with good views from garden; cosy beamed bar area, open fire, and decent food; no dogs in bedrooms; cl 25 Dec.

Frith Common SO6969 HUNT HOUSE FARM Tenbury Wells WR15 8JY (0299) 832277 £30; 3 rms. Friendly, 16th-c timbered farm on 180-acre arable and sheep farm, with beams and open fires, and lovely surrounding countryside; cl Christmas.

To see and do

Worcester SO8555 Though it's a busy commercial centre, this has some splendid medieval buildings dotted about, with lots of half-timbered houses, particularly around Friar St and New St. Kings like John and Charles II came to Worcester at various stages in their lives, and it's long been a place that interestingly combines industry (china and gloves, for instance) with the area's more established agriculture. Plenty of shops, including some nice specialist ones, and cafés in Hopmarket Yard, a former coaching inn. THE COMMANDERY (Sidbury) This timber-framed 15th-c building houses the only museum in the country wholly devoted to the English Civil War. With an impressive great hall and original stained glass, it was the headquarters of Charles II's army at the end of the conflict. Weaponry displays, spectacular audio-visual displays and tableaux of events throughout the war; regular displays by Worcester Militia. Teas, shop; cl 25-26 Dec; £3. ROYAL WORCESTER AND THE MUSEUM OF WORCESTER PORCELAIN (Severn St) Factory tours of the country's oldest continuous producer of porcelain; excellent collection of their products in the museum. Meals, snacks, shop, disabled access to museum only; cl Sun, 25-26 Dec, tours wkdys only; tours £3, museum £1.50. CATHEDRAL Founded on the site of a Saxon monastery, in a calm and peaceful setting overlooking the river. It took from 1084 to 1375 to construct the building, which sports an attractive 14th-c tower, and has a Norman crypt and the tombs of Prince Arthur and King John, the latter topped by the oldest royal effigy in the country. Also lots of Victorian stained glass and some monastic buildings. Snacks, shop, disabled access. The Farriers Arms nearby is useful for lunch. ELGAR'S BIRTHPLACE MUSEUM (Lower Broadheath) The cottage where the composer was born in 1857, now a museum of his life and work, with displays of musical scores and letters, and the desk where he did his writing. Shop; cl Weds, am Oct-Apr, 25-26 Dec, mid-Jan-mid-Feb; *£3. TUDOR HOUSE (Friar St) 15th-c timber-framed house with displays on local life, the Home Front of WWII, dolls, toys and an Edwardian bathroom. Shop, disabled access; cl Thurs, Sun; *£1.50. CITY MUSEUM AND ART GALLERY (Foregate St) Local and natural history, frequently changing art exhibitions, museums of local regiments and a complete 19th-c chemist's shop. Snacks, shop, disabled access; cl Thurs and Sun. GUILDHALL Handsome, early Georgian building with one of the best Queen Anne rooms in the country; meals, snacks, shop; cl Sun, Feb. WORCESTER WOODS COUNTRYSIDE CENTRE 140 acres of ancient woodland on the edge of the city, popular orienteering course or nature trails; not as interesting as woodlands elsewhere, but useful for strolling if you don't want to leave the city. Snacks, shop, disabled access. JOLLY ROGER BREWERY (Lowesmoor) Tours of cheerful, traditional micro-brewery with history of brewing process and samples; open normal licensing hours. GREYFRIARS (Friar St) Carefully restored, medieval timber-framed town house with delightful walled garden; open pm Weds, Thurs and bank hols, Apr-Oct; £1.60. BENNETTS FARM PARK (Lower Wick) Farm animals, vintage machinery museum and wknd milking parlour; also adventure playground, and fishing in season. Snacks, shop, disabled access; cl Sept-Easter; £1.

Other things to see and do

★ **Bewdley** SO7875 An attractive, small riverside town, with interesting side streets (and a very interesting pub, the Little Pack Horse, up towards the end of the old High St). SEVERN VALLEY RAILWAY Splendid steam train trips through the Wyre Forest and the Severn Valley between Kidderminster and Bridgnorth, both of which have lively, old-fashioned stations, with lots going on – this railway is run with great verve. The Bewdley station has a fine model railway called Wribbenhall Junction, and there are various special events and wknds. Meals, snacks, shop; tel (0299) 403816 for timetable; from £4.90. MUSEUM Museum of local crafts and industries in an 18th-c row of butchers' shops; displays of charcoal-burning, basket- and rope-making and coopering, restored brass foundry, working waterwheel and hydraulic ram pump. Shop, disabled access; cl Sat and Sun am, Mon, Tues, Oct-Easter; £1. WEST MIDLANDS SAFARI AND LEISURE PARK Wildlife park with exotic animals, sea lions, reptile house, parrot show, deer park and new drive-through lion reserve; lots of rides in the leisure area. Meals, snacks, shop, disabled access; cl Nov-Mar; £3.99.

Bromsgrove SO9670 AVONCROFT MUSEUM OF BUILDINGS Threatened buildings of historical interest are re-erected and restored here – anything from a 14th-c monastic roof through an 18th-c dovecot and icehouse to a 1946 prefab; demonstrations of traditional skills and building techniques as the buildings are restored. Snacks, shop, disabled access; cl Mon exc Jun, July and Aug, Fri in Mar and Nov, all Dec-Feb; £3, slightly less out of season. BROMSGROVE MUSEUM Past industries and crafts, with 15 shops in a Victorian street setting. Shop; cl Sun am, all Dec; £1. DAUB AND WATTLE'S POTTERY Largely unchanged pottery building with displays and shop; cl Sun.

Burcot SO9771 BURCOT FORGE has potters, stained-glass firing, wrought ironwork etc; usually at least something open exc Sun am.

Great Witley SO7664 WITLEY COURT Astonishing ruin of a Jacobean house transformed into an Italianate palace by the Earl of Dudley, and partly destroyed by fire in 1937. It's an elaborate place, with ceiling paintings, an enormous Perseus fountain, and balustraded garden – very atmospheric to wander through. The splendidly baroque CHURCH by the house, overlooking the lake, is one of the county's great finds; it has photographs of the house in its former glory. Snacks, shop; cl winter Mons; £1.20. EASTGROVE COTTAGE GARDEN (B4196 towards Shrawley) has interesting and unusual plants in a cottage-garden setting by an ancient timbered house (not open); good plants for sale. Disabled access; cl Tues, Weds, and all Aug; £1.

Hanbury SO9664 HANBURY HALL (NT) 18th-c country house with outstanding painted ceilings and staircase, fine porcelain, and contemporary icehouse and orangery in grounds. Snacks, shop, some disabled access; open pm Sat, Sun and Mon Apr-Oct; *£3. The CHURCH, high on a hill, has superb views over the countryside. THE JINNEY RING CRAFT CENTRE (B4091 Droitwich Rd) Twelve

varied craft workshops in beautiful timbered barns, inc glass, jewellery, pottery, woodturning, leatherwork and violin-making. Meals, snacks, shop, disabled access; cl Mon exc bank hols. They also organise regular craft courses. Nearby at Stock Green SO9858 WHITE COTTAGE has a profusion of interesting plants in colourful borders, pretty streamside, springtime wild garden; plant sales inc rare-species geraniums. Disabled access; cl Thurs, some Suns, phone (0386) 792414 to check, Oct-Easter; *£1.

Hartlebury SO8376 HEREFORD AND WORCESTER COUNTY MUSEUM Interesting museum in a wing of the castle, with unique collections of toys, costumes, and other elements of domestic life; also room settings, horse-drawn vehicles, reconstructed schoolroom and wheelwright's shop. Snacks, shop; cl am Fri, all Sat, Dec-Feb; £1.20. HARTLEBURY CASTLE STATE ROOMS Elegant rooms recounting history of the castle and the Bishops of Worcester, based here since 850. Shop, disabled access; open pm wknds and Weds, Easter-Sept; *75p.

Redditch SP0467 FORGE MILL NEEDLE MUSEUM AND BORDESLEY ABBEY VISITOR CENTRE The only remaining water-driven needle-

scouring mill, with demonstrations of 18th-c machinery and needlemaking, and displays of finds from the nearby 12th-c Cistercian abbey; very attractive grounds. Shop, disabled access with prior notice; cl am wknds, all Fri, and Dec-Feb; *£1.75.

Spetchley SO8953 Spetchley Park Gardens 140-acre gardens and park with both red and fallow deer, sweeping lawns and herbaceous borders, rose lawn, interesting trees and shrubs. Snacks, plant centre, disabled access; cl am Sun, Sat, Mon (exc bank hols), Oct-Mar; £2.

Stone SO8574 Stone House Unusual walled garden with colourful plants, esp climbers and tender flowering shrubs; interesting plant sales. Disabled access; cl Sun-Tues (exc Sun May-Jun), Nov-Feb; *£1.50.

West Hagley SO9080 Falconry Centre Frequent displays of falconry flights, with hawks, owls and other birds of prey. Meals, snacks, shop, disabled access; cl 25-26 Dec; *£2.50.

Wichenford SO7860 Dovecot (NT) Big, unusually constructed, timber-framed, wattle-and-daub 17th-c dovecot with nearly 600 nesting boxes; open daily Apr-Oct, winter by appointment, phone (0684) 850051; 60p.

Wychbold SO9265 Webbs Garden Centre (A38 towards Bromsgrove) is probably the best in the country, attractively laid out and recently extended, with a massive choice of things to buy, fine amusements for children and good disabled access; the thatched café is exemplary.

★ Other **attractive villages** inc Belbroughton SO9277 (the Queens is good for lunch); Chaddesley Corbett SO8973 (there's a fine, partly Norman church, and the Fox has a good carvery); Clifton-upon-Teme SO7162 (lots of quiet strolls above the orchards; the Red Lion's useful here); Feckenham SP0061, with an attractive green and some fine Georgian red brick; Ombersley SO8463, an attractive mix of handsome black-and-white timbered houses with elegant Georgian brick – both the Crown & Sandys Arms and Kings Arms are good for lunch; Upper Arley SO7680 on the Severn (the Severn Valley Railway, see above, stops at a station over the footbridge; the Harbour is useful for light lunches); and Wolverley SO8279, with quaint, steeply gabled cottages below a hilltop church – unusually, brick-built.

Correspondents reckon that the **Droitwich Spa** SO9063 brine baths are just the thing after an exhausting day's sightseeing; phone (0905) 794894 to book.

Walks

Paradoxically, it's over towards Birmingham that the topography is most interesting, with much of the land rising to over 1,000 feet. The **Lickey Hills Country Park** SO9975 is densely wooded, a fragment of primeval forest, with the views suddenly opening out over the sprawling city; waymarking makes the maze of paths and tracks less confusing. **Clent Hills Country Park** SO9379 is a fine hillscape, open and exhilarating; waymarked routes are provided. The Fountain at Clent SO9379 is useful for lunch.

Elsewhere, the **Wyre Forest** SO7575, on the Shropshire border, is a major broadleaved woodland, with numerous, ready-made Forestry Commission trails (leaflets available from the Visitor Centre; the Royal Forester nearby, if open, is useful for lunch). The **Abberley Hills** SO7567 near Stourport are far less trodden but rewarding, partly wooded, with good views and close to the extraordinary ruins of Witley Court (see above).

Pubs which are useful for **waterside walks** are the Camp House at Grimley SO8359 on the River Severn, the Fox & Hounds at Lulsley SO7455 for quiet Temeside orchards (and on up through Ravenshill Wood to Crews Hill, or instead along to the attractive Talbot at Knightwick SO5673), and on the Worcester & Birmingham Canal, the Firs at Dunhampstead SO9160, Navigation at Stoke Prior SO9468, Bowling Green at Stoke Works SO9468 (yes, it does have its own bowling green), and Queens Head at Stoke Pound SO9667.

Driving

This is not nearly such a rewarding area for leisurely country drives as either the Vale of Evesham and the Malvern Hills, or Herefordshire to the west. However, W of Worcester the B4197 through Martley has some quietly attractive views, and the B4204 crossing it is a pleasant country road. The B4194/B4196 S of Bewdley is quite a good road, though the Severn is not at its most engaging along here. The A456 has some worthwhile views, but can carry quite a bit of traffic.

Where to eat

Pensax SO7269 BELL Unspoilt and friendly 19th-c pub with good food, several changing real ales and open fires; dining room extension has a fine view over the hills to Wyre Forest; cl 25 Dec; fair disabled access (one step). **£17.50**|£2.25/£5.50.

Wychbold SO9265 THATCH (0527) 861412 Not a pub but part of Webbs Garden Centre (see above); open 9-7.30 (till 5 Sat, Sun and in winter) with wine licence, good-value snacks and meals in pleasant surroundings; cl 25-26 Dec; disabled access. **£14**|£1.90/£5.

Help this year from: *Pam Adsley, Derek and Sylvia Stephenson, D G Wood, Peter Lloyd, R B Crail, W H and E Thomas, Veronica Purcocks, Dr C A Brace, Tony and Lynne Gifford, Chris and Chris Vallely, N W Kingsley, C J Westmoreland, John Bowdler, Gordon Theaker, John and Beverley Bailey, John Bowdler, Phil and Sally Gorton, Ted George, Mr and Mrs P B Dowsett, A Y Drummond, Mrs C A Blake, Pat Bromley, Mrs V Nolan, Steve Thomas, Neil and Anita Christopher, David Wallington, Peter and Erica Davis, Mr and Mrs B H Robinson, Jill and Peter Bickley, P J Hanson, Graham Reeve, Peter Lloyd, Pauline Crossland, Dave Cawley, Alan and Heather Jacques, Dave Braisted, Roger Sherman, Chris Heathman.*

Hereford and Worcester Calendar

Some of these dates were provisional as we went to press.

JANUARY

1st **Bewdley** Duck Race – *plastic ducks dropped into the River Severn at Bewdley Bridge*

APRIL

2nd **Stoke Heath** Avoncroft in Steam *at Avoncroft Museum of Buildings – till Mon 4*; **Worcester** Civil War Encampment *at The Commandery – till Sun 10*

4th **Hartlebury** Easter Eggstravaganza *at Hereford and Worcester County Museum*

16th **Bewdley** Severn Valley Railway Steam Gala – *till Sun 17*

MAY

2nd **Leominster** May Fair

3rd **Hereford** May Fair – *till Thurs 5*

6th **Malvern** Spring Garden Show – *till Sun 8*

21st **Malvern** Festival – *till 4 Jun*

28th **Worcester** Oak Apple Day, *celebration of the restoration of King Charles II at The Commandery – till Sun 29*

30th **Redditch** Needlework Exhibition *at Forge Mill Needle Museum – till 30 Sept*

JUNE

5th **Hartlebury** Transport Day *at Hereford and Worcester County Museum*

11th **Worcester** Re-enactment of the Visit of King Charles I, *inc fair and procession at The Commandery – till Sun 12*

14th **Malvern** Three Counties Agricultural Show *at Three Counties Centre – till Thurs 16*

18th **Kidderminster** Carnival

24th **Upton-upon-Severn** Jazz Festival – *till Sun 26*

30th **Ross-on-Wye** Carnival – *till 6 July*

JULY

2nd **Worcester** Carnival

10th **Hartlebury** Victorian Street Market *at Hereford and Worcester County Museum*

15th **Harvington** Festival *at Harvington Hall, with jazz and baroque concert, Elizabethan afternoon and open-air concert on last day – till Sun 17*

17th **Redditch** Medieval Fayre *at Forge Mill Needle Museum*

AUGUST

3rd **Malvern** National Pony Society Show *at Three Counties Showground – till Thurs 4*

7th **Hartlebury** County Fair *at Hereford and Worcester County Museum*

Hereford and Worcestershire Calendar

August cont.

13th **Worcester** Tudor Festival *at The Commandery, to celebrate the visit of Queen Elizabeth I in 1575 – till Sun 14*

21st **Stourport-on-Severn** North Worcestershire Fuchsia Society Show *at Riverside Meadow*

29th **Ledbury** Street Carnival; **Leominster** Agricultural Show; **Ross-on-Wye** Regatta

29th **Ross-on-Wye** Regatta

September

8th **Worcester** Jolly Small Brewers Beer Festival *at Faithful City Brewery – till Sun 11*

October

1st **Redditch** Embroidery Exhibition *at Forge Mill Needle Museum – till 30 Nov*

6th **Ross** and District Arts Festival – *till Sun 9*

10th **Ledbury** Hop Fair

November

5th **Worcester** Fireworks

December

3rd **Worcester** Green Fair *at Woods Country Park*

HERTFORDSHIRE

St Albans justifies a short stay – otherwise this is mainly days-out territory.

There are quite a few destinations which make rewarding outings in Hertfordshire, including such highlights as Hatfield House, the unusual zoological museum at Tring, Knebworth, and the gardens of Benington Lordship. Children particularly enjoy the wildlife park at Broxbourne. Though Hertford's older parts are attractive, the only place here with real scope for a town-based weekend is St Albans: behind its undeniably modern face are the well-preserved remains of the Roman city, some other interesting old streets and historic corners, and – best in late June, but good all summer – great rose gardens.

Where to stay

Chipperfield TL0401 TWO BREWERS Kings Langley WD4 9BS (0923) 265 266 **£107**; 20 rms. Comfortably pubby Forte hotel with relaxing views of pretty village green; spotlessly kept, decent food and beers, and pleasant nearby walks.
St Albans TL1507 WHITE HART Holywell Hill AL1 1EZ (0727) 853624 **£45w**; 11 rms. Friendly but civilised hotel with lots of character and charm, and a long, entertaining history; comfortable bar with antique panelling, handsome furnishings, good restaurant.

To see and do

St Albans TL1407 was one of the most important Roman towns in Northern Europe, and has some fine, well-excavated remains in peaceful surroundings. There are other quiet quarters too, most notably in and around the CATHEDRAL. It did not come through the Reformation unscathed, but there are plenty of Norman features, some fine 13th- and 14th-c paintings in the nave, and even some Saxon traces (the transept pillars); up on a mound, it gives good views. Meals, snacks, shop, disabled access. The great 14th-c ABBEY GATEHOUSE beyond leads down to a neat park, its lake and willow-edged stream packed with ducks. This is the sort of town that repays a keen-eyed stroll, with interesting corners of considerable antiquity tucked between the modern shops which on first impressions seem to dominate it.

The visible remains of VERULAMIUM, as it was known, are down in the south-west corner of the town past the cathedral and park (coming from outside, most easily reached by the A4147 off the Hemel Hempstead exit from M1 junction 7). There is a carefully restored mosaic and hypocaust, while the well-organised MUSEUM has a lively interpretation of everyday life in a Roman city, as well as videos and jewellery, wall paintings and other domestic items found on the site. Shop, disabled access; £2.40. The ROMAN THEATRE is not large by the standards of some others in England (room for 1,600), but taking into account its good state of preservation is unique. First built around AD 160, though the

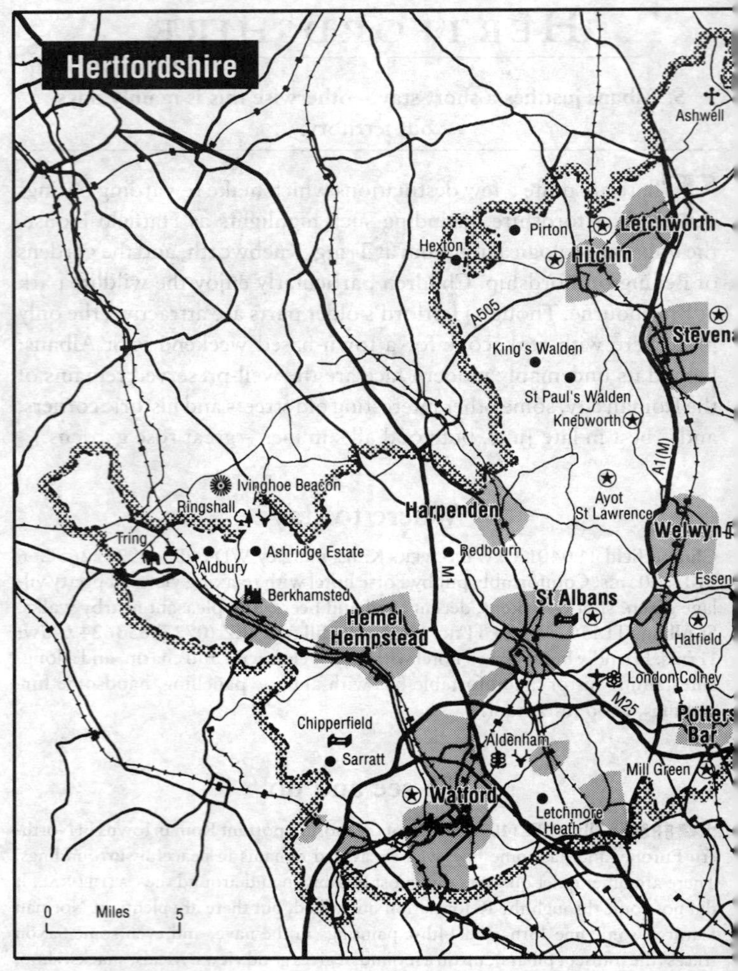

next two centuries saw various modifications. Shop, disabled access; cl Christmas and New Year; £1.

MUSEUM OF ST ALBANS (Hatfield Rd) History of St Albans since the departure of the Romans, taking in its development from medieval market town to commuter city. Also illustrates the natural history and geology of south-east Herts; shop, disabled access to ground floor only. KINGSBURY WATERMILL Half a mile from the city on the banks of the River Ver, this 16th-c watermill still has one working waterwheel, and now also houses a museum and art gallery incl a display of old farming implements. Meals, snacks, shop; cl Mon; *85p. GORHAMBURY Interesting collections in this charming 18th-c house inc an extensive assemblage of 17th-c family portraits and some 16th-c enamelled glass. Shop; open only pm Thurs May-Sept; £3. ORGAN MUSEUM (Camp Rd) Collection of automatically operated organs and other musical instruments inc Wurlitzer and Rutt theatre organs; recitals every Sun 2.15-4.30, other

concerts throughout the year. Teas, shop, disabled access (but no facilities); open Sun pm only; £1.50. GREBE HOUSE WILDLIFE CENTRE Home of regional nature conservation trust, with growing number of displays and activities centred around the local wildlife. Shop, disabled access; cl Sun am, wkdys Jan and Feb.

The most striking of the town's non-ecclesiastical buildings is the medieval stone CLOCK TOWER, almost unique; its bell, striking on the hour, is even older than the tower itself. Fine views over the city and surrounding country from the top; open wknds and bank hols Easter-mid-Sept; 25p. Nearby, French Row is a narrow alley of striking timbered buildings jettied out over the street, right by a modern shopping centre.

A mile or two outside the town, the GARDENS OF THE ROSE (B4630 S) have over 1,600 cultivars, many in mass plantings. These are the showgrounds of the Royal National Rose Society, and as well as old and modern roses, new roses are shown here in the International Trial Ground. Snacks, shop, disabled access; cl late Oct-early Jun; £3.50.

A stroll through the town in search of other notable buildings (the tourist information office in the Town Hall, Market Pl, has helpful guide maps) is rewarded by the surprisingly large number of decent pubs here. In French Row, the Fleur de Lys (though undistinguished as a pub) is a remarkable medieval building. Down between abbey gate and park, the Fighting Cocks is based on a building which had some connection with the abbey, and its interesting layout inc the clearly discernible shape of a cockpit. Down in the quietly attractive, largely Georgian St Michaels St, the Rose & Crown is very civilised. Other pubs well worth visiting if you pass them include the Goat in Sopwell St, Garibaldi in Albert St, Blue Anchor in Fishpool St and Crown in Hatfield Rd. The Cock is worth looking out because of its bizarre history; it seems to have been a charnel house, probably at the time of one of the battles of St Albans, as its floors were found to rest on thick foundations of human bones.

Other things to see and do

Aldenham TQ1398 COUNTRY PARK has plenty of space for children to run around in, with an adventure play area, nature trails and a herd of longhorn cattle.

★ **Ardeley** TL3027 Attractive thatched village where CROMER WINDMILL is the last remaining post-mill in the county, dating from the 13th c and now lovingly restored; open second and fourth Weds May-Sept, plus bank hols; 75p. The Jolly Waggoner is good for lunch.

Ayot St Lawrence TL1916 is a delightful little backwater, with a very picturesque, 12th-c ivy-covered RUINED CHURCH; the existing CHURCH is an incongruously grand neo-Grecian affair. SHAW'S CORNER The house and its contents have been kept much as they were when GBS lived here, from 1906-1950, and Shaw devotees will enjoy seeing his exercise machine, pen, spectacles, and even the soft homburg he wore for 60 years. Try and go on a wkdy when more is open; cl Sun am, all day Mon and Tues, Nov-Mar; £2.80. The Brocket Arms is good for lunch.

★ **Benington** TL3023 is one of the county's prettiest villages, its church lovely when the snowdrops are out in late Feb. BENINGTON LORDSHIP 7-acre, Edwardian terraced gardens kept well up to date; with many unusual plants – fine herbaceous borders, roses and rock garden, and a particularly lovely splash of snowdrops. The grounds inc a very picturesque, early 19th-c, 'Norman' ruined gatehouse, actually put together from stones of the genuine, moated, Norman ruined keep. Plant sales; open pm Weds Apr-Sept, Sun Apr-Aug, bank hols, pm Weds and Sun in Feb too; £2.20. The Bell here is useful for lunch.

Berkhamsted SP9807 BERKHAMSTED CASTLE Original earthen motte and bailey built by the half-brother of William the Conqueror, with ruins of a 12th-c stone keep. It was later owned by the Black Prince, Chaucer was clerk of works, and King John of France was imprisoned here. The Boat down by the canal is good for lunch.

☺ **Broxbourne** TL3707 PARADISE WILDLIFE PARK Friendly zoo and leisure park with animals such as lions, monkeys, camels and zebras, events all day from meeting the python to feeding the lions, and adventure playground, fun fair, crazy golf and woodland walk. Meals (they do a three-course carvery on Sun), snacks, shop, disabled access; *£4.

Hatfield TL2308 HATFIELD HOUSE Extensive rolling parkland and fine gardens surround this great Jacobean house, built in 1611 by Robert Cecil on the site of an earlier palace, a childhood home of Elizabeth I. Inside are plenty of items from this and later periods, inc fine furnishings and tapestries, portraits of the queen, and her silk stockings, perhaps among the earliest worn in this country. There's also a William IV kitchen and the National Collection of Model Soldiers, with over 3,000 exhibits. The gardens have been recreated in 17th-c style, with a scented garden and knot garden containing plants that were typical between the 15th and 17th c; also nature trails, wildlife and wildfowl. Meals, snacks, shop, disabled access; house cl am, Mon exc bank hols, Oct-Mar; park and gardens cl Sun, Good Fri, Oct-Mar; £4.50.

Hertford TL3212 has some quiet older parts, with handsomely pargeted buildings in the old main Fore St (inc the good Salisbury Arms). There are several antique shops in St Andrew St (one in a fine 15th-c house). The so-called CASTLE is in fact the 15th-c gatehouse for Edward IV's original moated castle, carefully restored and now occupied by the council; open pm first Sun in month (not Oct-Apr), with a brass band outside. The extensive riverside grounds, always open, inc the massive Norman flint walls of Henry II's castle, and a stone commemorating the first general synod of the English Church on 24 Sept 673. Opposite the castle remains, the White Horse is useful for lunch. MUSEUM Collections of local archaeology, history, geology and natural history in an elegant 17th-c building, with various temporary exhibitions and an elegant Jacobean knot garden. Shop, disabled access to ground floor only; cl Sun and Mon. SEED WAREHOUSE Four Roman ovens were excavated at Foxholes Farm just outside Hertford, and the best preserved is now installed in this 18th-c building (home of the Hertfordshire Archaeological Trust). The MCMULLENS BREWERY is a striking Victorian building on the river (the Woolpack nr it is good value; the Old Barge by the Lee Navigation Canal is also useful for lunch). Nearby Hertingfordbury is an attractive village, between river and beechwoods.

Hitchin TL1829 has a lot of Georgian and some older buildings rather lost among the new, esp along Tilehouse St and Bridge St. The 14th-c riverside CHURCH is very attractive. The MUSEUM AND ART GALLERY has an interesting, reconstructed Victorian chemist's shop among other displays on local working and domestic life; also the regimental collection of the Hertfordshire yeomanry, and a costume gallery covering two centuries. There's a physic garden outside, recreated as one might have been three centuries ago. Shop, disabled access to ground floor only; cl Sun am and bank hols.

Knebworth TL2520 KNEBWORTH HOUSE, GARDENS AND COUNTRY PARK Perhaps best known for providing a popular venue for various events and activities, the house and gardens themselves are well worth seeing. Sir Edward Bulwer Lytton was responsible for the spectacular high-Gothic decoration which radically altered the appearance of the original Tudor mansion. Of special interest is the splendid Jacobean great hall, esp its plaster ceiling and panelling; and the exhibition on the British Raj. The gardens were redesigned by Lutyens and the 250-acre park inc a miniature railway, extensive adventure playground and a deer park. Meals, snacks, shop, disabled access; house cl am, Mon (exc bank hols), Oct-Mar, with limited opening Apr, May and Sept – perhaps best to check first, phone (0438) 812661; £4. Along the outer edge of the park is the pretty little hamlet of Old Knebworth; the Lytton Arms here is particularly popular for its wide range of real ales.

Letchworth TL2232 was the country's first garden city, begun in 1903, a fact commemorated at the interesting FIRST GARDEN CITY HERITAGE MUSEUM, where the exhibits are displayed in the original thatched cottages of the architects, charting both the development of the town, and the whole thinking behind this uniquely 20th-c idea. Shop, disabled access; cl am exc Sat, Sun. STANDALONE FARM (Wilbury Rd) Working farm with plenty of traditional animals to stroke and feed, inc shire horse; also daily milking, working blacksmith and natural history displays. Snacks, shop, disabled access; cl Oct-Feb; £2.30. There's also a local MUSEUM AND ART GALLERY.

London Colney TL1803 MOSQUITO AIRCRAFT MUSEUM The Mosquito bombers were developed here in secret from 1939, and now the site houses a collection of 20 different de Havilland aircraft, as well as aero engines, full workshop, and other memorabilia. Snacks, shop, disabled access; open Thurs pm and wknds Mar-Oct; *£2. There are pretty riverside gardens down by the bridge; the Green Dragon here is useful for lunch. AYLETT NURSERIES Good garden centre specialising in geraniums, fuchsias and esp their award-winning dahlias. Meals, snacks, disabled access; cl four days at Christmas. The trial grounds for the dahlias have moved to Bowmans Farm, five mins away by car, and you can walk round from Aug to first frost of autumn.

Mill Green TL2409 MILL GREEN MUSEUM This water-powered mill has been producing corn for around 1,000 years; it's been well restored, and there's also a little local history museum, as well as demonstrations of crafts most Suns, from paper-quilling to love-spoon carving. Shop, disabled access to ground floor only; cl am wknds, all day Mon, milling Sun pm only.

★ **Much Hadham** TL4319 FORGE MUSEUM AND VICTORIAN COTTAGE GARDEN Based around a working blacksmith, the story of such craftsmen through the ages with examples of old equipment and tools; outside, the Victorian-style garden has an unusual bee shelter. Shop; open Sat and pm Sun all year, Tues, Fri and bank hols Apr-Sept (but cl Good Fri); *80p. The village is attractive, with fine Tudor and Georgian houses, and the Jolly Waggoners is useful for lunch.

Ringshall SP9814 Right on the county border, the ASHRIDGE ESTATE (NT) has 4,000 acres of unspoilt woodlands and open spaces, with plenty of deer and other wildlife (inc the dormouse, though you won't see it in daylight), and a monument erected for the Duke of Bridgewater. Teas summer wknds, shop and information centre, some disabled access; parking £1, monument £1.

† **Royston** TL3540 Though the town's largely modern there are some attractive Tudor buildings in Upper King St, and interesting ones to be tracked down among the modern shops. The local MUSEUM, tracing the history and development of the town, is housed in a former monastic chapel, and the partly 13th-c CHURCH was also a part of this pre-Dissolution large monastery. No doubt under the buildings of the town are a great many interesting remains, as it seems to have been a continuously occupied settlement on the crossing of the Roman Icknield Way and Ermine St. Right by this central crossing is an odd underground cavern with rough relief carvings; open summer wknds.

Sawbridgeworth TL4814 KECKSYS FARM Rare breeds of pig, as well as sheep, cattle, poultry and rabbits; right by the river, where coarse fishing is available. Disabled access; open Sun; *£2.

† **Stevenage** TL2325 STEVENAGE MUSEUM The story of this New Town from earliest times, housed in the undercroft of the parish church of St George; shop, disabled access; cl bank hols. In the Old Town, there are some old buildings around the 12th-14th-c CHURCH of St Nicholas. ROGER HARVEY GARDEN WORLD (Bragbury Lane) Garden centre in historic farmhouse, with lots of hardy trees, shrubs, roses, heather, and houseplant conservatory; also pets and animals to distract the children. Meals, snacks, shop, disabled access; cl 25-26 Dec.

Tring SP9211 WALTER ROTHSCHILD ZOOLOGICAL MUSEUM Largely consisting of the remarkably eclectic collections of the second Lord Rothschild, started when he was a little boy: extinct, rare and exotic specimens among thousands of mammals, insects, birds, fish, reptiles and domestic dogs – even a display of dressed fleas. Snacks, shop; cl 1 Jan, Good Fri, 24-26 Dec; £2. There's good access to the Grand Union Canal here, for long towpath walks.

! **Ware** TL3514 SCOTT'S GROTTO Extending 67 feet into the hillside under a modern housing development, with underground passages and chambers decorated with flints, shells, stones and minerals; it was built in the

1760s by the poet John Scott, and is one of the finest bits of romantic gothickry in the world. Visitors are advised to wear flat shoes and bring a torch; open pm Sat and bank hols Apr-Sept. Several of the private gardens running down to the quiet River Lee have gazebos over the water, neatly restored with crisp white paintwork.

Watford TQ1196 The local MUSEUM inc displays on the local industries of printing and brewing, as well as a wartime exhibition featuring the Watford Home Guard, the basis for local boy Jimmy Perry's TV series *Dad's Army*. Shop, disabled access; cl 1-2, Sun, bank hols. CHESLYN GARDENS are an unexpected pleasure, with 3½ acres of woodland and formal gardens, and an aviary; disabled access; cl 25-26 Dec. From Cassiobury Park there are CANAL BOAT TRIPS along the Grand Union Canal on Sun pm and bank hols Easter-Oct, as well as Tues and Thurs in Aug; £3.

Welwyn TL2316 ROMAN BATHS Excavated before the construction of the A1 and since then rather unusually preserved within the motorway embankment, this Roman bathhouse is all that remains of a 3rd-c villa. Very good condition, with explanatory displays. Shop, disabled access; cl am, all day Mon-Weds; *80p.

★ **Attractive villages** inc Aldbury SP9612 (with a perfect village green, stocks etc, teas; the Valiant Trooper's a good pub), Ashwell TL2639 (with an unusually tall church tower; the Bushel & Strike just beside it and the Rose & Crown are both useful for lunch), and Westmill TL3626 (a happy combination of neat green, tiled cottages and fine old church; the Sword in Hand here's good). Others, all with decent pubs, inc Braughing TL3925 (pronounced Braffing; its 14th-c riverside church is pretty), Great Amwell TL3712 (pretty conjunction of church, pre-Norman Emma's Well and pool with islets), Letchmore Heath TQ1597, Pirton TL1431 (the village green is actually the remains of a Norman motte and bailey), Redbourn TL1012 (despite motorway noise Church End with its workhouse and Norman church is pretty), Rushden TL3031 and Sarratt TL0499. The thatch and timbering of Great Hormead TL4030 is attractive, and Standon TL3922 has some good timbered buildings in its curving High St.

Walks

Large areas of this county are taken up by London's northward-stretching fingers through Rickmansworth, Chorleywood, Watford, Borehamwood, Potters Bar and the continuous Enfield/Cheshunt/Hoddesdon development, and also by the first early 20th-c 'new towns', the garden cities of Letchworth and Welwyn, and their more modern successors Hatfield, Hemel Hempstead and Stevenage. But between and beyond these there are good green windows of carefully preserved farmland and some more wooded countryside. These yield pockets of good walking terrain, though there is little that is really outstanding. In the east, the villages and rolling farmland have an East Anglian flavour, quite rural in many places such as around **Benington** TL3023, **Ardeley** TL3027, **St Paul's Walden** (birthplace of the Queen Mother) TL1922 and **King's Walden** TL1523. **Ayot St Lawrence** TL1916, west of Welwyn, is conveniently close to link to a walk along the **River Lea**, which has been dammed by Brocket Hall to form a lake (in view from the public right of way). Around **Essendon** TL2708 is much-walked, mildly hilly country, with pleasantly varied, village-to-village paths; the Candlestick is well placed for refreshment, and the Sailsbury Crest in the village itself is good for lunch.

In the extreme west of the county (indeed, actually in Bucks because of a wiggle in the county boundary), **Ivinghoe Beacon** SP9617, a protruding finger of the Chilterns, is the finish of the long-distance Ridgeway Path which begins in Wiltshire. The slopes, too steep for ploughing, comprise woodland, scrub and unspoilt downland; from the beacon itself you look down over eight counties. Aldbury SP9612 provides the nearest good pub, and those looking for a shorter stroll from here can explore the great woodlands of the **Ashridge Estate**, superb for autumn colours. The **Grand Union Canal**, nr Tring, SP9211 has a part-abandoned offshoot, the Wendover Arm, and the still-operational Aylesbury Arm; feeder reservoirs at Wilstone SP9014 and Marsworth SP9214 (again, just over the Bucks border) lie adjacent, both with waterside pubs within reach of the canal towpaths.

There's also canal access from the Boat at Gravel Path, Berkhamsted SP9807, Fisheries at Boxmoor TL0306 and the pretty Three Horseshoes at Bourne End TL0206.

Other pubs handy for walks inc the Alford Arms at Frithsden TL0110, Huntsman at Goose Green TL3509 (for Hertford Heath), Two Brewers on Chipperfield Common TL0401, Waggoners at Ayot Green TL2213, Two Brewers at Northaw TL2802 (the ancient Great Wood is very pretty) and the Greyhound at Wigginton SP9410 (where the landlord's very helpful with suggestions; the 18th-c summerhouse in the woods is an odd find). **Scales Wood** up near Anstey TL4133 is also good for walks, and in the woods above Hexton is an easily traced Iron-Age hill fort, Ravensburgh Castle TL1029 (the Live & Let Live in nearby Pegsdon is handy for refreshment).

Driving

There are no really scenic drives in this county, but there are several tranquil country outings. The back road through Dane End, Great Munden and on round past Wood End through Ardeley gives a good idea of the quiet, cut-off seclusion of this part of Hertfordshire, despite Stevenage being so close. Sandwiched between the M1 and the A1(M) N of Wheathampstead, the B651 runs through pretty countryside, as does the nearly parallel B656. An interesting back road is the Roman road through Coleman Green (where a ruined roadside chimney stack is preserved for its associations with John Bunyan – the nearby pub named after him is a useful stop).

North of Ware the A10, an old Roman road, doesn't carry that much traffic now and gives good views, with pleasant short detours to some of the villages mentioned above – and at Wadesmill there are some quaint, creeper-covered Norman ruins by the river, near the showy 19th-c bridge (the Sow & Pigs just S is a good stop).

There are quite a few roadside farm shops in the area, with massive glasshouse installations along the Lee Valley.

Where to eat

Ardeley TL3027 JOLLY WAGGONER Friendly and genuine country pub with thriving restaurant, two unspoilt bars, and wide range of good home-cooked bar food; cl evenings of 25 and 26 Dec; no under-12s. **£21**|£2.10/£10.50.

Puckeridge TL3823 WHITE HART (0920) 821 309 Lively but cosy village pub with floodlit garden full of animals; enormous choice of very good food in bar and restaurant (not Sun pm), emphasis on fresh fish, separate vegetarian and children's menus; children under 5 if prior permission given on the day; disabled access. £10|£1.60/£4.

Watton-at-Stone TL3019 GEORGE & DRAGON (0920) 830285 Sophisticated pub first licensed in 1603; antiques and daily newspapers, friendly, efficient service, and imaginative bar food inc lots of fresh fish. £3.90/£7.35.

Help this year from: *Charles Bardswell, Steve Bayley, JW, CW, Denise Plummer, Jim Froggatt, John Boylan, David Surridge, J A Boucher, Margaret and Allen Marsden, Stephen Brown, Stephen King, Michael and Alison Sandy, Clive Fry, Lesley Johnson, Richard Church.*

HERTFORDSHIRE CALENDAR

Some of these dates were provisional as we went to press.

JANUARY

8th **Tring** Wildlife Photographer of the Year Exhibition – *till 27 Feb*

21st **Hatfield** Antiques Fair *at Hatfield House – till Sun 23*

23rd **Hoddesdon** Wildfowl Guided Walk *at Ryehouse Marsh RSPB, 10-12 pm*

MARCH

27th **Hoddesdon** Beginners' Birdwatching Walk *at Ryehouse Marsh RSPB, 10-12 pm*

APRIL

3rd **Knebworth** Jousting Tournament *at Knebworth House – till Mon 4*

9th **Colliers End** Game and Countryman Fair *inc falconry, dog shows and fishing classes at St Edmund's College – till Sun 10*

22nd **Hatfield** Antiques Fair *at Hatfield House – till Sun 24*

24th **Hoddesdon** Returning Migrants Guided Walk *at Ryehouse Marsh RSPB, 10-12 pm*

25th **Hertford** Theatre Week – *till Sat 30*

MAY

1st **Hertford** Music Week *inc ballet – till Sat 7*; **Hoddesdon** Dawn Chorus Guided Walk *at Ryehouse Marsh RSPB, followed by coffee and croissants, 4-6 am*

2nd **Hertford** Art Society Exhibition *at the Corn Exchange – till Sat 14*

5th **Hatfield** Crafts Fair *at Hatfield House: 300 stands inc blacksmiths, spinners, furniture-makers, weavers; also maypole dancing, Morris men and Punch & Judy – till Sun 8*

22nd **Hoddesdon** Sunset Guided Walk, *maybe spotting cuckoos, at Ryehouse Marsh RSPB, 7-9 pm*

28th **Knebworth** Country Show *at Knebworth House – till Mon 30*; **Redbourn** Hertfordshire County Show *at The Showground – till Sun 29*

HERTFORDSHIRE CALENDAR

JUNE

5th **Hoddesdon** Sunset Guided Walk *at Ryehouse Marsh RSPB, 7-9 pm*; **Knebworth** MG Owners Club Rally *at Knebworth House*

11th **Great Amwell** Steam Rally *with fête and funfare at Hillside Farm – till Sun 12*

12th **Stevenage** Day

18th **Hatfield** Festival of Gardening *at Hatfield House – till Sun 19*

25th **Hatfield** Bentley Drivers Club Concourse, *about 350 cars, at Hatfield House*

JULY

2nd **Ware** Week, *with carnival and fête on opening day – till Sat 9*

9th **Stevenage** Cactus Show *at Roger Harvey Garden World – till Sun 10*

10th **Hoddesdon** Butterflies and Dragonflies Guided Walk *at Ryehouse Marsh RSPB. 10-12 pm*; **Knebworth** Pre-50 American Auto Club Rally *at Knebworth House*

17th **Redditch** Medieval Fayre *at Forge Mill Museum*

30th **Knebworth** National Street Rod Association, *hot rods at Knebworth House – till Sun 31*; **Stevenage** Fuchsia Show *at Roger Harvey Garden World – till Sun 31*

AUGUST

7th **Hatfield** Transport Spectacular *at Hatfield House – classic kit and American cars, military vehicles, buses and agricultural machinery*

27th **Hartham** Hertford Horse Show *on the Common*

28th **Great Amwell** Hertfordshire Motor Show

SEPTEMBER

2nd **Hatfield** Antiques Fair *at Hatfield House – till Sun 4*

10th **Hoddesdon** Carnival

OCTOBER

1st **Redditch** Embroidery Exhibition *at Forge Mill Museum – till 30 Nov*; **Royston** Festival Week *– till Sat 8*

NOVEMBER

4th **Hatfield** Antiques Fair *at Hatfield House – till Sun 6*

5th **Stevenage** Fireworks *at Fairlands Valley Park*

6th **Cheshunt** Fireworks *at Cheshunt Park*

12th **Letchworth Garden City** Craft Weekend *with animals at Standalone Farm – till Sun 13*

Humberside

Beverley and Hull are contrasting candidates for a weekend stay; there are several good places to visit outside, but the scenery is not outstanding.

Much of this area is too flat to stand out as a place for a satisfying countryside weekend. The sweeping landscapes of the rolling Wolds probably have the broadest appeal, though for most people suffer by comparison with the North York Moors a little to the north. However, north of the Humber, in what people here still think of as East Yorkshire, there are quite a few places worth visiting, including ones to amuse children.

Beverley is an archetypal quiet country town with fine old buildings and a magnificent minster church. Hull is a big port that has worked hard to make itself attractive and interesting for visitors. Both have a lot of character. As they are close to each other, you could stay in one and see the other too – as well as making forays into the countryside. Outside, our suggestions of places to visit would start with the Penny Arcadia in Pocklington, the fishing heritage centre in Grimsby, and three stately homes in splendid grounds – Burton Agnes Hall, Sledmere House and, at Sproatley, Burton Constable Hall. Bridlington has a certain charm.

Prices are generally low in the area – you get a lot for your money here.

Where to stay

Beverley TA0340 Beverley Arms HU17 8DD (0482) 869241 **£107**; 57 rms. Georgian-fronted, pleasantly modernised coaching inn; disabled access; pets welcome.

Hull TA0928 Forte Crest Castle St HU1 2BX (0482) 225221 **£69.40w**; 99 rms. Modern purpose-built hotel with fine views over the marina, bar-lounge with nautical decorations, and good restaurant food; disabled access.

To see and do

Beverley ★ ✝ Beverley is an attractive country town, in a way like a small-scale York, with much the same sort of appeal. Its minster is a wonderful 12th-14th-c building, with elegant buttressing and elaborately pinnacled towers. The W front is richly carved yet extraordinarily harmonious. Inside are several delights, inc the intricately carved Percy Tomb Canopy, and the unusual Saxon Fridstol, one of only two such seats in the country and connected with the minster's right of sanctuary. Shop, disabled access; cl Sun am, guided tours in summer only. The former wealth of the town can be guessed at from the magnificence of another subsidiary church not far away, St Mary's Church in Hengate; its interior decoration reflects the fact that it was paid for by the minstrels' guild – evidently songwriters were as well paid then as they are now. Opposite is the White Horse, a quaint old gaslit bare-boarded tavern; a more orthodox place for lunch is the Queens Head. There are many fine Georgian buildings in the partly pedestrianised city, and several antique shops and the like – though it's still very much an honest market town rather than a tourist place. Up to 1,000 animals, mainly pigs, are still sold at the Tues and Thurs cattle market.

MUSEUM OF ARMY TRANSPORT (Flamingate) A very militaristic atmosphere in this huge hangar, with realistic settings for some of the dozens of vehicles displayed – down to farm-building camouflage for the Second World War and scratchy sand for the Gulf War. Children like it a lot: being able to get into the jeeps and so on makes it much more fun for them than many museums, and there's a special area for them. Other exhibits include the story of women's involvement in the war. Meals, snacks, shop, disabled access; cl 24-26 Dec; £2.50.

GUILDHALL Now used for a county court and Mayor's parlour, the building was first established in 1500 and then rebuilt in 1762; exhibits inc civic regalia and ancient charters. Tourist information centre, disabled access on ground floor only; cl Sun in winter, 25-26 Dec. ART GALLERY AND MUSEUM Many and various local antiquities, pictures of Beverley and Victorian memorabilia, with a regimental museum and lots of works by Fred Elwell the woodcarver, most famous for his work in the minster; cl 12.30-2 pm, Thurs pm, all bank hols.

Hull Kingston-upon-Hull is the full name of this big port, which is surprisingly pleasant for visitors. On the waterfront the former docks have been well tidied up. The landing stage for the former Humber ferry is now an attractive pedestrian enclave with some solid well-restored Georgian buildings (and a good pub the Mine[illegible]a, brewing its own beer). Nearby, the original dock has become a yacht marina, with quite cheerfully buoyant modern buildings around it. Away from the water, some of the most ancient buildings in the narrow streets of the old town have survived, notably on the High St (where the Olde Black Boy is a useful port of call – its name recalls the slave-trade deals that were made here, just down the street from the house where Wilberforce was born). One of the most delightful old buildings is the Olde Whyte Harte just off Silver St; it was in its heavily panelled upper room that the town's Governor made the fateful decision to lock the town's gate against King Charles in 1642, depriving him of the arsenal that might otherwise have swung the Civil War in his favour. These two enclaves, the old town and former docks, are separated from each other by good main roads through to the modern container and ferry docks; the traffic just sweeps by, leaving them as self-contained islands – very quiet at weekends.

Most of the museums and so forth are concentrated in the old town, so it's easy to walk from one to another; several are currently developing quite enthusiastically. It's impossible to miss the TOWN DOCKS MUSEUM (Queen Victoria Sq), a massive yet solidly stylish three-domed Victorian building, well set up with good displays on various aspects of

Hull's maritime history, inc whales and whaling, ships and shipping – also a Victorian court room; shop, disabled access; cl Sun am, 25-26 Dec, Good Fri. OLD GRAMMAR SCHOOL (South Church Side) Rapidly expanding museum of local social history, following the story of Hull people from the 16th c to the present, from their birth and through their working lives; shop, disabled access; cl Sun am, 25-26 Dec, Good Fri. WILBERFORCE HOUSE (High St) Georgian and Jacobean rooms in this early 17th-c house, the birthplace of William Wilberforce, with interesting displays on slavery and the fight against it, and period costumes and chemist shop; shop; cl Sun am, 25-26 Dec, 1 Jan, Good Fri. WATER MUSEUM (Springhead Ave) Easy enough today to get water just by turning a tap, but this museum shows it wasn't always so simple; the main feature is a beam engine that in its day raised over 4,000 gallons of water a minute from the well below. Shop, some disabled access; cl am, all day Mon, Christmas week. FERENS ART GALLERY (Queen Victoria Sq) A good general collection, particularly strong on Frank Brangwyn, and enterprisingly run, with good visiting exhibitions. Meals and snacks, shop, disabled access; cl Sun am, 25-26 Dec, Good Fri. HULL MUSEUM OF TRANSPORT (High St) Another expanding collection, so far devoted to local public transport, and to bicycles, some weird and wonderful; meals and snacks, shop, disabled access; cl Sun am, 25-26 Dec, Good Fri. SPURN LIGHTSHIP Operating from the 1920s to the 1970s, and now moored in Hull Marina – interesting to go below decks and imagine being confined to this for weeks at a time, not going anywhere, tossed about in storms or blanketed in fog; shop; cl Sun am, Mon and Tues in winter. MAISTER HOUSE (High St) Only the staircase and entrance hall are open in this mid-18th-c rebuilding, but the staircase is splendid – Palladian stonework and wrought iron, while the doors are ornate and finely carved; cl wknds and public hols; 80p. NT. The HULL AND EAST RIDING MUSEUM, which has been very good, is closed until late 1995 for refurbishment.

Other things to see and do

Barton-upon-Humber TA0322 BARTON CLAY PITS A country park based around several old clay pits, with nature reserves, walks, fishing (extensive reed beds), sailing and other activities. Good views of the Humber Bridge.

★ **Blacktoft** SE8424 is an attractive village, and its pub the Hope & Anchor, with tables out by the waterside, is great for bird-watchers, being right by the RSPB marsh reserve. The SOUTH FARM CRAFT GALLERY has a pottery, doll's-house shop and other crafts; meals and snacks, good disabled access; cl Mon and Tues.

Broughton SE9608 MAYFIELD COURT CRAFTS is a decent craft shop; cl Weds and Thurs.

! **Bridlington** TA1766 had the image of being bracing in the heyday of the traditional seaside resort, and the way the country rolls down to the long sands of the shore still gives that feeling. The centre is a quay and small harbour, with the usual summer attractions, but the original core of the town is half a mile in from the sea, with some charming old houses among the more modern ones around the heavily restored but priory CHURCH; there's a separate 14th-c gateway which gives some idea of how imposing the priory must have been, before the Dissolution (it now houses a local history and regimental museum, open pm Tues-Thurs, Jun-Sept; £1). The HARBOUR MUSEUM AND

Aquarium is the best place to find out about the town's seafaring heritage; 40p. On the NE edge of the town SEWERBY HALL, in spacious parkland right on the coast, has a miniature zoo and aviary as well as a charming garden. The elegant house dates from 1714-1720 and houses an art gallery and museum of history and archaeology, including Amy Johnson memorabilia – the pioneer aviator lived nearby. Lots of events throughout the year; snacks, shop, disabled access (but not to the hall); open Sat-Tues Feb-Nov, also Weds-Fri Easter and May-Sept; £1.80 for entry to park, hall and zoo. There's a good MODEL VILLAGE nearby as well; disabled access; cl Oct-Apr; £2.50. A walk along the low cliff from here towards Flamborough Head soon brings you to a strip of woodland by a stream; if you follow the lane up from here past the car park and along the wood, you come to Iron-Age earthworks which cut right across the head – making it a pretty impressive defensive position. In the opposite direction by the leisure park at Carnaby the PARK ROSE POTTERY has factory visits and seconds shop, as well as 12 acres of parkland featuring play areas and an owl sanctuary; meals, snacks, shop, disabled access; cl Christmas week; site entry free, some individual attractions have charges. Also at this end of town is JOHN BULL'S WORLD OF ROCK, where you can tour a factory producing biscuits, chocolate and rock, the dentists' favourite.

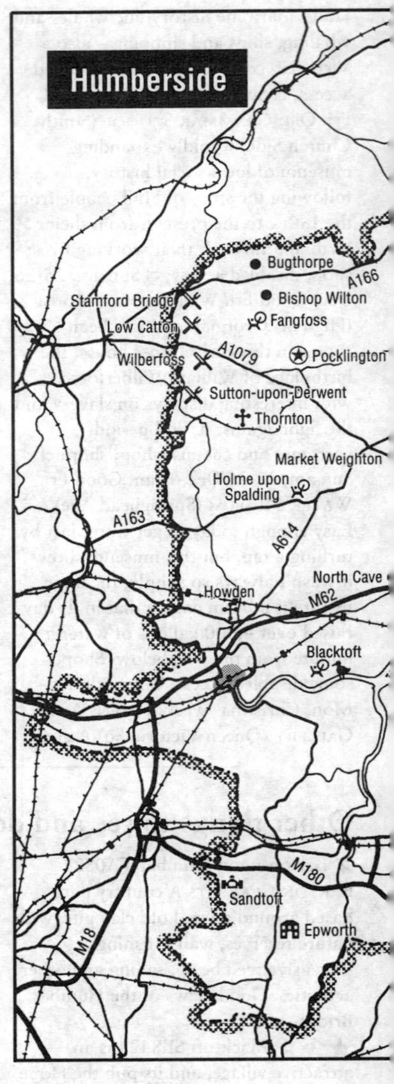

Burton Agnes TA1063

BURTON AGNES HALL The ghost of a young girl is said still to haunt the Elizabethan house and its grounds – a fine woodland garden, colourful borders, a topiary walk to an orangery – despite attempts to pacify her by reburying her skull in the hall she'd asked to be allowed to stay in for ever. The richly decorated house is full of interesting things to look at, from 16th-c antiques to Impressionist paintings; meals and snacks, shop, disabled access on ground floor only; cl Nov-Mar; *£3, grounds only £1.50. The Norman manor house which preceded the present one, refaced in brick but still showing its original structure, stands between here and the church. At nearby Kilham, the CHURCH is attractive, with a memorable

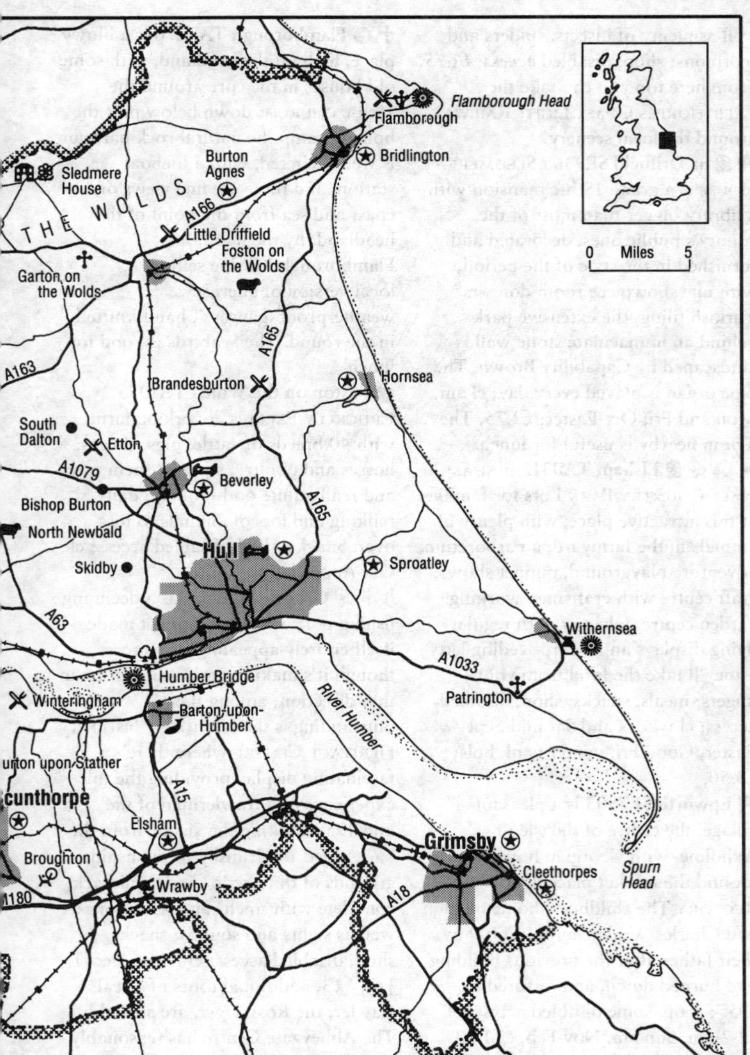

Norman door.

Cleethorpes TA3008 is a big traditional seaside resort with extensive gently shelving tidal sands, and all the entertainments you'd expect (as well as a surprisingly ancient church among some attractive older houses in its original core). The Smugglers and Willys (which brews its own beer) are useful for lunch.

Fuchsia Fantasy Garden centre with around 800 varieties of fuchsias for sale, and other plants according to season; disabled access. This lakeside area has a number of other attractions inc Jungle World and Mini-Beast Zoo, with lots of butterflies and birds flying through an indoor rainforest, as well as plenty of insects, spiders and scorpions; shop, disabled access; £1.75. From here too you can take the CLEETHORPES COAST LIGHT RAILWAY around the local scenery.

nr Driffield SE9365 SLEDMERE HOUSE is a grand 18th-c mansion with a library bigger than most of the county's public ones, decorated and furnished in the style of the period, with one showpiece room done in Turkish tiling; the extensive park behind an immaculate stone wall is landscaped by Capability Brown. The pipe organ is played every day; cl am, Mon and Fri, Oct-Easter; £2.75. The Triton nearby is useful for lunch.

Elsham TA0312 ELSHAM HALL COUNTRY PARK Lots for families at this attractive place, with plenty of animals in the farmyard, an arboretum, adventure playground, puppet shows, craft centre with craftsmen working, garden centre, falconry with regular flying displays and a carp-feeding jetty – they'll take the food from your fingers; meals, snacks, shop, disabled access; cl wkdys and Sat mid-Sept-Easter, Good Fri, winter bank hols; £3.50.

Epworth SE7803 is a pleasant village, the centre of the isle of Axholme, with Georgian houses around the market place. OLD RECTORY The childhood home of John and Charles Wesley, built in 1709 by their father after the previous building had burned down, and restored in 1957; shop, some disabled access; cl 12-2 pm, Sun am, Nov-Feb; *£1.50. Bed and breakfast is available there (by prior arrangement), and the whole village has become something of a Methodist centre.

Fangfoss SE7653 The ROCKING HORSE SHOP has moved here from Holme on Spalding Moor, with its splendid collection of antique rocking horses. You can watch them being constructed, and buy either a finished horse or plans for doing it yourself. Open by appointment.

✝ **Flamborough** TA2270 is a blowy place, high on the headland, with some old houses in the core around the 15th-c CHURCH; down below past the holiday camp the natural rock harbour is well sheltered, with a lifeboat station, and there are fine views of coast and sea from the point of the headland, by the lighthouse. Flamborough Marine sell a local version of guernseys, weatherproof 'ganseys', hand-knitted in the round. The Seabirds is good for lunch.

Foston on the Wolds TA1055 CRUCKLEY FARM is a working farm, with 40 breeds of cattle, pigs, sheeps, horses and poultry, some of them rare and really quite odd-looking; daily milking and lots of animals to fuss over. Snacks, shop, disabled access; cl Oct-Apr; £2.15.

Grimsby TA2710 is a declining fishing port which has not yet made itself entirely appealing to visitors, though it's making promising efforts in that direction; among them, outstanding is the NATIONAL FISHING HERITAGE CENTRE where there's a fascinating display providing the full experience of a trawlerman of the mid-1950s, taking the visitor from the backstreets of Grimsby to the fishing grounds of the Arctic Circle and back, complete with smells and sensations as well as sights and sounds; snacks, shop, disabled access; cl 25-26 Dec, 1 Jan; *£3, additional tours of a real trawler, the *Ross Tiger*, are available. The Abbeygate Centre has reasonably priced antique shops, also upstairs craft workshops inc lace-making; café. The Hope & Anchor and the Trawl are useful for lunch.

★ ✝ **Howden** SE7528 is an unpretentiously attractive place, with cobbled alleys, a fine market hall, a majestic MINSTER with a tall tower, the ruins of a charming medieval chapter house, and a small marshland country park down the lane opposite the minster, with ponds and raised walkways. The Plough is good for lunch.

Hornsea TA1947 MUSEUM Enthusiastically put together local-history museum in former farmhouse and its outbuildings, with good displays inc 19th-c farmhouse rooms and dairy, craft tools and farming implements. Various other activities and events such as craft demonstrations; snacks during July and Aug, shop, disabled access to most of the premises; cl Nov-Easter; £1.50. POTTERY LEISURE PARK Working potters and bargain factory shopping combined with family leisure attractions such as Butterfly World, Yorkshire Car Collection and Model Village, Birds of Prey centre and adventure playground. Meals, snacks, shop, disabled access; cl 24-26 Dec. Behind the town, Hornsea Mere, two miles long, is the biggest natural lake in this region.

The **Humber Bridge** TA0224 is the longest single-span suspension bridge in the world, nearly a mile between the towers, and a very impressive sweep of engineering (there's a footway across as well as the road). At the N end is the HUMBER BRIDGE COUNTRY PARK, with plenty of woodland and clifftop walks and an old mill from the days when this area was the centre of the chalk industry; meals, snacks, shop, good disabled access.

Market Weighton SE8742 is a neat and pleasant old market town with one or two useful antique shops; the Londesborough Arms is a civilised lunch stop.

North Newbald SE9136 NORTHERN SHIRE HORSE CENTRE (Flower Hill Farm) Lots to see at this busy place, a working farm with pedigree shire horse stud, displays of farming bygones, reconstructed rooms and period costumes, decent walks and plenty of other animals inc rare sheep and cattle; meals, snacks, shop, disabled access; cl Fri and Sat, all Oct-Easter; £2.

Pocklington SE8048 is an open-faced market town below the Wolds, with a good few handsome buildings; the Feathers is popular for lunch (and has decent bedrooms). PENNY ARCADIA Comprehensive collection of antique and veteran coin-operated amusement machines with lively tours and demonstrations exploring the fascinating and varied world of the slot-machine; shop, disabled access; cl am exc Jun-Aug, all Oct-Apr; *£3. A mile or two outside the town BURNBY HALL (Burnby Rd) is famous for its water lilies, dozens of varieties in two large ponds; also a splendid rose garden, and one of those intriguing colonial-days collections of all sorts of ethnic material and sporting trophies from across the world; snacks, shop, disabled access; cl mid-Oct-1st wk Apr; £1.50. From out here it's not far to the Plough at Allerthorpe – very good for lunch.

Sandtoft SE7408 TRANSPORT CENTRE Working trolley bus system and collection of over 60 trolley and motor buses from Britain and the Continent, with some working models, and other memorabilia; snacks, shop; open various dates Apr-Oct, best tel (0603) 300907 to check; £2.50.

Scunthorpe SE8910 BOROUGH MUSEUM AND ART GALLERY (Oswald Rd) Local history, natural history and archaeology with lots of fossils and reconstructed rooms; snacks, shop, disabled access to ground floor only; cl Sun am, all day Mon. NORMANBY HALL COUNTRY PARK 350 acres of grounds with deer grazing in the park, lots of wildfowl, nature trails, riding, other things to do. The Regency mansion itself has rooms decorated in period style, and a farm museum in the grounds; meals, snacks, shop, disabled access to ground floor only; cl am, Oct-Mar; charge for car parking, cheapest during the week.

Sproatley TA1934 BURTON CONSTABLE HALL Set in 200 acres of parkland landscaped by Capability

Brown, this Elizabethan house was extravagantly and splendidly remodelled in the 18th c. There's a sweeping long gallery, and its treasures include a wonderful collection of 18th-c scientific instruments; teas, disabled access to ground floor only; cl am, Fri, Sat, Sun, Oct-Easter; *£3. Camping, caravanning and seasonal fishing.

✝ **Thornton** SE7545 THORNTON ABBEY Ruins of Augustinian abbey founded in 1139, also a magnificent 14th-c gatehouse; shop, disabled access (not into gatehouse); shop; cl 1-2 pm, all day Thurs and Fri, wkdys Oct-Mar; £1.20.

Withernsea TA3427 LIGHTHOUSE Towers above the houses of this little resort, with fantastic views for those keen enough to climb the 144 steps. Varied displays and exhibitions cover the RNLI and the local lifeboat, as well as Captain Cook and especially the actress Kim Campbell – both of whom are linked to the family that own (and helped build) the lighthouse; snacks, shop, disabled access to ground floor only; open pm wknds Mar-Oct, daily July and Aug; £1.50.

WORKING WINDMILLS at **Wrawby** TA0209 (best to tel (0652) 653699 for opening times; 60p) and **Skidby** TA0133 (cl Sun am, Mon, and Oct-Apr; 80p), which has gentle country walks nearby, and brilliant filled Yorkshire puddings at the Half Moon.

★ **Attractive villages** include Bishop Wilton SE7955, Bugthorpe SE7758 (especially in spring; with a fine church), Garton on the Wolds SE9859 (another interesting church – 12th-c, and very high-church inside, with 19th-c mosaics and frescoes), North Cave SE8932 (for the view of the lake and park behind the church), Patrington TA3122 (a glorious church, with lovely carving inside – its graceful spire beckoning you from a long way off); and, all with decent pubs, Bishop Burton SE9939, Burton upon Stather SE8717 and South Dalton SE9645.

Walks

The area between Wolds, Humber and coast, known as Holderness, is flat: rich farming country with huge fields and not many buildings, though the fine village churches often with soaring towers or spires reflect the wealth that this fertile land has put into them in the past. The long southern stretch of coast is flat country too, without a great deal of appeal for walkers – except for long lonely off-season walks by the edge of the North Sea.

From Flamborough Head N, the hillier country coming down to the coast makes it more interesting. The coast is followed closely by a path nearly all the way. **Flamborough Head** TA2670 sticks its neck out over Bridlington Bay; the Head's most exciting moments occur around its N side, with the cacophany of thousands of kittiwakes sounding within the inlets; puffins can sometimes be seen on rock ledges. A level mile and a half from the lighthouse, along clifftops, leads to North Landing TA2273 (café and car park). A longer walk making the Head the midway point starts from Flamborough village TA2270 and heads around fields to join the coast path; to avoid anti-climax, walk the southern cliffs first and keep the real drama for later on.

A rough track open to cars makes it to the very end of **Spurn Head** TA4011, the vulnerable-looking spit which protrudes like a claw at the mouth of the Humber Estuary, a bleak place to some but a paradise for bird-watchers, who often wait here in spring and autumn for glimpses of rare migrant species. The estuary itself, looking a promising sight on the map, is actually not a beautiful piece of water, but grey, solemn and grim.

Inland the southern part of the **Wolds Way** (see also Yorkshire section) is the main attraction, with the start of the 79-mile route passing along the north bank of the Humber and getting close-ups of the Humber Bridge. The Gate pub at Millington SE8352 is by quite a steep path up on to the Wolds Way, and other walks above it, with good views, take you up on to the track of an old Roman road, and around some of the county's rare woods.

Driving

Distances here are long, but the roads have little traffic and are generally good, so that you can cover ground quickly.

People unfamiliar with the Wolds will enjoy any of the roads which sweep over these rolling stretches of farmland, with the views punctuated by distant clumps of trees and an occasional spire or tower proclaiming a village. The B1249 N of Driffield is one such (especially over the Yorkshire border, as it drops down over the Staxton Brow); on the way, it passes the Old Mill, a useful place to eat near Langtoft. Also out from Driffield, the B1252 has some handsome views, and the B1248 N from Beverley is of similar character. Towards the west the countryside becomes more picturesquely hilly, with pastures replacing some of the big-field arable farmland; the A163 passing Londesborough and the steeper B1246 between Driffield and Pocklington both take good account of this rather different scenery. Further S, the B1230 from Howden to Beverley, relieved of traffic pressure by the M62, has reverted to the more relaxed character of an old coach road.

The B1242 up the coast certainly gives you plenty of sea views, but tends rather to emphasise the monotony of the North Sea. A more interesting coast drive is the B1259 out to Flamborough Head, and then up the coast a bit on the B1229.

Where to eat

Winteringham SE9322 WINTERINGHAM FIELDS (0724) 733096 Restaurant-with-rooms in 16th-c manor house, comfortable Victorian furnishings, beams, open fires, excellent inventive food in no-smoking dining room, and warmly friendly service; fine breakfasts, individual bedrooms with period furniture; cl 2 wks Christmas, 1st wk Aug. **£38**|**£10**.

Stamford Bridge SE7155 THREE CUPS (0759) 71396 Former farmhouse with attractively furnished beamed bar and open fire, and good, popular food (carvery Tues-Sun); restaurant cl Mon. **£13.65**|**£1.65/£2.85**.

Sutton-upon-Derwent SE7047 ST VINCENT ARMS (0904) 608349 Cosily panelled front parlour, further lounge, dining room and restaurant, wide choice of popular bar food, lots of real ales, unusually good choice of wines by the bottle, and big garden; disabled access. **£12**|**£1.50/£2.50**.

Flamborough TA2270 SEABIRDS (0262) 850242 Friendly old pub with very good seafood dishes such as crab and lobster (in season), lots of wines; cl Sun/Mon pm in winter. **£11.10**|**£1.50/£4.20**.

Other good places for food include the Gold Cup at Low Catton SE7053, Dacre Arms at Brandesburton TA1247, Light Dragoon at Etton SE9843, Downe Arms at Little Driffield TA0158 and Oddfellows Arms at Wilberfoss SE7351. And this is a prime area for fish and chips.

Help this year from: C A Hall, R M Macnaughton, Allan and Ruth Sharp, A W Dickinson, Alan Wilcock, Christine Davidson, Dave Thompson, Margaret Mason, C W Elswood, Simon Dale, Roger Bellingham, Ivor Maw, Alf and Jane Ludlam, Miss J F Reay.

HUMBERSIDE CALENDAR

Some of these dates were provisional as we went to press.

JANUARY

6th **Haxey** Hood – *ancient game created in 13th c by Lady de Mowbray, whose hood was blown away and retrieved by labourers: she dedicated the area to the village, as Hoodland. The contest begins with a procession of the players, colourfully dressed 'Boggans', a king and a fool. The game resembles rugby played with leather hoods. The object is to get a hood away from the Boggans by throwing, kicking or carrying. When a Boggan touches the hood it is thrown again and the game continues until dusk*

MARCH

17th **Kiplingcotes** Derby – *starts at the Sandstone Post, 1 mile N of the old railway station: possibly the oldest flat race in the country, and surely the only race where the winner gets less money than the runner-up*

26th **Cleethorpes** Dance Festival – *till 4 Apr*

MAY

2nd **Cleethorpes** Gala

7th **Bishop Burton** Gardens Open Day – *at Bishop Burton College – demonstrations, advice, Victorian walled garden and conservatories*

12th **Beverley** Early Music Festival, *inc walks, talks, tea and candlelit concerts – till Sun 15*

23rd **Bridlington** Festival – *till 7 May*

28th **Cleethorpes** Folk Festival, *inc music, drama and workshops – till Mon 30*; **Ealand Crowle** Show

29th **Elsham** Children's Festival – *till Mon 30*

30th **Epworth** Wesleyan Market

JUNE

2nd **Hornsea** Spring Fair *at Hornsea Museum – inc demonstrations of Victorian crafts*

5th **Messingham** Show

11th **Bridlington** UK Jet-ski Championships *at North Bay – till Sun 12*; **Hull** Lord Mayor's Parade

12th **Hull to Bridlington** East-coast Vintage Vehicle Rally

17th **Beverley** Folk Festival, *inc concerts, ceilidhs, workshops, street shows, children's events, craft and music stalls – till Sun 19*

26th **Bishop Burton** Town and Country Day *at Bishop Burton College*; **nr Driffield** Vintage Car Rally *at Sledmere House*

Humberside Calendar

July

16th **Barton** Carnival; **Broughton** Show

24th **Grimsby** Edwardian Day

August

7th **Bridlington** Carnival

27th **nr Driffield** Flower Festival *at Sledmere House*

28th **Driffield** Sheepdog Trials and Craft Fair

29th **Brigg** Folklore Fayre and Dance Festival *at Elsham Hall Country Park*; **Epworth** Show

September

1st **Hornsea** Museum, Craft Fair

18th **Epworth** Ploughing Festival, *inc vintage machinery*

October

2nd **Cleethorpes** Harvest Football

7th **Hull** Fair – *till Sat 15*

23rd **Bridlington** Half Marathon

30th **Crowle** Scunthorpe Craft Fair and Agricultural Show

November

5th **Cleethorpes** Bonfire and Fireworks

17th **Hull** Christmas Lights – *turning-on ceremony*

20th **Cleethorpes** Victorian Christmas Fair

25th **Hornsea** Lights Night *inc craft stalls, mince pies and sherry*

December

3rd **Hornsea** Christmas Fair *at Hornsea Museum*

15th **Hull** Christmas Fair

Isle of Wight

The island has attractive countryside and coast and a great many places of interest; justly popular for summer family holidays, it's relaxing and uncrowded at other times, with a lot of potential for short breaks.

The Isle of Wight has long been a favourite for uncomplicated family seaside holidays, and for sailing. In summer, those are certainly the dominant elements here, but the island has a great deal of largely unknown potential for short breaks – especially at other times of year, when it feels fresh and is very uncrowded and leisurely. There are plenty of good coastal walks in fine scenery, and many places of interest. Top among these is Osborne House (with other places to visit close by); Ventnor, Arreton and Brading all have several worthwhile attractions, and Carisbrooke Castle is high on many people's list, as are the bird and animal attractions at Shorwell (a really nice farm park), Seaview, St Lawrence and Newchurch. Many of the more child-oriented features close for six months over winter.

In high summer, the main resorts and places to visit are very busy, with coach parties descending in droves on the prettiest villages (there are places, especially inland, where you can get away from them). Like so many other places, the island comes into its own out of high season. In May and June it's very peaceful, and its south coast is generally then the sunniest place in Britain. Right out of season really cold weather is rare on the island.

Once you're there, prices are rather on the low side compared with the mainland; but for a short stay the fare across does bump up the overall cost quite significantly. This has more impact if you're staying in a cheap place; even after you've added on the fare, hotels towards the top of the range are good value compared with ones of similar quality on the mainland. However, if you're planning to stay for two or three nights, it's always worth asking the hotel if they do a bargain package deal that includes the ferry fare; this can be good value.

The island has a bus service that would put this transport in most parts of the mainland to shame, especially between May and September, with route interconnections at many places (a timetable lets you make the most of these); a week's bus pass is good value.

We welcome reports from readers . . .

Readers who help us with reports for the Guide are offered a discount on the next edition: so please do help if you can!

Where to stay

Bonchurch SZ5778 Peacock Vane PO38 1RJ (0983) 852019 **£75**; 12 very comfortable and very individually decorated rms. Country-house hotel with relaxed atmosphere; comfortable lounge with Sat evening pianist, attractive breakfast room, conservatory, restaurant with good food, friendly service, and pleasant garden; cl Mon/Tues in Jan/Feb.

Ventnor SZ5677 Madeira Hall PO38 1NS (0983) 852624 **£70**; 8 rms. Once the home of Miss Dick (Dickens based Miss Havisham in *Great Expectations* on her), this attractive listed building has a friendly, relaxed atmosphere, appealing day rooms, swimming pool, putting green and lovely grounds; children over 7; disabled access.

Yarmouth SZ3589 George Quay St PO41 0PE (0983) 760331 ***£70**; 11 comfortable rms. Pleasantly relaxing panelled bars, one with nautical theme; log fires, good food, prompt, courteous service, own gardens to private beach, own fishing operation in Yarmouth and St Vaast.

Ryde SZ5992 Ryde Castle PO33 1JA (0983) 563755 ***£69**; 21 rms, most with four-posters. 16th-c castle with comfortable lounge, tapestries, and good food in restaurant designed to look like a galleon.

Totland SZ3286 Country Garden PO39 0ET (0983) 754521 ***£64**; 16 rms. Peaceful extended Victorian hotel overlooking the Solent; with friendly, attentive and personal staff and popular restaurant; undergoing major renovations as we went to press; children over 7; disabled access.

Seaview SZ6291 Seaview PO34 5EX (0983) 612711 ***£62**; 16 attractively decorated rms. Small and friendly hotel with fine ship photographs in the chatty and relaxed front bar, an old-fashioned back bar, good, freshly made bar food, and a highly regarded evening restaurant; children over 5 in evening restaurant.

Shanklin SZ5881 Luccombe Chine House PO37 6RH (0983) 862037 **£60**; 6 rms, all with four-posters. Very friendly small hotel at the end of a long drive and surrounded by large wooded grounds where you can watch foxes and badgers at night taking food left for them on the lawn; homely lounge, help-yourself drinks tray, beams and inglenook fireplaces, and very good food in cosy dining room; good walks; cl Dec-Jan; no children.

Bonchurch SZ5778 Lake PO38 1RF (0983) 852613 ***£40**; 23 rms. Early 19th-c country house in two acres of gardens with three lounges (one is a conservatory), bar, restaurant and enjoyable food; cl Nov-Feb; children over 3.

Yarmouth SZ3589 Bugle The Square PO41 0NS (0983) 760272 **£37**; 6 rms (best to have one not over the bar). Wide range of good food in bustling inn with real ales, bar decorated like galleon stern, restaurant, children's room, sizeable garden; cl 25 Dec.

Carisbrooke SZ4888 Great Park Farm Betty Haunt Lane Newport PO30 4HR (0983) 522945 **£30**; 3 no-smoking rms. Lovely old farmhouse on arable farm with panoramic views, good walks, dining room and sitting room; no dogs; cl Oct-Mar; children over 8.

To see and do

! ⛀ ❁ ⚘ ⌂ **Alum Bay** SZ3484 The Needles Pleasure Park has a chair-lift down the cliff to the beach, famous for its multi-coloured sands from the different rock strata in the cliff itself – pinks and greys and ochres. You can buy little glass tubes with the sands inside carefully layered – or set

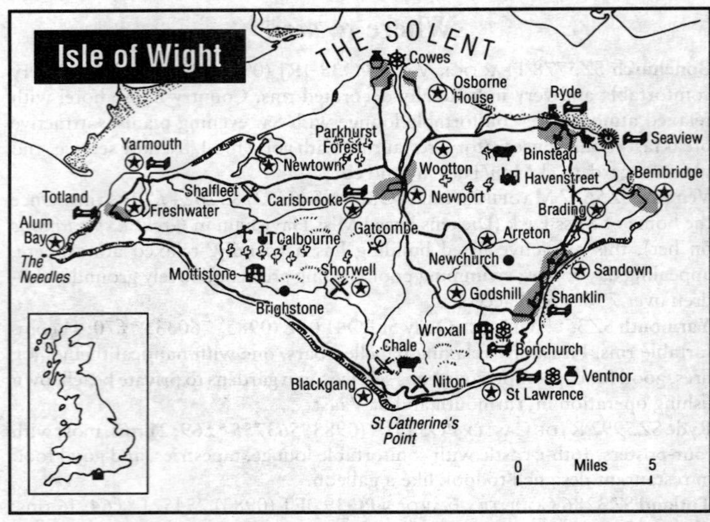

children to making them up themselves. Also glassworks, fun-park and other entertainments; meals, snacks, shop, disabled access; cl Oct-Mar. From the park a minibus goes up to the NEEDLES OLD BATTERY (you can't go by car). Here an extensive display in the powder house of the fort – built in 1862 and recently restored – illustrates the history of this headland. On the parade-ground are two 12-ton gun barrels which have been salvaged from the sea. From the fort itself a longish tunnel takes you to a look-out spot that gives spectacular views of the rock pinnacles of the Needles themselves, and their lighthouse; meals, snacks, shop; cl Fri and Sat (exc Jun-Sept and Easter hols), Nov-Apr; £2.20. ALUM BAY GLASS has glass-blowing demonstrations (not wknds), and a factory shop; disabled access; cl 2 wks over Christmas; *60p.

✝ ⌂ ⚱ ✿ ☺ **Arreton** SZ5386 is a pleasant place with a delightful 13th-c CHURCH (which has a brass-rubbing centre). The White Lion is useful for lunch. Around is lots for families to enjoy. ARRETON MANOR is a lovely old mellow stone house, dating from around 1600, with splendid period furnishings and panelling. It also contains a variety of museums, the most unusual of which is the NATIONAL WIRELESS MUSEUM – it was nearby that Marconi made his pioneering experiments. Also toys, dolls, doll's houses (inc a famous early 19th-c one), and costume and lace collections. Meals, snacks, shop; cl Sat (exc bank hol wknds); *£3. The nearby Arreton Country CRAFT VILLAGE has craft workshops and a restaurant with home baking; cl Sat exc bank hols, cl Nov-Mar; £1.60. HASELEY MANOR The largest and oldest manor house open on the island, it has some parts dating from the original foundation of 1310, and there are Tudor, Georgian and Victorian additions. After falling into misuse it was restored in the 1970s and now has around 20 rooms on show, decorated in period style and some with costumed figures. In the grounds is a reconstructed 18th-c farm with animals, as well as herb gardens, and play area; snacks, shop, disabled access; cl Nov-Easter; *£3.50. An associated CRAFT CENTRE has the island's biggest pottery studio, sweet-making (not wknds), pets' corner and teas. ROBIN HILL ADVENTURE PARK is a good place for children to let off steam, with a maze, commando assault course, toboggan ride, archery, snake-handling demonstrations in a tropical house, 10-acre walk-through wildlife enclosure – these are just a few of the huge number of activities and wildlife set in 88 acres of charming landscape; meals and snacks, shop, disabled access but rather hilly; cl Nov-Mar; £3.90.

Bembridge SZ6488 even in summer is quiet for a coastal place, though with plenty going on in its yachting harbour, and a lifeboat station nearby. SHIPWRECK CENTRE AND MARITIME MUSEUM The seafaring story of the island, with six galleries of displays of salvage and shipwreck items, models of ships and the harbour and early diving equipment; shop, some disabled access; cl Nov-Feb; £1.95. WINDMILL Built in 1700 and used until 1913, this is now the only surviving windmill on the island; shop; cl Sat (exc July-Aug) and Nov-Mar; *£1.20. NT. The school has a big collection of books, letters, manuscripts and drawings by John Ruskin and his associates; by appointment only – (0983) 872101. Out on the Foreland the rock pools are magnificent and would keep any beachcomber happy for hours. The clifftop Crab & Lobster (good views) and the Row Barge are useful for lunch.

Binstead SZ5791 BRICKFIELDS (Newnham Rd) is a working farm with shire and miniature horses, tame farm animals, carriage collection, agricultural bygones, and showjumping summer Weds evenings; also farrier, saddlery, cider-making and play area. Meals, snacks, shop, disabled access; *£3.50.

Blackgang SZ4971 BLACKGANG CHINE FANTASY PARK Attractive park tricked out with all sorts of different themed areas, inc Dinosaurland, Fantasyland and Jungleland, with a complete replica of a Victorian sawmill, and a display of woodland skills and traditional crafts. A museum on St Catherines Quay illustrates the local and maritime history of the area, and there are lots of lively events. Good views, and on a summer evening the gardens are well illuminated; meals and snacks, shop, disabled access; cl Nov-Apr, but winter exhibitions continue at the quay and mill; £3.99, sawmill and quay only £2.25.

Brading SZ6087 is a busy attractive place, with interesting monuments in its Norman CHURCH, and a pretty graveyard. The Bugle is good for lunch. The remains of a ROMAN VILLA have good mosaics (cl Oct-Mar; £1.50) and there's a little local-history museum in the town hall (cl Oct-Apr; 40p). LILLIPUT DOLL AND TOY MUSEUM Over 2,000 exhibits dating from as far back as 2000 BC with examples of almost every seriously collectable doll in Britain; shop, disabled access; cl Jan-mid-March for regular renovations; £1.25. WAX MUSEUM Set in the partly 11th-c Ancient Rectory Mansion, this is a superbly atmospheric place and one of the best of its kind – complete of course with the obligatory Chamber of Horrors; shop; £3.75. The price also covers admission to the ANIMAL WORLD OF NATURAL HISTORY, which has a huge collection of animals, birds and reptiles displayed in their natural surroundings; shop, access for disabled. MORTON MANOR 13th-c manor house, rebuilt in 1680 with further changes in the 18th c, and set in lovely landscaped gardens with ornamental ponds and a turf maze from the Elizabethan period. There's also a little vineyard, with an exhibition of winemaking relics; meals and snacks in thatched teashop, shop, disabled access; cl Sat, Nov-Mar; £2.75. NUNWELL HOUSE AND

GARDENS Lovely 16th-c house set in charming gardens; it has a Home Guard Museum as well as interesting furniture and family memorabilia. Charles I spent his last night of freedom here; snacks, shop; cl Fri, Sat, Oct-Jun; £2.30.

★ ✝ **Calbourne** SZ4286 is an attractive village with photogenic streamside thatched cottages and a 13th-c CHURCH; get there early to avoid the coach tours. WATERMILL AND RURAL MUSEUM The 20 ft waterwheel still powers this 17th-c mill – the latest of those which have stood on this site since 1299 – and the grounds have tame peacocks; home-baked snacks, shop with stoneground flour etc, disabled access; cl Nov-Easter; £2. The Sun is useful for lunch.

Carisbrooke SZ4888 CARISBROOKE CASTLE These impressive ruins are of the only medieval castle on the island and between 1647 and 1648 it was home to the imprisoned Charles I (his daughter died here in 1650). Originally the site of a Saxon fort, most of what's left are the remains of a Norman castle but there are also remnants of Elizabethan and Jacobean buildings. The site has two medieval wells – one in the 12th-c keep and the other in the 16th-c wellhouse in the courtyard, with entertaining demonstrations of the traditional method of driving the winding gear using a team of donkeys. A museum looks at the history of the castle, the wells and the donkeys; snacks, shop, disabled access to ground floor; cl 24-26 Dec, 1 Jan; £3.20. The Eight Bells, with good Solent views, is useful for lunch – and quite handy for the nearby DONKEY SANCTUARY.

Chale SZ4877 CHALE FARM A small farm producing ice cream in various flavours – inc Christmas Pudding. You can see the ice cream being made, and the cows being milked (around 4 o'clock); cl Sun am. The Wight Mouse is a good family pub.

Cowes SZ4995 is stylish and lively, very much centred on its yachting connections, with interesting buildings and shops inc fascinating ships' chandlers in the long narrow High St, and the battery of over 20 brass cannons used to start the yacht races down by the harbour. The Pier View is handy for lunch. COWES MARITIME MUSEUM (Beckford Rd) Thorough exploration of the island's maritime history, and especially of local shipbuilders and naval architects, told with photos, paintings, and models and housed in the public library; shop, mostly disabled access; cl Sun, Thurs, bank hols. More maritime memorabilia at the SIR MAX AITKEN MUSEUM; open 10 am to 2 pm wkdys Jun-Sept. The TOY & MODEL MUSEUM (High St) is largely ship-oriented, too, with masses of warship models alongside working steam-train models and so forth.

✝ **Freshwater** SZ3484 is a very extended rather sprawling village but has, tucked away, a charming quiet core with a partly Norman CHURCH, which includes quite a few Tennyson family memorials. There are craft workshops at GOLDEN HILL FORT, a former 19th-c fortified barracks block with splendid views from the battlements; local stone-polishing and fossils, pottery etc; £1.20 (free in winter). The famous Arch Rock collapsed into the sea last November, but there's an exhibition of pictures and photographs of it at the Mermaid Café. Hill Farm nearby has RIDING. The Red Lion is good for lunch, and the Vine has a pleasant terrace for warm days.

Gatcombe SZ4984 A TOUCH OF GLASS Traditional glassworks, with demonstrations and shop; disabled access; studio cl wknds. They also have a shop in Shanklin, cl Tues.

★ ✝ ! **Godshill** SZ5281 has famously pretty thatched cottages by a good 15th-c CHURCH – get there very early to avoid the coach parties descending on the teashops. OLD

SMITHY TOURIST CENTRE Various shops selling local crafts, gifts and fashions, an aviary of exotic birds, herb garden, and garden in the shape of the island itself, all centred around former blacksmith's forge; snacks, shop, disabled access; cl Sun Jan-Feb, 25-26 Dec, gardens cl end Oct-Easter; 75p. MODEL VILLAGE Shanklin, its Chine Valley and Godshill painstakingly recreated in miniature; they have to rethatch the tiny straw roofs on the cottages every few years. Shop, disabled access; cl Nov-Mar; *£1.90. NOSTALGIA TOY MUSEUM Lots of pre-war toys with plenty of die-cast model cars; shop, disabled access; cl Sat, all Nov-Easter; 95p. There's also a NATURAL HISTORY CENTRE with collections of minerals, fossils and precious stones; cl Nov-Mar; £1.25.

Havenstreet SZ5690 STEAM RAILWAY Restored by volunteers, the railway now runs a 10-mile trip from Wootton to Smallbrook Junction (where it's possible to change directly on to BR). Many of the engines and much of the rolling stock is vintage and there's a display of memorabilia at the old gas works at Havenstreet Station; meals and snacks, shop, disabled access if accompanied; phone for timetable, (0983) 882204; *£4.50. A good way of saving money is to buy the BR Island Line ticket, which for £6 gives you a day's unlimited travel on all BR trains and the Steam Railway.

Mottistone SZ4083 MOTTISTONE MANOR Medieval and Elizabethan manor house, with fine gardens; open pm Weds and bank hols mid-Mar-Sept; *£1.90. NT.

Newchurch SZ5685 ISLAND AMAZON ADVENTURE The exotic birds and animals you'd find in an Amazon rainforest, with monkeys, spiders, flamingos, crocodile and some other extremely odd-looking creatures in lively jungle and village settings; children can tunnel their way into the parrot enclosure, and there's also a playground and pets' corner. Snacks, shop, disabled access; cl 25 Dec; £2.50.

★ **Newport** SZ4989 has a good deal of character, with some fine old Georgian houses, and warm red-brick 18th-c buildings down by the quay. It's the main place on the island for antique shops. The Castle in the High St is useful for lunch. ROMAN VILLA Well-preserved baths and reconstructed rooms on the site of 3rd-c Roman villa, and a well-laid-out and informative museum houses some of the site finds; shop, some disabled access; cl Sat and Oct-Easter; £1.50. The Quay Arts Centre often has interesting displays of art and crafts, and the parish CHURCH OF ST THOMAS is worth a look – it has an interestingly carved Jacobean pulpit and a memorial to Charles I's daughter, constructed on the orders of Queen Victoria.

Newtown SZ4250 was for a while in the Middle Ages the island's capital, but a conflagration in 1377 brought it to its knees, and though it stumbled on for a few centuries it eventually faded out altogether – what used to be rich merchants' streets are now just grassy tracks. The OLD TOWN HALL, rebuilt in 1699 but now left stranded and unusually isolated from any houses, is all that's left to mark the once thriving town; open pm Mon, Weds and Sun Apr-Sept, plus Tues and Thurs in July and Aug; £1. NT. Just out of town the CLAMERKIN FARM PARK is a 30-acre working farm with lots of friendly animals, fine views, craft demonstrations and a golf driving range; meals, snacks, shop, disabled access; cl Oct-Easter; *£1.60.

Osborne House SZ5285 This was Queen Victoria's favourite house, and the state and private apartments have remained largely as they were when she died here in 1901. Designed by Prince Albert with professional help from Thomas Cubitt to resemble an Italian villa, the house is surrounded by terraced gardens, while the grounds are filled with every conceivable English tree. A horse-drawn carriage conveys you in style to the Swiss cottage, where the royal children learnt cooking and gardening. Snacks, shop, disabled access to ground floor only; cl Nov-Mar; *£5.40. Next to the house's fine GARDENS, which were originally laid out by Queen Victoria and Prince Albert, BARTON MANOR GARDENS AND VINEYARD covers about 10 acres, and is one of England's finest vineyards, with lovely gardens and plants, restored old farm buildings and the biggest rose-hedge maze on the island. Meals, snacks, shop, disabled access; open daily May-11 Oct and wknds and school hols in Apr; £3.50. Nearby WHIPPINGHAM CHURCH SZ5193 is said to have been another of Prince Albert's designs, and is a good deal more eccentric: a bizarre mix of different styles. Down on the River Medina, the Folly Inn is useful for lunch. There is nothing in East Cowes itself to lure a holiday visitor.

Ryde SZ5992 is now the biggest town here, with a long triple pier, good sandy beaches, a full set of holiday-resort amusements – just right for a straightforward family holiday.

St Lawrence SZ5376 TROPICAL BIRD PARK Over 400 birds in the beautiful grounds of Old Park, in the almost sub-tropical Undercliff; snacks, shop, disabled access; cl 25 Dec; *£2.50. The Park also houses ISLE OF WIGHT GLASS, with demonstrations and displays, and a shop; no glassmaking at wknds; *50p. RARE BREEDS AND WATERFOWL PARK Lots of rare breeds in 30 lovely secluded coastal acres, with cattle, sheep, pigs, ponies, miniature horses, donkeys and goats and waterfowl and poultry. They've recently added otters, which they hope to breed; meals, snacks, shop, disabled access; cl winter wkdys; *£2.40. The St Lawrence Inn is a popular dining pub with superb Channel views.

Sandown SZ5984 has grown up around its fine beach, with all the usual things for a family beach holiday, from pier to boat trips, canoeing lake and discos. MUSEUM OF GEOLOGY The prehistory of the island, going back millions of years, is examined here using interesting displays of fossils and rocks, with recently excavated dinosaur fossils; shop, some disabled access; cl Sun, 25-26 Dec. The ZOO has rare and endangered animals like tigers, panthers and leopards, as well as birds, spiders and snakes; cl Nov-Easter exc Sun; £3.99. Nearby ADGESTONE VINEYARD is one of the country's first commercial vineyards; walks round vineyard and part-underground winery (booking essential), tasting, shop; cl Sat pm, Sun.

Seaview SZ6291 is a quiet retreat, with sedate streets of unassuming villas; the Old Fort inn has good sea views, and the Seaview Hotel is good for lunch. Just out of town FLAMINGO PARK has hundreds of birds that can be fed by hand in good spacious landscaped grounds; also an aquarium. Snacks, shop, disabled access; cl Nov-Easter; £3.50.

Shanklin SZ5881 SHANKLIN CHINE Gorgeous natural gorge with magnificent 45 ft waterfall. A heritage centre gives details of rare flora, nature trails and life in Shanklin during Victorian times, and in 1994 will also feature a special D-Day exhibition; snacks; shop; cl mid-Oct-Easter; £1.45. The adjoining RYLSTONE GARDENS have a COUNTRYSIDE CENTRE with details and displays of the island's landscape and wildlife; shop, disabled access; cl Oct-Jun (exc Easter and spring half-term hols); 60p. They also organise guided walks. Down right on the beach, the Fisherman's Cottage is useful for lunch (but doesn't open at midday in winter). At the other end of the small resort town, the thatched Crab Inn makes a pretty picture.

Shorwell SZ4582, one of the few really pretty villages on the island to have escaped a flood of tourist interest, has charming streamside thatched cottages and a fine CHURCH; the attractive Crown is very good for lunch. YAFFORD MILL FARM PARK is most enjoyable: a seal lives in a special enclosure beside the millpond of the working 18th-c watermill, various species of waterfowl dwell in the pools of the stream, and rare breeds of sheep and cattle graze along its banks; there are nature trails along the sides. Also displays of old farm machinery, wagons and traction engines (sometimes in steam) and an adventure playground across the lane; meals and snacks, shop, disabled access; cl 25 Dec; *£2.50.

Ventnor SZ5677 is an interesting place, with a proper, relatively untouristy little town up on the cliff, a fairly restrained and decorous seafront down below linked to it by a tortuously steep loop of road, and between them perched on ledges among the trees quite a number of Victorian villas – many of them still private houses rather than guesthouses. Its great pride, developed over the last two decades or so, is the BOTANIC GARDEN, where an exceptional collection of suptropical plants make the most of the mild climate. The food at the Garden Tavern here has been praised by some readers. In the grounds (in fact, more correctly, under them) the MUSEUM OF SMUGGLING HISTORY is a unique and appropriately subterranean exhibition, with lots of interesting displays and tableaux showing the tricks various types of smugglers have used over the past 700 years, whether they were sneaking in wool, brandy, tobacco or drugs, as well as the more general story of smuggling; meals and snacks, shop; cl Oct-Mar; £1.50. HERITAGE CENTRE (Spring Hill) History of the town and surrounding area; cl 12-2 pm, pm Weds and Sat, winter Sun; *40p. The LONGSHOREMAN'S MUSEUM (Esplanade) has a similar exhibition of Ventnor's history, with a collection of model boats and various fossils; shop, disabled access; cl Jan and Feb; *50p. The Spyglass is an excellent pub with superb sea views. Nearby BONCHURCH is much quieter, with leafy lanes hugging the steep slopes and passing an unexpected tree-shaded pond; steep steps connect the different levels, and there's a quiet cove down below the cliff. The small 13th-c CHURCH has a lovely peaceful graveyard, and above the cliff St Boniface Down has tremendous VIEWS. For several miles along this section of coast, the cliffs have been and to some extent still are subject to massive landslides. The UNDERCLIFF along here is formed from the irregular masses of earth which have come to rest below, with often rocky chasms between each other and the cliff itself. Sometimes planted and sometimes with profuse natural vegetation, the resulting scenery is unlike anything else on the island, with quite a subtropical aspect. Some of the attractions along it we've listed under St Lawrence.

Wootton SZ5492 is a terminus for the STEAM RAILWAY – see Havenstreet. It has an attractive CHURCH, part Norman. BUTTERFLY WORLD, besides a five-acre garden centre, has free-flying butterflies in a subtropical house with water cascades, koi carp in a Japanese setting, an Italianate garden with fountains, and an insectarium; snacks, shop, disabled access; cl Nov-Easter; *£2.65. The Woodman's Arms is pleasant for lunch, as is the Sloop down overlooking the creek.

Wroxall SZ5480

APPULDURCOMBE HOUSE Intriguing Palladian ruin, on the site of a 12th-c one, nestling among grounds beautifully landscaped by Capability Brown; snacks, shop, disabled access (though the car park is a short distance away); cl 1-2 pm, probably Oct-Mar – worth checking first (0983) 852484; *£1.20.

Yarmouth SZ3589 is a lively place, its old harbour busy with yachts in summer. The CASTLE was built as part of Henry VIII's coastal defences; it's in an excellent state, and you can see the Master Gunner's surprisingly homely parlour and kitchen. There's also an exhibition of local watercolours and photographs; outside, the open gun platform has good views of the harbour; shop; cl 1-2 pm, Oct-Mar; £1.70. FORT VICTORIA COUNTRY PARK Overlooking the Solent, this country park surrounds the ruined 19th-c fort which was built to provide defence for Portsmouth and includes 50 acres of woodland and about 1 mile of pebbly beach. In the grounds are a maritime heritage centre, aquarium (£1.50) and planetarium (£2); snacks, shop, disabled access (though not yet in the planetarium); maritime heritage centre cl Oct-Easter, café and aquarium open wknds in winter period; park free. The Bugle and the George are both worthy inns, and the Kings Head and Wheatsheaf are useful for lunch.

Walks

The island's coastal walks equal and perhaps surpass anything else in the South-East: these alone would justify coming here for a break. The best place of all for walkers here is **Tennyson Down** SZ3285, Wight's western tip: a friendly grassy ridge and cliff walk rolled into one, with views over most of the island and across to the mainland. You pass the memorial to Alfred Lord Tennyson (who lived nearby) and the walk culminates in spectacular fashion above The Needles SZ2984, a group of wave-battered chalk pinnacles. There's a choice of start points, depending on how long you want to walk for. A close one is Alum Bay SZ3483; or you can walk the entire ridge from Freshwater Bay SZ3485 (summer bus service from Alum Bay to ferry you back), or walk the coast from Totland SZ3286 over Headon Warren.

Other good places for walking on this S coast include **Compton Down** SZ3785, east of Freshwater Bay, another hogsback grassy hill; circular walks can take in the coast path along Compton Bay. **St Catherine's Hill** SZ4977, capped by the ruins of a 14th-c lighthouse, is a short walk up from the coast path further east. The path skirts the undercliff of St Catherine's Point SZ4875, the isle's southern tip, which has a modern working lighthouse; there are several other paths through the undercliff here. Above Ventnor SZ5677, **Bonchurch Down** is somewhat dominated by unsightly radar installations but gives fine views. From Yarmouth SZ3589, the former railway line southward is now a footpath which skirts the unspoilt, reed-fringed **Yar estuary**.

On the north coast, the **Newtown Nature Reserve** SZ4191 has walks around the creeks of the Newtown/Clamerkin estuaries, although there are few circular routes; Newtown village SZ4290 is a good starting point.

The east coast is heavily developed; the coastal path sometimes follows roads and skirts large residential areas, but walk opportunities exist around **Bembridge** SZ6488, particularly S to **Culver Cliff** SZ6385. Inland, Wight is characterised by long, curving chalk ridges (tracks often follow the crests) and forestry plantations (with many signposted woodland trails). The hills north of **Brighstone** SZ4282 represent some of the pick of the scenery. The Countryman on Limerstone Rd at Brighstone itself is a good refreshment break, with fine views down to the sea; not far away the pretty thatched Sun in Hulverstone is another useful break.

Parkhurst Forest SZ4890, just west of the prison, is a couple of miles across, with plenty of paths and quite a good chance of seeing red squirrels.

Driving

The A3055 along the SE coast can, out of season, give the quite pleasurable feeling of driving out into the back of beyond, and starts by dropping down from a splendid viewpoint below St Catherines Hill (nervous drivers may or may not be reassured to know that this road has tiltmeters built into it, which are supposed to give automatic warning if there's a suddenly increased risk of a landslip dumping the road into the sea). The A3055 also has some fine sea and coast views best when driving from Ventnor to Shanklin. From Brading the road out over Bembridge Down to Culver Cliff has good views on the way, and ends at an isolated pub (the Culver Haven) which has terrific views in virtually all directions.

Inland, most of the roads give quietly attractive views, but particularly good are the back road between Brading and Newport – the one that tracks virtually the whole way down the island from Wootton Bridge through Downend to pass Bohemia Corner and track on down to Niton – and the one from Brighstone in to Calbourne.

Where to eat

Shalfleet NEW INN (0983) 78314 Partly flagstoned bar with roaring log fire, no-smoking restaurant, and good fresh fish dishes; cl Sun. £1.95/£4.25.
Shorwell SZ4582 CROWN (0983) 740293 The big back garden with its trout-filled stream, ducks, doves and lilies is a really lovely place to eat in summer; there's a small beamed two-roomed lounge with log fire, good food, and friendly staff; £1.60/£4.75.
Other useful places include the smuggling-theme Buddle Inn at Niton SZ5077 (splendid views down over St Catherine's Point) and Wight Mouse at Chale SZ4877, a very popular family place.

Help this year from: *B M Eldridge, HNJ, PEJ, M D Hare, Shirley Pielou, M and A Cook, J M Campbell, N Mortlock, Bill Edwards, Mark King, M Powys-Smith, Martyn and Mary Mullins, M and A Cooke, Theo Curtis, John Beeken.*

Isle of Wight Calendar

Some of these dates were provisional as we went to press.

April

4th **Brook** Easter Steam-up and Vintage Ploughing Match *at Compton Farm*

May

2nd **Arreton** Living History *at Arreton Manor – occupants dress in 17th-c costume and depict manor life as during the Civil War*

16th **Ventnor** Festival of Arts and Crafts – *till Weds 18*

23rd **Ventnor** Music-for-fun Festival – *till Sun 29*

27th **Cowes** Review of D-Day Veterans and Yachts – *from all Cowes yacht clubs as part of the commemoration of the Royal Yacht Squadron as the base for J Force*

29th **Bembridge** Festival – *till 4 Jun*

30th **Ventnor** Crab Fayre *at Botanic Gardens*

June

5th **Bembridge** Vintage Aircraft Fly-in *at Bembridge airport*

10th **Binstead** Isle of Wight Heavy-horse Festival – *till Sun 12*

11th **Ventnor** Smuggling Pageant – *till Fri 17*

18th **Cowes** Round the Island Yacht Race

19th **Niton** Mackerel Fayre

25th **Shorwell** Midsummer Fair

July

16th **Alum Bay** Fireworks Extravaganza *inc skydivers and live music at Needles Pleasure Park*

21st **Newport** County Agricultural Show *at Northwood Showground*

30th **Cowes** Yacht Racing *as part of Cowes Week – till 7 Aug*; **Mottistone** Open-air Jazz *at Mottistone Manor*

August

7th **Cowes** Children's Carnival Procession

8th **Arreton** Manor Pageant *with Morris men and country games*

10th **Sandown** Regatta *in the bay*

20th **Newchurch** Garlic Festival – *till Sun 21*

24th **Newport** Children's Carnival

25th **Newport** Carnival

26th **Havenstreet** Isle of Wight Steam Extravaganza *with steam displays, events, sheepdog trials and stalls – till Mon 29*

27th **Newport** Illuminated Carnival

28th **Cowes** Classic International Offshore Power-boat Race

29th **St Helens** Carnival and Sports Day

September

4th **Havenstreet** Morris Minor Owners Club Rally

November

5th **St Helens** Guy Fawkes Competition and Torchlight Procession

KENT

The west of Kent is quite a good area for an adult break, with charming houses and gardens to visit, villages with attractive tile-hung and weatherboarded dwellings and old stone-built churches, a good smattering of antique shops, teashops and so forth, and the attractive Wealden countryside of little hills and valleys, oak woods and some peaceful far views. The landscape in the west tends to be more open, the view often blocked anyway by the orchards' tall windbreaks. But this part of the county has a good number of excellent family attractions, besides Canterbury itself, that are very rewarding to the first-time visitor.

There's a reasonable choice of places to stay in both halves of the county – rather wider, as is the choice of places to eat, in the west than the east.

CANTERBURY AND EAST KENT

There are plenty of very good family attractions and some pleasant coastal resorts in this part of the county; Canterbury is well worth visiting.

Canterbury has many fine buildings besides the cathedral itself, and two interesting heritage centres – even if as a city it doesn't have the same overall sense of style as, say, York or Chester. Elsewhere, there are many interesting places to visit, including plenty attractive to families: best among them are the castle and heritage centre at Dover, enjoyable zoos at Bekesbourne and Lympne, the tropical bird park at Blean, and the famously quaint Romney Hythe & Dymchurch Railway. The coast has some pleasant resorts dating from pre-railway Victorian days, when boats brought well-to-do Londoners down the coast. When the early coastbound railways took many more people to the seaside elsewhere, these forerunners – most notably Broadstairs – settled into a tranquillity that at least to a degree they've kept till today. The inland countryside's undoubtedly at its best when the apple and cherry orchards are in bloom, generally April and early May; the many farm shops have local apples from September onwards – and that's a fine time to visit the extraordinary collection of rare apple and other fruit varieties at the Brogdale Trust near Faversham.

This year we've been able nearly to double the choice of recommended places to stay here – some nice finds.

Where to stay

Ashford TR0042 EASTWELL MANOR Eastwell Park, Broughton Lees TN25 4HR (0233) 635751 ***£110**; 23 prettily decorated, spacious rms. Fine Jacobean-style manor (actually built in the 1920s) in 62 acres of private grounds; grand oak-panelled rooms, open fires, comfortable leather seating, fresh flowers, very good service and extremely good food; snooker, croquet, pitch-and-putt, riding, tennis and lots of walks; disabled access.
Chartham TR1054 THRUXTED OAST Mystole Canterbury CT4 7BX (0227) 730080 ***£73**; 3 charming rms. Carefully converted 18th-c oasthouse, surrounded by hop gardens and orchards, with breakfast served in big farmhouse kitchen; pretty terrace, croquet, and their picture-framing workshop, gallery and gift shop; cl 24-26 Dec; children by arrangement.
Canterbury TR1557 THANINGTON 140 Wincheap CT1 3RY (0227) 453227 **£55**; 10 rms linked to main building by Georgian-style conservatory. Thoughtfully run and warmly welcoming hotel, with elegant little rooms, games room, walled garden, and indoor swimming pool; cl Christmas.
St Margarets at Cliffe TR3644 CLIFFE TAVERN HOTEL Dover CT15 6AT (0304) 852 749 **£54.80**; 12 rms, most in two little cottages across yard from main pub. Series of 17th-c buildings with popular, imaginative food.
St Margarets at Cliffe TR3644 WALLETT'S COURT Dover CT15 6EW (0304) 852 424 ***£50**; 7 rms. Fine old building – the cellars date back to Domesday – with antiques and comfortable seating, and very good seasonal food in the popular, simple restaurant; cl Christmas.
Barham TR2050 DUKE OF CUMBERLAND CT4 6NY (0227) 831396 **£35**; 3 rms. Pleasant and spacious two-bar local with big helpings of good-value straightforward lunchtime food.

To see and do

Canterbury You can't really rush a visit to Canterbury, with its wealth of historic buildings; it's best explored on foot. Many of its narrow streets are pedestrianised, with good car parks on the fringes of the old centre. There are good guided walks from the Visitor Information Centre, 34 St Margaret's St; if you're making your own way, don't miss Palace St, Burgate with the Buttermarket Sq, and St Peters St, all of which have fine buildings. Wherever you turn, there are antique shops, though prices here are not low.

✝ Since Roman times this ancient city has been at the forefront of political and religious events, and there are even older traces here – notably a prehistoric tumulus in Dane John garden. The ROMAN MOSAIC MUSEUM (Longmarket) is underground, by the remains of a Roman town house, with good reconstructions and hi-tech displays; shop, disabled access; cl Sun (exc Jun-Oct), Good Fri and Christmas week; £1.40. The oldest continuously used church in the country is ST MARTIN'S CHURCH, North Holmes Rd, in use before the mid 6th c; the Venerable Bede says it was built by the Romans, and there are certainly Roman bricks in the walls.

✝ The famous CATHEDRAL spectacularly lives up to expectations – for the most overwhelming first impression, it's best approached from Queningate. The earliest parts are Norman, with much added in the 15th c; there's a very impressive nave, fascinating stained glass, the Bell Harry Tower and the shrine of Thomas Becket, murdered here in the 12th c.

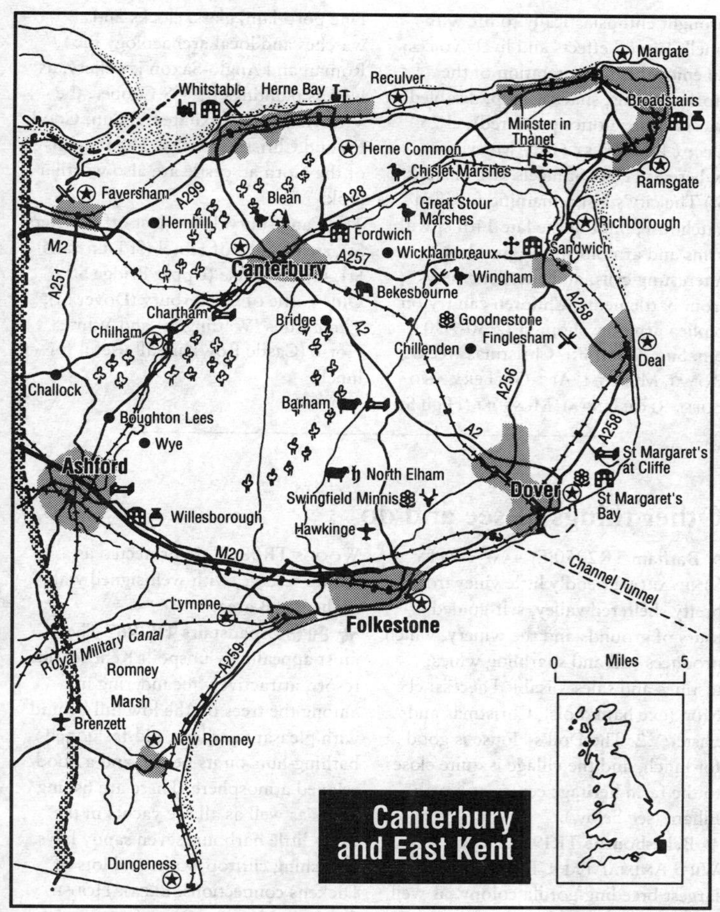

It's dramatically floodlit in summer, and there are concerts throughout the year; shop, disabled access; may be closed for services at certain times, cl am Sun. From the cathedral it's not far to the ruins of the former monastery and the medieval Kings School (The Borough). More ruins can be seen at St Augustine's Abbey (Longport) founded at the end of the 6th c and rebuilt in the 11th; it's the remains of the medieval Benedictine Abbey you can see today. Shop, disabled access; cl 1-2 pm, Mon; £1.20.

h ! ⚱ ▣ ♜ Canterbury Heritage Museum (Stour St) is housed in the fine medieval Poor Priests Hospital, where the story of the city is splendidly told with deft use of the most lavish and up-to-date display technology (even holograms), leaving many vivid visual impressions – one of the most rewarding places in the South East; shop, some disabled access; cl Sun (exc pm Jun-Oct), Good Fri and Christmas week; £1.40. Hidden away through an arch beside the building is the charming Greyfriars, above the River Stour. The Canterbury Tales (St Margaret's St) Chaucer's characters brought enthusiastically to life with smells, sound effects and lively voices; an enjoyable interpretation of the stories. Meals, snacks, shop, disabled access (prior notice preferred); cl 25 Dec; £4.25. West Gate Museum (where St Peters St meets St Dunstans St) The city's last remaining fortified gatehouse, built in the late 14th c, with arms and armour in the guardroom, interesting cells, and excellent views from battlements. Children can try on replica armour; shop; cl 12.30-1.30 pm, Sun, Good Fri, Christmas week. Royal Museum, Art Gallery and Buffs Regimental Museum (High St) Fine porcelain, glass, clocks and watches and local archaeology inc Roman and Anglo-Saxon jewellery, as well as paintings by T S Cooper, the Victorian animal painter; cl Sun, Good Fri and Christmas week. The remains of the Norman castle are also worth a look.

The Canterbury Tales (just off St Peters St), smart Falstaff Hotel (St Dunstans St), Flying Horse (Upper Bridge St), Olde Cittie of Canterbury (Dover St), Three Tuns (Watling St) and White Horse (Castle Row) are all useful for lunch.

Other things to see and do

Barham TR2050 Elham Valley Vineyards Friendly little vineyard in pretty sheltered valley, self-guided tours of grounds and the winery, which produces still and sparkling wines; tastings and sales, disabled access; cl Mon (exc bank hols), Christmas and Easter; £2. The Doll's House is good for lunch, and the village is quite close to the farm heritage centre at North Elham (see below).

Bekesbourne TR1955 Howletts Wild Animal Park The world's largest breeding-gorilla colony, as well as tigers, cats, deer, antelope, leopards, bison and the only herd of breeding elephants in the country; lots for children, who love it. Meals, snacks, shop, limited disabled access; cl 25 Dec; *£6.50. Evenhill House in nearby Littlebourne is good for lunch, and the Bow Window Hotel and King William IV there are both useful too.

Blean TR1260 Blean Bird Park Exotic tropical birds flying free in natural setting; largest collection of breeding macaws, cockatoos and parakeets in England, also owls, peacocks, animals and woodland walks. Snacks, shops, disabled access; cl Nov-Mar; *£2.65. Nearby Blean Woods TR0860 are protected as a nature reserve, with well-signed walks in the RSPB area.

★ **Broadstairs** TR3967 The most appealingly unspoilt Kent seaside resort, attractively meandering up among the trees on the low hill behind, with pleasant gardens, old-fashioned bathing-huts on its beach, and a good relaxed atmosphere. There are fishing boats as well as all the yachts in the lively little harbour, seven sandy bays, refreshing clifftop walks and lots of Dickens connections. Bleak House Dickens Maritime and Smuggling Museum The author's favourite seaside residence, where he wrote *David Copperfield* and other works; exhibitions on this as well as local wrecks and smuggling. Snacks, shop, some disabled access; cl Dec-Feb; *£1.75. Dickens House Museum Used as the home of Betsy Trotwood in *David Copperfield*, and the parlour is furnished as in the book; also Dickens' letters and possessions. Shop; cl am, third week in Oct-Apr; *80p.

★ **Chilham** TR0653 This lovely village square is the prettiest in Kent, and several antique shops reflect its popularity with visitors

– in summer, get there early to catch it at its most photogenic. Through the handsome stone gateway are CHILHAM CASTLE GARDENS in the spacious grounds of a Jacobean house, its red brickwork a fine contrast to the stone of the 12th-c castle keep. Rose, vegetable and herb gardens reflecting Tradescant's original design, wide lawns, lakeside and woodland walks in Capability Brown park, and birds of prey centre. Meals, snacks, shop; cl mid-Oct-Easter; £2.80. The perfectly placed White Horse, and the Woolpack just down the hill, are useful for lunch. Nearby BADGERS HILL FARM has pleasant gardens, cider-making, a craft centre, tame farm animals, a play area, pick-your-own and garden centre; disabled access; cl Jan.

Chislet Marshes TR2366 have thousands of geese and ducks; duck food by the bag from the nice little Gate Inn at Boyden Gate TR2265.

Deal TR3752 Pleasantly understated seaside resort, full of nice little streets and alleys; once the busiest harbour town in the South East, and Caesar's landing point in 55 BC. DEAL CASTLE The biggest in Henry VIII's chain of coastal defences, shaped like a Tudor rose with every wall rounded to deflect shot; Iron-Age weapons and local history on display. Snacks, shop; cl 1-2 pm in winter, and winter Mon and Tues, 24-26 Dec, 1 Jan; £2. WALMER CASTLE Built at the same time and for the same reason as Deal Castle, this later became the official residence of the Lord Warden of the Cinque Ports – there's a museum about past holders of the post inc the Duke of Wellington, with the original boot he left behind. Rooms are furnished in 18th-c style, and the pretty gardens were mainly laid out by a niece of William Pitt, another notable ex-resident; snacks, shop; cl winter Mon and all Jan and Feb, 24-26 Dec, 1 Jan; £2.70. TIME-BALL TOWER Museum of time, telegraphy and maritime communication with working time-ball dropping on the hour every day; shop; cl Mon, mid-Sept-May; £1.10. The Ship (Middle St) is useful for lunch.

Dover TR3141 Most familiar as the busiest ferry port in Europe and the gateway to France, Dover also has a long and fascinating history, thanks to its strategic importance. A useful way of exploring is with the Passport to Dover scheme, which gets you into most places more cheaply. The place to start is undoubtedly DOVER CASTLE, a magnificent and excellently preserved Norman fortress with its original keep, 242-ft well and massive walls and towers. Interesting exhibitions include a lively collection of secret-agent gadgetry and Hellfire Corner, the atmospheric complex of underground tunnels that played a vital role in WWII. Also within the walls is the PHAROS TOWER, a Roman lighthouse using a fourth-floor flaring brazier as a guide-light; there's a restored SAXON CHURCH right beside it. Meals, snacks, shop, disabled access; *£5. From the castle there are interesting VIEWS of the comings and goings down in the harbour, and out to sea. OLD TOWN GAOL An unusual opportunity to experience life behind bars in a Victorian prison, with hi-tech effects recreating courtroom scenes and cell life. And if you want to tease the children, they'll even lock you (albeit briefly) in a tiny cell; shop; cl Sun am, Mon and Tues Oct-May, Christmas; £3. WHITE CLIFFS EXPERIENCE A splendidly lively interactive museum telling the story of the port from the Romans to WWII; you can row in a Roman galley, talk to soldiers or walk through a 1944 blitzed street. Snacks, shop, disabled access; cl 25 Dec; £4.25. The same site also has a MUSEUM with more conventional displays. CRABBLE CORN MILL Beautifully restored working 19th-c water mill, still producing the flour that used to serve the troops; snacks (made using their own flour), shop;

times have varied recently – best to tel (0304) 823292; £2.50. ROMAN PAINTED HOUSE Well-preserved remains of a Roman hotel with wall paintings and elaborate underfloor heating system; shop, disabled access; cl Mon (exc bank hols), Nov-Mar; *£1.50. Blakes (Castle St) is useful for lunch.

Dungeness TR0916
DUNGENESS INFORMATION CENTRE AND POWER STATIONS Tours of either the A or the B power station, with hi-tech interactive displays, videos and models; cl Sat Nov-Mar, five days over Christmas; no children under 5, as everyone has to wear a hard hat. The RSPB NATURE RESERVE on the shingle headland is interesting for its unusual plants and in late spring for the nesting terns; cl Tues; £1. The Pilot right on the beach is useful for lunch, and a stroll away from OLD DUNGENESS LIGHTHOUSE, left stranded by the retreating sea and now redundant; it gives fine desolate views from the top.

★ **Faversham** TR0161
Delightfully photogenic village ideal for a stroll, plenty of colourwashed timbered old buildings such as the Elizabethan grammar school and the Guildhall (one of the few raised market halls still to shelter stallholders in the pillared market court beneath it – Tues/Fri/Sat). The very good FLEUR DE LIS HERITAGE CENTRE, all the better for the impetus given it by enthusiastic volunteers, is in another 16th-c building: the best way of discovering the town's heritage, with audio-visual show, colourful displays, reconstructions and working vintage-telephone exchange; shop (good for books on Kent); cl Sun Nov-Mar; *£1 for museum. Walking tours of Faversham leave here every Sat Apr-Sept and cost 50p. Read's is very good for lunch; the Elephant is simpler but good, and you might also try the Hole in the Wall. Outside among the orchards around Luddenham, the Mounted Rifleman's as unspoilt a traditional Kentish country tavern as you'll find anywhere and well worth a passing visit. BROGDALE TRUST (Brogdale Rd) A mammoth fruit farm that's a beautiful but baffling place to stroll through, its 30 acres of orchards producing hundreds of distinct varieties of every fruit imaginable. If you took the doctors' advice and had an apple a day you could go for nearly seven years here without ever having to have the same kind – there are no less than 2,500 variants. They also hold the National Fruit Collections, and are developing gardens to show how fruit farming has changed over the centuries. The shop sells trees and bushes and plenty of examples of their crop – from pears, plums and cherries to cobnuts, quinces and medlars; snacks, disabled access; cl Mon, Tues and all Dec-Mar; £2. Four miles west of town BELMONT is a pleasant 18th-c mansion, with a walled garden and an unusual collection of clocks; snacks, shop, disabled access; open pm wknds and bank hols Easter-Oct; £3.80.

! **Folkestone** TR2336
The second major cross-Channel port has developed a lot in the last 200 years. There is an intact pre-19th-c area called the Bayle around the interesting old CHURCH – very pretty and Kentish as far as it goes. Though the part around the harbour, previously a picturesque warren, was badly bombed in WWII, the fish stalls there contribute authentic local colour, and the Old High St has a certain Cornish-type quaintness. The remains known inaccurately as CAESAR'S CAMP show the town's history goes back much further. Particularly pleasant is a walk along the Leas, a clifftop expanse of lawns and flower gardens with good views. MUSEUM AND ART GALLERY The history of the town up to WWII, with fossils, archaeology, ceramics and glass, as well as regular art exhibitions; cl Weds pm, Sun and bank hols. ROTUNDA AMUSEMENT PARK Traditional fairground, with range of

family rides, lots undercover, also a big market Sun and bank hols; meals, snacks, shop, disabled access; cl Nov-Easter; £6 Mon-Sat, £7 Sun and bank hols. The Lifeboat (North St) and old-fashioned British Lion (by the parish church) are good for lunch.

EUROTUNNEL EXHIBITION CENTRE (out of town by M20, beyond Cheriton TR1936) The history, design and engineering of the Channel Tunnel and what it will be like to go through it, by car, bike or train; lively interactive displays. Meals, snacks (in French-style café), shop, disabled access; cl 25 Dec; £3. Out here, the Master Brewer is handy for lunch.

Fordwich TR1859 OLD TOWN HALL Tudor town hall and courthouse thought to be the oldest and smallest in England, overlooking River Stour; shop; cl am (exc Aug), Oct-May (exc Easter); 40p. The old jail can also be visited. The Fordwich Arms is good for lunch.

Goodnestone TR2553 GOODNESTONE PARK Old-fashioned roses in traditional walled garden recalling Jane Austen's stays in the fine 18th-c house (not open); also woodland garden with good trees. Teas Weds and Sun May-Aug, nursery, disabled access; cl Tues, Sat, Sun in Oct, Nov-Mar; £2.

Great Stour Marshes TR2262 are interesting for their thousands of geese and ducks; access from the good Grove Ferry pub just off the A28 near Upstreet TR2263.

Hawkinge TR2139 KENT BATTLE OF BRITAIN MUSEUM Aeroplanes in hangar, extensive collection of relics and memorabilia of British and German aircraft involved in the fighting; also uniforms and full-sized reconstructions. Snacks, shop; cl Nov-Easter; *£2.50.

Herne Bay TR1768 is a decorous and spaciously laid-out 19th-c resort. HERNE WINDMILL Early Kentish smock mill built at the end of 17th c, now restored and working, with original machinery; tel (0227) 361326 for opening details; 50p. There are other working windmills at Stelling Minnis TR1446 and Wittersham TQ8927.

Herne Common TR1865 BRAMBLES WILDLIFE PARK 20-acre woodland park with lots of animals inc deer, owls, foxes, wallabies and wildcats; also small rare-breed farm, walk-in rabbit enclosure and indoor garden. Snacks, shop, disabled access; cl Nov-Easter; *£2.

Hernhill TR0660 MOUNT EPHRAIM GARDENS Seven acres of pleasant gardens, with Japanese rock garden, topiary garden, water garden, woodland walk and small vineyard; good views. Craft centre on Sun (exc July); snacks, shop; cl Tues, Oct-mid-Apr; *£2. By the church and small green of this charming village, the ancient Red Lion is good for lunch.

Lympne TR1135 PORT LYMPNE WILD ANIMAL PARK, MANSION AND GARDENS 300-acre park with hundreds of rare animals inc the only pair of Sumatran rhinos in western world; also elephants, other rhinos, wolves, leopards, monkeys, and gorillas. The house has the Hexagonal Library used to sign the Treaty of Paris after WWI as well as lots of other interesting things to look at. Broad views over Romney Marsh, and beyond to the sea. Meals, snacks, shop, limited disabled access; cl 25 Dec; *£6.50. LYMPNE CASTLE Fortified medieval manor house remodelled in Edwardian times, with good Romney Marsh and Channel views from Norman tower.

Margate TR3571 Often rather brash seaside resort, but plenty of fun for families, and excellent sandy beaches. GROTTO 2,000 sq ft of winding underground passages and exquisitely decorated tunnels leading to a mysterious ancient shell temple, thought to be the only one in the world. An amazing place, it was found accidentally by schoolboys in 1835, and no one really knows its origins or what it was for; shop; cl Nov-Mar; *£1. OLD TOWN HALL LOCAL HISTORY MUSEUM Concentrates on the town's history from the 18th c to the present, and especially on its development as a Victorian resort; shop; cl Sun, all Oct-Apr; 80p. TUDOR HOUSE AND MUSEUM The oldest non-secular building in the town, a very well-preserved early 16th-c house with rich plaster ceilings and moulded beams, now housing a local-history museum. As we went to press the museum was open only to prebooked groups but it was hoped this would soon change – best to check first, tel (0843) 225511 DREAMLAND THEME PARK Lots of lively traditional fairground rides inc the tallest big wheel in Britain; meals, snacks, shop, disabled access; open wknds and school hols Apr-Oct; £7.50 for all-day pass covering all rides. To the east of town on College Rd there's a working WINDMILL.

New Romney TR0624 ROMNEY HYTHE & DYMCHURCH RAILWAY The world's smallest-scale public railway, with 13½ miles of 15-in-gauge track; New Romney station also has a toys and models museum with two magnificent model railways. Snacks, shop; cl wkdys Oct and Mar, all Nov-Feb; £7.10, inc the museum. The hillside town of HYTHE TR1634 is itself well worth a stroll around, for the attractive old houses to be found in its narrow High St and the pretty lanes around the church. Its beach stretches up to Sandgate, which is also pleasant to stroll through (with a couple of decent pubs, the Ship and, closer to Hythe itself, the Clarendon tucked up a steep cobbled track above the sea; the Lord Nelson in Hythe is also useful). Inland, ROMNEY MARSH is the most unspoilt corner of Kent, flat country laced with drainage ditches and isolated farmsteads: St Mary in the Marsh has a small but attractive church, and a good flagstoned pub – the Star. If you don't want to penetrate the Marsh quite so deeply, near Brookland TQ9825 (see West Kent map) on the main A259 (actually on Walland Marsh) the sign to the Woolpack leads you to another good pub with the right sort of atmosphere for the area. Standing quite alone in the marshes FAIRFIELD CHURCH TQ9626 is a tent-roofed brick-and-timber building, remarkable for its utterly lonely surroundings – and attractive inside.

North Elham TR1844 PARSONAGE FARM Rural heritage centre dating from medieval times, with traditional and rare breeds of pigs and cattle, cereal production, nature trails and old agricultural equipment; snacks, shop, disabled access; cl Mon (exc bank hols), Oct-Easter; £2.30. The Kings Head is useful for lunch.

Ramsgate TR3865 A quiet and civilised seaside resort, with some elegantly colonnaded Georgian buildings and other fine houses up on the cliffs (Pugin, the architect of the Houses of Parliament, designed the church – where he's buried – and the house next door), and a historic harbour (bustling now with its yacht marina and Hoverport). MARITIME MUSEUM Displays exploring maritime heritage of East Kent, with a collection of historic ships and boats; shop; cl winter wknds; £1. RAMSGATE LIBRARY ARCHIVE MUSEUM Local-history museum; shop, disabled access; cl Sun and bank hols.

Reculver TR2269 The 3rd-c ROMAN FORT was well preserved until the 18th c, when cliff erosion caused some of it to collapse into the sea; there are still some bits, though it's the proud pair of tall Saxon towers of the former church on the mound above the beach that stay in the memory. Surrounding these remains is a COUNTRY PARK, with a good visitor centre.

Richborough TR3461 RICHBOROUGH CASTLE Ruined Roman

castle, lots of walls, remains and a museum about the site; snacks, shop, disabled access; cl 1-2 pm, Mon Oct-Mar; *£1.50.

St Margaret's Bay TR3844 PINES GARDEN AND BAY MUSEUM Six acres of trees, shrubs, flowers and an ornamental lake, with a little local-history museum showing the area's long-established role as the gateway to Europe; disabled access; museum cl am, all day Mon and Fri, bank hol wknds and Sept-May, garden cl 25 Dec; *£1. The spectacularly sited Coastguard is useful for refreshments.

Sandwich TR3358 is a pleasant quiet town with a surprising number of medieval remains, including some sections of the old town wall and three handsome medieval CHURCHES, one part-Norman. In its day it was one of England's main commercial ports; the sea's now left it far behind. The best timbered buildings are in Strand St, with some by the attractive former quay on the River Stour (the old Bargate is very photogenic). As we went to press they were considering a festival for 1994, but had not decided (so no dates). There's a WINDMILL on the A258 just out of town.

Swingfield Minnis TR2142 BUTTERFLY CENTRE Tropical greenhouse garden with lots of colourful free-flying butterflies among exotic plants; snacks, shop, disabled access; cl mid-Oct-Mar; £1.95.

Whitstable TR1166 MUSEUM AND GALLERY (Oxford St) Exploration of the town's seafaring traditions, with features on divers, shipbuilding and oyster fishers, as well as various temporary exhibitions; shop, disabled access; cl 1-2 pm, Weds and Sun, Good Fri, Christmas week. CHUFFA TRAINS RAILMANIA MUSEUM is ideal for children, with model trains to play on, as well as other railway memorabilia; model-railway shop; cl Sun, Christmas-New Year; *£1.50. Whitstable also has an unusual ETHNIC DOLL AND TOY MUSEUM, with dolls and their houses from all over the world, as well as working railways and other toys; teas, shop; cl Christmas-end Jan.

Willesborough TR0241 has a restored working WINDMILL with lots to see and a small museum; snacks, shop, disabled access to ground floor only; open pm wknds and bank hols May-Oct; *£1.

★ **Wingham** TR2457 WINGHAM BIRD PARK Lots of endangered species of birds from all over the world here, with the emphasis on breeding; there are observation shelters by the lake so you can see waterfowl at close range. Also raccoons, wallabies and other animals; snacks, shop, disabled access; cl wkdys Nov-mid-Feb; *£2.75. The village is attractive, with a good restaurant (the Four Seasons); the Red Lion is also useful for lunch, as is the Eight Bells over at Wingham Well.

★ **Other attractive villages**, all with decent pubs, include Boughton Lees TR0247, Bridge TR1854, Challock TR0050, Chillenden TR2653, Wickhambreaux TR2158 and Wye TR0546.

Walks

Some of the most pleasant walks in this part of the county are on the **North Downs** – not that high, but steep enough along the escarpment to give some great views. The **Wye Downs** TR0745, designated a nature reserve for their chalkland flora that includes a variety of orchids (the 'green winged' is perhaps the commonest), look across the orchards below to both the Thames Estuary and the Channel.

The long-distance **Saxon Shore Way** also gives some good views and interesting walks. From Etchinghill TR1639, it crosses under an old railway line, heads up an unspoilt dry valley, and leads along the top of the slope for sightings of Dungeness and the French coast (Cap Gris Nez in Picardy). Elsewhere it takes in the Royal Military Canal TQ9630, built along the north fringe of Romney Marsh as a defence against Napoleon. The towpath from West Hythe TR1234 takes you up into Hythe itself, where a path from the junction of Station Rd (B2065) and Mill Lane enters parkland and continues up to Saltwood Castle TR1634, which still has its impressive medieval curtain wall.

From the east cliff at Folkestone you can walk out past the Martello Tower into **The Warren** TR2437, an intriguingly tumbledown undercliff; there's no way from here up on to the clifftop – which itself, on another occasion, makes for a good bracing walk, from Folkestone all the way to Dover for the train or bus back. At the Dover end, the famous **white cliffs** provide an exhilarating walk (and interesting views of the harbour – you can even see France on a clear day) from Dover Castle to St Margaret's at Cliffe TR3644, passing the Roman lighthouse above Dover and a curious scaled-down windmill at St Margaret's at Cliffe. There's a bus back to Dover (no point making a circuit, as the inland scenery here is not worth while), or you can press on to Kingsdown TR3748 or to Deal TR3752.

On the **Thanet coast**, there's a pleasant walk from **Broadstairs** TR3967 to **Ramsgate** TR3865.

Driving

One of the most notable roads here is the B2068 and its unclassified link with Canterbury, an old Roman road running straight as a die down to the coast (the detour to the nice country pub outside Stowting, the Tiger, is well worth while). More twistily, the B2065 down the lovely Elham Valley is a pleasant drive, passing several good pubs such as the Doll's House near Barham and (both good for families) the New Inn and Rose & Crown in Elham itself. The lanes above Wye also give a good taste of the quieter parts of the East Kent countryside; looping N of the Wye Downs and on past the Crundale Downs takes you past a pleasant country pub, the Compasses at Sole Street.

The orchard country inland from Kent's N coast is pretty to drive through at blossom time (and there may be pick-your-own soft fruit here in summer): between Gillingham and Boughton Street it's worth following any of the little lanes off the A2 (which carries relatively little traffic these days). There's a decent pub in Boughton Street itself (the White Horse), and others well worth working into a drive through this area include the Dove at Dargate, White Lion at Selling, and Carpenters Arms at Eastling.

Where to eat

Faversham TR0161 READ'S Painters Forstal (0795) 535344 Attractively decorated restaurant with imaginative, carefully prepared food and an excellent wine list; cl Sun/Mon, 2 wks end Aug; disabled access. **£33.50 evening, £19.50 lunch.**

Wingham TR2457 FOUR SEASONS (0227) 720286 Small restaurant, overlooking attractive garden, with a good choice of interesting food; cl 3-15 Jan. £20|£4.85/£8.

Whitstable TR1166 PEARSONS (0227) 272005 Consistently good and very fresh seafood inc shellfish and daily-changing fresh fish; traditional furnishings, and kind and quick service – even when very busy; upstairs restaurant; cl 25 Dec. £17.35|£1.50/£9.

Finglesham TR3353 CROWN (0304) 612555 Pleasant country pub with wide choice of reasonably priced bar food, popular old-world restaurant with inglenook fireplace and flagstones, and good, friendly service; cl am 25-26 Dec. £15.60|£1.30/£2.95.

WEST KENT

Here there are lovely houses and gardens to visit and the countryside is quietly attractive.

This part of Kent's greatest appeal is to adults. It's a good area for a quiet break, exploring villages (with their many antique shops) and countryside, taking in some of the 'sights' at the same time. The main draw for visitors here is the wealth of beautiful houses and gardens, especially Leeds Castle, the gardens of Scotney Castle near Lamberhurst, Sissinghurst Garden, Penshurst Place, Chartwell and Squerryes Court near Westerham, Ightham Mote and Hever Castle. The Finchcocks collection of keyboard instruments at Goudhurst is fascinating to anyone who's interested in music. None of these mentioned above is much fun for children, but other places here do have quite a lot for children to enjoy, most notably the Whitbread Hop Farm at Beltring, the farm park at Dartford, the little steam railway at Tenterden and, for older children, the Chatham dockyard.

The countryside is not dramatic, but has an intimate charm, with a wealth of detail in the village and country scenes, and some very pleasant walks. This is particularly true of the part known as the Weald, marked by the many villages whose names end in -den: to seem less of an outsider, you should know that the stress is always on the last syllable of these names, the reverse of how you'd guess they were pronounced. Any holiday in this part would almost certainly spill over, like the Weald itself, into neighbouring parts of East Sussex, which have a very similar appeal.

Tunbridge Wells is no longer the spa town that it once was, though the Pantiles there is still a pleasant spot, and the town usually has some interesting things going on – as well as comfortable places to stay. There's a good choice in other parts, too, though not cheap.

We welcome reports from readers . . .

This GUIDE depends on readers' reports. Please tell us what you think about places in it. And do recommend additions. Use the card in the middle, the report forms at the end, or just write – no stamp needed: THE GOOD WEEKEND GUIDE, FREEPOST TN1569, Wadhurst, E Sussex TN5 7BR.

Where to stay

Tunbridge Wells TQ5639 Spa TN4 8JX (0892) 520331 **£117**; 76 comfortable rms. Run by the same family for three generations, this Georgian hotel, set in 14 acres of landscaped gardens, has a comfortable, partly no-smoking lounge with panelling, popular and attractive bar, nice old-fashioned atmosphere and friendly, long-serving staff; leisure centre with indoor heated swimming pool, gym, beauty salon, and floodlit hard tennis court, children's adventure playground and games room; disabled access.

Boughton Monchelsea TQ7751 Tanyard Maidstone ME17 4JT (0622) 744 705 ***£80**; 6 beamed rms. Appealing medieval yeoman's house with fine views, cosy day rooms with log fires and beams, and garden; cl 21 Dec-1 Feb, children over 6.

Tunbridge Wells TQ5639 Mount Edgecombe Hotel TN8 8BX (0892) 526 823 **£80**; 6 attractive rms. Smart, well-run small hotel on the Common, with friendly staff, very good food in restaurant and characterful bar (built into the rock) and excellent wines with a choice of up to 20 by the glass.

Tenterden TQ8833 White Lion High St TN30 6BD (0580) 765077 **£60**; 15 rms. 350-year-old coaching inn, comfortably refurbished, with very good food in bar and dining room, and friendly, efficient service.

Warren Street TQ9253 Harrow Maidstone ME17 2ED (0622) 858727 ***£58**; 15 rms. Immaculate country inn with quietly low-key atmosphere; flowers, candles and big woodburning stove, extensive comfortably modernised low-beamed bar, attentive service and generous helpings of well-cooked food; cl 25 Dec.

Pluckley TQ9245 Elvey Farm Ashford TN27 0SU (023 3840) 442 **£55.50**; 9 rms, some in the oast house roundel, some in original barn and stable block. This 15th-c farmhouse is in a secluded spot on 75-acre working family farm with timbered rooms, inglenook fireplace, and French windows from lounge on to sun terrace; cl Christmas; lots of play areas for children; disabled access.

Shipbourne TQ5952 Chaser Stumble Hill TN11 9PE (0732) 810360 **£50**; 15 rms. Colonial-style building with porticoed front in a lovely spot by the village church and green; comfortable and homely atmosphere in well-kept bar, with a wide range of attractively presented good food in both the bar and the restaurant; restaurant cl pm, Mon; disabled access.

Sissinghurst TQ7937 Sissinghurst Castle Farm Cranbrook TN17 2AB (0580) 712885 **£46**; 3 rms, one with own bthrm. Victorian farmhouse in the grounds of Sissinghurst Castle, with spacious rooms and pretty garden; farm is mostly arable with cattle and sheep; children over 5.

Eastling TQ9656 Carpenters Arms Faversham ME13 0AZ (0795) 890234 ***£45**; 3 rms. Pretty pub with cottagey bric-a-brac and lace tablecloths, oak beams and big fireplaces; warm welcome, pleasant food in bar and restaurant, and decent wines; children over 12.

Penshurst TQ5243 Swale Cottage Old Swaylands Lane, Tonbridge TN11 8AH (0892) 870738 **£45**; 3 beamed rms. Careful conversion of 13th-c Grade II* listed barn and hayloft, with good breakfasts, cottage garden, and set a few yards from where the little girl 'Wendy' (Barrie's *Peter Pan* heroine) lived; children over 12.

Goudhurst TQ7238 Star & Eagle High St TN17 1AL (0580) 21152 **£40**; 11 character rms, most with own bthrm. Striking medieval inn with comfortable, Jacobean-style furnishings in heavy-beamed day rooms; pretty views, polite staff, and Whitbread's ales; disabled access.

Headcorn TQ8344 BLETCHENDEN MANOR FARM Ashford TN27 0JB (0622) 890228 *£37.50; 3 rms, most with own bthrm. 15th-c farmhouse surrounded by own farmland in Weald of Kent; big beamed dining room, own sitting room; cl Christmas; children over 12; self-catering also.
Charing TQ9549 BARNFIELD Ashford TN27 0BN (023 371) 2421 £36; 4 beamed rms, shared big bthrm. Delightful early 15th-c farmhouse with fine beams, big open fires, comfortable sitting rooms, lots of books, antiques, big garden, good food and friendly owners.
Pluckley TQ9243 DERING ARMS Ashford TN27 0RR (0233) 840 371 £36; 3 rms, shared bthrm. Friendly and relaxed bars, simply and attractively decorated with a variety of wooden furniture on wood and stone floors; wonderful food with emphasis on fish and gourmet evenings every six weeks; vintage-car rally once a month; cl 26 Dec.
Teston TQ7053 COURT LODGE The Street Maidstone ME18 5AQ (0622) 812570 *£36; 3 rms. Pretty garden, orchards and hop gardens surround this 16th-c house, which has inglenook fireplaces and beams; cl Christmas and New Year; children over 12.
Groombridge TQ5337 CROWN Tunbridge Wells TN3 9QH (0892) 864 742 £35; 4 rms, shared bthrm. Relaxed and chatty atmosphere in Elizabethan house set on village green; timbered and rough plaster walls and suitable traditional decoration, tasty and popular food, and quick service.
Smarden TQ8842 CHEQUERS Ashford TN27 8QA (0233) 770217 £34; 6 good-value rms, shared bthrm. Comfortable old-world pub full of character, with beams, log fire; varied choice of really good reasonably priced food inc vegetarian dishes and seasonal vegetables, exceptionally good breakfasts; cl 25 Dec.

To see and do

✝ 🏛 ✿ **Aylesford** TQ7359 AYLESFORD PRIORY Built in the 13th and 14th c and closed down in the Reformation, it is now restored and the home of a group of Carmelite Friars; fine cloisters, chapels, sculptures and ceramics by modern artists and potters, and beautiful grounds. Snacks, shop, disabled access; tearoom and shop cl Christmas and Easter. KITS COTY HOUSE up the road towards the A229 is a massive Stone-Age tomb chamber which 'mightily impressed' Pepys when he saw it. The Little Gem is a very quaint little pub.

🏰 **Bedgebury Pinetum** TQ7133 is a lakeside landscaped valley full of magnificent conifers, with walks up through forest plots designed to try out the commercial possibilities of all sorts of little-known species; £1.

🐑 🦆 ⚱ **Beltring** TQ6747 WHITBREAD HOP FARM Largest surviving group of Victorian oast houses and galleried barns, housing museums on hop-farming through the ages, rural crafts and farming machinery; also nature trails, birds of prey, shire horses, special events most summer wknds – a very popular family outing. Meals, snacks, shop, some disabled access; cl 25, 26, 31 Dec; £4.50.

★ ✝ 🐑 **Biddenden** TQ8438 This attractive village has several interesting old houses on the south side of the High St, and a handsome 13th-c CHURCH with a bold tower. Towards Benenden are BIDDENDEN VINEYARDS with pleasant strolls around thriving wine- and cider-producing vineyard, now covering over 20 acres. Samples of both wines and ciders, harvesting in Oct and bottling in Mar. Summer snacks, shop; cl Sun Jan and Feb, 24 Dec-2 Jan.

✿ **Borough Green** TQ6157 GREAT

Comp Garden (2 miles E) Interesting collection of trees, shrubs, herbaceous plants and heathers with fine lawns and paths; teas on Sun and bank hols, plant shop; cl Nov-Mar; £2.50. The Plough at Ivy Hatch a few miles south is very good for lunch.

❀ ✺ **Brasted** TQ4755 EMMETT'S GARDEN Charming hillside shrub garden with magnificent VIEWS – it's the highest garden in Kent; full of bluebells in spring and a riot of colour in autumn. Teas, shop, some disabled access; cl am, Mon (exc bank hols), Tues, Nov-Mar; £2.50. The White Hart Hotel and the Bull are both handy for lunch.

❀ **Brenchley** TQ6741 has some attractive old houses. MARLE PLACE has a pretty garden around a fine 17th-c house (not open), with interesting scented plants in the walled garden, a woodland walk, and showy bantams; herbs and other plants for sale, teas, disabled access; cl Nov-Mar; £2.

✈ **Brenzett** TR0027 AERONAUTICAL MUSEUM Wartime equipment and remains recovered from crash sites, along with aeroplanes inc a Vampire, and a Dambuster bomb; shop, disabled access; open Sun and bank hols Easter-Oct, plus pm Tues, Weds and Thurs July-Sept; £1.50.

☸ ✿ ⌂ ❀ **Chatham** TQ7567 HISTORIC DOCKYARD A Royal dockyard until 1984, now an 80-acre working museum set in the most complete Georgian dockyard in the world. Several museums, inc the Wooden Walls, showing through sights, sounds and smells how 18th-c warships such as HMS *Victory* were built here; also restorations, craft workshops and interesting Commissioner's House. Meals, snacks, shop, disabled access; cl Mon (exc bank hols) and Tues, as well as Thurs and Fri in winter; £5.20. FORT AMHERST The finest surviving 18th-c fort in the country, with massive ditches, gun emplacements, a warren of tunnels and a firing gun battery; 18 acres of parkland and live re-enactments most Sundays; snacks, shop; cl three weeks at Christmas; £2.50.

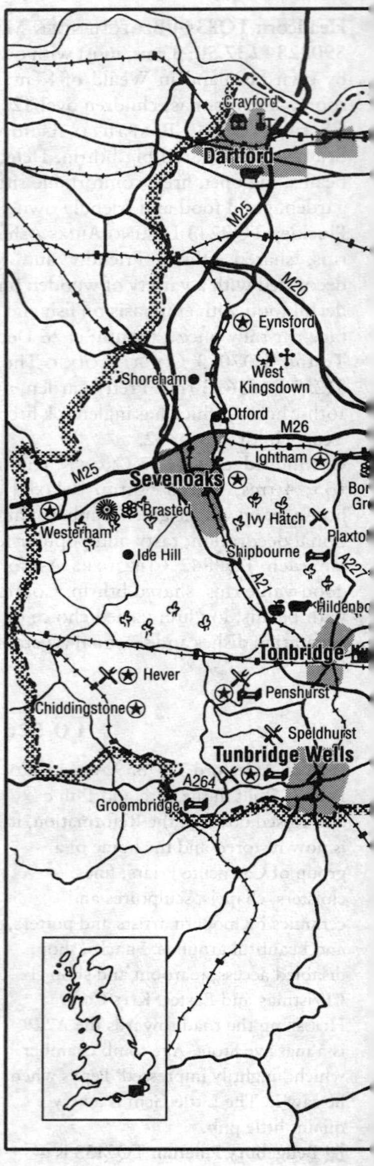

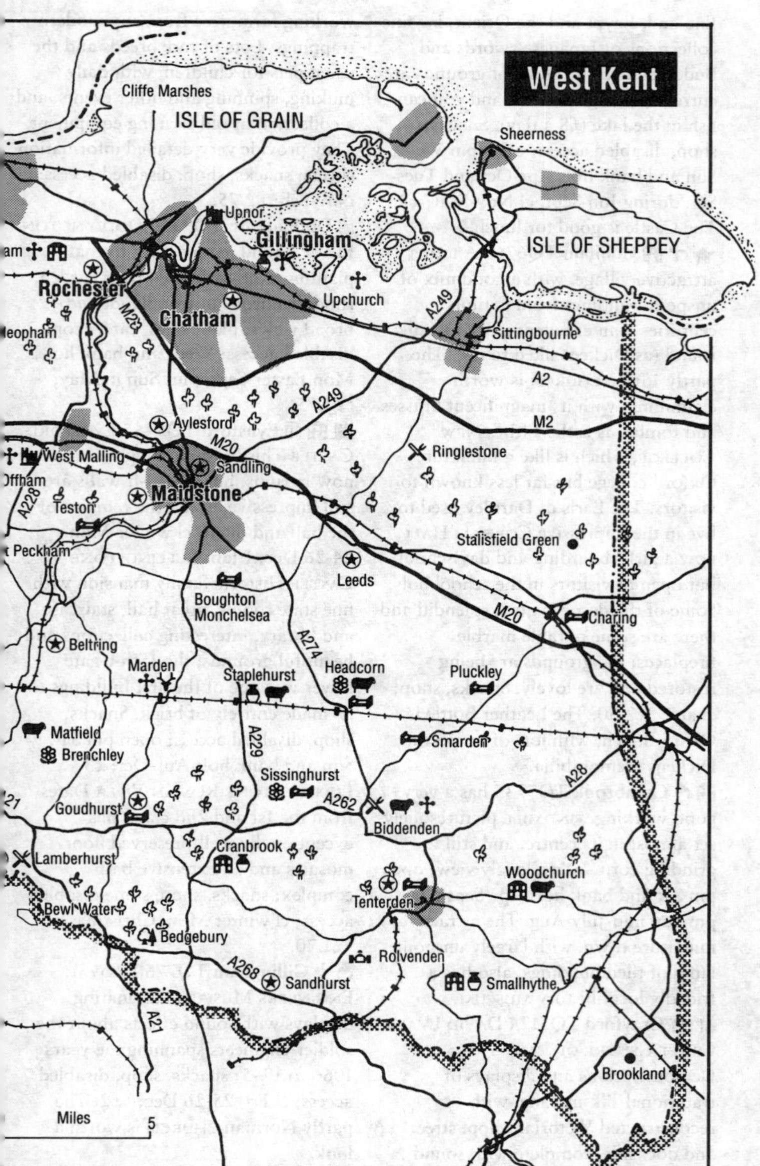

★ **Chiddingstone** TQ5045 A favourite Kentish village, an unspoilt cluster of Tudor houses and buildings owned by the NT. The church and the mysterious stone from which the village takes its name are worth a look. CHIDDINGSTONE CASTLE 17th-c house rebuilt in castle style at the start of the 19th c; renowned collection of paintings and antiquities from

England, Egypt and the Orient, inc fine collections of Japanese swords and Buddhist art. The pleasant grounds are currently being restored, and you can fish in the lake (£8 a day). Snacks, shop, disabled access; open pm Wed, Sun and bank hols Apr-Oct and Tues-Sun during Jun-Sept, cl Nov-Mar; £3. The Castle is good for lunch.

★ ✝ **Cobham** TQ6768 Another attractive village, with a good mix of unspoilt buildings from various centuries – an excellent place to walk round (as Dickens liked to do). The partly 13th-c CHURCH is worth examining, with its magnificent brasses and tombs, as is the 14th-c NEW COLLEGE, which is like a miniature Oxford college but far less known to visitors. The Earls of Darnley used to live in the impressive COBHAM HALL, now a girls' boarding and day school, but open to visitors in the school hols. Some of the decor is quite splendid and there are some notable marble fireplaces; the grounds are being restored and are lovely. Snacks, shop; cl am; *£2.50. The Leather Bottle is OK for lunch, with lots of interesting Dickens memorabilia.

Cranbrook TQ7735 has a very good working WINDMILL picturesquely set almost in its centre, and still grinding corn – it's a lovely view; open pm Sat and bank hols Apr-Sept plus pm Sun mid-July-Aug. The attractive miniature town, with largely unspoilt lanes of tiled buildings, also has a friendly local-history MUSEUM.

Crayford TQ5174 DAVID EVANS CRAFT CENTRE OF SILK Demonstrations and displays of traditional silk-making, with reconstructed Victorian shop, street and dockside, complete with sound effects. This is now the only company still producing the famous Madder silk; snacks, shop, disabled access; cl Sun and bank hols; £1. Tours of factory too by arrangement.

Dartford TQ5474 STONE LODGE FARM PARK Extremely well-organised working farm, free from any modern trappings. Lots of rare breeds and the usual pets for children, with daily milking, spinning and other events, and a collection of old farming equipment. They provide very detailed information sheets; snacks, shop, disabled access; cl Nov-Feb; £2.75.

Doddington TQ9357 DODDINGTON PLACE Grand garden with formal plantings, old-fashioned rock garden, rhododendrons in woodland, and broad views; plant sales, café, shop, disabled access; Weds and bank hol Mon Easter-Sept, plus Sun in May; *£1.75.

Eynsford TQ5465 EYNSFORD CASTLE This Norman knight's castle is now in ruins, but the 30-ft walls are still impressive, as are the remains of the hall and ditch; cl winter Mon, 24-26 Dec, 1 Jan. LULLINGSTONE CASTLE Historic family mansion with fine state rooms, great hall, staircase and library, interesting collections and beautiful grounds; the 15th-c gate tower was one of the first buildings to be made entirely of brick. Snacks, shop, disabled access; open pm Sat, Sun and bank hols Apr-Oct; £3. LULLINGSTONE ROMAN VILLA Dates from the 1st and 2nd c and has exceptionally well-preserved floor mosaics and an extensive bath complex; snacks, shop, some disabled access; cl winter Mon, Christmas; *£1.70.

✝ **Gillingham** TQ7768 ROYAL ENGINEERS MUSEUM Fascinating displays with sound effects about the soldier-engineers spanning the years 1066 to 1945; snacks, shop, disabled access; cl Fri, 25-26 Dec; *£2. The partly Norman CHURCH is worth a look.

★ **Goudhurst** TQ7237 Charming Wealden village, with quite a few antique shops and so forth, and spectacular views from the graveyard of the 14th-c hilltop church (but during the day too much traffic for comfort). FINCHCOCKS Attractive early Georgian house in extensive park with lovely recently developed gardens, and a large collection of working keyboard instruments from the 17th c onwards – some of which are played whenever the house is open; snacks, shop, some disabled access; open pm daily in Aug exc Mon and Tues, as well as pm Sun and bank hols Apr-Sept, and most other days Apr-Christmas by appointment (0580) 211702; *£5. There are various special events throughout the year, notably the concerts in Sept. The Spread Eagle up by the church, one of the village's most handsome old buildings, is useful for lunch.

Headcorn TQ8344 HEADCORN FLOWER CENTRE AND VINEYARD Enormous all-weather flower centre and vineyard, excellent chrysanthemums and orchid lilies in heated flower houses; wknd snacks, shop; £1.50. The simple George and Dragon is useful for lunch.

! **Hever** TQ4745 HEVER CASTLE AND GARDENS This double-moated 13th-c castle in 30 acres of beautiful gardens was the childhood home of Anne Boleyn. It was magnificently restored by the Astor family at the start of this century, and amongst its treasures has paintings, furniture and mementoes of the ill-fated queen as well as displays of Edwardian crafts. The grounds have lakes, an Italianate garden with antique sculptures, a walled rose garden and a maze, with a quarter of a mile of pathways. Meals, snacks, shop, some disabled access to castle, all gardens are ramped; cl early Nov-mid-Mar, castle cl am; £5, £3.60 gardens only. The Greyhound and Henry VIII are good for lunch.

Hildenborough TQ5648 RARE FARM ANIMALS OF HOLLANDEN Survival centre for rare breeds of farm animals, woodland trails, recreated Iron-Age settlement, adventure playground, pick-your-own fruit. Home baking, farm shop, some disabled access; cl Oct-Easter; *£3.40.

★ **Ightham** TQ5956 IGHTHAM MOTE One of the best remaining examples of a medieval moated manor house still with its moat, as well as fascinating great hall, Tudor chapel and 14th-c crypt. The drawing room has striking Jacobean fireplace, frieze and windows and hand-painted Chinese wallpaper; pretty courtyard, garden and woodland walks. Snacks, shop; cl am wkdys, Tues, Sat, and all Nov-Mar; £4. NT. The George & Dragon in the pretty village is useful for lunch, and the Rose & Crown at nearby Stone Street is good; snacks; shop; disabled access; cl Tues, Sat, Nov and March; £4.

✝ **Lamberhurst** TQ6736 SCOTNEY CASTLE Beautiful 19th-c gardens surrounding the ruins of a small 14th-c moated castle, with impressive rhododendrons, azaleas and roses – a really romantic place to stroll through; shop, some disabled access; cl Mon (exc bank hols, Tues, Sat and Sun am, Nov-Mar, Good Fri, castle open same hours May-mid-Sept; £3.20. NT. OWL HOUSE GARDENS 13 acres of sweeping lawns, flowers, shrubs and fruit trees around timber-framed 16th-c wool smugglers' house; sunken water gardens and woodlands; shop, disabled access; £2. BAYHAM ABBEY Technically in Sussex but more handy from here, impressive ruins of 13th-c Premonstratensian abbey and gatehouse in pretty wooded valley; cl Oct-Mar; £1.75. LAMBERHURST VINEYARD One of the biggest vineyards in the South East, also plants and home-made liqueur chocolates; disabled access; cl 25-26 Dec, 1 Jan; hourly guided tours, £2.85. TOY AND MODEL MUSEUM (Forstal Farm) Set in a typical Kent oast house above a working hop farm, a good nostalgic collection with teddies and dolls in period settings, a model railway, astonishingly detailed miniature fairground, lots of racing cars and various Rupert bear memorabilia. Nice walks around; snacks, shop, disabled access; £2. The Brown Trout, on the B2169 nearly opposite the entrance to Scotney Castle, does very good fish; the Elephants Head at Hook Green out near Bayham Abbey and Owl House is also useful for lunch.

Leeds TQ8253

LEEDS CASTLE Long renowned as one of the loveliest castles in the country, idyllically placed on two little islands in the middle of a lake in 500 acres of landscaped parkland. Dating from the 9th c, it was converted into a royal residence by Henry VIII – who always had to have a good thing when he saw it. Lots of paintings, furniture and tapestries, also unique dog-collar museum in gatehouse; the enormous grounds have gardens, a maze and grotto, duckery and aviary, a golf course, vineyard (with free tastings of English and country wines) and probably lots more that no one's quite noticed yet. Various special events throughout the year from wine festivals to open-air concerts; meals, snacks, shop, good disabled access; cl 25 Dec and before some special events; £6.50.

KENT GARDEN COSTUME DOLLS Demonstrations of the stages of creating reproduction antique porcelain dolls inc casting, polishing, painting, assembling and dressing; shop, disabled access; cl Mon-Weds, 25-26 Dec.

Maidstone TQ7555 is a busy modern town, but well worth penetrating on a weekend (when it's quieter) for its good museums.

ARCHBISHOP'S PALACE AND HERITAGE CENTRE Striking 14th-c palace used by the Archbishops of Canterbury as a stopping-place on their way from London. Recently very well restored, with a lively new heritage centre tracing the history of the building and the county; meals, snacks, shop, disabled access to heritage centre, but not all rooms of palace; cl 25-26 Dec; £2.95. Admission covers entry to the TYRWHITT DRAKE MUSEUM OF CARRIAGES in the Palace stables, which houses a notable collection of horse-drawn carriages and vehicles – official, state and private; shop, disabled access to ground floor only; cl as above; *£1.50 for this museum only. The site also includes the old parish CHURCH of All Saints. The MAIDSTONE MUSEUM AND ART GALLERY (St Faiths St) is in an Elizabethan manor house, with period furniture and fine pictures set out in original room settings; also Japanese art, ceramics, 20th-c fashions, Pacific ethnography, regimental museum and natural history; snacks, shop cl Sun am, 25-26 Dec. The Minstrel in Knightrider Rd is a useful wine bar, and the Pilot in Upper Stone St has decent bar food.

Marden TQ7444 has a 12th-14th-c ragstone CHURCH with a unique white weatherboarded tower, and other buildings going back to the 14th c; MARDEN MEADOW (Staplehurst Rd) is a lovely unimproved hay meadow, alive with wild flowers and butterflies in late spring and early summer.

Matfield TQ6541 BADSELL PARK FARM Originally built as a hunting lodge by the Earl of Westmorland, this site became an iron-working centre in the 18th c, before settling down as a typical Kentish hop farm. Now it has rare breeds of cattle, pigs, goats and sheep, poultry and pets, a butterfly house, pick-your-own soft fruits, a good farm shop, and a notable nature trail; meals, snacks, shop, disabled access; cl Dec and Jan; *£3.50.

Meopham TQ6466 has an unusual six-sided windmill, the base of which serves as a meeting place for the parish council; shop, disabled access to ground floor only; open pm Sun and bank hols May-Sept; 60p.

Minster in Thanet TQ9573

MINSTER ABBEY Site of one of the earliest nunneries in the country, with ruins and cloisters of the 7th-c building; the current house is still run by Benedictine nuns. Shop, disabled access; open 11-12 am all year exc Sun and also 2-4.30 pm May-Sept. The Mortons Fork is useful for lunch.

★ **Penshurst** TQ5243 is a pretty village, with antique shops, teas and so forth, and, above all, PENSHURST PLACE, a great medieval manor house, unchanged since the Sidney family first came here centuries ago. Interesting combination of architectural styles, huge chestnut-beamed baronial hall, state rooms with extensive collections of portraits and furnishings, toy museum and marvellous formal gardens with nature trails and adventure playground. Meals, snacks, shop, some disabled access; house cl am, and all Nov-Mar; £4.50, grounds £3. The Leicester Arms in the village is good for lunch, and above it up on Smarts Hill the Spotted Dog has lovely views down over Penshurst Place. The Bottle House and the Rock out in this direction are also both well worth tracking down if you're walking in the area.

Plaxtol TQ6053 OLD SOAR MANOR An ancient oak door at this 13th-c knight's dwelling has graffiti spanning the ages, and there's also a very well-preserved solar block, chapel, lavatorium and barrel-vaulted undercroft; cl Oct-Mar. This general area is attractive orchard country, with good-value apples from the farm shops, from Sept onwards; many here also have fresh cobnuts in Sept. The Golding Hop is useful for lunch.

† **Rochester** TQ7468 Partly because of its position on a promontory commanding the Medway, this has been an important city since Roman times, and it was here that Christianity gained one of its first footholds when the king of Kent, Ethelbert, was persuaded to set up a little chapel. It's a busy town, but well worth walking round, with several attractive buildings besides those we mention. The Norman CATHEDRAL is the most spectacular, with its original richly carved door, vaulted crypt, St Gundolphs tower, tombs and effigies and huge 15th-c window. ROCHESTER CASTLE dates from around the same time, and is one of the best examples of military architecture from this period, with an excellent storeyed keep and parts of the castle wall; all very dramatic. Snacks, shop; cl Mon, Oct-Easter, 24-26 Dec, 1 Jan; £1.70. CHARLES DICKENS CENTRE Late Tudor house used in both *Pickwick Papers* and *Edwin Drood*, now demonstrating scenes and characters from the author's books, displays on his career, local history and Victorian life; shop; cl over Christmas; £2.10. Dickens fans should also try and visit GAD'S HILL SCHOOL at Higham just out of town, the only house the writer ever owned and where he wrote many of his novels. He first saw the house as a boy, many years before he lived there, describing this first sight in *A Christmas Carol*; shop; open out of school hours by arrangement, tel (0474) 822366; £2. GUILDHALL MUSEUM Recently refurbished 17th-c building with impressive decorated plaster ceilings, local history and archaeology, dolls, toys and boats. The Coopers Arms in St Margarets St is cheap for lunch.

Rolvenden TQ8530 C M BOOTH COLLECTION OF HISTORIC VEHICLES The main feature is a unique collection of three-wheeled Morgan cars but there are also caravans, bikes, cars and toy and model-car displays. Shop; cl some Suns; *£1.20.

† **Sandhurst** TQ7928 has a fine 14th-c CHURCH with good views from the graveyard. SANDHURST VINEYARD (Hoads Farm, Crouch Lane) has tours of vineyard and hop gardens, inc hop-picking in Sept; tastings and shop; cl am wkdys, Nov-Easter. Nearby at Standen Street, Iden Green, TILE BARN NURSERY is the only one in the world to specialise in wild cyclamen, with four greenhouses filled with over two dozen miniature species, several of them hardy, in flower Sept-Apr; ring to confirm that they are open (0580)

240221.

Sandling TQ7558 MUSEUM OF KENT LIFE (Lock Lane) In 28 acres of exhibits, the story of the Kent countryside, as told by farming tools, gardens, a working oast house, machinery and animals; various crafts and regular special events; meals, snacks, shop, disabled access; cl Mon (exc bank hols), Oct-Easter; *£3. TYLAND BARN Well-restored 17th-c barn, now the headquarters of the Kent Trust for Nature Conservation, with displays and information of the many nature reserves they look after in the area; lots of events throughout the year. Snacks, shop, disabled access; cl Mon (exc bank hols), Jan. A good first stop for anyone planning to visit a wildlife site.

Sevenoaks TQ5255 This commuters' town is dominated by KNOLE, originally a simple medieval manor house but gradually transformed into a palace by a 15th-c Archbishop, followed by Henry VIII and then generations of the Sackville family. One of the largest houses in the country, it's said to be a calendar house, with 365 rooms, 52 staircases and 7 courtyards. The rooms are beautifully furnished and decorated, with splendid upholstered 17th-c furnishings, magnificent tapestries and paintings by the likes of Reynolds and Gainsborough, while outside are 26 acres of attractive grounds and a 1,000-acre deer park. Meals, snacks, shop, limited disabled access; cl Thurs am, Mon (exc bank hols), Tues, Nov-Mar; the garden is open only on the first Weds of each month May-Sept; £4, garden 50p. A really marvellous place to visit – but wrap up well, it can be a bit chilly. The WILDFOWL RESERVE (Bradbourne Vale Rd) has 135 acres of lakes, ponds, woodland and reedbeds, several viewing hides; snacks, shop, disabled access; open Weds, Sat, Sun and bank hols, cl Christmas; *£1.50. RIVERHILL HOUSE GARDENS (A225 S) Hillside gardens with rose and shrub terraces, woodland walks among fine trees, bluebells in spring, rhododendrons, and fine views; teas, plant sales; open pm Sun and bank hol wknds Apr-Jun; *£2. The Halfway House is good for lunch.

Sissinghurst TQ7937 SISSINGHURST GARDEN Several charming gardens themed according to season or colour and cared for by obviously loving hands, all offset by the lovely tall-towered Elizabethan gatehouse (not open); inc rose garden, nuttery, moat walk and Tower Lawn. The Three Chimneys on the way to Biddenden is good for lunch.

Smallhythe TQ8930 SMALLHYTHE PLACE Former Tudor harbour-master's house, later the final home of Dame Ellen Terry and now a museum of her life; cl am, Thurs, Fri, Nov-Mar; £2.50.

Staplehurst TQ7843 BRATTLE FARM MUSEUM Country museum on a working farm, with tools and skills from the past few centuries, and a pair of working oxen called Stuff and Nonsense; shop, disabled access; open Sun and bank hols Easter-Oct; *£1.50.

Tenterden TQ8833 is a busy small town with lots of attractive old buildings, especially 17th- and 18th-c character cottages on the north side of the High St. There's a small but interesting local history MUSEUM on Station Rd; cl am, Fri and all Nov-Mar; *75p. The KENT & EAST SUSSEX RAILWAY has steam trains running from here into Sussex, with lovely Weald views, recalling those halcyon days when few places were more than four miles from a railway station; regular Pullman dining-car runs are popular, as are the Christmas Santa Specials. Meals, snacks, shop, disabled access; trains daily and school hols, (058 06) 2943 for timetable; £5.50. The striking 15th-c Woolpack is good for lunch. TENTERDEN VINEYARD AND HERB GARDEN Acres of vines, attractive lakes ideal for picnics, winery, herb garden and agricultural museum; snacks, shop, some disabled access; £1.

Tonbridge TQ5846
TONBRIDGE CASTLE 13th-c castle gatehouse with models, scenes and audio-visual displays depicting events from that period; good views from the battlements and pleasant gardens; shop; cl 25-26 Dec, 1 Jan; £2.

Tunbridge Wells TQ5839
Very much a busy commuters' shopping centre nowadays, but parts still show its former character as a genteel spa town, from the 17th c onwards a popular summer resort for the court thanks to its allegedly health-restoring waters. The water still trickles through the Pantiles, the former centre of the town; rather like a Georgian pedestrian precinct, full of elegant buildings now housing interesting shops. A DAY AT THE WELLS Extravagantly recreates the town's Georgian heyday using very up-to-date display technology, lively period street scenes and tableaux; shop; cl 25 Dec; £3.50. The CHURCH of King Charles the Martyr is an interesting chapel built in the late 17th c for the gentry visiting the Pantiles; it has a remarkable plaster ceiling. MUSEUM AND ART GALLERY Local and natural history and archaeology, Tunbridge ware (the area's speciality woodware), toys and dolls, fine oil paintings, and regularly changing art exhibitions; shop, disabled access; cl Sun. Above the Pantiles the hillside Common is pleasant for strolls, with plenty of trees and rocks. The best place for a proper lunch is probably Sankeys fish restaurant (Mount Ephraim), though the bar lunches at the Mount Edgcumbe House Hotel on the Common are exceptionally good too – it has excellent wines.

Upnor TQ7670 CASTLE Elizabethan castle famous for failing to protect the Medway from the Dutch in 1667; attractive turrets, gatehouse and windows. Shop; cl Oct-Mar; *£1.50.

West Kingsdown TQ5762
CHURCH is largely Saxon, with a rare Saxon tower; given great appeal by its unique tranquil setting, secluded in the middle of a wood. In 1929 a property developer was about to buy this wood for building, but the Rector arranged its purchase instead by a trust; it's now owned and carefully preserved by the Parish Council. The yew tree by the west door looks very old indeed.

★ **West Malling** TQ6757
Attractive little village, most of which is a conservation area thanks to its many old timbered houses and wells; lots of nice alleyways to explore. Particularly worth a look are the ABBEY, one of the country's oldest ecclesiastical buildings, and ST LEONARDS TOWER, a fine Norman tower from an 11th-c castle.

Westerham TQ4454 This pleasant country town is perhaps best known to visitors for its proximity to CHARTWELL, the home of Winston Churchill from 1922 to his death and much as he left it; interesting rooms full of reminders of his career, and gifts he received from all over the world. Paintings of the statesman by notable artists, as well as several of his own pictures; very attractive gardens and lakes with famous black swans. Meals, snacks, shop, disabled access; house cl Mon (exc bank hols), Fri, and Tues after bank hols as well as Tues and Thurs in Nov and Mar, all Dec, Jan and Feb, gardens cl Nov-Apr; £4.20, gardens only £2, studio only 50p. Overshadowed by its altogether more famous neighbour but not to be missed is SQUERRYES COURT, a fine 17th-c manor house overlooking attractive grounds. It includes a garden first laid out in 1689 and now being painstakingly restored, and some magnificent lime trees as old as the house; excellent collections of paintings, china and furniture inside. Snacks, shop, some disabled access; cl am, Mon (exc bank hols), Tues, Thurs, Fri, Oct-Mar (exc Suns in Mar); £3.

QUEBEC HOUSE Gabled boyhood home of General Wolfe with exhibitions on his life and the battle that made his name; cl am, Thurs, Sat, and Oct-Mar; *£2. The Spinning Wheel and Fox & Hounds are useful enough for lunch.

Woodchurch TQ9434 SOUTH OF ENGLAND RARE BREEDS CENTRE Acres of Kentish farmland with one of the largest collections of rare animals in Europe; lots of pigs, cattle, horses, goats and poultry, plenty to touch and fuss over, as well as farm rides. Meals, snacks, shop, disabled access; cl 25 Dec; £3. There's also a well-restored WINDMILL, still grinding corn for demonstrations, and its sails turning whenever it's open; shop; open pm Sun and bank hols Easter-Sept; 50p.

★ **Other attractive villages**, all with decent pubs, include Groombridge TQ5337, Ide Hill TQ4851, Leigh TQ5446, Offham TQ6557, Pluckley TQ9243, Shipbourne TQ5952, Smarden TQ8842 (the Bell just outside is good, too – and very pretty), Speldhurst TQ5541, Stalisfield Green TQ9553, Upchurch TQ8467 (where the 13th-c church has a unique 'candle snuffer' tower) and West Peckham TQ6452. The church at Hadlow TQ6349 has the interesting Hop Pickers Memorial, dedicated to the 30 villagers who one wet day in 1853 drowned on their way back from the fields.

Walks

The area surrounding **Sevenoaks** TQ5255 has more walk potential than a glance at the OS map might suggest. The terrain is complicated, the Wealden villages unspoilt to a remarkable degree, and the path network dense and very well kept. Orchards, hop-gardens, pantile-clad timber-framed cottages and oast houses set the Kentish theme. Newcomers may be surprised to find such attractive and deeply rural countryside so close to London.

There are organised trails from the countryside centre at Lullingstone TQ5064, along the River Darent and into woods above the nearby golf course. **Shoreham** TQ5161 and **Otford** TQ5359 both have attractive village centres, linked by an easy track, with the downlands to the east giving scope for longer walks across Magpie Bottom and past Romney Street. Further east the farmland soon gets arable, and ploughed fields can be a tedious slog, but from **Trottiscliffe** (pronounced Trosley) TQ6460 the walk east to the Coldrum Stones TQ6560, a 4,000-year-old burial chamber, is recommended, with an extension on to the North Downs (Trosley Country Park), here densely wooded but open on the steep slope itself.

Knole Park TQ5454, just on the edge of Sevenoaks, is criss-crossed with paths and tracks encompassing the deer park and the great house of Knole itself.

One Tree Hill, reached from a somewhat obscure National Trust car park TQ5553 south of Godden Green, has a grand view over the Weald. From here the Greensand Way (look for 'GW' markers) follows the very edge of the lower greensand escarpment which dips gently down to Ightham Mote TQ5853, two miles east; Ivy Hatch TQ5854 and Stone Street TQ5754 have handily placed pubs to make this into a circuit. **Ide Hill** TQ4851, with its pubs and picture-book green, is also on the scarp slope and on the Greensand Way: other targets for walks here include Toy's Hill TQ4751, French Street TQ4552, Chartwell TQ4551 and Westerham TQ4454.

The Weald's most luscious lowlands include the vicinity of **Penshurst**

TQ5243, where the fields are predominantly pasture, the cottages characteristically pantile-hung and the paths just elevated enough to gain charming views. As with much of the rest of the area, route-finding is fiddly and patient map-reading is in order. One of the best circular routes is Penshurst-Chiddingstone Hoath TQ4942-Chiddingstone TQ4945, which passes several good pubs on the way. **Bewl Water** TQ6732, dissected by the Kent/East Sussex boundary, is skirted by a 14-mile path on the banks of the reservoir (can be very busy on bank hols; sailing, fishing etc too). A public footpath slices through the heart of the **Scotney Castle** Estate (from TQ6834), its pastures and woodlands, and can form a basis for circular walks from Kilndown TQ7035 to Lamberhurst TQ6736 and back.

There's an attractive round walk from Burnt House Farm on the Rye Rd E of **Sandhurst** TQ7928, via Cledge Wood and Marsh Quarter Farm to the Kent Ditch and the River Rother, to take you round to Bodiam Castle (see Sussex chapter) and back via Northlands Farm and Silverden. The walk from **Cranbrook** TQ7735 to **Sissinghurst** TQ7937 and back is pleasant.

The **Thames Estuary and North Kent coast** are not really of mainstream appeal. **Cliffe Marshes** TQ7278, N of Rochester, are bounded by a long sea wall cum footpath which feels (and is) extraordinarily remote and not a little surreal. The Isle of Sheppey has a brief moment of interest at its eastern end, where you can walk the dyke S from Leysdown-on-Sea TR0370 to Shell Ness TR0567 at the mouth of the Swale.

Pubs useful for walkers include the Wheatsheaf at Bough Beach TQ4846, Pepper Box at Fairbourne Heath above Ulcombe TQ8550, Woodman on Goathurst Common TQ4952, Bucks Head at Godden Green TQ5555, Ringlestone Inn TQ8755 N of Harrietsham, Cock at Ide Hill TQ4851, Golden Lion at Luddesdown TQ6766, Kentish Horse at Markbeech TQ4742, Horns and Bull at Otford TQ5359 (the ruined palace of the archbishops is well worth a look here), Rock at Hoath Corner TQ4943 and Harrow at Warren Street TQ9253.

Driving

All the B-roads in this area E of a line drawn up through Lamberhurst are worth taking, giving good views of the countryside without much traffic. W of this line, the B2188 through Groombridge and Fordcombe to Penshurst, and then left along the B2176 for a lovely view of Penshurst Place, is good.

In the Weald particularly, almost any side road will take you past ancient tilehung farmhouses, oast houses with their wind-vane cowl tops, and perhaps one of the declining number of hop yards with their twining hop bines climbing so high that men on stilts are needed to maintain the trellises.

Where to eat

Speldhurst GEORGE & DRAGON (0892 86) 3125 Distinguished old pub, based on a manorial great hall dating back to 1212, with striking first-floor restaurant under the original massive roof timbers, good food and a quite splendid wine cellar; cl Sat am, Sun pm, Mon. **£19.90**|£11.

Ringlestone TQ8755 RINGLESTONE (0622) 859900 Welcoming atmosphere in this popular country house, with very good food, especially the lunchtime buffet (no chips or fried food), and lots of real ales and country wines; no meals 25 Dec. **£19**|£3.50/£5.50.

Lamberhurst TQ6635 BROWN TROUT (0892) 890312 Very popular dining pub with friendly, prompt service and extremely good fish dishes – the daily specials are a bargain. **£17.85**|£3.15/£7.35.
Tunbridge Wells TQ5839 SANKEYS SEAFOOD RESTAURANT (0892) 511422 Refurbished pub with downstairs cellar bar and upstairs fish restaurant; fish is bought direct from source or kept in their seawater tank; no-smoking areas; cl 25 Dec. **£17**|£2.50/£6.50.
Ivy Hatch TQ5854 PLOUGH (0732) 810268 Relaxed and friendly tile-hung house serving good, imaginative and constantly changing food; summer barbecues. **£16.80**|£3.15/£7.35.
Biddenden TQ8538 THREE CHIMNEYS (0580) 291472 Busy, friendly country pub serving good, popular bar food from a large menu which varies seasonally; cl 25-26 Dec; children in garden dining room only. **£16**|£2.95/£5.
Newnham TQ9557 GEORGE (0795) 890237 Distinctive 16th-c pub furnished with great character; friendly staff and excellent imaginative food using fresh local produce; no credit cards; no food Sun pm, Mon; children tolerated, dogs welcome; disabled access. **£14**|£2/£6.50.
Hever TQ4744 GREYHOUND (0732) 8622221 Pleasant place to eat before musical or theatrical performances in Hever Castle; disabled access. **£11.95**|£1.50/£5.20.
Penshurst TQ5243 BOTTLE HOUSE (0892) 870306 Relaxed and friendly 15th-c pub with unpretentious bar and good popular food. £2/£4.

Help this year from: *B F Benson, Werner Arend, Wayne Brindle, A Church, Mr and Mrs M C Westley, Gregg Davies, Mr and Mrs Scholey, J Biesmans, Comus Elliott, Peter Hitchcock, S J Raine, R W Tompkins, R C Morgan, GB, F Tomlin, Michael Sarent, E G Parish, L M Miall, Nr Neil McBride, D H T Dimock, C P and M G Stent, Colin Laffan, Paul and Sue Davis, Pat and Andy Veitch, Miss J C Drumey, Miss M Byrne, D J Cross, Alan Jarvis, James Ryeland, Andrew and Ruth Triggs, Father D Glover, D C Eastwood, Richard Waller, Tracey Lovatt, Brian Kneale, Jim and Maggie Cowell, Tim and Pam Moorey, W J Wonham, E D Bailey, Hope Chenhalls, J G Smith.*

We welcome reports from readers . . .

This GUIDE depends on readers' reports. Do help us if you can – in return, we offer a discount on the next edition to people who've helped us with reports for it. Tell us what you think about places already in it, and anything extra you think we should say about them. And send us your ideas for inclusion in the next edition: places to visit, eat at or stay in, attractive drives or walks, maybe even unusual interesting shops you know of. Use the card in the middle, the report forms at the end, or just write – no stamp needed: THE GOOD WEEKEND GUIDE, FREEPOST TN1569, Wadhurst, E Sussex TN5 7BR.

Kent Calendar

Some of these dates were provisional as we went to press.

January

1st **Leeds** New Year's Day Treasure Trail *at Leeds Castle*

March

5th **Rochester** Dance Festival

12th **Rochester** Dance Festival

19th **Leeds** Spring Gardens Week *at Leeds Castle – till Sun 27*; **Rochester** Cathedral Chamber Choir Recital

26th **Sandwich** Craft Fair *at Guildhall*

April

2nd **Dover** Craft Fair *at Town Hall*; **Leeds** Easter-egg Hunt *at Leeds Castle – till Mon 4th*

3rd **Woodchurch** Easter (wooden) Bunny Hunt *at Rare Breeds Centre – till Mon 4*

30th **Rochester** Sweeps Festival, *celebrating the abolition of child chimney sweeps – till 2 May*

May

14th **Dover** Festival – *till Mon 30*; **Leeds** Festival of English Wines *at Leeds Castle – till Sun 15*

22nd **Ramsgate** Spring Festival – *till Sun 5*

28th **Sandwich** Garden Show *at Windmill Farm – till Mon 30*; **Sellindge** Steam Special – *till Mon 30*; **Woodchurch** Real Ale Festival *at Rare Breeds Centre*

29th **Goudhurst** Finchcocks Spring Garden Fair – *till Mon 30*; **Hernhill** Mount Ephraim Wine Weekend – *till Mon 30*

30th **Aylesford** Spring Fair *at Priory*; **Rochester** Organ Recital *in cathedral*

June

2nd **Rochester** Dickens Festival – *till Sun 5*

4th **Leeds** Balloon and Vintage Car Festival *at Leeds Castle – till Sun 5*; **Rochester** Concert *in the cathedral*

11th **Wrotham** Steam and Transport Rally – *till Sun 12*

18th **Broadstairs** Dickens Festival – *till Sun 25*; **Canterbury** Carnival

24th **Penshurst** Food and Drink Festival *at Penshurst Place – till Sun 26*

25th **Dover** Roman Festival; **Gravesend** Riverside Fayre – *till Sun 26*; **Leeds** Open-air Concert *at Leeds Castle*

July

1st **Rochester** Medway Sports Festival – *till Sun 10*

2nd **Leeds** Open-air Concert *at Leeds Castle*; **Sandwich** Craft Fair *at Guildhall*

6th Tour de France *passes through* **Dover, Folkestone, Canterbury, Ashford, Tunbridge Wells**

14th **Detling** County Show – *till Sat 16*

Kent Calendar

July cont.

16th **Woodchurch** International Sheep-shearing Contest *at Rare Breeds Centre – till Sun 17*

17th **Woodchurch** Rover Classic Car Rally *at Rare Breeds Centre*

23rd **Deal** Summer Music Festival – *till 6 Jun*; **Whitstable** Oyster Festival, *inc blessing and landing of the oysters, mud run, millers and sweeps competition at sea, raft race, music and Morris Men in local pubs – till Sun 31*

24th **Chatham** Heavy-horse Day *at the Historic Dockyard*

25th **Rochester** Arts Festival, *primarily concerts in the castle grounds – till Sun 31*

28th **Whitstable** Blessing of the Sea Ceremony: *a 150-year-old religious ceremony conducted on the foreshore by the Bishop of the Association of Men of Kent and Kentish Men, with an offshore boats gathering*

30th **Dartford** Show *at Central Park – till Sun 31*; **Maidstone** River Festival

August

5th **Broadstairs** Folk Week, *inc open-air arena, events in most pubs, workshops, children's activities, street theatre, dancing for everyone, torchlight procession and fireworks – till Fri 12*

13th **Ash** English Wine Weekend – *till Sun 14*

20th **Sheerness** Carnival

29th **Tunbridge Wells** Sedan Chair Race *in the Pantiles*

September

2nd **Faversham** Hop Festival – *till Sun 4*; **Goudhurst** Finchcocks Music Festival, *every Fri and Sat – till Sat 25*

4th **Ramsgate** Victorian Street Fair; **Woodchurch** Rare Breeds Show *at Rare Breeds Centre*

16th **Leeds** Flower Festival *at Leeds Castle – till Mon 19*

17th **Folkestone** Craft Fair *at Leas Cliff Hall – till Sun 18*

24th **Dover** Craft Fair *at Town Hall*

October

1st **Detling** Kent Motor Show – *till Sat 2*

7th **Goudhurst** Finchcocks Fair – *till Sun 9*

8th **Canterbury** Festival – *till Sat 22*

21st **Faversham** Brogdale Trust Apple Day – *displays, cider tasting, fruit doctor, cookery and cider-making demonstrations*

22nd **Margate** Craft Fair *at Winter Gardens – till Sun 23*

24th **Faversham** Brogdale Trust Apple Day – *displays, cider tasting, fruit doctor, cookery and cider-making demonstrations*

November

5th **Leeds** Fireworks Display *at Leeds Castle*; **Sandwich** Craft Fair *at Guildhall*

Kent Calendar

November cont.

6th **Cliftonville** Craft Fair *at Northdown House*

12th **Herne Bay** Craft Fair *at Kings Hall – till Sun 13*

19th **Folkestone** Craft Fair *at Leas Cliff – till Sun 20*; **Woodchurch** Christmas Gift Market *at Rare Breeds Centre – till Sun 20*

26th **Gravesend** Craft Fair *at Woodville Hall – till Sun 27*

December

3rd **Allington** Snow Queen Carnival and Old English Fayre; **Dover** Craft Fair *at Town Hall – till Sun 4*; **Rochester** Dickensian Christmas – *till Sun 4*

11th **Cliftonville** Craft Fair *at Northdown House*; **Woodchurch** Carols *in the barn at Rare Breeds Centre, with baked potatoes and soup*

17th **Deal** Craft Fair *at Astor Theatre – till Sun 18*

18th **Woodchurch** Carols *in the barn at Rare Breeds Centre, with baked potatoes and soup*

Lancashire (including Greater Manchester and Merseyside)

The little-known Forest of Bowland is the surprise here – good value for very quiet country breaks. The Silverdale area up towards Cumbria, even less well known, is also a possibility for country-lovers. Closer to Manchester, there is Pennine moorland of real beauty, with more places of interest to visit within easy reach. Manchester itself does have a great many interesting places to visit, as does Liverpool; but their appeal is probably more as somewhere to spend a day than as somewhere for a weekend or short holiday.

The famous traditional seaside resorts are a tremendous draw to some – Blackpool gets more visitors each year than does the whole of Spain. Out of season, when those long stretches of beach and dune are empty, they have a certain lonely charm.

There's also an element of fascination about the tidal sands of Morecambe Bay stretching for miles into the distance, north of Lancaster. Lancaster itself is a town of attractive streets and interesting buildings – some possibilities as a place to stay, even more as a place to visit for the day.

In general, prices in this area are appealing.

Lancaster and its Coast

There's good quiet countryside up by Cumbria; Lancaster itself is civilised and attractive; Blackpool offers boisterous summer fun.

The coast and its hinterland south of Lancaster is rather flat and featureless. This flatness is all part and parcel of the broad beaches which originally made Blackpool and its altogether more decorous neighbour Lytham St Annes popular beach resorts. Nowadays, with people more dubious about plunging into the Irish Sea, Blackpool has become more a place for young adults to have summer fun, with lots of discos, fun pubs and so forth as well as its vivid array of entertainments – an ideal place if that's the sort of thing you want.

North of Lancaster the countryside comes into its own. The Silverdale/Arndale area up by the Cumbrian border has a lot to recommend it for a quiet break: charming hilly countryside, by no means overrun with visitors even in summer, a coastline that's particularly interesting to bird-watchers and naturalists, and several places to visit.

Lancaster itself is an attractive town of considerable character, with a lot to do – and splendid countryside virtually on its doorstep.

There are quite a few things to see and do elsewhere here; highlights include Leighton Hall and the Carnforth steam railway centre.

Where to stay

Blackpool SD3035 IMPERIAL North Promenade FY1 2HB (0253) 23971 **£114**; 183 comfortable rms. Lots of Victorian features such as marble-pillared entrance hall and chesterfields, indoor swimming pool.
Lancaster SD4862 POST HOUSE LA1 3RA (0524) 65999 **£55.40w**; 115 well-equipped rms. Well-run bustling modern hotel with waterside garden, buffet-style restaurant and lots of leisure facilities; disabled access.
Bilsborrow SD5139 GUY'S THATCHED HAMLET Preston PR3 0RS (0995) 40010 ***£41**; 32 smartly modern rms. Bustling complex alongside canal, thatched old tavern, restaurant and pizzeria, outside terrace, children's play area and craft shops; good base for exploring the area; open all day; cl 25 Dec; disabled access.

To see and do

Blackpool SD3036 Few towns in the country can provoke such a strong reaction as Blackpool. Love it or loathe it, it's impossible to remain equivocal about it – so probably best to revel in the unashamedly boisterous summer atmosphere of the place (it's pretty dreary in winter). Though it's now more geared to young adults, most children love it, and there's plenty for them, from donkey rides along the beaches (they have a day off on Fri) to days at the SANDCASTLE leisure complex. BLACKPOOL TOWER now concentrates more on large exhibitions, inc a circus and laser shows; meals, snacks, shop, disabled access; cl winter wkdys; £5.95, more during the Illuminations. These famous autumn light displays are probably the best of their kind - if you don't mind travelling at a snail's pace along the Golden Five Hundred Yards (or Mile as they call it here). It's a town of extremes: where most towns have a pier Blackpool has three, and instead of a fairground it has BLACKPOOL PLEASURE BEACH, a sprawling mass of 150 quite spectacular and breath-taking rides. Begun in 1896, it's Britain's most visited attraction – crowded and noisy, but, if you can take it, an experience not to be missed. New this summer is the world's highest rollercoaster, 235 ft high, complete with aircraft-warning beacons and almost dominating the town's skyline. It's not all ice-creams and eyesores: the ZOO has over 400 animals, great and small, in spaciously landscaped gardens, as well as a miniature railway and play area; meals, snacks, shop, disabled access; cl 25 Dec; £3.65, half price Dec-Mar. SEA LIFE CENTRE Broadly similar to the other centres around the country, but this one has a bonus: the biggest display of tropical sharks in Europe; there's a walk-through tunnel underneath so you feel you're in there with them; meals, snacks, shop, disabled access; cl 25 Dec; *£4.25. GRUNDY ART GALLERY Works by 19th- and 20th-c artists, various temporary exhibitions; shop, disabled access to ground floor only; cl Sun and

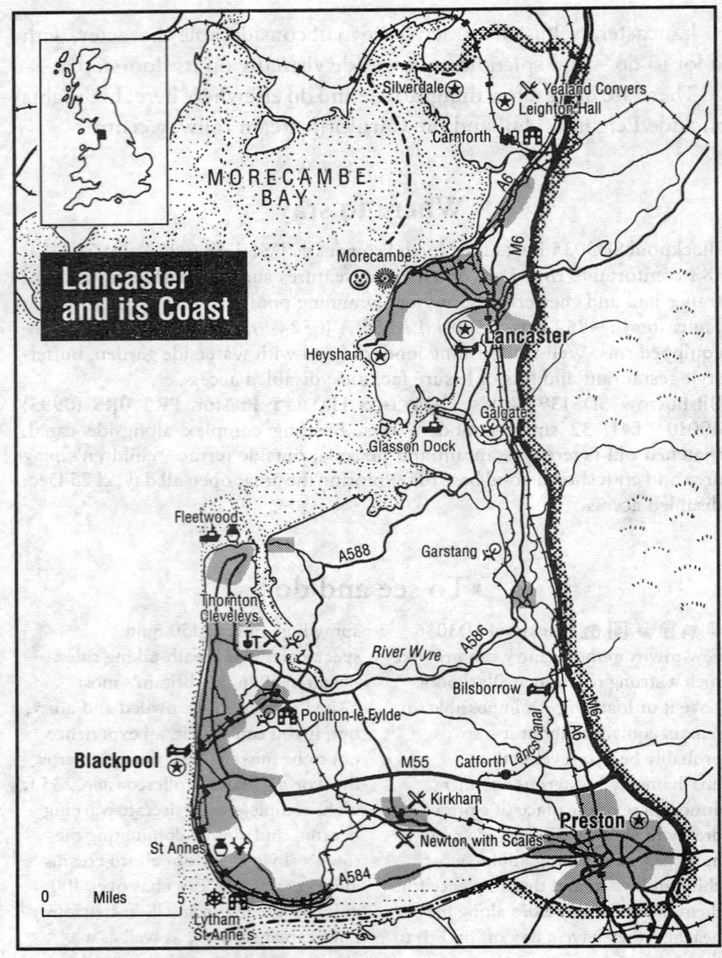

bank hols. No pilgrimage to this granddaddy of rollicking resorts would be complete without a visit to the factory where they make the famous BLACKPOOL ROCK: Coronation Rock Co, Cherry Tree Rd North; shop, disabled access; cl 1-2 pm, wknds. They shut at 3.30, an hour earlier on Fri. The Ramsden Arms opp Blackpool North station is the best of the town's pubs.

Carnforth SD4970 STEAMTOWN RAILWAY CENTRE Impressive collection of British and Continental locomotives, with regular steam days and miniature engines; snacks, shop, disabled access; cl 25-26 Dec; *£3.50 full steam days ((0524) 732100 for dates), £2.10 otherwise. A mile or so north, WARTON OLD RECTORY is the ruin of a 14th-c manor house – easy to trace the various living rooms among the attractively arched remains; disabled access; cl 25 Dec, 1 Jan.

Fleetwood SD3348 Developed as a rather elegant 19th-c resort, with landscaping by Decimus Burton, plenty of smart buildings, lively harbour (boat trips in summer), trams from Blackpool right through the town, and two elegant if not entirely practical lighthouses, one in the middle of the street; excellent market. There's a MUSEUM concentrating on the town's fishing history, with a hands-on trawler bridge, reconstructed salt mine and ship and dock models; shop; cl am Sat exc July, Aug and Sept, am Sun, Mon and Thurs, all day Weds exc in July, Aug and Sept, Nov-Easter; *£1. The Marine Hall exhibition centre on the front has a decent bar (the Wyre – no food) with excellent views of the harbour and Morecambe Bay. STANAH SD3542 some way up the Wyre has a stretch of waterside country with reedbeds, birds and views – attractive despite the ICI chemical works in the background; SKIPPOOL SD3540 has lots of yachting activity in an attractive boating area, with a decent small café.

Galgate SD4855 CANALSIDE CRAFT CENTRE Converted farm buildings by canal with various crafts inc woodturner producing unusual clocks, barometers and bowls; cl 25 Dec. The Plough is useful for lunch.

★ **Garstang** SD4845 is quite an attractive small market town, with a good deal of canal activity (and a fine aqueduct crossing the River Wyre); shop; disabled access; cl 25 Dec. The Old Post Office CRAFT CENTRE has some interesting workshops inc toy-maker; best on Sat, when most are likely to be open. The entertaining Owd Tithebarn is fun for lunch, and the more traditional Wheatsheaf and Kings Arms are useful too.

Glasson Dock SD4456, once an important port for Lancaster, still has the occasional coaster berthing, but is now a lively summer boating place, with attractive countryside around; good Sunday car-boot sales.

Heysham SD4160 HEYSHAM POWER STATIONS Hi-tech interactive exhibition on electricity generation, tours of power station and nuclear reactor, also nature reserve; disabled access; cl wknd am, 25-26 Dec, 1 Jan, tours in the afternoon. Useful for a trip out from Morecambe if it's raining. A tremendous contrast is the quaint squint-walled little village CHURCH, partly Saxon, with Norse-carved hogback tombstone inside. The waterside Golden Ball at Heaton with Oxcliffe off the Lancaster road (should be signposted Overton) is fun for lunch.

★ **Lancaster** SD4761 Lots to look at in this historic city, which always manages to seem friendly and relaxed despite the grandeur of many of its stone buildings; ambling down the cobbled streets and alleyways (much is pedestrianised), you find it hard to believe that this was once one of the major West Indies shipping ports. These days the water traffic is more sedate, and you can hire punts or cruises along the canal in the summer months; the Water Witch on the canal is useful for lunch, and other lunch spots worth knowing here include the Cross Keys, Mill Hotel and West Bank Hotel. The dramatic 12th-c Norman CASTLE famous for hangings and witch trials is owned by the Queen as Duke of Lancaster, and part of it is still used

We welcome reports from readers . . .

This GUIDE depends on readers' reports. Please tell us what you think about places in it. And do recommend additions. Use the card in the middle, the report forms at the end, or just write – no stamp needed: THE GOOD WEEKEND GUIDE, FREEPOST TN1569, Wadhurst, E Sussex TN5 7BR.

as a prison. The cells and the tower are open to the public, as is the 18th-c Gothic Revival Shire Hall, with a splendid display of heraldry, as well as grim exhibitions on prison life; shop; cl when Court in session, Oct-Easter; *£2. PRIORY CHURCH Dates back to before the Conquest but the present hilltop building is mainly 14th and 15th c, with very interesting medieval choir-stalls, needlework and Anglo-Saxon cross fragments; snacks, shop, disabled access. Nearby are the remains of a Roman bath house. CITY MUSEUM Grand Georgian former town hall with local history and archaeology, regimental museum; shop, some disabled access; cl Sun. COTTAGE MUSEUM Old cottage opposite the castle and furnished in the style of an early 19th-c artisan's house; cl am, Nov-Easter; 50p. MARITIME MUSEUM Fittingly sited in the old Customs house, history of local maritime trade and fishing industry and the Lancaster canal; snacks, shop, disabled access; cl am Nov-Apr; £1.50 summer, free in winter. JUDGES LODGING 17th-c house with museum of childhood inc doll collection, also Gillow furniture; cl Nov-Apr and am exc wkdys July-Sept; £1. WILLIAMSON PARK, ASHTON MEMORIAL AND BUTTERFLY PARK Famous and quite magnificent folly clearly visible from the motorway, set in 38 acres of lovely landscaped parkland; displays on Edwardian life and unrivalled views from upper galleries. The butterfly house has a good collection of plants and lepidoptera, and there are also free-flying birds; snacks, shop, disabled access; £2.50, more out of season.

Leighton Hall SD4974 LEIGHTON HALL Impressive neo-Gothic mansion, home of the Gillow family and with early examples of their furniture, as well as clocks and paintings. The grounds have a collection of birds of prey, with flying displays at 3.30 every afternoon; snacks, shop, disabled access; cl am, Sat, Mon (exc bank hols), Oct-Apr; £3.

Lytham St Anne's SD3627 has a splendidly restored WINDMILL in the centre of the green, with an exhibition of its history. There's also a little LIFEBOAT MUSEUM in the adjacent old lifeboat house; both open Tues, Thurs and wknds in season. The Taps is a good real-ale pub here.

Morecambe SD4364 Five miles of promenade and more of beaches to stroll along at this cheery resort, with pretty sunsets over the bay. FRONTIERLAND Wild West theme park with 30 family rides and attractions; rollercoasters, carousels and spectacular views across the bay from the Sky Ride. Meals, snacks, shop, disabled access; cl Nov-Easter; £5.99 for all-day ride pass. The New Inn is where to find some of the town's characters.

Poulton le Fylde SD3539 has quite an attractive pedestrianised market square, with a lovely church (as others in Lancashire, looking a good deal older than in fact it is), and several useful places to eat – the Old Town Hall is particularly good value. There's a good range of craft shops by the working WINDMILL at nearby Thornton SD3342; excellent tea shop.

Preston SD5329 HARRIS MUSEUM AND ART GALLERY Massively impressive if rather dour Greek revival building with good range of fine and decorative art, gallery of clothes and fashion and history of the town; snacks, shop, disabled access; cl Sun and bank hols. The town's also renowned for cheap shopping, and there's a good market on Tues and Thurs. COUNTY AND REGIMENTAL MUSEUM (Stanley St) The story of Lancashire up to the present with colourful displays, lively recreations of a trench, police cell and classroom, regimental collections and various changing exhibitions of art and history. They have had an interesting exhibition on the Somme, borrowed from the Imperial War Museum – it does run slightly into Jan this year so if you're quick you can still catch it; shop, disabled access; cl Thurs, Sun and bank hols; *£1. MOOR PARK OBSERVATORY is open the last two Fri evenings of the month Sept-Mar (exc Dec). Just out of town at Penwortham the CHURCH of St Mary's has a 14th-c chancel, and the scant remains of a motte and bailey castle in the churchyard. The Farmers Arms (Chainhouse Lane) is useful for lunch.

St Annes SD3228 TOY AND TEDDY BEAR MUSEUM Porritt-built Victorian building with big collection of old toys, dolls, trains, bears and other nostalgic children's items; shop, disabled access; open two weeks at Easter, then daily exc Tues Whit-Oct, and Sun all year; *£1.50. There's a sand dune NATURE RESERVE running alongside Clifton Drive North.

Silverdale SD4674 looks out over the tidal sands to the Cumbrian hills, with streets of quiet houses and a church that looks 14th-c but was built barely a century ago. There are good woodland walks behind the town, and the Silverdale Hotel on Shore Rd is worth knowing. LEIGHTON MOSS NATURE RESERVE (off Yealand Redmayne rd) RSPB reserve with several roomy hides looking out on to reedbeds where bitterns, bearded tits and marsh harriers breed; good walks, picnic areas; teas, shop, disabled access; £3. WOLF HOUSE GALLERY Old Georgian buildings selling paintings, knitwear, glass, rocking horses and other crafts; good views; snacks, disabled access; cl 1-2 pm, Mon, all wkdys 25 Dec-end Mar. Reginald Kaye's NURSERY has unusual alpine and other plants. Not far away, the FRIENDS' MEETING HOUSE at Yealand Conyers SD5074 is unobtrusively charming; the New Inn here is a good dining pub.

Thornton SD3342 MARSH MILL VILLAGE 18th-c flour and meal mill, now restored as the centrepiece of a bustling complex with various craft and gift shops and dried flower specialist; meals, snacks, shops, disabled access; cl 25 Dec; admission to the village is free, mill £1.20.

The **Lancaster Canal** which runs up the whole of this area from Preston to Carnforth is ideal for boating – 40 miles without a single lock; often through quiet countryside, with herons and even occasional kingfishers – best in spring or early summer, with abundant ducklings and cygnets bobbing about, and lots of lambs in the fields alongside. Boats can be hired by the day at Catforth SD4735 (0772) 690232, where there's a decent teashop.

! BALLOON TRIPS over Lancashire can be arranged on (0253) 736839; around £95.

Walks

The vast mudflats and sands of **Morecambe Bay** are home to 200,000 waders, and are famous for their galloping tides. Walks over them are described in the Cumbria chapter – foot access is easier from that side, though guided walks are also available from Hest Bank (details from local tourist information centres; the tides and stretches of quicksand do make a guide essential). Warton Crag SD4973 just north of Carnforth gives fine views over the bay and coast, and pleasant walking. **Leighton Moss Nature Reserve** (see above) is a short walk north, and is crossed by a public footpath.

The Preston-Carnforth canal towpath allows pleasant walks, largely through quiet countryside; Catforth SD4735 is a good departure point.

Driving

The Fylde is too low-lying to see much beyond the next bend. Once past Lancaster, there's a vivid change, with roads around Yealand Conyers and Silverdale looping through attractively wooded hilly countryside, and on the coastal side giving good views across Morecambe Bay.

Where to eat

Thornton Cleveleys SD3342 RIVER HOUSE Skippool Creek (0253) 883497 Delightful restaurant with very good honest cooking using the freshest ingredients; decent wine list, fresh flowers and log fires, and fine views (they also have lovely bedrooms); cl Sun pm, 25 Dec pm, 26 Dec; children must be well behaved. **£36|£3/£10.**

Kirkham SD4231 CROMWELLIAN 16 Poulton St (0772) 685680 Tiny evening restaurant with fixed-price menu in a classical French style – excellent food; cl Sun, Mon, 1st wk Apr, 2 wks Oct. **£27/£17 2 courses.**

Newton with Scales SD4532 PRACHEE Preston New Rd (0772) 685896 Classical Indian cooking in comfortable surroundings with consistently good standards over many years. **£16.25|£7.**

Yealand Conyers SD5074 NEW INN (0524) 732938 Welcoming creeper-covered pub handy for refreshment after walk on the fells; good lunchtime bar food and evening restaurant dishes; friendly service; no meals Mon pm Nov-May; children in dining room if eating lunchtime only. **£1.40/£5.50.**

THE LANCASHIRE HEARTLAND

Here there's lots to see, particularly in Manchester and Liverpool – though its best to base yourself outside; the heartland has plenty for sightseers and the moors are attractive for walkers.

Both Manchester and Liverpool are full of grand Victorian buildings, and interesting things to do and see – Manchester particularly so. To explore them, it might be best to stay outside and come in by day – particularly at the weekend, when traffic is very light and both are quite quick to get into by car, with easy parking. As they tend to be depressing in cold wet weather, a summer visit gives you most chance of seeing these two great cities at their best.

Southport, too, has a good many attractions. Elsewhere, highlights include Bramhall Hall, Speke Hall, the Martin Mere wildfowl reserve, Rufford Old Hall, the Camelot theme park at Charnock Richard, and the good re-creation of 1900s life at Wigan Pier. It's an easy area in which to find things to keep children amused.

There's magnificent countryside up on the moors here – plenty of exhilarating drives and some scope for walking.

Where to stay

Bury SD8010 NORMANDIE BL9 6UT (061) 764 3869 ***£69**; 24 attractive rms. Fine views, homely lounge and snug bar, excellent restaurant food, fine wine list, and professional service; cl Sun, last wk Dec, 1st wk Jan, 1st wk over Easter; disabled access.

Bromley Cross SD7213 DROP INN Hospital Rd Last Drop BL7 9PZ **£64.50**; 83 rms. Spacious, creeper-covered pub with lots of beamery and timbering; popular one-price hot and cold buffet, and heavy tables out on attractive flagstoned terrace; village is an odd pastiche of old-world stone-and-cobbles street complete with gift and tea shops, bakery, etc – all part of a big well-equipped Rank hotel complex; disabled access.

Darwen SD6922 OLD ROSINS Pickup Bank BB3 3QD (0254) 771264 **£59.50**; 15 well-equipped rms. Friendly old pub in centre of moors, ideal as base for exploring the area; good views from cosy bar, interesting bar and restaurant food.

Ashworth Valley SD8913 LEACHES FARM Rochdale OL11 5UN (0706) 41116 **£34**; 3 rms, shared bthrm. 17th-c hill farm with really wonderful views; beams, and log fires; cl 22 Dec-2 Jan.

To see and do

Manchester On a fine weekend it's a real pleasure just strolling around the city's very impressive buildings. Albert Sq is one of the finest areas, surrounded by the main cultural centres (and some lively café-bars), and the Town Hall is a massively impressive piece of Victoriana, facing colourful summer gardens. The CATHEDRAL is a very wide 15th-c church, with fine choir stalls. The council produce a good map detailing a walk round town; it's an excellent way of seeing the spectrum of Manchester's heritage and architecture, with so much to see that it's best taken in sections. Chinatown here, incidentally, is the second-largest Chinese community in England: lots of authentic restaurants and a Chinese Arts Centre. During 1994 Manchester has taken the title City of Drama, and the year-long festival will see local, national and international artists performing in theatres, streets and alongside canals. A creative ticketing policy means there should be good bargains about: 061-832 1994 for details and brochure.

! GRANADA STUDIOS TOUR (Water St) Not the least of the draws here is wandering down Downing Street, Baker Street and Coronation Street – three of the country's most famous thoroughfares all in one go. If peering through the window of the Rovers Return doesn't excite you, there are also shows, sets, rides and exhibitions covering all aspects of television and cinema. Meals, snacks, shop, disabled access; cl Mon (exc bank hols), winter Tues, 24-26 Dec and most of Jan; *£9.99 – one of the most expensive visits in this book, but great fun, lively and very slickly done; a visit can easily last all day.

MUSEUM OF SCIENCE AND INDUSTRY (Castlefield) On the site of the oldest passenger railway in the world, enormous museum with hours of things to do and look at; power hall, air and space gallery, electricity gallery, machine tools gallery, interactive science area and underground exhibition on sanitation and sewage are just some of the features. Meals, snacks, shop, disabled access; cl 23-25 Dec; *£3.50.

GALLERY OF ENGLISH COSTUME

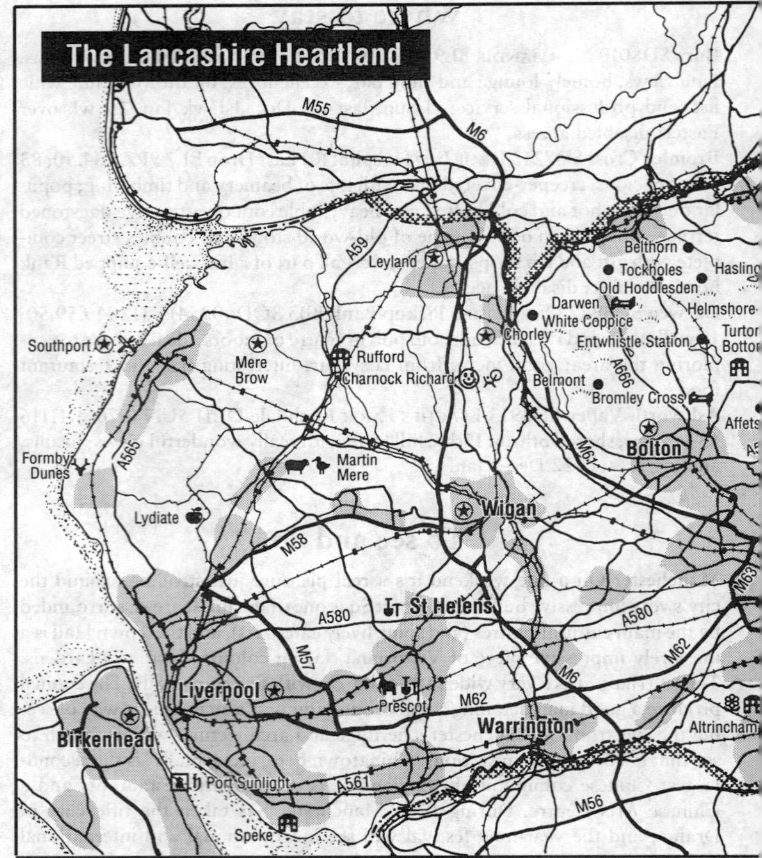

(Platt Hall) Georgian mansion displaying comprehensive examples of fashion styles over the last 400 years; they have such a large collection that all the displays are changed frequently. Also library by appointment; shop, disabled access to ground floor only; cl Sun am, Good Fri, 25-26 Dec.

CITY ART GALLERIES (Mosley St) The permanent displays are particularly strong on Pre-Raphaelite paintings; also lots of decorative and applied arts from early times to the 19th c, ceramics, silver and furniture, and various temporary displays; meals, snacks, shop; cl Sun am, Good Fri, 25-26 Dec.

JOHN RYLANDS LIBRARY (Deansgate) Magnificent neo-Gothic building with lovely old-fashioned reading-room and over five million books, among them splendid manuscripts and archival materials, inc parts of the Dead Sea Scrolls, several examples of medieval jewelled bindings, and the famous St John fragment. Shop; cl Sat pm, Sun, bank hols, 24 Dec-1 Jan.

MUSEUM OF TRANSPORT (Boyle St) Local transport through the ages inc over 70 buses and other vehicles, with photos, tickets and other items; Sun

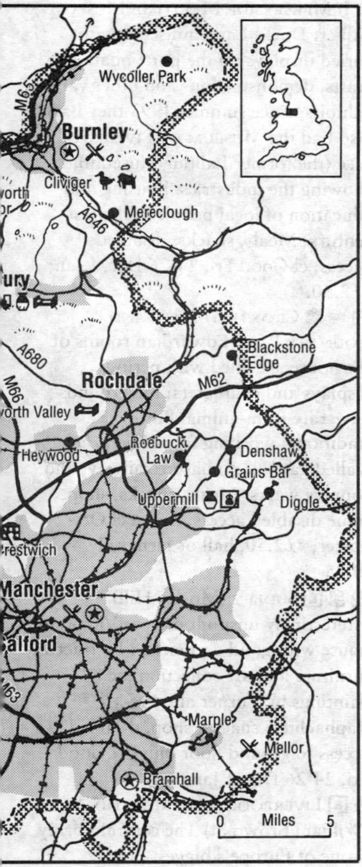

snacks, shop, disabled access; open Weds, Sat, Sun and bank hols; £1.25.

WHITWORTH ART GALLERY (Oxford Rd) Excellent assemblage of British watercolours from Sandby to Turner and plenty of modern art, with unusual collections of textiles and wallpaper. Items not currently on display can be viewed by appointment. Meals, snacks, shop, disabled access; cl Sun, Good Fri, Christmas wk.

PANKHURST CENTRE (62 Nelson St) The former home of Emmeline Pankhurst, who launched the Suffragette movement from here. The Edwardian parlour is furnished in period style, and displays show the story of the fight for the vote and other women's issues, as well as an interestingly planted garden and contemporary arts and crafts; meals, snacks, shop, disabled access; cl wknds.

MANCHESTER JEWISH MUSEUM Housed in a former synagogue, the story of Manchester's Jewish community over the last 200 years, with interesting recorded recollections of life earlier this century; shop, disabled access to ground floor only; cl Fri, Sat and Jewish holidays; £1.50.

MANCHESTER MUSEUM (Oxford Rd) Lots of displays on various subjects inc good Japanese collection, Egyptian relics, aquarium, beehive, local history and crafts; shop, disabled access; cl Sun, Good Fri, May Day, Christmas.

MANCHESTER UNITED MUSEUM AND TOUR CENTRE (Old Trafford) The country's first purpose-built football museum, covering the club's history from its foundation in 1878; hundreds of frequently changing exhibits and tours of the ground. Snacks, shop, disabled access; cl Mon, Christmas; £4.95 tour and museum, £2.95 museum only.

See also Salford and Prestwich, below.

Liverpool The fine 19th-c buildings which mark Liverpool's past as one of the world's great ports have in the last few years taken on a cleaner and prouder look. The Liver Building is still best viewed from the famous ferry across the Mersey, and other well-known buildings include the two cathedrals – the traditional Anglican one designed by Lutyens, and the more unusual modern Roman Catholic church. Shoppers are well catered for, as are art-lovers; the city has an impressive number of galleries well worth a look. The Cracke (Rice St) is a friendly pub for a bite to eat; by contrast the Philharmonic (Hope St) is probably the country's grandest late Victorian pub.

The ALBERT DOCK is a spectacular restoration of previously redundant warehouse buildings by the river, now a lively complex of shops, cafés and exhibitions with regular entertainers, performers, events and boat trips. The Pump House, one of the renovated buildings on the dockside, is good for lunch, and several of the main attractions described below are housed in the complex.

WALKER ART GALLERY (William Brown St) Excellent collection of European paintings and sculpture with especially notable Italian, Dutch and Pre-Raphaelite pictures; snacks, shop, disabled access; cl 1 Jan, Good Fri, 24-26 Dec.

LIVERPOOL MUSEUM (William Brown St) Very little left uncovered at this varied series of exhibitions, starting with dinosaurs and mummies and going right through all periods and continents and even beyond – there's a particularly good planetarium (shows 3.15 pm wkdys, around 1 pm, 2 pm and 4 pm wknds; cl Mon). Also lively natural-history centre (cl Mon) and aquarium; cl Sun am, Good Fri, 24-26 Dec, 1 Jan; free, planetarium £1.20.

TATE GALLERY (Albert Dock) Specialising in modern art, plenty of sculptures, paintings and various special events – so perhaps not the best place to take those with a traditional view of art; meals, snacks, shop, disabled access; cl Mon (exc bank hols), Good Fri, 25-26 Dec.

! BEATLES STORY (Albert Dock) Bouncy, dedicated to the group and the sights and sounds of the 1960s; shop, disabled access; cl 25 Dec; *£4.95.

! ANIMATION WORLD (Albert Dock) Lively hands-on displays and models about cartoons and animation; workshops, studios and sets featuring characters like Danger Mouse, Count Duckula, Toad of Toad Hall and Truckers. Shop, disabled access; cl 25-26 Dec; *£3.

MERSEYSIDE MARITIME MUSEUM (Albert Dock) Large museum with varied displays on the port; boats, crafts, demonstrations and other varied exhibits; since summer 1993 they have also had the MUSEUM OF LIVERPOOL LIFE (the former Labour Museum), showing the industries, housing and education of local people in the last century. Meals, snacks, disabled access; cl Good Fri, 24-26 Dec, 1 Jan; *£2.50.

CROXTETH HALL AND COUNTRY PARK Edwardian rooms of the house are filled with period displays and characters; the grounds have rare farm-animal breeds, a traditional working farm, Victorian walled garden, miniature railway, and country walks. Meals, snacks, shop, some disabled access; house cl Oct-Easter; *£2.50, hall or farm only £1.25.

SUDLEY (Mosley Hill) Interestingly unspoilt private Victorian house with good gardens and attractive furniture and art collection inc paintings by Turner and Pre-Raphaelites; snacks, shop, disabled access to ground floor only; cl Good Fri, 24-26 Dec, 1 Jan.

LIVERPOOL LIBRARIES AND ARTS (William Brown St) The central library is one of Europe's biggest public libraries, and the Picton Library, a circular reading room, is worth a look; tours to see first editions, prints and fine bindings; snacks, shop, disabled access; cl Sun, all bank hols and the Tues after spring and summer bank hols.

! LIVERPOOL FOOTBALL CLUB (Anfield Rd) Visitors Centre Museum has trophies and mementos of one of the country's most successful clubs, with videos of some of their greatest moments, and a look at the ground; shop, some disabled access; open pm wkdys exc when match on, (051) 263 2361 to check; *£1.50.

Other things to see and do

Altrincham SJ7687 DUNHAM MASSEY HALL Former 16th-c moated manor house extensively remodelled in the 18th c, with impressive collections of silverware, paintings and furnishings, and restored kitchen, pantry and laundry. The grounds have plenty of deer wandering about, formal avenues of trees and a working Elizabethan saw mill. Meals, snacks, shop, some disabled access; cl am, Thurs, Fri, Nov-Mar; £4 house and garden, £2 garden only. The Orange Tree has a good-value upstairs bistro.

Birkenhead SJ3288 Waterfront views over to Liverpool, of course, but a surprise in BIRKENHEAD PRIORY, a ruined 12th-c Benedictine priory with interesting visitor centre; good views from tower of neighbouring church. Some disabled access; cl 1.30-2 pm, Mon (exc bank hols), 25-26 Dec, 1 Jan. WILLIAMSON ART GALLERY AND MUSEUM English watercolours and art by the Liverpool school, sculpture and ceramics, and local history with collection of cars and motorcycles in period garage setting; shop, disabled access; cl Sun am and bank hols. The Shrewsbury Arms out in Claughton Firs is the best place for lunch, while at Shore Rd, Woodside, there's an unusual STEAM PUMPING STATION; cl 1.30-2 pm and all day Mon; £1.

Bolton SD7108 SWITHILLS HALL (Swithills Dean Rd) Beautiful old manor house with fine 14th-c Great Hall and splendid panelled drawing room; lots of Stuart furniture. Shop, disabled access to ground floor only; cl am Sun, Mon (exc bank hols), all Oct-Mar; £1.55. The nearby 15th-c HALL I' TH' WOOD was the home of Samuel Crompton and here he developed his Spinning Mule in 1779; there's a museum of his life. It was restored and refurnished by Lord Leverhulme at the start of this century; details as above, a joint ticket is available. BUTTERFLY WORLD Lots of different species of free-flying butterflies and moths, also fish pools, tarantulas, scorpions and locusts; snacks, shop, disabled access; cl Dec-Mar; £1.50. The Kings Head (Junction Rd), with a bowling green behind, is useful for lunch. LAST DROP VILLAGE Just outside Bolton, this former farm village has been transformed into a pastiche of an 18th-c village, very rustic and quaint, with cottages, shops, decent pub and craft centre.

Bramhall SJ8984 BRAMALL HALL One of the finest houses in the area, a splendid timber-framed 14th-c house with rare 16th-c paintings and furniture, and extensive parkland; snacks, shop, some disabled access; house cl am, winter Mon, 25-26 Dec, 2-31 Jan; *£3.

Burnley SD8432 TOWNELEY HALL ART GALLERY AND MUSEUMS A 14th-c house with displays of local crafts and industries, paintings, furniture and glassware, period rooms and natural-history centre with aquarium; meals, snacks, shop; cl Sat, Christmas. The CANAL WHARF (Manchester Rd) has a small museum with weaver's cottage etc, and short towpath walks along the Leeds & Liverpool Canal here give you a vivid impression of the towering old weaving mills; the raised canal embankment across the valley is a remarkable sight. ROCKWATER BIRD CONSERVATION CENTRE (Cliviger – A646 N) Pheasants, bantams, foreign birds and owls as well as rabbits, chipmunks and miniature sheep; snacks; cl Mon, Thurs, Nov-Easter; *£2. Nearby CLIVIGER GORGE has pleasant walks, with stream, woodland and farmland; moors above.

Bury SD8011 EAST LANCS RAILWAY Scenic 17-mile steam journeys along the pretty Irwell valley; station has various transport exhibits, mainly railway-related. Snacks, disabled access; cl wkdys; (061) 764 7790 for timetable. There's also a REGIMENTAL MUSEUM in Wellington Barracks; cl 12.30-1 pm, all Sun and Thurs; *50p. The Tap & Spile (Manchester Old Rd) is useful for a bite to eat, and the Lord Raglan up at Nangreaves SD8115 is a popular nearby moorland dining pub.

Charnock Richard SD5515 CAMELOT ADVENTURE THEME PARK 130-acre theme park recreating the mythical Camelot, with jousting and falconry displays, a medieval village and dozens of rides and attractions – rather better than other such places. Sun crafts; meals, snacks, shop, disabled access; open wknds and school hols Apr, May, Sept and Oct, and daily Jun-Aug; £8.99.

Chorley SD5817 ASTLEY HALL Timber-framed 16th-c house with extensive gardens and woodland; impressive carvings, plasterwork, pottery and paintings. Meals, snacks, shop, some disabled access; cl 12.30-1 pm, Mon-Thurs Nov-Mar, 25 Dec-2 Jan; *£2. The Malt 'n' Hops behind the station is useful for lunch.

Helmshore SD7821 HELMSHORE TEXTILE MUSEUMS Two stone mills with comprehensive collection of textile machinery, much of it in its original environment. Also working waterwheel and lots of explanatory displays on the wool and cotton industries; snacks, shop, disabled access; cl am (exc Sun Easter-Oct), Sat (exc July-Sept), all Nov-Easter (exc pm Sun); £1.50.

Leyland SD5422 BRITISH COMMERCIAL VEHICLE MUSEUM The biggest commercial-vehicle museum in Europe, with over 40 restored British vehicles; snacks, shop, disabled access; cl Mon (exc bank hols), wkdys in Oct and Nov, all Dec-Apr; £2. OLD GRAMMAR SCHOOL MUSEUM AND EXHIBITION CENTRE Sturdy 16th-c building with changing local-art exhibitions and displays of the area's industry, history and archaeology; open all day Tues and Fri, am Sat and pm Thurs. WORDEN ARTS AND CRAFTS CENTRE (Worden Park) Art displays and nine varied craft workshops, surrounded by 157 acres of parkland with ice-house, miniature railway, maze, arboretum, garden for the blind and play area; meals, snacks, shop, disabled access; cl Mon and 25 Dec. Leyland also has a pleasant little town trail, and the 15th-c church has some fine stained glass.

Martin Mere SD4310 WILDFOWL AND WETLANDS TRUST Natural open water habitats have been recreated in these 360 acres of marshland and now thousands of birds are regular visitors; wild geese, swans, ducks, flamingos and waders. In the winter swans come from Iceland and Siberia; good displays in the visitor centre. Meals, snacks, shop, disabled access; cl 24-25 Dec; £3.75. About 400 yards down the road, in **Burscough**, the WINDMILL ANIMAL FARM is a friendly 40-acre site with various animals and their babies to feed (inc rare breeds), as well as tractor rides and adventure playground; snacks, shop, disabled access; cl winter wkdys; *£2.25.

Mere Brow SD4118 TARLETON LEISURE LAKES Attractive lake and woodland area with 90 acres of countryside; watersports, fishing, golf, walks, nearby farm shop and pick-your-own fruit – good for summer strawberries. Meals, snacks, disabled access; £1.80.

★ **Port Sunlight** SJ3384 Picturesque garden village built by William Hesketh Lever for the workers in his soap factory. PORT SUNLIGHT HERITAGE CENTRE Tells the history of the village, factory and workers; shop; disabled access; cl winter wknds; *20p. LADY LEVER ART GALLERY Very good gallery with some interesting paintings; cl am Sun, Good Fri, 24-26 Dec, 1 Jan.

Prescot SJ4692 KNOWSLEY SAFARI PARK Five-mile drive through very natural-looking reserves of lions, tigers, elephants, rhinos, monkeys and other animals; also pets' corner and miniature railway. Meals, snacks, shop, disabled access; cl Nov-Mar; *£8. Museum of Clock and Watch Making Prescot used to be the centre of a thriving clock industry, and this 18th-c town house has exhibits on the clock, watch and tool-making industries, as well as a reconstructed watchmaker's workshop and examples of machinery and tools; shop; cl Sun am, Mon (exc bank hols), Good Fri, 25-26 Dec, 1 Jan. If you make an appointment they will also deal with any horological enquiries you may have. The Clock Face is a pleasant old mansion-house pub here.

Prestwich SD8104 Heaton Hall Splendidly decorated 18th-c neo-Classical house in extensive public parkland, fine paintings, plasterwork and furniture, unusual circular Pompeiian room, and various recitals and temporary exhibitions. Snacks, shop, disabled access; cl 1-2 pm, Sun am, Mon, Tues, Oct-Apr.

Rufford SD4615 Rufford Old Hall Lovely house built by the Hesketh family in the 15th c, with an intricate hammer-beam roof and movable wooden screen in the Great Hall, and impressive collections of 17th-c Lancashire oak furniture, 16th-c arms, armour and tapestries. Snacks, shop; cl am, Fri, Nov-Mar; *£2.70. NT.

St Helens SJ5195 Pilkington Glass Museum Famous glassmaking factory with the history of glass production over 4,000 years from Egyptian times; interactive displays and exhibitions; snacks, shop, disabled access; cl am, wknds and bank hols, Christmas-New Year.

Salford SJ8197 Mining Museum Georgian building with two reconstructed mines, and displays showing the history and development of coal-mining; shop; cl 12.30-1.30 pm, Sun am, Sat, Good Fri, 25-26 Dec. Ordsall Hall Museum Timbered Tudor manor house with local history and Victorian farmhouse kitchen; shop, some disabled access; cl 12.30-1.30 pm, Sun am, Sat, Good Fri, 25-26 Dec. Museum and Art Gallery Most notable for the unrivalled L S Lowry collection; also good collection of Victorian arts, and nostalgic reconstruction of industrial street scene; snacks, shop, disabled access; cl Sun am, Sat, Good Fri, Easter, 25-26 Dec, 1 Jan.

Southport SD3317 Smartish Victorian seaside resort, long famed as the most pleasant shopping town in the area, and as the place where the sea doesn't come in – in fact it comes in as often as anywhere else, but doesn't stay quite as long. Plenty of nice parks and gardens to stroll through, and it's a bracing trip down the Pier, either on foot or on the little train. Lord St is the elegant main shopping street, and there's an excellent secondhand and antiquarian bookshop down the Wayfarers Arcade. Southport Railway Centre Biggest centre of its type in the area; plenty of old locomotives, as well as local buses, tramcars, engines and other vehicles. Snacks, shop, disabled access; cl wkdys exc summer school hols, tel (0704) 530693 for times and details. Zoo Creatures great and small with chimp and tortoise houses, ducks, flamingos, aviaries, a new primate house and, more unusually, a reptile house with alligator beach; snacks, shop, disabled access; cl 25 Dec; *£2.40. Atkinson Art Gallery Specialises in 19th- and 20th-c watercolours, oil paintings, prints and sculpture; shop, disabled access; cl pm Thurs and Sat, 25-26 Dec, 1 Jan. Pleasureland Typical fairground, plenty of rides and attractions; cl wkdys out of season, Nov-Easter. British Lawnmower Museum (Shakespeare St) Slaves to the garden should think themselves lucky they don't have to mow the grass with some of the ancient machines displayed here. Fully restored examples dating from the 1830s to the present, with the workshop constructing what it's hoped will be the world's fastest; more bizarrely, there's also one of the first racing lawnmowers – the curator used to be a champion. Shop; cl Sun and bank hols; £1. CHURCHTOWN VILLAGE SD3618, the oldest part of town, has a number of pretty thatched cottages and the lakeside BOTANIC GARDENS, which are very attractive as well as being interesting to plantsmen; boats to hire, pets' corner. They include a MUSEUM, with varied collections of local history inc lifeboat display, Victorian parlour and Cecily Bate doll collection; shop, some disabled access; cl Mon (exc bank hols when cl following Fri), am Sat and Sun. The Hesketh Arms is good for lunch out here.

Speke SJ4383 SPEKE HALL A remarkable manor house built around a square courtyard, this is one of the most richly timbered black-and-white houses in the country; inside is a vast Tudor Great Hall, as well as interesting servants' quarters, intricate plasterwork and priest's hole. Snacks, shop, disabled access; cl am, winter Mon, Jan-Mar; *£3.20, 60p grounds only.

Turton Bottoms SD7315 TURTON TOWER 15th-c Renaissance house with Elizabethan buildings and earlier pele tower, major collection of carved wood furniture, interesting period rooms, and formal Victorian gardens; snacks, shop; open daily May-Sept (cl am wknds, and 12-1 pm for lunch), pm Sat-Weds in Mar, Apr and Oct, and pm Sun only in Nov and Feb; *90p. The White Horse at Edgworth nearby is useful for lunch.

★ **Uppermill** SD9905 This whole area of mill settlements in steep valleys cut through the moors is full of interest, and Uppermill itself is one of the most attractive places. SADDLEWORTH MUSEUM AND ART GALLERY Based around an old mill, displays on Victorian life, the textile industry and vintage vehicles, and regular days when the mill and weaver's cottage are brought to life by appropriately dressed volunteers; shop; cl Nov-Feb am, 25 Dec; £1. Up above the town is a lonely moorland church, with good walks around it; the ancient pub nearby, the Cross Keys, is good.

Wigan SD5805 WIGAN PIER Rather different from when Orwell knew it, now a dynamic museum on the wharf and in warehouses demonstrating local life at the turn of the century, with reconstructed coal mine, pub, school, music hall and house, with actors bringing it all vividly to life. Across the canal a textile mill has the world's largest working mill engine and other machines. Meals, snacks, shop, disabled access; cl Fri, winter Sat; *£4.10. The Old Pear Tree on Frog Lane is useful for lunch; the Orwell on Wigan Pier itself is atmospheric but can be noisy. HAIGH HALL COUNTRY PARK Once the home of the Earls of Crawford, now a 250-acre country park with a mini zoo, golf course, walled gardens and miniature railway; meals, snacks, shop, some disabled access; car-parking charge.

Pick your own is popular, with lots of places on the flat ground in the west of the area – soft fruit the speciality, late June to August; LYDIATE FRUIT FARM SD3604 (Pilling Lane) has a good farm shop in attractive 18th-c former stable buildings.

Walks

Rivington SD6214, just outside Horwich, lies close to **attractive reservoirs.** Lower Rivington Reservoir SD6213 has a waterside path along its eastern edge, and a curious mock-up of Liverpool castle built in 1912 as an adornment to the vast and atmospherically decayed gardens of Lever Park SD6313, which cover the hillside. A trail guides you around the undergrowth and up to the Pigeon Tower SD6314, within a few minutes of Rivington Pike, the summit. The Great House Barn SD6313 is the place to start, with a good information centre, maps, guides, etc.

From Marple SJ9588, the towpath along the **Peak Forest Canal** soon leaves suburbia for green countryside; to the north is the famous set of Marple locks SJ9689 and aqueduct over the River Etherow. To the south, you can leave the canal at Strines SJ9868 and climb on to Mellor Moor SJ9987.

Down on the coast, **Formby Dunes** SD2809 reached from the north-west edge of Formby is a large tract of sweeping sandy dunes which are in some areas being stabilised by pine plantations; broad beaches, good walks through the adjacent pinewoods, made interesting by the chance of seeing and even feeding red squirrels (you can buy nuts for them here). Best in spring and autumn – can be busy in summer; parking in some places may cost £1.50, but keep looking – a number of other spots are free.

Wycoller Park SD9339 is Lancashire Brontë country (the ruined hall at Wycoller features in *Jane Eyre*), and has walks along a beck to Clam Bridge, an Iron-Age slab, and up to Foster's Leap SD9439, a finely placed crag.

This area is outstanding for the number of pubs which are well placed as good jumping-off points for walks – or places to look forward to getting back to. Up on the moors, many of these are closed during lunchtime on Mon to Thurs. Good pubs for walkers include the Pack Horse at Affetside SD7513, Black Dog at Belmont SD6716, Dog at Belthorn SD7224, White House on Blackstone Edge SD9716, Owd Betts at Cheesden on Ashworth Moor SD8316, Rams Head near Denshaw SD9710, Diggle Hotel at Diglea Hamlet above Diggle itself SE0008, Strawbury Duck by Entwistle Station SD7217, Bulls Head on Grains Bar SD9608, Duke of Wellington on the B6232 west of Haslingden SD7522, Egerton Arms off the narrow Ashworth Rd above Heywood SD8513, Romper at Ridge End above Marple SJ9686, Kettledrum at Mereclough SD8632, Old Rosins at Pickup Bank, Old Hoddlesden SD6922, Roebuck on Roebuck Low SD9606, Royal Arms at Tockholes SD6623 (for Roddlesworth Valley woodlands, maybe on to the ruins of Hollinshead Hall and its restored curative well; the Victoria and Rock are also good, though slightly less well placed), Railway at White Coppice SD6118.

Driving

The best drives are over to the NE and E of the area. In the NE, the A635 out of Mossley quickly soars up on to Saddleworth Moor; the A670 takes you up over equally wild moorland countryside, over Standedge; the B6197 from Delph down to Grains Bar and then right along the A672 to Denshaw, where both the A672 and the A640 strike magnificently off into the moors. All these roads soon take you into Yorkshire.

The A675 N from Bolton is a fine drive, with attractive but narrow side roads branching off at Belmont; the back road forking off to the right through Tockholes is wider, and a pleasant drive. The A666 Bolton-Darwen, and the parallel loop of the B6391 out from Bromley Cross, are fine moorland roads; coming into Darwen you pass some very striking industrial relics such as the extraordinary campanile-style mill chimney and massive complex stationary steam engine. There are attractive views from the old Roman road heading N through

Edgworth. The B6232 from Haslingden to Blackburn has fine views. The moorland roads S from Burnley are quite attractive, with the best views from the back road angling off SE from the A52 to the junction of the A671 and B6238.

Perhaps best of all in this area are the old packhorse roads between Burnley and Hebden Bridge through Mereclough and over Stansfield Moor, and between Nelson/Colne and Hebden Bridge over Widdop Moor.

In the SE, the hill roads climbing up from Marple above the Goyt Valley yield good views, taking you quickly over the border into the high country of that part of Cheshire and Derbyshire.

West of the M6 there's a patch of surprisingly pleasant countryside around the area sometimes known over-generously as the Wigan Alps, with several popular dining pubs dotted around such as the Robin Hood on the Mawdesley-Croston road, the Stocks in Alder Lane, Parbold, the Farmers Arms at Bispham Green, and the Brook House on Barmskin Lane, the road between Wrightington Bar (which has yet more eating houses) and Mawdesley. Any of these will provide a decent meal, and the various roads looping between them make the most of this gently attractive and modestly hilly countryside – which also yields plenty of possibilities for quiet walks.

Where to eat

Manchester and Liverpool both have plenty of good ethnic restaurants – excellent for locals.

Burnley SD8332 KETTLEDRUM (0282) 24591 Pleasant atmosphere and wide choice of genuine home-cooking in friendly country local with good views; extraordinary collections inc gruesome knives; partly no-smoking gaslit upstairs dining room, and seats outside. **£15|£1.65/£2.95.**

Southport SD3376 SCARISBRICK HOTEL Lord St (0704) 543000 Smartened up recently, with decent reasonably priced restaurant; also bar food in comfortable lounge. **£11.80/£16.80|£1.60/£3.10.**

Mellor SJ9888 DEVONSHIRE ARMS Longhurst Lane (061) 427 2563 Relaxed and distinctive pub on the edge of the Peak District with truly home-made, interesting bar food; hope to open Mon-Weds pm also; children allowed if well behaved. **£4.50.**

Manchester SJ8398 ROYAL OAK 729 Wilmslow Rd Didsbury (061) 445 3152 Busy pub with exceptional choice of cheeses from around the world, rare to be given less than a pound of even the rare ones; bread, cheese and salad **£2.60.**

Manchester SJ8398 MARK ADDY Stanley St Salford (061) 832 4080 Smart pub in converted boat waiting rooms; very good food esp their range of cheeses, usually 50 at any time; extremely big helpings, doggy-bags provided; bread and cheese **£2.40.**

North Lancashire and the Forest of Bowland

Striking moorland, though with limited access, is the main feature here; it's a good area for a quiet break.

The Forest of Bowland is a striking area of Pennine moorland. It's less visited than most areas of comparable scenery, as much of the moorland, privately owned, is closed to walkers. Development in some of the villages (also in private hands) is controlled too strictly to allow for any significant expansion of holiday accommodation – let alone a proliferation of camp sites and so forth. Despite this, indeed in many ways because of this, the area does have a lot of appeal for people who want peace and quiet. There is at least some potential for walking here – for instance, along the pretty Rivers Hodder and Dunsop.

Elsewhere, Pendle Hill has always held the imagination, and other areas of fine countryside include the great whaleback of Longridge Fell, and the wooded Beacon Fell country park. Some of Lancashire's most attractive villages are to be found here, and there are plenty of places to visit.

Where to stay

Cowan Bridge SD6477 Hipping Hall Kirkby Lonsdale Carnforth LA6 2JJ (052 42) 71187 ***£75**; 7 pretty rms. Relaxed country-house atmosphere and delicious food in handsome small hotel with help-yourself drinks, open fire, beamed Great Hall with minstrel gallery where guests dine together, and four acres of walled gardens; cl Jan-Feb; children over 12.

Gibbon Bridge SD6342 Gibbon Bridge Country House Nr Longridge Preston PR3 2TQ (0995) 61456 **£70**; 30 rms. Family-owned country hotel with beautiful landscaped gardens and a quiet, relaxing atmosphere; good, straightforward English cooking, an excellent bakery, and very good service; a good base for walking and short driving trips; disabled access.

Slaidburn SD7152 Parrock Head Farm Clitheroe BB7 3AH (0200) 446614 **£57**; 9 rms – 3 in main house, 6 in garden cottages. Lovely converted 17th-c farmhouse in wonderful spot between moors and dales, with very good food, friendly staff, timbered library, open fire; disabled access.

Capernwray SD5371 New Capernwray Farmhouse Carnforth LA6 1AD (0524) 734284 **£55**; 3 comfortable rms. Pretty 300-year-old ex-farmhouse with helpful, friendly owners, cosy lounge, stone walls and beams, and candle-lit dinner in what was the dairy; children over 10.

Whitewell SD6546 Inn at Whitewell Clitheroe BB7 3AT (0200) 448222 ***£49**; 9 rms, some with open peat fires. Civilised stone inn in the Forest of Bowland, attractive setting and grounds with views down valley, interesting period furnishings, plenty of room, good food, lots of wines, and unusual facilities such as art gallery and six miles of trout, salmon and sea-trout fishing; friendly dogs welcome.

Slaidburn SD7152 Hark to Bounty Clitheroe BB7 3EP (0200) 446246 ***£45**; 8 attractive rms. Popular pub in lovely countryside; comfortable, cosy lounge, a wide range of decent bar food, professional service and a small, praised restaurant menu; lots of room to sit outside, fly-fishing can be arranged.

Clitheroe SD7441 Brooklyn Guest House BB7 2AH (0200) 28268 ***£38**; 4 rms. Very friendly and spotlessly kept Victorian town house with generous, well-cooked breakfasts; close to town centre and Forest of Bowland.

Colne SD8839 Higher Wanless Farm Red Lane BB8 7JP (0282) 865301 ***£38**; 2 rms, one with own bthrm. Warmly welcoming farmhouse with beams, log fires and lovely surrounding farmland used mainly for breeding of Shire horses, as well as sheep; cl Dec, Jan; children over 3.

Waddington SD7243 Peter Barn Cross Lane Clitheroe VV7 3JH (0200) 28585 ***£37**; 3 lovely rms. Converted old stone tithe barn with beamed sitting room, antiques, lovely home-cooking, warmly welcoming owners, a gentle atmosphere, and surrounded by a delightful garden; fine walking country; cl 23 Dec-1 Jan.

Waddington SD7243 Backford Cottage The Square Clitheroe BB7 3JA (0200) 22367 **£36**; 3 rms. Tiny 17th-c cottage in cobbled street, beautifully furnished with antiques; very good service, evening meals by arrangement; good walks in the Forest of Bowland nearby; cl 24-26 Dec; children at owner's discretion.

Hurst Green SD6838 Shireburn Arms Hotel Blackburn BB6 9QJ (0254) 826518 **£35**; 15 rms. Lovely old country hotel with a refined but friendly atmosphere; fine view of the Ribble Valley from the conservatory.

Newton SD6950 Parkers Arms Carnforth BB7 3DY (0200) 446236 **£34**; 3 rms, shared bthrm. Very friendly little pub in lovely setting between Waddington and Beatrix Fell; nice views towards river and hills, decent, generously served bar food.

Chipping SD6243 Carr Side Farm PR3 2TS (0995) 61590 **£34**; 3 comfortable, warm rms with magnificent Pennine views – as there are from the dining room. Immaculately kept B & B in farmhouse on a working farm with land that runs right up on to the fells; huge breakfasts and very good service; pony trekking; children over 3.

To see and do

Barnoldswick SD8746 Bancroft Mill Engine The last working steam mill in the area (not that long ago Barnoldswick had 13), with the engine and boilerhouse as they were in its glory days, and other machines, tools and documents related to the weaving industry; snacks, shop, disabled access; best to tel (0282) 813932 for dates of steam days; *£1.

Barrowford SD8539 Pendle Heritage Centre Local history and 18th-c walled gardens, 14th-c barn with pot-pellied pig, and displays on the Pendle witches – the house itself certainly looks appropriately witchy; farm and country trails; snacks, shop, disabled access; cl 20 Dec-2 Jan; *£1.50. The church at nearby unspoilt Newchurch SD8239 has the witches' grave.

Blackburn SD6827 Its history goes back over 1,000 years, but it was the Industrial Revolution that put Blackburn on the map. It's a fairly pleasant place to visit, with bustling shops and market, some fine buildings and lots of beautiful unspoilt countryside around. Lewis Museum of Textile Machinery Development of textile industry from the 18th c, displayed in period rooms with various

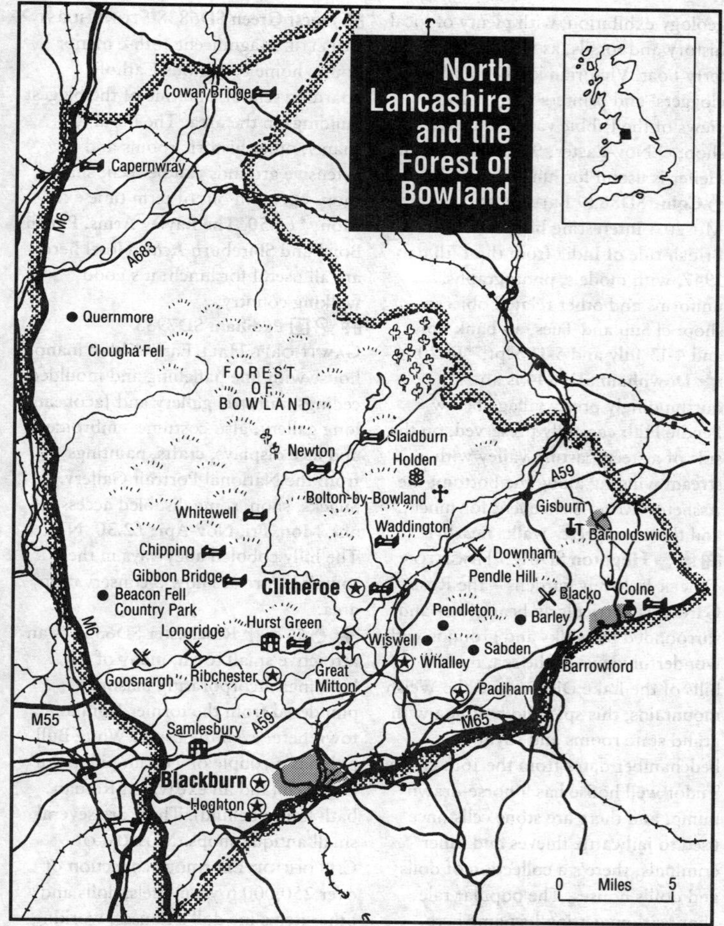

changing exhibitions; shop, some disabled access; cl Sun, Mon, bank hols and Christmas. MUSEUM AND ART GALLERY Fine books and manuscripts, paintings, prints, icons, coins and other features, with children's section and Asian centre; shop, disabled access to ground floor only; cl Sun, Mon, bank hols and Christmas. The parish CHURCH (actually now a cathedral) is very handsome – grand yet elegant. WITTON COUNTRY PARK 480 acres of attractive countryside with walks, nature trails, viewpoints, displays of carts and horse-drawn carriages, small mammal centre and other displays; wknd snacks, shop, some disabled access; visitor centre open pm Thurs, Fri and Sat, all day Sun and bank hols, cl Christmas – the park is always open.

Clitheroe SD7441 Bustling old market town, its high street dominated by the CASTLE perched on its limestone rock. One of the oldest buildings in Lancashire, it has one of the smallest Norman keeps in the country. CLITHEROE CASTLE MUSEUM The museum nearby has an extensive geology exhibition, with plenty of local history and fossils, as well as a restored ferry boat, Victorian kitchen and cloggers' and printers' shops; good views of the Ribble valley. Snacks, shop; cl Nov-Easter; 90p. The Craven Heifer is useful for lunch.

Colne SD8839 BRITISH IN INDIA MUSEUM Interesting history of the British rule of India from the 17th c to 1947, with models, photographs, uniforms and other related objects; shop; cl Sun and Tues, all bank hols and 4-13 July and 5-11 Sept; *£1.20.

★ **Downham** SD7844 is an outstandingly pretty village below Pendle Hill; carefully preserved, on the side of a steep pasture valley with a stream winding along the bottom; the Assheton Arms is excellent for lunch, and there are pretty walks nearby.

Hoghton SD6125 HOGHTON TOWER In lovely gardens – the Rose Garden is particularly beautiful – and surrounded by walks and grounds with wonderful views of the sea, moors, hills of the Lake District and the Welsh mountains, this splendid building with grand state rooms and royal bedchamber dates from the 16th c. The Tudor well house has a horse-drawn pump, and there are stone cells once used to jail cattle thieves and other criminals; there's a collection of dolls and doll's houses. The popular tale about sirloin getting its name here when the loin of beef was knighted during a particularly rumbustious feast is a myth – the word's much older; snacks, shop; open Easter-Oct Sun pm, plus Tues-Thurs July and Aug; £2.50, £1 garden only.

Holden SD7749 HOLDEN CLOUGH NURSERY Old-fashioned nursery with thoroughly up-to-date approach to raising interesting plants in Victorian kitchen garden of Holden Clough Hall; beds of alpines, trough gardens, herbaceous perennials, shrubs and rhododendrons. Shop; cl am (exc Sat), all day Fri, Sun (exc pm Apr and May), and 25 Dec-1 Jan.

Hurst Green SD6838 STONYHURST COLLEGE Magnificent 16th-c manor house, home to famous Catholic boarding school, and one of the biggest buildings in the area. The library, chapel, other historic rooms and the extensive grounds can be seen; snacks, shop; open pm out of term time exc Mon; *£3.50. The Bayley Arms, Punch Bowl and Shireburn Arms Hotel here are all useful for lunch; it's good walking country.

Padiham SD7933 GAWTHORPE HALL Early 17th-c manor house with fine panelling and moulded ceilings, minstrel gallery and Jacobean long gallery; also costume, embroidery and lace displays, crafts, paintings from the National Portrait Gallery. Snacks, shop, some disabled access; cl am, Mon, Fri, Nov-Apr; £2.30. NT. The hilly cobbled alleyways in the town's centre are now a conservation area.

★ **Ribchester** SD6335 is an attractive small town, many of its buildings incorporating masonry plundered from the former Roman town here: even the useful White Bull pub has a couple of Tuscan pillars for its porch (and an excavated Roman bath house behind). There are several small antique shops. MUSEUM OF CHILDHOOD Enormous collection of over 250,000 toys, models, dolls and other items inc doll's houses, working model fairground, various special displays and events. Best when it's not crowded; children enjoy it but adults will probably get the most out of it. Snacks, shop; cl Mon exc bank hols; £1.95. RIBCHESTER ROMAN MUSEUM On the site of a fort occupied by the Romans between the 1st and 4th c, it's an interesting little museum with lots of coins, pottery and the famous Ribchester helmet, as well as a new audio-visual display on the area's history; shop, disabled access; cl am wknds and all day Sat Nov-Feb; £1.25. There are also excavated granaries behind STYDD NURSERY, a specialist plant nursery with lots of old-fashioned roses and hardy perennials; cl am (exc Sat), Mon. The 15th-c CHURCH stands on the site of the Roman fort, and no doubt uses much salvaged material from it.

Sabden SD7837 PENDLE ANTIQUES CENTRE Several dealers selling varied goods such as furniture and pottery in converted mill; snacks, some disabled access; cl 25 Dec, 1 Jan; 50p.

Samlesbury SO5930 SAMLESBURY HALL Well-restored half-timbered 14th-c manor house; antiques, crafts and collector's items, and the windows from Whalley Abbey – see below. Meals, snacks, shop, disabled access; cl Mon exc bank hols, 15 Dec-20 Jan; *£2.

★ **Slaidburn** SD7152 in the Forest of Bowland is perfectly preserved: charming stone cottages, a green with the River Hodder running by, and at the opposite end an early 18th-c schoolhouse and a church with a very 18th-c feel inside. The Hark to Bounty is good for lunch.

† **Whalley** SD7336 WHALLEY ABBEY Striking remains of 14th-c Cistercian abbey – the monks' quarters, rather than the church which has virtually disappeared – in grounds of Blackburn Diocesan Retreat and Conference House, an interesting 16th-c manor house. Two gatehouses are intact, and there are cloisters, a chapter house and the abbot's lodgings and kitchen; snacks, shop, disabled access; cl Oct-Apr; *£1. Bed and breakfast is also available. The separate 13th-c parish CHURCH is very attractive, with interesting woodwork inside. There's also a nostalgic little MEMORY LANE MUSEUM with exhibits and displays of household objects from around the 1940s; cl am wknds, all day Mon, winter wkdys; £1.50. The Whalley Arms is useful for lunch.

★ **Other attractive villages** in or on the edges of the Forest of Bowland are Bolton by Bowland SD7849 (with a fine church tower), Gisburn SD8248, Newton SD6950 and Waddington SD7244. Elsewhere, we'd recommend Goosnargh SD5537 (where Chingle Hall, a little medieval manor, is reputedly one of the most haunted houses in Britain), and, on the slopes of Pendle Hill, Pendleton SD7539 and Wiswell SD7437. All these villages have decent pubs. Great Mitton SD7139 has an attractive church with an outstanding range of memorial tombs.

Walks

The major snag about the **Forest of Bowland** is its lack of legal access (Ramblers Association mass trespasses, the annual demonstration against denial of access for walkers, regularly takes place here) with only a few paths crossing the impressive massif that forms some of the county's most significant scenery. There are, however, rights of way allowing some fine walks – for instance, up Clougha Fell from Quernmore SD5259; above Tarnbrook Wyre SD5855; up Dunsop Fell from Slaidburn SD7152 or Dunsop Bridge SD6550; up Fairsnape and Wolf Fell from Chipping SD6143 or Bleasdale SD5745. Beacon Fell Country Park SD5642 is an atmospheric place to wander through.

You can walk round and almost all over **Pendle Hill** SD7941, so thorough is the path network, and although Pendle's witch-persecuting days are happily over the place still has a rugged appeal. The view that enraptured George Fox, the founder of the Quakers, is as good as ever. The quickest way up is from Barley village SD8240.

Driving

Crossing the Forest of Bowland, the B6478 takes in some of its most appealing if not grandest scenery; from Slaidburn the narrow old road N past Stocks Reservoir gives a sense of adventure. One of the nicest roads in this part is up from Clitheroe through Bashall Eaves and then the Trough of Bowland, eventually taking the right fork up towards Quernmore.

The back roads up over Longridge Fell give some fine views over much of Lancashire. Around Pendle Hill, the steep road up through Pendleton and down through Sabden also gives some splendid views, as does the road around the hill's eastern flank – passing through some very attractive scenery around Downham.

Where to eat

Longridge SD6037 PAUL HEATHCOTES 104 Higher Rd (0772) 784969 Very popular restaurant with excellent, imaginative cooking including wonderful puddings; cl Mon, 1st wk Jan; open Tues-Sun evenings, Fri/Sun lunchtimes; children over 5; disabled access. **£40.**

Goosnargh SD5537 BUSHELLS ARMS (0772) 865235 Friendly modernised pub close to Chingle Hall, excellent range of imaginative food (even soups are unusual), and good range of wines. **£15**|£2.50/£6.

Blacko SD8541 MOORCOCK (0282) 614186 Good popular bar food with quite a few continental dishes, efficient friendly service, and wonderful views from the picture windows in the comfortable lounge; cl 25 Dec, disabled access. **£12**|£2/£4.50.

Downham SD7844 ASSHETON ARMS (0200) 441227 Popular pub among peaceful pastures in prettily preserved village, rambling beamed bar, reasonably priced and generously served bar food, decent wines. £2.50/£5.95.

Help this year from: *C J Parsons, C A Brace, Drs Frank and Ann Bowman, MMD, Dilys Unsworth, David Craine, Brian Wainwright, Michael Butler, Doug Kennedy, Drs Frank and Ann Bowman, Graham Bush, Peter Atkinson, Brian Murphy, Ian Phillips, Karen Simpson, Paul Williams, A R Sayer, Andy and Jill Kassube, Basil Minson, Gill and Mike Cross, Robert and Gladys Flux, Andy Hazeldine, P A Legon, Lyn and Bill Capper.*

LANCASHIRE CALENDAR

Some of these dates were provisional as we went to press.

FEBRUARY

2nd **Carnforth** Antiques Fair *at Leighton Hall – till Sun 6*

4th **Blackpool** Ideal Home and Leisure Exhibition *at the Wintergardens – till Sun 6*

18th **Stonyhurst** Antiques Fair *at Stonyhurst College – till Sun 20*

19th **Liverpool** British Men's Team Gymnastics Championships – *till Sun 20*

Lancashire Calendar

February cont.

26th **Blackpool** British Magical Championships; **Southport** Thomas the Tank Engine Gala Weekend *at Railway Centre – till Sun 27*

27th **Blackpool** International Gala of Magic *at Opera House*

March

5th **Arkholme** Lambing *at Docker Park Farm Visitor Centre – till Thurs 31*

26th **Manchester** Transport Festival *at Transport Museum – till Sun* 27

28th **Morecambe** Children's Festival *with arts and sports workshops – till 8 Apr*

April

1st **Lancaster** Maritime Festival *– till Mon 4*; **Southport** Steam Trains *at Railway Centre – till Mon 4*

2nd **Bacup** Britannia Coconutters, *elaborately costumed black-face clog dancers in the streets from 9 am – thought to be pirate dances brought first to Cornwall and then to Lancs with miners moving north*

4th **Preston** Egg Rolling *at Avenham Park; when the brightly coloured eggs become too damaged to be rolled they are eaten – oranges, too, as a later addition to the pagan custom*

May

2nd **Marsh Mill Village** Mayday Clog Dancing *in the town square*

8th **Fylde** Red Rose Carriage Driving Club Event

22nd **Liverpool** Women's 10-kilometre Run

24th **Blackpool** Championship Dog Show *– till Sat 25*

27th **Blackpool** Dance Festival *– till 3 Jun*; **Morecambe** International Festival of Country Music *– till Mon 30*

28th **Churchtown** Children's Festival; **Glasson** Lancaster Canal Boat Club Annual Rally *at Glasson Dock, inc tall ships, trade stalls, bands and dog show – till Mon 30*; **Liverpool** Show *at Wavertree – till Mon 30*

30th **Garstang** Children's Festival

June

3rd **Cark-in-Carkmel** Garden and Countryside Festival *at Holker Hall*

4th **Bilsborrow** Gala; **Lancaster** Annual Punt Races; **Liverpool** Lord Mayor's Parade *at the City Centre;* **Slaidburn** Steam Traction Rally

5th **Morecambe** Carnival; **Thornton Cleveleys** Gala Horseshow *– till Weds 15, gala procession on Sat 11*

9th **Liverpool** Festival of Comedy *– till Sun 19*

11th **Calverdale** Children's Festival; **Southport** Thomas the Tank Engine *at Railway Centre – till Sun 12*

12th **Uppermill** Vintage Vehicle Gala *at King George Playing Field*

26th **Southport** Steam Day and Stationary Engines Display *at Railway Centre*

Lancashire Calendar

June cont.

30th **Old Trafford** England v NZ Test Match – *till 5 July*

July

2nd **Liverpool** Cathedral Festival – *till Sun 17*

9th **Winmarleigh** Gala

16th **Hambleton** Gala and Flower Show

17th **Fleetwood** Train Sunday

28th **Lancaster** Georgian Legacy Festival, *inc the smugglers' den, recruiting for the King's army, the trial of Hannah Smith, grand fair, prisoners in the castle cells, incident in the music room and sedan-chair racing – till Sun 31*

29th **St Helens** Agricultural Show *at Sherdley Park – till Sun 31*

August

6th **Garstang** Agricultural Show

13th **Fleetwood** Fireworks and Birdman Competition *on the Pier*; **Rochdale** Rush-bearing Ceremony; **Southport** Thomas the Tank Engine Gala Party *at Railway Centre – till Sun 14*

18th **Southport** Flower Show, *inc other events such as sheepdog trials, bowling competitions and firework display at Victoria Park – till Sat 20*

20th **Thornton Cleveleys** Arts, Crafts and Flower Show

26th **Liverpool** International Beatles Convention – *till Tues 30*; **Nateby** Lancaster Canal Boat Club Rally *at Bridgehouse Marina – till Mon 29*

27th **Fleetwood** Flower Show; **Old Trafford** 2nd One-day International, England v South Africa; **Southport** Enthusiasts Weekend *at Railway Centre – till Mon 29*

29th **Ramsbottom** World Black-pudding-throwing Championships

September

2nd **Fleetwood** Train and Transport Festival – *till Sun 4*

4th **Lancaster** Horticultural Society Summer Show

11th **Liverpool** Road Race

October

15th **Carnforth** Dolls Fair *at Leighton Hall*

29th **Southport** Thomas the Tank Engine *at Railway Centre – till Sun 30*

November

4th **Liverpool** Gymnastics Championships – *till Sun 6*

5th **Fleetwood** Fireworks and Birdman Competition *on the pier*; **Liverpool** River Mersey Fireworks

13th **Lancaster** Horticultural Society Late Show

23rd **Blackpool** Ideal Home and Gifts Exhibition *at Norbreck Castle – till Sun 27*

December

3rd **Southport** Santa Steam Specials *at Railway Centre – till Sun 4 and also following two wknds*

Leicestershire, Lincolnshire and Nottinghamshire

Leicestershire has the most broadly appealing countryside here, undulating enough to give good varied views. Parts of Lincolnshire have a somewhat similar rolling character, and, like Leicestershire, the county is studded with attractive villages and remarkably fine churches. Both these counties have plenty of grand houses and castles to look at, though rather less in the way of things to keep children entertained; that's where Nottinghamshire tends to score. This is not a part of Britain to come to if you want to spend the time looking around fine gardens.

Of the three county towns, Lincoln is the best bet for most people: it's preserved a more universally appealing character, and has lots to see. If you enjoy sightseeing, Nottingham might well be a choice – again with lots to see, and a gentler place at weekends than you'd expect. Though Leicester has a good many attractions, most people will probably find it too much of a big city to enjoy a weekend stay.

Leicestershire

Good for a civilised break, with rolling countryside and some interesting things to see.

The eastern side of the county has quite a lot to offer for a short break. The rolling countryside has long views and is pleasantly varied, with patches of woodland, attractive stone-built villages, many delightful churches, and several fine houses in handsome parkland. Among places to look around and things to do, we'd pick out Belvoir Castle, Stamford Hall at Swinford, the steam railway running from Shackerstone past the battlefield of Bosworth Field, followed by the ruined castles at Ashby-de-la-Zouch and Kirby Muxloe. There are other things for railway enthusiasts to enjoy at Loughborough and Cottesmore. Rutland Water is a reservoir, but now has the look of a huge natural lake, pleasant to walk around, with nature reserves at the western ends, bicycle and boat hire, and even launch trips. A smattering of things for children to enjoy elsewhere includes particularly the working farm at Oadby, the zoo at Twycross and the discovery park in Coalville. There's a good deal to see and do in Leicester itself, but it's a place for day visits and not for a stay.

Where to stay

Packington SK3614 SPRINGS HYDRO Ashby-de-la-Zouch LE65 1TJ (0530) 273873 **£139.90 inc lunch and dinner and body massage**; 41 rms. Britain's first purpose-built health hydro with all the facilities, good healthy food, and friendly staff; cl 5 days over Christmas; no children.

Stapleford SK8018 STAPLEFORD PARK Melton Mowbray LE14 2EF (057 284) 522 ***£125**; 35 rms. Luxurious country house, extravagantly restored, overlooking 500 acres of woodland, lots of mahogany, opulent furnishings, fine oil paintings, and impressive libary, good restaurant food, enthusiastic American owner and warmly welcoming staff; riding, stabling, tennis, croquet, miniature golf, coarse fishing, clay-pigeon shooting, hunting; cots/babysitting; dogs welcome.

Oakham SK8609 HAMBLETON HALL LE15 8TH (0572) 756991 **£115**; 15 luxurious rms. Set in beautiful grounds on the edge of Rutland Water, this grandly restored Victorian manor house has elegant day rooms with fine views, antiques, open fires and exceptional flower arrangements; professional, friendly staff, wonderful food, a grandly stimulating wine list and a marvellously pampering atmosphere; disabled access.

Rothley SK5812 ROTHLEY COURT LE7 7LG (0533) 374141 **£100.90**; 36 rms (the ones in the main house have more character). Mentioned in the Domesday Book, this carefully run manor house with its beautifully preserved 13th-c chapel has some fine oak panelling, open fires, a comfortable bar, conservatory, a terrace and garden, and courteous staff; disabled access.

Oakham SK8609 WHIPPER INN Market Pl LE15 6DT (0572) 756971 **£80**; 25 rms. Attractive and well-run 17th-c stone coaching inn with oak-beamed and panelled lounge – mainly a restaurant with good food; disabled access.

Market Harborough SP7388 THREE SWANS 21 High St LE16 7NJ (0858) 466644 **£55w**; 36 rms. Comfortable inn with plush furnishings and an exceptionally good range of quickly served bar food.

Stretton SK9416 RAM JAM INN Great North Rd LE15 7QY (0780) 410776 ***£56.40**; 8 comfortable and well-equipped rms. Actually on the A1, this is a civilised place with smart all-day continental-style snack bar from breakfast-time on, a comfortable airy modern lounge bar, a good choice of food quickly served from buffet counter, and useful small wine list; cl 25 Dec.

Lyddington SP8797 MARQUESS OF EXETER Oakham LE15 9LT (0572) 882477 **£55**; 17 rms. Rambling 16th-c family-run stone hotel in charming village, with beams, huge log fire surrounded by comfortable easy chairs – very tempting on a cold winter evening; excellent value bar food inc vegetarian dishes; disabled access.

Empingham SK9408 WHITE HORSE Main St LE15 8PR (078 086) 221/521 **£52**; 14 pretty rms, some in a delightfully converted stable block, and most with own bthrm. Refurbished, popular old pub on edge of Europe's largest man-made lake, relaxed and friendly atmosphere, big helpings of excellent food inc fine breakfasts, coffee and croissants from 8 am and cream teas all year round; log fire, attractive restaurant, and efficient, friendly service; cots/highchairs; disabled access.

Glooston SP7595 OLD BARN Market Harborough LE16 7ST (085) 884215 ***£49.50**; 3 rms. Attractively restored 16th-c pub with civilised décor – beamed main bar with pewter plates and Players cricketer cigarette cards on the walls; very good food inc breakfasts; cl 25 Dec.

Sibson SK3500 MILLERS Main Rd CV13 6LB (0827) 880223 **£48.85w**; 40 rms. Well-placed, clean hotel converted from a mill and village bakery with working millwheel and stream in lounge bar; cl 26 Dec; disabled access.

Breedon on the Hill SK4022 HOLLY BUSH Derby DE7 1AN (0332) 862356 **£45**; 2 attractive pine-furnished rms. Pleasant old pub with comfortable plush beamed bar and dining room, good food, and friendly service.

Wing SK8903 KINGS ARMS Top St LE15 8SE (057 285) 315 ***£42**; 4 rms. Close to Rutland Water, this simple early 17th-c inn, carefully refurbished, has a convivial atmosphere, coal fire, wide choice of good generous home-cooked food, and spacious restaurant; small but interesting medieval turf maze nearby; cl 25 Dec pm; disabled access.

Medbourne SP7993 NEVILL ARMS Market Harborough LE16 8EE (085 883) 288 ***£39.50w**; 3 rms. Old mullion-windowed inn just across footbridge over stream. Bright and busy with excellent food and friendly, prompt service; lots of bar games; cl 25-26 Dec; disabled access.

To see and do

Ashby-de-la-Zouch SK3516 ASHBY-DE-LA-ZOUCH CASTLE These impressive ruins are those of a Norman manor house and its later 15th-c extension, destroyed in the Civil War. Particularly notable features include the walls, solar and large kitchen, and above all the tower in which Mary Queen of Scots was imprisoned. The adjoining fields were the setting for Sir Walter Scott's *Ivanhoe*. Snacks, shop, some disabled access; cl 1-2 pm and winter Mon; £1.20. A little MUSEUM next to the tourist information centre on North St has displays on the castle and the rest of the town's history; shop, disabled access; cl 12-2 pm and Sun am, Oct-Easter; *25p. MOIRA FURNACE A central feature of the Industrial Heritage Trail, this site has a 19th-c blast furnace and foundations of engine house and casting shed along with a series of lime kilns; snacks, shop, disabled access; open pm weekends, Easter-Oct. A few craft workshops in the grounds. The Sun is useful for lunch. Just out of town in pretty Staunton Harold the FERRERS CENTRE has a number of notable craft shops and exhibitions; cl Mon. The church out here is now owned by the National Trust and is also worth a look.

Beacon Hill SK5114 above Woodhouse Eaves is one of the best viewpoints in the area – an intriguing mix of the industrial and the very rural; it's popular locally as a beauty-spot, rising almost like a volcano above its lower woodland slopes. The Wheatsheaf is useful for lunch.

Belvoir SK8133 BELVOIR CASTLE Overlooking the Vale of Belvoir, the house, rebuilt grandiosely in 1816, is a glorious fantasy of turrets and battlements, pinnacles and towers, surrounded by terraced gardens peopled with sculptures. The Dukes of Rutland have lived here since Henry VIII's reign, and the collections of furniture, tapestries and master paintings show that the eye of each successive generation has been unerringly tasteful. There is also the museum of 17th/21st Lancers and a collection of arms and armour; meals and snacks, shop, disabled access; cl Mon (exc bank hols), Fri and Oct-Apr (exc Sun in Oct); £3.50. The Peacock at Redmile not far off is very good for lunch, and the Wheel at Branston SK8129 is good too.

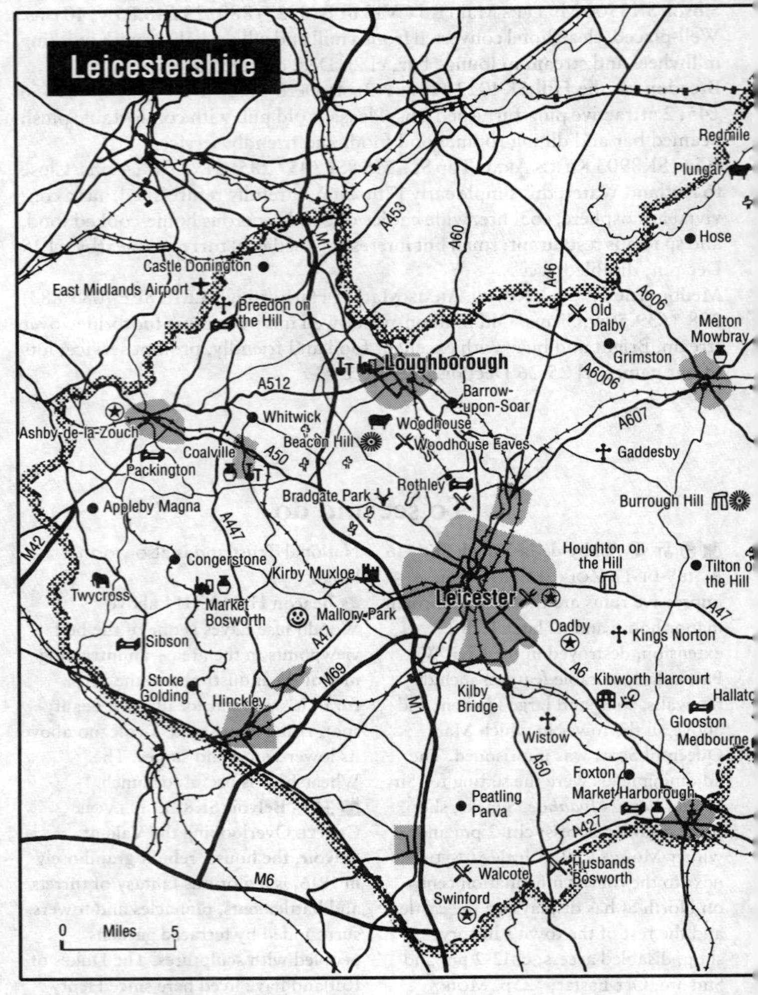

♆ **Bradgate Park** SK5209, on the edge of Newtown Linford, is an extensive tract of former hunting park, little changed over the last 750 years, around the ruins of a 15th-c house. Fallow deer still roam these heathy slopes among the rock outcrops, and below the park Cropston Reservoir has waterfowl. The Bradgate Arms at Cropston and Wheatsheaf above Woodhouse Eaves are handy for lunch.

Burrough Hill SK7611 is an imposing Iron-Age hill fort, its high ramparts still largely intact; a splendid viewpoint. The determinedly simple Stag & Hounds is useful for refreshment.

Coalville SK4214 SNIBSTON DISCOVERY PARK Originally a colliery (the first shaft was sunk by George and Robert Stephenson), this is now a thriving 100-acre centre with lots of fun exhibitions and interactive displays on the environment, weather, human

body, underground and overground engineering, transport, local history and fashion. Outside are reassembled wheelwright's and blacksmith's shops, a huge play area, nature trails, golf course and fishing lagoons. Enough here to keep most people busy for quite some time; meals, snacks, shop, disabled access; cl 25-26 Dec; £3.

Cottesmore SK9013 RUTLAND RAILWAY MUSEUM A collection of 28 industrial steam and diesel locomotives and 70 other wagons and vehicles used in the ironstone quarries and industry. Part of the former Midland Railway mineral branch, built for the quarries, is used to provide rides for visitors and to demonstrate the exhibits; snacks, shop; open weekends and bank hols Easter-Sept, and over Christmas period – best to tel (0572) 813203 for dates and prices of steam days. The Sun is good for lunch.

East Midlands Airport SK4525 on the Derbys border has a lively AEROPARK AND VISITOR CENTRE, with plenty of aeroplanes inc a Canberra, Vulcan and Lightning, and displays covering the history of flight and how a modern airport works. Viewpoints are just 180m away from the runways of the main airport; snacks, shop, disabled access; visitor centre cl winter weekdays; £2 a car. The Cap & Stocking just over the motorway in Kegworth SK4826 is a fine old tavern.

Egleton SK8707 RUTLAND WATER NATURE RESERVE is a strip of land stretching 9 miles around Rutland Water, sensibly divided into two parts. Lyndon Reserve is for the general public (with a useful visitor centre), and Egleton Reserve is aimed at the more serious birdwatcher. Both have observation hides overlooking the water; snacks, shop, disabled access. Lyndon Reserve is open wknds all year, plus Tues, Weds and Thurs in summer (£1), Egleton daily exc Thurs (£2.50). On the other side of the lake there are places to hire bikes to cycle round the water, and hourly BOAT TRIPS. The White Horse at Empingham is good for lunch, and other handy dining places are the Finches Arms at Upper Hambleton and Noel Arms at Whitwell.

Houghton on the Hill SK6703 The lane north brings you after a mile to the site, on its right, of Ingarsby DESERTED VILLAGE, its inhabitants evicted in the 15th c by the Abbot of Leicester who wanted their land for grazing sheep – which may still be seen here, among the clearly discernible mounds and hollows that mark the long-gone settlement.

Kibworth Harcourt SP6894 has the county's only remaining post mill, a fine example from the early 18th c. The Three Horseshoes is a civilised place for lunch. Other well-preserved WINDMILLS can be found at Arnesby SP6192, Shepshed SK4719 and Wymondham SK8518 (an unusual six-sailed mill with a tearoom and craft shops).

Kirby Muxloe SK5104 KIRBY MUXLOE CASTLE Started in 1480, this building was abandoned three years later when its founder, Lord Hastings, was executed. The peaceful ruins include an imposing gatehouse, water-filled moat and one tower which is still in good shape; shop, disabled access; cl winter Mon, 24-25 Dec; £1.10. The Royal Oak is useful for lunch.

Leicester SK5804 In this busy city's mix of ancient and modern, it's the modern which makes the most immediate impression. But a bit of digging around among the recently built shops, office blocks and traffic schemes does turn up quite a few interesting reminders of its long and varied past. JEWRY WALL MUSEUM AND SITE (St Nicholas Circle) The Roman city of Leicester was called Ratae, and the Jewry Wall is part of the Roman public baths. The museum uses models to give some insight into the lives of the town's citizens, besides showing some of the items found in the excavations, with excellent collections of mosaic pavements and painted wallplaster. The site itself consists of a courtyard excavated to reveal porticoes and shops sheltered by the remains of a massive stone wall, and there are useful displays of local archaeology from prehistoric to medieval times; shop, disabled access; cl am Sun, Good Fri, 25-26 Dec. A short walk away is WYGSTON'S HOUSE MUSEUM OF COSTUME where the display of English costume ranges from the 17th c to the present day, with entertaining reconstructions of various specialist clothing shops from the 1920s; meals and snacks, shop, disabled access; cl am Sun, 25-26 Dec, Good Fri. NEWARKE HOUSES show the story of Leicester folk from 1500 to the present day, with recreated scenes of domestic life and collections of clocks and musical instruments; shop; cl Good Fri, 25-26 Dec. In Church Rd, more on the edge of the city, is BELGRAVE HALL, a fine example of 18th-c architecture, furnished with period pieces; coaches and implements are shown in the stables, and there are also outbuildings and charming gardens; shop, limited disabled access; cl Sun am, Good Fri, 25-26 Dec. Nearby is the MUSEUM OF TECHNOLOGY, which focuses on Leicester's importance as an industrial centre throughout the centuries, inc a power-generation gallery, transport displays, and a galaxy of knitting machinery that makes the home version look decidedly primitive; shop, disabled access; cl Good Fri, 25-26 Dec. Other museums in the town include, in New Walk, the LEICESTERSHIRE MUSEUM AND ART GALLERY, with interesting displays of 18th- to 20th-c art, silver, geology, ceramics, Egyptology and natural history, and a collection of German Expressionist art that for this country must be unique; shop, disabled access; cl Good Fri, 25-26 Dec. In the same street the MUSEUM OF ROYAL LEICESTERSHIRE REGIMENT has military mementoes and relics; shop; cl Good Fri, 25-26 Dec. A more unusual exhibition is the GAS MUSEUM on Aylestone Rd, with a comprehensive study of the industry, and some unusual examples of its application; disabled access to ground floor only; open pm Tues-Fri. ECO HOUSE (Hinckley Rd) is an ordinary house converted to show over 100 ways to make the modern home more environment-friendly; cl am wkdys and all Mon and Tues. GORSE HILL CITY

Farm (Anstey Lane) is a friendly little place with the usual animals and activities, and a developing organic garden; meals, snacks, shop, disabled access; cl Weds; £1 donation requested. Towpath walks along both Grand Union Canal and the River Soar give a relatively tranquil back view of the city's industrial life. Besides the Tiffin (see Where to eat below), the Welford Place (on Welford Pl) is good for lunch here, actually serving food all through the day; the Melton on the A607 N is fascinating for its authentic Bombay cooking (Thurs-Sun evenings) rarely seen in view in an English pub.

Loughborough SK5354 BELL FOUNDRY MUSEUM demonstrates both the development of the craft and modern practices – the museum is part of the largest working bell foundry in the world, and the array of bells in the tuning room is quite remarkable; shop, disabled access; cl 12.30-1.30 pm, all day Mon (exc bank hols) and Sun; 75p. GREAT CENTRAL RAILWAY The locomotive depot at Loughborough Central is accompanied by a museum, while the line itself runs from Loughborough Central to Leicester; meals, snacks, shop, disabled access; cl wkdys Oct-Apr; £5.60. The Swan in the Rushes, very cheery, has better food than you'd expect from appearances, and down the line the Royal Oak at Rothley SK5812 is a useful journey break.

Lyddington SP8797 BEDE HOUSE A fine example of 15th-c architecture, this was a residence of the Bishops of Lincoln until the religious upheavals begun in Henry VIII's reign, and was later converted into an almshouse by the Earl of Exeter. There are notable carved ceilings in the Bishop's quarters upstairs, which still have 15th-c glass; also worth a look are the smaller rooms for the bedesmen downstairs and the tranquil garden; shop; cl 1-2 pm, Oct-Mar; £1.20. The Marquess of Exeter and Old White Hart are good for lunch.

Mallory Park SK4500 provides a complete change of mood, with motorsport meetings held every wknd Mar-Oct; meals, snacks, shop, disabled access; from £5.

Market Bosworth SK4003 This town used to specialise in the production of corsets – some bizarre, florid and even agonising examples of which can be seen in the town MUSEUM (Softleys and the Old Black Horse are useful for lunch). Now, however, the town is better known for the BOSWORTH BATTLEFIELD VISITOR CENTRE AND COUNTRY PARK to the south, where there are exhibitions, models and a film theatre which examine the Battle of Bosworth Field and the history behind it; meanwhile, in the field itself, you shouldn't need a horse to follow the downfall of Richard III along the Battlefield Trail, which uses models and displays to illustrate the details of the battle as it was conducted between Richard III and the future Henry VII; meals and snacks, shop, disabled access; cl Nov-May, cl am exc July and Aug, pre-booked parties at any time during the year – tel (0455) 290429; £1.50. From Shackerstone SK3706 the BATTLEFIELD STEAM RAILWAY LINE runs through Market Bosworth to Shenton by the battlefield, a return trip of just over 9 miles. A museum has enthusiastically mounted displays related to the age of steam; open wknds – tel for details of timetable, (0827) 880754; *£4.50 return. The Rising Sun here is useful for lunch, as is the Royal Arms at Sutton Cheney SK4100, at the battlefield end.

Market Harborough SP7387 The attractive town centre has some fine old Georgian buildings, and above them the gracefully soaring 14th-c spire of the church. HARBOROUGH MUSEUM Local council offices house this museum illustrating the varied history of the area; shop, disabled access; cl Sun am, Good Fri and 25-26 Dec. The Three Swans Hotel does good lunches.

Melton Mowbray SK7518 MELTON CARNEGIE MUSEUM Stilton cheese, pork pies and the Quorn hunt all originate here. The museum celebrates its fashionable 19th-c days and presents the present life of the area; shop, disabled access; cl Sun exc summer pm. Dickinson & Morris (Nottingham St) still make the pies to a traditional recipe (tours on Tues and Sat in season); and Websters at nearby Saxelbye SK7020 make stilton in their 19th-c dairy; tel (0664) 812223.

Oadby SK6200 FARMWORLD This working farm set in charming countryside has something for everyone in the family, with activities ranging from the Children's Farmyard and rare breeds to a milking parlour and a charming pastiche of an Edwardian alehouse, taking in crafts and walks along the way; meals, snacks, shop, disabled access; cl 25-26 Dec and 1 Jan; *£4. The UNIVERSITY BOTANIC GARDENS (Stoughton Drive South) are set around student halls of residence: 16 acres filled with a wide variety of plants in different and delightful settings, inc a hardy fuchsia collection; plant sales; cl wknds and bank hols.

Oakham SK8609, the capital of the former Rutland, is an attractive small town with a good sense of country bustle about it, and one or two interesting antique shops. OAKHAM CASTLE The magnificent Norman banqueting hall is all that remains of the late 12th-c manor house which once stood here, though earthworks and walls give a good idea of what it must have been like. The walls of the hall itself are decorated with a droll collection of extraordinary horseshoes, some grossly opulent, some simply enormously oversized – there's a tradition that royalty and peers of the realm should hand one over as they enter the lordship of Oakham; shop, disabled access; cl 1-2 pm, Mon (exc bank hols). RUTLAND COUNTY MUSEUM Good local-history museum with emphasis on rural life; displays of Roman and Saxon finds, and outside in the courtyard is a display of farming tools and wagons; shop; cl Sun am, Dec 25-26 and Good Fri. RUTLAND FARM PARK Lots of animals inc various breeds of cattle, pig, sheep and poultry, as well as old farming equipment and pretty walks round the woodland and stream, with fine trees and Victorian rockeries; snacks, shop, disabled access; cl am out of season, all day Mon and Oct-Easter; £2.30. The Whipper Inn, Waycotts and Barnsdale Lodge are all good for lunch.

Plungar SK7633 OUR LITTLE FARM Friendly little farm with traditional and rare breeds in the farmyard, an incubator and hatchery with tiny ducklings and the like, and 8-acre nature trail. Also events or craft displays at wknds; snacks, shop, disabled access; cl Mon, Nov-mid-Mar; £1.95.

Swinford SP5779 STANFORD HALL AND MOTORCYCLE MUSEUM The Cave family have lived here since 1430; the present house was built in the 1690s, with handsome state rooms and ballroom, and good collections of antique furnishings, costumes and paintings. The motorcycle museum is in the grounds, which also have a lovely 14th-c church with splendid stained glass, an old forge, walled rose garden, and a Sunday craft centre. Snacks, shop, some disabled access; open pm Sat, Sun, bank hols and Tues after bank hols from Easter Sat-end of Sept; house and grounds *£3.20, grounds *£1.80; museum extra *£1.

Tilton on the Hill SK7405 HALSTEAD HOUSE FARM A specialist poultry farm, with a display on poultry rearing, a nature trail, fishing lake and gardens. Meals, snacks, shop, disabled access; cl Mon and all Nov-Easter; £2 for displays.

Twycross SK3305 TWYCROSS ZOO PARK As well as the animals one would expect to find in a zoo, this specialises in primates, having an enormous and varied range of apes, gibbons, orang-utans, and chimpanzees – every shape, size and species; meals, snacks, shop, disabled access; cl 25 Dec; £4.

! **Welland Viaduct** SP9197 nr Seaton is one of the county's most striking sights: nearly a mile long, swooping across the pastures of the valley, it is the country's longest viaduct.

Wing SK8902 is a quietly attractive Rutland village, notable for its small medieval TURF MAZE. The Kings Arms is good for lunch.

Woodhouse SK5315 WHATOFF LODGE Just east towards Quorn, a decent nature trail starts from this working farm, where there's an exhibition of rural bygones and some farm animals; snacks, shop, disabled access; cl Mon; £2.

† Though not to quite such a degree as neighbouring Lincolnshire, this is church country, with many fine CHURCHES in both towns and villages. Among those well worth seeing are the ones at Breedon on the Hill SK4022 (on an Iron-Age hill fort), Exton SK9211 (beautifully placed in a park), Gaddesby SK6813 (elaborate 13th-c workmanship), Kings Norton SK6800 (graceful Gothic Revival), Normanton SK9306 (with Rutland Water and a museum nearby), Stoke Dry SP8596, Tilton on the Hill SK7405 and Wistow SP6496.

★ **Other attractive villages** here, all with decent pubs, include Appleby Magna SK3109, Ashby Folville SK7011, Barrowden SK9400, Branston SK8129, Braunston SK8306, Grimston SK6821, Hallaton SP7896, Hose SK7329, Knipton SK8231, Knossington SK8008, Lyddington SP8798, Medbourne SP7993, Peatling Parva SP5889, South Luffenham SK9402, Stoke Golding SP3997 and Whitwick SK4316.

Walks

The walk around **Rutland Water** totals 24 miles – information centres have details of shorter trails. The best walk, starting from Hambleton and touring the peninsula which protrudes into the reservoir, is little publicised.

The former great hunting park of **Charnwood Forest** has two good surviving chunks here: Bradgate Park SK5209 and nearby Beacon Hill SK5114. Surprisingly for the east Midlands, both have miniature patches of moorland with suitably scaled-down crags. Both are part of country parks, with general access, plenty of waymarked paths, and lots of opportunities for picnics. From the 800-ft summit of Beacon Hill, the Jubilee Walk heads N and E through partly wooded country. A trail S makes a small circuit around Broombriggs Farm SK5114, with boards explaining farming methods by the path. **Burrough Hill** SK7611 S of Melton Mowbray SK7518 has an enjoyable path along its escarpment. The summit has an Iron-Age hill fort, and a view indicator. **Foxton Locks** SP7090 on the Grand Union Canal nr Market Harborough SP7387 are a famous example of canal engineering, and next to an interesting inclined plane, now abandoned – a failed attempt at preserving water over this section. A handy pub, Bridge 61 (SP7090), is right next to the towpath.

The **Ashby Canal** towpath, which incidentally makes an ideal link between Bosworth battlefield and the steam railway to the N, has good countryside walking, with green fields and stone-arched bridges, as well as coots, moorhens, herons and maybe even the flash of a kingfisher. The best parts run from the tunnel under Snarestone SK3409 past Gopsall Park SK3505, and then on through Shackerstone SK3706 and Congerstone SK3505 to pass Shenton Park

SK3800 on an embankment, before heading into Warwickshire and its junction with the Coventry Canal.

Pubs useful for walkers here include the the Pear Tree and Bulls Head in Woodhouse Eaves SK5214, the Copt Oak SK4812 (for Charnwood Forest), and the Priest House at Kings Mills near Castle Donington SK4427 (for the River Trent); and, all handy for canals, the Three Horseshoes at Stoke Golding SP3997, Navigation and Soar Bridge in Barrow-upon-Soar SK5717, the Griffin at Congerstone SK3605, and the Navigation at Kilby Bridge SP6097 (canal).

Driving

Driving in much of Leicestershire is a pleasure, with good views from long-striding old coach roads, such as the one running below Belvoir Castle from Long Benington up in Lincolnshire through Bottesford, Harby and Hose; or the fine one from just below the castle NW of Knipton down through Eastwell and past Grimston all the way to Barrow-upon-Soar. The road N from Oakham through Ashwell, Wymondham and Waltham on the Wolds to Harby is very fine. Further S, a similar road runs easily across the county from Uppingham through Hallaton, Tur Langton and Kibworth Harcourt, past Wistow to Kilby, Countesthorpe and Cosby.

There are fewer views and more traffic over in the W of the county, though the road through Peckleton, Kirkby Mallory, Sutton Cheney and Fenny Drayton is quite good.

Where to eat

Leicester SK5904 TIFFIN London Rd (0533) 470420 Good Anglo-Indian food; cl Sun, Sat am, 4 days over Christmas. **£22**|£12.60.

Husbands Bosworth SP6484 FERNIE LODGE (0858) 880551 Warmly recommended by contributors. **£20.40**|£1.95/£5.

Old Dalby SK6723 CROWN (0664) 823134 Converted farmhouse, unspoilt and welcoming, serving a wide range of drinks (14 real ales and 20 malt whiskies), and big helpings of imaginative and completely fresh food (no freezers, microwaves or chips). **£17**|£3/£7.

Hallaton SP7896 BEWICKE ARMS (085 889) 217 Thatched cottage by village green with warm welcome and traditional feel; generously served bar food with particularly popular puddings and daily specials that change with the season; no dogs allowed. **£16.80**|£2.10/£8.40.

Redmile SK7935 PEACOCK (0949) 42554 Little village house opposite Belvoir Castle with extremely popular food and beer, aiming for a French flavour, generously and courteously served. Occasional special events inc cookery demonstrations and wine tastings; conservatory extension with painted mural by local artist. **£15.95**|£1.80/£4.50.

Walcote SP5683 BLACK HORSE (0455) 552684 Authentic Thai food cooked by Thai landlady, unusual drinks, chatty atmosphere, large open fire and seats out behind in summer; cl Mon/Tues am. **£14.50 for 5-course meal**|£5.

Woodhouse Eaves SK5214 PEAR TREE (0509) 890243 Full of Edwardian character, with a comfortably furnished and attractively decorated bar and dining area serving very good food; cl Sun pm. **£14**|£1.75/£5.25.

Rothley SK5812 ROYAL OAK The Green (0533) 302158 Situated on a village green nr Great Central Steam Railway and Bradgate Park; popular good-value food served in the bar. Warmly recommended by contributors; cl 24 Dec. 90p/£6.80.

LINCOLNSHIRE

A non-touristy area with some lovely houses, castles and villages, offering many possibilities for a quiet break; Lincoln and Stamford are enjoyable towns.

The best of the countryside is north and east of Lincoln: rolling wolds, attractive villages and small towns, soaring church spires, rich farmland with huge fields of arable crops – this is a good area for pleasantly long-winded country drives. Nearer the Wash, and up the coast towards Wainfleet and Coningsby, the land is very flat, reclaimed from the sea: pretty dull, except in springtime when the endless fields of bulbs around Spalding are very colourful.

Stamford and Lincoln in particular are interesting towns with a good deal of character. The county has some fine old mansions and castles to look at, most notably Burghley House (just outside Stamford), Belton House, Woolsthorpe Manor, and Tattershall and Grimsthorpe Castles. It's not an area that scores highly for a short family break, though there are things to entertain children, and of course the coast has its traditional family resorts, with good beaches: children also like the butterfly park at Spalding.

The county's main appeal is as a get-away-from-it-all break for adults, in a part of England that's got a decidedly different character from any other. It's best in late spring, summer, or autumn; in winter it can be one of England's chilliest areas. There's quite a good choice of places to stay, and to eat out in.

Where to stay

Lincoln SK9872 WHITE HART LB1 3AR (0522) 526222 **£107**; 50 rms. A mid-18th-c hotel with antique-filled lounges, beside the fine cathedral.

Stamford TF0207 GEORGE PE9 2LB (0780) 55171 **£100**; 47 rms. Some parts of this elegant building, a former coaching inn, may date back 1,000 years; quietly civilised atmosphere, sturdy timbers, broad flagstones, heavy beams and massive stonework, open log fires, wonderful food in Garden Lounge (tempting help-yourself buffet), restaurant and courtyard (in summer), excellent range of drinks – very good value Italian wines, and welcoming staff; well-kept walled garden and sunken lawn where croquet is played.

Sandilands TF5280 GRANGE & LINKS Mablethorpe LN12 2RA (0507) 441334 **£65**; 30 rms. Popular hotel, noted for good food and comfortable surroundings, plus own golf course; disabled access.

Lincoln SK9872 D'ISNEY PLACE LN2 4AA (0522) 538881 **£60**; 17 rms. Friendly 18th-c hotel with lovely gardens, fine furniture and relaxed atmosphere; disabled access.

Skegness TF5660 VINE Vine Rd Seacroft PE25 3DB (0754) 763018 ***£52**; 22 rms. 17th-c hotel with extensions built on in character, cosy lounges, oak-panelled bar, open fires, good food in dining room, and attractive grounds; close to golf course.

Woodhall Spa TF1963 DOWER HOUSE Manor Estate LN10 6PY (0526) 52588 **£48**; 7 rms, most with own bthrm. Edwardian hotel in its own grounds on a private road with friendly welcome, log fires, and comfortable lounge.

Barkston SP9241 BARKSTON HOUSE Grantham NG32 2NH (0400) 50555 **£45**; 2 rms. Warm and comfortable restored 18th-c house with open fires and beams, relaxed atmosphere, very good, imaginative English cooking, and 7 acres of grounds; cl 1 wk Christmas.

Alford TF4576 WHITE HORSE LN13 9DG (0507) 462218 **£40**; 9 prettily furnished and comfortable rms, most with own bthrm. Picturesque 16th-c inn, carefully restored over the years, with plush beamed lounge, superb range of vodkas (the licensee is from Poland), good range of well-prepared, reasonably priced bar food and popular communicating restaurant; cl 24-26 Dec.

Dyke TF1022 WISHING WELL Bourne PE10 0AF (0778) 422970 ***£38**; 7 rms, most with own bthrm. The wishing well is at the dining end of the long rambling bar – heavy beamed with dark stone, brasswork, candlelight and a big fireplace; excellent, popular food, helpful service, and a friendly atmosphere; disabled access.

North Hykeham SK9465 LOUDOR 37 Newark St LN6 8RB (0522) 680333 ***£36**; 10 rms. Family-run hotel with pleasant lounge, small bar, good, plentiful food, and quick, friendly service; disabled access.

Lincoln SK9872 EDWARD KING HOUSE LN2 1PU (0522) 528778 **£34.70**; 17 rms. Once the Bishop's palace and now a simple guesthouse in the centre of the city with Lincoln Cathedral views; cl 24 Dec-1 Jan.

Buslingthorpe TF0885 EAST FARM HOUSE Middle Rasen Rd Lincoln LN3 5AQ (0673) 842283 **£34**; 2 rms. 18th-c farmhouse surrounded by family farm, with beams, stripped pine, log fires and relaxed atmosphere.

Grantham SK9135 BLACK DOG Watergate NG31 6NS (0476) 66041 **£26**; 7 rms, shared bthrm. Old pub in the town centre with decent bar snacks and wide range of real ales, friendly staff; perhaps suited more to younger people.

To see and do

Lincoln SK9872 The cathedral and the castle, both very striking, share the hilltop in the centre of the town, with enough old buildings around them to keep a sense of unity. There's a lot to appeal to visitors up here, and in the steep streets (Steep Hill, and Strait St) of ancient buildings running down from them to the 15th-c Stonebow Gate at the top of the High St below. This lower part of the town is much more of a normal bustling shopping and working centre, though even here there are a good few interesting old buildings – several Saxon churches, the Norman guildhall, for example.

† CATHEDRAL On the site of a former Roman fort, the original building was largely destroyed in an 1185 earthquake, but the magnificent west front survived, and after nearly a century of rebuilding (and a hiccough in 1239, when the new central tower collapsed) it was complete by 1280. Spectacularly rising above the nearby rooftops, this is one of the finest Gothic buildings in the country. Its gorgeous triple towers dominate the town and its surroundings, particularly when lit up at night. Until the 16th c it was even more imposing, with an almost incredible spire above the central tower giving it nearly twice the height it has now; that proud feat of

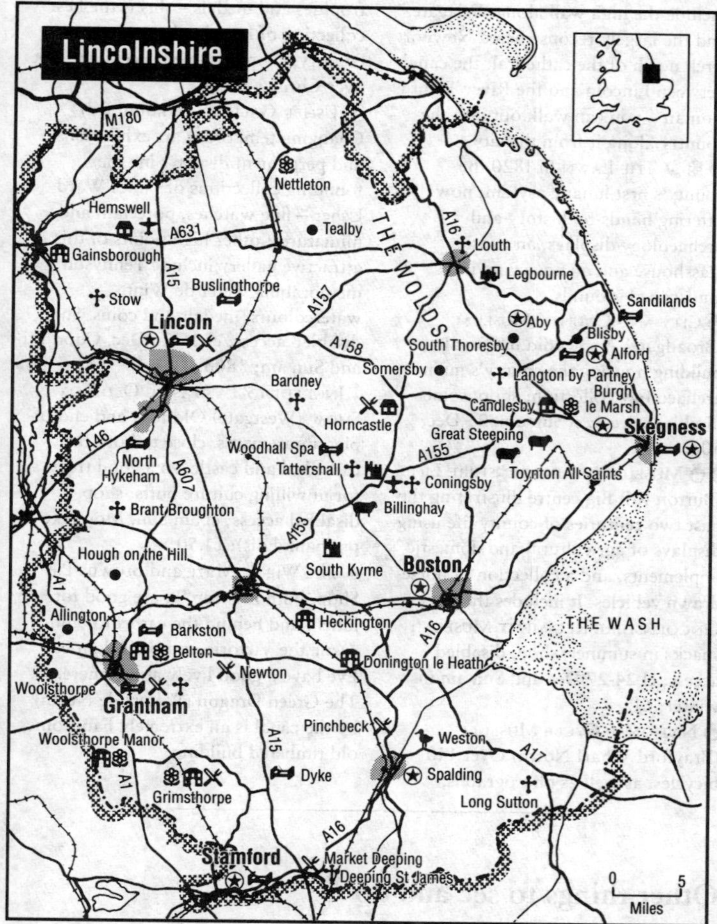

medieval engineering was clearly tempting fate, as a great storm eventually brought the spire down. Inside, the carvings and stained glass are stupendous, and the architecture gracefully harmonious; it is the home of the Lincoln Imp, a carving on one column in the choir. The Treasury has rare plate from the Diocese; snacks, shop, disabled access. From here you can visit the ruins of the once formidable Bishop's Palace.

CASTLE In beautiful surroundings on a formidable earthwork, the castle was originally built in 1068 for William the Conqueror, but only two towers and two gateways of what you see now date back to that original. Lots more has been added over the centuries, including a 19th-c prisoners' chapel (now with suitably gruesome exhibits), and there are good views from the ramparts. One of only four remaining originals of the Magna Carta is on display, and an exhibition fills in the background; snacks, shop; cl 25-26 Dec; £2.

Some ROMAN REMAINS in the city

include the high wall along Westgate, and the largely reconstructed Newport Arch north of the cathedral; the canal between Lincoln and the River Trent is Roman – you can walk out into the country along it from the city.

THE LAWN In 1820 the county's first lunatic asylum; now offering hands-on history and archaeology displays, an exotic glasshouse and an aquarium in its landscaped grounds.

CITY AND COUNTY MUSEUM (Broadgate) A splendid medieval building housing the county's main archaeology collection; shop, some disabled access; cl Sun am, 25 Dec; 50p.

MUSEUM OF LINCOLNSHIRE LIFE (Burton Rd) Big centre illustrating the past two centuries of county life using displays of agricultural and domestic implements, and a collection of horse-drawn vehicles. It includes the ROYAL LINCOLNSHIRE REGIMENT MUSEUM; snacks in summer, shop, disabled access; cl 24-27 Dec and Sun am in winter; £1.

NATIONAL CYCLE MUSEUM (Brayford Wharf North) Over 140 bicycles, as well as photographs, trophies and medals – this is the best collection of bicyclabilia in the country; shop; disabled access; cl 1 wk over Christmas; £1.

USHER GALLERY (Lindum Rd) Changing temporary art exhibitions and permanent displays inc the founding collections of James Ward Usher – fine watches, porcelain and miniatures; other high points of this attractive gallery include Tennyson memorabilia, Peter de Wint watercolours, medals and coins. Shop, disabled access; cl 25-26 Dec, Good Fri and Sun am; *80p.

! INCREDIBLY FANTASTIC OLD TOY SHOW (Westgate) Old toys and end-of-pier amusements, close to both the cathedral and castle, so a good treat for unwilling culture buffs; shop, disabled access; cl am Sun, Mon (exc pm bank hols); £1.50.

The Wig & Mitre and Browns Pie Shop, both in Steep St, are good for lunch, and behind the cathedral and castle the Victoria and the Adam & Eve have a good lively atmosphere. The Green Dragon (Waterside North) by the canal is an extremely handsome old timbered building.

Other things to see and do

Aby TF4178 CLAYTHORPE WATER MILL AND WILDFOWL GARDENS A pretty spot around an 18th-c water mill, with the grounds full of ornamental wildfowl and poultry, and animals such as rabbits and a miniature pony. Fun to wander through the woods too; meals, snacks, shop, mostly disabled access; cl Nov-Feb; *£2.

Alford TF4575 is a pleasant town with some attractive brick and thatch buildings, including the 17th-c ALFORD MANOR HOUSE, now a folk museum with displays recreating various shops and aspects of domestic life; snacks, shop; cl Sun am, Nov-Easter; 75p. In summer the town has a Friday crafts market. There's a tall restored WINDMILL on the road towards Sutton-on-Sea, and another a little further along at Bilsby. The White Horse Hotel is good for lunch, and beside it the Half Moon does simpler food.

✝ **Bardney** TF1468 Just off the B1190 south-east of the village are the remains of a 12th-c abbey, TUPHOLME ABBEY; interesting to wander around, and normally quite deserted.

Belton SK9339 BELTON HOUSE Set in a beautiful park, complete with orangery and formal Italian garden, this splendid mansion is full of wonderful carvings (some of them possibly by Grinling Gibbons), ornate plasterwork, sumptuous furnishings, tapestries, paintings and ceramics. Meals, snacks, shop, disabled access to gardens only; cl am, and Mon (exc bank hols), Tues, Nov-Mar; £4.

Billinghay TF1555 BILLINGHAY CHILDREN'S FARM is a small but very friendly place, where they take time to show you the differences between various breeds; snacks, shop, disabled access; cl Nov-Mar; *£1.

Boston TF3244 Still the county's leading port, this little town has a number of pretty spots and handsome historic buildings. The most famous is the BOSTON STUMP, the graceful tower of the magnificent 14th-c church St Botolph's. Climb to the top for far views over this flat landscape – it's the second-tallest parish church in the country (the tallest is mentioned below); the inside is spectacular too. Another prominent feature of the skyline is the MAUD FOSTER MILL, the tallest working windmill in the country, and surely one of the most photogenic – by the drainage canal running along the B1183 Coningsby road. GUILDHALL MUSEUM The main claim to fame of this 15th-c building is that in 1607 it became the prison of the Pilgrim Fathers after their unsuccessful attempt to flee to Holland (they did, of course, eventually escape further afield, taking their former town's name to one of their first settlements). Displays cover this and the rest of the town's history; shop, some disabled access; cl Sun am (all day in winter); 80p.

Burgh Le Marsh TF5065 LINCOLNSHIRE RAILWAY MUSEUM Lots of railway relics from a locomotive to signals, and a complete recreation of a station. Outside you can take the narrow-gauge railway through an adjacent conservation area; shop, disabled access; cl Sat and all Oct-Easter; *£1.60. There's a notable CHURCH here, and nearby is a WINDMILL with unusual left-handed sails; open pm 2nd and last Sun each month; 50p.

Candlesby TF4567 CANDLESBY HERBS Good range of herb plants for sale and on display in the garden, as well as hints and advice on all sorts of things you can do with them; cl Mon.

Coningsby TF2258 BATTLE OF BRITAIN MEMORIAL FLIGHT VISITOR CENTRE On display (though subject to operational commitments) are the aircraft of the Battle of Britain Memorial Flight – including the only flying Lancaster in Europe; summer snacks, shop, disabled access; cl wknds, bank hols, and 2 wks over Christmas; £2.50. The CHURCH has what's said to be the biggest dial of any clock with just a single hand. Just out of town, the interesting old Leagate Inn is useful for lunch.

Donington le Heath TF2035 DONINGTON LE HEATH MANOR HOUSE Built in around 1280, this house has been altered very little and is one of the very rare examples of an almost untouched medieval manor house; snacks, shop; cl am, Mon, Tues, all Oct-Easter.

Gainsborough SK8189 OLD HALL Visitors to this complete medieval manor house will be following in the footsteps of Richard III, Henry VIII, the Mayflower Pilgrims and John Wesley; interesting features include the Great Hall and original kitchen. Meals, snacks, shop, disabled access; cl winter Sun; £1.50. The Trent Port is useful for lunch.

Great Steeping TF4464 NORTHCOTE HEAVY HORSE CENTRE Demonstrations and talks; a collection of old vehicles and other animals besides the gentle giants themselves, from rare breeds of cattle and sheep to miniature ponies and working dogs; meals, snacks, shop, disabled access; open Sun, Weds and Thurs Mar-Oct, plus Tues May and Jun and every day exc Sat in July and Aug; *£3.

Grimsthorpe TF0422 GRIMSTHORPE CASTLE A patchwork of styles from its medieval tower and Tudor quadrangle to the baroque north front by Vanbrugh. It has eight state rooms and two galleries full of fine furnishings. Outside are formal gardens and parkland with lake and red deer tame enough for children to feed; meals and snacks, shop, some disabled access; open Easter Sun and Mon, then park and grounds Thurs, Sun and bank hols 2 May-5 Sept, castle Sun and bank hols 30 May-5 Sept; park and grounds £1, castle £2 extra.

Heckington TF1444 is an understated but pleasant small town, with a well-restored WINDMILL – the only one in Britain with eight sails; open pm Sun all year and Sat and bank hols in summer; 80p. The Nags Head here is good for lunch. Another fine restored mill, a splendid six-sailed model, is at Sibsey TF3550; £1.10.

Hemswell SK9391 BOMBER COUNTY AVIATION MUSEUM A small collection in a former RAF base, where you can see restoration work being carried out on Hunter, Vampire and Mystere planes; snacks, shop, disabled access; open Sun, and wkdys by appointment. Collectors should find something to interest them at the HEMSWELL ANTIQUES CENTRE close by – three buildings with around 270 shops selling books, period furniture, ceramics, rugs and jewellery.

Horncastle TF2669 A popular stop for antiques, with a number of shops, 30 of which are grouped together in the Bridge St Antiques Centre. You can still see parts of the town's ROMAN WALL.

Legbourne TF3684 RAILWAY MUSEUM Displays of varied Lincolnshire railway memorabilia, at the oldest preserved Great Northern Railway station; also a model railway and pets' corner. Snacks, shop, disabled access; cl Mon (exc bank hols), all Oct-Easter; *£1.50.

Nettleton TA1100 Potterton & Martin's NURSERY (Moortown Rd) has a lot of unusual and interesting plants – mainly alpines and small bulbs.

Skegness TF3663 was built as a late 19th-c resort, and has been an archetypal one, with the first Butlin's Holiday Camp just up the coast. It has the regular amusements, though it lost its pier in a storm 15 years ago. NATURELAND SEAL SANCTUARY is renowned for its seal rescuing activities. There's a public viewing area in the new seal hospital unit, as well as a specialised collection of animals and free-flight tropical butterflies (May-Oct), a seal life exhibition, floral displays and brass rubbing centre; snacks, shop, disabled access; cl 25-26 Dec, 1 Jan; £2.75. CHURCH FARM MUSEUM recreates daily farm life at the end of the 19th c, with displays of farming and domestic implements; there's also a timber-framed cottage and barn with changing exhibitions. Snacks, shop, disabled access; cl Nov-Mar; 80p. The Vine Hotel on the southern edge of the town was here long before the resort, welcoming Tennyson among others; it's useful for lunch.

South Kyme TF1749 has a fine 14th-c battlemented tower standing in a meadow quite near the road.

Spalding TF2422 BUTTERFLY AND FALCONRY PARK set in 15 acres right on the county border. It has butterfly and bee gardens with wildflower meadows, a nature trail, conservation ponds, farm animals and a pets' corner. This is one of Britain's biggest walk-through tropical houses with hundreds of butterflies flying freely, and also a creepy-crawly little insectarium. The falcons are displayed twice a day at the new falconry centre; meals and snacks, shop, disabled access; cl Nov-Mar; £3.20. SPRINGFIELDS GARDENS A 25-acre garden with glasshouses; there's a fantastic bedding plants display in summer, while in spring there are over a million bulbs in bloom. Meals and snacks, shop, disabled access; cl Oct-Mar; £2.50. MUSEUM OF ENTERTAINMENT Unusual and quirky collection tracing the development of entertainment from barrel and church organs to puppets and phonographs, taking in a history of the fairground along the way; many of the exhibits are working. Snacks, shop, disabled access; open wknds Easter-Oct plus pm wkdys July-Sept; *£2. All around this area, the flat fields by the roadside are a mass of colour in spring, first daffodils and then a multicoloured sea of tulips – very Dutch. In the town, the Olde Dun Cow is useful for lunch.

Stamford TF0307 Within its medieval walls are many fine buildings, including a good number of attractive medieval CHURCHES – particularly All Saints in the centre, St George's with excellent 15th-c stained glass, and St Mary's near it. The lasting impression is of timeless stonework, in a particularly attractive creamy buff. On the edge of the town is the splendid BURGHLEY HOUSE built by William Cecil and still the home of his family. Its exterior is Tudor at its most solidly showy. The inside was restyled between 1680 and 1700, and the state rooms are largely baroque with wonderful frescoes by Antonio Verrio – the Heaven Room is particularly impressive; notable paintings, furnishings, early Japanese ceramics and temporary exhibitions. The grounds, where the Burghley Horse Trials are held, were landscaped by Capability Brown; meals, snacks, shop; cl end of 1st wk Oct-Maundy Thurs, and, in 1994, Sat 3 Sept; £4.80. STEAM BREWERY MUSEUM vividly recreates what it must have been like to have been an employee of a Victorian brewery, with a sound system and extensive range of illustrations literally giving you the taste of things back then; snacks, shop, disabled access; cl Mon (exc bank hols), Tues, Nov-Mar. STAMFORD MUSEUM The history and archaeology of Stamford, with interesting displays ranging from local Roman iron manufactures to the town's steam-engine links. More unusual features are the life-size figures dressed in the clothes of Tom Thumb (only 3 ft 4 in when he died) and Daniel Lambert, a portly fellow who weighed 50 stone when he died on a racing outing here; shop, disabled access; cl 12.30-1.30 pm winter, all day Sun in winter and am in summer; 40p. The George, one of the town's grander old buildings with some parts going back to Saxon times, is good for lunch; the Bull & Swan and Lord Burghley are also good.

Tattershall TF2157 TATTERSHALL CASTLE The magnificent turreted keep of this castle, built in 1440, is 100 ft high and has fine heraldic chimneypieces on each of the four storeys; snacks, shop, some disabled access; cl 25-28 Dec; £2. The airy 15th-c CHURCH is also attractive, and just off the A153 towards Sleaford, on the left before you reach Tattershall Bridge, is a preserved steam engine which worked at keeping this area of fens drained for nearly a century.

Toynton All Saints TF3964 FENSIDE GOAT CENTRE Dairy farm with various breeds of goat and demonstrations of milking around 4 pm; also sheep, rare cows, pigs and other animals, spinning displays and a play area. Children are encouraged to touch the animals; shop, disabled access; cl am, all Tues and Sat, Oct-Mar; *£1.50.

Weston TF2924 BAYTREE OWL CENTRE Plenty of owls, many in a free-flying area; some can be handled. The entire centre is part of an expanding complex with ducks and rabbits in a landscaped glasshouse, a garden centre and plans for museum; meals, snacks, shop, disabled access; cl 25 Dec; £1.50.

Woolsthorpe SK9224 (this is the small village nr Colsterworth, not the bigger Woolsthorpe to the north-west) WOOLSTHORPE MANOR is the birthplace and home of Isaac Newton (1665-66), where he worked out the law of gravity and differential calculus, and analysed the nature of white light; some geometry workings in his handwriting are scratched into the plasterwork – and of course the garden has a venerable apple tree; cl am, Mon and Tues, Nov-Mar; £2.30. NT.

✝ This county has a remarkable collection of great churches. Even villages which are tiny now and can never have been very large are graced by buildings of often impressive power. The remarkable height of the spires is a particular feature, with the tallest of any parish church in Britain being the very elegant 16th-c church in Louth TF3387 (the tower can be climbed on summer afternoons; hundreds of steps for a fabulous view). Other notable spires are those in Grantham SK9135 (the early 19th-c jingle about it, 'Grantham, now two rarities are thine, A lofty steeple and a living sign', refers to the hive with living bees still used as an inn sign by the Beehive pub there), Brant Broughton SK9154 and Long Sutton TF4222 (the latter is unusual not so much for its sheer height as for the hundreds of tons of lead with which it's sheathed).

Other country **churches** worth seeing if you're near include those at Deeping St James TF1609, Langton by Partney TF3970 and Stow SK8882, while at Croyland you can see the remains of a once great abbey, part of which is still used as the parish church.

Apart, of course, from the Springfield display beds at Spalding, this is a disappointing county for large gardens, but in many of the villages the small gardens, easily seen from the road, add a very welcome splash of colour. This is particularly true of **Tealby** TF1590, making it perhaps the county's most delightful village. The stonebuilt cottages on the main street up the hill from a watersplash near a watermill to the 12th-c church, and those in the quaintly named side lanes, have neat and charmingly planted roadside gardens.

Other **attractive villages**, all with decent pubs, include Newton TF0436, Hough on the Hill SK9246, South Thoresby TF4077, Allington SK8540 (despite the proximity of the A1) and Woolsthorpe SK8435 (the one near Belvoir). Somersby TF3472 is also worth a visit.

Walks

The **Lincolnshire Wolds**, a tract of chalk hills in the E, rise gently: fields are mostly large (some like prairies), the scene interrupted by patches of woodland. The long-distance Viking Way assists village-to-village walks, with 'Tennyson country' a popular focus (Tennyson was born at the rectory in Somersby TF3472, when his father was rector at Bag Enderby). From Louth TF3387 a walk SW out of town enters **Hubbard's Hill** TF3186, not in fact a hill but a surprisingly deep river valley for the Wolds.

Driving

The most interesting drive in the county is probably the Bluestone Heath hill road off the A16, just N of its junction with the A1104 west of Alford. This runs past South Ormsby and then swings round N to reach the A157 W of Louth; fine views most of the way. In similar vein, if not quite so rewarding is the old road known as the High Street, which forks off the A158 about 3 miles N of

Horncastle and runs almost due N up past Ranby, Market Stainton and Ludford all the way to Caistor. Both these roads follow Iron-Age trackways. The A153 between Horncastle and Louth is a good road for getting a perspective on the rolling Wolds country, and doesn't usually carry heavy traffic. If you're prepared to take things gently, the B1398 northwards out of Lincoln has quite a few typically Lincolnshire views. Running S from Lincoln, the A607 through Leadenham (where the George is a pleasant stop) to Grantham follows the Lincoln Cliff, giving some good views.

Around Horncastle, an interesting day's drive includes Scrivelsby and its deerpark, the pretty market town of Horncastle itself, Belchford (Blue Bell useful for lunch), Fulletby (perhaps a stroll on the footpaths here), Somersby (Tennyson's birthplace – his bust is in the church), Old Bolingbroke (castle ruins), Spilsby (good delicatessen in the quiet market place with its statue of Sir John Franklin), and, if you've made good time, Wainfleet and Boston.

Over in the E and further S, driving is generally less interesting. The coast road is generally rather slow, with a lot of twists and turns. Even those side roads which look quite good on a map – straight, uninterrupted by towns – can turn out to be tryingly slow in practice, with agricultural vehicles too wide to pass trundling along slowly and muddily. Roads which are quite brisk in this part, though without a great deal of interest, include the B1183 from Boston up to Horncastle and the B1192 more or less parallel with it, up to Coningsby.

Where to eat

Market Deeping TF1310 CAUDLE HOUSE (0778) 347595 Georgian house with two small dining rooms and little bar area, friendly, helpful staff (the waitresses wear Victorian dress), a good choice of food, and decent wines; bedrooms, cl Mon, 1st 2 wks Aug, children over 12 only, disabled access. **£31.50.**

Grimsthorpe TF0423 BLACK HORSE (077 832) 247 Large open fire and rustic atmosphere in narrow bar, cosy Buttery Bar with another open fire, and intimate, candlelit dining room – all with excellent food; decent wine and pleasant, friendly staff; cl Sun, 1 wk over Christmas; children over 8; disabled access. **£21.50**|£3.15/£5.25.

Lincoln SK9771 JEWS HOUSE (0522) 524851 Small, intimate and elegantly furnished restaurant in one of the oldest buildings in the city; very good, imaginative food (lots of fish), professional, friendly service, and upstairs coffee lounge for those who want to smoke after the meal; cl Sun, Mon am, 25 Dec-1 Jan, bank hols. **£21**|£2.85/£9.95.

Newton TF0436 RED LION (052 97) 256 Full of charm and character, this pub specialises in choose-as-much-as-you-like salads – home-made soups are good too; also a couple of local specialities. **£18.90**|£2.10/£9.45.

Horncastle TF2669 MAGPIES 73-75 East St (0507) 527004 Warmly recommended by contributors; cl Mon; children over 10; disabled access. **£18 lunch, £24 dinner**|£11.50.

Pinchbeck TF2425 SHIP (0775) 723792 Well furnished with small lounge area and dining room, serving good-value food with occasional Oriental menus. Warmly recommended by contributors; children over 10 (though younger ones allowed if eating); disabled access. **£16**|£2.50/£5.25.

Lincoln SK9771 BROWNS PIE SHOP (0522) 527330 Spectacular pies (and lots of other food), helpful staff, comfortable seats and pleasant traditional atmosphere; cl eve 24-26 Dec, 31 Dec-1 Jan. **£15.75**|£2.35/£6.80.

Lincoln SK9771 WIG & MITRE (0522) 535190/523705 Attractively restored

14th-c building with imaginative food served all day (breakfast too), excellent puddings; more elaborate restaurant menu, interesting wine list, and consistently efficient, prompt service; cl 25 Dec. **£14**|£2.50/£5.50.
Grantham SK9135 BLUE BULL 64 Westgate (0476) 70929 Wonderful food in popular pub; cl 25 Dec, children lunchtimes only. **£12.60**|£1/£4.20.

NOTTINGHAMSHIRE

While Nottingham is a possible choice for a sightseeing break, there are attractive places and scenery elsewhere.

The county has some charming and interesting villages, one or two attractive old towns such as Newark-on-Trent and Southwell, and some pleasant countryside. In the north, the Dukeries, named for the noble families and their great seats which used to occupy the area, still have extensive tracts of landscaped, largely forested parkland left after the grand houses and families have gone – even quite close to the industrial and mining centres around Mansfield.

Nottingham itself has the lion's share of things to see and do here. Though it is a big, busy city, in the evenings and at weekends it settles back into a much quieter and more appealing frame of mind. It is a possibility for a sightseeing break, though perhaps not a front-runner. Elsewhere, there is a modest range of interesting places to visit, including several things for children to enjoy – the new World of Robin Hood at Haughton looks particularly promising.

Where to stay

Nottingham SK5640 ROYAL MOAT HOUSE NG1 5RH (0602) 414444 **£105**; 201 well-equipped rms. Large and very popular modern hotel with glass-roofed arcade of tropical trees and plants, lots of bars (one with fine city views) and four restaurants; cl 25-26 Dec, 1 Jan, disabled access.
Southwell SK7053 SARACEN'S HEAD Market Pl BG25 0HE (0636) 812701 **£97**; 27 well-kept rms. Interesting old THF hotel (Charles I spent his last free night here) with characterful main beamed bar, pleasant staff, straightforward bar lunches, and restaurant.
Barnby Moor SK6684 OLDE BELL Retford DN22 8QS (0777) 705121 **£64.50w**; 55 comfortable rms. Old coaching inn with open fires, beams, fine old furniture, and relaxed atmosphere.
Drakeholes SK7090 GRIFF Doncaster S Yorks DN10 5DF (0777) 817206 **£50**; 3 rms. Handsome brick house with beautiful landscaped gardens and excellent views over River Idle valley and basin of Chesterfield canal; wide range of bar food – carvery and salad bar open all week, substantial breakfasts and good vegetarian meals, friendly, helpful service; one bar is no smoking.
Bestwood Country Park SK5646 BESTWOOD LODGE Nottingham NG5 8NE (0602) 203011 **£40w**; 39 rms. Attractive Victorian hotel with minstrel's gallery, numerous coats of arms and suits of armour, and set in lovely parkland; cl 25 Dec.

To see and do

Nottingham SK5739 This busy industrial city has quite a few things to do, and on a weekend or a summer evening it quickly loses its 'big city' character, and is then easy to park in and stroll through, without the river of traffic that otherwise swarms so thickly along its inner ring road. It has an amazing number of decent pubs scattered through it – handy for the thirsty work of serious sightseeing. The parts around the parish church (which has some interesting carvings) and the Lace Market are particularly attractive. The rock on which the old town once stood is honeycombed with hundreds of galleries, cellars and passageways (one attractive old pub, the Olde Trip to Jerusalem, while nowhere near as old as it's claimed, does have a fascinating bar tunnelled right into the rock face).

Up on the summit is the CASTLE MUSEUM, with tours through some of the subterranean passages, a good history of the site, and displays of art and a museum. The building itself dates from the 17th c, but the gateway is from the earlier 13th-c fortress; meals, snacks, shop, disabled access; cl 25 Dec; free exc weekends and bank hols when £1. Cave tours are daily at 2 pm and 3 pm (and 4 pm in summer), but not Sun; £1. INDUSTRIAL MUSEUM (Courtyard Buildings, Woolaton Park) Nottingham's diverse industries are the focus of this museum, especially lace and hosiery, but also the pharmaceutical industry, engineering, printing and tobacco-making. The displays are housed in an 18th-c stable block with industrial and agricultural machinery in a new extension and Victorian street furniture in a yard outside; meals, snacks, shop, disabled access; cl Sun am, Oct-Mar open pm Thurs, Sat and Sun only; £1. CANAL MUSEUM (Canal Street) 19th-c warehouse recounting the history of the River Trent from the Ice Age, using interesting presentations. Shop, disabled access; cl 12-1 pm, am Mon, Tues and Sun, all day Fri, Oct-Mar. BREWHOUSE YARD MUSEUM (Castle Boulevard) Interactive and thematic displays inc rock-cut cellars tell the story of local life in post-medieval times. The 17th-c building is set in two acres planted with unusual local plants; shop, some disabled access; cl 25 Dec; *£1 wknds and bank hols. GREEN'S MILL AND SCIENCE CENTRE (Windmill Lane, Sneinton) Flour is still produced and sold at this restored tower mill whenever conditions allow, and you can try grinding corn on part of an old millstone. The life of George Green – miller and distinguished mathematician – is related via hands-on exhibits in the next-door Science Centre, and there's a weather satellite receiver showing pictures live from space. Shop, disabled access; cl Mon (exc bank hols), Tues and 25 Dec – best to tel (0602) 503635 to check the mill is working. The LACE HALL (High Pavement) not only tells the story of the local lace industry, but has demonstrations of lace-making, and lets you have a go yourself; a lively place, with a lot of commitment and surprisingly enthralling displays. Snacks, shop, disabled access; cl 25-26 Dec; £2. MUSEUM OF COSTUME AND TEXTILES (43-51 Castle Gate) Embroidery from all over the world, map tapestries, dress accessories and costume from 1730-1960; shops, some disabled access; cl 25 Dec. WOLLATON HALL AND PARK Splendidly ornate Tudor building, now home to the city's natural history museum; the 500-acre grounds are a delight; cl Sun am. THE TALES OF ROBIN HOOD (Maid Marian Way) Nottingham wouldn't be complete without a reference to the county's legendary heroine. Cars carry

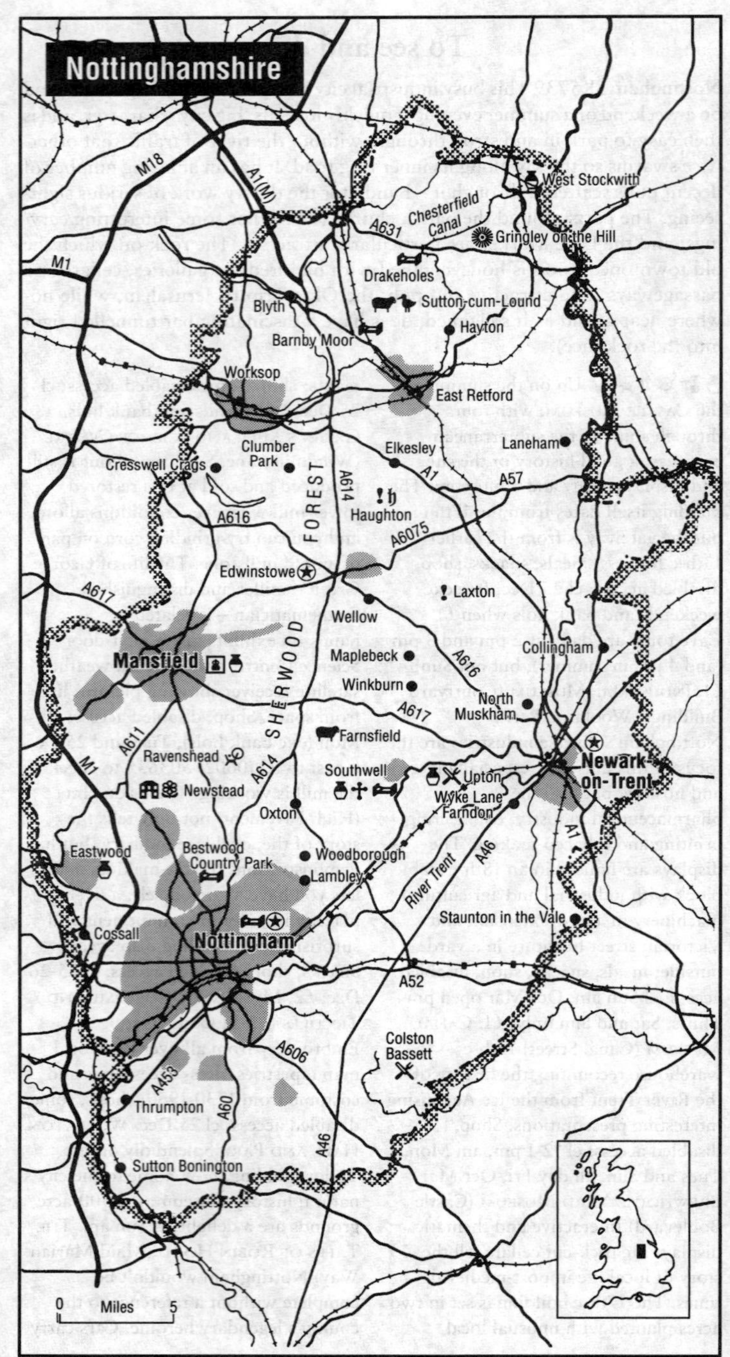

Nottinghamshire
M18
A1(M)
Chesterfield Canal
A631
West Stockwith
Gringley on the Hill
M1
Drakeholes
Sutton-cum-Lound
Blyth
Hayton
Barnby Moor
Worksop
East Retford
Laneham
Clumber Park
Elkesley
Cresswell Crags
A614
A1
A57
FOREST
Haughton
A616
A6075
Edwinstowe
Laxton
A617
Wellow
SHERWOOD
Maplebeck
Collingham
Mansfield
A616
Winkburn
North Muskham
A617
A611
Farnsfield
Ravenshead
M1
A614
Southwell
Upton
Newark on-Trent
Newstead
Wyke Lane Farndon
Oxton
A1
Eastwood
Bestwood Country Park
Woodborough
River Trent
A46
Lambley
Staunton in the Vale
Cossall
Nottingham
A52
Colston Bassett
A606
A453
Thrumpton
A60
A46
Sutton Bonington
0
Miles
5

you through recreated medieval Nottingham and Sherwood Forest, ingeniously designed so that the experience seems to surround you. Special events last wknd of every month; meals, snacks, shop, disabled access; cl 24-26 Dec; *£3.95. Useful lunch places are Fellows Morton & Clayton (Canal Rd), Limelight (attached to the Playhouse), Lincolnshire Poacher (Mansfield Rd), Royal Children (Castlegate) and Sir John Borlase Warren (Canning Circus). There's an unusual NATURE RESERVE down by Beeston at the extensive partly wooded Attenborough lakes SK5234; on the far side a path takes you along the narrow spit of land dividing them from the mighty Trent.

Other things to see and do

Eastwood SK4646 D H LAWRENCE BIRTHPLACE MUSEUM The writer's early experiences played an important formative role in his writing, and here you can explore the carefully restored Victorian working-class setting of that childhood. There are various craft workshops next door; meals, snacks, shop, some disabled access; cl 25 Dec-1 Jan; *£1.50. Another home of Lawrence's, furnished as he described it in *Sons and Lovers*, is open by appointment only on (0773) 719786.

Edwinstowe SK6266 SHERWOOD FOREST VISITOR CENTRE AND COUNTRY PARK The visitor centre includes a Robin Hood exhibition, slide shows, films and talks celebrating the legendary figure and the many stories surrounding him; snacks, shop, disabled access. It's a good springboard for the forest itself, only a fraction of what it once was but still miles across – and altogether more forested than the heathland that Robin himself would have known. It has good waymarked paths and footpaths. Near the village church the Church Farm CRAFT WORKSHOPS have various workshops in former farm buildings, inc knitwear, toy-making, doll's houses, lapidary; snacks, shops, disabled access. SHERWOOD FOREST FARM PARK has unusual breeds of traditional farm animals, foreign-bird aviaries, a pets' corner and colourful waterfowl on a sizeable lake; home-baked teas, shop, disabled access; cl mid-Oct-Easter; *£2.50. For lunch with a good view over the forest, the Bird in Hand at Blidworth SK5956 and perhaps the Black Bull are useful.

Farnsfield SK6456 WHITE POST MODERN FARM CENTRE With exhibits ranging from a mousetown through 20 acres of small demonstration arable crop plots to llamas, quails, snakes and fish, and lots of amiable farm animals to fuss over, this working farm provides a thorough presentation of a variety of farming techniques; snacks, shop, disabled access; £2.75.

Gringley on the Hill SK7391, an attractive village, gives magnificent VIEWS in all directions from Beacon Hill above the Chesterfield Canal; you can make out the towers of Lincoln cathedral on a clear day.

! Haughton SK6872 WORLD OF ROBIN HOOD A lively recreation of medieval times and the background to the tales of Robin Hood, with lots of settings and costumed characters giving the stories their historical perspective. Over the last year or so, an entire medieval town, with moated drawbridge, cobbled streets and authentic shops and houses, has been under construction – an ambitious project which should be ready in part by this summer. Meals, snacks, shop, mostly disabled access; cl Jan-Easter; *£3.95.

! Laxton SK7268 is unique for having kept the pattern of its MEDIEVAL FARMING, with different villagers each owning strips of the three great fields (which are now farmed for them by one farmer, but were once farmed by the villagers together). You can walk the grass paths or sykes which divide groups of these strips. The court of the manor, consisting of local villagers, does its rounds ceremoniously each year to check that boundaries and paths are being properly kept, and holds court in the Dovecote, a good village pub. In the pub's yard a small interpretation centre explains the system.

Mansfield SK5361 MUSEUM AND ART GALLERY Mainly local history with exhibitions inc William Billingsley porcelain and charming Buxton watercolours; shop, disabled access; cl Sun and bank hols.

Newark-on-Trent SK7953 is an attractive old market town with some interesting buildings in its side streets, a fine CHURCH, and walks by the River Trent with summer BOAT TRIPS. The Malt Shovel is useful for lunch. The CASTLE ruins date from the 11th c, and there's still a fair bit to see; it was destroyed during the Civil War when Newark had proved too loyal to Charles I for its own good. The history of the castle is well interpreted at the GILSTRAP HERITAGE CENTRE in the grounds, which has another permanent exhibition tracing the development of the town; shop, disabled access; cl 25-26 Dec, 1 Jan. AIR MUSEUM Over 40 assorted aircraft inc rare jet fighters and bombers, as well as a new Undercover Aircraft Display Hall and Engine Display; snacks, shop, disabled access; cl 24-26 Dec; £2.50. MUSEUM Various displays relating to local history and archaeology; shop; cl 1-2 pm, Thurs and Sun Oct-Mar. VINA COOKE MUSEUM OF DOLLS AND BYGONE CHILDHOOD This 17th-c house displays thousands of interesting objects related to childhood, prams, costumes, as well as dolls from all periods including Vina Cooke character dolls; meals, snacks, shop; cl 12-2 pm , 25-26 Dec; *£2. There's a lively event on Easter Mon, with Morris dancers, crafts and the like. MILLGATE MUSEUM OF SOCIAL AND FOLK LIFE A recreation of local domestic and working life from Victorian times through to the 1950s, with a variety of displays and reconstructed environments; teas, shop, some disabled access; cl am wknds (all day in winter).

Newstead SK5152 NEWSTEAD ABBEY Set in gorgeously romantic grounds, this splendid house was the home of Lord Byron, whose rooms here can be viewed. Other interesting things to look at include various rooms decorated in a variety of period styles ranging from medieval through to Victorian; meals and snacks, shop, disabled access; cl Oct-Mar; house and gardens £3.50, gardens only £1.50.

Ravenshead SK5755 LONGDALE CRAFT CENTRE (Longdale Lane) is set out as a Victorian village street, with rows of period workshops – carving, toy-making, jewellery and so forth, and a museum of craft tools; decent restaurant; cl 25-26 Dec; *£1.95.

Southwell SK7053 has a magnificent 12th-c MINSTER, a fine sight from miles around (especially at night when it's imaginatively floodlit), and glorious to walk through – it's well worth catching one of the regular concerts there. As well as being attractive in its own right, this small, quiet town is the home of the Bramley apple, developed by Henry Merryweather in the last century. The whole story is in an exhibition at his descendant's garden centre on Halam Rd, where the original tree still prospers. The aptly named Bramley Apple next door is useful for lunch.

Sutton-cum-Lound SK7285 WETLANDS WATERFOWL RESERVE AND EXOTIC BIRD PARK Two lagoons with over 32 acres full of birds ranging from ducks, through swans to flamingos, and many more wild birds inc parrots live in the surrounding countryside.

Also a children's farm on the site; meals, snacks, shop, disabled access; cl 25 Dec; *£1.50.

Upton SK7354 UPTON HALL is the home of the British Horological Institute, and a museum of clocks and timepieces from marine chronometers to the first telephone speaking clock; as some of the exhibits are over 300 years old don't expect all the ones that work to be keeping perfect time. Snacks, shop, disabled access; open pm Sun Apr-Sept; *£2.50. The Cross Keys is good for lunch, and the French Horn is also worth knowing.

★ **Wellow** SK6766 is an attractive village, unusual for being one of the only five in the country with a permanent MAYPOLE – which used to be the trunk of a Sherwood Forest tree, but is now metal. It stands on the only genuine village green in the county, kept that way since the village was founded in the 12th c (all the others were just open spaces used by the villagers and itinerant traders for buying and selling, which have been grassed over since all that stopped). The Olde Red Lion is good for lunch. There's a pleasant COUNTRY PARK nearby at Rufford SK6465.

West Stockwith SK7995 WORLD IN MINIATURE A museum housing all kinds of dolls from the 19th c onward, made from wood, wax and wool, with a number of their houses and tiny shops, gardens and furniture; meals, snacks, shop, disabled access; cl Mon and Tues, and all Jan; *£1.50.

The **River Trent** gives a tremendous sense of power even when it's on its best behaviour, sliding swiftly and massively along; its occasional floods are devastating, and most years it claims lives. Villages giving pleasant access to it include Laneham SK8076 and Thrumpton SK5031; the Lazy Otter in Wyke Lane Farndon SK7651 is in a good riverside spot, as is the Muskham Ferry at North Muskham SK7958.

★ Other interesting and **attractive villages** in the county include the delightfully rustic Maplebeck SK7160 (the Beehive's an attractive country tavern; nearby Woodborough is also worth a look – and Lambley, partly for its unusual unspoilt miners' tavern the Woodlark), Blyth SK6287 now that the A1's left it aside (the White Swan's good for lunch), Collingham SK8663, Cossall SK4842 (D H Lawrence country: he was once engaged to the girl who lived in Church Cottage), Elkesley SK6975 (working potter nr church; the Robin Hood is useful for lunch), Oxton SK6251 (the lane up hill northwards below the power lines takes you up to an Iron-Age hill fort), Sutton Bonington SK5025 (interesting spinning/weaving workshop on Bucks Lane; cl Weds pm, Sun and summer hols), Winkburn SK7158 (unusual in that its simple 12th-c village church is a temple of the Knights Hospitaller), and, with their more 'Leicestershire-ish' character, Colston Bassett SK7033 (the Martins Arms is excellent for lunch), and Staunton in the Vale SK8043 (the Staunton Arms is useful) over in the Vale of Belvoir.

Walks

Though the county is far from being ideal for walkers, it does have some pleasant forest walks. **Sherwood Forest** no longer covers a fifth of the county as in Robin Hood's day, and the heathland it once contained has been swallowed up into farmland. However, it is well endowed with trails, the most popular being to the Major Oak SK6267 (a huge tree in the heart of the forest). Of the great Dukeries estates, **Clumber Park** SK6275 is outstanding for its walks, with enough paths through its woodland and parkland for a full-day excursion. **Cresswell Crags**, E of Cresswell SK5374, occupy a wooded site beside Crags Pond and form the basis of a short there-and-back walk through woodland.

There's also scope for walks along the **Chesterfield Canal**; one quiet stretch is by the Boat at Hayton SK7384.

Driving

The best drives are in the N of the county: most notably, the B6034 from Edwinstowe through Sherwood Forest, left along the A616 for a mile or two, then right along the B6005, to turn right for Carburton and keep on through the fine landscapes of Clumber Park. A drive which runs with little traffic over the wolds in the S and along the Vale of Belvoir is the back road through West Leake, East Leake, Wysall, Widmerpool, Kinoulton, Colston Bassett, Granby and Orston. The B6386 coming into Southwell from the W, and connecting there with the A612 running E, is quite pleasant.

Where to eat

Upton SU7354 CROSS KEYS (0636) 813269 Atmospheric and heavily beamed 17th-c pub with rambling bar, lots of interesting pictures, enterprising and generously served food inc crepes and good vegetarian dishes; no chips, daily changing menu. **£12.60|£2.10/£5.25.**

Colston Bassett SK7033 MARTIN ARMS (0949) 81361 Homely, comfortable furnishings, lots of wine by the glass, open fire, good, interesting food, and civilised restaurant. £2.60/£7.50.

Help this year from: *John Woll, B M Eldridge, G and M Brooke-Williams, R T Moggridge, Dr C L Platt, Gwen and Peter Andrews, Tony and Rosemary Achurch, Neville Kenyon, M E A Horler, Mr and Mrs P A Jones, M and J Back, Mayur Sha, Rev Tim Haggis, Peter Burton, George Atkinson, Mike and Maggie Betton, Stephen and Julie Brown, Keith and Norma Bloomfield, Anthony John, Alan Wilcock, Christine Davidson, Dr C L Platt, John Baker, Peter Dowd, Roger Bellingham, John Knighton, George Mitchell, D S and J M Jackson, Nick Dowson, Dorothee and Denis Glover, S Howe, P J Caunt, Alan Mills, Jean and Anthony Lloyd, C A Brace, E J Locker, Paul Baxter, Rona Murdoch, Howard and Margaret Buchanan, F J Robinson, Jim and Maggie Cowell, Alan and Jackie Stuart, Caroline Wright, Joan and Michel Hooper-Immins, David and Ruth Hollands.*

We welcome reports from readers . . .

This GUIDE depends on readers' reports. Do help us if you can – in return, we offer a discount on the next edition to people who've helped us with reports for it. Tell us what you think about places already in it, and anything extra you think we should say about them. And send us your ideas for inclusion in the next edition: places to visit, eat at or stay in, attractive drives or walks, maybe even unusual interesting shops you know of. Use the card in the middle, the report forms at the end, or just write – no stamp needed: THE GOOD WEEKEND GUIDE, FREEPOST TN1569, Wadhurst, E Sussex TN5 7BR.

Leicestershire, Lincolnshire and Nottinghamshire Calendar

Some of these dates were provisional as we went to press.
There are frequent antique fairs at the Lincolnshire Showground, Grange de Lings, with quite a few too at the Winthorpe Showground.

March

12th **Newark-on-Trent** Spring Livestock Show *at Showground – till Sun 13*

13th **Winthorpe** Spring Exhibition *at Newark Showground*

April

1st **Goulceby** Redhill Good Friday Service, *cross-bearing parishioners lead procession up the hill and re-enact the erection of the crosses*

2nd **Grange de Lings** Horse Trials *at Lincolnshire Showground, with crafts and flower show – till Sun 3*; **Thoresby Park** Craft Fair *– till Mon 4*

3rd **Alford** Town Criers Championships *– till Mon 4*

4th **Hallaton** Hare Pie Scrambling *at Hare Pie Bank (pie given by the vicar) followed by the* Bottle Kicking Game *between villagers of Hallaton and Melbourne – the object is to kick all three 'bottles', in fact wooden barrels, over the boundaries of the village, inc general festivities*

22nd **Sutton Bonington** National Folk Festival *at School of Agriculture – till Sun 24*

May

1st **Elsham** May Day Festival *at Elsham Hall Country and Wildlife Park – till Mon 2*; **Leicester** Leicestershire County Show *at Braunstone Park*

2nd **Castle Donington** Medieval Market; **Gainsborough** May Fair *at Old Hall*

6th **Winthorpe** Nottinghamshire County Show *at Newark Showground – till Sat 7*

7th **Spalding** Flower Festival and Parade *with tulip-covered floats – till Sun 8*

14th **Skegness** Town Criers Gathering *at the Seacroft Hotel – till Sun 15*

21st **Nottingham** Lord Mayor's Show

22nd **Leicester** Historic Transport Pageant *at Abbey Park*; **Nottingham** Inland Boat Show *at Victoria Embankment – till Sun 22*

30th **Boston** Steam Day *at Carrington House*; **Melton Mowbray** Melton Day; **Woodhall Spa** Agricultural Show *at Jubilee Park*

June

2nd **Trent Bridge** England v NZ Test Match *– till Mon 6*

4th **Lincoln** Water Festival, *inc Mayor's parade*; **Market Deeping** Agricultural Show and Country Fair *at Stamford Road – till Sun 5*

5th **Melton** Open Day *at Brooksby College and Farm*

Leicestershire, Lincolnshire and Nottinghamshire Calendar

June cont.

9th **Nottingham** Crime, Mystery and Thriller Festival *at Broadway Media Centre – till Sun 19*

11th **Cadeby** Steam and Brass-rubbing Day *at The Old Rectory*; **Harborough** Carnival

18th **Winthorpe** Kit Car Show *at Showground – till Sun 19*

22nd **Grange de Lings** County Show *at Lincolnshire Showground*

July

3rd **Newark-on-Trent** Yester-year Rally *at Showground*

7th **Nottingham** Music Festival *at Wollaton Park – till Sun 10*

8th **South Kesteven** Folk and Food, Drink and Dance Festival *– till Sun 17*

9th **Sleaford** Carnival *– till Sun 10*; **Wymeswold** Rempstone Steam and Country Show *– till Sun 9*

10th **Market Bosworth** Agricultural Show

16th **Newark-on-Trent** Americana *at Newark Showground – till Sun 17*

22nd **Peckleton** Festival *– till Sun 24*

23rd **Nottingham** Rock and Reggae Festival *– till Sun 24*

30th **Heckington** Agricultural Show

August

1st **Edwinstowe** Robin Hood Festival *– till Sun 7*

6th **Nottingham** Riverside Festival *at Victoria Embankment – till Sun 7*

7th **Skendleby** Sheepdog Trials

13th **Market Bosworth** Medieval Fayre *– till Sun 14*; **Uppingham** Tug-of-war and Summer Fair *– till Sun 14*

14th **Newark-on-Trent** Half Marathon

21st **Grange de Lings** Steam and Vintage Rally *at Lincolnshire Showground*

27th **Breedon-on-the-Mill** Flower Festival, *also Mon 29*; **Stoke Golding** Flower Festival

29th **Alford** Craft Festival; **Louth** Vintage Racing Car Meeting *at Cadwell Park*

September

9th **West Bridgford** Rushcliffe Festival *– till Sun 25*

11th **Blyth** Bassetlaw Show; **Loughborough** Raft Race and Family Day

23rd **Osberton** Horse Trials *– till Sun 25*

25th **Nottingham** Robin Hood Marathon *at Victoria Embankment*

October

5th **Nottingham** 700th Goose Fair *– till Sat 8*

10th **Corby Glen** Sheep Fair

Leicestershire, Lincolnshire and Nottinghamshire Calendar

October cont.

15th **Thoresby Park** Craft Fair – *till Sun 16*

27th **Nottingham** Robin Hood Pageant – *till Sun 30*

28th **Castle Donington** Wakes – *till Mon 31 (not Sun)*

November

5th **Cadeby** Steam Day; **Leicester** Fireworks Display *at Abbey Park;* **Coalville** Fireworks; **Loughborough** Great Bonfire Night Special *at Great Central Railway*; **Nottingham** Bonfire Night

December

26th **Grange-de-Lings** Burton Hunt Meet *at Lincolnshire Showground*; **Swithland** Morris Dancing *at the Griffin Inn*

The Midlands (Warwickshire, West Midlands and Northamptonshire)

Stratford always keeps Warwickshire on the tourist map. The town certainly is great for Shakespeare lovers, though other people will find more to enjoy out in south Warwickshire. On the edge of the Cotswolds, this part of the county is given additional interest by the neighbouring parts of Gloucestershire and Oxfordshire.

North Warwickshire and the West Midlands have a lot of places to visit – and, indeed, offer the best choice in this area. However, many of the most interesting places are formidably ringed by urban areas that are not the ideal stuff of a weekend break. Birmingham and Coventry's rich pickings for visitors are best had by dipping in for a day, preferably on a weekend; Warwick and its closely coupled neighbour Leamington Spa do have more stay-put appeal.

For most people, we'd say that of this whole region Northamptonshire has the best to offer in terms of a short break – there's a good mixture of things to do and pleasant relatively undiscovered countryside to explore – though there's not as much to amuse children as there is elsewhere in the area. It has plenty of good places to stay, is the best for driving around, and price levels here represent good value for money. This is not very good countryside for walkers, however, though there are some pleasant strolls.

Birmingham, Warwick and North Warwickshire

There is plenty to see and do, particularly in and around Birmingham (best visited by the day); not recommended for a quiet break.

Birmingham has excellent art collections, lively museums, a surprisingly interesting factory visit at Bournville, good botanic gardens and many other things worth seeing. Though we have included one good-value hotel there for the determined sightseer, the city itself is not ideal for a weekend break: most people would find it better to go in by the day. Coventry also has quite a lot to see on day visits. Warwick, by contrast, does have the character and atmosphere to provide short-stay appeal, coupled as it is with its neighbour Leamington Spa – which still has the gardens, parks and spacious terraces of its heyday as a spa resort.

Outside these towns, the highpoints for most people are Kenilworth Castle and the open-air museum at Dudley. There are also strong attractions at Baddesley Clinton, Middleton, Farnborough, Packwood House, Arbury and Ryton-on-Dunsmore. There are many attractive villages.

Well endowed with canals, the area gives some of its better walking possibilities along their towpaths; otherwise, it has less to hold the attention of walkers, and is not a prime area for leisurely drives. It has quite a good choice of comfortable places to stay in.

Where to stay

Wishaw SP1794 BELFRY Sutton Coldfield B76 9PR (0675) 470301 **£145**; 219 rms in four wings named after famous golfers. Set in 360 acres of parkland and with two world-class 18-hole golf courses, this creeper-covered hotel has light, modern day rooms inc 8 bars and 4 restaurants, lots of plants, a floodlit driving range, putting green, golf centre, fine leisure complex, and nightclub; disabled access.

Leamington Spa SP3161 MALLORY COURT CV33 9QB (0926) 330214 **£140**; 10 wonderfully comfortable and luxurious rms. Fine, ancient-looking house – actually built around 1910 – with elegant, antique and flower-filled day rooms; really excellent food in the panelled restaurant, 10 acres of lovely gardens with outdoor swimming pool, tennis, squash, croquet; children over 9.

King's Norton SP0479 NORTON PLACE 180 Lifford Lane Birmingham B30 3NT (021) 433 5656 **£122**; 10 well-equipped rms. The outside of the blocky new brick building gives no hint of the stylish and individual elegance inside – much more what you'd expect from an old country house; conservatory with leisure facilities; children over 10.

Ansty SP3983 ANSTY HALL Coventry CV7 9HZ (0203) 612222 **£110**; 31 luxurious rms. Handsome 17th-c hotel with quiet, relaxing atmosphere, comfortable day rooms, and walled garden in 8 acres of ground.

Hockley Heath SP1573 NUTHURST GRANGE Nuthurst Grange Lane B94 5NL (0564) 783972 **£99**; 15 light, airy rms. At the end of a long drive through attractive parkland stands this handsome Edwardian house with warmly welcoming staff, excellent food, and comfortable day rooms with lots of flowers.

Sutton Coldfield SP1296 NEW HALL B76 8QX (021) 378 2442 **£93**; 60 lovely rms (the ones in the manor house are the best). The oldest moated manor house in England in 26 acres of beautiful grounds with luxuriously furnished day rooms; graceful, panelled restaurant with carefully cooked, imaginative food using very fresh (often home-grown) produce, and excellent service; children over 8; disabled access.

West Bromwich SP0091 MOAT HOUSE Birmingham Rd Birmingham B70 6RS (021) 553 6111 **£81.40**; 172 rms. Decent modern hotel, handy for the motorway, with good food (esp carvery), and attentive, helpful service; cl 24-31 Dec; playroom with nursery maid and childminder, disabled access.

Kenilworth SP2871 CLARENDON HOUSE CV8 1LZ (0800) 616883 **£50**; 31 cosy rms. Carefully restored 15th-c hotel with Cromwellian armour in the beamed public rooms, and set in the oldest part of town.

Sherbourne SP2661 OLD RECTORY Vicarage Lane CV35 8AB (0926) 624562 ***£40**; 14 rms, all with antique brass or brass and iron beds. Carefully furnished

Georgian house with cosy sitting room, big log fire, beams, flagstones, honesty bar and hearty breakfast; cl 23-27 Dec; good disabled access; dogs welcome; converted coach house is popular with families.

Birmingham SP0787 WHARF 20 Bridge St B1 2JH (021) 633 4820 **£39.50**; 54 rms. Decent place with plus point being that it's good value and overlooks the Worcester & Birmingham Canal; disabled access.

Avon Dassett SP4049 CRANDON HOUSE Leamington Spa CV33 0AA (0295) 770652 **£35**; 3 rms. Welcoming farmhouse on a small working farm with a variety of livestock, fine views, big garden, and comfortable sitting rooms (one with woodburning stove); evening meals by arrangement; cl Christmas; children over 8.

Birmingham SP0786 There are masses of things to see and do here, but for most people it is disqualified as a place to stay, because of its lack of an attractive town centre. However, the formidably efficient traffic system which ploughs through its heart means that, particularly at weekends, when of course it's all a lot quieter, you can easily tap in on this rich reservoir of things to see, just coming in as it suits you. The centre today may be mostly modern, but the city has a long heritage, dating back long before it was valued at £1 in the Domesday Book, and has a rich and varied industrial history taking in everything from buckles to chocolate buttons, and cloth to Crunchies. There's a surprising absence of that essential for big-city visits: good pubs. A few acceptable ones which do at least some lunchtime food include the Adam & Eve (Bradford St), Atkinson Bar (Midland Hotel), Crown (Broad St), Market Tavern (Moseley St), Prince of Wales (Cambridge St), Rope Walk (St Pauls Sq, Hockley), Rosevilla (Vyse St – handy for the jewellery quarter) and Station (High St, Kings Heath).

ASTON HALL (Aston) Impressive Jacobean mansion with panelled long gallery, balustraded staircase and magnificent plaster friezes and ceilings; snacks, shop; cl am, Nov-Easter. CITY MUSEUM AND ART GALLERY (Chamberlain Sq) houses perhaps the best collection of Pre-Raphaelite paintings anywhere, with plenty still looking as brilliantly, almost shockingly, fresh and detailed as when they were first painted, as well as other French, Dutch, Italian and English works from the 14th c on; excellent coins and archaeology sections and displays on local and natural history. Meals, snacks, shop, disabled access; cl Sun am, 25 Dec.

BARBER INSTITUTE (University) Excellent collection of paintings and sculptures, well housed in a very attractive gallery; just the right size to be enjoyable without being overwhelming. Shop, disabled access; cl Sun am.

MUSEUM OF SCIENCE AND INDUSTRY (Newhall St) Concentrating on the city's contribution to science and engineering, with displays of tools, equipment and working engines, and the oldest still-working steam engine in the world. Splendid Locomotive Hall and aircraft section with Spitfire and Hurricane steam days; meals, snacks, shop, disabled access; cl several days around Christmas and New Year.

BIRMINGHAM RAILWAY MUSEUM (Warwick Rd) Working railway museum with fully equipped workshop, many steam locomotives and several historic carriages, wagons and other vehicles; meals, snacks, shop, disabled access; cl 25-26 Dec and 1 Jan; £2.50 – tel (021) 707 4696 for details of steam days – and of their steam train driving lessons.

! CADBURY WORLD (Bournville SP0481) Displays on its origins, production and marketing of the world-famous chocolate, with plenty of samples along the way to satisfy the cravings created by the sumptuous smells. Watch out for the quite bizarre little cars shaped like Creme Eggs. It gets busy, so it might be a good idea to book in advance to avoid queues; very enjoyable. Meals, snacks, shop, disabled access; cl Mon and Tues exc in summer, 25 Dec; £4.50.

BOTANICAL GARDENS (Edgbaston) 15 acres featuring Tropical House with lily pool, bananas and cocoa, Palm House, Orangery, the National Bonsai Collection, Cactus House and the gardens themselves, filled with rhododendrons and azaleas and a goodly collection of trees. Bands play on summer Sun afternoons; meals, snacks, shop, disabled access; cl 25 Dec; *£2.90, *£3.20 summer Sun.

BIRMINGHAM NATURE CENTRE (Edgbaston) British and European animals in indoor and outdoor enclosures designed to resemble natural habitats, dry land and waterside; meals, snacks, shop, disabled access; cl wkdys from Nov-Mar.

WEOLEY CASTLE Ruins of 13th-c castle with interesting little museum; shop; cl am, Sat-Mon, Nov-Mar.

BLAKESLEY HALL (Yardley) Timber-framed 16th-c merchant's house, furnished according to an inventory of 1684. Displays on timber building, pottery and rural crafts; shop; cl am, Nov-Mar.

JEWELLERY QUARTER DISCOVERY CENTRE (Vyse St) Well-restored place tracing the history of the local jewellery industry, with interesting tours of jewellery factory, which remains unchanged since it was abandoned in 1914 and is still producing jewellery using the original equipment. The area's importance in the jewellery trade is much smaller than it used to be, but the Quarter is still Britain's biggest producer of gold jewellery. Snacks, shop, disabled access; cl Sun; *£2.

SAREHOLE MILL (Hall Green) Working 18th-c water mill, with several displays explaining the milling process; shop; cl am, Nov-Feb.

SELLY MANOR MUSEUM (Selly Oak SP0382) Two timber-framed medieval manor houses re-erected on new site, with herb garden, crafts and exhibitions; snacks, shop, some disabled access; cl wknds (though they hope this will change soon), Mon (exc bank hols), 15 Dec-15 Jan; *£1.

Warwick SP2865 Despite a major fire in 1694, many older buildings survive, and today's centre shows the benefits of the elegant Queen Anne rebuilding. Some of the oldest structures are to be found around Mill St, which is very attractive to stroll along; there are a good few antique shops.

! WARWICK CASTLE Begun by William the Conqueror, this is one of the most splendid castles in the country; the views from its parklands are dramatic, stirring stuff. It's a lively place, with lots of displays specially geared for families, such as the gruesome torture chambers in the dungeon or the Royal Weekend Party exhibition, both of which show the influence of Madame Tussauds, who own the site. It's also one of the busiest of the country's attractions, but definitely worth braving the crowds for; there are excellently preserved rooms such as the magnificent Hall, fine furnishings and art, and marvellous grounds designed by Capability Brown. Meals, snacks, shop, disabled access to grounds only; £6.75. The nearby MILL GARDEN is a delightful series of plantings in a super

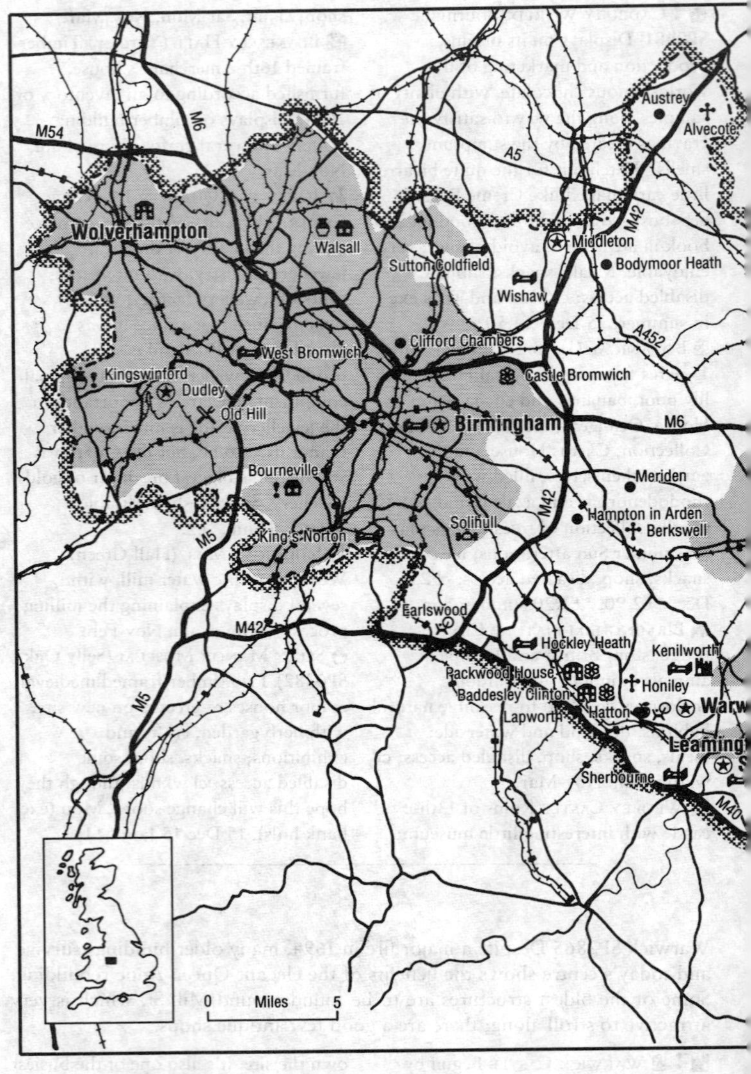

setting on the river beside the castle – a very nice place to stroll through, with plenty of old things to look at along the way; shop, disabled access; open pm Sun and bank hol Mons, mid-Apr-mid-Oct, some other days and times as well; donations.

✝ ❁ St Mary's Church Splendid medieval church on the town's highest point, Norman crypt, chapter house and magnificent 15th-c Beauchamp chapel; in summer you can go up the tower which has excellent views – small admission charge.

🏛 Lord Leycester Hospital (High St) Lovely half-timbered building built in 1383, still used as a home of rest for retired servicemen (there's a regimental

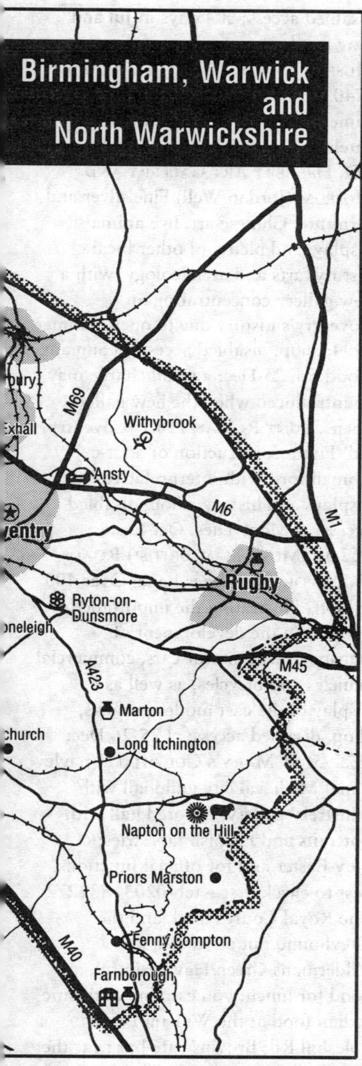

museum), and with the old Guildhall, chapel, gatehouse and courtyard on display; snacks, shop; cl Mon, Good Fri, 25 Dec; *£2.

St John's House (St John's) Fine 17th-c house with exhibits from the county museum, inc a reconstructed Victorian parlour, kitchen and schoolroom and the museum of the Royal Warwickshire Regiment; shop, disabled access to ground floor only; cl 12.30-1.30 pm, am summer Sun, all day Sun winter, Mon.

Doll Museum (Castle St) Carefully restored half-timbered Elizabethan house with comprehensive collection of antique and period dolls and toys; shop; cl Sun am, Oct-Easter exc Sat and local school hols; *£1.

Warwickshire Museum County museum in the 17th-c market hall, with local history and archaeology inc good fossils, habitat displays and Sheldon tapestry map of the county. Shop, disabled access to ground floor only; cl Sun exc pm Apr-Sept, Christmas and New Year.

Warwickshire Yeomanry Museum Militaria from the County Yeomanry, with some fine paintings and silver, and displays of the town's history; shop; open Fri-Sun and bank hols Easter-Sept, cl 1-2 pm. The Zetland Arms is good for simple lunches.

The impressive flight of canal locks on the Grand Union Canal west of the town can be reached most easily from Hatton SP2467, on the A4177 just past the hospital complex.

Other things to see and do

Alvecote SK2404 14th-c priory ruins, including a doorway and dovecot, in countryside by Coventry Canal – useful towpath walks.

Arbury SP3389 Arbury Hall They like to call this the 'Gothic Gem of the Midlands' and it is a splendid-looking place, the original Elizabethan house elaborately spruced up in the 19th c with soaring fan vaulting and filigree tracery in most of the rooms, and the outside additions making it one of the best examples of the Gothic Revival style. The writer George Eliot was born on the estate, and in her *Mr Gifgil's Love Story* describes some of the rooms – not unreasonably comparing the dining room to a cathedral. There's also some work by Wren in the stables (which now house a collection of vintage cycles) and the gardens are a pleasure; shop, limited disabled access; open pm Sun and bank hols Easter-Sept; £3. A major display on the life of George Eliot can be seen at the Museum in Nuneaton SP3592; cl Mon.

Baddesley Clinton SP2070 BADDESLEY CLINTON HOUSE Romantic 13th-c moated manor house, mostly unchanged since the 17th c; interesting portraits, priest's holes and garden with chapel and pretty walks. Meals, snacks, shop, disabled access; house cl am, Mon (exc bank hols), Tues, Nov-Feb; £3.80, grounds only £2. NT.

Castle Bromwich SP1489 CASTLE BROMWICH HALL GARDEN is an authentic collection of plants grown here in the 18th c, inc ancient vegetables as well as herbs and shrubs, in a classic 18th-c formal layout; snacks, shop, plant sales, disabled access; cl am, Fri, Oct-Easter; £2.

Coventry SP3378 Like Birmingham, more of a place to dip into than to fix as your full weekend-stay menu; its most interesting street is Spon St, with one or two ancient buildings that started their lives here and others that have been rescued from elsewhere and rebuilt here (the Old Windmill does cheap basic lunches). One of the town's most famous inhabitants was Lady Godiva, commemorated by a statue in Broadgate and the Coventry Clock – where she pops out in the pink every hour. CATHEDRAL (Priory Row) Bombed during the war, the old cathedral ruins have been carefully preserved, and parts of it such as the 14th-c tower remain intact. These have been joined by the new cathedral designed by Sir Basil Spence. It is in no way an orthodox church building, but is worth a look for unusual modern art and even holograms; the visitor centre has more, as well as a full history of its development. Meals, snacks, shop, disabled access; cl 4 days in Jul and Nov for degree ceremonies. TOY MUSEUM (Much Park St) Toys from 1740 to 1990, inc dolls, trains and games, housed in a 14th-c monastery gatehouse; shop; cl am and 25 Dec; *£1. HERBERT ART GALLERY AND MUSEUM (Jordan Well) Fine silver and furniture, Chinese art, live animals display, and plenty of other local history, arts and archaeology, with a new gallery concentrating on Coventry's history due to open summer 1994; shop, disabled access; cl Sun am, Good Fri, 25 Dec; a small charge may be introduced when the new gallery opens. LUNT ROMAN FORT (Coventry Rd) Fun reconstruction of a 1st-c Roman fort, with interpretative displays and history; shop, disabled access; cl Mon, Tues, Oct-Easter; *£2.50. MUSEUM OF BRITISH ROAD TRANSPORT (St Agnes Lane) Over 400 exhibits illustrating the importance of the area in the development of transport, with motor cars, commercial vehicles and bicycles, as well as a display of die-cast models; snacks, shop, disabled access; cl 25-26 Dec; *£2.95. ST MARY'S GUILDHALL (Bayley Lane) Medieval city guildhall with minstrels' gallery, restored hall with portraits and Flemish tapestries; cl Nov-Easter and for official functions, best to check first – tel (0203) 832272. The Royal Court Hotel, and the Greyhound out at Sutton Stop (Aldermans Green/Hawkesbury), are good for lunch; you can find authentic Indian food at the William IV on Foleshill Rd; Browns café-bar near the cathedral (Lower Precinct) serves food all day. Just south of town at the airport, the MIDLAND AIR MUSEUM has displays of civil and military aircraft spanning more than 70 years; snacks, shop, disabled access; cl Tues, Weds and Fri, and all Nov-Mar; *£2.50.

Dudley SO9490 BLACK COUNTRY MUSEUM Well-thought-out open-air museum giving a good feel of how things used to be in the Black Country, the heavily industrialised and proudly individual areas on the west part of the Birmingham conurbation. Reconstruction of typical turn-of-the-century Black Country village, complete with cottages, chapel, chemist, baker and pub. There's a canal boat dock with displays and trips into the Dudley Tunnel, you can go down a mine, or even back to school with classroom scenes brought to life in their new restored schoolroom. There are many displays in the workshops, and all the staff are in period costume. Plenty of things to do here – it could be a whole day out. Meals, snacks, shop, some disabled access; cl Mon and Tues in Nov-Feb, and wk before Christmas; £4.95. DUDLEY ZOO Popular traditional zoo in the wooded grounds of a RUINED CASTLE, with animals from all over the world; the remains are impressive, and there's a train up to the top of the hill. Meals, snacks, shop, disabled access; £4. MUSEUM AND ART GALLERY Good collection of 17th-, 18th- and 19th-c European paintings, furniture, and ceramics, with other local history and fossils in the lively new geology gallery; shop, disabled access; cl Sun. There's a properly Black Country feel in the British Oak in Salop St, Eve Hill, which brews its own beer and does cheap lunches.

Earlswood SP1173 MANOR FARM CRAFT WORKSHOPS (Wood Lane) Ceramics, furniture restoration, stained glass, print-making, needlework etc, also home-made ice cream; disabled access; cl Mon. The Bluebell (on the canal) and Bulls Head are popular for lunch.

Farnborough SP4349 FARNBOROUGH HALL Wonderful Palladian villa filled with splendid sculptures, paintings and rococo plasterwork; the staircase, hall and two main rooms are on show, and the gardens have a temple and views from the terrace walk – less impressive than they were thanks to the arrival of the M40. Open pm Weds and Sat Apr-Sept, also 1-2 May; terrace also open Thurs and Fri pm; £2.60; terrace walk only £1. NT. In the yard is the enthusiastic EDGEHILL BATTLE MUSEUM, commemorating the first major battle of the English Civil War, fought nearby in 1642. Weapons, uniforms, models and dioramas on the battle itself, and on the 17th-c life that it so rudely interrupted, with appropriate period music adding to the atmosphere; the friendly staff really are dedicated to their subject. Snacks, shop; open pm Weds and Sat Apr-Sept; *£1.

Hatton SP2367 COUNTRY WORLD (Dark Lane) Converted farm buildings now housing Britain's biggest crafts village, made up of some three dozen workshops; the 100-acre site also includes a collection of rare breeds of farm animals (some with walk-through paddocks), adventure playground, summer pick-your-own soft fruits, and a nature trail to the Stairway to Heaven – a flight of 21 canal locks over two miles. Meals, snacks, shop, disabled access; £2.50. Some of the craftsmen and women offer courses in their skills. Good FARM SHOP nearby at Windmill House Farm.

Kenilworth SP2871 KENILWORTH CASTLE Dramatic ruins of a castle begun in the 12th c and later transformed by John of Gaunt into a spectacular fortress. Its heyday was in the 16th c, when it became the property of the Earl of Leicester, but it was largely destroyed by Oliver Cromwell during the Civil War. Today the keep is still impressive, and there are various other buildings and remains within the sandstone walls, as well as a restored Tudor garden; snacks, shop, disabled access; cl winter Mon; £1.70. In the summer various re-enactments, plays and operas are performed in the grounds. The town itself has some pleasant strolls, especially around the castle area, where the Clarendon House Hotel is a civilised place for lunch.

! Kingswinsford SO8888 BROADFIELD HOUSE GLASS MUSEUM Focusing on glass from nearby Stourbridge, this has an excellent collection from the past few centuries; shop; cl Sat lunch, am exc Sat, all day Mon. Nearby Himley SO8791 has the CROOKED HOUSE, an extraordinary pub bent by mining subsidence into a three-dimensional optical illusion that'll have you imagining things roll uphill here, instead of down; perhaps surprisingly, it's a good pub too. Down by the canal, the Navigation (Greensforge) gives pleasant views of narrow boats working their way through the lock.

Leamington Spa SP3265 Elegant spa resort popularised by the rich who came to take the waters in the 18th c and 19th c. There are still many fine Regency buildings, though today the town is better seen as a civilised shopping centre, and perhaps as a base for sallies into the surrounding countryside – or into Warwick, across the River Avon. The JEPHSON GARDENS are beautifully laid out and well worth a look, with wild ducks on the lake; meals, snacks, shop, disabled access. WARWICK DISTRICT COUNCIL ART GALLERY AND MUSEUM Local history gallery, with collections of ceramics, pottery and glass, and British, Dutch and Flemish paintings from the 16th c to the present. Shop, disabled access; cl 1-2 pm, Weds, Sun, Good Fri, 25-26 Dec, 1 Jan.

Marton SP4068 MUSEUM OF COUNTRY BYGONES Country museum with tools used for traditional crafts, household and dairy equipment and heavy-horse harness; cl Nov-Mar; *75p.

Middleton SP1798 ASH END HOUSE FARM Friendly farm specifically set up for children; animals from shire horses to baby chicks and fluffy ducklings, as well as various rare breeds of goats, pigs and sheep. Snacks, shop, disabled access; cl 25 Dec; *£2.20 children, *£1.10 adults. MIDDLETON HALL Lots of styles of architecture here, from the recently restored 14th-c Hall to the grand Georgian wing. The grounds have a nature reserve, walled gardens, orchards and woodlands, and besides a smithy there is a craft centre in the stables – workshops inc lace bobbin makers, glassblowing, knitwear, jewellery, upholstery and ceramics. Snacks, shop, disabled access; house open pm Sun and bank hols Apr-Oct; £1.20. Craft centre cl Sun am, Mon, Tues. The Green Man is a good family dining pub.

★ **Napton on the Hill** SP4661 is an attractive village on a rounded hill above a curve in the Oxford Canal – perhaps the prettiest in this part of the world, with pleasant towpath walks. Great views of seven counties from the hill. CHURCH LEYES FARM is a 40-acre family-run organic farm with animals, walks and wild-flower conservation headlands by the hedges – lovely views; cl Sat and Jewish holy days; *£1. The Folly is good for lunch, and the Napton Bridge down by the canal is useful.

Packwood House SP1671 Friendly old house with origins as a 16th-c farmhouse, now carefully restored and not at all commercialised; interesting panelling, furniture and needlework, and in the garden unusual yew trees clipped to represent the Sermon on the Mount. Shop, some disabled access; cl am, Mon (exc bank hols), Tues, Nov-Mar; £3, garden only £2. NT. The Navigation by the canal at Lapworth is the best nearby place for lunch.

Rugby SP5075 JAMES GILBERT RUGBY FOOTBALL MUSEUM Gilbert's have made their famous rugby balls in this shop since 1842, and there are demonstrations of their production, as well as good displays and collections of other items connected with the game; shop; cl Sun and a few days over

Christmas. The Three Horseshoes not far off in Sheep St is useful for lunch.

Ryton-on-Dunsmore SP3874 RYTON GARDENS This is the home of the Henry Doubleday Research Association, the organic farming and gardening organisation, so the grounds are landscaped with thousands of organically grown plants and trees; herb garden, rose garden, garden for the blind, and shrub borders amongst the displays, and there are some free-range farm animals. Meals and snacks in very good wholefood café, shop, disabled access; cl over Christmas; *£2.50.

Solihull SP1679 NATIONAL MOTORCYCLE MUSEUM Five halls displaying over 650 gleamingly restored motorcycles covering a period of 90 years; all are British, from around 150 different factories. Also a permanent display on the Norton Racing team, Britains's first TT winners for nearly 40 years, and, more incongruously, the biggest theatre organ in Europe. Meals, snacks, shop, disabled access; cl 24-26 Dec; £3.75.

Walsall SP0198 JEROME K JEROME BIRTHPLACE MUSEUM House dedicated to life and work of the author of *Three Men in a Boat*, with a reconstructed 1850s parlour; cl 1-2 pm, Sat pm, Sun. WALSALL LEATHER MUSEUM 19th-c leather goods factory with tours of aromatic workshops and displays and demonstrations of leather production and development; meals, snacks, shop, disabled access; cl Mon (exc bank hols), 25-26 Dec, 1 Jan.

Wolverhampton SO9198 WIGHTWICK MANOR Wightwick (just off A454) Only a century old, but beautifully and unusually designed by followers of William Morris, this house is a fine testimonial to the enduring qualities of his design principles; good paintings, tiles and glass. Shop, some disabled access; open pm Thurs and Sat, bank hol wknds, cl up to Mar 1994 for maintenance; *£4. In the town, the Great Western in Sun St and the Press wine bar in Queens St are useful for lunch. Around 4 miles north of town, MOSELEY OLD HALL is a Tudor house famed as a hiding place for Charles II after the Battle of Worcester. The furnishings and atmosphere in its panelled rooms don't seem to have changed much since then and outside there's a 17th-c knot garden; teas, shop, limited disabled access; open pm Weds, wknds and bank hols Apr-Oct plus Tues in July and Aug; £3. NT.

Withybrook SP4384 CARRIAGE RESTORATION (Stable Cottage, Featherbed Lane) Coachwork on antique carriages and veteran cars; cl most weekends. The Pheasant is good for lunch.

★ **Other attractive villages** in the county include Priors Marston SP4857 (attractive old houses around the village green, unusual blue brick paths; good pubs – the Falcon and ancient Holly Bush; there's a walk up Marston Hill behind, and quite a good network of paths around nearby Priors Hardwick taking you down to the Oxford Canal); Austrey SK2906 (timbered houses and cottages); Berkswell SP2479 (pretty Norman church; the Bear is useful for lunch); Clifford Chambers SP1092 (timbered houses and a Tudor rectory which has some claim to being the true birthplace of Shakespeare); Exhall SP3385 (Shakespeare's dodging village, pretty black-and-white timbering and some pleasant gently hilly walks nearby despite the proximity of the M6); Hampton in Arden SP2081 (the White Lion is good for lunch); Honiley SP2472 (well, not exactly – the village has gone now, and there are only vestiges of the big house, but the surviving 18th-c church still makes this feel like a village); Meriden SP2482 (a cross on the green marks what the village feels is the centre of England – it's true that of the streams rising in the village pond one ends up in the Severn and the other over in the Humber);

and Stoneleigh SP3372 (sandstone Norman church, timber-framed houses – the one called Forsythia Cottage was a pub till 1890, when the local landlord closed it in disgust at the way the cyclists out from Coventry whistled at his daughter). Near Stoneleigh is the headquarters of the Royal Agricultural Society of England, and the showground for the Royal Show.

Walks

This is not notable walking country. The **canal towpaths** offer some possibilities; one of the prettier ones is the Ashby Canal heading off into the Leics countryside from its junction with the Coventry Canal at Marston Junction SP3688. Besides the places already mentioned, there are several useful canal-side pubs including the Navigation at Lapworth SP1670, Two Boats at Long Itchington SP4164 (the flight of Stockton Locks just E usually has plenty going on), George & Dragon at the Wharf nr Fenny Compton SP4152 (A423 – a popular family pub, with aviaries and so forth) and Dog & Doublet at Bodymoor Heath SP2096 (useful for the Kingsbury Water Park too). From the Stags Head in Offchurch SP3665 there's a pleasant walk W through the riverside parkland of Offchurch Bury.

Hayes Hill Country Park is a mixed woodland, opening out at the top of the site for fair-sized views towards the Peak District. The proximity of the Coventry Canal below enables extended rambles.

Driving

There are few pleasant country drives here, but the old drovers' road, the Welsh Road from Cubbington through Offchurch and Southam (a pleasant small town, where the ancient Old Mint is a good refreshment break) to Priors Marston and on into Northamptonshire gives a good taste of some of the quietest gently rolling farmland, getting hillier on the county boundary. A surprisingly quiet cross-country back road is that which follows the straight line of the Roman Foss Way down from the Leicestershire border through Brinklow (where the Raven is a useful stop), Stretton-on-Dunsmore and Princethorpe to Halford in the southern part of the county.

Where to eat

Old Hill SO9685 WATERFALL 132 Waterfall Lane (021) 561 3499 Small busy refurbished Black Country local with good value food, decent range of real ales from all over the country, and enthusiastic licensee; cl 25 Dec pm, disabled access. £10|£1/£3.35.

We welcome reports from readers . . .

This GUIDE depends on readers' reports. Please tell us what you think about places in it. And do recommend additions. Use the card in the middle, the report forms at the end, or just write – no stamp needed: THE GOOD WEEKEND GUIDE, FREEPOST TN1569, Wadhurst, E Sussex TN5 7BR.

SOUTH WARWICKSHIRE

Stratford is rewarding if you know and love your Shakespeare; elsewhere there is quietly appealing countryside.

Many of the things to see and do here are concentrated in Stratford, which is the tourist centre of the area which, while full of interest for people on the Shakespeare trail, can be disappointing to others. Around Stratford are quite a few pretty villages, with further Shakespeare connections for those who want to look for them: his wife's cottage at Shottery and mother's house at Wilmcote are both very attractive. There are three great houses in fine grounds worth visiting, at Alcester, Charlecote and Coughton. The countryside is not spectacular, but appealing in a quiet way, with some possibilities for leisurely drives and gentle strolls; there's very little to amuse children, though small boys may be riveted by the remarkable new motor vehicle collection at Gaydon. Nostalgia and music enthusiasts will also enjoy Ashorne.

The area has a reasonable choice of comfortable places to stay, though in Stratford prices are high. On the fringes of the Cotswolds, South Warwickshire has a lot to see and do, and better walking in nearby parts of Gloucestershire and Oxfordshire.

Where to stay

Stratford-upon-Avon SP2055 WELCOMBE Warwick Rd CV37 0NR (0789) 295252 **£145**; 75 rms with antiques and luxurious bthrms. Jacobean-style mansion in parkland estate with an 18-hole golf course and two all-weather floodlit tennis courts, deeply comfortable day rooms that include a fine panelled lounge, open fires and fresh flowers, and good service; cl 28 Dec-3 Jan; disabled access.

Stratford-upon-Avon SP2055 SHAKESPEARE Chapel St CV37 6ER (0789) 294771 **£127**; 63 comfortable, well-equipped rms. Smart Forte hotel based on handsome, lavishly modernised Tudor merchants' houses; comfortable bar with settles and armchairs, well-kept real ales and some bar food inc reliable cold table and hot dishes of the day; quick friendly service, tables in back courtyard, and civilised tea or coffee in peaceful chintzy armchairs by blazing log fires; 3 minutes' walk from theatre.

Stratford-upon-Avon SP2055 ARDEN THISTLE 44 Waterside CV37 6BA (0789) 294949 **£79**; 63 rms. Elegant Regency house opposite Royal Shakespeare and Swan Theatres and overlooking River Avon; private gardens and a relaxed, friendly atmosphere.

Stratford-upon-Avon SP2055 STRATFORD HOUSE Sheep St CV37 6EF (0789) 268288 **£78**; 11 comfortable rms. Georgian house close to Royal Shakespeare Theatre with open fire and lots of flowers in the lounge, fine food in airy restaurant; friendly, helpful service; disabled access.

Stratford-upon-Avon SP2055 COACH HOUSE 16 Warwick Rd CV37 6YW

(0789) 204109 £59; 24 comfortable rms. Not far from the Royal Shakespeare Theatre, this partly Georgian hotel has a cosy bar and restaurant, and good, reasonably priced food.

Wilmcote SP1657 SWAN HOUSE The Green CV37 9XJ (0789) 267030 ***£58**; 8 decent rms. Popular Georgian hotel overlooking the village green and Mary Arden's house; good home-cooked food and winter log fire; cl 3-7 Jan.

Stratford-upon-Avon SP2055 MELITA 37 Shipston Rd CV37 7LN (0789) 292432 **£54**; 12 well-equipped rms. Friendly family-run Victorian hotel with pretty, carefully laid-out garden, comfortable lounge, good food and some provision for no-smokers; close to town centre and theatres; cl Christmas; disabled access.

Ilmington SP2143 HOWARD ARMS Shipston-on-Stour CV36 4LN (0608) 682226 ***£50**; 2 rms. Neatly kept golden stone inn opposite village green with pleasant sheltered garden with seats, friendly service, very good food, and decent wines; no accom 25-26 Dec.

Wilmcote SP1657 PEAR TREE COTTAGE 7 Church St Stratford-upon-Avon CV37 9UX (0789) 205889 **£38**; 7 rms. Charming half-timbered Elizabethan house owned by the same family for three generations, with beams, flagstones, cosy atmosphere, good breakfasts; shady garden; self-catering also; cl Christmas-1 Jan; children over 2.

Little Compton SP2630 RED LION Moreton-in-Marsh GL56 0RT (0608) 74397 ***£36**; 3 rms, shared bthrm. Simple but civilised low-beamed Cotswold stone inn with separate dining area, big menu with speciality steaks, extensive wine list; large, attractive garden; children over 8.

To see and do

Stratford-upon-Avon SP2055 It is undoubtedly Shakespeare that's the miracle ingredient here. Visitors who look at the town just as a town can be disappointed, but for those who have a grounding in the plays, the genius of the man does somehow add a special gloss to everything, so that the interesting buildings seem that bit more interesting – and not so outnumbered by the workaday ones, the overpriced antique shops and the gift shops. There are, indeed, buildings of undoubted appeal here, and the gardens by the River Avon make a memorable setting for the Memorial Theatre. If you're looking forward to a good production at the theatre that evening, or, better still, able to run through much of the verse in your head, then you'll love Stratford. But if you've always thought Shakespeare overrated, then you'll think the same about Stratford, too. You can buy joint tickets for the places with the best Shakespeare connections.

The pub with the most theatrical Shakespeare connections is the Mucky Duck, or more properly White Swan (Southern Way) – traditionally where the RSC actors and actresses drink. Other useful places for lunch here include the quaint old Garrick (High St), Vintner Wine Bar, Lamplighters (Rother St), Slug & Lettuce (Guild St/Union St) and Shakespeare Hotel (Chapel St).

We welcome reports from readers . . .

Let us know what you think of places in the GUIDE, and any special tips you have. There are report forms at the back of the book, and a card in the middle.

SHAKESPEARE'S BIRTHPLACE (Henley St) The most logical place to start, the house where the writer is reputed to have been born in 1564; lots of exhibits from the period with good explanations and interpretative displays, as well as interesting garden and BBC TV costume exhibition; shop, disabled access to ground floor only; cl 24-26 Dec, am Good Fri and 1 Jan; £2.50.

NEW PLACE/NASH'S HOUSE (Chapel St) The place where Shakespeare died in 1616; the house was destroyed in the 18th c, but the Elizabethan knot garden remains, and the adjacent house, former home of the writer's granddaughter, has a good collection of furniture and local history. Some disabled access; cl Sun am in winter and 1 Jan, 25 Dec; £1.70.

KING EDWARD VI SCHOOL A half-timbered building where Shakespeare reputedly had his lessons; may allow visits in summer, tel (0789) 293351.

HOLY TRINITY CHURCH by the river was where Shakespeare was baptised and buried – many fine 15th-c features; 50p to enter the chancel where the grave is.

HALL'S CROFT (Old Town) Lovely gabled Tudor home of Dr John Hall, who married Shakespeare's daughter; good displays on the medicine of the time, and of Elizabethan and Jacobean furniture; snacks, some disabled access; cl am winter Suns and 1 Jan, 25 Dec; £1.70.

HARVARD HOUSE has no direct connection with Shakespeare, but it's a fine late 16th-c town house, a striking example of houses of his day; cl Sat, and Oct-late May; £1.

WORLD OF SHAKESPEARE (Waterside) A more modern feature of the town, but probably the best way of maintaining the interest of children less happy with real history; 25 life-size tableaux recreating Elizabethan life with the help of sound effects, music and dramatic lighting. Snacks, disabled access; cl 25 Dec; £3.

ROYAL SHAKESPEARE COMPANY COLLECTION (Waterside) Over 1,000 costumes, props, pictures and other items demonstrating the changes in staging from medieval times to the present; other exhibitions and displays. Meals, snacks, shop; cl 25 Dec; £1.50.

The town has a few other attractions that have nothing to do with Shakespeare at all:

! NATIONAL TEDDY BEAR MUSEUM Furry friends of all shapes and sizes – old ones, mechanical and musical ones, ones that belonged to famous people, and some that are famous themselves; shop; cl 25-26 Dec; *£1.90.

! BUTTERFLY FARM AND JUNGLE SAFARI (Tramway Walk) The difference from over the river couldn't be more striking – quaintly gabled houses here give way to cascading waterfalls and tropical forests, with up to 1,500 exotic butterflies flying free in a recreation of their own jungle habitat. Very interesting, with good explanations and knowledgeable staff – as well as a number of less friendly creatures in the Insect City, safely behind glass. Snacks, shop, disabled access; cl 24-25 Dec; £3.

SHIRE HORSE CENTRE AND FARM PARK Parades and demonstrations of the huge horses, as well as goats, pigs, rare breeds of sheep and cattle, owl sanctuary with falconry displays and an adventure playground; meals, snacks, shop, disabled access; cl 25 Dec; *£4.

Other things to see and do

Alcester SP0857 RAGLEY HALL Perfectly symmetrical Palladian house nicely set in 400 acres of parkland and gardens; excellent baroque plasterwork in Great Hall, fine paintings, and adventure playground, maze and woodland walks in the grounds. Meals, snacks, shop, disabled access; cl Mon, Fri, Oct-Easter; £4.50 house, garden and park; £3.50 park and garden. The village itself is attractive, and the nearby village of Arrow is also interesting to stroll around (despite some development) – as is the pretty stream that divides the two. Though fruit farming around here is much rarer than it used to be, you can still find delicious fresh dessert plums for sale in Sept. The Moat House is good for lunch.

! Ardens Grafton SP1153 The GOLDEN CROSS inn here is rather unusually decorated, with over 250 antique dolls, teddies and toys around the bar and restaurant; there's a small shop.

Charlecote SP2656 CHARLECOTE PARK 250 acres of parkland, full of deer (Shakespeare is said to have poached them from here), along with the descendants of reputedly the country's first flock of Jacob sheep. The Great Hall, Victorian kitchen and other well-furnished rooms can be seen in the house, and there's an impressive Tudor gatehouse; meals, snacks, shop, disabled access; cl Mon, Thurs, Good Fri, Nov-Mar, and house also cl 1-2 pm every day; £3.50. NT. By the park is a pretty little 19th-c estate village of timbered cottages, and a show Victorian church.

Ashorne SP3057 NICKELODEON A real treat for nostalgia buffs – a unique collection of mechanically played musical instruments such as self-playing harps, drums and violins and a vintage theatre, complete with organ rising from the floor, silent comedies and 1950s Pathé newsreels; various teas and events. The gardens of Ashorne Hall, where the collection is housed, are pleasant for a wander. Meals, snacks, shop, disabled access; open pm Sun Mar-Nov, and pm Fri and Sat May-Oct; £5.

Coughton SP0860 COUGHTON COURT Several priest's holes are hidden in this mainly Elizabethan house, renowned for its imposing gatehouse. Notable furniture, porcelain and relics inside, and a lake, two churches, pleasant walks, formal gardens and play area in the grounds; meals, snacks, shop, limited disabled access; cl am, Thurs, Fri, wkdys Oct and Apr, Nov-Mar; *£4. The Green Dragon at nearby Sambourne is good for lunch, and the Old Washford Mill at Studley is quite fun.

Gaydon SP3654 HERITAGE MOTOR CENTRE Busy new centre with the world's biggest collection of historic British cars – 300 of them in all from an 1895 Wolseley to the more familiar machines of the present. Also hundreds of drawings, photographs, trophies and related memorabilia, hi-tech displays and video shows, engineering gallery, demonstrations of four-wheel-drive vehicles, and a more peaceful nature reserve. Meals, snacks, shop, disabled access; cl 25-26 Dec; £5. The Malt Shovel is useful for lunch.

Long Compton SP2832 is a pleasant Cotswoldy village of thatched stone houses inc some antique shops. Nearby, a mile or so to the south, are the ROLLRIGHT STONES, the King Stone on one side of the lane, and on the other two groups of stones known as the King's Men and the Whispering Knights. Legend has it that this well-preserved stone circle is a king and his men, tricked by a witch into falling under her spell, and petrified. The stones straddle the Oxfordshire border, and just east at Rollright the Gate Hangs High is useful for lunch.

Shottery SP1854 ANNE HATHAWAY'S COTTAGE Substantial thatched Tudor farmhouse, the home of Anne Hathaway until her marriage to William Shakespeare; good displays of domestic life during the period, pleasant cottage garden. Snacks, shop; cl 25 Dec; £2.10. There's a craft centre next door.

Upton House SP3746 (A422 near Ratley) Late 17th-c house remodelled earlier this century, with exceptional art collection including paintings by Bosch, El Greco, Brueghel and Hogarth; also Brussels tapestries, Sèvres porcelain and woodland and terrace walks. NT have been carrying out work on the house, but it should be open again by Jun – until then you can still visit the grounds. Snacks, shop, disabled access; cl am, weekdays in Apr and Oct, Thurs and Fri, all Nov-Mar; *£4.

Wellesbourne SP2855 WELLESBOURNE WATERMILL Historic watermill in secluded rural setting, with the striking wooden wheel still producing flour; snacks, shop, some disabled access; open Thurs-Sun Easter-Sept, Sun pm only in Oct, Nov, Feb and Mar; *£2. WARTIME MUSEUM Housed in the underground HQ of a former RAF base, a collection of aeronautical archaeology and wartime memorabilia. Also a few restored aircraft inc a Vampire, Provost and Sea Vixen; limited disabled access; open Suns only; *£1.

Wilmcote SP1658 MARY ARDEN'S HOUSE Picturesque home of Shakespeare's mother, with the barns given over to countryside memorabilia; daily falconry displays, rare breeds. Snacks, some disabled access; cl am winter Sun and 25 Dec, 1 Jan; £3. The Swan House, overlooking it, is useful for lunch, as is the Masons Arms.

★ **Other attractive villages** in the area include Aston Cantlow SP1460 (timbered houses, fine guildhall, lovely church where Shakespeare's parents married); Lower Brailes SP3039 (lovely slender-spired church, pretty stone houses, good views; the George is useful for lunch); Shakespeare's 'Hungry Grafton', now Temple Grafton SP1255 (the Blue Boar is good for lunch); Hampton Lucy SP2557 (the Boars Head is useful for lunch); Honington SP2642 (church on edge of lawn of late 17th-c Honington Hall); Ilmington SP2143 (path to partly Norman church, lovely inside – and other walks in this relatively hilly part; Howard Arms good for lunch); Lighthorne SP3355 (the Antelope is good for lunch); Lower Quinton SP1847 (College Arms useful for lunch); Middle Tysoe SP3344 (with a very traditional cottage bakery); Preston-on-Stour SP2049; Radway SP3748, Ratley SP3847 and Warmington SP4147 (where the Plough is good; these last three are all below Edge Hill, where the castellated folly of the Castle Inn enjoys great views from its garden); Sutton under Brailes SP2937; and Welford-on-Avon SP1452 (the Bell is good for lunch). Shipston-on-Stour SP2450 is a small town with quite a busy shopping centre, but is rewarding to stroll through, with a good church and a good few handsome old stone buildings, antique shops among them; the Horseshoe seems currently best value for lunch here.

Walks

The S part of the county, just within the **Cotswolds**, has some pleasing countryside around Sutton-under-Brailes SP2937, and we've mentioned some other walking possibilities in this general area above. From Upper Tysoe SP3343 the walk S over Windmill Hill (which does have a windmill) takes you to the church on the edge of Compton Wynyates park, giving views of the attractive Tudor manor – a refreshing bit of brick building, in this Cotswold-edge stone country.

There's a short walk along the **River Avon** from the Ferry, a good dining pub in Alveston SP2356; and the Cottage of Content at Barton SP1051, which has day fishing tickets, also gives on to an Avon walk. The Fleur de Lys at Lowsonford SP1868 is a useful canalside pub.

Driving

Perhaps the nicest country drive here is the circular route around Alcester, through Walcote, Aston Cantlow, Wilmcote, Temple Grafton and Wixford, and then over the Gloucs border through Radford, Inkberrow, Holberrow Green, and back by New End and Kings Coughton. From its junction with the M40 (junction 13, near Bishops Tachbrook), the B4087 to Wellesbourne and then either on to Alderminster or turning right for Charlecote and Hampton Lucy is also quite attractive.

The coming of the M40 has turned the former A41, now the B4100, into a pleasantly empty road that gives a good general impression of the area, as does the Foss Way heading like a die up across country from Halford where it forks off the A429 – see North Warwickshire section.

Where to eat

Alderminster SP2348 BELL (0789) 450414 Very popular and rather civilised dining pub close to Stratford; excellent food relying on fresh local produce; disabled access. **£20**|£2.50/£8.

Lowsonford SP1868 FLEUR DE LYS (0564) 782431 Busy canalside bar with black beams; bar with several different areas, open fires, unusually elegant family room, good, interesting food (inc extensive children's menu) and lots of New World wines by the glass. **£15**|£2.50/£6.

Stratford-upon-Avon SP2055 THE OPPOSITION 13 Sheep St (0789) 269980 Small restaurant with generous helpings of very good food; handy for theatres and open for after-show meals; cl Sun Dec-Mar; no children in evening. **£18**|£3.50/£6.50.

Stratford-upon-Avon SP2055 CELLARS 16-17 Warwick Rd (0789) 204109 Renovated and attractive cellar restaurant in hotel (separate entrance) with a smoking and a no-smoking room and daily-changing, interesting home-cooked food; friendly service, and reasonably priced wine list; best to book Sat evenings; cl 25 Dec. **£18**|£2/£5.50.

NORTHAMPTONSHIRE

Delightful untouristy countryside, with pleasant drives and some fine houses to visit; good value for a peaceful break.

A great attraction of the countryside here is its untouristy feel – subtle landscapes of gentle hills, a fair amount of woodland, quietly attractive villages built in a warm stone that recalls the Cotswolds. Rockingham Castle, Castle Ashby House, Althorp Hall at Great Brington, Canons Ashby House, Sulgrave Manor, Deene Park, Cottesbrooke Hall, Lamport Hall and Boughton House make up a most impressive collection of grand houses to look at, most with interesting and handsome grounds. The gardens of Holdenby House and Coton Manor are delightful, the canal museum at Stoke Bruerne is interesting, and Oundle is a graceful small town. Along the wide valley of the River Nene, running across the county from Badby round Northampton and Wellingborough and then up past Oundle, some fine churches are to be found.

There are one or two things dotted around for children to do, though on the whole this county does not score as highly for family breaks as it does for older people going away for a relatively quiet weekend – in a part of the country that's not yet been 'discovered'. The choice of places to stay at and to eat out in is good, and prices are attractive.

Where to stay

Oundle TL0388 TALBOT Peterborough PE8 4EA (0832) 273621 **£97**; 39 most attractive big rms. Mary, Queen of Scots walked down one of the staircases in this carefully refurbished 17th-c hotel to her execution; attractive, cosy lounges, big log fires, good food in timbered restaurant, and garden; limited disabled access.
Weedon SP6046 CROSSROADS Northampton SP9 277 (0327) 40354 **£51.95**; 48 comfortable and attractive rms. Modern, main-road hotel with surprisingly flamboyant decor in main bar inc lots of bric-a-brac, light and airy separate coffee parlour, restaurant, and bar food; disabled access.
Towcester SP6948 SARACENS HEAD Watling St NN12 7BX (0327) 50414 **£50w**; 21 well-appointed rms. Handsome Georgian coaching inn with parts dating back to the 17th c, and strong *Pickwick Papers* connections.
Ashby St Ledgers SP5768 OLDE COACH HOUSE Rugby CV23 8UN (0788) 890349 ***£46**; 6 rms. Busy old inn in attractive village full of thatched stone houses; rambling atmospheric rooms, good bar food inc popular daily buffet, and at least 6 real ales; big gardens, large barbecue menu.
Sudborough SP9682 VANE ARMS High St Kettering NN14 3BX (0832) 733223 **£45**; 3 rms. Thatched inn on picturesque village street; attractive and welcoming, good range of freshly cooked food inc venison from nearby Rockingham Park, and lots of country wines.
Badby SP5559 WINDMILL Daventry NN11 6AN (0327) 702363 **£40**; 8 rms. Traditional, carefully modernised thatched stone inn with beams, flagstones and huge inglenook fireplace in front bar, cosy, comfortable lounge; good generously served bar and restaurant food, and decent wines; fine views of the pretty village from car park.
Culworth SP5446 FULFORD HOUSE The Green Banbury Oxon OX17 2BB (0295) 760355 **£40**; 3 pretty rms. Relaxing 400-year-old stone house with lovely views over the farmland, charming garden, beams, log fire in comfortable drawing room, and good food around circular Georgian table using fresh home-grown veg; cl mid-Dec-mid-Feb; children over 5.
East Haddon SP6668 RED LION Northampton NN6 8BU (0604) 770223 **£39**; 5 rms. Golden stone hotel with neat gardens and lawns, comfortable mix of furnishings, and decent daily changing food in bar and restaurant.
Old SP7872 WOLD FARM Northampton NN6 9RJ (0604) 781258 **£38**; 6 rms, 3 with shared bthrm. 18th-c house at the heart of beef and arable farm, with spacious, characterful rooms, good food in beamed dining room, attentive owners, and two pretty gardens; disabled access in one ground-floor room.

To see and do

Boughton SP7565 BOUGHTON HOUSE Very impressive old house often compared to Versailles; the largest in the county, richly furnished and decorated, with gorgeous paintings, tapestries and other art collections and beautiful parklands. Snacks, shop, disabled access; cl am, Nov-Apr, Fri (exc Aug); *£4, grounds only £1.50.
Brigstock SP9485 LYVEDEN NEW BIELD Unfinished 'new building' started in 1595 but abandoned after the owner Sir Thomas Tresham's son died in the Tower, where he'd been placed for his role in the Gunpowder Plot; intriguing and unusual, it was intended to celebrate the Passion of Christ, and is shaped like a Greek cross; *£1, NT. HILL FARM HERBS Popular herb nursery with plants

displayed in old farmyard; also selection of dried flowers. Snacks, shop; cl Jan and Feb. The CHURCH has a Saxon tower, and a bell that used to be rung three times a day to help anyone lost in the woods. BRIGSTOCK COUNTRY PARK is a good place for a wander. Another oddly designed building of Tresham's, the TRIANGULAR LODGE, can be seen at nearby Rushton SP8482. There are three walls, with three windows and three gables on three levels, and a three-sided chimney – logically, it represents the Holy Trinity

Canons Ashby SP5750 CANONS ASHBY HOUSE Exceptional little manor house, more northern-looking than Midlands, beautifully restored with Elizabethan wall paintings and glorious Jacobean plasterwork. The formal gardens have also been carefully restored over the last 20 years, and now closely reflect the layout of the early 18th c, with lovely stonework and plants that would have been used then rather than more recent introductions. A reasonably sized park has a hilltop 12th-14th-c PRIORY CHURCH. Brewhouse café, shop, disabled access; cl am, Mon (exc bank hols), Tues, Good Fri and all Nov-Mar; £3. NT. This is one of those houses that the Trust feels has almost too many visitors for its own good and deliberately under-publicises, so you may feel like confining any visit to a quiet time. The Crown at Weston SP5846 is quite handy for lunch.

Castle Ashby SP8659 CASTLE ASHBY HOUSE itself is not open, but is well worth seeing from outside, as it's one of the finest mansions in the Midlands, a splendidly palatial Elizabethan building at the end of a magnificent miles-long avenue planted nearly 300 years ago (William III would be proud of his suggestion, if he could see it today); the gardens, which can be visited, include grand Victorian terraces, sweeping lawns, Italianate gardens with an orangery, and lakeside parkland that may well be the prolific Capability Brown's most enduring achievement; nature trail, disabled access; £2. The CHURCH, within the park, is very attractive; there's a public path to it. CRAFT CENTRE AND RURAL SHOPPING YARD Variety of goods in restored farm buildings, inc farm produce, furniture, knitwear, toys and ceramics; snacks, shops, disabled access; cl Mon.

Coton SP6771 COTON MANOR Attractive views over countryside and Ravensthorpe Reservoir from charming gardens around 17th-c stonebuilt manor house (not open); interesting plantings, water gardens with flamingos, cranes and ornamental waterfowl wandering freely; teas, disabled access, plant sales; open pm Sun, Weds, bank hols Easter-Sept, as well as Thurs July and Aug; *£3.

Cottesbrooke Hall SP7173 COTTESBROOKE HALL Very attractive Queen Anne house reputed to be the model for Jane Austen's *Mansfield Park*, with a renowned collection of mainly sporting and equestrian paintings, and fine furnishings and porcelain. The lovely garden has formal borders, venerable cedars, greenhouses, extensive wild garden, and the separate cottage garden of Gamekeepers Cottage; teas, shop (some unusual plants for sale), disabled access to gardens only; open pm Thurs and bank hol Mon Easter-Sept; £3.50, gardens only £1.50. The CHURCH is the most interesting in the county, not nearly as grand as many others, but largely well-preserved Saxon, dating back 1,300 years, with a harmonious and very impressive charm.

Deene SP9492 DEENE PARK Lord Cardigan who led the Charge of the Light Brigade used to live in this interesting partly Tudor house, and his family still live here; attractive period furnishings (and one high-spirited contemporary portrait of him in full attack gallop). Outside are extensive

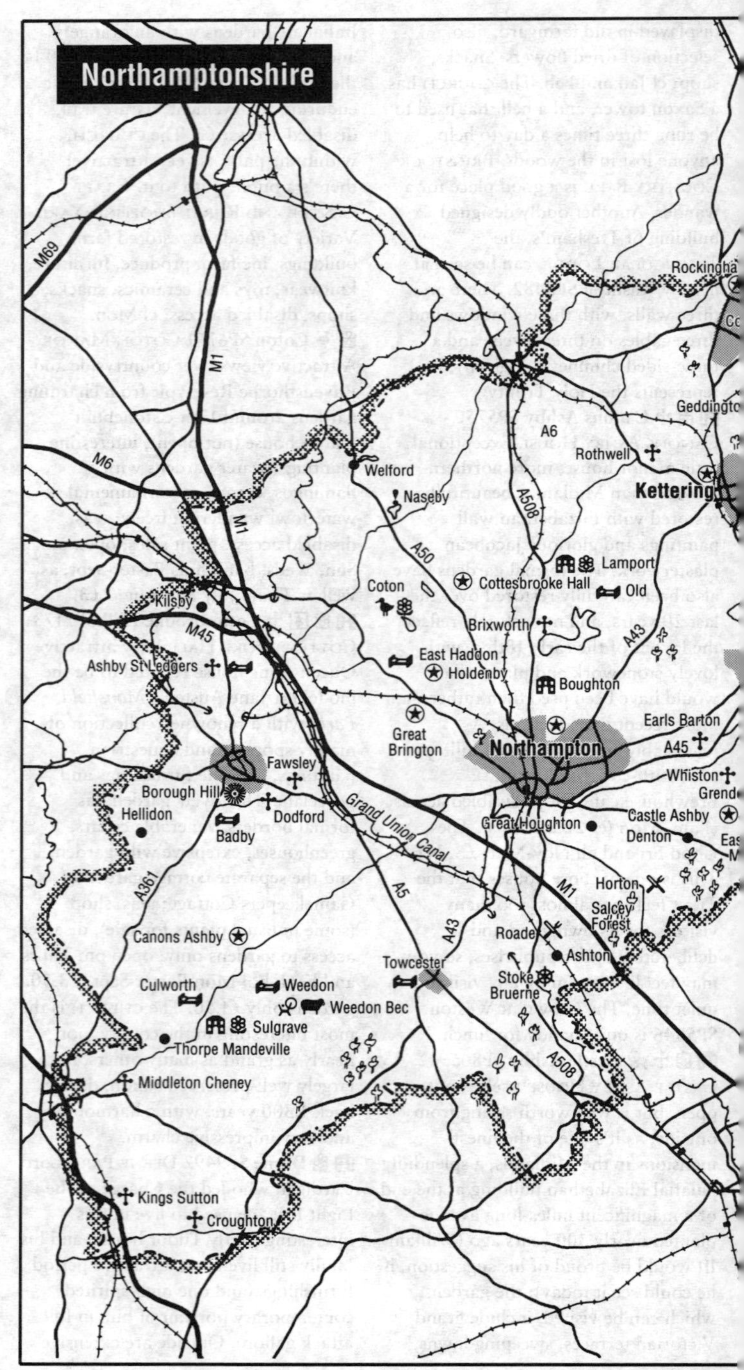
Northamptonshire
M69
M1
M6
M45
A6
Rothwell
Kettering
Welford
Naseby
A508
A50
Lamport
Cottesbrooke Hall
Coton
Brixworth
A43
East Haddon
Holdenby
Boughton
Kilsby
Ashby St Ledgers
Great Brington
Northampton
Earls Barton
A45
Whiston
Fawsley
Borough Hill
Hellidon
Dodford
Badby
Grand Union Canal
Great Houghton
Castle Ashby
Denton
A361
A5
Horton
Salcey Forest
Canons Ashby
Roade
Ashton
Towcester
Stoke Bruerne
Culworth
Weedon
Weedon Bec
Sulgrave
Thorpe Mandeville
Middleton Cheney
Kings Sutton
Croughton

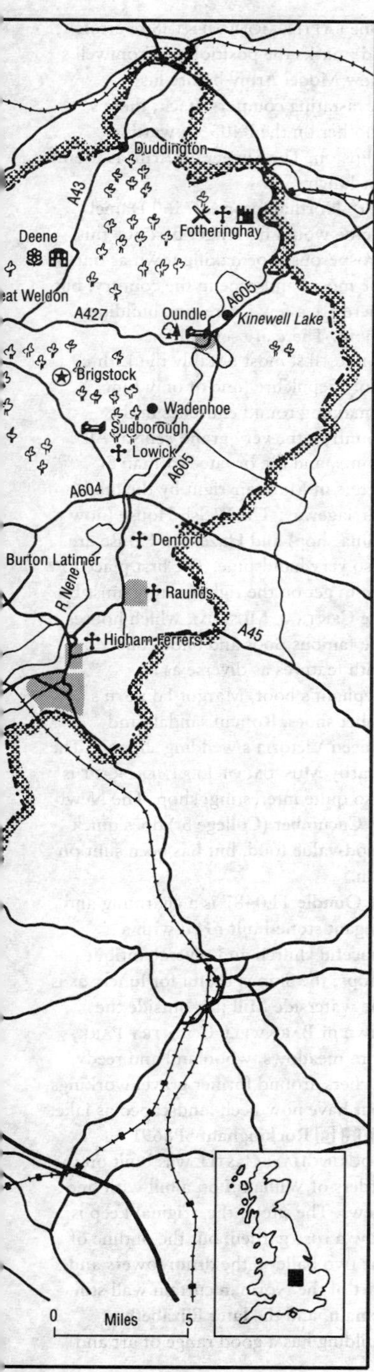

parklands with woodside and lakeside walks; the gardens have old-fashioned roses, rare trees and shrubs, and reflect continuing interest by the owners over the generations – there's a terrace designed by David Hicks. Snacks, shop, some disabled access; open pm Sun in Jun, July and Aug, also bank hol Sun and Mon in Apr and May; £3.50. KIRBY HALL Splendidly ruined Elizabethan mansion with a bizarre mixture of styles and design; it's a nice place for a picnic, and the 17th-c gardens are being restored to their original plan, with fruit and yew trees. Snacks, shop, disabled access; cl 24-26 Dec, 1 Jan; £1.20.

Fotheringhay TL0593 is a pretty village with a charming if slightly out-of-proportion 14th-c CHURCH (it was part of a small pre-Reformation college), across a watermeadow from the River Nene. There's only a fragment left of the CASTLE where Mary, Queen of Scots was imprisoned, beside the castle mound. The Falcon is excellent for lunch.

Geddington SP8963 has a 13th-c cross erected by Edward I where Queen Eleanor's funeral cortege rested on its way to Westminster. The pretty bridge is even older, and there's a 12th-c CHURCH.

Holdenby SP6967
HOLDENBY HOUSE GARDENS In Elizabethan times this was one of the biggest houses in the country, and the extensive gardens and grounds have been restored in the original style. There's also a museum, rare-breeds farm, and falconry centre with flying displays; snacks, shop, disabled access; cl am and Oct-Mar; *£2.50, less on Sat when only the falconry centre is open.

Great Brington SP6665
ALTHORP Since 1508 the home of the Spencer family, remodelled in the 17th and 18th c, with a splendid collection of furnishings and porcelain, and paintings by Rubens, Van Dyck and Lely – longer tours on Weds to linger over these. Snacks, shop, some disabled

access; 1994 opening times undecided as we went to press – it's usually open every day in Aug, but best to check on (0604) 770209; £4.50. On the edge of the estate there's public access to a sandy-floored area of pine woods and heathland known as Harlestone Firs SP7164, pleasant for walking. The village itself is charming, and the graveyard of the attractive CHURCH on the edge of the park has fine views. The Fox & Hounds here is a good pub, as is the Saracens Head in nearby Little Brington (which at least in summer does teas too).

Kettering SP8678 WICKSTEED PARK Big amusement park created in the 1920s; as then it has swings and slides, but these have been joined by more modern sophisticated rides. There are still train and steamer rides, also canoeing etc; meals, snacks, shop, disabled access; cl Oct-Easter. ALFRED EAST GALLERY National, regional and local art, craft and photography; shop, disabled access; cl Sun and bank hols.

Lamport SP7574 LAMPORT HALL Mainly 17th- and 18th-c house in spacious park, with tranquil gardens containing a remarkable alpine rockery – apparently the home of the first garden gnomes. Fine collections of art and furnishings, and frequent antique fairs; snacks, shop, disabled access to ground floor only; open pm Sun and bank hols Easter-Oct, and Thurs in July and Aug; *£2.80. In outbuildings local enthusiasts keep a collection of ancient tractors and agricultural bygones; similar opening hours, no extra charge. The Canadian-run Swan is useful for lunch.

! **Naseby** SP6878 The owner of Purlieu Farm has set out a model of the BATTLE OF NASEBY battle lines, using many hundreds of model soldiers, with a 10-minute commentary, also some battlefield relics. The site also has recreated period rooms, vintage farm machinery and tools, village history, and a spacious picnic area; open pm bank hol Sun and Mon Easter-Sept; £1. One BATTLE MONUMENT (Sibbertoft Rd) marks the position of Cromwell's New Model Army before his devastating counter-attack; there's another on the B4036 towards Clipston. The Fitzgerald Arms is useful for lunch.

Northampton SP7560 Daniel Defoe would no longer describe this prosperous shoemaking town as one of the most handsome in the country, but there are a few interesting buildings about. There are several fine CHURCHES, most notably the 12th-c Holy Sepulchre (one of only four remaining round churches in the country), the very grand central All Saints, and the ornate Norman St Peters in Marefair right by the dual carriageway. The Welsh House (now a china shop) and Hazelrigg House are also very handsome. The first place to see to get on the right footing must be the CENTRAL MUSEUM, which houses the famous Boot and Shoe collection, with features as diverse as an elephant's boot, Margot Fonteyn's ballet shoes, Roman sandals and Queen Victoria's wedding slippers. The nearby MUSEUM OF LEATHERCRAFT is also quite interesting; shop. The Newt & Cucumber (College St) does quick good-value food, but has been shut on Sun.

Oundle TL0487 is a charming and elegant stone-built town with a graceful church and several antique shops; the Ship is useful for lunch, as is the waterside Mill just outside the town nr BARNWELL COUNTRY PARK, with meadows, woodland and reedy corners around former gravel workings that have now been landscaped as lake.

Rockingham SP8691 ROCKINGHAM CASTLE was built on the orders of William I on a hill with fine views. The site of the original keep is now a rose garden, but the outline of the two baileys, the drum towers and part of the Norman curtain wall still remain, and the later Elizabethan building has a good range of art and furnishings. A very attractive place to visit. Teas, snacks, shop, disabled access; open Sun, Thurs, bank hols and Tues after bank hols Easter-Sept, as well as Tues in Aug; £3.50. The Sondes Arms in the village, also pretty despite the main road, is good for lunch, and has super views.

Stoke Bruerne SP7449 CANAL MUSEUM Close to a flight of locks on the Grand Union Canal, with fine old canal buildings (inc a useful pub, the Boat), and lots happening on the water, this is a handsome former corn warehouse housing a collection of canal memorabilia from over two centuries. There's a reconstructed traditional narrow boat complete with immaculately packed-in colourful furniture and crockery, as well as other working boats, interesting displays and trips through nearby tunnel. Shop, limited disabled access; cl winter Mon, 25-26 Dec; £2.30. Good towpath walks from here.

Sulgrave SP5544 SULGRAVE MANOR George Washington's family lived here until his grandfather emigrated to America, and there are several relics of the first president, as well as interesting furnishings, elegant period rooms and well-kept gardens. Lots of special events inc cavalry demonstrations and several jolly 'Living History' exhibitions, when for nine days the Manor is run exactly as it was in a particular era; snacks, shop; cl 1-2 pm, Weds, 25-26 Dec, Jan, Feb (exc by appointment), tel (029576) 205; £3. The Star is useful for lunch.

Weedon Bec SP6046 OLD DAIRY FARM CRAFT CENTRE has sheep, pigs, peacocks, ducks and donkeys, as well as craft workshops, antiques, farm shop, wool collection and Liberty materials; meals, snacks, shop, disabled access; cl 25 Dec, 3 Jan.

The county is notable for its lovely stone-built churches, many with elegant spires visible a long way off and a memorable feature of the county's landscape – particularly along the valley of the River Nene. A shortlist of these might include Ashby St Ledgers SP5768, Brixworth SP7470 (a particularly fine Anglo-Saxon church, mostly 7th-c with much reused Roman material), Burton Latimer SP9075, Croughton SP5433 (14th- and 15th-c murals), Denford SP9976 (for its nature-reserve churchyard by the River Nene), Dodford SP6160 (striking memorials), Earls Barton SP8563 (fine Saxon tower), Easton Maudit SP8858, Fawsley SP5556 (above Capability Brown's lakes), Great Weldon SP9289, Higham Ferrers SP9669, Kings Sutton SP4936, Lowick SP9780, Middleton Cheney SP4941, Passenham SP7739 (17th-c murals), Raunds SP9972, Rothwell SP8181 and Whiston SP8460. With many of these, the village is well worth seeing, too.

The **best views** in the region are from Borough Hill SP5862 above the golf course; an Iron-Age hill fort shares the top with a formidable array of television and telecommunications masts, but on a clear day the views are tremendous.

The county's enterprise agency runs a very full programme of guided **factory visits**, most free, covering all sorts of local manufacturing and service industries from the big shoe companies and places like Carlsberg or Barclaycard to helicopter makers, narrow-boat builders and blacksmiths. For a copy of their 1994 timetable (not fixed as we go to press) tel (0604) 671400 and ask for their 'Tours of the Unexpected' brochure.

Other attractive villages, all with decent pubs, include Ashton TL0588, Denton SP8358, Duddington SK9800, Geddington SP8963, Great Houghton SP7958, Grendon SP8760, Hellidon SP5158, Kilsby SP5671, Sudborough SP9682, Thorpe Mandeville SP5344, Wadenhoe TL0383 and Welford SP6480. Towcester SP6948 is a town not village (and pronounced Toaster not Towcester), but despite some light industry on the edge has regained something of a pleasantly villagey feel since its bypass, and has some attractive Georgian and Victorian building.

Walks

Gorgeous orange-coloured stone adds to the charm of buildings around Badby SP5658, where the well-waymarked **Knightley Way** takes a pleasant 12-mile course to Greens Norton SP6649. The finest part is between Badby Wood SP5658 and Fawsley Park SP5657, where the path drops to landscaped lakes by the hall and estate church. The bluebells in May in Badby Wood are lovely; though there's no right of way there is public access, and the Windmill and Maltsters Arms at Badby are both good for lunch.

Rockingham Forest SP9490 has enough country houses scattered around it to spice interest, and grey-stone cottages are a local feature. Other places for walks include the **Grand Union Canal**; Stoke Bruerne SP7450, with its waterside pub and waterways museum, is a popular jumping-off point, and other pubs handy for the towpath are the Royal Oak at Blisworth SP7253, Admiral Nelson at Braunston SP5466, New Inn at Buckby Wharf SP6065, Navigation at Thrupp Wharf near Cosgrove SP7942, Narrow Boat at Weedon SP6046 and Wharf in Welford SP6480. **Salcey Forest** SP8052 is a couple of miles of ancient forest, largely oak, now managed for nature conservation, with well-marked trails including one good for wheelchairs. **Kinewell Lake** SP9875 is a well-managed local nature reserve around former gravel-pit lakes by the River Nene.

Driving

Just E of Northampton, there's a pleasant drive around the northern edge of the Castle Ashby estates, through Cogenhoe, Whiston, Grendon and Easton Maudit.

Further N, the B4036 from off the A5 near Watford Gap through West Haddon, Naseby and Clipston to Market Harborough just over the Leics border gives a good feel of the quieter parts of the county. Up in the NE corner of the county pleasant back roads track through the Forest of Rockingham; though there are considerable stretches of woodland dotted about, this former hunting forest is now mostly farmland, with attractive stone villages.

The A5, relieved of much of its traffic by the M1 at least when that motorway is behaving itself, is a good road, swooping and gliding along the track of the old Roman Watling Street; the bit between the southern county boundary and Weedon is best.

Where to eat

Horton SP8254 FRENCH PARTRIDGE (0604) 870033 Lovely little evening restaurant run by the Partridges for nearly 30 years with consistently excellent food, a relaxed atmosphere, and fine wines; cl Sun, Mon, 2 wks around Christmas, 2 wks Easter, 3 wks mid-July/Aug; disabled access. **£28 for 4 courses.**
Fotheringhay TL0593 FALCON (08326) 254 Comfortable pub near interesting church and site of Fotheringhay Castle, neat garden, and very good, interesting bar food. **£18.90**|£3.15/£9.45.

Roade SP7551 ROADHOUSE 16 High St (0604) 863372 Very good food in attractive and comfortable popular restaurant; good wine list; cl Sat am, Sun pm, Mon, 26 Dec-5 Jan. **£15.75/£26.25.**

Help this year from: *John Wooll, B M Eldridge, David Brokensha, Peter Lloyd, CW, JW, Martin and Sarah Crossley, Mrs D J Restall, H M C Quick, Mrs B J Reynolds, Joan and Michel Hooper-Immins, George Atkinson, Mr and Mrs N A Spink, Graham and Belinda Staplehurst, Jill and Peter Bickley, Hazel Morgan, K H Frostick, Graham Reeve, Dorothy and David Young, Sir Nigel Foulkes, J D Rundle, D Stokes, Brian Jones, Dave and Jules Tuckett, R A Gabriel, H D Spottiswoode, Brian and Anna Marsden, Olive Carroll, I R Hewitt, Chris Raisin, Ian Phillips, Patrick Godfrey, Basil Minson, Graham Bush, Karen Simpson, Paul Williams, W A Wheeler, John Whitehead, David and Sheila, John Radford, J Barnwell, D C Eastwood, Stephen and Julie Brown, Tony Walker, Ann Griffiths, G T O'Connell, H R Bevan, Mr and Mrs R Wallis.*

THE MIDLANDS CALENDAR

Some of these dates were provisional as we went to press.

JANUARY

19th **Birmingham** Antiques and Fine Arts Fair *at the National Exhibition Centre (NEC) – till Sun 23*

23rd **Birmingham** Furniture and Lighting Show *at the NEC – till Weds 26*

FEBRUARY

5th **Sulgrave** Chamber Concert *at Sulgrave Manor*

6th **Birmingham** International Spring Fair *at the NEC – till Thurs 10*

15th **Atherstone** Shrovetide Football, *originating in the reign of King John as a Warwickshire/Leicestershire contest for a bag of gold; shop windows are boarded up, traffic diverted and a specially made large ball 'thrown out' by a celebrity*

MARCH

3rd **Birmingham** Innovation and Inventions Fair (contemporary) *at the NEC – till Sun 6*

5th **Sulgrave** Chamber Concert *at Sulgrave Manor*

10th **Birmingham** Crufts Dog Show *at the NEC*

18th **Sulgrave** Music Weekend *at Sulgrave Manor – till Sun 20*

The Midlands Calendar

April

2nd **Sulgrave** Chamber Concert *at Sulgrave Manor*

7th **Birmingham** Antiques Fair *at the NEC – till Weds 13*

15th **Stoneleigh** Heart of England Craft Market *at Stoneleigh Park – till Sun 17*

16th **Sulgrave** Living History 1643, *Sulgrave Manor run as it was a year after the Battle of Edgehill – till Sun 24*

23rd **Stratford-upon-Avon** Shakespeare Birthday Celebrations

29th **Birmingham** Home Show *at the NEC – till 2 May*

30th **Birmingham** BBC Top Gear Classic and Sports Car Show *at the NEC – till 2 May*

May

8th **Moulton** College Open Day, *milking, livestock and farm machinery displays*

15th **Sulgrave** Herb Fair *at Sulgrave Manor*

19th **Edgbaston** One Day International, England v NZ; **Stoneleigh** Midlands Woodworking Exhibition *at Stoneleigh Park – till Sat 21*

21st **Sulgrave** Needlework Festival *at Sulgrave Manor – till 5 Jun*

23rd **Corby** Pole Fair, *commemorating 1585 charter grant: celebrations start with sunrise charter reading, end with sunset toll gates closing and firework display; ox roasting, climbing a greasy pole for a side of bacon, carnival and dancing*

28th **Braunston** Boat Show *– till Mon 30*; **Rothwell** Rowell Charter Fair – till 4 Jun; **Stamford** Rainbow Craft Fair *at Burghley House – till Mon 30*

29th **Lamport** Country Festival *at Lamport Hall – till Mon 30*

June

1st **Birmingham** BBC Gardeners' World Live Broadcast *at the NEC – till Sun 5*

8th **Stoneleigh** Landscape Industries Exhibition *at Stoneleigh Park – till Thurs 9*

11th **Wellingborough** Festival *– till Sun 26*

18th **Stratford** Regatta

24th **Rushden** Festival *– till 3 July*

25th **Ryton** Organic Gardening Weekend *at Ryton Organic Gardens – till Sun 26*; **Thrapston** Charter Fair, *High St closed for the afternoon and filled with games and street performers*; **Warwick** Carnival

26th **Sulgrave** Farmyard Fair, *with rare breeds, at Sulgrave Manor*

July

2nd **Hollowell** Steam and Heavy Horse Show *– till Sun 3*; **Sulgrave** Living History 1746, *Georgian times at Sulgrave Manor – till Sun 10*; **Warwick** Midlands Art Festival *– till Sat 16*; **Wellingborough** Carnival *– till Sun 3*

The Midlands Calendar

July cont.

4th **Stoneleigh** Royal Agricultural Show *at Stoneleigh Park – till Thurs 7*

8th **Ryton** National Organic Food and Wine Fair *at Ryton Organic Gardens – till Sat 9*

9th **Kenilworth** Carnival; **Leamington** Carnival

10th **Silverstone** British Formula One Grand Prix

16th **Stratford-upon-Avon** Festival *– till Sun 31*

22nd **Sulgrave** Outdoor Theatre Productions *at Sulgrave Manor – till Sun 24*

23rd **Silverstone** Historic Racing Car Festival *– till Sun 24*

29th **Northampton** Town Show *family events, evening concerts and fireworks at the NEC – till Sun 31*

August

4th **Birmingham** Antiques Fair *at the NEC– till Sun 7*

5th **Warwick** Folk Festival *– till Sat 6*

6th **Ryton** Organic Gardening Weekend *at Ryton Organic Gardens – till Sun 7*

25th **Edgbaston** One Day International, England v South Africa

27th **Dudley** Canal Festival *– till Mon 29*; **Stoneleigh** Town and Country Festival *at Stoneleigh Park – till Mon 29*; **Sulgrave** Re-enactment of the 1644 Civil War Siege of Sulgrave Manor *– till Mon 29*

September

3rd **Stratford-upon-Avon** Shakespeare Run *at Coombe Abbey Countryside Park; over 350 vintage vehicles, food and entertainment – till Sun 4*

11th **Birmingham** Garden and Leisure Equipment Exhibition *at the NEC – till Tues 13*

October

1st **Sulgrave** Chamber Concert *at Sulgrave Manor*

8th **Sulgrave** Tudor Living History *at Sulgrave Manor – till Sun 16*

11th **Stratford-upon-Avon** Mop Fair *est over 600 years ago, once the main hiring fair for people seeking work in the district – till Weds 12*

15th **Warwick** Mop Fair

17th **Southam** Mop Fair

22nd **Birmingham** International Motor Show and Ideal Homes Show *at the NEC – till Sun 30*; **Ryton** Apple Weekend *at Ryton Organic Gardens – till Sun 23*; **Sulgrave** Apple Days *at Sulgrave Manor – till Sun 23*; **Warwick** Runaway Mop Fair *originally held so that unhappy servants hired at the mop fair could run away and be rehired without having to wait a year for the next fair*

25th **Stratford-upon-Avon** Runaway Mop Fair *– till Weds 26*

The Midlands Calendar

November

3rd **Stoneleigh** British Equine Event *at Stoneleigh Park – till Sat 5*

5th **Kenilworth** Bonfire *at Kenilworth Castle*; **Sulgrave** Chamber Concert and Fireworks *at Sulgrave Manor*

10th **Birmingham** Craft and Hobby Fair *at the NEC – till Sun 13*

11th **Ryton-on-Dunsmore** Wroth Silver Ceremony; *one of the oldest ceremonies in Britain, in which villagers gather to pay their dues to the Duke of Buccleuchs' representative, either in lieu of military service or to ensure rights of cattle-way from one village to another; followed by distribution of rum and milk and 'churchwarden' pipes at a local inn*

24th **Birmingham** BBC Good Food Cooking and Kitchen Show *at the NEC – till Sun 27*

December

1st **Birmingham** Clothes Show Live Event *at the NEC – till Tues 6*; **Warwick** Victorian Street Fair

2nd **Birmingham** Classic Motor Show *at the NEC – till Sun 4*

3rd **Sulgrave** Chamber Concert *at Sulgrave Manor*

Norfolk

The north part of the county has a great deal of appeal – especially for people who want to get away from it all. It certainly has a decided character of its own, for while there are traditional seaside resorts which pull the summer crowds, much of the coast is largely unspoilt, and one of the best places in England for bird-watchers. The hinterland has the feel of being undiscovered territory for visitors, yet there are interesting places to see within easy reach.

There is a wider choice of places to visit and things to do in the southern part of the county, though this has a rather less individual feel. The Norfolk Broads are a magnet for boating people and for land-based people do add interest to the countryside. The flat coast is largely given over to family beach resorts.

Norwich itself is an attraction for many, and can well support a weekend visit; it never seems visibly a 'tourist city', which is a big plus.

There's a good choice of places to stay here, covering a wide range of styles and prices – and no shortage of decent places to eat out in. Early spring, when the snowdrops are out, is a pleasant time for driving through the county; they crowd under many of the roadside hedges – and of course the more touristy parts of the county are virtually unvisited then.

North Norfolk

A largely unspoilt area of distinctive character, with places of interest for all ages and expansive coastal scenery.

This corner of Norfolk has a quite distinct character, with a real sense of style about even the simplest buildings, a coast that's full of fascination for bird-watchers, and a splendidly broad canvas of sea, saltings and sky for the rest of us.

Sandringham itself is a big draw. A varied roster of other places to visit is headed by three grander mansions – Holkham Hall, Houghton Hall and Felbrigg Hall – the castle at Castle Rising, the lavender gardens at Heacham, the Anglo-Catholic pilgrimage centre of Little Walsingham, the longest really narrow-gauge railway in Britain running from Wells next the Sea and another steam railway running from Sheringham (which has handsome parkland), and the splendid collection of steam organs and steam engines at Thursford Green. The shire horse centre at West Runton and open farm at Snettisham are fun, and Hunstanton and Cromer are civilised seaside resorts with a good deal of individuality.

We can recommend quite a good choice of reasonably priced hotels and inns to stay in here, and cooking in the area is above average, but we are still looking for the charming farm and country-house B & Bs which we feel sure must exist here – do please let us know if you've tracked one down!

The line we draw between here and the rest of Norfolk is the A148 to Cromer.

Where to stay

Blakeney TG0243 BLAKENEY HOTEL Holt NR25 7NE (0263) 740797 **£108**; 60 very comfortable rms, many with views over the salt marshes and some with own little terrace. Overlooking the harbour with fine views, this friendly hotel has appealing public rooms, good food, very pleasant staff, indoor swimming pool, saunas, spa bath, billiard room, and garden; good disabled access.

Grimston TF7222 CONGHAM HALL King's Lynn PE32 1AH (0485) 600250 ***£97**; 14 individually decorated rms. Warmly welcoming and handsome Georgian manor in 40 acres of grounds that include herb, vegetable and flower gardens (herbs for sale and garden open to public), paddock, orchards, and cricket pitch, fine day rooms, and a pretty orangery restaurant with excellent modern cooking; children over 12.

Great Snoring TF9434 OLD RECTORY Fakenham NR21 0HP (0328) 820597 ***£87.50**; 6 comfortable rms. Wonderfully tranquil Elizabethan hotel with church next door; lovely walled gardens, fresh flowers in the homely lounge, good food in beamed dining room with its stone mullioned windows, fine breakfasts, and courteous service; cl 24-27 Dec; children over 12.

Titchwell TF7543 MANOR HOTEL King's Lynn PE31 8BB (0485) 210221 **£76**; 15 rms. Smart but relaxed and comfortable hotel handy for RSPB reserve, pleasant views down to beach; ornithologist chef does good bar and restaurant food (esp local seafood), summer buffets.

Wells next the Sea TF9143 CROWN The Buttlands NR23 1EX (0328) 710209 ***£65**; 15 rms, most with own bthrm. Handsome 16th-c coaching inn in attractive square overlooking a village green with bustling front bar, friendly staff, and good, popular food in bar and restaurant.

Thornham TF7343 LIFEBOAT Hunstanton PE36 6LT (048 526) 236 – probably changing to (0485) 512236 **£65**; 13 rms, most with sea view. Well placed on the edge of coastal flats with very cosy atmosphere – especially in winter, when there are five fires and antique paraffin lamps; good bar and restaurant food; disabled access.

Burnham Market TF8342 HOSTE ARMS The Green King's Lynn PE31 8HD (0328) 738257 **£64**; 13 comfortable rms. Sited on the green of a lovely Georgian village; attractive bars, some interesting period features, good food, and friendly staff; disabled access.

King's Lynn TF6220 TUDOR ROSE St Nicholas St PE30 1LR (0553) 762824 ***£50**; 14 rms. Attractive half-timbered 15th-c inn with interesting medieval door, friendly and chatty atmosphere, decent food in bar and no-smoking raftered restaurant, and good breakfasts.

Dersingham TF6830 FEATHERS Manor Rd PE31 6LN (0485) 540207 **£40**; 5 well-furnished, comfortable rms. Solidly handsome Jacobean sandstone inn with relaxed and comfortably modernised dark-panelled bars opening on to attractive garden with play area; reasonably priced bar food, restaurant (not Sun pm), and pleasant service.

Hillington TF7225 FFOLKES ARMS King's Lynn PE31 6BJ (0485) 600210 *£35; 20 very good rms. Large, comfortable inn with good choice of food inc carvery, wide range of real ales, and country club; cl 25-26 Dec, disabled access.

To see and do

Brancaster/Scolt Head TF8045 Miles of these dunes, flat coastal saltings, broad tidal beaches and Scolt Head Island are owned by the National Trust: a fine lonely place, full of birds – the island is an important breeding ground, particularly for terns, and in good weather a boat takes people across from Brancaster Staithe. The Ship is useful for lunch.

Burnham Thorpe TF8441 has strong Lord Nelson connections, inc the pub named after him where he had several celebration dinners, and which is now richly decorated with really interesting Nelson memorabilia, though not losing sight of its unpretentious village character. The lectern in the village church uses wood from HMS *Victory*, and the church has other Nelson mementoes.

Castle Rising TF6624 CASTLE RISING CASTLE Massive earthworks surround this fine Norman keep, probably built by the Earl of Arundel, who married Henry I's widow, and now owned by the Duke of Norfolk. It's a marvellous setting for the summer jousting they stage here; snacks, shop; cl winter Mon, 25-26 Dec, 1 Jan; *£1.80. The Black Horse is a useful dining pub.

Cockthorpe TF9842 COCKTHORPE HALL TOY MUSEUM Comprehensive (and growing) collection of toys from 1860 onwards, with trains, dolls, teddies and, more unusually, Victorian magic lanterns; snacks, shop; cl winter exc pm wknds; *£2.

Cromer TG2242 Popular seaside resort since Victorian times, with lovely sandy beaches, more sun than average, bustling markets, golf courses, interesting shops and galleries and lots of entertainments. The pier is one of the last in the country to present an end-of-pier show – very popular, so worth booking early. The tower of the imposing CHURCH gives spectacular views of the surrounding countryside. By the church, the CROMER MUSEUM, in five 19th-c fishermen's cottages, gives a glimpse of the town's past, with pictures and exhibits from the Victorian period and displays exploring the local natural history, archaeology, social history and geology; shop; cl Mon 1-2 pm and Sun am, Good Fri, 23-26 Dec, 1 Jan; *£1. On the prom another aspect of the town's relationship with the sea can be seen in the LIFEBOAT MUSEUM. It presents the history of the RNLI in general and the history of the local lifeboat from 1804, when the first was stationed at the end of the pier. Exhibits include the many medals won by the famous local lifeboatman Henry Blogg, and the lifeboat *H F Bailer* which was in service from 1935 to 1945; shop, disabled access; cl Oct-Apr. Nearby you may find dressed crabs for sale; the crab boats still work from here, and Cromer crabs are the best on England's E coast. The Bath House on the Promenade and Red Lion in Tucker St are useful for lunch.

Felbrigg TG2039 FELBRIGG HALL Just 3 miles from Cromer, a magnificent 17th-c house in splendid grounds, inc an orangery with a wonderful collection of camellias and a colourfully restored walled garden overlooked by a dovecot that in its day held 2,000 birds. The house itself is decorated with paintings and

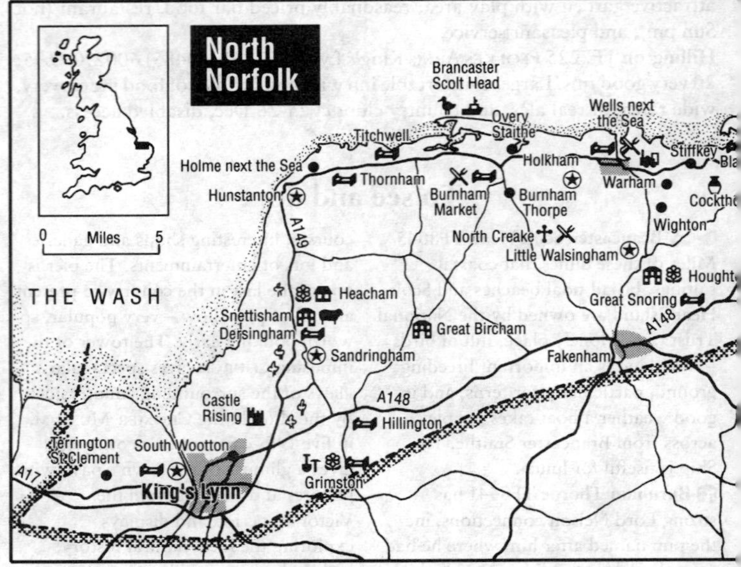

furnishings from the 18th c, and inc a wonderful library; meals, snacks, shop, disabled access; cl Tues and Fri, Nov-26 Mar, hall also cl am, grounds cl 25 Dec only; £4.30, garden £1.70. There's public access to the woods and lake.

Glandford TG0441 SHELL MUSEUM Curious little museum housing the sea shells and other interesting objects collected by Sir Alfred Jodrell, who lived in nearby Bayfield Hall; shop, disabled access; cl 12.30-2 pm Mon-Thurs, am Fri and Sat, and all day Sun, and Nov-Feb exc am Mon-Thurs in Nov and Feb; *50p.

Great Bircham TF7732 WINDMILL Not far from Houghton Hall, this great mill, the most striking in the county, is set atop a windy hill ensuring glorious views of the surrounding country. A well-explained account of the milling process and even bread baked at the mill's own bakery; snacks, shop, disabled access; cl Oct-Easter, tearooms and bakery also cl Sat; £2. The Kings Head Hotel is good for lunch.

Grimston TF7222 The HERB GARDEN of Congham Hall Hotel (see Where to stay, above) has 200-300 different herbs, in traditional layouts, with many unusual varieties for sale; open 2-4 pm, cl Sat and Oct-Mar. Besides the hotel itself, the Jolly Farmers is good for lunch.

Heacham TF6737 NORFOLK LAVENDER There are rose gardens and herb gardens here, but the focus is on the growing of lavender – it's the largest lavender-growing and distilling operation in the country. They also hold the National Collection of lavender species and cultivars; one place where the guided tour really adds interest. Snacks, shop, disabled access; cl 23 Dec-16 Jan.

Holkham TF8944 HOLKHAM HALL Splendid Palladian mansion set in delightful and very extensive tree-filled grounds with an ornamental lake and 18th-c walled garden. Very impressive state rooms inside, sumptuously furnished; among the many fine paintings are notable ones by Claude, Rubens, Van Dyck

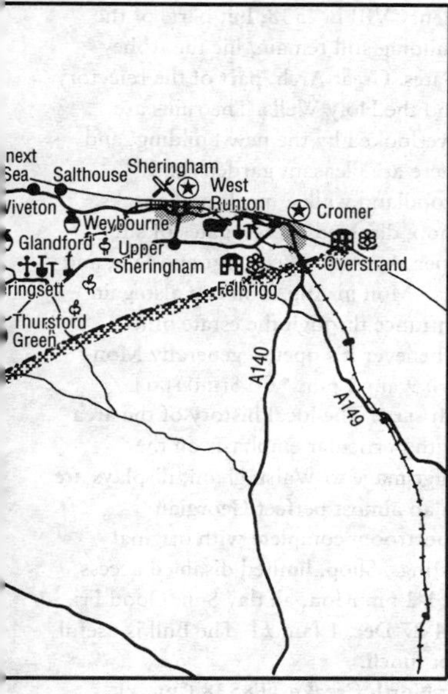

and Gainsborough. An ancestor of the present owner was Thomas Coke, whose revolutionary farming techniques are described in a new farming exhibition in the porter's lodge; also Holkham Pottery and a collection of agricultural and rural craft tools. Meals and snacks, shop, disabled access; cl am, all day Fri and Sat, Oct-Easter; £4.70 for everything, £2.70 hall only. The Victoria Hotel is good for lunch. The beach has a BIRD RESERVE, though spotters may get more twitchy than usual if they stray on to the adjacent nudist beach.

Houghton TF9235 HOUGHTON HALL Set in charming parkland, a Palladian mansion with state rooms decorated and furnished by William Kent. It was built for Sir Robert Walpole, and now houses an important collection of 20,000 model soldiers and other militaria. The stables have heavy horses, Shetland ponies and llamas; snacks, shop, disabled access; open pm Thurs, Sun and bank hols Easter-Sept; £4, grounds only £2.

Hunstanton TF6740 is a clean, fresh and well-kept resort with gently shelving tidal sands (donkey rides still), summer boat trips, pleasant dune walks past the golf course up to the BIRD RESERVE on Gore Point, and a hi-tech KINGDOM OF THE SEA. This puts you face to face with deep-water creatures as well as octopuses and toothy conger eels. There's also a seal hospital with pools of sick or injured animals; meals, snacks, shop, disabled access; cl 25-26 Dec; £3.99. There are also the more conventional resort entertainments, such as OASIS, a giant leisure park with tropically heated indoor and outdoor pools with both towering and toddler aquaslides, all sorts of games equipment for adults and children, and a tropical lagoon sun lounge; meals and snacks, shop; cl Dec-Feb; £2.80. The low cliffs around the town are quite colourful, with different rock strata. The Ancient Mariner, part of the Le Strange Arms Hotel in Old Hunstanton, is worth knowing for lunch.

King's Lynn TF6220 was once the fourth largest town in England; it is quieter now, with pleasant corners, some attractive Georgian brick buildings and a few much older places such as the 17th-c Custom House on the quay by the River Purfleet, the 15th-c CHURCH of St Nicholas, the South Gates, Red Mount Chapel and the two medieval Guildhalls. The handsome Trinity Guildhall is not open to the public, but the 14th-c King John Cup and other fabulous examples of civic paraphernalia housed in its Undercroft are included in the tour of the OLD GAOL HOUSE, a lively new journey through the town's rich history. Spirited models, and spooky sights, sounds and smells, particularly good for children; shop, disabled access; cl Weds and Thurs from Nov-spring bank hol; *£2. TRUES YARD These restored old fishermen's cottages are all that remains of the town's fishing community, the North End. The rooms give a good picture of what life was like living here in the last century, when families of up to 11 were often squeezed in the two little rooms, and there are displays of related relics; snacks, shop, disabled access; *£1.80. The newish TOWN HOUSE MUSEUM concentrates on the social history of the city from medieval times to the present, with room reconstructions and costumes and toys; shop, disabled access to ground floor only; cl Mon and Sun (exc pm May-Sept); *£1. LYNN MUSEUM has plenty of local history to draw on, going back to Bronze-Age weapons and the skeleton of a Saxon warrior; its collection of medieval pilgrim badges is surprisingly interesting, also natural history and geology; shop, disabled access; cl Sun, bank hols, 25-26 Dec, 1 Jan; *60p. The first of these, the 15th-c ST GEORGE'S GUILDHALL, is now the town's theatre, and home of the King's Lynn Festival; among the stories of its past uses is the tale that Shakespeare himself performed here; meals and snacks, shop, disabled access to galleries; cl Sat 12.30-2 pm and Sun, Good Fri, 25-26 Dec, 1 Jan and bank hols. The Tuesday Market in the main market place has some good crafts stalls. The Tudor Rose between there and St Nicholas is good for lunch, and in the market place the Maydens Heade is useful for food, as are the Lord Kelvin opposite the bus station and the Wildfowler on the Gayton rd.

✝ 🏛 **Letheringsett** TG0538 has a CHURCH with an unusual round tower, and a restored water-powered WATERMILL in a pretty setting, still milling flour from local wheat; cl 1-2 pm, all day Mon, Sat pm, Sun exc pm Whit-Sept, demonstrations are usually on Tues, Weds, Thurs and Sun pm; £2 when they're demonstrating, otherwise £1. The Kings Head is an attractive place for lunch.

✝ 🌳 🍵 **Little Walsingham** TF9336 WALSINGHAM ABBEY GROUNDS The original 12th-c priory was destroyed by Henry VIII in 1538, but parts of the building still remain, inc the Abbey Gates, Great Arch, part of the refectory and the Holy Wells. The ruins are overlooked by the new building, and there are pleasant gardens and woodland walks; meals and snacks, shop, disabled access; gates of site open Apr-Sept Weds, Sat and Sun, and also Mon in Aug. You can also gain entrance through the estate office whenever it's open – generally Mon-Fri, 9 am-5 pm; *£1. SHIREHALL MUSEUM The local history of the area with particular emphasis on the pilgrimage to Walsingham; displays are in an almost perfect Georgian courtroom complete with original fittings. Shop, limited disabled access; cl 1-2 pm Mon, all day Sun, Good Fri, 24-27 Dec, 1 Jan; £1. The Bull is useful for lunch.

✝ **North Creake** TF8538 CREAKE ABBEY This Augustinian priory was founded in 1206; now all that remains is the crossing and east arm, but it's still worth a passing look if you're here for the good food at the very traditional Jolly Farmers (see Where to eat below).

❀ 🏛 **Overstrand** TG2440 PLESAUNCE These gardens, laid out by Gertrude Jekyll, are currently being restored. You can also see a couple of rooms in the house designed by Lutyens, and admission includes cream tea; open pm Mon, Weds and Thurs May-Oct. Good beach walks nearby.

🏛 ✝ ❀ 🍵 🍎 🚂 **Sandringham** TF6928 For many people a main reason for coming to this part of Norfolk is its connection with the Royal Family. SANDRINGHAM HOUSE was bought by Queen Victoria for her son Edward in 1862 and has become the famous Royal Christmas residence; by permission of Her Majesty the Queen the 19th-c building, filled with their portraits and those of their European counterparts, is open to visitors. The parish CHURCH OF ST MARY MAGDALENE, as well as being full of treasures of its own, has a cross set into the chancel floor where the coffins of George V and VI rested before being transported to Windsor. The grounds are lovely; meals and snacks, shop, disabled access; open Easter Sun-Sun 3 Oct, exc during Royal visit 19 July-7 Aug; *£3. In summer pick-your-own lets you sample fruit that might otherwise have graced the Royal table – so a real case of food fit for a queen. On the journey to the house, the Royal Family often used the small building at WOLFERTON STATION to rest. Many of the original late 19th-c fittings survive, as well as period posters and Royal train furniture, letters and photos; snacks, shop, disabled access but no special facilities; cl am wknds, all Oct-Easter; £1.85. The Feathers on the Sandringham road out of Dersingham is useful for lunch.

Sheringham TG1443 still has a working fishing harbour, with some old buildings around it, though there's a lot of more modern building up behind. NORTH NORFOLK RAILWAY Full-size steam railway, chugging through five miles of lovely coastal scenery, with a museum of railway memorabilia at the station, and a collection of steam engines and vintage rolling stock such as Pullman carriages and ex-Great Eastern Railway engines; meals and snacks, shop, disabled access; steam train operates Mar-Dec – best to tel (0263) 825449 for dates and times; *£5 full return journey. The extensive parkland of SHERINGHAM PARK, gloriously landscaped by Humphrey Repton, gives excellent coastal views from viewing towers to let you see beyond the mature trees and fine rhododendrons (best late May/ June), with good walks to the coast; disabled access; free, but parking £2.20, NT. The Two Lifeboats and the Crown are useful for lunch. The 14th-c CHURCH in nearby Upper Sheringham is very attractive, and the Red Lion there is good for lunch.

Snettisham TF6834 PARK FARM Working farm offering a good insight into seasonal farming operations – lambing, shearing, and red deer calving. All the usual animals can be seen in a traditional farming environment, and there's also an adventure playground, indoor adventure area, craft centre and mini golf; snacks, shop, disabled access; cl Nov-20 Mar (exc shop and craft centre, open all year); *£3, and £3 for a 45-min guided ride around the deer park. There's also a restored working WATERMILL with pretty walks nearby (open Thurs pm July-mid-Sept; £1) and the Rose & Crown is good for lunch.

Terrington St Clement TF5419 AFRICAN VIOLET CENTRE This has a good range of plants besides the African violets it's developed so successfully as house plants.

Thursford Green TF9833 THURSFORD COLLECTION A rather jolly collection of organs – the musical kind, whether barrel, street or fairground. These are demonstrated every day, as is the Wurlitzer cinema organ, which also stars in Tues evening concerts in summer. As well as the organs there are showmen's steam engines, ploughing engines and a 2-ft gauge steam railway, and, for those seeking greater thrills, an adventure playground and Venetian Gondola switchback ride; snacks, shop, disabled access; cl am exc in summer, all Nov-Mar and bank hols; £4.20. The Crawfish is useful for lunch.

Wells next the Sea TF9143 WELLS & WALSINGHAM LIGHT RAILWAY Passing through delightful countryside, this railway is remarkable for being the longest track in Britain to use a 10¼-inch gauge track, with a steam locomotive built specially for it a few years ago; meals and snacks, shop; cl Oct-Easter; £3.50 return. The little village-sized town is a pleasant, quite gracious place, and the Crown is good for lunch.

West Runton TG1842 NORFOLK SHIRE HORSE CENTRE Extensive

collection of draught horses and moorland and mountain ponies (they have nine breeds). There's also an interesting range of horse-drawn machinery to show how to harness the animals and how they are used to work, and a museum of rural equipment. There's always something going on, with daily demonstrations and events such as sheepdog displays; meals and snacks, shop, disabled access; cl Sat all day; *£3.50. You can hire riding horses by the hour from West Runton Riding Stables throughout the year. The seaside village itself is attractive, and the Village Inn is useful for lunch.

Weybourne TG1042 MUCKLEBURGH COLLECTION World War II fighting vehicles and other matériel on the site of a former military camp, once the lynch pin of defences on this coast; tanks, trucks, guns, missiles and bombs from all over the world, right up to the Gulf War, with other local history items, model ships, and meals and snacks served in a NAAFI-style café; shop, disabled access; cl Nov-Easter; *£3.

This stretch of coast is particularly good for BIRD-WATCHING. We mention a few reserves elsewhere but other observation points that have been recommended to us include Holme next the Sea TF7043, Thornham TF7343, Titchwell TF7543 (a good RSPB reserve), and Blakeney TG0243 (which besides having a good pub, the Kings Arms, has a windmill, and boat trips out to see seals).

★ **Other attractive villages** here, all with decent pubs, include Burnham Market TF8342 (also gatehouse and 13th-c remains of Priory), Cley next the Sea TG0443 (handy for the bird-sanctuary marshes towards the Blakeney Point sandspit, and another windmill), South Wootton TF6422 and Wiveton TG0342. Decent pubs in other attractive coastal areas include the Red Lion at Stiffkey (pronounced Stukey) TF9743, Three Horseshoes at Warham TF9441, Sandpiper at Wighton TF9340 and Dun Cow at Salthouse TG0743.

Walks

Dutch-gabled buildings, flint walls, huge skies, saltmarshes and the odd windmill give the area a real sense of place and make it distinctive for walkers. The **North Norfolk Coast Path** follows the length of this coast, although not always right next to the sea. The weather is often kinder on the coast, when conditions a few miles inland can be quite different. Going over sand can be tiring, despite the lack of contours. The pearl of the coast is the section between Wells next the Sea TF9143 and Overy Staithe TF8444, where the sandy beach never quite looks the same from one day to the next; at Holkham there is a car park quite close to the beach, where pine trees meet the sands, while westwards the crowds rapidly thin out. From Overy Staithe, the path follows a zigzagging dyke – saltmarsh on one side, neat farmland on the other – to the dunes and beach. Another good stretch is Blakeney Point TG0046 which gets better as you walk along it, although the shingle bank needs patience and is hard on the ankles; pleasant dunes await at the far end. Less arduous is the dyke walk between Blakeney TG0243 and Cley next the Sea TG0443, with the birds on the mudflats for company in between.

Only **Beacon Hill** TG1841, near Cromer, rises to any height (a humble 300 ft); the coast path here detours over the sandy heath and through woodlands. Salthouse TF0743 and Kelling TG0942 back similar heathy hinterlands, where you can tie in a walk along the coast (here unvaryingly straight) as part of the same excursion.

The coastal **Holkham Hall** estate TF8842 allows walkers throughout the year on its driveways; the parkland is a bit gloomy, but impressively landscaped with a lake, a temple and an obelisk. Further west, another access point to a sandy beach is at Holme next the Sea TF7043, for a two-mile walk past a bird sanctuary and saltings to Thornham TF7343.

Most notable of the parkland walking areas is **Sandringham Country Park** TF6727, with its majestic trees and glades.

Driving

The A149 round the coast is not a quick road, except at quiet times of year, but does give the feel of the area very well indeed. The B roads are all quite good, with the roads north out of Fakenham (quite a pleasant small market town) passing through attractive villages.

Where to eat

Wells next the Sea TF9143 MOORINGS (0328) 710949 Pretty restaurant close to the harbour with locally caught seafood, good vegetarian dishes, and decent wines; cl Tues-Weds, Thurs am, 1st 2 wks Dec, 24-26 Dec, 1st 2 wks June; disabled access. £20|£9.95.

Blakeney TG0243 WHITE HORSE (0263) 740574 Good food inc fresh fish in popular bar with friendly, enthusiastic licensees, good reasonably priced wines, and attractive evening restaurant; bedrooms; disabled access (not bedrooms). **£18.50**|£1.50/£4.95.

Burnham Market TF8342 LORD NELSON (0328) 738321 Exceptional cooking by landlord, esp fish such as sea trout and mullet; popular restaurant; bedrooms; no food Tues/Sun pm except to residents; no children. **£16.50**|£3.50/£4.50.

Upper Sheringham TG1441 RED LION (0263) 825408 Simple, friendly little flint cottage with interesting bar food and Weds evening theme nights, and lots of malt whiskies. £3.10/£5.25.

Burnham Market TF8342 HOSTE ARMS Good bar food inc interesting vegetarian dishes in handsome old inn with warm-hearted bars, open fires, friendly staff and restaurant; bedrooms. £2/£5.25.

North Creake TF8538 JOLLY FARMERS Cosy and friendly little pub with chatty atmosphere, good fresh local fish, home-made puddings, and Thai food Weds and Fri evenings, buffet Weds evenings. £1.50/£4.75.

We welcome reports from readers . . .

This GUIDE depends on readers' reports. Do help us if you can – in return, we offer a discount on the next edition to people who've helped us with reports for it. Tell us what you think about places already in it, and anything extra you think we should say about them. And send us your ideas for inclusion in the next edition: places to visit, eat at or stay in, attractive drives or walks, maybe even unusual interesting shops you know of. Use the card in the middle, the report forms at the end, or just write – no stamp needed: THE GOOD WEEKEND GUIDE, FREEPOST TN1569, Wadhurst, E Sussex TN5 7BR.

South and East Norfolk

Norwich is good for a city break, and a fine choice of things to do and see elsewhere makes this area good for out-and-about weekends.

Norwich is a fine city for the visitor, very civilised, with interesting older parts and plenty to see – certainly one of Britain's dozen or so most rewarding places for a city break. Elsewhere, this part of the county has a lot to offer people who want to get out and about, visiting places of interest. Prime among these are Blickling Hall, the wildfowl centre at Welney, Bressingham Gardens and Steam Museum, Castle Acre, the extensive wooded water gardens at South Walsham, and the many animal and wildlife centres such as the South American zoo park near Thetford, the Asian one at Filby, the European one at Great Witchingham and the otter trust at Earsham.

In general the countryside isn't a major draw in this part of Norfolk. The famous Broads tend to hide away from land-based visitors unless you make a determined effort to penetrate to them. They are, of course, obviously best seen from a boat. Broads cruising is generally a week-long affair, but could be worked into a short-stay holiday, by the day or even a whole weekend. Wroxham is a popular centre for this, though one of the quieter bases in the north might make a better choice for just a day on the water.

The coast is strung with beach resorts, some large and lively (most obviously, Great Yarmouth), some relaxed and more individual. But for most people a weekend break here is more likely to concentrate on the interesting interior.

We've found some very civilised places to stay here, and there's no problem finding good food.

Where to stay

Hethersett TG1505 Park Farm Norwich NR9 3DL (0603) 810264 £70; 38 rms. Carefully extended Georgian house, now a hotel, with fine food in pretty restaurant and leisure complex with swimming pool; good disabled access.

Swaffham TF8109 Strattons Ash Close PE37 7NH (0760) 23845 £70; 7 interesting, pretty rms. Warmly welcoming, elegant Queen Anne house with delicious English food using home-grown herbs and vegetables from a family smallholding; a carefully chosen wine list illustrated with owner Mrs Scott's own watercolours, and comfortable drawing rooms with open fires and lots of china cats, dried flowers, and books; big cupboard full of toys and games for children; cl 25 Dec; dogs welcome.

Scole TM1579 Scole Inn Diss IP21 4DR (0379) 740481 *£75.50; 23 rms. Stately old coaching inn with colourful history, one of few pubs with a Grade I

The Good Weekend Guide

The Good Weekend Guide
FREEPOST TN1569
WADHURST
E. SUSSEX
TN5 7BR

Please use this card to tell us about anything which *you* think should or should not be included in the next edition of *The Good Weekend Guide*. Just fill it in and return it to us – no stamp or envelope needed. You can also use the report forms at the end of the book

ALISDAIR AIRD

YOUR NAME AND ADDRESS (BLOCK CAPITALS PLEASE)

☐ *Please tick this box if you would like extra report forms*

REPORT ON *(its name)*

Its address/location

Postcode: Telephone:

What is this? *(hotel, restaurant, garden, village, drive, walk etc)*

Description/why it appeals

REPORT ON *(its name)*

Its address/location

Postcode: Telephone:

What is this? *(hotel, restaurant, garden, village, drive, walk etc)*

Description/why it appeals

preservation listing, handsome beams and fireplace, good bar and restaurant food.

Shipdham TF9607 SHIPDHAM PLACE Thetford IP25 7LY (0362) 820303 **£65**; 8 rms. Relaxed Georgian rectory with old pine and antiques in the comfortable lounges, and good breakfasts.

Blickling TG1728 BUCKINGHAMSHIRE ARMS Norwich NR11 6NF (0263) 732133 **£50**; 3 rms. Handsome Jacobean inn in grounds of Blickling Hall, both owned by National Trust; civilised atmosphere, helpful staff, decent food in bar and restaurant (best to book), and good breakfasts.

Erpingham TG1631 SARACENS HEAD Norwich NR11 7LX (0263) 768909 ***£45**; 2 rms. Striking 19th-c brick inn, very smart and stylish; very good bar and restaurant food (wider choice in evening), and pleasant courtyard and walled garden.

Mundford TL8093 CROWN Crown St Thetford IP26 58Q (0842) 878233 **£45**; 5 good rms. Friendly small village pub, originally an ancient posting inn, rebuilt in the 18th c; attractive choice of good-value straightforward food, very welcoming staff, happy atmosphere, and well-kept real ales.

Winterton-on-Sea TG4919 FISHERMANS RETURN Great Yarmouth NR29 4BN (0493) 393305 ***£45**; 3 rms, 1 with shared bthrm. Traditional 300-year-old pub in quiet village, close to beach; very friendly and relaxed, decent bar food, and very good breakfasts.

South Lopham TM0481 MALTING FARM Blo'Norton Rd Diss IP22 2HT (037 988) 201 ***£38**; 3 well-furnished rms, some with own bthrm. Very good B & B in friendly, welcoming Elizabethan farmhouse on a working dairy farm; inglenook fireplaces with woodburning stoves in sitting and dining rooms; big breakfasts with home-baked bread and preserves around large table, small play area with toys, non-smokers preferred; the owner's passion is embroidery, patchwork, spinning and quilting; cl Christmas and New Year.

Northwold TL7596 GRANGE Thetford IP26 5NF (0366) 728240 **£36**; 6 rms, some with own bthrm. Lovely 18th-c rectory in 12 acres of garden behind the church, with log fire in drawing room, views over lawns with peacocks and ducks, and heated swimming pool; cl Christmas; no babies.

Shelfhanger TM1083 SHELFHANGER HALL Diss IP22 2DE (0379) 642094 **£32**; 3 rms. 16th-c moated farmhouse overlooking big garden and farmland with snooker table and table tennis; cl Christmas; children over 10; self-catering also.

To see and do

Norwich TG2308 There's quite a concentration of attractive streets and buildings in the old centre of this busy but civilised city. It has all sorts of surprises in the narrow streets and lanes that still follow its medieval layout – including plenty of antique shops and so forth. Elm St is particularly handsome. Even in the more commercial/industrial centre north of the River Wensum there are fine patches (such as Colegate). Norwich is the home of Colman's Mustard, and the Mustard Shop (Bridewell Alley) has some varieties you may not have come across before. Fortunately the visually disappointing university is hidden away out on the western edge, though in termtime its students do bring a good bit of life into the centre. The ancient Adam & Eve (Bishopgate) is good for lunch, and other central pubs and wine bars useful for a bite to eat without being overrun by students include the Edith Cavell (Tombland), Take Five (Bridewell Alley), Unthank Arms (Newmarket St) and Wild Man (St George St).

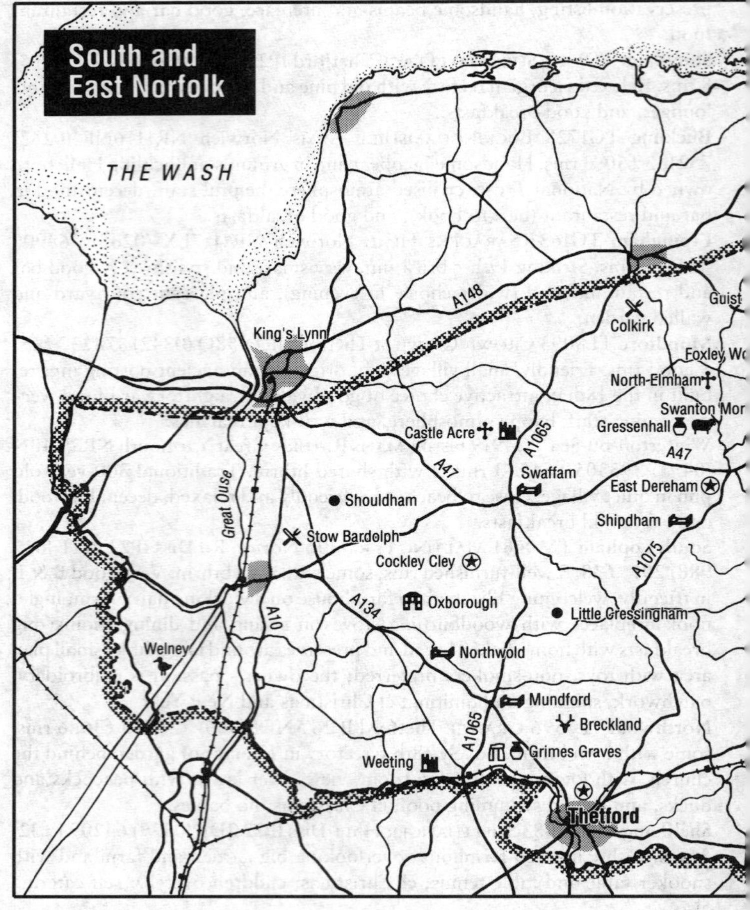

CASTLE (Castle Meadow) Set on the city hill, this impressive four-square Norman structure dominates the city. It houses the CASTLE MUSEUM, with guided tours of the dungeons, battlements and the 12th-c keep, and displays of art (with particular emphasis on the Norwich School), silverware (for which the town was famous) and ceramics, as well as archaeology and natural history. If you like stuffed birds, don't miss this part, which among countless other exhibits inc Norfolk's last pair of great bustards. Snacks, shop, disabled access; cl Sun am, Good Fri, 25-26 Dec, 1 Jan; *£1.80. Linked to this museum via a secret passage is a former courtroom in the historic Shirehall, now the ROYAL NORFOLK REGIMENTAL MUSEUM – the passage used to be used to transfer prisoners to court. The displays are more lively than in many regimental museums, and tell the story of the domestic and military life of a soldier in the county regiment from 1685; small shop; cl Sun am, Good Fri, Christmas period, 1 Jan; entrance is included in the Castle Museum ticket, or you can buy a ticket

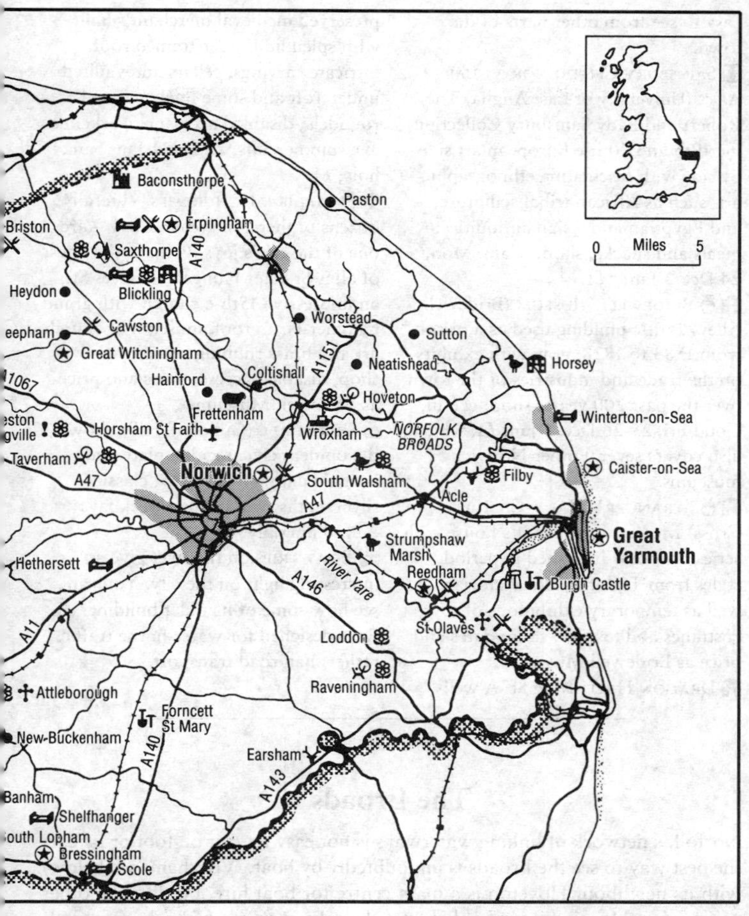

for £1 which covers this and several other Norwich museums.

✝ CATHEDRAL Magnificent, and with the cloisters and the many well-preserved buildings of its extensive precincts this makes an awe-inspiring impression behind the great medieval gateways that shut out the modern city. Basically medieval, the cathedral has some fine features from later periods – the flying buttresses for example, and the late-15th-c vaulted roof, spire and west window with Victorian glass; snacks, shop, disabled access. The precincts are delightful, with several closes, medieval alleys and secluded gardens, and all sorts of varied buildings from the cottages of Hooks Walk through the finer houses in the Upper Close to the buildings of Norwich School. The NORMAN CLOISTERS are the largest in the country, rebuilt after a serious riot between city and cathedral in 1272, and remarkable for the 400 bosses which are carved with scenes of medieval life (there are hundreds more in the cathedral itself, though less easy to see). The best view of the cathedral is from the river by Pulls Ferry; it's not easy to see from other parts of the town.

SAINSBURY CENTRE FOR VISUAL ARTS (University of East Anglia) The Robert and Lady Sainsbury Collection, inc 19th and 20th-c European art side by side with fascinating ethnographic art, such as African tribal sculpture, and Egyptian and Asian antiquities; meals and snacks, shop; cl am, Mon, 24 Dec-3 Jan; *£1.

BRIDEWELL MUSEUM (Bridewell Alley) 14th-c building used as a prison from 1583 to 1828, now with exhibits on the trade and industries of the town over the past 200 years; shop; cl Sun, Good Fri, 25-26 Dec, 1 Jan; £1, which also covers several other Norwich museums.

STRANGER'S HALL (Charing Cross) Medieval merchant's house with series of rooms furnished in period styles from Tudor to late Victorian, as well as temporary exhibitions of toys, costumes and textiles; shop; dates and price as Bridewell Museum.

DRAGON HALL (King St) A well-preserved medieval merchant's hall, with splendid timber-framed roof, intricate carvings, cellars and vaulted undercroft and some finely painted roundels; disabled access; cl weekends exc summer Sats, 23 Dec-1 Jan, bank hols; £1.

† MEDIEVAL CHURCHES – literally dozens of them, in great variety – are one of the city's joys. Perhaps the finest of all is St Peter Hungate (Princes St), an impressive 15th-c church with grand hammer-beam roof, museum of church art and brass rubbing centre; small shop, disabled access; dates and price as Bridewell Museum.

GUILDHALL (Guildhall Hill) Shows the opulent civic regalia, plate and insignia dating from 1549, classic silversmiths' work; open weekdays 2-3.30 pm only.

BOAT TRIPS on the river give an interesting light on the city. You can see how some of its older buildings were designed for water-borne traffic, rather than road transport.

The Broads

Norfolk's network of linking waterways is not easy to visit on foot or by car; the best way to see the Broads is undoubtedly by boat. Wroxham (see below) with its neighbour Hoveton is a main centre for boat hire, but like the other main centre Horning is probably better thought of as a base for longer spells afloat than short breaks or day trips. If you want a boat for just the day, the quieter reaches of the more northern Broads would probably suit you better – say, from Barton Turf TG3522, Hickling TG4123, Stalham TG3725 or Wayford Bridge TG3424.

Good places to get down to the Broads but stay on land include Hickling itself (with a pleasant path along the north shore) and Ormesby St Michael TG4614, where the Eels Foot pub has attractive waterside lawns, and the NORFOLK RARE BREEDS CENTRE has a good range of animals; cl Sat and Oct-Mar exc Sun; £2. Other waterside pubs handy for watching boating activity include the Rising Sun at Coltishall TG2719 (on a pretty bend of the River Bure); the Crown at Dilham TG3325; the Ferry, a busy Chef & Brewer at Horning TG3417; the quaint Walpole Arms at Itteringham TG1430; the Eels Foot at Ormesby St Michael TG4614 (spacious waterside lawn); the Old Bridge at Potter Heigham TG4119 (with a good riverside garden); the Ferry at Reedham TG4101 (the little car ferry here is fun); the Ferry House at Stokesby TG4310, the Ferry House at Surlingham TG3206 (there's still a rowing-boat ferry here) or the Coldham Hall with its lovely riverside garden nearby; the Sutton Staithe Hotel at Sutton Staithe TG3823 (a lovely quiet spot), or the Lock, a remote candlelit pub down by the River Waveney at Geldeston TM3991. For a sense of adventure you can take the long walk across the marshes from Wickhampton TG4205 or Halvergate TG4206 past former windpumps to the Berney Arms.

The Maltsters at Ranworth TG3514 is just across the lane from one of the few broads the boats can't get to, the conservation centre of Ranworth Broad (though you can take a different kind of boat across it). The BROADLAND CONSERVATION CENTRE here has nature trails and displays of local and natural history; disabled access; cl am Sat, all day Fri and all Nov-Mar; £1.

Other things to see and do

Attleborough TM0495 has PETER BEALES ROSE NURSERY, a specialist in old-fashioned roses that you won't find for sale elsewhere. The 15th-c CHURCH is interesting, with an unusual round tower and a screen decorated with the arms of the 24 bishoprics in England when it was built. The nearby Crown at Great Ellingham TM0196 is prettily placed and useful for lunch.

Baconsthorpe TG1237 BACONSTHORPE CASTLE The gatehouses, curtain walls and towers are all that's left of this moated and semi-fortified 15th-c house, but the displays on the site give a good idea of what it must have looked like in its glory. It's a very pretty peaceful spot, with swans on the lake adding to its charm. You can find information booklets at the nearby Post Office. The Hare & Hounds on the way to Hempstead is good for lunch.

Banham TM0688 BANHAM ZOO AND APPLEYARD CRAFT COURT Over 20 acres of parkland and garden with rare and endangered species, particularly monkeys and apes; also indoor activity centre, ice-cream parlour, play area, putting green and craft courtyard; meals, snacks, shop, disabled access; cl 25-26 Dec; £5.50.

Blickling TG1728 BLICKLING HALL Magnificent house dating mainly from early 17th c, though the hedges that flank it may be older. It has a dramatic carved oak staircase, splendid paintings inc a famous Canaletto, and intricate decor and furnishings. Best of all, perhaps, is the 125 ft Long Gallery with its ornate Jacobean plaster ceiling, though also worth a look is the Chinese bedroom, still lined with 18th-c hand-painted wallpaper. The gardens and grounds are lovely; meals and snacks, shop, good disabled access with a lift in the house; cl Mon (exc bank hols), Thurs, all Nov-Apr; £4.90. NT. There's free public access to the park on the west side of the pike-filled lake, with a pleasant walk from the Buckinghamshire Arms (which is good for lunch).

Breckland around Thetford is a region of poor, flat, sandy heathland with scattered shallow meres and originally scrubby mixed woodland, extensively planted now with pines instead; there are forest walks, for example from car parks on the A134 NW of Thetford, where you may disturb roe deer. A good place to see it as it was is the East Wretham Heath NATURE RESERVE TL9188 off A1075 NE of Thetford: plenty of wild flowers, and hides for watching the birds and deer; cl Tues.

Bressingham TM0780 BRESSINGHAM STEAM MUSEUM AND GARDENS The founder, Alan Bloom, has successfully combined his two interests to great effect at this site. The four steam-hauled trains run through the charming countryside – one running through 5 miles of the Waveney valley – and through parts of the 6 acres of informal gardens. These are planted with 5,000 species and cultivars of alpines and perennials in island beds, especially the dwarf conifers which Bloom has done so much to popularise. There are also 50 road and rail engines, mostly restored to working order, a steam roundabout and Norfolk fire museum; meals and snacks, shop, disabled access; cl Nov-Mar; £3.50. The Garden House is handy for lunch.

Burgh Castle TG4805 BERNEY ARMS WINDMILL This stands seven storeys high and dates from the 19th c when it was used to grind clinker and to drain the water from the marshes. The site is impossible to get to by car, so access is by foot, by boat, or by rail from Great Yarmouth; disabled access; cl 1-2 pm, Oct-Mar; £1.10. CASTLE You can still see sections of the massive walls of this coastal Roman fortress, built in the 3rd c to protect the coast from Saxon marauders. The bastions topping some parts of the walls were probably for ballistae, giant catapults which could sink or set fire to boats.

Caister-on-Sea TG5212, like all the other settlements down this coast, plays host to a good many summer visitors, with all the usual attractions, including long sandy beaches. It's also got a lifeboat station, right by the beach. The ruined moated CASTLE is set back from the town, a little way inland. Falstaff (the original behind Shakespeare's creation) built it on returning from Agincourt; its walls surround a 98-ft tower. The grounds contain a MOTOR MUSEUM with a good collection of vehicles from 1893 onwards – sorry, no time/price details from the management this year, but in the past it's been open mid-May to end Sept, and the last price we had for it was £4. The town contains various remains of an excavated ROMAN FORT inc the south gateway and a town wall.

★ ✝ **Castle Acre** TF8115 is a delightful village, with an 18th-c feel along the tree-shaded walk of Stocks Green (where the Ostrich is convenient for lunch). CASTLE ACRE PRIORY Twenty-five monks lived here in a gorgeous priory built for the Cluniac order by Earl Warren, William the Conqueror's son-in-law. Now it's largely in ruins, though there are extensive remains, inc the fine arcaded west front of the 11th-12th-c priory church, and a chapel and 15th-c gatehouse; all well laid out, and very picturesque. Snacks, shop, some disabled access; cl Mon exc Apr-Sept; £2. Beside these relics are the sparser yet still awe-inspiring ruins of a great CASTLE built at the same time. The site is on the Peddar's Way, a Roman road following the track of an earlier herding way – which is now a path extending the Norfolk Coast Path (see North Norfolk walks section). West Acre, 2 or 3 miles to the west, has a few further priory remains, and (like Castle Acre itself) picturesque fords over the River Nar.

! ✝ **Cockley Cley** TF7904 Lots of interesting historical things to see around this village (pronounced to rhyme with 'fry'). There's a MUSEUM of agricultural equipment, vintage engines and carriages, a 15th-c COTTAGE FORGE housing models and exhibits following local life from prehistoric times, and a 7th-c SAXON CHURCH. An unusual feature is the ICENI VILLAGE, built as and where it was believed to exist 2,000 years ago; shop, disabled access; cl July-Sept am, Nov-Mar; £2.50. The unusually named village pub, the Twenty Churchwardens, is useful for lunch (and handy too for Oxburgh Hall – see below).

Earsham TM3289 OTTER TRUST This charitable trust works towards re-introducing otters to rivers from which they've disappeared, but which now seem likely to support the animals again, thanks to cleaner water and the increase in fish that brings. You can see them here in a natural environment – obviously cheerful and intelligent, they don't perform on demand and you may have to wait a while to see anything. Snacks, shop; cl Nov-Apr; *£3.50.

East Dereham TF9913 BISHOP BONNER'S COTTAGE MUSEUM Quaint cottages that have miraculously survived two disastrous town fires and become a little local history museum, with good changing exhibitions on such themes as ladies' fashions, local industries and archaeological finds. There is no direct connection with the notorious Bishop of London it's named after, though he was in town for a few years from 1534; shop, disabled access to ground floor only; cl am, all day Sun and Mon, all Oct-Apr. The CHURCH has a medieval well, and there's a working WINDMILL on the Norwich rd, with useful displays; cl am, all Mon-Weds, Oct-Mar.

Erpingham TG1931 ALBY GARDENS Four acres of interesting shrubs, plants and bulbs, with a museum devoted to lace, another concentrating on bottles (over 2,000 of them), a bee observation hive, and various displays and demonstrations of crafts inc woodturning, stained glass, photography, furniture and ceramics; meals, snacks, shop, mostly disabled access; cl Mon, all wkdys Jan-mid-Mar (lace museum also cl Sat); crafts free, gardens £1, bottle museum 50p. The Ark, and the Saracens Head out at Wolterton, are both very good for lunch.

Filby TG4613 THRIGBY HALL WILDLIFE GARDENS 18th-c park filled with animals and birds from Asia, with tropical and bird houses, tree walk, willow pattern garden, and ornamental wildfowl on the lake. There is also a huge jungly swamp hall where you can watch somnolent crocodiles dozing under water; summer snacks, shop, disabled access; £3.80.

Forncett St Mary TM1694 INDUSTRIAL STEAM MUSEUM An unusual collection of stationary steam engines inc the one that used to open Tower Bridge; steam days usually first Sun of month, May-Dec; £2.50.

Foxley Wood TG0321 is a big block of ancient woodland, mainly deciduous and grown naturally for many centuries; lovely woodland spring flowers; cl Thurs.

Frettenham TG2417 HORSE SANCTUARY (Hill Top Farm, Hall Lane) Very dedicated and friendly place caring for hundreds of rescued horses and donkeys; snacks, shop, disabled access; open pm Sun and bank hols from Easter to mid-Dec, and maybe pm Mon in July and Aug; *£1.50.

Great Witchingham TF1021 NORFOLK WILDLIFE PARK 40 acres of gorgeous parkland contain a wealth of things to look at and activities. There's an electronic Theme Hall, narrow-gauge steam railway, trout pool and commando play areas. The park itself is home to a huge collection of British and European wildlife – there are also tame animals including a team of trained reindeer who take children for rides on a wheeled sledge; snacks, shop; cl Nov-Mar; £3.50.

Great Yarmouth TG5207 still has a fishing harbour, and most of the Broads cruising boats seem to end up passing through the town at one time or another. It's a cross between working town and resort, with lots of holiday entertainments – more a place for lively family holidays than for a weekend break. The first three attractions we list here are all good for families and holiday-makers, but the others might well tempt older visitors into the town if they were nearby. KINGDOM OF THE SEA (Marine Parade) Displays of the kinds of marine life found on the Norfolk coast, as well as underwater tunnels through shark-infested oceans and tropical fish; cl 25-26 Dec; £3.99. LIVING JUNGLE AND BUTTERFLY FARM (Sea front) An indoor tropical paradise, with butterflies, birds and fish in a recreated jungle environment – along with terrapins, tarantulas and scorpions; snacks, shop; cl Nov-Mar; *£3.

MERRIVALE MODEL VILLAGE (Wellington Pier Gardens) Attractive landscaped gardens with children's rides and remote-controlled cars, and the exceptionally detailed village – it covers an acre and features a railway, radio-controlled boats and over 200 models; meals and snacks, shop, disabled access; cl Oct-Easter; £2.50. ELIZABETHAN HOUSE MUSEUM This house is a patchwork of historical detail – built in 1596, it has a Georgian façade, 16th-c panelled rooms and, among features from later periods, some rooms decorated and furnished in 19th-c style; there are children's toys, Lowestoft porcelain and 18th-19th-c drinking glasses. Shop, disabled access to ground floor only; cl 1-2 pm, Sat and much of Oct-May, best to check first exactly when – tel (0493) 855746; *80p. MARITIME MUSEUM OF EAST ANGLIA explores various aspects of the sea and the fishing industry which have both played such important roles in the history of the area; shop; cl Sat and much of Oct-May, tel (0493) 842267 for details; *80p. TOLHOUSE MUSEUM This 13th-c building used to be the town's gaol and courthouse (you can still see the dungeons); it now has exhibits illustrating local history and archaeology and a brass rubbing centre; shop; cl 1-2 pm, wknds exc Sun Jun-Sept, Christmas, Good Fri, 1 Jan. OLD MERCHANT'S HOUSE 17th-c house standing among the narrow lanes or Rows near the waterfront, with displays of 17th- and 19th-c local building craft and some well-restored rooms; cl 1-2 pm and all Oct-Mar; £1.10. The White Swan (Caister Rd) is useful for lunch.

Gressenhall TF9615 NORFOLK RURAL LIFE MUSEUM AND UNION FARM Rare breeds of sheep, pigs, cattle and poultry can be seen at the farm which recreates a typical small farm of the 1920s. The museum, which is housed in what used to be the local workhouse, presents a history of the county over the last 200 years inc working reconstructions, particularly of rural and agricultural life; snacks, shop, disabled access; cl Sun am, all day Mon, Nov-Easter; £3.

Grimes Graves TL8189 GRIMES GRAVES It's advisable to bring a torch to this site in Breckland (see above), as you can climb into one of the 300 pits and vertical shafts which lead down into the galleries – some around 30ft deep – where the neolithic people mined their flint. The rough stone, not yet knapped into shape, would have travelled from this site to provide raw material for tool- and weapon-makers around the country; no lavatories at the site, but there are some within a mile; shop, disabled access; cl Apr-Oct 1-2 pm, cl Mon Nov-Mar, 25 Dec, 1 Jan; £1.10.

★ **Heydon** TG1127 is rather cut off from the surrounding countryside – a big green with an entirely unspoilt village around it; even the pub the Earle Arms, still with horses stabled in its yard, is the very basic sort of country tavern that died out years ago elsewhere.

Horsey TG4522 is in a quiet corner of the coast, below sea level – among the places most at risk of flooding if the sea defences are breached. There's a good path to the dunes and the sea from the lane past the Nelsons Head (good for lunch). On the other side of the main road, HORSEY WINDPUMP is a restored drainage windmill, now in full working order; small shop, teas; cl Sept-Mar; £1.20. NT. A path from here goes round the north side of quiet Horsey Mere, and on up the New Cut to another former drainage windmill, from where you can walk back to the village; the marshes on the far side of the cut have a lot of birds.

Horsham St Faith TG2114 NORWICH AVIATION MUSEUM Run by enthusiastic volunteers, this has displays of local aeronautical history, with exhibits including aircraft (there's a Vulcan bomber), engines, and other paraphernalia; as it's on the edge of Norwich Airport you get a good view of the live article too. Snacks, shop, disabled access; open Sun and bank hols, as well as other pms in summer – best to check first on (0603) 625309; £1.

Hoveton TG3018 HOVETON HALL GARDEN Large and attractive spring woodland garden with daffodils and rhododendrons, lakeside walk, walled old-fashioned herbaceous garden and kitchen garden; teas, shop, disabled access; open pm Weds, Fri, Sun and bank hols mid-Sept-Easter; £1.75. Wroxham Barns CRAFT CENTRE (Tunstead Rd) has several craft workshops in 18th-c restored farm buildings, inc pottery, boatbuilding and folk art, as well as a children's farm and traditional fair; teas, shop, play area, nice walks in parkland; cl 25-26 Dec; £1.50 for farm, otherwise free. The waterside Kings Head Hotel is useful for lunch.

Loddon TM3698 READS NURSERY (Hales Hall) has specialised for a century in unusual conservatory plants, inc a good range of lemon, orange and other citrus fruits, also nut trees etc; cl 1-2 pm, Sun and Mon (exc bank hol wknds).

✝ **North Elmham** TF9820 The CHURCH here is an attractive 13th-c building, odd in that there's a step down into it; a little further north are the interesting ruins of a SAXON CATHEDRAL. The Kings Head here is useful for lunch.

Oxborough TF7401 OXBURGH HALL Henry VIII stayed in this moated manor in 1487, and the room is now decorated with wall hangings worked by Mary, Queen of Scots. Unfortunately, most of the house was thoroughly refurbished during Victorian times but the 80-ft-high gatehouse remains as an awe-inspiring example of 15th-c building work; meals and snacks, shop, disabled access; cl am, Thurs and Fri, Oct-Mar; £3.60. NT.

Raveningham TM3996 RAVENINGHAM HALL GARDENS Victorian conservatory with interesting collection of rare shrubs, shrub roses, traditional kitchen garden and arboretum; open Sun pm late Mar-mid-Sept, nursery and arboretum open daily exc wknds in Nov-Feb; £2. RAVENINGHAM CRAFT WORKSHOPS (Beccles Rd) Victorian farm buildings with furniture-making and other workshops; shop, antiques, teas.

Reedham TG4101 PETTITTS FEATHERCRAFT AND ANIMAL ADVENTURE PARK A huge number of features here includes the gnome village, American-style locomotive ride around the grounds, half-mile miniature railway, large adventure playground, miniature horse stud, deer-petting park and crazy golf. Or you might choose to watch the demonstrations of the arts of feather craft and dip-and-carve American-style candles (products are on sale), and visit the aviaries of exotic birds; meals and snacks, shop; cl Sat, Nov-Easter; *£4.50. The Ferry is useful for lunch.

✝ **St Olaves** TM4599 ST OLAVES PRIORY This Augustinian priory was built in 1216 and is now just a ruin, but it's still possible to see the fine brick undercroft in the cloister – a remarkable early use of this material. The riverside Bell, very old indeed though much modernised, is useful for lunch.

Saxthorpe TG1130 MANNINGTON GARDENS AND COUNTRYSIDE The most beautiful feature of these gardens is the summer rose display, but they also have 20 miles of footpaths around the hall and woodland which are open all year round; snacks, shop, disabled access; open pm Sun Apr-Oct plus Weds-Fri May-Aug; *£2.50.

South Walsham TG3613 FAIRHAVEN GARDEN TRUST Small bridges link the waterways that make up these charming wooded water gardens, set beside the private South

Walsham Inner Broad. There are rare plants, masses of rhododendrons among the flowers and a tree – the King Oak – which is said to be 900 years old. It's a very extensive place, running to some 230 acres including a big BIRD SANCTUARY – to visit this part you need permission from the warden Mr Debbage; tel (0605) 49449; snacks, shop, disabled access – but paths are quite uneven; open daily exc Sat pm Good Fri-18 Apr, open Sun and bank hols to 3 May, 5 May-26 Sept Weds-Sun; £2.

Strumpshaw Marsh TG3306 (off Low Rd, Brundall) Partly drained water meadows and fen between woodland and River Yare; hides for watching marsh birds inc harriers and bearded tits, winter geese, maybe swallowtail butterflies in June; £2.50. RSPB.

Taverham TG1513 has a very large GARDEN CENTRE, with adjoining CRAFT WORKSHOP COURTYARD; teas.

Thetford TL8783 ANCIENT HOUSE MUSEUM Early Tudor house with fine oak ceilings, now a local history museum with finds going back as far as neolithic times. In the back courtyard there is a small period herb garden; shop; cl Mon 1-2 pm, Sun (exc am Jun-Sept), 25-26 Dec and 1 Jan; free exc in Aug, when 60p. THETFORD PRIORY You can easily make out the full ground plan of the cloisters of this ruined Cluniac monastery which was founded in 1103, while the 14th-c gatehouse still stands. WARREN LODGE was a 15th-c flint hunting lodge, worth a look. The Bell and Thomas Paine are both civilised places for lunch.

Weeting TL7788 WEETING CASTLE Remains of a three-storeyed cross-wing among the ruins of an 11th-c fortified manor house.

Welney TL5294 WILDFOWL AND WETLANDS TRUST Numerous hides and a spacious observatory allow visitors to take full advantage of this wonderful 1,000-acre nature reserve: in winter the sights include up to 4,000 migratory swans and numerous ducks of many species, while in spring the emphasis switches to waders and other birds, and in summer there is a nature trail to follow; snacks, shop, disabled access; £2.95.

! Weston Longville TG1115 DINOSAUR PARK 300 acres of unspoilt woodland with life-sized reconstructions of dinosaurs lying in wait around every corner – good for children to appreciate properly what the beasts looked like and just how big some of them were; also maze, adventure playground and rural bygones museum. Snacks, shop, disabled access; cl Nov-Mar; £3. The Parson Woodforde is useful for lunch.

Winterton-on-Sea TG4919 is one of the quieter seaside resorts scattered all along this coast, with a pleasantly villagey feel, and a particularly good beach over the dunes – a nice place for a wander by the sea; the 17th-c Fishermans Return is good for lunch.

Wroxham TG3017 is the main centre for BROADS BOAT CRUISING, and has several boat hire firms. So it's a good place to watch the boating activities from dry land, or to use as the start of a longer cruising holiday. The Bell here has kept more character than many places around.

We've already mentioned several WINDMILLS around the area; other fine examples are at Acle TG3910, Little Cressingham TF8700, Paston TG3134 and, best of all, Sutton TG3823 (the tallest mill in the country, nine floors high – cl Oct-Mar; £1).

★ **Other attractive villages**, all with decent pubs, include Colkirk TF9126, Coltishall TG2719, Hainford TG2218, Mundford TL8093, Neatishead TG3420, the interesting medieval New Buckenham TM0890, Reepham TG0922, Shouldham TF6708, Swanton Morley TG0116 and Worstead TG3025.

Walks

The **Peddar's Way** – the first half of the long-distance path that makes a strikingly straight bee-line across the county, and later metamorphoses into the more significant North Norfolk Coast Path – starts at Knettishall Heath TL9480 near Thetford, and follows ancient-feeling green ways and quiet lanes to reach the coast up in N Norfolk at Holme next the Sea TF7043, passing through Castle Acre TF8115 on the way. Some may find there is a little too much road-walking to sustain interest.

Few paths get close enough to the **Broads** themselves, often tantalisingly out of sight, and once away from the waterside and fenny woodlands you are immediately into the flat, humdrum agricultural landscapes found in much of the rest of the area. There is some scope for strolling along rivers, such as the reedy estuarine River Yare near Great Yarmouth, and the canalised parts of the Bure, Yare, Thurne and others; pumping-mills, birdlife and the boating scene are the principal features. Horsey TG4522 does have the ingredients for a varied round walk: a path along reed-fringed Horsey Mere (NT – owned for its wildfowl and otter population) and the New Cut, then for a total contrast joining the beach for sea views near Horsey Corner.

Elsewhere, the chief distinguishing marks are woodland plantations and parkland. Of the forests, the largest is **Thetford Forest** TL8783. This is mainly conifers and more conifers, though you may see the flash of a roe deer between the trees. The unforested part of the adjacent Breckland grasslands, largely army training area, can be appreciated from the 8-mile **Pingo Trail**, which starts from Stow Bedon TL9596, passes through three Sites of Special Scientific Interest (including Cranberry Rough, an alder swampland). It takes you along a disused railway line before joining the Peddar's Way at Hockham Heath TL9292.

Driving

The territory here is on the whole too flat to make driving interesting, as views tend to be rather repetitive and not very far-ranging. Some worthwhile roads N of Norwich include the B1149 from Norwich to Holt, the B1145 from King's Lynn right across to North Walsham and beyond, and the B1110 from East Dereham to Holt.

In the E of the county it's quite difficult to travel from S to N without going through Norwich – or at least around its ring road.

Where to eat

Norwich TG2308 ADLARDS 79 Upper St Giles St (0603) 633522 Warmly friendly restaurant serving delicious food; cl Sun/Mon, Sat am, 25 Dec and remaining wk; disabled access. **£40.**

Guist TF9925 TOLLBRIDGE Dereham Rd (036 284) 359 Fine food in relaxed and informal evening riverside restaurant with very good wine list; cl Mon; open for lunch Thurs/Fri May-Sept; disabled access. **£28**; 2-course lunch £5.

Stow Bardolph TF6205 HARE ARMS (0366) 382229 Good value, quickly served interesting lunchtime bar food in pleasantly refurbished country pub with cheerful licensees, prompt courteous service even when busy, fresh flowers, separate elegant evening restaurant, big conservatory for children (not allowed in main bar); cl 25-26 Dec; disabled access. **£25**|£1.20/£5.25.

Erpingham TG1631 Ark (0263) 761535 Lovely food inc home-made bread and home-grown vegetables in simple, relaxed cottage with log fire and courteous service; bedrooms; cl Mon, Sun pm, winter Tues pm, 25-26 Dec, and some time in October; disabled access. **£22.75**.

Cawston TG1324 Grey Gables (0603) 871259 Very good food (esp puddings) in little Georgian restaurant; bedrooms; cl 25-26 Dec; children over 5 in evening. **£22**.

Briston TG0532 John H Stracey (0263) 860891 Wide choice of notable but reasonably priced bar food in attractive, spotless pub with nicely set-out tables, friendly licensee, good real ales, and popular restaurant; cl 25 Dec pm; disabled access. **£19**|£1.85/£4.

Reedham TG4101 Ferry (0493) 700429 Perfectly placed pub beside River Yare, plenty of tables to watch boats or swans, very popular, good bar food. **£14.90**|£3.80/£5.95.

Colkirk TF9126 Crown (0328) 862171 Unpretentious but well-furnished pub with good plain but tasty food well presented; well-kept real ales, decent wines, restaurant, friendly landlord; own bowling green behind; disabled access. **£14.70**|£2.10/£3.15.

Swanton Morley TG0117 Darbys (0362) 637647 Way above average bar food (baked crab and Sunday roasts especially) in cosy beamed country pub that's almost a museum of farm tools and so forth; very well-kept real ales, log fire, and friendly staff, children's room and adventure playground; also bedrooms, self-catering, camping, caravan site, horse facilities, country trails; disabled access. **£14**|£2.75/£5.

St Olaves TM4599 Priory Farm (0493) 488432 Good, interesting food inc fresh fish and children's menu; right by St Olaves Priory; open all day, every day Jun-Sept. £2.25/£6.30.

Cawston TG1323 Ratcatchers (0603) 871430 Big helpings of very good food from enormous menu using local meat, fresh fish and home-grown herbs in cheery pub; cosy candlelit dining room too. £1.75/£5.

Help this year from: *M and J Back, R C Vincent, John Wilson, Andrew Preston, John Whitehead, JM, PM, Phil and Sue Pearce, Denise Plummer, Jim Froggatt, John Townsend, Derek and Sylvia Stephenson, John Wooll, Ian Louden, Tim Bishop, Charles Bardswell, Peter Griffiths, Hazel Morgan, John Baker, D J and P M Taylor, Mrs M C Barrett, Geoff Lee, Robert Gomme, G Atkinson, M G Hart, John Beeken, C R Whitham, J L Raker, Ann Reeder, BHP, Frank Cummins.*

Norfolk Calendar

Some of these dates were provisional as we went to press.

February

14th **King's Lynn** Mart: *originating in the Middle Ages, official opening by Mayor with proclamation, mace bearers, attendants in full regalia, town crier*

March

10th **Norwich** Blues Festival *at Norwich Arts Centre, performers from the US – till Sat 12*

Norfolk Calendar

March cont.

11th **King's Lynn** Fiction Festival – *till Sun 13*

April

3rd **Titchwell** Arts and Crafts Demonstrations *at RSPB Reserve*

8th **Norwich** Norfolk Furniture-makers Exhibition – *till Sun 10*

30th **Norwich** Mustard Week, *celebration of Norfolk food and drink – till 8 May*

May

29th **Norwich** Classic, Veteran and Vintage Car Event – *till Mon 30*

30th **Sandringham** Horse Trials

June

5th **Titchwell** Arts and Crafts Demonstrations *at RSPB Reserve*

11th **Hunstanton** and district Arts Festival – *till Sun 26*

24th **Sandringham** Country Weekend and Horse Driving Trial – *till* Sun 26

29th **Norwich** Royal Norfolk Show *at Royal Norfolk Showground – till Thurs 30*

July

3rd **Titchwell** Arts and Crafts Demonstrations *at RSPB Reserve*

8th **Norwich** Lord Mayor's Procession, *celebration of 800 years of Norwich, carnival floats and fireworks – till Sun 10*

15th **Weeting** Steam Rally *at Fengate Farm – till Sun 17*

16th **King's Lynn** Festival of Music and the Arts – *till Sat 30*

27th **Sandringham** Flower Festival *at Sandringham Park*

29th **Worstead** Festival – *till Sun 31*

August

10th **Holkham** Pageant and Son-et-lumière *at Holkham Hall in the evening – till Sat 13*

20th **Burnham** Market Craft Fair

29th **Aylsham** Agricultural Show *at Bickling Park*; **Sandringham** Craft Fair

September

11th **Norwich** Town and Country Show *at Royal Norfolk Showground*

23rd **King's Lynn** Poetry Festival *at King's Lynn Arts Centre – till Sun 25*

October

6th **Norfolk** and **Norwich** Festival, *events throughout the cities and countryside – till Sun 16*

24th **Norwich** CAMRA Beer Festival *at St Andrews Hall – till Sat 29*

November

6th **Titchwell** Arts and Crafts Demonstrations *at RSPB Reserve*

December

4th **Titchwell** Arts and Crafts Demonstrations *at RSPB Reserve*

25th **Hunstanton** Christmas Day Swim

Northumbria
(Durham, Northumberland, Cleveland, Tyne & Wear)

Durham is one of England's best four or five cities for a short stay. The Durham and Northumberland countryside, refreshingly uncrowded even in high summer, is also great for quiet breaks. People up here are among Britain's friendliest, prices are low, and the area is very good both for walking and for driving (there is less traffic than elsewhere in England).

Teesdale in County Durham and North Tynedale in Northumberland have the best of the countryside, but other areas here share the same basic qualities of interesting scenery enlivened by streams, high moorland, solid stone buildings, unhurried small market towns, and above all the sense of peace that comes from broad unspoilt landscapes. There is also a fine long coastline.

There are fewer places to visit here than in many other areas, but they are well worth tracking down, and well in tune with the expansive character of the region. The Calendar shows that there is quite a lot going on up here, if you want to pin your visit to a particular event. May and June are the most attractive months, with long days of generally dry weather, clean-coated young lambs, a dazzling variety of shades of green, and sparkling rivers. September can be delightful, but autumn tends to set in quite fiercely in October, and the weather in winter can make you want to stay indoors.

Northumberland and Tyneside

Grand lonely countryside and coast, lots of interesting castles, some other places well worth visiting – very good value for a quiet break.

The country areas here are rich in fine landscapes and seascapes, with many classic castles, ruined and inhabited – Bamburgh, Warkworth, Lindisfarne on Holy Island, Chillingham (with its ancient white cattle) and Alnwick prime among them. The magnificent Cragside at Rothbury, the villages of Ford and Etal linked by their little narrow-gauge railway, and perhaps Bede's monastery at Jarrow are also worth a visit. The best of the countryside is up in the empty Cheviots, though plenty of other parts are rewarding; the rocky sandy coast has many fine stretches, but its hinterland is less interesting. Newcastle has lots

of things to see and a great deal of character – making it good for day visits (preferably
on a weekend so as to avoid the traffic), but not so special for a longer stay. Hadrian's Wall and Kielder Water are discussed separately in the next section.

Where to stay

Cornhill-on-Tweed NT8639 TILLMOUTH PARK TD12 4UU (0890) 882255 **£86**; 14 spacious, pretty rms with period furniture. Solid stone-built country house, recently refurbished, in 15 acres of parkland with comfortable lounges, open fires, a galleried hall, and good food.

Belford NU1033 BLUE BELL NE70 7NE (0668) 213543 ***£80**; 17 comfortable rms. Pleasantly old-fashioned dining room overlooking an attractive garden, comfortable and relaxing lounge, family bar in former stables, plentiful bar food, and polite, friendly service; disabled access.

Longframlington NU1301 EMBLETON HALL Morpeth NE65 8DT (0665) 570249 ***£75**; 10 comfortable, pretty and individually decorated rms. Charming hotel in lovely grounds and surrounded by fine countryside; neat little bar, elegant lounge, log fires; excellent value bar meals and very good food in the attractive dining room; a particularly friendly, relaxed atmosphere, and courteous staff.

Powburn NU0617 BREAMISH HOUSE Alnwick NE66 4LL (066 578) 266 ***£65**; 11 well-furnished rms. Appealing hotel in neatly kept grounds with comfortable, relaxing lounge, and good food in the pretty dining room; cl Jan, 1st wk Feb; children over 12 except by arrangement.

Warkworth NU2506 WARKWORTH COUNTRY HOUSE Morpeth NE65 0XB (0665) 711276 ***£65**; 14 comfortably furnished rms. Warmly welcoming 16th-c hotel with comfortable lounge, a bar with real ales, and interesting *objets d'art* and paintings; very good food inc excellent breakfasts, and quick, efficient service; disabled access.

Bamburgh NU1835 LORD CREWE ARMS NE69 7BL (066 84) 243 ***£62**; 25 comfortable rms, most with own bthrm. Relaxing and comfortable old inn, beautifully placed in charming coastal village below magnificent Norman castle, with entertaining bric-a-brac and log fire in back bar; generously served straightforward food in bar and grill room, good breakfasts, and pleasant service; cl Nov-Mar; children over 5.

Seahouses NU2232 OLDE SHIP NE68 7RD (0665) 720200 ***£62**; 12 rms. Thriving harbourside inn full of nautical items and fishing memorabilia, popular bar food and good service; ideal for coastal walks; looks out towards the Farne Islands (boat trips bookable in harbour); cl Dec-Jan; no children.

Wylam NZ1265 LABURNAM HOUSE NE41 8AJ (0661) 852185 **£50**; 4 comfortable rms. Attractive 18th-c restaurant with pretty furnishings, generous helpings of unfailingly good modern French cooking (the fish is recommended), and unobtrusive service.

Chatton NU0628 PERCY ARMS Alnwick NE66 5PS (066 85) 244 **£40**; 7 rms. Stone inn with clean, comfortable and spacious bar, very good fresh fish, and 12 miles of private fishing for residents.

Edlingham NU1109 LUMBYLAW FARM Alnwick NE66 2BW (066 574) 277 **£33**; 3 rms, one with shower. Peacefully set working farm on 350 acres with sheep and South Devon cattle; marvellous views, warm welcome and good breakfasts; self-catering also available; cl Oct-Apr.

Newton by the Sea NU2426 JOINERS ARMS Alnwick NE66 3EA (0665)

576645 £28; 5 rms, shared bthrm. In easy walking distance of the best two beaches in Northumberland; village focal point; popular good food inc fresh fish in bar and lounge/restaurant, welcoming staff; cl wkdy lunchtimes Nov-Mar.

To see and do

Alnwick NU1813 has some attractive old streets near the market square. It's a busy town and the centre for the prosperous farming country around it. ALNWICK CASTLE The 'Windsor of the North' dates back to the 11th c, and is the second largest inhabited castle in the country – it's guarded by stone soldiers perched on the battlements. Numerous treasures inc paintings by Titian, Van Dyck and Canaletto, and there's an outstanding Claude, as well as the famous collection of Meissen china, a regimental museum and a display of Roman remains. Shop; cl mid-Oct-Easter; £3.60. The Market Tavern does good value lunches.

Bamburgh NU1735 BAMBURGH CASTLE Huge square Norman castle on a mighty cliff, above attractive village around cricket green – the castle clock serves as timekeeper. Impressive hall and armoury, with large collection of armour from HM Tower of London. Snacks, shop; cl am, Nov-Mar; £2.40. GRACE DARLING MUSEUM Pictures, documents and other reminders of the heroine, inc the boat in which Grace and her father rescued nine survivors from the wrecked SS *Forfarshire*. Shop; disabled access; cl Oct-Easter; free (donations to RNLI). The Lord Crewe Arms is useful for lunch.

Belsay NZ1079 BELSAY HALL, CASTLE AND GARDENS The same family have lived here for nearly 600 years, first in a medieval castle, then a Jacobean manor house and finally a grand mansion based on Greek classical temples – all can still be seen. The 30 acres of landscaped parkland are especially pleasant, with a rhododendron garden, formal terraces and woodland. Also an exhibition on the area and a video of Northumbrian castles; snacks, shop, disabled access; cl winter Mon, 25-26 Dec, 1 Jan; £2.20.

Berwick-upon-Tweed NT9953 The town walls, partly grassed over and easy to walk round, were a masterpiece of 16th-c military planning. The town is still largely unspoilt, nice to stroll in, with some handsome 18th-c buildings and a fine 17th-c CHURCH; everyone who comes here seems to while away at least a bit of time watching the swans on the River Tweed. BERWICK BARRACKS Built in the early 1700s, these are Britain's oldest surviving purpose-built barracks, their design attributed to Vanbrugh. They now house a museum and art gallery, with displays of local history, archaeology, fine art and decorative art, the museum of the King's Own Scottish Borderers, and an interesting exhibition tracing the history of the British soldier. Snacks, shop, disabled access; cl winter Mon, 24-26 Dec, 1 Jan; £2. WINE AND SPIRIT MUSEUM (Palace Green) The mainland base of Lindisfarne mead makers (see St Aidan's Winery listed under Lindisfarne), with a collection of objects from the wine and spirit industries, a traditional working potter, home-made pot-pourri, and a Victorian chemist shop; cl Sun and 24 Dec-5 Jan.

Cambo NZ0285 WALLINGTON HOUSE Built in 1688 and altered in the 1740s, with fine plasterwork, porcelain and doll's houses. Outside 100 acres of lawns, terraces, lakes and woodlands, with showpiece fuchsias in the conservatory. Meals and snacks, shop and plant centre, disabled facilities; house cl am, all day Tues, and Nov-

May; grounds and garden open all year; house, walled garden and grounds £4, grounds only £2. NT.

Chillingham NU0525 CHILLINGHAM CASTLE Striking old castle dating back to the 12th c, with great hall and state rooms full of interesting things to look at, inc fine antiques, tapestries, arms and armour. Formal gardens, woodland walks, lake and splendid views of the surrounding countryside; occasional concerts and special events. If you're feeling particularly brave, they'll let you rent one of their haunted rooms for a week. Snacks, shop, some disabled access; cl am, Tues, Oct-May; *£3.30. CHILLINGHAM WILD CATTLE PARK The famous large-horned white cattle have been here for the last 700 years, and are the only animals of their kind that still remain pure and uncrossed with domestic breeds. They are potentially aggressive, so tours are conducted by a warden, and binoculars are recommended for a closer view. Shop; cl 12-2 pm, am Tues and Sun, Nov-May; *£2. Above the park is Ross Castle HILL FORT NU0825, with great views.

Embleton NU2322 DUNSTANBURGH CASTLE Painted three times by Turner, this ruin is still a favourite with artists; its huge mass, partly built by John of Gaunt, stands imposingly on the cliff above the North Sea. Cl 24-26 Dec, 1 Jan and Mon Oct-Mar; £1.10.

★ **Ford** NT9437 is a very attractive village with one or two craft workshops. HEATHERSLAW LIGHT RAILWAY Steam or diesel journeys on narrow-gauge railway along the pretty valley of the River Till between here and Etal; snacks, shop, disabled access; cl wkdys Nov-Christmas, all Jan-Easter, tel (089 082) 244 for times; *£2.75. HEATHERSLAW CORN MILL 19th-c water-driven double corn mill, with displays and demonstrations of all aspects of production. Snacks, shop, some disabled access; open daily Easter-Oct, then wknds in Nov, Feb and Mar; £1.50. Etal NT9339, close by, is a pretty row of white cottages running down to a ford across the river, a working forge, the ruin of a small 14th-c CASTLE, and a decent thatched pub, the Black Bull.

† **Jarrow** NZ3065 ST PAUL'S CHURCH AND MONASTERY The church was part of the monastery where the 8th-c Venerable Bede lived for most of his life, producing his 37 books encompassing most fields of knowledge in those days – and much of what is now known of life in early Christian England. The site, along with the other half of the monastery at St Peter's, Monkwearmouth, is a major Christian shrine. The story of the building and the history of this great man are both told in BEDE'S WORLD, the museum, which houses finds from the excavations on the site. Very little remains of the original monastery, but there is some Saxon stained glass in the church (more in the museum too), and the chancel incorporates one of the churches where Bede worshipped. The site is developing rapidly, with a little herb garden behind the museum and further expansion on the way; snacks, shop, some disabled access; cl Sun am, all day Mon (exc bank hols), Christmas wk; £1.

† **Lindisfarne** NU1413, otherwise known as Holy Island, is linked to the mainland by a causeway which you can drive over at low tide; tide tables are posted at each end – or tel (0289) 89200. There are nature-reserve dunes, a restored tide-mill, fishermen's huts made of upturned former boats, old limekilns, a small extended village with tourist cafés and pubs, and good views from the close-grazed grassy crags. However, the main reason for most people coming here is LINDISFARNE PRIORY. The first monastery was founded in the 7th c by St Aidan and monks from Iona, and it was from here the seeds of Christianity were replanted in Dark Age England. The ruins with their graceful red sandstone arches and neat lawns inside

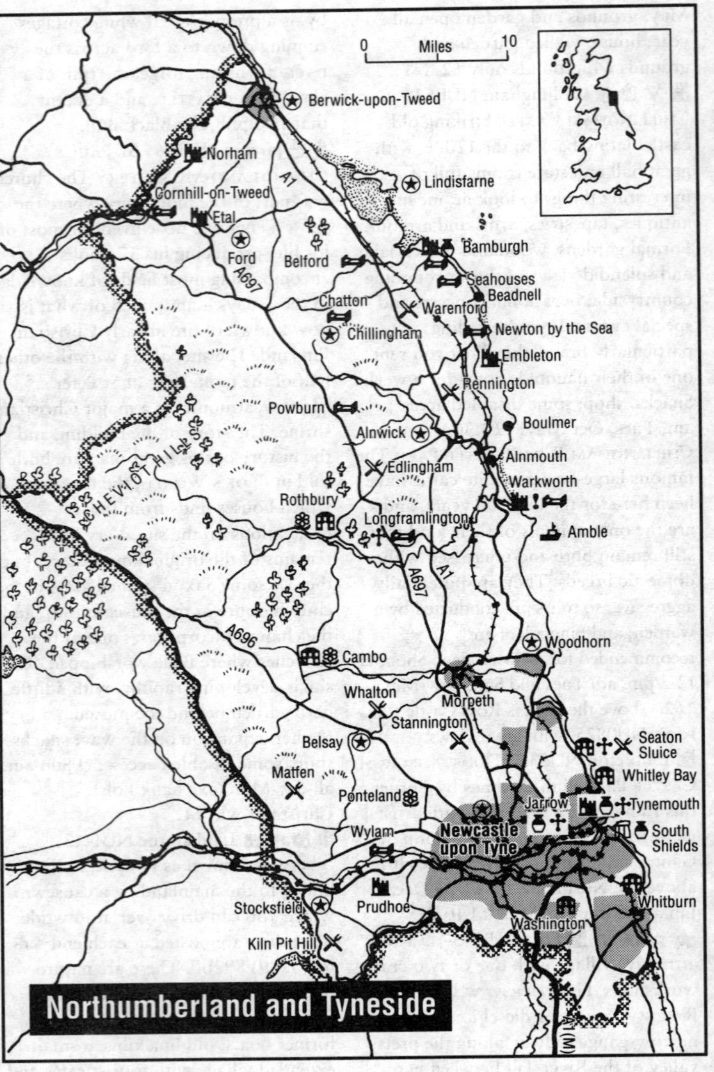

Northumberland and Tyneside

what was once the priory church date from the 11th c; the history of the priory is told at the nearby visitor centre. Snacks, shop, disabled access to visitor centre; cl 1-2 pm Oct-Mar, 24-26 Dec, 1 Jan; *£2. LINDISFARNE CASTLE The 16th-century castle was restored by Lutyens for the editor of *Country Life* in a suitably monolithic quasi-medieval style, with a sumptuous interior featuring a fine collection of antique oak furniture, and a walled garden designed to protect against the North Sea winds by Gertrude Jekyll. Shop; cl am, Fri (exc Good Fri), Nov-Apr; £3.20. NT. ST AIDAN'S WINERY Home of Lindisfarne Mead, a fortified wine made from grapes, honey, herbs and water from an island well. They make honey too, and the craft shop has a range of local pottery and jewellery. You can taste their mead here, and the Lindisfarne Hotel is useful for more conventional refreshment.

✝ **Longframlington** NU1201
BRINKBURN PRIORY Founded in 1153 on the River Coquet, it fell into disrepair after the Dissolution of the Monasteries, but was restored in 1858, and has just been reroofed. It still has medieval grave slabs, font and double piscina, and there are occasional services and concerts. Shop; cl 1-2 pm, Oct-Mar; £1.20. The Granby is useful for lunch.

Morpeth NZ2086 MORPETH CHANTRY BAGPIPE MUSEUM Tuneful collection of small pipes and bagpipes from the region and around the world. Headphoned sound displays explain the difference between a rant and a reel; shop; cl lunchtime, all day Sun and bank hols; £1.

✝ **Newcastle upon Tyne** NZ2464
There is a good combination here of stately 19th-c stone buildings with a lively atmosphere of regeneration, and a number of interesting places to visit. The centre is high above the River Tyne, memorable for its three great bridges – particularly what has become almost the city's trademark, the two-decker High Level Bridge for road and rail designed by Robert Stephenson in the 1840s. The 14th-15th-c CATHEDRAL is well worth a look. Though the CASTLE is largely Norman, it's spoiled as a potential attraction for visitors by the main railway line, which cuts the gatehouse off from the keep. You can trace some stretches of the medieval CITY WALL (especially from St Andrew's Church along the cobbled lane west of Stowell St – Chinese restaurants around here – and past the Heber Tower along Bath Lane).
Besides walking along the centre's lofty Victorian terraces, you can get a good bird's-eye view of them from the top of Grey's Monument, at the head of elegant Grey St; a steep climb, Sat only; Fitzgeralds down the street is useful for a bite to eat. Steep alleys and steps lead from the centre down to The Quay, the oldest part of the town, with several unexpected and quaintly attractive timber-framed medieval buildings; one of the oldest, the Cooperage, is a good pub.
Downstream, east of the 1920s Tyne Bridge, an area of recently refurbished 19th-c wharf buildings is also enjoyable to walk through, with crafts and bric-a-brac market on Sun, and a useful pub for food – the Baltic Tavern. The MUSEUM OF SCIENCE AND ENGINEERING (Blandford Sq) is a fascinating interactive museum, particularly strong on Newcastle's achievements, and includes an interesting perspective on the city in the 1920s; snacks, shop, disabled facilities; cl Mon and Sun. The HANCOCK MUSEUM (Barras Bridge) has magnificent collections of stuffed birds (particularly notable) and mammals from Northumbrian wildlife to big game, as well as insects, fossils, minerals, ethnography and egyptology, with special events and activities for children; meals, snacks, shop, disabled access; cl Sun am, 25-26 Dec, 1 Jan, Good Fri; £1.50. Smaller museums include JOHN GEORGE JOICEY MUSEUM (City Rd) in 17th-c almshouses, with audio-visual presentations on events such as the great flood of 1771 and great fire of 1854, and period rooms and some military exhibitions; shop; cl Sun and Mon (exc bank hols). The MUSEUM OF ANTIQUITIES (at the oldest University) houses finds from north-east England, especially from Hadrian's Wall; shop; disabled access; cl Sun, Good Fri, 24-26 Dec, 1 Jan.
Besides the pubs mentioned above, the Bridge Hotel (Castle Sq), Crown Posada (The Side, off Dean St), Duke of Wellington (High Bridge) and newly converted Waterline (Quayside) are all pleasantly civilised. On the south side of the Tyne, Gateshead's METRO

Centre (A1 just W) is a good family place for a rainy day. It's a massive modern shopping and leisure complex with several different themed undercover areas including all sorts of fairground attractions, and the Spitting Image hall of fame; the warning is that unless you remember exactly where you put your car it'll take you ages to find it – there are 12,000 parking spaces.

Norham NT9048 CASTLE On a steep sheep-terraced grassy mound stands this massive 12th-c ruined border fortress of the Prince Bishops of Durham, in their day the most powerful men in the north; a formidable keep and some more fragmentary outer defences; the locale for Scott's *Marmion*.

Ponteland NZ1773 KIRKLEY HALL GARDENS Very attractive and thoughtfully maintained gardens, with a big collection of herbaceous perennials, a Victorian walled garden, pretty sunken garden, woodland garden and lots of unusual trees and shrubs. New facilities are under construction; snacks, shop, disabled access; *£1.50.

Prudhoe NZ0962 PRUDHOE CASTLE 12th-14th-c ruined castle on an impressive mound commanding this crossing of the Tyne, once the stronghold of the powerful Percy family; the shattered keep stands in the inner bailey with a remarkable restored gatehouse on the outer bailey, and there's an exhibition centre in a nearby 19th-c manor house. Snacks, shop, disabled access; cl 1-2 pm, 24-26 Dec, 1 Jan, and Mon Oct-Mar; £1.70.

Rothbury NU0602 CRAGSIDE The opulent Victorian mansion of Lord Armstrong, the armaments king, with some spectacularly grand rooms; best of all are the miles of landscaped well-wooded grounds, with a walk showing the various elements of the hydro-electric scheme he devised to light the house, lakes, glorious rhododendrons, and a showy formal garden with fruit house and ferneries; meals, snacks, shop, disabled access inc fishing pier on trout lake; cl Mon exc bank hols, cl Nov-Mar (garden, grounds and visitor centre open Tues, Sat and Sun Nov and Dec); £5.40, grounds only £3.30. NT.

Seaton Sluice NZ3477 SEATON DELAVAL Vanbrugh's Palladian masterpiece, a fine design of central porticoed main block and massive outer wings, though not all of the interior has survived unscathed by fires and other ravages, and much of the original park and grounds have been submerged by surrounding developments; open pm Weds, Sun and bank hols, cl Oct-Apr; £1.50. The buildings around the Norman CHURCH are attractive. Down near the front, the Waterford Arms has excellent fresh fish.

South Shields NZ3567 ARBEIA ROMAN FORT Dates from the 2nd c when as a supply base it played a crucial role in the campaign against the Scots. Huge variety of remains, as well as recreated scenes of Roman life within the camp, and excellently displayed finds in the museum; snacks, shop, disabled access; cl Mon exc bank hols, cl Sun exc summer pm.

Stocksfield NZ0661 CHERRYBURN (Mickley) Well-preserved 18th-c farm, the birthplace of artist, engraver and naturalist Thomas Bewick, with an exhibition of his life and work, farm animals running about the yard, craft demonstrations and good views of the Tyne Valley; shop, some disabled access; cl am, all day Tues, Nov-Mar; £2.50.

Tynemouth NZ3669 CASTLE AND PRIORY The walls of the castle embrace the remains of the 11th-c Benedictine priory, built on the site of a Saxon monastery. The castle dates from between the 11th and 14th centuries – the gatehouse and parts of the curtain wall survive, while the church remains inc the church nave and chancel; snacks, shop; cl 1-2 pm Oct-Mar, Mon Oct-Mar, Dec 24-26, 1 Jan; £1.20.

Warkworth NU2403 is a quietly picturesque small town built around the main street that rises attractively from the Norman church by the river to the CASTLE on its hill above the River Coquet. This splendid ruin has a restored turreted 15th-c keep and early 13th-c curtain wall. Nearby is a 14th-c bridge with a rare guard tower. Disabled access; cl 24-26 Dec, 1 Jan, Mon Oct-Mar; £1.20. There's a pleasant riverside path upstream to the WARKWORTH HERMITAGE, a cell of retreat cut into the sandstone cliff in the 14th c; with tiny vaulted chapel, some crude wall carvings and two chambers, it was occupied for some 200 years. Disabled access difficult, as to get to the hermitage you take a rowing boat; open Apr-Sept, wknds only; 80p. In the town, the Warkworth House Hotel, Sun Hotel, Hermitage and Masons Arms are all useful for lunch, and there are one or two antique shops. In the other direction, this stretch of sea coast has some lovely beaches.

Washington NZ3156 WASHINGTON OLD HALL Well-restored stone-built 13th-c manor, long the home of George Washington's family, in the unspoilt old village that comes as a real surprise when you've penetrated the surrounding new town; snacks, shop; cl Fri and Sat, all Nov-Mar; £2. The nearby Washington Arms is good value for lunch.

Whitburn NZ4262 SOUTER LIGHTHOUSE When this red-and-white structure was built in 1870 it was the most advanced lighthouse of the day; the first to be powered by electricity, its light failed only twice in the first eight years of operation – one of these times because the keeper had fallen asleep. You can still see the rooms and equipment; meals, snacks, shop, disabled access (but not to tower); cl Nov-Mar; *£2.30. NT. The Trust also own the Leas, the spectacular stretch of coastline around here, leading to Marden Rock with its colony of kittiwakes, cormorants and fulmars.

Whitley Bay NZ3572 ST MARY'S LIGHTHOUSE Set by a small but diverse exhibition centre, the lighthouse, on St Mary's Island, is reached by causeway at low tide. When the lighthouse is closed the island is worth a visit for the rockpools alone. It's said that every exiled Geordie has a picture of this lighthouse; shop; adjacent café; cl wkdys Nov-May; £1. In the seaside town, the Briar Dene does good food, and the Foxhunters is good value too.

Woodhorn NZ3088 WOODHORN COLLIERY MUSEUM Excellent displays in former colliery buildings, with lifesize models, working machinery, period reconstructions and sound effects giving a vivid illustration of life in the pit and the communities around it. There's an interesting display of art by local miners, as well as several craft workshops and woodland walks. 1994 is the centenary of the start of work on this site, with special events planned most wknds; meals, snacks, disabled access; cl Mon and Tues. WOODHORN CHURCH close by is said to be the oldest on this coast and has fine Saxon and Norman features, as well as a MUSEUM of local history, art and craft, with weekend demonstrations; details as colliery but also cl 12.30-1 pm.

★ A number of attractive **coastal villages** and towns dotted along this underpopulated coast inc Amble NU2704 (solid old fishing harbour, new yacht marina; RSPB boat trips around nearby Coquet Island with its colourful eider ducks and puffins); Alnmouth NU2511 (attractive beaches, good coastal walks, a lot for summer visitors); Beadnall NU2329 (boats on the beach, and an interestingly restored waterside limekiln) and nearby Benthall, Boulmer NU2714 (active fishing boats), Craster NU2620 (tidal fishing harbour, good kippering factory, excellent pub), Newton by the Sea NU2426 (little more than a circle of houses above the sea, and a useful little inn, with a bird reserve near by) and Seahouses NU2232 (busy fishing harbour, overlooked by a good interesting pub, the Olde Ship. There are boat trips around the FARNE ISLANDS so you can see their eider ducks, thousands of other seabirds, and grey seals – breeding from the end of summer into autumn, with the plaintive-voiced pups staying on shore for only a few weeks. In fine weather landing may be possible on the Inner Farne, which has a lighthouse and 14th-c chapel, with a small exhibition about the islands in a former chapel beside it).

Walks

Rothbury Terraces NU0501, near Rothbury itself, and **Hulme Park** NU1414, just out of Alnwick's centre, are both excellent for parkland walks; in the latter, don't miss the whimsical Brizles Tower and hermit's cave.

The **Northumberland coast** has much of interest along its sandy and rocky shores, but the hinterland is rather dull, so it's better for pottering and for there-and-back walks than for round ones. A coast path covers the finest sections. These include Craster NU2620 to Dunstanburgh Castle NU2521, and the windswept solitude of Ross Back Sands NU1437. These overlook **Holy Island** NU1413, which itself has an easy but fascinating 3-mile walk around its shores.

The **Cheviots**, part of the Northumberland National Park, are strikingly empty and solitary, with only the characteristic local breed of hardy sheep for company in most places. The Pennine Way's penultimate stages take a long, lonely plod over the grassy moors, including a fine high ridge section along the English/Scottish border past the 2,036-ft summit of Windy Gyle NT8515. You have to walk some way from the road to attain this main ridge: start from Coquetdale NU0001, and walk along the Street, an ancient drovers' track. Gradients are mild but the peaty ground can get boggy after rain; not all routes are defined on the ground, but stone boundary walls and forest plantations are useful guides. Clennel Street, another drove road leading from Coquetdale, can be followed from near Alwinton NT9026, and offers much the same sort of scenery; there's a pretty way back, along a track by the River Alwin.

A stiff walk up the Pennine Way through the **Redesdale Forest** above Byrness NT7602 takes you to the spectacular earthworks of the little-visited Chew Green Roman camps NT7808, surrounded by wild country. The Pennines up here contain a great many more unspoilt prehistoric and other archaeological remains, many of them reached only by quite a long walk. This does set goals for walkers in these magnificent hills, which often reward you with remarkable views. Ordnance Survey large-scale maps show their position; Sheets 74 and 75 of the Landranger series are the most useful.

Berwick-upon-Tweed NT9953 has an extraordinary trio of bridges, and deserves to be approached along the Tweed: there are paths on both banks, starting from the East Ord picnic site by the A1 road bridge; the town ramparts, impressively intact, give good views. Industrial Tyneside provides a few reasonable coastal walks, including **Marsden Bay** nature reserve NZ4065 near South Shields.

Driving

Once clear of Tyneside, the traffic generally thins out a lot, so that getting to any of the places we've mentioned as worth visiting will normally be part of the pleasure.

The most attractive drive in the whole area is along Coquet Dale, on the B6344 through Rothbury, the B6341 to Swindon, and then on through Holystone, Harbottle and Alwinton. If you want you can keep right on to the end, along the increasingly desolate road to Blindburn.

Where to eat

Matfen NZ0372 BLACK BULL (0661) 886330 Striking stone building by the green with a local eating-out atmosphere in extended Turkey-carpeted bar; nicely presented good food (daily specials and puddings recommended), newly refurbished restaurant and efficient service; disabled access. **£29**|£1.95/£4.40.

Whalton NZ1382 BERESFORD ARMS (0670) 75225 Good food (waitress served) in pleasant bar or dining room inc range of proper pies, good service; attractive village; cl Sun pm, 25 Dec pm; children lunchtime only. **£24**|£3.95/£5.50.

Warenford NU1429 WARENFORD LODGE (0668) 213453 Very individual old, though rather modern feeling, pub with stripped stonework, big stone fireplace and serving really good unusual food and decent wines; cl Mon, Tues-Fri am, 25-26 Dec, 1 Jan; children only in evening dining room; disabled access. **£18.90**|£1.95/£4.50.

Stannington NZ2279 RIDLEY ARMS (0670) 789216 Spacious open-plan bars with cosy furnishings, quiet lounge, particularly good food in separate restaurant and pleasant bar; excellent A1 stop-off. **£15.50**|£2/£4.50.

Rennington NU2118 MASONS ARMS (0665) 577275 Friendly pub with wide choice of generously served bar food (fine puddings), comfortable lounge bar, cheery licensees, and decent breakfasts; bedrooms; children up to 8 pm; cl 25 Dec pm. **£15**|£2.25/£6.

Kiln Pit Hill NZ0454 MANOR HOUSE (0207) 55268 Warmly recommended by contributors; cl 25 Dec; disabled access. **£15**|£1.65/£5.85.

Seaton Sluice NZ3477 WATERFORD ARMS (091) 237 0450 Comfortably modernised pub with generous helpings of excellent food – their fish comes fresh from the harbour just down the road. **£12.60**|£2.10/£8.40.

HADRIAN'S WALL, TYNEDALE AND KIELDER WATER

Unspoilt quiet countryside plus Hadrian's Wall – a remarkable monument.

The charm of this area is its countryside, with the great Roman wall as an interesting bonus – indeed a fascinating one, if you've not seen it before. In high summer the wall does get hundreds of visitors and is popular to walk along, but even then its sheer length means that away from the excavated fortresses it's never crowded. At other times of year you can often look along great stretches without seeing anyone else.

The North Tyne valley has some extremely relaxing and fulfilling scenery (and good fishing), and would be ideal for a quiet weekend. But all the places to stay that we recommend in this area put you within easy reach of open spaces and high moors. There is a scattering of places with decent food. Apart from the wall and things associated with it, and the attractive recreational area around Kielder Water, there are very few places to visit in the area. In summer the evenings here are long; one tip is to stay away from water then, unless you're midge-proof.

Where to stay

Chollerford NY9372 George NE46 4EW (0434) 681611 £95; 49 rms. Quiet hotel with good food; 17th-c bridge over the North Tyne visible from the candlelit restaurant; thoughtful, attentive service; fine gardens sloping down to the river; swimming pool.

Allendale NY8456 Bishopsfield Country House Whitfield Rd NE47 9EJ (0434) 683248 £76; 11 individually decorated rms. Standing in 50 acres, this former farm and its outbuildings have been carefully converted into a charming hotel with two attractive lounges; good country cooking, friendly owners; garden, and game fishing; cl Christmas, New Year and Feb; disabled access.

Wall NY9168 Hadrian NE46 4EE (0434) 681232 £49; 10 rms. Well-run 16th-c house with Jacobean-style bars, well-kept beers; good helpings of imaginative good food; prompt, willing and cheerful service; lovely views; disabled access.

Tarset NY7985 Earls Lodge NE48 1LF (0434) 240269 £43; 4 rms. Licensed guesthouse (used to be a pub) with health-conscious food; attractive surrounding scenery, and three mountain bikes for residents' use (free of charge); cl 25 Dec, children over 14 only.

Barrasford NT9273 Barrasford Arms NE48 4AA (0434) 681237 £33; 5 rms. possibly cl Nov-Easter.

West Woodburn NY8987 Bay Horse NE48 2RX (0434) 270218 £32; 5 rms (share bthrm). Pretty, welcoming 18th-c coaching inn with curious Roman stone in garden which runs down to River Rede (good for trout and salmon fishing), comfortable bar with big horse collar over log fire.

To see and do

Hadrian's Wall The wall amazes people first seeing it. It's extraordinary to imagine those Roman military engineers, so far from their warm homeland, building this remarkable construction through such inhospitable surroundings. Much of it runs along the natural crag of the great Whin Sills, making it that much more formidable.

With its associated forts, the wall does have a lot to hold the interest, and an overall sense of grandeur that is a definite part of its appeal. The stone wall itself, with its turret watchtowers, milecastles and more sporadic forts, defines the northern side of a narrow frontier zone, bounded on its south side by a ditch between turf ramparts, with a military road running between wall and ditch. It was this whole installation rather than just the wall itself which the Romans used to control trade and cross-border travel.

We mention below some of the more striking and accessible features connected with the wall, including the bigger behind-the-lines forts and camps. The section at Cuddys Crag NY7868 is perhaps the most beautiful of all, very photogenic and giving glorious views.

Bardon Mill NY7868 VINDOLANDA This Roman fort and frontier town was started well before Hadrian's Wall, and soon became a base for 500 soldiers. Well-preserved remains include the headquarters building and a full-scale reconstruction of Hadrian's turf and stone wall, complete with turret and gate tower. The associated civilian settlement has also been excavated, and the museum at Chesterholme gives a vivid impression of life for both civilians and soldiers, with lots of rare finds and more dug up all the time. Shop; disabled access to museum but not site; museum cl Dec, Jan and first couple of wks in Feb; £2.60. The Milecastle Inn and the Twice Brewed Inn are useful for food; the Twice Brewed opens all day at busy times.

Carrawbrough NY8971 MITHRAIC TEMPLE On the line of the Roman wall near the fort of Brocolitia stand replicas of the three altars to Mithras which were found here. The originals, which date from the 3rd c, are in Newcastle's Museum of Antiquities.

Chollerford NY9365 CHESTERS ROMAN FORT The best-preserved example of a Roman cavalry fort in Britain, with a museum filled with sculptures and inscriptions from sites along the wall; attractive riverside setting. Snacks, shop, disabled access; cl 24-26 Dec, 1 Jan; *£2.

Corbridge NY9964 CORBRIDGE ROMAN FORT Granaries, portico columns and remains of what may be legionary headquarters survive among remains of Roman Corstopitum, built around 210; also museum inc the magnificent Corbridge Lion. Shop, disabled access; cl Nov-Apr, and Mon in Oct; £2. Corbridge itself is an attractive village (or very small town) above the Tyne; the Wheatsheaf here is good for lunch.

Gilsland NY6366 BIRDOSWALD ROMAN FORT Overlooking the Irthing Gorge (and in fact just over the Cumbrian border), this is one of the most impressive sites. Its visitor centre explores the area's Roman heritage, and follows the spot's history into the present. Snacks, shop, disabled access; cl Nov-Easter; £1.50.

Greenhead NY6666 ROMAN ARMY MUSEUM (Carvoran) A useful introduction to the Wall, with models, reconstructions and life-size figures recreating the life of the Roman legionary. Everything you could possibly want to know about his training, pay and off-duty hobbies, as well as an exhibition of the many finds made on the adjacent part of the great barrier itself; snacks, shop, disabled access; cl Dec and Jan; £2.50.

Housesteads NY7969 HOUSESTEADS ROMAN FORT AND MUSEUM The best known and most visited part of the Wall, it owes its fine state of preservation partly to the fact that in the centuries when farmers and priests were using other parts of the abandoned wall as a convenient source of free recycled quality masonry, this fort was base camp for a powerful group of border bandits. Woe betide anyone who tried to use their fortifications as material for cowsheds or churches. It's a compact 5-acre fort containing visible remains of granaries,

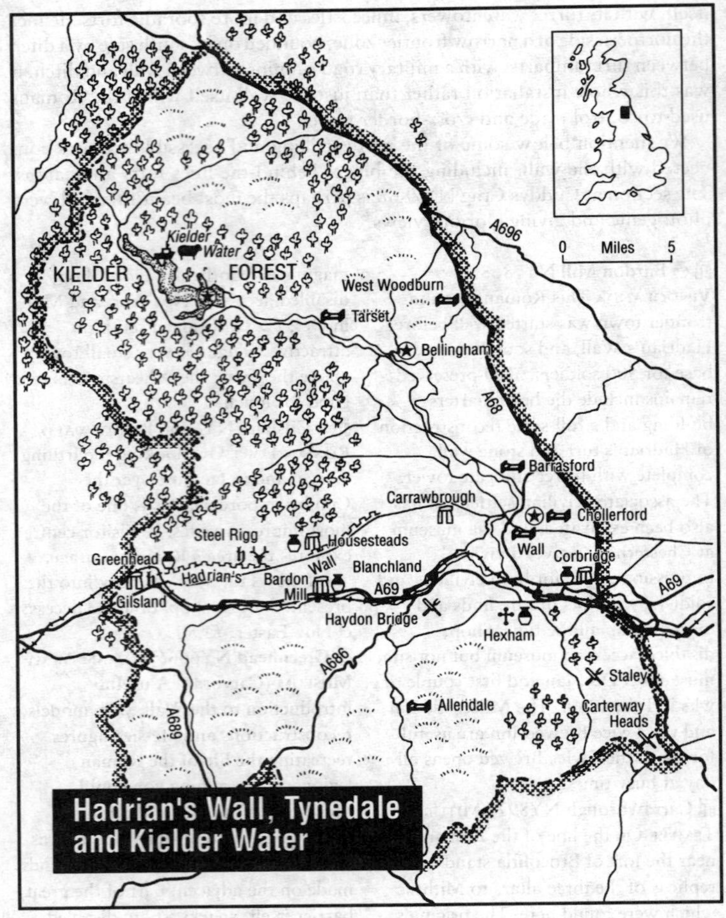

the commandant's house and latrines. The museum has altars, inscriptions and models. Snacks, shop; cl 24-26 Dec, 1 Jan; *£2.

Steel Rigg NY7667 ONCE BREWED Northumberland National Park Information Centre handy for Housesteads and Vindolanda, covering Hadrian's Wall area, featuring exhibitions and audio-visual presentations about the Wall and the park. Snacks, shop, disabled access; cl 7 Dec-13 Mar. The Once Brewed inn is useful for food.

Other things to see and do

Blanchland NY9750 is the archetypal border village, every house looking a stronghold, alone in a great bowl of magnificent scenery; the Lord Crewe Arms here is an interesting hotel, in parts very ancient indeed.

Chollerford SY9372 HEXHAM HERBS nr Chesters Fort (see above) Over 800 varieties of herbs are beautifully laid out in attractive walled gardens inc National Collections of thyme and marjorams; also old-fashioned roses, many other plants, woodland walk; some disabled access, plant sales; cl Nov-Easter exc by appointment, tel (0434) 681483; 80p.

✝ ⛫ **Hexham** NY9364 is the main town in the area, a pleasant market town with some attractive stone buildings – one now housing the BORDER HISTORY MUSEUM, colourfully charting the chequered contacts between the English and Scots over the centuries; cl Sun exc high summer, and Nov-Easter Mon and Tues from Feb. HEXHAM ABBEY Founded around 674 by St Wilfrid, this was once the largest church north of the Alps. Most of it was destroyed by Danish invasions in 875, and the bulk of what is seen today dates from the 12th c. As well as many interesting medieval features from this later building, there are two splendid Saxon survivals – the superb crypt, and the throne of the Bishop (St Wilfrid's Chair or Frith stool). Snacks (summer only), shop, disabled access; free, but donations welcome. The County Hotel is reliable for lunch. A little way north WARDEN CHURCH NY6265, down a lane by the Tyne, is a fine example of the sturdy northern churches that had to do double duty as holy places and watch-towers to warn of Border raiders.

Kielder Water NY6688 is an extremely large reservoir which has done quite a lot to open up a remote part of the Borders. It's an interesting shape, modelled by the steep folds of the land, and is already beginning to look as if it's always been tucked away in these forested hills. In summer there are water sports (with canoe and other BOAT HIRE from Leaplish Water Park (0434) 250203); CRUISES calling all around the lake (takes about an hour and a half); cycle and MOUNTAIN BIKE routes – hire from Kielder Bikes at Hawkhope car park (0434) 22039; and LOG CABINS to rent by the week (0502) 500500. Nearby the HIGH YARROW FARM is a working farm with spring lambing, also tame animals, ornamental pheasants, even free-ranging hand-feeding reindeer; some disabled access; cl Oct-Mar; *£1.50. The Kielder Heavy Horse Co, based in the village of Kielder NY6293, may do HORSE-DRAWN WAGON TRIPS: (0434) 250319. The surrounding miles of pine forests give a good chance of seeing red squirrels, as well as deer.

North Tynedale is one of the least known and most unspoilt parts of Northumberland. Between the Pennines and the Cheviots, it's a peaceful river valley surrounded by wild moorland, with fine scenery and a particularly unrushed atmosphere – very relaxing. The main town of the upper North Tyne is Bellingham (pronounced Bellingjum) NY8383, a small country town with an attractive 13th-c church, stone-roofed to protect it against arson-minded Border raiders; there's a pretty walk just north of the town, to the 30-ft cascade of Hareshaw Linn. There's summer PONY-TREKKING from Brown Rigg Farm (0434) 220210.

Walks

Hadrian's Wall has easy access from the parallel B6318 and numerous car parks on the way. The best-preserved sections include those around Walltown Crags NY6666, Cawfield Crags NY7167 and Housesteads Fort NY7969. There's not a lot of point trying to make walks into circuits: all the interest is along the Wall itself, although in places you may prefer to drop down beneath the switchback Whin Sill (the ridge of hard rock on which the Wall stands), which itself can be quite tiring. The views are bleak and exhilarating. Even in fine summer weather the wind can be chilly on the Wall, so go well wrapped up.

The great tract of **Kielder Forest** has been set up as a recreational area, with self-guided forest walks (easy to follow).

Driving

In Kielder Forest, there is a 12-mile forest drive with some open views among the millions of conifers, from the Forestry Commission's visitor centre at 18th-c Kielder Castle. The approach roads to Kielder Water from Bellingham also make an attractive drive, passing several isolated villages, and the B6320 from Wall through Wark to Bellingham traces through a lovely part of the North Tyne valley.

The B6318 from Humshaugh to Gilsland follows old Roman military road along the line of Hadrian's Wall, and gives some good views of it, while the B6295 down Allendale has some fine scenery.

The A68 runs through increasingly grand scenery in Redesdale as it approaches the Scottish border.

Where to eat

Haydon Bridge NY8464 General Havelock (0434) 684283 Very civilised old stone terraced house without machines or piped music, stripped-stone back dining room overlooking the Tyne; good, popular food; cl Mon, Tues, 2 wks beg Jan, 2 wks beg Sept. **£22 dinner, £16 lunch**|£1.50/£5.50.

Carterway Heads NZ0552 Manor House (0207) 55268 Simple slate-roofed stone house with pleasant view over moorland pastures, plentiful and imaginative food with a menu that changes daily. **£16.80**|£2.10/£6.30.

Slaley NY9858 Rose & Crown (0434) 673263 Friendly family-run inn with decent bar food and good interesting restaurant food inc several vegetarian dishes and a good-value Sunday lunch; bedrooms; disabled access (not bedrooms). **£15**|£1.10/£3.85.

We welcome reports from readers . . .

This Guide depends on readers' reports. Do help us if you can – in return, we offer a discount on the next edition to people who've helped us with reports for it. Tell us what you think about places already in it, and anything extra you think we should say about them. And send us your ideas for inclusion in the next edition: places to visit, eat at or stay in, attractive drives or walks, maybe even unusual interesting shops you know of. Use the card in the middle, the report forms at the end, or just write – no stamp needed: The Good Weekend Guide, FREEPOST TN1569, Wadhurst, E Sussex TN5 7BR.

DURHAM

Durham City is good for a weekend stay; the county has grand unspoilt scenery, especially in Teesdale; Beamish open-air museum is an outstanding attraction.

The city of Durham has much character, a good atmosphere and plenty to see besides its cathedral, which is one of the three most impressive in Britain; it's an enjoyable place for a short stay. In a county which has a great deal of fine countryside, Teesdale above Barnard Castle stands out for its beautiful peaceful scenery and it gives good access to the high moors (with splendid fishing, too).

The magnificent open-air museum at Beamish stands out as Britain's most appealing and rewarding attraction, excellent for keeping children interested, though fun whatever your age. The Bowes Museum at Barnard Castle is also tremendously worth while, a surprisingly under-visited storehouse of treasures. There is an expanding range of other interesting places to visit here, from Raby Castle at Staindrop to the lead-mining relics in Weardale and the mining museum at Skinningrove, but the county's prime attractions are its scenic beauty and the fact that it's not touristy.

We include Cleveland in this chapter, though the possibilities for a weekend stay in that predominantly industrial area are limited.

Where to stay

Durham NZ2743 ROYAL COUNTY DH1 3JN (091) 386 6821 **£110**; 150 rms. Close to the centre of the city with views of the castle and cathedral, this extended hotel has attractively furnished rooms, several restaurants, and lots of leisure facilities; disabled access.

Easington NZ4143 GRINKLE PARK Belford TS13 4UB (0287) 610515 ***£80**; 20 individually decorated rms. Charming country house in 35 acres of parkland between moors and coast, croquet, all weather tennis court; comfortable lounges, open fire; friendly and efficient service and enjoyable food using local produce when possible; full-sized snooker table.

Romaldkirk NY9922 ROSE & CROWN Barnard Castle DL12 9EB (0833) 50213 ***£75**; 12 rms, the ones in the main house have lots of character. Interesting old coaching inn by green of delightful Teesdale village, with beamed traditional bar, Jacobean oak settle, log fire, old black-and-white photographs, lots of brass; excellent, unusual food inc wonderful home-made puddings in fine oak-panelled restaurant; cl 25-26 Dec.

Headlam NZ1819 HEADLAM HALL Darlington DL2 3HA (0325) 730238 ***£70**; 26 rms. Jacobean mansion with elegant rooms, fine carved oak fireplace in the main hall; attractive restaurant with good food; indoor swimming pool, snooker; cl 25-26 Dec.

Greta Bridge NZ0813 MORRITT ARMS Barnard Castle DL12 9SE (0833) 27232 **£66**; 17 rms. Characterful old coaching inn where Dickens stayed in

1838, Dickensian bar with colourful mural, comfortable lounge; garden, coarse fishing; no children in evening dining room.

Cotherstone NZ0119 Fox & Hounds Barnard Castle DL12 9PF (0833) 50241 **£55**; 3 no-smoking rms. Attractive building in lovely setting overlooking Teesdale village green with comfortably furnished cosy beamed bar with alcoves and recesses, local photographs, open fire; good food, no-smoking dining room and courteous, friendly service; handy for walks; children over 9.

Middleton-in-Teesdale NY9526 Teesdale Barnard Castle DL12 0QG (0833) 40264 **£49.50**; 14 rms. In summer, this warm, pleasant and comfortable place is a riot of colour with really lovely hanging baskets, window boxes and borders; well-presented very good, fresh food in the attractive dining room (wonderful fresh wild Scottish salmon), decent bar food, and fine service.

Shincliffe NZ2941 Seven Stars Durham DH1 2NU (091) 384 8454 **£39w**; 8 rms. Small but comfortably smart inn in attractive village, traditionally furnished in one half, remarkable fireplace in the other; friendly staff and quiet atmosphere; decent bar and restaurant food and big breakfasts; cl 24 Dec-2 Jan.

High Force NY8728 High Force Hotel Barnard Castle DL12 0XH (0833) 22222 **£36**; 6 rms (shared bthrm). Close to England's highest waterfall (for which it's named), this is a cheerful, friendly place, robustly furnished; decent food and lots of malt whiskies; it includes a mountain rescue post.

Tow Law NZ1138 Greenwell Farm Bishop Auckland DL13 4PH (0388) 527248 **£32.50**; 3 rms. 300-year-old farmhouse with fine views, sitting and dining rooms; good food using naturally reared meats and locally grown produce; spring lambs, calves and chicks, nature trail and conservation areas; can bring own horse or mountain bike; self-catering also.

Bowes NY9112 Ancient Unicorn DL12 9HA (0833) 28321 **£30**; 4 comfortable rms. Coaching inn with *Nicholas Nickleby* connections; welcoming open-plan modernised bar with good, honest bar food; self-catering in well-converted stables block.

To see and do

Durham NZ2743 The ancient core of the town stands on a crag defended by an almost complete loop of the River Wear. There's an unforgettable view of the cathedral's magnificent pinnacled towers soaring above the trees from the far bank of the river, by the old corn mill across the weir from the archaeology museum (see below). The old part of town is largely pedestrianised, with attractive cobbled alleys and narrow medieval lanes, and fine medieval buildings among the Georgian and later ones, particularly around the 12th-c pedestrians-only Elvet Bridge. There are several medieval churches, and interesting little shops. You can hire rowing boats near Elvet Bridge, which is also the departure point for launches; and paths track along the riverside.

✝ ☕ The Cathedral is among the places which our contributors say they prize above all in Britain. It's a fiercely beautiful Norman building, breathtaking and very masculine inside, with many treasures including the shrine of St Cuthbert. The Treasury contains many valuable and beautiful objects representing 900 years of cathedral history, including relics of the saint, fine altar plate and clerical robes and jewellery; the 15th-c monks' dormitory now houses the cathedral's collection of rare books and manuscripts. Meals and snacks, shop, disabled facilities; monks' dormitory open 11 am-3 pm Mon-Sat, 2-4 pm Sun, admission 20p; Treasury open 10 am-4.30 pm Mon-Sat, 2-4.30 pm Sun, admission £1. There are handsome old houses around the close behind the cathedral.

The CASTLE nearby started as an early Norman motte and bailey; it's seen a lot of action over the centuries but is still a proud building, its chapel dating from about 1080 and its great hall from 1284. Shop; guided tours Easter and spring bank hol 2-4.30 pm, Sun 2-4.30 pm, other times of the year Mon, Weds, Sat 2-4.30 pm; £1.50.

UNIVERSITY MUSEUM OF ARCHAEOLOGY In a former fulling mill on the river bank below the cathedral's south-west corner, now showing material of international importance from excavations in and around the city. Shop; cl 25-26 Dec; *80p.

ORIENTAL MUSEUM (Elvet Hill) Remarkable display of oriental artefacts spanning ancient Egypt to Japan, with special exhibitions throughout the year. Shop, some disabled access; cl 1-2 pm, am wknds, Christmas-New Year; *£1.

UNIVERSITY BOTANIC GARDENS (Hollingside Lane) 18-acre garden in mature woodland with exotic trees from America and Himalayas, tropical house, cactus house and visitor centre, as well as a garden with sculptures by Colin Wilbourne celebrating the heritage of County Durham. Snacks, shop, disabled access to visitor centre and part of gardens; open daily Apr-Nov, and pm the rest of year, weather permitting.

HOUGHALL COLLEGE GARDENS The county's main horticultural training centre, with 10 acres of hardy plants, a water garden, woodland garden, Alpine rock garden and arboretum. This area records some of the lowest temperatures in the country so they like to say that if something grows here, it'll grow anywhere. The latest addition is a parterre and formal pond; snacks, disabled access; open daily 2-4 pm.

FINCHALE PRIORY St Godric chose this site as a place to meditate in 1110, and the priory was begun in 1180; there are considerable remains of the 13th-c church. Snacks, shop, disabled access; 75p.

ST AIDAN'S COLLEGE GROUNDS (Windmill Hill) At their best in July when shrub beds are in flower; good views of the cathedral. Facilities for disabled; cl Christmas, New Year and Easter wk.

DURHAM LIGHT INFANTRY MUSEUM AND ART GALLERY (Aykley Heads) Models, medals and more militaria telling the history of the regiment, while the art gallery hosts temporary exhibitions. Meals, snacks, shop, disabled access; cl Sun am, Mon (exc bank hols), Christmas hols; *75p.

Other things to see and do

Acklam NZ4917 BOTANIC CENTRE Thriving environmental demonstration centre, with organic gardens and wildlife areas and an exhibition centre. A number of natural habitats (moorland, wetlands etc) are under construction; meals, snacks, shop, disabled access; cl Mon and Tues in winter; £1.50.

Barnard Castle NZ0516 is a pleasant market town, still coming to life on Weds market day, with several attractive buildings. Most notable is the BOWES MUSEUM – not so much a museum as a beautiful French-style château in appropriately formal and meticulously kept grounds running to some 20 acres. Bowes and his

French wife were avid collectors, though the sumptuous exhibits here probably owe more to her taste than to his. Oddities include a silver swan that bends its neck to fish. The 40 rooms are filled with an outstanding display of paintings by Canaletto, Goya, El Greco and others (the biggest collection of Spanish paintings in Britain); also children's room and local history section. Because of its location, very few people visit this treasure-house, and on a cold winter's day you'll have it and its frost-sparkling grounds virtually to yourself. Snacks, shop, disabled facilities; cl Sun am, 20-25 Dec, 1 Jan; £2.30. CASTLE Built in 1125 in a dramatic site on the rocks above the Tees, most of this is now ruined, but the 12th-c keep and 14th-c hall survive; snacks, shop, disabled facilities; cl winter Mon, 24-26 Dec, 1 Jan; £1.70. Near it the White Swan is an ancient pub, perched in a similarly striking position over the river. In the centre, the Old Well is useful for lunch, and nearby there are good places like the Morritt Arms Hotel at Greta Bridge and Fox & Hounds at Cotherstone. The riverside walk a couple of miles downstream to EGGLESTONE ABBEY is well worth while (it can also be reached by car). In a serene spot above the River Tees, this ruined Premonstratensian abbey has left church walls with gracefully arched windows, and some remnants of the monastic buildings.

Beamish NZ2253 THE NORTH OF ENGLAND OPEN AIR MUSEUM Set in 300 acres, this amazingly ambitious museum thoroughly recreates life in the North of England at the turn of the century, exploring social, industrial and agricultural aspects on a grand scale, and constantly adding to its exhibits and displays. Shops, workshops, dentist, houses, trams, omnibus, colliery, drift mine, vintage fairground, Victorian bandstand, shire horses – something for everyone, though best on a dry day. Deservedly

winner of European Museum of the Year and British Museum of the Year Awards; it's the best open-air museum we've seen, and more of our contributors rate it among Britain's top attractions than any other place to visit. Meals and snacks, good shop, disabled access; cl Mon and Fri Nov-Mar, phone for details of Christmas opening times (0207) 231811; summer £5-£6, winter £3, when there's less to see – though of course the plus side is there are fewer people too, so guides can take more time to explain things. The Shepherd & Shepherdess not far from the gate is useful for lunch.

Binchester NZ2332 ROMAN FORT Quite a bit to see of this 10-acre fort, built around AD 80 to guard the road between York and Hadrian's Wall. The remains of the commandant's bath house contain the most complete hypocaust system in the whole country; shop; cl Thurs and Fri, all

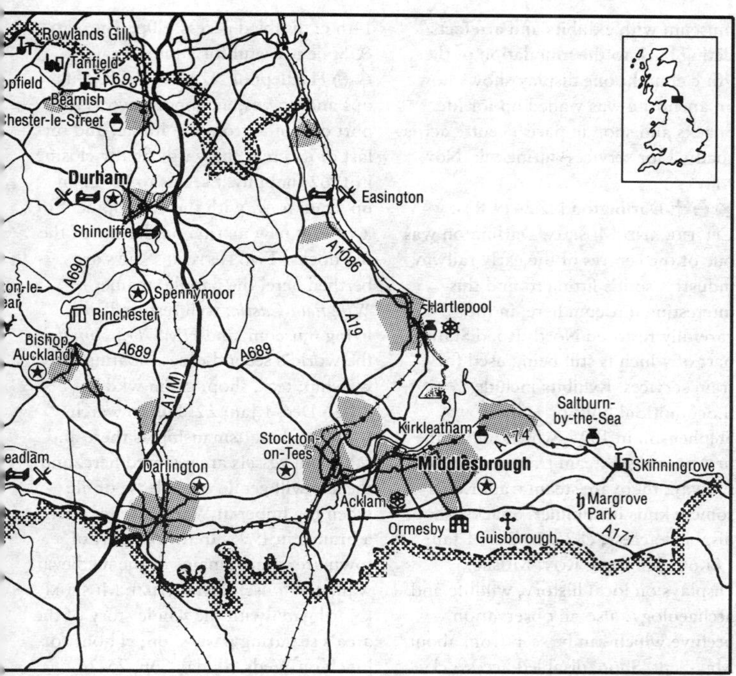

Oct-Mar; *80p. A 3rd-c fort can be seen at Piercebridge NZ2116 (where the George is good for lunch), and finds from both sites are shown at the Bowes Museum in Barnard Castle (see above).

Bishop Auckland NZ2130 Auckland Castle was for eight centuries the main country residence of the Bishops of Durham; it's a grand series of buildings with a rich history, entered through a splendid Gothic gatehouse in the town's market place. Some of the rooms are relatively stark, but the highlight is the chapel, splendidly transformed from a 12th-c banqueting hall by John Cosin from 1660. The grounds outside are attractive, with an unusual 18th-c deercote; shop; open May-mid-Sept, all day Tues, pm only Sun, Weds, Thurs, bank hols and Sat in Aug; £1.50.

Bowes NY9913 Bowes Castle Great Norman keep three storeys high among the ruins of the castle, which stands inside the earthworks of a Roman fort.

Burnopfield NZ1757 Leap Mill Farm 18th-c working farm and watermill, with very little changed since then – even the pigsty is a listed building. Rare breeds of cattle, old-fashioned roosters, ganders and goats in the farmyard, and handsome mature trees around the mill, recently restored to working order; snacks, shop; open pm Sun and bank hols Apr-Sept; *£1.25. Also worth a look here are the Gibside Chapel and Grounds, a marvellous Palladian mausoleum for the Bowes family in an 18th-c landscaped park, with the ruins of a hall and other estate buildings dotted around; snacks, shop, disabled access; cl Mon (exc bank hols) and Nov-Mar; *£2.50. NT.

Chester-le-Street NZ2751 Anker's House Museum Good local-history museum with exhibits and artefacts dating back to the foundation of the 9th-c church; one display shows how an anchorite was walled up for life. Snacks and shop in parish centre across road; cl for services during wk, Nov-May.

Darlington NZ2419 RAILWAY CENTRE AND MUSEUM Darlington was one of the centres of the early railway industry, so it's fitting to find this interesting museum here, in the carefully restored North Road Station, part of which is still being used for train services. Exhibits include 'Locomotion' built by Robert Stephenson in 1825, which pulled the first passenger steam train on a public railway; there are steam train rides some wknds in summer. Snacks, shop, disabled access; cl 25-26 Dec, 1 Jan; *£1.60. TUBWELL ROW MUSEUM Displays on local history, wildlife and archaeology; also an observation beehive which can be seen from about May-Sept. Shop, disabled access; cl lunchtimes, Thurs pm, Sun, also Good Fri, May Day, Christmas, 1 Jan. DARLINGTON MUSEUM is a friendly little museum covering local history and agriculture, with an observation beehive in summer and a few railway exhibits; shop, disabled access to ground floor only; cl 1-2 pm, Thurs pm, all day Sat. St Cuthbert's is an interesting early English CHURCH.

Eggleston NY9924 EGGLESTON HALL GARDENS Good example of updated 19th-c country-house garden, with rare and unusual plants and seven greenhouses; plant sales, also organically grown herbs, fruit and vegetables from the walled kitchen garden. Disabled access; 50p. The Three Tuns is good for lunch, and this is an attractive moorside Teesdale village.

Guisborough NZ6115 GISBOROUGH PRIORY The priory was founded in the 12th c, but the remains which stand so dramatically on this site belong to the east end of a church built here in the 14th c; disabled access; 90p. The Tap & Spile is useful for a bite to eat.

Hartlepool NZ5133 has had its ups and downs, its importance as a port declining from the 16th c, and the last of its great shipyards finally closing in 1962; happily it seems to be on an up again now, with the development of a vibrant new marina on the site of the old docks. Two HISTORIC SHIPS are berthed here, the paddle steamer *Wingfield Castle*, well restored as a living museum, and HMS *Trincomalee*, the world's second-oldest floating warship; teas, shop; cl am wkdys, 25-26 Dec, 1 Jan; £2. Fun to watch traditional craftsmanship as these and other old vessels are restored here, and the site will get an extra lease of life when the Imperial War Museum open a branch in 1995. In the old part of town are some remains of the medieval wall, and a useful MARITIME MUSEUM (Northgate) with the whole story of the area's seafaring past; shop; cl hour for lunch on Weds, all day Sun, 25-26 Dec, 1 Jan, Good Fri.

Kirkleatham NZ5922 OLD HALL MUSEUM Grand old school building displaying the history, archaeology and natural history of the area, with an exhibition on ironstone mining, a reconstructed sweet and rock-making shop, lifeboat and maritime memorabilia, and various temporary shows. Meals, snacks, shop, disabled access; cl Tues and Weds. The village has a few other old buildings, many associated with the family that used to live here, inc an unusual mausoleum – it looks even odder with the views of the area's modern industrial heritage behind.

Margrove Park NZ6516 MARGROVE HERITAGE CENTRE Right on the edge of the moors, so concentrating largely on the natural history and environment of the area, with other displays of fossils, archaeology and wildlife. They organise walks and nature trails; shops, disabled access; cl Sun am, all day Fri and Sat and every am in winter.

Middlesbrough NZ4920 Though the town itself is not a particular attraction for visitors, it does contain several places worth seeing. CAPTAIN COOK BIRTHPLACE MUSEUM Set in impressive grounds which also include a conservatory of tropical plants and various animals and fowl, this museum presents a detailed account of the early life of James Cook and his discoveries; snacks, shop, disabled access; cl Mon exc bank hols; £1. There's a decent ART GALLERY in Linthorpe Rd, and the CLEVELAND GALLERY in Victoria Rd has a notable range of modern art (and local lace). The CLEVELAND CRAFT CENTRE in Gilkes St has a good collection of traditional and contemporary crafts (esp pottery and jewellery) and various changing exhibitions; all cl Mon. The town's social history, industry, archaeology and wildlife are explored at the DORMAN MUSEUM (Linthorpe Rd); cl Sun and Mon. NEWHAM GRANGE LEISURE FARM (Coulby Newham) The site has been continuously farmed since Domesday, and now has a number of rare breeds, an agricultural museum, reconstructed vet's surgery and merchant's shop, and plenty of other animals and poultry; snacks, shop, disabled access; cl winter exc Sun; £1.20. The Transporter Bridge across the Tees is unique, with the central section serving as a ferry shuttling cars and pedestrians across the river; cl Sun am; car 57p, pedestrian 18p.

Ormesby NZ5416 ORMESBY HALL Elegant 18th-c house with elaborate platerwork, newly renovated Victorian laundry and kitchen, pleasant gardens and grounds; snacks, shop, disabled access; cl am, Mon, Tues, Fri, Nov-Mar; £2.

Rowlands Gill NZ1759 DERWENTCOTE STEEL FURNACE (on A694 between Rowlands Gill and Hamsterley) The earliest and most complete steel-making furnace to have survived, with an exhibition on steel production and this site's role in the development of the industry; shop, disabled access; cl Oct-Mar; £1.20.

Saltburn-by-the-Sea NZ6722 Originally a superior Victorian seaside resort, with traces of those days still in the Italianate valley garden and water-operated sloping tramway by pier. The SHIP INN, right by the boats pulled up on the beach and worth knowing as a pub, is probably the most ancient building, and the old cottages alongside it house a vivid exhibition on the town's smuggling heritage; cl Oct-Easter; £1.50. The beach is sheltered by the great headland of Warsett Hill to the south.

Skinningrove NZ7119 TOM LEONARD MINING MUSEUM The site of the old Loftus mine is the setting for this museum, where visitors can experience the reality of work underground. Not only are there the more usual kinds of exhibits – collections of tools, safety equipment and old photos – but also you can see how the stone is drilled, charged with explosives and fired; snacks, shop; cl am, Nov-Easter; *£1.50. This industrial village with its steel-rolling mill is far from picturesque but has strong local colour.

Spennymoor NZ2634 WHITWORTH HALL AND GARDENS When Bobbie Shafto went to sea it was from this neat old house, dating back in part to 1183. As well as the period furnished rooms and miniature village there's a clock museum and a vineyard and brewery, and the handsome grounds have been restored to their original state; teas, shop, some disabled access; open wknds and bank hols Easter-Sept, plus Mon, Tues and Weds from spring bank hol, hall cl am; £3. Bonnie Bobbie is buried in the parish church.

Staindrop NZ1220 RABY CASTLE Imposing old castle with Saxon origins, and since the 17th c the home of Lord Barnard's family. The current structure is largely 14th-c, with parts added almost every century, and impressive features include the vast medieval hall, the recently spruced-up Victorian octagonal drawing room and a 14th-c kitchen with collection of Victorian copper utensils. Also interesting furniture, paintings and china, walled gardens and deer park; snacks, shop, disabled access (prior notice appreciated), tel (0833) 60202; open all bank hol wknds to following Weds, Weds and Sun in May and Jun, daily except Sat July-Sept, castle pm only; £3.

Stockton-on-Tees NZ4419 GREEN DRAGON MUSEUM (Theatre Yard) The main attraction is a lively audio-visual presentation on the birth of the railways here in 1825, though there are also displays of other pieces of local history, from shipbuilding and a working steam engine to Lonnie Donegan's hairbrush; shop, some disabled access (prior notice preferred), tel (0642) 781184; cl Sun and bank hols. PRESTON HALL MUSEUM (2m S) Reconstructions of period rooms and a street with working craftsmen are just some of the ways this fascinating museum illustrates Victorian social history; snacks, shop, disabled access; cl Sun am, Good Fri, 25-26 Dec, 1 Jan. On the same site BUTTERFLY WORLD has a recreated jungle environment with hundreds of exotic butterflies flitting between the trees, rocks and waterfalls; snacks, shop, disabled access; *£2.50. There's a railway heritage trail around town.

Tanfield NZ1855 TANFIELD RAILWAY The world's oldest surviving railway, set in a picturesque wooded valley, with a stationary steam engine to haul the vintage carriages by cable. Display boards tell the story of the early railway and collieries; also machine tools, and often a blacksmith forging new parts for restoration work. Summer snacks, shop, facilities for the disabled; phone for train timetable (091) 274 2002; from £3 for trains.

Teesdale has the best of the county's scenery, with England's most powerful WATERFALL at High Force NY8728 dropping into a craggy cauldron at the end of a striking wooded gorge (the nearby High Force Hotel is useful); the attractive villages of Middleton in Teesdale NY9526, Romaldkirk NY9922 and Eggleston NN9924 (all with good pubs and inns); side tracks with rewards at their end such as the cosy Strathmore Arms in Holwick NY9027 or the Cow Green reservoir (a short drive or walk above the pleasant Langdon Beck Inn NY8631, with the 200-ft cascade of Caldon Snout below it); good fishing on the river or the reservoirs above it, and fine landscapes all the way along.

Weardale runs through the heart of the county, and was the source of much of its wealth, with lead and iron mining along its length and in the moors above. There's little reminder of those days now, but high up at the top of the dale near the Cumbrian border at Cowshill is the KILLHOPE WHEEL lead mining centre NY8243, probably the best-preserved lead mining site in Britain, showing the extraction process powered by a huge waterwheel, and the way the fell ponies used to bring the lead down from isolated moorland mines. Also working smithy and exhibition giving an insight into the lives of the miners and their families; snacks, shop; cl Nov-Mar; £2. At Ireshopeburn NY8639, near the source of the river, the WEARDALE MUSEUM recreates life in the mining days, with period rooms and furnishings and displays of local rocks, minerals and wildlife. There's also an exhibition on John Wesley, who often preached in the adjacent chapel; shop; cl am, all day Mon, Tues and Fri (exc in Aug and bank hols), and Oct-Easter; 80p. Along the dale is a string of attractive villages like Stanhope NY9939 (the 'capital' of Weardale, with odd fossil tree stump in churchyard) and Wolsingham NZ0737, and pleasant waterside and moorland walks.

♈ **Witton-le-Wear** NZ1730 LOW BARNS NATURE RESERVE 100-acre reserve with nature trails, woodland, grassland, lake and lots of interesting wildlife; snacks, shop, disabled access. The village is attractive, with a tree-lined sloping green; the Victoria is useful for lunch.

Walks

Though this county can't quite compete with Northumberland for serious walking, it does have a good many very enjoyable walks in fine scenery. **Upper Teesdale** has much of the best walking in the Durham Pennines. Most popular of all is the short path from the main road to the High Force waterfall NY8728. From Bowlees Visitor Centre NY9028 you can make more of a walk of it, first detouring north to Gibson's Cave NY9028, a pretty waterfall at the top of a gorge, and then heading south to cross the Tees for an easy two miles upriver, passing Low Force NY9028 on the way. Beyond High Force, the **Pennine Way** encounters some truly wild landscape as the Tees rushes along a gorge beneath Cronkley Scar NY8329 and tumbles down Caldron Spout NY7930, a cascade which can be reached from the dam at Cow Green Reservoir NY7930 (where there is also a nature trail).

There is more gorge scenery around **Barnard Castle** NZ0516, here wooded, romantic and unmistakably lowland in character; the valley path west eventually climbs above the river and follows field routes as it leads towards Cotherstone NZ0119. Similar pockets of scenery are found along the River Greta, south of town, and the Deepdale Beck, to the west; both have attractive paths along them.

Cleveland, though solidly built up and much industrialised, has rural fringes, including the northern flanks of the **North York Moors**, where Roseberry Topping NZ5712 is a memorable viewpoint reached by a walk over moors from Gribdale Gate car park east of Great Ayton NZ5611; a popular circuit goes by way of Airy Home Farm NZ0453, the childhood home of Captain Cook. Eston Nab NZ5618, outside the National Park, has a massive view over industrial Teesside. The **Cleveland Way**, most of which is actually in North Yorkshire, begins its grand coastal finale at Saltburn-by-the-Sea NZ6722, passing Skinningrove NZ7199 (an odd shantytown of pigeon-fanciers' sheds spreads over the cliff) and ascending Boulby Cliff NZ7619, the highest point on the east coast, before re-entering North Yorkshire and the national park. The county council's environment department runs a busy programme of guided walks throughout the county, with some emphasis on country pursuits, local history and geology; tel (091) 386 4411 ext 2354 for programme.

Driving

One of the finest drives in the north is the B6277 through Teesdale right over to Alston in Cumbria. Others include the B6278 from Barnard Castle through Egglestone to Stanhope, and then on to Edmondbyers where a left turn on to the B6306 takes you down through Blanchland and over the border into Northumberland; and the A689 up Weardale. If you are passing through on the way to or from Scotland, a splendid route is to turn off the A1 just N of Scotch Corner down in Yorkshire, then take the B6275 through Piercebridge to join the A68 and plunge on over the hills into and through Northumberland.

Where to eat

Romaldkirk NY9922 KIRK (0833) 50260 Country pub with good food inc interesting veg; landlord does cooking, wife tends bar; cl Tues am, no food Tues pm. £2.50/£5.
Eggleston NY9924 THREE TUNS (0833) 50289 Good helpings of decent food, very attractive surroundings. £1.45/£4.80.
Good food is also to be found in the places we recommend in Where to stay, above.

Help this year from: *Derek and Sylvia Stephenson, Dilys Unsworth, John Oddey, Stephen Savill, WAH, SS, M and J Back, Barbara and Mike Williams, Andy and Jill Kassube, Jennie and Malc Wild, Barry and Anne, Bob Shand, Mrs J R Thomas, Mary and Peter Clarke, R J Herd, Roger Bellingham, D Maplethorpe, Scott and Anne Foringer, M G Hart, CW, JW, Roxanne Chamberlain, R C Lewis, R T Moggridge, Mrs P Arnold, Anthony John, Graham and Karen Oddey, Nigel and Teresa Brooks, Klaus and Elizabeth Leist, Mike and Wendy Proctor, G Taylor, Neil and Angela Huxter, Alan Wilcock, Christine Davidson, Graham Bassett, R S Dancey, Gill and Maurice McMahon, Andrew and Ruth Triggs.*

NORTHUMBRIA CALENDAR

Some of these dates were provisional as we went to press.

MARCH

24th **Crook** Wear Valley Duathlon; *run, bike, run*

APRIL

1st **Shildon** Extravaganza *at Timothy Hackworth Victorian and Railway Museum, to celebrate its redevelopment*

3rd **Lanchester** Lambing Time *at Hall Hill Farm – till Mon 4*; **Ormesby** Hall, Easter Eggstravaganza *at Ormesby Hall*

8th **Morpeth** Northumbrian Gathering, *festival of Northumbrian traditions, inc concerts, films, street events, clog dance and workshops – till Sun 10*

10th **Lanchester** Lambing Time *at Hall Hill Farm*

24th **Barnard Castle** Teesdale Country Fair *inc main ring events, falconry, vintage cars and crafts at Lartington Park*

29th **Barnard Castle** Teesdale Thrash; *craft fair, swing-arounds, ceilidh, folk concert and workshops – till 2 May*

MAY

1st **Berwick-upon-Tweed** Riding the Bounds; *ancient and colourful ceremony run without break since the reign of Henry VIII. Starting from Guildhall, Mayor's party, mounted riders and foot-followers perambulate the 10 miles around the town's boundaries. The ceremony is of special significance as part of the boundary of Berwick forms the frontier with Scotland. Races and games*; **Ormesby** May Day Merriment *at Ormesby Hall*; **Prudhoe** Falconry Event *at Prudhoe Castle*

Northumbria Calendar

June cont.

7th **Durham** Gardens Open Weekend *at Houghall College of Agriculture and Horticulture – till Sun 8*

23rd **Seaham** Gala

27th **Berwick-upon-Tweed** May Fair *dating from 1302, starting at 12 when the Mayor and Council walk the streets*

28th **Eastgate** Show; **North Shields** Fishquay Festival *– till Mon 30*

30th **Corbridge** Northumberland County Show *at Tynedale Park*

June

4th **Allendale** Fair; **Mickleton** Carnival

11th **Durham** Regatta, *50 events – till Sun 12*

12th **Berwick-upon-Tweed** Spittal Gala Day, *traditional entertainment*; **Morpeth** Town Fair

17th **Newcastle** Hoppings; *biggest funfair in Europe at Town Moor, Grandstand Rd – till Sat 25*

18th **Ovingham** Goose Fair, *trad fair with proclamation, Morris men and pipers*

19th **Stocksfield** British Field Sports Country Fair *at Bywell Hall*

26th **Alnwick** Medieval Fair *– till 2 July*

July

9th **Durham** Miners Gala; *commonly known as the 'big meeting' this annual gathering began in 1871 as a demonstration of solidarity. Each lodge of Durham miners marches behind its own colliery band and banner from the outskirts of the city into Durham. Culminates in trade union rally, gala and dancing*

16th **Chester-le-Street** County Agricultural Show *at Lambton Park – till Sun 17*

17th **Woodhorn** Open Day *at Colliery Museum*; *animal fun day with bands, jugglers and sports*

23rd **Middlesbrough** Cleveland County Show

29th **Hartlepool** Town Moor Fair *– till Sun 31*

August

5th **Kielder** Festival *– till Sun 7*

6th **Hartlepool** Carnival; **Middleton-in-Teesdale** Carnival

7th **Alnwick** Tournament Day *at Alnwick Castle*; **Kirkleatham** Country Fair, *with arena entertainment*; **Saltburn** Victorian Festival *– till Sun 14*

13th **Billingham** International Folklore Festival, *10 countries represented, song, dance and craft fair – till Sat 20*; **nr Hexham** Slug Show *(bring your own) at Dipton Mill pub or possibly on Sat 20*

17th Bishop Auckland Teddy Bears Picnic *at Deer House, inc Punch & Judy*

20th **Allendale** Agricultural Show; **Falstone** Border Shepherds Show; **Darlington** Agricultural Show, *at South Park*

NORTHUMBRIA CALENDAR

AUGUST cont.

27th **Allendale** Floral, Horticultural and Industrial Society Show; **Bellingham** Show; **Eastgate-in-Weardale** St John's Chapel Agricultural Show; **Glendale** Agricultural Show; **Weardale** Agricultural Show

29th **Blanchland** Agricultural Show; **Newcastle** Free Festival, *open-air events, music, dance, circus, concerts, comedy – till 3 Sept*; **Seaham** Gala; **Weardale** Triathlon

SEPTEMBER

1st **Durham** CAMRA Beer Festival – *till Sat 3*

3rd **Harbottle** Country Show; **Wolsingham** & Wear Valley Agricultural Show *at Scotch Isle farm – till Sun 4*

10th **Bowes** Agricultural Show; **Stanhope** Agricultural Show – *till Mon 12*

17th **Eggleston** Agricultural Show

OCTOBER

8th **Alwinton** Border Shepherds Show; *sheep show, fell race, hound trail, dog trials*; **Middlesbrough** Literary Festival

NOVEMBER

4th **Bishop Auckland** Fireworks and Funfair

5th **Alnwick** Northumbrian Gathering, *small pipes, fiddles, concert and ceilidh*; **Stockton** Fireworks Display

DECEMBER

26th **Sunderland** Boxing Day Dip *at Coastal Road; over 1,000 dippers in fancy dress are hosed by the fire brigade before braving the sea*

31st **Allendale** Baal Festival: *local men 'guisers' in fancy costumes assemble 11.30 pm by Golden Lion, at 11.45 tar barrels are lit and carried on their heads around the perimeter of the village; at midnight the burning barrels are thrown on a bonfire, 'Auld Lang Syne' is sung and the traditional 'first footing' is begun*

OXFORDSHIRE

Oxford itself is one of the best half-dozen or so English cities for a short break. Just to the north of the city are Blenheim and its small town of Woodstock, where you could easily spend a day.

Away from these two places, the county's appeal is primarily rural. The very varied countryside includes the fringes of the Cotswolds in the north of the county, and, in the south, part of the Chilterns, the lush Thames valley, and the much emptier northern crest of the downs. Many of the county's villages and small towns have great charm, ideal to potter around: Great Tew in North Oxfordshire is one contender for the title of England's prettiest village. There are great houses to visit, with a few fine gardens, though not many of the more organised types of visitor attractions. This is a particularly good county for eating out.

OXFORD

A vibrant bustling city, Oxford is packed with memorable medieval university buildings and magnificent collections.

Oxford is not a restful city: the ancient university buildings in their medieval lanes are surrounded by a bustling largely industrialised town, and a formidable amount of traffic. Yet there are many tranquil corners, and idyllic moments when a hush seems to suffuse the whole centre – perhaps at dusk on a summer evening, or on a dark winter night.

The one-way system and difficulties in parking away from the NCPs combine to make it a driver's nightmare; if you can, it may be best to leave your car at the Park and Ride, on the ring road. Walking is anyway the best way to see Oxford, and the only way you can see more than tantalising glimpses of college quads through the tiny doorways.

Most of the oldest or most interesting colleges are grouped around the centre of town, particularly around the Bodleian Library, the Sheldonian Theatre and the splendid domed Radcliffe Camera (also a library). The cluster of ancient buildings around this partly cobbled area makes it one of the most attractive parts of the city, and easily the most photographed.

Besides the colleges themselves, the art collections of the Ashmolean Museum, the extraordinary Pitt Rivers Museum and the Bodleian Library are all extremely rewarding; the university's botanic garden is the oldest in the world.

As well as the following recommended places to stay, several of those listed in North and South Oxfordshire are within easy reach of the city.

Where to stay

Oxford SP5305 RANDOLPH OX1 2LN (0865) 247481 **£161**; 109 rms. Fine Victorian hotel, facing the Ashmolean Museum, with elegant, comfortable day rooms, grand foyer, and graceful restaurant; disabled access.

Oxford SP5305 OLD PARSONAGE 1 Banbury Rd OX2 6NN (0865) 310210 **£140**; 30 stylish modern rms. 17th-c parsonage with very courteous staff, good breakfasts and light meals in cosy bar (Browns Restaurant – under the same ownership – is over the road), small lounge, and pretty little garden; they have their own punt.

Headington SP5407 CONIFER GUEST HOUSE 116 The Slade Oxford OX3 7DX (0865) 63055 ***£45**; 8 rms, some with own bthrm. Very friendly, spotlessly kept B & B with outdoor swimming pool; cl Christmas/New Year; disabled access.

To see and do

A TOUR BUS from St Aldates or the High St is good value for the first-time visitor; the tours take in all the best sites and last about 1½ hours; *£5. GUIDED WALKS leave from the corner of Catte St on the High St.

A look round a few colleges is almost compulsory, and most allow visitors into some of the quads, although this may be more limited in term time, and some are starting to charge. The chapels are often the best buildings.

MAGDALEN is the most beautiful college, its tower a dramatic sight for visitors entering the city from the south. The quads and cloisters are very pleasant to stroll through, but the chief attraction is the DEER PARK. There's a circular path around this called Addison's Walk, in spring a mass of snowdrops and daffodils, and full of wildlife. Over a small bridge is the Fellows' Garden with a small ornamental lake – a very peaceful, sheltered spot.

CHRIST CHURCH is better known: a magnificently stately place begun by Cardinal Wolsey in the 16th c, but soon taken over by Henry VIII. The main entrance into the main quad is through Tom Tower, designed by Christopher Wren and named after its famous bell that rings out 101 times at nine o'clock every night – in less liberal times the hour when students were due back in their rooms. The Hall is worth a look, with its remarkable hammerbeam roof, paintings of alumni and benefactors by all the most expensive portrait-painters of the period, and the long tables laid out with silver for meals. The elaborate little CATHEDRAL, which also doubles as the college chapel, has some excellent stained glass by Burne-Jones as well as some of the original Norman priory work. The PICTURE LIBRARY has important Old Master paintings and drawings, as well as various temporary exhibitions; cl Sun am; *80p.

Other interesting colleges are NEW, with its impressive chapel, atmospheric wisteria-covered cloisters, and remains of the city wall; MERTON, the most ancient buildings with the first quad and the country's oldest library (tours available); UNIVERSITY, which has an interesting monument to Shelley despite having thrown him out; the brightly Victorian very red-brick

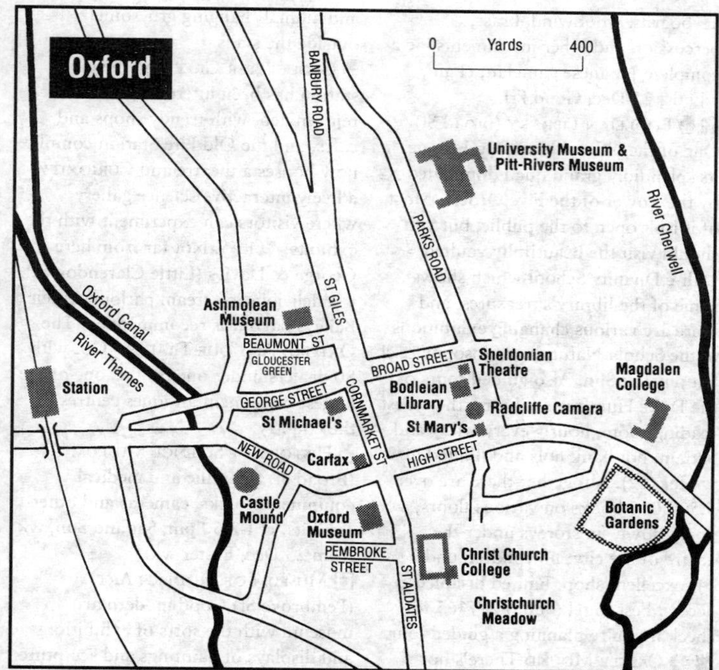

KEBLE (with perhaps the most famous Pre-Raphaelite painting of all, Holman Hunt's *Light of the World*, in its chapel); and ST EDMUND HALL, the only surviving medieval college, complete with Norman crypt. Amble down some of the town's prettiest streets and there are more, such as charming EXETER, JESUS and LINCOLN down Turl St, and CORPUS CHRISTI and ORIEL around Merton Lane and Oriel Sq. This latter college has a very attractive and unusual entrance to its dining hall. TRINITY on Broad St is very grand. Around Radcliffe Sq BRASENOSE is quaint (and has good views of the surrounding skyline from its quads), and Hertford has its BRIDGE OF SIGHS over New College St, in itself worth exploring for some more unusual and less busy views and a good look at the gargoyles on the backs of some of the buildings. Colleges with particularly nice GARDENS include Worcester and the more modern St Hugh's.

Other things to see and do

⛑ ◙ ASHMOLEAN MUSEUM (Beaumont St) The first museum in the country, opened in 1683 and rehoused in this imposing building from 1845; well-arranged galleries displaying marvellous European paintings, antiquities from ancient Egypt, Greece and Rome, and coins, medals, porcelain, ceramics and pottery from all over the world. A fascinating place to spend an afternoon. Shop, disabled access; cl am Sun, Mon (exc bank hols), Good Fri-Easter Sun, during Sept St Giles Fair.

⛑ BATE COLLECTION OF MUSICAL INSTRUMENTS (St Aldates) Early

keyboards, woodwind, brass, percussion and other instruments inc a complete Japanese gamelan; cl am, wknds, 25 Dec, Good Fri.

BODLEIAN LIBRARY (Broad St) One of the oldest libraries in Europe, its splendidly grand quad dominated by the Tower of the Five Orders. Most of it isn't open to the public, but you should visit the beautifully vaulted 15th-c Divinity School which shows some of the library's treasures, and there are various changing exhibitions in the Schola Naturalis Philosophiae; cl Sat pm and Sun. Also guided tours of the Duke Humfrey's Library, the oldest reading room, hourly every wkdy and Sat am, not bank hols and limited in winter (£2). Altogether there are over 5,500,000 books on various floors, going down six storeys under the centre of the city; no children under 14; excellent shop; limited disabled access; best to tel (0865) 277165 to check if you're planning a guided tour.

CASTLE MOUND There's not much left of Oxford's Norman castle other than the tower and crypt of the castle church, and an underground medieval well chamber, but the Mound gives quite good views over the city and its surroundings; tours on Weds pm twice a month July-Sept, possibly Sun too – tel Mrs O'Neill on (0865) 815559 for dates.

CHRISTCHURCH MEADOW is an unspoilt expanse of green astonishingly close to the busy city streets. You can gaze across the fields of grazing Christchurch cattle to the spires in the distance, or walk under overhanging trees along the banks of the river to the boathouses. From here you can usually see college eights rowing down the water. This really is a marvellous place to explore or, if it's a nice day, somewhere just to relax.

The COVERED MARKET is a maze of stalls with something different at every turn; chic boutiques, speciality shops, cafés and old-fashioned butchers and poultry merchants with whole birds and animals hanging gruesomely outside the stalls.

GLOUCESTER GREEN by the bus station has been interestingly rejuvenated, with trendy shops and cafés, and the Old Fire Station complex now houses a theatre and CURIOXITY, a lively interactive science gallery where visitors can experiment with the exhibits; *£1.75. Not far from here George & Davies (Little Clarendon St) is a delicious ice-cream parlour – their Baileys flavour is recommended. The OXFORD ANTIQUE TRADING CO, with 80 dealers under one roof, is one of the largest permanent antiques centres in the country.

HISTORY OF SCIENCE MUSEUM (Broad St) Scientific and medical equipment, clocks, cameras and other exhibits; cl 1-2.30 pm, Sat and Sun, wk from 23 Dec, Easter wk.

MUSEUM OF MODERN ART (Pembroke St) Good modern art museum with the sorts of exhibitions and displays of paintings and sculpture not often found in galleries outside London; snacks, good bookshop, disabled access; cl am Sun, Mon; £2.50.

MUSEUM OF OXFORD (St Aldates) Interesting little museum about the archaeology and history of the city, with recreated rooms, models, maps, relics, period music and sound effects; shop; cl Sun, Mon.

ST MICHAEL AT THE NORTH GATE (Cornmarket St) Oxford's oldest building, a Saxon church, with interesting displays of silver, clocks and bells; you can climb the tower, which has quite a good view from the top; cl during services; £1.

THE OXFORD STORY (Broad St) Lively exhibition with the sights, sounds and smells of the university's history. Great fun – you ride around in a desk, with a commentary by either Magnus Magnusson or Timmy Mallett. Ideal for families, and a good introduction to the city; shop, disabled access; cl 25 Dec; £4.25.

PITT RIVERS MUSEUM (Banbury Rd) Shrunken heads, totem poles and fertility rites – a fascinating ethnological museum off the tourist track, with art and ingenuity from all cultures and periods. Don't miss Captain Cook's Pacific Islands Collection and the 18th-c ship models, nor the eskimo coat made from seal intestines, and the severed fingertip. Disabled access, shop; cl am and Sun. The adjacent BALFOUR BUILDING has a gallery of archaeology and a large collection of musical instruments.

PUNTING is good fun in sunny weather; once you've got the knack it's a very nice way of spending a lazy afternoon. You can hire boats from Magdalen Bridge or Folly Bridge; usually about £5 an hour, but you'll probably have to put down a big deposit. From Folly Bridge, Salters also run steamer trips to Abingdon; £5.25.

ROTUNDA MUSEUM OF ANTIQUE DOLL'S HOUSES (Grove House, Iffley Turn) Private collection of over 40 historic houses, dating from 1700-1900, with period furniture, carpets, dinner services, books and inhabitants; no under-16s; open pm Sun May-mid-Sept; £1.50.

SHELDONIAN THEATRE (Broad St) A grand classical building, with a lovely painted ceiling. In its time it's been used for parliaments, but nowadays university ceremonies are held here; you may be lucky enough to see students heading for these on some wknds, though the theatre is closed to the public then.

UNIVERSITY MUSEUM (Parks Rd) Victorian Gothic building specialising in natural history – fossils and dinosaurs, a popular working beehive and even Alice's dodo; shop; cl Sun and some days over Easter and Christmas.

UNIVERSITY OF OXFORD BOTANIC GARDEN (High St) Founded in 1621, with 8,000 species of plant from all over the world. It's a lovely relaxing place to sit for a while, or to wander through on the way to the river; disabled access; cl Good Fri and 25 Dec; £1 in July and Aug, no charge at other times. The 55-acre UNIVERSITY ARBORETUM outside town is also worth visiting; some disabled access; cl am Sun, all Nov-Apr.

The best place to go for VIEWS is up, and there are plenty of places that facilitate this. The interesting university church ST MARY'S has fine views from its old tower (shop, snacks; cl 25 Dec; *£1), as does CARFAX TOWER, all that remains of a 14th-c church. There are some exhibits on display here as well, and the bells in the tower are interestingly designed; shop; cl Nov-Mar; *£1.

Walks

Most of the walking you do here will be from college to college and building to building, but there are more countrified walks almost from the city centre.

The UNIVERSITY PARKS are the closest place to the centre for a good stroll – and you can watch first-class cricket matches for free.

The best outlying area is **Port Meadow**, a fen-like and often misty expanse of waterside common land with grazing horses and flocks of geese, which extends north from Jericho and can be reached on the far side of the Oxford canal via Walton Well Road (near the University Press), crossing the Thames and turning right along the west bank. Just beyond the far end of Port Meadow is the ruin of 12th-c Godstow Nunnery, where Fair Rosamund the mistress of Henry II is buried; nearby, the riverside medieval Trout pub is attractive, with peacocks wandering around. A second well-sited riverside pub, the Perch at

Binsey, is another popular objective in this direction. **Iffley Meadows** on the other side of the centre are conserved for wildlife, and in late spring are a sea of purple snakes-head fritillaries.

The rivers **Thames** and **Cherwell** make strikingly rural corridors through the city, though walks along the Cherwell may be impeded by closed college gates. Climb round them, as the locals do, or try mid-afternoon when they are most likely to be open.

Where to eat

15 NORTH PARADE (0865) 513773 Smart French-style restaurant, run by women, with comfortably cushioned chairs, changing paintings on the walls and a calm, informal atmosphere; very good food, inc delicious home-baked bread and a vegetarian dish, decent wines, and the service is efficient, friendly and unobtrusive; cl Sun pm, 25 Dec, 1 Jan, disabled access. £23|£12.

TIBERIO 260 Banbury Rd, Summertown (0865) 54117/67210 Welcoming Italian restaurant with good food and pleasant, efficient and friendly service; cl Sun; disabled access. £20|£4.50/£7.95.

CAFÉ MOMA Museum of Modern Art Pembroke St (0865) 722733 Clean, light and very popular self-service café in the museum basement, simple modern furnishings, exhibitions on walls, largely vegetarian food, excellent cakes, and efficient and friendly service; free entry to gallery Weds am/Thurs pm; cl Mon, 25-28 Dec; disabled access. £10|£1.80/£4.

As well as these, the city is full of useful stop-offs.

The ancient Turf Tavern in Bath Pl between Holywell St and New College Lane is the most interesting pub, and other decent pubs include the Bear (Alfred St), Rose & Crown (North Parade), Kings Arms (Holywell St) and Tolkien's old stamping-ground, the Eagle & Child (St Giles). The Victoria Arms at Old Marston on the Cherwell is a popular punters' destination.

In Cowley Rd there's COCO'S, a busy pizza parlour with generous toppings and marvellous carrot cake; the ice-bucket is unusual; and the BLUE COYOTE, popular with young professionals and moneyed students for its modern dishes. The High St has QUEEN'S LANE CAFÉ, family-run, efficient and friendly, with huge cooked breakfasts, muffins, rich chocolate brownies and sandwiches, but often long queues; BETJEMANS, a small chintzy place with exotic teas and coffees, honey in proper pots, boiled egg and toast; and ROSIE LEE'S, a good tea shop.

Several places in the covered market include L'ESCARGOT, which is a smartish French restaurant with a tapas bar underneath; GEORGINAS, very fashionable upstairs restaurant with self-service food – huge salads, loud music, and tea in mugs; BEATONS (next door), very trendy with good sandwiches (not cheap); BROWNS, firmly run by Greeks with simple, attractive decor and good home-made cakes; and HI-LO, which is atmospheric and has fine Jamaican dishes.

The HOT POT in St Clements is small, popular and very friendly, with straightforward decent food – lovely custard. RIMINI is a plush, softly lit Italian place with very good pasta and good-value pizzas. MORTONS in Broad St is mostly take-away but you can sit upstairs or in the garden; tasty good-value sandwiches. CHIT-CHATS serves good-value Italian pizzas, fresh salads in wooden bowls, and lovely hot chocolate-fudge brownies. HEROES in Ship St is a popular sandwich bar with newspapers to read.

St Michaels St has NOSEBAG, which is popular with students' parents –

generous salads, interesting hot meals (esp vegetarian) all served in heavy earthenware crockery, civilised, relaxed atmosphere, and yummy cherry bakewell tarts and éclairs; and MICHAELS – decent French cooking (not cheap) and good wine list.

FREUDS in Great Clarendon St is in a huge abandoned Methodist church and specialises in cocktails and little tasty snacks – best in the evening with live jazz, candlelit metal tables, friendly people, and unusual sculptures. BROWNS in Woodhouse Rd down St Giles does a wonderful bloody mary, serves good-value, decent food, has a friendly fun atmosphere, and is extremely busy. Further up St Giles is ST GILES CAFÉ – a good, simple café with a wide mix of people and wonderful chips, egg and cheese sandwiches and cappuccino. BATH PLACE HOTEL in Bath Pl is smart, with lovely food.

Some reliable ethnic restaurants are MUNCHY-MUNCHY in Park End St (Indonesian); the OPIUM DEN (George St), good Chinese food but not cheap; LIAISON (Castle St), also Chinese; JAMALS (Walton St), Indian; and MAMA MIA (South Parade), authentic pizzas.

Good TAKE-AWAY places: Mexican food and Italian sandwiches from the covered market; the PIZZA EXPRESS in the Golden Cross is in a medieval building with original timbers – and frescos can be seen on walls.

NORTH OXFORDSHIRE

This region has attractive Cotswolds countryside in the west, some good places to visit, civilised places to stay and good eating out.

The villages and countryside have a distinctly Cotswolds flavour over in the west, and up in the north-west corner of the county many of the buildings use a particularly beautiful golden stone. There are some beautiful villages, and a special pleasure here is tracking down ones that are far less well-known than the famous visitor honeypots such as Burford: Great Tew is very special. Most of the small towns and even the larger villages have antique shops and craft shops that are at least worth a look.

Blenheim is the county's great showpiece; it's genuinely a palace, with memorable lakeside grounds, as well as lots of things to do if you (or your children) want to be amused. Nearby Woodstock is an attractive small town. Elsewhere, the gardens at Waterperry (and those of Cornwell Manor, if you can time your visit right), Broughton Castle and Rousham House are all particularly appealing.

There are a few things to take children out to, but on the whole this area is not well served in this respect.

A good choice of places to stay includes quite a few charming old small inns and a couple of friendly family farmhouses that seem particularly to suit the character of the area. Besides the restaurants we list, a great many of the local pubs have decent food.

Where to stay

Weston-on-the-Green SP5318 WESTON MANOR Bicester OX6 8QL (0869) 50621 **£105**; 37 rms. Manor house in 13 acres of informal gardens, with fine oak-panelled Baronial Hall dining room complete with minstrel gallery, carefully furnished lounges, and outdoor swimming pool, squash and croquet; 10 mins to North Oxford; disabled access.
Horton-cum-Studley SP5912 STUDLEY PRIORY Oxford OX9 1AZ (086 735) 616 ***£98**; 19 rms. Once a Benedictine nunnery, this lovely 12th-c building (which has little changed since Elizabethan times) stands in 13 acres of wooded grounds; fine panelling, 16th- and 17th-c stained-glass windows, antiques and open fires in the elegant drawing room and cosy bar, seasonally changing menus, and attractive restaurant.
Woodstock SP4416 FEATHERS OX20 15X (0993) 812291 **£98**; 17 rms. Lovely old building with relaxing drawing room and study, open fires, first-class friendly staff, a gentle atmosphere, daily-changing imaginative food inc lovely puddings, and a sunny courtyard with attractive tables and chairs.
Chadlington SP3222 MANOR Chipping Norton OX7 3LX (060 876) 711 – will be changing to (0608) 676711 ***£95**; 7 attractive rms. In a pretty village, this small Cotswold-stone manor house has comfortable, graceful lounges, a relaxed atmosphere, open fire, very good seasonally changing food, and excellent wine list.
Minster Lovell SP3111 OLD SWAN Witney OX8 5RN (099 377) 4441 **£90**; 60 rms. Ancient Cotswolds inn, now rather smart, with restful and attractive low-beamed rooms opening off a small central bar, antiques, good china in corner cupboards, log fires in huge fireplaces, good food in the restaurant (housed in what used to be the brewhouse), and pretty garden with a medieval well.
Kingham SP2523 MILL HOUSE Chipping Norton OX7 6UH (0608) 658188 ***£80**; 23 good rms. Carefully renovated 17th-c flour mill with antique furniture in the comfortable lounge and bar, original features such as two bread ovens, open fires, cosy, popular restaurant, and very good, interesting food; children over 5; disabled access.
Charlbury SP3519 BELL Chipping Norton OX7 3AP (0608) 810278 ***£75**; 14 spotless, attractive rms. Small 17th-c hotel with quiet and civilised flagstoned bar, huge open fire, notable bar lunches, decent restaurant, and friendly service; disabled access.
Burford SP2512 LAMB OX18 4LR (0993) 823155 **£80**; 15 rms, 12 with own bthrm. 500-year-old Cotswold inn with lovely restful atmosphere; spacious, beamed, flagstoned and elegantly furnished lounge, civilised public bar with antique handpump beer engine, bunches of flowers on oak and elm tables, three winter log fires in inglenook fireplaces, antiques, good food, and pretty little garden; cl 25-26 Dec.
Shipton-under-Wychwood SP2717 LAMB Chipping Norton OX7 6AQ **£65**; 5 rms. Ancient Cotswold sandstone pub with friendly and helpful licensees, relaxed and civilised atmosphere and extremely good food, especially breakfasts; no children.
Chipping Norton SP3127 CROWN & CUSHION OX7 5AD (0608) 642533 **£55**; 40 splendid rms. Old coaching inn with civilised and attractive flagstoned bar, flower-filled conservatory, decent bar food, sheltered garden and suntrap terrace, restaurant, and swimming pool/sports complex.
Duns Tew SP4528 WHITE HORSE Bicester OX6 4JS (0869) 40272 **£55**; 13 rms. In a pretty village, this inn has lovely flagstones, old oak panelling on stripped

masonry, ancient beams and enormous inglenook fireplaces; friendly staff, real ales, and good food in bar and restaurant; own golf course; disabled access.

Kidlington SP4914 Bowood House OX5 1EB (0865) 842288 **£55**; 22 rms. Small, modern hotel with friendly atmosphere and good service; cl 2 wks over Christmas; disabled access.

Chipping Norton SP3127 Fox OX7 5DD (0608) 642658 ***£50**; 6 comfortable rms. Ancient old inn with open fire in rambling lounge, good-value bar food, upstairs restaurant; cl 25 Dec.

Asthall SP2811 Maytime Burford OX18 4HW (0993) 822068 **£48**; 6 quiet, cottage-style rms. Very welcoming landlord; comfortable, relaxing bar, good food and decent wines, huge breakfasts; worth an early spring-morning walk through the pretty village, across the fields to Swinbrook and back along the river; disabled access.

Burford SP2512 Angel OX18 4SN (0993) 822438 **£45**; 2 rms. Pleasantly unassuming old inn with one attractive flagstoned bar and another charmingly cosy one; generous home-made bar food, inventive evening meals in restaurant inc lots of fish and seasonal theme menus, and pretty secluded garden and dining terrace.

Church Enstone SP3724 Crown Chipping Norton OX7 4NN (0608) 677262 **£42**; 4 well-appointed rms, most with own bthrm. Cotswold-stone inn in pretty village; attractive horseshoe bar, good atmosphere, friendly staff, bar food and restaurant, and good breakfasts; children over 2.

Charlbury SP3519 Danbury Mill Farm Chipping Norton OX7 3JH (0608) 810314 **£40**; 3 rms. Cotswold-stone farmhouse with lovely views to Wychwood Forest; friendly atmosphere, decent food, and good service; can watch animals.

Minster Lovell SP3111 Hill Grove Farm Witney OX8 5NA (0993) 703120 **£40**; 2 rms. Friendly B & B on mixed, family-run, 300-acre working farm; no smoking; cl Christmas.

Clifton SP4831 Duke of Cumberlands Head Banbury OX15 0PE (0869) 38534 ***£35**; 3 rms with own showers in new sympathetically built extension. Simply but stylishly refurbished 17th-c stone inn with friendly atmosphere, an emphasis on good wine, beer and food, and helpful service.

North Leigh SP3813 Woodman Witney OX8 6TT (0993) 881790 **£29.50**; 2 rms, shared bthrm. Friendly little village pub with wholesome food all freshly prepared and cooked (vegetarian dishes, too), real ales, daily papers, and big garden; no food Mon.

To see and do

Banbury SP4540, a busy shopping town, was actually without its famous cross for 250 years, between the Puritans destroying it in 1602 and the construction of its replacement in 1859. Also interesting is the tomb in the church graveyard from which Jonathan Swift borrowed the name Gulliver for his traveller. Banbury Museum Interesting little museum with local history, archaeology and photography; snacks, shop, disabled access; cl Sun and winter Mon. The Reindeer and Wine Vaults, both in Parsons St, are useful for lunch. Out on the B4035 towards Broughton, there's good summer pick-your-own.

Broughton SP4138 Broughton Castle Striking early 14th- and 16th-c house with proper moat and gatehouse, originally owned by William of Wykeham but in the hands of the present owner's family for over 600 years; exceptional oak panelling, period furniture, paintings and Civil War relics (in the Civil War an ancestor of the present Lord Saye and Sele was known as Old Subtlety, for his political skills). Snacks, shop, disabled access; open Easter and 18 May-14 Sept pm Weds, Sun and bank hol Sun and Mon, also Thurs in July and Aug; £3. The Elephant & Castle at Bloxham is useful for lunch, and there's a decent little village MUSEUM too.

★ † **Burford** SP2512 Lovely little Cotswold town with interesting shops and teas along its pretty main street. The CHURCH is particularly intriguing, with a super graveyard (some of the rich wool merchants who lived here had stone woolpacks as gravestones), and 17th-c graffiti by some of the 400 Leveller mutineers imprisoned here by Cromwell; there remain bullet-holes in the wall, where some were shot. The town also has an interesting little MUSEUM, and is full of attractive pubs: the best for food and atmosphere are the Lamb and the Angel. Just outside town the COTSWOLD WILDLIFE PARK has animals, birds and reptiles from all over the world in re-creations of their natural environment, with an aquarium, tropical and insect houses, brass-rubbing centre, adventure playground and train rides, all set in acres of attractive parkland. Penguin-feeding every day (exc Fri) at 11 am and 4 pm; meals, snacks, shop, disabled access; cl 25 Dec; £4. In an area not especially rich in family attractions, this should prove popular with children. Burford does get very busy indeed with visitors, and it's worth noting that several smaller and altogether quieter nearby villages are, in their way, as pretty: TAYNTON SP2313, the BARRINGTONS SP2013 (just over the Gloucestershire border), FULBROOK SP2513, SWINBROOK SP2712 and ASTHALL SP2811. All except the first have the additional attraction of a decent pub. You can walk between these, along the River Windrush for much of the way.

† **Chipping Norton** SP3127 Very pleasant old stonebuilt wool town with unusually wide market place, and a good few antique shops. The pretty CHURCH is one of the longest in the country, and has some interesting brasses. Among other attractive buildings, there are also some fine 17th-c ALMSHOUSES. An interesting little MUSEUM is open Weds, Sat and Sun; 50p. There are some unusual old carved heads under a shop called the Playpen, usually on view Thurs pm. The Fox is good for lunch.

Combe SP4115 COMBE MILL Mid-19th-c sawmill with working steam beam engine, original Cornish boiler and a working blacksmith's forge; an exhibition on the first floor has tools and models. Snacks, shop, limited disabled access; open only occ Sun in summer – best tel (0993) 891785 for dates; £1.

Deddington SP4631 DEDDINGTON CASTLE Not much left of this 12th-c castle, but the huge earthworks of the outer and inner baileys can still be seen. There are some attractive stone buildings around the village square, and the Holcombe Hotel and Kings Arms are good for lunch.

★ **Great Tew** SP3929 is the most charming village in the area (some would say in all England). It's an outstanding series of golden stone 17th- and 18th-c cottages, some thatched and others with stone-slabbed roofs, around an attractive sloping green and among ancient trees, with wooded slopes above; the Falkland Arms here is a classic country tavern.

Little Rollright SP2930 ROLLRIGHT STONES Dramatic and mysterious Bronze-Age stones, chiefly in a circle about 100 ft across, dating from around 1800-550 BC; as they straddle the border with Warwickshire, we've mentioned them in the Midlands

chapter too. The Gate Hangs High near here is useful for lunch.

Long Hanborough SP4214 OXFORD BUS MUSEUM Around 40 vehicles, from Oxford horse trams to more modern machines up to the 1960s, some roadworthy, others in the course of restoration; disabled access; open Sun only; £1. The George & Dragon is useful for lunch.

★ ✝ **Minster Lovell** SP3111 is one of the prettiest and most unspoilt old villages in the area; there's an attractive 15th-c CHURCH and village green, and a 15th-c bridge over the River Windrush narrow enough for the Welsh drovers to use for counting the sheep in the flocks they brought this way each year. MINSTER LOVELL HALL Once home to the Lovell family, the 15th-c house was being used as ramshackle farm buildings until its 'restoration' as neat ruins in the 1930s – imposing and attractively set. Enough survives to make it easy to believe the story about Richard III's favourite, Lord Lovel, being hidden in a secret room here after the king's downfall at Bosworth Field, and then dying of starvation with his dog when a trusted servant stopped feeding him; or even the Mistletoe Bough tale, about the girl playing party games on her wedding night, and hiding herself in a chest which unfortunately locked on her, leaving her hidden till the discovery of her skeleton decades later. The medieval DOVECOT has been well restored; snacks, shop; cl 1-2 pm, Mon-Weds, all Oct-Mar; £1. The Old Swan Hotel does good light lunches, and the White Hart up on the main road is good value.

✝ **North Leigh** SP3813 ROMAN

VILLA Occupied between the 2nd and 4th c, when it was a very grand place with several dozen rooms; there's little left now beyond a tessellated pavement and some of the walls; open Apr-Sept. The medieval village CHURCH, with a Saxon tower, is lovely inside. The Woodman is good for lunch.

Otmoor SP5615 is several square miles of flatland, so poorly drained that in very wet weather its river actually flows backwards. Because serious farming is virtually out of the question, it does have more natural wildlife than most places in the county; there are several paths through it. The Abingdon Arms at Beckley is one good starting point. On one edge, the PICK-YOUR-OWN fruit farm at Elsfield SP5410 has good views over the wilderness, as well as an unusually wide range of varieties.

Rousham SP4724 ROUSHAM HOUSE 17th-c house embellished by court artist and architects, and remodelled in the 18th c by William Kent to give the external appearance of a Gothic Tudor mansion; 150 paintings, fine period furnishings. Excellent 18th-c classically landscaped garden with buildings, cascades, statues and vistas in 30 acres of hanging woods above the River Cherwell, and walled flower and vegetable gardens. A Royalist garrison in the Civil War, it still has shooting holes in the door; no children under 15; disabled access grounds only; house open pm Weds, Sun and bank hols Apr-Sept, gardens all year; £2.50 house and £2.50 garden. There's a 12th-c CHURCH. The Red Lion at Steeple Aston is good for lunch (no children here, either), and the Gardiners Arms at Tackley is also handy.

Swalcliffe SP3737 SWALCLIFFE BARN Constructed between 1400 and 1409, one of the best-preserved barns in the country, with much of its medieval-timber half-cruck roof intact; there's a display of agricultural and trade vehicles. Disabled access; open pm Sun Apr-Sept, bank hols and Sat Jun-Aug. The village is pretty, and the Stags Head is useful for lunch.

Waterperry SP6206 WATERPERRY GARDENS Peaceful gardens and nurseries, between 1932 and 1971 the home of a celebrated horticultural school; fine herbaceous borders, a rock garden, riverside walk, shrub borders, lawns, trees and useful nurseries. The wonderfully tranquil little CHURCH is Norman, but incorporates some Saxon work, and has fine ancient glass and brasses: a really beautiful place to visit. Snacks, excellent garden shop, good disabled access; cl Christmas and New Year and several days in July; £1.95. The Clifden Arms in Worminghall just over the Buckinghamshire border is nice for lunch.

Witney SP3510 Saxon kings used to hold their meetings, or witans, here, which is where the name comes from. It was a prosperous town in the Middle Ages, thanks to its position on the main London to Gloucester road, and is well known for its blankets, made here since medieval times. A quiet and relaxed place, the market square still has the ancient butter cross, with its 17th-c clock, and there are quite a few interesting old buildings such as the 13th-c church and 18th-c blanket hall. The Three Horseshoes in Corn St is useful for lunch. COGGES FARM MUSEUM Victorian living farm museum with interesting manor house displaying farmhouse kitchens, dairy, walled gardens, local breeds of farm animals, and lots of other displays and exhibits; daily feeding, agricultural and craft demonstrations. Snacks, shop, disabled access; cl am wknds, Mon (exc bank hols), Nov-Mar (exc Advent weekend, tel (0993) 772602 for details of this and other special wknds when aspects of the farming year are illustrated); *£2.50. Great fun.

Woodstock SP4416 BLENHEIM PALACE One of the most impressive stately homes in the country, Blenheim was given to the Duke of Marlborough by Queen Anne as a reward for his military achievements against the French. Fantastically grand, the house itself covers 14 acres, and the grounds stretch for well over 2,000. There's a lot to see: sumptuous State Rooms and 183 ft Long Library, an exhibition about Churchill, born here in 1874, and tapestries, sculpture and fine furnishings. The grounds, landscaped by Capability Brown, have an enormous maze and lots of other children's play areas, a walled garden and butterfly house. Rowing boats can be hired for the lake. Very much geared for visitors, and all carried out with great efficiency, yet it hasn't moved too far downmarket; this really is a splendid place for a day out. Meals and snacks, several shops and plant centre; disabled access in house, but limited in garden; house cl Nov-Mar; £6.50. At the gates, the small town of Woodstock is also very civilised and prosperous, with good antique shops and fine stone buildings. Besides the excellent if pricy Feathers Hotel, the Bear Hotel and cheaper Woodstock Arms are all good for lunch.

OXFORDSHIRE COUNTY MUSEUM
Elegant town house with pleasant gardens and good displays of the county and its people; snacks, shop, some disabled access; cl Sun am, Oct-Apr Mon. The graveyard of BLADON CHURCH, where Churchill is buried, has views over Blenheim Park.

✝ Among the county's many fine **churches**, one of the most interesting is at Widford SP2612 just outside Burford: very simple, but notable for three things – its medieval wall paintings, the remains of a Roman pavement at the west end of the chancel, and its surroundings, a former village that's now virtually disappeared. The one house that's left was in the past, in turn, a fulling mill, paper mill and flour mill.

Other attractive villages here, all with decent pubs, include Shenington SP3742, Shipton-under-Wychwood SP2717 (interesting bookshop, lovely green, two good pubs – one very ancient), Adderbury SP4635, Cropredy SP4646, Duns Tew SP4528, Epwell SP3540, Souldern SP5131 and Wroxton SP4142.

Walks

Opportunities for walking are more limited here than over in the Gloucestershire Cotswolds, and there's rather more for walkers in the south of the county. However, there are quite a few attractive shorter walks in the area.

Blenheim SP4416 has plentiful paths and tracks through its huge estate, including a public right of way. The wilderness of **Otmoor** SP5615 too is interesting to walk through: see To see and do, above.

The **Oxford Canal** towpath closely parallels the railway as well as the River Cherwell, so you can walk from one village to another – for example, from Lower Heyford SP4824 to Nethercott SP4820, and return by train. There's also access from the Boat at Thrupp SP4815.

Over in the west, the **Cotswolds** offer a handful of good walks, such as along the Windrush from Burford SP2512 or Swinbrook SP2712, and around Sibford Gower SP3537 (the thatched Wykham Arms is good for lunch here).

Closer to Oxford, there are several pleasant walks from the White Horse on **Forest Hill** SP5807.

Driving

Some of the nicest country drives in this part of Oxfordshire are along the back roads around the valley of the River Windrush just N of the A40, W of Witney. These are all worth exploring, with a succession of attractive views.

The A44 (formerly the A34) N out of Oxford through Woodstock and on to Stratford (changing to the A3400 as it passes Chipping Norton) is probably the best road of all for giving an overview of the rolling North Oxfordshire scenery with its Cotswold overtones, but does carry quite a bit of traffic.

The B4035 from Banbury to Sibford Ferris, or the more northerly unclassified road looping off it through North Newington, Shutford and Epwell, takes you through attractively hilly farming country, very quiet; you can then track down through Hook Norton to Chipping Norton for a Cotswoldy drive, and on down to Charlbury and Witney on the B4026/B4022.

Since the opening of the M40 extension, the A4260 Oxford-Banbury road carries much less traffic and is a reasonably quick way of getting an overall picture of much of the area, with worthwhile detours into Tackley, Steeple Aston, Duns Tew, Deddington and Adderbury (all of which have decent pubs).

Where to eat

Woodstock SP4416 VICKERS (0993) 811212 Restaurant with good snacks; cl 25 Dec pm. **£23**|£4.15/£9.45.

Adderbury SP4635 RED LION Pleasantly civilised 16th-c coaching inn with comfortable, attractive rooms, decent bar food, good wines, and friendly licensees; also bedrooms. **£18.90**|£1.60/£4.75.

Barnard Gate SP4010 BOOT (0865) 881231 Very popular pub with bar food, restaurant, good coffee and friendly staff; cl 25 Dec; disabled access. **£15**|£2.50/£5.95.

SOUTH OXFORDSHIRE

Prosperous and civilised, this part of the county has some fine hotels and restaurants, but it's not cheap to visit.

This area has rather more varied countryside than in the north of the county, including as it does long reaches of the Thames, the edge of the Chilterns, and the altogether more open sweeping downland south of the B4507/A417; it offers a wider range of possibilities for walkers. Like the rest of the county, it has attractive small towns and villages, and a fair number of places to visit, prime among them Stonor House, Buscot Park, Mapledurham House, the railway collection at Didcot, Greys Court at Henley-on-Thames, and Dorchester Abbey. Children enjoy the bird and animal collection at Ipsden, the model landscape at Long Wittenham, and trips on the river. It's one of the more expensive places for a short stay, though there's a fine choice of hotels and good food.

Where to stay

Great Milton SP6202 LE MANOIR AUX QUAT' SAISONS Oxford OX44 7PD (0844) 278881 ***£174.50**; 19 opulent rms. Luxurious Jacobean manor in 27 acres of parkland and lovely gardens with heated pool and kitchen garden (providing many of the cooking ingredients), gracious lounges with fine furniture, and perfectly presented superb food (at a price); disabled access.

Abingdon SU4997 UPPER REACHES OX14 3JA (0235) 522311 **£106**; 25 rms. Former corn mill with the River Thames on one side and old mill stream on the other; preserved waterwheel, comfortable and cosy public rooms, and good food.

North Stoke SY6086 SPRINGS Wallingford OX10 6BE (0491) 836687 **£100**; 36 well-furnished spacious rms. Grand mock-Tudor hotel with old-fashioned panelled lounge and snug bar, fresh flowers, good restaurant food, friendly, helpful staff, and 30 acres of grounds with spring-fed lake; children by arrangement only; disabled access.

Moulsford SU5983 BEETLE & WEDGE Wallingford OX10 9JR (0491) 651381 **£95**; 10 pretty rms, most with lovely river view. Delightful riverside inn where Jerome K Jerome wrote *Three Men in a Boat* and where H G Wells lived for a time (it was The Potwell in *The History of Mr Polly*); elegant, spacious dining room with fine food, informal old beamed Boathouse bar with more hearty dishes, carefully chosen wine list, open fires, fresh flowers, riverside terrace and waterside lawn with moorings, and a warmly welcoming atmosphere; no food 25 Dec; disabled access.

Stonor SU7388 STONOR ARMS Oxford RG9 6HE (0491) 638345 **£92.50**; 9 rms. Carefully restored 18th-c hotel with elegant restaurant and pretty conservatory, relaxed flagstoned bar, friendly staff, and good, imaginative food; disabled access.

Henley-on-Thames SU7882 RED LION RG9 2AR (0491) 572161 **£83**; 26 rms, half of which have been newly refurbished. Handsome family-run 16th-c riverside hotel with comfortable public rooms, and very good, interesting food in the elegant Regency-style restaurant.

Clanfield SP2801 PLOUGH Bampton OX8 2RB (036 781) 222 **£80**; 6 rms. 16th-c inn with beamed bar, open fire, friendly, helpful staff and very good food.

Dorchester SU5794 GEORGE Wallingford OX10 7HH (0865) 340404 **£75**; 18 rms. Lovely 500-year-old building with comfortably old-fashioned and civilised bar, old beams, big fireplace, exceptionally good wines, good food, and pleasant service; first used as brewhouse for Norman Abbey opposite.

Wallingford SU6089 SHILLINGFORD BRIDGE OX10 8LX (086 732) 8567 **£65**; 42 rms. Very pretty riverside setting; comfortable, bustling bars and restaurant (all with fine views), coarse fishing, squash, and swimming pool; dinner-dance every Sat evening; disabled access.

Checkendon SU6582 HIGHWAYMAN Exlade St Reading RG8 0UA (0491) 682020 **£55**; 4 rms. 17th-c pub in magnificent rolling countryside with fine views, an interesting variety of furniture in unusual rambling low-beamed rooms, and friendly, courteous service.

Newbridge SP4000 ROSE REVIVED Oxford OX8 6QD (0865) 300221 **£55**; 7 rms, 3 with own bthrm. Big stone inn on a quiet reach of the upper Thames; lots of Victoriana, dining room with 16th-c stone fireplace, no-smoking area, good wines and ales, and spacious garden.

Clifton Hampden SU5495 PLOUGH Abingdon OX14 3EG (086 730) 7811 **£45**;

4 rms with thoughtful extras included. Quaint little village pub close to Thames and run by extraordinarily obliging Turkish couple; relaxed and friendly atmosphere, cosy bar with beams and panelling, two civilised lounge areas, no-smoking restaurant, and good fresh food (no chips).

Faringdon SU2895 CROWN SN7 7HU (0367) 242744 **£39.50**; 12 rms, most with own bthrm. Flagstones and panelling, decent bar and restaurant food, friendly staff, roaring log fires, and lovely courtyard; children sharing parents' room are only charged for meals.

To see and do

★ ✝ **Abingdon** SU4997 Until 1974 the county town of Berkshire, this is an attractive Thames-side town, much expanded around its old partly pedestrianised centre, which originally rose to prominence as the easternmost centre for the area's wool industry. There's a fine old gatehouse, several attractive old buildings and almshouses around the impressive 15th-16th-c Wren-style CHURCH OF ST HELEN off Thames St, the 17th-c former county hall which has now become a good MUSEUM, and the unusual CHURCH OF ST MARY, wider than it's long. The remains of the partly Norman Benedictine ABBEY, which was once the second most powerful in England, have been restored, with part now housing a local theatre; you can visit other parts. The delightfully placed Old Anchor is useful for lunch.

Bix Bottom SU7288 WARBURG RESERVE is an extensive area of wildflower-rich rough grassland and ancient beech wood, good for wild orchids and butterflies, besides birds and maybe deer. The Fox is good for lunch.

Buscot SU2298 BUSCOT PARK What makes this 18th-c house really special is the amazing collection of art and furnishings amassed by its owners; paintings by Reynolds, Gainsborough, Rembrandt, Murillo and several of the Pre-Raphaelites (including a splendid series by Burne-Jones), with some more recent pictures too. The attractive grounds have formal water gardens and a mouthwatering kitchen garden; teas; open Apr-Sept Weds-Fri pm, also open every 2nd and 4th wknd in each month; £3.80. NT. The Trout at St Johns Bridge on the Lechlade road is useful for lunch.

Didcot SO5290 DIDCOT RAILWAY CENTRE The biggest collection anywhere of Great Western Railway stock, housed under cover, inc 20 steam locomotives, a diesel railcar and lots of passenger and freight rolling stock; snacks, shop, disabled access; open wknds all year and wkdys Easter-Sept; non-steam £3, steam days £4; the town itself has nothing to detain a visitor.

★ ✝ **Dorchester** SU5794 DORCHESTER ABBEY Very impressive and well-preserved old abbey, with 12th-c nave and font, and other parts from the next few centuries. The tower was rebuilt in 1605 and has a 14th-c spiral staircase, as well as a very rare Jesse window from the same period, and some mosaic-like 12th-c glass in other windows. The adjacent former guesthouse is now a MUSEUM about the abbey and the area. Very English and unusually served teas (Weds-Sun pm), shop; museum cl 12.30-2 pm, am Sun, Mon, Oct-Easter (exc first two wknds in Oct). The whole Thames-side village is a lovely place to explore, with interesting antique shops. The handsome old George is good for lunch.

Filkins SP2304 COTSWOLD WOOLLEN WEAVERS Working woollen mill demonstrating traditional production methods in 18th-c buildings; snacks, shop, disabled access; cl 25-31 Dec. The Lamb is useful for lunch. Craft workshops in the village include natural dyers (Filkins Farmhouse, appointment only (0367) 860253), traditional chairmakers (Calf Pens, Cross Tree) and saddlers (Oxleaze Farm).

Great Coxwell SU2693 GREAT COXWELL BARN 13th-c stonebuilt tithe barn 152 ft long and 44 ft wide, with beautifully crafted timbers supporting the roof. Built for the Cistercians, it was described by William Morris as being as noble as a cathedral; small admission charge. The Woodman at Fernham on the other side of the A420 is an interesting old country tavern, nice for lunch.

Henley-on-Thames SO7682 Pleasant well-heeled Thames-side town famed for its summer regatta, and you can usually see other rowing races or practices on the river throughout the year. GREYS COURT The gabled Jacobean house and the ruins of its medieval predecessor are interesting, but the gardens are the best feature, with white and rose gardens, ancient wisterias, a kitchen garden, wheelhouse and brick maze. Inside are some good 18th-c furnishings and decor, as well as a pre-medieval kitchen; teas; open Apr-Sept, house pm Mon, Weds and Fri, garden pm daily exc Mon and Thurs; £3.80 house and gardens, £2.80 gardens only. NT. The Three Tuns has good food, and the Old White Hart is useful too. You can hire river boats here: phone (0491) 572035.

! Ipsden SU6385 WELLPLACE BIRD FARM Hundreds of different kinds of birds and animals inc lambs, goats, otters, donkeys and monkeys – a great place for children, as you can feed lots of the animals; snacks, shop, disabled access; cl wkdys Oct-Easter; £1.50. They have car-boot sales on bank hols. The King William IV at Hailey nearby is an excellent country pub, full of old farm tools which the landlord really knows about; he also has a shire horse which pulls a brewer's dray. A friend of his, Ian Smith (0491) 641364, can arrange for you HORSE-DRAWN WAGGON RIDES through these pretty Chilterns fringes. Most fine summer days he runs two-horse waggons from the old brick kiln by the main road through Nettlebed SU7086.

Kingston Bagpuize SU4098 KINGSTON HOUSE Charming 17th-c manor house with lovely panelling, fine staircase, attractive furnishings and a friendly unstuffy feel; peaceful garden with mature flowering shrubs, woodland walks, Georgian gazebo over former Elizabethan cockpit. Snacks, shop; open pm Sun and bank hol Mon Apr-Sept; £2.50, 50p garden only. The Lamb & Flag is useful for lunch.

Long Wittenham SU5493 PENDON MUSEUM OF MINIATURE LANDSCAPE AND TRANSPORT Charming exhibition showing a highly detailed model railway and 1930s model village scenes; you can often see modellers working on the exhibits. Snacks; shop; disabled access on certain days only – check first; open pm wknds and bank hols, cl mid-Dec-early Jan; *£2. The Machine Man is good for lunch.

★ **Mapledurham** SU6776 Very attractive little community with lovely beechwoods full of birds. The best way to reach it is by boat from the Caversham Promenade at Reading, operating whenever MAPLEDURHAM HOUSE is open. This is an impressive Elizabethan mansion in pretty parkland running down to the Thames, with lots of paintings and family portraits, great oak staircases and moulded Elizabethan ceilings. In the grounds is the MAPLEDURHAM WATERMILL, the last mill on the Thames to use wooden machinery, still fully operational and producing flour, bran and semolina and grain. Teas, shop, disabled access to ground floor only; open pm Sat, Sun and bank hols Easter-Sept; £4 house and watermill,

£3 house only, £2.50 watermill only.

Milton SU4892 MILTON MANOR Elegant 17th-c manor house with splendid Strawberry Hill Gothic library and interesting wings, chapel, stables, walled garden and grounds; unusual collections of teapots and fine china. Snacks; open pm wknds and bank hols Easter-Oct; £2.50. The Fish at Sutton Courtenay nearby does good lunches.

Milton Hill SU4790 is surrounded by CHERRY ORCHARDS, a fine sight when the white blossom is out in spring, and with plump red-black fresh cherries from roadside stalls around July.

Nuffield SU6687 NUFFIELD PLACE The home of Lord and Lady Nuffield from 1933-1963, with the original thirties furnishings; very good gardens with mature trees and shrubs inc rhododendrons, lawns, pond and rockery, as well as Lady Nuffield's own Wolseley. Teas; open pm 2nd and 4th Sun each month May-Sept; £2.50. The Crown pub here has good food.

Rycote SP6604 RYCOTE CHAPEL Small private chapel founded in the 15th c and visited by both Elizabeth I and Charles I; still has original font and fine 17th-c interior; shop; disabled access; open 11 Apr, 2 May, 13 Jun, 18 July, 29 Aug, 19 Sept; 95p.

Segsbury Camp SU3884, reached by the dead-end lane up past the Sparrow in Letcombe Regis, is a big Iron-Age hill fort, also used by the Romans, with good views.

Sonning Common SU7080 HERB FARM Extensive range of herb plants and products, with over 3,200 different species in the display garden. A restored 19th-c granary has an exhibition of agricultural implements and there's a maze; cl Mon (exc bank hols and in Dec); 60p for maze.

★ **Stanton Harcourt** SP4105 is an attractive village, with the medieval MANOR HOUSE really rather unusual and well worth a look. The conical Great Kitchen has no chimney – the smoke from ovens and fireplaces

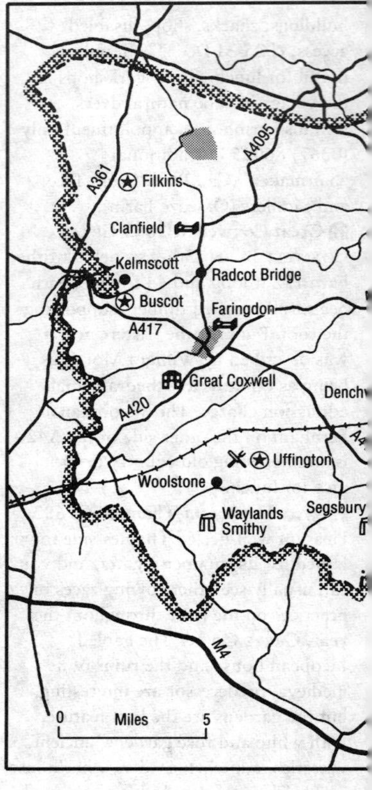

collected in the cone of the roof and drifted out through wooden louvres; the gardens too are attractive. Disabled access; open roughly pm Thurs and Sun fortnightly from Easter-Sept, plus bank hols, tel (0865) 881928; £3, garden only £1.50. The Harcourt Arms nearby does good meals.

Stonor SU7388 STONOR HOUSE AND PARK Despite the stately Tudor façade this ancient house actually dates back to 1180, and there are beautiful furnishings, paintings, sculptures and tapestries from all over the world. The lovely gardens have an unusual exhibition of sculpture from Zimbabwe, and there's a wooded deer park. Snacks, shop, disabled access; open Apr-Sept Sun pm, plus May-Sept Weds pm, July/Aug Thurs pm and Aug

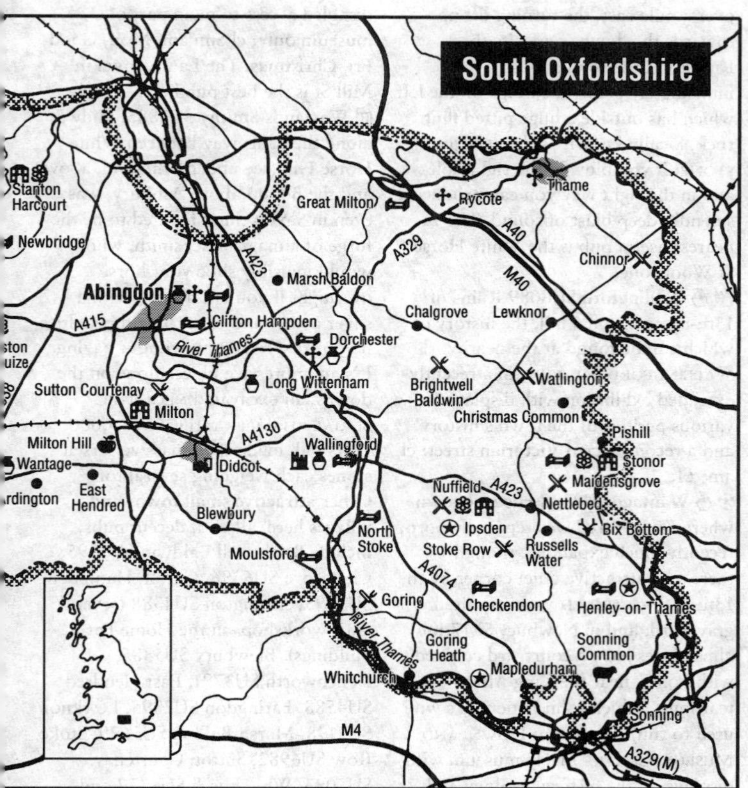

Sat pm; £3.30, garden only £1.20. The Stonor family still use the chapel to celebrate Roman Catholic mass, as they have for 800 years; St Edmund Campion used it in 1581. The smart Stonor Arms is useful for lunch.

★ ✝ **Thame** SP7005 is worth a look for its splendid range of unspoilt architecture. The main street is very wide and has escaped any significant development this century, so there are a number of medieval timber-framed buildings next to stately Georgian houses; the 13th-c CHURCH is attractive. The 15th-c Birdcage Inn used to be the town lock-up; the Abingdon Arms and Six Bells are useful for a bite to eat.

! Uffington SU3089 CASTLE Iron-Age fort that covered eight acres but had only one gateway; great views over the vale below. On the hillside is a 375 ft WHITE HORSE carved into the chalk, very Celtic in style, and now thought to be at least 2,000 years old. If you stand in the centre of the eye and turn around three times with your eyes closed, any reasonable wish will be granted. This is one good setting-off point for the Ridgeway – see Walks, below. Down in the village is TOM BROWN'S SCHOOL MUSEUM Young Mr Brown's schooldays must have been based on those the author Thomas Hughes passed here; the building now has an exhibition on his life and work and of other local history; shop, disabled access; open pm wknds and bank hols Easter-Oct; *30p. Off the B4507 below the White Horse, a bit over a mile east, the turning off up towards the downs opposite the Kingston Lisle road almost immediately passes a cottage on the left which has outside a huge pitted flint rock, locally known as the BLOWING STONE: if you blow in the right hole and in the right way you can produce a splendid deep blast of sound. The nearest useful pub is the White Horse at Woolstone.

Wallingford SU6089 Ruins of 13th-c CASTLE on a hill, the history of which can be found at the nearby WALLINGFORD MUSEUM, in a recently extended exhibition with displays on various periods of the town's history, and a reconstructed Victorian street; cl am; £1.

✝ **Wantage** SU9388 Historic town where King Alfred was reputedly born; recently much expanded, though there's an attractive quiet corner by the 13th-15th-c CHURCH with its raised graveyard, and in Newbury St 17th-c almshouses have a courtyard cobbled with bones, near the King Alfred tearooms (which John Betjeman's wife used to run). VALE AND DOWNLAND MUSEUM CENTRE Lively museum with displays on the history, geology and archaeology of the Vale of the White Horse; meals and snacks; shop; disabled access to main part of museum only; cl Sun am, Mon, Good Fri, Christmas. The Lamb down in Mill St is the best pub here.

Waylands Smithy SU2885, midway along the Ridgeway between White Horse Hill (see under Uffington, above) and the B4000 above Ashbury, was even in Saxon times reputed to be the forge of a magic blacksmith, who would invisibly shoe your horse overnight if you left it there with a silver coin – and exact horrid penalties if you tried to slip by without paying. It's an impressive place, alone on the downs, an excavated NEOLITHIC BURIAL CHAMBER rather over 5,000 years old, made with massive sarsen stones each weighing several tons.

Other attractive small towns and villages here, all with decent pubs, include Brightwell Baldwin SU6595, Chalgrove SU6396, Clifton Hampden SU5495, Ardington SU4388 (several craft workshops in the Home Farm buildings), Blewbury SU5385, Denchworth SU3791, East Hendred SU4588, Faringdon SU2895, Lewknor SU7198, Marsh Baldon SU5699, Stoke Row SU6982, Sutton Courtenay SU5093, Whitchurch SU6377 and Woolstone SU2987.

Walks

South-east of Oxford **the Thames** passes Dorchester SU5790, a fine old town with timber-framed houses and a venerable old coaching inn (the George SU5794). Paths lead from here to the river, which can be crossed at Day's Lock SU5693; a short walk brings you to Sinodun Hills SU5692 (alternative access from adjacent car park), a pair of hillocks which look across the Chilterns and Berkshire Downs. The **Thames Valley** proper, shared with Berkshire and Buckinghamshire, has a classic, very English sort of beauty, with boating scenes, superb trees and riverside architecture. Riverside walks on the Oxfordshire side are possible only in places, notably between Henley SU7682 and Sonning SU7080.

The **Upper Thames** west of Oxford flows through low-lying country, not outstanding for walking along although the towpath itself is pleasant enough, with Cotswold villages making good focal points: from William Morris's house at Kelmscot SU2899, for example, it is a straightforward mile and a half east to the Swan at Radcot Bridge SU2899. Other useful pubs for pleasant if undramatic riverside strolls here are the Trout on the unclassified road between Bampton and Buckland at Tadpole Bridge SP3300, Maybush or Rose Revived on the A415 at Newbridge SP4001, and Ferry off the B4449 south of Stanton Harcourt at Bablock Hythe SP4304.

The **Chilterns** have numerous possibilities for exploring the beechwoods and farmlands, though the chalk hills' more memorable viewpoints and landscapes mostly lie outside the county (see Buckinghamshire chapter). Stonor Deer Park is skirted by an attractive right of way from Stonor village SU7388, and you can link this with the famous Maharajah's Well at Stoke Row SU6884; or you can continue east to Turville SU7690 (see Buckinghamshire chapter). At Cowleaze Wood SU7295 between Christmas Common SU7193 and the M40, forest art exhibits are scattered around as part of a sculpture trail. Useful pubs for walkers in and around the Oxfordshire Chilterns include the Crown at Pishill SU7389, Five Horseshoes at Maidensgrove SU7288, Fox at Bix SU7285, King Charles Head on Goring Heath SU6678, Beehive at Russells Water SU7089, Carpenters Arms at Crocker End just outside Nettlebed SU6986, Fox & Hounds on Christmas Common SU7193, Black Horse or Four Horseshoes at Checkendon SU6683, and Crooked Billet at Stoke Row SU6883. A particularly good short walk with a palpable sense of peace is the one from the lane out of Bix past Bix Hall to Valley End Farm SU7286, along the Oxfordshire Way.

Near the northern crest of the downs, the **Ridgeway** tracks right across the county from Wiltshire to Berkshire. This broad grassy trackway was used as a herding highway for some 2,000 years before the Romans came, and after the break-up of the Roman empire came back into use for the same purpose, well into medieval times. It's now part of the long-distance path network, and gives good walking with fine views.

Driving

On the whole this area is not very good for country drives: there is least traffic in the W of the area, and the downland roads from here S into Berkshire have some long views. The B4507 below the downs W of Wantage has some attractive views of the downs above it. Another good downland road is the A417 through Blewbury, but it does carry rather a lot of traffic.

Over towards the Chilterns, the B480 Henley-Watlington through attractive rolling countryside, some wooded, is fairly quiet. Side roads in this same part are rewarding – for instance, the loop largely through woodland from off the B481 S of Nettlebed at Highmoor Cross, through Stoke Row and back up to Nuffield. The road steeply uphill from Watlington through Christmas Common and over the Buckinghamshire border to Northend is pleasant; going back down, there are fine views out over Oxfordshire. The car park beside it gives access to Watlington Woods SU7093, with good views and a mass of bluebells in spring. Below the Chilterns escarpment, the B4009 running along on the edge of the plain from Watlington to Chinnor and beyond gives good views of the hills above. Though the A423 Henley-Wallingford goes through attractive scenery, it does carry quite a bit of traffic.

Where to eat

Chinnor SP7500 SIR CHARLES NAPIER 10 mins from Exit 6 M40 (0494) 483011 Though most of the emphasis in this civilised pub is on the very good stylish back restaurant, decorated with works by local artists, you can enjoy fine food from the short bar menu as well; really good wine list, homely furnishings, winter log fire, and relaxed, friendly service; you can eat on the terrace in summer; it gets busy at wknds; cl Sun pm, Mon; children over 7 in evening; disabled access. £25/£5.50.

Goring SU6080 LEATHERNE BOTTEL (0491) 872667 Smart restaurant overlooking a quiet stretch of the Thames, with excellent food using home-grown herbs, local game and vegetables, and fresh fish delivered daily; cl 25 Dec. **£30**|£12.50.

Stoke Row SU6784 CROOKED BILLET (0491) 681048 Food-oriented country pub with a wide choice of interesting home cooking, a good choice of decent wines and good coffee; cl 25 Dec pm. **£26.25**|£8.35.

Sutton Courtenay SU5093 FISH (0235) 848242 Outstanding food using very fresh ingredients, always a vegetarian dish, good wines, and lovely nibbles; cl Tues pm, 24-29 Dec; disabled access. **£25.20.**

Brightwell Baldwin SU6595 LORD NELSON (0491) 612497 17th-c inn with comfortably modernised furnishings and nautical theme in bar; menu covers both bar and restaurant at lunchtimes (separate in evening), with daily fish dishes and good puddings; popular 3-course Sun lunch, and friendly courteous service. **£18.90**|£3.15/£9.45.

Watlington SU6894 CHEQUERS (0491) 612874 Rambling, candlelit pub with very good food and pretty garden; no children. **£18**|£2.50/£5.

Maidensgrove SU7288 FIVE HORSESHOES (0491) 641282 17th-c inn with rambling bar, winter log fire and low ceiling in main area covered in banknotes from all over the world; efficiently served and very popular food from imaginative menu; summer barbecues in nice garden; children in new conservatory only. **£16**|£3.30/£6.

Nuffield SU6687 CROWN (0491) 641335 Brick-and-flint pub in fine countryside with roaring winter log fires, reasonably priced good food, decent wine, friendly and prompt service; cl 25 Dec, pm 26 Dec/1 Jan; children over 14 in evening, in family room only at lunchtime; disabled access. **£16**|£2/£5.75.

Uffington SU3087 BRITCHCOMBE FARM (0367) 820667 Working farm, in lovely spot right underneath White Horse Hill, offering afternoon teas on Sat and Sun with home-made scones, cream teas, cakes and so forth; very friendly service, log fire in winter, tables outside amongst the geese and sheep in summer; some fruit and vegetables, home-made mohair knitwear and crafts, mobile home for hire, and certified camping/caravan site; cl Nov-2 wks before Easter; disabled access. £2.50.

Help this year from: *Joan Olivier, Walter Reid, HNJ, PEJ, Robert Crail, Mark Shutler, Viv Middlebrook, Basil Minson, Steve Goodchild, Wayne Brindle, Mr and Mrs Carlyle-Lyon, Harold and Alys Daubney, Mrs L Powys-Smith, JM, PM, Lynn Sharpless, Bob Eardley, Jenny and Brian Seller, David Campbell, Vicky McLean, Tom Macdonald, Klaus and Elizabeth Leist, Susan and John Douglas, Keith Mills, F M Bunbury, G W A Pearce, Ted George, George Atkinson, TBB, P Ware, Alan Skull, Pat Woodward, A M Atkinson, Michael and Alison Sandy, Mrs G Teall, Andy Stone, M L Clarke, Maureen Hobbs, Simon and Caroline Turner, Tim and Ann Newell.*

Oxfordshire Calendar

Some of these dates were provisional as we went to press.

JANUARY

13th **Oxford** Julian Bream Concert *at Sheldonian Theatre*

MARCH

5th **Didcot** Thomas the Tank Engine and Friends *at Railway Centre – till Sun 6*

APRIL

30th **Woodstock** Craft Fair *at Blenheim Palace – till 2 May*

MAY

1st **Oxford** May Morning: *medieval celebration, choristers sing from Magdalen College tower at 6 am, Morris dancers in Radcliffe Sq and Broad St, pubs and restaurants open early for breakfast*

12th **Oxford** Beating the Bounds *at St Michael's Church, custom celebrated since 1428: 11 am priest, choir and parishioners set off round 22 boundary stones, some of which are in pubs, ending at Lincoln College, where hot pennies are thrown to the choir boys*

22nd **Shenington** Hay Strewing *at Holy Trinity Church, (also 29 May and 5 Jun, freshly cut grass strewn on church floor; on Mon after second strewing, club tours village with enormous banner, beer and buns in village hall*

30th **Blenheim** Palace Charity Cricket Match, *celebrity team play a team from Oxford University*; **Oxford** Lord Mayor's Parade

JUNE

5th **Shenington** Hay Strewing (*see above*); **Stonor** VW Car Rally *at Stonor House*

12th **Banbury** Vintage Motorcycle Run *at Drayton School*; **Didcot** and **Oxford** 150th Anniversary Steam Shuttle *between stations Oxford-Didcot*

18th **Abingdon** Election of Mayor of Ock St (*tradition since 1700 fight over an ox), votes counted 4 pm, new mayor invested with the regalia of office, drinks from 200-year-old mace, and is chaired down Ock St, Morris dancing into evening*; **Buscot Park** Mozart Summer Festival

28th **Henley** Regatta – *till 3 July*

JULY

6th **Henley** Festival of Music – *till Sat 9*

9th **Oxford** Oxford Races *(formerly Sheriff's horse races) at Wolvercote Common inc boot sale, dog show and family amusements*

14th **Wheatley** Art in Action *at Waterperry Gardens, international craftsmen, artists and musicians – till Sun 17*

17th **Didcot** Teddy Bears' Picnic *at Railway Centre*

AUGUST

6th **Claydon** Vintage Fayre *at Granary Museum – till Sun 7*

7th **Abingdon** Horse Show *at Rye Farm Meadow*

26th **Towersey** 30th Village Festival – *till Mon 29*

Oxfordshire Calendar

August cont.

27th **Woodstock** Craft Fair *at Blenheim Palace – till Mon 29*

28th **Uffington** White Horse Show – *till Mon 29*

29th **Bletchingdon** Heathfield Show; **Ducklington** Flower Show

September

2nd **Woodstock** Autumn Flower Show *at Blenheim Palace – till Sun 4*

5th **Oxford** St Giles' Fair

9th **Beckley** Otmoor Country Show and Fair *at Lower Woods Farm – till Sun 11*

10th **Henley** Agricultural Show

11th **Abingdon** Works Car Show; **Didcot** Thomas the Tank Engine and Friends *at Railway Centre*

15th **Thame** Agricultural Show

October

19th **Banbury** Michaelmas Fair

November

5th **Bodicote** Fireworks, Bonfire and Fair

Shropshire

The Ironbridge museums, especially the lively open-air one, are among Britain's most enjoyable places to visit, and the Severn Valley Railway running out of Bridgnorth is perhaps the liveliest and most fun of all the country's steam railways. Shrewsbury is one of England's dozen or so most interesting cities, with plenty to fill a weekend stay, and Ludlow is a classic picturesque small town. Other particularly interesting places to visit here are the aerospace museum at Shifnal and nearby Shifnal Park, the working farm at Acton Scott, Attingham Park at Atcham, the gardens of Hodnet Hall, Hawkstone Park, and Stokesay Castle.

It is, however, the unspoilt countryside which is the county's really distinctive feature. There are several hills of decided character, most notably the Long Mynd (partly heather-covered; the country's southernmost grouse moor), with the much smaller but very striking Caer Caradoc facing it across the valley; the rather eery Stiperstones west of the Long Mynd, outcrops of harder quartzy rock leaving strange-shaped boulders, tors and crests on the skyline – and strange tales among the people living nearby; Wenlock Edge to the east, long and smoother, wooded along its flanks; the rather volcanic-looking Titterstone Clee north-east of Ludlow, and the aptly named Brown Clee north of that; and the bold Wrekin towering over Telford. All these hills give remarkable views; though some are quarried, the quarries don't obtrude too much.

In between the hills, and benefiting from them as background, are valleys of farmland, woods and streams. Buildings are often of stone, with a lot of black-and-white timbering, giving a picturesque look to many of the villages and towns.

The county scores for value, with prices low for eating out and for places to stay. Besides a large range of comfortable hotels and inns, it has quite a few comfortable and charmingly set farm and country-house B & Bs.

Where to stay

Ludlow SO5175 Feathers Bull Ring SY8 1AA (0584) 875261 **£104**; 40 comfortable rms. Hotel with exquisitely proportioned and intricately carved timbered frontage, Jacobean panelling and carving, period furnishings; decent food in bar, artistically presented restaurant dishes, and efficient, pleasant service; disabled access.

Shrewsbury SJ4912 Lion SY1 1UY (0743) 353107 **£92**; 59 comfortable rms. Imposing old coaching inn with cosy oak-panelled bar and sedate series of high-ceilinged rooms opening off; obliging staff and decent food in bar and restaurant.

Ludlow SO5175 DINHAM HALL SY8 1EJ (0584) 876464 *£89.50; 13 well-equipped rms. Graceful Georgian hotel, opposite the castle, with comfortable lounge, courteous service, very good food in the restaurant, lighter meals in terrace bar, and secluded gardens.

Shrewsbury SJ4912 ALBRIGHT HUSSEY Ellesmere Rd SY4 3AF (0939) 290571 £85; 5 rms. Fine moated medieval manor house, partly timber-framed and partly stone-and-brick, with good food and excellent service in panelled restaurant and 4 acres of gardens; children over 5.

Worfield SO7595 OLD VICARAGE Bridgnorth WV15 5JZ (074 64) 497 *£85; 14 rms. Restful and carefully restored Edwardian house with an airy conservatory-style lounge, parquet floors, good, interesting food, and friendly service; cl 2 wks from 26 Dec; disabled access.

Norton SJ7200 HUNDRED HOUSE Craven Arms TF11 9EE (095 271) 353 £69; 9 rms. Carefully refurbished mainly Georgian inn with quite a sophisticated feel; old quarry-tiled floors, beamed ceilings and oak panelling; popular food served all day inc excellent breakfast and afternoon tea, and elaborate evening meals using inn's own herbs.

Cleobury Mortimer SO6775 REDFERN Kidderminster DY14 8AA (0299) 270395 *£68; 11 rms. Small Georgian hotel run by friendly couple; disabled access, children £10 if sharing parents' rm.

Hopton Wafers SO6476 CROWN Kidderminster Worcs DY14 0NB (0299) 270372 £60; 8 rms. Attractive creeper-covered stone inn in pleasant countryside; interestingly furnished bar, inglenook fireplace, good food, decent house wines, beers and malt whiskies, friendly, efficient service, and streamside garden.

Much Wenlock SO6299 TALBOT TF13 6AA (0952) 727077 *£60; 6 rms. Dating from 1360 and once part of Wenlock Abbey, this converted 18th-c malthouse is very civilised, with lovely flower arrangements, prints and engraved songsheets on the walls (landlord is an expert on old music-hall tunes; very quiet music from thirties and forties dance bands), very friendly, helpful staff, and justifiably popular food inc good puddings; no smoking; cl Christmas; children over 12.

Church Stretton SO4593 MYND HOUSE SY6 6RB (0694) 722212 *£58; 8 rms, most with extensive views. Friendly Edwardian hotel at the foot of the Long Mynd; comfortable lounges, cosy bar, log fire, caring staff and good food and fine wines in candlelit restaurant; lots of walks; cl Christmas, Jan, 2 wks Aug.

Hopesay SO3883 OLD RECTORY Craven Arms SY7 8HD (058 87) 245 *£56; 4 comfortable rms. Neatly kept rectory, with 17th-c core, overlooking Hopesay Hill and Common and standing in two acres of immaculately maintained gardens; warmly friendly atmosphere, comfortable lounge and dining room, lots of books, and excellent food (unlicensed, so bring your own wine); cl Christmas; no children.

Cleobury Mortimer SO6775 TALBOT High St DY14 8DQ (0299) 270036 *£55; 8 comfortable rms. Tastefully refurbished and very welcoming 16th-c inn serving well-cooked and nicely presented food, inc good breakfasts.

Hodnet SJ6128 BEAR Market Drayton TF9 3NH (0630) 84214 *£55; 6 rms. Clean, comfortable 16th-c hotel, serving a good range of reasonably priced and imaginative food in the big main bar and the restaurant (small no-smoking area); cocktail bar with unusual sunken garden in the former bear pit, and Baronial-style room for Medieval banquets; cl 25 Dec pm for meals.

Wenlock Edge SO5796 WENLOCK EDGE INN Much Wenlock TF13 6DJ

(074 636) 403 ***£48**; 4 rms, showers only. Family-run and warmly friendly inn by the Ippikins Rock viewpoint, with lots of walks through NT land that runs along the Edge; good fresh home-made bar food (not Mon), fine breakfasts, good old-fashioned puddings, and wide range of drinks; 2nd Mon evening of month is story-telling night; cl 24-26 Dec; no children.

Llanfair Waterdine SO2476 RED LION Knighton LD7 1TU (0547) 528214 **£45**; 3 rms, 1 with own bthrm. In an area of outstanding beauty and overlooking the River Tene, this pub is determinedly traditional – no noisy machines, music or children.

Gretton SO5295 COURT FARM Cardington Church Stretton SY6 7HU (0694) 771219 **£42**; 4 rms, 3 with own bthrm. Large, comfortable, stone-built farmhouse on 325-acre arable stock farm with warm welcome, big woodburning stove in inglenook fireplace and good food; no smoking; cl Dec-Jan; children over 12; no pets.

Ludlow SO5174 CHURCH INN SY8 1AW (0584) 872174 **£40**; 8 rms. Georgian stuccoed building opening behind on to a quiet walk by the parish church; well-served, popular bar food.

Ludlow SO5174 UNICORN Lower Corve St SY8 1DU (0584) 873555 **£40**; 5 rms. Pleasantly refurbished inn with good, popular food in bar and restaurant, real ales; cl 25 Dec.

Wrockwardine SJ6212 CHURCH FARM Telford TF6 5DG (0952) 244917 **£40**; 6 rms, some with own bthrm. Friendly Georgian farmhouse, built on very ancient site overlooking the attractive garden and church, with relaxed atmosphere, beams and log fire in lounge, and good home-cooked food.

Woolstaston SO4599 RECTORY FARM Church Stretton SY6 6NN (0694) 751306 ***£38**; 3 rms. Lovely half-timbered 17th-c farmhouse on the lower slopes of the Long Mynd, with fine views, friendly welcome and hearty breakfasts; no evening meals; cl Dec-Jan; children over 12; no dogs.

Ludlow SO5175 WHEATSHEAF Lower Broad St SY8 1PQ (0584) 872980 **£35**; 5 oak-beamed rms with showers. Attractively furnished small 17th-c pub spectacularly built into medieval town gate; traditional atmosphere, wide range of good bar food, real ales and farm ciders, and friendly owners.

Hampton Loade SO7586 OLD FORGE HOUSE Bridgnorth WV15 6HD (0746) 780338 **£34**; 3 rms, 2 with own bthrm. Family-run, homely Georgian house close to River Severn, with fine breakfasts, friendly owners, and lovely quiet garden; cl 25 Dec.

Strefford SO4485 STREFFORD HALL FARM Craven Arms SY6 6NN (0588) 6722383 ***£34**; 3 rms. Stone-built Victorian farmhouse surrounded by 360 acres of working farmland; woodburning stove in sitting room, no smoking, lots of walks; cl Christmas and New Year.

Clun SO3081 NEW HOUSE FARM Craven Arms SY7 8NJ (0588) 638314 **£32**; 3 rms. Up in the hills, friendly and very comfortable 18th-c farmhouse of stock-rearing farm, with its own Iron-Age hill fort; excellent walks, breakfasts inc own honey, and evening meal (by arrangement) using home-grown produce; riding and fishing (lake and fly-fishing) nearby; cl Christmas and New Year; children by arrangement.

Wentnor SO3893 CROWN Bishops Castle SY9 5EE (058 861) 613 **£26**; 4 rms. Well-kept and welcoming pub with wide choice of well-priced good food in bar and cosy, pleasant restaurant, decent wines, and good coffee; camping/caravan facilities; cl 25 Dec, no children.

To see and do

Acton Burnell SJ5302 ACTON BURNELL CASTLE Ruined manor house built in the 13th c but almost abandoned by 1420.

Acton Scott SO4589 ACTON SCOTT WORKING FARM A vivid introduction to traditional rural life, with rare breeds of lots of different farm animals and the kinds of crop they used to grow around the turn of the century, cultivated using old rotation methods. All the work is done by hand or horse power, with period farm machinery. Lots of different craft demonstrations, and daily buttermaking; meals and snacks, shop, disabled access; cl Mon and Nov-Apr; £2.50. Nearby places for decent lunches include the Plough at Wistanstow (which brews its own beer), Ragleth and Green Dragon in Little Stretton and, perhaps best of all, up on Wenlock Edge the Wenlock Edge Inn.

Atcham SJ5409 ATTINGHAM PARK A splendidly grand late 18th-c house on the site of an old Roman town, with an imposing three-storey colonnaded portico and elaborate and intricate decor. The extensive picture gallery was designed by Nash, who made imaginative use of early curved cast iron and glass for the ceiling; attractive mature gardens and deer park outside. Snacks, shop, disabled access by prior arrangement; house cl am, all day Thurs and Fri, all Nov-Mar; house and grounds £3.20, grounds only £1.20. NT. The HOME FARM has rare breeds of farm animal and traditional farm machinery; you can watch the milking of the Jersey cows, and play with the pets. Farmhouse teas, shop, limited disabled access; cl am, all Thurs and Fri, Nov-Mar; £2. The handsome Mytton & Mermaid, and the Corbet Arms at nearby Upton Magna, are useful for lunch.

Billingsley SO7185 RAYS FARM COUNTRY MATTERS Traditional farm in pleasant countryside with pigs, sheep, cattle, a llama, and a good collection of owls and other animals. Also decent woodland walks, and bicycles can be hired for exploring the surrounding scenery (£3 an hour); snacks, shop, disabled access; cl 25 Dec; £1.50.

★ **Bridgnorth** SO7193 A picturesque old market town on the River Severn, divided into the High Town and Low Town and connected by the hair-raising CLIFF RAILWAY. High Town has lots of fine timbered buildings, such as the odd town hall built on a sandstone-arched base that straddles the road in the high street. The old CASTLE was mostly destroyed in the Civil War, but part of the keep remains, left at a lopsided angle by the constant bombardment; the grounds are now a park with good views. The unusual CHURCH nearby was designed by Thomas Telford. SEVERN VALLEY RAILWAY The leading standard-gauge steam railway, with a great collection of locomotives, a splendidly lively atmosphere, and trips through beautiful scenery; for full details see entry under Bewdley, in Hereford and Worcester chapter. It's worth taking the excellent return dining trip, and there should be just enough time to stop for a swift pint at the Railwayman's Arms on the station. Other useful pubs for food here are the Hollyhead opposite the station, and Kings Head in Whitburn St. MIDLAND MOTOR MUSEUM Over 100 well-restored sports cars, racing cars and motorcycles in converted stables of beautiful grounds of Stanmore Hall; also steam traction engines; snacks, shop, disabled access; open wknds and bank hols and daily July-Sept; £3.50. COSTUME AND CHILDHOOD MUSEUM Lots of old costumes, and a Victorian nursery; also collections of art and minerals, and a witch's house for children to play in. Meals, snacks, shop; cl Tues and 25 Dec; *£1.25. DANIEL'S MILL The biggest waterwheel powering a working corn mill in the country; the mill museum has a good collection of country tools and old maps and documents. A picturesque old place, run by the same family for 200 years; snacks, shop; open wknds and bank hols Easter-Sept, cl am Apr and May; £1.50.

Broseley SJ6701 BENTHALL HALL Elizabethan sandstone house with fine oak woodwork and panelling, decorative plasterwork, interesting garden, and 17th-c church (services 3.15 pm most Suns); shop, some disabled access; open pm Weds, Sun and bank hols Apr-Sept; £2.50. NT. The Foresters Arms and Cumberland Hotel are both useful for lunch.

Buildwas SJ6204 BUILDWAS ABBEY Beautiful remains of 12th-c Cistercian abbey in nice setting – apart from the roof it's practically all still here; shop, disabled access; cl winter Mons; £1.10. The best places for lunch are in nearby Much Wenlock.

Bury Ditches SO3384 is an Iron-Age ring fort, high up on a hill, with superb views of south Shropshire and north Herefordshire.

★ **Clun** SO3081 is an attractive stonebuilt village on the edge of the CLUN FOREST, a peaceful pastoral area of rolling partly wooded hills. The ruined Norman CASTLE gives fine views from the castle mound. Down by the River Clun, the 16th-c stone bridge is very picturesque. The Sun is useful for lunch.

Cleobury Mortimer is a civilised small town, most notable perhaps for its church's CROOKED SPIRE, though timbered Tudor buildings among its more elegant Georgian ones are picturesque. A restored WATERMILL produces its own stoneground flour. The Bell is pleasant for lunch.

Dudleston Heath SJ3736 ERWAY FARM HOUSE Small woodland garden with interesting profusion of snowdrops, hellebores, daphnes and shade-loving plants; unusual plant and seed sales. Open pm last Sun of month Feb-Sept, as well as Easter Sat and Sun; *£1. The nearby Ellesmere Inn is useful for lunch.

Harmer Hill SJ4922 PIM HILL FARM (Lea Hall) Rare breeds of farm animal, picnic site, a friendly donkey, and organic produce shop; snacks; cl Sun, Mon, Tues. The Bridgewater Arms is useful for lunch.

Haughmond Abbey SJ4414 (off B5062 E of Shrewsbury) HAUGHMOND ABBEY Ruined Augustinian abbey, partly converted into house after Dissolution. Fine Norman doorway in chapter house, and well-preserved lodgings and kitchens; cl winter Mon; £1.10.

! **Hawkstone Park** SJ5830 Created in the 18th c by the Hill family, this remarkable parkland with its magnificent series of follies was for a while one of the most visited attractions in the country, though this century it became neglected and mostly forgotten. It's now been restored to its original grandeur, and has spectacular views from the monuments dotted around its 100 acres. There are the ruins of a medieval red castle, intricate arches and pathways, a hermit in his hermitage and a fantastic underground grotto; it's a rewarding place to stroll around – the full circuit can easily take over three hours, and sensible shoes are recommended. Meals, snacks, shop, limited disabled access; cl Weds and Nov-Mar; *£4. It's not far from Hodnet – see below.

Hodnet SJ6218 HODNET HALL GARDENS Sixty acres of landscaped gardens with spacious lawns, lush pools, plants and trees; also a 17th-c dovecot and an astonishingly decorated tearoom, full of big-game trophies. A very pleasant place to spend an afternoon; snacks, shop, disabled access by prior arrangement; cl am, and Oct-Mar; £2.50. The Bear Hotel opposite is good for lunch.

Ironbridge SJ6703

This early industrial area, like others using both minerals and water, is in lovely surroundings – in this case, the Severn Gorge, with woods and steep grassy slopes running down to the river. Many of the former industrial monuments and buildings have now been linked into the IRONBRIDGE GORGE MUSEUM, more a collection of museums in fact, several of them scattered over six square miles along the gorge. It includes the biggest open-air museum of its kind, a hugely enjoyable series of reconstructions, displays and museums on a variety of sites. Iron rails, wheels, boats, trains and the metal bridge were all first made here, thanks to the pioneering techniques of the Darby family, and the valley soon became the biggest iron-making area in the whole world. The MUSEUM OF IRON illustrates all this, and you can still see the original working furnace. Other museums cover Coalport china, tiles, and the river, there are old houses belonging to the Darby family, and you can even go down the Tar Tunnel. By far the most popular part is the BLISTS HILL OPEN AIR MUSEUM, a complete reconstructed Victorian village, showing everything from the offices, houses and machinery to the shops, pubs and pigsties. In summer a bus service can take you between the sites; they are some distance apart. You don't have to visit all the component parts of the complex at once to take advantage of the special-offer passport ticket, which includes all at a reduced price, as it remains valid indefinitely until you've seen all the bits you want – you could easily spend a weekend here. Meals, snacks, shop, disabled access; cl 24-25 Dec; £8 for a passport ticket. There are plenty of other things to see around the area, such as the TEDDY BEAR MUSEUM, displaying lots of bears and other furry animals made here by the long-established Merrythought Company; shop too. IRONBRIDGE TOY MUSEUM Lots of Meccano, and plenty

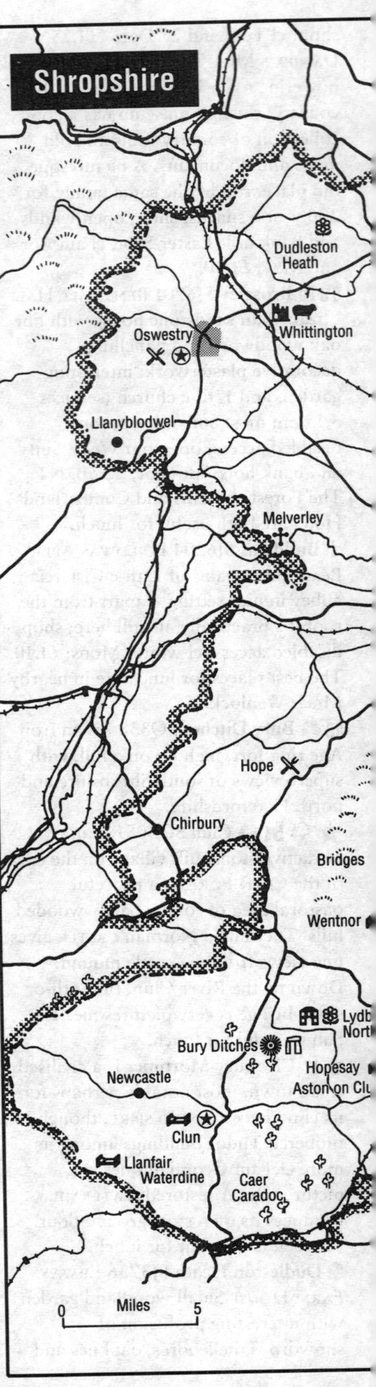

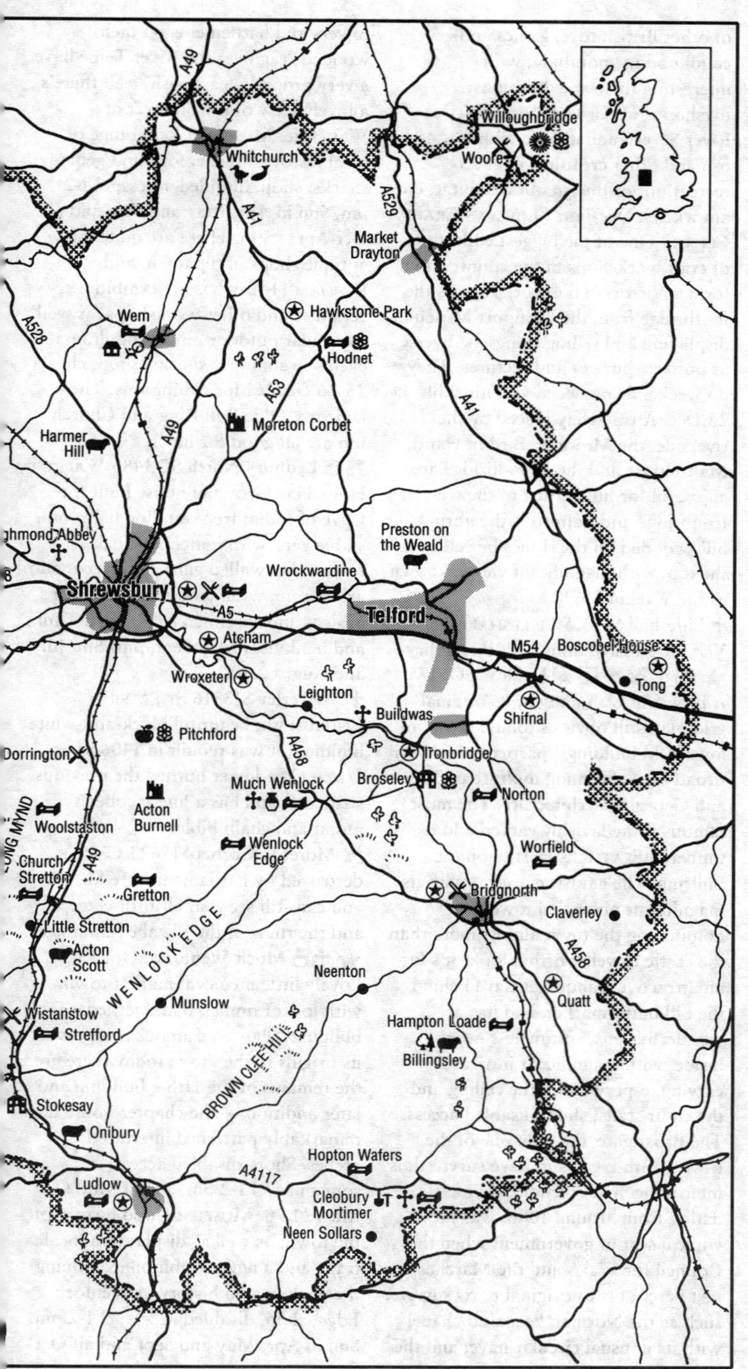
Willoughbridge
Woore
Whitchurch
A49
A41
A529
Market Drayton
Wem
Hawkstone Park
Hodnet
A528
A53
Moreton Corbet
Harmer Hill
A41
Preston on the Weald
Wrockwardine
Shrewsbury
A5
Telford
Atcham
M54
Boscobel House
Tong
Wroxeter
Leighton
Shifnal
Buildwas
Pitchford
A458
Dorrington
Ironbridge
Much Wenlock
Broseley
Norton
Acton Burnell
Woolstaston
Wenlock Edge
Worfield
Church Stretton
Gretton
Bridgnorth
Claverley
Little Stretton
A458
Acton Scott
WENLOCK EDGE
Neenton
Quatt
Wistanstow
Munslow
Hampton Loade
Strefford
BROWN CLEE HILL
Billingsley
Stokesay
Onibury
Hopton Wafers
A4117
Ludlow
Cleobury Mortimer
Neen Sollars

of other British toys, games and childhood memorabilia, with interesting themed exhibitions; toyshop; *£1. Underwater World River Severn aquatic life with lots of fish and other creatures in good recreations of their natural habitat; cl am wkdys, Dec-Jan; £1. Maws Craft Centre One of the biggest collections of craft workshops in the country, in a former Victorian tile works across the footbridge from the Coalport Museum, displaying and selling things as diverse as pottery, puzzles and pictures. They do weekend courses in various skills; cl 25 Dec. Attractively placed by the riverside, the Meadow, Bird in Hand, Malt House and the Woodbridge are all useful for lunch. Just to the west of Ironbridge and Telford is the abrupt hill, wooded on the slopes but clear at the top, with magnificent views, known as the Wrekin SJ6208.

✝ **Lilleshall** SJ7315 Lilleshall Abbey Very impressive ruins of 12th-c abbey.

★ ✝ **Ludlow** SO5175 A beautiful 12th-c town, its original grid plan still obvious today. Plenty of lovely old buildings, particularly down Broad St, a charming mixture of Tudor and Georgian architecture. The most famous is the lavishly carved and timbered Feathers Hotel on the Bullring. The parish church with its magnificent pinnacled tower dominating the town almost more than the castle is well worth a look; it's in an attractive tranquil enclave behind the old buttermarket, and has a wonderful sense of timeless peace inside, with magnificent intricate carving, especially on the ceiling and the choir stalls; shop, disabled access. The Broadgate, the only one of the town's 13th-c gates to have survived, is interesting. The splendid old castle, dating from around 1086, was for a while a seat of government when the Council for Wales and the Marches met here. Lots of original parts survive, such as the Norman keep and chapel with its unusual circular nave, and the towers and battlements on their wooded crag over the River Teme have a very properly 'castle-ish' feel; there's a lovely view of it from over at Whitcliffe. Museum Good range of local history, archaeology and geology; snacks, shop, disabled access; cl 1-2 pm, Sun in Apr, May and Sept and all Oct-Apr; *50p. There are quite a few antique shops in the town, and Dinham House has art exhibitions, ceramics and other workshops, as well as regular outdoor music and drama events in summer; snacks, shop; cl 25-26 Dec; £1 for exhibitions. The Unicorn, Olde Bull Ring and Church Inn are all good for lunch.

Lydbury North SO3486 Walcot Hall Fine Georgian house built for Clive of India; free-standing ballroom, stable yard with matching clock towers, big walled garden, dovecot and arboretum, with good rhododendrons, azaleas and specimen trees; open Thurs and bank hols May-Sept, plus Sun July and Aug; £2.50.

✝ **Melverley** SJ3316 St Peter's Church is a beautiful black-and-white building; it was rebuilt in 1406 after Owen Glendower burned the previous structure, and has a fine Jacobean pulpit and chain bible.

Moreton Corbet SJ5623 Castle destroyed by Parliament in 1644, but you can still see a small 13th-c keep and the ruins of the Elizabethan house.

★ ✝ **Much Wenlock** SO6299 Lovely little medieval market town, with lots of timbered and jettied buildings. Priory Famous priory with its origins in the 7th c; today there are the remains of the 11th-c building and later additions – the chapter house has remarkably patterned interlaced arches. Shop, disabled access; sometimes cl 1-2 pm, and cl Mon Oct-Mar; £1.70. Museum Good history of the town, as well as displays on local trade and a new exhibition examining the geology and history of Wenlock Edge; shop, disabled access; cl 1-2 pm, Sun in Apr, May and Sept and all Oct-

Mar; *50p. The Talbot is good for lunch.

Onibury SO4579 WERNLAS COLLECTION OF RARE POULTRY Mostly large fowl, also rare breeds of pheasant, unusual European species, several breeds of animal. About 6,000 chicks are hatched each year so there are usually plenty about for children to handle or feed; attractive surroundings. Snacks, shop; cl Mon mid-July-mid-Sept, 25 Dec; £2.75. The Hollybush is adequate for lunch.

Oswestry SJ2929 CAMBRIAN RAILWAY MUSEUM and OSWESTRY CYCLE MUSEUM Joint museum with lots of old bicycles and a history of cycling through the ages, as well as steam engines and railway memorabilia; on bank hols and some weekends there may be locomotives in steam. Shop, disabled access; *£1.50. OLD OSWESTRY Iron-Age hill fort covering 68 acres; elaborate western defensive entrance and five ramparts remain. The ancient black-and-white timbered Fox is good for lunch.

Pitchford SJ5303 GOLDING GARDEN Steeply terraced 16th-c gardens, tender plants in sheltered corners, views; pick-your-own asparagus in May/June; cl mid-June-mid-Apr; £1.50.

Preston on the Weald SJ6815 HOO FARM ANIMAL KINGDOM All the ingredients you'd expect on a traditional working farm, animals, pets, nature trails and sheep shearing, but they race the sheep too, and there are other unusual features such as ostriches, pheasant-rearing and bee-keeping. Children can bottle-feed the lambs, and there's also a maze; snacks, shop, disabled access (but no special lavatories); cl Mon (exc bank hols) and Tues, mid-Sept-Easter exc month up to Christmas for trees; £2.

Quatt SO7588 DUDMASTON 17th-c house in extensive parklands with lakeside and woodland walks; fine furnishings and paintings, inc the old flower-painting collection of Francis Darby of Coalbrookdale, and a collection of modern sculpture. Snacks, shop, disabled access to house, parts of garden and woods; open pm Weds and Sun Apr-Sept; *£3 house and garden, £2 garden only. The Lion of Morfe over at Upper Farmcote is fairly handy for lunch.

Shifnal SJ7407 AEROSPACE MUSEUM Spectacular collection of planes inc the Victor and Vulcan bombers, Hastings, York and British Airways airliners, the last airworthy Britannia and lots of other aircraft; snacks, shop, disabled access; cl Christmas; *£4.30. WORKING POTTER (1 Newhouses, Aston Rd) using Raku firing; cl Sat pm, Sun. Nearby WESTON PARK (Weston under Lizard SJ8080) is a particularly striking and richly decorated 17th-c stately home, with a fine collection of furnishings, tapestries and porcelain and paintings, inc works by Van Dyck, Rubens, Gainsborough and Constable, and a number of letters from Disraeli. The deer park and grounds were landscaped by Capability Brown, and have a restored 18th-c terrace garden, brightly planted broderie garden, and interesting trees and shrubs inc a good southern beech collection and big rhododendrons; also pets' corner, woodland adventure playground and miniature railway. Meals and snacks in former stables restaurant, shop, some disabled access; cl Oct-Easter; £3 (plus £1 for house). In Shifnal, the White Hart is good for lunch.

Shrewsbury SJ4912 still has a largely medieval central street layout, with oddly named streets (such as Shoplatch, Murivance, Wyle Cop), plenty of quiet corners up narrow alleys and courtyards, and several timbered Tudor buildings among its more modern shops and offices. The 14th-c ABBEY with its statue of Edward III is impressive, as is the church of ST MARY'S, with one of the tallest spires in England. The 12th-c CASTLE was refurbished by Thomas Telford in

1790, but parts of the earlier building remain, such as the Norman gateway and the Great Hall. It's being restored at the moment, so may not be open, but much can be seen from the pleasant grounds. CLIVE HOUSE MUSEUM (College Hill) Old town house associated with Clive of India, with excellent displays of Coalport and Caughley porcelain, fine paintings in period room settings, a walled garden and various other displays and exhibitions; shop, disabled access to ground floor only; £1. ROWLEY'S HOUSE MUSEUM Impressive timber-framed building housing local archaeology, geology and social and natural history, as well as interesting Roman remains, a new medieval gallery and a costume gallery; shop, disabled access to ground floor only; cl Sun exc pm in summer; *£1. It's a rewarding town to walk around, with several attractive riverside parks. Among other interesting shops is a good CRAFT CENTRE (St Alkmonds Sq, top of High St) in 12th-c St Julian's church, with several cheery workshops, a bustling craft fair every Sat and a good restaurant (esp useful for vegetarians); some disabled access; cl Thurs (exc school hols) and Sun. The Castle Vaults, one of the black-and-white timbered buildings, surprises by having a decent Mexican restaurant.

Stokesay SO4381 STOKESAY CASTLE Largely unspoilt 13th-c manor house in charming setting; excellent timbered Tudor gatehouse, solar and hall with cruck-framed roof and early English windows. Good views from the top of the tower; snacks, shop; cl Mon and Tues Oct-Mar; *£2.20.

Nr Tong SJ7907 BOSCOBEL HOUSE Several hiding places were included in this house when it was built in 1600, and they were put to good use later in the century when Charles II was fleeing from the Battle of Worcester. It's an interesting place with an unusually well-preserved 17th-c garden and cobbled courtyard, and 19th-c decor giving a romanticised view of the King's drama; meals, snacks, shop, disabled access to gardens only; cl winter Mon, 25 Dec, all Jan. The ROYAL OAK here is said by some to have been the hiding place of the king, by others to be a descendant, and by still others to be just a fine old tree. WHITELADIES PRIORY Ruins of Augustinian nunnery destroyed in the Civil War. The Bell is good for lunch.

Wem SJ5128 ROCKING HORSE WORKSHOP An interesting opportunity to watch the production of traditionally styled rocking horses; the workshop also has horses at various stages of renovation, and a display of period toys. Shop; cl 25 Dec, check first at wknds, tel (0939) 232335.

Willoughbridge SJ7540 DOROTHY CLIVE GARDEN Seven-acre hillside woodland garden created from old gravel quarry; rock and water gardens, rare trees and shrubs, splendid rhododendrons, fine views. Snacks, disabled access; cl Nov-Mar; £2. Actually just over the Staffordshire border, but usually listed under nearby Market Drayton – so we've included it in this chapter instead.

Whitchurch SJ5441 SHROPSHIRE BIRD AND AQUATIC CENTRE Hundreds of birds from finches to parrots, taking in a few more exotic creatures; also aquatic fish and outdoor fish pond. Snacks, limited disabled access; cl 25 Dec. The canalside Willey Moor Lock pub just north of the town is a pleasant spot for lunch.

Whittington SJ3331 PARK HALL WORKING FARM MUSEUM The powerful shire horses here still work the land as they have for decades. The Victorian stables also have lots of livestock from that period inc cattle, sheep and several breeds of pig, and there are examples of vintage farm machinery and equipment, especially with an equine theme; snacks, shop, disabled access; cl Fri exc July-mid-Sept, all Nov-Easter; £2.50. Nearby are the handsome remains of a CASTLE.

Wroxeter SJ5608 ROMAN TOWN Excavated remains of the Roman town of Virconium, probably dating from the 2nd c, when this was the fourth-largest Roman town in the country; the MUSEUM has finds from the town and the earlier fortress, and there is a well-preserved colonnade and municipal bath. Snacks, shop, disabled access; cl 12-2 pm and winter Mon; £1.70. There's also a Roman wall on the neighbouring ROMAN VINEYARD, a friendly little place producing several wines – it's the most northerly producer of red wine in the world. Also a lavender farm (Romans used lavender to keep insects off their vines), rare breeds and some interesting glacial stones; shop (with various lavender-based products), disabled access; cl Mon and Oct-Mar, shop open all year; £1.50 tour.

The local tourist information centres have details of a number of imaginative trails round the region, centring on the work of Thomas Telford, haunted villages and even the novels of Ellis Peters. They can also give details of BALLOON TRIPS over the largely unspoilt countryside.

★ **Other attractive villages,** almost all of them with decent pubs, include Aston on Clun SO3982, Bridges SO3996, Chirbury SO2698 (with its famously haunted graveyard), Claverley SO7993, Leighton SJ6105, Little Stretton SO4392, Llanyblodwel SJ2423, Lydbury North SO3586, Munslow SO5287, Neen Sollars SO6672, Neenton SO6488, Newcastle SO2582, Tong SJ7907, Wentnor SO3893 and Worfield SO7696.

Walks

South Shropshire's hills rise to nearly 1,800 ft, and have a real Welsh Marches feel. The **Stiperstones ridge** SJ3600, reached from a nearby car park or from a longer walk up from spoil-heap-dominated Snailbeach SJ3702, is crowned by dramatic rocks and has a splendid view. The **Long Mynd** SO4092 is best reached from Church Stretton SO4593; this bracken-and-bilberry-clad massif has a flat plateau-like top, crossed by the Port Way, an ancient track dating from Neolithic times. Its sides are cut into by a series of narrow, remote-feeling valleys, of which Cardingmill Valley is best known because of its relative accessibility. East of Church Stretton SO4593, **Caer Caradoc** SO3075 has a pleasingly compact summit, and the pick of the local views. The best start is Hope Bowdler SO4792, not far from the county's oldest pub, the Royal Oak at Cardington SO4792. **Brown Clee Hill** SO5985, Shropshire's highest point, has a disappointingly flat top but a certain solitary grandeur.

The industrial monuments in the **Severn Gorge** are spaced close enough together, and in what is charming scenery despite the Buildwas cooling towers to the west, to make them ideal for a tour on foot. Steep lanes and paths connect Ironbridge SJ6703 and Coalbrookdale SJ6604, and an old railway track and a path along the base of Benthall Edge Wood SJ6603 assist routes along the gorge. A fine linear walk can be taken from Broseley SJ6701, descending north-west into the gorge via Corbett's Dingle to Coalport SJ6902. From Coalport, you can follow the river all the way south to Bridgnorth SO7193. Just west of Telford SJ6810, the **Wrekin** SJ6208, so useful for limerick-writers, is no Everest (a respectable and easily attained 1,334 ft) but commands a huge panorama over points over 100 miles apart by virtue of its isolation on the edge of the Shropshire uplands. Further east, the Lion at Hampton Loade SO7586 by the **River Severn** is a good base for walks – and quiet, except when the Severn

Valley Railway has one of its weekend steam spectaculars.

North Shropshire is in general less interesting for walkers, but does have some places well worth seeking out. Around **Ellesmere** SJ3934 are a number of meres or lakes – the Mere by Ellesmere itself, Blake Mere SJ4133, and Cole Mere SJ4333, which has a country park around it. This is close enough to the **Shropshire Union Canal** to include a walk along the towpath, with Colemere village SJ4332 a suitable starting place. **Grinshill Hill** SJ5223, between Grinshill SJ5223 and Clive SJ5124, has much wider views than you'd expect from its modest height, and quite an atmospheric summit, where woods open out by sheer quarried rock-faces.

Driving

Driving in Shropshire is made pleasurable by the relative lack of traffic – and by the fact that a good many roads take you through attractive scenery and past attractive houses and villages. There are pleasant views from the old coaching road SW from Shrewsbury, through Longden, Pulverbatch and beyond, with increasingly attractive scenery the further you go. Other enjoyable roads include the B4371 from Much Wenlock to Church Stretton, along Wenlock Edge, with bracing views except in places where woods line it; and the back road from Wigmore through Leinthall Starkes to Ludlow, giving lovely views as you approach the town. The back roads up over the top of the Long Mynd from Church Stretton are attractive but steep.

Even the trunk roads tend to be quite civilised here, though once they hit towns like Shrewsbury and Ludlow the traffic does tend to pile up. The busiest seems to be the A49, and even that is tolerable.

Where to eat

Dorrington SJ4703 COUNTRY FRIENDS (0743) 718707 Cosy, pleasant restaurant with good interesting food; cl Sun, Mon, last 2 wks July, 24-27 Dec. **£22.40**|£2.10/£5.90.

Woore SJ7342 FALCON (0630) 647230 Fairly plain interior but with wide choice of generous well-presented good food and good friendly service; cl 25 Dec, children over 12 in restaurant. **£17**|£1.40/£8.50.

Hope SJ3401 STABLES (0743) 891344 Warmly welcoming charming cottage with promptly served, particularly good food (fine home-made ice-creams), and good view to Long Mountain from the front, and over Hope Valley to the Stiperstones at the back. One of our favourite places; cl Mon, end Feb; children lunchtimes only. **£15**|£1.50/£5.

Wistanstow SO4385 PLOUGH (0588) 673251 Brightly lit, with lots of chairs and tables, home of Woods beers brewed in separate older building nearby, popular home-made food with fuller evening menu, and good selection of drinks; cl Mon; children over 8 in evenings. **£15**|£1.25/£4.75.

Bridgnorth SO7293 MAGPIE HOUSE (0746) 763977 Little timbered evening restaurant backing on to River Severn with excellent food from a smallish menu, and very attentive staff; resident ghost; open Thurs, Fri, Sat. **£14.70**|£9.45.

Shrewsbury SJ4912 CASTLE VAULTS (0743) 358807 Mexican restaurant attached to black-and-white pub, with generous helpings of good-value food; cl Sun pm, 25-26 Dec. **£14.20**.

Oswestry SJ2929 Fox (0691) 653311 Low ceilings, big log fire, very friendly, obliging staff, well-kept beer and big helpings of very good, wholesome food – extremely good value; cl Sun am, 25 Dec pm. **£12.60**|£1/£5.75.

Help this year from: *Graham and Belinda Staplehurst, Frank Cummins, Mary Davies, Julie Peters, Richard and Maria Gillespie, E H and R F Warner, C A Brace, John Greenwood, Diane Tailby, Paul and Janet Waring, John and Beryl Knight, Miss R M Tudor, Jason Caulkin, Bill and Beryl Farmer, Andrew and Barbara Sykes, R C Smail, DH, Mary Davies, Pat and John Millward, R A Harris, Basil Minson, TOH, L G and D L Smith, P J Keen, Dave Braisted, H K Dyson, C Roberts, Dr Richard Fry, Bernard Phillips, Mrs P J Pearce, Bob Alton.*

We welcome reports from readers . . .

This GUIDE depends on readers' reports. Do help us if you can – in return, we offer a discount on the next edition to people who've helped us with reports for it. Tell us what you think about places already in it, and anything extra you think we should say about them. And send us your ideas for inclusion in the next edition: places to visit, eat at or stay in, attractive drives or walks, maybe even unusual interesting shops you know of. Use the card in the middle, the report forms at the end, or just write – no stamp needed: THE GOOD WEEKEND GUIDE, FREEPOST TN1569, Wadhurst, E Sussex TN5 7BR.

Shropshire Calendar

Some of these dates were provisional as we went to press.

February

8th **Shrewsbury** Shropshire Antiques Fair – *till Thurs 10*

April

3rd **Newport** Driving Society Rally, *women wearing Easter bonnets*

16th **Ludlow** Point-to-point

May

1st **Telford** Kids International, *activities for all the family at Town Park – till Mon 2*

2nd **Ironbridge** Blists Hill Open Air Museum, *street entertainment inc maypole dancing*

20th **Shrewsbury** West Midlands Agricultural Show – *till Sat 21*

28th **Ludlow** Craft Fair *at Ludlow Castle – till Mon 30*

29th **Aston-on-Clun** Arbor Tree Dressing – *as part of an ancient ritual a 250-year-old poplar tree is decorated with flags on Royal Oak Day*

30th **Ludlow** Carnival; **Market Drayton** Carnival

June

5th **Ironbridge** Coracle Regatta

11th **Lydbury North** Shropshire Game Fair *at Walcot Hall – till Sun 12*

19th **Shifnal** Cosford Air Show, *at Aerospace Museum*; **Shrewsbury** Tudor Dancing *performed in the Square at 2 pm*

25th **Ludlow** Festival – *till 10 July*

July

3rd **Bishops Castle** Carnival

8th **Much Wenlock** Olympian Games – *till Sun 10*

17th **Shrewsbury** Tudor Dancing

23rd **Church Stretton** Arts Festival – *till 6 Aug*; **Long Ashton** Bristol Community Festival *at Ashton Court Estate – rock, jazz, folk, classical, art and theatre tents, and 150 stalls*; **Wem** Sweat-pea Festival *at Town Hall and Market Hall – till Sun 24*

August

4th **Burwarton** Agricultural Show

6th **Oswestry** Agricultural Show

12th **Shrewsbury** Flower Show – *till Sat 13*

21st **Shrewsbury** Tudor Dancing

28th **Lydbury North** Traction Engine Rally *at Walcot Hall – till Mon 29*

September

18th **Shrewsbury** Tudor Dancing

24th **Hopton** British Isles Horse and Tractor Ploughing Championships

November

5th **Ironbridge** Traditional Gaslight Night *at Blists Hill Open Air Museum culminating in firework display*

Somerset and Avon

Bath is excellent for a weekend break – sophisticated and elegant, it is one of Britain's three or four most rewarding cities. Bristol is lively and vigorous, with lots of things to see and do: great for day visits, though not for a stay. In East Somerset, Wells is a charming largely unspoilt small cathedral city; Glastonbury has the pull of its Arthurian legends; and the Mendip Hills have the best of the county's walking, and some spectacular scenery. West Somerset seems more secluded, with the Quantock Hills having the most attractive countryside; on the whole, it's an area for quieter breaks.

Throughout the area, there are plenty of places to visit, with attractive villages and small towns, and a profusion of church towers, pinnacled, turreted and gargoyled, landmarks both in the flatlands and among the trees of the hills and valleys. In the hillier areas, buildings are generally of stone, varying in colour and character from the Cotswold-style of Avon, through the pale limestones of the Mendips and the golden warmth of South Somerset's Ham stone, to the rugged and stolid greys of the hamlets tucked into the folds of the Quantocks.

Right over in the west, Somerset includes a large part of Exmoor. We have covered this in a separate Exmoor section, included at the end of the Devon chapter.

Bath

Excellent for a short stay, it is a lovely city with lots to see.

Graceful and elegant, Bath's mellow squares, crescents and terraces of fine 18th-c buildings gain added appeal and even a touch of drama from the steepness of the hills they cling to. They were built for people planning to enjoy themselves, and a strong sense of this still runs through the atmosphere here: you feel it's somewhere to be entertained and pampered, that there's a lot going on that is fun.

Many places here enjoyably recall the days of Beau Nash and the building of Bath as a fashionable resort. Other attractions go back to the Roman Baths, and come right up to date with the city's interesting and unusual shops.

In the Walks section we note the greatest of the Regency buildings to look at; just strolling around the city is a special pleasure, but among many places to visit we'd pick out particularly the Roman Baths, Pump Room, Museum of Costume at the Assembly Rooms, Building of Bath Museum, Industrial Heritage Centre, No 1 Royal Crescent, and Bath Abbey. The American Museum on the edge of the city at Claverton is very special.

This is not a cheap city to stay in, but the places we recommend, all stylish and comfortable, give you the feeling that you're getting value for money.

In midsummer, during the week the centre floods with school parties, sometimes from other countries. Weekends are better; but for a weekday summer visit it might be best to wait until the school holidays.

If you want to go during the early summer Festival, book accommodation well ahead.

Where to stay

Bath Priory Weston Rd BA1 2XT (0225) 331922 **£170**; 21 rms. Victorian Gothic hotel with friendly, informal atmosphere, antiques and paintings, comfortable lounge opening on to the neat walled garden, and good food in the three cosy rooms of the restaurant.

Bath Royal Crescent Royal Crescent BA1 2LS (0225) 319090 **£160**; 42 luxurious rms. Elegant Georgian town house with comfortable, antique-filled lounges, very attractive garden room (with its own menu), open fires and lovely flowers; excellently presented, very well-prepared fine food in the Dower House Restaurant with its own relaxed spacious drawing room and well-balanced, extensive wine list; impeccable service; a special place; disabled access. **£34 3-course set dinner, £24 3-course set lunch.**

Bath Queensberry Russel St BA1 2QF (0225) 447928 ***£93**; 22 rms. Three beautifully decorated Georgian town houses in quiet residential street, with attractive restaurant, good food (inc vegetarian), and professional service; may shut Christmas.

Bathford ST7964 Old School House 3 miles from city centre, Church St BA1 7RR (0225) 859593 ***£62**; 4 rms. Quietly relaxed hotel in early Victorian village school house with winter log fires; candlelit dinner (24 hrs notice); no smoking; disabled access.

Bath Haydon House 9 Bloomfield Park BA2 2BY (0225) 427351 ***£55**; 4 good rms with thoughtful extras. Unassuming-looking Edwardian house with comfortable, elegant and restful rooms, antiques, excellent breakfasts (no evening meals), and pretty garden; no smoking; children by arrangement.

Bath Brocks 32 Brock St BA1 2LN (0225) 338374 ***£52**; 8 rms. Good B & B in Georgian house with fine breakfasts and service; close to some shops, restaurants, secondhand bookshops and theatre; cl 24-26 Dec, 2 wks Jan.

Bath Dorian House 1 Upper Oldfield Park BA2 3JX (0225) 426336 **£52**; 7 individually decorated rms. Gracious and neatly kept Victorian house with fine views of the city (only 10 mins stroll away); charming, friendly owners, small bar, comfortable sitting room and elegant little dining room.

To see and do

† Bath Abbey was started in 1499 and is the third great church to be built on this site. Called the Lantern of the West by the Elizabethans, the building is particularly famous for its fan vaulting and its great east window.

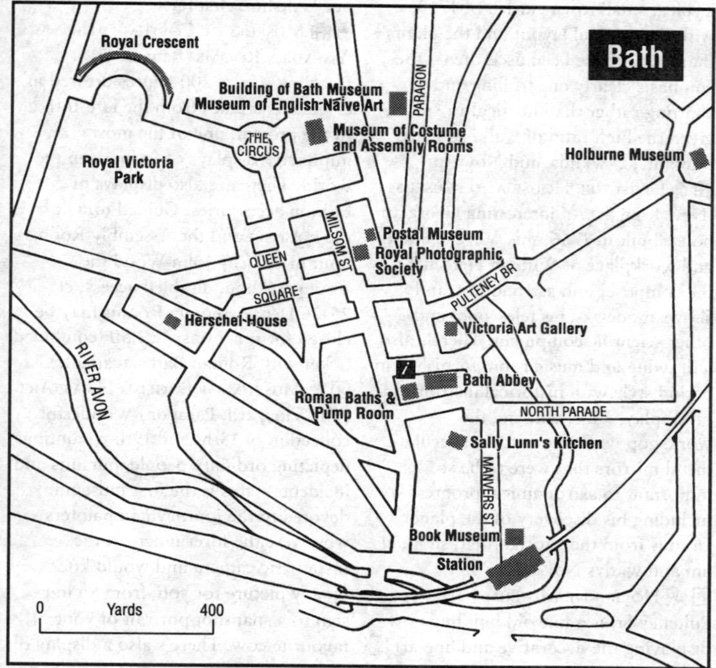

This depicts 56 scenes from the life of Christ and has on one side the finely carved memorial to Bartholomew Barnes (1608), and on the other the beautiful medieval carving of the Prior Birde Chantry; shop; cl Good Fri, 25 Dec; £1.

BATH POSTAL MUSEUM (Broad St) Development of the postal system since the days of Henry VIII, inc the Air Mail service, and a full-scale replica Victorian post office (it was from Bath's Central Post Office that the first postage-stamp, the Penny Black, was posted); shop, disabled access; cl Sun, 25 Dec, bank hols; £2.

BOOK MUSEUM (Manvers St) Bath's elegant atmosphere has long proved popular with book buyers and writers, and part of this museum celebrates the city's connections with literature, with displays and first editions relating to authors who lived or worked here, esp Jane Austen and Charles Dickens. There's a reconstruction of Dickens' study at Gadshill Place. The other half of the exhibition is devoted to the history and art of bookbinding. Next door is GEORGE BAYNTUN, who has been binding and selling antiquarian books for 50 years; cl 1-2 pm, Sat pm, all day Sun and bank hols.

BUILDING OF BATH MUSEUM (The Vineyard, Paragon) How the city was transformed in the 18th c, with exhibits ranging from the tools used for the building through a fabulous city model to full-sized mock-ups. The museum is housed in a chapel, and those who have difficulty walking might find the floor slightly uneven; shop, disabled access but no facilities; cl Mon, and 16 Dec-1 Mar; *£2. (The Naive Art Museum, see below, is also on this site.)

GEORGIAN GARDEN (Gravel Walk, between Royal Crescent and Queen Sq)

Typical small town garden of 1760, with the original layout and the plants that would have been used then – the emphasis clearly on strolling and chatting rather than horticulture itself, given the high ratio of walking-space to plants; cl wknds, and Nov-Apr.

HERSCHEL HOUSE AND MUSEUM (New King St) An interesting Georgian house built in 1766, this was the home and workplace of William Herschel, the composer and astronomer, and shows models of his telescopes and other scientific equipment. There's also a drawing and music room furnished in period style with historical instruments on display, a kitchen, and the workshop where he cast the specular metal mirrors that were to be so important to astronomical progress – including his discovery of the planet Uranus from the back garden; shop; cl am and wkdys Nov-Mar; *£2.

HOLBURNE MUSEUM (Gt Pulteney St) is a fine old building now displaying the decorative and fine-art collection of Sir Thomas William Holburne (1793-1874), as well as works by 20th-c artists and craftsmen in the Crafts Study Centre. Meals, snacks, shop, disabled access; cl Sun am, Mon Nov-Easter; *£2.50.

INDUSTRIAL HERITAGE CENTRE (Julian Rd) The story of Bath stone, with a replica of a mine face before mechanisation. It also includes a Bath cabinet-maker's workshop complete with original drawings and tools, and the engaging MR BOWLER'S BUSINESS, a brass founder's established in 1872 to provide various plumbing, engineering, gas-fitting, bell-hanging and other services, including not just his entire stock-in-trade but even an antique soda fountain turning out rather charmingly named drinks such as Cherry Ciderette. Snacks, shop, disabled access if advance warning given; cl Nov-Easter; *£2.80. (For more on the infrastructure of Bath's 18th-c revolution, see also the Underground Quarry, included under Corsham in our Wiltshire chapter.)

MUSEUM OF COSTUME AND ASSEMBLY ROOMS (Bennett St) Dazzling – over 200 figures dressed in original costumes from the late 16th c to the present, one of the most impressive displays of fashions in the world. There are also displays of fashion accessories. Guided tours of the museum and the Assembly Rooms built in 1771 by John Wood the Younger; shop, disabled access; cl 25-26 Dec, Assembly Rooms may be closed for functions; *£2.50 (combined ticket with Roman Baths available).

MUSEUM OF ENGLISH NAIVE ART (The Vineyard, Paragon) Wonderful collection of 18th- and 19th-c paintings depicting ordinary people, pursuits and incidents – this is the first museum devoted to the journeyman painters who were the forerunners of the Instamatic camera and would knock up any picture for you, from an inn sign to a snapshot portrait of your favourite cow. There's also a display of shop signs, weathervanes and country furniture; shop; cl Sun am, Mon, 22 Dec-1 Jan, Easter; *£2.

NO 1 ROYAL CRESCENT, built in 1768 as part of Bath's most regal terrace, has two floors restored and furnished in the style of that time; there is also an interesting kitchen. Shop; cl Mon, mid-Dec-Feb; *£3.

PUMP ROOM The stylish 18th-c mecca for the fashionable, it is built directly above the Roman temple courtyard, and now has a restaurant serving morning coffee, lunches and teas to the gay strains of the Pump Room trio. Meals and snacks, shop, disabled access (but not to the baths themselves); cl 25-26 Dec; £4.

The ROMAN BATHS were founded by AD 75; north of the spring the Romans laid out a colonnaded precinct containing the temple of Sulis Minerva, while to the south a range of cleansing and curative baths was built. The Sacred Spring was both a focus for worship – receiving the required offerings – and also a reservoir supplying the baths with spa water. In August the baths are open at night and quite beautifully floodlit. The MUSEUM shows finds made during excavations of the spring, including the Gorgon's Head pediment which symbolises the merging of the classical and celtic tradition on this site, also altars, tombstones and fascinating curse tablets; there's a model of the baths, temple and Sacred Spring as they would have appeared in the 4th c.

ROYAL PHOTOGRAPHIC SOCIETY (the Octagon, Milsom St) Five galleries with major international exhibitions; meals and snacks, shop, disabled access; cl 25-26 Dec, bank hols; £3 (free to members).

SALLY LUNN'S KITCHEN (North Parade Passage), called 'the oldest house in Bath', is a charming partly timbered medieval structure, and in its cellars is the original kitchen of the legendary Sally Lunn, preserved as it would have been in the 17th c, when resourceful Sally created her famous brioche bread buns. Extensive excavations have revealed Roman and Saxon remains below the present house. The house itself; meals and snacks – inc of course the buns, shop; cl Sun am; 30p.

VICTORIA ART GALLERY (Bridge St) The city art collection includes European Old Masters and 18th- to 20th-c British paintings and drawings, as well as decorative arts such as porcelain, glass and watches of the 18th and 19th c; shop, disabled access to ground floor only; cl Sun, 25-26 Dec and bank hols.

BOAT CRUISES leave on the hour from the landing stage by Pulteney Bridge (not Oct-Easter), and boats and punts can be hired in summer from the Boating Station on the River Avon, Forester Rd, Bathwick: (0225) 466407.

! To see the city as it's shown in the great architectural drawings, and go as much further afield as the wind will allow, you can book hot-air BALLOON TRIPS, subject to weather, perhaps taking off from the Royal Victoria Park; (0225) 466888.

Shopping Bath is famous for shopping – yet it's all too easy for strangers here for the day to end up near the Roman Baths paying high prices for things they could get in any other High Street. Here are some suggestions for things you won't so easily find elsewhere.

BARTLETT ST MARKETS (both sides of street) Every day: from junk to top-drawer antiques, often buzzing with dealers from elsewhere.

CHINA DOLL (Walcot St) Excellent collection of doll's-house accessories, not cheap – probably best to keep children's noses glued to the window rather than letting them loose inside.

FINE CHEESE CO (Walcot St) Huge range of interesting cheeses, mouthwatering olive bread, helpful staff.

GUINEA LANE MARKET Very early Weds am, antiques changing hands quickly.

HITCHCOCKS (Chapel Row) Specialised craft gallery on four floors.

ROOKSMOOR GALLERY (Brock St) Modern limited-edition prints, sculpture, light and well presented.

ST JAMES GALLERY (Margaret Buildings) Fine British crafts, wide range; small – don't try to squeeze a pushchair in.

SHEPHERDS PURSE (John St) Long-established knitting wool/patterns shop.

THE GREEN SHOP (Green St) Vetted environmentally sound products, from unbleached cotton bedclothes to long-life light bulbs – lots of gift ideas for 'green' friends.

WALCOT ST FLEA MARKET is best of all for bargains; Sat, occasional Sun.

Other things to see and do near Bath

Claverton ST7862 American Museum in Britain (Claverton Manor) Quite a contrast to the rest of Bath's attractions, a fascinating illustration of American history and life in lovely gracious surroundings. Eighteen rooms are decorated to recreate the style of American homes from the 17th to the 19th c, while the grounds include a replica of part of George Washington's garden at Mount Vernon, as well as an American arboretum. Collections of pewter, glass, Folk Art, patchwork quilts and maps, with special sections on the Indians and the Shakers, various special events and changing exhibitions; snacks, shop, disabled access; cl am, all day Mon, end Mar-end Oct; £4.50.

Farleigh Hungerford ST8057 Ruined 14th-c castle, with monuments in the chapel to the Hungerford family, who once owned the land from here to Salisbury; shop; cl 1-2 pm and all day winter Mon; *£1.20.

Priston ST6960 Priston Mill Set in charming countryside, this mill has supplied flour to the citizens of Bath for centuries, and was once run by the monks of Bath Abbey. Staff describe the workings of the mill, and there are children's play areas, a trailer ride and a nature trail; meals and snacks, shop; cl am, Oct-Mar exc pre-booked groups; £2.50.

Walks

Walking around Bath is a delight; there are flat parts, though to make the most of it you have to be prepared to climb some of the steeper streets. Places not to be missed include the great showpieces of 18th-c town planning, Queen Sq, The Circus and the Royal Crescent; the quieter Abbey Green and cobbled Abbey St and Queen St; and the great Pulteney Bridge (there's a fine view of it from the bridge at the end of North Parade, or the riverside Parade Gardens, where brass bands play in summer). The narrow little lanes between the main streets can be fascinating. In summer lots of informal eating places have tables outside.

The revivified **Kennet & Avon Canal** is one of Bath's pleasures, with quiet towpath walks along to Bathampton (where the George is popular for lunch); it has quite a few colourful narrowboats in summer.

Driving

Not recommended. Bath's streets were laid out for travel by sedan chair, not car, and a tortuous one-way system seems designed to deter drivers rather than to make traffic flow more easily.

Where to eat

Bath ST7464 Woods Alfred St (0225) 314812 Bustling bright restaurant with horse-racing pictures, excellent set menus as well as interesting daily specials (good fish), and cheery staff; cl Sun, 24 Dec pm, 25-26 Dec, 1 Jan; disabled access. £20|£6.30.

For somewhere really special see the Dower House Restaurant in the Royal Crescent Hotel, Bath, under the Where to stay section.

Bathford ST7966 CROWN Bathford Hill (0225) 852297 Four or five attractively decorated rooms lead off main bar; good food with nice puddings, wide choice of drinks inc good cafetière coffee with fresh cream; no-smoking garden room; cl Mon am, 25-26 Dec; disabled access. £15|£2.25/£5.95.

There's no shortage of entertaining snack places, and good pubs providing at least some decent food here include the Old Green Tree (Green St), Crystal Palace (Abbey Green) and Hare & Hounds (Lansdown Hill – great views).

AVON

Avon has a few splendid country-house hotels; Bristol is lively and interesting for day visits, and elsewhere there are one or two other worthwhile attractions.

The three country-house hotels we list are excellent retreats for a cosseted weekend stay, and, like the humbler but good-value inn, would make good bases for excursions into Bath or down into Somerset, as well as for Avon itself. Here, there's some pleasant countryside down towards the Mendips, and Dyrham Park is attractive. It's Bristol which is the real focus of attention in the county, though. Bristol has masses of things to do, and is well worth a day visit: it's too busy an industrial city to use as a base for an enjoyable stay.

On the coast, Weston super Mare has possibilities as an undemanding family resort, and Clevedon is also quite attractive.

Where to stay

Hunstrete ST6462 HUNSTRETE HOUSE Pensford Bristol BS18 4NS (0761) 490490 **£120**; 24 individually decorated rms. Handsome country-house hotel, on the edge of the Mendips, in 92 acres of grounds including a walled garden and deer park; comfortable, elegantly furnished day rooms with antiques, log fires, flowers, and paintings; tranquil atmosphere, excellent service, and very good enjoyable food using produce from the garden when possible; children over 8; disabled access.

Thornbury ST6390 THORNBURY CASTLE Bristol BS12 1HH (0454) 281182 **£100**; 18 opulent rms, some with big Tudor fireplaces or fine oriel windows. Impressive and luxuriously renovated early 16th-c castle with deeply comfortable seats, antiques, tapestries, huge fireplaces and mullioned windows in the baronial public rooms; two restaurants (one in the base of a tower), fine cooking, extensive wine list (including their own wine from their expanding vineyard), thoughtful, friendly service, and vast grounds; cl 2 days Jan; children over 12.

Stanton Wick ST6162 CARPENTERS ARMS Pensford Bristol BS18 4BX (0761) 409202 **£52.50**; 12 no-smoking rms. Warm and attractively furnished tile-roofed inn with big log fire, woodburning stove, a wide choice of good food inc good breakfasts, and friendly, efficient staff.

To see and do

Bristol Bristol has quite a different sort of vitality from that which marks Bath – it's down-to-earth whereas Bath is elegantly fanciful, activist whereas Bath prefers to be more of a spectator, radical whereas Bath has traditionally been conservative. The city's prosperity still stems from its port, where facilities have been kept up-to-date so as to accommodate increasingly sophisticated vessels, and it is still a major industrial centre, with aerospace predominating among many other manufacturing interests.

It is more a place to dip into for small doses by the day than a place to choose for a stay. Day visits are made easy to achieve by the motorway that plunges right into the city's heart. Besides some of the city's grand buildings, it's worth having a look at the recently refurbished parts of the dockside, the SS *Great Britain*, and the church of St Mary Redcliffe; children like the Hands-On Science Centre, and the zoo. The Red Lodge, Georgian House and good City Museum and Art Gallery make up a worthwhile combined ticket. Useful central pubs for a lunchtime bite to eat are the Bridge (Passage St), Cottage (Baltic Wharf) and Shakespeare (Prince St); a little further out, the Highbury Vaults (St Michaels Hill, Cotham) is the best in the city, and out in Clifton the Somerset House (Princess Victoria St) is also useful. In the evening Millwards (see Where to eat) is good.

🏛 ✝ Two of the finest buildings are the CORN EXCHANGE (Corn Street), built in 1743, and the OLD COUNCIL HOUSE (Corn Street) built in 1827 – one in a series standing on that spot since 1552; in Broad Street, there is the Grand Hotel (1869), the Guild Hall (1843) and the art-nouveau façade of the former Edward Everard printing house built in 1900. Also in this area are the famous CHRISTMAS STEPS dating from 1669, quaintly lined by steep buildings: this is a good area for antiques and old books. At the top of these steps is the CHAPEL OF THE THREE KINGS OF COLOGNE dating from the 1480s (the 'three kings' are the three wise men whose shrines are in Cologne cathedral). The warden of the nearby Almshouses will provide access to this tiny chapel. At the bottom of the steps is the lodge of ST BARTHOLOMEW'S – all that remains of the 13th-c hospital and almshouse which once stood on this site.

🏛 Houses that can be viewed inside include the RED LODGE (Park St), built in the 16th c and then altered in the 18th, with interior features and furnishings from both periods. On the first floor is the last surviving suite of 16th-c rooms in Bristol, as well as a wonderful carved stone chimney-piece, plasterwork ceilings and fine oak panelling; other rooms contain walnut and gilt furniture and portraits from the early 18th c. Cl 1-2 pm, all day Sun, possibly Mon too – best to check first; £2. For £2.50 you can buy a combined ticket to view also the nearby GEORGIAN HOUSE (Great George St), one of several examples in this street of 18th- and early 19th-c architecture. Built in 1790 by the Bristol architect William Paty for a wealthy sugar merchant, it's a fine illustration of a typical late 18th-c town house, with three floors of the house still decorated in period style, inc the below-stairs area with kitchen, laundry and housekeeper's room; times and price as for Red House. Another ticket at £3 covers both of these and the City Museum.

✝ JOHN WESLEY'S CHAPEL (Broadmead Shopping Centre), built in 1739 and rebuilt in 1748, is the oldest methodist chapel in the world. Both chapel and living rooms are preserved in their original state and include the famous double-decked pulpit from which John Wesley preached; shop, disabled access to ground floor only; cl 1-2 pm, Sun, Weds Oct-Apr. The LORD MAYOR'S CHAPEL (Park Street) is all that remains of the medieval Hospital of the Gaunts founded in 1220. Since 1722 this has been the Corporation's official place of worship – the only civic church in the country. The 16th-c stained-glass windows, floor tiles and fan-vaulted ceiling are glorious.

✝ Nearby, and supposedly on the very spot where St Augustine met the Celtic Christians in the early 7th c, is the imposing edifice of the CATHEDRAL. This was originally founded as an Augustinian monastery but by 1542 had become the cathedral church, and is a real mix of architectural styles down the ages. Well worth seeing are the Chapter House (one of the finest Norman rooms in the country), and also the candlesticks given in thanks by the privateers who rescued Alexander Selkirk (whose adventures inspired Daniel Defoe to write *Robinson Crusoe*); meals and snacks, shop, disabled access but no facilities.

✝ Another fine church in this city, one among many, is the CHURCH OF ST MARY REDCLIFFE (Redcliffe Hill) – the earliest parts of which date back to about 1180 – which was described by Elizabeth I as 'the goodliest, fairest and most famous parish church in England'. Most of the building visible today dates from the work begun in 1280 – for example, the glorious hexagonal outer porch. Notable features within the church include the tomb of Admiral Sir William Penn, who founded Pennysylvania, and the Handel Window, where eight passages of the Messiah commemorate the great composer's ties with this church; disabled access.

The DOCKS are being restored in a way that's making them increasingly attractive to visitors. Ferries (Apr-Sept) link several points around the harbour – the complexity of the docks is better understood when viewed from the water. The old part around King Street, between the waterfront and the Bristol Old Vic, has quiet cobbled streets of Georgian buildings, pleasant to wander through, and elsewhere some of the bigger warehouses are being pressed into service as museums, café-bars and the like. One bar's in a converted lightship, another steamer's become a restaurant/bar, and a former coaster has become the Old Profanity, an entertainment showboat popular with students. The ARNOLFINI, a big former tea warehouse, is now a contemporary arts complex with bar, restaurant, exhibitions, cinema, theatre and so forth. BRISTOL INDUSTRIAL MUSEUM (Floating Harbour off Wapping) Obviously the city's role in trade and industry has meant involvement with many forms of transport, and this museum provides a comprehensive presentation of that history. Housed in a converted dockside transit shed, exhibits include locally built aircraft, steam locomotives, histories of various Bristol-centred transport-manufacturing companies, a presentation of the development and trades of the port since the 18th c, and reconstructions of an old warehouse and workshop. Lots of special events; shop, disabled access; cl 1-2 pm, Thurs and Fri (though this may soon change to Mon instead – best to check first on (0272) 251470), 25-26 Dec, 1 Jan, Good Fri; £2.

On the dockside outside, during the summer, is a small steam railway, the BRISTOL HARBOUR RAILWAY, which for 70p has a return trip down along the old cargo route to the SS *Great Britain*. This ship was the first iron, screw-propelled, ocean-going vessel, designed by Isambard Kingdom Brunel, and still has the power to surprise one with the extent to which it was a departure from what had gone before; snacks, shop; cl 25 Dec; £2.90. Also moored here are the 1860s steam-tug *Mayflower* (running every hour in summer), diesel-powered firefloat *Pyronaut* (1934) and Fairbain steam-crane (1876).

From April to October the PLEASURE STEAMERS *Waverley* and *Balmoral* run fairly frequent day cruises from here, along the Avon and Severn or to Devon, Wales or Lundy; (0272) 260767 for programme.

Bristol's long heritage of ship-building is well shown at the MARITIME HERITAGE CENTRE (Floating Harbour), where displays include original machinery, full-sized reconstructions, models and videos; snacks, shop, disabled access; cl 25 Dec. This too is on the harbour rail link, with the entrance at the SS *Great Britain*.

CITY MUSEUM AND ART GALLERY (Queens Rd) has collections falling into several categories – applied art, fine art, Oriental art, archaeology and history, geology and natural history – all of which contain impressive exhibits well worth seeing; snacks, shop, disabled access; £2.

The BLAISE CASTLE HOUSE MUSEUM is a branch of this museum, and houses its collections of agricultural and social history. Displays include many unusual and for once carefully explained items of farming equipment, a section devoted to household activities, an interesting collection of costumes from the 18th and 19th c, and a room devoted to dolls. This is out on the BLAISE CASTLE ESTATE (Henbury, about 4 miles out), which also has a spacious and locally popular undulating park with some woodland and refreshments. The museum is in the house, which was built in 1795. The castle itself is a Gothic folly built in 1766 within the now scarcely discernible ramparts of an Iron-Age hill fort, which in its busy life has also been the site of a Roman temple and a medieval chapel dedicated to the patron saint of woolcombers – St Blasius. The grounds are full of interesting features; shop; cl 1-2 pm, Thurs and Fri – though in common with other Bristol museums this may change to just Mon, best to check first, tel (0272) 506789 – bank hols, 25 Dec, Good Fri, 1 Jan.

! EXPLORATORY HANDS-ON SCIENCE CENTRE (By Templemeads Railway Station) A great place for children (and of course adults) to get their fingers

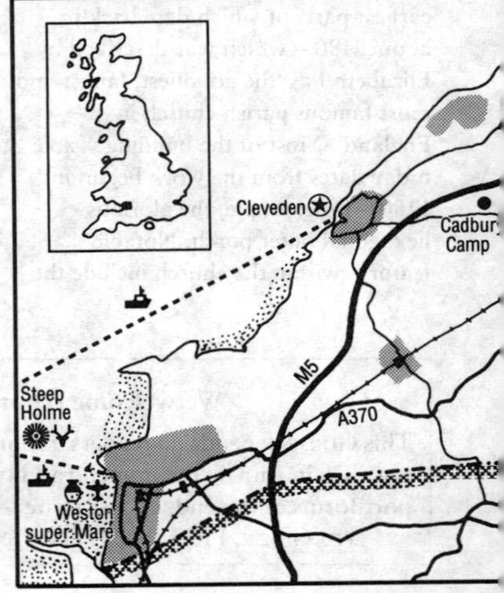

into all kinds of science, and there are very lively displays; snacks, shop, disabled access; cl Christmas week; £3.75.

The CABOT TOWER, in attractive gardens at the top of Brandon Hill, gives good views of the city, but there are hundreds of steps; snacks, cl 25-26 Dec. Nearby ST GEORGES has good Thurs lunchtime concerts, rarely booked up completely in advance.

CLIFTON is the quiet side of Bristol, with some fine late 18th- and 19th-c terraces, an antiques market (Mall, cl Sun, Mon), a big park right on the spectacular Avon gorge facing the NT woodlands on the crags opposite, and the remarkably modern-looking Suspension Bridge, based on an 1836 design by Brunel and finished in 1864.

BRISTOL ZOO in Clifton is the fourth most visited zoo in the country, a traditional one, nicely set in 12 acres of pleasant gardens. There are over 400 mammals of all shapes and sizes and over 500 birds in the aviaries, while the aquarium incorporates a walk-through tank with many fantastic species of tropical, freshwater and saltwater fish. There's also a new Insect House, and a hands-on exhibition centre; meals and snacks, shop, disabled access; cl 25 Dec; £4.80.

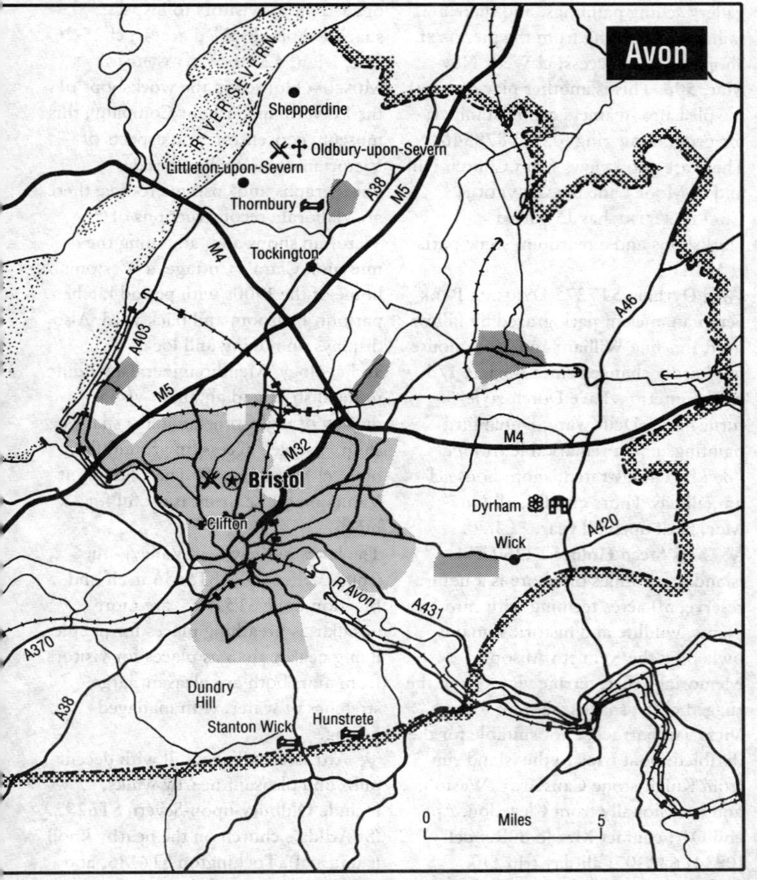

Other things to see and do

Clevedon ST4071 CLEVEDON COURT Most of the original structure of this manor house, built in 1320, is still intact, though there are interesting additions from other periods inc a charming 18th-c garden; snacks, limited disabled access but welcome to try; open pm Sun, Weds, and Thurs Apr-Sept; £3.20. CLEVEDON PIER This Victorian pier partially collapsed in 1970 but has since been lovingly restored – rebuilding of the Victorian pavilions and pierhead should be completed by this year. Upstairs, above the tollhouse, is a gallery selling paintings, and there are sailings and fishing from the pier itself. Shop, disabled access; cl Weds Nov-Mar; 50p. This is another place where the pleasure steamers call in summer; for programme ring (0275) 878846. There are good views from Church Hill and in Moor Lane the CLEVEDON CRAFT CENTRE has 15 varied workshops and a tearoom; some parts cl Mon.

Dyrham ST7375 DYRHAM PARK Set in an ancient park grazed by fallow deer, this fine William and Mary house has hardly changed since the late 17th c. The interiors have Dutch-style furnishings, Delft ware, Dutch bird paintings and a remarkable *trompe l'oeil* by Hoogstraten; shop; house cl am, all day Thurs and Fri, all Nov-Mar, park open all year; *£4.70.

Steep Holm ST2260 This island a few miles off shore is a nature reserve, 50 acres teeming with rare plants, wildlife and historic remains, owned by the Kenneth Allsop Memorial Trust; terrific views from the rugged cliffs; snacks, shop in former Victorian barracks; not suitable for the disabled; boat trips to the island run from Knightstone Causeway, Weston, and occasionally from Clevedon, Apr-end Oct; contact Mrs Joan Rendell (0934) 632307; all-day trip £10.

Weston super Mare ST3261 This friendly seaside resort has long been popular with families for its beaches and wide opportunities for leisure and entertainment, its Latin epithet added in the 19th c in an attempt to be one up on the fashionable French resorts. One less-expected thing to see is the INTERNATIONAL HELICOPTER MUSEUM, with over 50 helicopters and autogyros on display, as well as photographs, models and explanations of how the various parts of the machine work. On the second Sun each month they have an Open Cockpit Day, when some of the helicopters are opened up for visitors to inspect; snacks, shop, disabled access; cl 25-26 Dec, 1 Jan; £2.50. WOODSPRING MUSEUM Housed in the workshops of the Edwardian Gaslight Company, this museum concentrates on aspects of Victorian domestic life: besides photographs and costume rooms, there are elaborate reconstructions of Victorian shops and, adjoining the museum, Clara's Cottage, a Westonian home of the 1900s with period kitchen, parlour, bedroom and back yard. Also displays on mining and local archaeology, Mendip minerals, wildlife in the district and an audio-visual display of night-time animals; snacks, shop, disabled access on ground floor only; cl Mon; *£1.50. The Claremont Vaults on the seafront is useful for lunch.

The **lakes** in the Chew Valley – the Chew Valley Lake ST5656 itself and Blagdon Lake ST5159 – are more popular as breathing places for people living nearby than as places for visitors from afar; both are pleasant large stretches of water, with managed fishing.

★ **Attractive villages**, all with decent pubs and pleasant nearby walks, include Oldbury-upon-Severn ST6292 (St Arilda's church on the nearby knoll is unusual), Tockington ST6186, and Wick ST7072.

Walks

The north edge of the **Mendips** (which marks the boundary with Somerset) offers good walks, and useful starting points include the Crown at Churchill ST4459 and Ring o' Bells at Compton Martin ST5457, both in East Somerset. The great limestone gorge of **Burrington Combe** ST4858, an easy walk by the B3134, can be combined with walks over the adjacent heather and cranberry moors and on to Dolebury Warren ST4558, also in East Somerset, where the site of an Iron-Age hill fort marks a splendid Mendip viewpoint.

The attractively restored **Kennet & Avon Canal** has a good footpath alongside. The canal runs across the county from Bristol through Hanham ST6472, Saltford ST6867 and Bath to the spectacular aqueduct at Avoncliff ST8059 (and beyond, across Wiltshire and into Berkshire).

From the Black Horse in Clapton in Gordano ST4773 the lane past the church leads to a footbridge high over the M5, from where you can walk up to the Iron-Age hill fort of **Cadbury Camp** ST4572 (not to be confused with the altogether more famous Cadbury Castle in Somerset).

The White Hart in Littleton-upon-Severn ST5990 and Anchor in Oldbury-on-Severn ST6292 are useful for lonely walks along the sea wall of the **Severn estuary**, with power station cooling towers emphasising the emptiness of the tidal flats; the Windbound at Shepperdine ST6295 is right on the embankment.

Dundry Hill ST5566 just beyond Bristol's southern suburbs has views over the city, Chew Magna and Blagdon lakes and the Mendips.

Driving

The steep wooded hills and valleys around Bath, particularly towards the south, are very picturesque. The A36 from Bath towards Warminster has some fine views of the richly wooded Avon valley, but except at very quiet times is too busy for pleasure. Better is the B3110 to Norton St Philip, but best of all, to view this steep and intricate scenery, are the narrow side roads such as the one through South Stoke (where the Pack Horse is an interesting ancient pub) or the one between Monkton Combe and Combe Hay (the Wheatsheaf here is good).

In the Chew Valley, the B3130 and B3114 are quite pleasant drives. The B3134 up into the Mendips is one of the prettiest roads in the area.

In the north of the county, the B4160 north of Chipping Sodbury quickly comes into more Cotswoldy scenery, as does the A46 and the side road off it through Hillesley to Wotton under Edge in Gloucestershire.

Where to eat

Bristol ST5872 MILLWARDS 40 Alfred Place Kingsdown (0272) 245026 Small candlelit no-smoking vegetarian evening restaurant with simple, clean furnishings, very good imaginative food, decent wine list inc many organic choices, and smiling service; cl Sun, Mon, 1 wk Christmas/Easter. **£17**|£8.

Oldbury-on-Severn ST6292 ANCHOR Church St (0454) 413331 Attractively modernised village pub with good, daily-changing bar food, enterprising puddings, friendly service, no-smoking dining room; children in dining room only; disabled access. **£14**|£1.90/£4.75.

East Somerset

This area has some interesting countryside and places to visit; Wells and Glastonbury are very popular.

Wells cathedral is glorious; it, Glastonbury, the Wookey Hole Caves and Cheddar Gorge do attract a good many summer visitors, but they are all much quieter out of season, and there's plenty to see elsewhere if you want to avoid the summer crowds. Highlights include Castle Cary (with Hadspen Gardens), Lytes Cary Manor at Kingsdon, and the Fleet Air Arm museum at Yeovilton; Ebbor Gorge is a quieter alternative to the Cheddar one, and throughout the region there are pretty villages and interesting small towns. The edge of the Mendips has the best of the area's scenery (and offers the county's best walking), but the marshy grazing lands of the dead-flat Somerset Levels provide an interesting contrast, and the richer more rolling farmland with small secluded valleys and wooded hillsides towards the east offer some gentle country drives.

There's enough to keep children entertained (and Longleat's just over the Wiltshire border), though on the whole it's adults who will enjoy this area most. And of course Bath itself is within easy reach.

Where to stay

Ston Easton ST6253 Ston Easton Park Bath BA3 4DF (076 121) 631 **£151**; 21 really lovely rms. Majestic Palladian mansion of Bath stone with beautifully landscaped 18th-c gardens in 26 acres of parkland; elegant day rooms with antiques and flowers, attractive restaurant with good food (much grown in the kitchen garden), and extremely helpful, friendly and unstuffy service; babies and children over 7 welcome by prior arrangement.

Freshford ST7859 Homewood Park Bath BA3 6BB (0225) 723731 ***£95**; 15 rms. On the edge of the ruins of Hinton Priory stands this charming Victorian hotel; graceful day rooms with flowers and fine furniture, elegant restaurant with very good, imaginative food, and ten acres of gardens and woodlands; tennis, croquet; disabled access.

Ansford ST6333 Bonds Hotel Bath BA7 7JP (0963) 50464 ***£60**; 7 rms. Small listed Georgian house, once an inn, with antiques, personal caring service, and lots of charm; interesting weekly changing food (many local cheeses on the cheeseboard), and good wine list; cl 1 wk over Christmas; children over 8.

Glastonbury ST5039 Who'd A Thought It 17 Northload St BA6 9JT (0458) 834460 ***£55**; 6 cosy rms. A friendly welcome and a good atmosphere with a 1920s feel; serves popular food including good breakfasts; cl Christmas.

Croscombe ST5844 Bull Terrier Wells BA5 3QJ (0749) 343658 **£44**; 3 rms. One of the oldest pubs in Somerset, with neat, civilised decor, warm, courteous service, decent choice of wines, and consistently good food inc enterprising daily specials and imaginative particularly good puddings; no children or pets.

Axbridge ST4255 LAMB The Square BF26 2AP (0934) 732253 **£40**; 3 spacious old-world rms. Interesting rambling old place just right for its position on the partly medieval market square; good-value bar food, real ales, pretty little garden with cockatiels, and quite handy for M5; cl 25 Dec.
Milborne Port ST6718 QUEENS HEAD Sherborne DT9 5DQ (0963) 250314 **£35**; 2 cosy rms, shared bthrm. Old coaching inn with beamed lounge, good food, friendly service, quiet restaurant, well-kept beers, and tables in sheltered courtyard and garden.
Polsham ST5142 SOUTHWAY FARM Wells BA5 1RW (0749) 673396 ***£35**; 3 rms, some with own bthrm. Friendly Georgian farmhouse with open fire in comfortable lounge, attractive dining room, good breakfasts and pretty garden; cl Dec-Feb.
Horsington ST7023 HALF MOON Templecombe BA8 0ED (0963) 70140 **£32**; 4 rms, in chalets with showers. Nicely refurbished, with stripped stone, oak floors, beams and inglenook fires, and garden with play area; restaurant cl Sun-Weds.
Emborough ST6151 REDHILL FARM Bath BA3 4SH (0761) 241294 ***£28.50**; 3 rms, shared bthrm. Friendly old farmhouse high on the Mendips, with animals and poultry to amuse the children and good fresh food; riding, sailing, fishing nearby; no dogs.

To see and do

Axbridge ST4354 This pleasant small town has a narrow winding medieval high street, unusual in this part of the world for its jettied timber-framed buildings. One of them is KING JOHN'S HUNTING LODGE, actually built around 1500 so having no connection with King John (nor in fact with hunting) – but no less attractive for that. It now houses a museum of local history; disabled access to grounds; cl am, all Oct-Easter; £1. NT. The little market square is a tranquil place, and the rambling old Lamb on the corner is good for lunch.
★ † **Bruton** ST6834 Fascinating little town; worth looking out for are the Bartons, narrow alleys leading down from the High Street to the river (which you can cross either by footbridge or by using stepping stones); also St Mary's CHURCH which stands on the site of a medieval Augustinian priory and abbey – the old abbey wall with its buttresses still stands in Silver Street. The church has a spectacular altar-piece, and in the chancel is a fine effigy of Sir Maurice Berkely, a great survivor who was standard-bearer to Henry VIII, Edward VI and Queen Elizabeth. Interesting and individual shops – antiques, books and prints. The Castle Inn is good for lunch.
Burnham-on-Sea ST3050 is in summer a bustling low-cost family seaside resort with its wide beaches, sandy dunes, and the usual holiday facilities. Children will enjoy the ANIMAL FARM COUNTRY PARK AND THE LAND OF LEGENDS at nearby Berrow ST2952, where there are animals and conservation trails, and displays of folk tales and other myths and stories; cl Nov-Mar; £2.80.
Burrington Combe ST4758 is a steeply wooded roadside combe on the north flank of the Mendips, with good viewpoints above it.
★ **Castle Cary** ST6332 HADSPEN GARDENS Covering about eight acres, these beautiful gardens surround a fine 18th-c house. A delightful 17th-c walled garden has all sorts of herbaceous plants and old-fashioned roses. Also a lily pond and ancient flower meadow; there are many old favourite plants, but also

many exotics. Sunday snacks, nursery, some disabled access; cl 1-2 pm, Mon-Weds and Oct-Feb; *£2. The village itself is also very attractive, basically a bustling medieval market town, now offering a useful range of traditional family-run shops, hotels and inns. The Castle Cary VINEYARD produces decent wine (cl Sun am and Nov-Apr), and also worth seeing are the ROUNDHOUSE, Britain's smallest prison, built in 1779, and the local MUSEUM.

Cheddar
ST4553 CHEDDAR SHOWCAVES Two beautiful caves beneath the picturesque limestone cliffs of Cheddar Gorge; quite cathedral-like with spectacular stalagmites and stalactites joining to form columns. Jacob's Ladder affords a spectacular view of this conservation area. There is also an exhibition devoted to 'Cheddar Man', Britain's oldest complete skeleton, with a re-creation of his world of 9,000 years ago. Lots of activities, specially for children, inc an adventure playground; snacks, shop; cl 24-25 Dec; £4.90. CHEDDAR GORGE CHEESE CO RURAL VILLAGE Collection of shops and traditional craftsmen based around a factory that thanks to its location claims to make the only really genuine cheddar cheese in the world. You can watch each stage of the seven-hour process, and of course taste the matured product. The whole village is quite an appetising place to visit, with demonstrations (and, again, tastings) of fudge-making, scrumpy sampling at the cider exhibition, and a reconstructed 1920s sweet factory. Also cooperage, pottery, dairy and lacemaker; meals, snacks, shops, disabled access; cl Nov-mid-Mar; *£2.45. There's an AQUARIUM near here too. The older part of the extended village is attractive, with some interesting shops and a 14th-15th-c CHURCH with a fine tall tower, and outside there are roadside strawberry stalls and pick-your-own in

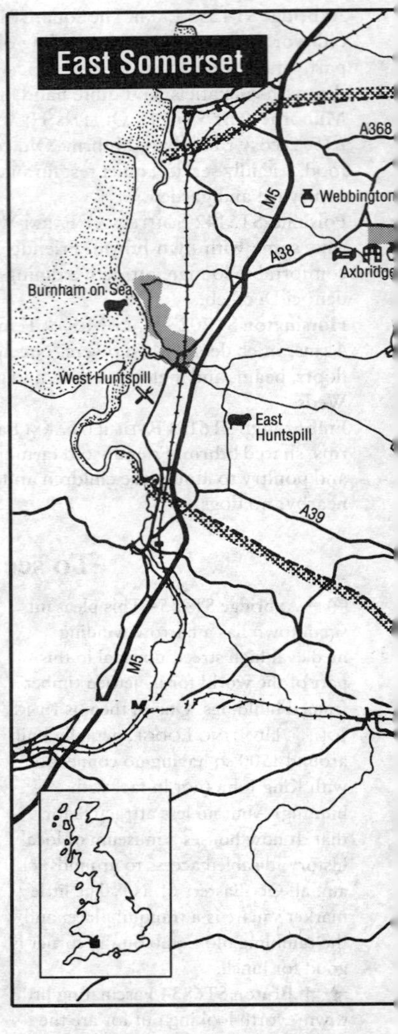

summer. The Galleries is quite useful for lunch.

Chewton Mendip ST5953
CHEWTON CHEESE DAIRY Another traditional cheese dairy, one of the few process, and of course taste the matured product. The whole village is quite an appetising place to visit, with demonstrations (and, again, tastings) of fudge-making, scrumpy sampling at the cider exhibition, and a

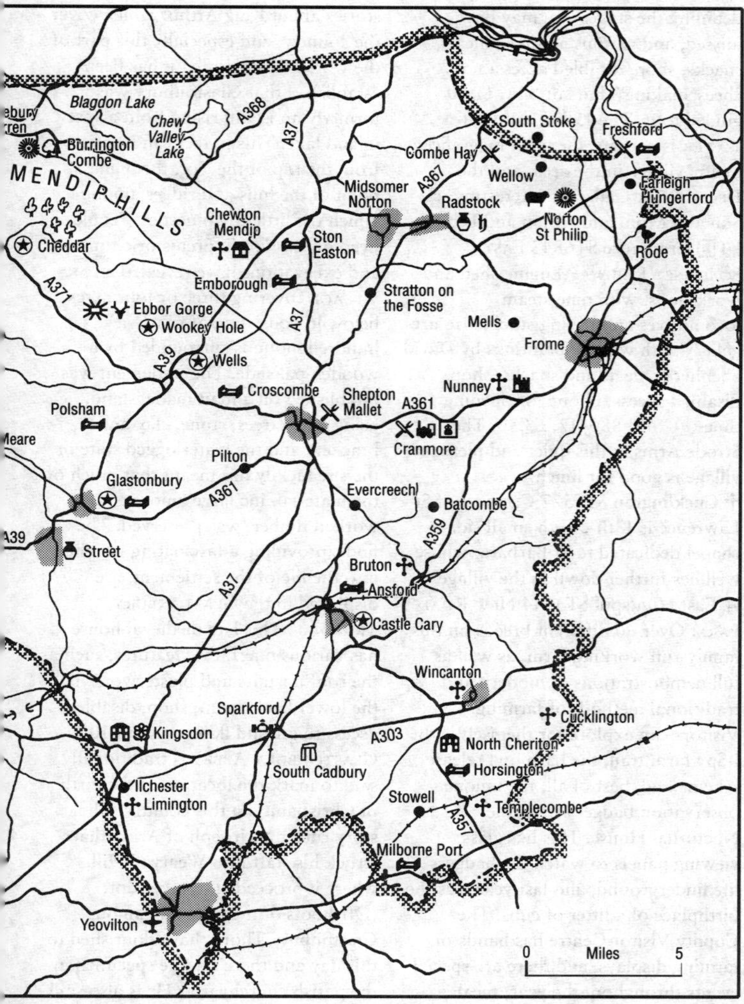

reconstructed 1920s sweet factory. Also cooperage, pottery, dairy and lacemaker; meals, snacks, shops, disabled access; cl Nov-mid-Mar; *£2.45. There's an AQUARIUM near here too. The older part of the extended village is attractive, with some interesting shops and a 14th-15th-c CHURCH with a fine tall tower, and outside there are roadside strawberry stalls and pick-your-own in summer. The Galleries is quite useful for lunch.

Chewton Mendip ST5953
CHEWTON CHEESE DAIRY Another traditional cheese dairy, one of the few to mature their cheeses properly, so producing not just the characteristic rind but also the true depth of flavour. They start at 7 am and go on till 3 pm, with the best time to watch between 11.30 am and 2.30 pm. Also a video

detailing the stages you may have missed, and various animals; meals, snacks, shop, disabled access; no cheesemaking Thurs or Sun; £1.50 guided tour. The 15th-c CHURCH TOWER is perhaps the most magnificent in any village in the area, and the Decoy Duck Gallery is interesting; cl Sun and Mon, and all Jan and Feb.

Cranmore ST6843 EAST SOMERSET RAILWAY Engine shed and workshops, with nine steam locomotives and rolling stock, also art gallery with wildlife paintings by David Shepherd; meals and snacks, shop, disabled access; phone for opening times, (0749) 880417; £3.30. The Strode Arms in this quiet and pleasant village is good for lunch.

✝ **Cucklington** ST7527 CHURCH of St Lawrence is 13th-c with small side chapel dedicated to St Barbara, whose well lies further down in the village.

East Huntspill ST3444 NEW ROAD FARM Over 60 different breeds on this family-run working farm, as well as full demonstrations of modern and traditional methods of farming. Visitors can explore for themselves the I-Spy farm trail, the barn owl release scheme and, best of all, the unique observation badger sett in the Nocturnal House. This has glass viewing panels to watch the badgers' life underground, and last year was the birthplace of a litter of cubs. The County Visitor Centre has hands-on farming displays, and there are special events throughout the year; meals, snacks, shop, disabled access; cl Nov-mid-Mar; £3. The Crossways Inn over at West Huntspill is good for lunch.

Ebbor Gorge ST5248 If you like Cheddar Gorge but don't like the souvenir stall, coach parties and all, then Ebbor Gorge is for you. It's the same sort of thing, above Wookey Hole, but altogether more unspoilt.

✝ **Glastonbury** ST4938 This town and its immediate surrounding area is rich in myth and legend, a major strand in the web of stories about King Arthur which cover the country, and especially this part of the world. Historically, it has been established that Glastonbury was formerly an island rising from a vast inland lake. This in fact can be seen from the top of the Tor, the highest point of the hills and ridges among which the little town nestles. People lived on the Tor in prehistoric times, and excavations have revealed a LAKE VILLAGE covering three or four acres below it, consisting of nearly a hundred mounds surrounded by a wooden palisade. The settlement was established on a man-made island, using felled trees, stone, clay and bracken, and the waterlogged state of the site luckily has meant that much of the material, inc large amounts of worked timber, was preserved. The finds, providing a fascinating insight into the life of the settlement, are displayed in the GLASTONBURY TRIBUNAL. This late medieval house has various fine 15th-c features, such as the roof upstairs and plasterwork in the lower back room; shop, disabled access to ground floor only; £1.10. GLASTONBURY ABBEY is traditionally said to mark the location of the birth of Christianity in this country. The story runs that Joseph of Arimathaea struck his staff into Wearyall Hill, where it proceeded to take root. (Offshoots of the tree, the famous Glastonbury Thorn, have flourished to this day and there's a fine specimen in the parish churchyard.) He is also said to have brought with him the Holy Grail, the chalice from the Last Supper, which Arthur's table of knights heroically sought through so many famous tales. The connection of the site with Arthur becomes almost historical in 1191, when bones, apparently those of King Arthur and Guinevere, were exhumed and reinterred before the high altar in the choir. The great abbey church dates mainly from 1524 though the Lady Chapel is much older (part of an earlier church which had been largely destroyed by fire in 1184). The massive roof timbers and richly decorated gable ends and porches testify to the enormous wealth of the order who ran it. After the Dissolution, the abbey fell into disrepair and finally ruin, but its passing was not easy – the last abbot is said to have refused to give in to Henry VIII's demands and so was dragged to the top of the Tor where he was hanged, drawn and quartered. A new interpretation area recounts these and many more tales of the site; shop, disabled access; *£2. Legend has it the chalice of the Holy Grail was hidden in the CHALICE WELL, now set amidst a colourful 2½-acre garden, the spring unsurprisingly possessing healing powers ever since; disabled access, shop; cl am winter; *60p. The Abbey Barn and outbuildings comprise the SOMERSET RURAL LIFE MUSEUM, where displays present traditional regional skills such as cider-making, peat-cutting and basket-weaving, and examine the life of a 19th-c Somerset labourer. There's also an orchard, rare breeds, a bee garden with hives and lots of special events; summer snacks, shop, disabled access ground floor only; cl am wknds and all day Sun in winter, 25-26 Dec, 1 Jan, Good Fri; £1.20. The George & Pilgrims, its medieval carved façade one of the sights of the town, is quite useful for lunch, as is the Who'd A Thought It. ADAMS & JONES near the abbey car park will hand-make shoes to measure.

★ **Ilchester** ST5222 Charming, with a useful range of well-stocked little shops. Used to be a Roman town, and one of the houses has a piece of Roman paving. The whole of the green fronting the Town Hall is said to be the burial ground of Plague victims. The Ivelchester Hotel is useful for lunch.

Kingsdon ST5126 LYTES CARY MANOR Most of the surviving building dates from the 16th c, though it was the home of the Lyte family even earlier, and they stayed here 500 years until the 18th c. Interesting architectural features include the 14th-c chapel, and the Great Hall, with its stained glass, added in the 15th c. The gardens were designed and stocked by Henry Lyte, a notable Elizabethan horticulturist and writer on gardening, and are being brought back to their original state, using plants which he described and recommended; plant sales, limited disabled access; open pm Mon, Weds and Sat Apr-Oct; *£3.50. NT. The Kingsdon Inn is good for lunch.

✝ **Limington** ST5422 Worth seeing is the fine CHURCH with effigies of the Giverney family dating back to the 1300s.

North Cheriton ST6825 Close by the church are the remains of a court with five walls where Napoleonic officers imprisoned in 'The Dogs' (manor house at Wincanton) used to play Fives.

Norton St Philip ST7755 NORWOOD RARE BREEDS FARM Friendly farm on high open land with good views, and plenty of traditional and rare breeds of cattle, sheep, pigs, goats and poultry. You can go right up to the animals, and watch the pigs being fed at 4.15 pm; meals, snacks, good farm shop, disabled access; cl Oct-Mar; *£3. The George is useful for lunch – and one of the most interesting ancient inn buildings in Britain.

★ ✝ **Nunney** ST7345 NUNNEY CASTLE Reduced to ruins by the Parliamentarians during the Civil War, this 14th-c crenellated manor house has one of the deepest moats in the country; it and its feeder stream running through the green of this quaint and quiet village are very popular with ducks. The castle's layout and round towers were supposedly modelled on France's Bastille. The CHURCH, as usual in so many Somerset villages, is well worth a look.

Peat Moors Visitor Centre ST4341 This VISITOR CENTRE (just west of

Meare) is in the heart of the peat-cutting area of the Somerset Levels. It provides a fascinating insight into its archaeology, history and natural history, with an excellent exhibition on peat-cutting and a reconstructed Iron-Age village; meals and snacks, shop, disabled access with help; cl 25-26 Dec; £1.

Radstock ST6854 MUSEUM Once a dairy and cheese-making farm set in the old North Somerset coalfield, now a local-history museum, with features inc reconstructed coalface, miner's cottage, workshop and schoolroom, a model railway, agricultural implements, blacksmith's shop and 1930s Co-op shop; snacks, shop, disabled access; cl wkdys (exc bank hols), Sun/bank hols am, all Dec; £1.50.

Rode ST8053 TROPICAL BIRD GARDENS Over 240 species of colourful and exotic birds flying through 17 acres of grounds, with ornamental lakes, ponds and masses of trees and shrubs. For children there is also a pets' corner and, from Easter to mid-Sept, a woodland miniature railway; summer meals, snacks, shop (inc sales of clematis, of which they have a notable collection), disabled access; cl 25 Dec; £3.70. The Red Lion nearby at Woolverton is useful for lunch.

★ **South Cadbury** ST6325 CADBURY CASTLE The Arthurian connections crowd this area; the legendary King and his knights are still said to sleep in the castle, waking on Christmas Eve to ride down the hill, along what is still called King Arthur's Hunting Causeway, and through the village on their pilgrimage to Glastonbury. The castle, covering about 18 acres, is in fact a massive Iron-Age camp: many relics have been found there – especially Roman artefacts. The village huddled below it has some attractive houses around the church with its strikingy gargoyled tower. While in this area, it's worth going to COMPTON PAUNCEFOOT ST4625, about a mile away. The village is in a conservation area and comprises a scatter of golden cottages, including a crescent built in 1815 for farmworkers – 'Waterloo Crescent'.

Sparkford ST6026 HAYNES SPARKFORD MOTOR MUSEUM Lots of cars and motorcycles restored to working condition, where possible using original parts; meals, snacks, shop, disabled access; cl 25 Dec, 1 Jan; £3.50.

Street ST4836 SHOE MUSEUM Footwear from Roman times to the present day, as well as machinery, tools and advertising material, in the oldest part of the shoe factory, established in 1825. It now forms the centrepiece of the Clarks Village, made up of over 20 factory outlets; meals, snacks, shop, disabled access; cl Sun, and Nov-Easter. The Mullions opposite is useful for lunch.

✝ **Templecombe** ST7022 Ancient village with stocks still standing in place; gets its name from medieval order of Knights Templar who were dedicated to the protection of pilgrims and religious treasures. The church, founded by King Alfred's daughter, houses a 13th-c painting of Christ, found by accident 30 years ago in an outhouse which had once formed part of the priest's house; possibly an early copy of the Turin Shroud, which the Knights Templar may have had in their possession for a while. The Half Moon at nearby Horsington is useful for lunch.

Webbington ST3855 WHEELWRIGHTS WORKING MUSEUM AND GYPSY FOLKLORE COLLECTION Wheels, carriages and caravans next to working old workshop, as well as Edwardian fairground and Romany museum; snacks, shop, disabled access; cl Mon (exc bank hols) and Tues (exc Aug); £2.

✝ **Wells** ST5445 With a population of only 9,500 this delightful place wouldn't normally even qualify as a big town, but in fact it's England's smallest city. The CATHEDRAL that grants it this honour is a stunning structure right in the centre, its three towers stretching up against the Mendip foothills. Certainly, this is the way cathedral cities were meant to be, their skylines dwarfed by the grandeur of the cathedral itself. The spectacular west front is the first sight to greet you as you come through one of the several surviving medieval gateways. This dates from the 13th c, and carries 293 pieces of medieval sculpture, a façade unique in Europe. Inside be sure to see the wonderful inverted arches – scissor-shaped and designed to take the additional weight of the tower which was heightened in 1338. In the nave the austere lines of the perpendicular minstrels' gallery help make up one of the earliest completely Gothic designs. The clock in the north transept dates from 1390, and horsemen still joust on it every quarter of an hour; while in the south transept is an opportunity to enjoy that marvellous medieval gift for caricature – two of the eleven carvings in the church showing men suffering toothache are to be found here, as well as four graphic scenes of an old man stealing fruit and getting what for. The embroidered stallbacks in the choir (1937-1948) are a riot of colour – a labour of love for needleworkers across the country. The chapter house is a gem of the Decorated style, while archives and documents from as early as the 10th c are housed in the library which, at 168 ft long, is possibly the largest medieval library building in England. Meals, snacks, shop, disabled access; donations. The Chain Gate (1459/60) links the cathedral with the Vicars' Close, where the Vicars Choral still live, in the original medieval houses. It's said to be one of the oldest complete medieval streets in Europe. The moated BISHOP'S PALACE nearby is surrounded by fortifications, and can be approached only through the 14th-c gatehouse – it's quite dramatic as you go across the drawbridge. A beautiful series of buildings with some original 13th-c parts, notably the banqueting hall and undercroft, as well as several other interesting state rooms and a long gallery hung with portraits of former bishops; meals, snacks, shop, disabled access; open Tues, Thurs, bank hols and Sun pm Apr-Oct, daily in Aug; *£2. The grounds are the site of the famous wells that give the town its name, bubbling up from the pool below the cathedral and producing on average 40 gallons of water a second. There's also a decent arboretum and a rather clever flock of swans, trained to ring a little bell under the gatehouse window when they want feeding. The MUSEUM building in Cathedral Green is Tudor, and houses good local history displays and notable embroidery samplers; disabled access to ground floor only; cl Mon and Tues in winter; £1. There are a good few other attractive old buildings, many now used as offices and shops (inc several antique shops), and several grouped around the Market Place; the Fountain and the City Arms near here are good for lunch, and there's a big cheese shop not far away.

★ ✝ **Wincanton** ST7128 Fine Georgian houses and many of the multitude of inns and hotels survive from the coaching era; many still have old coach-entry gates. CHURCH PORCH has medieval relief of St Eligius.

Wookey Hole ST5145 WOOKEY HOLE CAVES AND PAPERMILL Guided tours of half a mile of dramatic subterranean tunnels and caverns, using remote-controlled lighting to spotlight the geological features and illustrate the history and myths associated with the caves. Just along the river the papermill demonstrates paper production, as well as housing an authentic Edwardian fairground, a Victorian portrait studio, a Magical Mirror Maze and an Old Penny Arcade. A bustling place, and all under cover, so ideal for a day when the sun's not shining; meals and snacks, shop, disabled access exc the caves; cl 17-25 Dec; £5.20. The Burcott Inn nearby is useful for lunch, and in Burcott itself there's a working WATERMILL with several craft shops and animals; cl Mon and Tues, no milling wkdys; £1.80.

Yeovil ST5516 MUSEUM OF SOUTH SOMERSET (Hendford) Good range of local-history exhibits from prehistoric and Roman remains to 19th-c clothes and industries. Reconstructed rooms from Roman and Georgian times; disabled access to ground floor only; cl Sun and Mon. This big town otherwise has little to interest visitors.

Yeovilton ST5422 FLEET AIR ARM MUSEUM A big, bustling place concentrating on the story of aviation at sea from 1908, and the history of the Royal Naval Air Service. Various exhibitions on topics as diverse as the WRENS, the Falklands and Gulf Wars, and jets and helicopters, as well as nearly 50 historic aircraft, lively displays and reconstructions, and lots of models, paintings, letters, weapons and photographs. The museum is housed in the Royal Naval Air Station, and there are viewing galleries where you can watch the aircraft using this busy base. Also children's adventure playground and a hi-tech flight simulator; meals and snacks, shop, disabled access; cl 24-26 Dec; £4.80.

★ **Other attractive villages** in this area are Batcombe ST6838, Cheddar ST4653, Combe Hay ST7359, Croscombe ST5844 (great 17th-c woodwork in its 15th-c church), Evercreech ST6438, Mells ST7249, Pilton ST5940, South Stoke ST7641, Stowell ST6822, Wellow ST7458, Winscombe ST4157 and, particularly, Stratton on the Fosse ST6550 is notable for the spectacular modern (though not modern-looking) Downside Abbey.

Walks

Excluding Exmoor (discussed separately, in the Devon chapter), the **Mendips** have the county's most interesting walks – not on the top, which is mostly unremarkable farmland, but along its edges, particularly in the two great limestone gorges. Burrington Combe on the north side has been mentioned above, under Avon. The **Cheddar Gorge** ST4553 is also a straightforward walk along the road. It rapidly loses its commercialised trappings, and when you reach the far end two worthwhile paths leave the road. On the east side is a quiet dale with two nature reserves, Black Rock ST4854 and Velvet Bottom ST4955. On the west side, the West Mendip Way climbs through woods and gives access to another path which skirts the top of the gorge (the views into it are hair-raising). Close to Wells is an attractive nature trail in **Ebbor Gorge** ST5248, altogether quieter than Cheddar Gorge. The **West Mendip Way** (Wells to Weston super Mare) crosses the Mendip plateau and ascends some medium-sized hills, such as Wavering Down ST4055. Below the Mendips at **Winscombe** ST4257, the abandoned railway nicknamed the Strawberry Line is now a footpath.

Brent Knoll ST3450, a detached Mendip outlier, has a path to its summit from Brent Knoll village (the Red Cow here is useful), while **Brean Down** ST2958, sandwiched between Weston super Mare and acres of holiday camps, protrudes into the Bristol Channel and provides the finest coastal walk in east Somerset.

There's a pleasant walk to **Wells** from Croscombe ST5844, with the cathedral growing in stature as you approach.

Driving

The best road into the Mendips is the B3135 up through the Cheddar Gorge, passing the dramatic limestone cliffs, and then coming out on the plateau of the Mendips. Here, poor windswept soils are good for grazing sheep but not for cropping – so the land is left grassy and green, pocked with unseen caverns used by potholers, and more visible Bronze-Age funeral barrows.

Many of the back roads in the east part of the area, towards the borders with Wiltshire and Dorset, take you through countryside with a very secluded feel, the rolling farmland giving way to secret valleys and wooded hillsides. A good part for exploration, more open, is east of Bruton and up towards Alfred's Tower.

The B3139 through Wells and Wedmore is an old coach road running along land which rises very slightly above the flood-prone Somerset Levels: roads off on either side show the dead flatness of the Levels, with the B3151 down to Glastonbury giving a good view of the town below the Tor as you approach.

Where to eat

Knapp ST3025 RISING SUN (0823) 490436 Fine 15th-c longhouse with friendly atmosphere, stripped beams and stonework and good, popular food inc lots of fish dishes; cl 25 Dec. **£19**|£1.90/£8.

Shepton Mallet ST6143 BLOSTINS 29 Waterloo Rd (0749) 343648 Friendly candlelit evening bistro with reasonably priced, very good food; cl Sun, Mon, 2 wks Jan, 2 wks Jun, 1 wk Nov. **£18.95**|£10.95.

West Huntspill ST3044 CROSSWAYS (0278) 783756 Popular, spacious dining pub with lovely atmosphere and very good food (esp puddings). **£16.80**|£3/£5.25.

Cranmore ST6643 STRODE ARMS (0749) 880450 Carefully run former farmhouse with charming country furnishings and generous helpings of good home-made dishes; also excellent puddings; cl Sun pm; children in restaurant only; disabled access. **£16.50**|£1.50/£7.

Combe Hay ST7359 WHEATSHEAF (0225) 833504 Pleasantly old-fashioned rooms, sloping lawn looking down to church and ancient manor stables, wide choice of good food (lots of game and fish), and friendly staff; summer barbecues. **£15.75**|£3/£5.25.

Blagdon Hill ST2217 WHITE LION (0823) 142296 Gently refurbished village pub with good china ornaments, log fire, very pleasant service, and a wide choice of good home-made food; cl 25 Dec; children in dining room. **£15.50**|£1.95/£4.50.

Freshford ST7859 FRESHFORD INN (0225) 722250 Picturesque three-storey building with comfortable, interestingly decorated bar, good generous bar and restaurant food, well-kept ales and helpful staff. £1.50/£5.

We welcome reports from readers . . .

Do send us reports on places in the GUIDE, or ones you think should be in. Use the card in the middle, the report forms at the end, or just write – no stamp needed: THE GOOD WEEKEND GUIDE, FREEPOST TN1569, Wadhurst, E Sussex TN5 7BR.

West Somerset

Here there are many interesting places to visit, good-value places to stay and some very unspoilt if undramatic countryside.

A good many interesting places to visit here include particularly Montacute House, Dunster and its castle, Barrington Court with its lovely gardens, the fine old gardens of Clapton Court at Crewkerne, the Cricket St Thomas wildlife park, the garden of Lambrook Manor at East Lambrook, the unusual indoor jungle at Washford, and one of the enjoyable cider mills at Dowlish Wake or Bradford-on-Tone. It would be a shame to come here and not venture into the quieter and unspoilt parts of the countryside, which do have a special appeal. What strikes visitors most about much of the countryside in this part of Somerset is its secluded and self-contained nature: without the splendid church towers peeking up out of the trees, you'd often not know a village was there at all. The Quantock Hills, above all, exemplify the private feel of Somerset, with their small valleys each seeming to be a little individual world.

Minehead is a pleasant traditional resort, most notable perhaps for the steam railway which runs up below the Quantocks, a much longer route than usual for private railways.

A wide choice of places to stay runs from a good many little country inns and civilised farm or country-house B & Bs, which seem particularly to suit the area's character, to very comfortable small hotels; prices in this part of the county represent good value for money.

The Somerset parts of Exmoor have been described in the section devoted to Exmoor, in the Devon chapter.

Where to stay

Dunster SS9943 Luttrell Arms Minehead TA24 6SG (0643) 821555 **£112**; 27 rms. Comfortably modernised THF hotel in ancient building of great character with individual atmosphere, good popular food and interesting evening meals; cannon emplacements in the garden date from the Civil War; close to Exmoor National Park.

Hatch Beauchamp ST3220 Farthings Taunton TA3 6SG (0823) 480664 ***£94**; 6 rms with thoughtful extras. Charming little Georgian house in three acres of gardens, caring, friendly owners, open fires, and good food using fresh local produce; cl late Dec-early Jan; children by arrangement.

Middlecombe SS9645 Periton Park Minehead TA24 8SW (0643) 706885 **£88**; 8 rms with views of surrounding countryside. Fine Victorian country house on the edge of Exmoor; comfortable lounge, books, log fire, a relaxed atmosphere, friendly service, and good food; excellent walks and very good riding centre next to hotel; children over 12; disabled access.

Langley Marsh ST0729 LANGLEY HOUSE Wiveliscombe Taunton TA4 2UF (0984) 623318 **£79**; 8 individually decorated, pretty rms. Spotlessly kept Georgian house with 16th-c heart; charming lounge and dining room, antiques, fresh flowers, log fires, friendly service, very good carefully cooked food using home-grown herbs and vegetables, and neatly kept landscaped gardens; cl Feb.

Kilve ST1442 MEADOW HOUSE Bridgwater TA3 1EG (027 874) 1546 **£75**; 10 rms, 5 of them in cottage in courtyard. Beautifully kept Georgian house with relaxed atmosphere; fresh flowers, antiques and comfortable seats, fine wines, landscaped gardens, croquet, streamside walks, and sea fishing (5 mins); cl 2 wks over Christmas.

Barwick ST5613 LITTLE BARWICK HOUSE 2 miles south of Yeovil BA22 9TD (0935) 23902 **£72**; 5 rms. Listed Georgian dower house in pretty garden; excellent food, lovely relaxed atmosphere, open fire in lounge, and good service; cl Christmas, New Year.

Kilve ST1422 HOOD ARMS Bridgwater TA5 1EA (0278) 741210 ***£62**; 5 rms. Popular village inn with straightforwardly comfortable main bar, woodburning stove decorated with horse brasses, cosy little lounge, attentive service and excellent food; cl 25 Dec.

Holford ST1541 COMBE HOUSE Bridgwater TA5 1RZ (0278) 741382 **£58**; 20 rms. Warmly friendly hotel in pretty spot, with comfortable rooms, good home-made food, and relaxed atmosphere; cl Nov-Feb.

Somerton ST4228 LYNCH COUNTRY HOUSE 4 Behind Berry TA11 7PD (0458) 722316 **£45**; 5 prettily decorated rms. Carefully restored, homely Georgian house with comfortable lounge, open fire, books, and good breakfasts (no evening meals) in airy room overlooking grounds and lake, where there are black swans and exotic ducks; cl Christmas.

North Perrott ST4709 MANOR ARMS Crewkerne TA18 7SG (0460) 72901 ***£44**; 5 rms. Comfortable and attractive little inn with friendly, helpful licensees, good home-made food in bar and restaurant, and garden with play area; cl 25 Dec; disabled access.

Waterrow ST0425 ROCK Taunton TA4 2AX (0984) 23293 ***£44**; 7 rms. Welcoming pub prettily placed in small valley village; log fire, smallish bar, civilised lunchtime dining room that doubles as smart evening restaurant, wide choice of good food, decent coffee, real ales; no accomm 24-26 Dec.

Wiveliscombe ST0827 DEEPLEIGH Taunton TA4 2UU (0984) 23379 ***£44**; 5 cottagey rms with lovely views. Pink-washed 16th-c house in 3 acres; beams, panelling, log fire in inglenook fireplace, comfortable drawing room, cosy bar and attractive dining room with good food; lots of walks; riding or clay-pigeon shoots can be arranged.

Lower Vellow ST0938 CURDON MILL Williton Taunton TA4 4LS (0984) 56522 ***£42**; 6 smallish but pretty and individually furnished rms. Charming and beautifully furnished hotel on the edge of Exmoor National Park; very good evening meal in antiques-filled dining room, substantial breakfasts, friendly staff (and other guests); lovely garden – as well as 200 acres of working farm to wander over; the waterwheel and mill shaft have been carefully preserved and still work; outdoor heated swimming pool; children over 8.

Roadwater ST0338 WOOD ADVENT FARM Watchett TA23 0RR (0984) 40920 ***£37**; 5 rms. Relaxed, spacious farmhouse on 340 acres of working farm; log fire in comfortable lounge, good country cooking, grass tennis court, outdoor heated swimming pool, and clay-pigeon- and pheasant-shooting.

Stogumber ST0937 HALL FARM Taunton TA4 3TQ (0984) 56321 **£37**; 6 rms,

5 with own bthrm. Old-fashioned B & B with evening meals (bring your own wine) – wonderfully unpretentious, and warmly friendly staff; cl 23 Dec-mid-Jan.

Bradley Green ST2438 MALT SHOVEL Blackmoor Lane, Cannington TA5 2NE (0278) 653432 **£36**; 4 comfortable rms. Friendly, welcoming pub with wood-burning stove in comfortably furnished main bar, family room, dining room, simple and popular home-made food and real ales; cl 25 Dec.

Stoke St Gregory ST3527 ROSE & CROWN Taunton TA3 7EW (0823) 490296 ***£35**; 3 rms, shared bthrm. Warmly friendly 17th-c cottagey inn with a cosy and pleasantly romanticised stable theme, generous helpings of particularly good-value food, excellent breakfasts, decent wine list, and popular skittle alley; children over 12.

West Bagborough ST1633 RISING SUN Taunton TA4 3EF (0823) 432575 **£35**; 4 rms. Pleasant quiet little place in tiny Quantocks village; short choice of fresh generously served food inc big breakfasts, well-kept real ale, and big log fires; disabled access.

Pinksmoor ST1320 PINKSMOOR MILLHOUSE Wellington TQ21 0HD (0823) 672361 **£34**; 3 rms. Though the old mill is no longer in use, you can walk along the millstream (conservation area with lots of wildlife) or around family-run dairy farm; log fire, 2 lounges (one no-smoking), friendly welcome, and farmhouse cooking; cl Christmas/New Year.

Isle Brewers ST2224 BUSHFURLONG FARM Taunton TA3 6QT (046 08) 219 **£32**; 4 rms, 2 with own bthrm. Hamstone farmhouse, dating from early 1700s, on family-run arable farm with fine country views; breakfast room with access to garden, and guest lounge; no smoking, no evening meal; bikes for hire, fishing.

To see and do

Barrington ST3918 BARRINGTON COURT In the grounds of a splendid 16th-c house, a magnificent series of gardens influenced by Gertrude Jekyll, inc a rose garden and traditional walled kitchen garden, the produce from which is on sale in the shop; snacks, shop, disabled access; house open pm Weds Apr-Oct only, garden pm daily in same period exc Fri and Sat; £3, house extra 50p. NT. The village itself is attractive, and the Royal Oak is useful for lunch.

Bradford-on-Tone ST1722 SHEPPY'S CIDER (Three Bridges) The Sheppys have been making cider since the early 19th c, and here you can follow the process all the way through – walk around the 42 acres of orchards, see the cider press and sample the product itself, before buying some in the farm shop. There is also a museum with exhibits relating to the business of producing cider; snacks, shop, disabled access; cl Sun Christmas-Easter (other Suns open only 12-2 pm); £1.50, or £3 for guided tours.

Bridgwater ST3037 ADMIRAL BLAKE MUSEUM Now the town museum, this picturesque house was the birthplace of the Admiral in 1598, and shows his personal possessions (inc his sea chest) and a diorama of his great victory over the Spaniards at Santa Cruz. Also displays on the Battle of Sedgemoor in 1685, and other local history, archaeology and industry; shop; cl am Sun, 25-26 Dec.

Burrow Bridge ST3630 SOMERSET LEVELS BASKET CENTRE have been making baskets from local materials cut on the surrounding Levels for nearly 150 years; also other crafts. Shop; cl Sun.

Chard ST3208 This town was founded in 1234 and has a rich history, involving many industries from woollen and cloth-making to lace-making and more recently agricultural engineering – all of which is amply illustrated in the MUSEUM, which also has a reconstructed dairy, laundry, schoolroom and cobblers and lots more unusual displays, inc a bizarre collection of locally made artificial limbs. Shop, disabled access; cl Sun (exc in July and Aug) and mid-Oct-early May; £1.50. There are a couple of places to hire bikes; the local tourist board do good cycle routes. Just north of town HORNSBURY MILL is a 200-year-old watermill, with landscaped water garden, trout lake, play area and craft shops; meals, snacks, shop, disabled access; £1.50 museum. FORDE ABBEY nearby is listed under Dorset – particularly worth visiting, just over the border.

Cannington ST2539 CANNINGTON COLLEGE HERITAGE GARDENS Over 10,000 different types of plant in these extensive gardens, with eight National Collections, display and ornamental beds, tropical and sub-tropical glasshouses, and gardens of bees and butterflies. Meals, snacks, shop, disabled access; cl am, and Oct-Mar; *£1.50.

Cheddon Fitzpaine ST2427 HESTERCOMBE GARDENS Raised walks, sunken lawns and a water garden are all part of the grand design which Lutyens and Gertrude Jekyll created for this garden (now beautifully restored) set around the headquarters of the Somerset Fire Brigade; cl wknds exc pm May-Sept; £1.50 .

Crewkerne ST4409 CLAPTON COURT GARDENS Ten acres of beautifully laid-out formal and woodland gardens with a particularly fine old ash tree among the many rarer trees and shrubs; it's full of flowering bulbs in spring; snacks; cl Sun am, Sat exc Easter, all Nov-Feb; £3. The 15th-c CHURCH is magnificent, with an imposing Tudor gateway and some fine carving on the west front and in the main porch.

Cricket St Thomas ST3708 WILDLIFE PARK This great house was once the home of Alexander Hood; now its park is home to a multitude of wild and wonderful creatures, their enclosures designed to blend in with the surroundings as far as possible. Also the National Heavy Horse Centre and a woodland railway; meals and snacks, shop, disabled access; £5.50.

Dowlish Wake ST3713 PERRY'S CIDER MILLS They've been making Zummerzet Zider here for centuries, and during the autumn you can watch it being produced. The cider mill is in a group of thatched 16th-c buildings around a yard with brightly painted old farm waggons and so forth, with more agricultural bygones under cover; enthusiastically run, with liberal tastings and half a dozen different ciders for sale, in old-fashioned earthenware flagons if you want. Shop, disabled access; cl 1-2 pm, pm Sun, 25-26 Dec, 1 Jan. The nearby New Inn is good for lunch.

East Lambrook ST4319 EAST LAMBROOK MANOR GARDEN This well-loved cottagey garden around a 15th-c house (not open) is now Grade 1 listed; it was started by Walter and Margery Fish in 1937, and Margery Fish described the process in her book *We Made A Garden*, which became immensely popular; snacks, plant sales, shop; cl Sun, and all Nov-Feb; *£2. The Rose & Crown opposite is useful for lunch.

! Dunster SS9943 DUNSTER CASTLE A dramatically placed castle near Exmoor, and set in a 28-acre park teeming with exotic flora and even subtropical plants. The castle's current appearance is largely 19th-c, but there are older features inside such as the 17th-c oak staircase and gallery with its brightly painted wall hangings; shop in 17th-c stables, limited disabled access; cl Thurs/Fri,

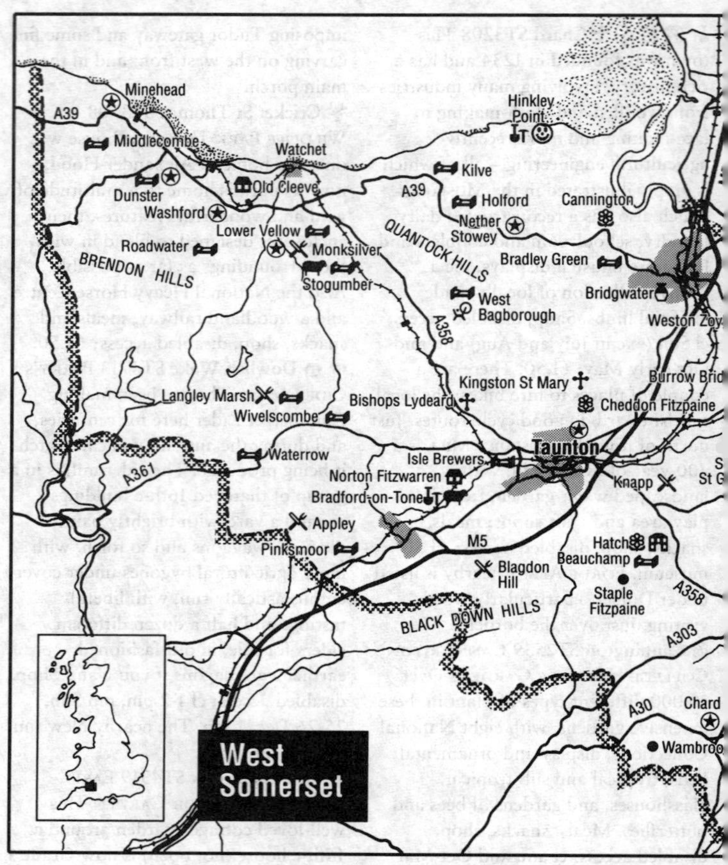

2 Nov-2 Apr; £4.50, £2.50 garden and park only, NT; tremendous views. Below the castle and the wooded hill on which it stands, the village has fine medieval houses along its wide main street, an 18th-c WATERMILL still producing stoneground flour for sale (teas; cl Sat exc July, Aug and Easter, all Nov-Mar; £1.40), a handsome former yarn market and market cross, a lovely 15th-c priory CHURCH with particularly tuneful bells, a doll museum, and the OLD DOVECOTE. Built as part of the priory, this dates from the 12th c and is particularly special for still having its 'potence' or revolving ladder, used for harvesting the plump squabs from the nesting boxes; cl mid-Oct-Easter. The handsome old Luttrell Arms Hotel is good for lunch.

Hatch Beauchamp ST3220
HATCH COURT is a fine Palladian mansion with an impressive hall, as well as walled kitchen garden, deer park, plenty of china and a small military museum. The advantage of visiting less familiar private homes such as this is that care is taken showing you round and often exhibits are enlivened by plenty of anecdotes; teas; open pm Thurs mid-Jun-mid-Sept, and garden only Fri pm in same period; £3, £1.50 garden only. The Hatch Inn is useful for lunch.

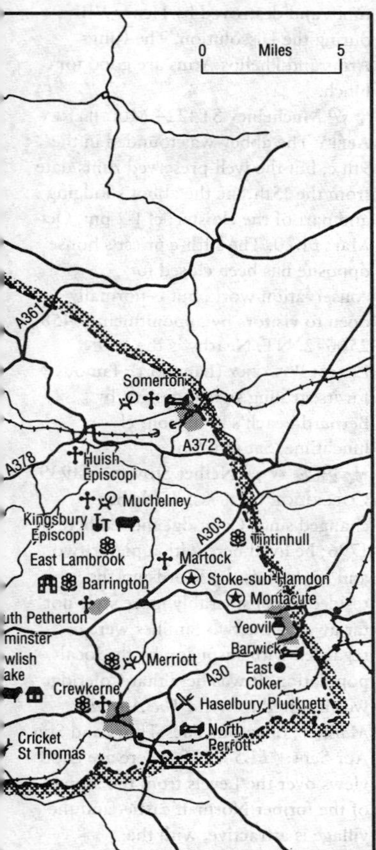

Hinkley Point ST2646 POWER STATION Quite a contrast to most of the other places we recommend in this region, with hi-tech displays and interactive videos explaining how electricity is generated, and information on local ecology and wildlife (there are nature trails from here); cl winter Sat. There are tours of the station too, which must be booked in advance: (0278) 652461.

★ ✝ **Huish Episcopi** ST4226 Attractive village with a fine CHURCH, and a quaint old pub, the Rose & Crown.

Kingsbury Episcopi ST4321 SOMERSET CIDER BRANDY CO England's first fully licensed cider distillery, with huge copper stills, oak vats and wooden presses, and traditional cider orchards to stroll through; shop; cl Sun. The village green has an ancient lock-up, and the Wyndham Arms is useful for lunch.

✝ **Martock** ST4819 Magnificent CHURCH with splendid roof; look out for old Court House turned into Grammar School by William Strode in 1661, with inscription above the door 'Martock neglect not your opportunities' in English, Latin, Hebrew and Greek.

Merriott ST4412 SCOTTS OF MERRIOTT Perhaps the last of the big general retail nurseries to raise and grow most of their own trees and shrubs, on 90 acres – a sea of colour when the 500 varieties of roses are in flower in July; snacks, shop, disabled access. In the village D B POTTERY (Highway Cottage, Church St) make attractive teapots and other stoneware; shop, disabled access; cl lunchtime wkdys. The Poulett Arms on the attractive main street of nearby Hinton St George is good for lunch.

Minehead SS9746 is a spacious resort, its beach and promenade sheltered by the wooded hills to the north-east. It has the usual attractions, a lively harbour, a sizeable holiday camp, and up above the modern shopping area (which serves the surrounding countryside as much as the resort itself) an older core with some thatched cottages and steep winding streets. There's an unusual POTTERY SHOP (cl Sun) on Park St, and a little SHOE FACTORY you can visit on North Rd (cl 1-2 pm and wknds exc Sat am). Minehead is the terminus for the WEST SOMERSET RAILWAY, whose steam trains run along the coast to Watchet and then inland to Bishops Lydeard – a splendid long run stopping at several little stations (the one at Washford – see below – has a museum devoted to the old Somerset & Dorset Railway); meals and snacks, shop, very good disabled access, with a specially adapted coach; cl wkdys in Mar, Nov and Dec, and all Jan and Feb, best to check on (0643) 707650 for dates and times; *£2-£8 depending on the length of the journey. From the harbour you may be able to catch the *Waverley* (paddle steamer) or *Balmoral* to various destinations.

Monksilver ST0737 COMBE SYDENHAM COUNTRY PARK The Elizabethan-style garden has a corn mill, children's play area and woodland walks in 580 acres of Exmoor-edge woodland. The recently restored 16th-c house was once home to Francis Drake's second wife, and you can see the meteorite which crashed to her feet as she was about to go into church to marry another while Drake was away at sea – stopping the ceremony and leaving her free to marry Drake; meals and snacks, shop; cl Sat, but shop open Sat am, cl Nov-Easter; £3. The Notley Arms is good for lunch.

★ **Montacute** ST4916 MONTACUTE HOUSE Set in a beautiful little village, this magnificent 16th-c house with its honeyed stone contains a wealth of interesting things to look at – tapestries, furniture, paintings and ceramics set in rooms with decorated ceilings, ornate fireplaces and fine wood panelling. Not to be missed is the collection of paintings in the Long Gallery, which is on permanent loan from the National Portrait Gallery and portrays members of the Tudor and Jacobean courts. The house itself stands in impressive formal gardens; the main body of the house is original but the heraldic beasts and fluted columns were added in the 18th c. Meals and snacks, shop, limited disabled access; cl am, Tues, Good Fri, Nov-Mar; £4.60. NT. In the village, features worth seeing include the Borough – a square of two-storey houses – which is quite charming, while Abbey Farm and the Monk's House are all that remain from the Cluniac Priory founded in Norman times and destroyed by Henry VIII during the Dissolution. The Kings Arms and Phelips Arms are good for lunch.

✝ **Muchelney** ST4224 MUCHELNEY ABBEY The abbey was founded in the 9th c, but the well-preserved ruins date from the 15th, inc the abbot's lodging and part of the cloister; cl 1-2 pm, Oct-Mar; £1.20. The 14th-c priest's house opposite has been closed for conservation work, but is normally open to visitors by appointment (0458) 250672. NT. Nearby is the JOHN LEACH POTTERY (Langport), famous for its striking signed designs by Bernard Leach's grandson; cl lunchtime, Sat pm, Sun.

★ **Nether Stowey** ST1939 COLERIDGE COTTAGE Little has changed since Coleridge moved here in 1796; he lived here with a pig or two, and his friends the Wordsworths resided in considerably more style not far away – the two families were regarded with suspicion by the local population. It was here that Coleridge was inspired to write *The Ancient Mariner*; open pm Tues-Thurs and Sun Apr-Sept; *£1.50. NT. There are good views over the Levels from the mound of the former Norman castle, and the village is attractive, with the QUANTOCK HILLS INFORMATION CENTRE in Castle St a valuable source of information. New Stowet Farm has a SHEEP-MILKING CENTRE, and the Cottage Inn at Keenthorne just east of the village is good for lunch. Up at Over Stowey ST1838, QUANTOCK WEAVERS (Old Forge, Plainsfield) carry out hand spinning, knitting and weaving using natural dyes, in former 17th-c forge; cl am wknds.

Norton Fitzwarren ST1925 TAUNTON CIDER MILL Tours of working cider mill, with samples at the end and an exhibition of the history of the drink, so deeply rooted in Somerset life that workers used to receive it as part of their pay; shop, disabled access; tours Easter-Sept every Thurs at 3 pm, plus Tues at 3 pm and Fri at 11 am; £2.75.

Old Cleeve ST0342 John Wood (Old Cleeve Tannery) is a SHEEPSKIN FACTORY with wkdy guided tours (not Nov-Mar; 50p), café, and a shop selling rugs, coats, slippers etc inc cheap seconds; cl Sun, best to check first for Christmas opening, (0984) 40291.

Somerton ST4828 has a long history – Roman settlement, claimant to title of capital of ancient Wessex, birthplace of King Ine, predecessor of King Alfred. ST MICHAEL'S CHURCH is stupendous, its roof supposedly created by monks of Muchelney from 7,000 fetter pieces, among which is a beer barrel – apparently a reference to Abbot Bere. Fine old Georgian buildings in quiet main square (misleadingly called Cow Sq) with 17th-c market cross. The ICELANDIC TAPESTRY SCHOOL (Little Lynch, Behind Berry) teaches medieval Icelandic embroidery, with wknd courses and kits for sale; disabled access; cl Sun and 25 July-25 Aug. The Red Lion and White Hart are useful for lunch.

South Petherton ST4316 This houses the HQ and two shops of Global Village, a company importing ethnic art and low-technology products from over 30 countries, including many of the Third World. The CHURCH has the second-highest octagonal tower in the country. Opposite Nat-West in the High Street is Market House, where three local men were hanged in the courtyard after the Monmouth Rebellion.

Stogumber ST0937 BEE WORLD AND ANIMAL CENTRE Friendly little bee farm with observation hives, good displays and videos on beekeeping, and demonstrations of the uses to which the honey can be put, from candles to face cream. Also rare breeds and other animals to fuss over, pony rides for children at 12 pm and 2.30 pm, and nature trails; snacks, shop, disabled access; cl Nov-Easter; *£2.75. The village, like so many round here, is pretty, and the White Horse is good for lunch.

Stoke-sub-Hamdon ST4419 This village is overlooked by Ham Hill, which has provided the stone for many of the villages in the area, producing that distinctive warm honey-coloured look. The former 14th- and 15th-c STOKE SUB HAMDON PRIORY manor house is also built of this stone. The priests of the chantry of Beauchamp manor used to live here – the manor itself has long vanished, but its fine thatched barn and the screens, passage and Great Hall of the chantry can still be seen. NT. Montacute is the best nearby place for lunch, and on the way is a striking folly, St Michael's Tower; it's one of three, all built by neighbouring friends in the 18th c – whenever one had a flag up it was an invitation for the others to go round for a hearty evening. Just south, HAM HILL COUNTRY PARK has 140 acres of grassland and woodland. Once an Iron-Age fort, it's full of wildlife and plants, and the views from the top of the hill are really quite splendid.

Stoke St Gregory ST3426 WILLOW AND WETLANDS VISITOR CENTRE Shows how this area – the most important area of wetland in the country – developed from marsh and swamp, also its flora and fauna, and the various industries that have used its products; shop; cl wknds (exc shop Sat), Easter Mon; £1.75. Nearby, the ENGLISH BASKET CENTRE produces baskets from its own willow plantations, and art charcoal; here too are a blacksmith and a display of willow sculptures; shop, disabled access; best to check first out of season, (0823) 69418. The Rose & Crown at Woodhill on the edge of the village is good for lunch.

Taunton ST2324 A prosperous country town with a lively Saturday cattle market. The 13th-c portcullised gatetower of its former castle is now absorbed into the County Hotel, though another part now houses the SOMERSET COUNTY MUSEUM. This has local history and archaeology exhibits as well as ceramics, glass, and dolls, and a Military Museum with relics of the Somerset Light Infantry. Judge Jeffrey conducted some of his Bloody Assizes after the Monmouth rebellion of 1685 in the castle's Great Hall; shop, disabled access to ground floor only; cl Sun, Good Fri, 25-26 Dec; *£1.20. There are a few other interesting old buildings dotted around, inc the Tudor House on Fore St, and the CHURCH of St Mary Magdalene has a lovely pinnacled tower and a lofty Perpendicular chancel. SOMERSET CRICKET MUSEUM (Priory Ave) Balls, bats and blazers, cards, cuttings and caps, with a cricketing reference library too. The exhibition is housed in a medieval barn, one of the town's oldest buildings, thought to have been the gatehouse for the priory that once stood on the cricket ground; shop, some disabled access; open wknds, Christmas and Easter hols and whenever there's a first-class cricket match; *60p. Just behind Riverside Place the SHAKESPEARE GLASSWORKS have demonstrations of glassblowing (not Sun or Mon), and in Bath Pl MAKERS is a decent craft shop selling local hand-made crafts; cl Sun. The Vivary Arms, across the park from the centre, is useful for lunch, as is the Masons Arms in Magdalene St.

❀ **Tintinhull** ST4919 TINTINHULL HOUSE GARDEN Colourful and attractive formal garden sheltered by walls and hedges, around 17th-c house with Queen Anne façade; teas, shop, disabled access; open pm Weds, Thurs, Sat and bank hols Apr-Sept; £3.20. NT.

❀ ✝ **Washford** ST0441 TROPIQUARIA Amazing transformation of a 1930s BBC transmitting station – now the main hall houses an indoor jungle with a 15-ft waterfall, tropical plants, free-flying birds and all sorts of weird and wonderful-looking animals. The more dangerous exhibits are caged, while local and tropical marine life can be found in the crypt. Outside are aviaries, landscaped gardens and an adventure playground, and there's also a puppet show; meals and snacks, shop, disabled access (exc to aquarium); cl all Dec and wkdys Nov, Jan and Feb; £3.25. CLEEVE ABBEY The gatehouse, dormitory and refectory of this 12th-c Cistercian Abbey are all in good condition, and there's a fine timbered roof, wall paintings and traceried windows. The rest of the complex of buildings is ruined; snacks, shop; cl 1-2 pm; *£1.70. The Notley Arms at Monksilver not far off is good for lunch.

Watchet ST0743 is a small working port, with fishing boats and coasters using its tidal harbour, and enough industry to keep it from being too touristy – though it's by no means unattractive.

West Bagborough ST1633 QUANTOCK POTTERY Traditional working pottery with demonstrations and shop; meals and snacks.

✝ Some of the CHURCHES in this area have very finely carved 15th- and 16th-c bench ends, their quality explained by the prosperity brought about by the wool trade. The most interesting are at Kingston St Mary ST2229 (a pretty village), Milverton ST1225 (where there's also a little pottery on the High St), Hatch Beauchamp ST3220 and Bishops Lydeard ST1629; the tourist board do a trail inc several more.

Other attractive villages in the area, all with decent pubs, include East Coker ST5412 (T S Eliot's ashes are buried here), North Perrott ST4709, Staple Fitzpaine ST2618, Stogumber ST0937, Wambrook ST2907 and Waterrow ST0425. Weston Zoyland ST3534 is also a pretty village. East Quantoxhead ST1343 with its archetypal duckpond, tiny church with fine oak carvings, and walks to the coast, is delightful; the Hood Arms over at Kilve is good for lunch.

Ilminster ST3514 is decidedly a town rather than a village, but for anyone who has developed a taste for Somerset's fine church towers it is worth a visit for its magnificent 15th-c specimen, all turrets, pinnacles and gargoyles.

Walks

In this region, only the **Quantocks** have anything substantial to offer the walker. The hills' secretive quality is illustrated by the dense broad-leafed woodlands on the northern side, where shady combes display splendid spring and autumn colours. The village of Holford ST1541 is a good starting point: the paths begin with helpful signposts, although you may soon get bemused by the complexity of the path junctions; Holford Combe ST1540 is reasonably easy to find, and a map will get you to the ancient hill-fort site capping Dowsborough ST1639, from where a moorland track leads gently north to Holford.

The less-wooded western slopes have some attractive valleys enclosed by plunging slopes, with tracks along the bottom: Bicknoller ST1139 is a good start point. The moorland tops are quite a different world, where ancient trackways lead past prehistoric cairns and burial mounds; Exmoor, the Bristol Channel, South Wales and the Mendips are in sight. The tiny road from Nether Stowey ST1939 to Crowcombe ST1336 crosses the ridge and gives easy access on to the moor.

Down towards the Blackdown Hills south of Taunton, the well-marked woodland walks around **Castle Neroche** ST2715, an isolated ruined Norman fortification with more the aspect now of a hill fort than a castle, are well worth it for the fine views at the top.

Driving

This area is full of little lanes winding quietly around without getting you anywhere very significant: you can stop almost anywhere and feel surrounded by peace. It's around the Quantocks that they give the greatest sense of exploration, and the most attractive views, particularly on the gentler slopes of the western side. The road up wooded Cockercombe from Nether Stowey seems to be taking you right into the unknown. In this same general area, there's a nice road running from Cannington on the A39 west of Bridgwater to Combwich, then round to Stogursey (worth a stop to look at the charming carved pew ends in the church), and then on to rejoin the A39 either at Nether Stowey or further on near Kilve.

The countryside of the Vale of Taunton is mostly rich well-hedged farmland, not so interesting for drivers; there are increasingly, more pastures, well broken-up by woodland, as you head westwards. The A358 south from Taunton looks attractive on the map, but this winding road carries quite a lot of heavy traffic, and is to be avoided if possible; the B3170 is a better alternative.

Inland, a quiet road with good views is the one forking off the B3170 past the Holman Clavel Inn (a useful stop), over Culmhead and the Blackdown Hills, to pass the Wellington Monument above Wellington itself.

Where to eat

Dowlish Wake ST3713 New Inn (0460) 52413 Neatly kept 17th-c stone pub with good-value basic snacks as well as a fuller à la carte menu inc Swiss specialities; decent range of drinks especially Perry's ciders – it's possible to visit the nearby 16th-c stone cider mill; no credit cards; children in family room; disabled access. **£20**|£1.25/£3.50.

Appley ST0621 Globe (0823) 672327 Unspoilt 15th-c pub with generous helpings of delicious food inc adventurous daily specials and vegetarian meals, gorgeous puddings; cl Mon lunch exc bank hols; limited disabled access. **£17**|£1.25/£7.

Haselbury Plucknett ST4711 Haselbury Inn (0460) 72488 Popular and inviting pub with very wide choice of food inc all-day brunch and ten daily specials. **£14.70**|£3.15/£5.25.

Monksilver ST0737 Notley Arms (0984) 56217 Relaxed and friendly, with popular food that includes imaginative vegetarian dishes, wonderful puddings and good home-made pasta; neat garden runs down to small stream; cl 25 Dec, 1st 2 wks Feb; limited disabled access. **£14**|£1.60/£3.95.

Langley Marsh ST0729 Three Horseshoes (0784) 23763 Popular red sandstone pub with imaginative, daily-changing food; vegetables from the pub's garden, no chips; children must be well behaved; disabled access. **£10**|£1.50/£4.

Help this year from: *M G Hart, Pat and John Millward, Hazel Morgan, Joan Olivier, Dr and Mrs A K Clarke, Margaret and Douglas Tucker, Judith Chegwidden, J Ferguson, Roger and Judy Tame, Phil and Heidi Cook, Richard Chew, Beryl and Bill Farmer, Y Cotterill, Andrew Latchem, Helen Reed, Veronica Purcocks, KC, J R Williams, Bob and Maggie Atherton, M D Green, Barry and Anne, Patrick Godfrey, E C Daniels, Richard Dolphin, Clive Waldron, Adrian Pitts, Gwen and Peter Andrews, Mr and Mrs A E McCully, C E T Smith, Maj D A Daniels, Chris and Sue Heathman, Michael and Alison Sandy, John Boylan, Nan and David Johnson, Barbara Hatfield, R Shelton, Joy Heatherley, Alastair Campbell, Steve and Carolyn Harvey, Mrs S H Richards, T H G Lewis, M D Green, Tony Gayfer, J Gowers, Mike Walters, Margaret Drazin, Maj and Mrs J A Gardner, K R Harris.*

We welcome reports from readers . . .

This Guide depends on readers' reports. Do help us if you can – in return, we offer a discount on the next edition to people who've helped us with reports for it. Tell us what you think about places already in it, and anything extra you think we should say about them. And send us your ideas for inclusion in the next edition: places to visit, eat at or stay in, attractive drives or walks, maybe even unusual interesting shops you know of. Use the card in the middle, the report forms at the end, or just write – no stamp needed: The Good Weekend Guide, FREEPOST TN1569, Wadhurst, E Sussex TN5 7BR.

SOMERSET AND AVON CALENDAR

Some of these dates were provisional as we went to press.

JANUARY

17th **Carhampton** Wassailing the Apple Trees *(the old Twelfth Night). Locals gather round one of the largest trees in the cider orchard to beat it and sing an incantation: 'Old apple tree, old apple tree, we've come to wassail thee'; cider-soaked toast left in the tree, cider poured on its roots, shots fired through the branches creating a din to drive away evil spirits which might harm the crop*

MARCH

5th **Bath** Competitive Festival *for children and adults, literary competitions, speech, drama and music – till Sat 19*

APRIL

4th **Yeovil** Easter-bunny Road Race

9th **Taunton** Arts and Crafts Fayre *at County Hotel*

23rd **Rode** Railway Weekend *at Tropical Bird Gardens – till Sun 24*

30th **Bath** Spring Flower Show, *marquees, bands, Morris dancing and crèche facilities – till 2 May*; **Bridgwater** Arts and Crafts Fayre *at Town Hall*; **Minehead** Hobby Horse Parade: *horse (maybe originally to scare away Danish invaders) made of painted canvas, with ribbons and a long tail, goes through the streets accompanied by musicians; 'bootee' on last day with dancing in the streets – till 2 May; also* Spring Steam *at West Somerset Railway Station – till 1 May*

MAY

1st **Horsington** Jack-in-the-Green Festival, *traditional festival with Morris men*

5th **Badminton** Horse Trials, *3-day event at Badminton House – till Sun 8*

6th **Cheddar** May Fair and Folk Festival *– till Sun 8*

7th **Minehead** D-Day Preparation Weekend *at West Somerset Railway Station, with military vehicles – till Sun 8*

8th **Cricket St Thomas** Custom and American Car Show *at Wildlife and Leisure Park, nr Chard*

14th **Taunton** Arts and Crafts Fayre *at County Hotel*

26th **Yeovil** Floral Society Show *at Octagon theatre*

27th **Bath** International Festival of Classical Music, Jazz and the Visual Arts *– till 12 Jun*

29th **Cricket St Thomas** Heavy Horse Show *at Wildlife and Leisure Park;* **Watchet** May Fair

JUNE

1st **Shepton Mallet** Agricultural Show *at Royal Bath and West Showground – till Sun 4*

4th **Bridgwater** Arts and Crafts Fayre *at Town Hall*

11th **Shepton Mallet** Collett Day Festival

12th **Bristol** to Bournemouth Vintage Vehicle Run *to Bournemouth; starts Ashton Court Estate*

Somerset and Avon Calendar

June cont.

13th **Burnham-on-Sea** South West Counties Amateur Golf Championships *at Burnham and Berrow golf club – till Sat 18*

18th **Chiselborough** Church Flower Festival, *afternoons – till Mon 20*

20th **Montacute** Carnival Week *with procession on Sat evening – till Sat 25*

24th **Pilton** Glastonbury Music Festival *at Worthy Farm – till Sun 26*

25th **Cricket St Thomas** Wessex Game Fair *at Wildlife and Leisure Park – till Sun 26*; **Glastonbury** Church of England Pilgrimage *at the Abbey; Roman Catholic pilgrimage on Sun 26*

July

2nd **Bath** 'Recent British Sculpture' *at Victoria Art Gallery, a touring exhibition from the South Bank Centre – till 13 Aug*

3rd **Watchet** Carnival

8th **Somerton** Summer Arts Festival, *music, drama, talks and exhibitions – till Fri 15*

9th **Bristol** Steam Weekend – *till Sun 10*; **Montacute** Horse Trials – *till Sun 10*; **Wincanton** Steam and Country Fair – *till Sun 10*

10th **Cricket St Thomas** Classic Car Day *at Wildlife and Leisure Park*

16th **RNAS Yeovilton** International Air Day; **Rode** Clematis Weekend *at Tropical Bird Gardens: questions answered and demos by British Clematis Society – till Sun 17*

23rd **Long Ashton** Bristol Community Festival *at Ashton Court Estate, rock, jazz, folk, classical, theatre and arts, 150 stalls – till Sun 24*; **Weston super Mare** Carnival and Fun Day *at Beach Lawns, helicopter fly-in and display, pleasure flights, stalls and entertainment – till Sun 24*

30th **East Huntspill** Secret World *at New Road Farm; steam rally, classic cars, crafts and fair – till Sun 31*; **King Weston** Somerton Horse Show and Exemption Dog Show; **Three Bridges** Craft and Cider Country Fayre – *till Sun 31*; **Wambrook** Flower Show

August

6th **Bishops Lydeard** Traction Rally – *till Sun 7*; **Bristol** Harbour Regatta and Fireworks – *till Sun 7*; **Dunster** Flower Show

13th **Clapton** Wayford and District Horticultural Show; **Yeovil** Festival of Transport – *till Sun 14*

20th **Frome** St Catherines Medieval Fayre; **Shepton Mallet** Mid-Somerset Show; **Whitchurch** Bristol Festival of Transport *at Hengrove Park – till Sun 21*

26th **Glastonbury** Children's Festival, *performances and participation events – till Mon 29*

28th **Bristol** Avon Rowing Regatta

29th **Hunters Bridge to Yeovilton Weir** Raft Race; **Watchet** Summer Fair; **Yeovil** Games

Somerset and Avon Calendar

September

3rd **Shepton Mallet** Countryside Cavalcade, *inc heavy horses, crafts, vintage cars and carriage driving – till Sun 4*

9th **Long Ashton** International Balloon Fiesta: *150 balloons, crafts, fair, live music, arena events – till Sun 11*

17th **Bridgwater** Arts and Crafts Fayre *at Town Hall*; **Minehead** Steam Weekend *at West Somerset Railway Station – till Sun 18*; **Rode** Steam Attractions Weekend *at Tropical Bird Gardens – till Sun 18*

21st **Frome** Cheese Show

24th **Frome** Illuminated Carnival; **Wellington** Carnival

28th **Bridgwater** St Matthew's Fair, *since 1400, first day farmers' day – till 1 Oct*

October

1st **Ilminster** Carnival Procession, *illuminated floats and bands*; **Weston super Mare** Speed Trials and Vintage Sprint – *till Sun 2*

8th **Taunton** Arts and Craft Fair *at County Hotel*

15th **Taunton** Illuminated Carnival and Cider Barrel Rolling Race

22nd **Minehead** Friends of Thomas the Tank Engine *at West Somerset Railway Station – till Sun 23*

24th **Bath** Antique and Fine Art Fair *at the Assembly Rooms – till Sun 30*

27th **Hinton St George** Punkie Night – *lanterns made from hollowed mangel-wurzels carried by children from house to house*

29th **Minehead** Diesel Weekend *at West Somerset Railway Station – till Sun 30*

November

3rd **Bridgwater** Guy Fawkes Carnival – *procession of over 80 brilliantly lit floats; 10 pm 'squibbing display', long hand-held fire-fountain poles*

4th **Bridgwater** Arts and Crafts Fair *at Town Hall – till Sat 5*

5th **Dunster** Firework Display *at Dunster Castle*; **Durdham Downs** Firework Fiesta; **North Petherton** Guy Fawkes Illuminated Procession

7th **Burnham-on-Sea** Illuminated Procession

9th **Shepton Mallet** Illuminated Procession

11th **Wells** Illuminated Procession

12th **Glastonbury** Illuminated Procession

14th **Weston super Mare** Illuminated Procession, *bands and balloons*

December

3rd **Taunton** Arts and Crafts Fayre *at County Hotel*

10th **Bridgwater** Arts and Crafts Fayre *at Town Hall*

24th **Dunster** Burning the Ash Faggot *at 10 pm at the Luttrell Arms, cider served – ceremony dates from witchcraft days*

SUFFOLK

Suffolk is good for a short break, with largely unspoilt seaside scenery along the coast, delightful villages in the interior, quite a lot of interesting things to see and do, and pleasant places to stay in. The countryside is not spectacular but has a gentle charm, underlined by some delightful colour-washed and timbered farmhouses and other buildings.

It's not a particularly cheap county, but the budget is helped by the fact that so many of the area's pubs do decent food in pleasant surroundings, and at sensible prices.

Whichever area you are in, the Museum of East Anglian Life at Stowmarket, described in the West Suffolk section but centrally placed for all three areas, is well worth a visit.

SOUTH SUFFOLK

An area of low-key appeal, with harmonious ancient village buildings and some houses and gardens worth a visit.

This area's quiet attraction is summed up in the four classic English villages, fairly close to one another, which draw visitors from all over the world for their charming ancient buildings, very picturesque with the subtle colours of their timbered plasterwork. Long Melford, Lavenham, Cavendish and Clare are all pleasant places to potter about in. The first two in particular have plenty of places to visit, besides the antique and craft shops which have come on the heels of the visitors (many of the larger villages all over the region have antique shops).

Constable country, along the border with Essex, is also a lure for visitors, with East Bergholt its centre; very pretty indeed. Elsewhere, Ickworth at Horringer is the most interesting place to visit, and there are several attractive gardens in the area. It's not a good place for determined walkers, but there is a decent choice of places to stay.

Where to stay

Lavenham TL9149 SWAN High St CO10 9QA (0787) 247477) **£127.90**; 47 rms. Handsome and comfortable Elizabethan hotel with a pubby little bar, lots of cosy seating areas and alcoves with beams, timbers, armchairs and settees; lavishly timbered restaurant, bar food, afternoon teas, and good evening meals, and friendly, helpful staff. Children free in parents' room (pay for meals only).

Long Melford TL8645 BULL Hall St CO10 9JG **£102**; 25 rms, ancient or comfortably modern. An inn since 1580, this fine black-and-white building was originally a medieval manorial hall; handsome and interesting stripped woodwork and timbering, large log fire, old-fashioned and antique furnishings, decent food, and pleasant, friendly service; beautiful village.

Hintlesham TM0843 HINTLESHAM HALL Ipswich IP8 3NS (047 387) 334 **£97**; 33 thoughtfully furnished rms. Elegantly furnished, mainly Georgian house with antiques, books and comfortable seating, and very good cooking; 18-hole golf course, outdoor heated swimming pool, tennis court, pool, snooker, sauna and steam room.

Ipswich TM1744 MARLBOROUGH Henley Rd IP1 3SP (0473) 257677 **£65**; 22 rms. Comfortable, very well-run Victorian hotel with attractive public rooms and imaginative restaurant food; disabled access.

Stoke-by-Nayland TL9836 ANGEL Colchester CO6 4SA (0206) 263245 **£55**; 6 rms. Elegant dining pub in Stour Valley, busy but relaxed; Tudor beams in cosy bar, decent wines, and imaginative and reasonably priced bar food; cl 25-26 Dec, 1 Jan; children over 10.

Bildeston TL9949 CROWN Ipswich IP7 7EB (0449) 740510 **£55**; 15 rms. Reputedly haunted Tudor inn, with welcoming, courteous service, good food, comfortable, well-furnished lounge, open fire, and busy restaurant; cl 25 Dec pm; disabled access.

Needham Market TM0855 PIPPS FORD Norwich Rd Ipswich IP6 8LJ (0449) 79208 **£53**; 6 pretty rms with antiques and fine old beds; 4 rms in converted Stables cottage. Lovely 16th-c farmhouse in quiet garden with log fires in big inglenook fireplaces and good, imaginative food served in conservatory with subtropical plants; home-baked bread, home-produced ham and pork and own honey, eggs, and preserves with organically home-grown veg and herbs; surrounded by farmland and set on beautiful stretch of River Gipping; cl Christmas/New Year; babies and children over 5 welcome.

Lavenham TL9149 ANGEL CO10 9QZ (0787) 247388 **£50**; 7 well-equipped rms. 15th-c inn in the heart of an excellently preserved medieval town; still has original cellar and pargeted ceiling; civilised atmosphere, very good food, lots of decent wines, and good for families; cl 25 Dec; disabled access.

Chelsworth TL9848 PEACOCK The Street IP7 7HU (0449) 740758 **£40**; 5 rms, share bthrm. Elegantly restored 14th-c inn with plenty of exposed Tudor brickwork and timbers, close to Chelsworth Hall, craft shop behind, friendly service, and decent bar food; no credit cards.

Lawshall TL8654 BRIGHTHOUSE FARM Melford Rd Bury St Edmunds IP29 4PX (0284) 830385 **£40**; 4 rms. Homely B & B in timbered Georgian farmhouse with log fires, lounge and games room; self-catering and camping also.

Cavendish TL8046 GEORGE High St CO10 8BA (0787) 280248 **£35**; 2 rms. Picturesque setting, well-presented, reasonably priced food, pleasant atmosphere, good service, and jazz Tues; cl 24-25 Dec, children over 12 only.

Hintlesham TM0843 COLLEGE FARM Ipswich IP8 3NT (0473) 652253 **£35**; 3 rms. Late 15th-c house on farm with neat garden, comfortably furnished rooms, lots of beams, log fire in inglenook fireplace, and friendly owners; no pets; walks around the farm (beef and arable), and riding and golf nearby; cl Christmas and New Year; children over 5.

To see and do

✝ 🐄 🏛 **Cavendish** TL8046 is a lovely sight, its green framed by colourfully plastered timbered houses with behind them the tower of the attractive MEDIEVAL CHURCH. CAVENDISH MANOR VINEYARDS AND NETHER

HALL A 15th-c manor house nicely surrounded by vineyards; the house has paintings and interesting old exhibits, and there are tours and tastings in the vineyard. Shop; cl 25 Dec; *£2.50. Nearby PENTLOW FARM is a children's farm with lots of baby animals – unusually, it's free; open pm Sun and bank hols Mar-Aug.

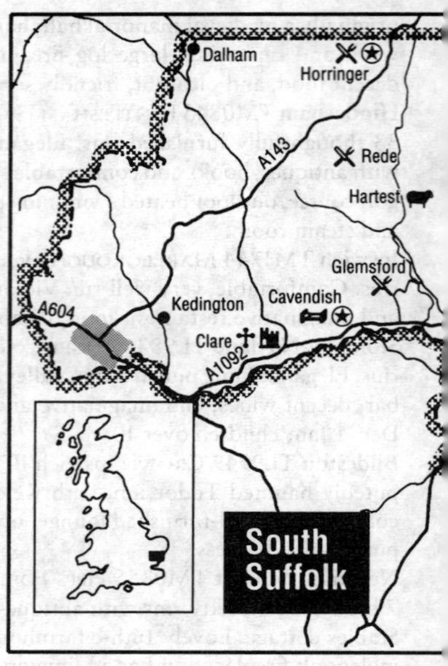

Clare TL7645 is another of the area's charming timber-and-plaster villages, with a huge CHURCH, the sketchy ruins of a CASTLE on a former Iron-Age earthwork above the River Stour, and some remains of a 13th-c Augustinian priory; nature trails around the castle. There's a three-storey antiques warehouse, and the Bell is good for lunch.

East Bergholt TM0734 BRIDGE COTTAGE, FLATFORD A 17th-c cottage near the mill immortalised by Constable. Inside is a good interpretative centre for his paintings, with information on those which had a local theme; teas; cl Mon, Tues, Nov-Easter. You can hire ROWING BOATS for trips along the River Stour – very relaxing if you can persuade someone else to man the oars. The mill itself and its famous partner Willy Lott's House are both owned by the National Trust and leased by them to the Field Studies Council, which runs arts courses here – tel (0206) 298283. The Kings Head nearby is attractive for lunch, and the CHURCH with its uncompleted tower has a unique 16th-c timber-framed bell cage.

Hartest TL8352 GIFFORDS HALL 33 acres with vineyard and winery, wild-flower meadows, rare breeds of sheep and domestic fowls, and a rose garden. It's perhaps best known among gardeners for its sweet peas, and they have a Rose and Sweet Pea Festival the last weekend in Jun; snacks, shop, disabled access; cl am, and Nov-Easter; £1.25-2.75, depending on season. The Crown is a pleasant place for lunch.

Hintlesham TM0843 HILLSIDE NURSERIES Farm shop with organically grown veg, pick-your-own, plant sales; cl Sun, Mon. Hintlesham Hall does marvellous lunches (see Where to stay, above); on a humbler level, the George here is good.

Horringer TL8261 ICKWORTH A very untypical stately home, a 100-ft-high oval rotunda with two curved corridors filled with a fascinating art collection and other treasures: fine furniture, porcelain, pictures by Gainsborough amongst others, and an exceptional collection of Georgian silver. The gardens have fine trees and a deer enclosure; meals, snacks, shop; house cl am, all day Mon (exc bank hols) and Thurs, Nov-Mar (exc shop and restaurant open wknds to Christmas), park open all year; £4.30, the park on its own is free. NT. The village is attractive, and the Beehive is good for lunch.

Ipswich TM1644 A regional centre since the Stone Age, Ipswich flourished as a port sending cloth to the continent after King John granted it a charter in the 13th c. It's too busy to compete with other places

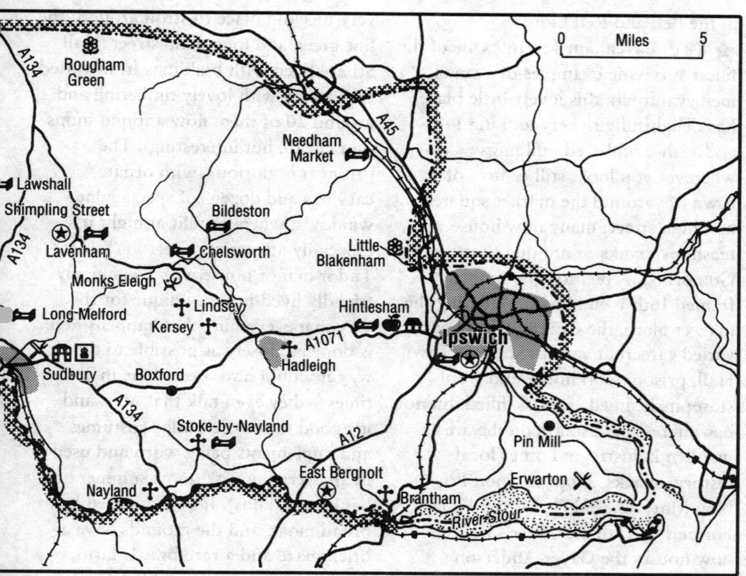

here as a base for a short holiday, but has quite a few things to look at on briefer visits (the traffic makes getting in and out rather slow). Cardinal Wolsey set up a college here, but all that remains is the 16th-c GATEHOUSE in College St. The Ancient House in the Butter Market (now a bookshop) has some 15th-c carvings and exceptionally neat pargeting. CHRISTCHURCH MANSION (Soane St) The original 16th-c house was altered in the following century after a fire, but since then it's escaped any further redevelopment. The rooms are furnished in period style, with a Victorian wing inc servants' quarters, and the Suffolk Artists' Gallery has the best collection of works by Constable and Gainsborough outside London, all set in a pleasant park. Shop, disabled access to ground floor only; cl Sun am, Mon, 24-26 Dec, 1 Jan, Good Fri. Attached is the Wolsey Art Gallery, with various changing exhibitions. IPSWICH MUSEUM (High St) Local history and archaeology from prehistoric to medieval times, with a special emphasis on Roman Suffolk; also a natural history gallery. Shop, disabled access to ground floor only; cl Sun, Mon, 24-26 Dec, 1 Jan, Good Fri. TOLLY COBBOLD BREWERY (Cliff Rd) Striking waterside Victorian brewery, with tours taking in the whole brewing process. They've got some particularly interesting old equipment, inc a Victorian steam engine, and there are beer tastings in the Brewery Tap (which functions as a separate pub, with decent meals and snacks); shop; tours at 11.30 am and 2.30 pm daily exc 25 Dec; £2.75. Dotted about the town are several attractive medieval CHURCHES, especially the 15th-c St Margaret's; St Mary at the Elms has the town's oldest cottages behind it. If you're there on a winter's night five medieval churches are nicely floodlit. The port is quite busy.

✝ Kersey TL9944 is a very pretty village, full of timbering and attractive and colourful plasterwork, running from the fine 14th-c CHURCH down to a ford with ducks, and up again; craft and antique shops, and decent lunches at the Bell and Red Lion.

★ **Lavenham** TL9149 One of the finest surviving examples of a small medieval town, this lovely little place has delightfully rickety-looking 14th- and 15th-c timbered buildings wherever you look, still centres of town life around the market square and high street; many now house teashops, banks or antique shops. GUILDHALL A picturesque timber-framed 16th-c building dominating the market place, the Guildhall has had a varied career, at various stages a Town Hall, prison, workhouse and wool store; its beamed and oak-filled interior has interesting displays on the area's woollen industry and other local history; snacks, shop; cl Good Fri, Nov-Mar; £2.30. NT. LITTLE HALL Formerly a 15th-c clothier's house, now houses the Gayer-Anderson collection of books, pictures and antiques, and has a pleasant enclosed garden; cl am, Mon (exc bank hols), Tues, Fri, all Nov-Easter; £1. THE PRIORY Very well-restored Benedictine house with interesting drawings and Elizabethan wall-paintings, fascinating stained glass by Ervin Bossanyi, and a uniquely designed herb garden; meals, snacks, shop; cl Nov-Easter; *£2.50. The old wool hall has been incorporated into the Swan Hotel, itself well worth seeing. Both it (at a price) and the Angel are good for lunch.

✝ **Lindsey** TL9745 ST JAMES'S CHAPEL Charming little thatched flint and stone chapel, built some time during the 13th c but inc some earlier work too. The Red Rose in nearby Lindsey Tye is useful for lunch.

Little Blakenham TM1048 BLAKENHAM WOODLAND GARDEN Woodland garden richly planted with camellias, rhododendrons, magnolias and the like; lovely in May when the bluebells are out too; open pm Weds, Thurs, Sun and bank hols Apr-Sept; £1.

✝ **Long Melford** TL8645 A very nice old place to stroll around: the fine green and long main street (Hall St) are lined with buildings from varied eras, many with lovely timbering and around 20 of them now antique shops (not cheap, but interesting). The CHURCH is glorious, with ornate carvings and dozens of spectacular windows; when floodlit at night it's especially attractive. KENTWELL HALL Tudor manor house with a genuinely friendly lived-in feel, unique for the way that everything that happens here is done as closely as possible to the way it would have been done in Tudor times – they even talk that way, and it's good to see the Tudor costumes and implements being worn and used in an everyday way (most summer and bank hol wknds). It's surrounded by a broad moat, and the grounds have a brick maze and a rare-breeds farm; meals, snacks, shop, disabled access; open Sun Apr-Sept, daily Easter wk and mid-July-Sept; *£4, more on costumed days. MELFORD HALL Mostly unchanged since Elizabeth I (with a retinue of 500, and 1,500 servants) stayed here in 1578, this turreted Tudor house still has its original panelled banqueting hall; also worth a look are the later drawing room, library and bedrooms. Displays include a collection of Chinese porcelain, and a series of exhibits relating to Beatrix Potter, who was related to the owners and often stayed here; the gardens have a Tudor pavilion. Some disabled access; open Sat and Sun pm end of Mar-Oct and Weds and Thurs pm May-Sept; *£2.60. NT. The Bull Hotel, one of the finer old buildings here, does good light lunches; the Green Dragon and at the end of the truly long village the Hare are also useful for food.

Monks Eleigh TL9647 CORN CRAFT Demonstrations – by appointment, tel (0449) 740456 – and displays of traditional corn dollies and their production, and in Aug and Sept you can walk through the fields and pick the flowers; snacks, big shop, disabled access. The Swan Hotel is good for lunch.

Pin Mill TM2037 below the wooded slopes by the River Orwell has Thames barges on tidal moorings, and is a nice spot; the Butt & Oyster here is attractively placed for a bite to eat.

❀ **Rougham Green** TL9061
NETHERFIELD COTTAGE (towards Hessett) shows that you don't have to have a massive garden to make it very special indeed: hundreds of different herbs, beautifully yet sensibly grouped by how you'd use them, with two small knot gardens.

✝ **Stoke by Nayland** TL9836 has a lovely 15th-c CHURCH with a very familiar-looking tower, and several handsome Tudor buildings; the Angel is very good for lunch, but get there early.

Sudbury TL8741
GAINSBOROUGH'S HOUSE The famous painter was born here in 1727, and the house has a collection of work by him and his contemporaries. There's plenty of period furniture and china too, with displays of contemporary arts and crafts; shop; cl Sun am, Mon (exc pm bank hols), Good Fri; *£2. This is a pleasant market town (good Saturday market stalls); the Waggon & Horses is good value for lunch.

✝ Apart from the places already mentioned, lots of villages have Constable and Gainsborough connections, as both were raised in the area. Constable painted altarpieces for the churches at Brantham TM1034 and Nayland TL9734, and often painted the church at Stoke by Nayland TL9836, while Gainsborough painted the church at Hadleigh TM0242 (which has some other striking old buildings and a woodland RSPB reserve nearby). There are also nice churches at Kedington TL7046 (Saxon crucifix) and Needham Market TM0855, where the marvellous hammer-beam roof has been described as 'a whole church seemingly in the air'.

★ **Other attractive villages** in the area, all with decent pubs, include Boxford TL9640, Chelsworth TL9848, Dalham TL7261 and Shimpling Street TL8752.

Walks

The views immortalised by Constable make the walk from **East Bergholt** TM0734 along the water-meadows by the Stour East Anglia's most famous walk – picturesque and well worth while, though there is no real point in leaving the path to make a circular route. Elsewhere, unfortunately, the Stour Valley's attractive villages don't quite compensate for the humdrum scenery in between, and although it is possible to find field paths, it's difficult to work these into circular walks.

Shotley Gate TM2433, at the meeting of the Stour and Orwell estuaries, is at the hub of a rewarding walk that follows the two rivers, with good views across to Harwich and its shipping. Start inland at Shotley TM2335 and cross the fields either north to the Orwell or south to the Stour, then follow the waterside. Another fine stretch of the broad Stour estuary can be enjoyed just south of **Stutton** TM1534.

Driving

The classic drive is the back road between Long Melford and Lavenham, and then the A1092 along to Cavendish and Clare, linking these four lovely villages.

The back roads in the triangle between these and the A143 and A134 up to Bury St Edmunds all give plenty of pleasing views of colourwashed old houses, generally set close enough to the road to enjoy.

In the opposite direction, the A1141 E of Lavenham through Monks Eleigh, and then the B1115 through Chelsworth and Bildeston to Hitcham, are attractive, as is the back road through Buxhall and Rattlesden to Woolpit.

Where to eat

Sudbury TL8741 MABEYS BRASSERIE 47 Gainsborough St (0787) 74298 Simple restaurant with very good cooking using first-class ingredients; relaxed atmosphere, friendly service, and good wine list; cl Sun, Mon (inc bank hols), 25-26 Dec. **£21**|*£5.20*.

Rede TL8055 PLOUGH (028 489) 208 Welcoming, partly thatched cottage in lovely spot, lots of fresh fish and game in season, imaginative daily specials, and good evening restaurant; no food Sun pm. **£16**|*£5.95*.

Horringer TL8261 BEEHIVE (0284) 735260 Pretty ivy-covered pub with friendly atmosphere and good, often adventurous bar meals; no food Sun pm; disabled access. **£15**|*£1.85/£5.95*.

Glemsford TL8247 BLACK LION (0787) 280684 Wide choice of very good food cooked by the obliging young landlord's German wife; pleasant bar, good service, small restaurant; cl Sun pm, 25 Dec pm. **£13.65**|*£1.20/£5*.

Erwarton TM2134 QUEENS HEAD (0473) 787550 Remote and unspoilt little pub with homely atmosphere, lovely views, good well-priced bar food inc fresh fish and game in season. *£1.95/£5*.

EAST SUFFOLK

A good place for quiet breaks, East Suffolk has an unspoilt interesting coast, pleasant small towns and villages and attractive places to visit.

This area has a lot of appeal for quiet breaks, with a largely unspoilt coast giving wide sea and skyscapes that most would say constitute Suffolk's loveliest scenery, and plenty for nature-lovers. Even in summer you can walk for miles along fairly empty beaches and coast. Southwold, Walberswick, Aldeburgh and Orford are all relatively unspoilt, very pleasant for anyone wanting to be by the sea without being too seasidey.

Inland there are attractive villages and small towns, with prettily timbered and plastered buildings (though not so many as you'll find in the southern part of the county), and a fair number of antique shops. Interesting places to visit include the farm park at Easton, Helmingham Hall, Framlingham Castle and the wildlife park at Kessingland; there are several things in the area that children like. Lowestoft, England's busiest fishing port, doubles as a summer beach and boating resort, and has plenty to do.

Where to stay

Framlingham TM2863 CROWN Woodbridge IP13 9AN (0728) 723521 **£102.90**; 13 comfortable rms. Bustling and friendly little black-and-white Tudor coaching inn with comfortable lounge and open fire, cosy bar with heavy beams and log fire, attractive small courtyard with winter-flowering cherry, decent food (also bar meals), and friendly, helpful staff. A Forte hotel, though pleasantly individual and old-fashioned.

Woodbridge TM2749 SECKFORD HALL IP13 6NU (0394) 385678 ***£99**; 34 rms. Handsome Tudor mansion with beams, flagstones, big fireplaces, comfortable panelled lounge with antiques, cosy bar, good food and service, and 32 acres of gardens and parkland with trout-filled lake; indoor heated pool, gym, 18-hole pay-and-play golf; cl 25 Dec; disabled access.

Southwold TM5076 SWAN Market Place IP18 6EG (0502) 722186 ***£81**; 45 rms. 17th-c inn with comfortable, airy front lounge, good food, well-kept real ales, decent wines, ambitious restaurant, and efficient staff; children over 5 in evening restaurant.

Aldeburgh TM4656 WHITE LION Market Cross IP15 5BJ (0728) 452720 **£75**; 38 rms, some with sea view. Popular, rather smart family-run hotel on the sea-front with good bar and restaurant food.

Brome TM1376 OAKSMERE Eye IP23 8AJ (0379) 870326 **£74.50**; 11 rms. Warmly friendly, partly 16th-c hotel with bustling bar, lovely restaurant, good food, conservatory, and neatly kept gardens.

Westleton TM4469 CROWN Saxmundham IP17 3AD (072 873) 777 **£67.50**; 19 rms, some with jacuzzis. Very comfortable inn in excellent walking country near Minsemere bird reserve, pretty landscaped garden and floodlit terrace, smart no-smoking dining area, good restaurant food, decent wines.

Halesworth TM3877 ANGEL IP19 8AH (0986) 873365 ***£60**; 7 rms. 16th-c hotel carefully refurbished in keeping with the building, decent bar and restaurant food, and good, friendly service.

Southwold TM5076 CROWN High St IP18 6DP (0502) 722275 **£57**; 12 rms, 2 with shared bthrm. Outstanding old pub in centre of town; smart but relaxed, elegant main bar; excellent, imaginative food in bar and no-smoking restaurant; lots of wines, properly kept, by the glass, and friendly, helpful staff; cl 1 wk Jan.

Beccles TM4290 WAVENEY HOUSE NR34 9LP (0502) 712270 **£55**; 13 rms. Pleasant, well-kept riverside inn with own moorings and decent food; cl 24-27 Dec, 31 Dec-2 Jan.

Lowestoft TM5492 BAYFIELDS 159 High St NR32 1HU (0502) 568617 ***£50**; 10 rms. Pleasant hotel within walking distance of town and beach with good value fresh fish straight from the market.

Campsea Ashe TM3255 OLD RECTORY Woodbridge IP3 0PU (0728) 746524 **£45**; 6 comfortable and pretty rms. This is more of a restaurant with bedrooms: very relaxed and informal 17th-c house with lovely food – there's no menu so you have to give some choices when booking; cl Christmas.

Great Glemham TM3361 CROWN Saxmundham IP17 2DA (072 878) 693 **£35**; 3 rms. Welcoming and pleasantly placed old brick house, neat garden, decent wines, and imaginative bar food.

To see and do

★ **Aldeburgh** TM4656 Fishing village with quaint little streets running down to the shingle beach where the fishermen still haul in and sell their catch; quite touristy, especially at Festival time, but not at all garishly so. MOOT HALL MUSEUM 16th-c brick and timber Moot Hall with an outside staircase leading up to the Council Chamber displaying old maps and other items of local history, with an emphasis on maritime history and coastal erosion. There are items from the Snape Anglo-Saxon ship burial; cl am Sun and every day in Sept, wkdys and Sat Apr-Jun, all Oct-Easter; 40p. The attractively placed Cross Keys is good for lunch, and there's an RSPB reserve just north at North Warren.

Aldringham TM4461 CRAFT MARKET Three galleries with extensive stocks of locally made crafts and fine art; teas, disabled access; cl 12-2 pm Sun (and all day in winter), 25-28 Dec, 1 Jan. The Parrot & Punchbowl is useful for lunch.

Ashbocking TM1654 JAMES WHITE Cider brewery recently moved from nearby Brandeston; cider and apple juice making and tasting, and pick your own in season. Snacks, shop, disabled access; shop open all year, production viewing wkdys Jun-Sept.

Beccles TM4289 WILLIAM CLOWES PRINT MUSEUM Interesting museum illustrating the development of printing from 1800 onwards, with a wide range of machinery, woodcuts and books; open 2-4.30 pm Mon-Fri in Jun, July and Aug, or other times by appointment on (0502) 712884. Down the same road there's a good local history museum; open pm Sun, plus Weds and Sat in Apr-Oct. The Kings Head Hotel is useful for lunch.

Bungay TM3389 Ruins of Norman CASTLE right in the centre of this little market town, with twin towers and massive flint walls. Bungay straddles the border with Norfolk, and we've described the nearby Otter Trust in our Norfolk chapter, under Earsham. The Green Dragon is useful for lunch.

Butley TM3650 BUTLEY POTTERY Working pottery showroom, with shop, tearoom and restaurant; cl 25 Dec, restaurant and tearoom cl Christmas-Mar. The Oyster Bar is good for lunch – and does have local oysters. South of here by the quiet back road to Capel St Andrew are the remains of a medieval abbey gatehouse.

† **Debenham** TM1763 is an attractive village with a fine partly Saxon CHURCH, and a POTTERY (Carters Ceramics, Low Rd; cl lunch and Sun – best to tel first (0728) 860475).

Dunwich TM4770 is slipping slowly beneath the waves; most of what was once quite a sizeable town is now under the sea, and there's a tale that on quiet nights, when there's a swell running after a previous storm, you can hear the bells of one of the submerged churches tolling. There are some fragmentary ruins of a friary, but more interesting is the MUSEUM on the subject of the village's gradual erosion. Excellent coastal walks along the cliffs, beaches and heathland of DUNWICH HEATH, which has an NT tearoom. The Ship is good for lunch, as are the Flora Tearooms.

Easton TM2858 EASTON FARM PARK There is plenty to see at this farm park which deftly combines learning with a fun and friendly approach. There are demonstrations of milking and other operations at the Victorian dairy set up by the Duke of Hamilton – and in the more modern version alongside – as well as animals and rare breeds to feed, a display on food production, a working blacksmith, adventure playground, nature trails and other exhibitions. Meals, snacks, shop, disabled access; cl Oct-mid Mar; *£3.70. The White Horse is good for lunch.

Felixstowe TM3034 LANDGUARD FORT AND MUSEUM Early 18th-c coastal-defence fort, with displays of its history and an explanation of how the other forts in the area (several of which can also still be seen) linked in; also materials from RAF and HMS *Beehive*. Shop, disabled access; open pm Weds, Thurs and Sun end of May-Sept; 30p. The town has quite a busy port, with a ferry (passengers, not cars) across to Harwich, and thanks to its beaches and relatively dry climate has developed into a popular low-price family resort. Along the coast north of the town, past another Martello Tower, golf course and quiet sand dunes, is the gently attractive and altogether quieter little settlement of FELIXSTOWE FERRY, with another foot-ferry across the estuary of the River Deben.

Flixton TM3186 NORFOLK AND SUFFOLK AVIATION MUSEUM Aircraft and related items from the Wright Brothers to the present day, with aeroplanes displayed outside and in the Blister Hangar; shop, disabled access; open Sun and bank hols Easter-Oct, plus some Weds and Thurs eves in July and Aug.

Framlingham TM2863 CASTLE This 12th-c castle was the place where Mary I heard that she had become Queen. Unusually the entire curtain wall has survived, and there are also 13 towers, some 17th-c almshouses and an array of Tudor chimneys; good views, and an interesting museum. Shop, disabled access to ground floor only; cl Mon Oct-Mar, cl 25-26 Dec, 1 Jan; £1.70, museum 30p extra. The CHURCH has an excellent hammer-beamed roof. The town's sloping market square is quite attractive, and the Crown at its head is useful for lunch, as is the Castle Inn.

Helmingham TM1957 HELMINGHAM HALL GARDENS The beautiful gardens here are still much as they were in Tudor times, and in the 500 years since have never fallen into disrepair. They stand around a grand battlemented house, very harmonious, based on an attractive Tudor core and carefully adapted over the centuries; it's ringed by a moat, over which the drawbridge is still raised each night. There's also an extensive deer park with magnificent old oak trees, and Highland cattle and Soay sheep as well as the hundreds of red and fallow deer; Constable painted a number of views of the woodlands – it is a pretty spot. Cream teas, shop (inc Helmingham produce), disabled access; open (gardens only) Sun pm 2 May-12 Sept; *£2.50.

Horham TM2072 The CHURCHYARD here has been conserved as natural grassland around its older graves for generations, just scythed for hay in the first week of July; so from spring onwards it's a mass of wild flowers, with plenty of butterflies (and beehives).

Kessingland TM5286 SUFFOLK WILDLIFE AND RARE BREEDS PARK Over 100 acres of very attractive grounds filled with lions, leopards, camels, antelope and other animals, some of them very rare, as well as owls, parrots and other birds. Good roadtrain journeys round the park; meals, snacks, shop, disabled access; cl 25-26 Dec; £5.

Laxfield TM2972 EAST OF ENGLAND BIRDS OF PREY AND CONSERVATION CENTRE Aviaries with hawks, falcons, eagles and owls, three flying displays a day, and closed-circuit TVs to watch young birds in their nests; meals, snacks, shop, disabled access; *£3.25. Laxfield also has an interesting old CHURCH, and the old Guildhall has the DISTRICT MUSEUM, with cottage kitchen, village shop and observation beehive; shop; open pm wknds and bank hols late May-Sept.

Leiston TM4462 LONG SHOP MUSEUM Good museum concentrating on local history and Richard Garrett engineering, with steam engines, steam

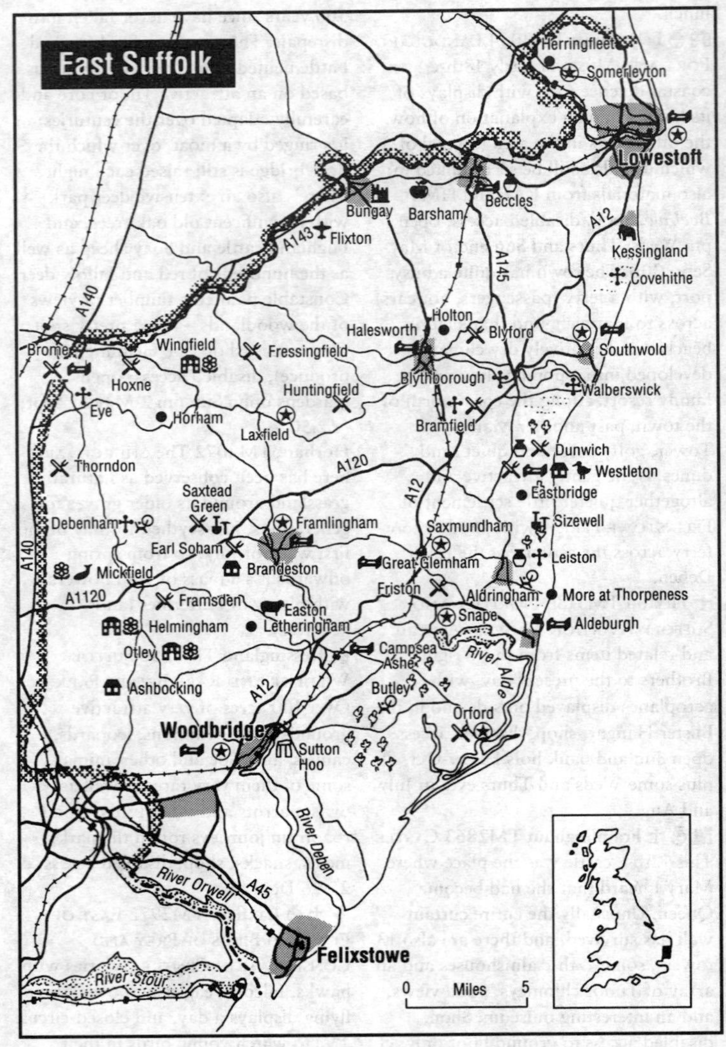

rollers, traction engines and memorabilia from the nearby WWII air base; shop, disabled access; cl Nov-Mar; *£1.50. Nearby are the remains of the 14th-c ABBEY.

☩ ⛴ ❀ ☺ Lowestoft TM5493 The country's main fishing port, so there's always lots to see in the harbour, but it has also developed as a resort thanks to its beaches and proximity to the Broads. Cobbled streets of old buildings survive in the part known as The Scores, and the early medieval CHURCH is imposing and attractive. In the High St the Bayfields Hotel and Volunteer are useful for lunch. There are regular summer harbour tours and sea BOAT TRIPS; details from Tourist Information Office, Esplanade (0502) 523000. Also in the harbour is the

Lydia Eva Steam Drifter, the last surviving herring drifter, with an exhibition on life aboard and the herring industry in general; cl July-Easter. At Boatworld (Oulton Broad) you can watch boats being made in the traditional manner; cl wknds, £1.90. East Anglia Transport Museum (Carlton Colville) The best part of this museum is the reconstructed 1930s street scene used as a setting for working vehicles such as trams, trains and trolley-buses, but there are lots of other vehicles displayed on the three-acre woodland site. Snacks, shop; open Sun May-Sept, Sat Jun-Sept and wkdys in summer hols; £2.50. Maritime Museum (Whapload Rd) Displays of ancient and modern fishing and commercial boats, as well as fishing gear, tools, an art gallery and a lifeboat display; shop, disabled access, cl Oct-Apr; *50p. There's also a Royal Naval Museum in Sparrow's Nest; cl 12-2 pm, all day Sat, mid-Oct-mid-May. Pleasurewood Hills American Theme Park (Corton Rd) Lots of exciting rides and attractions such as the Waveswinger and the Tempest, as well as fairytale features for younger visitors, and parrot and sealion shows. Trains and chairlifts speed up travel round the grounds; meals, snacks, shop, disabled access; open daily May-Sept and some wknds in Apr and Oct, tel (0502) 513626 to check; from £8.75.

Mickfield TM1361 Fish and Water Garden Centre Two acres of ornamental water gardens and working nursery, with displays of tropical, marine and freshwater fish; wknd teas, garden centre, disabled access; cl 25 Dec.

Orford TM4250 Orford Castle When Henry II commissioned this castle it was right on the shore, but since then the river has silted so much that it's now slightly inland. It has an amazing 18-sided keep rising up to 90 ft, supported by three extra towers, and there are good views from the top; shop; cl occasionally 1-2 pm for lunch, Mon Oct-Apr, 25-26 Dec, 1 Jan; £1.70. The process of coastal erosion is well illustrated at the Dunwich Underwater Exploration Exhibition at the Craft Shop in Front St, and there are displays on other aspects of marine life; cl 25-26 Dec; 40p. The Kings Head down here is good for lunch. There's a long lane down to the shore, looking across to the desolate Orford Ness, where avocets breed. In the village, the church has the ruined chancel arches of a Norman predecessor in the graveyard.

Saxmundham TM3863 Bruisyard Vineyard (signed off B1119 Framlingham rd) Picturesque 10-acre vineyard producing decent English wine, with herb garden, water gardens and woodland picnic area; meals, snacks, shop, some disabled access; cl Christmas wk. Entry is free but tours of the site with a Walkman commentary are £2.50. This is an attractive village with yet another fine church, and Yoxford TM3968 2-3 miles further north has a couple of good craft workshops.

Saxtead Green TM2564 Saxtead Green Post Mill Traditional Suffolk post mill dating from 1854, although there's been a similar mill on the site for much longer. It's a steep climb up the staircase, but once inside you'll see that the gearing, millstones and other equipment have been meticulously brought back into perfect working order; cl 1-2 pm, all day Sun, Oct-Mar; £1.20. Attractive surroundings, and the Volunteer opposite is good for lunch.

Sizewell TM4762 Sizewell Visitor Centre Interactive displays and exhibitions of energy, nuclear power and the environment, with tours of the Sizewell B power station (must book for tour, on (0728) 642139); cl winter Sun, and Christmas and New Year. Nearby, the long Sizewell Beach is generally virtually deserted out of season, and a pebble-hunter's dream (you may even find scraps of amber after a spell with strong east winds). At its south end is the curious village of THORPENESS, built as a holiday village in a deliberately fanciful olde-worlde style, with quite a few attractive mock-Tudor houses (one even masking a water-tower); it has a sizeable artificial but now thoroughly natural-looking picturesque lake, and the windmill here was brought over from Aldringham.

Snape TM3959 MALTINGS Converted 19th-c maltings, home of the Aldeburgh Music Festival begun by Benjamin Britten, as well as other concerts throughout the year. The centre has unusual shops and galleries, and in summer there are one-hour BOAT TRIPS down the River Alde. The Plough & Sail just outside is good for lunch. Up in Snape village, the Golden Key is also good.

Somerleyton TM4897 SOMERLEYTON HALL Interesting Jacobean house rebuilt in the Anglo-Italian style in 1840; inside it's still very much lived-in, and there are period furnishings and paintings. The lovely gardens have a maze and miniature railway; snacks, shop, disabled access; open pm, Thurs and Sun only in Apr, May, Jun and Sept, Tues and Weds too in July and Aug – cl Oct-Easter; *£3.50. Nearby, with access from the Hall, is the interesting FRITTON DECOY on Fritton Lake, which attracts numerous wildfowl, particularly in the autumn and winter. In summer, it's a popular place for boating and pottering about, with a play area and children's rides. The Plough at Blundeston, home of Barkis the carrier in *David Copperfield*, is useful for lunch.

Southwold TM5076 Once an important fishing port, this is now a pleasant and civilised little resort with a distinctive lighthouse as its main landmark, and no end of good pubs and inns supplied by the local Adnams brewery (their wholesale wine shop has interesting stock). For food, the Crown is outstanding, and though more straightforward the Kings Head is good, as is the smart Swan Hotel. Southwold Jack on the church tower is worth a look. MUSEUM 17th-c Dutch gabled cottage with good local-history museum, offering items on the Southwold light railway and a local battle against the Dutch in 1672; open pm spring bank hol-Oct, as well as Easter and May bank hol wknd. LIFEBOAT MUSEUM Small museum with RNLI related material and models; open pm daily spring bank hol-Sept. Across the golf course or along the breezy sea wall you come to the harbour, a tidal inlet, with its cheerful mix of beached fishing boats and multitudes of sailing boats. There's a footbridge over to Walberswick on the other side of the water – an attractively decorous seaside village, popular with artists ever since Wilson Steer's days there in the 1890s. The Bell here is an attractive if very informal old inn, and the 15th-c CHURCH, parts now destroyed and other bits looking shaky, is attractive. (The drive round by car between Southwold and Walberswick is several miles.)

Sutton Hoo TM2849 One of the most famous archaeological sites in the country, where in 1939 the discovery of an Anglo-Saxon ship burial caused historians to reinterpret the period completely. Knowledge of the Dark Ages is still patchy in parts, and you can't help wondering if there's another hoard of treasure waiting to be discovered that will have a similarly dramatic effect on current theories. Most of the treasure from here is in the British Museum, but you can go round the site and see the burial mounds, and there's an exhibition centre explaining its importance; shop; tours at 2 pm and 3 pm wknds only, Apr-Oct; *£1.50. Further down the B1083 the Plough at Sutton itself is good for lunch; or you can turn off down to Ramsholt and have lunch among the pine woods by the waterside, at the

Ramsholt Arms, with quiet walks along the Deben estuary.

Westleton TM4369 MINSMERE RESERVE Big RSPB reserve with lots of different species among the heath, woods, marshes and lagoons, and good observation hides to see them from; snacks, shop, disabled access; cl Tues; £3 for non-RSPB members. Nearby there are public walks over similar country, heath and pine woods; Dunwich itself is within quite an easy walk. The Eels Foot at Eastbridge is the pub favoured by bird-watchers; the Crown on Westleton Green by those who like to fortify themselves with more stylish food. FISK'S CLEMATIS NURSERY has many varieties of clematis on show and for sale; cl winter wknds.

Wingfield TM2277 WINGFIELD COLLEGE It's quite a surprise when you enter this seemingly Georgian country house – the frontage is just a disguise hiding away a splendid medieval timber-framed college building. Founded in 1362, the college flourished in the 15th c, but after the Reformation declined and became a private house. One of its 18th-c owners constructed the Palladian exterior to make his home more fashionable, using false ceilings, floors and windows so skilfully that for 200 years the house's earlier parts were forgotten. Now it's a fascinating mix of medieval and Georgian styles, with a striking great hall, and outside topiary and kitchen gardens; snacks; open pm wknds and bank hols Easter-Sept; *£2.20. They also organise Wingfield Arts, a varied programme of events in churches, halls and other everyday buildings all over the region – tel (0379) 384505 for details and programme.

Woodbridge TM2649 A quietly attractive and rather dignified market town, with many fine buildings and interesting book and antique shops, and a CHURCH of great style and interest. MUSEUM The history and archaeology of the area inc the ship burial at Sutton Hoo close by, and the recent Anglo-Saxon finds at Burrow Hill; cl Sun am, Mon (exc bank hols and summer hols), Tues (exc summer hols), Weds, all Nov-Easter; 50p. TIDE MILL This restored 18th-c mill on a busy quayside has photographs, drawings and demonstrations of the machinery used at the time. Shop, disabled access to ground floor only; open Easter, then daily May-Sept and wknds in Oct; 80p. On Burkitt Rd BUTTRUMS MILL is a six-storey tower mill, now fully restored, with displays of its history; open pm Sun and bank hols May-Sept; 50p. The Melton Grange Hotel is good for lunch, and the Cherry Tree opposite Notcutts Nursery (off A12) is useful.

Woolpit TL9762 BYGONES MUSEUM Small museum showing life in a Suffolk village with annually changing displays and an exhibition on brickmaking; shop, disabled access; open pm wknds and bank hols Oct-Easter. The village has a medieval tradition that in the 12th c two slightly strange-looking green-skinned children were found by a pit that was suddenly blasted in the earth one night; the boy soon died, but the girl lived, was taken in by the priest and learned English. She never said more about her origins than that she'd come from a land far far away, and grew up to marry a local lad and have children. The Brewers Arms at nearby Rattlesden does good food.

Lots of Suffolk's famous WINDMILLS are found in this coastal region, and although many fell into disrepair earlier this century a large number have been painstakingly restored. As well as those already mentioned there's a good example at Letheringham TM2757, which also has nice gardens (open pm Sun and bank hols Apr-May, July-Aug, £1.50); and others at Herringfleet TM4797 and Holton TM4077, though you can't often get into these.

† Interesting old churches can be found at Blythburgh TM4475 (a

magnificent building in a lovely setting above the marshes), Bramfield TM3973 (unusual detached round tower), Covehithe TM5282, and Eye TM1473 (beautiful stonework and rood screen).

★ **Other attractive villages** here, all with decent pubs, include Blyford TM4277, Eastbridge TM4566, Fressingfield TM2677, Hoxne TM1777 and Huntingfield TM3374.

Walks

Large areas of the flat formerly heathy land near the coast have been covered with pine plantations, which are also pleasant for undisturbed walks, with the chance of seeing red squirrels, and in summer with that lovely fresh foreign pinewood smell. In some places the heath and marshy ground below it has been left undisturbed, and these reserves are interesting for bird-watchers. **Minsmere** bird reserve TM4369 is perhaps the best-known feature, where the lake, surrounding heathlands and woods, and the coast supply walks for all seasons. The reserve is skirted by public paths, and a hide is available for public use, but you need a permit for entry to the rest of the reserve. Approach points are Dunwich TM4770 and Eastbridge TM4566.

Among the broad **rivers** that have delightful waterside paths close to the coast are the River Blyth near Southwold TM5076 and the River Deben near Shottisham TM3144. Sizewell nuclear power station dominates the landscape rather gracelessly around Thorpeness TM4759, but the **coast walk** south to Aldeburgh TM4656 is still pleasurable, and diverse heathland, an old railway track walk and The Meare (Thorpeness's lake) justify detours inland.

Among the plantations off the B1084 towards Woodbridge is the **Tangham Nature Trail** TM3450, a short trail specially designed for disabled people; there are longer walks through the pine woods here too.

Driving

From this part of Suffolk, the A1120 – quite a pleasant drive passing some attractive villages with little traffic – would get you down to Lavenham in about 1¼-1½ hours: so the delightful villages around there are well within reach.

Within this northern area, the B1077, an old coach road up through Debenham and Eye, is considerably more interesting than the A140 for north-south trips. The B1116 through Framlingham and Fressingfield is another pleasant north-south coach road. An attractive back road is the one NE of Wickham Market, through Easton, Brandeston and Cretingham to Debenham. Nearer the coast, the B1084 from Woodbridge to Orford is a pleasant drive, as is the little-travelled good road from Orford past the pine woods of Iken Heath to Snape. The farming country up past Halesworth has plenty of quiet back roads through it, though the scenery is not that striking.

Most of the A12 is now a good road, getting you quickly across this area and giving a good impression of the countryside as you go: it gives perhaps the finest view in the area, approaching Blythburgh from the S.

Cycling is one of the best ways to get around this area, as it's so relatively flat, without too much traffic on the back roads; bicycles of all kinds can be hired from Byways Bicycles in Saxmundham – tel (0728) 77459.

Where to eat

Fressingfield TM2677 Fox & Goose (037 986) 247 Early 16th-c timbered inn with a very wide choice of dishes from all over the world, lovely puddings and fine wines; cl Mon/Tues, Weds am, 25-26 Dec. **£23.60/£6.30.**
Orford TM4250 Kings Head (0394) 450271 Friendly mainly Tudor inn, some parts older, with decent food in bar and restaurant inc lots of fresh fish; handy for the castle; restaurant cl Sun pm (open bank hol wknds). **£16**|£3.50/£6.
Orford TM4250 Butley Orford Oysterage (0394) 450277 Simple restaurant with its own oyster beds, fishing boat and smoke house; very popular locally and with the yachting fraternity for its wonderfully fresh fish, decent wines, and brisk, friendly service; cl 25-26 Dec, Nov-Mar no evening meals exc Fri/Sat; disabled access. **£12/**£4.90.
Friston TM4160 Old Chequers (0728(688270 Friendly pub in interesting village – a useful stop for promptly served hot and cold buffet lunches, bar food, and decent wines; limited disabled access. **£11.60**|£3.25/£6.50.
Hoxne TM1777 Swan (0397) 975275 Efficient and civilised historic pub, nice tree-filled garden, and promptly served, interesting bar food. £2.10/£4.20.
Framsden TM1959 Dobermann (0473) 890461 Charmingly restored thatched pub with twin-facing fireplace separating the friendly, spotlessly kept bars, decent choice of beers and spirits and good popular food.
Dunwich TM4770 Flora Tearooms (072 873) 433 Little tearoom on the beach serving huge helpings of good-value, really fresh fish – take your own wine; little museum is worth a look; cl Dec-Feb. /£3.70.
Earl Soham TM2363 Victoria (0728) 685758 Unassuming pub with particularly friendly landlord, welcoming atmosphere, very interesting own-brewed beers, and good, reasonably priced home-made food. £1.15/£4.15.
Other places with decent food include the Queens Head in Blyford TM4277, the Queens Head at Bramfield TM4073, the Oaksmere at Brome TM1376, the Huntingfield Inn in Huntingfield TM3374, the Volunteer at Saxtead Green TM2665, the Black Horse in Thorndon TM1469, the Four Horseshoes at Thornham Magna TM1070, and the White Horse at Westleton TM4469.

West Suffolk

Not a particularly alluring area, apart from racing at Newmarket, but there are several interesting places to visit if you're staying nearby.

This is not in general the most appealing part of the county, though anyone at all interested in racehorses could spend a very enjoyable weekend based at Newmarket. For others, the most interesting place in the area is the lively Museum of East Anglian Life in Stowmarket, though West Stow country park, with its reconstructed Anglo-Saxon village, and Euston Hall are also well worth visiting. The collection of music machines at Cotton is fun. Bury St Edmunds itself has quite a lot to see, and though busy during the week quietens down at weekends when its very pleasant to stroll through. On the whole, this area is best seen as an adjunct to a stay in Suffolk or Cambridge.

Where to stay

Bury St Edmunds TL8564 ANGEL IP33 1LT (0284) 753926 **£99**; 42 rms. Thriving 15th-c country-town hotel with good atmosphere in relaxed bar which has long been a meeting-place for the county's upper crust; comfortable lounge, and two restaurants – one in 12th-c vaults.

Newmarket TL6463 RUTLAND ARMS CB8 8NB (0638) 664251 ***£50**; 45 rms. Recently refurbished Georgian coaching inn built around lovely cobbled courtyard with elegant and gracious two-room bar, good restaurant, friendly, efficient service and happy mix of customers in cheerful bar; no accomm Christmas.

Newmarket TL6463 WHITE HART CB8 8JP (0638) 663051 **£48.45**; 23 rms. Comfortable central hotel with racing pictures and open fire in spacious lounge, traditional restaurant, reliable bar food, friendly staff, front bar where the trainers meet, and solid back cocktail bar where they take their more important owners.

To see and do

Brandon TL7886 BRANDON HERITAGE CENTRE Brandon used to be the centre of the flint industry, and among the local history of the area here is a reconstructed flint-knappers' workshop; also displays on the fur industry and Thetford Forest. Shop, disabled access; open Thurs, Sat, Sun pm, and bank hols, Easter-mid-Dec; 50p. BRANDON COUNTRY PARK, largely pine woods, is pleasant to stroll around.

Bury St Edmunds TL8564 The old monastery became an abbey in the 12th c, famous for its illuminated manuscripts, but though the precincts themselves have remained as a tranquil enclave in what's become a busy shopping town, a fire and the Dissolution have left little of the structure except for the 12th and 14th-c gatehouses, and the old church building that in 1913 was given the status of CATHEDRAL. Parts are 15th-c, but the hammer-beamed ceiling is 19th-c, and work still goes on. The SAMSONS TOWER MUSEUM, opening at the end of 1993, has a full history and remains of the earlier abbey; cl Sun am, 25-26 Dec, Good Fri. MANOR HOUSE MUSEUM (Honey Hill) Recently reopened Georgian house with a marvellous collection of watches, clocks and other timepieces, as well as prints, ceramics, paintings, furniture and costume; some interesting hands-on displays; snacks, shop, disabled access; cl Sun am, 25-26 Dec, Good Fri; *£2.50. MOYSE'S HOUSE MUSEUM (Cornhill) Unusual 12th-c flint and stone house with good range of Suffolk history, archaeology and natural history; trips up the clock tower can be made by arrangement. Shop, disabled access; cl Sun am, Good Fri, 25-26 Dec. A Robert Adam building is now the ART GALLERY; shop, disabled access; cl Sun, Mon and

We welcome reports from readers . . .

This GUIDE depends on readers' reports. Please tell us what you think about places in it. And do recommend additions. Use the card in the middle, the report forms at the end, or just write – no stamp needed: THE GOOD WEEKEND GUIDE, FREEPOST TN1569, Wadhurst, E Sussex TN5 7BR.

bank hols; 50p. An oddity near the abbey is the pretty little Nutshell (Traverse), probably the country's smallest pub, with long church connections – it closes on Sundays and Holy Days. The THEATRE ROYAL on Westgate St is Britain's third oldest working theatre, built in 1819 by William Wilkins, the designer of London's National Gallery. Now owned by the National Trust, you can look round the handsome building when productions or rehearsals are not in progress. The town has several antique shops. The Masons Arms (Whiting St) is good for a quick lunch, and the Queens Head (Churchgate St), Bushell (St Johns St), Fleetwoods Restaurant (Lower Baxter St) and Dog & Partridge (Crown St) are also useful.

Cotton TM0666 MECHANICAL MUSIC MUSEUM A big collection of instruments and musical items from the expected organs, street pianos, polyphons and gramophones to dolls, fruit bowls and even a musical chair. A reconstructed cinema has an unusual Wurlitzer theatre pipe organ; teas and shop, disabled access; open Sun pm Jun-Sept, and first Sun in Oct; *£2. The Greek-run Trowel & Hammer is good for lunch.

Euston TL8979 EUSTON HALL An elegant old house built by Charles II's Secretary of State Lord Arlington. The highlight is probably the excellent art collection, with several portraits of the King and his family and court inc ones by Lely and Van Dyck. The grounds were laid out by John Evelyn, William Kent and Capability Brown, so reflect centuries of development, with stately terraced lawns, fine trees, a lake, lovely rose garden and classical temple; there's also a 17th-c church in the style of Christopher Wren. Teas in former kitchen, shop, disabled access to grounds and tea room; open pm Thurs Jun-Sept, as well as pm the last Sun in Jun and 1st Sun in Sept; £2.25.

Great Barton SUFFOLK BARN A restored old barn with local crafts, and a pretty herb and wild flower garden with 200 plant species; teas; cl Sun am, all day Mon (exc bank hols) and Tues, all Jan and Feb. The Flying Fortress (a nearby pub) does food.

Newmarket TL6463 Newmarket has been the centre of racing since James I used to slope off here from 1605, and in the early morning people driving through are quite likely to have to give way to a string of racehorses. NATIONAL HORSERACING MUSEUM Recently extended museum telling the stories and scandals of the sport's development through the centuries, with art, trophies, videos of classic races, a display on the history of betting, and all sorts of racing relics from saddles to skeletons of notable horses. Meals, snacks, shop, disabled access; cl Sun am, Mon (exc bank hols), Dec-Mar; *£2.50. They also organise tours of the local breeding and racing scene with a look at horses at work on the gallops, and visits to a training yard, stud and to the handsome Georgian Jockey Club itself; there are variously priced tours, for all of which booking is essential – tel (0638) 667333. To book a tour of the National Stud (A1304 W), tel (0638) 663464; guided tours are at 11.15 am and 2.30 pm wkdys, and 3 pm Sun, cl bank hols and Sat (exc when Newmarket Races on, when they have an 11.15 am tour), and all Oct-Mar. The Rutland Arms across the road from the Jockey Club is useful for lunch and another place you'll see racing people; the Kings Head out past the paddocks at Dullingham is also good.

Stanton TL9673 WYKEN HALL GARDENS Formal herb, knot and woodland gardens, walled old-fashioned rose garden, and woodland walk to 7-acre vineyard; meals, snacks, shop, disabled access; open Thurs, Sun and bank hols May-Sept; *£1.50.

Stonham Aspal ST1359 The garden centre at STONHAM BARNS has an

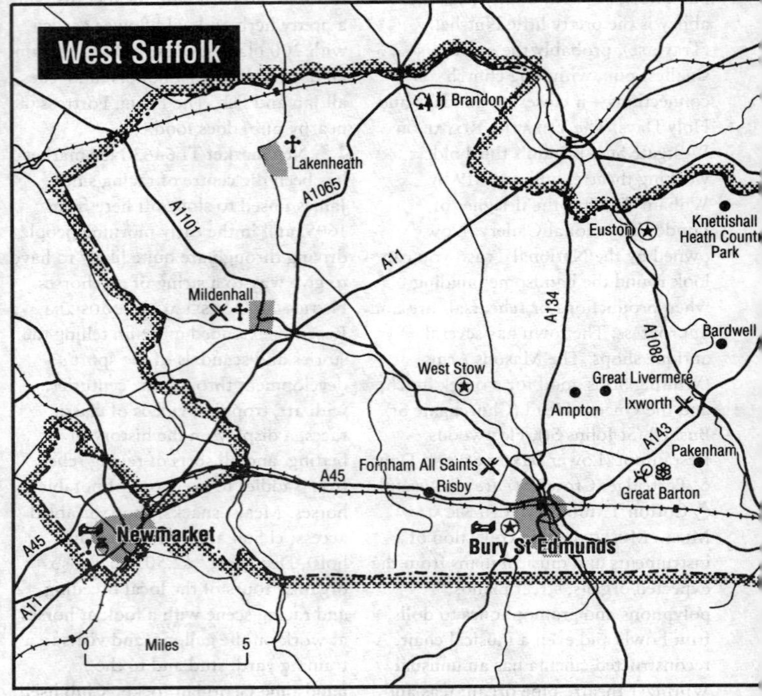

orchid centre, as well as various other little businesses such as picture framing and glass engraving.

Stowmarket TM0458 MUSEUM OF EAST ANGLIAN LIFE A very good and growing open-air museum, now covering 70 acres, with reconstructed buildings inc a water mill, chapel smithy and wind-pump, and demonstrations of traditional crafts and skills such as woodturning and basket-making. There are also displays on Victorian domestic life, gypsies, farming and industry, with working steam engines, horses and the only surviving pair of Burrell ploughing engines. Lots of events throughout the year from steam engine displays to demonstrations of spinning or corn dolly making; meals, snacks, shop, disabled access; cl Nov-Easter; £3.50.

West Stow TL8171 WEST STOW ANGLO-SAXON VILLAGE An expanding reconstruction of an Anglo-Saxon settlement from around the 5th c, with the buildings constructed by the same methods and tools as originally used; crops, crafts and costumed characters. Snacks, shop, disabled access; cl Christmas; *£2.50 for a taped guide. WEST STOW COUNTRY PARK, where the village is based, is attractive to explore, with 125 acres of heath and woodlands bordered by the River Lark. Over 120 different species of bird have been sighted here, and 25 species of animal; the visitor centre often has art and craft exhibitions. COW WISE Working dairy farm with cows, goats, lambs and hens; plenty to touch and feel, milking and feeding every afternoon; open pm Sun and bank hols from 1 Mar-11 July, pm daily 22-30 Aug; £1.70.

Suffolk is notable for its WINDMILLS, and this area has fine ones at Bardwell

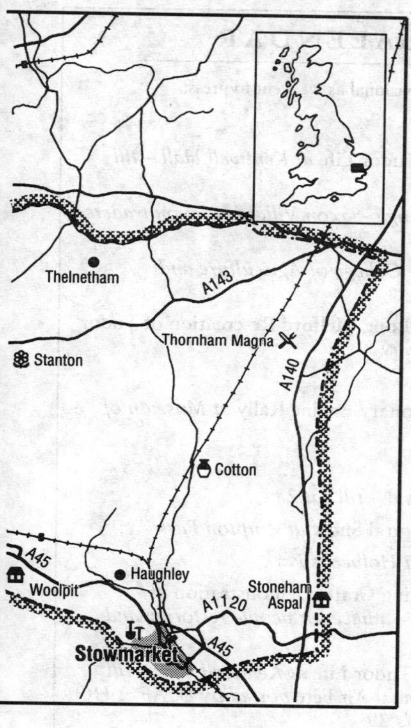

TL9473 (cl am Sun, Sat and Mon), Pakenham TL9267, and Thelnetham TM0178 (open every Sat, Easter wknd and then Suns and bank hols from July to Sept; 60p).

† ★ Attractive old churches around here can be found at Mildenhall TL7174 and Lakenheath TL7182; pleasant **villages** include Risby TL8066 (with a decent antique centre), Haughley TM0262 and Ixworth TL9370.

Walks

Apart from the one or two places mentioned above, there's little interesting walking here. **Knettishall Heath Country Park** TL9480 has some pleasant strolls. There's a nice shortish walk from Great Livermere church TL8871 across the Ampton Water lake to Ampton church TL8671. A longer path leads up through farmland to Great Livermere from Ixworth TL9370.

Driving

A good road across Thetford Heath is the B1106 from Bury to Brandon, carrying much less traffic than the busy A11. The A1101, though not a quick road, and the B1112 forking off it, also give a good impression of these relatively unyielding flatlands. East of the A1088, the countryside's more rolling, with a few decent patches of woodland, richer farming country, and lots of small villages.

Where to eat

Ixworth TL9370 THEOBOLDS 68 High St (0359) 31707 Imaginative food, cosy rooms with log fires, very good wine list; cl Sun pm, Mon, Sat am, bank hols, 25-26 Dec, 1 Jan, children in evening over 8 only. **£21/£29|£8.35.**
Other places with decent food include the Three Kings in Fornham All Saints TL8367 and the White Hart at Mildenhall TL7174.

Help this year from: *Mrs S A Greenwood, Mrs S Burrows-Smith, Gwen and Peter Andrews, J G Smith, Neville Kenyon, Richard Goss, Shirley Pielou, Sarah and Jamie Allan, Richard Fawcett, John Townsend, Steve Goodchild, Jeremy Williams, Anne Hyde, Hazel Morgan, Sylvie Weston, Derek Patey, Rita Horridge, Mike and Joyce Bryant, C H Stride, TBB, C G Bolton, Keith and Janet Morris, Mrs M C Barrett, Brian Allt, D O Hamilton, John Evans, George Atkinson, Susan and John Priestley, George Rumsey, Steve and Sarah de Mellow, Neville Kenyon, Andrew McKeand, Frank Gadbois, D J and R A Parish, Peter and Jean Brooks, John Baker, Tony and Lynne Gifford, M L and B S Rantzen, Romey Heaton, Anthony Barker.*

Suffolk Calendar

Some of these dates were provisional as we went to press.

April

1st **Long Melford** Re-creation of Tudor Life *at Kentwell Hall – till Mon 4*

3rd **West Stow** Saxon Market *at Anglo-Saxon Village – Saxon traders on Mon 4*

16th **Otley** Open Weekend *at Otley College of Agriculture and Horticulture – till Sun 17*

30th **Beccles** Festival – *till 21 May*; **Long Melford** Re-creation of Tudor Life *at Kentwell Hall – till 2 May*

May

1st **Stowmarket** Tractor and Stationary Engine Rally *at Museum of East Anglian Life – till Mon 2*

2nd **Mendlesham** Street Fayre

12th **Bury St Edmunds** Music Festival – *till Sat 28*

14th **Ingham** South Suffolk Agricultural Show *at Ampton Park*

21st **Hadleigh** Agricultural Show *at Holbecks Park*

22nd **Stowmarket** Traditional Building Crafts Demonstration *at Museum of East Anglian Life – advice for people restoring and repairing historic buildings*

28th **Long Melford** Re-creation of Tudor Life *at Kentwell Hall – till Mon 30*; **RAF Mildenhall** Annual Air Fête *hosted by USAF at HQ of US 3rd Air Force – till Weds 29*

29th **Long Melford** Red Rose Rent *at Hadleigh Guildhall – Sir William de Clopton gave the Guildhall to the town of Hadleigh in 1451 for an annual rent of one red rose; though the Clopton family emigrated to America a rose is placed on Sir William's tomb in Long Melford Church, with the Mayor and Council in attendance*; **West Stow** Country Park Open Day, *nature activity trails and talks*

June

1st **Ipswich** Suffolk County Agricultural Show *at the Suffolk Showground – till Thurs 2*

10th **Snape** Aldeburgh Festival of Music and the Arts *at the Maltings – till Sun 26*

11th **Long Melford** Country Fair *at Melford Hall, inc rare breeds, thatcher, carriage driving, lurcher and terrier racing*

19th **Long Melford** Re-creation of Tudor Life *at Kentwell Hall; 200 participants dress, speak and live like Tudors – till 17 July*

25th **Great Waldingfield** Farm Machinery Preservation Society Vintage Rally – *till Sun 26*

30th **Bury St Edmunds** Cakes and Ale Ceremony *at St Mary's Church in memory of Jankyn Smyth who provided in his will for an annual service for the almshouse residents followed by cakes and ale – now it's coffee, sherry and fruit cake in the Guildhall for the Board of Trustees, residents and councillors*

Suffolk Calendar

July

8th **Wangford** Music Festival – *till Mon 18*

9th **Carlton Colville** London Event *at East Anglia Transport Museum with old coaches and buses – till Sun 10*

10th **Kessingland Beach** Fun Day and Fête; **Stowmarket** Carnival Week *– till Sat 16 (procession day)*

16th **Framlingham** Horse Show, *inc driving*; **Hadleigh** East Anglian Summer Music Festival *– till 7 Aug*

29th **Beccles** Regatta Carnival *– till 1 Aug*; **Westleton** Wildflower Festival, *exhibition and demonstrations – till 1 Aug*

August

1st **Snape** Proms *at the Maltings – till Weds 31*

13th **Aldeburgh** Carnival *– till Mon 15, dancing in the street on Sat 20*

26th **Long Melford** Re-creation of Tudor Life *at Kentwell Hall – till Mon 29*

27th **Mildenhall** Cycling Rally, *largest in the south of England, inc indoor roller racing, cyclo-cross and cycle jumble – till Mon 29*

28th **West Stow** Saxon Market *at Anglo-Saxon Village – Saxon traders on Mon 29*

29th **Oulton Broad** Gala Day, *arena events, land, air and sea displays*

September

3rd **Felixstowe** Fuchsia Festival, *displays, advice, demonstrations, sales – till Sun 4*

25th **Stowmarket** Farming Open Day, *with steam threshing, cultivating and ploughing – till Sun 25*

November

5th **Ipswich** Firework Display *at Christchurch Park*

Surrey

Some really quiet attractive countryside, with lots of places to visit; not a cheap county.

There is a lot to see in this county. Highlights include Polesden Lacey at Great Bookham, Wisley Garden, Loseley House near Guildford, Hatchlands at East Clandon, the arboretum at Winkworth, Clandon Park at West Clandon and, among many pretty villages, Shere, Outwood and Chiddingfold. Some popular family attractions are headed by the zoo and theme park at Chessington, the zoo at Charlwood, Thorpe Park at Chertsey, the rural life centre at Tilford and the Horton Park Rare Breeds Farm near Epsom.

The main surprise is the countryside – large expanses of beautifully preserved scenery, with relatively free access for walkers, and good quiet back roads through some of the best of it. This is a tremendous bonus, given its proximity to London. Surrey is, in fact, the most heavily wooded county in England.

Where to stay

Bagshot SU9163 Pennyhill Park GU19 5ET (0276) 71774 **£157.50**; 76 spacious rms. Impressive country house in over 100 acres of well-kept gardens and parkland with friendly, courteous staff, comfortable lounges and little bar, and very good, imaginative cooking; outdoor swimming pool, tennis, 9-hole golf course, riding, stabling, game fishing, and clay pigeon shooting; indoor pool and gym planned; disabled access.

Haslemere SU9032 Lythe Hill GU27 3BQ (0428) 651251 **£110**; 40 individually decorated rms, 5 in the house, the rest in beautifully converted farm buildings. Lovely 14th-c timbered house in spacious grounds with good food in two restaurants, and fine antiques in the lounges; tennis, croquet, coarse fishing; limited disabled access.

Dorking TQ1649 Burford Bridge RH5 6BX (0306) 884561 ***£105**; 48 well-equipped rms. At the foot of Box Hill, this mainly 18th-c hotel has flowers and antiques in the day rooms, a relaxed atmosphere, friendly staff, and lovely gardens with outdoor swimming pool.

Chertsey TQ0466 Crown 7 London St KT16 8AP (0932) 564657 ***£58**; 30 rms. Bustling, friendly place with large bar and conservatory, good bar and restaurant food, lovely big garden; disabled access.

Reigate Hill TQ2552 Bridge House Reigate RH2 9RP (0737) 246801 **£55w**; 37 rms. Modern hotel with comfortable lounge, popular restaurant (especially Sun lunch), and good wines; disabled access.

Albury TQ0547 Drummond Arms The Street GU5 9AG (0483) 202039 **£50** (continental breakfast only); 7 rms. Attractively furnished pub with wide choice of good, quickly served food and pretty garden; children over 10.

Farnham SU8446 Trevena House GU10 5ER (0252) 716908 **£49**; 20 rms. Beautiful and comfortable Victorian Gothic manor house, good food, quick service; set well back from the road in 5 acres of garden with swimming pool, tennis; good disabled access.

To see and do

The countryside is one of the main reasons people – and particularly Londoners – come to this county. The National Trust owns several thousand acres of the finest places here. These include the steep juniper and boxwood slopes of BOX HILL TQ1850 (great views, wild orchids and butterflies in early summer, and field mushrooms in early autumn; the attractively placed King William IV at Mickleham is excellent for lunch); LEITH HILL TQ1342 (heather, sandy walks, steep pinewood, and tremendous views; an 18th-c tower on top of the hill, the highest point in south-east England, is the best viewpoint of all, and is open with teas on Weds pm and Sat, Sun and bank hols, but cl Oct-Mar exc fine weekends – 50p; the Parrot on Forest Green below is useful for lunch); parts of wooded NETLEY HEATH above Gomshall TQ0848; HEADLEY HEATH TQ2053 (sandy walks and rides through heather, birch woods and rather too much bracken; the Cock at Headley is good for lunch); HOLMWOOD COMMON TQ1745 (undulating oak and birch woods, lots of good paths; the Plough at Blackbrook is good for lunch); RANMOOR COMMON TQ1451 (downland slopes with sheep, wild orchids, and woodlands; the Ranmore Arms is useful for lunch and Walton Poor sell herb, scented and foliage plants Weds-Sun, not Oct-Easter, and open their pretty garden by appointment (048 65) 2273); FRENSHAM COMMON SU8540 (heather and woodland around a lake formed in the 13th c for fish breeding); and the DEVIL'S PUNCHBOWL SU8936 (a spectacular wooded fold of the downs, with nature trails, and fine views from Gibbet Hill above).

Another notable area is THURSLEY COMMON SU9040, with more heather, unusual birds, and boggy patches with shallow ponds where dragonflies breed; the Three Horseshoes at Thursley is useful for lunch.

Somewhere to start an acquaintance with the county's rich natural history, and in particular the sandy heathlands, is the LIGHTWATER COUNTRY PARK AND HEATHLAND VISITOR CENTRE SU9362, which has lots of information and interpretative environmental displays; shop, disabled access; park open all year but visitor centre may be cl at times – tel (0276) 479582.

Other things to see and do

Bletchingley TQ3250 TILGATES (Little Common Lane) Sizeable garden enthusiastically planted with a very wide variety of well-labelled rare trees and shrubs, with the National Collection of magnolias and an exceptional display of daffodils in spring; disabled access, teas, soup in Jan, plant sales; cl 25 Dec, all Jan and Feb; £1.50. The village itself has a good few attractive old houses and cottages, tile-hung or timber-framed, especially on the road up to the Norman CHURCH. The Plough, Whyte Harte and William IV are all useful for lunch.

Camberley SU8860 SURREY HEATH MUSEUM Good local-history museum, with plenty of geology, archaeology and crafts from the area; shop, disabled access; cl Sun and Mon, 25 Dec, 1 Jan.

Charlwood TQ2441 GATWICK ZOO AND AVIARIES Hundreds of mammals and birds, many in big naturalistic settings – some of which visitors can walk through, inc the two big tropical houses with plants and butterflies from around the world; meals and snacks, shop, disabled access; cl wkdys Nov-Feb, 25-26 Dec; *£3.50.

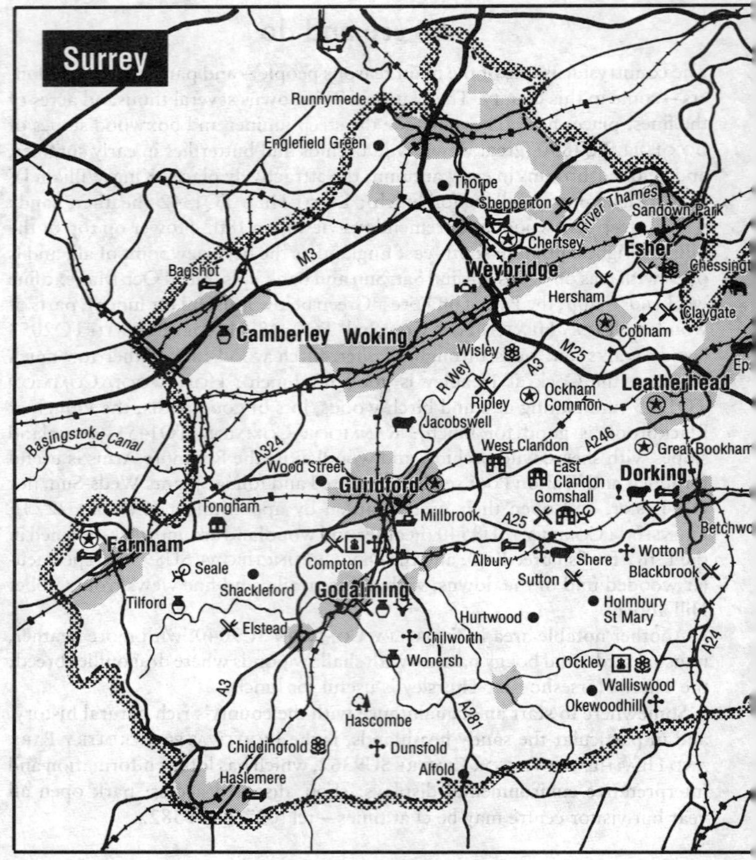

Chertsey TQ0466 has a good few Georgian buildings in its main streets, the remains of a medieval ABBEY, and pleasant walks by the Thames. The Golden Grove and Crown are useful for lunch. The late Georgian MUSEUM has a collection of costumes and accessories, displays of local history, glass, silver and dolls, and a pleasant little garden; shop; cl Sun, Mon, 25 Dec and bank hols. Slightly north-west at Lyne, the GREAT COCKROW RAILWAY is a notable miniature steam railway, with a unique signalling system; snacks; open Sun pm May-Oct; £1.20 ride. THORPE PARK An enormous 500-acre amusement park around former gravel pits, with lots of rides and attractions, many of them water-based – for example the Loggers' Leap, the highest log flume in the country. Miniature trains and waterbuses ferry you round the park, with various reconstructions recalling invasions from Stone Age to Norman, and models of famous buildings in Britain and abroad. More unusually for such a site, there's a working farm with rare breeds, birds, and craftsmen and women; meals and snacks, shop, disabled access; cl Nov-spring – as we go to press reopening date not fixed – tel (0932) 562633 to check; £8.95.

☺ **Chessington** TQ1863

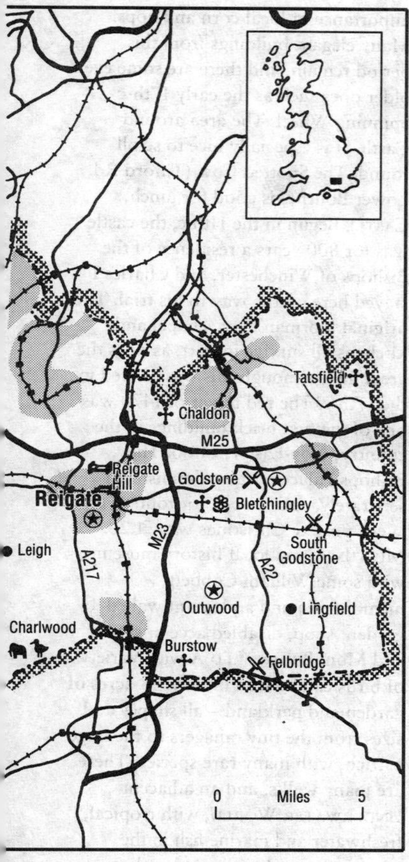

CHESSINGTON WORLD OF ADVENTURES Over 100 rides and other attractions and amusements in this spacious park, plus a circus and the famous zoo; meals and snacks, shop, disabled access; cl Nov-Mar; £11.50.

❀ **Chiddingfold** SU9635 is a lovely village in fine surroundings, with one window of its church made up from locally excavated fragments of 13th-c glass made here. RAMSTER (A283 S) has a splendid Edwardian woodland spring garden; wknd teas, plant sales, disabled access; open pm late Apr-2nd wk Jun, or by appointment; £1.50.

❀ **Cobham** TQ1060 is quite a busy shopping town, with some attractive older buildings around the church and in Church St; just outside Downside Common there is a classic cricket green, with cottages scattered around it, and a good pub – the Cricketers. PAINSHILL PARK has 18th-c landscape gardens, now beautifully restored. It's a continual surprise, with Gothic temples, Chinese bridges and other follies at every turn, and a lake with seemingly endless bays and inlets. Lots of unusual trees and shrubs; snacks, shop, limited disabled access; usually open Sun only, Apr-Oct, but in 1994 they may be open more often – best to tel (0932) 868113 to check; £3. Almost opposite the gates, the Little White Lion is useful for lunch. BUS MUSEUM Private collection of London buses from the 1930s to present; open wknds and bank hols. The SURREY WATER MILL has been restored and is now working for the first time in 60 years.

† **Compton** SU9546 (nr Guildford) WATTS PICTURE GALLERY A memorial gallery to the Victorian painter and sculptor G F Watts, filled with his work; snacks, shop, disabled access; cl am, all day Thurs. Just down the road the art nouveau tomb built by his widow is worth a look, and the village CHURCH is attractive. The Harrow is good for lunch, if not cheap.

! **Dorking** TQ1649 DENBIES (London Rd) Britain's biggest vineyard – at 250 acres it's bigger than many of the famous French ones it resembles. The tour is quite unlike any you'd find elsewhere, at times a cross between a fairground ride and a theme park. A train takes you through the working winery to an audio-visual show called 'Seasons of the Vineyard', and then on to a 3-D theatre, where four months of vine growth is condensed into four minutes. With 3-D glasses moving vines take on a Triffid-like air, and when the grapes are loaded on to the lorry they look as if they're flying out of the screen. There are tastings at the end. Good fun, and you don't have to be a wine buff to get something out of it; meals and snacks (in unusually designed restaurant), big shop, good disabled access; cl 25 Dec; *£4. Fine views and walks nearby. CHAPEL FARM TRAIL A working farm with lots of animals in lovely countryside; children can go right up to the animals, and there are pleasant walks. Disabled access; cl Nov-Feb; *£1.50. Dorking is a pleasant market town, with a lot of antique shops, and a local museum, in West St. The Cricketers (South St – A2003 towards Horsham) is very good value for lunch.

East Clandon TQ0651
HATCHLANDS A handsome 18th-c brick house, actually on seven levels, but from outside looking as if there are fewer, thanks to ingenious use of false windows. The grand rooms are especially notable for their fine ceilings and fireplace, early examples of the work of Robert Adam. The house also contains the Cobbe Collection of keyboard instruments inc a Stein pianoforte once played by Mozart, as well as paintings and furnishings; meals and snacks, shop, disabled access; cl am, Sat (exc in Aug), Mon, Fri, Nov-Mar; £3.60. NT. The Queens Head is useful for lunch.

Epsom TQ2160 HORTON PARK FARM (B280 W) A rare-breeds farm with adventure playground and craft shops; snacks, shop, disabled access; cl 25-26 Dec; £1.70.

Esher TQ1364 CLAREMONT LANDSCAPE GARDEN The oldest surviving landscaped garden in the country, laid out by Vanburgh and Bridgeman before 1720 and extended and naturalised by Kent; 50 colourful acres to lose yourself in. Meals (not Mon), snacks, shop, disabled access; cl Mon Nov-Mar; £1.70, going up to £2.50 on Sun and bank hols. NT.

Farnham SU8346 The Romans and Saxons both had settlements here, but it was in Georgian times that this handsome town had its heyday, thanks to the importance of local corn and hops. Many elegant buildings from this period remain, and there are some even older ones such as the early 17th-c Spinning Wheel. The area around Castle St is especially nice to stroll round. The Spotted Cow (Tilford Rd, Lower Bourne) is good for lunch. CASTLE Begun in the 11th c, the castle was for 800 years a residence of the Bishops of Winchester, and Charles I stayed here on the way to his trial. The original Norman keep, chapel and kitchens all survive in part, as does the great hall, although this was altered in the 17th c. The red tower of 1470 was one of the first brick buildings in the country; Nov-Easter; £1.60. The Bishops Palace part is administered separately, and is open for tours every Weds pm exc Christmas wk, £1.20. MUSEUM Good local-history museum, with some William Cobbett memorabilia and a pleasant walled garden; shop, disabled access; cl Sun and Mon. BIRDWORLD A wide variety of birds can be seen in these 18 acres of garden and parkland – all shapes and sizes from the tiny tanagers to the huge ostrich, with many rare species. There are many walks, and an adjacent UNDERWATER WORLD, with tropical, freshwater and marine fish in the aquarium; meals and snacks, shop, disabled access; cl 25 Dec; £3.65. The JOHNSON WAX KILN GALLERY in Bridge Sq has diverse arts and crafts, with workshops and demonstrations; cl Sun and bank hols.

Godalming SU9643 is an attractive town with a good few interesting buildings and, because of its narrow streets, a more old-fashioned feel than most in Surrey. Opposite the town hall, known affectionately by the locals as the Pepper Pot, is a 15th-c house with an interesting local-history MUSEUM, with Gertrude Jekyll-style walled garden; shop; cl Mon, Sun, 25-26 Dec. The town is the terminus for the River Wey & Godalming Navigation, a 17TH-C CANAL extended here in 1763. Its original locks and towpath have been restored for the National Trust; the wharf here has some fine Georgian buildings (you can walk all the way to Weybridge, some 20 miles). BUSBRIDGE LAKES (Hambledon Rd, off B2130) A very pretty spot set on three lakes in fine parkland, with exotic waterfowl, peacocks, ornamental pheasants and 100 other kinds of bird, as well as follies and grottoes throughout the grounds. In spring there are lambs and newly hatched ducklings and chicks; wknd snacks, shop; open (1994) 1-10 Apr, 1-2 pm, 29-30 May, and 21-29 Aug; *£3. The Inn on the Lake (A3100 S) is good for lunch, and in the High Street the interesting old Kings Arms & Royal Hotel, and the Red Lion at the south end, are also useful.

Godstone TQ3551, despite its main roads, is attractive, spread around a broad green with a duck pond, and a pretty group of houses around the imposing CHURCH, 14th/15th c with a Norman tower. The Bell and the Hare & Hounds are useful for lunch. PILGRIM HARPS (Stansted House, Tilburstow Hill Rd) make and restore harps of all sorts; best to ring first, (0342) 893242. GODSTONE FARM (Tilburstow Hill) Small 40-acre working farm where children are encouraged to learn about and touch the animals; snacks, shop, disabled access; cl Nov-Mar; £2.55. FLOWER FARM (Quarry Rd, just off the A22 towards Oxted), looking up to the downs, has organically grown pick-your-own produce and a vineyard; snacks, shop, disabled access; cl Nov-May (exc vineyard, open all year).

Gomshall TQ0848 GOMSHALL MILL is a restored and working two-wheeled watermill dating back to 1086, with the mill pond converted to riverside gardens and the buildings housing various craft shops; meals and snacks (not Sun eve), disabled access. The GOMSHALL GALLERY in Station Rd has contemporary arts and crafts; cl Sun am. The Compasses is useful for lunch.

Great Bookham TQ1354 POLESDEN LACEY (2 miles S) This attractive Regency house was at the centre of high society life during Edwardian times, and later Her Majesty Queen Elizabeth the Queen Mother spent part of her honeymoon here. There are photographs of some of the notable guests, as well as the Greville collection of tapestries, porcelain, old masters and other works of art. The spacious grounds have a walled rose garden and an open-air theatre; meals and snacks, shop, disabled access; house cl am, all Mon and Tues, Dec-Feb; £2.50 Weds-Sat, £3.50 Sun. NT. North of the extended commuter village, the Bookham Commons, with a mixture of thorny scrub (full of birds), small lakes, marshy bits and oak woods, are well wooded and attractive.

Guildford SU9949 The biggest town in the area, Guildford is older than you might at first think; although most of the buildings are Georgian-fronted, what's behind often dates back much further. The sloping High Street is most attractive, and the Kings Head and Star (both Quarry St) are useful for lunch. Interesting buildings include the GUILDHALL, which has one of the few existing sets of Elizabethan standard measures, ABBOT'S HOSPITAL, the GRAMMAR SCHOOL with its notable chained library, and GUILDFORD BOAT HOUSE, now an art gallery. More recent is the CATHEDRAL, begun in 1936 and one of the only two entirely 20th-c cathedrals in the country – it's otherwise unremarkable. Good shopping facilities are usually briskly modern; for a change of pace, you can hire a boat on the river. GUILDFORD CASTLE Not quite in the centre, but there are fine views of the town from the hill where this ruined 12th-c building stands. In its grounds, a royal wine cellar which had been sealed for

600 years was discovered and being excavated as we went to press. The castle ditch now has a garden, and the museum has a brass-rubbing centre and displays on the writer Lewis Carroll, who died here in 1898; shop; open week after Easter-end of Sept; 65p. MUSEUM Interesting little local-history museum, with archaeology and needlework displays; shop, limited disabled access; cl Sun, Good Fri, 24-26 Dec. LOSELEY HOUSE (3 miles SW) Most people are familiar with the name from the heavenly ice cream and yoghurts produced here (the butterscotch ice cream is delicious), and you can tour the dairy farm that makes them. The stately Elizabethan country house was built in 1562 from stone taken from the older Waverley Abbey, and has fine panelling, ceilings, paintings and tapestries. Afternoon tours usually feature milking; meals and snacks, shop; limited disabled access; house and farm cl am, Sun-Tues, Oct-May; £3.50 house and grounds, £2.50 farm tours.

Hascombe TQ0039 WINKWORTH ARBORETUM Nearly 100 acres of lovely hillside woodland, with fine views over the North Downs – especially nice in spring, and with unusual flaring colours in the autumn; meals and snacks, shop, disabled access; £2. NT. The White Horse is good for lunch, and the village church is very interesting.

Jacobswell TQ0053 BURPHAM COURT FARM PARK (Clay Lane) Over 75 acres of countryside with rare breeds of cattle, sheep, goats, pigs and poultry; good explanations and interpretative displays. Also more familiar breeds, pets' corner, play area and pretty riverside walks; snacks, shop; cl Mon, Nov-Jan; £2.

Leatherhead TQ1656 FIRE AND IRON GALLERY has unusual exhibitions of ornamental metalwork; shop, disabled access; cl 1-2 pm, Sat pm, all day Sun. The MUSEUM OF LOCAL HISTORY is in a pretty 17th-c timber-framed cottage with garden; open Sat and Fri am Apr-Christmas. BROCKETTS FARM PARK at nearby Fetcham is a new working farm in a pretty historic setting; meals, snacks, shop, disabled access; cl 10-26 Jan; £2. The Star (out on the Chessington Rd) is popular for lunch.

nr **Ockham Common** TQ0858 CHATLEY HEATH SEMAPHORE TOWER (entrance on Old Lane, off A3 to Effingham) Once part of a chain of 13 stations sending messages between the Admiralty in London and Portsmouth, this is now the only restored one left. It's a unique tower, like a lighthouse, with living accommodation for the signalling lieutenants, and gives excellent views from the top of the 88 steps. The tower is surrounded by 700 acres of heath and woodland, with good walks and a nature trail – indeed, it's 20 minutes' walk from the car park to the tower; shop; open pm wknds and bank hols wk before Easter-Sept, plus Weds in school hols; £1.50. The Black Swan at Martyrs Green is useful.

Ockley TQ1439 HANNAH PESCHAR GALLERY AND GARDEN (Black and White Cottage, Standon Lane) A lush garden filled with contemporary sculpture: the watergarden is now more like a tropical rainforest than the cottage garden it started off as, and the atmospheric sculptures and ceramics blend in perfectly with its unusual design. The sculptures are the only man-made features in the gardens (except the cottage) and change regularly; there's also a small indoor gallery. Disabled access (but no lavatory); open Fri, Sat and Sun pm May-Oct; *£4. The Punch Bowl out at Okewoodhill is useful for lunch.

Outwood TQ3145 THE POST MILL The oldest working windmill in England, built in 1665, and one of the best preserved. It's a very nice spot, 400 ft above sea level, with ducks, goats and horses all wandering freely about its grounds; there's a small museum and a collection of coaches. Shop, disabled access; cl wkdys exc bank hols, Nov-Easter; *£1.50. The village, spread around the common, is attractive, with an antique shop; the Dog & Duck out towards Coopers Hill is good for lunch.

Reigate TQ2550 Few of the town's original buildings have survived the trampling boots of progress, although there are a couple of timber-framed houses around the high street. PRIORY MUSEUM Now a school, this Tudor mansion has a notable hall fireplace and 18th-c stucco painting, as well as a small museum; shop, disabled access; open 2-4.30 pm Weds and Sat during term-time only. OLD WINDMILL AND CHURCH On the Heath just outside town, this 220-year-old former windmill was converted into a church in 1882; services are still held there the 3rd Sun each month in summer. Disabled access; open all year – if closed, key at golf club clubhouse. Near it, the Skimmington Castle, an archetypal country tavern, is good for light lunches.

Runnymede SU9972 is a field by a main road; not worth visiting unless you are quite fascinated by Magna Carta, though up the hill beyond the trees, the nearby memorials to John F Kennedy and, with their names, to the aircrew who died during World War II, are dignified and touching.

Seale SU8947 MANOR FARM CRAFT CENTRE Farmyard craft centre with furnishings, woodturning, jewellery and general crafts; meals, snacks, shop, disabled access; cl am wknds, all day Mon (exc bank hols).

Shepperton TQ0867 is one of the best places to watch the comings and goings on the RIVER THAMES, with the Wey Navigation joining the river here; the waterside Red Lion is useful for lunch, and away from the water there's a quiet and attractive 18th-c village square with a pleasant church.

★ **Shere** TQ0747 Very picturesque village, with 17th-c timber-framed cottages, a grassy-banked stream with ducks and ford, and lots of interesting corners. In the partly Norman CHURCH a quatrefoil blocked hole in the chancel wall marks the spot where a 14th-c anchorite had herself walled in, being fed through another hole outside. The ancient White Horse nearby is useful for lunch (as is the Prince of Wales), and the Malt House is a decent local history museum. THE OLD FARM has informative and unusually comprehensive demonstrations of various aspects of farming, from rope-making to sowing corn and even milling flour, with lambs for children to feed whenever one is available; shop; open pm wknds Apr, May and Aug and bank hols; *£3. The village is within reach of both the North Downs around Ranworth Common and the greensand hills to the south (see Walks, below).

Tilford SU8743 RURAL LIFE CENTRE Good collections of farm implements and machinery, and examples of the related crafts and industries; also a smithy and wheelwright's shop, and an arboretum in the pleasant grounds. Snacks, shop, disabled access; cl Mon (exc bank hols), Tues, and all Oct-Easter; *£3. The village has a massive oak tree, thought to be 800 years old; the Barley Mow between the river and the goose-cropped village green is good for lunch, and it's not far from here to the remains of Waverley Abbey.

Tongham SU8848 HOG'S BACK BREWERY There are tours of this friendly little brewery, which still uses traditional 'Full Mash and Top Fermentation' methods to produce its six distinctive ales. The shop sells not only their own beer but over 500 different English, Belgian and German varieties, alongside English wines and farm ciders; tours Weds evening at 6 pm, other times by arrangement – tel (0252) 782328, shop cl Sun; tour *£3.

West Clandon TQ0250 CLANDON PARK There is a fine collection of furnishings, porcelain and paintings in this 18th-c house, which also has a regimental museum in the basement and regular concerts in the grand two-storeyed Marble Hall. The gardens have a Maori house which was brought over from New Zealand in 1892; meals and snacks (restaurant open for Christmas), shop (open for Christmas shopping), disabled access to the ground floor; cl am, Thurs and Fri exc Good Fri, Nov-Apr; £3.60. NT. The smart Onslow Arms is good for lunch, and the Bulls Head is good value.

Weybridge TQ0764 BROOKLANDS MUSEUM Motoring records were being set here even before the first race was held in 1907. It later became the place where man first travelled at 100 mph, where the first British-made plane was flown, and the site of the first British Grand Prix. The racing circuit's heyday was in the fashionable 1920s and 1930s, and those days have been recreated at the museum, where the restored clubhouse, sheds and other buildings display racing cars, motorbikes and bicycles, and tell the story of aircraft production at the site, with a collection of Vickers and Hawker aircraft. Demonstrations and events most wknds; snacks, shop, disabled access; cl Mon; *£4.

Wonersh TQ0145 BRITISH RED CROSS MUSEUM AND ARCHIVES records the history of the Red Cross from its foundation in 1863, especially the British branch formed in 1870, with uniforms and other material from both World Wars; open wkdys by appointment – tel (0483) 898595. The Grantley Arms is useful for lunch.

Wisley TQ0659 WISLEY GARDEN These 300-acre gardens have come a long way since they were set up in 1904 as experimental gardens for the Royal Horticultural Society; half the area is devoted to garden, some to vegetables, and the rest to farm, orchard and woodland, with lots of unusual plants, shrubs and trees. The gardens get very busy (esp at wknds) but are quite big enough to cope. Meals and snacks, shop (lots of hard-to-get gardening/plant books), garden centre (good plants from wide range of nurseries, but expensive), disabled access; cl 25 Dec, members only Sun; £4.20. The canalside Anchor at Pyrford Lock (turn left down exit road) is useful for lunch if the queues at the good café here daunt you; and the pub is well placed for walks along the prettiest section of the Wey Navigation Canal.

If you fancy a day at the races, some of the country's most famous courses are in this area: Sandown Park TQ1364, Kempton Park TQ1168, Lingfield TQ3843 and of course Epsom TQ2160. All have good facilities, and some have various exhibitions throughout the year.

Boat hire is possible on the **Wey Navigation,** from Farncombe Boat House, Godalming, (0483) 421306, or Guildford Boat House, Millbrook, (0483) 504494; the canal passes through some fine scenery.

Other **attractive villages,** all with decent pubs, include Albury TQ0547 (where the Victorian mansion Albury Park is famed for its chimneys), Alfold TQ0334, Betchworth TQ2049, Dunsfold TQ0036, Englefield Green SU9970 (handy for Savill Garden – see Berkshire chapter), Holmbury St Mary TQ1144, Hurtwood TQ0845, Leigh TQ2246, Shackleford SU9345, Thorpe TQ0268, Walliswood TQ1138 and Wood Street SU9550.

✝ Though Surrey's village churches are not as notable as those in, say, Somerset, Lincolnshire or Suffolk, and though you'll usually have to get the key from a local keyholder, most are at least worth a look. A shortlist, for the intrinsic appeal of the churches themselves or for their surroundings, would include Burstow TQ3140, Chaldon TQ3155, Chilworth TQ0247, Dunsfold TQ0036, Okewoodhill TQ1337, Ockham TQ0756, Tatsfield TQ4156 and Wotton TQ1247.

Walks

In this well-wooded and surprisingly hilly county, it's easy to escape from the suburbia that covers much of its northern part. Even quite close to the M25, the traffic is out of earshot at popular strolling-grounds such as **Banstead Wood** TQ2657 and **Marden Park** TQ3655.

Further west, the **North Downs** have a more untouched rural character. **Box Hill** TQ1850 is the most popular viewpoint, with a summit car park and walks among its famous box trees. On the other side of the Mole Gap, the North Downs Way continues along **Ranmore Common** TQ1451, a densely wooded chalk escarpment within close range of Polesden Lacey.

The **upper greensand** country to the south, though much wooded, displays some satisfying variety and is arguably Surrey's best walking territory. Around **Hurt Wood** TQ0943 large areas of private forest are open to walkers; relatively unfrequented, so it's a good place to spot birds and wild animals. The Royal Oak and Kings Head at Holmbury St Mary TQ1144 are handy for walkers. Friday Street TQ1245, with a pleasant pub and a lake, is one starting point for switchback routes south through a series of brackeny summits to **Leith Hill** TQ1342, the highest point in the south-east (refreshments at wknds at the Prospect Tower). It has a surprising view of south London – which feels 100 miles away. Leigh Hill can also be approached from the south, from Ockley TQ1440 or Forest Green TQ1241 – this approach through attractive farmland may be preferable for people who like open country. There's a similarly open approach from Ewhurst TQ0950 to **Pitch Hill** TQ0842.

St Martha's Hill TQ0248, E of Guildford, has a church on its summit that can be reached only on foot, and by starting from Chilworth TQ0247 you can see the long-abandoned gunpowder mills by the Tilling Bourne (even if you don't find the tawny balsam J S Mills found there in 1822, when retreating from a tiresome house party at Albury Park). Further SW the terrain is lower but unspoilt in the vicinity of **Winkworth Arboretum** SU9441 near Godalming; more dramatic (despite road-building proposals) at the **Devil's Punchbowl** SU8936 near Hindhead. This is a great hollow in a landscape characterised by mixed woodlands, quiet valleys, scattered ponds and sandy heaths. The area is quite developed but the woods and intricacy of the landscape give it a wholesome rurality, and the footpath network is dense. **Gibbet Hill** SU9035, above the A3, gets a view over most of it.

As we've said, the best waterside walks are to be had along the **Wey Navigation** towpath in the W of the county. The **Basingstoke Canal**, formerly derelict, has been undergoing a tremendous programme of rehabilitation over the last 15 years or so. In its Surrey section it does not pass through such fine scenery as the Wey Navigation, but its towpath has been well restored. A new visitor centre has just opened at Mytchett SU8855, explaining the restoration.

The Environment Unit of the County Council's Planning Department coordinates an ambitious programme of guided walks throughout the year, generally exploring some historical or more usually natural history theme; on a typical Sunday there might be eight or more different walks to choose from. For the current programme, tel 081-541 9454 and ask for the Environment Unit.

Driving

The county's best drives are over on the W side of the A24, with all the side roads that lead S off the A25 between Dorking and Albury giving enjoyable views and little other traffic. The road from Shere dropping steeply down over Pitch Hill towards Ewhurst is particularly memorable. Further W, there's a pretty drive from Godalming down through Hascombe on the B2130, turning off on the side road to Dunsfold and on to Chiddingfold.

The A3 coming into Hindhead gives a good passing view of the Devil's Punchbowl, and the A31 between Guildford and Farnham has good views from the Hog's Back ridge; both, however, are scarcely roads you'd seek out for a quiet country drive.

The roads around and steeply over Box Hill are attractive, and nearby is a pleasant route off the A25 through Betchworth and Brockham, then S through Newdigate and on to Rusper over the Sussex border.

Where to eat

Claygate TQ1563 LES ALOUETTES High St (0372) 464882 Particularly fine French cooking in attractive, civilised restaurant, lovely puddings, and courteous service; cl Sat am, Sun pm, last wk Aug-1st wk Sept, 24-30 Dec, 1 Jan; limited disabled access. **£35**|£9.

South Godstone TQ3749 LA BONNE AUBERGE (0342) 892318 Comfortable, quietly set Victorian house with very good food and helpful staff; cl Sun pm, Mon, 27-29 Dec. **£27.30**|£10.50.

Esher TQ1464 GOOD EARTH 14-18 High St (0372) 462489 Consistently good Chinese food and quick, attentive service in comfortable modern restaurant; cl 4 days over Christmas. **£26.25**|£7.

Dorking TQ1649 PARTNERS WEST STREET 2, 3 and 4 West St (0306) 882826 Cosy popular restaurant in 16th-c building with very good food inc good-value set meals and well-thought-out wine list; cl Sun pm, Mon; children over 5; disabled access. **£24.95**.

Ripley TQ0556 MICHELS 13 High St (0483) 224777 Fine modern cooking in attractive restaurant with good wines and professional service; cl Sun pm, Mon, Sat am, 1 Jan. **£22.50/£40**.

Hersham TQ1164 THE DINING ROOM The Village Green (0932) 231686 Five little rooms with log fires, very good English food, a relaxed atmosphere, and cheerful, friendly staff; cl Sat am, Sun pm, 24 Dec-3 Jan; limited disabled access. **£21**|£8.

Godalming SU9743 INN ON THE LAKE (0483) 415575 Ockford Rd Comfortable and attractive restaurant surrounded by lawns, gardens and lake, with very good and popular modern British cooking; cl 25 Dec pm. **£21**|£1.95/£3.95.

Shepperton TQ0867 EDWINNS RESTAURANT (0932) 223543 Very good, popular food; cl Sat am, Sun pm, 25-27 Dec; disabled access. **£19.70/£22.25**|£9.50.

Sutton TQ1046 PARTNERS BRASSERIE 23 Stonecot Hill (081 644) 7743 Cosy and pretty restaurant with really good modern cooking and carefully chosen wines; cl Sun/Mon, Sat am, 25 Dec-1 Jan; disabled access. **£18.60**|£7.95.

Gomshall TQ0847 MULLIGANS Station Rd (A25) (0483) 202242 Friendly staff in attractively decorated and relaxed fish restaurant with live French café music on Thurs; cl 25-26 Dec; disabled access. **£17**|£3/£8.

Compton SU9546 HARROW (0483) 810379 Smart dining pub in interesting

village close to North Downs Way with very popular bar food. £4/£7.35.
Elstead SU9143 WOOLPACK (0252) 703106 Cheerfully old-fashioned pub, bustling but still atmospheric, with huge helpings of interesting, tasty bar food, real ale tapped from the cask, family room, and garden; disabled access (though one step to lavatory). **£17.45**|£3.75/£4.50.
Felbridge TQ3639 WOODCOCK (0342) 325859 Spacious pub with lots to look at and some unusual touches in the various differently styled areas, good home-made food using fresh hand-picked produce from the markets inc cream teas Easter-Oct (emphasis on fresh fish, too), and hardworking, helpful staff; bedrooms; disabled access. **£16.95 in restaurant, £14 in bar**|£1.50/£4.50.
Blackbrook TQ1846 PLOUGH (0306) 88603 Colourful pub in attractive walking country, very friendly service, good bar food with imaginative specials and decent wines by the glass; no food Mon pm, 25-26 Dec, 1 Jan; no children; disabled access. **£15**|£2.95/£4.45.

Help this year from: *A H Denman, John Evans, Brian and Jenny Seller, Ian Phillips, Mr and Mrs C Holmes, J E Lloyd, R M Sparkes, Doreen and Brian Hardham, Andy Stone, P J Keen, Win and Reg Harrington, J T Charman, Clem Stephens, Pat and Tony Martin, WFL, Father Robert Davies, D J Underwood, Mr and Mrs R J Foreman, DWAJ, Patrick and Patricia Derwent, John Pettit, John and Joan Wyatt, Lyn and Bill Capper, Ron Corbett, Roger Taylor, E G Parish, Miss M K Hankins, Romey Heaton, Doug Kennedy.*

SURREY CALENDAR

Some of these dates were provisional as we went to press.

JANUARY

6th **Guildford** Wassailing, *Twelfth Night pub tour by Morris men who act out the old tiptearers' or mummers' play and drink spiced beer from the wassail bowl*

27th **Guildford** Dicing for the Maid's Money *at the Guildhall – 1674 will instructed that two maids of long service were to throw dice competing for a year's income (the loser gets money from another charity)*

MARCH

31st **Guildford** World Speed Track Skating Championships *at the Spectrum Centre – till 2 Apr*

APRIL

30th **Abinger Hammer** Teddy Bears' Picnic; **Farnham** Folk Day *at the Maltings*; **Guildford** Procession – *the Summer Pole is carried up High St to castle green where it is put up; folk dancing around pole and elsewhere*

MAY

1st **Guildford** May Celebrations, *at 5.30 Morris dancing greets sunrise on St Martha's Hill*

2nd **West Ewell** Festival of Fun

5th **Banstead** Arts Festival – *till Sun 15*

SURREY CALENDAR

MAY cont.

20th **Farnham** Maltings Southern Counties Craft and Design Show – *till Sun 22*

28th **Mickleham** Country Craft Fair *at Norbury Park – till Mon 30*

30th **Guildford** Surrey County Show *at Stoke Park*

JUNE

1st **Epsom** Derby *at the racecourse – till Fri 3*

11th **Abinger** Old Fair; **Caterham** Carnival

19th **Farnham** Blues Festival *at the Maltings, 12 hours' non-stop blues*

22nd **Dorking** Merchant of Venice *at Polesden Lacey Open Air Theatre – till Sat 25*

29th **Dorking** Broadway Pirates *at Polesden Lacey Open Air Theatre – till 2 July*

JULY

6th **Dorking** Marriage of Figaro *at Polesden Lacey Open Air Theatre – till Sat 9*

9th **Chertsey** Black Cherry Fair

10th **Dorking** Fair *at Polesden Lacey Open Air Theatre, inc Kenny Ball jazz evening*

13th **Esher** Claremont Landscape Garden Fête Champêtre – *till Sun 17*

31st **Tilford** Rustic Sunday *at Old Kiln Museum Rural Life Centre Rustic Sunday*

AUGUST

6th **Cranleigh** Agricultural Show, *inc showjumping, carnival parade, duck racing and events for children*; **Guildford** Classic Car Show and Country Fayre *at Loseley Park – till Sun 7*

12th **Wisley** Flower Festival – *till Sun 14*

28th **Lingfield** Edenbridge and Oxted Agricultural Show *at Ardenrun Showground – till Mon 29*

SEPTEMBER

10th **Chertsey** Agricultural Show *at Chertsey Meads – till Sun 11*

OCTOBER

21st **Farnham** Southern Counties Craft and Design Show *at the Maltings – till Sat 23*

NOVEMBER

20th **Farnham** Blues Festival *at the Maltings, 12 hours' non-stop blues*

We welcome reports from readers . . .

Please send us your ideas for inclusion in the next edition: places to visit, eat at or stay in, attractive drives or walks, maybe even unusual interesting shops you know of. Use the card in the middle, the report forms at the end, or just write – no stamp needed: THE GOOD WEEKEND GUIDE, FREEPOST TN1569, Wadhurst, E Sussex TN5 7BR.

SUSSEX

This county has all that one might want from a weekend break. Attractively varied scenery includes the expansive views of the South Downs, the sparsely wooded high heathland of the Ashdown Forest, and the more intricate countryside of the Weald. There is well above average walking (and plenty of it), and a wide choice of interesting places to visit. It's difficult to choose between the county's two halves.

West Sussex has one of Britain's most interesting open-air museums, and the pick of the county's rich collection of great houses and fine gardens, though by no means a monopoly of them. It also has a wider choice of really splendid country-house hotels than East Sussex. However, East Sussex does have some outstanding attractions, too, including rather more for families, and plenty of good places to stay; Rye is a particularly attractive town for a short visit.

EAST SUSSEX

With lots to see and do, attractive scenery and plenty of variety, East Sussex is ideal for a short stay.

The excellent choice of places to visit and things to do here is topped by Bodiam Castle, Sheffield Park garden, the Bluebell steam line nearby, Drusillas zoo (a children's favourite), nearby Alfriston, and, for culture-minded people, the trail of Bloomsbury, around Firle and Rodmell. Among many other family attractions, the sheep centre at East Dean and Bentley at Halland have been much enjoyed. On the coast, Eastbourne stands out as an unusually civilised old-fashioned seaside resort, well placed for a lot of the places to see out in the countryside.

Brighton, of course, has its own unique style, combining elegant Regency architecture with a more shamelessly vulgar side; it's a great place for antiques, and the newly restored Royal Pavilion is well worth seeing. Rye, also by the sea, is a really interesting old town of great character; very good for a short stay or day visit.

The most picturesque countryside here is in the Weald towards the Kent boundary: there are steep slopes and valleys, fine woods, pretty villages, tile-hung or weatherboarded oast houses and ancient wood-and-tile Sussex barns with their long 'cats'-slide' roofs. Walkers find more scope, though, in the open downland culminating on Beachy Head that towers above the sea, or in the open sandy heaths and woodland of the Ashdown Forest.

Where to stay

Eastbourne TU6199 GRAND BN21 4EQ (0323) 412345 ***£150** (minimum stay is 2 nights); 164 rms, many with sea views. Well-run, impressive Victorian seaside hotel with chandeliers and marble pillars, spacious lounges, flowers; excellent, imaginative food, very good service, and good leisure facilities; disabled access.

Uckfield TQ4721 HORSTED PLACE TN22 5TS (0825) 750581 **£135**; 17 individually decorated spacious rms. Imposing Victorian country house in 23 acres of grounds; luxurious lounges with antiques, flowers and log fires; delicious food and good wine list in no-smoking dining room; croquet, tennis, and indoor heated swimming pool; children by arrangement and must be over 7 in restaurant; disabled access.

Alfriston TQ5103 STAR Polegate BN26 5TA (0323) 870495 ***£120 inc dinner**; 34 rms. Fascinating and atmospheric Forte hotel, built in 15th c as guest-house for pilgrims; lots of medieval carvings, sanctuary post in bar, decent food and drinks, and excellent service; disabled access.

Battle TQ7416 NETHERFIELD PLACE TN33 7PP (0424) 774455 **£95**; 14 lovely rms. Handsome hotel in 30 acres of gardens and park with light, attractive day rooms, really lovely flowers, and imaginative food using home-grown produce from the garden; cl last 2 wks Dec or 1st 2 wks Jan.

Alfriston TQ5103 DEANS PLACE Polegate BN26 5TW (0323) 870248 **£85**; 36 rms. Lovely old hotel with pleasant lounge and bar, good food, spacious old-fashioned gardens, swimming pool and tennis court; popular with older people; good walks in every direction; disabled access.

Rye TQ9220 GEORGE High St TN31 7JP (0797) 222114 **£80**; 22 rms. 16th-c coaching inn with friendly staff, beams, and log fires.

Brighton TQ3105 TOPPS 17 Regency Sq BN1 2EG (0273) 729334 ***£79**; 14 comfortable rms. Carefully furnished and well-kept Regency town house near the seafront with good food and friendly, helpful service; cl 25 Dec, 1 Jan pm.

Telham TQ7614 LITTLE HEMINGFOLD FARMHOUSE Battle TN33 0TT (0424) 774338 ***£70**; 13 rms, most with own bthrm. Partly 17th-c, partly early Victorian farmhouse in 40 acres of woodland, with trout-filled lake, gardens, and lots of walks; comfortable sitting rooms, open fires, restful atmosphere and very good food using home-grown produce – either in style of dinner party or at own candlelit table; children can feed farm animals; tennis court.

Wallcrouch TQ6630 SPINDLEWOOD COUNTRY HOUSE Wadhurst TN5 7JG (0580) 200430 **£62.50**; 8 comfortably old-fashioned rms. Late Victorian building in 5 acres of gardens, ponds and woodland; big rooms with comfortable recent furnishings, log fires, friendly service and relaxed atmosphere; fishing and golf nearby, hunting and shooting can be arranged; cl 4 days over Christmas.

Sedlescombe TQ7718 BRICKWALL Battle TN33 0QA (0424) 870253 **£58**; 23 rms. Well-run hotel with happy atmosphere, very good food, lively bar, and outdoor swimming pool; good base for exploring the area.

Mayfield TQ5827 MIDDLE HOUSE TN20 6AB (0435) 872146 **£55**; 8 rms. Old-world Elizabethan hotel with lovely panelled restaurant, leather chesterfields and armchairs in the morning coffee/afternoon tea area, chatty locals bar with open fire (maybe spit roasts), attractive back garden, and pleasant views.

Rye TQ9220 JEAKES HOUSE TN31 7ET (0797) 222828 ***£55**; 12 rms overlooking the rooftops of this medieval town or across the marsh to the sea, 10 with own bthrm. Fine 16th-c building, well run and friendly, with good breakfasts, lots of well-worn books, comfortable furnishings, linen and lace, and lovely peaceful atmosphere.

Fletching TQ4423 Griffin Uckfield TN22 3SS (0825) 722890 **£50**; 4 rms, some with four-posters. Extremely civilised and genuinely old country inn in pretty village on edge of Sheffield Park, very good friendly service, attractive rooms, lots of wines, and good food.

Hartfield TQ4735 Bolebroke Mill TN7 4JP (0892) 770425 ***£50**; 4 rms. Attractively converted family-run watermill and barn, very comfortable and spotlessly clean, with particularly good breakfasts and evening meals, and excellent, personal service; children over 7; cl Jan, Feb, Dec.

Frant TQ5835 Old Parsonage Tunbridge Wells Kent TN3 9DX (0892) 750773 **£49**; 3 very pretty rms, 2 with four-posters. Carefully restored imposing former Georgian rectory with antiques, watercolours and plants in elegant sitting rooms, spacious Victorian conservatory, good food in candlelit dining room, and balustraded terrace overlooking quiet 3-acre garden.

Mayfield TQ5827 Rose & Crown TN20 6TE (0435) 872200 **£48**; 5 attractively furnished, comfortable beamed rms. Pretty weatherboarded 16th-c inn with unspoilt oak-beamed bars, two log fires, lots of real ales, very good food, cosy little restaurant; decorated with flowering tubs and baskets in summer.

Ditchling TQ3215 Bull Hassocks BN6 8SY (0273) 843147 **£42.50**; 3 well-equipped rms. Attractive 14th-c inn in charming old village with decent bar food, very relaxed atmosphere, nice garden, and many nearby walks and views; cl 25 Dec pm.

Offham TQ4012 Ousedale House Lewes BN7 3QF (0273) 478680 **£42**; 3 rms. Small castellated house with good views, 3½ acres of garden and woodland; friendly owners and traditional cooking using home-grown seasonal produce; children over 10.

Arlington TQ5407 Bates Green Polegate BN26 6SH (0323) 482039 **£40**; 3 rms. Originally an 18th-c gamekeeper's cottage, a quietly set no-smoking farmhouse on a working sheep and turkey farm of 130 acres; very neatly kept, with beams and log fire, home-made cake and hot drinks on arrival, big breakfasts and good evening meal cooked on Aga using home-reared lamb and turkey and fresh local produce; good walks; no children or pets.

Eastbourne TU6199 Seacroft 9 St Aubyns Rd BN22 7AS (0323) 735433 **£39**; 6 rms, showers. Small, comfortable hotel close to pier, theatres and shopping centre; cl 2 wks over Christmas; children over 10.

Poynings TQ2612 Manor Farm Brighton BN45 7AG (0273) 857371 **£37**; 3 rms, shared bthrm. Quietly set old manor house in 260-acre family-run arable/sheep farm; evening meals by arrangement; lovely walks; cl Jan, Feb, Dec.

Lewes TQ4110 Dorset Arms BN7 2RD (0273) 477110 **£37**; 2 comfortable rms, showers. Popular 17th-c pub with friendly service, good bar food (esp fresh fish Fri lunch), restaurant, well-equipped family room, and terraces.

Gun Hill TQ5614 Gun Heathfield TN21 0JU (0825) 872361 **£32**; 3 rms, 1 with own bthrm. Run by the same people for 21 years, this charmingly furnished pub has a very nice country feel, lots of flowers, generous helpings of home-cooked bar food, several wines by the glass, and real ales; very attractive surroundings and big garden with swings for children.

Winchelsea TQ9017 New Inn TN36 4EN (0797) 226252 **£30**; 6 rms. Rambling 18th-c pub in interesting and historic village, comfortable furnishings; hearty, popular food with local, fresh fish specialities and home-made pies, and good views of interesting church from bars; cl 25-26 Dec pm.

To see and do

✝ ⛫ ⛪ ♄ ⚘ 🐘 **Alfriston** TQ5103 has thatched, tiled and timbered houses in a sheltered spot below the Downs – it strikes some as the prettiest village they've ever seen. Its fine CHURCH is built on a Saxon funeral barrow, by a large green just off the single main street. Near the church, CLERGY HOUSE, a 14th-c priest's hall house, was the first building to be taken over by the National Trust. Carefully restored, it now gives a faithful impression of what it must have been like to live in medieval times; shop; house cl Nov-Mar, shop cl Jan-Mar; £2. NT. HERITAGE CENTRE In an adjoining 15th-c forge, with local crafts, bygones, and history; shop, disabled access; cl Nov-Easter; *£1.20. One of the most engaging buildings in the village is the Star Inn, with its 'Old Bill', a bright red figurehead lion on one corner taken as a trophy from a 17th-c Dutch ship, and some intricate painted 15th-c carvings among its handsome timbering: what looks like St George and the dragon is actually St Michael killing a basilisk. In high summer the ice-cream eaters, teashops and curio shops somewhat blunt the appeal of the village, but at quieter times it's very special. Besides the Star, the Market Cross and George are good for lunch. Nearby DRUSILLAS (up towards the A27) is an excellent small zoo, very popular with children, featuring many different specialist areas including an otter valley, world of owls, meerkat mound and flamingo lagoon; good meals and snacks, shops, disabled access; cl 24-26 Dec; *£4.80. On the other side of the Cuckmere valley the small village of Litlington TQ5201 is notable for its CHURCH down a footpath – so small that there can scarcely be room in it for a congregation of more than about 15.

✝ ⛪ **Battle** TQ7415 Following the actual route into Battle used by William (taking the old London Road and turning east in Ore along The Ridge), our research officer had a re-enactment of the famous fracas that gives the place its name, involving a collision between his car and another vehicle – the driver of which bizarrely turned out to be called William Norman. It's easy to visualise the battle itself from the terrace in the grounds of BATTLE ABBEY, which the earlier William built four years later in penance for the bloodshed. Surviving ruins of the solid golden stone building include the excavated foundations of the abbey, other later remains such as the monks' dormitory and common room, and the great gatehouse which looms over the small market square. Inside is an interesting new exhibition about the site, with an interactive video on daily monastic life; snacks, shop, disabled access; cl 24-26 Dec, 1 Jan; £2.70. The battlefield itself has been kept much as it was at the time, and there's a mile-long walk around it, with models demonstrating what actually happened. The main streets (carrying a fair bit of traffic, so not exactly peaceful) have a lot of attractive old buildings, some now antique shops and cafés; beyond them the town extends into spreading new estates. BATTLE AND DISTRICT HISTORICAL SOCIETY MUSEUM Local-history exhibits including a diorama of the Battle of Hastings and a reproduction of the Bayeux Tapestry; shop; cl 1-2 pm, Sun am, Oct-Easter; *80p. A similar exhibition is at the historic old ALMONRY, which also has teas and a pretty little garden; shop, some disabled access; cl am Sun, 25-26 Dec; *£1. BUCKLEYS YESTERDAY WORLD Over 100,000 exhibits exploring the shopping and social habits of the past, with reconstructed Victorian chemist, sweet shop, railway station and the like; snacks, shop; may cl weekdays in Jan; £3.50. The Olde Kings Head, Senlac and 1066 are all useful for lunch, and the CHURCH of St Mary has some 13th-c wall paintings.

Bexhill TQ7407 BEXHILL MUSEUM OF COSTUME AND SOCIAL HISTORY Set in the rather delightful grounds of the Old Manor House, this recently refurbished museum provides something of a social history of the period 1740-1960, augmenting the collection of costumes with many other domestic items and clothing accessories; shop, disabled access; cl am weekends; *£1. This seaside town is not otherwise vividly interesting.

Bodiam TQ7825 BODIAM CASTLE Surrounded by its romantic moat, this dramatic old place, proudly standing guard over the crossing of the Rother, is the perfect picture-book castle, and a classic example of 14th-c fortification at its peak. The massive walls still rise sheer from the moat, with round drum towers at each corner, and an internal court. One of the three portcullises defending the gatehouse still survives. Despite being gutted during the Civil War, the castle was preserved by conservation-minded landowners against the 19th-c depradations which ravaged so many other fortresses, so much of the interior structure survives. There are over 30 fireplaces and 28 garderobes to see, as well as the remains of the chapel, great hall, chambers and kitchens. The view from the battlements is splendid; the best view of the castle itself is from up on the Ewhurst road. Meals and snacks, shop, disabled access; cl Mon in Oct-Mar, 25-29 Dec; £2.50. NT. Nearby Quarry Farm has a collection of STEAM ENGINES and associated antique machinery in an attractive country setting; open weekends, bank hols and Weds, Easter-Sept; £2.50. Up the hill in Ewhurst, BODIAM BONSAI grow, show and sell these miniature trees. Subject to weather, 45-minute BOAT TRIPS run to the castle through peaceful countryside from Newenden (where the White Hart is a useful pub); £6 return; not late Oct-Mar – tel (0797) 280363 for times. This can link with a STEAM TRAIN on the Kent & East Sussex Railway (see Tenterden, in the West Kent section of the Kent chapter).

Brighton TQ3105 Despite its many more modern blocks, huge shopping centre and vast modern sports halls, Brighton still has plenty of glistening white Regency buildings dating from its fashionable days in the early 18th c. Its atmosphere gets a real kick from its vigorous young university and from its several language schools for foreign students. Its most lively part is the Lanes – 17th-c fishermen's cottages squeezed together in narrow twisting byways, now crammed with jewellery and antique shops, restaurants and bars. Paramount among things to see is Nash's flamboyant Indianesque ROYAL PAVILION, the most eccentric of all royal palaces, a riot of chinoiserie inside. Years of restoration are now over, and you can once again see the apartments of Queen Victoria (the last monarch to own the Pavilion) in their full glory, while the gardens too have been restored to the original Regency plan; meals and snacks, shop, disabled access to ground floor only; cl 25-26 Dec; *£3.60. The SEA LIFE CENTRE (Marine Parade) presents excellent lively displays of creatures found off the British coast, with a new walk-through tunnel and pools where you can actually touch the creatures; meals and snacks, shop, disabled access; cl 25 Dec; £4.25. BOOTH MUSEUM OF NATURAL HISTORY (Dyke Rd) has thousands of butterfly and insect specimens, geology galleries with fossils, rocks and local dinosaur bones, plus a magnificent well-presented collection of animal skeletons. There's also the Victorian collection of birds which the museum was first built to house; shop, disabled access; cl am Thurs and Sun, 25-26 Dec, 1 Jan, Good Fri, bank hols. MUSEUM AND ART GALLERY (Church St) The Prince

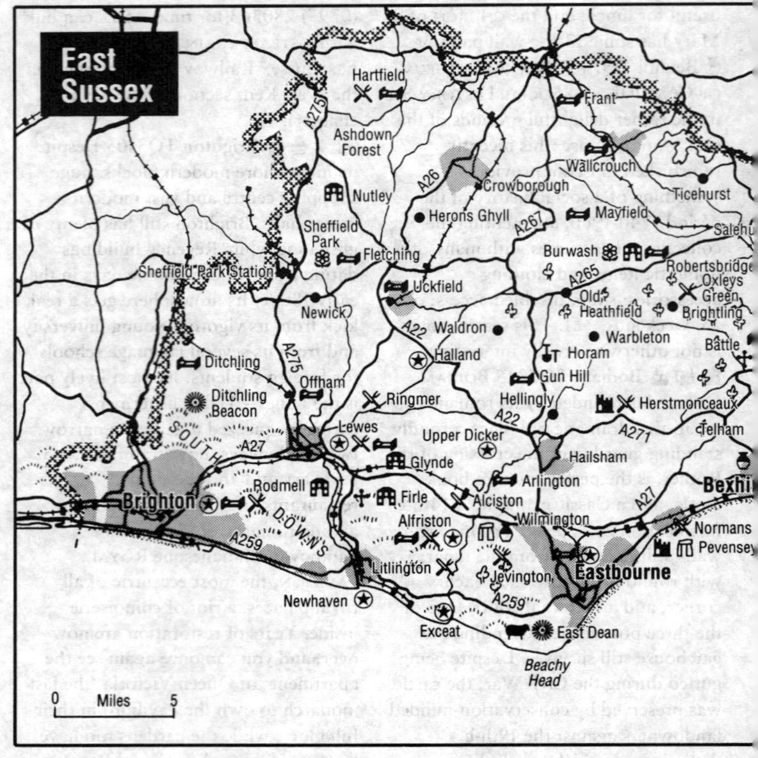

Regent's stables and riding school, now housing paintings and displays of musical instruments, as well as local history, folklore and archaeology. Snacks, disabled access to ground floor only; cl Sun am, Weds, 25-26 Dec, 1 Jan, Good Fri. BRITISH ENGINEERIUM (Nevill Rd, Hove) Traction engines, fire engines and many other engines, also restored Victorian water pumping station with original working steam beam engine of 1876, used to supply the town with well water, and a prize-winning 1889 French Corliss horizontal engine; good instructive displays, snacks, shop, limited disabled access; cl wk before Christmas; £3. There's a CAMERA OBSCURA near here at Foredown Tower. PRESTON MANOR Built in about 1738, with major alterations and additions in 1905, this is an entertaining and vivid illustration of life in Edwardian times, with fully furnished period rooms including the nursery and basement servants' quarters, and there are pleasant gardens; shop; may be cl 1-2 pm, cl Mon exc bank hols, Sun am, 25-26 Dec, Good Fri; £2.50. The modern MARINA, east of the centre, is lively in summer, with lots of boutiques, bars, tables out by the water and so forth. On Sunday mornings there's a good STREET MARKET by the station approach; you do have to get there well before breakfast for the bargains, as it's become a major source of supply for the countless Brighton antique dealers. There's no shortage of simple places to eat here. Pubs with decent food include the Cricketers (Black Lion St), Queens Head and Royal Standard

(both Queens Rd).

Burwash TQ6724 The single main street of this ridge village has many attractively restored tile-hung cottages, inc a good antique centre and tea shop, with lime trees along its brick pavement. The graveyard of the Norman-towered church gives fine views over the Dudwell Valley. Just outside the village is BATEMAN'S. Set in attractive gardens with a quaint operating watermill (grinding flour every Sat at 2 pm in season), this handsome stonebuilt 17th-c ironmaster's house was home to Rudyard Kipling from 1902 to 1936. His study is preserved much as it was then, as is the hefty pipework he installed for a hydro-electric plant to light the house. Lots of his possessions can be seen around the estate, including his 1928 Rolls-Royce, and a couple of friendly donkeys are paddocked opposite; meals and snacks, shop, disabled access to ground floor only; cl Thurs and Fri (exc Good Fri), Nov-Mar; £3.50, Sun and bank hols £4. NT. The Bell is useful for lunch, and there are good, little-used walks along the wholly unspoilt valley from here, where you can recognise Kipling landmarks such as Pooks Hill.

Ditchling Beacon TQ3313 right by the road gives superb views all around, especially out over the villages and towns to the north; a nice area of preserved sheep-cropped unimproved downland, with chalk hill blue butterflies in summer. The village below is pleasant, and the Bull is useful for lunch.

Eastbourne TU6199 Built largely in the second half of the 19th c, this civilised and restrained resort has a splendid line of imposing white-faced edifices along its long seafront. The Duke of Devonshire still owns much of the town, which was built for his ancestors; as he prohibits seaside tat, the place has a more dignified and solid feel than most seaside resorts. MUSEUM OF SHOPS AND SOCIAL HISTORY (20 Cornfield Terrace) offers a fascinating stroll through 20 reconstructed Victorian shops, a rare chance to see what sort of items featured in the weekly shopping 100 years ago; there are also other displays such as wartime rationing, Royal mementoes and seaside souvenirs. Shop, disabled access on ground floor only; cl after New Year for rest of Jan; *£2. Eastbourne's Martello Tower, one of 100 or so built to provide coastal defence against Napoleon, and interesting in itself, houses the COASTAL DEFENCE MUSEUM where displays are related to methods of defence and equipment from the Napoleonic Wars to World War II. This tower also houses an interesting exhibition of model soldiers from Norman times to World War II, ranging from toys to valuable collectors' items; shop; cl Nov-Easter. REDOUBT FORTRESS The Sussex Combined Services Museum is housed in this old fortress – another of those built during the Napoleon invasion scares of the early 19th c. Marine and freshwater fish in an aquarium grotto; meals and snacks, shop; cl 6 Nov-Easter; £1.70. LIFEBOAT MUSEUM (Grand Parade) This enthusiastic museum tells the story of the RNLI and in particular its service in this area. Models, parts and sails of the last boat at the station, along with descriptions and photographs of famous rescues; shop, disabled access; cl early Jan-week before Easter. On the prom is the BUTTERFLY CENTRE (Royal Parade), a tropical house with lush poolside plantings and free-flying butterflies; café; cl Nov-Easter; £2.25.

East Dean TV5597 SEVEN SISTERS SHEEP CENTRE (Birling Manor Farm) Family-run downland sheep farm with compact visitor centre, and paved paths between pens of many breeds of sheep, some rare; lambing (mid-Mar-early May), ancient flint barn with demonstrations of shearing (Jun-mid-July), spinning, milking and cheese-making, as well as plenty of young animals (goats, calves, pigs, rabbits and chicks) for children to cuddle, and baby lambs to bottle-feed. The farm shop has sheep cheeses, yoghurts and souvenirs; snacks, disabled access; cl am, all Oct-Feb, and may be restricted opening May – tel (0323) 423302 to check; £2. The village itself is very prettily set around a sloping green, with a useful pub for lunch, the Tiger. The road past the farm continues to the BIRLING GAP TV5595, a cleft in the coastal cliffs famous since smuggling days, with a lighthouse and coastguard station; and on to BEACHY HEAD TV5995, the towering cliffy edge of the Downs which is such a landmark for miles around: terrific views, including the lighthouse dwarfed far below, and an unspoilt spot with nature trails and a small local exhibition.

Exceat TV5199 LIVING WORLD Set in two 18th-c barns in lovely countryside above Cuckmere Haven, this has a remarkable collection of small creatures, ranging from snails through scorpions to marine life; meals and snacks, shop, disabled access; cl Nov-mid-Mar exc weekends and school hols; £2.20. Also information about the SEVEN SISTERS COUNTRY PARK all around, running down to the sea by the River Cuckmere – protected meadow, saltings, shingle and the flanking chalk headlands; you can hire bikes to go round it. The Golden Galleon is good for lunch.

Firle TQ4704 FIRLE PLACE A beautiful house, with some real treasures of European and English painting, and wonderful furnishings from renowned English and French factories. The house itself is essentially Tudor but was extensively remodelled in the 18th c; the home of the Gage family, it has some interesting mementoes of General Gage, commander of the British forces at the start of the American War of Independence. Snacks, shop; open pm Weds, Thurs and Sun May-Sept, as well as Easter and spring and summer bank hols, with longer unguided tours the first Weds each month so you can linger over some of the treasures; £3.25. In the village, the Ram is useful for lunch. The beautiful 17th-18th-c CHARLESTON FARMHOUSE (over towards Alciston, where the Rose Cottage does good food) was the home of Duncan Grant and Clive and Vanessa Bell; decorated by them, it and its magical garden still evoke the atmosphere of those Bloomsbury days; snacks (summer Suns only), shop; cl am, all day Mon (exc bank hol), Thurs and Fri (exc 23 Jul-3 Sept), all Nov-Mar; £3.75. Off the A27 a couple of miles east, BERWICK CHURCH TQ5105 has murals by the Bloomsbury Group; see also Rodmell, below.

Glynde TQ4509 GLYNDE PLACE An Elizabethan manor house in a beautiful setting. The exterior has been largely left alone but the interior was extensively remodelled in the 18th c; snacks; open pm Weds and Thurs, Jun-Sept; £3, less for garden only.

Halland TQ4916 BENTLEY WILDFOWL AND MOTOR MUSEUM The house itself is worth seeing – a Tudor farmhouse converted into a Palladian mansion, filled with fine furnishings and paintings, inc 150 watercolours by local artist Philip Rickman. The motor museum includes gleaming veteran, Edwardian and vintage vehicles, while the lakes and ponds surrounding the building are home to a countless variety of exotic wildfowl (thought to be one of the biggest collections in the country), and there's a small children's farm. Also narrow-gauge railway (to be extended by half a mile), adventure playground, licensed tearoom, shop, disabled access; cl all Jan, and wkdys Nov-late Mar, house cl am and winter; £3.40. The Forge is useful for lunch.

Hastings TQ8205 The Old Town up on the cliff at the east end is very attractive – two medieval churches, a couple of streets with raised pavements, lots of medieval buildings, and relatively unobtrusive more recent infilling. Down below, the fishermen still haul their boats up on to the beach and sell excellent fresh fish by the unusual tall black wooden net huts. The rest of the town is less interesting – a typical busy shopping town, with 19th-c resort buildings nearer the seafront, seaside hotels and B & Bs, a good prom, pier and shingle beach, pleasant enough if not remarkable. HASTINGS CASTLE AND 1066 Standing on the crumbling cliffs, the ruins of the Norman castle are close to the site of William the Conqueror's first motte and bailey castle in England. The grounds have the STORY OF 1066, a lively audio-visual exhibition on the battle and its aftermath; shop; cl Jan-mid-Feb; *£2.30. HASTINGS MUSEUM AND ART GALLERY (Johns Pl, Cambridge Rd) Local history, archaeology and wildlife, with examples of ironwork and pottery from the area; shop, disabled access; cl 1-2 pm Sat, am Sun. MUSEUM OF LOCAL HISTORY (Old Town Hall, High St) Explorations of the archaeology and history of Hastings, with particular emphasis on the fishing industry and the town's role as one of the Cinque Ports; shop; cl 1-2 pm, all day Mon, Oct-Easter. FISHERMEN'S MUSEUM (Rock-a-Nore, Harbour) Paintings, photographs, model craft and the last of Hastings' luggers built for sail are all housed in the former fishermen's chapel; shop, disabled access; open late May-Oct, cl am weekends. Nearby the SHIPWRECK HERITAGE CENTRE has an audio-visual display of 500 years of dramatic wrecks as well as plenty of rescued treasures; cl Oct-Apr; £2. The SEA LIFE CENTRE here is another in the lively chain – see entry under Brighton for details. HASTINGS EMBROIDERY (in the Town Hall, Queens Rd) An ambitious 80-yard tapestry depicting great events in British history, created by the Royal School of Needlework: also dolls in period costume and a scale model of the famous Battle itself; shop, disabled access; cl Sat, bank hols, 24-26 Dec; £1.25. SMUGGLERS ADVENTURE A labyrinth of caverns and passages deep below West Hill, with models, museum and life-size tableaux demonstrating what life as an 18th-c smuggler would have been like; shop; cl 25 Dec; £3.50. At each end of the cliffs there is an unusual sloping tracked lift down to sea level (55p). The First In Last Out in the Old Town is useful for lunch.

Herstmonceux TQ6312 The extensive gardens around this very handsome 15th-c brick-built castle (which some 50 years ago was rebuilt internally for the Royal Observatory) are generally open in summer – tel (0323) 833913 to check.

Horam TQ5818 is the home of MERRYDOWN VINTAGE CIDER, who make it in the traditional way; audio-visual show and tours. Shop; cl Mon and weekends; booking required – tel (0435) 812254. The Gun is useful for food.

Lewes TQ4110 The administrative capital of East Sussex, this is a pleasantly unrushed country town below the quarried white edge of the South Downs. It has some attractive old buildings, mainly Georgian though with a few older stonebuilt or timber-framed specimens, particularly along its steep main street and in the little narrow alleys and other streets alongside. This is where you'll see Sussex tile-hanging at its best; there are several decent antique shops, and an attractive complex of CRAFT SHOPS in a former candlemaker's factory in Market Lane; café, cl Sun. Strategically sited on the mouth of the River Ouse, the town was an important place in Saxon times, and an obvious place to build a Norman stronghold. William gave it to his son-in-law William de Warenne, whose CASTLE was unusual for being built on not one but two artificial mounds (Lincoln is the only other such place we know of). Much of the surviving walling still stands, and the best view of the town is obtained from the roof of the keep; the tall-towered outer gatehouse dates from the early 14th c, with later architectural additions. Near this barbican is the MUSEUM, with displays on prehistoric, Roman, Saxon and medieval Sussex. The town's history is explored in a 25-minute tape/slide show; shop; cl Christmas; £2.50. ANNE OF CLEVES HOUSE Not all Henry VIII's wives were able to come away from the marriage with anything to show for it, but Anne of Cleves received this fine 16th-c house as part of her divorce settlement. Its rooms give an idea of what life was like here over the following two centuries, and displays include arts, crafts and costumes of the area, as well as aspects of local agricultural, industrial and domestic life; shop; cl Sun am, all Nov-Apr; £1.60. The Dorset Arms, Pelham Arms, Chalk Pit and Rainbow are useful for lunch.

Newhaven TQ4401 NEWHAVEN FORT Built 120 years ago in case of French attack, this is a big place to explore, with underground installations and tunnels burrowing into the cliffs, and super views from its ramparts. There's a comprehensive museum about the site and its part in the two World Wars, and an assault course for children; snacks, shop; cl Mon and Tues, all Nov-Mar; *£3. GARDEN PARADISE AND PLANET EARTH Gardening centre with new exhibition designed to bring 4,500 million years of change and development dramatically to life. Also desert, tropical and subtropical plant houses, and a miniature railway through the grounds; meals, snacks, shops, disabled access, cl 25-26 Dec; £2.99 for exhibition. You can take the four-hour FERRY TRIP to Dieppe in France from here.

Northiam TQ8324 GREAT DIXTER Timbered house dating from the 15th c, carefully restored and added to by Lutyens in the early part of this century. Particularly worth a look is the great 15th-c hall, its hammerbeams carved with armorial bearings inc the arms of the Dalyngrygges who built nearby Bodiam Castle. The gardens, also designed by Lutyens, are attractive. Originally arranged as a series of distinct areas, they were later stocked more informally with interesting plants by the gardening writer Christopher Lloyd who lives here; plant sales; house and gardens open pm Apr-10 Oct (open earlier Sun in July and Aug), cl Mon exc bank hols; £3.30, £2.20 gardens only. Another fine old building here is BRICKWALL HOUSE, dating back 500 years, with splendid 17th-c plastered ceilings; shop, disabled access; open pm Sat and bank hols Easter-Sept; *£2. The Juggs at Kingston on the way from Lewes is good for lunch.

Nutley TQ4427 The 300-year-old WINDMILL here is the only working open trestle post mill in the country, saved from decline by enthusiastic locals before such action became more common (until then it was precariously propped up by telegraph poles).

Pevensey TQ6404 PEVENSEY CASTLE The castle is based on a 4th-c Roman fort, covering some 10 acres, with massive bastions and walls of Roman masonry still up to 30 ft high in places. There's also the Norman keep built by William the Conqueror and 13th-c additions, and you can see interesting interior details inc fireplaces, dungeons and an oubliette; snacks, shop, some disabled access; cl 1-2 pm, and Mon Oct-Mar; *£1.70. The Royal Oak & Castle, right by the gate, is useful for a bite to eat, and the nearby Smugglers is an appropriate-feeling sort of place.

Rodmell TQ4106 MONKS HOUSE Just a quiet lived-in village house, in a pleasant village, but a beautifully kept place of pilgrimage for followers of the Bloomsbury Group, as Leonard and Virginia Woolf lived here from 1919 until their deaths; open pm Weds and Sat only, Mar-Nov; £2. The Juggs at Kingston on the way from Lewes is good for lunch.

Rye TQ9220 is an enchanting town, easily worth spending a day or longer wandering through, its interesting history strongly bound up with its relationship with the sea. Before the wind and sea currents did their work, the town was virtually surrounded by sea, and as one of the Cinque Ports played an important part in providing men and ships for coastal defence – most notably in the 13th and 14th c. There are still plenty of impressive remains of the fortifications. The town is built on a hill crowned by a partly Norman CHURCH (with a very early turret-clock, two quarter-jacks by it striking the quarter-hours); up here the largely cobbled streets still follow a 12th-13th-c narrow layout, with most of the houses lining them dating from the 16th c (when the town was rebuilt following a series of devastating French raids). The views from up here are lovely, and steep Mermaid Street in particular is famously photogenic (the Mermaid itself is a grand old inn). The town is still almost encircled by three rivers, and its unique and peaceful atmosphere has inspired artists in all media. LAMB HOUSE (West St) was built in 1723 for James Lamb, who, like his son, was mayor of the town. It's chiefly devoted now to mementoes of the author Henry James, who lived here from 1898 to 1916; after his death E F Benson, who also became mayor, moved here; open pm Weds and Sat Mar-Nov; £2. NT. RYE MUSEUM This 13th-c Ypres Tower (as in Wipers) was originally built to defend the town, but later became the courthouse, and for 300 years after that was used as a prison. It's now a local history museum with Cinque Ports material, militaria, toys, dolls and medieval pottery; shop; cl Nov-Mar; *£1.50. The town is full of antique shops, book shops and craft shops – mostly good stuff, not tat. The Hope & Anchor is useful for food. The HARBOUR, because of the build-up of shingle along this coast, is now a mile or two from the town, though yachts and fishing boats do still come right up the river to the pretty quay at the bottom of the town. Tony Easton will take you SEA FISHING for the day: tel (0797) 252104. The expanse of shingle stretching around the river mouth is now preserved as a NATURE RESERVE, with hides to watch the sea birds. CAMBER CASTLE, a massive Tudor fort right on the coast, is now stranded a mile or so inshore by the encroaching shingle; it's undergoing restoration work and has not yet been reopened.

Sheffield Park TQ4124 Covering 200 acres, this wonderful garden was landscaped by Capability Brown and has since been imaginatively planted with many varieties of tree unknown to him, especially chosen for their autumn colours – each of the several hundred black gums, for instance, seems to flare into a different colour in September and October, despite their all being a single species (*Nyssa sylvatica*); there are also marvellous rhododendrons, azaleas and waterlilies on the lakes. Snacks, shop, disabled access; cl Mon, mid-Nov-Apr; £3.50-£4 depending on season. NT. The Griffin at Fletching nearby is good for lunch.

Sheffield Park Station TQ4023 BLUEBELL LINE Recently extended steam railway, with 9-mile trips through Horsted Keynes to Kingscote (where there are period bus connections to BR East Grinstead). The journey goes past woodlands that are a mass of bluebells in late spring, usually at their best in mid-May – hence the name of the line. Part of the station is a museum and houses the region's largest railway collection, including some 30 locomotives and many carriages. Pullman dining specials, Santa specials, shop, café; some trains all year, daily Jun-Sept – best to tel (0825) 722370 for dates and times; *£7.50. The Sloop at Scaynes Hill not far off is good for lunch.

✝ **Upper Dicker** TQ5510 MICHELHAM PRIORY The Augustinian priory here was founded in 1219, and the site has a 14th-c gatehouse by the moat (spaciously encircling the grounds, with plenty of waterfowl), and a charming 16th-c house based on the original building, with interesting furniture, tapestries and local ironwork. The grounds also have examples of many traditional local crafts, for example a blacksmith's and wheelwright's shop, working watermill, and museum on the local industry of ropemaking; meals and snacks, shop, disabled access to ground floor only; cl Nov-Mar exc Sun in Mar and Nov; *£3.30. The Plough is good for lunch.

Wilmington TQ5403 Famous for its LONG MAN, a gigantic chalk-cut figure so far impossible to date – guesses hover anywhere between the early 18th c and the Bronze Age. Below the hill with a view of the Long Man is WILMINGTON PRIORY, a largely Tudor house based on a 12th-c Benedictine priory, with a small folk museum including a Tudor kitchen and agricultural bygones; sizeable garden, disabled access; cl am Sun, all Tues and Sat, all Nov-Feb; £1.50. The recently reopened Giants Rest has good home cooking, and the Sussex Ox at Milton Street is a good family pub.

✝ **Winchelsea** TQ9017 The original port was smashed by storms in the 13th c and rebuilt around 1300, though a series of French raids over the next 150 years meant that few old buildings and little of the original fortifications have survived. With the river silting up it lost its role as a port, and is interesting now for the way it's so obviously shrunk: a quiet and pleasant little place, dwarfed by the distances between the three surviving town gates around it. The ROYAL MILITARY CANAL runs from here to Hythe in Kent, a never-used Napoleonic defence that was meant as a sort of glorified coastal moat – now a peaceful spot for coarse fishermen. The New Inn is good for lunch, and the CHURCH has some fine old stained glass and medieval tombs.

Among several flourishing **vineyards** here, notable ones that do tours or vineyard trails and tastings include ST GEORGES at Waldron TQ5419 (attractively laid out for visitors, with changing art and craft exhibitions in a 15th-c tithe barn, a pleasant restaurant, craft shop, charming village and scenery; adopt-a-vine scheme; cl wkdys Mar-Easter, Nov-Feb); BARNSGATE MANOR at Herons Ghyll TQ4828 (attractive restaurant with great views from terrace – good for parties; also llamas, donkeys, shop, good disabled facilities); BARKHAM MANOR near Newick TQ4321 (attractive grounds around Manor House, 18th-c thatched barn, shop; cl Mon, cl Christmas-Easter); and CARR TAYLOR at Westfield TQ8115 (one of England's most successful commercial vineyards, producing sparkling wine as well as still; cl Christmas/New Year, cl weekends Jan-Easter).

★ **Attractive villages,** all with decent pubs, include Brightling TQ6921 (though Jack Fullers on Oxleys Green is now more restaurant than pub), Fletching TQ4223, Frant TQ5835, Hartfield TQ4735, Hellingly TQ5812, Mayfield TQ5827, Old Heathfield TQ5920 (not Heathfield itself, a mile or two W), Robertsbridge TQ7323, Salehurst TQ7424, Sedlescombe TQ7718, Ticehurst TQ6830 (the best pub is the Bull, up a side road at Three Legged Cross) and Warbleton TQ6018 (more pre-1750 Sussex barns here than anywhere else in the county).

Walks

The South Downs Way has the area's best or at least most expansive walks. There is a fine stretch with distant views up over **Ditchling Beacon** TQ8813 (easy access from the road) and **Firle Beacon** TQ4805 E of Lewes. At Alfriston TQ5103 the Way splits into two. The coastal route joins the sea at **Cuckmere Haven** TV5196 for a march along the **Seven Sisters** TV5396, a series of chalk cliffs which, together with Beachy Head, are the spectacular finale of the South Downs; for an interesting circular route you can head inland by Friston Forest TV5499, Westdean TV5299 and East Dean TV5597. **Beachy Head** TV5995, the giant of these cliffs, has a lighthouse far below, and is within close reach of Eastbourne TV6199. From the Old Town in the E of Hastings TQ8205, a path climbs on to the sandstone cliffs for a rugged couple of miles towards **Fairlight Cove** TQ8711. The coast here has a tumbled appearance and cliff-falls occur occasionally.

The inland South Downs Way route from Alfriston bound for Jevington TQ5601 and Eastbourne passes **Lullington Heath** TQ5401, a rare survival of downland untampered with by modern farming practices, and managed as a National Nature Reserve for its chalkland and heathland flora; a diversion to Wilmington TQ5403 gives a view of the enigmatic chalk figure, the Long Man of Wilmington.

A major inland attraction is the **Ashdown Forest,** part forest, part heathland. Don't be put off by the OS map: there are far more walking routes than it suggests. Sandy tracks, clumps of Scots pines, secretive glades and exhilarating views comprise the key factors. It looks just like the E H Sheppard drawings for A A Milne's *Winnie the Pooh* stories, which were set here. **Five Hundred Acre Wood** TQ4832 is the Hundred Acre Wood of Pooh's world, and with a little searching you can find, SE of Hartfield TQ4735, the **Poohsticks Bridge** and, by the B2026, **Gills Lap** TQ4631 (the 'enchanted place' at the top of the Forest, near Piglet's house), where a memorial to Milne has been placed near the triangulation point. **Camp Hill** TQ0311, near Nutley Windmill, is one of the best walking areas in the Ashdown Forest. Handy pubs for Ashdown Forest walks include the Foresters Arms at Fairwarp TQ4646 and Hatch at Colemans Hatch TQ4533.

In May, there are pleasant walks through bluebell woods near the Old Oak at Caneheath TQ5507. East Sussex shares Bewl Water with Kent – see West Kent section of Kent chapter.

Driving

Attractive downland routes include the clifftop road E from Fairlight to Winchelsea, the busy A27 between Polegate and Brighton along the N slope of the South Downs, for the views of the Downs themselves; the B2116 from Polegate to Ditchling, for quieter Downs views; the back road S of Ditchling up over the Downs towards Brighton, for terrific views over both the Weald and then Brighton itself and the coast.

In the Weald, the back road from Northiam through Ewhurst Green and Bodiam towards Hurst Green, but taking the southwards loop through Salehurst, is good. The B2096 from just W of Battle towards Heathfield gives views S to Beachy Head from its highest points, near Netherfield and just before Dallington. Off this road any of the narrow side roads N into the countryside between Burwash and Dallington take you into what is probably the most unspoilt expanse of hilly Wealden woods-and-pasture anywhere.

In the Ashdown Forest, the B2026 right across its heart is good.

Where to eat

Herstmonceux TQ6312 SUNDIAL (0323) 832217 17th-c cottage with excellent, varied food, very good wine list, and terrace and garden in which to eat during summer; cl Sun pm, Mon, last 3 wks Aug, 25 Dec-middle Jan. **£25/£36 – though set meals are about £10 cheaper**|**£16.**

Ringmer TQ4412 COCK (0273) 812040 Civilised, heavily-beamed bar with good inglenook log fire, freshly prepared good food, decent wines, 2 lounges (one is no smoking), and seats on good terrace and attractive fairy-lit garden; cl 25 Dec. **£26.25**|£5.25.

Jevington TQ5601 HUNGRY MONK The Street (0323) 482178 Celebrating 25 years under the same ownership (and many of the same staff) this popular candlelit evening restaurant (they do Sun lunch) has 3 sitting rooms, bar, little dining room, open fires, beams, a friendly, dinner-partyish atmosphere, and good, interesting food. **£24.**

Alfriston TQ5103 MOONRAKERS (0323) 870472 Reliably good food in cosy little cottage with log fire, good wine list, and friendly staff; cl Sun, Mon, 25 Dec, no under-10s. **£21.**

Hastings TQ8109 ROSERS (0424) 712218 Extremely good imaginative food (lots of fish dishes) in cosy little restaurant opposite pier; fine wines, too; cl Sun/Mon, Sat am, 1st wk Jan; disabled access. **£20**|£10.95.

Brighton TQ3105 IL BISTRO 6 Market St The Lanes (0273) 324584 Friendly place with wide choice of popular food, decent wine list, and efficient, friendly service; cl 25-26 Dec. **£18**|£4.50.

Brighton TQ3105 IL TEATRO 7 New Rd (0273) 202158 Friendly and enjoyable Italian restaurant next to Theatre Royal; cl Sun, 25 Dec. **£17.85**|£4.95/£7.

Litlington TQ5201 LITLINGTON TEA ROOMS (0323) 870222 Established 150 years ago, these tearooms still retain their quaint Victorian elegance, with seating on an attractive sheltered lawn, under a copper beach or ginko, in renovated beach huts with open fronts or tearoom/restaurant; colourful hanging baskets and flowering tubs, quick, efficient service, and snacks, proper English teas, and weekend French 'gourmet' lunches; handy for Alfriston; cl Nov-Mar, disabled access. **£17**|£1.20/£4.50.

Oxleys Green TQ6921 JACK FULLERS (042 482) 212 Smart pub, now really a restaurant, with very good food inc interesting pies and fine steamed puddings, vegetarian dishes, lots of wines (English ones, too), and pleasant service; cl Mon, Tues, Sun pm, sometime in Jan. **£16**|£6.

Lewes TQ4110 LA CUCINA Station St (0273) 476707 Good Italian restaurant with pine tables; cl Sun, cl Mon-Weds am, 2 wks over Christmas. **£13**|£6.50.

Alciston TQ5005 ROSE COTTAGE (0323) 870377 In the same family for over 30 years, this charming wisteria-covered cottage is popular for its home-made, traditional food (inc local fish and game), real ales and good house wines; small no-smoking evening restaurant as well as bar. £3.50/£5.25.

Normans Bay TQ6805 STAR (0323) 762648 Friendly ex-smugglers pub with spaciously modernised bar, friendly atmosphere and huge helpings of popular food inc lots of puddings; paths inland to the marshy nature reserve. £3/£5.50.

Hartfield TQ4735 ANCHOR (0892) 770424 Relaxed and friendly pub nr good walks, popular front verandah, and very good seafood; cl 25 Dec pm. £2/£3.50.

WEST SUSSEX

There's lots to interest visitors here, especially magnificent gardens and fine houses; plus some luxurious places to stay.

The open-air museum at Singleton and the chalk pits museum at Amberley are both most enjoyable, and West Sussex has some of England's most gorgeous gardens, the larger ones beautifully laid out in settings of great natural beauty, with many of the finest specimen trees and shrubs to be found anywhere, and many species which are either too tender or simply too rare to turn up elsewhere. The greatest are Wakehurst Place at Ardingly, Leonardslee at Lower Beeding, Nymans at Handcross and Borde Hill near Haywards Heath. The Roman villas at Bignor and Fishbourne are very splendid in their way, and Arundel Castle, Goodwood House, Parham House at Pulborough and Petworth House are all marvellous places to visit. Rejectamenta at East Wittering is an engaging utter contrast. Chichester and Arundel are both pleasant and rewarding places to spend time strolling around, and the area has many attractive villages besides. There's a good range of countryside from the rich woodlands up in the north towards Haslemere to the downlands north of Chichester, while south and west of Chichester the flat countryside around the great sea inlet of Chichester Harbour has some very quiet places by the shore.

There are some lovely hotels, at a price, as well as a decent selection of less expensive places to stay.

Where to stay

East Grinstead TQ3938 Gravetye Manor RH19 4LJ (0342) 810567 **£176**; 18 lovely rms. Elizabethan manor house in beautiful grounds with lovely antiques and fine paintings in spacious panelled public rooms; excellent restaurant using home-grown produce (inc spring water and free-range eggs) and their own home-smoked fish and meats; an exceptional wine list, and a relaxed, almost old-fashioned atmosphere; children over 7.

Turners Hill TQ3435 Alexander House Crawley RG10 4QD (0342) 714914 **£165**; 16 luxurious rms. Standing in 135 acres, this magnificent country mansion has grand day rooms with hand-painted silk wall panels, crystal chandeliers, fine antiques and paintings; courteous, friendly service, lovely flowers, and good, modern cooking; no children.

Amberley TQ0111 Amberley Castle Arundel BN18 9ND (0798) 831992 **£95**; 14 well-equipped, charming rms. Magnificent 900-year-old castle with day rooms filled with suits of armour and weapons as well as antiques, roaring fires and panelling; friendly service, imaginative cooking and well-kept gardens; disabled access.

Rusper TQ2037 Ghyll Manor Horsham RH12 4XX (0293) 871571 **£95**; 25 rms in the main house, converted stable block or extension. Fine old manor house in 40 acres of grounds with log fire in the oak-panelled library-cum-lounge, and attractive candlelit restaurant; croquet, outdoor swimming pool; disabled access.

Cuckfield TQ3025 Ockenden Manor RH17 5LD (0444) 416111 **£90**; 22 rms. Lovely views and a pretty garden surround this mainly Tudor building with its panelled bar, elegant lounge, and attractive restaurant; disabled access.

Bosham SU8003 Millstream Chichester PO18 8HL (0243) 573234 ***£89**; 29 rms. Warmly friendly small family-run hotel with very good hot and cold buffet lunch; close to the sea and 1,000-year-old church; disabled access.

Climping TQ0002 Bailiffscourt Littlehampton BN17 5RW (0903) 723511 **£80**; 20 rms, mainly with real fires in winter. Mock 13th-c manor built only 60 years ago but with tremendous character – fine old iron-studded doors, huge fireplaces, heavy beams and so forth; garden with outdoor swimming pool, tennis and croquet.

Storrington TQ0814 Abingworth Hall Pulborough RH20 3EF (0798) 813636 **£80**; 21 rms. Country hotel with warm family atmosphere, good food, decent wines, excellent service, small outdoor heated swimming pool, and musical evenings and wine tasting events; disabled access.

Midhurst SU8821 Spread Eagle GU29 9NH (0730) 816911 **£78**; 41 rms. Historic old inn dating back in part to 1430; impressive beamed and timbered lounge, handsome furnishings, very good food, and friendly service; disabled access.

Lancing TQ1804 Sussex Pad VN15 0RH (0273) 454647 **£72**; 20 rms. Comfortable refurbished hotel with wonderful views of the Adur Valley and Sussex Downs, a relaxing atmosphere, good, reasonably priced food, fine wine list, and impeccable but friendly service; by Shoreham airport.

Bognor Regis TQ2623 Royal Norfolk PO21 2LH (0243) 826222 **£70**; 51 rms. Comfortable Regency hotel on seafront with good food and pleasant service; outdoor swimming pool, tennis, croquet.

Arundel TQ0107 Norfolk Arms BN18 9AD (0903) 882101 **£69.90**; 34 rms. Comfortable genuinely old hotel with good food and service, pleasant bar, lounge, and restaurant.

Chichester SU8605 BEDFORD PO19 1DP (0243) 785766 **£62**; 23 comfortable rms. Family-run Georgian hotel in centre of city, with friendly atmosphere, comfortable lounge and restaurant opening out on to quiet terrace.

Chichester SU8605 SUFFOLK HOUSE PO19 1PD (0243) 778924 **£60**; 10 comfortable, spacious rms. Warmly friendly 18th-c town house in quiet back street with relaxed atmosphere, extremely helpful, thoughtful service, very good food, and little walled garden; close to cathedral, theatre and station; they are kind to children; disabled access.

Sutton SU9715 WHITE HORSE The Street Pulborough RH20 1PS (079 87) 221 **£58**; 5 rms. Attractive creeper-covered inn in pretty village nr Bignor Roman villa, with log fires, pleasant garden, and good South Downs walks.

Fittleworth TQ0118 SWAN Pulborough RG20 1EN (079 882) 429 **£55**; 10 rms. Attractive 15th-c inn with big inglenook log fire in comfortable lounge, friendly service, decent food, attractive panelled side room, sheltered back lawn; good nearby walks.

Rogate SU8023 MIZZARDS Petersfield GU31 5HS (0730) 821656 **£46**; 3 rms. 16th-c house in quiet country setting with comfortable elegant sitting room, vaulted dining room, outside swimming pool, landscaped gardens and lake, and fine farmland views; no evening meals and no smoking; cl Christmas; children over 7.

Wisborough Green TQ0526 OLD WHARF Billingshurst RG14 0JG **£45**; 4 rms with views over farmland and canal. Carefully restored canal warehouse with fine old hoist wheel, comfortable sitting room with log fire, breakfasts using free-range eggs from the farm, walled canalside garden, and friendly atmosphere; no smoking, no pets; cl Christmas/New Year; children over 12.

Bosham SU8003 KENWOOD PO18 8PH (0243) 572727 ***£40**; 3 large rms. Comfortable and well-kept Victorian house with harbour views, plushly furnished lounge, pleasant dining room, heated swimming pool, and free-range poultry; fitness equipment; disabled access.

Arundel TQ0107 BRIDGE HOUSE BN18 9JG (0903) 882142 ***£38**; 19 rms, most with own bthrm. Very pleasant bedrooms, overlooking Arundel Castle; cl 1 wk Christmas; disabled access.

Shipley TQ1422 GOFFSLAND FARM Horsham RG13 7BQ (0403) 730434 **£28**; 1 family rm. Friendly 17th-c farmhouse in the Sussex Weald on 260-acre family farm; good walks.

To see and do

Amberley TQ0313 AMBERLEY CHALK PITS MUSEUM Set in a 36-acre former chalk quarry and limeworks, this carefully thought-out museum examines many of Britain's traditional industries, with craftsmen and recreated workshops inc pottery and cobbling, concrete exhibition, engineering workshop, lime kilns and grinding mill among a host of others; there's also a miniature railway and collection of vintage buses; meals and snacks, shop, disabled access; cl Mon and Tues (exc school hols), all Nov-Mar; £4.20. The Black Horse in the delightful thatched village nearby is good for lunch.

Ansty TQ2923 LEGH MANOR The garden was designed by Gertrude Jekyll, and in the charming house (reworked by Lutyens) three rooms and the hall can be viewed; open every 2nd and 3rd Weds, every 2nd Sat, Jun-Sept; 40p. The White Harte in nearby Cuckfield is good value for lunch.

Ardingly TQ3429 WAKEHURST PLACE GARDEN Tremendous variety of interesting trees and shrubs including many tender rarities; lakes and water gardens, steep Himalayan glade, woodland walks and fine rhododendron species in peaceful and large garden which is now the 'Southern Kew', administered by the Royal Botanic Gardens. Meals and snacks, plant and book sales, disabled access; cl 25 Dec, 1 Jan; *£3.50. NT. The appropriately named Gardeners Arms is good for lunch (children in garden only).

Arundel TQ0101 The town itself dates back to pre-Roman days, and is dominated by the magnificent walls and towers of the castle, on a mound high over the River Arun. Attractive buildings, including antique shops and so forth, cluster along the sides of the steep main street climbing up from the bridge to the castle itself. The MUSEUM AND HERITAGE CENTRE along here has a good potted history; shop; cl 1-2 pm, am Sun, all day Mon (exc bank hols), weekdays in Apr, May and Sept and all Oct-Easter; £1. The CASTLE was built at the end of the 11th c, and has been the seat of the Dukes of Norfolk for over 700 years (a plaque in the main square says 'Since William Rose and Harold Fell, There have been Earls at Arundel'). It's a magnificent sight, a great spread of well-kept towers and battlements soaring above the village and the trees around it. The keep is the oldest part; much of the rest of the building dates from the 19th c, and its treasures include portraits by Van Dyck, Reynolds, Lely and Gainsborough, as well as furniture dating from the 16th c, and personal possessions of Mary Queen of Scots; meals and snacks, shop; cl Sat, Nov-Mar; £4. The new (well, 19th-c) Roman Catholic CATHEDRAL built to complement the castle does so very well, giving rather a French feel to the whole small town. TOY AND MILITARY MUSEUM Full of curiosities and interesting little things to look at, this has a private collection of games, toys, dolls, bears, rocking horses, lead soldiers, puppets, fancy egg-cups, boats and Goss miniatures collected from all over the world, housed in an attractive small Georgian cottage in the heart of the town. Shop, disabled access to ground floor only; cl am, weekdays Oct-May exc some school hols; *£1.25. ENGLISH COUNTRY CRAFTS, in a converted chapel in Tarrant St, has a good range of local crafts – they have another branch in Worthing. WILDFOWL AND WETLANDS TRUST 55

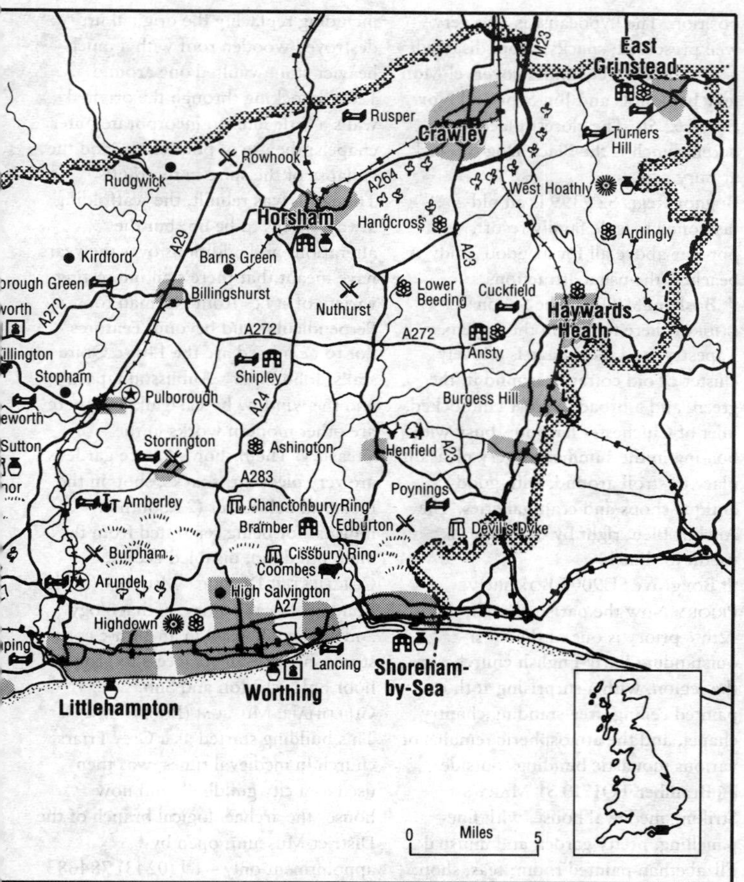

acres of well-landscaped pens, lakes, and paddocks are home to over 1,000 ducks, geese and swans from all over the world, and the site also acts as a sanctuary for wild birds. Hides overlooking the different habitats make observing the birds easier, and the site also has a large viewing gallery and education complex; meals and snacks, shop, disabled access; cl 25 Dec; £3.75. The lane past the Trust ends at a little cluster of houses by an isolated church and former watermill. On the way to the Trust, the Black Rabbit has a superb location and does food; in the town, the Bridge House, Red Lion and White Hart have decent food.

Ashington TQ1315 HOLLY GATE CACTUS GARDEN Over 30,000 succulents and cactus plants from both tropical and arid habitats all over the world – all kept in over 10,000 sq ft of greenhouses – a cactus enthusiast's prickly paradise. Snacks, plant sales, disabled access; cl 25-26 Dec; *£1.50. The Franklands Arms at Washington is useful for lunch.

Bignor SU9814 ROMAN VILLA AND MUSEUM One of the largest villas yet discovered, this has marvellous mosaics including the longest in Britain – 82 ft long, and still in its original position. The hypocaust is also very well preserved; snacks, shop, disabled access, and largely under cover; cl Mon (exc bank hols and Jun-Sept), all Nov-Feb; *£2.50. The closest place for a decent lunch is the Black Dog & Duck at Bury.

Bognor Regis SZ9399 is an old-fashioned seaside family resort, popular above all for its good sandy beaches; the usual attractions.

✝ **Bosham** SU8003 The Saxon CHURCH here figures in the Bayeux Tapestry, and the village is a lovely cluster of old cottages around it, the green, and a broad, almost landlocked, inlet of Chichester harbour, busy with boating in the summer. A very pleasant place to stroll around, with good antique shops and craft galleries. The Anchor Bleu, right by the water, is useful for lunch.

✝ **Boxgrove** SU9007 BOXGROVE PRIORY Now the parish church, this 12th-c priory is one of the most outstanding Early English churches in the region, with a surprising 16th-c painted ceiling, free-standing chantry chapel, and the atmospheric remains of various monastic buildings outside.

Bramber TQ1710 ST MARY'S Striking medieval house, with fine panelling, pretty garden and unusual Elizabethan painted room; teas, shop; open pm Sun, Thurs and bank hols Easter-Sept, plus pm Mon July-Sept; £3.30.

✝ **Chichester** TQ1811 With a heritage reaching back as far as the Romans who called it Noviomagus, this handsome small city, now partly pedestrianised, is one of the country's finest examples of Georgian town planning and architecture. The CATHEDRAL is Norman, begun some time after 1091, although building continued throughout the 12th c, and it's unusual for rising straight out of the town's streets rather than a secluded close. It's had structural problems down the centuries, aggravated by ad hoc alterations, including replacing the original fire-destroyed wooden roof with a much heavier stone-vaulted one around 1200; knocking through the original walls a little later to incorporate outer chapels; the use of poor stone, and the collapse of the spire in the 1860s. Though it was rebuilt, the scaffolding always seems to be up; but the alterations and additions over the years have meant that there's an interesting variety of styles from Norman to Perpendicular and beyond. Features not to be missed are the 14th-c Quire stalls, John Piper's Aubusson tapestry and the window by Chagall, and there are other modern works in the Treasury. The Bishop's Palace gardens are very pleasant; snacks, shop in the medieval bell tower (23 South St – unusual for being separated from the main building), disabled access.

CHICHESTER DISTRICT MUSEUM (Little London) Local history, archaeology and geology housed in an 18th-c corn store; shop, disabled access to ground floor only; cl Mon and Sun.

GUILDHALL MUSEUM (Priory Park) This building started as a Grey Friars church in medieval times, was then used as a city guildhall, and now houses the archaeological branch of the District Museum; open by appointment only – tel (0243) 784683 – though they hope this will change.

MECHANICAL MUSIC AND DOLL COLLECTION (Church Rd, Portfield) There are many interesting curiosities in this museum, a former Victorian church: stereoscopic viewers, vintage cycles, natural history exhibits and a doll collection with a great many French and German dolls. But the main feature is the multitude of barrel, fair and Dutch street organs, music boxes and phonographs – all restored and ready to play. Shop, disabled access; cl am, all day Sat, Oct-Easter exc Sun (not Dec); £2. PALLANT HOUSE (North Pallant) A Queen Anne town house with an Edwardian kitchen and fine furnishings. The gallery has a fine collection of Bow porcelain, and a good range of extremely carefully chosen 20th-c art – Sutherland, Klee, Leger, Ben Nicholson and the like. The garden is planted in 18th-c style; shop; cl Sun and Mon; £2.50. In St Pauls St, the White Horse is useful for lunch. South of Chichester is flat country with nurseries and huge glasshouses; there's also the peaceful NATURE RESERVE of Pagham Harbour SZ8796, largely silted marshy tidal flats, full of wading birds and wildfowl, particularly in spring and autumn. The Crab & Lobster at Sidlesham on the edge of the reserve is handy for lunch. Peter Adams runs BOAT TRIPS from Chichester Harbour, full of yachts and dinghies in summer; from Itchenor SU8001 (where the Lamb is useful for lunch), timetable (0243) 786418 – best at high tide, £3.50; and there's an hourly passenger ferry between there and the landing at the end of the lane south from Bosham (not weekdays Oct-Easter).

Coombes TQ1908 CHURCH FARM also organise trailer rides over farmland and through conservation areas – you have to book (tel (0273) 452028), but it's great fun, especially in the lambing season; cl mid-Oct-Feb; £2. They also have a coarse fishing lake, open in summer and also some winter eves.

Dell Quay SU8302 APULDRAM ROSES Over 300 kinds of old-fashioned and new roses in harbourside field and gardens made from former orchards; the shop sells various types, and everything needed to look after them. They have a sale at the end of the season in Sept; shop all year, field from Jun. The attractive waterside hamlet has the remains of a Roman quay.

East Grinstead TQ3938 The town itself is really to be avoided, with long weekend traffic queues, but its main attractions are actually just outside, off the B2110 just west. STANDEN Designed by Philip Webb, a friend of William Morris, and little changed since, this house is a fine example of the many talents of the 19th-c Arts and Crafts Movement. The interior is decorated with several different William Morris wallpapers, while many of the furnishings are of the period, even down to the unusual light fittings designed by Webb; snacks, shop, limited disabled access; cl am, Mon and Tues, Nov-Mar; *£3.80, *£2.30 garden only. NT. INGWERSENS NURSERY (Birch Farm, Gravetye) is a very long-established alpine plants specialist; disabled access; cl 1-1.30 pm, weekends Nov-Feb. Out this way, the Cat in the pretty village of West Hoathly TQ3632 (see below) has good food, and the White Hart at Selsfield and Crown at Turners Hill are also useful for lunch.

East Wittering SZ7997 REJECTAMENTA NOSTALGIA MUSEUM (Church Rd) has over 25,000 everyday objects from this century, collected over 22 years by an ex-art student who says she just can't stop; everything from gasmasks through knickers to pre-war lavatory paper, with period music and television programmes like Andy Pandy and Bill and Ben. The museum is unusually located in an old CHURCH, parts of which date back to the 12th c; shop, disabled access; cl Sat and all Nov-Easter; *£1.80.

Fishbourne SU8304 ROMAN PALACE This magnificent villa with its 100 or so rooms was occupied from the 1st to the 3rd c, and is the largest known residence from the period in Britain. The museum details the villa's history, while on the site itself you can see 25 of the mosaic floors, and a garden has been laid out according to its 1st-c plan; meals and snacks, shop, disabled access; cl mid-Dec-mid-Feb; £3.20.

Fontwell SU9507 DENMANS GARDEN A colourful series of vistas over 3½ acres, inc exuberantly Oriental-feeling areas with a gravel stream, ornamental grasses, bamboos and flowering cherries, as well as a beautiful richly planted walled garden; meals, snacks, plant sales, disabled access; cl Jan and Feb; £2.25. The George at Eartham nearby is good for lunch.

Goodwood SU8808 GOODWOOD HOUSE Set in beautiful downland countryside, the house contains some marvellous treasures, especially its 18th-c furniture, with fine Sèvres porcelain, tapestries, and paintings by Canaletto and Stubbs. The focus of the house is riding – the house was acquired by the first Duke of Richmond in 1697 so that he could ride with the local hunt, and the stables added during 18th-c alterations are grander even than the house. The racecourse is the setting for Glorious Goodwood; snacks, shop, some disabled access; open pm Sun and Mon Easter, then May-Sept plus pm Tues-Thurs in Aug; £3.40. The Anglesey Arms at Halnaker is useful for lunch.

Handcross TQ2629 NYMANS Some very impressive rare trees here, inc magnificent southern beeches and eucryphias, as well as fine camellias, rhododendrons and magnolias, countless other interesting flowering shrubs, a secluded sunken garden, pretty ruins and an extensive, artfully composed wilderness; snacks, plant sales, shop, disabled access; cl Mon and Fri, and Nov-Feb; £3.30. NT. The Fountain and Royal Oak are both useful for lunch.

Haywards Heath TQ3324 BORDE HILL (Balcombe Rd, north) Forty-acre gardens with woodland walks through rare maples, oaks, conifers and many other fine trees, as well as a lake, herbaceous borders and magnificent rhododendrons; meals and snacks, plant sales, disabled access; cl Nov-Feb; *£3, £3.50 bank hol weekends Apr and May. The Cowdray Arms at Balcombe is useful for lunch.

Henfield TQ2116 WOODS MILL COUNTRYSIDE CENTRE 18th-c watermill with wildlife exhibitions and nature trails over 15 acres of the surrounding countryside; snacks, shop; open Sun, bank hols and Sat pm Apr-Sept, plus pm Tues, Weds and Thurs in school hols; £2.

Highdown TQ0904 HIGHDOWN HILL There are excellent views to be had from this famous garden, which differs from most of the other famous Sussex gardens in that it's on very uncompromising chalk – laid out in and around a chalk pit high on the Downs above Angmering; many rarities, inc unusual Chinese plants; some disabled access; cl winter wknds. The Spotted Cow at the foot of Highdown Hill is useful for lunch.

High Salvington TQ1206 WINDMILL Early 18th-c black post mill, currently being restored; shop; open pm first and third Sun Apr-Sept; 50p.

Horsham TQ1730 MUSEUM Timber-framed Tudor house with various wonderful collections inc locally found dinosaur bones, an extraordinary collection of early bicycles, recreated wheelwright's and blacksmith's workshops, a new Shelley gallery, and an exhibition of shops and shopping; it's all laid out in an enticing way, and the small but pretty garden has some unusual wild cyclamen. Shop; limited disabled access but full facilities; cl Mon and Sun, cl 25-26 Dec. Though the town has seen considerable development, a particularly attractive quiet corner is The Causeway, by the church. The Black Jug (North St) and the Boars Head (Tower Hill, S towards Worthing), are useful for lunch.

Littlehampton TQ0202 Considering that the town figured as a port of some importance for several centuries up to the 1500s, it shows little sign of real age, but its long sandy beaches make it a popular simple family resort. MUSEUM Early 19th-c manor house with local archaeological finds, ship paintings, old photographs and other material of local interest; shop, disabled access; cl Sun and Mon. Towards the west, beyond the River

Arun, there's quite an extensive area of unspoilt dunes between beach and golf course. The Arun View right on the river does decent lunches.

Lower Beeding TQ2227
LEONARDSLEE An enormous Grade 1 listed garden set in a 240-acre valley with six beautiful lakes; marvellous rhododendrons, magnolias, oaks and unusual conifers, a delightful rock garden, extensive greenhouse and Japanese garden and bonsai exhibition, wallaby and deer. The gardens are set on the edge of the ancient St Leonard's Forest and were landscaped by Sir Edmund Loder of rhododendron fame; meals and snacks, plant sales, limited disabled access; cl Nov-Mar; May *£4 (exc bank hols and Sun *£4.50), Apr, Jun, Oct *£3.50, July-Sept *£3. The Crabtree at Lower Beeding does excellent food.

Lurgashall SU9327 This attractive small village, with an unusual loggia outside the church where parishioners walking in from a distance could eat their sandwiches, houses the unusual LURGASHALL WINERY which produces a wide range of traditional country wines, meads and cordials; tastings, open daily but only 12-3 pm Sun; weekend tours £1.25. The Noahs Ark here is good for lunch.

Petworth SU9721 PETWORTH HOUSE A quite splendid stately home, the present building is the result of 17th-c rebuilding – the chapel is all that's left of the original 13th-c house. The rooms are magnificent, with period furnishings and one of the most impressive painting collections in the country. Among its treasures are great works by Dutch masters and 20 paintings by Turner, a frequent visitor to the house. Other highlights are the grand staircase with its frescoes and the carved room, elegantly decorated by Grinling Gibbons. Meals and snacks, shop, disabled access; cl am, all day Mon and Fri (exc bank hols), the Tues after bank hols, Nov-Mar; £4. NT. The deer park, with stately trees and prospects still recognisable as those glorified by Turner, is free. The village, clustered by the great stone wall of the park, has narrow streets of attractive old houses, including a good few antique shops. The nearby Black Horse at Byworth and Horseguards at Tillington are best for lunch.

Pulborough TQ0418
PARHAM HOUSE A charming Elizabethan house, still a family home, its panelled rooms are full of notable portraits, furniture, Oriental carpets and lots of rare needlework. The grounds that surround it are really very special – they include a rose garden and a vegetable garden, the produce from which is for sale in the shop. There is also a deer park, and a maze designed with children in mind; snacks, shop; open pm Weds, Thurs and Sun Easter-Oct; £3.50, gardens only £2.
NUTBOURNE VINEYARDS An 18-acre vineyard with tours and tastings and a new visitor centre in a former windmill; shop; cl Nov-Easter. The town has some attractive buildings down towards the river, and the White Hart at Stopham just along the Petworth road does decent food. There's an RSPB RESERVE nearby.

Selsey SZ8593 By this busy holiday village, NORTHCOMMON FARM CENTRE has a wide range of friendly animals, with pony rides; snacks, shop; open daily Easter week and summer hols, weekends in between; £1.50.

Shipley TQ1422 Striking working WINDMILL, a smock mill built in 1879 and once owned by Hilaire Belloc; teas, shop; tel (0243) 777100 for opening dates.

Shoreham-by-Sea TQ2105
Though not one of England's more famous ports, this is quite a busy one, and there are several attractive buildings around the harbour which show by their age that this has always been so. One such is MARLIPINS MUSEUM – a Norman building which may once have been a customs house: the collection includes a maritime

gallery and exhibits relating to local history and archaeology; shop; cl Sun am, Mon all day, all Oct-Apr. Inland, in Old Shoreham, the early Norman CHURCH is accompanied by some handsome old houses, and the Red Lion here is good value for lunch.

Singleton SU8713 WEALD AND DOWNLAND OPEN AIR MUSEUM A fascinating and unusual museum of rescued historic buildings from all over the south-east, dismantled and re-erected here. The buildings are arranged to form a village, with outlying farm and agricultural buildings, a Tudor market hall, blacksmith's forge, a tollhouse and Victorian schoolroom; you can even buy flour from the medieval farmstead's working watermill. There are also displays of rural industries and traditional local crafts; snacks, shop; cl Mon and Tues Nov-Feb; *£4. CHILSDOWN VINEYARD A 13-acre vineyard and winery based around an unusual Victorian station; shop; cl Oct-Apr; £1.50. The Fox Goes Free at Charlton is handy for lunch.

Tangmere SU9006 MILITARY AVIATION MUSEUM Good collection of photographs, models and uniforms, aircraft and aircraft parts relating to Tangmere and air conflicts in this area of the country. It's based on a former RAF base, interesting for the role it played during both World Wars (H E Bates finished *Fair Stood the Wind for France* while he was stationed here); meals and snacks, shop, disabled access (but no lavatory); cl Dec-Jan; *£2.50. This is poised between the Anglesey Arms at Halnaker and the quaint Gribble at Oving, both useful for lunch.

Tillington SU9621 NOAH'S FARMYARD (Grittenham Farm) Lambs, calves, goats, rabbits etc for children to pet, along with a nature trail and riverside picnic area; snacks, shop; cl mid-Sept-mid-Apr; £2. The Horseguards is quite stylish for lunch, and the village is pretty.

West Dean SU8512 WEST DEAN GARDENS Old roses, 100-yard pergola, wild garden, kitchen garden and interesting collection of stately mature conifers in park and arboretum, already visibly recovering from the 1987 storm; a splendid downland setting. Snacks, shop, some disabled access, plant sales; cl Nov-Feb; £2.25. The Fox Goes Free at Charlton is quite handy for lunch.

West Hoathly TQ3632 This attractive village, tucked quietly away from the road past it, has tremendous views from the lane downhill past the Cat (a good pub with authentic Italian food). On a clear day you can see the whole sweep of the South Downs between Chanctonbury Ring and the Long Man of Wilmington. Near the 13th-c church is the 15th-c timbered PRIEST HOUSE, now a folk museum with country furniture, domestic implements and needlework and a little cottage garden; shop; cl Sun am, Tues, Nov-late Mar; *£1.70.

Worthing TQ1402 A restrained but rather charming town, with a pleasant seafront, in the same mould as Brighton but altogether quieter and less gaudy. In the formerly separate village of West Tarring are some attractive old cottages, a 250-year-old fig garden by the 14th-c parish hall, and a folklore museum in a row of 15th-c cottages; nearby, the Vine is an entertaining little tavern. MUSEUM AND ART GALLERY (Chapel Rd) Collections of 18th- to 20th-c costume, toys, pottery and pictures, as well as an extremely rich archaeological collection, with artefacts from prehistoric to Anglo-Saxon times, and a new sculpture garden; shop, disabled access; cl Sun, 25-26 Dec, 1 Jan, Good Fri.

The BRITISH SCHOOL OF BALLOONING at Ebernoe, just north of Petworth SU9721, organises champagne balloon trips over the countryside – tel (0428) 707307; £120 – cheaper if more people.

★ **Attractive villages** in the area, all with decent pubs, include Barns Green TQ1227, Burpham TQ0308, Easebourne SU8922, East Dean SU9013, Elsted SU8119, Fittleworth TQ0118, Funtington SU7908, Henley SU8925, Kirdford TQ0126, Rudgwick TQ0833, South Harting SU7819, Stopham TQ0218 and Sutton SU9715.

Walks

The chalk South Downs dominate much of this part of the county, and have the best of its walks. The **South Downs Way** makes for quick progress along their crest. **Harting Downs** SU9718 involve no more than a level stroll from the road near South Harting SU7819. **Kingley Vale** SU8210 needs much more stamina, whether you approach via the nature trail on the S side or from Stoughton SU8011 to the N. This nature reserve is Europe's largest yew forest, a magical place where the trees create some eerie pools of darkness on the S slopes of the Downs; above, you can look over Chichester Harbour from a prehistoric burial mound. At **Bignor Hill** SU9813, the trees that obscure views for much of the way hereabouts give way to open ground; Stane St, a Roman road here relegated to a path, takes a strikingly straight course SW over a woodland and pasture landscape.

At **Arundel** TQ0107, you can walk along the canalised River Arun and into Arundel Park, with its lakes and woodlands beneath the slopes of the Downs. From Amberley TQ0313 you can climb on to the Downs or take a path across **Amberley Wild Brooks** TQ0314, a large expanse of watermeadows which form an important habitat for wetland plants and birdlife.

N of Worthing TQ1402 are two of the great landmarks of the Downs, both of them ancient hill forts: **Chanctonbury Ring** TQ1312, now a prominent hilltop clump of trees, is reached from Steyning TQ1711 or Washington TQ1212, while the huge ramparted site of **Cissbury Ring** TQ1308 is within close access of Findon TQ1208 (where the Village House and Gun are both good for lunch). The Downs above Brighton are open; arable farming and the presence of pylons rather distract from the pleasure of walking, but the steep northern slopes are still impressive, as at **Devil's Dyke** TQ2611 (with its tremendous view over Brighton, even more startling at night than by day), **Wolstonbury Hill** TQ2813 and the **Jack and Jill windmills** near Clayton TQ3014.

Up in the NW of the county there is some nicely varied countryside around **Fernhurst** SU8928; much is densely wooded, but there are some chances to get out on to the open hillsides as on **Woolbeding Common** SU8625 and the S tip of **Black Down** SU9129. Further E you can stroll by the shore of **Ardingly Reservoir** TQ3229, or plan a longer walk around the elevated farmland and woodlands surrounding **Wakehurst Place** TQ3331 and **Balcombe** TQ3130. Another reservoir walk can be had along the north side of **Weir Wood Reservoir** TQ3934, with paths leading up to Standen House TQ3835.

The coast is densely developed, but **Chichester Harbour** still has unspoilt waterside. A shoreside path skirts the peninsulas of Thorney Island SU7503 and Chidham SU7903. East Head SZ7694, an NT-owned promontory on the E entrance of the harbour, is a sandy spit, with dunes overlooking the marshes and mudflats of the estuary. The only other appreciable stretch of undeveloped coast is between Littlehampton TQ0202 and Middleton-on-Sea SU9700, which includes an attractive few miles along **Climping Beach** SU9902.

Driving

Good downs roads include the B2141 from Chichester to South Harting, the B2146 S from South Harting past Uppark (a splendid NT property, still being restored after a fire) to Walderton, and the back road up the valley from there through Stoughton (good walks from the Hare & Hounds here) and East Marden, where you can either go on to meet the B2141 again, or keep round to the left behind Telegraph Hill and rejoin the B2146 near Compton. From South Harting taking the back road through East Harting and then a right turn in Elsted to take you slowly through the little villages of Treyford, Didling and Bepton, joining the A286 at Cocking, gives good views of the steep wooded N slope of the downs, on your right. All the back roads around Goodwood are pleasant mainly open country drives, and to the E of that area the B2139 between Houghton and Storrington has lovely views of a fine stretch of downland.

The A272, though not a quick road, gives a good cross-section of West Sussex, and goes through Midhurst, Petworth and Pulborough, all of them attractive small towns. The A286 N and S through Midhurst carries relatively little traffic for a trunk road, and passes through some splendid countryside.

Where to eat

Chilgrove SU8214 White Horse (024 359) 219 An 18th-c pub in the South Downs with very good, generously served wholesome food and a superb wine list; cl Sun pm, Mon, last wk Oct, Feb, 25 Dec pm, 26 Dec; children in restaurant only. **£30.50 dinner, £24.50 lunch**|£1.75/£5.50.

Storrington TQ0814 Old Forge (0903) 743402 Good imaginative food in converted beamed forge and excellent choice of sweet wines to go with the rich puddings and home-made ice-creams; cl Sat am, Sun pm, Mon, Tues am; children must be well behaved; **£29; £23 set dinner.**

Burpham TQ0308 George & Dragon (0903) 883131 Smartly comfortable old pub with splendid views down to Arundel Castle and river, popular with walkers; good, promptly served bar food with unusual specials inc good vegetarian dishes, and elegant restaurant; cl 25 Dec. **£17.50**|£2.20/£5.

Edburton TQ2311 Tottington Manor (0903) 815757 Cosy country pub with good bar food, international restaurant menu inc lovely fresh fish, and a relaxed atmosphere; bedrooms; cl winter Sun pm, 1st wk Jan; children over 5. **£17**|£3.50/£6.

Elsted SU8119 Elsted Inn (073 081) 3662 Simple but very friendly country inn, excellent daily-changing bar food, and very well-kept real ales. **£16.50**|£6.50.

Easebourne SU8922 Olde White Horse (0730) 813521 Neatly kept old stone local; imaginative food made with real care by landlady inc good puddings, and decent range of wines. **£14.70**|£2.85/£5.75.

Lodsworth SU9223 Halfway Bridge (079 85) 281 Cottagey old pub with upmarket feel and inventive home cooking inc lots of fish. £3.10/£6.25.

Rowhook TQ1234 Chequers (0403) 790480 Pleasantly rustic and old-fashioned atmosphere, good lunchtime bar food, and evening steaks. £3.10/£5.80.

Nuthurst TQ1926 Black Horse (0403) 891272 Warmly welcoming black-beamed pub with good, promptly served bar food, well-kept real ales and country wines. £3.15/£5.25.

Elsted SU8119 THREE HORSESHOES (0730) 825746 Cosy Tudor pub in lovely setting, fine views of South Downs from garden, decent bar food, good puddings, and several wines by the glass. £2.60/£6.30.

Help this year from: *Peter Churchill, C and C Stevens, Mr and Mrs LaFayette Noah, Mr and Mrs Michael Boxford, N H Purslow, Jeff and Barbara Stratton, Betty Darvall, David Shillitoe, John Townsend, Annette Tress, Gary Smith, Rob and Doris Harrison, G Washington, Belinda Mead, Jim and Maggie Cowell, Graham Reeve, Paul Forziati, Dave Lands, John Beeken, D H T Dimock, C and C Stevens, C T Laffan, Shirley Pielou, Margaret Drazin, A W Stratton, Susan Lee, John and Joan Wyatt, Mrs C Archer, Jeff and Barbara Stratton, Alain and Rose Foote, W J Wonham, Mrs D M Gray, Mrs J E Hilditch, Sarah and Peter Adams, A E R Albert, Terry Buckland, Ian Blackwell, R T and C E Moggridge, Andrew and Ruth Triggs, T G Thomas, M F Goodwin, Andy and Jill Kassube, John and Joy Winterbottom, Paul Weedon.*

We welcome reports from readers . . .

This GUIDE depends on readers' reports. Do help us if you can – in return, we offer a discount on the next edition to people who've helped us with reports for it. Tell us what you think about places already in it, and anything extra you think we should say about them. And send us your ideas for inclusion in the next edition: places to visit, eat at or stay in, attractive drives or walks, maybe even unusual interesting shops you know of. Use the card in the middle, the report forms at the end, or just write – no stamp needed: THE GOOD WEEKEND GUIDE, FREEPOST TN1569, Wadhurst, E Sussex TN5 7BR.

SUSSEX CALENDAR

Some of these dates were provisional as we went to press.

JANUARY

1st **Chichester** Sleeping Beauty *at Festival Theatre and Minerva Studio Theatre*; **Hastings** Foreign and Colonial Chess Congress *at Cinque Ports Hotel and Pier Ballroom – till Sun 9*

3rd **Chichester** Swan Lake *at Festival Theatre and Minerva Studio Theatre – till Sat 8*

5th **Brighton** Holiday on Ice *at the Centre – till Sun 30*

FEBRUARY

13th **Hastings** Dance Festival *at White Rock Theatre*

28th **Hastings** Musical Festival *inc dance and drama at White Rock Theatre – till 26 Mar*

MARCH

13th **Hastings** Half Marathon

14th **Bognor Regis** International Clowns Convention *– till Sun 20*

APRIL

1st **Arundel** Easter Egg Hunt *at Wildfowl and Wetlands Centre – till Mon 4*; **Tinsley Green** British Marbles Championships *at Greyhound Hotel*

3rd **Singleton** Traditional Food Fair *at Weald and Downland Open Air Museum – till Mon 4*

4th **Handcross** Daffodil Day *at High Beeches Gardens, inc plant sale, wine tasting*

5th **Bognor Regis** Folk Festival *at South Coast World – till Fri 8*

23rd **Brighton** UK Coach Rally *– till Mon 25*; **Haywards Heath** Festival of Gardening *at Borde Hill Garden – till Sun 24*

30th **Hastings** 'Jack-in-the-Green' Festival of Morris Dancing *– till 2 May*; **Mayfield** Festival of Music and the Arts *– till 15 May*

MAY

1st **Bexhill** Festival of Motoring *– till Mon 2*; **Handcross** Bluebell Day *at High Beeches Gardens*

4th **Battle** Festival *– till Sun 15*

6th **Brighton** Horse Driving Trials *at Stanmer Park – till Sun 8*; *also* International Arts Festival *– till Sun 29*

7th **Brighton** Madeira Drive Festival of Family Fun; **Lower Beeding** Bonsai Exhibition *at Leonardslee Gardens – till Sun 8*

8th **Newhaven** Five Star Club Classic Car Rally *at Newhaven Fort*

11th **Hastings** Rogationtide Blessing of the Sea Ceremony, *at the Fishmarket, foreshore service with lifeboat pulpit*

15th **Brighton** Madeira Drive MG Car Rally

27th **Brighton** Old Ship Royal Escape Race, *yacht racing starting on beach in front of the Old Ship, Kings Rd*

28th **Heathfield** Agricultural Show *at Broad Oak*

29th **Handcross** Azalea Day *at High Beeches Gardens*; **Selsey** Donkey Derby *on football field*

SUSSEX CALENDAR

JUNE

1st **Arundel** Corpus Christi Carpet of Flowers and Floral Display *at Cathedral – till Thurs 2*

3rd **Brighton** University Carnival – *till Sun 5*

9th **Ardingly** South of England Show – *till Sat 11*

11th **East Preston** Festival Week – *till Sun 19*; **Eastbourne** International Ladies Tennis Championships – *till Sat 18*

12th **Newhaven** Mark 4 Zodiac Club Rally *at Fort*; **Singleton** Heavy Horse Day, *working demonstrations at Weald and Downland Open Air Museum*

18th **Pulborough** Parham Park Steam Rally – *till Sun 19*

24th **Petworth** Open Air Concerts *in the Park – till Sun 26*

25th **Crawley** Festival – *till 10 July; also* Folk Day *at the Hawth – till 10 July*; **Lower Beeding** Country Craft Fair *at Leonardslee Gardens – till Sun 26*

JULY

2nd **Petworth** Festival, *inc kites, cross-country race, pram race and square dancing – till Sun 10*

3rd **Chichester** Festivities, *inc classical, comedy, jazz, street entertainment and children's events – till Tues 19*

6th **Brighton** Tour de France *English leg ends on Madeira Drive after run through Ashdown Forest and gruelling climb up Ditchling Beacon*

7th **Hastings** Beer Festival *at Alexandra Park – till Sat 9*

9th **Bodiam** Quarry Farm Rural Experience Steam Fayre – *till Sun 10*; **Goodwood** Fireworks Concert *at Racecourse*

16th **Lamberhurst** Firework and Laser Symphony Concert *at Bewl Water*; **Littlehampton** Armed Forces Day *at Smarts Amusement Park*

22nd **Petworth** National Trust Craft Festival, *entertainment, bands, Morris dancing at Petworth House and Park*

23rd **Ebernoe** Horn Fair and Cricket Match; **Lamberhurst** Have-a-go Day *at Bewl Water, outdoor sports inc windsurfing, sailing, rowing, sub-aqua diving and archery – till Sun 24*

24th **Bexhill** Carnival Week – *till Sat 30*; **Singleton** Show for Rare and Traditional Breeds of Animal *at Weald and Downland Open Air Museum*

25th **Eastbourne** LTA County Cup Grass Court Championships – *till Fri 29*

29th **Worthing** Seafront Fair and Gaslight Market, *inc torchlight procession, fireworks and vintage cars – till Sun 31*

30th **Bognor Regis** Carnival

AUGUST

1st **Eastbourne** Family Tennis Festival – *till Mon 8*

7th **Hooe** Old Motor Club Vintage Car Rally

Sussex Calendar

August cont.

13th **nr Chichester** Sussex Game and Country Fair *at St Michael's School (Burton Park) – till Sun 14*; **Hastings** Town and Country Fair – *till Sun 14*

22nd **Eastbourne** South of England Tennis Championships – *till Sat 27*

26th **Arundel** Festival – *till 4 Sept*; **Worthing** All British Country Music Festival – *till Sun 28*

27th **Bognor Regis** Illumination Gala – *till Mon 29*

28th **Selsey** Carnival – *till Mon 29*

September

1st **Rye** Carnival, *also Sat 3*

3rd **Alfriston** English Wine and Regional Food Festival *at English Wine Centre – till Sun 4*; **Hastings** National Town Criers Championships; **Uckfield** Torchlight Procession and Firework Display

4th **Battle** Car Show

10th **Crowborough** Torchlight Procession and Firework Display; **Findon** Sheep Fair

17th **Mayfield** Torchlight Procession and Firework Display

23rd **Eastbourne** Orchestra Festival *for amateur musicians at Sandhurst Hotel, book in advance – till Sun 25*

24th **Burgess Hill** Torchlight Procession and Firework Display

October

8th **Newhaven** Torchlight Procession and Firework Display

20th **Chichester** Sloe Fair *at Oaklands Park*; **Handcross** High Beeches Gardens Autumn Colour

22nd **Singleton** Steam Threshing and Ploughing *at Weald and Downland Open Air Museum with heavy horses and vintage tractors – till Sun 23*

29th **Littlehampton** Torchlight Procession and Firework Display

November

5th **Hastings** Guy Fawkes Celebration; **Lewes** Torchlight Procession, *commemorates the Gunpowder Plot and remembers the 17 local Protestants burned at the stake in the reign of Mary I: the best of Britain's bonfire celebrations; town closed to traffic at 5.30, spectacular celebrations inc a 'no popery' banner, bands, fireworks, effigies, large bonfires and burning tar barrel race*

12th **East Hoathly** Torchlight Procession and Firework Display

December

25th **Eastbourne** Band Concert *at Grand Parade*

26th **Eastbourne** Open Air Dancing *at Grand Parade*

WILTSHIRE

A good many attractive and interesting places to visit in this county include, in the south, one of England's two or three most appealing cathedrals (in the elegant and civilised old city of Salisbury), and the wonderful grounds of Stourhead – again, one of the country's most attractive places. The north of the county has Castle Combe, which most people would say is England's prettiest village, as well as Lacock, which would also be very high on any shortlist of outstanding places. On the whole, the countryside in the north is slightly more appealing than in the south, and in Longleat the south has a fine all-day family attraction, but otherwise honours are very evenly divided between the two halves of the county, with both having their share of fine houses and gardens to visit as well as more unusual places of interest.

For people who enjoy wandering around pleasant small towns and villages, and looking at beautiful houses and gardens and the like, Wiltshire can hardly be bettered. It's not too touristy even in summer, and a good choice of places to stay runs from B & B in comfortable cottages and farmhouses to luxurious country-house hotels.

SOUTH WILTSHIRE

Here there's an ample variety of places to stay in and to visit; Salisbury is good for a cultivated short break.

Besides its gloriously elegant cathedral, Salisbury has a lot of appeal as a place for a civilised quiet break, and makes a good base for exploring the surrounding countryside. The pick of the area's places to visit includes Stourhead at Stourton, Longleat near Warminster, Stonehenge and Wilton House. Among less well-known places, the pretty village of Teffont Magna has an enjoyable farm visit and a charming garden, and the imposing ruins of Old Wardour Castle near Tisbury are very peaceful.

The Salisbury Plain is an almost unbroken expanse of rolling high ground, a mixture of pasture and broad unhedged arable fields intersected by military training tracks – too monotonous for walkers, but on the right scale for driving through. The most attractive scenery is along the valleys of the chalk streams – a quite private landscape of stone or flint houses and lusciously clear-water rivers. There are a good many attractive villages.

Where to stay

Warminster ST8744 BISHOPSTROW HOUSE Boreham Rd BA12 9HH (0985) 212312 **£123**; 32 sumptuous rms. Charming Georgian house in 27 acres inc frontage of the River Wylye; homely, informal atmosphere, log fires, fresh flowers, antiques, and fine paintings in elegant day rooms; very good food; heated indoor and outdoor swimming pools, indoor and outdoor tennis courts and fishing on own stretch of river.

Salisbury SU1429 ROSE & CROWN Harnham Rd SP2 8JQ (0722) 327908 **£95**; 29 rms in the original building or smart, modern extension. It's almost worth a visit just for the view – well-nigh identical to that in the most famous Constable painting of Salisbury cathedral; elegantly restored inn with friendly beamed and timbered bar, good bar and restaurant food, and charming Avonside garden; disabled access.

Salisbury SU1429 RED LION Milford St SP1 2AN (0722) 323334 **£80**; 56 rms. Handsome old hotel with a mix of antique settles, leather chairs and modern banquettes in small two-roomed panelled bar, spacious old-fashioned lounge with interesting furnishings inc clock with skeleton bellringers; medieval restaurant, seats outside; disabled access.

Salisbury SU1429 OLD MILL Town Path, W Harnham SP2 8EU (0722) 327517 ***£65**; 11 comfortably converted rms. Based on a former mill and warehouse – there's been a mill here since 1135; terrace out by mill pool, meadow walks with classic views of Salisbury cathedral; good food in evening restaurant and beamed bar.

Warminster ST8744 OLD BELL Market Pl BA12 9AN (0985) 216611 ***£58**; 20 rms. Old-world country-town hotel with traditional bar food, bistro and restaurant, good choice of wines, and efficient service; cl 25-26 Dec.

Stourton ST7734 SPREAD EAGLE Church Lawn BA12 6QE (0747) 840587 **£56**; 5 comfortable and spacious rms. Fine position at the head of Stourhead Lake and popular with mostly older customers; old-fashioned furnishings, straightforward waitress-served food in bar and restaurant, and good residents' lounge; an NT pub; cl 25 Dec.

Hindon ST9132 LAMB Salisbury SP3 6DP (074 789) 573 ***£55**; 13 rms. Solidly built, welcoming and civilised old inn with log fires, attractive lounges, imaginative food, friendly, helpful service, and no-smoking restaurant.

Horningsham ST8141 BATH ARMS Warminster BA12 2LY (0985) 844308 ***£52**; 6 well-equipped and clean rms. By the entrance to Longleat House, this comfortable old inn has been modernised without being spoilt; good interesting food, pleasant service, and well-kept real ales; restaurant cl Christmas.

Heytesbury ST9242 ANGEL High St BA12 0ED (0985) 40330 ***£49**; 4 comfortable rms. Beautiful little coaching inn with superb service from very friendly staff; good home-made innovative food inc in-house patisserie with home-made croissants and so forth, and restaurant; cl 25 Dec.

Semley ST8926 BENETT ARMS Shaftesbury Dorset SP7 9AS (0747) 830221 ***£46**; 5 rms. Friendly little local village inn with cheery service, traditional often home-made bar food using local produce, and extensive range of drinks; cl 25-26 Dec; disabled access.

Ansty ST9526 MAYPOLE Salisbury SP3 5PY (0747) 870607 ***£40**; 3 rms. White-shuttered brick-and-flint pub overlooked by the tallest maypole in the country, continuing the tradition from the 15th c. Dark-green hessian walls with old prints and photographs, very friendly welcome and good, popular food; children over 10; no dogs.

Ebbesbourne Wake ST9824 Horseshoes Salisbury SP5 5JG (0722) 780474 *£35; 2 rms. Simple, attractive and sparklingly clean secluded village pub serving popular home-made bar food and good breakfasts; new children's room, and pets' corner in paddock at bottom of garden: 4 goats and a Vietnamese pot-bellied pig; cl pm 25 Dec.

West Grafton SU2460 Rosegarth Marlborough SN8 3BY (0672) 810288 *£33; 2 rms. 16th-c thatched and half-timbered cottage with comfortable lounge, good breakfasts, friendly owners, and big garden; free taxi service for guests taking supper at any of 4 local pubs.

Corsley ST8246 Lane End Cottage 72 Lane End Warminster BA12 7PG (0373) 832392 *£32; 3 rms, 1 with own shower. Quiet and secluded 17th-c cottage, very well kept, with delightful atmosphere, pleasant furnishings, excellent breakfasts, caring service, and neat garden; children over 11.

To see and do

Salisbury SU1429 A beautiful and gently relaxed city, with a good many fine old buildings, particularly around the lovely cathedral close. The most extensive close in the country, it's always been a distinct area of town, and the gates to it are still locked every night. The buildings cover a variety of architectural styles from the 13th c to the present, and of course its great glory is the elegant cathedral itself. Outside the close, there are some interesting antique and other shops, and the Market Square still has a traditional market each Tues and Sat – parking in town can be tricky on those days. The Haunch of Venison (Minster St) is a quite delightful old town tavern, while the Red Lion (Milford St), New Inn (New St) and Avon Brewery (Castle St) are all good for lunch, as is the waterside Old Mill out at West Harnham.

✝ Cathedral Begun in 1220, this took just 38 years to build, making it one of the only cathedrals to have a uniform style throughout. The tower and magnificent spire were added in 1334; at 404 ft, the spire is the tallest in the country. Christopher Wren discovered it was leaning, but successfully corrected it, a feat now commemorated by a brass plaque. Also notable is the clock made in 1386, now the oldest working mechanical clock in the world, and the tomb of the first Earl of Salisbury, who gave the church one of only four surviving copies of the Magna Carta; it's still on display. Snacks, shop, disabled access.

There's a good view of the cathedral from outside the 13th-c Bishop's Palace, though the one immortalised by Constable, and still much as then, is from across the meadows by the River Avon over by West Harnham.

Mompesson House (Cathedral Close) Exquisite Queen Anne building, probably the most interesting in the cathedral close, with period furnishings, china and paintings, a remarkable collection of 18th-c drinking glasses, and an interestingly carved oak staircase; teas; cl am, all day Thurs and Fri, Nov-Mar; *£3. NT.

Salisbury and South Wiltshire Museum (Cathedral Close) Lots of good local history and archaeology in lovely building, with displays and models of Old Sarum and Stonehenge, a fascinating and very miscellaneous ethnology exhibition, and collections of Wedgwood, costume, lace and embroidery; snacks, shop, disabled access; cl Sun exc pm July, Aug and during the Salisbury Festival, 24-27 Dec; £2.25 – the ticket gives unlimited visits all year. Smaller museums in the city range from the Bishop Wordsworth School Museum to an exhibition in the library relating to crime writer John Creasey.

Also worth a look in the close are NORTH CANONRY GARDENS, a peaceful place for a stroll near the river (summer only), ST ANNE'S GATE, MALMESBURY HOUSE, and the regimental museum (this year has D-Day Juno Beach display, Feb-Nov). Nearby, the CHURCH of St Thomas was built for the cathedral workers so is slightly older than the cathedral itself; it's notable for the medieval Painting of Doom.

OLD SARUM (A345 on northern outskirts) This substantial and easily defended Iron-Age hill fort held a township right on through the Roman occupation and Dark Ages into Norman times, when a castle and cathedral were built. In the early 13th c, either because of sheer shortage of space or because of shortage of water, the clergy started a general move to the much more fertile site of the present city, which under its original name of New Sarum soon developed as an important trading centre. The fort gradually fell into decline and became a quarry for the new centre; consequently there's not much left of the old cathedral and castle, but the views are splendid, and the foundations give interesting clues to ancient architecture and styles; snacks, shop; £1.20.

Other things to see and do

You can't really visit Wiltshire without taking in some of the ANCIENT SITES AND MONUMENTS. There are around 4,500 of them, more than anywhere else in the country, and they range from the familiar Stonehenge to less well-known barrows and hill figures. The major sites are described in the alphabetical listing below, but others worth a look if passing can be found near Corston ST9284 (in North Wilts), Enford SU1351, Norton Bavant ST9043 and White Sheet Hill ST8034 (its traditionally maintained downland now a nature reserve), with a white horse near Pewsey SU1560. Not all these places have much for the non-archaeologist to notice other than a few mysterious humps in the ground, but they're peaceful spots, generally with interesting unchanging views.

Brokerswood ST8352 WOODLAND HERITAGE MUSEUM AND WOODLAND PARK 80 acres of woodlands, with lakes, wildfowl, an adventure playground, walks, and little railway; snacks, shop, disabled access; park open every day, museum cl Sat (exc pm in summer) and Sun am in winter; *£2.

Cholderton SU2242 CHOLDERTON RARE BREEDS FARM A living museum of farm animals and poultry through the ages, with lots of pigs, goats, sheep and cattle to feed; also 50 breeds of rabbit, water gardens and some lovely views. Meals, snacks, shop, disabled access; cl Nov-Mar; *£3. The Crown is useful for lunch.

East Knoyle ST8830 WATERDALE HOUSE (Milton) Woodland garden at its best in late spring/early summer, with long-established camellias, rhododendrons and magnolias; also other plants inc water garden; teas if fine; open Sun only, Apr-May; *£1.50. The plasterwork in the chancel of the CHURCH was designed by Wren's father; he was the parish priest. The Seymour Arms is useful for lunch.

Ludgershall SU2650 CASTLE A ruin since the 16th c, this was once a royal castle and hunting palace, and you can still see some of the original large Norman earthworks, as well as the later flint walling. The village CHURCH too is Norman. The nearby area is very pretty and unspoilt, the little villages of the Chutes, Tangley and Vernham Dean straddling the Hampshire border all worth a look (with the pubs over that way worth exploring too).

Middle Woodford SU1136 HEALE GARDENS Eight acres of lovely formal gardens beside the River Avon, with lots of varied plants; the water garden is particularly nice in spring and autumn. Snacks, specialist plant sales with many rare types propagated from the main gardens, shop, disabled access; *£2. The Wheatsheaf in nearby Lower Woodford is good for lunch.

Pepperbox Hill SU2124, 5 miles south-east of Salisbury, is named after the strangely shaped 17th-c tower on its summit. You can't get into the tower, but the site commands fine views over Salisbury itself, and southwards as far as Southampton. Another viewpoint over Salisbury is the Iron-Age hill fort of **Figsbury Ring** SU1833.

Stockton ST9738 LONG HALL A series of meticulous formal gardens laid out along Gertrude Jekyll lines, set against lovely partly medieval hall (not open); also fine trees with profusion of spring bulbs, hellebores. Plant sales; open Weds Apr-Sept; *£2. The Bell at Wylye is good for lunch.

Stonehenge SU1142 One of the most famous prehistoric monuments in the world; everyone knows what it looks like, and the mechanics of getting the stones here (the larger ones local, the smaller ones all the way from Wales) have been pretty much sorted out, but no one's really sure exactly what Stonehenge with its careful astronomical alignments was for. All very mysterious, and that's part of the attraction – though if you've made a long journey to see it you may find it slightly disappointing. The best views are very early in the morning from the track from Larkhill, on the other side of the A344, or on a cold clear winter evening looking west past the monument towards the sunset. Silhouetted against the sky the massive ancient stones are very impressive – just as well, as in the interests of conservation you can't get right up to them any more. In broad daylight when the crowds are there (not to mention the busy traffic on the nearby trunk road), the place loses much of its power to inspire awe, and at the best of times is not somewhere to impress young children. Plans for a new visitor centre represent at least some attempt to resolve the virtually unresolvable contradictions posed by a site whose grandeur depends on loneliness and isolation but must cater for the crowds who want to visit it. Museum, snacks, shop, disabled access; *£2.70. At **Woodhenge** SU1541 nearby can be seen the scant traces of another prehistoric monument, which consisted of six rings of timber posts in a ditch; the positions are today marked by concrete posts, and a cairn marks the central spot where the tomb of a little girl ceremoniously axed to death was found. There's good PICK-YOUR-OWN fruit from late June to late July at Rolleston Manor Farm on the B3086 north-west of Stonehenge.

Stourton ST7734 STOURHEAD Marvellous gardens, laid out in Italian style by the banker Henry Hoare II over the decades following his return from an Italian tour in 1741. A beautifully harmonious landscape of temples, lakes, bridges and splendid trees and other plants; fine views from the very tall 18th-c folly at the far end of the estate. The early Georgian house has some good Chippendale furniture, and the church in the grounds has a lovely hillside setting; snacks, shop, disabled access; house open pm daily exc Thurs and Fri Apr-Oct, folly open pm daily exc Mon and Fri (but open bank hols), grounds open all year; £4 house and gardens. NT. STOURTON HOUSE GARDEN An informal garden nearby, profusely planted with interesting and colourful shrubs, trees and other plants, inc unusual daffodils; plant and dried-flower sales, snacks, shop, disabled access; open Weds, Thurs and Sun, Mar-Dec; £2. The Spread Eagle at the entrance to Stourhead is useful for lunch.

★ **Teffont Magna** ST9932

FARMER GILES FARMSTEAD A working dairy farm with 150 cows milked every afternoon, as well as calves, cattle, shire horses, donkeys, pigs, goats, rabbits and poultry; children can feed the lambs in late spring and early summer, fuss over the other animals and play on the tractors. There are also historical exhibitions and an adventure playground; meals and snacks, shop, disabled access; cl Nov-Mar exc wknds up to Christmas; *£3. The stonebuilt village is very attractive, and among the charming cottages with their neatly banked stone-walled gardens is FITZ HOUSE, its peaceful and sheltered streamside gardens full of flowering plants, many scented, inc old-fashioned roses and honeysuckles, all beautifully laid out and charmingly set off by the mellow 16th-17th-c stonework of the house itself (not open), formerly the home of Siegfried Sassoon; gardens open pm wknds only, Apr-Oct; £2. The Black Horse is good for lunch.

★ **Tisbury** ST9429 Charming small town, left behind by the main roads so largely unspoilt, with some fine old buildings, riverside church, and just outside to the east an immensely long medieval tithe barn. OLD WARDOUR CASTLE, a couple of miles south, is the remains of a substantial 14th-c castle, badly damaged in the Civil War when a formidable elderly chatelaine with a handful of servants and estate workers held off a thousand Roundheads for quite a time before surrendering. The walls still stand to their original 60 ft, and you can walk

almost to the top. It's a lovely peaceful setting; disabled access; cl 24-26 Dec, 1 Jan and wkdys Oct-Mar; £1.30. The South Western Hotel is useful for lunch.

! **Warminster** ST8745

LONGLEAT (off A362 W) Lots to do on this lively estate, its handsome house one of the first still lived-in stately homes to open its doors to the public. Since then it's all become firmly geared to visitors, but not so much that the attractive grounds have lost any of their appeal. Fine beech trees fill the parklands, which also include formal

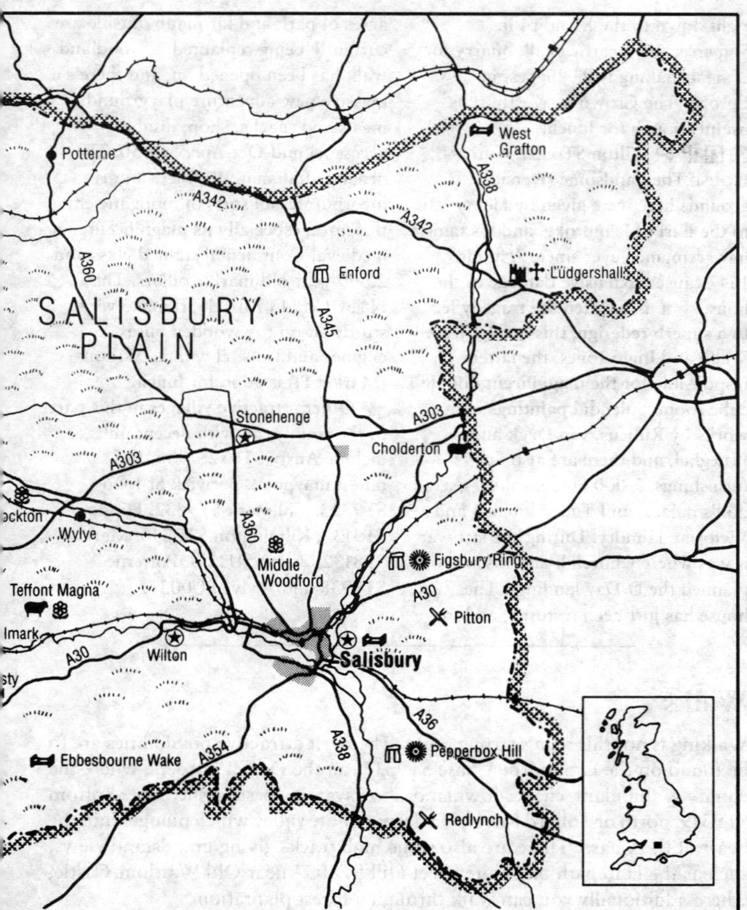

gardens laid out by Capability Brown, and the safari park with its famous lions and white tiger. The 16th-c house has impressive libraries and family portraits, with an interestingly restored Victorian kitchen. Also on the site are an adventure castle, narrow-gauge railway, and what may be the world's biggest maze; meals, snacks, shop, disabled access; park cl Nov-Mar, house cl only 25 Dec; £10 for all 17 attractions (individual tickets available, but the all-in ticket works out much cheaper). The Bath Arms at Horningsham at the south entrance to the park is good for lunch; in the town (not really a notable place for visitors) a GLOVE MUSEUM is open by arrangement, (0985) 212741.

Westbury ST8751 To the east you can see the huge Westbury WHITE HORSE cut into the chalk of the downs; late 18th-c, it was an 'improvement' on an altogether older one which may have been Saxon, or even as old as the prehistoric Uffington white horse in Oxfordshire – the original horse here even faced in the opposite direction. Above the white horse is an extensive Iron-Age hill fort, with good views right down to the Mendips in Somerset; the nearby chalk quarry for cement-making is the biggest in Europe. The Crown in Westbury is useful enough for lunch.

Wilton ST0931 WILTON HOUSE The handsome riverside grounds here were given by Henry VIII to the Earl of Pembroke, and his family have remained ever since. A fire in 1647 caused extensive damage to the house, but as so often the tragedy led to a superb redesign, this one by John Webb and Inigo Jones, the latter responsible for the magnificent double cube room. Splendid paintings inc works by Rubens, van Dyck and Brueghel, and there are also fine furnishings, 7,000 model soldiers, a doll's palace, and Tudor kitchen and Victorian laundry. During the last war it was where Churchill and Eisenhower planned the D-Day landings. The house has just been restored, and the acres of park and farmland outside are currently being replanted; a woodland walk has been opened up, and there's a massive new adventure playground; meals and snacks, shop, disabled access; cl mid-Oct-Apr; *£5.50. The ornately Italianate 19th-c CHURCH incorporates all sorts of more ancient treasures, especially its magnificent medieval Continental stained glass and 2,000-year-old marble pillars. The NIPPY CO (43 Russell St) make very sturdy sit-on toy wooden buses, engines and vans; cl wknds. Wiltons (Market Pl) is good for lunch.

★ **Other attractive villages** in this part of the county, all with decent pubs, include Ansty ST9526 (England's tallest maypole), Berwick St John ST9323, Chilmark ST9632, Hindon ST9132, Kilmington ST7736, Mere ST8132, Pitton SU2131, Potterne ST9938 and Wylye SU0037.

Walks

Walking is not this area's strong point. The most attractive possibilities are to be found on the **Cranborne Chase** ST9317, on the Dorset borders, where the county's abundant chalk downland shows at its best. Ashcombe Bottom ST9319, north of Tollard Royal, is a deep, remote valley which plunges into the heart of the Chase. There are also some high tracks giving grandstand views, such as the Harepath on White Sheet Hill ST8034 near Old Wardour Castle, where additionally you can walk through a forest plantation.

On **Haydown Hill** SU3156, reached from the east by a walk up from Vernham Dean SU3456 (itself in Hampshire), are the ramparts of a hill fort bounded by steep gradients on its southern side; the three counties of Berkshire, Hampshire and Wiltshire meet close by at SU350590.

For the **Salisbury Plain**, the County Council has a leaflet mapping out clearly way-marked walks around the edges of the Army's Imber firing range, totalling some 30 miles for the complete circuit: generally peaceful countryside with large-scale arable farming, but some wide views and maybe the sight of tank and infantry training.

Driving

The area's prettiest drives are those through the valleys of its chalk streams, particularly the following: the back road which takes the opposite side of the Avon valley to the main road, and runs down the E side from Upavon through East Chisenbury to Amesbury, then switches to the W bank for the run down to Salisbury through Wilsford and the Woodfords; the back road along the S side of the Wylye Valley, through Great Wishford, Wylye itself, Stockton and Corton; and the delightful road winding narrowly along the Ebble Valley, through euphoniously named villages such as Odstock, Stratford Tony, Stoke Farthing and Ebbesbourne Wake. W of Salisbury, the B3089 through Dinton, Chilmark and Hindon is attractive – a pleasantly quiet alternative to the east-west trunk roads on either side of it.

The A360 smack across Salisbury Plain gives a good feel of its emptiness, and carries little traffic (though you may possibly be held up by tank manoeuvres). The B3098 tracking along below the Plain's N lip is quite a pleasant drive.

Where to eat

Redlynch SU2020 LANGLEY WOOD (0794) 390348 Very good innovative food and decent wines in creeper-covered restaurant set in its own grounds; cl pm Sun, Mon/Tues, am Weds-Sat; children welcome Sun lunch or must be over 11; disabled access. **£24**|£11.75.

Pitton SU2131 SILVER PLOUGH (072 272) 266 Stylish, pleasant inn, well run, myriad things to look at; decent snacks and more elaborate meals with emphasis on imaginatively done fresh fish and seafood, with substantial helpings. **£21**|£3.15/£5.25.

Berwick St John ST9323 TALBOT (0747) 828222 Well-run and friendly village pub with simply furnished, heavily beamed bar, huge inglenook fireplace and decent food in bar and restaurant. **£16.80**|£2/£5.25.

Potterne ST9958 GEORGE & DRAGON (0380) 722139 Much restored 15th-c thatched cottage with welcoming atmosphere, good food, pleasant service, and unique antique indoor rifle range. £2/£5.25.

NORTH WILTSHIRE

This area has pleasant small towns, charming quiet villages and attractive great houses and gardens.

This part of the county has many charming quiet villages – including Castle Combe and Lacock, two of the country's prettiest (and most visited). As well as its little streets of attractive buildings, Lacock has other things well worth seeing. Elsewhere the most rewarding places to visit are Bowood House at Calne, Littlecote Manor at Chilton Foliat, Corsham Court and the nearby underground quarry centre, Sheldon Manor at Chippenham and the intriguing gardens of Hazelbury Manor at Box. Several attractive small towns with a good deal of character include particularly Bradford-on-Avon (rich in places to visit – and antique shops), Devizes, Marlborough and Malmesbury. The Avebury stone circle is in its way as impressive as Stonehenge, and gives you altogether more scope for pottering around; other remarkable prehistoric sites are within easy reach of it.

The countryside, though undramatic, is quite attractive and offers a fair range of pleasant walks. The area does have year-round possibilities for an enjoyable quiet break, and this year we've nearly doubled the number of places where we can recommend you to stay, which include a good few country places of real character.

Where to stay

Colerne ST8171 Lucknam Park Chippenham SN14 8AZ (0225) 742777 ***£161**; 42 rms. Noble Georgian house, reached by a long beech-lined driveway, with extensive grounds and carefully furnished, elegant day rooms and panelled library; lovely flowers, antiques and paintings; excellent food and extremely good service in charming restaurant; leisure spa with indoor swimming pool, gym, beauty salon, hairdresser, snooker and floodlit tennis courts; croquet; children over 12 in evening restaurant; disabled access.

Castle Combe ST8477 Manor House Chippenham SN14 7HR (0249) 782206 ***£155**; 36 lovely rms. Twenty-six acres of garden and parkland, including an Italian garden, are the setting for this 14th-c manor house with its gracious day rooms, panelling, antiques, log fires and fresh flowers; very good innovative food; disabled access.

Easton Grey ST8787 Whatley Manor Malmsbury SN16 0RB (0666) 822888 **£112**; 29 rms with antique furniture, 18 in manor house, 11 in Court House across courtyard. Lovely Cotswold manor house in quiet gardens with paddocks by the River Avon; spacious and rather fine oak-panelled drawing room, pine-panelled lounge, log fires, relaxed atmosphere, lots of books in the library-bar, and attractive dining room overlooking garden; tennis court, swimming pool, croquet lawn, putting green, billiards, sauna, solarium and jacuzzi.

Malmesbury ST9287 Old Bell SN16 0BW (0666) 822 344 ***£98**; 34 rms. With some claim to being one of England's oldest hotels and standing in the shadow of the Norman abbey, this fine wisteria-clad building has traditionally furnished rooms with Edwardian pictures, an early 13th-c hooded stone fireplace, two good fires, cheerful and helpful service, and attractively old-fashioned garden.

Bradford-on-Avon ST8261 Woolley Grange BA15 1TX (0225) 864705 ***£95**; 20 rms. Civilised Jacobean manor house with a relaxed, informal atmosphere; log fires, antiques and comfortable seating in the day rooms, and a pretty conservatory; delicious food using local (or home-grown) produce, often organic, inc home-baked breads and muffins and home-made jams and marmalades for breakfast; very good for children – nursery with full-time nanny, games room, and their own sort of food; disabled access.

Nettleton ST8277 Fosse Farmhouse Nettleton Shrub Chippenham SN14 7NJ (0249) 782286 **£95**; 6 rms. 18th-c Cotswold-stone house extensively restored with French decorative antique furniture and pretty English chintzes; morning coffee, lunch and afternoon cream teas served on the lawns or in very attractive dining room; antique shop with dried flowers and decorative items in former dairy behind the house.

Crudwell ST9592 Crudwell Court SN16 9EP (0666) 577194 ***£88**; 15 rms. Delightful, warmly welcoming 17th-c rectory with attractive day rooms, log fires, good food in pleasant dining room, friendly staff, and neatly kept walled gardens; swimming pool; disabled access.

Beanacre ST9066 Beechfield House Melksham SN12 7PU (0225) 703700 ***£80**; 20 rms. Victorian mansion of Bath stone with very comfortable lounges, antiques and ornate moulded ceilings, and seven acres of well-kept gardens; disabled access.

Purton SU0887 Pear Tree Church End Swindon SN5 9ED (0793) 772100 ***£80**; 18 very comfortable, pretty rms. Impeccably run former rectory with elegant, comfortable day rooms, fresh flowers, fine conservatory restaurant with good food using home-grown herbs, and 7½ acres of grounds inc a traditional Victorian garden; disabled access.

Lacock ST9367 At the Sign of the Angel SN15 2LA (0249) 730230 ***£75**; 9 rms. This fine 15th-c house in a lovely NT village is full of character, with heavy oak furniture, beams and big fireplaces; good food in candlelit restaurant; cl 23-30 Dec; disabled access.

Ford ST8374 White Hart Chippenham SN14 8RP (0249) 782213 ***£62**; 11 rms. Attractive ivy-covered inn in lovely spot by trout stream; old-fashioned atmosphere, unusual and popular food, day rooms of real character, good service, and secluded small swimming pool; disabled access.

Burbage SU2361 Old Vicarage Marlborough SN8 3AG (0672) 810495 **£60**; 3 rms. Carefully run Victorian house in two acres of lovely grounds; log fires, books and magazines in very attractive, solidly comfortable drawing room, and good food using fresh local produce and home-grown veg (summer picnic hampers, too); croquet; cl Christmas/New Year; no children.

Devizes SU0061 Bear SN10 1HS (0380) 722444 **£60**; 24 rms. An old-fashioned feel to this inn which dates from the 16th c and is very much at the town's heart; wide choice of food from snacks to more elaborate meals served in the oak-panelled Lawrence room, two more formal restaurants, and prompt service.

Corsham ST8670 Methuen Arms SN13 0HB (0249) 714867 **£59**; 25 rms. Georgian inn (a former nunnery) with mullioned windows, heavy oak beams, comfortable seats, good food, and friendly staff; pretty walled garden and fine skittle alley; cl 24-25 Dec; disabled access.

Willesley ST8488 Tavern House Tetbury Glos GL8 8QU (0666) 880444 **£55**; 4 pretty rms. Carefully restored and neatly kept 17th-c Cotswold-stone house, once an inn and staging post; elegantly furnished rooms, antiques and flowers, and charming walled garden; children over 10.

Alderton ST8382 Manor Farm Chippenham SN14 6NL (0666 840271) **£46**; 3 rms, 2 with own bthrm. Warmly friendly 17th-c house, on busy working farm with homely lounge and good breakfasts; children over 10.

Wilcot SU1360 Golden Swan Pewsey SN9 5NN (0672) 62289 ***£35**; 4 rms, shared bthrm. Ancient and very picturesque steeply thatched village inn in the quiet Vale of Pewsey, with lots of china jugs and mugs hanging from beams in two small rooms, a friendly atmosphere, bar food and dining room, and pretty front lawn; cl Christmas.

Rowde ST9762 Lower Foxhangers Farm Devizes SN10 1SS (0380) 828254 **£34**; 3 rms, showers. An 18th-c farmhouse on a 90-acre working beef farm; dining room and lounge; boating, fishing and walking on Kennet & Avon canal; mobile homes also; cl Oct-Apr.

Gastard ST8868 Boyds Farm Corsham SN13 9PT (0249) 713146 **£30**; 3 rms. Friendly and handsome 16th-c house on family-run working farm with pedigree herd of Herefords; homely lounge, woodburning stove, and traditional breakfasts; no evening meals.

To see and do

★ Avebury SU1069 Stonehenge has had all the glory, but it's this prehistoric stone circle covering over 28 acres that's the largest one in Europe, and is also probably older than its southern cousin. In its way it's just as spectacular, but hasn't had the same hordes of tourists, so you can still get close to the 200 stones which are enclosed in a massive earthen rampart nearly a mile in circumference. The big difference from Stonehenge is that here the stones share their site with a village. With all the fuss about preserving Stonehenge, it seems quite remarkable that the main road still runs right through here, with no bypass. An interesting MUSEUM shows finds from the area, as well as from WINDMILL HILL ST9623, a Neolithic enclosure a little over a mile away, but still on the same property; shop, disabled access; £1.20. GREAT BARN MUSEUM OF WILTSHIRE LIFE Close by, in the pretty village, this big 17th-c thatched barn has interesting displays on various aspects of rural life, with demonstrations of cheesemaking, thatching, saddlery and other local crafts; also occasional craft and food fairs. Snacks, shop, disabled access; cl wkdys mid-Nov-mid-Mar; *95p. The barn itself is magnificent. AVEBURY MANOR Very well restored house dating from before the Conquest, but mainly 16th-c; rambling layout with oak-panelled rooms, and similarly intriguing gardens outside. The gardens are open every day exc Mon and Thurs, while the house's opening times depend on the continuing restoration work – best to tel (067 23) 388 to see what's open when; garden £2. NT. Right on the site, the Red Lion is useful enough for lunch.

Many more prehistoric remains around Avebury include the strange SILBURY HILL, the largest man-made mound in Europe, which would have taken a thousand men about ten years to build; as with all the best of such sites, no one knows just what it was for. Also close by is the 5,000-year-old chambered tomb and barrow at WEST KENNET, where several dozen people were buried – take a torch if you want to venture in behind the massive entrance stone: the chamber with two side chapels runs some 30 ft or more into the barrow. There's also the 1½-mile avenue of stones known as WEST KENNET AVENUE – a good stretch leading out of Avebury has now been restored. The Waggon & Horses at Beckhampton (of *Pickwick Papers* fame) is quite handy for these.

★ ✝ **Box** ST8268 is an attractive up-and-down village, its interesting parts hidden down the steep valley below the A4, with cottages and houses using the same stone that's been quarried near here since Roman times. There's a story that on 9 April, Brunel's birthday, the rising sun shines right through the great railway tunnel he quarried through the hill above here, in its day the longest in the world (you can see the restored grand entrance from the A4). HAZELBURY MANOR (off B3109 just E of centre) Richly varied landscaped gardens, with a medieval archery alley, stone and yew circles, fountain, waterfall, pond, large rockery, formal areas, laburnum walk and many other treasures laid out as a sort of giant maze, around the 15th-c fortified manor house (not open). Best during the week when you can explore it on your own; some disabled access, plant sales; open daily May-Sept, wknds only in Apr and Oct; £2.80. In Chapel Plaister ST8367 on the way, look out for the 15th-c CHAPEL for Glastonbury pilgrims on the little hilltop 'green'. The Quarrymans Arms tucked away on Box Hill is good for lunch.

★ ✝ **Bradford-on-Avon** ST8261 is an attractive town given a distinguished air by the golden stone as used to build Bath; like parts of Bath, it's very steep, and has some handsome buildings reflecting its past wealth as a wool town. There are quite a few serious antique shops. Near the Norman parish CHURCH is a tall narrow late Saxon church, unusual in its having virtually no later additions. The Barge down by the canal, and the Canal on the Frome Rd, are useful for lunch. A medieval TITHE BARN can be seen at nearby Barton Farm down by the river and canal, its massive stone-slab roof supported by an impressive network of great beams and rafters. A short walk along the canal from here is AVONCLIFF, quite a steep gorge shared by canal, river and railway, the canal disdainfully stepping over the river by way of an aqueduct. The Cross Guns has good views over all of this, and is a good place for lunch. Up the hill from here, just south-east of Bradford itself, is WESTWOOD MANOR, a fully furnished 15th-c stone manor house with its original Gothic and Jacobean windows, fine 17th-c plasterwork, and a modern topiary garden; open pm Sun, Tues and Weds Apr-Sept; £3.20. The New Inn in Westwood village is good for lunch. Just past here is IFORD MANOR, notable for its stylish Edwardian Italianate riverside terraced garden, with romantic cloisters, colonnade and statues; house not open; teas Sun and bank hols; cl am, all day Mon and Fri, Oct-Apr (exc Sun in Oct and Apr – no teas then); £2. Out to the north-east of town, past Bradford Leigh, is GREAT CHALFIELD MANOR, a beautiful moated manor house, restored in 1920 and still with its original Great Hall; open Tues-Thurs Apr-Oct, guided tours only from 12.15 pm; £3.50. Next door is a small 13th-c church.

Bromham ST9665 SANDRIDGE FARM Farm curing bacon and Wiltshire ham using traditional recipes – not pumping them full of slimy water; exhibition, viewing window shows curing process; sales, disabled access. The Greyhound in the village is good for lunch.

Calne ST9870 BOWOOD A very civilised and stately Georgian house, with a notable library by Robert Adam, fine displays of art and sculpture, and the laboratory where Joseph Priestley discovered oxygen in 1772. Perhaps Bowood's best feature is the extensive parkland laid out by Capability Brown, featuring temples, cascades and a hermit's cave among the colourful pleasure gardens, and shielded from the outside world by further miles of partly wooded grounds. There's a good adventure playground; meals, snacks, shop, limited disabled access; cl Nov-Mar; £4.50. The Lansdowne Arms at Derry Hill, near the house, is good for lunch, and Calne also has a MOTOR MUSEUM.

★ † **Castle Combe** ST8477 Voted the 'prettiest village in Britain we've ever seen' by our contributors, this has a classic group of stone-tiled Cotswoldy cottages by the turreted CHURCH at the bottom of the tree-clad hill that descends to the trout stream and its ancient stone bridge. Preservation of the village is taken so seriously that you won't even see television aerials on the houses. Some of the villagers open their beautifully kept gardens for charity on the afternoon of the wknd of 25-26 Jun. Best of all during the week out of season; at other times it does get a great many visitors, even though the car park is sited some way up the hill. The Castle opposite the old market cross does food all day, at least in summer.

Chilton Foliat SU3070 LITTLECOTE MANOR Handsome red brick gabled Tudor house in lush Kennet Valley parkland (once stayed in by Elizabeth I, and where Henry VIII courted his wife Jane Seymour), with Civil War armour in the oak-panelled great hall, fine collections of period furniture, china and glass and some intricately hand-painted Chinese wallpaper. Within the grounds, which comprise gardens and lush parkland, are a collection of classic cars, a pets' corner, a rare-breeds farm and an adventure playground for children, as well as a little Roman museum, around the remains of a villa, containing a beautiful 4th-c mosaic. Meals, snacks, craft shops and garden centre; some disabled access; cl Oct-Easter; £4.95.

Corsham ST8770 CORSHAM COURT Fine house and park begun in 1582 but subsequently added to and developed by those busy masters Capability Brown, John Nash, Robert Adam and Humphrey Repton. The collection of beautiful old-master paintings is among the best in any stately home in the country and there are also fine statues and furnishings, while, in the gardens, the peaceful lake and a Georgian bath house are patrolled by a number of peacocks – if they haven't decided to have a wander off into the village. A very interesting place to spend an afternoon; shop, disabled access; open pm Tues-Thurs and wknds Sept-Nov and Jan-Easter, then open Fri and bank hols Easter Thurs-30 Sept; *£3. Nearby there are some attractive former weavers' cottages; the CHURCH, on the edge of the park, is largely 12th-c, partly Saxon. UNDERGROUND QUARRY (Park Lane) The only shaft stone mine open to the public anywhere in the world; you can don a miner's helmet and descend hundreds of steps (well, over a hundred at least) into a fascinating and impressive labyrinth of tunnels and galleries, to see for yourself where the gorgeous Bath stone comes from, and how it's extracted. Wrap up well – it always stays chilly down there; shop; open Easter Sun and Mon, Sun in Apr and Oct, and daily exc Fri May-Sept; guided tours roughly every hour and a half from 10.15 am (11.45 am Sat); £3.20. The town has a surprising number of antique shops, some very fine, and the Methuen Arms, which includes parts of a former priory, is

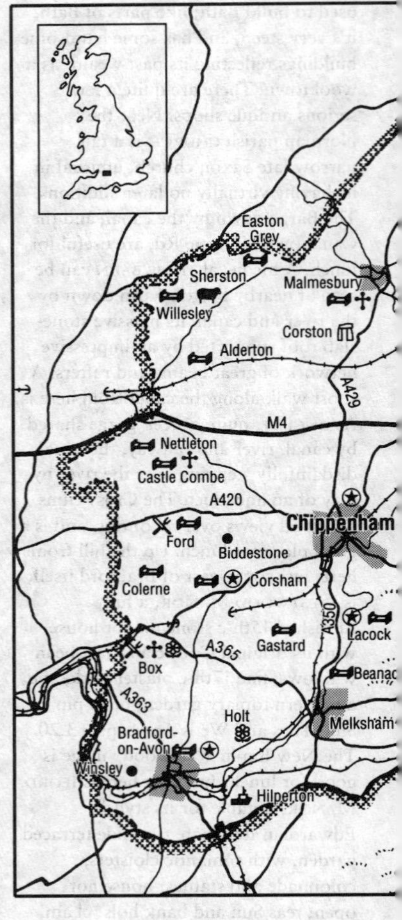

good for lunch; anyone who likes real ale will enjoy the Two Pigs.

Chippenham ST9173 SHELDON MANOR This charming 13th-c manor house is the oldest inhabited manor house in the county, and still has its original (and unusual) porch, as well as a 15th-c CHAPEL. The panelled rooms have a range of oak furnishings and collections of glass and porcelain; the lovely terraced gardens have a mass of old-fashioned roses, yew trees as old as the house, and other interesting trees. Good meals and snacks, shop with plant sales, disabled access; open pm

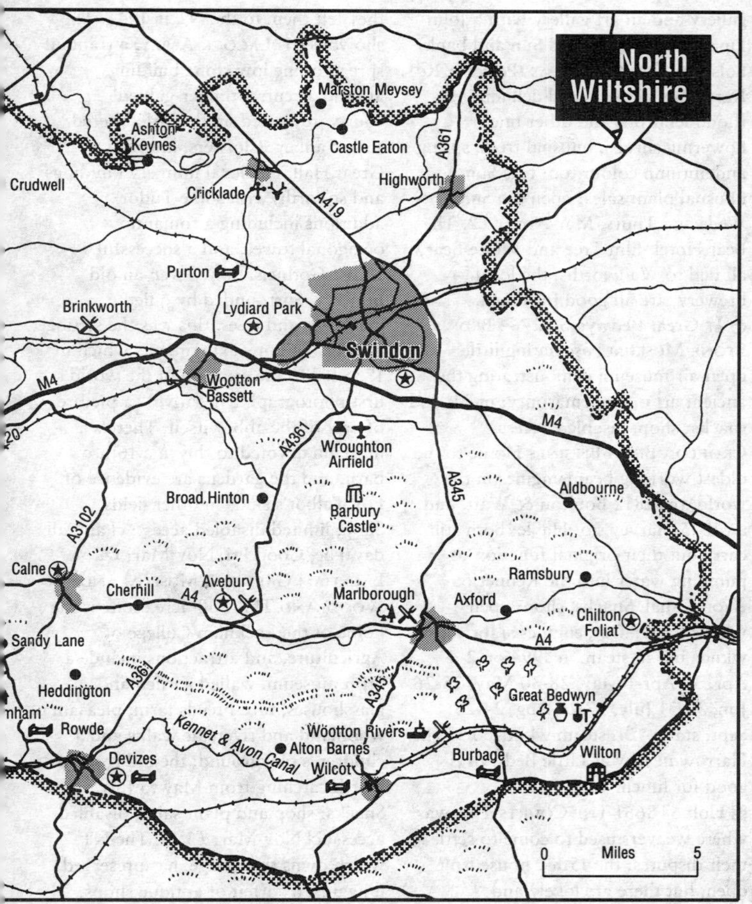

Sun, Thurs and bank hols, Apr-Oct; £3.

✝ ⚘ The small town of **Cricklade** SU1093, quietly separated from the busy A419, has some attractive buildings and a fine parish CHURCH with a glorious tower; at the end of the high street, just north of the Thames, a path on the left off the slip road heading back towards the A419 leads to a broad RIVERSIDE MEADOW which has been kept unimproved for decades, and is mown only in July after the numerous wild flowers have seeded.

Devizes SU0061 Lots of grand old buildings in this interesting and friendly town, and a good town trail takes most of them in. The 29 locks of the Kennet & Avon Canal coming up Caen Hill from the west form one of the longest flights of locks in the country; recent droughts have made it difficult to maintain an adequate water flow here, and an appeal has been launched for funds to build a new pumping station. The headquarters of the Canal Trust on the Wharf has a museum and information centre; £1. MUSEUM Local history, geology and archaeology, with a good Bronze-Age gallery and an art gallery with a John Piper window; shop; cl Sun and bank hols; *£1.75. BROADLEAS (Potterne Rd) Rare plants in secluded dell among rhododendrons and other fine flowering shrubs, unusual trees, spring and autumn colour too; teas Sun, unusual plant sales; open pm Sun, Weds and Thurs, Mar-Nov; *£2. The Bear Hotel, Elm Tree and White Bear, all tied to Wadworths, the local brewery, are all good for lunch.

Great Bedwyn SO2764 BEDWYN STONE MUSEUM Fascinating little open-air museum demonstrating the ancient art of stonemasonry; meals and snacks; shop, disabled access. CROFTON BEAM ENGINES Home to the oldest working beam engines in the world, the 1812 Boulton & Watt, and an 1845 Harvey's of Hayle; both still carry out their original function of pumping water into the Kennet & Avon Canal. Snacks, shop; open wknds Easter-Oct, engines static most wknds but in steam in 1994 on 2-4 Apr, 30 Apr-1 May, 28-30 May, 25-26 Jun, 30-31 July, 27-29 Aug, 24-25 Sept; static *£1, steam wknds *£3. The Harrow nearby at Little Bedwyn is good for lunch.

Holt ST8661 THE COURTS This was where weavers used to come to settle their disputes; the 15th-c house isn't open, but there are lovely and extensive formal gardens full of yew hedges, pools and borders, with the other half of the grounds given over to wild flowers among interesting trees; disabled access; cl am, all day Sat and Nov-Mar; £2.50.

★ **Lacock** ST9168 A favourite village, this has a grid of quiet and narrow streets which are a delightful harmony of mellow brickwork, lichened stone and timber-and-plaster; the CHURCH is 15th-c, and nothing in the village looks more recent than 18th-c. It's remained so remarkably unspoilt because most buildings in the village were owned for centuries by the Talbot family, until they left them to the NT in 1944. The showpiece is LACOCK ABBEY, a tranquil spread of mellow stone buildings, around a central timber-gabled courtyard, based on the little-altered 13th-c abbey. Cloisters, impressive Great Hall, medieval nunnery buildings and so forth, with some Tudor additions including a romantic octagonal tower, and a successful 18th-c Gothicisation – even an old brewery. Surrounded by quiet meadows and trees, this was the setting for Fox Talbot's experiments which in 1835 led to the creation of the world's first photographic negative – a picture of part of the abbey itself. There's a museum devoted to this in a 16th-c barn, and the gardens are evidence of Fox Talbot's skills in other fields. Shop, limited disabled access; cl am, all day Tue, Good Fri, Nov-Mar; £4. LACKHAM GARDENS, MUSEUM AND WOODLAND This 500-acre estate is the home of the Lackham College of Agriculture, and attractions include a farm museum, walled garden and glasshouses, rare-breeds farm, pleasant woodland and riverside walks and a children's playground; the old roses are worth catching from May to July. Snacks; shop and plant sales; disabled access; cl Nov-Mar; £3.15. The NT, which owns the village, has preserved it against a surfeit of antique shops, but you'll find all you want in the nearby old market town of Melksham ST9063. The village does on the other hand have a splendid collection of pubs and inns – all good in their way.

✝ **Lydiard Park** SU1085 After a period of neglect up to World War II, this grand Georgian house has been painstakingly restored to its original impressive condition – with interesting early wallpaper and rare painted glass window, and elegant furnishings much as they would have been when first installed. Outside are extensive lawns, lakes and well-wooded parkland, with nature walks and adventure playgrounds. The adjacent parish

CHURCH of St Mary's has interesting monuments to the St John family, who lived in the house for 500 years; snacks, shop, disabled access; cl 1-2 pm, Sun am, Good Fri, 25-26 Dec; up to the end of March 1994 the cost is just 50p, to mark the house's 250th anniversary, but it will go up after that.

★ ✝ **Malmesbury** ST9287 Yet another charming old town, especially around the green facing its serene Norman ABBEY, from the tower of which a medieval monk called Elmer made one of the earliest semi-successful attempts at flight – he covered a couple of hundred yards, but did break both legs when he crash-landed. The Suffolk Arms out on the Tetbury road is probably the best place here for lunch, though we've recently been getting good reports on the Whole Hog (which has been doing food all day); the picturesque Old Bell is almost as old as the abbey, which is alongside.

★ **Marlborough** SU1868 One of the area's most attractive towns, this has a very pleasing wide High St, scene of the annual autumn Mop Fair which used to be held in most market towns for the hiring of servants, but which has been revived here as a general celebration – there's also a regular market each Weds and Sat. The street is a harmonious mix of Georgian and Tudor buildings, with even the more modern additions not looking obtrusively out of place, and some interesting shops. The side streets are well worth exploring, too. To the north, the downs give great open spaces, not all turned over to monotonous arable farming (see Walks, below); to the east there are woody walks through the surviving miles of SAVERNAKE FOREST. The Wellington Arms and Sun are useful for lunch.

Swindon SU1484 Today known as a business and industrial centre, this bustling hill-top market town is much older than you might think, and is mentioned in the Domesday Book. Later it was caught up with a vengeance in the railway age, and in the Railway Village had one of the earliest examples of a planned workers' estate. GREAT WESTERN RAILWAY (Faringdon Rd) Excellent rail museum, with lots of locomotives and related train memorabilia, inc the historic Dean Goods and Lode Star; shop; cl Sun am; £1.80; also an exhibition on the GWR village itself, with recreated workshop displays. RAILWAY VILLAGE HOUSE AND MUSEUM (34 Faringdon Rd) Restored foreman's house furnished in typical turn-of-the-century working-class style; shop; cl Christmas and New Year, museum cl Sun am; £1.80. MUSEUM AND ART GALLERY (Bath Rd) Small local-history collection; also pictures by important 20th-c artists such as Moore and Sutherland; shop, limited disabled access; cl Sun am, bank hols. SWINDON AND CRICKLADE RAILWAY One of the only live steam projects in the area, gradually being restored, with trips through the countryside, and a museum; open wknds; (0793) 721252 for train times.

Wilton SU2661 (not to be confused with the larger town in the south of the county) WILTON WINDMILL The only working windmill in the county, built in 1821 after the construction of the Kennet & Avon canal had taken away all the water previously used to power mills. It's now been restored, and on quite a prominent chalk ridge is beautifully floodlit every evening; shop; open pm Sun Easter-Sept, plus Mon and Sat bank hol wknds; 80p.

✈ **Wroughton Airfield** SU1378 SCIENCE MUSEUM Growing national collections of aircraft, rockets, hovercraft, with road transport from carriages through steam lorries to cars, farm machinery and occcasional live steam runs. So far the collection's more of specialist interest, and hasn't yet really been aimed at entertaining the general public – it's only open about five times a year, but when it is they generally have air displays or other lively events; tel (0793) 814466 for 1994 dates.

As well as the places we've mentioned, there are ANCIENT SITES at Barbury Castle SU1677 (a splendidly remote and atmospheric place) and several near Marlborough, with good WHITE HORSES at Alton Barnes SU0962, Broad Hinton SU1076 and Cherhill SU0370.

The recently restored **Kennet & Avon Canal** runs right across this part of the county (see also Devizes above), and there are pleasant boat trips from several places along its route. Several of our correspondents have particularly enjoyed boats hired at Hilperton ST8759 and Bradford-on-Avon ST8261, and you can also embark from Devizes SU0061 or Wootton Rivers SU1963, though we've had no reports on these. In the canal's restoration, a great deal of attention has been paid to the natural environment, and it's attractive for walks alongside; in winter you may even see a kingfisher flashing along it.

★**Other attractive villages in this part** of the county, all with decent pubs, include Aldbourne ST2675, Ashton Keynes SU0494, Axford SU2370, Biddestone ST8773, Castle Eaton SU1495 (by a quiet stretch of the upper Thames, pleasant for strolling), Heddington ST9966, Highworth SU2092, Marston Meysey SU1297, Ramsbury ST2771, Sandy Lane ST9668, Winsley ST7961, and Wootton Rivers SU1963.

Walks

Castle Combe ST8477 has surroundings that are as appealing as the village, and attractive paths along peaceful valleys.

Much of the Wiltshire chalklands are unvarying green mono-agricultural expanses, but the **Marlborough Downs** harbour archaeological bounties which you can use to punctuate walks around Avebury SU1069 – for example, to the major prehistoric sites of Silbury Hill SU1068, West Kennet Long Barrow SU1067 and the neolithic camp on Windmill Hill SU0871. **Fyfield Down** SU1470 is primeval-feeling and unkempt, scattered with outcrops known as Sarsen stones, the raw material of Avebury stone circle and of part of Stonehenge. At the northernmost point of the Marlborough Downs, **Barbury Castle** SU1476 is an ancient hill-fort site with formidable ramparts, on the long-distance Ridgeway Path. There is a car park nearby, but you can also walk up to it from Ogbourne St George SU1974 along Smeathe's Ridge SU1775, a preserved stretch of downland (gorse and all).

The **Kennet & Avon Canal** has a long flight of locks on the west side of Devizes SU0061, and can form part of a river and canal walk around Barton Farm Country Park at Bradford-on-Avon ST8261. At Alton Barnes SU1062, the canal lies close enough to **Pewsey Down** nature reserve for an afternoon's walk to incorporate both features; the spine of the downs here is followed by the Wansdyke, an ancient earthwork which runs across the downs for miles from Morgans Hill SU0267 nr Calne nearly as far as the Savernake Forest.

Driving

The back road from Marlborough over the downs to Broad Hinton gives a good view of the open downland farming country – and covering the ground at car speed rather than walking speed, the scenery seems altogether more varied.

Another quiet downland road, giving a view of one of the area's several white horses cut into the chalk of the downs, is from Marlborough to Alton Priors, where a right turn takes you along a pleasant valley road through Allington and Horton to Devizes.

Up towards the Gloucestershire border, the topography tends generally to be too flat to make for interesting drives, but all the B roads radiating from Malmesbury are quite pleasant.

The A4/A420 paralleling the M4, and for the most part a good wide road, does not carry a great deal of traffic, and has some good views.

Another relatively quiet main road through attractive countryside is the A342 out of Devizes; a left turn at Sandy Lane takes you on a very pretty back road to Lacock.

The countryside is not bad for cycling, with some quite quiet and not too hilly roads – good routes and maps are available from the County Council, and you can hire bikes in most of the towns in the area (though you need a permit to ride on the canal towpath).

Where to eat

Brinkworth SU0184 THREE CROWNS The Street (0666) 510366 Friendly atmosphere in villagey pub with good-sized helpings of unusual and elaborate dishes as well as a wide range of snacks, good choice of drinks, and garden that looks out towards church and over rolling country. **£20 for 2 courses**|£3/£9.

Wootton Rivers SU1963 ROYAL OAK (0672) 810322 Prettily thatched 16th-c pub with relaxed, friendly atmosphere, huge reasonably priced and popular menu with elaborate daily specials and good home-made dishes; bedrooms with help-yourself breakfasts; cl Christmas. **£18**|£1.50/£6.50.

Ford ST8374 WHITE HART (0249) 782213 In lovely spot by trout stream; unusual and tempting meals, and good service. **£12.60**|£5.25/£7.35.

Marlborough SU1869 POLLY TEAROOMS (0672) 512146 Warmly recommended by contributors as a nice place for lunch or tea; cl 25-27 Dec. **£9.45**|£6.

Avebury SU0969 STONES RESTAURANT (0672) 3514 Relaxed but civilised restaurant with very good, generously served vegetarian food and friendly service; open all day (not evenings), wknds only Nov-Easter, cl Christmas-end Jan; disabled access. **£9**|£2.25/£4.75.

Box ST8268 QUARRYMANS ARMS (0225) 743569 Tucked-away unspoilt hillside pub with fine views; two small knocked-together rooms with quarrying memorabilia, wide choice of good home-cooked food, well-kept real ales, and very friendly staff; children welcome; bedrooms. £2/£4.

Help this year from: *HNJ, PEJ, P Gillett, G J Evans, R H Crawcour, John Knighton, P M Woodger, John Evans, George Atkinson, Gerrit and Martine, S J Rix, Mr and Mrs N J Dorricott, John and Beryl Knight, Mr and Mrs P Wildman, Jean Minner, M A Watts, Don and Thelma Beeson, D Barr, W F C Phillips, Belinda Mead, Jerry and Alison Oakes, Tony Gayfer, Neil Andrews, T G Saul, Roderic Plinston, W K Struthers, Tim Bucknall, Chris Elias, Maysie Thompson, June and Tony Baldwin, Colin Laffan, Paul Weedon, M E Cleaver, P Gillett, Viv Middlebrook, Nigel Gibbs, Peter Cleaver.*

Wiltshire Calendar

Some of these dates were provisional as we went to press.

FEBRUARY

15th **Bradford-on-Avon** Great Pancake Race

27th **Warminster** Husky Races *at Longleat House*

MARCH

26th **Wilton** Antiques Fair *in the Cloisters, Wilton House – till Sun 27*

APRIL

1st **Devizes** *to Westminster* International 125-mile Canoe Race

4th **Bradford-on-Avon** Duck Race

MAY

2nd **Devizes** May Day Fair

14th **Castle Combe** Vintage Rally *at Castle Combe Circuit – till Sun 15*

21st **Devizes** Boto-cross

22nd **Lacock** Country Day *at Lackham College of Agriculture*

27th **Chippenham** Folk Festival *– till Mon 30*; **Warminster** Steam Engine and Vintage Vehicle Rally *at Longleat House – till Tues 31*

28th **Wilton** D-Day Celebrations *at Wilton House (HQ of Southern Command), inc military rally and bands – till 5 Jun*

29th **Castle Combe** Classic Run *at Castle Combe Circuit*

30th **Calne** Pro-am Tournament *at Bowood Golf Course*

JUNE

4th **Amesbury** Carnival; **Warminster** Horse Trials *at Longleat House – till Sun 5*

16th **Devizes** Festival *– till 3 July*

21st **Stonehenge** Druid Summer Solstice Ceremony *at midnight, vigil till dawn when service celebrates first rays of sun on altar, Presider crowned at noon: public welcome to watch*

23rd **Warminster** Goldwing Motorbike Rally *at Longleat House*

26th **Stourton** Delphinium Day; **Warminster** Amateur Radio Rally *at Longleat House*

JULY

2nd **Heddington and Stockley** Steam Rally *at Home Farm, Heddington – till Sun 3*

9th **Bradford-on-Avon** Festival *– till Sun 10*; **Crudwell** Strawberry Fayre and Craft Market *at village green and school – till Sun 10*; **Marlborough** Festival *– till Sun 17*

16th **Devizes** Canal Festival and Boat Rally *– till Sun 17*; **Warminster** Harley Davidson Motorbike Meet *at Longleat House – till Sun 17*

20th **Stourton** Stourhead Fête Champêtre, *song, music and dance, firework finale – till Sat 23*

22nd **Trowbridge** Village Pump Festival *– till Sun 24*

30th **Castle Combe** VW Beetle Action Display *at Castle Combe Circuit*

Wiltshire Calendar

August

5th **Marlborough** Wiltshire Artists Annual Exhibition *at St Peter's Church – till Sat 13*

13th **Castle Combe** Classic Cars Action Display *at Castle Combe Circuit*

21st **Edington** Music Festival, *music within the liturgy – till Sun 28*; **Salisbury** and South Wilts Agricultural Show

27th **Castle Combe** Super Car Test Day *at Castle Combe Circuit*

28th **Neston** Vintage Rally – *till Mon 29*; **Wroughton** Great Warbirds Air Display *at Science Museum, inc massed formation flypasts, 1940s nostalgia and marching bands*

29th **Corsham** Flower Show

September

2nd **Salisbury** Festival – *till Sun 18*

3rd **Bradford-on-Avon** Wharfside Show – *till Sun 4*; **Chippenham** Garden and Allotment Society Annual Flower Show *at Neeld Hall*; **Devizes** Carnival Procession; **Pewsey** Carnival, *inc race of 100 decorated wheelbarrows from pub to pub, procession on Sat 17*

10th **Trowbridge** Carnival Procession; **Warminster** Dog Agility Show *at Longleat House – till Sun 11*; **Westbury** Medieval Fayre

16th **Melksham** Festival – *till Weds 28*

17th **Castle Combe** Kit Car Action Day *at Castle Combe Circuit*

24th **Castle Combe** Mini Action Day

30th **Cricklade** Music Festival – *till 8 Oct*

October

8th **Marlborough** Little Mop Fair

15th **Marlborough** Big Mop Fair

November

26th **Westbury** Craft Trail

December

23rd **Salisbury** Christmas Carol Service *at Cathedral*

YORKSHIRE

York itself is difficult to beat as a place for a civilised yet lively short stay – it stands head and shoulders above all other English cities for that. The Yorkshire Dales are among Britain's very best areas for a weekend break, and perhaps the best of all for a quiet stay in glorious countryside. Both they and the North York Moors (which also have some interesting coastal scenery) are ideal for walking holidays, though very rewarding too for people who want to get around by car instead. Yet, besides its magnificent scenery, this county – the largest in Britain – has romantic ruined abbeys and castles, grand houses, and some magnificent landscaped gardens. It's one of the friendliest places in Britain, and there's no shortage of most enjoyable places to stay in.

Harrogate, very civilised, is perhaps best seen as a comfortable base for exploring other areas, though would be appealing if what you want is a very soporific and idle stay without doing much more than the gentlest local pottering. The area we've called East Yorkshire, less well known to visitors than the Dales and the Moors, has a quietly untouristy appeal.

South and West Yorkshire is the part where you'll find the most places to visit, including some outstanding museums; the west particularly has great possibilities if you want to spend quite a busy time combining sightseeing, museum visits and so forth with the ability to get out into magnificent countryside quickly.

YORK

Outstanding for a short stay: largely pedestrianised medieval walled centre, with lots to interest visitors.

The magnificent Minster is one of Britain's great sights, and the Jorvic Centre among the country's best heritage centres. The National Railway Museum and the Castle Museum are also impressive, and there are many other things well worth visiting here. But the city's particular appeal is that it's so pleasant just to be in and stroll through. Much of the centre, enclosed in 13th-c city walls, is pedestrianised and filled with lovely medieval buildings, fascinating twisting snickleways and alleys, and interesting shops. It's very civilised, but lively too, the atmosphere brightened up by the students at its flourishing university. They help to support a dense network of lively cafés, pubs and bars, and bring warmth and colour into the streets, especially on warm summer evenings. Particularly in the summer, York does flood with visitors, but fortunately it's one of those cities, like Paris but unlike London, where all the other visitors actually seem to add to the atmosphere, rather than detracting from it.

Where to stay

York SE5951 MIDDLETHORPE HALL YO2 1QB (0904) 641241 **£134.90**; 29 rms, most in the converted stables. Lovely, immaculately restored William III country house just south of the city, with fine gardens and parkland, comfortable, quiet day rooms, and excellent food and service; no under-9s.

York SE5951 VIKING YO1 1JF (0904) 659822 **£112.50**; 188 rms. Smart and comfortable modern hotel on the banks of the River Ouse with fine city views.

Shipton by Beningbrough SE5559 SIDINGS York (0904) 470221 **£95**; 8 rms in two converted coaches. A railway enthusiast's paradise, based on restored former railway carriages with excellent food served at Pullman-style tables; decent wine list, railway viewing platform, models, videos, and paintings and artefacts; disabled access.

York SE5951 4 SOUTH PARADE YO2 2BA (0904) 628229 **£75**; 3 lovely rms with Edwardian-style furnishings, original fireplaces and fresh flowers. Beautifully decorated house in small elegant Georgian terrace on private cobbled street 15 mins from Minster and 5 mins from station; pretty drawing room; very helpful owners, good breakfasts and candlelit suppers by arrangement in delightful dining room; no smoking; cl Christmas; children over 12.

York SE5951 MOUNT ROYALE YO2 2DA (0904) 628856 **£75**; 23 rms. Near the racecourse, this William IV hotel has warmly friendly staff, a relaxed atmosphere, good food, decent wines, and garden with swimming pool; cl 24-31 Dec.

Dringhouses SE5849 CURZON LODGE 23 Tadcaster Rd York YO2 2QG (0904) 703157 **£56**; 10 rms, some in former old coach house and stables. Charming early 17th-c house in marvellous spot overlooking Knavesmire Racecourse with attractive, comfortable drawing room, sunny farmhouse dining room, and secluded walled garden; cl Christmas/New Year; children over 8.

York SE5951 HOLMWOOD HOUSE 114 Holgate Rd YO2 4BB (0904) 626183 **£55**; 8 pretty rms, some are no smoking. Carefully restored mid-19th-c hotel 5 mins to city walls; open fire and books in homely lounge and very good breakfasts; you are given keys and can come and go as you please; own car park; cl 2 wks early Jan; children over 8.

York SE5951 GRANGE YO3 6AA (0904) 644744 **£50**; 29 rms. Close to the Minster, this Regency town house has elegant public rooms, open fire, newspapers, good breakfasts, excellent restaurant food (there's also a brasserie), and warmly friendly staff; car park; disabled access.

Bishopthorpe SE5947 MARCIA York YO2 1RA (0904) 706185 **£40**; 6 rms, some with own bthrm. Just outside the city, but well recommended by contributors as good value; new restaurant and large garden.

We welcome reports from readers . . .

Readers who help us with reports for the GUIDE are offered a discount on the next edition: so please do help if you can!

To see and do

The ARC (St Saviourgate) presents the study of archaeology in a refreshing and interesting way, using hands-on interactive displays that give you a chance to play archaeologist yourself. You can decipher Viking-age writing, learn to make a Roman shoe, and sift through the remains of the past – all with professional archaeologists there to give information and advice. This is very much on the school-trips circuit, so best out of term-time. The building itself is also well worth a look – the medieval CHURCH OF ST SAVIOUR, which has been beautifully restored, with an interesting old-fashioned garden; shop, disabled access; cl am wknds, 18-31 Dec; *£3.20. The Archaeological Trust that run the ARC (and the Jorvik Centre) also have a Georgian coffee-house THOMAS GENT'S (off Stonegate), serving appropriate snacks on three candle-lit floors furnished in period style; cl Sun. It joins on to BARLEY HALL, a medieval family home currently being restored. As there are 11 rooms the full process will take some time, but the completed rooms are already open; there's a useful Walkman tour, with glass panels letting you see some of the restoration work being carried out; cl Sun, Good Fri, 20 Dec-1 Jan; *£3.50.

BAR CONVENT (Blossom St) Still used as a convent, this elegant Georgian building is also a museum illustrating the early history of Christianity in the north of England, and in particular the inspiring story of Mary Ward who founded the Institute of the Blessed Virgin, and pioneered women's education and apostolic orders; snacks, shop, disabled access; cl Sun, Mon, Good Fri, all Jan; *£1.75.

The city has a good few fine medieval CHURCHES, though many are no longer used for services. Among the finest are Holy Trinity (Goodramgate) and St Helens (St Helens Sq).

CASTLE MUSEUM (Tower St) Housed in 18th-c prison buildings on the site of the former castle (part of the outer wall still stands), this popular place has a huge range of everyday objects from the past four centuries, shown in convincingly reconstructed real-life settings, from individual rooms and craft workshops to whole cobbled streets of shops. There's even a watermill, by the river outside. Among many other collections that you could go back to again and again, the museum has one of the finest collections of militaria in the country, inc one of only three Anglo-Saxon helmets in the world – it was found here in York in the 1980s. This again is a favourite for school trips, so is best out of school term-time; snacks, shop, disabled access ground floor only; cl 25-26 Dec, 1 Jan; £3.80. A REGIMENTAL MUSEUM for the Royal Dragoon Guards and the Prince of Wales's Own Regiment is nearby; cl Sun and bank hols; 50p.

CITY ART GALLERY (Exhibition Sq) Good collections, well displayed, run from Old Masters to the lusciously romantic nudes of William Etty (who was largely responsible for thwarting an early 19th-c plan to knock down the city walls), with some very handsome stoneware pottery – a veritable treasure house of paintings from over seven centuries; shop, disabled access; cl Sun am, 25 Dec, 1 Jan, Good Fri.

CLIFFORD'S TOWER (near the Castle Museum in the castle precints) After the Minster, perhaps York's most interesting building, originally the 14th-c castle keep. You can walk around the top of the walls, which enclose a garden, and there are good views of the city. It's seen its fair share of violence, and indeed gets its name from Roger de Clifford who was hanged from it by chains. Subsidence of the mound it stands on has split it in two, and it got a battering in the Civil

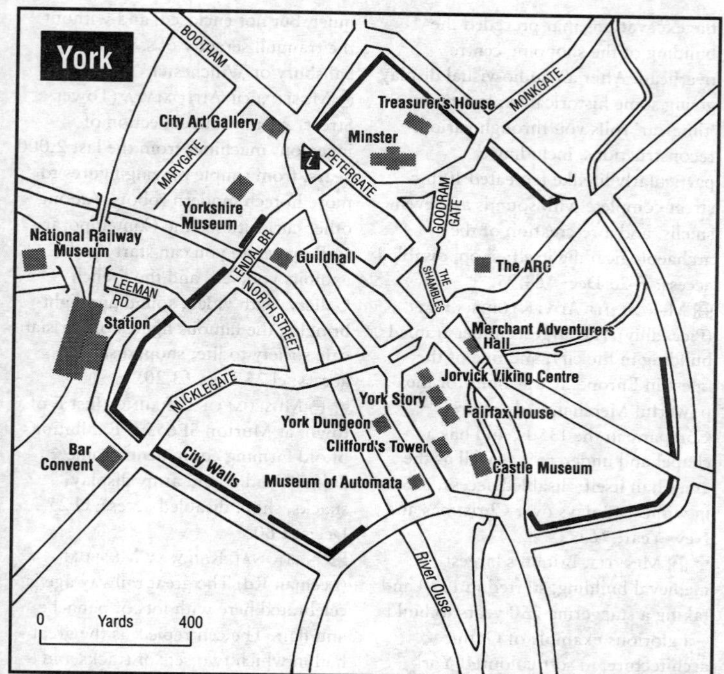

War, followed by an explosion which blew off the roof; shop; cl winter 1-2 pm, and 24-26 Dec; *£1.20.

FAIRFAX HOUSE (Castlegate) After periods as a cinema and a dance hall, this mid-18th-c house was magnificently restored, and now boasts a richly decorated interior. Much of the splendid collection of paintings, pottery, clocks and Georgian furniture was donated by the great-grandson of the confectionery baron Joseph Terry. Among some very interesting displays is a recreated meal of 1763; shop, some disabled access; cl Sun am, all day Fri, Jan and Feb; £3.

! FRIARGATE MUSEUM (Lower Friargate) A rather jolly wax museum, with over 60 lifesize models, all posed, often wittily, in realistic sets to illustrate moments in history, from Alfred the Great through Drake to the Yeti. There is also an unusual and infectious display of laughter machines; shop, disabled access; Dec-Feb; £2.50.

GUILDHALL (St Helens Sq) An exact replica of the original building of 1446, destroyed in a 1940 air raid. The stone walls of the earlier building survived and form the framework of the new one, the details of which are all as the original – there's an interesting arch-braced roof supported by solid oak pillars and decorated with colourful bosses, and some 17th-c glass in the west window; disabled access; cl Sun am in summer, all day in winter when cl Sat too, Good Fri, Easter Mon, Christmas period.

JORVIK VIKING CENTRE (below Coppergate Shopping Centre) Be warned, the queues for this can be horrifically long, but almost everyone finds the wait well worth while; for the shortest wait, get there early or late. The Centre displays over 15,000 of the Viking artefacts which were found in the excavations that preceded the building of the shopping centre overhead. After an audio-visual display giving some historical explanations, a 'time-car' rolls you through various reconstructions, including a particularly lifelike recreated 10th-c street complete with sounds and even smells, and a re-creation of the archaeological dig itself; shop, disabled access; cl 25 Dec; *£3.95.

MERCHANT ADVENTURERS HALL (Piccadilly) The largest timber-framed building in the city, and one of the finest in Europe. It was built for the powerful Merchant Adventurers' Company in the 1350s, and has a chapel and undercroft as well as the great hall itself; disabled access; cl Sun in winter, 10 days over Christmas and New Year; *£2.

MINSTER Britain's largest medieval building, started in 1220 and taking a staggering 250 years to build – a glorious example of Gothic architecture, in soft-coloured York stone. Look out for the beautiful ceilings of the central tower and the chapter house, and the splendid glass of the five sisters window in the north transept, or the great east window which shows Genesis and Revelation in 27 panels. The choir stalls are 19th-c copies, but still worth looking out for, and the choir screen has 15 niches containing statues of the kings of England from William the Conqueror to Henry VI. The interior is extremely rich in detail, as is the chapter house, and it's well worth buying the guide book to help you spot at least some of the delights. The south transept vault has now been restored after the disastrous 1984 fire. In the Foundations and Treasury a display explains the Roman origins of Eboracum, and events in Christian history to which the church relates, as well as its own hair-raising history. Shop, disabled access; cl Sun am, and occasionally for major services. Largely traffic-free, the Close outside is fairly quiet, but not enclosed, and without the tranquil serenity of say Exeter, Salisbury or Winchester.

MUSEUM OF AUTOMATA (Tower Street) An unusual collection of ingenious machines from the last 2,000 years, from simple moving figures to more hi-tech modern robots. Among other curiosities is the Contemporary Gallery where you can start up the exhibits yourself, and the French Gallery, with video, sound and light bringing the famous figures of Parisian café society to life; shop, disabled access; cl 25 Dec; £3.20.

MUSEUM OF FARMING (just E of town, at Murton SE6552) Exhibitions of old farming equipments, some animals and a land army display; snacks, shop, disabled access; cl 25-26 Dec; £2.60.

NATIONAL RAILWAY MUSEUM (Leeman Rd) The great railway age is celebrated here with lots of panache and flair. The centrepiece is the great hall in which two sets of tracks and platforms radiate from central turntables, one with a changing display of two dozen great locomotives from the museum's collection of a hundred or so, the other with all sorts of carriages and waggons, from the humblest and most utilitarian to Queen Victoria's sumptuous royal coach – all there for you to step up into. In the background is a well-reproduced soundtrack of recorded station noises from the steam era, and alongside is a mass of material vividly illustrating the 200-year history of rail and how it changed the world, from a lock of Robert Stephenson's hair to the Channel Tunnel trains. There are also timetabled working demonstrations and rides – one place where the trains are always on time; meals and snacks, shop, disabled access; cl 24-26 Dec, 1 Jan; £4.

TREASURER'S HOUSE (Chapter House St) There's been a house here since Roman times – this one dates from the 17th c, although the staircase dates from the 18th, and the basement has an exhibition of the site's history. The timbered hall is very fine, as is the period furniture, useful as an indication of how the officials of the nearby Minster used to live. Snacks, shop; cl Nov-Mar; £2.80. NT.

! YORK DUNGEON (Clifford Street) Full of grue and gore, but of course all true – this carefully researched exploration of superstition, torture and various forms of death accurately portrays the sort of punishments our ancestors received in the days when justice really did need reforming; shop, disabled access; cl 24-26 Dec; *£3.

YORK MODEL RAILWAY (York BR Station, Tearoom Sq) Extensive model railway in painstakingly recreated miniature town and country landscape, running as many as 20 trains at the same time; a second much smaller model shows a typical German town at night; shop, disabled access; cl 25-26 Dec; £2.30.

† YORK STORY (Castlegate) Elaborate exhibition tracing York's last thousand years, with a big 3-D model of the city and comprehensive audio-visual display. It's based in the partly 15th-c Church of St Mary, whose spire at 152 ft is the tallest in the city; shop, disabled access ground floor only; cl Sun am, 25-26 Dec, 1 Jan; *£1.40, joint ticket with castle £4.70.

YORKSHIRE MUSEUM (Museum Gardens) A real treasure-trove, crammed with myriad archaeological finds and riches from Roman, Anglo-Saxon, Viking and medieval times, including the fabulous and recently discovered medieval Middleham Jewel, the Ormside bowl and the marble head of Constantine the Great. It's all set out very sympathetically, working through the ages and effectively putting the exhibits into the context of how people lived. One especially good display is the reconstruction, complete with sound effects, of part of the abbey which stood here. Summer snacks, shop, disabled access; Oct-Mar cl Sun am, cl 25-26 Dec, 1 Jan; £3. Outside are ten acres of botanical gardens by the wall: peaceful and attractive, around a shapely group of ruins inc the Benedictine St Mary's abbey and the Multangular Tower (medieval, on a Roman base), as well as a working observatory.

Walks

Inside the city walls, York is largely pedestrianised: it's the most rewarding of all English cities to walk around. You can do the circuit of the 13th-c **city walls** and their many towers in a couple of hours or so, mostly on top. One of the best stretches, with good views of the Minster, is between the Monk Bar, the most striking of the turreted medieval gateways, and Bootham Bar. If you plan on doing the whole circuit it's well worth using one of the Walkman guides rented by the helpful Tourist Office (Exhibition Sq).

Around **The Shambles**, jettied medieval buildings leaning towards each other across the alleys are enlivened by witty architectural details such as the red figure of the printer's devil almost opposite the courtyard entry to the Olde Starre (a touristy pub, but genuinely old, with a view of the Minster from seats in its yard). This area has some of the city's most interesting shops, inc good bookshops, all sorts of unusual specialist shops, and, especially in Stonegate, nearer the Minster, and in elegant Micklegate, some serious silver and antique shops.

The **River Ouse** flows right through the centre: the staithe below Clifford St is one quiet place beside it (with a decent pub, the Kings Arms).

Driving

This can be summed up in one word – don't. It's best not to drive into the centre, within the walls, and there's a dreadful morning and evening rush hour, though once the evening rush hour is over you can find parking even in the centre fairly easily. There's a good park-and-ride from the Tesco superstore (A64 SW). All the hotels we list have parking.

Where to eat

York SE5951 MELTONS 7 Scarcroft Rd (0904) 634341 Smart little restaurant with very good modern and more straightforward dishes, seafood specialities Tues evenings, and a relaxed, friendly atmosphere; cl Sun pm, Mon am, 3 wks over Christmas, last wk Aug. **£25**|*£4.50/£9*.
York SE5951 19 GRAPE ST (0904) 636366 Close to the Minster, this neat timbered restaurant serves a good mix of traditional and imaginative dishes (lovely nursery puddings) in a warmly friendly atmosphere; cl Sun-Mon, last 2 wks Sept, 1st 2 wks Feb, 25-26 Dec, 1-2 Jan; children over 8 in evening. **£23.45**|*£2.50/£7.75*.
York SE5951 ST WILLIAMS COLLEGE RESTAURANT College St (0904) 634830 Enjoyable, varied food (inc vegetarian dishes) in pleasant self-service restaurant in fine building with enclosed courtyard for eating outside in summer; open 10-5; cl 25-26 Dec, Good Fri. **£13.25**|*£1.45/£4.50*.
York SE5951 MAMA MIA 20 Gilligate (0904) 622020 Reasonably priced, decent Italian food; cl 25-26 Dec, 1 Jan; disabled access. **£12**|*£5.95*.
Useful bars, cafés and food pubs include Bettys (St Helens Sq), the 15th-c Black Swan (Peaseholme Green), Brigadier Gerard (Monkgate), Hansom Cab (Market St), Red Lion (Merchantgate), Royal Oak (Goodramgate), Spread Eagle (Walmgate) and Tap & Spile (Monkgate).

THE NORTHERN DALES

Magnificent scenery, friendly places to stay, attractive prices.

Wensleydale is the main focus of interest here for visitors, with very beautiful and varied scenery including some magnificent waterfalls, a succession of attractive villages and small towns, and a good few pleasant places to stay in – generally not grand, but comfortable, warm, very friendly and invitingly priced.

The upper reaches of Swaledale up in the north are largely unspoilt and with a remote feeling, more dramatic if more austere than Wensleydale, with a quieter road running through; we haven't yet found a place we can recommend to stay in up here, but it's within easy reach for drives and day walks from places we recommend to the south and east, including the pleasant and interesting town of Richmond downriver.

Apart from the scenery itself, which is unquestionably the area's main draw, places to visit in these dales and in the flatter country to their east tend to be relatively low-key. Among the most rewarding, we'd include the ruined abbeys of Jervaulx and Easby, the castle remains at Richmond, Middleham and Castle Bolton, and Aysgarth for its waterfalls and carriage museum.

Where to stay

Simonstone SD8791 Simonstone Hall Hawes DL8 3LY (0969) 667255 **£90**; 10 pretty rms. Carefully restored, warmly welcoming country house in beautiful countryside with spacious panelled drawing rooms, antiques, paintings and old maps of the area; fine views, good food, and interesting wines; cl 2 wks Jan; dogs always welcome; limited disabled access.

Newby Wiske SE3688 Solberge Hall Northallerton DL7 9ER (0609) 779191 **£85**; 25 rms. Country house in 16 acres of gardens and woodland with homely lounge, attractive wood-panelled reception area and good food; croquet; disabled access.

Hawes SD8789 Cocketts Market Pl Hawes DL8 3RD (0969) 667312 ***£84**; 8 warm rms, 6 with own bthrm. Friendly, hardworking owners make this a most attractive and enjoyable place to stay with woodburning stove in small bar, candlelit restaurant, and residents' lounge with books; children over 10; disabled access.

Richmond NZ1801 Howe Villa Richmond DL10 4TJ (0748) 850055 ***£70**; 5 spacious rms. Late Georgian house with public rooms on the first floor to make the most of the views over the lovely garden, River Swale and surrounding NT land; comfortable, light and airy; good, enjoyable home-made food, and efficient, caring service; cl Dec-Mar; children over 12.

Askrigg SD9591 Kings Arms Leyburn DL8 3HQ (0969) 50258 **£66**; 9 rms. Smart Georgian former manor house with three distinct bars, one used in the television series *All Creatures Great and Small*; attractive furnishings, beams, oak panelling, fine green marble fireplace; imaginative restaurant dishes and excellent bar food.

Sedbusk SD8891 Stone House Hawes DL8 3PT (0969) 667571 ***£60**; 18 rms. Small, warmly friendly Edwardian hotel with country-house feel and appropriate furnishings, magnificent views, attractive oak-panelled drawing room, billiard room, winter log fire; pleasant dining room with good food, super breakfasts and reasonable choice of wines; tennis lawn in the grounds, wonderful walks; P G Wodehouse stayed here as a guest of the original owner who employed a butler called Jeeves – it was on him that Wodehouse based his famous character; cl wkdys mid-Nov-Christmas (open then and New Year), cl Jan; good disabled access.

Middleham SE1288 Greystones Market Pl Middleham DL8 4NR (0969) 22016 **£56**; 4 rms. Friendly, family-run guesthouse in Georgian house with generous helpings of good food using home-grown vegetables; cl Nov-Mar but open Christmas and New Year; babysitters available.

Bainbridge SD9390 Rose & Crown Leyburn DL8 3EE (0969) 50225 **£50**; 12 comfortable rms. Overlooking lovely village green with antique settles and other old furniture in beamed and panelled front bar, big wine list, and bar and restaurant food; cl 25 Dec, 1 Jan.

Leyburn SE1191 Golden Lion Market Pl Leyburn DL8 5AS *£50; 15 good-value rms, most with own bthrm. Two comfortable knocked-together rooms with bay windows, light squared panelling, armchairs, pale country tables and chairs in airy eating area; good-value evening restaurant and bar food, good beer brewed to their own recipe, and helpful service; popular for coffee too; cl 25-26 Dec; no children; disabled access.

Thornton Watlass SE2486 Buck Ripon HG4 4AH (0677) 422461 **£45**; 5 rms. Warmly friendly country pub overlooking cricket green in very attractive village, interesting beamed and panelled rooms, open fire, live music wknds in function room, excellent food, and lots of walks.

West Burton SE0186 Fox & Hounds Leyburn DL8 4JY (0969) 663279 **£44**; 8 rms. Unspoilt, simple local in idyllic Dales village around long green, with homely welcoming atmosphere; small bar with extension, generous wholesome home-cooked food in residents' dining room and in bar, good service from friendly staff; no children; disabled access.

Pickhill SE3584 Nags Head Thirsk YO7 4JH (0845) 567391 **£42**; 17 rms. Cheerful and popular old inn with lots of ties, ale-yards, jugs and such around bar, stylish no-smoking restaurant, good bar food, huge breakfasts, well-kept beer, lots of malt whiskies, and fine wine list.

Richmond NZ1801 Whashton Springs Farm Richmond DL11 7JS (0748) 822884 **£40**; 8 comfortable rms. Attractive Georgian stone-built farmhouse on 600-acre mixed farm with comfortable sitting room, log fire, country home-cooking using home-produced meat, fruit and veg, and lovely surrounding countryside; cl Christmas-New Year; children over 5.

East Witton SE1586 Holly Tree Leyburn DL8 4LS (0969) 22383 **£40**; 4 good rms. Very attractively decorated, partly 12th-c house in peaceful village with very good food, homely, welcoming atmosphere, open fire in sitting room, TV lounge, and small garden; cl Jan-Feb; children over 10.

Middleham SE1288 Black Swan Market Pl Middleham DL8 4NP (0969) 22221 **£39**; 7 rms. Handsome 17th-c inn with heavy-beamed bar, stripped stonework, very sturdy furniture inc high-backed settles built in by big stone fireplace, separate dining room, cheerful local atmosphere and wide choice of filling food; charming village; no accom 24-26 Dec.

Richmond NZ1801 Black Lion Finkle St Richmond DL10 4QB (0748) 823121 **£34**; 14 rms, shared bthrm. Old coaching inn with cosy fires and beams, and very good, generously served food.

Danby Wiske SE3499 White Swan Northallerton DL7 0NQ (0609) 770122 *£30; 3 comfortable rms, shared bthrm. Cosy little pub in the middle of nowhere, handy for walkers on coast-to-coast footpath; very friendly licensees, and decent choice of good-value food inc free-range eggs from their chickens.

To see and do

Aysgarth SE0088 is most famous for its romantic series of waterfalls, easily reached from the National Park Centre (which explains the history and natural history of the Yorkshire Dales, using maps, walks and guides; there's a café beside it; shop; disabled access; limited wknd opening Nov-Mar). The Lower Fall is the most spectacular, via the path on the opposite side of the road. The waterfalls do get crowded, particularly through August (when even parking can be a problem here). They're better in late spring or early autumn, when there tends to be more water in the river and therefore a better show. In severely cold weather they become spectacular, with wonderful ice sculptures building up. YORKSHIRE CARRIAGE MUSEUM Some magnificent coaches and carriages among this collection of over 60 horse-drawn vehicles, with a decent crafts and pottery shop; cl Nov-Good Fri; £2. The George & Dragon Hotel is good for lunch.

Bainbridge SD9390 is a delightful village, its broad sloping green still ringing with the blowing of a buffalo-horn to guide shepherds down through the mists each night at 9 from the end of Sept till late Feb, as it has done for centuries. The Rose & Crown is good, and there's a restored 18th-c CORN MILL, with a collection of fully furnished hand-made doll's houses, all produced on the premises; shop sells assembled houses or plans to make your own; open pm bank hol wknds and Weds and Fri July-mid-Sept, or by appointment; *75p.

Bedale SE2687 BEDALE HALL Displays of domestic items give a strong impression of what life in this restored house must have been like in the days when its later use as council offices and now as a community centre could scarecly have been dreamed of; a main focus of interest is the Bedale fire engine dating from 1742. The house itself is 17th-c, but has grander Georgian and Palladian extensions; disabled access; cl Sun, and Oct-Easter. The BIG SHEEP AND LITTLE COW at Aiskew is a small-scale dairy farm, with friendly sheep and Dexter cows (Britain's smallest), and pigs and chicks – the family in charge love talking to visitors; shop; cl Oct-Easter; £2.50. A little way south is THORPE PERROW, a well-laid-out 60-acre landscaped lakeside collection of rare trees and shrubs among some splendid mature specimens that have been growing here for over 400 years; particularly strong on oaks, ornamental cherries, willows and hazels, and lovely in spring when the bulbs are out; £2.20.

Castle Bolton SE0392 14th-c BOLTON CASTLE, home of the powerful Scrope family (pronounced Scroop), is a massive structure towering over the little village built for it. Considering it was partly dismantled in 1645 and has been empty ever since, it's still in fine shape, its 100-ft towers giving a great view; they'll show you Mary, Queen of Scots' bedroom – she was locked up here in 1568. Snacks, shop; cl Dec-Feb; *£2.50.

Crakehall SE2490 MUSEUM OF BADGES AND BATTLEDRESS Private collection of the battledress and equipment of the British soldier from 1900 to the present, many displayed on dummies, with related ephemera; shop; cl am wknds, Mon (exc bank hols), Oct-Easter; *£1. Nearby the 17th-c CRAKEHALL WATERMILL stands on the site of a still earlier one; restored in 1980, it's now producing flour again; snacks, shop; cl Mon and Fri; *90p.

Croft NZ2909 Right on the border with Co Durham is a pleasant CHURCH, where Lewis Carroll's father was parson; there's a plaque in memory of the writer, complete with an enamelled White Rabbit, and an unusual family pew, reached by a staircase. If the church is closed, the key is kept at the hotel across the road, and there are nice river views.

Hawes SD8789 Busy in summer with hikers and coach-parties, but pretty, and a proper market town, its Tuesday mart alive with cattle and sheep in late summer. DALES COUNTRYSIDE MUSEUM AND NATIONAL PARK CENTRE explains how man has changed and developed the area over the last 10,000 years, with displays of farming implements, domestic and industrial life and other bygones; shop, disabled access; cl Nov-Mar; £1.20. Outhwaites ROPEMAKERS have been making them for 200 years – see how it's done; shop (not just great hawsers, useful things too like dog-leads), disabled access; cl Sat (exc July-Oct and Easter) and Sun. The White Hart and Board are useful for lunch. Just north is HARDRAW FORCE SD8691, England's tallest waterfall cascading over a 100-ft lip – best after rain, though the paths can be muddy then; the nominal fee (around 50p) is paid at the Green Dragon pub. The valley above the falls is attractive, and this can be a good start for the long day's walk to Great Shunner Fell.

✝ **Jervaulx Abbey** SE1785 is less imposing than Fountains, Rievaulx and Bolton, but in some ways even more appealing – perhaps because the rough-cropped grass and wild flowers around the shattered walls emphasise the slightly melancholy atmosphere of a place of great worldly wealth and power that's come to nothing. The Blue Lion at East Witton nearby is very good for lunch.

Middleham SE1288 Attractive and civilised basically Georgian stonebuilt village, still with the style that came from its days as the country's top racehorse-training centre in the 18th and early 19th c, before Newmarket took over. It's still the flourishing centre of Yorkshire's racehorse-training country, and often seems to have more horses than people: pick up breeding and gallops gossip in the bar of the good Black Swan. The village is dwarfed by 12th-c MIDDLEHAM CASTLE, which was for a time the home of young King Richard III and but for Bosworth Field might have become one of England's most powerful fortresses (beware of criticising him here). The castle's period of greatest prosperity was during the Wars of the Roses; now only the huge keep and some later buildings remain but there are marvellous views from the top. Snacks, shop, disabled access; cl 1-2 pm, Mon Oct-Mar; *£1.70. This is a good area for self-catering accommodation.

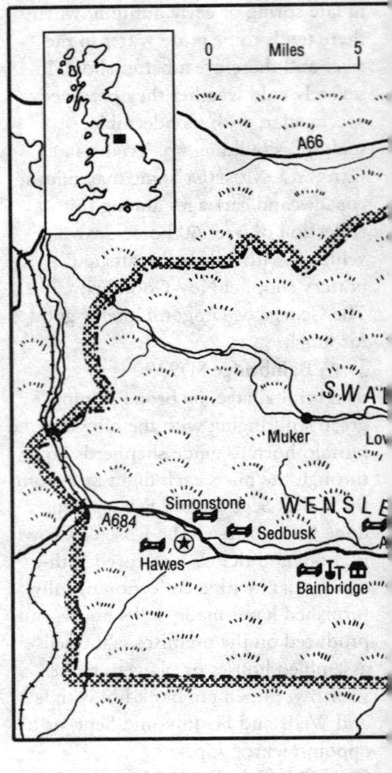

Richmond NZ1701 is a most attractive riverside country town, with steep and pretty streets of old stone buildings, and a splendid broad sloping market square (still cobbled, and perhaps the biggest in the country; market day is Sat). It's dominated by the austere and intricate ruins of RICHMOND CASTLE, which overlook the River Swale from a high rocky outcrop. The castle was begun in 1071 and the 100-ft triangular keep still stands, as do two of the towers on the curtain walls; some disabled access, shop; cl winter Mon, 24-26 Dec, 1 Jan; £1.70. Scollards Hall, which was built in 1080, is possibly the oldest domestic building in Britain. GREEN HOWARDS MUSEUM The story of one of Britain's oldest and most famous regiments, nicely set in a converted 12th-c church; uniforms, medals, paintings, photographs, regimental and civic plate, weapons and the blood-stained

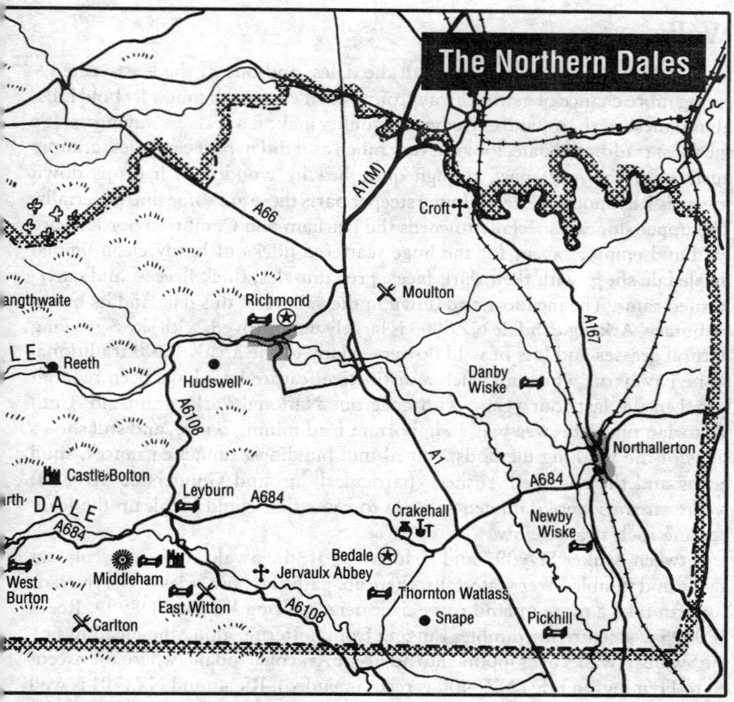

pistol holsters of the Grand Old Duke of York. The army connection with the town is still strong; nearby Catterick Camp is the biggest in the north. Shop; cl Sun exc pm Apr-Oct, Sat in Feb and all Dec and Jan; £1.25. GEORGIAN THEATRE ROYAL The oldest theatre in the country still in its original form and used for live performances, with its original gallery, boxes and pit. Built in 1788, the theatre closed in 1848 but was immaculately restored and reopened in 1962; snacks, shop; cl Sun am, museum cl Nov-Easter, theatre Jan-Mar; *£1. The Black Lion in Finkle St is good value for lunch.

★ Particularly attractive villages here include Askrigg SD9591 – a delightful collection of elegant stone houses around neat streamside greens, walks to nearby waterfalls, fine 15th-c church, and good pub, the Kings Arms; and Reeth SE0499, with another high, wide, sloping green (the Kings Arms is best for lunch here). Other pretty villages, all with decent pubs, inc East Witton SE1586, Hudswell NZ1400, Langthwaite NZ0003, Low Row SD9897 (popular with potholers), Muker SD9198 (woollens shop), Snape SE2784, Thornton Watlass SE2486 and West Burton SE0186. Leyburn SE1191 is a bustling little agricultural town rather than a village, but a good stop, with a proper country atmosphere and lively Friday market: the Sandpiper's the nicest pub.

Walks

Swaledale is the northernmost of all the dales, and one of the least visited – giving more chance of getting away from it all at even peak times. Its bold hills, abundant stone barns and extreme tranquillity make it a walkers' favourite. It's the most traditional dale, looking very much as it did in past centuries, grandly austere for the most part, though quite heavily wooded as it drops down towards Richmond NZ1801. In the steeper parts there are some fine waterfalls. The upper slopes, especially towards the Durham and Cumbrian borders, are wild and empty, except for the huge scattered flocks of hardy clean-limbed Swaledale sheep with their dark faces, grey muzzles, thick fleeces, and curly-horned rams. The meadowland down in the valleys of this dale and its broad 'tributary' **Arkengarthdale** NZ0003 is largely unimproved, with slow-growing natural grasses and lots of wild flowers. Many of the area's 1,200 traditional stone hay barns which are such a distinctive feature here have been rehabilitated in the last four years, with generous National Parks grant aid. Until Victorian times the area was an important lead-mining centre, and still shows signs of the working methods: ruined mill buildings, tunnel entrances, spoil heaps and the so-called 'rushes' (particularly around Gunnerside SD9598) where streams were dammed to form torrents that could break up the lead-bearing rock strata below.

Between **Muker** SD9097 and **Keld** NY8901, the Swale enters a deeply cut valley and tumbles over waterfalls; there are paths on both sides of the river, or you can take a more upland route over neighbouring Kisdon SD8999. **Reeth** SE0499 is a centre for rambles ranging from pottering along the meadows by the Swale to walks over moors into adjacent Arkengarthdale (where the ascent on to Fremington Edge NZ0400 is recommended). **Richmond** NZ1701 is well placed for walks, along the riverside beneath the towering bulk of its castle – E to Easby Abbey NZ1800, or W through Hudswell Woods NZ1400, with an extension to Whitcliffe Scar NZ1302, a cliff above the Swale with an exciting path along its top.

Wensleydale is more expansive in character and not quite as dramatic as Swaledale, but its scenery is richly picturesque, and its unspoilt villages and numerous waterfalls make for pleasurable walking. It was in the past one of the richest dales, its broad pastures and countless sheep supporting the wealthy abbeys and castles whose ruins now add so much interest to its scenery. The upper dale around and W of Hawes SD8789 is steep and wild; E of here the valley starts broadening out, with richer lower pastures, and more regular farmland below Middleham SE1288. **Hardraw Force** SD8691, a 96-ft waterfall, is, as we've said, reached through the Green Dragon at Hardraw, but a longer excursion follows the Pennine Way from Hawes SD8789 and over the River Ure. **Aysgarth Falls** SE0888, the National Park's chief visitor honeypot, involve a short amble from the car park; or you can contrive longer routes along the S bank of the Ure from the delightful village of West Burton SE0196. A 3-mile plod up tracks NW of Castle Bolton reaches **Apedale Head** SE0095, which feels like the top of the world on fine days; views encompass both Wensleydale and Swaledale.

For walkers, the most interesting of Wensleydale's subsidiary valleys is Raydale SD8288 nr Bainbridge SD9390. Its lower neck is quite narrow, but it broadens out into quite a broad sheltered bowl of valley, with **Semer Water** SD9187, a sizeable glacial lake which legend has was conjured up by a wandering beggar to drown a village which had spurned him. It's Yorkshire's third largest natural lake, and has a path along its half-mile long S sides, but the local path network requires some road-walking for circular routes. The walled track (a Roman road) just N has wide-ranging views as it descends to Bainbridge. **Widdale** SD8288, with extensive conifer plantations above it, **Sleddale** SD8586 above Hawes SD8789, and the broader **Bishopdale** SD9885 are steep-sided and dramatic. **Coverdale** SD0582, Wensleydale's major tributary valley, is relatively very quiet; fairly gentle in its lower reaches, climbing high into a wild and untamed-feeling world of lonely high sheepfarms. Wensleydale sheep are very distinctive, with long fleecy dreadlock curls.

Driving

It seems almost cheating to spend one's time driving through what is such marvellous countryside for walking – but in fact you can see a great deal of this area without stepping out of your car.

All the side roads off the A684 W of Leyburn are well worth exploring, particularly the Coverdale road over to Kettlewell (see next section); the B6160 up Bishopdale and into the top of Upper Wharfedale – after you pass Cray there's a pretty turning off on the right which brings you back to Hawes via Hubberholme; the B6255 up over Newby Head; the B6259 N into the headwaters of the Eden Valley in Cumbria; the steep and spectacular Buttertubs Pass road up to Swaledale (stop to look at the Buttertubs themselves, deep ferny holes near the summit where carriers used to cool their butter in hot weather); and the hill road through Carperby and Castle Bolton up to Reeth. Though the A684 itself is quite busy in summer, it does have better views than the parallel road that runs along the other side of Wensleydale between Redmire and Hardrow.

The B6270 along Swaledale is less travelled yet a very fine drive, with a splendid lonely loop off it up through Arkengarthdale to the Tan Hill Inn NY8906 (Britain's highest pub), where a left turn brings you back down to rejoin the B6270 near Keld.

Roads over in the E of the area can't match the grandeur of these routes, but the back road more or less paralleling the A66, through Newsham, Gayles and Kirby Hill to Richmond, is quite pretty and carries very little traffic.

Where to eat

East Witton SE1586 Blue Lion (0969) 24273 Stylish and civilised dining pub with distinctive old rooms, enterprising food, decent wines, and good restaurant (not Sun pm); bedrooms; disabled access. **£23.50**|£1.70/£4.95.

Moulton NZ2404 Black Bull (0325) 377289 Decidedly civilised, well-run pub with old-fashioned style and standards of service, memorable bar snacks (excellent smoked salmon), conservatory restaurant or one in the Brighton Belle, and good wines. **£17**|£2.25/£7.

Carlton SE0684 Foresters Arms (0969) 40272 Reasonably priced good food in bar and restaurant, pleasant atmosphere and very friendly staff. £2.95/£6.95.

CENTRAL DALES

Outstanding countryside for walkers and for drivers, with a good few beautifully located places to stay.

Walking is the main thing in this wonderful countryside: most of the places we recommend to stay in let you walk straight from their door into fine scenery, and are very quietly placed indeed – perfect for a relaxing quiet break. Though you have to get your boots on to make the most of the area, you can take in a great deal without ever leaving your car – yet so far it has not been overrun with coach tours, so even in summer driving here can be a real pleasure.

The individual dales are described in the Walks section. To summarise, Wharfedale has the most varied scenery and is the most visited. Ribblesdale above Settle climbs into austerely impressive countryside with challenging walks, and does have some fine scenery, though is relatively tame in its lower reaches. Malhamdale, quite small, has some of Yorkshire's most striking landscape features and is a magnet for day visitors. Nidderdale has fewer paths than the other dales, but plenty of walking to fill a short stay, and though like the others it has lovely scenery it has the advantage of being rather off the tourist track.

Though the area has few places to visit, Skipton Castle, the show cave at Ingleton, and Bolton Abbey are all memorable, and the railway over the Pennines from Settle to Carlisle is a wonderful ride on a clear day. Many of the villages are delightful places to while away a bit of time, and the larger ones and small towns generally have craft shops and the like, and sometimes interesting bookshops.

Prices represent good value for what you get. On the whole, food here is robust and heartening rather than specially imaginative, though there are one or two outstanding exceptions.

Where to stay

Bolton Abbey SE0754 DEVONSHIRE ARMS COUNTRY HOUSE Skipton BD23 6AJ (0756) 710441 ***£120**; 40 individually furnished rms with thoughtful extras. Close to the Priory itself and in lovely countryside, this country house is owned by the Duke of Devonshire and has been carefully furnished with fine antiques and paintings from Chatsworth; log fires, good service, and decent breakfasts; disabled access.

Ramsgill SE1271 YORKE ARMS Harrogate HG3 5RL (0423) 755243 **£69**; 13 rms. Carefully refurbished and civilised old inn with interesting antique furnishings, and decent food; short walk from bird sanctuary.

Settle SD8264 FALCON MANOR Skipton Rd BD24 9BD (0729) 823814 **£66**; 19 rms. Quietly set, imposing hotel in its own grounds with spacious public rooms, log fires, fine food, and good service; a good touring base; disabled access.

Buckden SD9278 Buck Skipton BD23 5JA (0756) 760228 **£62**; 15 rms, most with own showers. Busy pub with views of surrounding moors, snug original bar area, good wines, and decent food which is served by smartly uniformed staff.

Burnsall SE0361 Red Lion Skipton BD23 6BU (0756) 720204 **£59.90**; 12 rms. Busy 16th-c family-run ferryman's inn overlooking river and village green with tall maypole, attractively panelled bar, log fires and beams, decent bar and restaurant food, and big gardens and terrace on river banks; 75 yds of private fishing and permits for further 7 miles.

Grassington SE0064 Black Horse Garrs Lane BD23 5AT (0756) 752770 **£54**; 15 rms. Good-value traditional home-cooked bar food in busy but comfortable open-plan modern bar, open fires, friendly staff, small but attractive restaurant, and sheltered terrace; cl 25 Dec.

Wigglesworth SD8157 Plough Skipton BD23 4RJ (0729) 840243 **£51.50**; 12 good, well-equipped rms. Pleasant and well-run country inn with highly regarded barn/conservatory restaurant (good bar food, too), lots of little rooms surrounding bar area, some smart and plush, others spartan yet cosy; good, friendly service, big breakfasts, and views of the Three Peaks; disabled access.

Wath in Nidderdale SE1467 Sportsmans Arms Harrogate HG3 5PP (0423) 711306 **£50**; 7 simple rms. Friendly 17th-c hotel with elegant bar, good range of wines, excellent lunchtime bar food (esp fish) and no-smoking evening restaurant; lots of fine cheeses. A smashing place to stay if you're after good-value rooms and really enjoy fine food; cl 25 Dec.

Elslack SD9249 Tempest Arms Skipton BD23 3AY (0282) 842450 **£50**; 10 rms. Characterful 18th-c inn, very comfortable, lots of wines, and excellent bar and restaurant food; disabled access.

Malham SD8963 Buck Skipton BD23 4DA (0729) 830317 **£48**; 10 rms. Comfortable and homely country hotel overlooking Malham Beck in small village with oak-panelled lounge, homely atmosphere, open fires, spacious bar for hikers/ramblers, good food, and friendly service; wonderful walking country; self-catering also.

Kilnsey SD9767 Tennant Arms Skipton BD23 5PS (0756) 752301 ***£47**; 10 rms. In a nice spot by the River Wharfe, this spacious beamed and flagstoned inn has open fires (one fireplace made from an ornate carved four-poster), friendly service and atmosphere, weapon collection, maps and stuffed or skeleton animals and fish; good-value food, and views over spectacular overhanging Kilnsey Crag from restaurant; cl 25 Dec.

Darley Head SE1959 Wellington Harrogate HG3 2QQ (0423) 780362 **£45**; 12 well-furnished rms. Tastefully extended old pub with decent food in restaurant and big bar with open fire, smaller day rooms too; disabled access.

Malham SD8963 Miresfield Farm Skipton BD23 4DA (0729) 830414 **£44**; 13 rms, 12 with own bthrm. Spacious old farmhouse with good, freshly prepared food, big conservatory, two lounges and lovely garden by stream and village green; disabled access.

Arncliffe SD9473 Falcon Skipton BD23 5QE (075 677) 0205 **£40**; 5 rms, 1 with own bthrm. Friendly walkers' pub with functional little rooms and a fire, homely front lounge, airy conservatory, no-smoking dining room, and good simple food inc enormous breakfasts; cl end Oct-mid-Mar for residents.

Starbotton SD9574 Fox & Hounds Skipton BD23 5HY (0756) 760269 **£40**; 2 rms. Prettily placed and rather smart little Upper Wharfedale village inn with flagstones, beams, big log fire, decent food, and no-smoking dining room; cl 21 Dec-18 Feb.

Cray SD9379 WHITE LION Skipton BD23 5JB (0756) 760262 ***£40**; 5 rms. Friendly little pub 1,100 ft up with super views of countryside, lots of walks, traditional feel with flagstones, beams, and log fires, and decent bar food; pleasant to sit by stream; disabled access.

Austwick SD7668 GAME COCK Lancaster LA2 8BB (052 42) 51226 **£40**; 4 rms, shared bthrms. Prettily placed inn with views over Dales National Park, notably friendly welcome, and good low-priced bar food.

Feizor SD7867 SCAR CLOSE FARM Austwick Lancaster LA2 8DF (0729) 823496 ***£34**; 4 clean, well-appointed rms. Friendly converted barn on working farm with big guest lounge, books, magazines and TV, and good breakfasts (evening meal available); lovely quiet surrounding countryside; cl 25-26 Dec, disabled access.

Stainforth SD8267 CRAVEN HEIFER Settle BD24 9PB (0729) 822599 **£33**; 4 good-value rms, shared bthrm. Small cosy village pub with friendly licensees, log fire, and reasonably priced bar food; a good base for walking in this Upper Ribblesdale area; cl 24-26 Dec.

Chapel le Dale SD7477 OLD HILL Carnforth Lancs LA6 3AR (052 42) 41256 **£30**; 5 warm, basic but well-furnished rms; shared bthrms. Popular with walkers and pot-holers, this inn has stripped stone walls, flagstone floors, old woodwork and partitions with wagon wheels in the bar, roaring log fire in cosy back parlour, and popular food inc good breakfasts.

To see and do

✝ **Bolton Abbey** SE0754 In lovely rolling wooded parkland on a knoll above the River Wharfe is an extensive and beautiful group of graceful PRIORY RUINS dating from the 12th to the 16th c, with some 19th-c additions inc stained glass (some by Pugin) and murals oddly not striking a false note. It's a popular place, and the car park does get full in summer. There are most attractive walks from here, and the Devonshire Arms is very fine for lunch.

Brimham Rocks SE2164 Spectacular and extraordinarily weathered gritstone pinnacles, tors and boulders facing the winds at a height of 950 ft, conjuring up people, animal heads and other strange figures. A Victorian guidebook declared they were 'wrecked with grim and hideous forms defying all description and definition'. Children like them a lot – Henry Moore said that when he was a boy they sculpted quite a few ideas in his imagination. Meals and snacks, shop; open wknds Easter-Oct, and daily in school hols; parking *£1.20. NT.

Clapham SD7569 is an attractive village that has turned walking and caving into something of an industry. The outdoors centre of Ingleborough Hall was formerly the family home of the great plantsman Reginald Farrer, who in his short life (besides introducing a great many notable plants from the Himalayas and China) wrote about them with unsurpassed gusto. A NATURE TRAIL leads past his own woods and small lake to the entrance to INGLEBOROUGH CAVE, one of the most easily visited of the vast network of caverns plunging into the limestone hills around here; snacks, shop, disabled access; cl wkdys Nov-Feb; £3.50. The New Inn is useful for lunch (and a good place for walkers to stay in).

Embsay SE0053 EMBSAY STEAM RAILWAY has steam trips from the village along a couple of miles of railway prettily set below the limestone crags. It's being extended and hopefully will before too long run to Bolton Abbey. Back at the Embsay end is a ticket office originally at Ilkley, and a collection of old locomotives and carriages; meals, snacks, shop (remarkable collection of books), disabled access; usually open Sun all year as well as Tues and Sat in July and daily in Aug – best to tel (0756) 795189 for full dates and timetable; £2.70. The Elm Tree is good for lunch.

★ **Grassington** SE0064 is a pleasant small town or large village around a sloping cobbled square, depending a lot on walkers and other visitors, with some attractive shops and a few interesting old buildings. The Black Horse and Devonshire Hotel are both useful for lunch.

✝ **Hubberholme** SD9178 has a good 13th-c CHURCH, built on an ancient burial site, with Norman tower, unusual rood loft and pews by Thompson of Kilburn – with their little carved mouse trademark. The George is useful for lunch.

Ingleton SD6973 WHITE SCAR CAVERN (B6255 towards Hawes) The country's biggest show cavern and easily one of the most spectacular, with underground waterfalls and streams and an Ice-Age cavern. There are some amazing sights and atmospheric formations, and stunning stalactites and stalagmites that have been here for 100,000 years. Snacks, shop, some disabled access; cl 25 Dec (and sometimes after heavy rain); £5. The Wheatsheaf and Bridge both do generous food.

Parcevall Hall Gardens SE0661 Surrounding an Elizabethan house, these beautiful and extensive woodland gardens are charmingly set on a hillside east of the main Wharfedale Valley; good views. Snacks; cl Nov-Easter exc by appointment, tel (0756) 720311; *£2. The Craven Arms at nearby Appletreewick is good for lunch; snacks; plants for sale in spring; cl Nov-Easter; *£1.50.

Settle SD8264 The SETTLE-CARLISLE RAILWAY has a magnificent 70-mile route carved up through Ribblesdale across the wild moors between here and Cumbria, and then dropping down through the lovely Eden Valley; tel (0228) 44711 for times. There are some steam runs, and throughout the year a programme of Sat walks connecting with its moorland stops. Mary Milnthorpe & Daughter is a good antique jewellery and silver shop. Market day (on Tues) is particularly attractive.

✝ **Skipton** SD9851 CASTLE A properly romantic old-fashioned castle, with sturdy round towers, broad stone steps, and a lovely central flagstoned and cobbled courtyard with a seat around its venerable central yew tree. It's one of the best-preserved medieval castles in Europe, though there was some restoration after partial damage in the Civil War. It really is remarkable how much is left, interior and all – very few other castles have kept their roofs and stayed habitable. The original Norman arched gateway still stands – the word 'Desormais' carved above it is the family motto of the Cliffords, who lived here from 1310-1676. Shop; cl Sun am, 25 Dec; *£2.90. A 14th-c CHURCH nearby has a 16th-c rood screen and interesting stained glass. On Sat Skipton's main street leading up to the castle and its 12th-c church has a colourful market (at least some stalls here on most other days too, exc Sun and Tues). A canal runs through the town, and the Royal Shepherd in an attractive spot beside it is good for lunch; the Greenbank Hotel also does good lunches.

★ Numerous **attractive villages or tiny hamlets** in the area, all with decent pubs and most in delightful surroundings, include Appletreewick SE0560, Arncliffe SD9473 (the inspiration for Kingsley's *Water Babies*), Askwith SD1648, Austwick

SD7768, Buckden SD9477, Burnsall SE0361, Cray SD9379, Gargrave SD9354, Kettlewell SD9772, Kirkby Malham SD8961, Linton in Craven SD9962, Middlesmoor SE0874, Ramsgill SE1271, Stainforth SD8267, Starbotton SD9574, Thornton in Lonsdale SD6873, Wath SE1467 and Wigglesworth SD8157. A quaint spot for lunch in Nidderdale is the Watermill just north of Pateley Bridge SE1466; a converted flax mill with one of the largest waterwheels in Britain.

There are National Park Centres in Malham SD9062, Clapham SD7469 (cl Nov-Mar) and Grassington SE0064. Besides local information, maps, leaflets with suggested walks etc, the centres have displays on the natural history of the area, the life of the local community, and conservation work.

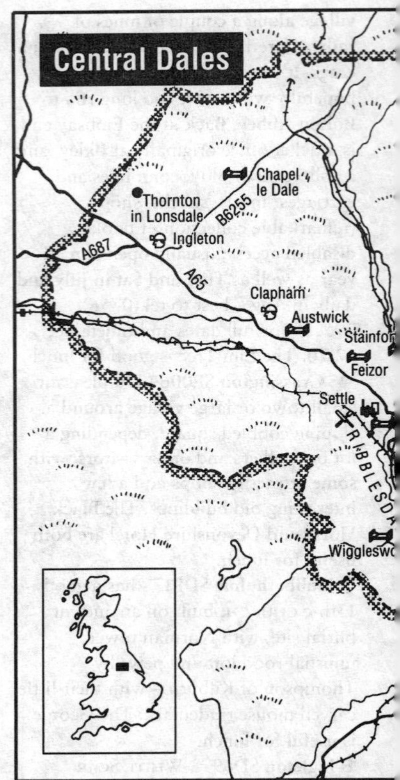

Walks

Wharfedale, with its tributary valley Littondale and its headwaters up in the steep conifer plantations at the top of Langstrothdale, is one of England's most popular areas for walkers, and very beautiful indeed in parts. The Dales Way follows the River Wharfe for the length of the dale, except between Kettlewell SD9772 and Grassington SE0064. **Upper Wharfedale** above Grassington has a level floor of sheltered well-drained pastures with the river winding through, a few grey stone barns, and steep sides laced with dry stone walls, gnarled woodland and occasional austere crags, climbing up to high fairly level tops some 1,200 ft above the valley floor. Kettlewell and particularly Grassington are sizeable villages, major bases for walkers; the smaller villages are delightfully private and unspoilt, their grey or whitewashed stonework blending perfectly with the long scars of the limestone terraces above them. Away from the valley floor, stone-walled grassy tracks are the easiest ways of gaining height: you can return over the high land, after a walk along the river, from Starbotton SD9574 to Kettlewell, or follow less obvious paths W to Arncliffe SD9473 in Littondale – which is very similar to the parent valley, though with a flatter damper valley floor. The high headwaters on either side above quaint and ancient Hubberholme SD9178 are very pretty. From Hubberholme a walk not to be missed is

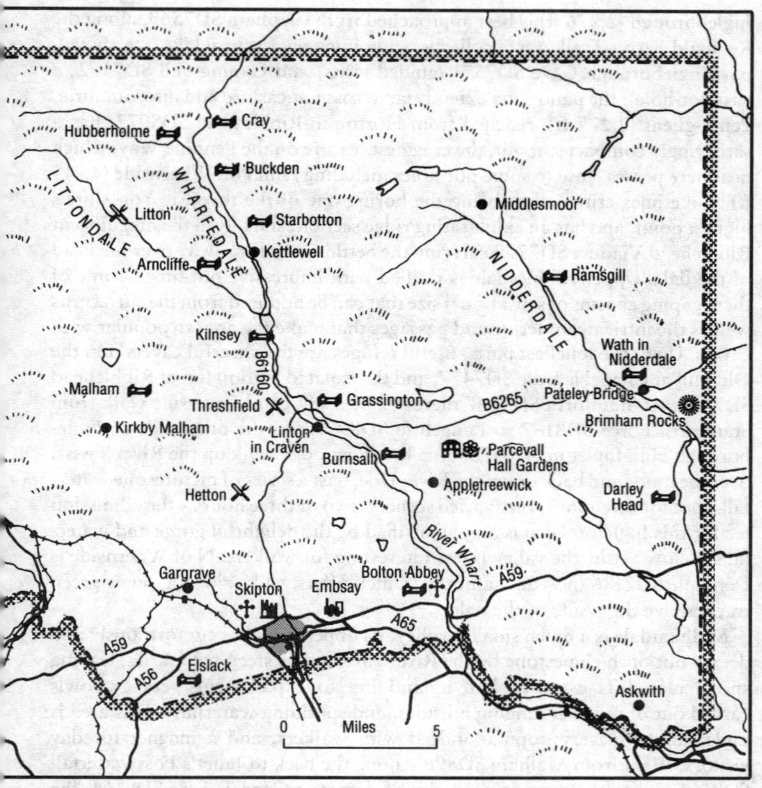

up to Scar House SD8998 and along a level turfy terrace, which commands magnificent views down the dale, to Cray SD9379; both hamlets have inns, and the walk can be expanded to include Buckden SD9447.

Below Grassington there's an extremely pretty stretch where the valley winds more sinuously past Burnsall SE0361, Appletreewick SE0560 and Bolton Abbey SE0574, below hills which though less grand are more varied in shape, with rather sensitively laid-out conifer plantations adding a slightly subalpine feel to some of the views. There's a pleasant walk from Hebden SE0263 down to the Burnsall-Appletreewick stretch. Around **Bolton Abbey** the landscape has a lowland beauty: the ruined abbey, the turf banks of the Wharfe and the oaks of the Strid Wood SE0656, where a leaflet detailing nature trails is available. A steep ascent from Howgill SE0659 is rewarded by views from Simon's Seat SE0759, an unmistakably upland perch on the edge of moors.

Ribblesdale, although partly marred by quarrying in its lower southern portions, climbs above Settle into severe and grand mountain scenery, craggy and remote: this is a major magnet for walkers on the Three Peaks Walk, a 24-mile 'challenge route' taking in the summits of Ingleborough SD7474, Pen-y-ghent SD8473 and Whernside SD9975. This is a tough undertaking in its entirety, but each of the peaks on its own is a manageable half-day excursion: choose a clear day – not just for the magnificent views but for your own safety.

Ingleborough (2,376 ft) is best approached from Clapham SD7569, along the Reginald Farrer Trail (a tree collection adjoining an artificial lake, see above), past Ingleborough Cave SD7571 (guided visits) and Gaping Gill SD7572 (a vast pot-hole); the panorama extends far across Lancashire and into Cumbria. **Pen-y-ghent** (2,277 ft), reached from Horton-in-Ribblesdale SD8072, has a satisfyingly compact summit, the craggiest feature on the Pennine Way, which near here passes close to some pot-holes including Hull Pot. **Whernside** (2,415 ft), sometimes criticised as being the boring one of the three, is Yorkshire's highest point, and has an exhilarating ridge section; start from the magnificent Ribblehead Viaduct SD7779 carrying the Settle-Carlisle railway over the head of the dale. Upper Ribblesdale is riddled with impressive pot-holes, some of them gaping chasms of sensational size that can be admired from the surface, as well as the intricate underground passages that make the area so popular with cavers. Up in the loneliest parts, useful refuges are the cheerful cavers' inn the Old Hill at Chapel le Dale SD7477, and the isolated Station Inn at Ribblehead SD7779. At **Stainforth** SD8267 there is a pleasant gentle riverside walk from Stainforth Force SD8167 to Langcliffe SD8971. On the other side of Ingleborough Hill, Ingleton SD6973 has a lovely wooded walk up the River Twiss, over the moor and back down the River Doe, past a series of picturesque waterfalls; not too strenuous, very varied scenery, two or three hours – the admission fee for this Ingleton Glen is amply justified by the delightful gorge and waterfalls. Below Settle, the valley is less interesting for walkers. N of Whernside is Dentdale SD7186 (now in Cumbria), which offers walks along a lonely green track above the S side of the dale.

Malhamdale is a much smaller valley, its upper stretches cut tortuously and deeply out of the limestone by the River Aire and its steep tributaries, leaving spectacular cliffs, extensive bare upland limestone 'pavements', craggy bowls carved out of the overhanging hillsides, and sparkling waterfalls. This area is understandably very popular indeed with walkers, and a magnet for day visitors. Walk from Malham SD8963 along the beck to Janet's Foss waterfall SD9163 and to the romantic severity of dramatic **Gordale Scar** SD9164, the dale's most memorable natural feature, where a beck makes a spectacular leap from the rocks. The Pennine Way N of Malham waterfall ascends the side of **Malham Cove** SD9864, a great cliff, then crosses a natural rock pavement and heads over a landscape of limestone scars, disappearing streams and green turf to **Malham Tarn** SD8966, a lovely mountain lake skirted on its E side by a nature trail.

Nidderdale is a quiet yet beautiful valley with an impressive solitary grandeur. Just outside the National Park, it and the hills above are less liberally laced with footpaths and open-access moorland than the other two dales here, and attract far fewer visitors – yet certainly have a sufficiency of relatively unfrequented walks, often on good paved but untarred tracks. The **Nidderdale Way** allows a fine fairly gentle walk of a couple of hours or so, up on to the high pastures (see lambs being born in spring) and moorland at Glasshouses SE1764 and back, with spectacular views almost all the way. It's well signposted with yellow arrows or 'Nidderdale Way' signs; start from Dacre Banks SE1962 and take the lane a couple of hundred yards past the church. The stretch between the attractive small town of Pateley Bridge SE1666 and the little village of Lofthouse SE1073 is dominated by the sheltered two-mile waters of **Gouthwaite reservoir** SE1269, serenely set below the hills with some tall trees alongside. From Lofthouse SE1073 a path runs along beside the River Nidd, with picturesque tracks among small woods and ruined farmhouses, to **Scar House**

Reservoir SE0576, quite exposed at the valley head (there's also a toll road up to it); high, exposed routes line the N side of the dale up here. To the W of Lofthouse, **Howe Stean Gorge** SE0673 is a spectacular ravine pocked with potholes and caverns; a footpath snakes between miniature cliffs, with bridges giving views into the gorge; there's also a visitor centre.

Driving

The B6160 along Upper Wharfedale is a fine drive, with better views than from the narrow back road between Grassington and Kettlewell, and without any nerve-wrackingly steep bits even keeping right on to West Burton. The side roads from Kettlewell over into Coverdale and past Hubberholme up to Hawes both have exhilarating views. The road up Littondale is pretty, and from Arncliffe the steep mountain road over to Langcliffe in Ribblesdale takes you through some very wild countryside. The B6479 up Ribblesdale itself is good, as is the relatively long-winded B6255 from Ribblehead down to Ingleton.

Over towards the E, the B6265 from Grassington to Pateley Bridge, once past the high-walled bends out of Grassington itself, is a good road with some memorable views (and passes the colourfully lit underground Stump Cross Caverns SE0863, well worth a look if you're passing; £2.50). The moorland road from the head of Nidderdale up to Masham is a splendid expedition.

Where to eat

Hetton SD9558 ANGEL (075 6730) 263 Extremely popular dining pub with old-fashioned rambling rooms, consistently excellent imaginative food, very good service from hard-working, friendly staff, well-kept real ales, and over 300 wines; cl 25 Dec pm, 1 Jan pm, 3rd wk Feb; disabled access. **£27**|£3.50/£6.50.

Settle SD8264 ROYAL OAK (0729) 822561/823102 Wide choice of popular food in well-kept low stone inn; ground floor is almost one huge room with a few walls dividing it into separate areas, dark oak panelling, and pleasantly relaxed atmosphere. **£15**|£2.70/£4.70.

Threshfield SD9763 OLD HALL (0756) 752441 Very busy pub handy for Dales walks, comfortably unfussy rooms, and huge helpings of good imaginative food relying on seasonal produce; no food Sun pm, Mon (exc bank hols); disabled access. **£15**|£2/£5.

Litton SD9074 QUEENS ARMS (0756) 770208 Welcoming 17th-c inn with good popular food, main bar with big collection of cigarette lighters, another room with more of a family atmosphere, two coal fires, and newish restaurant. £2/£5.60.

We welcome reports from readers . . .

Do send us reports on places in the GUIDE, or ones you think should be in. Use the card in the middle, the report forms at the end, or just write – no stamp needed: THE GOOD WEEKEND GUIDE, FREEPOST TN1569, Wadhurst, E Sussex TN5 7BR. Readers who help us with reports for the GUIDE are offered a discount on the next edition.

North York Moors

Attractive moors, valleys and villages, interesting cliffy coast; not that many places to visit, but plenty for a weekend or rather longer stay.

It's the valleys rather than the moors themselves which most visitors spend time in here: rich pastures, with red-tiled stone farmhouses, twisting rivers, quiet roads, and few villages. The higher moorland is generally very grand and empty, mile after mile of heather scoured by breath-snatching winds, where the few walkers have for company scatterings of hardy sheep and the occasional harsh cry of a grouse.

Though this area is not quite so rich in memorable walks as are the Dales, it does have an excellent choice – plenty to occupy anyone on a walking holiday. In one sense, the countryside here has more variety, too, in that besides the moors and the lovely valleys that cut through them, there is a splendid stretch of cliffy coast, with some delightful little fishing villages, the interesting working fishing port of Whitby, and the attractive traditional seaside resort of Scarborough.

There are good places to stay in the valleys themselves: ideal for walks straight from the door. If however you want to explore the area more widely, Helmsley, Pickering or one of the villages just off the A170 might be a better bet, as that road can get you around much more quickly than crossing from a village high in one valley to another. Of these two towns, Helmsley is probably the more attractive.

The ruins of Rievaulx Abbey are the area's crowning glory. There's a handful of other interesting places to visit, and there are a good few attractive villages, but the area's chief attraction is the countryside – even in high summer a good bit quieter than the Yorkshire Dales, and in low season very peaceful indeed.

Where to stay

Hackness SE9790 Hackness Grange Scarborough YO13 0JW (0723) 882345 **£118**; 28 rms. Set in acres of grounds in the heart of the North York Moors National Park, this Victorian country house has efficient, friendly service, fine food, and indoor heated swimming pool, 9-hole pitch-and-putt golf and hard tennis court; disabled access.

Helmsley SE6184 Black Swan Market Pl YO6 5BJ (0439) 70466 **£116**; 44 well-equipped and comfortable rms. Striking Georgian house and adjoining Tudor rectory with beamed and panelled hotel bar, attractive carved oak settles and Windsor armchairs, cosy and comfortable lounges with a good deal of character, and charming sheltered garden.

Lastingham SE7391 Lastingham Grange York YO6 6TH (075 15) 345/402 **£104.75**; 12 rms. Very attractive stone-walled country house in 10 acres of well-kept gardens and fields with the moors beyond; homely, relaxed atmosphere in spacious lounge, open fire, no bar (though it is licensed), very good breakfasts and dinner and extremely helpful service; marvellous walks; cl Dec-Feb.

Scalby TA0191 Wrea Head Scarborough YO13 0PP (0723) 378211 **£99**; 21 rms. Victorian country house in 14 acres of parkland and gardens with friendly staff and open fires in the panelled lounge and library; cl 24-26 Dec, disabled access.

Great Ayton NZ5611 Ayton Hall Middlesbrough TS9 6BW (0642) 723595 **£79**; 9 rms. Handsome building with elegant day rooms, paintings and antiques, cosy restaurant with good, interesting food, and neatly kept grounds.

Whitby NZ9011 Bagdale Hall 1 Bagdale YO21 1QL (0947) 602958 **£78**; 6 rms. Handsome medieval manor hotel with fine restaurant and good bar lunches; children under 5 free and under 12 half-price if share parents' rm.

Rosedale Abbey SE7396 Blacksmiths Arms Pickering YO18 8EN (075 15) 331 ***£70**; 18 rms. Spacious extended modernised bars and lounges in attractive surroundings at the foot of Rosedale; nicely furnished, log fires, helpful service, and imaginative food; lovely walks all round; cl 22-25 Dec; disabled access.

Pickering SE7984 White Swan Market Pl YO18 7AA (0751) 72288 **£70**; 13 rms. Inviting small and quiet plush hotel bar, friendly staff and locals, good chip-free bar food, and good restaurant with fine clarets.

Dunsley NZ8611 Dunsley Hall Whitby YO21 3TL (0947) 83437 **£70**; 7 spacious rms. Imposing hotel in 4 acres of grounds with croquet, hard tennis court, and 9-hole putting green; lots of oak panelling, comfortable furnishings, quietly relaxed atmosphere, billiard table, fitness room and indoor heated swimming pool; cl 25-26 Dec; disabled access.

Goathland NZ8301 Mallyan Spout Whitby YO22 5AN (0947) 86206 **£70**; 24 rms. Warmly friendly, creeper-covered Victorian hotel overlooking the moors on the edge of the village green, with homely public rooms, and a cosy restaurant; cl to residents 2 days over Christmas; limited disabled access

Helmsley SE6184 Feversham Arms 1 High St YO6 5AG (0439) 70766 ***£70**; 18 comfortable rms. Pleasant, welcoming hotel in an acre of walled gardens with comfortable, cosy bars, and good bar food (superb seafood) served by smart waitresses; hard tennis court, good outdoor heated swimming pool; children under 16 sharing parents' rm free; disabled access.

Pickering SE7984 Forest & Vale Malton Rd YO18 7DL (0751) 72722 **£66**; 17 rms (the main building ones are nicest). Pleasant hotel with good service and very good food inc fresh fish from Whitby; an excellent base for exploring the area.

Rosedale Abbey SE7395 Milburn Arms Pickering YO18 8RA (0751) 417312 ***£66**; 11 rms. Friendly 18th-c inn surrounded by fine steep moorland with traditionally furnished bar, good food and decent wine list.

Helmsley SE6184 Carlton Lodge Bondgate YO6 5EY (0439) 770557 ***£65**; 12 rms. Pleasant hotel in National Park with very good food, convivial owners, and garden; disabled access.

Rosedale Abbey SE7396 White Horse Farm Pickering YO18 8SE (0751) 5239 **£60**; 15 rms. An inn rather than a farm, this friendly place has fine views and eleven acres of land around it; cosy beamed bar and log fire, comfortable lounge, generously served food, and decent range of wines and malt whiskies; marvellous walks; cl 24-26 Dec.

Helmsley SE6184 Feathers York YO6 5BH (0439) 70275 **£53**; 17 rms, most with own bthrm. Handsome and atmospheric old inn, heavy old beams and dark panelling, attractive garden; lots of wines, tasty and good-value bar and restaurant food; disabled access.

Blakey Ridge SE6897 LION Pickering YO6 6LQ (075 15) 320 ***£49**; 9 clean rms. Said to be the fourth highest inn in England, this has spectacular moorland views, characterful rambling bars, good fires, generous helpings of decent food served all day, good breakfasts and candlelit restaurant, 8 real ales, and genuinely friendly licensees and staff; fine walking country; cl 25 Dec; disabled access.

Egton Bridge NZ8105 HORSE SHOE Whitby YO21 1XE (0947) 85245 **£46**; 6 rms. Beautifully placed inn by River Esk (stepping stones big enough for children to sit on), lots of friendly wild birds, pleasant sheltered lawn, English and New World wines, and decent bar food.

Cropton SE7588 NEW INN Pickering YO18 8HH (075 15) 330 ***£46**; 7 rms. Comfortably modernised village inn with interesting own-brew beers, elegant little restaurant, and big helpings of good-value bar food; disabled access.

Egton Bridge NZ8105 POSTGATE Whitby YO21 1UX (0947) 85241 **£36**; 6 rms, shared bthrms. Relaxed and informal pub, super views looking down hill, and decent daily-changing bar food inc several vegetarian dishes; fishing and riding can be arranged. Very handy indeed for the quiet country station with trains to Whitby (connecting at Grosmont with the North Yorkshire Moors Railway).

Lastingham SE7391 BLACKSMITHS ARMS York YO6 6TL (075 15) 247 **£35**; 4 rms. Cosy little village pub in lovely countryside near interesting ancient church, comfortable oak-beamed bar, and decent food served all day.

Aislaby NZ8608 COTE BANK FARM Egton Rd Whitby YO21 1UG (0947) 85314 **£32**; 3 rms, shared bthrm. Comfortable 18th-c farmhouse with fine views, big garden, log fires, and good home cooking; lambing March/April; cl Christmas; children over 5.

Chop Gate SE5699 HILL END FARM Middlesbrough TS9 7JR (0439) 798278 **£32**; 2 rms, shared bthrm. Friendly 17th-c farmhouse with good farm cooking, comfortable lounge and dining room, and fine walks; on the farm is part of one of the last remaining ancient oak forests; cl Oct-Easter.

Robin Hood's Bay NZ9505 COBLE Covet Hill YO22 4SN (0947) 880042 **£32**; 3 rms, showers. Homely little cottage overlooking the bay with warmly friendly, caring owners and extremely good, very large breakfasts (8 courses).

Ainthorpe NZ7008 FOX & HOUNDS Whitby YO21 2LD (0287) 660218 **£30**; 8 rms, shared bthrms. 16th-c inn with oak beams, horsebrasses, coal fire and homely atmosphere in lovely dark old room; good food inc vegetarian and vegan dishes, friendly cat; cl 25 Dec.

Cloughton TA0096 HAYBURN WYKE Scarborough YO13 0AU (0723) 870202 **£30**; 3 well-equipped rms. Friendly inn by rugged cliffs with obliging licensees, log fire, huge helpings of good food (steaks and Sunday carvery highly recommended), character restaurant, and big breakfasts; cl 2 wks over Christmas, children over 10.

Fadmoor SE6789 PLOUGH Kirkbymoorside YO6 6HY (0751) 31515 ***£28**; 4 rms, shared bthrm. Hearty little pub in a stunning location and overlooking quiet village green, with spick-and-span bar, crackling open fire, simple old furnishings, cheery landlady, straightforward bar food (inc vegetarian dishes), and restaurant like a private dining room; children over 12.

To see and do

Brompton SE9582 WORDSWORTH GALLERY (Gallows Hill) The former home of Mary Hutchinson, who married William Wordsworth at Brompton Church in 1802. The medieval barn has an exhibition on the poet and Samuel Coleridge, as well as an exhibition of paintings and prints; meals, snacks, shop, disabled access; cl 25-26 Dec and 10-31 Jan; £1 for Wordsworth exhibition.

Danby NZ7008 THE MOORS CENTRE Surrounded with terraced riverside and woodland grounds, this centre has exhibitions, videos and a bookshop information desk devoted to the North York Moors National Park. Also a children's play area and brass-rubbing centre; meals and snacks, shop, disabled access; cl wkdys Oct-Easter. The Duke of Wellington is useful for lunch.

Easby NZ5708 EASBY ABBEY Extensive remains of the monks' domestic buildings survive on this, the peaceful site of a Premonstratensian Abbey, which was founded in 1155 and dedicated to St Agatha; a pretty walk along the Swale from Richmond; disabled access; cl winter Mon, 24-26 Dec, 1 Jan.

Goathland NZ8301 in the heart of the moors has a short walk from opposite the church to a wooded smooth-rocked gorge where the MALLYAN SPOUT waterfall is a fine sight. The hotel named after the waterfall is useful for lunch. A rather longer walk south from here, or reached direct by the narrow moorland lane south from Egton Bridge NZ8105, is WADE'S CAUSEWAY, a mile-long stretch of broad paved Roman road up over the moors, well restored and maintained.

Hayburn Wyke TA0097 From the very well-sited hotel here, steep Victorian woodland paths wind down to the cliff-sheltered cove; a clifftop path to the south gives fine views.

Helmsley SE6183 This attractive small market town, in its spacious setting below the moors, has a large cobbled square (the busy market day is Friday), enough antique shops and craft shops to please a visitor without seeming too touristy, and lanes running straight up on to the moors. A lively and bustling place, with a lot of class. It's dominated by the 12th-c CASTLE, ruined in 1644, and standing within enormous earthworks; shop; cl 1-2 pm, winter Mon; *£1.70.

DUNCOMBE PARK Beautifully restored house, first built in the early 18th c and then rebuilt after a fire at the turn of this century. The early 18th-c landscaped gardens are magnificent, covering 30 acres and set in 300 acres of memorable parkland; meals, snacks, shop, disabled access; cl Fri and Sat, Nov-Apr exc Easter wknd and Sun in Apr; £4.40, gardens only £2.75.

Besides the hotels and inns we recommend, the courtyard café outside the Edinburgh Woollen Mill does imaginative light lunches.

Hutton-le-Hole SE7090 is a very neat and pretty streamside village at the mouth of Farndale, with an interesting FOLK MUSEUM – old buildings from the area re-erected inside the museum itself, inc recreated workshops and even a gipsy caravan, as well as an Edwardian photographic studio and well-displayed everyday articles going back to Roman times; shop, disabled access; cl Nov-Easter; £2.50. The Crown here is useful for lunch.

Kirkdale SE6886 has a Saxon church with unique Saxon sundial, and 7th-c Celtic crosses and carved stones.

Osmotherley SE4596 MOUNT GRACE PRIORY More than usual dedication was needed to be a Carthusian monk, as not only did they have a vow of silence but they rarely emerged from their own individual cells. One of the cells at this ruined 14th-c priory has been fully restored, and gives a good illustration of how the monks must have worked and lived; there's also an exhibition of pottery found here. The ruins are better preserved than those of any other Carthusian establishment in England, and in the spring an impressive display of daffodils makes it an especially attractive spot; snacks, shop, disabled access; cl lunchtimes and every Mon from Oct-Easter, as well as 25-26 Dec, 1 Jan; £2. Beside the ruins stands a 17th-c house. The town, or large village, is quietly attractive. The Golden Lion, Kings Head, Queen Charlotte and Three Tuns are all useful for lunch.

Pickering SE7983 is another attractive small town, usually very quiet, with vivid medieval murals in the splendid tall-spired CHURCH. NORTH YORKSHIRE MOORS RAILWAY Steam trains (and some diesel) run between Pickering and Grosmont – a distance of 18 miles, through nostalgically restored stations and lovely countryside. The line was originally built by George Stephenson. At Grosmont you can look at locomotives and antique carriages, even watch repairs; there's also a model railway. Meals, snacks, shop, disabled access; limited service early Nov-late Mar, tel (0751) 73535 for timetable; *£7.90. PICKERING CASTLE Ruins of 12th-c keep and later curtain walls and towers, much pillaged for building stone, and with fine views from its imposing castle mound above the town; snacks, shop; cl 1-2 pm, winter Mon; £1.70. The BECK ISLE MUSEUM in a 17th-c riverside house has a wonderful collection of local bygones set out (with costumes) as the contents of shops and workshops – blacksmith, wheelwright, photographer, barber, pub and so forth, with more to see outside; shop, disabled access to ground floor; £1.50. The White Swan is good for lunch.

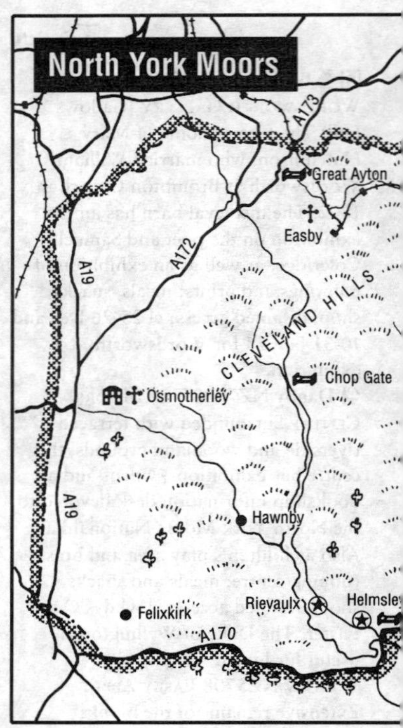

Rievaulx SE5785 RIEVAULX ABBEY Superbly atmospheric ruins of a magnificent and once highly prosperous abbey, set among the wooded hills of Rye Dale. It was first started by twelve Cistercian monks in 1131, and the nave, dating back to 1135, is one of the earliest built in England by the Cistercian order. Also among the extensive remains is the choir, which is a fine example of 13th-c work. The graceful colonnades, arches and lancet windows, lovely at any time, are extremely moving if you get there early or late on a wkdy out of season (when the absence of crowds adds a great deal to the site's appeal); snacks, shop, disabled access; cl 24-26 Dec; £2. RIEVAULX TERRACE AND TEMPLES Dramatic views of the abbey can be obtained from the half-mile-long, grass-covered 18th-c terrace overlooking it. Each end of the terrace

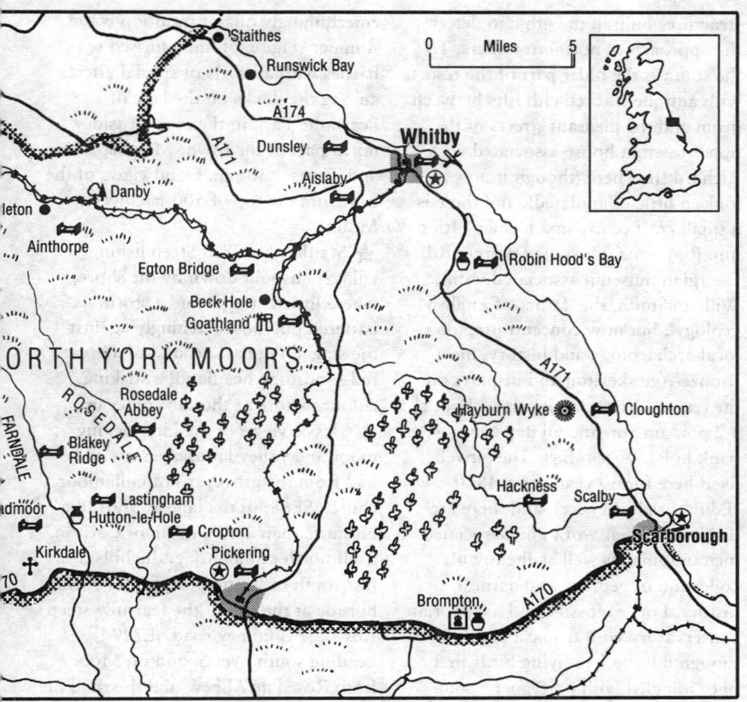

is adorned with a classical temple; one a small Tuscan rotunda built to while away the hours in peaceful contemplation, the other, an elaborate Ionic creation, for hunting parties; shop; cl Nov-Mar; £1.80. Besides the many places in Helmsley not far off, the Hare over in Scawton (a pleasant drive) is useful for lunch.

Robin Hood's Bay NZ9505 is a steep, picturesque fishing village, largely unspoilt (though there are quite a few shops and cafés for visitors now), its cottages clustered close together on the slopes above the rocky shore – a rich hunting-ground for pottering at low tide, when a surprising expanse of sand is exposed too. It was a popular haunt of smugglers, and the SMUGGLING EXPERIENCE has the whole story. The Olde Dolphin above the seafront does good freshly caught fish, and the Bay is good for food too.

Scarborough TA0388 This famous resort has all the usual seaside attractions, aquariums and so forth, but is also a place of some style, its two great curves of firm sandy beach separated by the small harbour and by a high narrow headland. The once impressive CASTLE is up here, on the site of British and Roman encampments. Thought to have been built by Henry II, it remained a royal palace until the reign of James I, and one of some importance – King John spent what was then the unheard-of sum of £2,000 on it. It was seriously damaged in the Civil War, and now all that remains are the 13th-c barbican, medieval chapels and house, and the shell of the original 12th-c keep; shop, disabled access; cl winter Mon; *£1.70. Between the castle and the cliff edge are the remains of a Roman signal station, one of five such structures built in the 4th c to detect the approach of northern raiders. To the south is the older part of the resort, with antique tracked cliff lifts between prom and the pleasant streets of the upper town; a house associated with Richard III is here (though it now looks a little dilapidated), and there is a small craft centre in a former 14th-c inn. ROTUNDA MUSEUM (Vernon Rd) Georgian museum associated with William Smith, the 'father of English geology', but now concentrating on local archaeology and history, inc a Bronze-Age skeleton and displays on the resort's Victorian heyday; shop; cl 1-2 pm, am Sun and all day Mon (exc bank hols). WOOD END The Sitwells lived here for 60 years from 1870 (Edith was born here), and there are displays of their work and associated memorabilia, as well as the town's collection of geology and natural history. Lots of fossils, and a Victorian conservatory with tropical plants – though not the free-flying birds that once mingled with partygoers; some disabled access. Times as above, and the same for the ART GALLERY, with paintings from the 17th c to the present in a striking Italianate villa. AMAZING WORLD OF HOLOGRAMS (Foreshore Rd) Ideal for children, a lively new exhibition with over 200 holograms coming to life, from bodies in the bog through Viking helmets to film stars; shop; open wknds Apr-Oct, daily late May-Sept; *£1. Interesting CHURCHES include the medieval St Mary's, where Anne Brontë is buried, and the 19th-c St Martin's with elaborate work by Burne-Jones, William Morris and other Pre-Raphaelite artists. The SEA LIFE CENTRE (Scalby Mills) offers the same lively mixture we've described in several other resorts; cl 25 Dec; £4.25. A LIGHTHOUSE has a little fisheries museum. Shows are still an essential ingredient in the Scarborough cocktail, from the more old-fashioned concerts to the theatre now linked to Alan Ayckbourn. One unique and entertainingly quaint tradition is the summer staging of miniaturised sea battles with all sorts of special effects among the ducks on the lake of Peasholm Park in the more seasidey north part of the town; May-Sept Mon and Thurs 3.30 pm. Good views of the bay from the top of 500-ft Oliver's Mount.

★ **Staithes** NZ7818 Steep fishing village, unspoilt down by the shore, where little cottages and a storm-battered pub pose fetchingly against the staggering background of a great red-sandstone headland, a striking colour picture as the sun comes up.

❁ Classic **views** of the interlocking moor and valley landscapes are to be had from the graveyard of Gillamoor church SE6890; the lane at SE6188 a bit more than a mile north of Carlton, itself north of Helmsley; the hillside just south of Lastingham SE7290; the hillside at the top of the fearfully steep Rosedale Chimney road SE7294 heading south over Spaunton Moor from Rosedale Abbey; and the road on either side of Blakey Ridge SE6899.

✝ ⛑ ❄ **Whitby** NZ8910 Famous as the port at which Count Dracula came ashore; Bram Stoker got the idea for the book in the fishermen's churchyard of St Mary's partly Norman CHURCH, 200 steps up from the harbour, with lovely woodwork. The town is steep and away from the bright waterfront is attractive, with picturesque old buildings (now often rather smart shops) and some quaint cobbled alleys in its original core east of the busy harbour, where excellent fresh fish is sold straight from the catch. Whitby's important historical connections are illustrated in the well-stocked MUSEUM (Pannett Park), full of all sorts of bits and pieces, among them some fascinating finds (this part of the world is rich in fossils). Many exhibits relate to Captain Cook and his great endeavours (his ship was built here), and there are also other maritime mementoes and relics inc plenty of model ships, fossils, jewellery, toys and costume. Shop, disabled access; cl Sun am, pm Mon and Tues Oct-Apr, Christmas and New Year; *£1. The CAPTAIN COOK MEMORIAL MUSEUM (Grape Lane) is more specifically devoted to the famous explorer, in the house where he lived as an apprentice in the shipping trade from 1746; the rooms are furnished in period style with models, letters and drawings from Cook's later voyages; shop; cl wkdys and all Nov-Mar; *£2. WHITBY ABBEY Dramatically overlooking the harbour from their windswept clifftop setting, these 13th-c ruins are an impressive sight, with the skeletal remains of the magnificent 3-tiered choir and the north transept. (These date from the rebuilding of the abbey after it was refounded following the Norman Conquest; the first religious building here had been the wooden abbey of St Hilda, erected in 657, where the dating of Easter was thrashed out in 664 at the Synod of Whitby.) Snacks, shop; cl winter lunchtimes, 24-26 Dec, 1 Jan; *£1.20. And a visit here probably wouldn't be complete (certainly not for children at least) without a visit to the DRACULA EXPERIENCE, a vividly spooky retelling of the classic tale; cl Fri, and Oct-Easter; *£1.75. Besides good lunches at Bagdale Hall (see Where to stay), and the excellent fish and chips from the Magpie café, the Duke of York (Church St) is useful for food.

Other attractive villages here, all with decent pubs, include Ainthorpe NZ7008, Beck Hole NZ8202, Castleton NZ6908, Cloughton Newlands TA0196, Egton Bridge NZ8105, Fadmoor SE6789, Felixkirk SE4785, Great Ayton NZ5611, Hawnby SE5489, Lastingham SE7391, Rosedale Abbey SE7395 and Runswick Bay NZ8217.

Walks

The **Cleveland Way**, meticulously waymarked and signposted, is a great help in selecting and following there-and-back walks here. It follows the W, N and E margins of the Moors National Park, leaving it at one point to enter Cleveland (see also Northumbria section). Starting from Helmsley SE6184, it passes Rievaulx Abbey SE5785 (itself more dramatically viewed from approach routes down Rye Dale from the north) and **Sutton Bank** SE5182, a steep escarpment with an enthralling view. The most popular section along this escarpment is S from the A170 along the level clifftop to the white horse hill figure SE5181. Immediately N of the A170 you can combine the path along the top of the slope with a venture down the nature trail into Garbutt Wood SE5374, a nature reserve abutting Gormire Lake SE5083, the only natural lake in the National Park. Past here, there's a lonely stretch with some road access over the **Hambleton Hills** SE5187 to Osmotherley SE4597. A fine section on the N slopes of the moors can be enjoyed from the B1257 S of Great Broughton NZ4506, where the path westwards takes in rock outcrops.

Along the **coast** the Cleveland Way is consistently interesting – and so much more rewarding than the immediate hinterland that there-and-back walks keeping to the Way itself are more fun than trying to work out circular walks heading inland. The village of Runswick Bay NZ8217 makes a pretty start point for the path to Staithes NZ7818, or you can begin closer from tiny Port Mulgrave NZ7197. A bus service is useful for the section linking Whitby NZ8190, Robin Hood's Bay NZ9505 and Scarborough TA0388. At the famous village of Robin Hood's Bay the foreshore is a fascinating place for rock-pools, except at high tide; or you can walk along a fine section of cliffs to Ravenscar NZ9801, where a geological trail takes in old alum quarries; an abandoned railway provides an easy walkway back.

Off the Cleveland Way, **Farndale** and **Rosedale** have characteristic North York Moors scenery – lush green fields and red-roofed yellow-stone houses beneath the brooding moorland plateau. Farndale, the largest dale, is famous for its miles of wild daffodils in April, probably introduced and naturalised here many centuries ago. They're at their best around Low Mill SE6795, and any walk to enjoy them gives the chance of coming back down the ancient 'green lane' of Rudland Rigg, for spectacular views. The Feversham Arms at Church Houses SE6697 is usefully placed near the daffodil reserve. Rosedale now seems to typify the quiet pastoral countryside of the area, though until 60 or 70 years ago it was a busy iron-working site. The old railway track that once served the quarries loops around the moor above, and makes an easily followed stroll. Hutton-le-Hole SE7090 and Lastingham SE7391 are two charming villages, an hour or so apart on foot.

The E part of the National Park has large forest plantations with colour-coded trails in **Dalby Forest** SE8788, but the scenery is open around Levisham SE8390, with a track across the blustery moors and an attractive valley making two routes to the Hole of Horcum, just below the A169. From **Grosmont** NZ8205 you can walk a historic rail trail along the abandoned line that preceded the current North Yorkshire Moors Railway route to **Goathland** NZ8301, where a popular walk is from the Mallyan Spout Hotel to Mallyan Spout, a waterfall which tumbles into the side of a fine gorge. Close to the village is Wade's Causeway NZ8312, Britain's best-preserved stretch of Roman road (open to walkers only).

Driving

This is fine driving country, with relatively little traffic. High roads with good moorland views, though sometimes steep and narrow, include the one N from Hutton-le-Hole over Blakey Ridge to Castleton; the road straight up from Kirkbymoorside (a pleasantly old-fashioned small market town) forking left through Fadmoor to take you over the unpopulated wilds of Rudland Slack, looping round Cockayne and heading back to Helmsley; and the road branching off the B1257 N of Rievaulx Abbey, taking you through Hawnby and over to Osmotherley. The road from East Ayton to Hackness through the ancient woodlands of Forge Valley is pretty, and any of the valley roads N of the A170 are well worth taking: the Rosedale Abbey road through Cropton from Wrelton and the B1257 N from Helmsley are perhaps the most rewarding.

The attractive drive from Helmsley past Rievaulx Abbey to Old Byland and Cold Kirby brings you out by the top of Sutton Bank (for the outstanding view). If you turn left along the A170 and then take the next right turn down the steep road past the gliding club, you get a good view of the white horse cut into the hillside, and at Kilburn you can link with the drive we mention in the East Yorkshire section, through Coxwold, Byland Abbey and Ampleforth, to bring you back to Helmsley for a pleasant and very varied round trip.

Outside peak periods even the trunk A170 itself is quite a free-flowing road, and has some good views; at the top of the steep ascent of Sutton Bank a car park gives access to some memorable vistas over the Howardian Hills. The A169 N of Pickering is a fine fast moorland road with sweeping views.

In the north of the area, it's very difficult indeed to follow Esk Dale by road, but driving down into it is well worth while: one of the prettiest parts is around Egton Bridge.

Where to eat

Whitby NZ8911 is famous for its fish and chips, and the MAGPIE CAFÉ, which overlooks the town and river, is warmly recommended by contributors as perhaps the best in England – where else could haddock taste so delicious? Lots of wonderfully evocative sepia photographs on the walls, cheerful service; cl late Nov-Mar; children's menu. £10|£2.10/£4.95.

Apart from this and the places we suggest in the text above, many of the places we suggest in the Where to stay section have good food.

EAST YORKSHIRE

Quiet and untouristy; not a front-runner, but a distinct possibility for a gentle stay.

This very civilised part of Yorkshire has in Coxwold one of England's prettiest villages (with Newburgh Priory well worth a visit), and in Castle Howard one of the country's most magnificent houses. Sutton Park and Nunnington Hall also deserve to be explored, as do the stricken remains of Byland Abbey and Kirkham Priory. Flamingo Land at Kirby Misperton is fun as a family outing, and Eden Camp just outside Malton is an unusual re-creation of World War II experiences.

The countryside is altogether more muted than in those parts of North Yorkshire described above, and much less interesting for walkers, though the gentle generously wooded Howardian Hills between Coxwold and Malton present a series of quiet but attractive landscapes; more open wolds roll on between there and Flamborough Head. It's pleasant scenery to drive through.

Less well known than other parts of North Yorkshire, the area does have a quietly untouristy appeal, and some unshowy but attractive places to stay in.

Where to stay

Hovingham SE6775 WORSLEY ARMS York YO6 4LA (0653) 628234 £84; 23 pleasant bedrooms with swifts and house-martins nesting under the eaves. Comfortable lounge, good-value food, nice tables out by stream.

Harome SE6582 PHEASANT York YO6 5JG (0439) 771241 *£73; 12 rms. Family-run hotel with relaxed, homely lounge and traditional bar with beams, inglenook fireplace and flagstones, good very popular food, efficient service, and indoor heated swimming pool; cl Christmas, Jan-Feb; children over 12; disabled access.

Kilburn SE5179 Forresters Arms York YO6 4AH (0347) 868386 **£56**; 10 rms. Friendly old coaching inn opposite pretty village gardens, sturdy but elegant furnishings made next door at Thompson furniture workshop, and decent food.

Wass SE5679 Wombwell Arms York YO6 4BE (0347) 868280 **£47**; 3 individually furnished rms. Attractive, warmly welcoming small inn with cosy central bar, good imaginative food and decent wines; cl Mon; children over 8.

Coxwold SE5377 Fauconberg Arms York YO6 4AD (0347) 868214 ***£45**; 4 rms. Civilised old stone inn in pretty village, cosy and comfortably furnished rooms, extensive wine list, decent bar food, fine restaurant, and good breakfasts.

Crayke SE5670 Durham Ox York YO6 4TE (0347) 821506 **£35**; 3 rms. Carefully run and warmly friendly village inn opposite church, marvellous views from neighbouring hill, antique furnishings and panelling in bar, winter log fire and summer flowers, and good bar food.

Ampleforth SE5878 Carr House Farm Shallowdale York YO6 4ED (0347) 868526 **£30**; 2 rms. In peaceful undulating farmland and surrounded by an acre of garden, this 16th-c stone farmhouse has beams and oak panelling, flagstoned dining room with woodburning stove in inglenook fireplace, separate lounge; good breakfasts using home-made butter and preserves and fresh farm eggs; no smoking; cl Christmas-New Year; children over 7; no dogs.

To see and do

✝ **Byland Abbey** SE5579 The fraggle-toothed ruins of this abbey, built for the Cistercians, date from the 12th and 13th c. Enough of the structure, and indeed of the finer detail of the buildings, exists to show what a fine place this must have been: look out for the well-preserved floor tiles and carved stone; Oct-Mar Mon, some parts cl 1-2 pm; £1.10. The nearby Abbey Inn is very good for lunch.

✝ 🏛 ❀ ⚘ **Coxwold** SE5377 A neat and very attractive little stonebuilt village, very harmonious, and the site of Laurence Sterne's quaint Shandy Hall (open pm Weds and Sun Jun-Sept; £2), and the attractive 15th-c church of which he was curate – it still has the box pews it had in his day. The Fauconberg Arms is good for lunch. Just S, Newburgh Priory is one of those charming houses that have grown – but not too big – over the centuries; its origins are Norman, and there are Tudor and Georgian additions. One of the family married Oliver Cromwell's daughter, who rescued her father's headless corpse and had it reburied here; the room with the tomb is on the tour. Outside is a lovely 40-acre lakeside and riverside garden with a fine collection of dogwoods, splendid formal borders and lots of unusual plants; also miniature railway, children's adventure garden, woodland trail and 19th-c statuary walk. Plant sales, shop, meals and snacks, disabled access; grounds open pm Weds and Sun Apr-Aug, house same times Apr-Jun; £3, grounds only £1.50. Take some stale bread for the grateful waterfowl (even if you're just passing through – the lake's right by the road). There's a good working pottery.

Filey TA1180 is a much quieter seaside resort than Scarborough, its neighbour up the coast, with the main road dropping down a steep little valley between the church and the old town (and under a footbridge linking the two) to the beach, where fishermen still beach their boats. There's a small and attractively homely summer local

MUSEUM in former medieval fishermen's cottages (Queen St; cl am and all day Sat). The rock reef north of the town beyond the sands is interesting; to the south there are holiday camps.

✝ **Kirkham** SE7365 KIRKHAM PRIORY The remains of this Augustinian priory are in an attractive quiet spot by the River Derwent, and include a finely sculpted lavatorium, graceful arcaded cloister, and handsome 13th-c gatehouse. Shop, disabled access; cl 1-2 pm, Mon Oct-Easter; £1.20. The Stone Trough overlooking the ruins is good for lunch.

Kilburn SE5179 This quiet village is almost a place of pilgrimage, to the Robert Thompson FURNITURE WORKSHOP, famous for the unobtrusive little mouse carved as a trademark that you'll see all over North Yorkshire, on church pews and in the better inns and pubs. Lovely simple furniture, made by generations of this family for nearly a century, from oak that you can see all around, seasoning over the years; shop, disabled access; cl 12-12.45 pm, Sat pm, all day Sun, 2 wks at Christmas and Easter wk. It's not cheap (for a wider choice you might try the Old Mill at nearby Balk SE4881, where the craftsmen include ex-Thompson employees and prices seem lower). The Singing Bird near the church does good refreshments.

☺ **Kirby Misperton** SE7779 FLAMINGO LAND ZOO AND FAMILY FUN PARK Huge adventure park with massive choice of rides and activities, a large lake and over 1,000 species of animals. Useful enough for children to let off steam; meals, snacks, shop, disabled access; cl Nov-Easter; £7.

Malton SE7871 CASTLE HOWARD (outside, to the W) A really quite magnificent 18th-c palace designed by Sir John Vanbrugh, who up to then had no architectural experience whatsoever, but went on to create Blenheim Palace. Evelyn Waugh's Brideshead was based on Castle Howard, and it wouldn't be surprising if visitors left forming as deep an attachment to the place as Charles Ryder did to its fictional counterpart. It boasts a striking façade 300 ft long topped with a marvellous painted and gilded dome, an unforgettable sight beyond the lake as you approach from the north. Inside are splendid apartments, sculpture gallery, long gallery (192 ft to be exact), and a magnificent chapel with stained-glass windows by Burne-Jones. Beautiful paintings include a portrait of Henry VIII by Holbein and works by Rubens, Reynolds and Gainsborough. The grounds are impressive but inviting, and include the family mausoleum designed by Hawksmoor, the domed Temple of the Four Winds by Vanbrugh, and a beautiful rose garden; Ray Wood covers 30 acres and includes rare trees, rhododendrons and other shrubs. The Stable Court has a fantastic collection of period costume, and there's a good and unobtrusive adventure playground. Meals and snacks, shop, disabled access; cl Nov-Mar; £5.50. EDEN CAMP (just N of town, A64/A169) Elaborately recreated wartime scenes in buildings of former prisoner-of-war camp, very well done with sound and even smoke effects – and smells. Covers a wide range of World War II experiences, from the rise of the Nazis to the blitz and Bomber Command ops room; children's commando assault course; NAAFI, shop, disabled access; cl Christmas-mid-Feb; £3. Malton itself is a comfortable market town with some interesting side streets, in prosperous farming and racehorse-training country. Sat is a busy market day (the lively livestock mart is on Tues and Fri). The Wentworth Arms is useful for lunch.

Nunnington SE6679 NUNNINGTON HALL There's a magnificent staircase in this big 16th- to 17th-c house nicely set on the banks of the River Rye, and some fine panelling in the Hall.

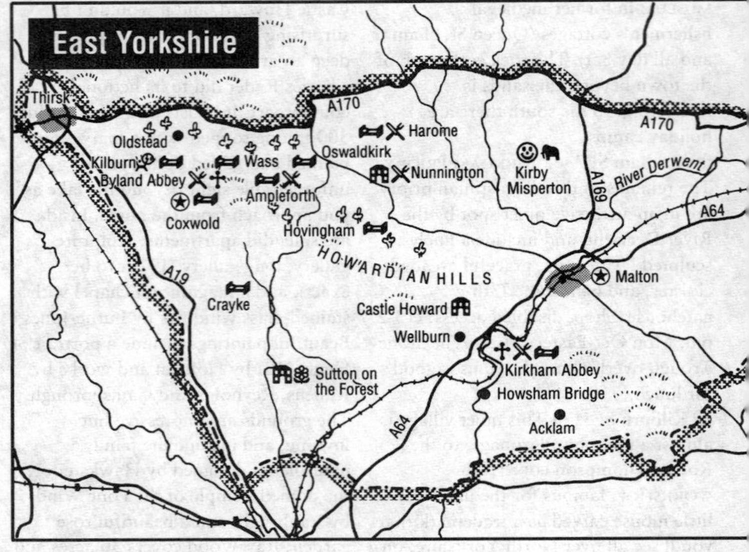

A family home for nearly 400 years, perhaps the most intriguing feature is the unique Carlisle Collection of miniature rooms, each of them 1/8th life size; snacks, shop; cl am, all day Mon and Fri (exc bank hol Mon in Aug), Nov-Mar; £3.30, garden only £1.60. NT. The Royal Oak is good for lunch.

Sutton on the Forest SE5864 SUTTON PARK A friendly 1730s manor house with furniture by Chippendale and Sheraton and a fine porcelain collection. The delightful grounds have terraced gardens, a Georgian ice house and a lily pond and there are also a number of pleasant woodland walks and nature trails; snacks, shop, disabled access to grounds only; house open Easter wknd then pm Sun, Weds and bank hols till Sept; £3.50.

★ **Attractive villages**, all with decent pubs, include Acklam SE7862, Ampleforth SE5879, Crayke SE5760, Hovingham SE6775, Seamer TA0284, Weaverthorpe SE9771, Oldstead SE5380 and Welburn SE7268.

Walks

The **Howardian Hills** protrude mildly from the surrounding plain, with a path along their N flanks giving intermittent views across to the North York Moors. Castle Howard SE7871 is of course the principal feature of the area, its vast estate threaded by a few public footpaths which gain glimpses of the great house and the landscaped parts of its grounds. From Kirkham SE7365 a path meanders S by a placid stretch of the **River Derwent**, to Howsham Bridge SE7362 and beyond.

The **Yorkshire Wolds** are quiet, agricultural chalk country, unfortunately suffering a dearth of footpaths. The most useful are to be found on the well-

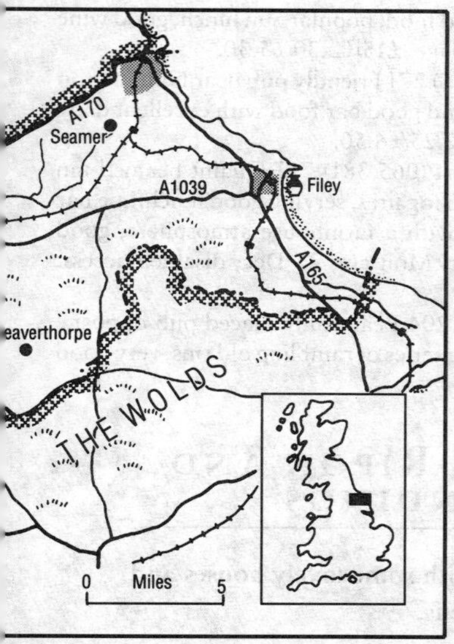

signposted long-distance Wolds Way from Hessle Haven TA0325 down in Humberside to Filey Brigg TA1381 on the coast, where it meets the inland Wolds Way. Thixendale SE6841 is perhaps the best starting point, with a characteristic dry valley to the S and some elevated land to the N, where the Way passes within sight of the abandoned medieval village of Wharram Percy SE8564.

The **coast** between Scarborough TA0388 and Filey TA1180 is followed by the Cleveland Way – an agreeable few hours' walk, although of less scenic significance than the cliffs further N, described in the North York Moors section. Oddly, the Way stops just short of Filey, at the headland of Filey Brigg, although there is nothing to prevent you from walking on into town.

Driving

Striding over this gently rolling countryside are some good long-legged back roads with attractive country views, particularly the one S from Hovingham through Sheriff Hutton and Flaxton, the estate road slicing S from Slinsgby through the grounds of Castle Howard, and the old high road slightly west of S out of Norton, which runs down parallel to the A64 and joins the A166 near Gate Helmsley.

A very attractive slower road is the one which runs through Bagby (SE of Thirsk) through Kilburn to Coxwold, where a left turn takes you up to Byland Abbey, and on through Wass and Ampleforth to Oswaldkirk. This road gives good views of the prettily varied hills rising to the north.

Where to eat

Harome SE6582 STAR (0439) 70397 Civilised thatched pub with deeply polished dark rustic tables, cushioned old settles, lots to look at, good bar food, evening restaurant, and garden; cl winter Mon am. **£18**|£2.25/£4.95.
Ampleforth SE5878 WHITE SWAN (043 93) 239 Big, neatly run modernised

We welcome reports from readers . . .

This GUIDE depends on readers' reports. Please tell us what you think about places in it. And do recommend additions. Use the card in the middle, the report forms at the end, or just write – no stamp needed: THE GOOD WEEKEND GUIDE, FREEPOST TN1569, Wadhurst, E Sussex TN5 7BR.

pub with wide choice of generously served food, popular Sun lunch, good wine list and very friendly staff; attractive village. **£15**|£2.30/£5.30.

Nunnington SE6779 ROYAL OAK (043 95) 271 Friendly pub near Nunnington Hall with carefully chosen furnishings, and good bar food with excellent daily specials; cl Mon; children over 8. **£15**|£2.25/£6.50.

Kirkham Abbey SE7466 STONE TROUGH (065 381) 713 Quaint beamed inn with small, cosy and interesting bars with log fires, serving good lunchtime bar food, and an old-fashioned restaurant with a farmhouse atmosphere, good outside sitting area with valley views; cl Mon am, 25 Dec; disabled access. **£12.50**|£2.95/£5.50.

Byland Abbey SE5579 ABBEY (034 76) 204 Beautifully placed pub opposite ruins of abbey, big garden and interesting series of rambling old rms, very good bar food. £3.15/£7.30.

HARROGATE, RIPON AND SURROUNDINGS

Comfortable and civilised, with some lovely houses and gardens.

This area has more for sightseers than any other part of North Yorkshire except for York itself (which of course is within very easy reach). Its particular high points are Fountains Abbey, one of Yorkshire's best-loved places, Ripley Castle, Newby Hall and Beningborough Hall, all with grand gardens. The most interesting gardens are those at Harlow Carr just outside Harrogate (believe it or not, they recently changed the name from Harlow Car in case people thought they sold cars). Little known to visitors or even to locals, Markenfield Hall is a lovely place to look round. Ripon is an attractive and largely unspoilt market town with one of Britain's largest cathedrals, very well placed for several of the area's major attractions. Harrogate is an extremely civilised former spa resort, a pleasant place to spend a leisurely morning or afternoon; with its many hotels, good restaurants and relatively central position, it makes a good base for excursions further afield if you want the comforts of an up-market town around you. It has some of Yorkshire's smartest shops, and is said to have more millionaires per acre than anywhere north of the Bishops Avenue in London. Knaresborough is fun for a family outing. The countryside is less dramatic than neighbouring areas to the north, but there are pleasant places for strolls.

Where to stay

Ripley SE2861 BOARS HEAD Harrogate HG3 1AY (0423) 771888 **£98**; 25 individually decorated rms. Beautiful old coaching inn with comfortable sofas in the attractively decorated lounges, long flagstoned bar, notable wines by the glass, good food in bar and restful dining room, and unobtrusive service; disabled access.

Harrogate SE3155 OLD SWAN Swan Rd Harrogate HG1 2SR (0423) 500055 **£90w**; 135 rms. Close to the centre in quiet gardens, this fine hotel is very well run, with attractive day rooms, and good food.

Bilbrough SE5346 BILBROUGH MANOR York YO2 3PH (0937) 834002 ***£85**; 12 pretty rms. In a quiet village, this handsome country house has a comfortable, wood-panelled lounge, log fire, good library, good food, and courteous service; cl 25-29 Dec; children over 10.

Markington SE2865 HOB GREEN Harrogate HG3 3PJ (0423) 770031 **£80**; 12 well-equipped rms. Pretty gardens and over 800 acres of rolling countryside surround this stone hotel with its attractively decorated and comfortable lounge and garden room, and there are fresh flowers, a relaxed atmosphere, good food, and friendly service.

Boroughbridge SE3967 CROWN York YO5 9LB (0423) 322328 **£74.50**; 42 rms. 17th-c coaching inn with good food and service; cl 26-31 Dec; disabled access.

Ripon SE3171 RIPON SPA HG4 2BU (0765) 602172 **£69.60**; 40 rms. Neatly kept, friendly and comfortable hotel with seven acres of gardens, yet only a short walk from the centre; attractive public rooms, and good food in bar and restaurant; disabled access.

Harrogate SE3155 RUSSELL Valley Dr Harrogate HG2 0JN (0423) 509866 **£55**; 35 rms. Overlooking Valley Gardens, this pleasant Victorian hotel has good restaurant food, a relaxed atmosphere, and friendly service.

Masham SE2381 KINGS HEAD Market Sq Ripon HG4 4EF (0765) 689295 **£55**; 10 rms. Tall and handsome Georgian stone inn on market square in attractive small town; lots of flowers and hanging baskets, comfortable furnishings, decent food.

Aldborough SE4166 SHIP Boroughbridge York YO5 9ER (0423) 322749 **£40**; 5 rms, showers. Friendly 14th-c pub near ancient church and Roman town, neat heavily beamed bar, and decent food.

Masham SE2381 WHITE BEAR Ripon HG4 4EN (0765) 689319 **£30**; 2 rms. Busy pub that's part of Theakstons old stone headquarters buildings with bric-a-brac in the traditionally furnished public bar, comfortable lounge, and decent bar food; cl 24-26 Dec, 30 Dec-1 Jan.

To see and do

Harrogate SE3155 This is an elegant and self-confident inland resort, a spa town which has kept a Victorian atmosphere despite now filling many of its handsome hotels with very up-to-date conference visitors. The layout of the town is very gracious and you couldn't ask for better shops, including many selling interesting antiques, and a surprising number of top-notch specialist shops. Though the darkish stone of the buildings does not itself do much to shrug off the gloom of a dour day, the town has always recognised that this is so, and fills almost every available space with colourful plant displays – even floral petticoats for lampposts.

The first thing a visitor notices is the great sweep of The Stray, open parkland which runs right along and through the south side of the centre. The elegant buildings of the compact central area sweep down from here to the pleasantly laid-out Valley Gardens, very Victorian, their curlicued central tea house run by a friendly Italian family.

The relaxed tempo of the place, and the clean bracing climate (it stands 400 ft up on the moors), have made it a popular retirement area.

❀ HARLOW CARR BOTANICAL GARDENS (W edge of town) Ornamental and woodland gardens over 68 acres, with streams, pools, rockeries, rhododendrons, spring bulbs and many interesting plants, inc the Northern Trial grounds. Also a museum of gardening and a model village. Rarely busy, a place of real peace and fresh moorland air, and lovely out of season when it's virtually deserted and the excellent collection of heathers comes into its own. Snacks, plant centre; Mar-Oct £3, Nov-Feb £1. Out this way the Squinting Cat at Pannal Ash is useful for lunch.

ROYAL PUMP ROOM MUSEUM The central sulphur wells (there are other outlets all over the town) are housed here, enclosed by glass to control the smell, and you can still order a free glass of the water at the original spa counter, now the ticket counter for the museum. Remember that though it smells dreadful, it's good for you. The octagonal pump room building now contains displays of 19th-c fine china and jewellery, as well as the bath chairs and other impedimenta of the golden spa days, and other local history displays; shop, disabled access; cl Sun am, 25 Dec; £1. Next door the elegant ASSEMBLY ROOMS are kept much as they were, very genteel and palm-courtish; you can stroll around, sit down for musical coffee and cakes, or plunge into a (non-sulphurous) Turkish bath. The very first sulphur well was discovered in the 16th c and named the TEWIT WELL after the local word for the lapwings which led a local sporting gent to ride into what was then a smelly bog. It's up on The Stray, grandly encased in what looks like an Italianate mausoleum.

Besides the places mentioned in Where to eat, the Drum & Monkey (fish restaurant/wine bar, Montpellier Gardens), Hedleys (wine bar, Montpellier Parade), the Regency (off East Parade), and that venerable Yorkshire institution Bettys Tea Room (Parliament St) are all good for lunch or a snack; the café of the Theatre Royal is also a pleasant place.

Other things to see and do

Aldborough SE4066 ROMAN TOWN The northernmost civilian Roman town was on this site. The houses, courts, forum and temple were all surrounded by a 20-ft-high, 9-ft-thick wall, but all that remains today are two pavements, the position of the wall and, in the museum, some of the finds from the site; shop; cl Oct-Mar; *£1.20. The Ship is good for lunch.

❀ **Beningborough** SE5257 BENINGBOROUGH HALL Early 18th-c house full of treasures, with a large collection from the National Portrait Gallery, fine carvings in several of the rooms, and a marvellous staircase with balusters carved in imitation of wrought iron. The big Victorian laundry has been restored for a taste of life below stairs, and the fine formal gardens feature a conservatory and wilderness play area; meals and snacks, shop; disabled access ground floor only; cl all day Thurs, Fri (exc July and Aug), and all Oct-Mar; *£4.50, garden only ticket available. NT. The Dawnay Arms at nearby Newton-on-Ouse is good for lunch.

✝ ❀ **Fountains Abbey** SE2768 FOUNTAINS ABBEY AND STUDLEY ROYAL WATER GARDEN The largest monastic ruins in the country, this

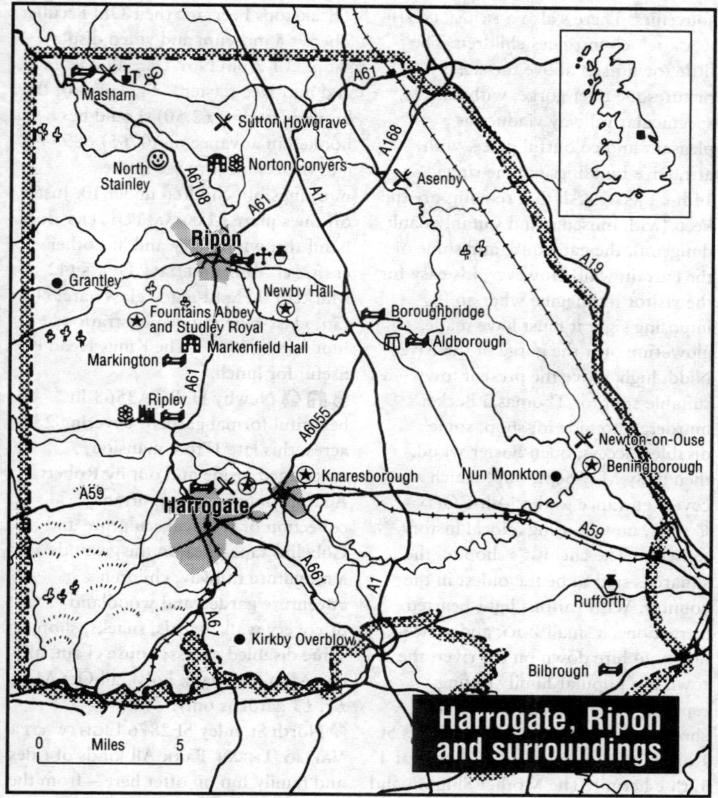

romantic place was founded in 1132 by Cistercian monks, in a delightful riverside setting. Most of the remains are 12th c, but the proud main tower is 15th c. Much of the stone from the abbey was taken to build FOUNTAINS HALL nearby up on the valley side, a charming unusually tall building. Around the ruins are the lovely landscaped gardens begun by William Aislabie in 1768. They include ornamental temples and follies, formal water gardens, lakes aflutter with waterfowl, and 400 acres of deer park. The most beautiful approach is through the extraordinarily ornate Victorian CHURCH at the far end, and this 'back door' entrance is the most tranquil too. A new visitor centre has been added; it's an interesting modern design, skilfully constructed so that it blends into the site and doesn't spoil the view. Meals and snacks, shop, good disabled access; cl Fri Nov-Jan, 24-25 Dec; *£4. NT. The abbey gets a great many visitors and the park is free. The very prim and proper Sawley Arms in Sawley just west does good food.

Knaresborough SE3557 Harrogate's more raffish sister, with quite a little tourist industry concocted around the alleged 16th-c prophecies of Mother Shipton, the cave she lived in, and a nearby limestone spring, the PETRIFYING WELL, which quickly coats teddy-bears and other unlikely objects in rock so that they can be sold as souvenirs. There's also a HOUSE IN THE ROCK which intrigues children. The little town itself above the steeply picturesque river gorge, with its spectacular railway viaduct, is a pleasant and colourful place, with attractive buildings inc the ruined 14th-c CASTLE. All that remains are the keep (with museum and suitably dank dungeon), the gatehouse and some of the curtain wall. However, it's easy for the visitor to imagine what an imposing sight it must have made, glowering over the gorge of the River Nidd, high above the present town – a suitable spot for Thomas à Becket's murderers to hide in; shop, some disabled access; open Easter wknd, then daily May-Sept; 80p, which also covers entrance to the 14th-c OLD COURT, now housing a local history museum. The chemist's shop on the square is said to be the oldest in the country. With various light-hearted attractions, a small ZOO, and ROWING BOATS to hire down on the river, the town is a popular family outing, especially on its Weds market day. A short walk away down Abbey Rd is St Robert's Cave, the riverside home of a 12th-c hermit. The Mother Shipton and Blind Jacks are useful for lunch.

Markenfield Hall SE2967 is one of the area's hidden treasures, which can be reached by a longish walk along a riverside track south from Ripon, or its main drive, another track turning right off the A61 heading south from Ripon, just past the drives to Hollin Hall on the left. It's a secluded fortified and moated medieval manor house around a charming courtyard, with lovely original rooms; disabled access; open Mon Apr-Oct, cl 12.15-2.15 pm; £1.50.

Masham SE2280 (pronounced Mazzum) is a civilised small market town, dignified Georgian houses around its broad market square, which wakes up on Weds. THEAKSTON BREWERY VISITOR CENTRE Situated next to the brewery, this centre explains the brewing process behind Theakstons beer, inc their Old Peculier. There's a museum and video display; shop; cl 1-2 pm Nov-Dec, all day Tues, and mid-Dec-Easter; *£1. Tours of the brewery itself (*£2.50) should be booked in advance on (0765) 689544, and there's most to see in the mornings; no children under 10. Just off the square MASHAM POTTERY does hand-thrown pottery and has other crafts; cl Mon. UREDALE GLASS (42 Market Pl) Hand-made glassware; cl Jan; glass-blowing demonstrations £1 (not Sun or Mon). The Kings Head is useful for lunch.

Newby Hall TA3568 In beautiful formal gardens covering 25 acres, this late 17th-c mansion, redesigned inside and out by Robert Adam, contains an important collection of classical sculpture and Gobelins tapestries. In the grounds are a miniature railway, children's adventure garden and woodland discovery walk. Meals, snacks, shop, some disabled access; house cl am, all day Mon (exc bank hols), all Oct-Mar; £5, £3 gardens only.

North Stainley SE2876 LIGHTWATER VALLEY THEME PARK All kinds of rides and family fun on offer here – from the white-knuckle, green-faced thrills of one of the world's biggest roller coasters through a traditional big-top circus to the more nostalgic pleasure of a steam train; meals, snacks, shop, disabled access; open wknds and bank hols Apr-Oct and daily in Jun, July and Aug; £8.50. The Bruce Arms in the quite attractive village of West Tanfield just north is useful for lunch.

Norton Conyers SE3176 (3½ miles NW of Ripon) This late medieval house is very much a family home – it's belonged to the same family for 370 years, and the furniture and pictures reflect that. Visitors follow in the footsteps of James I, Charles I and James II, while Charlotte Brontë used the building as one of her models for Thornfield Hall. Attractively planted 18th-c walled garden; shop (with unusual plants and in season garden fruits); house open pm Sun, Mon and bank hols, 25-30 July (no high-heels); garden open pm 3 Apr-4 Sept, cl Mon (exc bank hols) and Tues; tours by arrangement, tel (0765) 640333; house £2.80, garden free. The White Dog at Sutton Howgrave just north is good for lunch (not Mon).

Ripley SE2860 RIPLEY CASTLE A beautifully picturesque castle, in the same family for an amazing 26 generations, with guests during that time including Cromwell and James I. Most of the current building dates from the 16th c, including the tower, housing a collection of Royalist armour, and there's also a priest's hole, discovered by accident in 1964. For many visitors the main attraction though is the spendid gardens, the setting for the national hyacinth collection and (under glass) a fine tropical plant collection; there's also a birds-of-prey centre; meals and snacks, shop, disabled access to ground floor of house only; open wknds Apr-Oct as well as Tues, Weds and Thurs May-Sept, and bank hols; castle and garden £3.75, gardens only £2.25. The attractive village, rebuilt in the 1820s, has a superb delicatessen. The fine old Boars Head is good for lunch, and another good place a little way east is the Malt Shovel at Brearton SE3261.

✝ **Ripon** SE3171 The best time to come here is on Thurs, when colourful stalls fill the attractive and ancient market square (quite a few stalls too on Saturday, including bric-a-brac); it's largely unspoilt, lined with specialist shops and old inns and hotels. Going from there down one of the town's engagingly narrow old streets you are faced with the magnificent and elegant Early English west front of the CATHEDRAL. It's one of the largest half-dozen in the country, and has plenty to see, inc very fine carving indeed in both stone and wood, and a 7th-c crypt – the oldest surviving part of any British cathedral building (and probably the oldest surviving crypt outside Italy). The cathedral is spectacularly floodlit at night; shop, disabled access. A pleasant town to wander through, with a nicely chilling little PRISON MUSEUM, which also looks at the history of the local police; cl am exc Mon-Sat July and Aug, all Nov-Mar; £1. At nine each night the Wakeman, a red-coated bugler, blows a buffalo horn in the market place, as one has done for centuries. The Water Rat (Bridge Lane) down by the river, with a charming view of the cathedral, is good for lunch, and the Golden Lion just off the market square is useful too. Fountains Abbey and Markenfield Hall are within a walk from here, and Newby Hall and Norton Conyers are also quite close.

Rufforth SE5351 MUSEUM OF MECHANICAL MUSIC (Bradley Grange) A collection of ornate European organs which play anything from Brahms to the Beatles; fairground, street and cinema organs from 1870 to the present day. Snacks, shop, disabled access; open Sun pm Jun-Sept; £3.99.

★ **Attractive villages** with decent pubs in the area include Grantley SE2369, Kirkby Overblow SE3249, Nun Monkton SE5058, and Ogden SE0730.

Walks

This is not the part of Yorkshire to come to for serious walking, though it's within easy reach of both the Dales and the Moors – from Harrogate you can drive to Grassington or to Helmsley in about 45 mins. Closer at hand, the grounds of Studley Royal are excellent for strolling, as is Harlow Carr on the edge of Harrogate. The moorland W of Harrogate has some possibilities for more stretching walks, for instance on Stainburn Moor SE2352 from the car park by the woods along the side road W from Beckwithshaw, or on Denton Moor above the reservoirs S of Blubberhouses SE1655.

Driving

This is not so rewarding for drives as the parts of the county to the west, north and east, and for an afternoon out in the car you'd be best to head out there instead.

Where to eat

Harrogate SE3155 LA BERGERIE 15 Mount Parade (0423) 500089 Delightful unassuming French evening restaurant with freshly prepared, interesting food, and very good French staff; cl Sun, 2 wks Aug, 25 Dec; disabled access. **£23**|£10.

Harrogate SE3155 MILLERS 1 Montpellier Mews (0423) 530708 Attractive little restaurant with very good English and French cooking – lots of fish, a fine wine list, and good service; cl Sun, Mon, 1st 2 wks Aug, 25 Dec-3 Jan. **£22**|£9.45.

Masham SE2381 FLOODLIGHT (0765) 689000 Warmly recommended by contributors; cl Mon, cl Tues-Thurs am **£21**|£10.

Asenby SE3975 CRAB & LOBSTER (0845) 577286 Old thatched pub with a relaxed, informal atmosphere, cosy L-shaped bar with interesting furnishings, lots of bric-a-brac, really delicious food, and good wines by the glass; cl Sun pm; disabled acccess. **£20**|£3.50/£7.95.

Sutton Howgrave SE3279 WHITE DOG (0765) 640404 Pretty village pub with comfortable beamed bar, good bar lunches and no-smoking evening restaurant; cl Sun pm, Mon; children over 8. **£20**|£3.75/£5.45.

Harrogate SE3155 TANNIN LEVEL 5 Raglan St (0423) 560595 Very good wine bar also serving continental breakfasts and early evening tapas; cl Sun, 25-26 Dec, 1 Jan, bank hol am; limited disabled access. **£18**|£5.80/£7.95.

Harrogate SE3155 STUDELEY HOTEL Swan Rd (0423) 560425 Very good restaurant in homely hotel with generous helpings of good-value food – lots of chargrills; cl 25-26 Dec. **£15.75**|£1.40/£10.50.

Harrogate SE3155 GIANI'S Mount Parade (0423) 566453 Lively Italian restaurant with good pasta, pizzas and fresh fish; good with children; cl 25-26 Dec, 1 Jan. **£15.75**|£5.25.

Harrogate SE3155 WILLIAM & VICTORIA Cold Bath Rd (0423) 521510 Wine bar with upstairs evening restaurant and serving hearty helpings of decent country cooking – excellent roast lamb; cl Sun, Sat am, 1-7 Jan; children over 12. **£15**|£1.50/£4.95.

Newton-on-Ouse SE5160 DAWNAY ARMS (0347) 848345 Attractive listed building with lots of beams and timbers in comfortable rooms, very good food in bar and restaurant, and moorings at bottom of garden; cl Mon am; disabled access. **£12.95**|£2.50/£4.95.

Harrogate SE3155 TIFFINS (0423) 504041 Very good value vegetarian food (lovely puddings), take your own wine; cl Sun, Mon, 25 Dec. **£10.50**|£5.20.

SOUTH AND WEST YORKSHIRE

The west is good for a busy sightseeing weekend – lots of interesting and unusual places to visit (with the moors for a quieter escape).

This has far more places to visit than the north and east. It would make an unusual, if not exactly restful, weekend break. Some of the big industrial cities are very rewarding: Bradford in particular stands out as Britain's most surprisingly interesting urban area. Its film and photography museum is one of the most enjoyable museums in the country – and it's free. Bradford has several other interesting places to visit: we have not yet tracked down somewhere in the city that we can recommend as an enjoyable place to stay in, but can firmly tip it as a place well worth visiting by the day.

Other places which stand out as particularly worth a visit here are Harewood House, Halifax (appealing cleaned-up mill town), Ilkley (attractive small spa town), the mining museum at Middlestown, Conisbrough Castle, the pioneering industrial village of Saltaire at Shipley, Nostell Priory and Bramham Park. We have also very much enjoyed four less well-known places – the postcard museum in Holmfirth, East Riddlesden Hall at Keighley, the Bagshaw Museum in Batley and the Colne Valley Museum at Golcar. The busy cities of Leeds and Sheffield both have a lot of things worth tracking down, and Haworth makes the most of its Brontë connections. The picturesque Keighley & Worth Valley Railway is fun for family outings.

The west of the area is blessed with great moorland and mountain scenery coming right up to and indeed embracing the towns, and offering plenty of well above average walking – if not up to the exceptionally high standards of the Dales. It has a good few attractive stonebuilt villages (and a remarkable number of pubs that seem to have been placed with a perfect eye for making the most of the countryside); but the real reason for coming to the area would be to make the most of its very considerable sightseeing possibilities – either with an eye to its rich industrial heritage, or to take in some of the stately homes and the like.

In general, the west of the area scores hands down both for interest and for beauty over the east. With the present counties of South and West Yorkshire, we have included the bottom corner of North Yorkshire, below York itself and the A64.

Where to stay

Halifax SE0826 HOLDSWORTH HOUSE HX2 9TG (0422) 240024 **£90w inc £20 per person towards meal**; 40 comfortable, attractive rms. Lovely 17th-c house a few miles outside Halifax with friendly, helpful staff, comfortable lounges, oak-panelled restaurant, good food, and garden; cl 24-30 Dec; disabled access.

Sheffield SK3687 CHARNWOOD S11 8AA (0742) 589411 ***£90**; 22 comfortable, well-equipped rms. Friendly extended Georgian house with peaceful lounges, conservatory, two restaurants and extremely good food; cl 3 days over Christmas; disabled access.

Monk Fryston SE5029 MONK FRYSTON HALL Leeds LS25 5DU (0977) 682369 **£89.50**; 28 comfortable rms. Grand manor house in attractive grounds with antiques and flowers in the oak-panelled bar and lounge, log fires, and friendly staff; disabled access.

Leeds SE3033 42 THE CALLS (0532) 440099 **£80**; 41 extremely attractive rms using original features such as old beams and maybe an old winch, CD stereo with complementary library, satellite TV, and work desk. Stylish modern hotel in converted riverside grain mill with genuinely friendly staff; no restaurant but they have an arrangement with several leading local restaurants; cl 5 days over Christmas; limited disabled access.

Otley SE2045 CHEVIN LODGE Otley LS21 3NU (0943) 467818 **£74.50w**; 52 rms. Built of Finnish logs with lots of walks through the 50 private acres of birchwood (free mountain bike too), and good restaurant food; tennis, fishing, and free membership of nearby leisure club: indoor swimming pool, gym and supervised crèche; disabled access.

Wentbridge SE4817 WENTBRIDGE HOUSE Pontefract WF8 3JJ (0977) 620444 **£55w**; 12 rms. Early 18th-c, pleasantly furnished house in 15 acres of grounds with helpful, friendly staff and good food and good choice of very sound wines; the restaurant and cocktail bar are being refurbished; cl 25 Dec pm.

Escrick SE6343 BLACK BULL York YO4 6JP (0904) 728245 **£48**; 10 comfortable rms. Unchanging pub with cheerful fire, quickly served straightforward bar food and pleasant dining room.

Haworth SE0337 OLD WHITE LION Keighley BD22 8DU (0535) 642313 ***£45**; 14 comfortable rms. Warmly friendly 300-year-old inn with three bars, cosy restaurant with good vegetarian dishes, and oak-panelled residents' lounge; close to Brontë Museum, parsonage and church and the Keighley & Worth Valley Steam Railway.

To see and do

Batley SE2424 BAGSHAW MUSEUM In a beautiful Victorian Gothic mansion surrounded by a pleasant lakeside park, this has one of those excellent very personal and miscellaneous collections based on the curio-hunting of an individual enthusiast. All sorts of oddities from the byways of local history, natural history, and oriental arts, with a recent gallery of Egyptology; shop, disabled access; cl am wknds.

Bradford SE1633 is the area's great surprise for the uninitiated. Its 19th-c buildings, all in a solidly unifying northern stone, are a staggering monument to the days when its wools, woollens and worsteds ruled the world: gigantic and confidently Renaissance-style woollen and velvet mills, the imposing Wool

Exchange, the opulent city-centre cliffs of heavily ornate merchants' warehouses in Little Germany behind the mostly 15th-c cathedral, and the florid exuberance of the municipal buildings such as the Gothic city hall, the neo-classical St George's concert hall, the showily baroque Cartwright Hall (see below) given to the city by one of its textile magnates, even the great Undercliffe cemetery. The city's been through very bad times this century with the loss of much of the market for its textiles to competitors abroad (after some recovery what's left of its resilient textile industry is again under pressure), and has suffered some of the same heavy-handed traffic-management and redevelopment assaults that have for example so weakened Birmingham's appeal to visitors. Yet here there is a palpable feeling of underlying vigour and zest which do make Bradford exciting to visit. It's been lucky in its influx of Asian immigrants who have brought a vivid and visible dash of cultural diversity. And it has some quite excellent museums and galleries.

NATIONAL MUSEUM OF PHOTOGRAPHY, FILM AND TELEVISION (Princes View) You can be a newsreader for the day, ride a magic carpet or have a go at vision mixing at this remarkable museum. Its changing displays are both entertaining and thought-provoking (you'll never take a newspaper photograph of a politician at face value again). Also here is the massive IMAX – at over five storeys high, it's the country's largest cinema screen. The museum has its own theatre company which performs highlights from the galleries, and there's a new exhibition of favourite TV programmes that have passed away; snacks, shop, disabled access; cl Mon (exc bank hols), Christmas; £3.65 for IMAX and Cinerama, otherwise free.

INDUSTRIAL MUSEUM (Moorside Rd, Eccleshill) A former spinning mill well illustrating the growth of the woollen and worsted textile industry. A tramway carries you up and down the Victorian street, which is complete with workers' cottages and working Victorian stables with three shire horses. There's also the mill owner's house, providing a taste of what life at the top of the textile tree was like at the turn of the century, and a number of transport exhibits, including three- and four-wheeler cars made locally; meals and snacks, shop, disabled access; cl Mon (exc bank hols).

COLOUR MUSEUM (Grattan Rd) An interesting and award-winning study of the use and perception of colour, with imaginative interactive displays on the effects of light and colour in general, and particularly the story of dyeing and textile printing; shop, disabled access; cl am (exc Sat – but cl then 12.30-2 pm), all day Mon and Sun; £1.

TREADWELL'S ART MILL contains painting and sculpture by local and more familiar artists from the area, inc the largest collection of Superhumanist art in one building. At the time of going to press they were moving, but weren't sure exactly where to.

CARTWRIGHT HALL ART GALLERY (Lister Park) Dramatic baroque-style building in an attractive floral park, housing the Brown Boy by Reynolds as well as a good representative selection of late 19th- and early 20th-c paintings, and contemporary art and prints; snacks, shop, disabled access by prior arrangement, tel (0274) 493313; cl Mon exc bank hols.

BOLLING HALL (Bowling Hall Rd, one mile S) A classic Yorkshire manor house, dating mainly from the 17th c, but parts of it are medieval and parts 18th c. Look out for the panelling in the rooms, as well as for the plasterwork, the huge 15th-c heraldic stained-glass window representing great Yorkshire families, 17th-c oak furniture in the stylish local pattern –

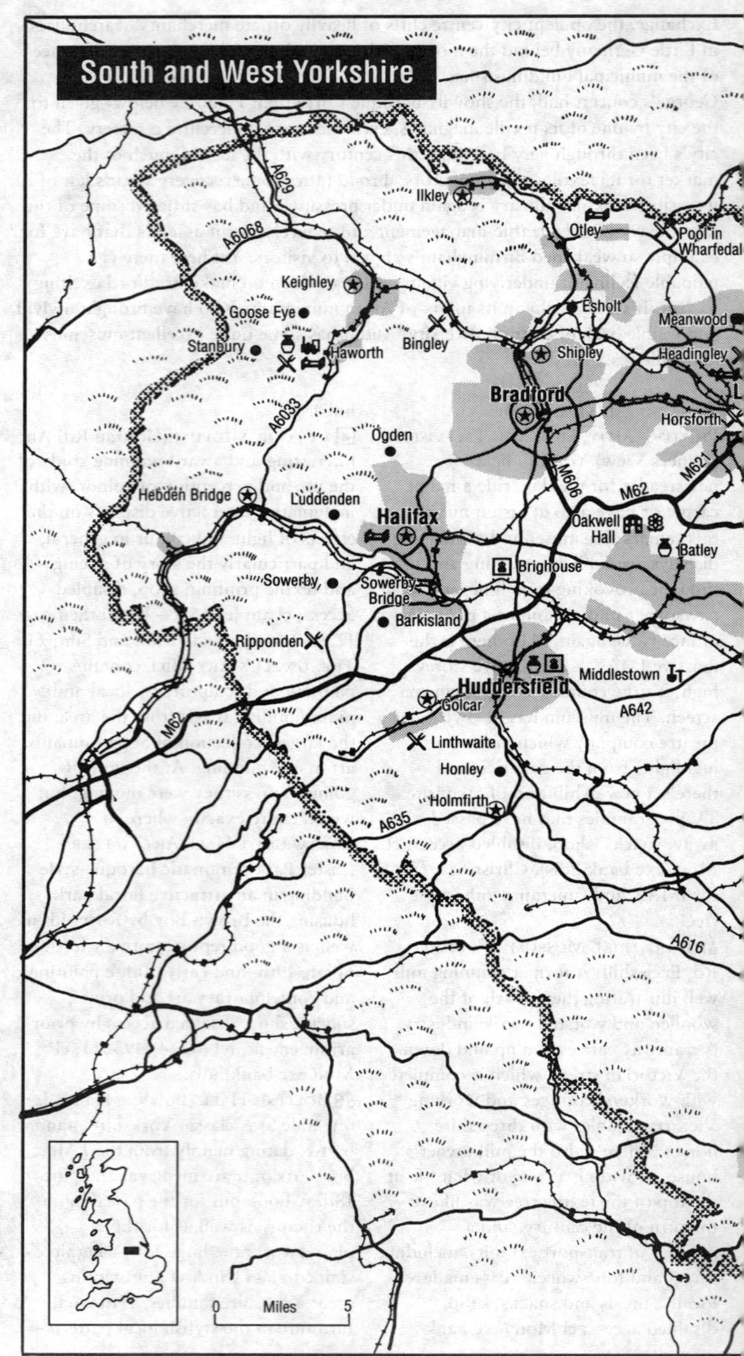
South and West Yorkshire
A629
Ilkley
Otley
Pool in
Wharfedal
A6068
Keighley
Goose Eye
Esholt
Meanwood
Stanbury
Haworth
Bingley
Shipley
Headingley
Bradford
A6033
Horsforth
Ogden
M606
M621
M62
Hebden Bridge
Luddenden
Halifax
Oakwell
Hall
Batley
Brighouse
Sowerby
Sowerby
Bridge
Barkisland
Ripponden
Middlestown
Huddersfield
Golcar
A642
M62
Linthwaite
Honley
Holmfirth
A635
A616
0
Miles
5

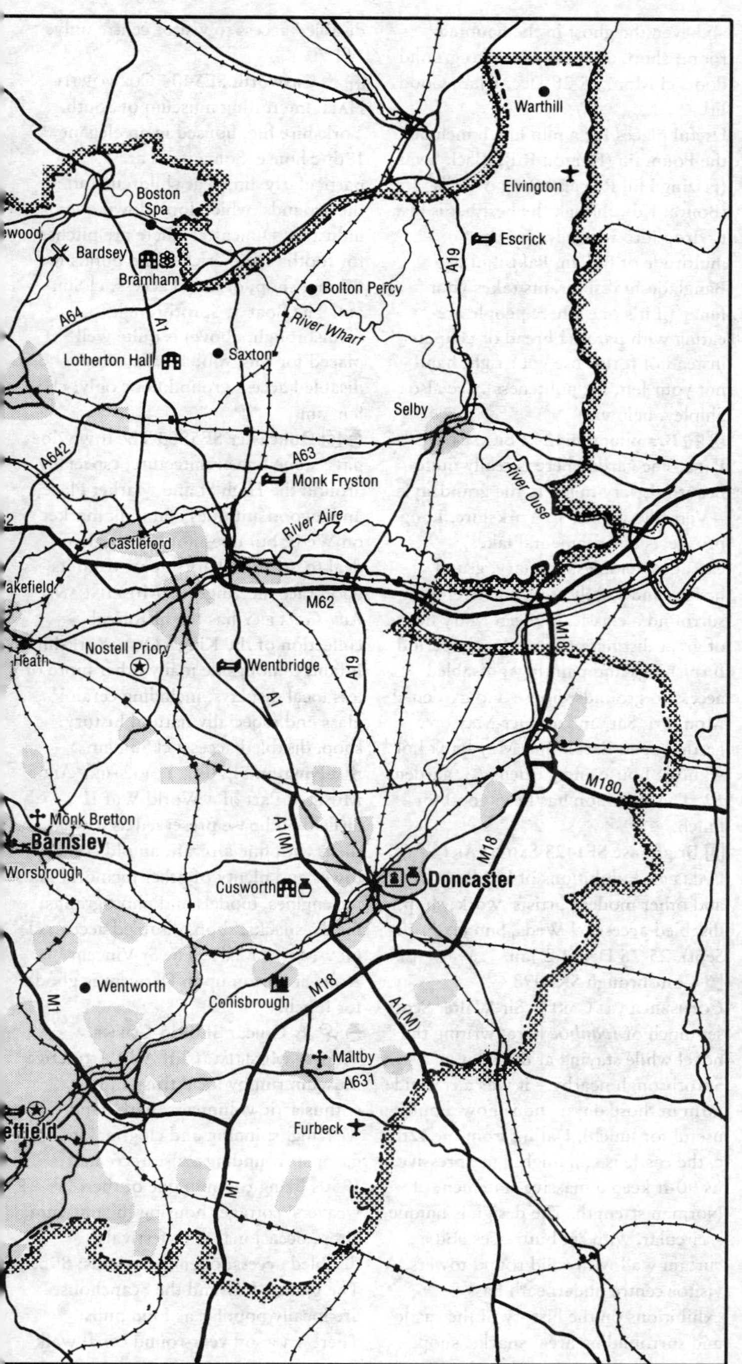
Warthill
Elvington
Escrick
A19
Boston Spa
ewood
Bardsey
Bramham
Bolton Percy
A64
A1
River Wharf
Lotherton Hall
Saxton
Selby
A642
A63
Monk Fryston
River Ouse
River Aire
Castleford
akefield
M62
M18
Nostell Priory
Heath
Wentbridge
A19
A1
M180
Monk Bretton
Barnsley
Worsbrough
A1(M)
M18
Cusworth
Doncaster
Wentworth
Conisbrough
M18
A1(M)
M1
Maltby
A631
Furbeck
effield
M1

and even the ghost in the haunted room; shop, disabled access to ground floor; cl Mon, 25-28 Dec, 1 Jan, Good Fri.

Useful places for a pub lunch include the Fountain (Heaton Rd), Black Swan (Frizing Hill Rd) and Ring o' Bells (Bolton Rd), though the best bet is just to drop into whichever of the multitude of Indian, Pakistani or Bangladeshi restaurants takes your fancy (if it's one where people are eating with paratha bread or chapatis instead of forks, use your right hand not your left, for politeness). See also Shipley, below.

Bramham SE4242 BRAMHAM PARK The garden here is really quite beautiful, very much in the grand style – Versailles comes to Yorkshire. Long prospects of ornamental lakes, cascades, temples, statuary, grand hedges and stately trees and avenues surround a classical Queen Mary house of great distinction, with lovely period furnishings and paintings; disabled access to grounds; house and garden cl Mon, Fri, Sat, and all Oct-May (exc garden open Easter and May bank hol wknds); house and gardens £3, gardens £2. The Red Lion has been good for lunch.

Brighouse SE1423 SMITH ART GALLERY Exhibitions of local work and other modern artists' work; shop, disabled access; cl Weds, Sun (exc Apr-Sept), 25-28 Dec, 1-2 Jan.

Conisbrough SK5098 CONISBROUGH CASTLE Sir Walter Scott set much of *Ivanhoe* here (writing the novel while staying at the Boat at Sprotbrough nearby – it was a riverside farm in those days, and is now a pub, useful for lunch). Dating from the 12th c, the castle is still mightily impressive, its 90-ft keep a massive statement of Norman strength. The design is unique – circular, with six buttresses and a curtain wall with solid round towers. A visitor centre underneath has exhibitions on the history of the castle and surrounding area; snacks, shop, disabled access to visitor centre only; *£1.70.

Cusworth SE5404 CUSWORTH HALL Interesting museum of South Yorkshire life, housed in an elegant 18th-c house. Some parts are particularly aimed at children, and in the grounds, which look down over industrial Doncaster, there are pitches for football and cricket and ponds for fishing; shop, disabled access; cl Sun am. The Boat at Sprotbrough (see Conisbrough, above) is quite well placed for this, too; snacks; shop; disabled access ground floor only; cl Sun am.

Doncaster SE5803 The town does have some fine architecture, especially around the High St and Market Place, and a good antiques and junk market on Weds, but does not have a great deal to attract visitors apart from its good race meetings. Its MUSEUM AND ART GALLERY has the historical collection of the King's Own Yorkshire Infantry, alongside many other more or less local displays, including ceramics, glass and especially natural history; shop, disabled access; cl Sun am.

Elvington SE7047 YORKSHIRE AIR MUSEUM Part of a World War II airfield and base preserved as it was then, with fine aircraft, an old control tower and plenty of other memorabilia inc engines, models and photographs; meals, snacks, shop, disabled access; cl Nov-Mar; *£2.50. The St Vincent Arms at Sutton upon Derwent is good for lunch.

Golcar SE0915 COLNE VALLEY MUSEUM (Cliff Ash) Attractive museum run by local trust and enthusiastic volunteers, with hand weaving, spinning and clog-making in gaslit surroundings, also recreated 1850s living room in one of the weavers' cottages housing the museum. Shop, occasional craft festivals, disabled access; open pm wknds; 80p. The Golcar Lily and the Scapehouse are locally popular as food pubs. There's a good year-round canal walk along the restored towpath between here and Marsden SE0412 in *Last of the Summer Wine* country, where a small TUNNEL END MUSEUM has canalia, café and summer BOAT TRIPS; the Tunnel End pub here is useful for food, as are the Carriage House and Olive Branch a little further off.

✈ **Firbeck** SK5688 SOUTH YORKS AIRCRAFT MUSEUM (Home Farm) Recently opened little museum in former RAF Officers' Mess buildings, taking a modest look at the area's aviation history: relics from crashes, 20 aero engines, a couple of planes and helicopters, uniforms and other memorabilia; shop, some disabled access; open Sun, or anytime by appointment, tel (0709) 812168.

Halifax SE0925 Another town with some mighty relics of textiles wealth, interesting to drive through when it's quiet on a summer evening or a Sunday, and surrounded by a splendid ring of moorland. The centre's been cleaned up and partly pedestrianised, which makes it pleasant to potter through. CALDERDALE INDUSTRIAL MUSEUM (Central Works, Square Rd; off Piece Hall, see below) The sights, sounds and even smells of the 1850s in reconstructed street scenes, shops, pubs and basement dwellings. There is also a thorough presentation of the area's many industries, using over a hundred machines; meals and snacks, shop, disabled access; cl Sun am, Mon (exc bank hols); £1.50. EUREKA! (Discovery Road) Good fun for children, for whom it's specially designed, a lively discovery centre with hi-tech hands-on science displays as well as themed exhibitions on how the body and senses work, daily life, and inventing and creating – wherever you go there's something to touch, smell or listen to. Meals, snacks, shop, disabled access; cl 25 Dec; *£4.50. BANKFIELD MUSEUM (Ackroyd Park, Boothtown Rd) was built in the 1860s, and has a fascinating collection of textiles and costumes from many periods and parts of the world, as well as the museum of the Duke of Wellington's regiment and a display on toys. Shop, disabled access on ground floor only; cl Sun am, Mon, 25-26 Dec. The 250-ft folly of WAINWRIGHT TOWER (off A646 just W) was originally a dyeworks chimney, now gives good views if you can manage all those steps. SHIBDEN HALL AND FOLK MUSEUM (Listers Rd) The rooms of this fine 15th-c house have been refurbished to illustrate different periods from its history. In the barn the folk museum has an interesting collection of horse-drawn vehicles, and around it is a reconstruction of a 19th-c village, with workshops, a cottage and even a pub; snacks, shop, limited disabled access; cl Sun am, all Dec-Feb; *£1.50. PIECE HALL (Centre) This magnificent Renaissance-looking galleried and arcaded building was put up in 1775 by the merchants of Halifax as a market for their cloth. Now its merchants' rooms are filled with specialist shops selling books, antiques and bric-a-brac, as well as an art gallery and lively museum; meals, snacks, disabled access; cl 25-26 Dec. The Italianate courtyard comes to life on Thurs with 160 bustling stalls. Close by, the 12th-15th-c CHURCH with its proud spire is one of England's grandest, with fine carving. Look out for Old Tristram, the life-size painted carving of a beggar which was used to collect alms. The enormous DEAN CLOUGH carpet mill, faced with demolition when it closed down some years ago, is now quite a lively complex of small businesses. The Shears (Paris Gates, Boys Lane) right among the mill buildings is a pub that embraces much of Halifax's past and atmosphere.

Harewood SE3245 HAREWOOD HOUSE Undoubtedly the area's grandest stately home, this magnificent 18th-c pile contains some real treasures – fine Chippendale furnishings, exquisite Sèvres and

Chinese porcelain, paintings by such artists as Turner, El Greco, Bellini, Titian, and Gainsborough, and glorious Robert Adam plasterwork decorated by Angelica Kaufmann and others (his Gallery is particularly impressive). The 1,000-acre grounds were designed by Capability Brown with very pleasing lakeside and woodland walks, as well as a magnificent collection of rhododendron species; there are very relaxing views of the gardens from the terrace designed by Charles Berry, designer of the Houses of Parliament. While exploring the grounds try to visit the 15th-c CHURCH, with a splendid array of tombs, and a curious tunnel under the wall of the churchyard, so that servants could arrive unseen by sensitive souls. Other notable features include over 150 types of bird in the aviaries, a tropical house, and demonstrations and sales of the work of various contemporary craftsmen and printmakers; meals and snacks, shop, disabled access; cl Nov-Mar; £5.75 bird garden, house, grounds, £5 house only, £4 bird garden only, £2.50 grounds and terrace gallery only.

Haworth SE0337 takes the Brontës very seriously, with their former home the PARSONAGE MUSEUM attracting some 120,000 visitors a year. It's very carefully preserved, with period furnishings and displays of the family's possessions, books and manuscripts; shop; cl 11 Jan-5 Feb, 24-27 Dec; £3.50. The steep cobbled main street is lined with souvenir shops devoted to the family, at least in name, with some antique shops too, but does have quieter more atmospheric side alleys. MUSEUM OF CHILDHOOD Wide range of toys, dolls, trains and teddies; shop, disabled access (with help); cl wkdys Nov-Jan; £1. KEIGHLEY & WORTH VALLEY RAILWAY Passing through the heart of Brontë country, this line, now staffed entirely by volunteers, was really built to serve the valley's mills. It begins at Keighley, where it connects with BR trains, then to Haworth and the railway HQ, and then on to Oxenhope, where the terminus houses the museum and restoration building. The prettiest station is Oakworth (familiar to many from the film *The Railway Children*); trains include Santa Specials. Snacks, shop, disabled access; open daily mid-Jun-Sept, Sun all year and most school hols – tel (0535) 647777 for talking timetable; *£4. The moors above here are very grand. The Fleece and Old Hall are useful for lunch; and see Where to eat, below.

Hebden Bridge SD9927 An engaging small town deep in a valley below the moors, and stepped very steeply up the hillsides, with quite a lively subculture of art and craft shops. Sylvia Plath is buried in the churchyard in the ancient village of Heptonstall SD9728, a steep climb above the town; it has a small museum and decent pubs. AUTOMOBILIA TRANSPORT MUSEUM (Billy Lane, Old Town) Austin and Morris cars, motorcycles and bicycles and other memorabilia from the humbler days of the motoring past, all housed in this three-storey textile warehouse. You can arrange chauffered days out in an old Bullnose Morris; shop, disabled access; cl Mon exc bank hols, Sat from Nov to Feb, all winter wkdys; *£2.20. MAUDE-WALKLEYS CLOG MILL (A646) An enormous number of different kinds of clogs made here from heavy-duty steel-toed industrial numbers to more fashionable frippery; you can see the range and watch them being made. Also craft and specialist shops; meals, snacks, shop, disabled access; cl 25-26 Dec. HEBDEN CRYPT (Valley Rd) Children especially will love this creepy journey through myth, legend and horror – the gruesome exhibits are all too realistic; snacks, shop; cl Mon (exc bank and school hols); £2. WORLD OF THE HONEY BEE (Hebble End Mill) Those busy little bees at close quarters, with working hives, demonstrations, video and displays, and free samples of over 30 different types of honey. They've just added a new Insect World feature, with similar microscopic explanations; wknd snacks, shop, some disabled access; cl Jan; £1. Next door are several working craftsmen, with demonstrations of skills inc glass-making. In summer there are HORSE-DRAWN BARGE BOATS from the canal basin, tel (0422) 845557 for times; from £2.50; the hold of one barge has been converted into a VISITOR CENTRE with a real boatman's cabin. Stubbings Wharf at Thistle Bottom is useful for lunch, as is the Nutclough House, above the town and on the way to HARDCASTLE CRAGS SD9630 – a pretty spot above the wooded river valley, for walks or picnics.

Holmfirth SE1408 Famed as the setting for TV's *Last of the Summer Wine*, with evocative little alleys, several good pubs (the Old Bridge is probably the best for lunch), a handsome Georgian CHURCH, and its POSTCARD MUSEUM. The first of its kind, this displays an excellent selection of Bamforth & Co sentimental postcards and lantern slides, and demonstrates their pioneering work with silent films. Also some local history, and this year special exhibitions to celebrate the centenary of the picture postcard in 1994; shop, disabled access; cl Sun am, 25-26 Dec, 1 Jan; £1.

Huddersfield SE1416 has a great sense of style in many of its buildings, especially around the station and central square, and much of the centre is closed to traffic. TOLSON MEMORIAL MUSEUM (Ravensknowle Park) This former mansion of a wool baron has local history and archaeology collections, toys and folk exhibits, displays on the development of the cloth industry, and a good collection of horse-drawn vehicles; shop, disabled access; cl Sun am, Christmas, 1 Jan, Good Friday. ART GALLERY (Castle Hill, Almondbury) Drawings and sculpture, oil paintings and watercolours are among the permanent collections. The gallery, above the town, gives you an excellent view of it in its moorland setting; shop, disabled access; cl Sun, bank hols, Christmas period; the Castle Hill Inn up here is useful for lunch.

Ilkley SE1147 owes its Victorian and Edwardian spaciousness and style to the mid-19th-c and later craze for hydropathic 'cures', which produced quite a rash of luxurious hydros using the town's pure moorland spring water. Their forerunner was the simple little bath-house built in mid-18th c around the ice-cold spring up on the moor just south of the town at WHITE WELLS – you can still follow the paths the infirm took by donkey. The group of characterful rocks known as the Cow & Calf up here also makes a pleasant short walk above the town. MANOR HOUSE GALLERY AND MUSEUM One of the few buildings in town to predate the 19th c, this Elizabethan manor house has a good history of Ilkley's Victorian heyday, as well as a 17th-18th-c farmhouse parlour, local art and crafts, Roman relics and displays on archaeology. It's built on the site of a Roman fort, and part of the Roman wall can be seen. Shop; disabled access ground floor only, no facilities; cl Mon exc bank hols, Christmas, Good Fri. The CHURCH has three lovely Saxon crosses, and just beside it are more traces of the Roman fort. There are a good few prehistoric remains around the town, the best known of which is the Bronze-Age SWASTIKA STONE, a symbol of eternity carved on a flat rock by a moorland path SE of the town, above wooded Hebers Ghyll; the stone is marked on the Ordnance Survey 1:50,000 map, at SE095469. Hebers Ghyll itself is a picturesque area of steep Victorian walkways, and the town with its attractive gardens and interesting shops (you can see chocolate being made at Humphreys) makes a nice stop. Useful places for lunch include the Ilkley Moor Vaults (Stockel Rd/Stourton Rd), the Wheatley Arms (Ben Rhydding), and the pleasantly situated Riverside Hotel.

Keighley SE0641, pronounced Keithly, is a busy working town, but has a pleasant centre. The Grinning Rat on Church Green is useful for lunch. CLIFFE CASTLE MUSEUM AND GALLERY A 19th-c mansion with a good collection of French furniture, much of it from the Victoria & Albert Museum, as well as displays relating to local issues – everything from minerals through archaeology to dolls. Though quite close to the centre, this is set in a park well above the main road, with an aviary and greenhouses; snacks in park, shop, disabled access ground floor only; cl Mon (exc bank hols), 25-28 Dec, 1 Jan. EAST RIDDLESDEN HALL (Bradford Rd) is an interesting early 17th-c oak-panelled stone manor house with attractive plasterwork, good collections of period textiles and furniture, and a formal walled garden. A huge medieval tithe barn in the grounds, probably built for the monks of Bolton Priory, now has a collection of agricultural wagons, machinery and other bygones; there's still a medieval monastic fishpond. Meals, snacks, shop; cl am, all day Thurs and Nov-Mar; £2.80. NT. YORKSHIRE CAR COLLECTION (Grange St) Cars that have been in films, that have belonged to famous people, or that just bring a feeling of nostalgia; over 70 vehicles from 1894-1983. Teas, shop, disabled access; cl winter wkdys; *£3.

Leeds SE3034 has an excellent and quite compact centre for the walker – freedom from traffic, lots of splendid covered arcades (Victorian, Edwardian and modern), and all sorts of interesting and engaging Victorian architectural details to spot (why did they put so many owls on their buildings?). Shopping is elevated almost to an Olympic sport here, so much energy is put into it – especially in the exuberantly Venetian/Oriental glass-roofed MARKET, the biggest in Yorkshire. The nearby impressive 1860s CORN EXCHANGE is now filled with neat little specialist shops and designer shops, including interesting places like the fresh continental bread stall. There's a stamp market on Sun and often a small jazz group at teatime – there are plenty of places for tea, coffee and so forth; well worth going to. The imposing TOWN HALL is perhaps the high point of Leeds' essentially Victorian centre; and there are good gardens and open spaces. The CITY MUSEUM (Claverley St) is a good starting point; shop, disabled access; cl Sun and Mon. CITY ART GALLERY (The Headrow) Changing displays of art with a Henry Moore gallery. It's linked by a footbridge to the new HENRY MOORE CENTRE, with sculpture from Roman times to the present; shop, disabled access; cl bank hols. The University of Leeds has a MUSEUM OF THE HISTORY OF EDUCATION; cl 12.30-1.30 pm, wknds, bank hols and Tues following. ARMLEY MILLS MUSEUM (Canal Rd) Once the largest woollen mill in the world, this building is now a huge working museum, its floors given over to a massive display of all sorts of machinery used in or connected with the textiles industry. Also reconstructions of turn-of-the-century tailors' shops, a buying room and a clothing factory, presentations of the history of cinema projection, and demonstrations of static engines, steam locomotives and underground haulage. Snacks, shop, disabled access; cl Mon exc bank hols, Sun pm, 25-26 Dec; £1.20. In summer you can take a canal BOAT TRIP from the city centre to here, booking necessary on (0532) 456195. THWAITE MILLS (Stourton, 2 miles S of centre) This water-powered mill was the focus of a tiny island community perched between the River Calder – which drives the mill wheels – and the Aire & Calder Navigation. The

Georgian mill-owner's house has been restored and has displays on the site's history; snacks, shop, disabled access; cl Mon, 25-26 Dec, 1 Jan; £1.20. MIDDLETON COLLIERY RAILWAY This railway from Turnstall Rd roundabout to Middleton Park was the first to be authorised by Parliament, after a 1758 Act passed in order to make it easier to get coal to Leeds. It's got other claims to fame too: in 1812 it was the first railway to succeed with steam locomotives, and in 1960 it became the first standard-gauge line to be operated by enthusiasts. With a picnic area, fishing, nature trail and playgrounds as well as the trains, there's plenty for families here; snacks, shop, disabled access; trains wknds Apr-Sept as well as Weds in Aug and Sun Oct-Nov; £1.60. KIRKSTALL ABBEY (A65 towards Ilkley) This is the most complete example of a Cistercian abbey in the country, the ruins now standing among trees in a quiet suburban park. The massive arches of the Norman nave are impressive, and you can wander through several of the quite well-preserved ancillary buildings. An interesting museum in the 15th-c former gatehouse includes lots of full-size Victorian shops, workshops and cottages, as well as a notable collection of costumes and fashion and a number of toys; shop, disabled access to ground floor only; cl Sun am, 25-26 Dec, 1 Jan; *£1.20. TEMPLE NEWSAM HOUSE That trusty old faithful Capability Brown designed the wonderful 1,200 acres of landscaped parkland and gardens in which this house stands, an extraordinary asset for any city. The house itself dates from Tudor and Jacobean times, and the rooms are being restored to their former glory. There's an exceptional Chippendale collection, and rare breeds in the grounds; snacks, shop; cl Mon, 25-26 Dec, 1 Jan; £1.20. In the centre, Whitelocks (Turks Head Yard, off Briggate) is a marvellous old city tavern, very much a Leeds institution.

Lotherton Hall SE4436 (B1217 Garforth-Tadcaster) Edwardian house with a wide variety of displays ranging from oriental art to British fashion, as well as collections of paintings, silver and ceramics and some lovely furnishings. Snacks, shop, disabled access ground floor only; cl 1-2 pm, all day Mon, 25-26 Dec, 1 Jan; *£1.20. The White Swan at nearby Aberford is good for lunch.

✝ **Maltby** SK5392 ROCHE ABBEY (off A634 SE) A fine gatehouse to the north-west and the still-standing walls of the south and north transepts are all that's left of this 12th-c Cistercian abbey, but they make an impressive sight; cl wkdys Oct-Mar, 24-25 Dec, 1 Jan; *£1.20.

Meanwood SE2937 MEANWOOD VALLEY URBAN FARM Small working farm on regenerated waste land, not far from Leeds centre; meals and snacks (not Mon), shop, good disabled access; *50p.

Middlestown SE2617 THE YORKSHIRE MINING MUSEUM Dress sensibly for this visit – there's the opportunity to sample something of what it's really like to be a miner. 450 ft underground, down one of Britain's oldest working mine shafts, models and machinery have been set up to depict the methods and working conditions of miners from the 1800s to the present. For the faint-hearted (and under 5s), on the surface there are pit ponies, 'paddy' train rides, steam winder and an adventure playground; meals and snacks, shop, disabled access and excellent facilities – helpful to arrange it in advance on (0924) 848806); cl 25-26 Dec, 1 Jan; *£5.25. The Kaye Arms at Grange Moor does good food and is fairly handy.

✝ **Monk Bretton** SE3607 MONK BRETTON PRIORY Remains of an important Cluniac house, founded in 1135, with gatehouse, church and other buildings, as well as some unusually well-preserved drains; shop; cl winter Mon; *80p.

Nostell Priory SE4018 A sumptuous Palladian mansion dating mainly from the 18th c, but with an additional wing built by Adam in 1766. Elegant inside and out, it has perhaps the best collection of Chippendale furniture anywhere, all specially designed for this house, and other highlights include the tapestry room, the charming saloon, and the grand 18th-c doll's house said also to have been furnished by Chippendale. The grounds are most attractive, with lakes, woodland walks, and a lovely rose garden. There's an interesting medieval CHURCH near the entrance, and a craft centre in the stables; meals, snacks, shop, disabled access; open pm wknds and bank hols only Apr-Jun and Sept-Oct, and pm daily exc Fri in July and Aug; £3.50 house and grounds, £2.20 grounds only.

Oakwell Hall SE2127 (signed off A651/A652 S of Birkenshaw) Set in extensive grounds with formal gardens, an equestrian arena and adventure playground, this moated Elizabethan manor house is furnished to look as it must have done in the 1690s. Lots of wknd events throughout the year; snacks, shop; cl am weekends; £1.

Sheffield SK3587 is a town which has made great strides over the last decade or two towards making life, cultural and otherwise, a lot of fun for people who live there. Though you do have to be a local to know what's going on there, and how to make the most of its lively cultural side, there are several places that are rewarding to visit, though needing a street map and quite a bit of – journeying. ABBEYDALE INDUSTRIAL HAMLET (Abbeydale Rd S) was one of the first examples of an industrial archaeological site to be made accessible to the public. The main feature is the 18th-c and early 19th-c water-powered scythe and steelworks, but there are also restored workers' houses and managers' houses, and some days when you can see workmen at their forges; meals, snacks, shop; cl Mon exc bank hols; £2. KELHAM ISLAND INDUSTRIAL MUSEUM (around Alma St; and signed from centre) Lively exploration of Sheffield's industrial development over the last 400 years, with all sorts of buildings, workshops and machinery collections (including formidable working engines), and traditional cutlery craftsmen at work; meals, snacks, shop, disabled access; cl Fri, Sat and all Dec-Feb; *£2.20. More about the city's industrial heritage at the CITY MUSEUM (Weston Park) with a particularly splendid display of cutlery and antique Sheffield plate. Other local industries are also represented in displays of clocks, watches, ceramics and sundials; shop; disabled access; cl Mon, 25 Dec, 1 Jan. The real thing can be seen out at SHEPHERD WHEEL (Whiteley Woods – A625 towards Chapel-en-le-Frith), an early cutlery grinding works established in 1584 and using the same dangerous methods up to the 1930s; shop, disabled access; cl 12.30-1.30 pm, all day Mon and Tues, 24-26 Dec. BISHOPS' HOUSE (Meersbrook Park, S of centre) nearby gives a good impression of the lives of the people involved in such industries. It's a striking 15th- and 16th-c yeoman's house, now reopened as a museum of social history, with regularly changing exhibitions and events; shop; cl Mon and Tues; 80p. The Fat Cat (Alma St, very handy for Kelham Island) is a good place for an informal lunch. North of the centre at Tinsley the SHEFFIELD BUS MUSEUM has a varied collection of buses and even pre-war milk floats, with related memorabilia and a big model railway layout; open pm wknds for members of their Trust to restore the vehicles, with special open days every couple of months when the displays are more lively; 50p.

! Shipley SE1437 is famous above all for Saltaire, the pioneering industrial village Joseph Salt developed here in the 1850s. Salt's beautifully thought-out and classically designed village was so successful that even now it's a favoured place to live. It's well worth looking around, and you might want to try the antique CABLE RAILWAY. REED ORGAN AND HARMONIUM MUSEUM (Victoria Hall, Victoria Rd, Saltaire) If you play the organ then you may get the chance to try some of those on display. If not, there are still some eye-opening exhibits here, the only reed organ museum in Europe. The organs range from one no bigger than a family bible, to the largest which has three manuals and pedals; shop; cl Fri, Sat, 2 wks at Christmas; *£1.50. COMMONWEALTH INSTITUTE NORTHERN REGIONAL CENTRE Also in the heart of historic Saltaire, this centre organises programmes of visual arts and crafts exhibitions, educational workshops and cultural events, designed to make the 50 countries of the Commonwealth more familiar; shop, disabled access; cl Sat, 25 Dec, bank hols. The 1853 GALLERY in part of the original magnificent mill building has a good collection of paintings by David Hockney; shop, disabled access. SOOTY'S WORLD (Leeds Rd, Windhill) A shrine to perhaps one of the century's most important cultural icons; politicians and film stars may come and go but Sooty and Sweep carry on undaunted. The eccentric puppet's 40-year history is all here with scripts, photos, cuttings and props displayed in rather jolly animated sets, and there are continual showings of some of the little bear's finest moments; snacks, shop, disabled access; cl Fri in term time, 25-26 Dec, 1 Jan; £2. There's a splendid flight of locks on the Leeds-Liverpool Canal here.

✝ ⛫ ▣ ❀ **Wakefield** SE3320 has a number of handsome buildings, including its CATHEDRAL, much restored in Victorian times but with some fine 15th-c masonry and carvings (and a marvellous spire – the tallest in Yorkshire), its rare 14th-c BRIDGE CHAPEL over the River Calder, some Georgian and Regency houses most notably around Wood St and St John's Sq, and its imposing civic buildings. MUSEUM (Wood St) The Waterton collection is housed here – a unique collection of preserved animals and exotic birds; also displays of local history and archaeology; shop. ART GALLERY (Wentworth Terrace) Good collection of 20th-c painting and sculpture, internationally famous for its galleries devoted to two famous local sculptors – Barbara Hepworth and Henry Moore; shop; cl Sun am, Christmas, Easter Sun. YORKSHIRE SCULPTURE PARK (Bretton Hall College, West Bretton) Carefully and imaginatively displayed series of major contemporary sculpture set in fine 18th-c landscaped parkland; meals, snacks, shop, disabled access; cl 25 Dec. There's a museum of psychiatry in the Stanley Royd Hospital, formerly a lunatic asylum; open Weds only, cl 1-2 pm. The Ferry Boat on Ferry Lane has a useful carvery, and the Beer Engine (Westgate End) is fun for a light lunch on Friday or Saturday; the Kings Arms up at Heath is good, an interesting old place.

❀ 🐄 ⛏ **Worsbrough** SE3503 COUNTRY PARK, FARM AND MILL MUSEUM Once a busy industrial area, now a peaceful country park, the noise of foundries replaced by the sounds of wildlife, and the railway tracks transformed into nature trails. Some of the 200 acres are used as pasture for the farm, which has a number of traditional and rare breeds, and several beehives. The only sign of the site's former activities is at the working corn mill, now a museum but still producing a range of stoneground flour; snacks, shop, disabled access; mill cl Mon and Tues and over Christmas. Events throughout the year, particularly on bank hols.

★**Attractive or attractively placed villages** with decent pubs include

Barkisland SE0420, Bolton Percy SE5341, Boston Spa SE4345, Esholt SE1840 (the Commercial Hotel has now been formally renamed the Woolpack, to take account of the leading role it and the village has played in television's *Emmerdale* series), Luddenden SE0426 (the enormous Oats Royd Mill in the valley is a remarkable sight), Stanbury SE0037, Goose Eye SE0340, Heath SE3519, Honley SE1312, Ripponden SE0419, Saxton SE4736, Sowerby SE0423, Sowerby Bridge SE0623 (the canal basin here always has a lot going on, and the Moorings is good for lunch), Warthill SE6755 and Wentworth SK3898.

Other useful **pubs in fine positions** or with good views include Dick Hudsons on the Otley Road at High Eldwick above Bingley SE1240, the Strines near Strines Reservoir above Bradfield SK2692, the Stanhope Arms on Windle Edge Lane nr Winscar Reservoir by Dunford Bridge SE1502, the Scapehouse on Scapegoat Hill above Golcar SE0915, the Cow & Calf up Skew Hill Lane at Grenoside above Sheffield SK3293, the Malt Shovel at Harden SE0838, the Robin Hood at Pecket Well outside Hebden Bridge SD9928, the Cherry Tree on Bank End Lane at High Hoyland SE2710, the Fleece at Holme SE1006, the Buckstones on the A640 towards Denshaw high above Huddersfield SE1416, the Blacksmiths Arms on Heaton Moor Rd at Kirkheaton SE1818, the Shepherds Rest on Mankinholes Rd at Lumbutts SD9523, the Will's o' Nat's on Blackmoorfoot Rd and perhaps the Travellers Rest on Slaithwaite Rd at Meltham SE0910, the Mount Skip nr Midgley perched high over Hebden Bridge SE0027 (a super place to watch Guy Fawkes Night down in the valley from), the Hobbit up Hob Lane, Norland SE0723, the Grouse on Harefields Lane, Oldfield, nr Oakworth SE0038, the Causeway Foot on the Keighley Rd by Ogden Reservoir SE0631, the Waggon & Horses on the A6033 nr Oxenhope SE0335, the Clothiers Arms in Station Rd, Stocksmoor, nr Shepley SE1810, the Blue Ball nr Soyland SE0120, the Sportsmans Arms at Hawks Stones, Kebcote on Stansfield Moor SD9227, the Ring o' Bells on Hill Top Rd at Thornton SE0933, the Royal Oak on Turnshaw Rd, Ulley SK4687, the Freemasons Arms on Hopton Hall lane at Upper Hopton SE1918, the Delvers on Cold Edge Rd at Wainstalls SE0428 and the Pack Horse at Widdop SD9333.

Walks

West Yorkshire has this area's best walking, particularly on the Pennine moors. The Brontë country around **Haworth** SE0337 is a favourite stamping-ground, with a good walk W through Penistone Hill Country Park SE2403 to the much-visited Brontë Waterfalls SD9935, and on through a remote valley to Withins SD9835, the original Wuthering Heights. Paths are plentiful hereabouts, although finding the way across fields frequently entails searching for unprominent stone stiles over the dry-stone walls.

From **Hebden Bridge** SD9927, you can tackle a fearsomely steep cobbled lane up to Heptonstall SE9278 (you can get up there by car); from Heptonstall, a scenic path along the cliffs above the wooded valley of Colden Water SD9429 is the reward. Hardcastle Crags SD9630, a beauty spot to the N of Hebden Bridge, protrude above the trees that shelter Hebden Water. The Rochdale Canal lines the bottom of adjacent **Calderdale**. For effortless views into Calderdale, take the Calderdale Way over Norland Moor SE0621, S of Sowerby

Bridge SD0623 (road access close by).
Ilkley Moor S of Ilkley SE1147 has potential for satisfying high-level walks, while closer to Ilkley the Swastika Stone (see Ilkley in To see and do) makes an interesting objective beyond the pretty ravine of Heber's Ghyll SE0947. Behind Otley SE2045, **The Chevin** SE2044, though not a high hill, gives a grand view of Wharfedale.

Numerous **reservoirs** on the moors are served by footpaths, including Ogden Reservoir SE0630 (N of Halifax) and Withens Clough Reservoir SD9822 (S of Hebden Bridge).

South Yorkshire does not have much good walking country, though the moors and reservoirs of the Pennines W of Sheffield have a certain rugged austerity. The high lands just touch the **Peak District National Park**, including Carl Wark hill fort SK2561, set in a great bowl fringed by gritstone outcrops. The **Anston Brook**, accessible on foot from South Anston SK5183, flows through a wooded valley that interrupts the monotony of the flat farmlands SE of Rotherham.

Driving

West Yorkshire has some fine drives with interesting views often combining grand scenery with antique industrial settlements clinging to steep hillsides. Easy and relatively quiet main roads through attractive countryside include the A640 west of Huddersfield, the A6033 from Hebden Bridge to Haworth, the B6188 south of Mytholmroyd across the moors to join the A58, the B6113 above Ripponden and the nearby B6114 through Barkisland. Other interesting drives include the high road out of Haworth through Stanbury and up over the moors towards Nelson and Colne, the several moorland and valley roads around Goose Eye above Keighley (a very picturesque area, this), the old packhorse roads from Hebden Bridge into Lancashire (one up through Heptonstall and Widdop and the other through Blackshaw Head), and the back moorland roads between Guiseley and Otley around The Chevin. Further east, it's either too busy or too flat for driving to be much of a recreation.

Where to eat

Pool-in-Wharfedale SE2445 Pool Court Restaurant with Rooms Pool Bank; 9 miles to Leeds/Bradford/Harrogate (0532) 842288 Fine Georgian house – popular for miles around – with extremely good, fairly priced, imaginative food, fine wines, and helpful, friendly service; bedrooms; cl lunchtimes except by prior arrangement, Sun, Mon, 25 Dec for 2 wks; limited disabled access. **£25.75.**
Ripponden SE0419 Old Bridge (0422) 822295 Well-kept medieval inn by pretty bridge over River Ryburn with interesting rooms, good wines and real ales, and very popular cold buffet wkday lunchtimes (best to book); good evening restaurant just over the bridge; no bar food Sat pm, Sun (restaurant only then); no children; disabled access. **£22.50 4 courses in restaurant**|£1.80/£4.
Haworth SE0337 Weavers 15 West Lane (0535) 643822 Charming evening restaurant made up of weavers' cottages with very good hearty (not heavy) food, cheerful service, and lovely puddings; cl Sun, Mon, 26 Dec for 2 wks, 2 wks July. **£17.50; they do a 7 pm special for £16.**

Horsforth SE3033 OUTSIDE INN (0532) 581410 Bustling, friendly evening restaurant with good atmosphere, consistently good food, and welcoming service; cl 25-26 Dec; disabled access. **£16.70|£7.**

Bardsey SE3643 BINGLEY ARMS (0937) 572462 Ancient pub and decorated in keeping, full of interest and atmosphere, with very wide range of decent bar food, picturesque restaurant, and charming terrace. **£16|£2.25/£5.**

Headingley SE2836 SALVOS 115 Otley Rd (0532) 755017 Welcoming, family-run Italian restaurant with good food and cheerful service; cl Sun, bank hol Mon am, 25 Dec, 1 Jan. **£14.50.**

Leeds SE3033 LEODIS Victoria Mill (0532) 421010 Sister restaurant of the Paris in Horsforth, this attractive place on the ground floor of the old mill serves very good and carefully cooked elegant Anglo-French food, and decent wines; cl Sun, Sat am; disabled access. **£14.**

Horsforth SE3033 PARIS Town St (0532) 581885 Very popular, imaginative French food with an excellent value, early evening 3-course meal; first-class service; cl lunchtimes, 25-26 Dec, 1 Jan. **£13.60|£5.15.**

Leeds SE3033 HANSA'S GUJARATI VEGETARIAN RESTAURANT 72/74 North St (0532) 444408 Very good and carefully prepared Indian vegetarian food from the state of Gujarat, helpful service, and a relaxed atmosphere; cl Sun, Sat-Weds am, 25-26 Dec; disabled access. **£13|£1.95/£4.**

Bingley SE1039 FISHERMANS Dowley Gap (0274) 564238 Carefully restored inn on River Aire (handy for the Five Rise Locks) with convivial atmosphere, and very good value decent food; cl Sat-Sun pm, 25 Dec pm, disabled access. **£11|£1.50/£4.15.**

Linthwaite SE1014 BULLS HEAD (0484) 842715 Popular pub looking out over moors, unassuming rooms, good daily-changing bar food, and lovely puddings. **£2.60/£4.70.**

Help this year from: *L A Moignard, Dilys Unsworth, Derek and Sylvia Stephenson, Neil and Angela Huxter, Mr and Mrs Peter Dowsett, Miss D Baker, Mike Simpson, Neil and Anita Christopher, Clive and Michele Platman, Mr and Mrs D Darby, W and S Rinaldi-Butcher, Stephen and Julie Brown, Nick and Alison Dowson, Michael Marlow, R T Moggridge, David Varney, Brian Skelcher, Giles Quick, Doug Kennedy, G Olive, David Atkinson, Julie Peters, David Logan, Roger Bellingham, John Allsopp, Mr and Mrs J G Whitaker, Gwen and Peter Andrews, Paul and Ursula Randall, C J McFeeters, Prof R N Orledge, Carol and Phil Byng, Dr and Mrs D A Everest, Richard W Chew, K Harvey, Geoffrey and Eddi Cowling, I T Parry, John Walker, D R Shillitoe, Consuelo Littlehales, Trevor Scott, John Fazakerley, Richard Waller, Andy and Jill Kassube, Paul Lightfoot, M Joyner, J E Rycroft, T Nott, John Henderson, Anthony Bayes, Neil and Jenny Spink, R T Stanton, Mark Bradley, Beverley Cummins, Ray Cuckow, Julian Price, Heather Berry, Neil Barker, Mrs M J Kingston, Mrs M Taylor, C J Westmoreland, Mrs D Craig, D P Pascoe, P R Morley, Mike and Wendy Proctor, John and Joan Wyatt, Kim Schofield, S V Bishop, D Stokes, D M Kirke-Smith, Stephen Oxley, Anna Cwajna, C F Walling, G S and A Jaques, Ian Boag, R Hole, R M Sparkes, M J Morgan, Paul Williams, Viv Middlebrook, Dr and Mrs B D Smith, Amanda Dauncey, Neville Kenyon, Paul and Gail Betteley, M L Clarke, Mrs Margaret Mulgrew, H K Dyson, D A Cash, Simon Dale, Tony and Pat Martin, Alan Wilcock, Christine Davidson, Miss B Mattocks, Brian Bannatyne-Scott, J R W Bune, Prof S Barnett, J R Smiley, R M Macnaughton, M G Hart, Andrew and Ruth Triggs, D H T Dimock.*

Yorkshire Calendar

Some of these dates were provisional as we went to press.

January

1st **Embsay** Steam Railway Family Day *at Embsay station*

3rd **Hubberholme** Land Letting *at The George, 8 pm: ancient form of auction determined by the length of a burning candle; pub split into House of Commons and House of Lords, controlled by vicar – when the candle has burnt out the last bid gains the church lands grazing*

7th **Sheffield** British Ice Dance Championships *at the Arena – till Sun 9*

16th **Heslington** Concert by Lindsay String Quartet *at University of York*

February

4th **York** Jorvik Viking Festival, *inc combat, feasts, boatburning, crafts, lectures and music – till Fri 19*

15th **Scarborough** Shrovetide Skipping Festival: *noon curfew bell at Rotunda Museum rung as signal to start pancake cooking, ¾-mile of Foreshore Rd closed to traffic for skipping in the road, till 5 pm*

March

10th **Ilkley** Literature Festival *at Ilkley Playhouse – till Mon 13*

11th **Ilkley** Complementary Medicine Festival *at Kings Hall and Winter Gardens – till Sun 13*; **Sheffield** Industrial Hamlet Working Days *at Abbeydale – till Sun 13*

30th **Harrogate** International Youth Music Festival *– till 6 Apr*

April

1st **Harrogate** International Festival of Country Music *at Exhibition Centre – till Mon 4*; **Scarborough** Easter Hockey Festival *– till Mon 4*

3rd **Harewood** Giant Easter Egg Hunt *at Harewood House*; **Keighley** Revels *at East Riddlesden Hall, various entertainments on first Sun of month till Oct*; **Overton** nr Wakefield Easter Egg Hunt *at Yorkshire Mining Museum*; **Worsbrough** Open Days *at Wigfield Farm and Worsbrough Hall – till Mon 4*

4th **Ossett** World Coal-carrying Championship

16th **Sheffield** World Championship Snooker *at Crucible Theatre – till 2 May*

21st **Harrogate** RHS Spring Flower Show *at Valley Gardens – till Sun 24*

23rd **Bridlington** Festival *– till Sat 7*

24th **Horton-in-Ribblesdale** Three Peaks Race

May

2nd **Harewood** Yorkshire Festival of Transport *at Harewood House – till Tues 3*; **Ilkley** Carnival

7th **Gawthorpe** Maypole, Feast and Procession, *starts 2.15*

Yorkshire Calendar

May cont.

8th **Mytholmroyd** World Dock Pudding Championships (*made of dock leaves, nettles, oatmeal, onions, butter and seasoning*); **Sheffield** Chamber Music Festival – *till Sun 22*

11th **Whitby** Upper Harbour Planting of the Penny Hedge (*corruption of penance hedge), orig 1159 when a boar pursued by hounds took refuge with a monk in Eskdaleside chapel, hunters mortally injured a monk who begged Abbot of Whitby to spare their lives if they and their successors did penance by building a hedge of stakes at the water's edge strong enough to 'stand three tides without removing by the force of water'; the Penny hedge is planted at or as soon after 9 am as tides permit*

14th **Ilkley** Music Festival – *till Sat 21*; **Sheffield** Chamber Music Festival *at Crucible Studio Theatre – till Sat 28*

21st **Otley** Agricultural Show *at The Showground, Bridge End*

26th **nr Keld** Tan Hill Inn Show, *inc Swaledale sheep, quoits, music*

28th **Harewood** Dalesway Craft Fair *at Harewood House – till Tues 31*; **Sheffield** Fulwood Booth Sheepdog Trials – *till Mon 30*

29th **Nostell** Cavalcade of British and Classic Motorcycles *at the Priory*; **Worsbrough** Open Days *at Wigfield Farm and Worsbrough Mill – till Mon 30*

30th **Helmsley** Country Fair *at Duncombe Park*

June

3rd **Richmond** Folk Festival – *till Sun 5*

4th **nr York** Archery Weekend *at Clifton Park – till Sun 5*; **Skipton to Whitby** Vintage Car Run – *till Sun 5*

9th **Bramham** *nr Wetherby* Horse Trials and Country Fair – *till Sun 12*

11th **Fountains Abbey and Studley Royal**, Music *ending with fireworks – till Sun 12*; **Whitby** Festival *at the Pavilion Theatre and Pavilion – till Sun 26*

16th **Ilkley** Literature Festival – *till Sun 19*

17th **Bradford** Festival – *till 9 July*; **Grassington** Festival – *till 2 July*; **Holmfirth** Harden Moss Sheepdog Trials – *till Sun 19*

18th **Otley** Carnival; **Wakefield** Yorkshire Chamber Choir *in Cathedral*; **Wetherby** Agricultural Show *at Orange Park*

25th **Rotherham** Motoring Weekend and Tattoo *at Herringthorpe Leisure Centre*; **Thirsk** North Yorkshire County Show *at Rybeck Farm*

26th **Easingwold** Open Gardens; **Skipton** Dalesman Game Show *at Broughton Hall*

July

1st **Cleckheaton** Folk Festival – *till Sun 3*; **Whitby** Boatman's Angling Festival – *till Sun 10*

2nd **Helmsley** Greater Yorkshire Traction Engine Club Steam Fair and Rally *at Duncombe Park – till Sun 3*; **Long Marston** Re-enactment of the Battle of Marston Moor – *till Sun 3*

YORKSHIRE CALENDAR

JULY cont.

3rd **Oxenhope** Straw Race

8th **Fountains Abbey and Studley Royal** Music by Moonlight, *picnic and dance with a theme – till Sat 9*; **York** Early Music Festival – *till Sun 17*

9th **Wetherby** Bramham International Horse Trials and Yorkshire Country Fair – *till Sun 12*; **Huddersfield** Carnival

10th **Barnsley** Metropolitan Vintage Vehicle Rally; **Harewood** Jaguar Rally *at Harewood House*; **Whitby** Blessing of the Boats *by the Bishop of Whitby, inc sail-past at 2.30*

12th **Harrogate** Show *at Great Yorkshire Showground – till Thurs 14*

16th **Masham** Steam Engine and Fair Organ Rally *at Low Burton Hall – till Sun 17*

17th **RAF Church Fenton** Air Display

22nd **Rydale** Festival – *till 7 Aug*

26th **Rydale** Show *at Welburn Park*

27th **West Witton** Burning of Bartle, *the effigy of a legendary outlaw who lived in the forest above the village*

28th **Harrogate** Festival – *till 11 Aug*

30th **Ripon** St Wilfrid's Feast Procession, *orig 1108*

AUGUST

2nd **Egton Bridge** Old Gooseberry Show (*the most famous of the great gooseberry shows*); **Littlebeck** Garden Fête and Rose Queen Ceremony

3rd **Thornton Dale** Agricultural Show

4th **Headingley** England v South Africa Test Match – *till Mon 8*

6th **Ripon** St Wilfrid's Procession *at 2 pm*; **Whitby** Regatta and Carnival – *till Mon 8*

10th **Danby** Agricultural Show *at Vicarage Field;* **Sheffield** World Championships Modern Pentathlon *at Arena – till Tues 16*

14th **Danby** Embroidery and Painting on Silk *at The Moors Centre Exhibition – till Tues 16*

20th **Leyburn** Wensleydale International Brass Festival *at Aysgarth Falls – till Mon 29*; **Whitby** Folk Week *–till Fri 26*

21st **Bridlington** Vintage Car Rally *at Sewerby Park*; **Overton** nr Wakefield Horse Day *at Yorkshire Mining Museum*

27th **Leyburn** Wensleydale Agricultural Show; **Ravenscar** Bonfire, Barbecue and Music *at National Trust Centre*; **Ripley** Live Crafts Show *at Ripley Castle – till Mon 29*; **Thongsbridge** Torchlight Procession

28th **Birstall** Country Fair *at Oakwell Hall and Country Park*; **Danby** Longbow Display *at The Moors Centre*; **Worsbrough** Open Days *at Wigfield and Worsbrough Mill – till Mon 29*

29th **Burniston** Horticultural and Agricultural Show *at Showground*; **Epworth** Show *at Showground*; **Hovingham** 18th-c Street Fair; Gardens Open *at Hovingham Hall*

Yorkshire Calendar

September

3rd **Filey** Fishing Festival – *till Sun 11*; **Keighley** and District Agricultural Show; **Warley to Sowerby Bridge** *on Sat and* **Sowerby to Ripponden** *on Sun 4* Rushbearing: *ancient ceremony providing clean rushes for church floors – procession of Morris dancers leaves a token branch of rushes at a number of churches, markets and entertainments*

4th **Great Smeaton** Vintage Working Day *at Thorpe Farm*

10th **Castleton and Danby** Show *at Castleton Cricket Field*

11th **Hardraw** Brass Band Contest *at Green Dragon Inn*; **Sheffield** Transport Rally

16th **Harrogate** RHS Great Autumn Show – *till Sat 17*

17th **Finningley** RAF Air Show; **Stokesley** Show *at Showfield*

18th **Worsbrough** Festival of the Horse *at Country Park*

19th **Pateley Bridge** Nidderdale Show *at Beverley Park*

October

1st **Masham** Sheep Fair *inc the Bishop Blaise procession*

7th **Hull** Fair – *till Sat 15*

13th **Leeds** Film Festival – *till Fri 28*

21st **Calder Grove** *nr Wakefield* Crafts at Christmas *at Cedar Court Hotel – till Sun 23*

November

5th **Embsay** Steam Railway Bonfire, *fireworks and steam trains at night*; **York** Firework Spectacular

17th **Huddersfield** Contemporary Music Festival – *till Sun 27*

December

1st **York** St Nicholas Fayre – *till Sun 4*

3rd **Grassington** Dickensian Christmas, *also on Sat 10 and Sat 17*

4th **Birstall** Christmas Craft Fair and Tree Celebration *at Oakwell Hall and Country Park*

18th **Haworth** Father Christmas, *torchlight procession and carol service*

26th **Ripon** Pilgrimage *from Cathedral to Fountains Abbey*

31st **Ripon** Watchnight Service and Torchlight Procession *at Cathedral*

We welcome reports from readers . . .

Do send us reports on places in the Guide, or ones you think should be in. Use the card in the middle, the report forms at the end, or just write – no stamp needed: The Good Weekend Guide, FREEPOST TN1569, Wadhurst, E Sussex TN5 7BR. Readers who help us with reports for the Guide are offered a discount on the next edition.

London

Unrivalled for sightseeing, shopping and shows; superb choice of restaurants, excellent places to stay (at high prices); but undeniably suffers from noise, litter and congestion, and has seen better days.

London ranks supreme for the vast range of things you can find to do, see, watch, visit, buy and eat in a relatively small area, and for the ease of walking from one interesting thing to the next. It's let down by its high restaurant and accommodation prices (a saving grace is that many of the places to visit are free). Like most big cities, it's impersonal rather than friendly, has noisy and smelly traffic problems (not in the City, noticeably quieter and fresher since its security cordon has been in place; and there are peaceful enclaves in many other parts), and there's a distinct feeling that it's seen better days: many visitors will feel there's too much dirt and delapidation (though again not in the City, nor in much of Westminster).

London sprawls for miles and miles, but almost all the things visitors might want to see are concentrated in its relatively small central part. We have divided this centre into a few general areas of a size to facilitate quite a bit of sightseeing in a day or so. As these central areas are clustered so closely, you can very quickly get from one to the other – so the place you choose to stay in needn't necessarily be in the area you are most interested in exploring. We have recommended only those hotels which we know to be comfortable and to have some individuality – places that would definitely add something to the enjoyment of your stay. If all you want is a bed for the night, there's an almost endless range of cheaper places, especially around Bloomsbury, Bayswater, South Kensington and Victoria.

The only parts of outer London that we have included are those which would really add something significant to a stay in the centre – Greenwich, Kew and Richmond, Hampton Court, Hampstead and Highgate. Generally, though, outer London does not appeal as a choice for a weekend stay.

Among the tremendous choice of places to visit, highlights in the West End might include Covent Garden, Trafalgar Square and the National Gallery, Leicester Square/Piccadilly Circus/Piccadilly with the Museum of Mankind and the Royal Academy; in Westminster, the newly opened Buckingham Palace (quite stunning), the abbey and its cloisters, and the walk across St James's Park between them – perhaps also Westminster Cathedral; in Knightsbridge, the three great South Kensington museums – and Harrods seems irresistible to most visitors; in Bloomsbury, the British Museum, and south of the river the Museum of the Moving Image, the Imperial War Museum, a walk along the south bank for its views across the river, and perhaps the Design Museum. Further afield, Greenwich, Kew and Hampton Court are all inviting, especially in fine weather. Children particularly enjoy the Science Museum and Natural History Museum (South Kensington), Regent's Park Zoo, the Tower of London (City) and the Museum of the Moving Image and London Dungeon (south of the river).

There's a magnificent choice of restaurants, from the simplest to the most grandiose or places with the most delicious food (often not the same). Again, we've restricted our recommendations to a manageable number of places that have real character.

Unless you are familiar with London's roads or entirely confident about driving in a big city with too much traffic, poor local signposting and a lot of unpredictable drivers, don't come by car. For seeing much of London, a car is actually an encumbrance, because of the traffic and the expense of parking. The two exceptions to this general rule are that on a Sunday Central London's roads are relatively quiet, with parking generally free; and that very early on a fine late spring or summer morning – say, between 4 or 5 and 7 o'clock – it can be idyllic driving around the broad and empty streets and avenues of the centre, especially around Westminster and Buckingham Palace, seeing the stately buildings waking up in the early sunshine, without a single tourist to be seen around them.

London's 'tube', the underground railway, is the most straightforward way of getting around, and easy for even first-time visitors. The routes are all colour-coded, on the same system used in that masterpiece of 1920s design, the pocket tube map (free from ticket offices); this is a big help in finding the platform you want, particularly in those busy stations that serve more than one line. In the text, we have grouped things to see and do under the heading of the most convenient tube station, using the ⊖ symbol.

Except in dismally cold wet weather, most people find the buses more pleasant, and of course they allow you to sightsee as you go. One of the first things you do is to get a free London Transport bus map, and spend a bit of time checking out the lie of the land as far as the bus network is concerned, to see which routes are likely to be useful to you. The routes are all numbered, and each bus shows its route number.

A one-day travelcard is an excellent investment for the visitor, and you can even buy them in advance from newsagents. It's valid on both buses and the tube, for as many journeys as you want to make during the day (it does not cover the night buses which run in the small hours, and is not valid during the morning rush hour). A particular joy of this is that you can hop on and off buses for even quite short trips, say just to the end of the road you're in, without bothering about the cost. If you're coming up to London by train, you can add a one-day travelcard to the rail fare at a big discount.

Taxis could scarcely be more convenient, but are expensive for just one or two people: anything except a very short trip will cost £5 or more.

The West End

The area around Covent Garden, Soho, Piccadilly, Mayfair, Regent St and Oxford St is bursting with things to do. There are plenty of interesting places to shop, ranging from the daunting bustle of Oxford St, through the bookshops of and around Charing Cross Rd, the specialist food and cookery shops of Soho, and the elegant stores of Regent St and Piccadilly, to the ultra-smart clothes shops of South Molton St and Bond St. There are great opportunities for window-shopping, too, in the small galleries and auction houses. There's food to suit almost every pocket, and every taste as well: Chinatown has become a particularly vivid enclave, Neal St is a focus for vegetarian restaurants, there are staunchly old-fashioned institutions of Englishness like Rules or Simpsons, and you can find superbly imaginative, less conventional cooking. There are the theatres and cinemas, of course, which this area's name has become virtually synonymous with. And there are some intriguing, tucked-away specialist museums and other places of interest, as well as the great national galleries.

Where to stay

THE CONNAUGHT Carlos Pl W1Y 6AL 071-499 7070; 90 lovely, individually decorated rms. A very special place with fine, old-fashioned values – there's no brochure, and prices are on application; elegant, restful day rooms filled with lovely flowers and antiques, exemplary service, and marvellous food in the two formal restaurants; disabled access.

LE MERIDIEN 21 Piccadilly W1V 0BH 071-734 8000 **£276**; 263 comfortable, well-equipped rms. The very best in modern French hotel-keeping; attractive, quiet public rooms with professional and friendly service, popular afternoon tea, fine restaurant food, and free membership of the good health-club downstairs; one child under 12 free in parents' room.

BROWNS Albemarle St/Dover St W1A 4SW 071-493 6020 **£238.50**; 102 comfortable rms (some at the back have a dull 'view' – say if this matters to you). Fine hotel with panelling, deeply comfortable seats, flowers and antiques in the elegant public rooms, cosy bar, popular afternoon tea (best to book), and good food.

CLARIDGES Brook St W1A 2JQ 071-629 8860 **£220w**; 190 excellent rms. Grand hotel long used by royalty and heads of state; with liveried footmen, lift attendants and valets, elegant and comfortable day rooms, civilised colonnaded foyer where the Hungarian Quartet plays; lovely formal restaurant with mirrored mural and terrace, and more intimate smaller restaurant called the Causerie; complimentary golf at Wentworth and tennis at Vanderbilt Racquet Club; disabled access.

THE LANGHAM HILTON 1 Portland Pl W1N 3AA 071-636 1000 **£217**; 379 rms. Beautifully refurbished Victorian hotel opposite the BBC's Broadcasting House, with many original features, champagne and caviar bar, clubby Chukkha Bar, very good service; free use of gym; disabled access.

SAS PORTMAN 22 Portman Sq W1H 9FL 071-486 5844 **£170.35**; 272 attractive and well-equipped modern rms. Efficiently run, smart hotel with clubby atmosphere, and very friendly service; creative and imaginative cooking in the Truffles restaurant, fine lunch and buffet in the Bakery; afternoon tea in comfortable lobby; disabled access.

THE CUMBERLAND Marble Arch W1A 4RF 071-262 1234 **£140**; 890 comfortable, well-equipped rms. Very well-run, popular hotel with 3 restaurants inc carvery and café and 3 bars; disabled access.

HAZLITTS 6 Frith St W1V 5TZ 071-434 1771 **£135**; 23 rms with 18th- or 19th-c beds and free-standing Victorian baths with early brass shower mixer units. Behind a typically Soho façade of listed early Georgian houses, this is a well-kept and comfortably laid-out little hotel which could scarcely be handier for the West End; good continental breakfasts served in your bedroom, and you can get snacks in the sitting room – lots of restaurants all around; kind, helpful service; cl 25-26 Dec.

ST GEORGE'S Langham Pl W1N 8QS 071-580 0111 ***£135**; 86 light rms with marvellous views over London. Popular hotel, a stone's throw from Oxford Circus, with fine rooftop restaurant and dinner-dance every Fri and Sat; disabled access.

DURRANTS George St W1H 6BJ 071-935 8131 ***£110.50**; 96 well-equipped rms, most with own bthrm; the quietest are at the back. Managed by the same family for over 70 years, this surprisingly quiet, privately owned central hotel, behind a delightful Georgian façade, has fine paintings and antiques, a clubby bar, relaxing lounges; cosy panelled restaurant with essentially English cooking, and helpful, pleasant staff; disabled access.

FIELDING 4 Broad Court WC2B 5QZ 071-836 8305 ***£94.50**; 26 rms, showers. Carefully renovated, well-run, little 18th-c hotel opposite the Royal Opera House and charmingly lit at night by the preserved 19th-c gas lamps; cl 24-26 Dec.

To see and do

⊖ Leicester Sq/Covent Garden
We've grouped these stations together because so many of the things worth seeing in the area can be reached just as easily from either of them. It's always worth being flexible in your tube stops – the gap between stations in the centre is much smaller than it seems on the map, and the walk above ground is always more pleasant. Leicester Sq, particularly, is handy for all manner of places (Covent Garden, Trafalgar Sq, Soho, Charing Cross Rd, Piccadilly . . .) giving it a strong claim to be right at the heart of London. It generally feels like it too – when stuck

for a place to meet, many Londoners settle on one of the exits from the tube station, so there are always people milling around, anxiously looking for the friends they finally discover they've been standing next to for half an hour.

A short walk from Leicester Sq up Cranbourn St and into LONG ACRE brings you to Stanfords, the best map and guidebook shop in Britain, with helpful, knowledgeable staff, as well as books and maps on aspects of London you'd never even dreamed of, not to mention guides and maps for every other part of the country and the world.

COVENT GARDEN Partly pedestrianised, the former vegetable, fruit and flower market with its elegant buildings is now made over to smart café-bars, boutiques and stalls, such as those in the covered PIAZZA, selling good but expensive handmade clothes and craft items. There's also the JUBILEE MARKET which specialises in different wares on different days. The many bars and restaurants are always lively at night, but again they're not cheap.

† ! ST PAUL'S CHURCH, also called the Actors' Church, is full of interesting memorials to stars of stage and screen. Pepys watched the first-ever Punch and Judy show here in 1662. Outside its back gate, facing the covered market, the theatrical tradition continues, with jugglers, clowns, mountebanks and unusual musicians performing on the cobbles. A little way along from here, the Lamb & Flag (Rose St) is an attractive, 300-year-old pub which has a Dickensian feel – even Marley's ghost would feel at home – with decent snacks.

The LONDON TRANSPORT MUSEUM on the site of Covent Garden's Flower Market has been closed for most of 1993 for a complete overhaul, and when it reopens in December 1993 should be much more lively. They promise even more of their collection of original vehicles and related artefacts (it was already pretty comprehensive), with new touch-screen exhibits and videos, some traditional displays and a chance to climb into the driving seat of a bus or tube train – if you're there early enough to grab it. Meals, snacks, interesting shop, disabled access; cl 24-26 Dec; *£4. Attractively housed in another part of the old market buildings, off Russell St, is the THEATRE MUSEUM where a variety of theatre memorabilia, from posters to puppets to props, provide an interesting and lively illustration of events and personalities on the stage. Snacks, shop, disabled access; cl Mon; *£3.50. Knutz nearby has everything for the practical joker.

Just around the corner in CATHERINE ST is Suttons seed shop: you'd never imagine so many different varieties of plant could be grown from seed. WELLINGTON ST behind has Penhaligons, selling lovely old-fashioned toiletries with scents like Bluebell. It leads on into Bow St, where you can't miss the imposing, creamily massive-columned edifice of the OPERA HOUSE; you don't have to pay your £50 a seat to see the great performances here – major events are relayed to a giant screen outside in the Piazza, where you can watch free; five are planned for 1994. The Marquis of Anglesea opposite is quick for food, with a good-value, upstairs restaurant.

North of here interesting and unusual shops are set in a labyrinthine network of attractively rejuvenated alleys and streets; you will get lost, but wandering around is great fun, and they all lead back out into roughly the same area. NEAL ST is rewarding for its small craft and specialist shops, kitchen shops, and NEAL'S YARD, full of healthy living – it's delightful in summer with its fresh paint and tubs of flowers. FLORAL ST has elegant and expensive clothes and shoe shops (don't miss the Tintin shop – from cards to key-rings, paradise for the Tintin fan).

At the bottom, turn right into Garrick St, then left into St Martin's Lane, again with smart little restaurants and cafés, theatres and bars, and various little courts leading off, their shop-windows filled with posters of dancers, rare stamps and postcards, or antique scientific instruments. It's got a splendid Victorian pub, the Salisbury, all velvet and cut glass (and a useful food counter); the Chandos here is also good, with big windows to watch the world go by and food all day. In the early evening this area gives an impression of affluence, coming into its own as a centre of theatrical London, but later at night it shows London's down side – shop fronts crammed with blankets, cardboard boxes and huddled figures sleeping or begging.

A walk past the Coliseum, home of the English National Opera, takes you to the elegant church of St Martin-in-the-Fields with its unmistakeable blue clock-dial – the only clock in this part of London that seems always to keep the right time. There are frequent lunchtime concerts here; phone 071-930 0089 for programme. The crypt has a busy coffee bar, shops and occasional exhibitions. A market at wknds usually has a few bargains. Spreading below the church is Trafalgar Sq, London's most famous square. Designed by Nash early in the 19th c, the square was named for the great naval victory of 1805. Look out for the gifted roller-skaters who perform in the evenings around the base of the central Nelson's Column – and, of course, for the pigeons.

The National Gallery here is quite magnificent. You'll probably enjoy it most if you're firm with yourself and restrict yourself to just a few of the galleries, rather than trying to rush round all of it. It can get very busy, esp when you get to the Impressionists and esp on a Saturday. Don't miss the exciting new Sainsbury Wing, which gives perfect lighting and viewing conditions for its treasure-trove of early Renaissance works. From the steps of the building, a neo-Classical affair opened in 1838, you get one of the best views of London – not just the buildings, but the people and buses at their most vibrant. Meals, snacks, shop, disabled access; cl Sun am, 24-26 Dec, 1 Jan, Good Fri, 1 May.

Just around the corner is the National Portrait Gallery, literally illustrating British history, with paintings of kings, queens and other notable characters arranged in chronological order from the top floor (medieval) to the present. Shop, disabled access; cl Sun am, 24-26 Dec, 1 Jan, Good Fri, 1 May.

Cutting round the back of Trafalgar Sq brings you into pedestrianised Leicester Sq itself, attractively cleaned up in the last few years, with lots of pubs and restaurants. The Swiss Centre on the far corner sells exquisite chocolates and Swiss groceries. The cut-price theatre ticket booth is a collaborative venture involving the major West End theatres themselves, selling surplus tickets cheaply; you'll have to queue, but there's generally a decent choice of shows. There are four huge cinemas.

Running between the striking Charing Cross station and Leicester Sq, Charing Cross Rd is justifiably famous for its bookshops, specialist and general, new and secondhand, inc Foyles (the biggest city bookstore – but trying to find what you want is time-consuming) and Waterstones (very friendly, informed staff, relaxed atmosphere); at the bottom end, the side alleys between here and St Martin's Lane have good secondhand bookshops, several with specialisations such as the occult, antique children's books, or the theatre. Covent Garden Records at the famous address of 84 Charing Cross Rd is excellent for classical CDs.

⊖ **Piccadilly Circus** Another lively hub of London life, with famous streets radiating off in every direction, each quite different in character. The famous statue of EROS, while no longer in the middle of Picadilly Circus, is still where all the foreign students sit to be photographed, despite suggestions it should be replaced by a copy. Big stores on opposite sides of the traffic islands are Tower Records, three floors of pop, classical and jazz (open till midnight); and Lillywhites, the long-established sports clothes and equipment store.

! ROCK CIRCUS (London Pavilion) A lively trip through the history of rock and roll, with wax figures and animated models of stars from Elvis to Bono, and a hi-tech musical accompaniment supplied via headsets. Shop, disabled access; cl Tues am, it's open most nights till 9 or even 10; £6.25. The adjoining Trocadero is rather gaudy, an exception being the GUINNESS WORLD OF RECORDS, which uses videos, life-sized models and the latest audio-technology to bring to life sporting and all sorts of other sometimes quite extraordinary world records. Shop, disabled access; cl 25 Dec; £5.50. The Glassblower in Glasshouse St is handy for lunch.

PICCADILLY stretching westwards from here has some very handsome buildings and fine shops. Simpsons has several floors of good classic British clothes, for men and women. Friendly Hatchards is a nicely old-fashioned bookshop where you can order any book you want in the unlikely event of their not having it in stock; and the staff are very good at turning your vague 'I think it may have had "yellow" in the title, and it's about a stern grandmother' into an actual book. Almost next door, Fortnums (or Fortnum & Mason as people who don't shop there call it) has excellent if expensive clothes, as well as the foods for which they're world-famous. On the other side of the road is the magnificent Burlington House, with the ROYAL ACADEMY OF ARTS, which has excellent, changing exhibitions of international importance during the year, and from Jun to Aug holds its famous (often notorious) Summer Exhibition of works by living artists great and small. Meals, snacks, shop, disabled access by prior arrangement; cl 24-25 Dec, Good Fri; admission charge varies – always a few pounds.

⊖ **Green Park** (also see below) is very handy for this end of the area.

Nearby, the BURLINGTON ARCADE is an elegant Regency covered arcade of expensive but good shops (excellent cashmere and knife/scissors shops, for instance), with a delightful set of rules, still enforced, that stop people whistling, singing or running in its confines. At the far end, Burlington Gardens has the MUSEUM OF MANKIND, its vast and interestingly displayed collections detailing the customs, art and material culture of inhabitants of the non-Western world. It generally consists of a series of changing exhibitions – go back each year and you'll rarely see the same things. Meals, snacks, shop, disabled access; cl Sun am, Christmas, 1 Jan, Good Fri and first Mon in May.

Behind Piccadilly's south side is JERMYN ST, where among other splendid but top-of-the-range shops you can buy fine cheeses at Paxton & Whitfields, briar pipes at Astleys, hand-made shoes at Trickers, hand-made shirts from Turnbull & Asser, flat hats at Bates, and old-fashioned toiletries at Floris. The Red Lion in Duke of York St just off here is a little gem of a pub, with decent snacks (but very busy on wkdy lunchtimes).

HAYMARKET, south from Piccadilly Circus, has smart theatres and the DESIGN CENTRE, with changing exhibitions of modern British products that have won awards for a combination of beauty and efficiency. A landmark here is one of the two branches of Burberrys (the other's in

Regent St), whose characteristic pattern for the linings of their macs, originally such a staple of the prep-school uniform, has so unaccountably become a *sine qua non* of world fashion.

! To the north is SOHO, Georgian terraces that are often rather run-down, with peepshows and naughty video shops stuffed into basements and ground floors, and too many taxis and cars using these narrow streets as rat-runs. But there are parts that have had much of their original quiet charm restored, like SOHO SQ and MEARD ST. And CHINATOWN has developed its own character, inviting despite the locals' obvious complete indifference to outsiders; the supermarkets and shops along pedestrianised GERRARD ST and in neighbouring streets are fascinating, with their weird and wonderful vegetables, strange squidgy things in little cellophane packets, and odd-smelling dried meats and fish. Soho's also still good for restaurants, and excellent for shops connected with food or cooking. OLD COMPTON ST has a good few interesting shops – Italian delicatessens (I Camisa is the best, with fabulous salamis), the Algerian Coffee Store which also sells lots of fruit teas, and two cheap but good wines and spirits shops. Milroys in GREEK ST has a wonderful collection of hundreds of different malt whiskies. Ferraris in WARDOUR ST, the most traffic-plagued of Soho's streets, is excellent for kitchen equipment, particularly knives. BERWICK ST is a daily fruit and vegetable market – the lower half is more expensive but has better produce. The little Dog & Duck in Frith St is one of the nicest Soho locals. ⊖ **Tottenham Court Rd** and **Leicester Sq** are both just as handy for here.

⛫ One of the grandest streets in this whole area is REGENT ST (⊖ **Oxford Circus** or ⊖ **Picadilly Circus**), curving away from Piccadilly Circus and straightening out for its grand run up to Oxford Circus, and beyond to the imposing yet rather bullying bulk of the BBC's BROADCASTING HOUSE. Though there was great controversy when the original Regency buildings were demolished and replaced in the 1910s and 1920s, it now seems a harmonious street of considerable character. The fine shops here definitely enhance its appeal, even if all you want to do is browse. Liberty's is a splendid, art nouveau, timbered building full of gorgeous soft furnishings and clothes, Oriental and leather goods, jewellery, and a good gift department. Other high points inc Mappin & Webb for fine china, glass, and jewellery; Hamleys, a marvellous toy shop (not cheap, though); Aquascutum, great for expensive English classic clothes; Garrards the royal jewellers; and Waterford/ Wedgwood, for lovely china and glass in quite a wide range of prices. The Old Coffee House in Beak St around the corner from here, and the Red Lion in Kingly St, are useful for lunch. CARNABY ST, tucked away behind, has some rather florid men's shops but is mainly full of small boutiques with trendy accessories, leather goods and tacky souvenirs; not really worth seeking out, apart from 1960s nostalgia, though some good street-fashion houses seem to be coming back here.

Busy and noisy OXFORD ST doesn't have a lot of character, but is full of good stores such as Selfridges, John Lewis (the self-service restaurant next to babywear is excellent for lunch), Marks & Spencer (two major outlets), BHS, Debenhams, the two giant music shops HMV and Virgin Megastore, as well as the usual high street shops. Down at the altogether quieter far end of the long street, past Tottenham Court Rd and the eye-catching tower of Centre Point, is James Smith & Sons, a splendid old place full of interesting umbrellas and walking sticks. SOUTH MOULTON ST and ST

CHRISTOPHER'S PLACE on either side of Oxford St are full of designer clothes shops and smart cafés, and are fun to wander along; St Christopher's Place also has quite an interesting antiques market.

⊖ Bond St WALLACE COLLECTION (Hertford House, Manchester Sq) Excellent art collection in an elegant 18th-c house – once used as the Spanish Embassy, and then passing to the Hertford family in 1797. Sir Richard Wallace, the son of the 4th Marquis, bequeathed the incredible paintings to the nation in 1897. It's visually very seductive, with luscious paintings from the French school by Watteau, Boucher and Fragonard, great Canalettos, fine works by Rembrandt, Rubens and Van Dyck, and works by British painters; also furniture – mostly 18th-c French, Sèvres porcelain, Italian majolica, and an amazing array of arms and armour, both Oriental and European. Shop, disabled access with prior warning; cl Sun am, 24-26 Dec, Good Fri, 1 Jan, May Day bank hol.

⊖ Marble Arch is also handy for Oxford St, and for SPEAKERS CORNER in Hyde Park (see also Hyde Park Corner in Knightsbridge section), where every Sun morning you can still hear impassioned diatribes on all sorts of causes – or indeed on nothing at all. This tube station has so many exits it's a real initiative test finding your way out.

⊖ Green Park MAYFAIR west of Regent St and north of Piccadilly (and only the shortest of strolls from them) is mostly a discreet area of elegant town houses, smart, well-established hotels, and the offices of companies which are so prosperous that they don't need to consider accommodation expense – or at least are trying to look that way. It lets its hair down in SHEPHERD MARKET, a lively and colourful place, no longer a market but busy with cafés, decent wine bars, good pubs (the Bunch of Grapes and Kings Arms), and little lanes to wander down. Despite their famous names, Berkeley Sq and Grosvenor Sq don't really have any special appeal to attract the visitor. BOND ST with its continuation New Bond St is the area's main shopping street, and a good place to spend a great deal of money on shoes and designer clothes. It also has plenty of interesting shops to wander around: silver, antique jewellery, Oriental rugs, art and antique galleries, and a good indoor antique market (124 New Bond St). Aspreys is a remarkable place, with the most expensive fantasies created in rich and beautiful materials around the most everyday objects – if you've always wanted a diamond-studded gold and titanium potato-peeler, this is where you're most likely to find it. There are many more conventionally beautiful things here, including luscious antiques. SOTHEBY'S AUCTION ROOMS are fascinating to wander around. Other small and prestigious art galleries are dotted throughout Mayfair, particularly in nearby DOVER ST and CORK ST; Grays antique market off 58 Davies St has hundreds of indoor stalls. SOUTH AUDLEY ST has Hobbs of Mayfair, a delicious, smart delicatessen, and Goodes, a magnificent glass and china shop. Higgins in DUKE ST is Her Majesty the Queen's coffee-man. Good Mayfair pubs are the Red Lion in Waverton St, Audley in Mount St and Guinea in Bruton Pl.

Where to eat

NICO AT NINETY 90 Park Lane W1 071-409 1290 Nico Ladenis is one of the country's best-known chefs, and in this latest venture his legendary food is as sophisticated as ever; cl Sat am, Sun, 23 Dec-2 Jan; children over 7; disabled access. **£60 dinner, lunch £35**. There's also NICO CENTRAL 35 Great Portland St W1 071-436 8846; cl Sat am, Sun, 23 Dec-2 Jan. **£30**; and SIMPLY NICO 48a Rochester Row SW1 071-630 8061 – same closing hours. **£23.**

ALASTAIR LITTLE 49 Frith St W1 071-734 5183 Beautifully presented, imaginative modern cooking in very popular, unpretentious restaurant; fine wines; cl Sat am, Sun, bank hols. **£45**|£13.

MIYAMA 38 Clarges St W1 071-499 2443 Restful Japanese restaurant with carefully prepared, delicious food served by courteous, efficient staff in national costume – a favourite with Japanese over here; downstairs are private rooms, and teppan-yaki counter; cl Christmas, New Year, bank hols; disabled access. **£37 dinner**; the **set lunches** are extremely good value at around **£18.**

GAY HUSSAR 2 Greek St W1 071-437 0973 Hungarian restaurant still popular with literati and publishers even though most have moved out of Soho, with bags of atmosphere and generous helpings of good, authentic food; cl Sun, bank hols. **£31.50**|£12.

SIMPSON'S 100 The Strand WC2 071-836 9112 Marvellously old-fashioned place with traditional English cooking inc nursery puddings, and roasts carved as you want them at your table on silver-domed trolleys; all very decorous, the surroundings and atmosphere more memorable than the food; cl 25-28 Dec, 1 Jan, disabled access. **£30**|£13.50.

RULES 35 Maiden Lane WC2 071-836 5314 Smart, very British, old restaurant, very popular with the Establishment, serving extremely good English food inc game and oysters in season; cl 24-28 Dec. **£30**|£12.75.

BISTROT BRUNO 63 Frith St W1 071-734 4545 Extremely good innovative food in delightfully decorated restaurant – lots of reworking of traditional dishes and fine fresh fish; cl Sat am, Sun, 24 Dec-2 Jan. **£25**|£10.

CORK & BOTTLE 44-46 Cranbourn St WC2 071-734 6592 Popular basement wine bar (now open till midnight), with good food inc interesting salads and unusual hot dishes; cheerful service, and very good wines – esp Australian; open all day Sun; cl 25 Dec, 1 Jan. **£22**|£3.25.

RASA SAYANG 10 Frith St W1 071-734 8720 Consistently reliable Malaysian/Singaporean restaurant with good-value, freshly cooked food; cl Sat am. **£21**|£5.70.

MON PLAISIR 21 Monmouth St WC2 071-836 7243 Good-value, well-prepared French food in busy bistro, popular for pre-theatre meals; cl Sat am, all day Sun, bank hols; partial disabled access. **£20, set lunch £13.95**|£10.

TAPPIT HEN 5 William IV St London WC2 071-836 9839 Cosy and atmospheric little wine bar, very old-fashioned feeling, with good snacks and good-value wines – excellent for quick, pre-theatre light supper (the smoked salmon sandwiches are lovely) or lunch; there's also a downstairs restaurant; cl Sat, Sun, bank hols, no children. **£19.50**|£3.15/£6.30.

MUSEUM OF MANKIND CAFÉ, Café de Colombia 6 Burlington Gdns W1 071-287 8148 Smart, no-smoking café with freshly prepared food inc fine coffee and morning/afternoon cakes; cl evenings, Sun, bank hols. **£16.50**|£2.40/£5.95.

I VESPRI 33 Southampton St WC2 071-379 7585 Comfortable and as thoroughly Italian as you'd want; cl Sun, bank hols; disabled access. **£14**|£1.80/£6.

GABYS 30 Charing Cross Rd WC2 071-836 4233 Ideal for a quick snack before the theatre, with promptly served, perfect salt beef sandwiches and other good snacks, generous wine, too; very friendly, popular with actors. **£12.60**|£2.10/£4.70.

POONS 27 Lisle St WC2 071-437 4549 WC2 Atmospheric, unlicensed and unmodernised Chinese restaurant with extremely good-value, tasty food; cl Good Fri, 24-26 Dec; late opening Sun till 5.15. **£12.60**|£1.35/£5.25. Other branches (more modern and expensive) at 4 Leicester St WC2 071-437 1528 and 41 King St WC2 071-240 1743.

CAFÉ IN THE CRYPT St Martin-in-the-Fields, Trafalgar Sq WC2 Sq 071-839 4342 Good, freshly prepared food as well as a shop, art gallery (frequent exhibitions) and brass-rubbing centre; cl Sun, Maundy Thurs, Good Fri, 25 Dec, 1 Jan pm; disabled access. **£10.75**|£2.50/£5.50.

FORTNUM & MASON 181 Piccadilly W1 071-734 8040 On the corner of the famous store, with separate entrance, the Fountain Restaurant with its attractive murals is spacious, airy and very civilised – the perfect place for tea (though they also do good breakfasts and brunch); cl Sun, Good Fri, Easter Sun, 25-26 Dec, bank hols; disabled access. £8.95.

POLLO 20 Old Compton St W1 071-734 5917 Cheap and very crowded basement, serving good Italian food; cl Sun, 25 Dec. **£7.35**|£1.35/£3.15.

AROMA St Martin's Lane W1 071-730 7734 Fashionable, bright little café, serving exceptionally good coffee; hand-painted crockery on sale; cl 25 Dec, 1 Jan. **£6.80**|£1.15.

FOOD FOR THOUGHT 31 Neal St WC2 071-836 0239 Long-established and consistently good, unlicensed vegetarian restaurant with take-away service upstairs and communal eating at long tables downstairs – you can now also eat at tables outside; special discounts between 3-5pm for students, OAPs and unemployed; no corkage; cl 24 Dec-1 Jan; partial disabled access. **£6**|£2.50/£2.

BUNJIE'S COFFEE HOUSE 27 Litchfield St WC2 071-240 1796 Cosy basement café with good vegetarian food; cl Sun. £3.15/£4.14.

WESTMINSTER

Westminster, the site of the Court and the seat of government, has plenty to see related to the long and varied history of both monarchy and government. It's a pleasant area to walk around, much of it with only light traffic, and with few shops to add extra people to the wide pavements. Two parks bring a further feeling of space, and add an attractive longer perspective to the grandeur of the buildings themselves.

Where to stay

ROYAL HORSEGUARDS THISTLE 2 Whitehall Court SW1 4HP 071-839 3400 **£130.50**; 376 spacious rms. Comfortable hotel ideally placed for the area's sights, with elegant public rooms and a fine marbled entrance; foyer, coffee shop, bar and restaurant; disabled access.

EBURY COURT 24-32 Ebury St SW1W 0LU 071-730 8147 *£100; 42 cosy rms, most with own bthrm. Small, charmingly old-fashioned hotel made up – as you'd guess from the address – of several town houses; with friendly atmosphere, attractive lounges, good food in the elegant restaurant, and decent wines; cl 22 Dec-4 Jan; disabled access.

To see and do

St James's Park ST JAMES'S ST, running down to St James's Palace, has more gentlemen's clubs than shops, and those there are are very upmarket indeed: cigar shops, hand-made shoes at Lobbs, hats at Locks, and fine wines at Berrys, or Berry Bros & Rudd to give it its full name. It's well worth a visit, the only shop in London still to look both inside and out just as it did in the early 19th c; and they are very helpful even if you want just one humble bottle. Just around the corner, KING ST has Spinks with wonderful antiques and antiquities to drool over, as well as CHRISTIE'S AUCTION GALLERIES just across the road, and some other interesting top-of-the-market antique and book shops nearby, up Duke St for instance. Off King St, the Red Lion in Crown Passage is a useful and friendly pub for a snack. At the far end of King St is gracious ST JAMES'S SQ, with a peaceful central garden and often a man who'll wash cars while they're parked on the meters.

Walking down St James's St, most streets to the right will take you to GREEN PARK, the smallest of the parks in Central London. It is not a formal garden but, watered by the Tyburn stream which runs below the park, does stay genuinely green in summer when London's other grassy spaces are getting dry and dusty. At its top end is the relentless torrent of traffic around Hyde Park Corner; you can cross by subway, for a look at the Duke of Wellington's elegant APSLEY HOUSE, and at the engaging and glittering neo-baroque gates recently erected in honour of the Queen Mother on the edge of Hyde Park behind it.

PALL MALL has yet more gentlemen's clubs in very stately buildings; and, at opposite ends, Hardys the fishing shop, and Farlows, fishing too – but also almost anything you might need for that expedition up the Limpopo or into the Gobi Desert. There's a first-class antiquarian bookshop along here; and tucked away between here and St James's Park are the discreetly imposing and impregnable Establishment cliffs of CARLTON HOUSE TERRACE – often a place to find a parking space when everywhere else is full.

Parallel to Pall Mall, with three splendid cuts through (past St James's Palace at the bottom of St James's St, down the stately ceremonial steps at the end of Lower Regent St, or past the magnificent ADMIRALTY ARCH), is THE MALL, the 3,412-ft-long ceremonial route laid out from 1660 by Charles II, with St James's Park on one side, and a grand line of buildings on the other. These inc ICA with cinemas and galleries devoted to contemporary arts, and a wonderful little informal restaurant and bar (see below); this is an excellent place to spend an afternoon, and possibly the evening as well. THE MALL GALLERIES Eight art societies administered by the Federation of British Artists exhibit interesting and varied work, with other displays by independent individuals and groups. Disabled access; may close when exhibitions are changing; *£2.

Looking down The Mall you'll see one of the most famous views in the world – towards the relatively recent frontage of BUCKINGHAM PALACE, now opened to the public for the first time. For years people have stood staring expectantly through the gates that guard the palace, and now at last they can do the same from the other side. The main attraction is that this is where the Queen actually lives – it's her official London residence, and where she meets other heads of State; the Royal Standard flies above it when she's there. But beyond that, it does pile a magnificent series of opulent sights into your walk through the state rooms; it's definitely somewhere that repays a bit of homework before you go, so that you know the background to some of the things you're going to see. Surprisingly, it's not a guided tour: you can theoretically take your own pace through the 18 different areas open to visitors, though in practice you're likely to be carried along in the stream of other people. You enter the great inner courtyard through the Ambassadors Entrance: this courtyard is itself a surprise, in many ways more genuinely majestic and certainly more elegant than the familiar, more modern façade. Once up the spectacular Grand Staircase you are into the throne room and other chambers of state where the predominant impression is of gold, red and splendour. The highlight for many is the beautiful Picture Gallery, 150 ft long and filled with priceless master paintings from the royal collection. The range of rooms following this, overlooking the garden (and perhaps a glimpse of a full-dressed footman walking corgis), were designed by Nash, and have plenty of interesting and even ironic touches. Finally, you get a chance to walk round the edge of the garden, keeping to a covered walkway. It's not been decided yet how entrance will be organised in 1994 – in 1993 a few thousand tickets were sold each day from a little booth on the corner of St James's Park, with each ticket restricted to a certain time to avoid overcrowding, and sales limited to no more than four tickets for each person in the queue. This year you may be able to get them in advance – phone 071-930 5526 for details. Shop, disabled access (and advanced booking for disabled); open Aug-Sept; £8. The former chapel of the palace is now the QUEEN'S GALLERY, showing a changing selection of more of the magnificent paintings and other works of art from the royal collection. Shop; cl Sun am, all day Mon, Jan and Feb; £2.50. The ROYAL MEWS lets you view the State Coaches, private driving carriages and even sleighs of the royal family, as well as the immaculately turned out Windsor greys and Cleveland bay carriage horses. Shop, disabled access; open pm Weds 6 Jan-22 Dec, pm Tues and Thurs Apr-Sept; £2.50.

You can also reach the palace very easily from ⊖ Victoria (and ⇌ main line station), and if you're coming this way, the Grouse & Claret in Little Chester St, Belgravia, is a civilised place for a light lunch. Perhaps the best approach of all, though, is from Parliament Sq through St James's Park.

! ⛫ ❀ Outside the palace the CHANGING OF THE GUARD can be seen daily at 11.30 am. Another good vantage point for this is outside the altogether more domestic-looking and much older ST JAMES'S PALACE. This was built on the site of a leper hospital by Henry VIII, and parts of the original building still remain, inc the gatehouse. Charles I spent his last night here before walking down to Whitehall to meet his fate. Much of the palace comprises apartments of the royal family, and it's not open to the public. Between the palace and Whitehall is ST JAMES'S PARK, which has undergone a variety of facelifts in its long history. The oldest of the royal parks in London, it was drained and converted into a deer park by Henry VIII, redesigned in the style of Versailles by order of Charles II (who often went for walks through it), and then recreated by Nash for George IV – this is the park which we see today, its relaxing lakeside environment particularly enjoyed by lunch-breaking office workers.

✝ ⛑ ⊖ **Westminster** It was Edward the Confessor who first transformed what had been a tiny Roman settlement into one of major and enduring importance by building WESTMINSTER ABBEY. His body now lies in the great shrine of the present building, which was erected in the 13th c on the site of his original, and is surely one of the most impressive pieces of architecture to survive from the Middle Ages. It looks better at the moment than it has for a very long time, with restoration and clean-ups revealing its full glory. Although constructed over a period of about a century, the original design was adhered to throughout, so that, with its huge rose window and flying buttresses, this church is closer in design to French Gothic architecture than any other English church. Look out for the superb 13th-c sculpture – for example the angels high in the transepts, and the arcading around the walls in the Chapel of St Faith. As well as Edward the Confessor, pretty much every king and queen up to George II is buried here; the chapel for Henry VII is particularly impressive, and there are splendid tombs erected by James I for his mother Mary, Queen of Scots, and his predecessor Elizabeth I, under whose orders Mary had been executed. Perhaps it's in revenge for this that Elizabeth was lumped in with her sister Mary I, with whom she never got on. Other notable historical and literary figures are here too, from Chaucer to Handel (both in the loosely named Poets' Corner) – it's great fun to stroll through the hushed hall peering at the tombs, plaques and effigies. Hawksmoor designed the harmonious addition of the west towers, working on them from 1735-40. Don't miss the precincts and cloisters, shared with Westminster School: great tranquillity, and the sense of unchanging values in contrast to the flickering mutability of political expediency over the road in Parliament. Shop, disabled access (but not to Henry VII chapel); royal chapels cl Sun. If you're interested in history the museum in the crypt underneath shouldn't be missed – it has effigies of many ancestors of the royal family made from their death masks, and often wearing their own clothes; £1. ST MARGARET'S CHURCH nearby is worth a look too – Sir Walter Raleigh is buried here.

🏛 Until Henry VIII moved to Whitehall Palace in 1529, the HOUSES OF PARLIAMENT were the main residence of the monarch, and this is why this building is often referred to as the Palace of Westminster. The present building is the result of an architectural competition held in 1834 after a catastrophic fire destroyed the original medieval palace. It stands 940 ft long and covers eight acres, with the lofty Victorian Tower at one end – which flies the Union Jack when Parliament is in session – and at the other end the clock tower which contains BIG BEN. The Gothic detail which has given so much life to what would otherwise be rather a tiresomely deadpan Classical façade is by Pugin. Inside there are over two miles of passages which link the central hall and two chambers – the House of Lords and Commons to the north and south of the building respectively; queue 5.30 Mon-Thurs or 9.30 Fri for entrance to the Strangers' Galleries – or at any time if you have a letter from your MP. Meals, snacks, shop, disabled access. A letter from your MP can also give access to what's called the Line of Route, going through both Houses, and the Members' Lobby and Divisions Lobby, to WESTMINSTER HALL, from 1224-1882 the chief law court of the country. It witnessed such trials as those of Sir Thomas More and Charles I. It's worth going to the trouble to see inside, even just to admire the magnificent hammer-beam roof, the earliest surviving example of its kind.

Heading up Whitehall towards Trafalgar Sq, the CABINET WAR ROOMS (King Charles St) are a series of 21 rooms built to provide Sir Winston Churchill, the War Cabinet and his Chiefs of Staff with a safe place from which to plan their strategies during WWII. The Cabinet Room, Map Room and Prime Minister's Room have all been preserved as they were at the end of the war, while other rooms have been restored to their original appearance; authentic sound-effects. Shop, disabled access; cl 24-26 Dec, 1 Jan; £3.80.

BANQUETING HOUSE (Whitehall) This is the only surviving part of the Palace of Whitehall, designed by Inigo Jones and built in 1619; it was a royal residence until late that century. The present hall was erected after a fire, and has a sumptuous interior with a gorgeous ceiling painted by Rubens. Charles I was executed here, and symbolically it was also the site of his son's restoration. Shop, some disabled access; cl Sun, and sometimes cl at short notice for State occasions – tel 071-930 4179 to check; *£2.75.

! While you're walking up Whitehall, stop to admire the CENOTAPH – the national memorial to the dead of both world wars, designed by Sir Edward Lutyens. You won't be allowed into DOWNING ST, where the Prime Minister lives at No 10 and the Chancellor of the Exchequer at No 11, but you can at least have a passing look at its surprisingly modest buildings. At HORSE GUARDS PARADE, the daily spectacle is the changing of the Queen's Life Guard, on their splendid black horses; at 11 am Mon-Sat and 10 am Sun. A useful nearby pub is the Westminster Arms in Storey's Gate – popular with politicians and civil servants.

† ⊖ **Victoria** A detour from the glassy cliffs of Victoria St brings you to the Byzantine splendour of the Roman Catholic WESTMINSTER CATHEDRAL, with the best views over Central London from its tall tower. There are some interesting mosaics and marblework inside, as well as Eric Gill's *Vision of the Cross*. Behind here you'll find VINCENT SQ, where the ROYAL HORTICULTURAL SOCIETY has regular flower shows filled with beautifully arranged displays by specialist nurserymen; phone 071-828 1744 for information. At other times their halls are often used for other exhibitions.

⊖ **Pimlico** TATE GALLERY (Millbank) Designed in Classical style to house the collection of Sir Henry Tate, the sugar refiner, and now containing the national collection of British art. It covers all important British artists for the past 450 years, with a large number of works by Turner and Constable; also annually changing displays, and plenty of contemporary sculpture. The collection has been enlarged this century to embrace foreign 20th-c art, esp French Impressionists and Post-Impressionists. Major displays for 1994 inc exhibitions of Picasso (Feb-Apr), R B Kitaj (Jun-Aug) and Whistler (Oct-Jan 1995). Meals, snacks, shop, disabled access; cl Sun am, 24-26 Dec, 1 Jan, Good Fri, May Day bank hol. Though the Tate Gallery restaurant is a particularly good one, you might find the Morpeth Arms nearby useful, with its views of the stunning new MI6 building across the river.

Where to eat

TATE GALLERY Millbank SW1 071-834 6754 Smart and upmarket restaurant with fine range of traditional dishes as well as some imaginative ones; good classic wine list; cl Sun and evenings, 24-26 Dec, 1 Jan, Good Fri, May Day; disabled access. **£25.25|£7.50.**

KEN LO'S MEMORIES OF CHINA 67 Ebury St SW1 071-730 7734 Fine Chinese food in attractively simple restaurant, with interesting set menus and courteous staff; cl Sun am, bank hols; disabled access. **£25|£8.**

FOOTSTOOL RESTAURANT St John's Smith Sq SW1 071-222 2779 Converted church in pleasant political square, offering good, interesting food in the crypt; chamber music most evenings upstairs, also some lunchtimes; restaurant evenings only (cl alternate Thurs); cl wknd am. **£20|£6.**

ICA The Mall SW1 071-930 0493 Informal, serve-yourself restaurant with short choice of good-value, honest food; cl 24 Dec for 2 wks, disabled access. **£9.45|£1.60.**

EBURY WINE BAR 139 Ebury St SW1 071-730 5447 Good imaginative food in bustling wine bar. **£4.20/£7.85.**

KNIGHTSBRIDGE, CHELSEA AND KENSINGTON

This area is one of contrasts – to the west are the looming Victorian façades of the various great museums and the splendid beauty of the former royal apartments of Kensington Palace, while to the south-east a placid network of clean-cut, subdued Georgian terraced houses suddenly gives way to the ostentatious bustle of the Kings Rd. The shopping opportunities vary as widely, from the elegant materialism of Harrods to the hubbub of the Portobello Rd market, with a liberal dose of interesting and unusual antique shops.

Where to stay

CONRAD Chelsea Harbour SW10 0XG 071-823 3000 **£195**; 160 suites with a spacious, light living room area, current hardback novels, and free caviar where other hotels give you a couple of biscuits. American-owned, Europe's first purpose-built, luxury 'suite hotel' is tucked away in the quiet modern enclave of the Chelsea Harbour development and overlooks its small marina; good food served in the Brasserie (harbour views) or the Long Gallery, friendly service, evening pianist, and health club; disabled access.

BASIL STREET HOTEL 8 Basil St SW3 1AH 071-581 3311 **£177.70**; 100 pleasant, decent-sized rms. Handy for Harrods and Hyde Park, this privately owned Edwardian hotel has a relaxed atmosphere, antiques and paintings in the public rooms, a panelled restaurant with reliably good food, a cellar wine bar, coffee shop and ladies' club; helpful, courteous service.

L'HOTEL 28 Basil St SW3 1AT 071-589 6286 ***£125**; 12 well-equipped rms. Small, family-owned, French-style city hotel, close to Harrods and above the neatly kept, well-run Metro wine bar where English and continental breakfasts are served, as well as good, modern French café food; friendly staff; disabled access.

To see and do

High St Kensington
KENSINGTON PALACE (Kensington Gardens) A once-humble town house remodelled by Sir Christopher Wren and then enlarged by William Kent. The birthplace of Queen Victoria and principal private royal residence until the death of George II, it's now the London home of the Princess of Wales, Princess Margaret and Prince and Princess Michael of Kent. Some of the rooms are quite magnificent, with elaborate furnishings, decor and *trompe l'oeil* (the domed ceiling is effective, though the cognoscenti don't consider this anything like the best), while others are interesting for their comparatively restrained understatement – and a couple of the older ones could even be described as downright poky. Make sure you look up at the ceilings: some are exquisitely painted (a couple of the patterns transfer very nicely to stationery in the gift shop). Also pictures and furniture from the royal collection, and the court dress collection with changing displays of the many magnificent costumes worn at royal ceremonies since 1750. The guides are very friendly and know their stuff. Snacks, shop, disabled access to ground floor only; *£3.90. The palace is set in lovely gardens, themselves worth a wander, if less lush than neighbouring Hyde Park. There's a toy boats lake, playground, a fetching statue of Peter Pan and a tree trunk carved with all sorts of little painted animals. On a sunny day you could be forgiven for thinking you'd stumbled on a beach club, as the grass is covered with prone bodies soaking up the radiation.

Further up KENSINGTON HIGH ST the COMMONWEALTH INSTITUTE is an excellent place to learn about the history, landscapes, crafts and people of the Commonwealth, with three floors of uniquely designed galleries divided into sections for each of the 50 countries. It can be a bit dry, and younger children probably won't find too much to amuse themselves, but it's astonishingly comprehensive, and if you allow enough time to explore properly – quite fascinating; also temporary exhibitions. Meals, snacks, shop, disabled access; cl Sun am. Behind it down Holland Walk is HOLLAND PARK, one of London's least-known open spaces, a wooded park with peacocks, summer open-air theatre, and an airy restaurant. Nearer the tube station, there are jolly clothes and street-fashion markets: Hyper Hyper is smart and designerish, Kensington Market more bohemian to say the least; cl Sun. Good food pubs in this area inc the Britannia (Allen St), Scarsdale Arms (Edwardes Sq), and (a walk up Kensington Church St, which has some interesting antique shops) the Churchill Arms – surprisingly good Thai food.

South Kensington
VICTORIA & ALBERT MUSEUM (Cromwell Rd) Britain's national museum of art and design is one of the finest in the world; it was founded in 1851 by Prince Albert, and houses all manner of decorative arts, from Oriental carpets to Italian sculpture to fine jewellery. The galleries run to over seven miles, so whatever *objets* are your own particular interest, you should find superb examples of them here, on the way to find them passing tantalising collections devoted to subjects you didn't even know existed. While children like the Great Bed of Ware dating from the 16th c, a current favourite with adults is the Toshiba Gallery of Japanese art, and other highlights are the world's greatest collection of Constables, and a splendid collection of dresses from the 17th c on. Temporary exhibitions during 1994 will focus on Fabergé and Pugin. Meals, snacks, shop, disabled access; cl am Mon; donations. Nearby

the Roman Catholic Brompton Oratory has a heavy magnificence, sombre despite the pallor of its marble. Beside it the gardens of Holy Trinity Brompton lead you into a very peaceful corner of residential London, with a decent pub in Ennismore Mews (the Ennismore Arms, which does Sun lunches).

Natural History Museum (Cromwell Rd) Here you can feel what it's like to be in the womb, see creepy-crawlies clambering all over the place, or meet a life-size blue whale. The whole place has been very successfully jazzed up in recent years, and everyone who goes gets a real kick out of it. This was where everyone used to go to see the dinosaurs, and they're still at the forefront of that fad, with a new high-tech exhibition that even has robotic versions of the monsters. The elaborate Romanesque building, which covers four acres, also houses the Earth Galleries, containing the largest exhibition on basic earth science in the world, inc a piece of the moon (entrance in Exhibition Rd – but one ticket covers both museums). Meals, snacks, shop, disabled access; cl 24-26 Dec, 1 Jan, Good Fri, May Day bank hol; *£4.50. Science Museum (Exhibition Rd) Like its neighbour, this is a museum you shouldn't have any trouble getting children interested in. It covers all aspects of science and industry, with over 600 working exhibits, inc the very successful Launch Pad, a high-tech interactive gallery where you can have great fun carrying out your own experiments. Exhibits elsewhere range from Stephenson's *Rocket* to the Apollo 10 space capsule, with lively displays on food, flight and pharmaceuticals. Various temporary exhibitions and special events like their all-night camp-ins. Meals, snacks, shop, disabled access; *£4.

The Royal Albert Hall in Kensington Gore is the home of the summer Promenade Concerts, and many other concerts throughout the year; finished in 1871, this huge oval arena was built in honour of Prince Albert. Below the massive metal and glass domed roof is a terracotta frieze which shows the progress of Man in the arts and sciences throughout the ages. Before modern technology got to grips with its acoustics, the hall used to be famous for its echo – it was said that this was the only hall where it was possible to hear the works of modern composers twice. Across the road should be the Albert Memorial, but it's rather pointlessly covered up at the moment, and we could find no-one prepared to say if or when it will be properly restored.

⊖ **Knightsbridge** Harrods is a wonderful place to browse, and has most things anyone could want – there's even a personal shopper available to help you choose. But it's the food halls that visitors to London really enjoy; they're divided up into fruit and vegetables, an interesting delicatessen, grocery, meat, poultry, fish (the display of fresh fish at the end of the room is legendary), bread and cakes, flowers, and wines – and the downstairs pantry is not as expensive as you might think. The Scotch House, almost opposite, is not cheap but does have lovely cashmeres, fine woollens, kilts and so forth; tucked away just behind in Montpelier Sq is a good quiet dining pub, the King George IV. Harvey Nichols is a stylish department store, strong on classic English clothes and high fashion. Sloane St stretching down from here starts with a run of very expensive shops – chic clothes shops and jewellers. Then there's a long stretch by the private but attractively laid out Cadogan Place gardens before nearing Sloane Sq (see below). In Knightsbridge itself, the Paxtons Head has decent food upstairs, and in the handsome terraces on the far side of Sloane St can be found the charming little Grenadier (Wilton Row; no food in the bar, but a snug little restaurant) and the useful Nags

Head (Kinnerton St).

❀ ▣ ⛴ ⊖ **Hyde Park Corner** HYDE PARK This 340-acre park used to be a royal hunting park, and in 1851 it was used as the site of the Great Exhibition. In the grounds of the park near the boating lake is the SERPENTINE GALLERY, which often has interesting exhibitions concentrating on younger contemporary artists; it has a fine reputation for its choice of sculptural and allied arts; phone 071-402 6075 to hear what's on. You can hire boats on the lake (£5.50 an hour), or even swim in parts of it.

⊖ **Sloane Sq** The heart of Chelsea, with Peter Jones, the mecca of the Sloanes, on the square itself (a sister department store of John Lewis, it's good value for money). Just around the corner, the Antelope in Eaton Terrace is a useful lunch stop. The bottom end of Sloane St has two interesting though expensive shops: Partridges, a fancy food shop; and the General Trading Company, for a fine collection of oddities, besides stylish kitchenware, soft-furnishings, antiques, glass and so forth. Sloane Sq's most famous offshoot is the KINGS RD: not what it used to be, and a few places are now standing empty, though it's still possible to find some really individual clothes and shoe shops, and three good antique markets (Chenil Galleries has some fine specialist stalls; the other two go further down the price range but have interesting stuff). Off to the left is CARLYLE'S HOUSE (NT) (Cheyne Row), the home of the writer from 1834 till his death, with lots of letters and personal possessions, and an early piano played by Chopin. Cl Mon (exc bank hols), Tues, all Nov-Mar; £2.80. Down at the far end, and on into the NEW KINGS RD, an interesting series of specialised antique shops and shops selling books and maps, with unexpected treasures in the way of lovely old clocks, model ships (some 6 ft long), garden furniture and ornaments going back to the 16th c, and two shops specialising expensively but magnificently in mirrors; there's also Christopher Wray's enormous lighting shop which largely fuelled the vogue in Tiffany-style lamps and has almost any sort of lamp fitting you could possibly want. On the way, refresh yourself at Henry J Beans (197 Kings Rd; a rather stylish American-style bar with good quick snacks), La Bersagliera (a pleasantly clattery, matriarch-run pizza house just past Beaufort St) or the Sporting Page (Camera Pl/Limerston St).

⛫ Going from Sloane Sq towards the river, a little way south of the square, off the bottom of Lower Sloane St, the PIMLICO RD has an interesting collection of antique and other small shops (and Peter's Restaurant, a very good-value, all-day Italian-run café which has been a taxi-drivers' haunt for 20 years or more). The Orange Brewery here is a pub with attached pie shop, brewing its own beers. Keeping on along to Ebury Bridge brings you to a classic photographic view of BATTERSEA POWER STATION, beyond a sinuous network of railway lines.

⛫ ⚱ ❀ ✝ In the opposite direction, the Royal Hospital Rd passes the ROYAL HOSPITAL, Christopher Wren's most glorious secular building, which still houses some 400 Chelsea Pensioners; cl lunchtime, Sat am, Sun (though you can go to the full dress service in chapel at 11 am on Sun). Further along is the NATIONAL ARMY MUSEUM, surprisingly little visited but well and honestly presented – the history of the men of the British, Indian and Colonial armies from 1485, with displays in chronological order of militaria, photographs, uniforms, prints and other mementoes. There are pictures of battle scenes and of the Indian regiments, as well as portraits by Gainsborough and Reynolds, with a new gallery on the Victorian army opening at the end of 1993. Snacks, shop, disabled access; cl 24-26 Dec, 1 Jan, Good Fri, May Day bank hol. The MUSEUM OF THE WOMEN'S ROYAL

ARMY CORPS is soon to be incorporated into this museum; snacks, shop, disabled access. Nearby is the CHELSEA PHYSIC GARDEN – if you're tired of the braying crowds of Chelsea, take refuge here. A real haven of peace, it was started in 1673 and forms the second-oldest botanic garden in the country. Its aim was to provide and study the plants used in medicine by the Society of Apothecaries, and by the late 18th c it was famous for its rare and unusual plants. It's still used for botanical and medicinal research, but is also full of lovely and unusual plants which thrive here in Thames-side London's warm microclimate, inc an ancient, fruiting olive tree. Snacks, shop, disabled access; open pm Weds and Sun Apr-Oct; £2.50. Where the road joins the river embankment, near the elegant CHELSEA OLD CHURCH, streets up on the right take you quickly to two very good pubs, the Cross Keys (Lawrence St) and Front Page (Old Church St; particularly good food).

CHELSEA HARBOUR A monument to the recession, this smart waterside shopping centre is like a ghost town, with untenanted shops and little action except for popular Deal's Restaurant and the Canteen (see below), and the cheerfully relaxed Matt's café. Children like the glass-sided lifts which swoop up into the big dome; there's also a marina. On Sun afternoons they often have jazz.

⊖ **Fulham Broadway** is the best station for the clutch of good-value antique shops towards the bottom end of Fulham Rd (or you can cut quickly through from the far end of the Kings Rd); and for the unfrequented, rather melancholic tranquillity of the somewhat overgrown BROMPTON CEMETERY near them. The Fox & Pheasant in Billing Rd is a very pleasant pub, for a break. The station is also handy for Chelsea Football Club, and Chelsea Harbour (see above) is not too far away.

Where to eat

TANTE CLAIRE 68 Royal Hospital Rd SW3 071-352 6045 Exceptionally fine, modern French cooking in Pierre Koffmann's stylish restaurant – the lunchtime set menu is good value and very popular; courteous service, and some good-value French country wines; jacket and tie are required; cl wknds, Christmas and New Year; children over 8. **£64 dinner, lunch £24.50.**

BIBENDUM 81 Fulham Rd SW3 071-581 5817 Housed in the carefully renovated old Michelin building, this is a light, spacious and fashionable restaurant with excellent and enjoyable, robust French food – it's more elaborate in the evening; the downstairs oyster bar is very popular too. **£60 dinner, lunch set menu £25.**

MR WING 242 Old Brompton Rd SW5 071-370 4450 Opulent, impressive surroundings with plants and aquarium and very good Chinese food. **£35.**

BLUE ELEPHANT 4-6 Fulham Broadway SW6 071-385 6595 Luxurious Thai food eaten amongst waterfalls and exotic jungle greenery, with produce flown in weekly from Thailand; the set meals are better value; cl Sun am, 24-26 Dec; disabled access. **£35, buffet lunch £19.50|£8.95.**

CANTEEN Chelsea Harbour SW10 071-351 7330 Airy and rather functional inside, but pleasantly so, and informal, with your money clearly going on food quality – which is excellent – instead of extra waiters or excessively plush surroundings; you may spot other trendy restaurateurs sitting chatting to the boss, Marco White. **£30|£10.**

BOMBAY BRASSERIE Courtfield Close Courtfield Rd SW7 071-370 4444 Big restaurant and conservatory with grand, colonial-style furnishings; very good Indian food using recipes from all over India (lots of vegetarian dishes), and courteous, helpful staff; it's cheaper at lunchtime when there's a buffet; cl 25-26 Dec; disabled access. **£30**|£9.50.

CHUTNEY MARY 535 Kings Rd SW10 071-351 3113 Interesting Anglo-Indian food in light conservatory and two dining rooms, also a bar; buffet only Sun; disabled access. **£29**|£3.25/£9.50.

BILL BENTLEYS Beauchamp Pl SW3 071-589 5080 Though there's a decent upstairs fish restaurant, the nicest place is the crowded little bar, very popular with well-off local residents for good wine, highly individual service and choice nibbles such as fresh ham or oysters; cl Sun and bank hols. **£26.25**|£5.25.

WODKA 12 St Albans Grove W8 071-937 6513 There's a choice of 13 vodkas to accompany the authentic Polish food at this simple, pleasant restaurant; cl Sat am, Sun pm, bank hols. **£25**|£3/£7.

SAN FREDIANO 62 Fulham Rd SW3 071-584 8375 Consistently good (and very popular) Italian food with lots of interesting daily specials; cl Sun, bank hols. **£23.50**|£7.

JULIE'S 137 Portland Rd W11 071-727 7985 Well run and most attractively decorated, long-standing wine bar with lots of different sitting areas, antiques, lovely flowers and plants; good, imaginative food, and friendly service; cl 4 days Christmas, 3 days Easter; **£22.75, set lunch/9.95**|£7.95.

DEALS Chelsea Harbour SW10 071-352 5887 Bustling café-restaurant with good food ranging from hamburgers to sizzle platters and some Far Eastern touches (the Japanese vinaigrette is recommended and the prawns are heavenly), generous glasses of decent house wine, good cocktails, and very friendly service; best at lunchtime when it's less frenetic; cl 24 Dec pm, 25-26 Dec, 1 Jan; great for children – esp Sun – when they have magician going from table to table, plus face-painter; disabled access. **£22**|£3.50/£7.

SCANDIES WINE BAR 4 Kynance Pl SW7 071-589 3659 Relaxed wine bar with good food, relaxed, friendly service; Sunday newspapers, and unlimited coffee; cl Sat am, 25-26 Dec, 1 Jan. **£18**|£2.95/£6.50.

KALAMARES MICRO 66 Inverness Mews W2 071-727 9122 (Not to be confused with its larger sister restaurant at No 76). Tiny, close-packed authentically Greek restaurant (though all the waitresses seem to be Czech), with very good cheap food and friendly service; unlicensed, take your own wine; cl Sun, am, and bank hols; **£16.80**|£5.25.

ADAM'S CAFÉ 77 Askew Rd W12 081-743 0572 Decorated with lots of colourful Tunisian tiles, ceramics and plates, this daytime café turns into evening Tunisian restaurant with Tunisian wine (sole importers to UK); cl Sun, bank hols, 2 wks Aug. **£14**|£1/£3.

WINE GALLERY 49 Hollywood Rd SW10 071-353 7572 Consistently good, nicely presented food, fairly priced wines, and helpful, friendly service; for fine-weather eating – attractive back courtyard with enormous black cat; quieter at lunchtime; **£12**|£5.50.

LUBA'S BISTRO 6 Yeoman's Row off Brompton Rd SW3 071-589 2950 Unlicensed, very long-standing Russian evening restaurant in converted stable; with gingham tablecloths, candles in bottles, friendly Russian or Polish waitresses, and good, generously served food. **£11.55**.

VICTORIA & ALBERT MUSEUM Tasty, good-value food in airily spacious restaurant; newspapers to read and jazz brunches Sun morning; cl pm, 24-26 Dec; disabled access. **£7.50**|£1.80/£3.50.

LADBROKE ARMS 54 Ladbroke Rd W11 071-727 6648 Unusually good food for a pub – proper home cooking inc good traditional, Sunday family lunches; comfortable, with open fire; cl 25 Dec pm; disabled access. £2/£5.
By the time this book is published Marco Pierre White will have opened a restaurant in the Hyde Park Hotel, 66 Knightsbridge SW1 071-235 2000; should be interesting.

THE CITY

Although the buildings are for the most part Victorian and Edwardian, the ground-plan essentially comprises the narrow, twisting streets and alleys of medieval times, and some churches and a handful of other buildings also date from the medieval or Tudor period. Around St Paul's and the Tower, the layout is more open – and far less affected by the City's human tides: most of the rest of the area is packed with worried financial workers during weekdays, then when they leave goes into a catatonic trance in the evening and at weekends. For every person who actually lives in the City, another 60 or 70 flood in each day to work there, then flood out again at night.

This is the hub of the country's trade and finance. Originally, particular streets came to be associated with particular crafts and trades, and this is reflected in street names throughout the City – Carter Lane, Hosier Lane, Cloth Fair, Ropemaker St, Milk St, Silk St, Coopers Lane and so forth. The great City Livery Companies representing the various trades have effectively ruled the City for 800 years or more, with the right to appoint the Lord Mayor who heads the Corporation of London. This form of local government is quite different from that of any other town in Britain (and it certainly works – here, you won't find the dirt and dereliction that marks most other parts of London). Now, many of the Livery Companies have only a tenuous connection with the original crafts involved in their trades – you won't see many members of the Worshipful Company of Skinners actually skinning an animal. But in a couple of places you can still see the old trades being carried on in much the same way as ever. The ancient Fishmongers Company still control Billingsgate (West India Dock Rd, early morning Tues-Sat), and if you get up really early you can watch the Bummerees lugging huge carcases around at Smithfield Market (Mon-Fri).

Though the halls of the City Livery Companies may have been rebuilt since they were first established in the Middle Ages, they still house some remarkable treasures. Some are open to visit, but only by prior arrangement: you'll have to book well ahead, through the City of London Information Centre, St Paul's Churchyard, EC4; 071-332 1456.

Where to stay

TOWER THISTLE St Katharine's Way E1 9LD 071-481 2575 **£155.50**; 826 rms (ask for one with a view). In a marvellous location next to Tower Bridge and the Tower of London, this busy modern hotel has stylish public rooms, and several eating areas – the coffee shop (good views over Tower Bridge) doubles as an understated nightclub; disabled access.

To see and do

⊖ Tower Hill The most notable building to survive the Great Fire is the TOWER OF LONDON. It's a picturesque, classic castle, and a lot of fun to look at even superficially. But a closer look at its architecture can show the development of the medieval defence system in a more interesting light. The White Tower (finished about 1097) stands at the centre of the edifice, just inside the Roman city wall which had probably been used for defence right through the dark ages. This central core was then encircled by two lines of new walls in the 13th c. Almost every period of English history has witnessed certain famous or infamous characters sent to the Tower, for years or just briefly before execution, inc Walter Raleigh, Lady Jane Grey and two of Henry VIII's wives. From the reign of Charles II it housed the Royal Mint, but there's still ample evidence of the Tower's days as a prison (such as prisoners' graffiti on walls) – days not in fact that far off, as it reverted to its former role in both world wars. There's a mass of things to see here, inc enough armour and medieval weaponry to glut the most bloodthirsty small boy's appetite, the Crown Jewels, the Beefeaters, and the ravens. This year they've also opened two towers that were part of Edward I's medieval palace, with the rooms furnished in period style and peopled with appropriately costumed guides recreating 13th-c court life. To show what an extensive task the restoration was, one of the rooms has been left untouched. Meals, snacks, shop; jewel house cl some of Jan; £6.70.

TOWER BRIDGE is a distinctive sight, and gives wonderful views from its glass-covered walkway, 142 ft above the Thames. A new state-of-the-art exhibition has just opened to celebrate the bridge's centenary in 1994, and you can also see some of the older Victorian machinery for raising it (*The Times* newspaper shows when it's to be raised each day). During recent restoration work the bridge was found to be more damaged than had previously been thought, and there's some doubt as to whether traffic will be able to go on using it. Snacks, shop, disabled access; cl Jan-July for refurbishment; £2.50. Tower Hill is also the best tube station for visiting St Katharine's Dock (see Docklands, below), and outside there's an appropriately castellated McDonalds.

⊖ Monument The MONUMENT (Monument St) is a 202-ft-high, fluted doric-style column, designed by Wren and Hooke to mark the start of the Great Fire of London. For perfect symmetry they placed its base exactly 202 ft from Pudding Lane. There are splendid views from the top (311 steps up), but it's now closed for restoration, and could be for the next couple of years.

⊖ Bank The CUSTOM HOUSE in Lower Thames St is the HQ of the Collector of Customs for the Port of London. The building has an early 19th-c neo-Classical façade, and the Long Room where the ships' masters and agents come to register can be viewed by appointment; tel 071-283 5353. The BANK OF ENGLAND (Bartholomew Lane) This neo-

Classical, windowless fortress does still contain oodles of gold – though you can't see it, let alone get your hands on it. There's a small but interesting museum, which even shows how computerised currency speculators work. Disabled access; cl Sat and winter Suns. ROYAL EXCHANGE (Cornhill) This is the third building erected on this site (the first two were both destroyed by fire, in 1666 and 1838 respectively), and like its predecessors is Renaissance in style. Fronted by proud columns, it's constructed round a quadrangle, which was roofed over in 1882. Since further enlargement in 1991 most of the sections open to the public have closed, but it's a handsome building, and has a restaurant. Cl wknds. Moving west, there is the glorious aspect of the MANSION HOUSE (Bank, EC4), the official residence of the Lord Mayor of London. If you apply in writing in advance, you can view a suite of sumptuous 18th-c rooms inc the fabulous Egyptian Hall. LLOYD'S OF LONDON (Lime St) This hugely controversial building is the headquarters of the world's leading insurance market. Though it's no longer open to casual members of the public, it's at least worth seeing from outside if you're nearby. More fun and altogether more stylish is LEADENHALL MARKET (Whittington Ave, off Gracechurch St), a Victorian, iron and glass covered market, alive with Cockney humour yet quite smart, and filled with seafood, game, vegetables and fruit; cl afternoonish, wknds.

St Paul's ST PAUL'S CATHEDRAL looms out at you suddenly from amongst the crowded streets, despite the attempts of brasher, taller modern buildings to take over, its huge dome a pleasing shape after the stolid self-satisfaction of the Victorian and Edwardian masonry which still dominates this area. Originally the cathedral was Gothic in style, with a towering 500-ft spire. It fell into disrepair and though Wren started to work on renovation in 1660 it was only after the Great Fire, from 1675 onwards, that his plans came to fruition. The cathedral has of course been the setting for various State occasions and is full of interesting monuments – the one to John Donne was the only complete figure to be salvaged after the Great Fire. Look out for the wonderful carving on the exterior – some of which is by Grinling Gibbons, who also did the choir stalls. Try the Whispering Gallery, and visit the crypt, full of magnificent tombs and memorials to notable figures from British history, as well as a display illustrating the history of the cathedral itself. Shop, disabled access; *£2.50. The GUILDHALL (off Gresham St) was built with money raised by the Livery Companies in 1411. Here the Court of Common Council, over which the Lord Mayor presides, administers the City of London. The Lord Mayor's Banquet is held in the great hall, which is hung with the banners and shields of the 90-odd livery companies. Underneath the building is the largest 15th-c crypt in the City, and there is also a clock museum with fascinating and intricate displays, and a library with an unrivalled collection of manuscripts and books which bear some relation to the City; cl Sun, and Oct-Apr; may cl for civic occasions, ring 071-606 3030 ext 1460 to check.

Barbican MUSEUM OF LONDON (London Wall) When this fascinating museum, adjoining a stretch of the original Roman wall, originally opened in the late 1970s it was considered to be the most advanced of its day. Museum technology has of course moved on enormously since then, and younger children esp might find some of the earlier exhibits a little dull. That said, anyone with just a passing interest in history should find it compelling, with comprehensive coverage of the city's development told through chronological reconstructions and period clothes, music and various remains, from a medieval hen's egg to an early (and quite different) tube map – ever heard of the station called Post Office? There's a rather jolly, audio-visual presentation showing the spread of the Great Fire, and the 18th-, 19th- and 20th-c sections have almost too much to take in. It livens up considerably as it goes on, and you should allow plenty of time to explore it properly. Londoners should enjoy looking at the old maps to see exactly when their street was built. Meals, snacks, shop, disabled access; cl Sun am and all Mon (exc bank hols); *£3 – ticket valid for three months, and it certainly is the sort of place you want to come back to. NATIONAL POSTAL MUSEUM (King Edward St) Guaranteed to tickle any philatelist's fancy, a comprehensive collection of stamps from all over the world, as well as a history of the postal system. Shop, disabled access by prior arrangement; cl wknds and bank hols. The BARBICAN could be called the North Bank's equivalent to the South Bank Centre – certainly its aesthetic equal. This complex includes cinemas, theatres, exhibition halls and galleries, and there is often free entertainment in the foyers.

Farringdon MUSEUM OF THE ORDER OF ST JOHN (St John's Lane) Housed in a 16th-c gatehouse and 12th-c crypt are silver, paintings and furniture belonging to the medieval Order, and displays relating to the history and work of its more modern offshoot, the St John's Ambulance Brigade. Shop, some disabled access; cl Sun, Christmas and Easter. Tours of the gatehouse and priory church on Tues, Fri and Sat at 11 and 2.30.

✝ **Old St** WESLEY'S HOUSE (49 City Rd) The father of Methodism had his house and chapel built here in 1778, and they're still much as they were then, with plenty of his personal possessions. Wesley's tomb is here, and a museum in the crypt of the 1778 CHAPEL presents the development of Methodism from the 18th c. Shop, disabled access – limited in house, but good in museum; cl Sun am (exc for services); *£3.

! **Aldgate East** Once the terror-stricken haunt of Jack the Ripper, Whitechapel is still one of London's poorest areas. However, if you visit the market in BRICK LANE – a riot of colour, smells and sound – you will get a taste of the vibrancy and cheerfulness of the people who live here, and there are plenty of bargains for early risers. The community is largely Asian, so much of the food and other wares are quite exotic; Sun 5 am-2 pm.

! **Bethnal Green** MUSEUM OF CHILDHOOD (Cambridge Heath Rd) This very special little museum houses the V & A's collection of toys, dolls, dolls' houses, games, puppets and children's costumes. Shop, disabled access with prior notice; cl am Sun and all Fri, 25 Dec, Good Fri, May Day bank hol.

✝ The City as a whole is full of striking **churches**; among the more interesting ones are St Anne and St Agnes (Gresham St), particularly worth knowing for the Bach cantatas that may grace its Lutheran Sun services (071-373 5566); St Bartholomew-the-Great (West Smithfield), partly Norman, with a 13th-c gateway into the market precincts, lunchtime recitals and choral evenings (071-606 5171 for programme); St Brides (Fleet St), a Wren masterpiece, with a partly Roman crypt, good Sun choir and frequent short lunchtime recitals (071-353 1301 for programme); St Mary-le-Bow (Cheapside), with the famous Bow Bells and Thurs lunchtime early-music concerts (071-248 5139); 13th-c St Ethelredas (Ely Pl); and St Helens (Great St Helens, Bishopsgate), also 13th-c, but badly damaged by the IRA Bishopsgate bomb.

! If you want to visit the **Docklands** area, it's worth getting in touch with the London Docklands

Visitor Centre, 3 Limeharbour, E14, 071-512 1111, who offer information, free maps and an audio-visual show. The most visitor-friendly area of revivified dockland on the north bank is ST KATHARINE'S DOCK, which has a lively marina, a quite cheerful pastiche of a Victorian pub, and quite a few things going on. CANARY WHARF is an all-too-obvious landmark, but you can't go up or see anything inside save a small display on the ground floor. You can view many other parts of the area from the DOCKLANDS LIGHT RAILWAY. Further down river is the gigantic, closeable THAMES FLOOD BARRIER (the Visitor Centre is in Unity Way, Woolwich SE18, 081-854 1373; there are also cruises around the barrier, 081-854 5555), recently built to protect London from freak tides.

Where to eat

The restaurants and wine bars in the City tend to be full at lunchtime with businessmen entertaining clients on expense accounts – and both service and price reflect this. Pubs and wine bars tend to empty at 2.20 – a good time to go if you can hold out till then. At the wknd, the City is much quieter and a great many of the restaurants and even pubs are shut. BALLS BROTHERS and DAVYS wine bar chains are both reliably good for snacks or larger meals and decent wine.

ROUXL BRITANNIA in Triton Court 14 Finsbury Sq EC2 071-256 6997 Run by the Roux brothers, this is a busy, rather cramped brasserie with very good food; cl evenings and wknds. **£27**|£3.95/£6.75.

OLDE WINE SHADES 6 Martin Lane EC4 One of the few buildings to have escaped the Great Fire of 1666, and much as it was when Dickens used it as a tavern – heavy black beams, dignified alcoves, dark panelling and old-fashioned, high-backed settles; good wine and good-value, traditional lunchtime snacks; packed with smart City types; cl pm and wknds; no children; jacket and tie are required. **£15.75**|£2/£3.15.

BLOOM'S 90 Whitechapel High St E1 071-247 6001 Strictly kosher Jewish restaurant with enjoyable food – most fun on Sun lunchtime when it's packed with Jewish families; cl Fri evening, all Sat and on Jewish hols. **£12.60**|£5.25/£7.35.

HAMILTON HALL Bishopsgate EC2 071-247 3579 Part of the new Liverpool St Station development, with terrific Victorian-baroque decor, lots of space, and decent range of food all day; cl Sun pm, 25-26 Dec. **£11**|£3.95.

Some good City pubs inc the Blackfriar (Queen Victoria St/Blackfriars Bridge EC4: stunning Edwardian decor); Eagle (Farringdon Rd EC1: interesting Italian food); Hand & Shears (Middle St EC1: very traditional Smithfield pub); Olde Mitre (Ely Pl, off Hatton Garden EC1: ancient-feeling enclave); and Rising Sun (Rising Sun Court, Cloth Fair EC1).

We welcome reports from readers . . .

Do send us reports on places in the GUIDE, or ones you think should be in. Use the card in the middle, the report forms at the end, or just write – no stamp needed: THE GOOD WEEKEND GUIDE, FREEPOST TN1569, Wadhurst, E Sussex TN5 7BR. Readers who help us with reports for the GUIDE are offered a discount on the next edition.

Bloomsbury/Holborn/ Regent's Park

Between the City and Westminster is a civilised and genteel, if slightly faded area of Georgian squares, gardens and courts – legal and academic London. We have included with it the area over towards Marylebone, with Regent's Park on its northern border – doctors' and dentists' territory, then the largely residential area around the shopping streets of Marylebone High St and Baker St.

Where to stay

The hotels we have recommended for the West End make good bases too for this area, which is very easily reached from them. Bloomsbury does have a large number of hotels, especially for the more budget-conscious visitor, though many are on the tawdry side. Ones which can be recommended include the Academy (17 Gower St WC1E 6HG 071-631 4115), the Morgan (24 Bloomsbury St WC1B 3QJ 071-636 3735) – both handy for the British Museum – and the George (60 Cartwright Gardens WC1H 9EL 071-387 6789).

To see and do

Russell Sq BRITISH MUSEUM Spectacular collections in monumental building dating from 1823-1857, with priceless man-made objects from all over the world, some of them over 3,000 years old. The range is staggering, in which just a few highlights are the Elgin Marbles, the log-book of Nelson's *Victory*, the wonderful and intriguing Egyptian galleries, the comprehensive galleries of Greek vases, the Oriental antiquities, the Amaravati sculpture. There are also changing displays of historic books and documents (they often have a document of the month), administered by the British Library. Don't try to take it in all at once – decide what interests you most and stick to that, or your head will start reeling with the extent of this treasure-house before you've got even a tenth of the way through. Meals, snacks, shop, disabled access; information about current special exhibitions 071-637 7384; cl Sun am, 25 Dec, 1 Jan, Good Fri, 1 May. Though it's normally free, you can avoid the crowds (worst at wknds) by paying £5 for the late-night opening on the first Tues of the month (not Jan).

DICKENS' HOUSE Dickens lived at 48 Doughty St during his 20s, and during that period wrote the *Pickwick Papers*, *Oliver Twist* and *Nicholas Nickleby*. The drawing room has been reconstructed to appear as it was then, and there are a number of original manuscripts and first editions, pictures and personal possessions. His wife's sister died here in 1837, an event which greatly affected the young writer, and which he later used as the model for the death of Little Nell in *The Old Curiosity Shop*. Shop; cl Sun and Christmas week; £3. JEWISH MUSEUM (Woburn House, Tavistock Sq) Jewish life, history and religion are illustrated here using displays of ceremonial art, portraits and antiques, and various audio-visual programmes. In spring they're planning to move to a new site in Albert St, NW1. Shop, disabled access; cl pm Fri and Sun in winter, all

Sat, Mon, and Jewish hols; *£1. The Museum Tavern (Museum St) usefully does food all day.

! ⛫ ⊖ **Goodge St** POLLOCK'S TOY MUSEUM (1 Scala St) The displays – from all over the world and from all periods – are housed in a rather charming setting, almost as if lots of enthusiastic children had just left them scattered through these little rooms. Mechanical and optical toys, folk toys and nursery furniture, teddy bears and toy furniture, board games and toy theatres, and a proper toy shop downstairs, with some reproduction Victorian toys. Disabled access to ground floor only; cl Sun; £2.

❀ ⛫ ⛫ ⊖ **Holborn** LINCOLN'S INN FIELDS is a perfect example of the tranquil architecture of this area – a large open space with trees and lawns surrounded by handsome houses; there are also tennis courts and, in summer, various band concerts – a pleasant place to spend a summer afternoon. On the south side is the impressive edifice of the ROYAL COLLEGE OF SURGEONS, while to the north is SIR JOHN SOANE'S MUSEUM, containing the architect's collection of paintings, drawings and books, inc Hogarth's acid series on *The Rake's Progress* and his fine election cartoons. Sir John was responsible for some of the most magnificent buildings in the City, and his collection of architectural drawings can be viewed by appointment, phone 071-405 2107. Shop; cl Sun, Mon. A splendid semi-legal institution is the Cittie of York (22 High Holborn), an enormous and very atmospheric basement pub with little private booths down one side – and masses of lawyers. Another fine pub in this area is the opulent Victorian gin palace, the Princess Louise (208 High Holborn; good Thai food upstairs, not wknds).

⛫ ⊖ **Temple** Just off this end of the Strand, the COURTAULD INSTITUTE GALLERIES in Somerset House display an excellent collection of Impressionist and Post-Impressionist paintings by artists inc Monet, Renoir, Degas and Cezanne, as well as works by Michelangelo, Rubens and Goya. Meals, snacks, shop, disabled access; cl am Sun; *£3. Somerset House is also the Public Records Office and you can have great fun searching for those skeletons in the family closet.

⛫ ⊖ **Chancery Lane** FLEET ST, once the hub of newspaperland, is now merely a passage between the law courts and the City – but look out for relics of the newspaper kingdoms such as the black-glass DAILY EXPRESS BUILDING. You may even find one or two of the last surviving genuine journalists on the Street (from Associated Press), in the Punch pub. The Gothic Royal Courts of Justice are impressive, and at No 17 there's an interesting half-timbered house. Behind Fleet St is 17 Gough Sq where DR JOHNSON'S HOUSE is a perfect example of early 18th-c architecture, just as Dr Johnson himself was a perfect example of 18th-c barbed gentility. Between 1749 and 1759 he wrote his great *English Dictionary* here, and a first edition of this is on display, along with various memorabilia from his learned life. Shop; cl Sun and bank hols; *£2. The passages and walkways around here are a good reminder of how London's streets used to be laid out. Another writer is remembered at LUDGATE CIRCUS, where the memorial to Edgar Wallace stands – famous journalist and even more famous detective story writer. A prolific author, he was said to be capable of dictating two tales of mystery and suspense simultaneously to the same secretary. Many famous literary figures lived at the TEMPLE INN OF COURT, including Lamb, Thackeray and for a while Dr Johnson too. Most of the buildings date from after the reign of Elizabeth I or the Great Fire, but the name points to an older history: the land was owned by the Knights Templar from about 1160. MIDDLE TEMPLE HALL is a fine example of

Tudor architecture, with a double hammer-beam roof and beautiful stained glass. There is a table made from timber from Sir Francis Drake's ship the *Golden Hind* – he was a member of the Middle Temple – while a single oak tree from Windsor Forest supplied the wood for the 29-ft-high table. Open 10-11.30 am and 3-4 pm Mon-Fri exc bank hols; cl over vacations – all Aug, 10 days each at Christmas and Easter and 9 days at Whitsun.

❀ 🐘 ⛴ ⊖ **Baker St** The area around REGENT'S PARK has plenty to offer. The park itself, covering over 400 acres, is the culmination of a glorious swathe of Regency terraces designed by John Nash, which can be seen almost all around it, though the buildings of Park Crescent are among the finest. It was originally intended to be the setting for a palace for the Prince Regent, after whom it was named: now it contains an open-air theatre where Shakespeare's plays are performed in the summer, the lovely Queen Mary's Rose Garden, a boating lake and of course the LONDON ZOO. After a period of doubt, the zoo seems to have set its sights on a more coherent and more attractive identity, and has just begun a 10-year redevelopment programme. Most of this is still under wraps, but already this year you should be able to see a few changes. They've slimmed down the collection of over 5,000 animals, birds, fish and insects, to concentrate on particularly endangered species or those which can be expected to breed here, from the tiniest creatures to elephants and gorillas. So while you may think the lions are the same as anywhere, they in fact represent a particular subspecies of which there are probably no more than 400 left in the world. Exhibits inc the Clore House where day and night are reversed so that you can watch nocturnal creatures such as vampire bats, and the African aviary. Also a children's zoo where animals can be handled, a new aviary for rare parrots, and a centre specialising on lemurs, fruit bats and other animals from Madagascar. Meals, snacks, shop, disabled access; cl 25 Dec; *£6. The London Waterbus Company – one of several companies who now run CANAL BOATS along the stretch of Regent's Canal between Little Venice and Camden Lock – make a stop for passengers who want to get off at the zoo.

⚱ **!** To many people the world over, the words Baker St call to mind only one thing – Conan Doyle's great detective. The famous address of 221b now has a SHERLOCK HOLMES MUSEUM, with various Holmes paraphernalia, and something of the atmosphere of the books recreated. Shop; cl 25 Dec; *£5. You can probably see Sherlock himself not far away, at MADAME TUSSAUD'S in Marylebone Rd, with its huge and constantly changing range of lifelike waxwork figures. Everyone from John Paul I to John, Paul, George and Ringo – but be warned that the queues are also huge and usually slow-moving (esp in school hols). This year you get more for your money than last, in the shape of a new dark-ride – the Spirit of London, which sends you rolling past moving and even speaking historical figures telling the story of London in non-stop, rollercoaster fashion. Meals, snacks, shop, disabled access; £7.40. Next door is the LONDON PLANETARIUM – recently installed displays incl a Space Trail with touch-sensitive screens telling you about the solar system, and the good shows now incorporate stunning lasers. No under-5s; shows every 40 mins; snacks, shop; £4.

Where to eat

WAGAMAMA 4 Streatham St WC1 071-323 9223 Attractive, simply furnished Japanese basement restaurant with long tables and benches for communal eating; very friendly, cheerful service (using interesting computerised order pads), chatty, informal atmosphere, good healthy food – raw salads, ramens (huge bowls of noodles with meat, vegetables and Japanese additions), rice dishes, saké, grape and plum wines, beer, and free green tea; exceptionally good value; cl Sun, 24-26 Dec, 1 Jan. £10.50|£4.20.

This area is only a short walk from the West End, so many of the restaurants we have mentioned there (see above) will be useful for this area too.

SOUTH OF THE RIVER

The South Bank arts centre with its magnificent riverside site should be a magnet for visitors, but in fact the unappealing, concrete blocks which house the complex are bleakly discouraging, and the hinterland too is unprepossessing (typified in the squalor of Lambeth). However, the South Bank walkways give marvellous views across the river – the best views of the Houses of Parliament are from the quiet riverside walk between Westminster Bridge and the ancient palace of the Archbishop of Canterbury by Lambeth Bridge. Dotted about the area are several places well worth visiting, including the Museum of the Moving Image, one of the most satisfying museums in the country, and the excellent Imperial War Museum. And besides the excellent shows and performances in the various halls and theatres of the South Bank complex, there is usually something going on in their foyers – including free entertainment.

Where to stay

Places on this side of the river are best visited from a base on the other side; somewhere in the West End or Westminster would be preferable.

To see and do

⊖ Lambeth North/ Westminster LAMBETH PALACE Despite much rebuilding in the 19th c, a large part of this building is original – inc the chapel (1230 – the stained glass is modern), the crypt (the earliest part of the palace, dating from 1200), and the late 15th-c, red-brick exterior which from across the river is such a refreshing antidote to the ostentatious stonework of governmental London. The hall, 93 ft long with a spectacular hammer-beam roof, dates from Cromwell's Commonwealth. The building is still the official residence of the Archbishop of Canterbury, though in practice is now used mainly to conduct church business; the adjacent ST MARY'S CHURCH has the tombs of several archbishops, and Captain Bligh of the *Bounty* is buried here too. Just by the south gateway here is the little MUSEUM OF GARDEN HISTORY founded in memory of John

Tradescant, Charles I's gardener, with a small area planted with nothing introduced since his time. Tradescant himself is buried here. Snacks, shop; cl Sat and second Sun in Dec-first Sun in Mar. FLORENCE NIGHTINGALE MUSEUM (St Thomas's Hospital, Lambeth Palace Rd) On the site of the first School of Nursing, a recreated hospital ward in the Crimea, and various artefacts and possessions of the Lady with the Lamp. Snacks, shop, disabled access; cl Mon; *£2.50. IMPERIAL WAR MUSEUM (Lambeth Rd) Recently brilliantly refurbished, this museum is now top-notch, using very up-to-date presentation techniques to give a vibrant and sometimes even nerve-wracking exploration of aspects of all wars involving Britain and the Commonwealth since 1914. The Blitz Experience vividly recreates London's darkest days (a similar Trench Experience gives WWI the same treatment), and there's a chance to fly with the RAF on Operation Jericho (£1.30 extra). The Gulf War official paintings are very moving, as are the archive recordings of people's experiences of war. Meals, snacks, shop, disabled access; £3.70, free after 4.30.

⊖ Waterloo Just beyond the JUBILEE GARDENS is the SOUTH BANK CENTRE, an ill-conceived design of walkways, theatres, cinemas and galleries in hideous stained concrete that yields multifarious cultural treasures. There are sometimes open-air festivals between the attractions, with stalls of books, clothes and jewellery going down to the river, or free performances in the foyers of the various halls. The NATIONAL THEATRE, as well as its incomparable productions in its three different-sized auditoria, also features interesting artistic exhibitions, guided tours behind the scenes, and good places to eat – often accompanied by live music in the foyer of the Olivier theatre. The NATIONAL FILM THEATRE also has a nice little café, with many bookstalls set up in front of it. The HAYWARD GALLERY specialises in world-class art exhibitions. The ROYAL FESTIVAL HALL often has free performances in the foyer as well as a full programme of music and dance; it too has good cafés, inc a useful place for lunch. MOMI or the Museum of the Moving Image is also here, providing a romp through cinematic history which everyone really enjoys. Lively displays trace moving pictures from magic lanterns to today's hi-tech special effects, taking in clips from favourite films, TV shows and cartoons along the way. You can learn how to operate a television studio, read the news or fly like Superman, while older visitors should find the montage of old Pathe newsreels particularly nostalgic. The costumed actors work really hard with their performances, and there are various temporary themed exhibitions – it really is a fun place, and a visit can easily last several hours. Meals, snacks, shop, help for disabled – contact reception when you get there; cl 24-26 Dec; £5.50.

⊖ Blackfriars Between Southwark and Blackfriars Bridge is Bankside – the site of Shakespeare's GLOBE THEATRE, open from 1599 to 1642 (when the Puritans closed it down), and soon to have a complete reconstructed version. At the time of going to press they'd reached the third stage of their ambitious plans, and the wooden bays were already beginning to look like a theatre. The vagaries of the weather make it impossible to say for sure when it will be finished, but it should be some time in 1994. By then it will be a three-tiered, O-shaped theatre, 100 ft in diameter, capable of seating audiences of 1,000 with a further 500 promenaders. They hope to perform some of the plays the way they were done in the early 1600s – no spotlights, canned music or eleborate sets. Already there have been performances on the site, as well as in the theatre in the museum, four converted Georgian warehouses with exhibitions on Elizabethan London and its theatre, the life of Shakespeare, and the Globe itself, old and new. That the project has gone so far owes a great deal to the enthusiasm of actor Sam Wanamaker, who had a real struggle convincing sceptics of its viability. His success is perhaps best illustrated by the fact that Southwark council, who initially opposed the plans, have renamed the adjacent street New Globe Walk. Shop, disabled access; museum cl am Sun; £3 museum, site free. There is the most wonderful view of St Paul's Cathedral from here – indeed it's said that Sir Christopher Wren himself watched the building operations from here.

❄ ✹ ⚱ ! ✝ ⊖ **London Bridge** Moored or rather marooned down by London Bridge is the last of this country's three-masted topsail schooners, the *Kathleen & May* from Bideford: you can go on board, where there are various displays and exhibitions; cl Sat and Sun; £1. It's in an attractive dockland redevelopment worth wandering around, with good Thames and City views from the quay, a useful bar doing lunches (the Old Thameside), and the medieval remains of the Bishop of Winchester's palace (Clink St), once said to be the biggest building in Europe but now reduced to a single wall and atmospheric Rose Window. In those days this area was the sleazy side of the city, taking in all sorts of entertainments – as well as the theatres there were 22 brothels officially licensed by the bishop. The story of this less salubrious side of London life is told at the Clink Exhibition next door, on the site of the prison that gave its name to all others. It's a fascinating tale, but very much a traditional museum with pictures, models and lots to read, so not ideal for children – and thanks to some of the subject matter there are parts they say aren't suitable for them at all! Included is one of the few working armourers in the country, making armour and chainmail on the site; if you think your wardrobe's missing that extra something decent suits made to order start at around £1,000. Shop, disabled access once in, but entry down a few steps; *£2. Southwark Cathedral This was originally the church attached to the priory of St Mary Overy, founded in 1106. The first church on this site burnt down and the present building was its replacement, begun in 1208-9. The design is a mixture of English and French – compare the very English proportions of the choir with the more continental detail on it, for example the vaulting and use of a triforium passage. Interesting memorials to William Shakespeare (whose brother is buried here), and John Harvard, the founder of the American university. The nave dates from the late 19th c. Meals, snacks, shop, disabled access. London Dungeon (Tooley St) Certainly not for the squeamish, this museum celebrates the seamier side of London through the ages: witchcraft, torture, black magic and death are all presented in glorious and life-like scenes using wax figures, and there's a new Jack the Ripper Experience. All very atmospheric, and genuinely historical, whatever the critics suggest. Snacks, shop, disabled access; cl 24-26 Dec; *£6. An attractive ex-dock shopping arcade is Hays Galleria (off Tooley St), which has places to eat inc a comfortable pub with river views, and a fascinating whimsical pirate-ship working sculpture by David Kemp. HMS Belfast On the east side of the bridge, docked permanently in the pool of London, is the largest preserved cruiser ever built for the Royal Navy. Now it acts as a floating naval museum, with seven decks complete with sound and light displays, exhibitions, art gallery and cinema. It's recently been repainted in 1942 camouflage; snacks, shop, limited disabled access; *£4. DESIGN MUSEUM (Butlers Wharf) Interesting museum showing how design is used in the mass production of everyday objects, with good temporary exhibitions. Meals, snacks, shop, disabled access; cl 25-26 Dec; £3.50. Nearby the Anchor Tap (just off Shad Thames) is a handy refreshment stop.

! ⊖ Elephant and Castle CUMING MUSEUM The history of Southwark, along with the worldwide collections of the Cuming family; exhibitions inc finds from Roman and medieval Southwark, and a selection of medieval charms and superstitions. Shop; cl Mon and Sun. Get up very early on Fri for the bargains at BERMONDSEY MARKET (Bermondsey St/Long Lane): when the antique-dealers start arriving around 5, other dealers literally pounce on the choice items while they're being set out, and by 8 or 9 things are more ordinary. It's probably the biggest primary source of antiques and bric-a-brac in London, and can be the most exciting. Take a torch in winter.

Where to eat

RSJ 13a Coin St SE1 071-928 4554 Relaxed and friendly restaurant with fine, modern British cooking and exceptional Loire wines in simple surroundings; handy for the South Bank shows; cl Sun, 4 days over Christmas. £23.20|£2.95/£10.95.

REBATO'S 169 South Lambeth Rd SW9 071-735 6388 Busy, high-ceilinged tapas bar with friendly barman and waiters, and good choice of tapas; also Spanish restaurant; cl Sun, Sat am, bank hols, disabled access. £18.90|£4.20/£8.40.

PHUKET 246 Battersea Park Rd SW11 071-223 5924 A bit of an expedition, but very good Thai food in friendly and extremely unpretentious little restaurant, more café in style really – though the food is of far better quality than that; ask to sit upstairs; cl 24-26 Dec, 1 Jan, lunchtimes. £15.75|£3.90/£5.82.

There's a clutch of useful tapas bars and the like up past the Imperial War Museum, around the junction of Kennington Rd and Kennington Lane. Near the Old Vic just south of Waterloo, La Barca (81 Lower Marsh St) is an enjoyably theatrical Italian restaurant; and Caesars (103 Waterloo Rd) is a decent, burger-style place. The café of the Young Vic (The Cut) does very good-value light lunches, but you'll feel centuries old if you're out of your 20s. Besides those already mentioned, decent pubs in this area inc the ancient Anchor on Bankside, the Founders Arms on Bankside (spectacular views of St Paul's) and, above all, the George off 77 Borough High St, the closest thing to an old-fashioned coaching inn left in London.

FURTHER AFIELD

We include here those places which despite being away from the centre appeal so much at least to some people that, for them, even a short stay in London would be incomplete without them. The most generally appealing of these places are Greenwich and Kew. Other parts of London do have many treasures tucked away (the Horniman Museum in Forest Hill for instance, or the Whitechapel Gallery in Whitechapel

High St east of the City, or Osterley Park and Sion House out in west London). But getting to them would take too much of a chunk out of your time to justify including them in a short-stay itinerary, when there's so much else to see closer in.

Camden Town This part of north London has come up in the world tremendously in the last decade or two. It's now something of a bohemian's idyll, with a very wide variety of unusual shops from radical bookshops to fashion workshops, from comic shops to one of London's best brassware and ironmongery shops. There are lots of restaurants and cafés too, and good delis serving the area's Italian and Greek communities; try the Parkway Deli for Italian, and Chris Milia (Pratt St) for Greek. What makes the area worth a visit is its wknd series of lively markets, particularly the interesting craft, handmade fashion and other stalls around the attractively converted, former warehouses of Camden Lock. There's also a covered market by the Bucks Head pub on Camden High St, the Inverness St market for fruit and veg, and the Stables, where the best food stalls are to be found. Go and browse, but be warned that you may never again see such huge crowds. Don't miss the Parkway Cinema – which may be closed down soon despite a storm of protests. It's glorious, with an art-deco exterior, a grand piano and chandeliers within. The Princess of Wales up towards Primrose Hill (Chalcot Rd/ Regents Pk Rd) does good bistro food.

Greenwich Most of the interesting things to look at in this area are related to the River Thames, with museums, boats and grand old ships still reflecting Greenwich's long and illustrious maritime connections. It also used to be the site of a favourite residence of the royal family, though the original magnificent palace was demolished in the 17th c – the only surviving part is the vaulted crypt beneath what's now called Queen Anne's Block. This later building was designed by Inigo Jones for Anne of Denmark, and it was finished for the wife of Charles I, Queen Henrietta Maria, who lived here for a while. Still called the QUEEN'S HOUSE today, it was completed in the mid-17th-c, the first Palladian-style villa in the country, and has recently been grandly (and expensively) refurbished to show how it was when first built. Sumptuous silks and furnishings on display, as well as a collection of Dutch seascapes; there's an accompanying commentary provided via a hand-held recorder. Shop, disabled access; cl 5 Jan-5 Feb; *£3.75. It's the focal point of a glorious group of buildings designed, successively, by Webb and Wren and augmented by Vanbrugh, Hawksmoor and Ripley. They were used as a naval hospital until 1873, when they were given over to the ROYAL NAVAL COLLEGE, and form a magnificently preserved part of old London. The college buildings have an interesting chapel and a particularly notable painted hall. Shop; cl am, all day Thurs, Good Fri, 25 Dec. The view from across the river (there's a pedestrian tunnel under the Thames here) looks like an 18th-c print come to life. NATIONAL MARITIME MUSEUM (Romney Rd) is good fun, telling the story of Britain and the sea, with plenty of boats, details of past royal fleets and vessels, great masterpieces of naval battles, and even Nelson's uniform. There's also a new 20th-c gallery. Meals, snacks, shop, disabled access; cl Sun am, 24-26 Dec; *£3.75. GREENWICH PARK Wonderful views from this carefully landscaped park sloping down towards the river, which was laid out by Le Nôtre – whose love of symmetry is clear. A herd of deer graze in a smallish area of woodland and wild flowers known as the Wilderness, and there's the largest children's playground in any royal park (and even the preserved trunk of a tree in which the young Elizabeth I is said to have played). The park's chiefly famous for the OLD ROYAL OBSERVATORY, the original home of Greenwich Mean Time – standing as it does on zero meridian longitude. The brass line marking the meridian is still there set in the ground: standing with one foot on each side is almost irresistible. The Wren-built observatory was founded by Charles II in 1675 'for perfecting navigation and astronomy'; it now houses a comprehensive collection of historic instruments for time-keeping, navigation and astronomy – recently spruced up, with good views from the top. The Time Ball is rather confusing – it can go down and up so fast you barely notice it. Shop; cl Sun am, 24-26 Dec; *£3.75. The park is a great place for a picnic. Sir Francis Chichester was the first to sail around the world single-handedly, and his yacht *Gipsy Moth IV* is moored here by Greenwich Pier; cl 1-2 pm wkdys, Sun am, Nov-Mar; 50p. You should be able to get BOAT TRIPS from here up to Westminster (around £4). Nearby is the clipper *Cutty Sark*, built in 1896 and the fastest of her time – she once sailed 363 nautical miles in a single day. On board, you can watch a video telling the story of the vessel. Shop, some disabled access; cl Sun am, 24-26 Dec; £3.25. The pub named after the vessel, nearby in Lassell St, is an attractive old place for lunch; other reliable Thames-view pubs here are the Trafalgar (Park Row) and Yacht (Crane St), and there's a decent wknd arts and crafts market. You can buy joint tickets for many of Greenwich's attractions, or even a season ticket which allows unlimited visits all year – quite good value, as Greenwich really is a place worth coming back to (some of our contributors rate it more highly than anywhere else in the country). It's not far from here to **Blackheath**, a civilised place good for a pleasant stroll, with RANGERS HOUSE a lovely stately home with fine furnishings, portraits and a collection of musical instruments.

⊖ Hampstead

Hampstead prides itself on its villagey atmosphere, and off the main streets its maze of fashionable, twisting lanes is very picturesque and seductively charming. It's home to artistes of all kinds, and well-heeled bohemians in general. Past inhabitants inc Aldous Huxley, George Orwell, John Masefield and Katherine Mansfield. Down in Keats Grove (past the little Downshire Hill church, which has lovely, candlelit Christmas carol services), Keats and his lover and nurse Fanny Brawne lived in two fine Regency houses; KEATS HOUSE now has interesting displays relating to his life, with manuscripts, letters and personal mementoes (and maybe a recorded nightingale out in the garden on summer nights). Shop; cl 1-2 pm, Sun am, am every wkdy Nov-Mar. SIGMUND FREUD'S HOUSE (20 Maresfield Gardens) Extraordinary collection of antiques from various ancient cultures, as well as his working library, papers and indeed his desk and couch. The pioneering work of his daughter is also illustrated. Shop; open Weds-Sun pm; £2.50. FENTON HOUSE is a William-and-Mary merchant's mansion, set in a walled garden, with fine Oriental, English and European china and an exceptional collection of early keyboard instruments. The period-music concerts on some summer Weds evenings are well worth catching (phone 071-435 3471 for programme). Cl am wkdys, Thurs and Fri, all Nov-Mar (exc pm wknds in Mar); £3. The Flask in Flask Walk is a good pub (and a long-standing favourite of the local actors), as is the gaslit Holly Bush, prettily tucked away up Holly Mount.

Particularly attractive areas inc Church Row, and Squires Mount (where the Regency-looking house at the end on the left, in fact built in the 1950s, belonged to Richard Burton and Elizabeth Taylor). Across the road from here is Hampstead Heath, north London's best open space, with lakes, hilly prospects, and some wonderful views of the city skyline – Parliament Hill has a direction-finder pointing out various landmarks. Walk across the heath to Kenwood: the house achieved its present splendid proportions in the 18th c at the hands of Robert Adam, while the surrounding wooded grounds form the most beautiful part of the heath. The house contains a fine collection of paintings, inc old masters and 18th- and 19th-c portraits by Reynolds and Gainsborough; in the garden is Dr Johnson's summerhouse, moved here from Ashgrove when the house was demolished. On summer Sats there are concerts in the garden, idyllic when it's fine, with the music drifting across the lake with its Japanese bridge, and a fireworks finale (phone 081-348 1286 for programme; virtually impossible to park anywhere near then). Meals and snacks, shop; disabled access.

Highgate Highgate, on the far side of the heath (you can easily walk across from Hampstead), dates largely from the Victorian period and still keeps a villagey atmosphere, centred as it is around the High St. The village is dominated by Highgate School (which Betjeman attended and where T S Eliot taught). There are lots of pubs in this area, and some smart little cafés. The Grove, a row of very elegant Victorian houses, is home to such diverse musicians as Yehudi Menuhin and Sting. On the outside wall of the park on the west side of Highgate High St, just north of Lauderdale House, is a weather-beaten plaque recording the site of the cottage where Andrew Marvell once lived. Highgate Cemetery is the most impressive of a series of landscaped and formal cemeteries started in the early decades of Victoria's reign on the outskirts of the city. You'll find it hard to miss the tomb of Karl Marx – a monstrous head, frequently daubed with paint and slogans. It's more difficult to search out the graves of Christina Rossetti and George Eliot in the wonderfully atmospheric tangle of trees, shrubs and crumbling ivy-covered monuments. We should add that this is still an active cemetery – there are a number of burials each year. The east cemetery is open most days, the west by guided tour only (phone 081-340 1834 for details); east cemetery £1, west cemetery £3.

Hampton Court Perhaps most famous today for its maze, Hampton Court was started by Cardinal Wolsey in the early 16th c, based around an estate belonging to the Knights Hospitallers. As often happened its splendour proved dangerous, pricking Henry VIII's jealousy so that Wolsey felt compelled to present the house to his king in an attempt to appease him. Successive monarchs have left their architectural marks: the hammer-beamed hall and kitchens were Henry's addition, the Fountain Court was designed by Wren for William and Mary, and much comes from the work of the Victorians (the chimneys mostly date from then). The rooms from each of these periods have managed to keep their distinctive styles, from the starkly imposing Tudor kitchens (themselves taking up 50 rooms) to the elaborate grandeur of the Georgian chambers. It's an amazing place, just as a royal palace should be, with countless sumptuous rooms and elaborately landscaped gardens and parkland. The King's Staircase is wonderfully over the top, and the Picture Gallery has the finest Renaissance works from the royal collection, inc the fascinating *Massacre of the Innocents* by Brueghel the elder. Look out too for the carvings by

Grinling Gibbons and the cartoons by Mantegna in the Lower Orangery. One of the oldest parts, Henry VIII's Great Watching Chamber, has just been restored after the 1986 fire to its original splendour. Meals (in summer), snacks, shop, disabled access; cl 24-26 Dec; *£6.50. The Kings Arms, next to the Lion Gate, is good for lunch. BUSHEY PARK nearby is another royal park, formerly reserved for hunting. Wren laid out its famous double chestnut avenue, which runs from the great house to the Teddington Gate. There are pleasant Thames-side walks around Hampton Court, and summer CRUISE BOATS from here back down to Westminster (phone 071-930 4721).

Kew Bridge KEW GARDENS were started here in 1759 by George III's mother, and consisted of nine acres landscaped by Capability Brown. By 1904, they had grown to cover 300 acres, with the foundations of the present wonderful collection firmly laid in the previous century by Sir Joseph Banks and the head gardener William Aiton. The glasshouses inc the magnificent modern Princess of Wales range and the remarkable, restored Palm House (with a new marine display in the basement). The gardens nr the entrance are largely formally arranged, and drift into attractively landscaped woodland, glades and tree collections further out. Look out for the many interesting buildings which have been constructed among all this greenery, for example the 163-ft-high Chinese Pagoda (too dodgy structurally to go inside now); there's also a gallery, and on some summer evenings jazz concerts with fireworks. Meals, snacks, shop, disabled access; £3.50. A wonderful place you can come back to time and time again – always discovering something new. In the grounds too is KEW PALACE, built in 1631 and used by members of the royal family until Queen Charlotte's death in 1818. It's a Dutch-style, brick building that seems remarkably unroyal, and remains much as it was during George III's reign, with family paintings, furniture and tapestries. Shop; cl Oct-Apr; *£1.20. The garden has been planted to appear as it would have done in the 18th c. Kew was at that time one of the royal family's favourite residences, somewhere they could enjoy quiet times as a family. In the gardens they built a rusticated summerhouse, QUEEN CHARLOTTE'S COTTAGE, its interior designed to look like a tent. Open wknds and bank hols; 70p, or joint ticket with Kew Palace *£1.50. The Kings Arms on Kew Green is quite handy for lunch. In summer you can come by CRUISE BOAT from Westminster – see the numbers we give for Hampton Court above and Richmond below.

Richmond RICHMOND PARK is the most country-like of all London's parks, and with its great rolling spaces and wildlife (inc herds of deer) is wonderful for Londoners to clear the cobwebs out of their lungs, but probably not the sort of thing you'd think of coming up to London to visit – even with the temptation of sailing model boats on Adam's Pond, or fishing in the 18-acre Pen Ponds. There's a good formal garden at Pembroke Lodge, and the Isabella Plantation's rhododendrons and azaleas are a must-see in season. In Richmond itself there are quite a few good dining pubs, inc the riverside White Cross, and the White Swan (Old Palace Lane), Racing Page (Duke St) and Orange Tree (Kew Rd). There are summer CRUISE BOATS from here back down to Westminster (phone 071-930 2062).

More Specialised Expeditions

⊖ **Angel** Camden Passage and the surrounding streets have a great collection of antique shops, well worth the expedition if that interests you. The nearby Island Queen (Noel Rd) does good food in its bar and upstairs restaurant.

✈ ⊖ **Colindale** RAF Museum (Grahame Park Way) The story of flight from early times, with 70 full-size aeroplanes and other exhibits, a flight simulator, films, and an interesting examination of the impact of flight on history and politics. Excellent for enthusiasts and flying-minded children, it's warmly recommended by several of our contributors, and for 1994 (mid-May-Oct) has a D-Day exhibition inc many British, US and German planes. Meals, snacks, shop, disabled access; cl 24-25 Dec, 1 Jan; £4.90. If you're up this way and have time to spare, the newspaper section of the British Library is fascinating – though you have to allow them time to find what you want.

⊖ **Putney Bridge** Start with a pleasant riverside stroll. The Bishop's Park opposite the boathouses has lovely views and the interesting little Bishop's Palace (open pm Sun). The Duke's Head is a civilised riverside pub, from where you should be able to see some rowing (the crêpe stall outside Putney ⇌ station is useful too if you happen to be here at night).

⊖ **St John's Wood** At Lord's Cricket Ground the MCC Museum has a very good collection of cricket memorabilia, inc the Ashes urn and 18th-c paintings of the sport. Shop; disabled access by prior arrangement. The grounds themselves are open to spectators during cricket season 3 May-12 Sept, otherwise by tour only, booking essential (phone 071-266 3825); £4.50. On the far side of this sober residential area, take a stroll through Primrose Hill, which was once part of the same hunting park as Regent's Park. From the summit there are breathtaking views of the city.

⊖ **Southfields** Wimbledon Lawn Tennis Museum The only museum of its type, with trophies, pictures and other tennis memorabilia tracing the development of the game throughout this century. Particularly interesting displays on the changes in fashion during this period, and you can also see the famous Centre Court outside. Teas, shop, disabled access; cl am Sun and all Mon; *£2. Incidentally if you're in London during the Wimbledon fortnight it's always worth popping along to the club in the early evening around 5.30 or 6 – lots of people leave then and they resell the seats at a cheaper price.

⊖ **Walthamstow Central** William Morris Gallery (Lloyd Park, Forest Rd) William Morris lived here from 1846-1858 and the house has an unrivalled collection of his work: fabrics, furnishings and wallpaper, much of which is still fashionable today. They've recently reorganised the exhibition, with more on display than ever before. Upstairs are paintings and work by the Pre-Raphaelites, inc pictures by Burne-Jones and Rossetti. Shop, disabled access to ground floor only; cl 1-2 pm, Mon and Sun (exc first Sun in month – cl 12-2 pm then).

! ⊖ **Wembley Central** Wembley Stadium Tours of the most famous football stadium in the land, going from the dressing rooms through the players' tunnel and on to the pitch itself, with an audio-visual show and displays of trophies and related memorabilia. Snacks, shop, disabled access; cl 25 Dec; £4.

⇌ **West Dulwich** Dulwich Picture Gallery (College Rd) The country's oldest public picture gallery, and though not large one of the best; a good range of European old masters with works by Van Dyck, Gainsborough and Rembrandt. Summer teas, shop, disabled access; cl Sun am and all Mon; *£2.

Where to eat

ODETTE'S 130 Regent's Park Rd NW1 071-586 5486 Slightly quaint, cellar wine bar with lots of pictures on the walls, bags of character, and good food; cl Sat am, Sun pm. **£25, set lunch £10**|£10.
SEASHELL 49-51 Lisson Grove NW1 071-723 8703 Take-away and straightforward restaurant selling excellent fresh fish and chips; disabled access; cl Sun. **£15.20.**
EVERYMAN CAFÉ Hollybush Vale NW3 071-431 2123 Sophisticated and busy, but still relaxed, with almost a continental feel; cl 25 Dec. **£14.45**|£3.15/£4.20.

Walks

Central London is fun to explore on foot, though the traffic and stop-start rhythm can be wearying. There is no end of potential walks of architectural/historic/royal/sociological/whatever interest. One of the best overviews of the capital is had by walking along the **south bank** of the Thames from Lambeth Bridge to Tower Bridge, giving mostly traffic-free panoramic views of the West End, St Paul's Cathedral, the City, the Tower of London and finally the Docklands. Unfortunately you can't yet walk along the river east of HMS *Belfast* to Tower Bridge; the path is blocked by a huge, undeveloped building site which has been empty for years, so you have to divert into Tooley St – but can soon rejoin the river.

Daily guided walking tours are given by Citisights of London (081-806 4325), City Sights of London (071-837 2841) and Original London Walks (071-624 3978). Walks last about two hours, usually starting from a tube station; you don't need to book, and the cost is around £4.

Out of the centre, London has idyllic verdant stretches around **Kew** and **Richmond** – the old villages along the riverside have considerable charm and some good pubs. The Thames towpath can be combined with a walk in Richmond Park and to Ham House. The towpath between Putney and Kew Bridge (you have to cross the river a few times) has train stations at either end, and gives opportunities to take in Chiswick Mall, Chiswick Park (a necessary diversion from the river at a point where there is no towpath on the north bank), and Strand-on-the-Green, as well as Kew Gardens.

Hampstead Heath is the airy escape for north Londoners, with lots of paths, ponds, glades and hollows, and views of Central London from Parliament Hill. The **Regent's Canal** offers an excellent walk from Little Venice to Camden Lock (with its huge wknd market), passing by Regent's Park and Primrose Hill (another good viewpoint); boat cruises also operate along here – one-way tickets available.

The south-east fringes of London give way to surprisingly rural **North Downs** countryside, still within the London borough of Bromley, around Knockholt, High Elms and Downe; paths are plentiful and well maintained. Only the view over south London from behind Knockholt church shows how close you are to the capital.

Help this year from: *Michael Bechley, Lt Col J H Parker Jones, A L Morrison, Nigel Gibbs, Dilys Unsworth, David Unsworth, G and M Brooke-Williams, Mark Walker, Bill and Edee Miller, Wayne Brindle, Ian Phillips, A J Frampton, A Vermeul, Graham and Karen Oddey, TBB, Brian Jones, T Nott, G Walsh, P Smith, Simon Collett-Jones, Dr and Mrs A K Clarke, D Cox, Eric Locker, John Scarisbrick, Tom Thomas, Mick Hitchman, Brian and Jenny Seller, Howard and Margaret Buchanan, Rob and Helen Townsend, John Fazakerley, D C Eastwood, Prof S Barnett, Susan and John Douglas, K P Smith, Andy Stone, Paul Cartledge, John Evans, A Y Drummond, M Clarke, Dr and Mrs Rackow.*

London Calendar

Some of these dates were provisional as we went to press.

JANUARY

1st **Westminster Abbey** Lord Mayor of Westminster's Parade

6th **Earls Court** International Boat Show *at Exhibition Centre – till Sun 16*

13th **Kensington** Antiques Fair *at Town Hall – till Sun 16*

30th **Whitehall** Charles I Commemoration *at Banqueting Hall*

FEBRUARY

1st **Wembley** Holiday on Ice *at Arena – till Sun 27*

3rd **Alexandra Palace** Road Racing and Superbike Show *– till Sun 6*

6th **Wembley** Snooker Tournament *at Conference Centre*

13th **Soho** Chinese New Year Celebrations

19th **Twickenham** England v Ireland Rugby Union

24th **Olympia** Motor Racing Show *– till Sun 27*

27th **Kensington** British Teddy Bear Festival *at Town Hall*

MARCH

1st **RHS Halls,** *Greycoat St*, British Philatelic Exhibition

8th **Chelsea** Antiques Fair *at Old Town Hall – till Sat 19*

17th **Earls Court** Ideal Home Exhibition *at Exhibition Centre – till 10 Apr*

19th **Twickenham** England v Wales Rugby Union

20th **Olympia** International Book Fair *– till Tues 22*

26th **Putney to Mortlake** Oxford v Cambridge University Boat Race

31st **Olympia** International Spring Gardening Fair *– till 4 Apr*

APRIL

2nd **Alexandra Palace** Craft Fair *– till Mon 4*

4th **Regent's Park** London Harness Horse Parade

5th **Goldsmiths Hall,** *Foster Lane*, London International String Quartet Competition *– till Sun 10*

13th **City,** *Gresham St*, Spital Sermon *is delivered to the Lord Mayor after a colourful procession, inc the Lord Mayor from Guildhall House to church by Guildhall*

17th **London** Marathon

London Calendar

April cont.

24th **Old Bailey to Tyburn Convent, Marble Arch** *Catholic bishop leads thousands in silent procession in memory of Catholics martyred in 16th and 17th c; benediction from balcony of Tyburn Convent nr spot where gallows stood; 1 am*

28th **RHS Halls**, *Greycoat St*, Antiques Fair – *till 1 May*

30th **Wembley Stadium** Rugby League Cup Final

May

7th **Twickenham** Rugby Union Cup Final

14th **Kensington** Doll's House Festival – *till Sun 15*; **Wembley FA Cup Final**

21st **Lords** One-day International, England v New Zealand

24th **Chelsea** Flower Show – *till Fri 27*

June

1st **Horse Guards Parade** Beating Retreat – *till Thurs 2*

2nd **Olympia** Art and Antiques Fair – *till Sun 12*

5th **St James Church, Picadilly and Wigmore Hall** Festival of Baroque Music – *till Sun 26*

9th **Grosvenor** House Hotel Antiques Fair – *till Sat 18*

11th **Horse Guards Parade** Trooping the Colour

16th **Lords** Test Match, England v NZ – *till Mon 20*

20th **Wimbledon** Lawn Tennis Championships – *till 3 July*

July

3rd **City of London** Festival – *till Weds 20*

6th **Hampton Court Palace** Flower Show – *till Sun 10*

16th **Royal Festival Hall** Jazz Parade – *till Sun 24*

19th **Earls Court** Royal Tournament *at Exhibition Centre*; **Kew Gardens** Jazz *in the evening – till Thurs 21*

21st **Lords** Test Match, England v South Africa – *till Mon 25*

August

4th **Hyde Park**, *Park Lane opp Dorchester Hotel*, Queen Mother's Birthday Gun Salute

7th **Hyde Park**, *Rotten Row*, London Riding Horse Parade

16th **RHS Halls**, *Greycoat St*, RHS Flower Show – *till Weds 17*

18th **Kensington** Antiques Fair *at Town Hall – till Sun 21*; **Lords** Test Match, England v SA – *till Mon 22*

19th **South Bank Centre**, *Purcell Room*, Folk Week – *till Fri 26*

28th **Kensington** British Teddy Bear Festival *at Town Hall – till Mon 29*; **Ladbroke Grove** Notting Hill Carnival, *Europe's largest street festival – till Mon 29*

September

6th **City** of London Flower Show, *rare opportunity to see the Guildhall interior*

London Calendar

SEPTEMBER cont.

9th **Hampton Court** Merrie Olde England Country Craft Fayre – *till Sun 11*

10th **London Docklands** Seafood Fair – *till Sun 11*

13th **Chelsea** Antiques Fair *at Old Town Hall – till Sat 24*; **RHS Halls,** *Greycoat St*, Great Autumn Flower Show – *till Weds 14*

15th **Royal Albert Hall** BBC Henry Wood Promenade Concerts – *till 10 Sept*

OCTOBER

2nd **Covent Garden Piazza** Punch and Judy Fellowship; **Trafalgar Square** Pearly Harvest Festival Service *at St Martin-in-the-Fields, best occasion to see the Pearly Kings and Queens*

4th **Wembley** Horse of the Year Show *at Arena – till Sun 9*

15th **Albert Hall** National Brass Band Championships

NOVEMBER

6th **Hyde Park** London to Brighton Veteran Car Run *starts early am*

12th **The City** Lord Mayor's Procession and Show, *Lord Mayor elect is driven in state to the Royal Courts of Justice where he takes the oath to perform his duties faithfully*

27th **Earls Court** Royal Smithfield Show *at Exhibition Centre – till Weds 30*

DECEMBER

15th **Olympia** International Show Jumping Championships – *till Mon 19*

25th **Hyde Park** Peter Pan Cup Swimming Race *in The Serpentine at 8 am*

We welcome reports from readers . . .

This GUIDE depends on readers' reports. Do help us if you can – in return, we offer a discount on the next edition to people who've helped us with reports for it. Tell us what you think about places already in it, and anything extra you think we should say about them. And send us your ideas for inclusion in the next edition: places to visit, eat at or stay in, attractive drives or walks, maybe even unusual interesting shops you know of. Use the card in the middle, the report forms at the end, or just write – no stamp needed: THE GOOD WEEKEND GUIDE, FREEPOST TN1569, Wadhurst, E Sussex TN5 7BR.

Scotland

Edinburgh has great appeal for a short city holiday at any time of year – either during the Festival if you want a culturally stimulating time, or emphatically not during the Festival if you want to see the city in comfort. Glasgow does have possibilities for a lively and thought-provoking visit, and Stirling deserves consideration if you already know Edinburgh well. In the countryside, the deeply indented west coast from Strathclyde northwards has the broadest-based appeal, but almost every part of Scotland has some attraction for a short stay. In every part, except the North, there are a lot of places to visit – particularly castles, lived-in or ruined, but also some magnificent gardens (especially on the west coast, where they tend to be at their best in late May and June).

Much of Scotland is good for driving holidays, with roads considerably emptier than in most of England; however, at the height of summer the most beautiful main roads do tend to attract too many other drivers for comfort. This brings home the quite important point that as Scotland's uncrowded scenery is a major attraction, the best time to enjoy it is precisely when it is uncrowded. North of the Forth, this generally means out of high season. May and June tend often to be ideal months in this part of Scotland. The Borders and the south-west corner of Scotland stay fairly quiet year-round.

For a short stay, the snag for many people in England is the sheer scale of the distances involved. As a rough guide, a three-hour drive will get anyone living north of Manchester or York well into the southern parts of Scotland. If you're coming from further south than that, the driving does become rather daunting. Trains and aeroplanes put much more of Scotland within reach for a short stay. There are direct flights from London and some regional airports to Edinburgh, Glasgow, Inverness and Aberdeen, with some local connections from there. The fastest trains do the London-Edinburgh run in around four hours, and it's fair to say that by rail, and with sleepers from both London and Plymouth/Poole/Bristol, someone really determined to get to Scotland – even a distant part of Scotland – for a short stay can do so from virtually any part of England. For instance, if you boarded the night sleeper for Inverness at nine o'clock in the evening in London, a hire car could get you on to Skye by about 11 o'clock the next morning.

South Scotland

Edinburgh is excellent for a city break, while the countryside is good for quiet touring or for a walking break, especially the Borders.

Edinburgh is the biggest lure for a weekend break here: a beautiful city, with lots to do within a conveniently compact area – most of the main things to see are within an easy, interesting and pleasant walk of each other. There are some great things to see in Glasgow too, which has an edge of vitality that can be very appealing.

The countryside does have possibilities for a quiet break, with some of Scotland's best walking. The Borders' scenery is grand without being austere, and very pleasantly varied, with no end of little-visited ancient castles, romantic ruined abbeys, and other things to look at. It has civilised small towns and a good choice of comfortable places to stay, but has not become overly touristy. The south-west corner of Scotland is one of the friendliest parts of Britain, particularly Galloway, and though it doesn't have quite such memorable scenery as the Borders, it does have at least some interesting old monuments, attractive places to potter around in (particularly on the coast), and relatively few visitors. Ayrshire has some great golf courses, and Scotland's most popular racecourse, but its main appeal might be to people wanting to follow the Robert Burns trail.

Outside Edinburgh and Glasgow, some of the most enticing places to visit are the many great romantic castles such as those at Hermitage, Caerlaverock, Peebles and Castle Douglas; the ruined abbeys such as those on Inchcolm (boats from South Queensferry) and at Glenluce and New Abbey; and the rich gardens, prime among them those near Stranraer, at Port Logan, Stobo and Kirkbean, and at Brodick on Arran. There are many remarkably fine houses in the area, especially those we describe under Traquair, Selkirk, Thornhill, Duns and South Queensferry; Culzean Castle is a favourite Scottish family outing. The Newton Grange mining museum and the preserved printworks at Innerleithen are surprisingly interesting.

Where to stay

Edinburgh NT2574 CALEDONIAN Princes St EH1 2AB 031-225 2433 **£252.50**; 239 rms. On the site of the old Caledonian railway station, this is a grand hotel with elegant lounge and cocktail bar, and very good food in the stylish restaurant; disabled access.

Edinburgh NT2574 BALMORAL Princes St EH2 2EQ 031-556 2414 ***£195**; 189 fine rms. Lovely hotel with wonderfully opulent entrance hall, elegant day rooms, friendly staff, and very good food in several restaurants; excellent leisure facilities; good disabled access.

Edinburgh NT2574 HOWARD 36 Great King St EH3 6QH 031-557 3500 **£180**; 16 luxurious rms. Fine, civilised 18th-c hotel with comfortable, elegant public rooms, courteous, efficient service, and good food; disabled access.

Bonnyrigg NT3065 DALHOUSIE CASTLE Midlothian EH19 3JB (0875) 820153 **£150**; 24 rms, some of great character. Turreted red sandstone castle with some fine historic features such as the dungeon restaurant and oak-panelled library bar; children under 12 free if in parents' rm and meals half-price.

Gullane NT4882 GREYWALLS East Lothian EH31 2EG (0620) 842144 **£150**; 23 individually decorated rms. Overlooking the Muirfield Golf Course, this beautiful Lutyens family-run house has antiques, open fires and flowers in its comfortable lounges and panelled library, very good food and fine wines in the restaurant, and impeccable service; cl Nov-Apr; disabled access.

Maybole NS3009 LADYBURN Ayrshire KA19 7SG (065 54) 585/586 **£140**; 8 rms. Quietly set family home in lovely wooded countryside with antiques, books and open fires in comfortable day rooms, and friendly staff; shooting and fishing can be arranged; s/c flat also; may cl mid-Dec-mid-Jan; no children; disabled access.

Kelso NT7334 SUNLAWS HOUSE Roxburghshire TD5 8JZ (0573) 450331 **£128**; 22 good rms. Splendid hotel in 200 acres of garden and parkland with relaxed and comfortable lounge, library and conservatory, and open fires; tennis, croquet and shooting; disabled access.

Glasgow NS5865 ONE DEVONSHIRE GARDENS G12 0UX 041-339 2001 **£125w**; 27 huge, opulent rms. Elegant hotel not far from city centre with luxurious Victorian furnishings in the public areas, fresh flowers, friendly staff, and very good food in the stylish restaurant; disabled access.

Uphall NT0571 HOUSTOUN HOUSE Broxburn West Lothian EH52 6JS (0506) 853831 **£121**; 30 comfortable rms. 17th-c house in fine grounds with a quiet lounge, panelled dining rooms, cellar bar, and good food.

Edinburgh NT2574 ROXBURGHE Charlotte Sq EH2 4HG 031-225 3921 ***£120**; 75 rms. In an elegant square, this is a fine example of Adam architecture with quiet public rooms, attractive restaurant, and good service; cl 25-26 Dec.

Gatehouse of Fleet NX5956 CALLY PALACE Castle Douglas Kirkudbrightshire DG7 2DL (0557) 814341 **£118 inc dinner**; 55 comfortable rms. 18th-c mansion in extensive grounds with lovely views, comfortable, rather splendid public rooms, and good food; outdoor swimming pool; cl Jan-Feb; disabled access.

Newton Stewart NX4165 KIRROUGHTREE Newton Stewart Wigtownshire DG8 6AN (0671) 2141 ***£111**; 18 spacious rms. Early 18th-c mansion in 8 acres of carefully landscaped gardens on edge of Galloway Forest Park; oak-panelled lounge with rococo furnishings and French windows leading to terrace and croquet lawn, formal dining rooms (one is no smoking) with very good food – puddings come in for special praise – and friendly staff; free golf on 5 local courses and fishing, shooting and stalking can be arranged; cl Jan-Feb; children over 10.

Dirleton NT5184 OPEN ARMS North Berwick East Lothian EH39 5EG (062 085) 241 **£110**; 7 rms. Run by the same family for over 45 years, this friendly hotel has a very comfortable lounge with log fire and nice little bar, and overlooks the ruins of Dirleton Castle; cl 31 Dec, 1 Jan; disabled access.

Portpatrick NX0154 KNOCKINAAM LODGE Stranraer Wigtownshire DG9 9AD (077 681) 471 ***£100**; 10 individual rms. Lovely, very neatly kept, little hotel with comfortable, pretty rooms, open fires, wonderful food, and friendly, hotel with comfortable, pretty rooms, open fires, wonderful food, and friendly, caring service; the surroundings are dramatic and there are lots of fine cliff walks; cl 3 Jan-15 Mar; children over 12 in evening restaurant (high tea at 6); disabled access.

Quothquan NS9939 SHIELDHILL Biggar Lanarkshire ML12 6NA (0899) 20035 **£98**; 11 pretty rms. Partly 13th-c hotel in a fine setting with deeply comfortable oak-panelled lounge, open fires, library, particularly good food in the no-smoking restaurant, and warm, friendly service; children over 10.

Kilwinning NS3043 MOUNTGREENAN MANSION HOUSE Ayrshire KA13 7QZ (0294) 57733 **£92**; 21 rms. Grand Georgian-style mansion with fine public rooms, friendly service, and extensive grounds; croquet.

Rockcliffe NX8453 BARONS CRAIG Dalbeattie Kirkcudbrightshire DG5 4QF (055 663) 225 **£90**; 26 rms, 21 with own bthrm. 12 acres of gardens and woodland surround this imposing Victorian house with its relaxing lounges and fine views; lots of golf courses within easy reach; cl Nov-Mar; disabled access.

Selkirk NT4728 PHILIPBURN HOUSE TD7 5LS (0750) 20747 ***£90**; 16 rms. A particularly good place for families, this very relaxing 18th-c hotel has Austrian-style furnishings, very good food, wine and friendly service; fine walks in the surrounding grounds and woods; disabled access.

Peebles NT2540 CRINGLETIE HOUSE EH45 8PL (0721) 730233 **£86**; 13 pretty rms. Surrounded by 28 acres of garden and woodland and with fine views, this turreted baronial mansion, run by the same couple for over 20 years, is very welcoming and quiet, with delicious food using home-grown vegetables, extensive Scottish breakfasts, and excellent service; cl 2 Jan-1st wk Mar; disabled access.

Skelmorlie NS1967 MANOR PARK Ayrshire PA17 5HE (0475) 520832 **£85**; 22 rms. In lovely gardens with fine views, this country house has a spacious, quiet lounge and well-stocked bar.

Auchencairn NX7951 BALCARY BAY Castle Douglas Kirkcudbrightshire DG7 1Q7 (055 664) 217 **£76**; 17 rms with fine views. Charming hotel with wonderful views over the bay, neat grounds running down to the water, comfortable public rooms, friendly service, very good, enjoyable food, and lots of walks; cl mid-Nov-1st wk Mar.

Clarencefield NY0968 COMLONGON CASTLE Dumfries Dumfriesshire DG1 TNA (038 787) 283 ***£75**; 10 rms. Country house with suits of armour in oak-panelled great hall, good food in Jacobean dining room, and relaxing drawing room, and right next door to a large border stronghold with dungeons, lofty battlements, archers' quarters and haunted long gallery – candlelit tour before dinner if you like; cl Christmas and half Jan.

Canonbie NY3976 RIVERSIDE Canonbie Dumfriesshire DG14 0UX (038 73) 71512 **£72**; 6 notably comfortable, well-decorated rms. Peacefully civilised hotel with pleasant, no-smoking restaurant, charming communicating bar rooms, excellent food using organic or naturally fed produce, marvellous breakfasts with home-made breads, oatcakes and preserves, award-winning wines, good beers, and sympathetic service; fishing permits; cl 2 wks Nov, Feb; children over 5.

Lockerbie NY1381 DRYFESDALE HOTEL Dumfriesshire DG11 2SF (0576) 202427 ***£72**; 15 rms, 6 on ground floor level. Relaxed and comfortable with good food in pleasant restaurant, nice gardens, and lovely surrounding countryside; cl 25-26 Dec; good disabled access.

Beattock NT0905 AUCHEN CASTLE Moffat Dumfriesshire DG10 9SH (068 33) 407 **£70**; 25 pleasantly decorated rms. Smart but friendly country-house hotel in lovely quiet spot with a trout-loch and spectacular hill views, delicious food and peaceful, comfortable bar; cl 3 wks over Christmas.

Melrose NT5434 BURTS HOTEL Roxburghshire TD6 9PN (089 682) 2285 *£70; 21 rms. Welcoming 18th-c inn in delightfully quiet village and close to ruined Abbey with consistently popular, imaginative food, good breakfasts, decent wine list, and comfortable lounge; cl for accomm 24-26 Dec (open for meals then).

Minnigaff NX4166 CREEBRIDGE HOUSE Newton Stewart Wigtownshire DG8 6NP (0671) 2121 **£70**; 18 rms. Country-house hotel in 3 acres of gardens with huntin' and shootin' feel in comfortable bar, friendly atmosphere, big choice of very good, popular bar food inc fine local fish and seafood.

Auchencairn NX7951 COLLIN HOUSE Castle Douglas Kirkcudbrightshire DG7 1QN (055 664) 292 **£68**; 6 rms with period furniture. Attractive pink-washed stone house in 20 acres looking across to Hestan Island and the Solway Firth; fine views from the drawing room and dining room, relaxed sitting room, imaginative food and carefully chosen wines; cl 4 Jan-12 Mar.

Glasgow NS5865 RAB HA'S G1 1SH 041-552 2206 **£68**; 4 rms. Sensitively converted Georgian town house with delightfully informal ground floor bar, basement restaurant, well-cooked seafood, and good service; younger brother of Babbity Bowster.

Portpatrick NX0154 CROWN Stranraer Wigtownshire DG6 8SX (077 681) 261 **£66**; 12 rms. Atmospheric harbourside inn with attractive bedrooms, rambling old-fashioned bar with interesting furnishings, airy 1930s-ish dining room, good food with an emphasis on local seafood, excellent breakfasts, carefully chosen wines.

Glasgow NS5865 BABBITY BOWSTER 16-18 Blackfriars St G1 1TE 041-552 5055 **£63.50**; 6 clean simple rms, showers. Warmly welcoming, rather continental place with decent breakfasts (served till late), attractively decorated airy bar, and a cheery first-floor restaurant, which hosts a gallery as well as a programme of musical and theatrical events.

Gifford NT5368 TWEEDDALE ARMS Haddington East Lothian EH41 4QU (062 081) 240 **£60**; 18 rms. Civilised old inn in quiet village with comfortable sofas and chairs in tranquil lounge, gracious dining room, wide choice of good daily-changing food, and charming service.

Kelso NT7334 EDNAM HOUSE Roxburghshire TD5 7HT (057 322) 4168 **£60**; 32 rms. Homely and relaxed Georgian mansion with pleasantly old-fashioned rooms, good service, and gardens running down to the banks of the River Tweed; cl 25 Dec-10 Jan.

Innerleithen NT3336 TRAQUAIR ARMS Peeblesshire EH44 6PD (0896) 830229 **£54**; 10 good rms. Very friendly pub with interesting choice of good food, comfortable lounge bar, friendly service, the superb local Traquair on handpump, and nice breakfasts; cl 25-26 Dec, 1-2 Jan.

Swinton NT8448 WHEATSHEAF Duns Berwickshire TD11 3JJ (089 086) 257 **£54**; 4 rms, showers. Warmly friendly inn with exceptionally good food (emphasis on fish), pleasantly decorated, relaxed main lounge plus small pubby area, separate locals' bar, and no-smoking front conservatory; garden play area for children.

Tweedsmuir NT0924 CROOK INN Biggar Lanarkshire ML12 6QN (089 97) 272 **£52**; 7 rms. Old drovers' inn on lonely road through grand hills with large, airy lounge, simply furnished back bar, sun lounge, various art-deco features, good food, and friendly service; attractive garden across the road, petanque and putting in adjoining field, and glassblowing centre in old stableblock (open daily); fishing permits.

Kirkbean NX9859 Cavens House Dumfries Dumfriesshire DG2 8AA (0387 88) 234 **£48**; 6 rms. Comfortable mansion in 11 acres of mature gardens and woodland with friendly atmosphere and good food; disabled access.

Gatehouse of Fleet NX5956 Anwoth Hotel Castle Douglas Kirkcudbrightshire DG7 2JT (0557) 814217 **£44**; 9 decent rms. Welcoming hotel with a riverside garden, good-value home cooking and pleasant bar.

Annanwater NY1966 Corehead Farm Moffat Dumfriesshire DG10 9LT (0683) 20973 ***£42**; 2 rms. Welcoming farmhouse on working hill sheep farm with woodburning stove in lounge, and good food using home-grown and local produce and their own naturally reared lamb and beef; excellent hill walking; children over 10.

Melrose NT5434 Dunfermline House Roxburghshire TD6 9LB (089 682) 2148 **£38**; 5 rms. Neatly kept Victorian terraced house, close to Melrose Abbey ruins, with good breakfasts and friendly owners; cl 24-26 Dec.

Kirkcowan NX3260 Craighlaw Arms Newton Stewart Wigtownshire DG8 0HQ (067 183) 283 ***£35**; 3 clean, comfortable rms, shared bthrm. Carefully modernised old coachhouse in quiet village, with comfortable residents' lounge, imaginative choice of good home-cooked food including huge T-bone steaks, rod-caught salmon and wild brown trout; shooting and fishing; s/c also.

Ettrick Valley NT3018 Tushielaw Selkirk TD7 5HT (0750) 62205 **£34**; 3 rms, one with own bath. Friendly little inn in lovely spot on Ettrick Water, imaginative restaurant food, intimate bar, fine views, own loch, shooting and fishing (as well as birdwatching and walking).

Innerleithen NT3336 Caddon View 14 Pirn Rd Peeblesshire EH44 6HH (0896) 830208 ***£32**; 5 well-equipped rms, most with own bthrm. Warmly welcoming and relaxing grey stone Victorian villa with attractive candlelit dining room, really good, piping hot home-made food, comfortable lounge, and caring service; private parking; cl last 2 wks Jan; disabled access.

Nenthorn NT6838 Whitehill Farm Kelso Roxburghshire TD5 7RZ (0573) 470203 **£32**; 4 rms, 3 with shared bthrm. Comfortable farmhouse on mixed farm with fine views, big garden, log fire in sitting room, and good home cooking; cl Christmas/New Year.

Ayr NS3321 Trees KA6 6EW (0292) 570270 **£28**; 3 rms. B & B in quiet, secluded farmhouse with welcoming owners, good Scottish breakfasts, and new riding school attached to the farm; cl 25 Dec, 1 Jan.

Dumfries NX9776 The Hollies 255 Annan Rd Dumfriesshire DG1 3HB (0387) 67196 **£26**; 3 rms. Very good B & B, warmly commended by contributors.

To see and do

Edinburgh NT2574 Part of Edinburgh's charm lies in the fact that in the 18th c the city authorities decided to develop it not by knocking down the crowded and outmoded narrow streets of largely medieval buildings in the Old Town and replacing them with new smart Georgian streets, but instead to create an entirely new part of the city, working from scratch. So the New Town, a masterpiece of spacious Georgian town planning that's a real pleasure to stroll through (especially since most of its grand stone buildings have been cleaned up), stretches out handsomely below the steep crag of Castle Rock and its medieval skyline. It's been given great visual appeal by later additions in the classical style, columns and all – most notably the great neo-Greek temples at the foot of The Mound climbing from the New Town to the Old, and the romantic Doric colonnade which is a prominent landmark at the top of Calton Hill to the east. The whole of the New Town is dominated by the ancient silhouettes of Edinburgh Castle atop its castle cliff and of the long erratic line of tall, narrow Old Town buildings stretched along beside it. Up here narrow streets and alleys with steep steps between them and courtyard closes leading off have a real flavour of the distant past, with a good many interesting ancient buildings (and a lot of the city's antiquarian bookshops and other interesting specialist shops). As in most cities, there's a hop-on hop-off tour bus, and the ticket gives discounts to some of the places to visit. Edinburgh does put on its best clothes and best events for its Festival. It's easier to see, and truer to itself, at other times of year.

EDINBURGH CASTLE Perched on its hill and dominating the centre, the castle is a place of great magnetism – a series of buildings, constructed over various centuries, with plenty of history and things to see. There are the apartments of Mary, Queen of Scots, the room where James I of England and VI of Scotland was born, a room where the polished bare rock bulges up through the floor and the Scottish Crown Jewels – centuries older than the English ones. The site has been a fortress since the 7th c but the oldest surviving building is the beautiful little St Margaret's Chapel in one of the courtyards, which dates back to the 11th c. In 1314 the early buildings were destroyed to make the fortress useless to the invading English, so most of the castle is a series of later accretions inc the King's Lodging and James IV's Great Hall which date from the 15th and 16th c; further alterations were made in the 17th c. Highlights are Mons Meg, the 15th-c Belgian cannon with which James II cowed the Black Douglases; the Scottish National War Memorial built on the site of the castle's church; and the glorious views from the battlements, over the New Town, the Pentland Hills and the Firth of Forth to Fife beyond. Though you can wander around on your own, this is one place where the official guides are a great bonus; shop, disabled access; cl am Sun in winter; *£4. Also in the castle is the SCOTTISH UNITED SERVICES MUSEUM. And at 1 pm there's the ritual of firing of the One o'Clock Gun from the parapet. Disabled access; entrance free once in castle.

From the castle follow the ROYAL MILE, a largely medieval street, down to the PALACE OF HOLYROODHOUSE, an imposing old palace that has its origins in the Abbey of Holyrood, founded by David I. Later the court of Mary, Queen of Scots, it was used by Bonnie Prince Charlie during his occupation of Edinburgh, and of course is still a Royal residence for part of the year. The oldest surviving part is James IV's tower, with Queen Mary's rooms on the second floor, and a plaque on the floor there marks where her secretary Rizzio was murdered in front of her. The throne room and state rooms have period furniture, tapestries and paintings from the Royal Collection, while the picture gallery is interesting for its series of portraits of Scottish monarchs. The building has an almost domestic scale that makes it more inviting than many English palaces; shop, limited disabled access by prior arrangement; cl winter Sun, 2 wks mid-late May, 3 wks late Jun-early July and occasional other days – it may be best to check first on 031-556 1096; £3.

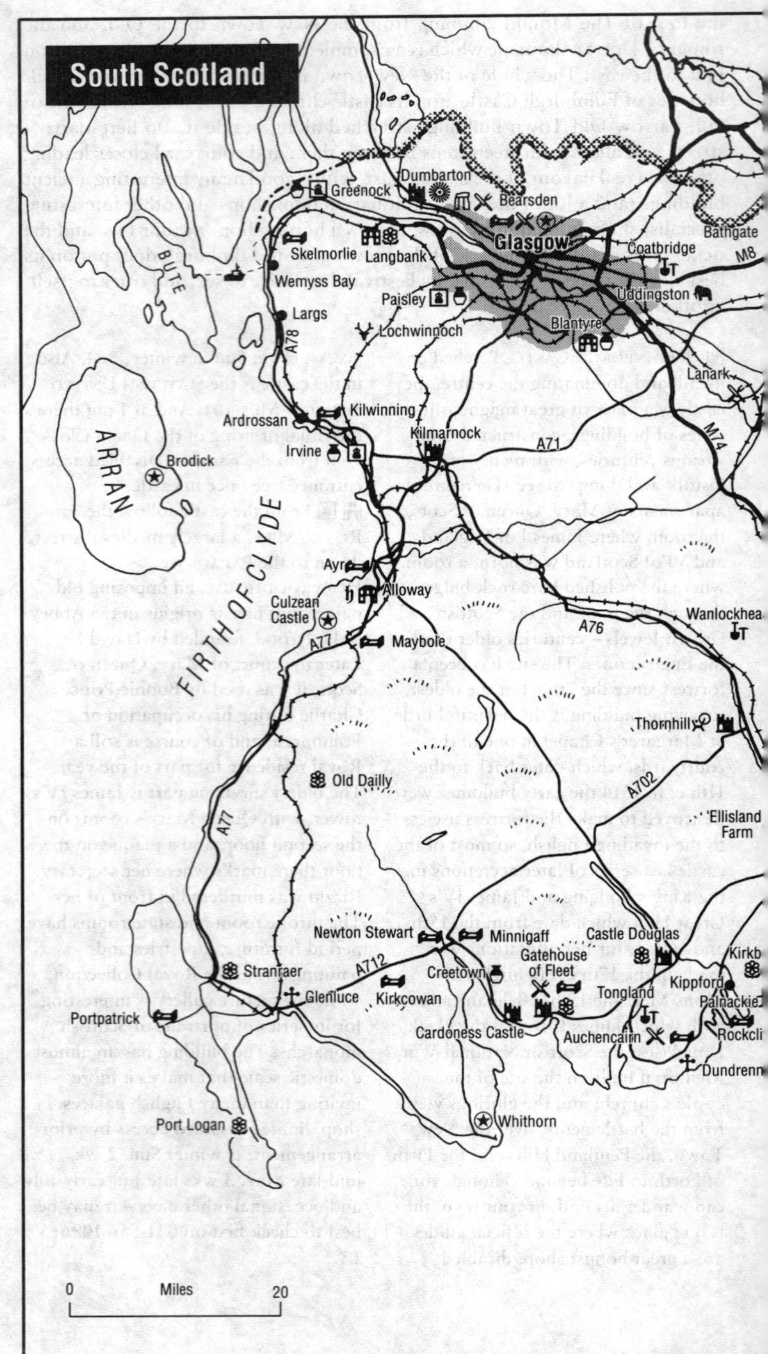
South Scotland
Greenock
Dumbarton
Bearsden
Glasgow
Bathgate
Coatbridge
M8
Skelmorlie
Langbank
BUTE
Wemyss Bay
Paisley
Uddingston
Largs
A78
Lochwinnoch
Blantyre
Lanark
M74
Kilwinning
Ardrossan
Kilmarnock
Irvine
A71
ARRAN
Brodick
FIRTH OF CLYDE
Ayr
Alloway
Culzean Castle
Wanlockhea
A76
A77
Maybole
Thornhill
Old Dailly
A702
A77
Ellisland Farm
Newton Stewart
Minnigaff
Castle Douglas
Gatehouse of Fleet
Kirkb
A712
Creetown
Kippford
Stranraer
Tongland
Palnackie
Glenluce
Kirkcowan
Portpatrick
Cardoness Castle
Auchencairn
Rockcli
Dundrenn
Port Logan
Whithorn
0
Miles
20

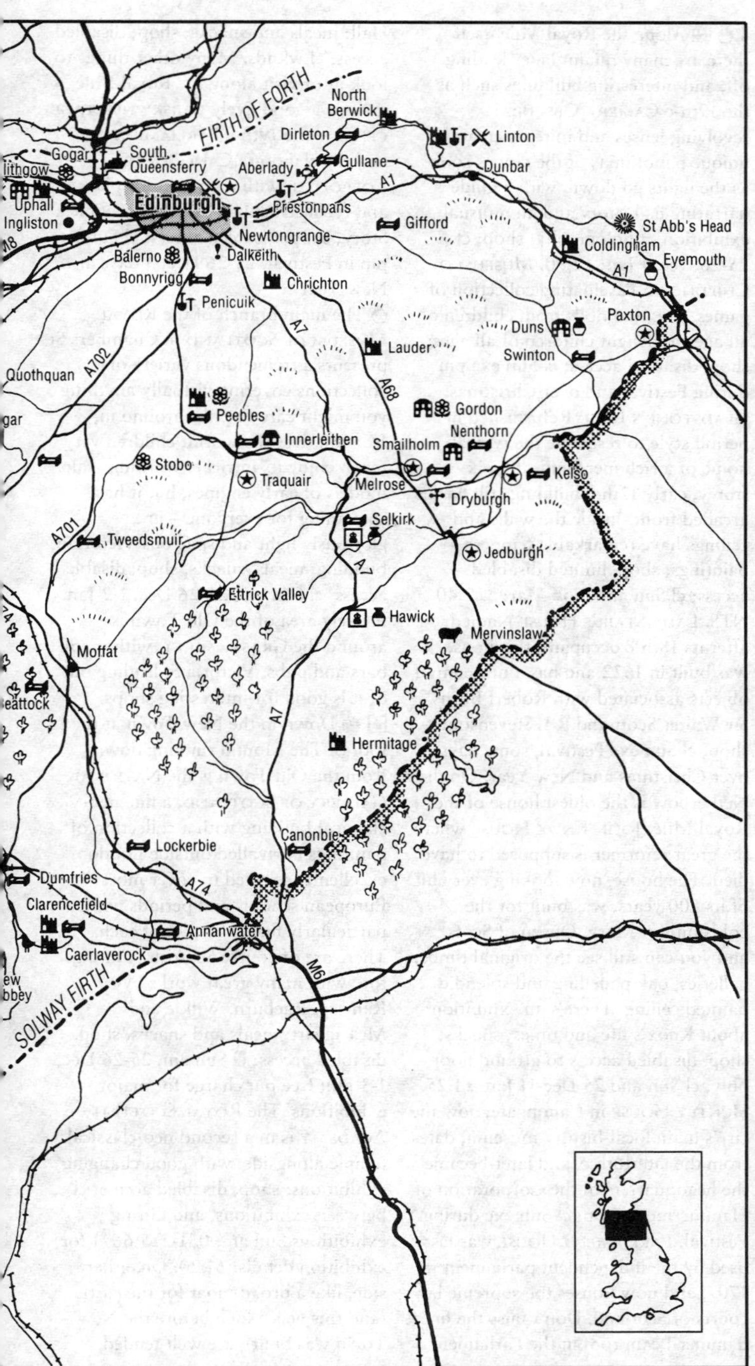
FIRTH OF FORTH
North Berwick
Dirleton
Linton
Gogar
South Queensferry
Gullane
Aberlady
Dunbar
lithgow
A1
Uphall
Edinburgh
Prestonpans
Ingliston
Gifford
St Abb's Head
Newtongrange
Coldingham
M8
Balerno
Dalkeith
Eyemouth
Bonnyrigg
Chrichton
A1
Penicuik
Paxton
Duns
A7
Lauder
Swinton
Quothquan
A702
A68
Gordon
Peebles
Nenthorn
gar
Innerleithen
Smailholm
Stobo
Traquair
Melrose
Kelso
Dryburgh
A701
Selkirk
Tweedsmuir
Jedburgh
Ettrick Valley
Hawick
Mervinslaw
Moffat
eattock
A7
Hermitage
Canonbie
Lockerbie
Dumfries
A74
Clarencefield
Annanwater
Caerlaverock
ew
bbey
SOLWAY FIRTH
M6

! Along the Royal Mile itself there are many quaint lanes leading off, and interesting buildings such as the 19th-c CAMERA OBSCURA: revolving lenses and mirrors create unique panoramas of the city as soon as the lights go down, with a guide narrating its history and an unusual exhibition of holography; shop; cl 25-26 Dec, 1 Jan; £2.90. MUSEUM OF CHILDHOOD Fascinating collection of games, toys and dolls from children of all ages to delight children of all ages; shop, disabled access; cl Sun exc pm during Festival and over Christmas. GLADSTONE'S LAND Refurnished in period style to resemble the typical home of a rich merchant, this six-storey, early 17th-c building still has its arcaded front. Inside the walls and ceilings have remarkable tempera paintings; shop, limited disabled access; cl Sun am, Nov-Mar; *£2.40. NTS. LADY STAIR'S HOUSE Named after its 18th-c occupant, this house was built in 1622 and has a museum of objects associated with Robert Burns, Sir Walter Scott and R L Stevenson; shop; cl Sun exc Festival, some days over Christmas and New Year. On the Netherbow is the oldest house of the Royal Mile, JOHN KNOX HOUSE where the great reformer is supposed to have died. The house, now looking every bit of its 500 years, was built for the goldsmith of Mary, Queen of Scots, and you can still see the original timber galleries, oak panelling and splendid painted ceiling. There's an exhibition about Knox's life and times; snacks, shop, disabled access to ground floor only; cl Sun and 25 Dec-11 Jan; £1.25. HUNTLY HOUSE in Canongate, now the city's main local-history museum, dates from the late 16th c, and later became the headquarters of the Corporation of Hammermen; shop; cl Sun exc during Festival. PARLIAMENT HOUSE was last used by the independent parliament in 1707, and now houses the supreme law courts of Scotland. Don't miss the fine hammer-beam roof in the Parliament Hall; meals and snacks; shop; disabled access; cl wknds. Many other things to look at or visit along the Royal Mile include a good lively WHISKY HERITAGE CENTRE, the 19th-c PARLIAMENT SQ, and the elaborate CANONGATE TOLBOOTH, with a series of displays and reconstructions called the People's Story; shop, disabled access; cl Sun exc pm in Festival, 25-26 Dec, 3 days at New Year.

The main branch of the ROYAL MUSEUM OF SCOTLAND in Chambers St presents a tremendous variety of collections covering virtually anything you might care to poke around in, from all over the world; children very much enjoy its intricate working scale models of early engines, but it has something for everyone – in a gloriously light and spacious Victorian building; meals, snacks, shop, disabled access; cl Sun am, 25-26 Dec, 1-2 Jan. A lively area of the Old Town is around the GRASSMARKET, with many bars and pubs. Victoria St leading out of it is good for interesting shops.

Down in the New Town at the foot of The Mound running down from the Old Town is the NATIONAL GALLERY OF SCOTLAND, a fine neo-classical building with a collection of paintings unrivalled outside London, excellently selected to cover most European schools and periods with particularly fine examples of each. There are of course Scottish paintings too, with many great works by Ramsay, Raeburn, Wilkie and McTaggart; meals and snacks, shop, disabled access; cl Sun am, 25-26 Dec, 1-3 Jan; free but charge for major exhibitions. The ROYAL SCOTTISH ACADEMY is in a second neo-classical temple alongside, with good changing exhibitions; shop, disabled access; cl between exhibitions, and during exhibitions Sun am; 031-225 6671 for exhibition details; £1.20. On either side, like a broad moat for the castle (and this was a loch before the New Town was built), are well-tended gardens, and facing them runs PRINCES ST, the city's main shopping street – its tall, mainly Georgian buildings lining just the one side, giving an expansive view across the sunken gardens to the castle. The NELSON MONUMENT dominates the end of Princes St, with glorious views if you can face the climb to the top. Every day at 1 pm the time ball drops as the gun from the castle goes off; shop; cl am Sun (all day Sept-Apr) and Mon; £1. Also on Princes St is the remarkably ornate SCOTT MEMORIAL, for many people Edinburgh's most memorable single building after the castle. It, too, gives terrific views from the top – though it takes 287 steps to get there; cl Sun; £1. Parallel with Princes St are GEORGE ST (some good superior shops) and beyond it QUEEN ST, with the very handsome CHARLOTTE SQ at their eastern end. Below Queen St, beyond a further strip of gardens, is a quiet further Georgian area with some interesting shops (for instance in Dundas St; for malt whiskies, Hoggs in the alley behind stately Great King St has the best combination of low prices with wide choice). Another fine Georgian area is the series of crescents around Moray Place above the Water of Leith, west of here. The WATER OF LEITH itself is worth exploring, often very picturesque and ravine-like; surprisingly close to Edinburgh's centre by its banks is the quaint little Dean Village, unaffected by all the New Town building above it.

For a structured introduction to the New Town's smart terraces and clean-cut Georgian houses, try the CONSERVATION CENTRE near the top of Dundas St. You can get a closer look in the archetypal GEORGIAN HOUSE, part of Robert Adam's magnificent terrace along the north side of Charlotte Sq. The rooms and servants' quarters have been refurbished in the style of 1800, and there are two interesting videos; shop, disabled access to ground floor only; cl Sun am, all Nov-Mar; £2.80. NTS.

SCOTTISH NATIONAL PORTRAIT GALLERY illustrates the history of Scotland through a huge collection of portraits in a variety of media; snacks, shop, disabled access; cl Sun am, 25-26 Dec, 1-3 Jan. It shares a building with the antiquities branch of the ROYAL MUSEUM OF SCOTLAND, where old-fashioned displays show a very rich collection of artefacts, jewellery and so forth from the Stone Age to the present; there's also a presentation on Stuart rule in Scotland; snacks; shop; disabled access; cl Sun am.

ROSE ST is an alley between Princes St and George St, quite lively, with lots of pubs and cafés.

SCOTTISH NATIONAL GALLERY OF MODERN ART (Belford Rd) A breathtaking collection inc good works by Picasso, Magritte, Barbara Hepworth and Lichtenstein, as well as the national collection of Scottish modern art; meals, snacks, shop, disabled access; cl Sun am, 25-26 Dec, 1-3 Jan.

Not far from the city centre is the ROYAL BOTANIC GARDEN, founded as a physic garden in 1670 at Holyrood and then transplanted to this site in the early 19th c. Covering 72 acres, it has various splendid themed areas, with a woodland garden, peat garden, arboretum and the Glasshouse Experience, including palm houses, fern house and aquatic house. It has the most comprehensive rhododendron collection in the country, and grows many other rare asiatic plants – particularly primulas, and lilies and their more awkward relatives – to perfection. It's a lovely place; meals and snacks, shop, disabled access; cl 25 Dec, 1 Jan. Overlooking the city and providing glorious views, even as far as the Braid Hills, is Scotland's ROYAL OBSERVATORY. In 1994 a special exhibition commemorates its centenary, and celebrates the latest discoveries about the universe and the work carried out here; collection of telescopes and astronomy books; shop; disabled access; cl am, 25 Dec, 1 Jan; £1.50. Out along the Corstophine Rd is EDINBURGH ZOO, yet another place with fantastic views of the city. An entertaining place, the zoo is especially noted for its penguin colonies (don't miss the penguin parade every day at 2 pm) with underwater viewing windows, and, as well as plenty of other animals, has various exhibitions explaining how zoos can help with research, education and conservation; meals and snacks, shop, disabled access; *£4.80.

Out beyond Holyrood is the great saddle-back hill of ARTHUR'S SEAT, a pleasant place for wandering, with the largely unspoilt Duddingston village below it (the Sheep Heid here is a good pub).

Edinburgh's pubs and bars are a special delight, chatty places often of great character. Among the best for atmosphere are the Bow Bar (Victoria St), Bannermans Bar (Cowgate), Café Royal and Guildford Arms (both W Register St), the Diggers (properly the Athletic Arms, Angle Park Terrace/ Kilmarnock Rd), Kays Bar (Jamaica St W), and the Rose Street Brewery (Rose St); for food too, the Abbotsford and Kenilworth (both Rose St), Starbank (Laverockbank Rd), Baille (Stockbridge), T G Willis (George St), Kings Wark (The Shore, Leith), Ocean Mist (a retired steam yacht in the Old Harbour there) and Steadings (Biggar Rd – A702).

Glasgow NS5865 Glasgow's been making huge strides recently in its crusade to convince a sceptical world that it's outgrown its former rather rough image. But in fact it's always had a solid cultural underpinning: the city-owned collection of paintings at the Kelvingrove Gallery is excellent, Glasgow had Scotland's first museum, and it now houses the Royal Scottish Orchestra (with a fine-sounding new concert hall), the Scottish Opera and the Scottish Ballet. Its Mayfest is good, and, like the Edinburgh Festival, is developing entertaining fringes; other festivals take you virtually right through the year. There's a zing and vitality about the place that shows most in the wealth of entertainment from street theatre and pub singers to big shows, the self-confidence and enormous civic pride of the people who live here, and even the huge modern development projects.

Though there is a mass of places to see and visit, they are not clustered conveniently around a compact and attractive centre. Instead, they are rather scattered about what is a big sprawling city. So it's a place to learn to love over a long period or repeated visits, rather than letting you feel you've immediately understood all its charms.

✝ The city was founded by St Mungo, and the 12th-c CATHEDRAL is dedicated to him. It is well preserved, though most of the fittings date from the 19th c; the best parts are the crypt and the Blackadder aisle. Nearby is the oldest house in the city, PROVAN'S LORDSHIP, which was used by the Prebend of Provan – a canon of the cathedral. This dates from 1471 and has a long and mixed history. Now, after careful restoration, the house has been redecorated using furnishings from various different periods of history; shop; cl Christmas/New Year. The country residence of the Prebend, PROVAN HALL is in Auchinlea Park, which has a variety of formal and informal gardens inc a garden for the blind. The house is virtually unchanged since the 16th c; disabled access; cl wknds.

It often strikes people as unexpected that there are so many green areas in the city: one of the best is POLLOK COUNTRY PARK which covers 361 acres, with waterside and woodland trails, a rose garden, advice for gardeners, and herd of highland cattle. But its great glories are the two museums in the grounds, the Burrell Collection and Pollok House, both not to be missed if you have the chance of coming to Glasgow; snacks; shop; disabled access. The BURRELL COLLECTION is splendidly and imaginatively housed in a modern building created especially to show its different parts to perfection, and the fact that it's out of the city centre means it's very uncrowded. The huge collection – far too much to see at one go – includes Egyptian alabaster, Chinese jade, oriental rugs, remarkable tapestries, medieval metalwork and stained glass, even medieval doorways and windows set into the walls; and paintings by, among others, Degas, Manet and Rembrandt; meals and snacks, shop, disabled access; you may have to pay for parking. POLLOK HOUSE treasures inc silver, ceramics and porcelain, and paintings (there's a collection of Spanish masters such as Goya and El Greco cannily acquired in the days when they were greatly undervalued); snacks, shop; cl Christmas-New Year.

! TENEMENT HOUSE (Buccleuch St) is a one-floor late 19th-c flat giving a vivid impression of what life was like for many Glaswegians at the turn of the c. The same woman lived here from 1911 to 1965 and in that time scarcely changed a thing; its time-capsule quality was preserved by a subsequent owner, and then the flat, with parlour, bedroom, kitchen and bathroom, original beds and coal bunker, kitchen range and rosewood piano, was left to the NT. Shop, disabled access; cl am, and probably from 1994 all Nov-Mar; £2. A further and more in-depth look at the work and leisure of the people of Glasgow is displayed at the PEOPLE'S PALACE (Glasgow Green) where exhibits very enjoyably illustrate the Jacobite risings, the industries of Glasgow, material from the campaigning days of the citizens, even football games, boxing matches and Billy Connolly's boots; meals, snacks, shop, disabled access; cl 25 Dec, 1 Jan. The WINTER GARDENS with huge tropical plants housed in a massive conservatory is just nearby. The MUSEUM OF TRANSPORT in Kelvin Hall in Argyle St contains a huge number of vehicles, from trams even to ships. Features include a reconstruction of a Glasgow sidestreet in 1938, and a walk-in car showroom with cars dating from 1930s to the present; snacks; shop; disabled access; cl Christmas-New Year. HAGGS CASTLE (St Andrews Drive) was built in the 1580s, and now is a museum specifically aimed at children, who are encouraged to explore the house and try to find out its history; shop; cl Christmas-New Year.

The UNIVERSITY OF GLASGOW VISITOR CENTRE does tours around some of the university's grander features, such as the Lion and Unicorn Staircase, Bute and Randolph Halls and Memorial Chapel; snacks, shop, disabled access; cl Sun exc pm May-Sept, and Christmas-New Year. Also part of the University is the HUNTERIAN MUSEUM which houses collections of ethnographic, palaeontological and anthropological material, and lots of archaeology and minerals. The present exhibitions started from the collection of Dr William Hunter, the 18th-c physician, who also bequeathed the core of fine paintings which form the basis of the HUNTERIAN ART GALLERY'S beautifully hung collection. This now includes a grand range of works by Whistler, and interesting and well-chosen contemporary British art and sculpture among a growing collection of 19th- and 20th-c paintings, as well as an amazing re-creation of the home of Charles Rennie Mackintosh, the designer/architect whose exuberant yet very disciplined and clean-lined art nouveau buildings stand out among the more traditional solidity of much of Glasgow; snacks, shop, disabled access with prior notice – tel 041-330 5431; cl Sun, all public hols. His most famous building is the GLASGOW SCHOOL OF ART (Renfrew St), and the decoratively mirrored WILLOW TEA ROOM (Sauchiehall St; open till 5) is furnished to his designs, too. More space is devoted to his work at the GLASGOW ART GALLERY AND MUSEUM (Kelvingrove Park) in the 'Glasgow Style' section (and you can buy works after him at the Glasgow Style Gallery, Gt Western Rd). Other sections in this huge Victorian building have sculpture, silver, porcelain, armour, also archaeology, ethnography and natural history. It has an amazingly rich collection of paintings inc familiar masterpieces from Rembrandt's *Man in Armour* to Dali's *Christ of St John of the Cross*. It's especially strong in works by the French Impressionists, Post-Impressionists, and Scottish artists from the 17th c; meals and snacks, shop, disabled access; cl Christmas-New Year. Major and international displays usually feature at the spacious and well-lit McLELLAN GALLERIES; shop, disabled access; cl between exhibits; charge varies according to exhibitions.

The area around St George's Sq and Buchanan St has been polished up, as elsewhere the dour grime of the proud Victorian buildings wiped away to show a fresh and appealing warm sandstone; this is Glasgow's smart shopping quarter. There are café-bars and bistros off Princes Sq, antique stalls in Victorian Village (West Regent St), and an entertaining weekend flea-market at the Barras (barrows: between Gallowgate and London Rd, past the Tolbooth) – here, try the plump fresh clappie doos (mussels).

The BOTANIC GARDENS (Queen Margaret Drive, off Great Western Rd) slope gently down to the River Kibble and are famous for their fantastic glasshouses, particularly the half-acre Kibble Palace, with its soaring tree ferns interspersed with Victorian sculpture; disabled access; main glasshouse cl am. The Empire Exhibition of 1938 was held at BELLAHOUSTON PARK, 3 miles from the centre, which covers about 171 acres, comprising a walled garden, sunken garden and sweeping lawns. An additional attraction is the Charles Rennie Mackintosh-designed house built here; disabled access. GREENBANK GARDEN aims to encourage and help owners of small gardens, so has lots of different shrubs and flowers to spark ideas. There's also a garden and greenhouse designed to meet the needs of disabled gardeners, with advice on specially designed tools; tearoom and shop (both cl weekdays Oct-Apr), disabled access; £2. ROUKEN GLEN PARK is a place of great tranquil beauty, with a walled garden, gorgeous lawns, and woodland walks along the river to a waterfall at the head of the glen; snacks. Slightly more historical is tree-lined VICTORIA PARK where fossil remains, some of them 230 million years old, were discovered by workmen digging a path in the late 19th c. Lots to do in LINN PARK with riverside walks, nature trails, children's zoo, golf course and collections of British ponies and highland cattle – even a ruined 14th-c castle, and an adventure playground for the disabled (prior arrangement preferred – tel 041-637 1147).

A walkway tracks along the Clyde now, its waterfront cleaned up. The veteran pleasure steamer *Waverley* makes some summer runs from here – 041-221 8152 for dates and times – and there are other summer boat trips; disabled access.

The Horseshoe (Drury St) is a classic Glasgow pub, not at all daunting, and Babbity Bowster and Rab Ha's (see

Where to stay) are very good. Other pubs and bars to try are the Blackfriars (Bell St), Bon Accord (North St), Chip Bar (off Byres Rd, nr University) and Stirling Castle (Old Dumbarton). Besides the restaurants we've mentioned, Glasgow is full of places to eat out in, formal and informal.

Other things to see and do

Aberlady NT4679 MYRETON MOTOR MUSEUM Wide-ranging collection of cars, motorbikes and military vehicles from the mid-19th c onwards, as well as lots of period advertising, posters and enamel signs; shop, disabled access; cl 25 Dec-1 Jan; *£2. The Green Craigh on the seashore is useful for lunch, and this seaside town has good golf.

Alloway NS3318 LAND O'BURNS CENTRE Alloway is a key stop on the Burns Trail, and this centre is a good introduction to both the poet and the area; various exhibitions, an audio-visual display and landscaped gardens outside; snacks, shop, disabled access; cl Christmas and New Year; audio-visual show 60p. More personal remains can be seen at BURNS' COTTAGE, the little thatched cottage where the writer was born in 1759; there's now a little museum of his life. Not far away and included in the admission price is the BURNS MONUMENT, built in 1823 to a fine design by Thomas Hamilton Jr, adorned with characters from Burns' poems sculpted by James Thorn; this is a monument as monuments should be, very much alive. Summer snacks, shop, disabled access; cl Sun am exc Jun-Sept, all Oct-Mar; *£1.80 (combined ticket).

The island of **Arran** is just under an hour by ferry from Ardrossan NS2342 (two ferries a day in winter, more in season), with summer ferries from Claonaig on Kintyre too. It has a marvellous variety of scenery from subtropical gardens to mountain deer forest. **Brodick** NS0136 here has a fine old CASTLE, built on a site fortified since Viking times. Now magnificent 18th-c formal gardens surround the impressive 13th-c building, full of treasures and fine furnishings, with extensions added in 1652 and 1844. The highlight is the woodland garden started in 1923 by the Duchess of Montrose, which includes many lovely, rare, tender rhododendrons; meals, snacks, shop, disabled access; cl Nov-Mar; castle open daily mid-Apr-Sept, Mon, Weds and Sat only early Apr and Oct; £3.50, just garden and Goat Fell £2.50. The nearby ISLE OF ARRAN HERITAGE MUSEUM in an 18th-c croft farm has farming and shipping displays as well as a 'smiddy' where a blacksmith worked until the 1960s, and a cottage furnished as it would have been in the 1920s; snacks, shop; cl Sun and all Oct-Apr; £1. Arran has a good circular walk up and down Goat Fell, prominent for miles around, and you can follow the shore right around the north tip, the Cock of Arran.

Balerno NT1666 MALLENY HOUSE GARDEN Charming gardens that are home to the National Collection of 19th-c shrub roses (best in late Jun), as well as four clipped old yew trees – the survivors of a dozen planted in 1603; disabled access; *£1.

Near **Bathgate** NS9758 CAIRNPAPPLE HILL (just E of Torpichen) One of the most important prehistoric sites in the country, a stone circle and series of successive burial cairns that seems to have been used for around 3,000 years from neolithic times to the first c BC, and especially during the second millennium BC. Extraordinary views from this raw and atmospheric hilltop site, known locally as 'windy ways'; cl all winter; £1.

Bearsden NS5471 ROMAN BATH HOUSE Probably the best surviving visible Roman building in Scotland, originally for the garrison at Bearsden Fort, part of the Antonine Wall defences.

Biggar NT0438 GLADSTONE COURT MUSEUM A 19th-c coachhouse housing an entire reconstructed village street, with shops, a bank, photographer's booth and telephone exchange; snacks, shop, disabled access; cl 12.30-2 pm, Sun am, all Nov-Easter; *£1. GREENHILL'S COVENANTERS HOUSE This 17th-c farmhouse was originally at Wiston but was moved piece by piece and reassembled on its present site. Rare breeds of sheep and poultry, and relics of the Covenanting period when the right to Presbyterian worship was fought for with grim ferocity; shop; cl am, and mid-Oct-Easter; 50p. The history and geology of the Upper Clyde and Tweed valleys are comprehensively dealt with at the MOAT PARK HERITAGE CENTRE; snacks; shop; disabled access; cl Sun am; £1.50. You can get a joint ticket for all three museums.

Blantyre NS6857 DAVID LIVINGSTONE CENTRE The famous explorer was born in a little one-roomed building in this row of houses, all of which have now been converted into a museum about his life and work in Africa. An African Pavilion also examines the continent today; snacks, shop, some disabled access; cl Sun am; *£2.

Bute The popular Glasgow holiday island is a half-hour ferry trip from Wemyss Bay/Skelmorlie NS1967; it has a thorough mix of open country (lovely in the north), fresh air and ebullient summer entertainments.

Caerlaverock NX9968 CAERLAVEROCK CASTLE The ancient seat of the Maxwell family, dating from the 13th c, protected not just by its moat but by the wild swampy marsh around it. The triangular inner courtyard is unusual, and the elaborate projecting tops for dropping missiles on assailants were added to the towers in the 15th c; shop, disabled access; £1.70. The surrounding saltmarshes are a reserve of the WILDFOWL AND WETLANDS TRUST, with outstanding hide facilities and observation towers over its 100 acres. Countless wildfowl flock here, especially barnacle geese – between Oct and Apr there are generally around 13,000 of them, and they make a dramatic sight when they're all in flight. Snacks, shop, limited disabled access; cl 24-25 Dec; *£2.95 – as well as the usual concessions, they'll offer you a discount if you come by bike!

Castle Douglas NX7662 THREAVE GARDEN is the National Trust for Scotland's horticulture school, with plenty to see throughout the year in its walled garden and glasshouses. If you're there in spring, don't miss the massed display of over 200 varieties of daffodil; meals, snacks, shop, disabled access; *£2.80. The Black Douglas, Archibald the Grim, built THREAVE CASTLE in the 14th c; four storeys high, it stands on an islet in the River Dee and you have to get a ferry across; shop; cl all winter; 60p.

Cardoness Castle NX5956 overlooks the Water of Fleet and dates from the 15th c – it was once the home of the McCullochs of Galloway; cl winter wkdys; £1.

Clarencefield NY0968 COMLONGON CASTLE dates from the 15th c but is unusually well preserved, indeed so much so that it's a popular spot for weddings; it's closed to visitors during these so you have to check in advance: (038 787) 283. Interesting original features include dungeons, kitchen, great hall and even privies; by appointment only – cl Dec-Apr; *£2.

Coatbridge NS7265 SUMMERLEE HERITAGE TRUST The story of the

Industrial Revolution and its effect on Scottish culture and history illustrated over 25 acres of a former iron works, with a working tramway, underground coalmine and miners' row-houses; snacks, shop, disabled access; cl 25-26 Dec and 1-2 Jan.

Coldingham NT9066 FAST CASTLE on the coast to the north isn't much more than a storm-battered pinnacle precariously tethered to the mainland cliffs by a dizzy walkway; the site is impressively defiant – it was the model for Wolfs Crag in Scott's *The Bride of Lammermoor*.

Creetown NX4758 GEM ROCK MUSEUM Recently refurbished and expanded, an enormous private collection of gem stones and minerals from around the world, some displayed in an atmospheric crystal cave; snacks, shop, disabled access; cl Thurs and Fri in Dec, 2 wks over Christmas and wkdys in Jan and Feb (exc by appointment); *£2.

Culzean Castle NS3309 CULZEAN CASTLE AND COUNTRY PARK A day here is one of the most popular outings in the region. The 18th-c mansion is one of great presence and brilliance, and the 563 acres of grounds are among the finest in Britain. Lushly planted and richly ornamental, Culzean was Scotland's first country park, and has bracing clifftop and shoreline walks, with woodlands and an 18th-c walled garden. The house was splendidly refashioned by Robert Adam, and it's been well restored recently to show off his work to full effect; particularly worth a look are the oval staircase and circular drawing room. Meals, snacks, shop, disabled access; cl Nov-Mar; house £3.30, country park £6 per car, pedestrians free. NTS.

! **Dalkeith** NT3367 EDINBURGH BUTTERFLY AND INSECT WORLD NT3367 Gloriously coloured exotic butterflies, with displays of other interesting and sometimes dangerous creatures like scorpions and tarantulas; snacks, shop, disabled access; cl Nov-8 Jan; *£2.95. It's set in a big garden centre slightly north of Dalkeith itself.

Dirleton NT5184 DIRLETON CASTLE Besieged by Edward I in 1298, this old castle was grandly rebuilt, only to be destroyed again in 1650. It has a charming garden planted in the 16th c, with ancient yews and hedges around a bowling green; cl am Sun, 25-26 Dec, 1-2 Jan; £1.70. The Castle and Open Arms in this pleasant golfing village are both useful for lunch.

† **Dryburgh** NT5932 DRYBURGH ABBEY One of David I's monasteries in a lovely setting among old cedars by the River Tweed – its graceful cloisters are very peaceful; shop, disabled access; cl 25-26 Dec, 1-2 Jan; £2.

Dumbarton NS4075 DUMBARTON CASTLE Perched on a rock 240 ft above the River Clyde, with dramatic views of the surrounding countryside. Most of what can be seen dates from the 18th and 19th c, though there are some earlier remains; snacks, shop; cl Sun am and in winter Thurs pm and all day Fri; £1.50.

Dumfries NX9776 is another place with good Burns connections. The ROBERT BURNS CENTRE provides an exhibition and audio-visual display about the poet, as well as an interesting scale model of the town at the time he wrote; snacks, shop, disabled access; cl 1-2 pm winter, all day Sun (exc pm summer) and Mon; 70p for the audio-visual exhibition. BURNS HOUSE (Burns St) is where he lived for the three years before his death, and has original letters and manuscripts, and the chair in which he wrote his last poems and songs; shop; times as for Centre; 70p. Neatly rounding off the tale is the BURNS MAUSOLEUM in the churchyard, in the form of a Greek temple and containing the tombs of Robert Burns, his on-and-off wife Jean Armour, and their five sons; you can make an appointment to visit at the Burns House, tel (0387) 55297. The GLOBE TAVERN has two rooms still very much as they were when this was his regular haunt (Anna Park, the barmaid, bore his child).

Dunbar NT6778 The harbour here is pretty, with some picturesque fragments of the medieval castle, and good walks nearby.

† **Dundrennan** NX7447
DUNDRENNAN ABBEY Ruined Cistercian abbey famous as the place Mary, Queen of Scots is thought to have spent her last night in Scotland, in ragged disguise with her head roughly shaved. Still hounded by her rebel pursuers, she then sought shelter in England where she was imprisoned for so long before her eventual execution; cl all winter; £1.20.

Duns NT7954 MANDERSTON A splendidly lavish house which features the world's only silver staircase. It was built for the millionaire racecourse owner Sir James Miller, who told the architect to spare no expense. Other gloriously extravagant parts are the painted ceilings and a ballroom decorated in Miller's racing colours. Vivid presentations of Edwardian life both above and below stairs, with stable block and marble dairy, fine formal gardens, and an unusual biscuit-tin museum; meals, snacks, shop, disabled access; open pm Thurs and Sun, Apr-Oct and English bank hols in May and Aug; £3.90 house and grounds, £2 grounds only. In the small town the poignant JIM CLARK ROOM shows the motor racing trophies the champion driver won, along with photographs and other memorabilia; shop; disabled access; cl 1-2 pm, Sun am, all Nov-Easter; 50p.

East Fortune NT5579 MUSEUM OF FLIGHT A good range of aircraft, with 35 aeroplanes from a Spitfire to a Vulcan bomber, and displays on famous flyers and air traffic control; snacks, shop, disabled access; cl Sept-Easter; £2.

East Linton NT5977 HAILES CASTLE Another brief stopping point for Mary, Queen of Scots; dressed as a man, she was brought here by Bothwell when they were fleeing from the rebels who had surrounded Borthwick Castle (now a hotel). It's now in ruins, but is lovely in spring, with wild flowers along the stream; cl am Sun and in winter Weds pm and all Thurs.
PRESTON MILL is one of the oldest working water-driven oatmeal mills surviving in Scotland; shop (pm wknds only, daily in July and Aug), limited disabled access; cl 1-2 pm, all Nov-Mar; £1.50. NTS. There's a dovecot a short walk away.

Ellisland Farm NX9385 is where Robert Burns lived from 1788 to 1791 and tried to introduce new farming methods, but failed. There are displays of material associated with the poet (who wrote *Tam o' Shanter* and *Auld Lang Syne* while living here), and cattle and sheep wander around much as they must have done then; disabled access; cl 25 Dec; donations.

Eyemouth NT9564 is an understated family holiday seaside town around a busy fishing port, with a decent beach, and a local MUSEUM commemorating the great fishing disaster of 1881, when 23 boats were smashed by a sudden storm and 129 fishermen were drowned, many in sight of their helpless families on shore; shop, disabled access; cl Sun am (all day in Oct), all Nov-Mar; *£1.

† **Glenluce** NX1957 GLENLUCE ABBEY Ruined Cistercian abbey founded in the late 12th c, set in beautiful surroundings. Remains include a vaulted chapter house; disabled access; cl winter wkdys; £1.20.

Greenock NS2776 MCLEAN MUSEUM AND ART GALLERY Various exhibitions relating to James Watt who was born here, as well as changing art exhibitions, a collection of model ships and engines, and exotic and very miscellaneous animals and artefacts brought from overseas by local travellers; shop, disabled access to ground floor only; cl 12-1 pm, all day Sun.

Gogar NT1672 SUNTRAP GARDEN AND ADVICE CENTRE Splendidly informative as well as sumptuous to look at, with several different gardens (Italian, Japanese, rock, peat, herbaceous and woodland), and free advice and tips; plant sales (wkdys only), disabled access; *£1.

Gordon NT6543 MELLERSTAIN HOUSE William Adam and his son Robert both worked on this striking Georgian house, which has impressive plasterwork and furnishings, and paintings by Van Dyck and Gainsborough. The terraced gardens and parkland are very pleasant, with fine views towards the distant hills; snacks, shop, limited disabled access; cl am, all day Sat, Oct-Apr exc Easter; £3.

Hawick NT5014 HAWICK MUSEUM AND SCOTT ART GALLERY Nicely placed in the beautiful Wilton Lodge Park, displays on the history, trade and wildlife of the Border area; shop, some disabled access; cl 12-1 pm, all day winter Sat, Christmas and New Year; *80p.

Hermitage NY5095 HERMITAGE CASTLE Well-restored but very forbidding remains of a 14th-c stronghold reeking of dire deeds; shop; cl winter wkdys; £1.20.

Hunterston NS4621 NUCLEAR POWER STATION Interesting visitor centre and tours of the nuclear power station itself; snacks, disabled access to visitor centre only; cl Dec-Feb exc by appointment.

Ingliston NT1473 SCOTTISH AGRICULTURAL MUSEUM (Royal Highland Showground) The rural history of the area, with tools and equipment used through the ages, and displays of domestic life; snacks, shop, disabled access; cl Sun, Oct-spring.

Innerleithen NT3336 ROBERT SMAILS PRINTING WORKS A fully restored Victorian printers with a water-powered press; you can try your hand at metal typesetting and hand-print your own bookmark. Shop, limited disabled access; cl 1-2 pm, Sun am, cl Nov-Mar; £2. NTS.

Irvine NS3239 GLASGOW VENNEL MUSEUM AND BURNS HECKLING SHOP Art gallery and museum, and behind, a reconstruction of the Heckling Shop where, as a young man, an unwilling Burns tried to learn the filthy trade of flax dressing. Happily for him, during a New Year's Eve party his aunt knocked over a candle and burnt the building to ashes. Also a reconstruction of his lodgings; disabled access; cl 1-2 pm, Sun am, all day Weds and in winter cl Mon and Sun too.

Jedburgh NT6521 12th-c JEDBURGH ABBEY is the most complete of the ruined Border monasteries founded by David I, and is an impressive sight, despite its town setting. Ransacked and burned with alarming regularity during its turbulent life, it was partly restored by the Victorians, who still used the roofless nave for services. The 86-ft tower is imposing, and the west door is splendid. Also a video show and the remains of some of the domestic buildings; shops, disabled access; £2. MARY, QUEEN OF SCOTS HOUSE A charming 16th-c castle house or fortified dwelling where Mary had to prolong her 1566 stay because of a near-mortal fever (during her long confinement at the hands of her cousin Queen Elizabeth, she later said she wished she'd died back in Jedburgh). It now presents a good interpretation of her life; look out for the left-handed spiral staircase which allowed the men of the Ker clan – traditionally all left-handed – to use their sword hands; shop; cl Nov-Easter; *£1.20. CASTLE JAIL AND MUSEUM Built in the 1820s on the site of the medieval castle, this is one of the few surviving prison buildings with different blocks for different types of offender. It now houses a local-history museum; disabled access; cl am Sun and all Oct-Mar; 90p. Just off the A68 S of town are the ruins of FERNIEHURST CASTLE.

✝ 🏰 ⚱ **Kelso** NT7334 The greatest and wealthiest of the four famous Border abbeys was at Kelso, though today not much of the building remains. A nearby MUSEUM explains the history of the abbey, as well as that of the town, with a reconstructed 19th-c marketplace; shop; cl 12-1 pm, Sun am, all Nov-Easter; *80p. NTS. FLOORS CASTLE is a magnificent building designed by William Adam in 1721, now the home of the Duke of Roxburgh. There's a window for every day of the year, a splendid collection of tapestries, and a magnificent walled garden; meals and snacks, shop, disabled access; open Easter wknd, then open late Apr-Oct, cl Fri and Sat exc by appointment; £3.20. Kelso is an attractive place to wander round, with lots of interesting events almost all year – its Sept ram sales are altogether more fun than you could imagine they'd be, with all sorts of agricultural side events. The Queens Head is good for lunch.

❀ **Kirkbean** NX9859 ARBIGLAND GARDENS Extensive woodland, formal and water gardens based around a lovely sandy bay. The US Admiral John Paul Jones worked here as a boy (his father was the gardener), and his birthplace nearby has been turned into a little museum; snacks, shop, disabled access; cl Mon exc bank hols, all Oct-Apr; *£2.

🏰 **Kilmarnock** NS4337 DEAN CASTLE The ancestral home of the Boyd family, now housing a wonderful collection of medieval arms and armour, musical instruments, tapestries, and a display of Burns' manuscripts. A good restoration means the 15th-c house and the 14th-c keep are shown almost in their original splendour, and the grounds outside are pleasant; snacks, shop; cl am, 25-26 Dec, 1-2 Jan; *£2.

🏛 ❀ **Langbank** NS3873 FINLAYSTONE The home of the chief of the Clan Macmillan, with the main attraction the garden – formal and walled with woodland walks and adventure playgrounds. Also worth a look are the interesting displays in the house, inc an exhibition of Victorian flower books and international collection of dolls. The house has connections with Robert Burns and John Knox – unlikely partners; snacks wknds and wkdys May-Sept, shop, disabled access; £1.50.

Largs NX6755 is the pick of the traditional Clydeside resorts, with boats across the narrow strip of water to the island of Great Cumbrae. The pleasure steamer *Waverley* also calls here in summer.

🏰 **Lauder** NT5347 THIRLESTANE CASTLE Charming old castle with an interesting collection of old dolls and toys and some of the best plasterwork in the country in the 17th-c state rooms; snacks, shop; open pm Weds, Thurs and Sun May-Sept, daily (exc Sat) July and Aug; *£3.50. The Lauderdale Hotel and the Eagle are useful for lunch.

🏰 🏛 **Linlithgow** NS9976 LINLITHGOW PALACE was the birthplace of Mary Queen of Scots – it burned down in 1746 and now makes a magnificently sombre ruin standing beside the loch. You can still see the chapel, great hall and a quad with a fountain; shop, limited disabled access; cl Sun am; £1.70. In the town a pleasant old tavern, the Four Marys, is named for her maids-in-waiting Mary Carmichael, Mary Hamilton, Mary Beaton and Mary Seaton, with relevant memorabilia. HOUSE OF THE BINNS Interesting 17th-c laird's house built by Thomas Dalyell, and the home of his family ever since. Some splendid plaster ceilings and a varied collection of furniture and porcelain, much of it from the Regency period; disabled access; cl am, Fri, Oct-Apr; *£2.80. NTS.

🐦 **Lochwinnoch** NS3559 RSPB NATURE CENTRE Fine views of the reserve from the observation tower, and nature trails through the woodland and marshland to observation hides, one of which has been specially designed for disabled visitors; wknd snacks, shop, disabled access; cl Christmas and New Year; *£2.

Melrose NT5434 PRIORWOOD GARDEN Specialising in flowers suitable for drying, with a display orchard illustrating apples through the ages; shop, disabled access; cl Sun am, all Jan-Apr; *£1. Memorabilia, relics and the mammoth 9,000-volume library of Sir Walter Scott can all be seen at his mansion ABBOTSFORD HOUSE, set grandly on the River Tweed slightly west of town. He lived here until his death in 1832, collecting all sorts of oddities like Rob Roy's gun and Bonnie Prince Charlie's quaich (drinking cup); snacks, shop, disabled access; cl Sun am, all Nov-mid-Mar; £2.50. Further connections with the writer can be made at the ruins of MELROSE ABBEY, probably the country's finest Cistercian abbey – and as Scott says, best in moonlight. Look out for the wonderful stonework on the 14th-c nave (and the pig playing the bagpipes). The heart of Robert the Bruce is buried somewhere in the church; shop; disabled access; cl Sun am; £2.30. The MUSEUM here is housed in a 16th-c abbey official's house, with material from the Trimontium Roman fort. While in this area the two dozen vintage cars of the MELROSE MOTOR MUSEUM are worth a look; shop, disabled access; cl Nov-Apr; £2. Besides the Burts Hotel, the Kings Arms is useful for lunch.

Mervinslaw NT6713 JEDFOREST FARM PARK Working hill farm with deer as well as other animals, good for children; cl Nov-Apr.

Moffat NT0805 still has some of the poise of its former days as a spa; the Moffat House, Star (Britain's narrowest hotel), Balmoral and Black Bull are all useful for lunch.

New Abbey NX9666 has one of the most romantic ruins in the area, both in its lofty arched nave open to the sky, and in its story: SWEETHEART ABBEY was built by Lady Devorgilla in memory of her late husband (she also founded Balliol College in Oxford). On her death, she was buried in front of the high altar, with the heart of her husband resting on her bosom – hence its name; shop, disabled access; cl winter Thurs pm and Fri; £1. The recently reopened and much extended SHAMBELLIE HOUSE OF COSTUME has costumes from the late 1700s to the early part of this c; snacks, shop; at the time we went to press opening times hadn't been decided – tel (038 785) 375; £2. There's also a restored 18th-c WATERMILL in this pretty village; shop; cl Thurs, and Fri in winter; £1.50.

Newtongrange NT3364 SCOTTISH MINING MUSEUM Excellent coverage of mining history; the Lady Victoria Colliery has been restored and developed as a vivid re-creation of mining days, both at the pithead and back home, even in the tearooms; meals, snacks, shop, limited disabled access; cl Oct-Mar; *£1.95.

Old Daily NX2289 BARGANY GARDENS have fine ornamental trees, woodland walks winding through springtime glades of snowdrops, bluebells and daffodils, and a lilypond enveloped by azaleas and rhododendrons; disabled access, cl Nov-Feb; £1, £1.50 May and Jun.

Paisley NS4864 MUSEUM AND ART GALLERIES 19th-c Scottish artists receive most emphasis here, and there's a marvellous collection of antique and more modern paisley shawls, along with the looms on which they were made; shop; cl Sun and public hols. COATS OBSERVATORY Recently re-equipped with good displays covering astronomy, meteorology and space flight; shop; cl am Mon, Tues, Thurs (when open till 8), all day Sun.

Paxton NT9453 PAXTON HOUSE Built in 1758 by the lovestruck Patrick Billie, who hoped to marry a daughter of Frederick the Great; the marriage never took place, but the result was a splendid neo-Palladian mansion, designed by the Adam family and furnished by the Chippendales. The gallery shows Scottish art and among the other treasures are a frail pair of gloves given to Billie by his heroine. Outside are woodland and riverside walks and an adventure playground designed by the Territorial Army; snacks, shop, disabled access; cl Nov-Easter; £3.50.

Peebles NT2540 Attractive if sedate Border town, with quite a lot for visitors; the Tontine is useful for lunch. To the west is spectacularly set NEIDPATH CASTLE, converted from the original 14th-c tower in the late 16th and early 17th c to make it more comfortable for the family living there. There's a rock-hewn well, a small museum and a pit prison – not much chance of escape, some of the walls are 11 ft thick. Nice views from the parapets; shop; cl Sun am, Nov-Easter, Oct open Tues only; £1.50. KAILZIE (2 miles SE) Extensive grounds with lovely old trees flanked by azaleas and rhododendrons, formal rose garden, walled garden, and small art gallery; meals, snacks, shop, disabled access; £2.

Penicuik NT2360 EDINBURGH CRYSTAL VISITOR CENTRE You can watch the techniques of glass-blowing here, as well as cutting, polishing, engraving and sand etching. There's also an exhibition of the history of the crystal; meals, snacks, shop, disabled access; tours Mon-Fri all year and wknds May-Sept, cl Dec 24-27, 1-2 Jan; *£2.

Port Logan NX0940 LOGAN BOTANIC GARDEN just out of the village is another specialist garden of the Royal Botanic Garden of Edinburgh, containing a wide range of plants from the warm temperate regions of the southern hemisphere; meals and snacks, shop, disabled access; cl Nov-mid-Mar; £1.50. The village itself has a natural sea pool where fat fish will eat from your fingers; and for food, we've been getting very good reports recently on The Inn.

Prestonpans NT3874 was the setting for Bonnie Prince Charlie's 1745 rout of the Hanoverians. The MINING MUSEUM is located on the oldest documented coal mining site in Britain, and is being redeveloped as an Industrial Heritage Museum, taking in other industries of the area as well as the existing reconstruction of a coal face and colliery workshop, and a Cornish beam engine. Industrial steam locomotives are put through their paces on the 1st Sun of each month; snacks, shop; cl Oct-Mar.

The **Rinns of Galloway** – the hammerhead of land in the extreme west of the area – is largely empty even in high summer, a very peaceful place, with cliffs (especially on the south point), rocks and small coves.

St Abb's NT9167 on the east coast is a steep and pretty little seaside village by a sandy beach and the old fishing harbour, little used now. The cliffs of ST ABB'S HEAD are noisily crowded with breeding seabirds in late spring, with high breezy walks, and a LIGHTHOUSE which is often open for visits.

Selkirk NT4728 is good for bargain-hunting for the tweeds, woollens and cashmeres which are woven and knitted here; the Woodburn House Hotel and Queens Head are useful for lunch. BOWHILL HOUSE (3 m W) has an outstanding collection of paintings, inc works by Canaletto, Van Dyck and Claude, as well as impressive furnishings and porcelain, and memorabilia relating to Sir Walter Scott and Queen Victoria. The restored Victorian kitchen is worth a look, and children will enjoy the adventure playground and surrounding country park. You can hire bicycles; snacks, shop, disabled access; grounds open pm May-Aug (exc Fri), house pm in July only; *£3.50 park and house, park only £1.

Smailholm NT6435 BORDER TOWER HOUSE (just S, signed off the B6404 NE of St Boswells) Classic 15th-c Border tower house, very well preserved – all 57 ft of it. Display based on Sir Walter Scott's book *Minstrels of the Borders*, and an exhibition of dolls; shop; cl Sun am, Oct-Mar; *£1.50.

South Queensferry NT1477 Notable for its views of the two great Forth bridges on either side, with piers to potter on; the Hawes Inn is useful for lunch. HOPETOUN HOUSE is probably Scotland's best example of the work of William and Robert Adam. The magnificent reception rooms have a wonderful art collection with works by Canaletto and Gainsborough. The superb and extensive grounds include a deer park and a flock of rare sheep, and you can play croquet or petanque; snacks, shop, some disabled access; cl 3 Oct-early Apr; *3.50, £1.80 grounds only. DALMENY HOUSE Despite its Tudor Gothic appearance this splendidly placed house dates only from the 19th c – there's a superb hammer-beamed roof, as well as fine furnishings, porcelain and portraits. Good walks in the grounds and on the shore; snacks, disabled access; open May-Sept Sun, Mon, Tues pm only; £3.20. By ferry you can get to INCHCOLM ABBEY, an Augustinian abbey founded by Alexander I. It's in a better state of preservation than any other in Scotland, with a fine 13th-c octagonal chapter house and a wall painting from the same period. A lovely trip on a fine day; ferries 11.45, 1 and 3, summer only, though if you can get there yourself the abbey is open in winter too; £5.75 ferry and abbey.

Stobo NT1838 DAWYCK BOTANIC GARDEN is a specialist garden of the Royal Botanic Garden, particularly noted for its arboretum which is very rich in mature conifers (inc a larch believed to have been planted in 1725), with notable Asiatic silver firs and many rarities; other trees include the original of the fastigiate Dawyck beech, and a good collection of maples. Meals, snacks, shop, disabled access; cl 22 Oct-15 May; *£1.

Stranraer NX0660 CASTLE KENNEDY GARDENS Prettily set between two lochs (with lots of good walks around), these gardens were first laid out in the early 18th c, then after years of neglect were restored and developed in the 19th. They're especially admired for their walled garden and flowering shrubs, esp the rhododendrons, azaleas and embothriums; snacks, shop, limited disabled access; cl Oct-Mar; *£2.

Thornhill NX8795 DRUMLANRIG CASTLE An unusual pink sandstone castle built in the late 17th c with a glory of fine panelling and furnishings (mainly Louis XIV), and splendid paintings by Leonardo da Vinci, Holbein, Rembrandt and Murillo; there are craft workshops in the stables, and extensive woodland walks. Meals, snacks, shop, disabled access; cl am wknds, all day Thurs, and castle all Sept-Apr (grounds cl Oct-Apr); *£4.

Tongland NX6953 TONGLAND TOUR Tours of part of the Scottish Power Galloway hydro-electricity scheme, which has a salmon-jumping ladder; shop; cl early Sept-mid-May; tel to check tour times (0557) 30114.

Traquair NT3334 TRAQUAIR HOUSE One of the longest-inhabited and for many the most romantic houses in the country. It dates back to the 10th c and has a rich history: 27 English and Scottish kings have stayed here, and there are strong associations with Jacobite risings. The Bear Gates have remained closed since 1745 when Bonnie Prince Charlie passed through them for the last time – they won't open again until the Stuarts regain their rightful place on the throne. The house has a bed said to have been used by Mary, Queen of Scots and there's an 18th-c brewery, recently restored to working order. This is particularly popular with our contributors – with a maze, antique and craft shops and an art gallery as well as the house and gardens there's plenty to see; meals and snacks, shop, some disabled access; open Easter wk, then pm May-Sept, and am too in July and Aug; *£3.50. The Traquair Arms is good for lunch.

Uddingston NS6960 GLASGOW ZOO Growing open-plan zoo, specialising in cats and reptiles, with other rare mammals and birds on display; summer meals and snacks, shop; disabled access; cl 25 Dec; £3.60.

Remote **Wanlockhead** NS8713 is Scotland's highest village. The MUSEUM OF LEAD MINING has guided tours of an 18th-c lead mine and miners' cottages furnished in the styles of 1740 and 1890. A new visitor centre also has mineral displays; meals and snacks, shop, limited disabled access; cl Nov-Mar exc by appointment, tel (0659) 74387; *£2.75.

Whithorn NX4440 WHITHORN DIG An archaeological dig on the spot where Scotland's first-recorded Christian settlement was established by St Ninian 1,500 years ago. There are the remains of several later churches that sprang up when the site became a centre of pilgrimage, and a visitor centre with an audio-visual display; snacks, disabled access; cl Nov-4 Apr; *£2.50. The PRIORY on this site dates from 1297, but was the last in a series built on this spot since 397. The good museum has some fine Celtic crosses and explains its importance – it was once a holy place of pilgrimage, with kings walking the 130 miles from Edinburgh; disabled access; cl Mon-Fri; £1.20.

There are many more CASTLES as well as the ones we've described: imposing ones include ORCHARDTON TOWER at **Palnackie** NX8256, CRICHTON CASTLE at **Crichton** NT3862 and TANTALLON CASTLE at **North Berwick** NT4585, a 14th-c Douglas stronghold.

The coasts have some fine stretches, with some attractive villages. On the west coast, the harbour towns of Isle of Whithorn NX4736 and Portpatrick NW9954 are attractive, usually with something going on down by the water, and Kippford NX8354 and Rockcliffe NX8453 are pretty yachting places; there's a vast stretch of tidal sands backed by dunes just around the headland from Rockcliffe. All have useful pubs serving food.

★ **Other attractive villages** with decent pubs in the area include Auchencairn NX7951, Cramond NT1876, Dunure NS2515, Eskdalemuir NY2597 (it also has an unexpected Tibetan Buddhist temple), Gifford NT5368, Kirkcowan NX3260 and Larkhall NS7651. Some Clydeside pubs with decent food and good sea views include the Cardwell at Cardwell Bay in Gourock NS2477 and the Spinnaker there, and the Lookout in Troon Marina NS3230. Besides those we've mentioned as places to eat at or stay in, inns where you can get a decent bite to eat and which are particularly well placed for walkers, drivers or just strollers in these parts include the Angel and Murray Arms at Gatehouse of Fleet NX5956, Golf Hotel at Gullane NT4882, Breadalbane Hotel at Kildonan NS0231, Border at Kirk Yetholm NT8328, Selkirk Arms at Kirkcudbright NX6851 and Buccleuch Arms at St Boswells NT5931.

Walks

The **Border hills** have plentiful solitary hill-walking. The **Southern Upland Way** (coast to coast over S Scotland) is a good basis for day walks. Large distances between places often make it hard to find focal points for walks, but the

Eildon Hills above Melrose NT5434 are splendidly compact, giving a very pleasing ridge walk along the top. The E shore of **St Mary's Loch** NT2422 (where Tibbie Shiels Inn is very handy) is followed by the Southern Upland Way; a short drive to the S, there is a car park and starting point for a pretty walk up a narrow glen to the spectacular Grey Mare's Tail waterfalls NY0195. You can continue beyond them along Tail Burn to Loch Skeen NT1716.

The **Dumfries and Galloway coast** is long and unspoilt. Good peaceful walks include going from Rockcliffe NX8453 E to **Castle Hill Point** NY9169 and beyond; or to **Balcary Point** NX8249 on the W side of Auchencairn Bay; or around the **Mull of Galloway** NX1530, Scotland's SW toe. You can get an astonishing view of the English Lake District over the Solway Firth from the summit of **Criffel** NX9562, S of Dumfries; the best access point is New Abbey NX9666. There's energetic hill walking on the **Rhinns of Kells** ridge from Forrest Lodge NX5586 NW of New Galloway. Galloway Forest Park offers trails around **Loch Trool** NX4179 and a walk up Merrick NX0054, the highest point in SW Scotland.

Edinburgh adjoins bumper walking territory. **Arthur's Seat** (also called Holyrood Park – actually Arthur's Seat is strictly just the summit) is the mountain virtually in the city centre – a great volcanic mass giving a wonderful panorama over the city. The **Firth of Forth** has dull hinterland, but excellent shoreside walks along the sands from Aberlady NT4679 to North Berwick NT5485, with stop-off possibilities at Dirleton NT5184 and Gullane NT4882; a good bus service connects the shoreside villages between North Berwick and Edinburgh.

W of the city, from the Cramond Brig Hotel on the A90, you can walk along the wooded **River Almond** to Cramond NT1876, cross the Almond by ferry, then go along the shore past Dalmeny House, and finish below the Forth Bridge at South Queensferry NT1477. There are frequent buses back to the start, and to Edinburgh. The **Pentland Hills** NT1358 are the nearest uplands to Edinburgh, with some good high-level walks and attractive reservoirs.

Just outside Lanark, the **Falls of Clyde** are dramatic when the hydro-electric station upriver opens the sluices; a path snakes around river cliffs from New Lanark NS8842, the 'model' early industrial revolution village of social reformer Robert Owen (well worth a look). The **Culzean Castle** estate NS3309 near Ayr is a country park, with woods, landscaped grounds, a lake, and the adjacent coast adding up to a worthwhile outing, with an abundance of paths. Level walks can take in the early stages of the **West Highland Way**, which starts at Milngavie NS5574 and takes glen routes to Fort William (up in the area we discuss next), the scenery getting better all the way. Above Greenock NS2776, meandering **Greenock Cut** (part of an elaborate, now abandoned, water scheme for Greenock) makes a level walk around a hillside terrace giving views into the Highlands. Around Glasgow are a number of country parks with lots of short walks, for example around Mugdock NS5576, N of the city, which has two castle ruins, a view over Glasgow, and an attractive loch.

The best of the E coast is around St Abbs Head NT9169 (walk from Eyemouth or St Abbs).

Driving

Heading S from Edinburgh, you almost immediately climb into fine scenery. The A70 and A702 heading SW from the city run through fine scenery, but both carry a fair amount of traffic. Another north-south trunk road out of Edinburgh, the busy A7, also has a lot of fine mountain and river scenery; but for pleasure the B709 which virtually parallels it is greatly preferable, taking you over the Moorfoot Hills and into desolate moorland, with attractive and altogether gentler interludes at Innerleithen, Traquair, Mountbenger in Yarrow (where the Gordon Arms is a very welcoming stop), and the Tushielaw Hotel, then plunging on through grand hills to head S into Eskdale, with the River Esk bowling along beside the road. Another attractive alternative to the A7, at least S of Hawick, is the B6357/B6399 through peaceful Liddesdale, which more or less parallels it.

It is up in these southern hills that the finest drives are to be found. The B7009 which runs from the B709 at Tushielaw down the Ettrick Valley to the softer country around Selkirk is very rewarding; you can follow the River Ettrick in the opposite direction too, high into the forests around its headwaters. Another notable drive is the A708 between Selkirk and Moffat: fine hill scenery, the still waters of St Mary's Loch, and a view of at least part of the tremendous waterfall of the Grey Mare's Tail (worth getting out for a closer and more impressive view).

From Moffat the A701 climbs up past the path to the Devils Beef Tub (a huge crater where the border raiders hid cattle they'd rustled, rather an awesome sight on a dour day), then drops gently down through grand scenery along the valley of the upper River Tweed, among hills where the high sheep pastures shade into heather above. To follow the Tweed, a right turn on the B712 takes you to the A72 and the richer well-wooded valley country around Peebles and Innerleithen.

Off all these roads little back roads delve off into lonelier places, often tracking a stream, sometimes climbing into the clouds – almost always worth exploring, if you've the time. Near the English border, the little roads delving off to the E of the A68 (itself a grand road) between Jedburgh and Carter Bar are very rewarding.

On the E side of this area the Lammermuir Hills make for an attractive drive between Duns and Gifford, either along the riverside B6355 (more varied scenery), or on the more direct hill road through Longformacus (lonelier).

Over in the W the countryside is milder, though the A747 from Glenluce down to the Isle of Whithorn and the A715 down to Drummore and the Mull of Galloway are both pleasant coastal roads, and if you're not allergic to landscapes consisting largely of spruce plantations, the Glentrool road forking off the A714 N of Newton Stewart certainly takes you up into very remote countryside.

If you've reason to be around that area anyway, the A78 between Gourock and West Kilbride does give glorious views over the Clyde. Even close to Glasgow there are some surprises – like the pleasant A760 from Lochwinnoch to Largs, and the back hill road from there to Greenock.

Where to eat

Glasgow NS5865 ROGANO 11 Exchange Place 041-248 4055 Excellent restaurant decorated in splendidly sustained art deco style – emphasis on fish, though not exclusively so. **£40**. There's also an oyster bar (**£15**|£2.90/£5.50) as well as a very good value café which is open all day; cl Sun am, bank hols; disabled access.

Linlithgow NS9977 CHAMPANY (0506 83) 4532 Wonderful Aberdeen Angus beef as well as lovely fresh fish (they also have their own smoke-house), home-made ice creams, and good wines; cheaper bistro-style meals in Champany Chop and Ale House next door; main restaurant cl Sun, 2 wks fr 24 Dec; children over 8; disabled access. **£35**|£18.50.

Glasgow NS5865 UBIQUITOUS CHIP 12 Ashton Lane 041-334 5007 Very popular downstairs restaurant (no chips, hence the name) with friendly, efficient service, excellent Scottish food, very good wine cellar, and no-smoking areas; cl Sun am, 25-26 Dec; disabled access. **£27.30**. Upstairs is a convivial pub with good-value bar food; cl 25-26 Dec. **£7.35**|£2.60/£4.20.

Linton NT5977 DROVERS EH40 3AG (0620) 860298 18th-c pub with attractively furnished bar and fresh, interesting food inc local fish; no children; **£26**|£10.50.

Bearsden NS5471 FIFTY-FIVE BC 128 Drymen Rd 041-942 7272 Very good, interesting modern cooking using good local produce in attractive and stylish restaurant; friendly staff; cl Sun, 25-26 Dec, 1-2 Jan, disabled access. **£21**/£3.70.

Edinburgh NT2574 PIERRE VICTOIRE 38-40 Grassmarket EH1 2JV 031-226 2442 Reasonably priced French restaurant with particularly good soups and fish; popular at lunchtime, cl Sun. **£21**|£5/£7.50.

Lanark NS8843 LA VIGNA 40 Wellgate (0555) 664320 Very good Italian food; cl Sun am, 1 wk Jan. **£20**|£3/£7.

Glasgow NS5865 CUL DE SAC 44-46 Ashton Lane 041-334 4686 Lively crèperie, close to Byres Rd and the fashionable west end and University; cl 25 Dec-1 Jan. **£19**.

Lanark NS8843 EAST INDIA COMPANY 32 Wellgate (0555) 663827 Simply but attractively decorated Indian restaurant with exceptionally good, carefully prepared food, and helpful, friendly service. **£14**/£4.50.

Edinburgh NT2574 KALPNA 2-3 St Patrick 031-667 9890 Extremely good Indian restaurant with very efficient service; cl Sun, Christmas; **£12.70**|£3.50/£8.50.

Glasgow NS5865 SANNINOS 61 Elmbank St 041-332 3565 Very good pasta and pizzas and warmly recommended by contributors; cl Sat/Sun am, 25 Dec, 1 Jan; children can have half helpings. **£12.50**/£4.90 (2-course lunch).

Glasgow NS5865 DI MAGGIOS 61 Ruthven Lane 041 334 6000 Warmly recommended by contributors; other restaurants in the same chain at 21 Royal Exchange Sq 041-248 2111/4443 and at 1038 Pollokshaws Rd, Shawlands 041-632 8888; cl Sun am, 25 Dec, 1 Jan. **£12**/£4.

Auchencairn NX7951 SMUGGLERS Main St (0556) 64331 18th-c inn with comfortable, clean, bright, recently redecorated lounge bar and eating area serving good food inc outstanding puddings and cakes; disabled access. **£10**|£1/£3.80.

Glasgow NS5865 HORSESHOE BAR 17 Drury St 041-221 3051 Excellent and unspoilt Victorian pub with horseshoe motif throughout, popular with lawyers and journalists, and amazingly cheap food; no bar food on Sun; **£1.80** (3-course lunch)|40p/£1.

We welcome reports from readers . . .

Readers who help us with reports for the GUIDE are offered a discount on the next edition: so please do help if you can!

The West, Argyll and Loch Lomond

Here, you can find mainland Scotland's finest scenery, especially on the coast; some lovely gardens to visit; best of all in May and June.

Glorious scenery is the overriding reason for coming here, and the pick of it is on the west coast. It's not an area to come to for a lively time: drive, walk, potter around a great garden or two, unearth some prehistoric sights, go looking for seals or deer, and simply enjoy the glorious views. It's great for exploring by car (though don't expect to go at any speed): the roads twist and turn around the intricate edges of the lochs and sea lochs, making endlessly varying combinations of water, trees and mountains. It's also got some of Scotland's most rewarding walking, and the West Highland Line steam train from Fort William takes you through some of the finest scenery.

May and June are the best months here, when the great gardens are at their best, the midges have not yet got into their stride, the roads and the sites are empty, and the days are very long. It's not too crowded in the main holiday season, but road travel can then become painfully slow, and it's difficult to find places that you can really have to yourself. Late September and October or even November can be lovely, with spells of good fine weather, the heather still a glorious colour on the hills, and the midges in retreat; but the days start to shorten dramatically. Many places close over the winter, when the days are too short to make much of the scenery – though near the sea and sea lochs the area stays very mild.

Dunoon has all you'd expect of a long-standing summer resort, and Oban is a lively sea-town, but otherwise even Fort William is pretty quiet, and the smaller places have a very relaxed and gentle pace of life: Inveraray is the most interesting. There are some very civilised hotels, and some very good value, simpler places. You can find excellent fresh seafood.

Where to stay

Port Appin NM9045 The Airds Argyll PA38 4DF (063 173) 211 **£220 inc dinner**; 12 rms. Instantly relaxing 18th-c inn with lovely views of Loch Linnhe and the islands of Lismore, blissfully comfortable day rooms, friendly and helpful service, and charming owners; the food is exceptional (as is the wine list) and there are lots of surrounding walks, with more on Lismore (small boat every two hours); cl mid-Jan-end Feb.

Eriska NM9042 Isle of Eriska Hotel Ledaig Oban Argyll PA37 1SD (0631) 72371 **£215 inc dinner**; 17 rms. In a wonderful position on a tiny island linked to the mainland by a bridge, this impressive hotel is run along old-fashioned lines with formal dress for dinner, very good food inc marvellous breakfasts, exceptionally good, professional service, and lovely surrounding walks; cl Dec-Mar; children over 10 in evening restaurant (high tea provided); disabled access.

Tiroran NM5834 TIRORAN HOUSE Isle of Mull PA69 6ES (068 15) 232 **£180 inc dinner**; 9 rms. Carefully modernised sporting lodge in 15 acres of gardens and woodlands on the shores of Loch Scridain; comfortable, homely sitting room with family antiques and pretty flowers, log fires, and fine food using home-grown produce, meat from the estate, and island fish; cl early Oct-mid-May; children over 10.

Kilmore NM8824 GLENFEOCHAN HOUSE Oban Argyll PA34 4QR (063 177) 273 **£124**; 3 rms. Scottish Baronial home at the head of Loch Feochan in 350 acres inc a fine six-acre garden open to the public, with elegant hall, staircase and drawing room, lots of fresh flowers, and excellent food; cl 1 Nov-7 Mar; children over 10.

Crinan NR7894 CRINAN HOTEL Lochgilphead Strathclyde PA31 8SR (054) 683261 **£110**; 22 rms. Rather smart hotel by start of coast-to-coast canal, marvellous views from neat cocktail bar and stylish, formal top-floor restaurant, nautical decorations in lounge bar, lots of local fish and large wine list.

Tarbert NR8668 STONEFIELD CASTLE Argyll PA29 6YJ (0880) 820836 **£108**; 32 rms. With wonderful views and surrounding wooded grounds, this Scottish Baronial mansion has comfortable public rooms, and decent restaurant food; disabled access.

Strachur NN0901 CREGGANS Cairndow Argyll PA27 8BX (036 986) 279 **£98**; 21 rms, 19 with own bthrm. Smart inn in extensive grounds overlooking sea loch and hills (deer-stalking, fishing and pony-trekking arranged), attractive lounge, conservatory and cocktail bar, lively locals' bar, popular food, coffee bar, and gift shop; disabled access.

Onich NN0261 ALLT-NAN-ROS Fort William Inverness-shire PH33 6RY (085 53) 210 **£95**; 21 rms. Victorian shooting lodge with fine Scottish food, a friendly atmosphere, bright rooms, and magnificent views across Loch Linnhe and the gardens; cl Nov-2 wks before Easter, disabled access.

Arduaine NM7910 LOCH MELFORT Oban Argyll PA34 4XG (085 22) 233 **£90**; 27 rms, gorgeous sea views. Comfortable hotel popular in summer with passing yachtsmen (hotel's own moorings), nautical charts and marine glasses in airy, modern bar, own lobster pots and nets so emphasis on seafood, pleasant foreshore walks, lovely springtime woodland gardens.

Duror NM9854 STEWART Appin Argyll PA38 4BW (063 174) 268 ***£80**; 19 rms. Family-run Victorian country house with splendid views towards Loch Linnhe, five acres of splendid gardens (lovely in May/June), comfortable lounge with open fire, good food using local fish and game; own boat moorings and 31-ft sloop; cl 15 Oct-Easter.

Kilchrenan NN0322 ARDANAISEIG Taynuilt Argyll PA35 1HE (086 63) 333 **£75 inc dinner**; 14 rms. Delicious food using local supplies (esp seafood), quiet day rooms with stunning views of Loch Awe, friendly service, and fine gardens; cl mid-Oct-Easter, no under-8s.

Fort William NN1074 FACTORS HOUSE Inverness-shire PH33 6SN (0397) 705767 ***£70.50**; 6 rms. Carefully run and warmly friendly little hotel beneath Ben Nevis, with good food, comfortable lounge, and fine walks; cl Nov-Feb; children over 6 in evening dining room.

Kilchrenan NN0222 TAYCHREGGAN Taynuilt Argyll PA35 1HQ (086 63) 211

*£68; 15 rms. Civilised hotel with fine garden running down to Loch Awe, comfortable, airy bar with stuffed birds and fish, attractively served lunchtime bar food, polite efficient staff, good, freshly prepared food in no-smoking dining room, careful wine list, lots of malt whiskies, and pretty inner courtyard; children over 6.

Kilfinan NR9379 Kilfinan Hotel Tighnabruaich Argyll PA21 2AP (070 082) 201 ***£68**; 11 rms. Friendly ex-coaching inn, popular locally, in fine scenery with sporting activities such as shooting, fishing and stalking; very good restaurant food, decent bar food, and log fires; cl Feb.

Tobermory NM5055 Tobermory Isle of Mull PA75 6NT (0688) 2091 **£68**; 17 rms. Friendly, recently refurbished family-run hotel on the waterfront with flowers in the comfortable, homely lounges, and good relaxed atmosphere; good disabled access.

Ardrishaig NR8485 Allt-na-Craig Tarbert Rd Lochgilphead Argyll PA30 8EP (0546) 3245 **£56**; 6 rms. Victorian mansion overlooking Loch Fyne with big lounge and dining area, log fire, and evening meals by request; cl Christmas/New Year; s/c also.

Kilberry NR7164 Kilberry Inn Tarbert Argyll PA29 6YD (088 03) 223 **£55**; 2 newly opened grd floor, no-smoking rms. Homely and warmly welcoming inn on west coast of Knapdale, fine sea views, outstanding country cooking; cl Sun, mid-Oct-Easter (but open New Year); disabled access.

Connel Ferry NM9133 Falls of Lora Oban Argyll PA37 1PB (063 171) 483 ***£49**; 30 comfortable, well-modernised rms. Well-kept Victorian hotel on edge of village, across road from Loch Etive with several spacious communicating bar areas, good solidly comfortable modern furnishings, big watercolour landscapes, free-standing Scandinavian-style log fire, no-smoking areas, and well-presented food; cl 25 Dec, 1 Jan; disabled access.

Inveraray NN0908 George Argyll PA32 8TT (0499) 2111 **£46**; 14 rms. Friendly hotel with decent restaurant, stripped-stone bar, flagstones, exposed joists and log fire, good choice of whiskies; cl 24-26 Dec, 1-3 Jan.

To see and do

❀ **Arduaine** NM8010 The seaside gardens here, a very sheltered spot with lovely views of the islets and islands, are almost subtropical, with many rarities beside the rhododendrons and magnolias which flourish so in this part of the world. The Loch Melfort Hotel does good bar lunches.

Barcaldine NM9642 Sea Life Centre Lively underwater centre (part of a chain with several in England and one in St Andrews), with one of Britain's biggest collections of native marine life, and a new exhibition of seal puppies. Hi-tech features inc a tidepool touch tank and intertidal dump tank; meals and snacks, shop, limited disabled access; cl wkdys Dec-mid-Feb; £3.95.

❀ **Benmore** NS1385 Younger Botanic Garden An outstation of the Royal Botanic Garden in Edinburgh, with attractive woodland and glorious rhododendrons; there are some enormously tall and magnificent conifers here, and a good many rarities. Nice views as well; meals and snacks, shop, disabled access; cl Nov-mid-Mar; *£1.50.

Cairndow NN1810 Strone House The pinetum here includes the tallest tree in Britain, a 208-ft grand fir, still growing very quickly, among a group of other noble trees. Also rhododendrons, azaleas and other exotic plants, and daffodils in spring; disabled access; cl Oct-Mar. The Loch Fyne Oyster Bar at the head of Loch

Fyne is good.

Colintraive NS0374 is an attractive village spread out along the shore of the sea loch, with lovely views across the narrow Kyles of Bute. There's a short ferry crossing to Rhubodach on Bute.

The **Crinan Canal** NR8390 was cut through the 9 miles at the top of the Kintyre peninsula at the end of the 18th c, to save coastal sailors many miles of dangerous waters; the end at Crinan is attractive, usually with one or two yachts or even a rare fishing boat waiting to enter the first lock, and the Crinan Hotel is a comfortable lunch stop.

Dunoon NS1776, brought in easy reach of Glasgow by frequent ferries from Glasgow, is a late Victorian resort with pleasant views from its fine long promenade; very busy in Aug.

Fort William NN1174 is a largely Victorian town that doubles being the hospital, schools and shopping centre for many miles around with being a holiday base, particularly for solid Ben Nevis which rises above it, and for the Caledonian Canal which leads on up into the Great Glen and across eventually to the North Sea. WEST HIGHLAND MUSEUM One of the most interesting features is a secret Jacobite portrait of Prince Charlie that requires a curved mirror to decode it. Lots more exhibits relating to Flora MacDonald, Prince Charlie and the Hanoverian garrisons; shop; cl lunchtimes, all day Sun (exc July and Aug), and Mon Nov-Mar; *£1. The battle between Montrose and the Campbells was fought at INVERLOCHY CASTLE just NE of town in 1645. The castle was begun in the 13th c, but added to over the ages; key-keeping arrangement, cl Oct-Mar. The Alexandra Hotel, Ben Nevis and Nevis Bank Hotel are useful for food. In summer you can take steam train journeys on the WEST HIGHLAND LINE from here – it goes right up into the Highlands and the views are quite superb (see also North of Scotland section).

Gigha Island NR6436 3 miles offshore is linked by frequent ferries from Tayinloan on the A83 down the west coast of Kintyre, and is a perfect place for really getting away from it all. There's a small hotel, and rooms at the Post Office and other places, and you can hire bicycles to explore it properly. The island was bought in 1944 by Sir James Horlick, who created here ACHAMORE GARDENS, a garden of woodlands filled with rhododendrons and azaleas, bringing over many of the plants from his home in Berkshire in laundry baskets. There are many subtropical plants, as the climate and soil are perfect for them; meals, snacks, shop; best to tel (058 35) 254 for times of opening and for ferries out to the island; *£2.50. Try to see the strange old stones, some of which are supposed to have mysterious powers.

Glencoe NN1058 The scenery around here is some of Scotland's most beautiful and wild. It's understandably popular with walkers and climbers, who share it with deer, wildcats and golden eagles. It's most famous for the massacre of 1692 when billeted troops tried to murder all their MacDonald hosts. Close to where this happened, the GLENCOE VISITOR CENTRE has the whole story, as well as useful information about the area and its wildlife. It's in awesome surroundings; snacks, shop, disabled access; cl 18 Oct-Mar; 30p. The Clachaig is useful for lunch.

Helensburgh NS2982 THE HILL HOUSE In an area short of many great houses, this is a wonderful example of the work of Charles Rennie Mackintosh; the site has an exhibition about his life, and the gardens are being restored to their original form. Snacks, shop; cl am, all Jan-Mar; £2.80. NTS. The dignified resort town, attractively placed on the Clyde, has some good views from its broad streets.

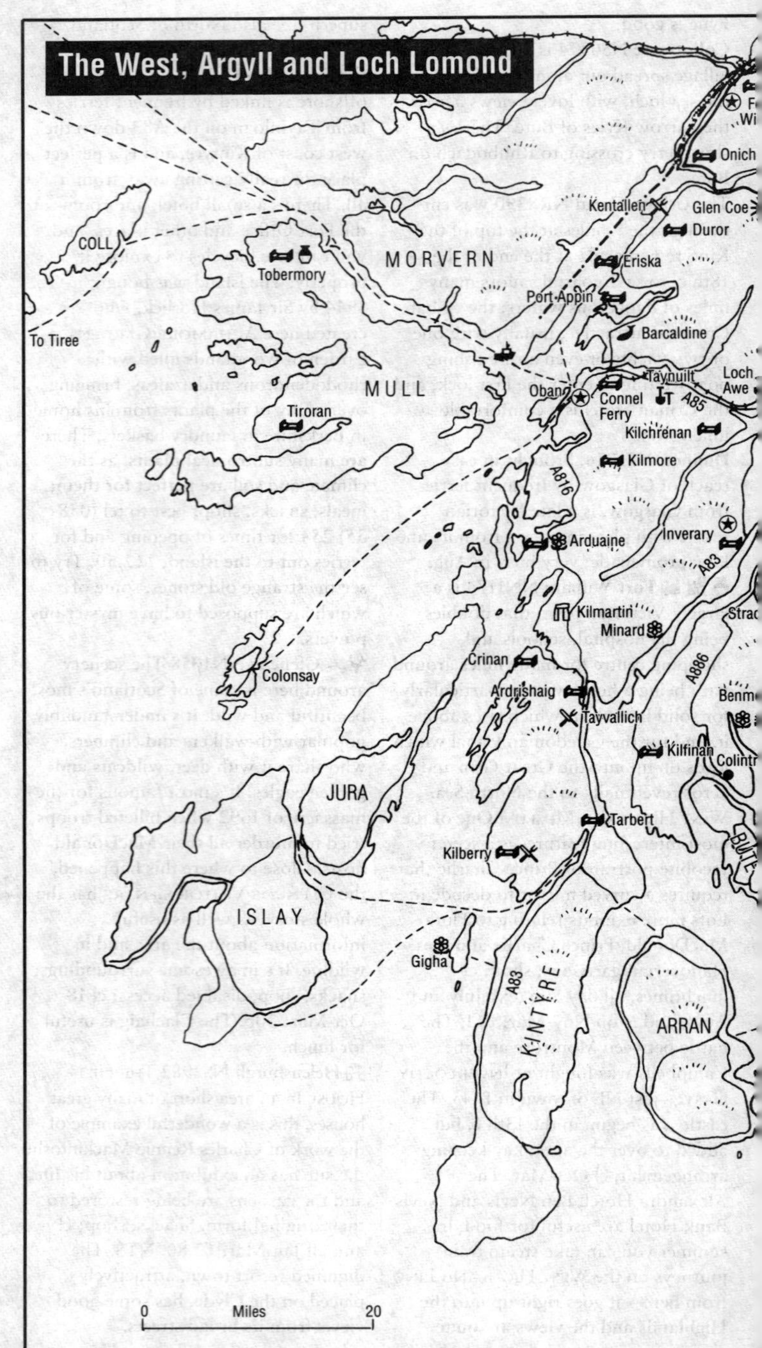
The West, Argyll and Loch Lomond
COLL
To Tiree
Tobermory
MORVERN
MULL
Tiroran
Colonsay
JURA
ISLAY
Gigha
Kentallen
Onich
Glen Coe
Duror
Eriska
Port Appin
Barcaldine
Oban
Connel Ferry
Taynuilt
Loch Awe
A85
Kilchrenan
Kilmore
A816
Inverary
A83
Arduaine
Kilmartin
Minard
Crinan
A886
Ardrishaig
Tayvallich
Kilfinan
Tarbert
Kilberry
A83
KINTYRE
ARRAN
0
Miles
20

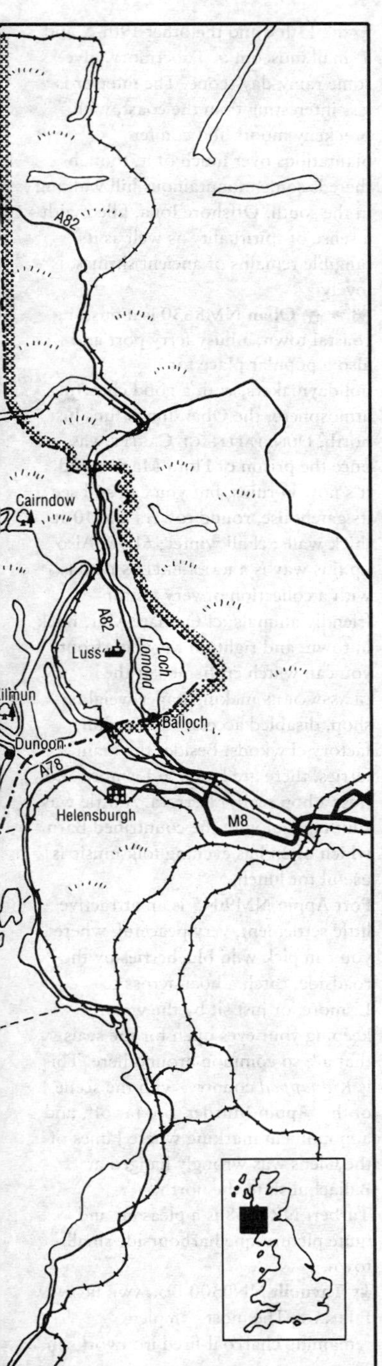

Inveraray NN0908 Beautifully placed and rather self-consciously elegant, with lots to see. The bell tower of ALL SAINTS' CHURCH has the world's third-heaviest ring of ten bells, installed as a Campbell War Memorial in 1931. It has exhibitions on campanology; cl 1-2 pm Mon-Sat, Sun am, all Oct-mid-May; £1. The CASTLE was built in 1743 and is still the home of the Duke and Duchess of Argyll; it's filled with rich furnishings, tapestries and paintings – particularly worth seeing are the great armoury hall and state rooms. Snacks, shop, disabled access; cl 1-2 pm, all day Fri, all mid-Oct-Apr; *£3.50. Less elegant is the nearby JAIL, where you can watch a trial in the 1820 courtroom, find out from the prisoner himself how to pick oakum or make herring nets, listen to the matron about the various charges – lunatic, pregnant mother and thieves – in her care, and experience the sights, sounds and smells of the prison cells; shop; cl 25 Dec, 1 Jan; *£4. Nearby the ARGYLL WILDLIFE PARK has a collection of the sorts of creatures found here not so long ago, from wild boars to wildcats – with some eminently tame wild creatures wandering around; meals and snacks; shop; disabled access; cl Nov-Mar; £2.95. The Loch Fyne Hotel is pleasant for lunch.

Kilmartin NR8398 DUNADD (3 miles S) This prehistoric hill fort was one of the ancient capitals of Dalriada from which the Celtic kingdom of Scotland was formed. Look out for the carvings nearby of a boar and a footprint, which probably mark the spot where early kings were invested with royal power. Between here and the village (where the simple Kilmartin Hotel is useful for lunch) are several other well-signed prehistoric monuments, and the rough roads W to the N shore of Loch Crinan take you past several more.

Kilmun NS1781 has wonderful FOREST WALKS among rare conifers, an arboretum of great beauty, and some striking gum-trees.

Lochawe NN1227 CRUACHAN POWER STATION Hydroelectric plant inside a vast cavern in the depths of Ben Cruachan, driven by water from a high-level reservoir on the mountain. Tours around the site are conducted in a minibus; snacks, shop; cl mid-Oct-Easter; *£1.80.

Loch Lomond NS3957 is the one place in this area that everyone's heard of. Remarkably, in spite of being so close to Glasgow and on every coach company's hit list, it does have a serene beauty that seems unspoilt by the visitors – and it's often calm enough to reflect the mountains. The best views are from the narrower N end, the quietest spots along the E shore. Beside Loch Lomond is BALLOCH CASTLE COUNTRY PARK at **Balloch** NS3881. The early 19th-c house contains a visitor centre with an introduction to local history and the wildlife which you're likely to find in the country park. There are woodland trails, a walled garden and lawns to wander through, with fine views; disabled access; cl Nov-Apr. **Luss** NS3952 is a good place to hire a boat for pottering about on the water; there are regular cruises around it, too. Past the north end of the loch, the Inverarnan Drovers Inn is an entertaining stop.

Minard NR9796 CRARAE GARDENS Lovely gardens noted for their rare ornamental shrubs and rhododendrons, azaleas and conifers. It's a beautiful hillside setting overlooking Loch Fyne; snacks, shop, some disabled access; visitor centre cl Nov-Easter; *£2.50.

Mull NM5834 For most people this island takes a bit of getting to for a weekend break, but if you are within reach, its unspoilt coasts are certainly a dramatic lure. There's a good ferry service from Oban and Lochaline (and in summer from Kilchoan). A couple of castellated mansions, one going back to the 13th c and the other 19th-c, and a small museum in Tobermory, give some rainy-day scope. The interior is less interesting than the coast, with brackeny moors and conifer plantations over much of it, though there is some mountainous hill walking in the south. Offshore Iona, filled with a sense of spirituality as well as its tangible remains of ancient shrines, is lovely.

Oban NM8630 is a bustling coastal town, a busy ferry port and also a popular place for holidaymakers, with a good cheerful atmosphere; the Oban Inn is fun. Just north, DUNSTAFFNAGE CASTLE was once the prison of Flora MacDonald. It's now in ruins, but you can still see its gatehouse, round towers and 10-ft-thick walls; cl all winter; £1.50. Also up this way is a RARE-BREEDS FARM with a collection of very visitor-friendly animals; cl Oct-late Mar. Back in town, and right on the waterfront, you can watch craftsmen at the GLASSWORKS making paper weights; shop, disabled access; shop cl Sun, factory cl wknds. Besides the main ferries, there are boats to Lismore and (just a hop really) Kerrera. A little way south at Cologin, the countrified Barn which often has evening folk music is useful for lunch.

Port Appin NM9045 is an attractive little settlement, very peaceful, where you can pick wild blueberries by the roadside, catch a boat across to Lismore, or just sit by the water keeping your eyes open for the seals that are so common around here. This is *Kidnapped* country, with the scene of the 'Appin Murder' not far off, and a monument marking where James of the Glens was wrongly hanged at Ballachulish to the north.

Tarbert NR8668 is a pleasant and quite picturesque harbourside small town.

Taynuilt NN0300 BONAWE IRON FURNACE The most complete remaining charcoal-fired ironworks in

Britain, established in 1753 and worked until 1876. Displays show how iron was made here, and the uses it was put to – inc the cannonballs for Nelson's ships; shop; cl Sun am, all Oct-Mar; *£1.70. The Polfearn Hotel on the lochside does good food, and the station is a surprising location for a pub brewing its own beer.

Besides those we've mentioned in the text above, or as places to eat at or stay in, inns where you can get a decent bite to eat and which are particularly well placed for walkers, drivers or just strollers in these parts include the Ardentinny Hotel at Ardentinny NS1887, Galley of Lorne at Ardfern NM8004, Ballachulish Hotel at Ballachulish NN0858, Tigh an Truish at Clachan Seil near the bridge linking the little island of Seil NM7718 to the mainland, Kilchrenan Inn at Kilchrenan by Loch Awe NN0222, Portsonachan Hotel on the opposite side of that loch NN1227, Inverbeg Inn at Luss on Loch Lomond NS3593, Whistlefield Hotel by Loch Eck NS1493 and Loch Gair Hotel on Loch Gair NR9190.

Walks

For non-mountaineers the Highlands can be tantalising but problematic: compared to the uplands of England and Wales there are few obvious walking routes (OS maps show hardly any), and the scale of the scenery is often so vast that you need to walk for hours before the views change. The high peaks are mostly for the dedicated (and fit) enthusiast. An informal tradition of allowing general access exists on the mountains, but there are few rights of way, and areas are often closed for at least part of the grouse-shooting season (12 Aug-10 Dec), particularly its first few weeks, or the deer-stalking season (1 July-20 Oct for stags, 21 Oct-15 Feb for hinds).

There are attractive walks along many lochs, and around the complex coast and sea lochs. The area has a fair amount of forestry walks, sometimes taking in viewpoints and waterfalls. There's good scope for walking along many of the valleys (always called glens in Scotland). **Glen Nevis** NN1570 near Fort William NN1174 is probably the best known, with splendid gorge scenery for an easy long mile to Steall Falls. There's also a fine walk through semi-wooded terrain along the glen of the **River Leven,** from **Kinlochleven** NN1861, to the dam of the gigantic **Blackwater Reservoir** NN3059 – and an awesomely bleak view ahead of empty hills.

In **Glen Coe** NN1556 you can discover the Lost Valley, a secret pasture-ground used by the MacDonalds for stolen cattle in times of clan warfare; it involves an ascent from the **Meeting of the Three Waters** NN1756. From **Altnafeadh** NN2256 at the top of the glen, the West Highland Way takes a zigzag route N up the Devils Staircase and through the mountains to Kinlochleven; another hill walk from Altnafeadh heads E up Beinn a' Chrùlaiste, one of Glen Coe's more manageable peaks. From Glen Coe, a squelchy walk along glens, with close-ups of mighty peaks for company, leads into **Glen Etive** NN1650.

Ben Nevis NN1671, though Britain's highest mountain, is one of the more easily managed summits, with a long, safe path up it: expect big crowds in season. Munro-baggers (a 'munro' is any 3,000-ft peak – the nickname comes from Sir Hugh Munro, who tabulated them all) say it's far from being the best viewpoint mountain, though. The **Pap of Glencoe** NN1259 and the succession of peaks in the largely unwooded **Mamore Forest** NN1565 (access from Glen Nevis) are more interesting; they don't require rock-climbing expertise, just reasonable fitness and plenty of time.

Woodland trails around **Inveraray Castle** NN0908 have a view over Loch Fyne from Dunchuach Tower.

Loch Lomond, surprisingly, hasn't a lot of paths: the shoreline track, partly metalled, on the quieter E side, comes closest to the water. There's a good ascent of **Ben Lomond** NN3602, the southernmost munro, from **Rowardennan** NS3699 on this E side of the loch.

The **Caledonian Canal** leading NE from Fort William NN1074 has straightforward towpath walks with mountain backdrops. The **Crinan Canal** between Crinan and Lochgilphead provides a gentle stroll. Just to the N, tracks link a succession of ancient burial mounds near **Kilmartin** NR8398.

Islands within reach of Oban have a few shoreside walks and the odd castle, e.g. Lismore (also ferry from Port Appin) and Kerrera. There are a few good walks on Mull – but there's the usual problem of not many defined paths.

Driving

The A82 twisting along Loch Lomond's W side carries too much traffic to let the driver see much of the loch itself, but passengers always enjoy this drive – and there are plenty of places to stop. There's also a much quieter road up the E side, but it does not go the whole way round.

W and N of here, almost every road is a delight, though none is quick except at quiet times. The roads that hug the shores of the sea lochs give particularly enchanting views, changing constantly – and have the great advantage over mountain roads that the weather has to be very bad indeed before the views lose all their charm. The circuit of the Mull of Kintyre makes a glorious drive, though very slow in summer. Other memorable moments here include the approach to Inveraray on the A83; the good A8003 down the Cowal Peninsula with great views over the Kyles of Bute to the island of Bute itself; the B8024 round the coast of the Knapdale Peninsula, looking across a translucent summer sea to Islay and the mountains of Jura turning deep purple with an early autumn sunset behind them; the sea views, studded with smaller islands, from several places along the A816 S of Oban; just N of Oban, the view from the A85 of Dunstaffnage Castle moulded in rock on its wild promontory; and some miles N of here, the sight of Castle Stalker on its offshore islet from the A828, one of Scotland's most romantic views. Inland, the B8074 up Glen Orchy is very pretty, with plenty of places to stop by the stream (much loved by midges in late summer). The A82 is a magnificent road, both through the awesome Pass of Glencoe and over the stern moorlands E and S of there.

Where to eat

Kentallen NN0057 HOLLY TREE (063 174) 292 Super food in carefully converted railway station, cosy public rooms, lovely shoreside setting (best to book in winter); bedrooms, disabled access. **£26**|£1.60/£9.45.
Kentallen NN0057 ARDSHEAL HOUSE (063 174) 227 Particularly good food in attractive conservatory dining room of fine hotel set in 900 acres; very comfortable rooms, antiques, and relaxed atmosphere; lovely bedrooms; cl 3 wks Jan. **£22**|£4/£9.
Tayvallich NR7386 TAYVALLICH INN (054 67) 282 Simple pub overlooking yacht anchorage with emphasis on local seafood, though other decent dishes, too; dining conservatory (no smoking). **£21**|£4.70/£9.50.

Fort William NN1074 ALEXANDRA The Parade (0397) 702241 Popular hotel in the town square with meals and snacks in the Great Food Stop (open all day) and the evening restaurant; disabled access. **£19.95 for 4 courses**|£1.45/£4.95.

Many of the places in the Where to stay section, above, also offer extremely good food.

NORTH OF THE FORTH: CENTRAL HIGHLANDS AND EAST COAST

This area provides good scope for mixing sightseeing with memorable Highland scenery.

The area's best scenery is in the north: both Highland, and the more varied beauties of the valleys – the well-known Spey, Dee and Don, and the lesser-known places such as the Angus glens of Glen Clova, Glen Esk and Glen Isla. The coast from Nairn to New Aberdour and Rosehearty and even right on round to Aberdeen is full of picturesque little coves, boiling seas around terrifying cliffy crags (Slains Castle and the nearby Bullers of Buchan are fine examples), unexpected sandy beaches and interesting small towns and villages: a part of Scotland that's much underrated. On the southern fringes of the Highlands, Tayside has civilised towns such as Perth and on a much smaller scale Crieff, Pitlochry and Aberfeldy, with some tremendous richly forested valley scenery as well as its Highland hills.

Further south, the countryside is a lot milder. Over in Fife it's largely agricultural, with quite a bit of industry dotted through it, but there are some attractive fishing villages, and splendid coastal golf courses (particularly at St Andrews, of course, and at Elie). More centrally, the interesting town of Stirling does have the real moorland of Sheriff Muir nearby, as well as the Trossachs: a sort of Highlands in miniature, with lovely if small-scale landscapes of loch, river, forest, moor and mountain – but not the emptiness or the grandeur of the true Highlands.

Thoughout the area, there are a good many interesting places to visit – especially castles and great houses: Craigievar, Cawdor, Fyvie (near Turriff), Blair, Glamis, Crathes and Brodie are all outstanding castles, and Scone Palace and Falkland Palace are very rewarding. St Andrews, Perth, Stirling, Aberdeen, Dundee and the much smaller Anstruther and Culross are all worth considering for a day or half-day visit. Good family attractions include the Highland wildlife park at Kincraig, the Storybook Glen at Maryculter, the Bo'ness steam railway (other things there too), the safari/leisure park at Blair Drummond, and deer parks at Glengoulandie and Cupar. Of several distillery tours, the Glenturret one at Crieff is particularly enjoyable.

In high summer, the fact that there are not that many roads in the remoter parts does mean that the people visiting the Highlands tend to be concentrated into the same strips of territory along these roads – so to feel at all remote then you either have to set off ambitiously on foot or search out the less well-known corners. But it's worth remembering that in June, when the days up here are very long indeed and it's still light as midnight approaches, the whole area is altogether quieter. This is also true of late September; though the days then are much shorter, the heather on the hills is still looking spectacular.

There's a fine choice of places to stay, and quite a good choice of places to eat – though they thin out as you head north.

Where to stay

Advie NJ1235 TULCHAN LODGE Grantown-on-Spey Morayshire PH26 3PW (0807) 510200 **£350 full board**; 10 rms. Extremely civilised Edwardian sporting lodge with fishing on one of the best stretches of the Spey (each beat has its own ghillie and luxurious fishing cabin) and game shooting on 4,500 acres; fine paintings and antiques in gracious drawing room and comfortable panelled library. Good food, using much produce from the estate and kitchen gardens, served at one long candlelit table; billiards room, tennis; no children.

Auchterarder NN9413 GLENEAGLES Perthshire PH3 1NF (0764) 662231 **£205**; 236 individually decorated rms. Grand hotel in lovely surroundings with attractive gardens and outstanding leisure facilities: golf courses (inc a new championship one designed by Jack Nicklaus), shooting, riding, fishing, a health spa, tennis, squash, bowling green, and croquet, and the British School of Falconry now have a base here; comfortable, elegant high-ceilinged day rooms, several bars, professional but friendly service, live pianists, and good food using local produce (much is home-grown); disabled access.

Dunkeld NO0243 KINNAIRD HOUSE Kinnaird Estate Perthshire PH8 0LB (0796) 482440 **£170**; 9 spacious, individually decorated rms. 18th-c country-house hotel in lovely 9,000-acre estate with very restful, civilised atmosphere in deeply comfortable, antique-filled rooms, lovely flowers, family mementos and pictures, log fires, good, creative food in no-smoking dining room with its early 19th-c hand-painted frescoes, and very fine wine list, not cheap; excellent fishing on River Tay and 3 hill lochs, and shooting; cl Feb; children over 12; good disabled access.

St Andrews NO5116 RUFFLETS Fife KY16 9TX (0334) 72594 **£164 inc dinner**; 26 well-equipped rms, many no smoking (5 luxury rms should be ready mid-1994). The spacious and attractively furnished public rooms all overlook the award-winning gardens of this privately owned, creeper-clad hotel; good food using home-grown or fresh local produce, efficient, friendly service, and relaxing atmosphere; disabled access.

Ballater NO3695 TULLICH LODGE Aberdeenshire AB35 5SB (033 97) 55406 ***£160**; 10 individually decorated rms. Characterful Baronial-style pink granite house, well run by the same owners for over 20 years, with fine views from handsome first-floor drawing room, chintzy little sitting room, open fire in informal bar (light lunches served here), and carefully prepared food using first-class ingredients in slightly formal panelled no-smoking restaurant; high tea for children; good hill walking and lots of nearby golf courses; cl Dec-Mar.

Blairgowrie NO1745 KINLOCH HOUSE Perthshire PH10 6SG (025 084) 237 **£144.90 inc dinner**; 21 individually decorated rms. Creeper-covered 19th-c country house in 25 acres of parkland with highland cattle and fine views; relaxed lounges, comfortable bar, pretty conservatory with lots of plants, and fine choice of carefully prepared food in an elegant dining room; popular Sportsman's room with own entrance, drying facilities, gun cupboard, deep freeze, game larder and so forth; cl 15-31 Dec; disabled access.

Banchory NO6995 INVERY HOUSE Kincardineshire AB3 3NJ (033 02) 4782 ***£140**; 14 comfortable rms. Peaceful, well-run Georgian house surrounded by 47 acres with elegant, very comfortable public rooms, fine food and wines, and friendly service; walled garden, tennis, putting, croquet, and fishing; cl Nov-Feb.

Elgin NJ2162 MANSION HOUSE Morayshire IV30 1AQ (0343) 548811 **£140**; 20 rms. Relaxed and friendly Scottish baronial mansion with prettily furnished public rooms, lovely food inc fine breakfasts, and good wine list; country club facilities.

Kinclaven by Stanley NO1436 BALLATHIE HOUSE Perth Perthshire PH1 4QN (0250) 883268 ***£140**; 28 fine rms. Overlooking the River Tay, this turreted mansion has fresh flowers in the comfortable, carefully furnished day rooms, very good, interesting food in elegant dining room, and friendly service; cl 2 wks Feb, disabled access.

Dunblane NN7801 CROMLIX HOUSE Perthshire FK15 9JT (0786) 822125 ***£135**; 6 comfortable rms, 8 spacious suites. Walking, loch and river fishing or shooting are available on the 5,000 acres of land around this rather gracious country house; relaxing day rooms with fine antiques, furniture and family portaits, very good food using estate game and local meats and fish, and courteous service; cl 24-28 Dec, 6 Jan-end Feb.

Auchterarder NN9413 AUCHTERARDER HOUSE Perthshire PH3 1DZ (0764) 663646 **£130**; 15 individually furnished rms, some in turret, most with fine views. Baronial mansion with warm, homely atmosphere, lovely day rooms with open fires, lots of fresh flowers, fine panelling and antiques, good, imaginative food, and 17 acres of grounds; children over 10; disabled access.

Peat Inn NO4509 PEAT INN Cupar Fife KY15 5LH (033 484) 206 **£130**; 8 luxurious rms. This is really a very good and popular restaurant with rooms; beams and white plaster walls, friendly service, fine, interesting food, and excellent wine list; cl 25 Dec, 1 Jan; disabled access.

Scone NO1226 MURRAYSHALL HOUSE Perth Perthshire PH2 7PH (0738) 51171 ***£130**; 19 rms. Handsome mansion in 300 acres of parkland and very popular with golfers (it has its own course); comfortable, elegant public rooms, warm, friendly staff, relaxed atmosphere, imaginative food, and good wines; cl 23-28 Dec.

Newtonmore NN7199 ARD-NA-COILLE Kingussie Rd Inverness-shire PH20 1AY (0540) 673214 ***£126 inc dinner**; 7 rms, those on first floor have fine views. Carefully run, little Edwardian hotel in 2 acres of pine woodland with quiet country-house atmosphere, marvellous views of the Cairngorm Mountains from the public rooms, homely touches, attentive staff, extremely good 5-course set dinner, and thoughtful, very reasonably priced wine list; cl mid-Nov-end Dec.

Ballater NO3695 CRAIGENDARROCH HOTEL AB3 5XA (033 97) 55858 ***£125**; 50 rms. In lovely countryside, this popular hotel has lots of leisure facilities, comfortable public areas, friendly service, and very good food; cl 4-11 Jan, disabled access.

Whitebridge NN7754 Knockie Lodge Inverness Inverness-shire IV1 2UP (0456) 486276 **£125 inc dinner**; 10 rms. Alone in the hills with lovely views of Loch Nan Lann, this country house has a relaxed atmosphere, caring, personal service, and very good food; cl Nov-Apr; children over 10.
Callander NN6208 Roman Camp Perthshire FK17 8BG (0877) 30003 **£120**; 14 rms. Former hunting lodge rather like a small French chateau with characterful and comfortable lounges, open fires, an interesting little turret chapel, and 20 acres of grounds; disabled access.
Alloa NS8893 Gean House Gean Park Tullibody Rd Clackmannanshire FK10 2HS (0259) 219275 **£120 inc dinner**; 8 luxury rms. Carefully restored mansion house in mature parkland with views of the Ochil Hills; elegant drawing room with inglenook fireplace, minstrel's gallery and marvellous windows, cosy library, and very good food in no-smoking, walnut-panelled dining room overlooking the formal rose garden; disabled access.
Kildrummy NJ4617 Kildrummy Castle Alford Aberdeenshire AB33 8RA (097 55) 71288 **£110**; 17 comfortable rms. Overlooking the ruins of the original 13th-c castle and set in lovely gardens, this castellated hotel has a fine oak-panelled Grand Hall, gracious drawing room, convivial bar, relaxing library, fresh flowers and open fires, good food using the best beef, game and fish, and welcoming, friendly staff; lots of fishing; cl Jan.
Inverness NH6645 Bunchrew House Inverness-shire IV3 6TA (0463) 234917 **£105**; 11 rms. Warmly friendly hotel on the shore of Beauly Firth with fine views and landscaped gardens, open fires in the public rooms, and good food using local produce.
Ardeonaig NN6635 Ardeonaig Killin Perthshire FK21 8SY (0567) 820400 **£98**; 10 rms. Hotel in lovely setting with good food and pubby atmosphere in nice bar; cl Nov-Dec, disabled access; £10 per day for using the outdoor activity centre.
Aberfeldy NN8549 Farleyer House PH15 2SE (0887) 820332 ***£95**; 11 rms. Charming country house with fine views over the Tay Valley, log fires, antiques and flowers in the library and drawing room, and excellent food.
Auchterhouse NO3337 Old Mansion House Dundee DD3 0QN (082 626) 366 **£95**; 6 attractive rms. Carefully converted 16th-c baronial house with fine entrance hall, comfortable day rooms, open fires, and very relaxed atmosphere; garden with outdoor swimming pool, croquet and tennis; cl 25-26 Dec, 1st wk Jan; children over 12 in evening dining room.
Nairn NH8856 Clifton House IV12 4HW (0667) 53119 ***£95**; 12 individually decorated, comfortable rms. Lovely, civilised, flower-filled old family hotel (the present owner has lived in the house all his life and has been running it as a hotel since 1952), individually furnished with antiques, paintings and sculptures; extremely good food using their own eggs, lovely fish, home-made jams and bread, late breakfasts, and exceptional wine list; during the winter they stage some 20 concerts, plays and recitals; cl mid-Dec-mid-Jan; pets welcome.
Pitlochry NN9162 Killiecrankie PH16 5LG (0796) 473220 **£88**; 11 rms. Comfortable country hotel in spacious grounds with putting course and croquet lawn, splendid mountain views, mahogany-panelled bar with stuffed animals and fine wildlife paintings, plants and flowers, friendly owners and helpful staff, and good, well-presented and often unusual food; cl Jan-Feb.
Fintry NS6186 Culcreuch Castle Glasgow G63 0LW (036 086) 228 ***£86**; 8 individually decorated rms with lovely views. Scotland's oldest inhabited castle, nearly 700 years old, in beautiful 1,600-acre parkland and surrounding

hills and moors, with log fires and antiques in the public rooms, good freshly prepared food in candlelit panelled dining room, and a friendly, relaxed atmosphere; 8 modern Scandinavian holiday lodges, too.

Cleish NT0998 NIVINGSTON HOUSE Kinross KY13 7LS (0577) 850216 ***£80**; 17 rms. Civilised small country-house hotel with relaxing bar and library, interesting food; sweeping lawn with distant hill views; cl 2 wks beg Jan; disabled access.

Dulnain Bridge NH9925 MUCKRACH LODGE Grantown-on-Spey Morayshire PH26 3LY (047 985) 257 **£78**; 12 rms. 19th-c hunting lodge with comfortable, relaxed lounge, open fire, and cosy little bar with decent lunchtime snacks; cl Nov, disabled access.

Kenmore NN7745 KENMORE Aberfeldy Perthshire PH15 2NU (0887) 830205 **£67.50**; 38 rms. Scotland's oldest inn with relaxed atmosphere, friendly staff, open fires, good food in the no-smoking restaurant, a poem in Burns' own handwriting on the plaster of one wall, river and loch fishing (salmon and trout), and own golf course; access to leisure centre; disabled access.

Crianlarich NN3825 ALLT-CHAORAIN COUNTRY HOUSE Perthshire FK20 8RU (083 83) 283 **£66**; 8 rms. Comfortable small hotel with homely atmosphere, log fire in lounge, honesty bar, sunroom with marvellous views, and good home-cooked food in wood-panelled dining room; lots of fishing, golf and walks nearby; cl 1 Nov-20 Mar; children over 12; disabled access.

Alyth NO2548 LANDS OF LOYAL Blairgowrie Perthshire PH11 8JQ (082 83) 3151 **£65**; 14 rms. Mansion house in its own grounds with lovely panelled hall/lounge, roaring fire and staircase off to galleried bedroom floor; attractive dining rooms, delicious, innovative food, excellent local service, and fine views; good base for the area; cl 25-26 Dec.

Fochabers NJ3458 GORDON ARMS Morayshire IV32 7DH (0343) 820508 ***£65**; 13 rms. Comfortable, traditional, small hotel with good food in restaurant and bars using fresh local produce, and good choice of whiskies; can arrange stalking and fishing; disabled access.

Glendevon NN9904 TORMAUKIN Dollar Clackmannanshire FK14 7JY (0259) 781252 **£64**; 10 rms, some in converted stable block. Comfortable, neatly kept inn in good walking country, loch and river fishing, lots of golf courses in reach; beamed dining room, softly lit bar, very good food (soup and coffee all day), decent breakfasts; cl 2 wks mid-Jan; disabled access.

Lundin Links NO4002 OLD MANOR Leven Fife KY8 6AJ (0333) 320368 ***£64w**; 19 rms. Overlooking Lundin Links golf course, this recently refurbished extended hotel has friendly staff and good local seafood in its two restaurants; disabled access.

Monymusk NJ6815 GRANT ARMS Inverurie AB51 7HT (046 77) 226 **£62**; 15 rms, most with own bthrm. Smart old inn with decent food using local game and fish, dark-panelled lounge bar divided into two areas by a log fire in the stub wall, simpler public bar, and exclusive right to 15 miles of good trout and salmon fishing on the River Don; ghillie available; cl 1 Jan, disabled access.

Spean Bridge NN2491 LETTERFINLAY LODGE Inverness-shire PH34 4DZ (0397) 712622 **£60**; 13 rms. Secluded and genteel family-run country house with picture window in extensive modern bar overlooking loch; elegantly panelled small cocktail bar, good, popular food, and friendly, attentive service; grounds run down through rhododendrons to the jetty and Loch Lochy; fishing can be arranged; cl Nov-Mar.

East Haugh NN9656 EAST HAUGH HOUSE Pitlochry Perthshire PH16 5JS (0796) 473121 ***£58**; 8 rms. Turreted stone house with lots of character, delightful conservatory bar, house party atmosphere, helpful, cheerful owners, and very good popular food inc local seafood and game in season; excellent shooting, stalking and salmon and trout fishing on surrounding local estates; cl 23-28 Dec.

Lower Largo NO4102 CRUSOE Leven Fife KY8 6BT (0333) 320759 ***£58**; 12 spacious rms with good sea views. Friendly and efficient service and good choice of decent food, separate family bar.

Aberdeen NJ9305 FERRYHILL HOUSE AB1 2UA (0224) 590 867 **£50w**; 10 rms. Well-run, small hotel with restaurant, wide choice of bar food, comfortable communicating spacious bar areas, very good choice of real ales and malt whiskies, and lots of tables on the neat, well-sheltered lawns; cl 1 Jan.

Kirkton of Glenisla NO2160 GLENISLA Blairgowrie Perthshire PH11 8PH (057 582) 223 **£50**; 6 rms. Prettily placed 17th-c coaching inn, beautifully restored, with natural unpainted wood throughout, happily unmatched furniture, bar with open fire, good bar suppers inc lovely Aberdeen Angus beef, and a cheerful, warm atmosphere – very much a local for the community; cl 24-26 Dec, disabled access.

Balquhidder NN5320 MONACHYLE MHOR Lochearnhead Perthshire DK19 8PQ (087 74) 622 ***£46**; 5 rms with fine views overlooking Voil and Doine lochs. 18th-c farmhouse/hotel in 2,000-acre estate with prettily furnished rooms and good food using own game and herbs; private fishing and stalking for guests; children over 10.

Dulnain Bridge NH9925 MUCKRACH LODGE PH26 3LY (047 985) 257 **£45**; 12 rms. Secluded, Victorian, former shooting lodge with good restaurant, notable bar lunches, hearty breakfasts, and friendly service; cl Nov, disabled access.

Crail NO6108 GOLF Anstruther Fife KY10 3TB (0333) 50206 **£40**; 5 clean if basic rms. Village inn with simple but tasty bar food, good breakfasts, plenty of atmosphere in bustling little public bar, quieter lounge, and coal fire.

Findhorn NJ0464 STRATHIOLAIRE Forres Morayshire IV13 7HA (080 82) 359 **£38**; 3 rms. Modern bungalow in quiet rural position overlooking fields and near river with excellent service, and very good food (home-grown vegetables); may see ospreys fishing as one contributor did; cl Nov-Easter, no under-12s.

Dalcross NH7650 EASTER DALZIEL FARM Inverness Inverness-shire IV1 2JL (0667) 462213 **£34**; 3 rms. Early Victorian farmhouse on 210 acres of family-run mixed farm (beef cattle and grain) with friendly, helpful owners, log fire in lounge, good Scottish breakfasts in big dining room and – when farm commitments allow – evening meal using own beef, lamb and veg; holiday cottages, too; cl Dec-Feb.

Inverness NH6645 CRAIGSIDE GUEST HOUSE 4 Gordon Terrace Inverness-shire IV2 3HD (0463) 231576 **£32**; 6 rms. Pleasant Victorian house near castle with friendly owners and good breakfasts; warmly recommended by contributors; disabled access.

Carronbridge NN8182 LOCHEND FARM Denny Stirlingshire FK6 5JJ (0324) 822778 **£31**; 2 rms, shared bthrm. 18th-c farmhouse in lovely position beside Loch Coulter on 650-acre upland sheep farm with sitting room, dining room and carefully prepared farmhouse cooking using own and local farm produce; cl Nov-Feb; no children.

To see and do

Aberdeen NJ9305, Scotland's third-largest city, has a large and interesting HARBOUR, well worth pottering around, and some interesting old buildings dotted among its more modern ones (especially around the pedestrianised High St of the Old Town above the River Don). The MARITIME MUSEUM (Shiprow) is in the town's third-oldest building, and has displays on the city's nautical heritage and on the North Sea oil industry. There are big plans for expansion this year; shop, limited disabled access; cl Sun, 25-26 Dec, 1-2 Jan. SATROSPHERE (Justice Mill Lane) A lively hands-on science and technology centre, where everything is there to be touched; lots of changing displays and exhibitions; snacks, shop, disabled access; cl Sun am, all day Tues (exc school hols), 25-26 Dec, 1-2 Jan; *£3. ART GALLERY (Schoolhill) First-class collection of Scottish and English painting since the 16th c, with good displays of sculpture, silver and other decorative arts; meals, snacks, shop, disabled access; cl Sun am, 25-26 Dec, 1-2 Jan. The 19th-c CRUIKSHANK BOTANIC GARDEN covers 11 acres with various smaller gardens – rock, water, rose and herbaceous – as well as trees and shrubs and a small terrace garden; disabled access; cl wknds exc pm summer Suns. The Athol (Kings Gate) is useful for lunch, and the Silver City does have this part of Scotland's best proper pub, the Prince of Wales (St Nicholas Lane).

Aberfeldy NN8549 is a nice, quiet Highland shopping town, with a fine 18th-c stone bridge designed by William Adam. Weem, for a good lunch at the Ailean Chraggan, is close by.

Alford NJ5716 GRAMPIAN TRANSPORT MUSEUM Big collection of vintage vehicles from the area, from horse-drawn sledges and carriages to motorcycles, cars and steamers; shop, disabled access; cl Nov-Mar; £2.30. More vintage transport at the ALFORD VALLEY RAILWAY, a narrow-gauge passenger railway with trips in two one-mile sections; shop, disabled access; open pm wknds and daily Jun-Aug – trains in steam peak wknds only; £1.50.

Anstruther NT1985 A pretty village with the interesting SCOTTISH FISHERIES MUSEUM in a little cobbled courtyard by the harbour: restored and model boats, an aquarium and an old fisherman's cottage in a series of buildings built between 16th and 19th c; snacks, shop, disabled access; cl am summer, 25-26 Dec, 1-2 Jan; £2. The Cellar is good for lunch, and the Craws Nest and Haven are also useful.

Aviemore NH8912 Famous for its ski-slopes, but the scenery can be enjoyed less energetically from the STRATHSPEY STEAM RAILWAY, covering the 5 miles from the Boat of Garten to Aviemore; meals, snacks, shop, disabled access; cl Nov-Mar – best to tel (0479) 810725 for train times; *£4. There are plenty of places to get something to eat in the extended village, now a sizeable tourist development, and a useful springboard for the Cairngorms and Glen More.

Balmoral Castle NO2588 is the Royal Family's Highland residence. Prince Albert bought the property four years after he and Queen Victoria had first rented it in 1848, and had a new castle built here by 1855. You can't go inside, but you can explore the wonderful gardens and woodlands, and there are various exhibitions; snacks, shop, disabled access; open Mon-Sat May-July; *£2.

Ballindalloch NJ1636 GLENLIVET DISTILLERY The first distillery in the Highlands to be licensed; the famous Smith was actually a Jacobite bootlegger who changed his name from Gow, the Scottish equivalent, to seem more Hanoverianly law-abiding. Tours and tastings; snacks, shop, disabled access; cl Sun, Nov-Easter. The Croft, a few miles south on the B9008, is good for lunch.

Banff NJ6864 MUSEUM As well as local history and armour, this has an award-winning exhibition on British birds set out as an aviary; shop, disabled access to ground floor only; cl am, Thurs, Oct-May. DUFF HOUSE is an especially fine Georgian baroque house, though it was never finished as intended.

Blair Atholl NN8765 BLAIR CASTLE Scotland's most visited privately owned house, dating back to the 13th c, although it was largely renovated in the 18th. It's the home of the Duke of Atholl and his unique private army, shown off in their annual parade in May. Thirty-two rooms are open, with interesting collections of arms and armour, china, paintings and embroidery. A piper outside every day in summer adds to the atmosphere; meals and snacks, shop, disabled access to ground floor only; cl Nov-Mar; *£4.50.

Blair Drummond NS7399 SAFARI AND LEISURE PARK Wild animals in natural surroundings, with an unusual aerial walkway above the big cats' reserve and a boat trip round the chimps' island. As well as often playful animals, there are rides, playgrounds and shows – it's set up very much as a family day out; meals, snacks, shop, disabled access; cl Oct-Mar; *£5.50.

Bo'ness SK0410 has the interesting if not extensive remains of a ROMAN FORTLET; shop; cl 12.30-1.30 pm, Oct-Apr exc Sat. The adjacent KINNEIL HOUSE has a museum with an audio-visual display on the history of the site, and other exhibitions on the area and estate, housed in a converted stable block. The house itself has decorated ceilings and wall paintings, and James Watt developed the steam engine in its grounds. BO'NESS & KINNEIL RAILWAY Re-creation of the days of steam complete with relocated railway buildings and Scotland's

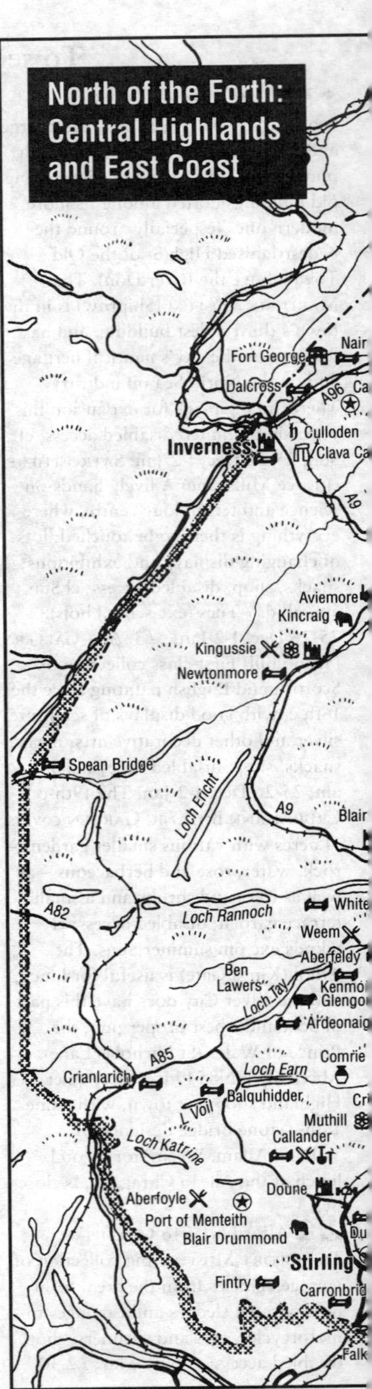

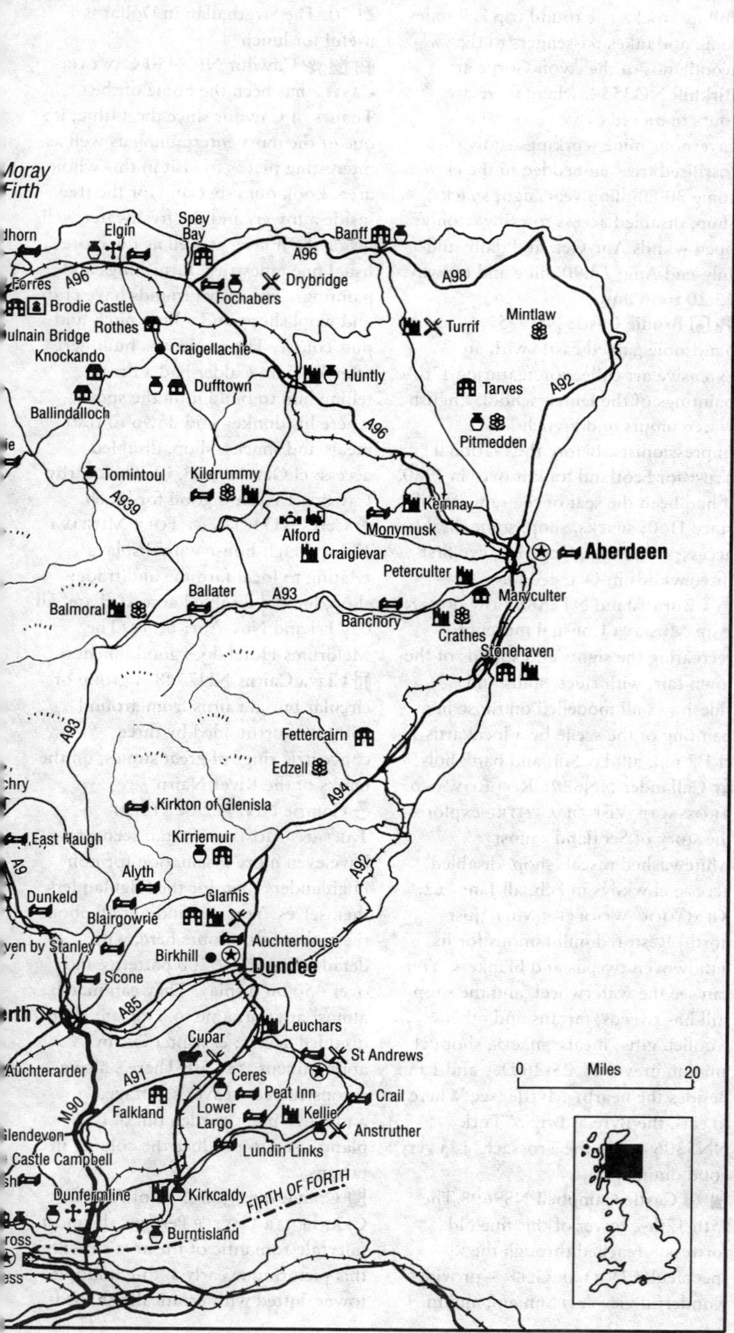
Moray Firth
Elgin
Spey Bay
Banff
A96
A98
Forres
Drybridge
Fochabers
Brodie Castle
Rothes
Mintlaw
Turrif
Craigellachie
Knockando
Huntly
Dufftown
Tarves
A92
Ballindalloch
A96
Pitmedden
Tomintoul
Kildrummy
A939
Kemnay
Alford
Monymusk
Craigievar
Aberdeen
Peterculter
Ballater
A93
Maryculter
Balmoral
Banchory
Crathes
Stonehaven
A93
Fettercairn
Edzell
A94
Kirkton of Glenisla
East Haugh
Kirriemuir
A92
A9
Alyth
Dunkeld
Glamis
Blairgowrie
Auchterhouse
Birkhill
Dundee
Scone
A85
Leuchars
Cupar
St Andrews
Auchterarder
A91
Ceres
Peat Inn
Crail
Falkland
M90
Lower Largo
Kellie
Anstruther
Lundin Links
Castle Campbell
Dunfermline
Kirkcaldy
FIRTH OF FORTH
Burntisland
0
Miles
20

largest collection of locomotives and rolling stock. The round trip is 7 miles long, and takes passengers to the woodlands of the Avon Gorge at **Birkhill** NO3534, where there are tours of an old CLAY MINE. The cavernous mine workings show the fossilised trees embedded in the clay some 300 million years ago; snacks, shop, disabled access to railway only; open wknds Apr-Oct, and daily mid-July-end Aug; £4.90 mine and railway, £3.20 train only.

Brodie Castle NH9757 A handsome gabled castle with an extensive art collection featuring 17th-c paintings of the Dutch school, English watercolours and French Impressionists. Before the National Trust for Scotland took it over in 1980, it had been the seat of the same family since 1160; snacks, shop, some disabled access; cl Sun am, Oct-Mar, exc first three wknds in Oct; £3.30.

! **Burntisland** NT2386 EDWARDIAN FAIR MUSEUM Unusual museum recreating the sights and sounds of the town fair, with rides, stalls and sideshows all modelled on those in a painting of the scene by a local artist; cl 1-2 pm, all day Sun and bank hols.

Callander NN6208 ROB ROY AND TROSSACHS VISITOR CENTRE explores the story of Scotland's most whitewashed rascal; shop, disabled access; cl wkdys in Feb, all Jan; *£2. KILMAHOG WOOLLEN MILL (just north) Restored mill famous for its handwoven tweeds and blankets. You can see the waterwheel, and the shop still has tweeds, tartans and other woollen gifts; meals, snacks, shop; cl am Sun in winter, 25-26 Dec and 1 Jan. Besides the nearby Myrtle (see Where to eat), the Byre at Brig o' Turk NN5306 out in the Trossachs is a very good dining pub.

Castle Campbell NS9698 The 15th-17th-c tower of this fine old fortress – reached through the spectacular DOLLAR GLEN – provides wonderful views; cl Sun am, and in winter Thurs pm and all day Fri; £1.70. The Strathallan in Dollar is useful for lunch.

Cawdor NH8450 CAWDOR CASTLE has been the home of the Thanes of Cawdor since the 14th c; it's one of the most entertaining as well as interesting places to visit in this whole area. Look out especially for the tree inside a tower, and the freshwater well inside the house, as well as the more usual fine tapestries, furnishings and paintings. The busy grounds have craft and wool shops and a little pitch-and-putt course. The castle was built here after William Calder had a dream telling him to build it on the spot where his donkey laid down to rest; meals and snacks, shop, disabled access; cl Oct-Apr; £3.50. The nearby Cawdor Tavern is good for lunch.

Ceres NO4011 FIFE FOLK MUSEUM 17th-c weigh-house with displays relating to local farming and trade; shop, limited disabled access; cl am, all day Fri and Nov-Apr; £1.30. The Meldrums Hotel does good lunches.

Clava Cairns NH7748 A group of circular burial cairns from around 1600 BC surrounded by three concentric rings of great stones, on the banks of the River Nairn.

Comrie NN7722 SCOTTISH TARTANS MUSEUM Tartan seems to have even more fascination for non-Highlanders than for the Highlanders themselves. You can find out all about these clannish colours here, with details of nearly 2,200 patterns and over 450 on display. They can match almost any surname to a tartan; shop, disabled access; cl winter exc by appointment; *£1.50. There's also a reconstructed weaver's cottage, and a dye-plant garden full of the plants used to produce the colours in tartans.

Craigievar NJ5509 (S of Alford) CRAIGIEVAR CASTLE Perhaps the most fairytale-romantic of the area's castles, this picturesque early 17th-c multiple tower dotted with erratically shaped windows soars to a mushrooming of corbels, turrets and crow-stepped gables, and inside the warren of narrow staircases takes you into a rich series of ornately beamed and plastered rooms. The National Trust for Scotland are worried that too many people come here, and for your own sake, too, you should avoid busy times, as it's not a place to absorb coach parties comfortably; cl am, cl Oct-Apr; £3.50. NTS.

Crathes NO7596 CRATHES CASTLE The beautiful 16th-c tower house has wonderful interiors – especially its ceiling paintings, and royal associations dating back to the early 14th c. The surrounding gardens include a four-acre walled garden with a remarkable series of carefully toned colour borders, nature trails, wild gardens and an interesting collection of unusual plants; meals, snacks, shop, some disabled access; cl Nov-Mar; *£3.80, £2.60 garden only.

Crieff NN8621 GLENTURRET DISTILLERY Scotland's oldest distillery, dating from 1775 and using the pure water of the Turret Burn. In its earlier days it was run by smugglers keen to avoid paying English taxes, but a more recent claim to fame is that the distillery cat Towser, who died in 1987, is still listed in the *Guinness Book of Records* as World Mousing Champion – challengers have 28,899 to beat. There's a particularly good visitor centre here; good meals and snacks, shop, limited disabled access to distillery; cl Sun am, 25-26 Dec, 1-2 Jan; £2.30. The town perched on the edge of the Highlands is a pleasant stop.

Culloden NH7345 The site of the gruesome massacre in which the 25-year-old Duke of Cumberland destroyed the Highland army of Bonnie Prince Charlie. On the moor a cairn marks this last bloody battle fought on mainland Britain. You can see the Graves of the Clans and the Wells of the Dead, and there is also the Old Leanach Cottage around which the battle was fought: this has now been refurbished in period style. Meals, snacks, shop, disabled access; visitor centre cl Jan; *£1.50. NTS.

Culross NO3714 is a fascinating small town on the Forth, virtually unchanged since the 16th and 17th c. Until the 1930s this was because no one could afford any improvements, and since then its red pantiled-roofed houses have been carefully restored and preserved by the National Trust for Scotland (they are still lived in). There's a visitor centre in the TOWN HOUSE (shop, disabled access, cl 1-2 pm and all Oct-Apr; £1, NTS) while the house called the STUDY is open for visitors to see the Norwegian painted ceiling in the drawing room; shop; cl am, and all Oct-Apr; 60p. NTS. The Palace, the first building the Trust purchased here, is officially closed for restoration, but there are occasional guided tours – ask at the Town House.

Cupar NO3714 SCOTTISH DEER CENTRE You can stroke the deer and even feed the young fawns here, and there are also nature and heritage trails, aerial walkways and observation platforms, an adventure playground and a new falconry centre, with daily displays of owls, hawks and falcons; meals and snacks, shop, disabled access; cl Nov-Mar; *£3.95. The Ostlers Close is good for lunch.

Doune NN7201 DOUNE CASTLE A 14th-c stronghold with two fine restored towers on the banks of the River Teith. It has strong associations with Bonnie Prince Charlie and with Sir Walter Scott; shop; cl Sun am and in winter Thurs pm and all Fri; £1.70. Close by, the DOUNE MOTOR MUSEUM has around 50 cars on display; meals, snacks, shop, disabled access; cl Nov-Mar; £2.50.

Dufftown NJ3240 GLENFIDDICH DISTILLERY Run by the Grant family since 1886, this is the only Highland distillery where you can follow the entire whisky production process from barley to bottle; shop; disabled access; open wkdys all year and wknds Easter-Oct, cl Christmas and New Year; shop, disabled access. Dufftown also has a useful MUSEUM.

Dunblane NN7801 is a small town of ancient origin, with old buildings in its narrow streets, especially around the close of its elegant 13th-c cathedral.

Dundee NO0430 is a bustling busy city, its distinguished heritage amply demonstrated in a number of museums. The main one is the MCMANUS GALLERIES MUSEUM (Albert Sq), with displays of local history, industry, archaeology, silver, ceramics and furniture, with the art gallery showing important works by 19th-c Scottish and English artists; shop, disabled access; cl Sun, Christmas-New Year. BARRACK STREET NATURAL HISTORY MUSEUM (Barrack St) Wildlife of the Scottish Lowlands and Highlands, inc the skeleton of the great Tay whale; shop; cl Sun. BROUGHTY CASTLE MUSEUM (Broughty Ferry) A 15th-c seaside castle rebuilt in the 19th c to defend the estuary, with displays on the city's maritime history. Plenty of harpoons and whaling exhibits – whaling used to be one of Dundee's major industries, with most of Britain's whaling ships built here; shop; cl 1-2 pm, all day Fri and Sun (exc pm summer). MILLS OBSERVATORY (Balgay Park) Built in 1935, this is Britain's only full-time public observatory, now housing exhibits on space research and astronomy, as well as a small planetarium (by prior arrangement only on (0382) 67138), and a variety of instruments inc a splendid 10-inch refracting telescope; there's a good audio-visual display. Shop; cl Sat am, all day Sun, and till 3 every day Oct-Mar (when open till 10 at night). Down at the DOCKS the Royal Research Ship *Discovery* was the first British purpose-built research vessel, commissioned for the ill-fated expedition by Scott to the Antarctic. The guides are very good, and they've just added a new visitor centre looking at the ship's history and the various people who used her; shop, disabled access; cl 1-2 pm and 25 Dec; *£3.85. Also in Victoria Dock is the 1824 frigate *Unicorn*, the oldest British-built warship still afloat, now containing a museum of naval life in her days in commission; snacks, shop, limited disabled access; cl 25-26 Dec, 1-2 Jan; £2. CAMPERDOWN COUNTRY PARK Based around the 19th-c Camperdown House, 400 acres of fine parkland with a variety of attractions, inc a golf course, wildlife centre, nature trails and woodland footpaths. Also a good adventure play area with the theme of the defeat of the Dutch at the 1797 Battle of Camperdown; meals and snacks, shop, disabled access; charge for wildlife centre. CLAYPOTTS CASTLE is a fine example of the tower house kind of castle; cl Sun am and all Oct-Mar; £1.20.

† **Dunfermline** NT0987 ABBEY Remains of Benedictine abbey, with later church buildings, pleasantly set in quiet precincts away from the busy centre. The foundations of the original 11th-c church are still under the more elaborate Norman nave, and the grave of King Robert the Bruce is marked by a modern brass in the choir stalls. The monastery guest house was a Royal palace for a while, and was the birthplace of Charles I; shop, disabled access; cl pm Thurs and Fri in winter; *£1.50. The DISTRICT MUSEUM includes an interesting explanation of the local manufacture of damask linen, and there's also a little gallery; shop; cl Sun and public hols. ANDREW CARNEGIE MUSEUM Explains the work of the Carnegie Trust and tells the story of the man who founded it, from his humble origins here to his fortune in Pittsburgh steel, and his work as a philanthropist on a grand scale – he gave away over $350 million but claimed he didn't believe in charity; summer snacks, shop, disabled access;

cl am Sun and winter wkdys, 25 Dec, New Year. On the first Fri of each month in summer there are weaving demonstrations. PITTENCRIEFF HOUSE MUSEUM (Pittencrieff Park) Fine 17th-c mansion in a rugged glen, with displays of local history and costume; shop, disabled access; cl Tues and all Nov-Apr.

Edzell NO5969 EDZELL CASTLE The walled garden here was planted in 1604 by Sir David Lindsay; heraldic sculptures unique to Scotland alternate with recesses for flowers and nests for birds. Disabled access; cl winter Thurs pm and Fri; £1.70.

Elgin NJ2162 is a shopping town of some poise, with ancient buildings as well as its ruined 13th-c cathedral, and is handy for the north coast. There's still quite a lot to see of the ruined CATHEDRAL, founded in 1224 and known as the Lantern of the North and the Glory of the Kingdom because of its extraordinary architectural beauty and great fine-traceried windows. Although rebuilt after a fire in 1390, it fell into disrepair after the Reformation. The 15th-c nave has some ancient Celtic cross slabs with Pictish symbols; shop; cl Thurs pm and all Fri; £1.20. The MUSEUM in the High St has a justifiably world-famous fossil collection; cl Mon and Sun and all Oct-Mar; £1.20.

Falkirk NS8880 ROUGH CASTLE Not too much left of the Roman fort that was here, only the mounds on which the barracks, granary and bath buildings stood. The military road which once linked this fort with all the others on the Antonine Wall runs among these buildings.

Falkland NO2507 FALKLAND PALACE set below the Lomond Hills was the hunting palace of the Stuart Kings and Queens. The rooms are beautifully decorated, especially the King's bedchamber and the Chapel Royal. The French Renaissance architecture of the south range is very impressive, and the 1539 tennis courts are the oldest in the country; shop; cl Sun am, all Nov-Mar; *£3.50 palace and garden, £2 garden only. The Covenanter Inn is useful for lunch.

Fettercairn NO6473 FASQUE (just N) still belongs to the Gladstones, and the Prime Minister lived here from 1830-1851. The main rooms look as if they've scarcely been changed (let alone modernised) since he moved to Wales, and the servants' quarters are also an extraordinary period survival, complete with a touching gallery of servants' portraits. All very unrestored; snacks; shop; disabled access; cl am, Fri, cl Oct-April; £2.50.

Fochabers NJ3458 FOLK MUSEUM The largest collection of horse-drawn vehicles N of the Forth, as well as displays of village life; shop, disabled access; cl 1-2 pm; *60p.

Forres NJ4265 SUENOS STONE Mysterious 9th- or 10th-c stone that may have been erected to commemorate a forgotten battle. It's 20 ft high, and is carved with a cross on one side and groups of warriors on the other. Bequests by two brothers – Alexander and Hugh Falconer – founded the FALCONER MUSEUM, which displays the fossil collection of Hugh who was a distinguished scientist and friend of Darwin; shop; disabled access; cl 12.30-1.30 pm, Sun am. DALLAS DHU is a fine old Victorian distillery, which you can wander around on your own. It's been cleverly adapted using animatronic models to explain what's happening; shop, disabled access; cl Sun am, and in winter Thurs pm and all day Fri; £1.50.

Fort George NH7657 One of three fortresses built after 1745, when the Hanoverians were taking no risks in keeping this area firmly under their thumb. It's one of the finest examples of an 18th-c artillery building, and the Lieutenant Governor's house has the regimental museum of the Queen's Own Highlanders; shop, disabled access; cl Sat, Sun exc pm Apr-Sept; £2.50.

Glamis NO3848 GLAMIS CASTLE The family home of the Earls of Strathmore, and the childhood home of the Queen Mother – a splendid creation, utterly suitable as the setting for Shakespeare's murder of Duncan in *Macbeth* (one of the oldest parts of the building is known as Duncan's Hall). Notable features include the chapel with its painted panels and ceiling and the drawing room, and of course there are those stories about what's locked away in one of the towers; meals, snacks, shop, some disabled access; cl Oct-Apr; £4. The Strathmore Arms is good for lunch.

Glengoulandie Deer Park NN7652 Herds of red deer and other wild creatures kept in surroundings as close to their natural habitat as possible, yet keeping the animals within sight; snacks, shop; cl Oct-May; £3.50 with car, 90p walking.

Huntly NJ5240 CASTLE The original medieval castle here was destroyed and rebuilt several times, once by Mary, Queen of Scots. Reconstructed for the last time in 1602, the ruins are now worth a look for their ornate heraldic decorations; shop; cl winter Thurs pm and all Fri; £1.80. In the square is a little local-history museum.

Inverness NH6645 is the biggest town up here, and the main shopping town for the whole of the N of Scotland (Melvens is a good book shop). It doesn't have many things that make it an obvious tourist town, but has an attractive riverside setting, and is a handy centre. Looking over the Moray Firth a few miles E, CASTLE STUART was built for the Earl of Moray in 1621 when his family, the Stuarts, ruled the United Kingdom, and it has recently been restored to include decorations and furnishings that reflect its days of glory. You can stay by appointment, tel (0463) 790745; shop; £3.

Kellie NS5805 KELLIE CASTLE A fine example of 16th- and 17th-c domestic architecture, though parts date from the 14th c, with good collections of plasterwork, panelling and furniture. Also 4 acres of gardens, inc a Victorian walled garden and a woodland area with adventure playground; snacks, shop; cl am, Nov-Apr; £2.80.

Kemnay NJ7212 CASTLE FRASER The architectural embellishments here are the work of two remarkably talented families of stonemasons, who helped to make it one of the grandest castles of Mar. The z-shaped building incorporates the remains of an earlier building; snacks, shop; cl wkdys Apr and Oct, all Nov-Mar; £3.30. NTS.

Killiecrankie NN9162 Queen Victoria is just one of the people to have found this romantic spot beguiling, but it wasn't always so serene. In 1689 it was the site of a fierce battle when the Highlanders routed the troops of King William, and there's now a VISITOR CENTRE to tell the tale. It also has displays on the area's natural history; snacks, shop, disabled access; cl Nov-Apr; *50p. The Killiecrankie Hotel is a nice spot for lunch.

Kildrummy NJ4617 KILNDRUMMY CASTLE was the seat of the Earls of Mar. Now in ruins, though there are still the original 13th-c round towers, hall and chapel, as well as some later remains; £1.20. It provides a spectacular backdrop to the GARDENS, which are very beautiful indeed and of some botanical interest. There's an alpine garden in an old quarry, a water garden, walks in the woods and a video showing the changes in the garden through the seasons; shop, disabled access; cl Nov-Mar; *£2.

Kincraig NH8305 HIGHLAND WILDLIFE PARK Animals native to the area such as reindeer, bears, wolves, wildcats and bison, as well as aviaries and a pets' corner – all in lovely surroundings; snacks, shop, disabled access; cl Nov-Mar; £11 for full car, £9 for 2 passengers.

Kingussie NH7501 (pronounced Kinoossie) has a HIGHLAND FOLK MUSEUM with craft demonstrations, displays of domestic life, a reconstructed mill and a farming exhibition; shop, disabled access; cl Sun am and all wknds in winter; *£2. The Cross is good for lunch.

Kinross NO1102 LOCH LEVEN CASTLE Mary, Queen of Scots was imprisoned in this fortress on an island in the loch, though she managed to escape. The loch itself is rather undramatic, but in the winter the evening flights and sounds of the thousands of ducks and geese here seem a mournful echo of those days; cl all winter. You need to get a ferry across to the castle. KINROSS GARDENS Rather fine and formal, with yew trees, roses and herbaceous borders; cl Oct-Apr; £2.

Kirkcaldy NT2791 RAVENSCRAIG CASTLE 15th-c ruin in a park, perhaps most notable for its symmetrical shape. It was one of the first British castles designed to be defended by firearms, and has great views over the Firth of Forth. The MUSEUM here is worth a look, though the town itself has little to interest visitors.

Kirriemuir NO3954 BARRIE'S BIRTHPLACE The birthplace of the writer of *Peter Pan*: the upper floors are furnished in the style of the period, and next door are displays relating to his work, both literary and theatrical; cl Sun am, all Oct-Apr exc Easter; *1.50. NTS.

Knockando NJ1842 TAMDHU DISTILLERY Interesting displays and tour of the distillery, with tastings; shop; cl Sun, Nov-Apr.

Leuchars NO4521 EARLSHALL CASTLE Grand old castle with an especially elaborate painted ceiling in the Long Gallery; it's adorned with mythological beasts and the heraldic devices of the principal families of Scotland. Other notable features include the bedchamber of Mary, Queen of Scots, dozens of broadswords, and lovely gardens (famous for their topiary chessmen) where children are encouraged to run around; snacks, shop; cl am, all Nov-Mar; *£2.90, *£2 gardens only.

! **Maryculter** NO8599 STORYBOOK GLEN Children should enjoy it here, with various fictional characters brought to life in 20 acres of beautiful Deeside countryside; meals, snacks, shop, disabled access; cl winter wkdys; *£2.40.

Marypark NJ1938 GLENFARCLAS DISTILLERY This distillery produces one of the traditional top three malts, and there are interesting displays on how it's done; shop, limited disabled access; cl wknds exc Sat Jun-Sept, Christmas and New Year; £2. The other two malts are Smith's Glenlivet, and the glorious sherry-casked Macallan, from Craigellachie NJ2844, who allow visits only by appointment, tel (034 05) 471.

Mintlaw NJ9948 ADEN COUNTRY PARK More than 200 acres of lovely woodland and farmland, criss-crossed with nature trails and with plenty of wildlife. The NE SCOTLAND AGRICULTURAL HERITAGE CENTRE here illustrates two centuries of farming history in a restored and now working 19th-c estate farm; meals, snacks, shop, disabled access; cl wkdys in Apr and Oct and every day Nov-Apr; £1.

Muthill NN8617 (pronounced 'mewtle') DRUMMOND CASTLE GARDENS Splendid gardens originally laid out in 1630 by John Drummond, 2nd Earl of Perth. Lovely views from the upper terrace, and the centrepiece sundial was designed and built by the master mason of King Charles I; cl am, Oct-Apr; £2.

Nairn NH8856 is a quiet, relaxed and rather discreet old-fashioned resort on the north coast, with good sheltered beaches.

Perth NO1123 is spaciously laid out along the broad River Tay; it has a popular craft centre in the Fair Maid's House, and an excellent specialist rhododendron nursery, Glendoick Gardens. There are a couple of decent museums, inc one devoted to the Black Watch Regiment; cl am Sun and all Sat. BRANKLYN GARDEN only covers about 2 acres but seems much bigger, thanks to a remarkable planting of interesting rhododendrons, small trees, asiatic primulas, meconopsis, lilies and the like; shop, limited disabled access; cl Nov-Feb; *£2. CAITHNESS GLASS You can watch all aspects of paperweight-making from a viewing gallery, and there's a collectors' museum and factory shop; meals and snacks, disabled access; cl Sun Nov-Mar, no glass-making at wknds. Just west is HUNTINGTOWER CASTLE with an interesting painted ceiling, and there's another castle a little south-east at ELCHO beside the river. Timothys is good for lunch.

Peterculter NJ8301 DRUM CASTLE built in the late 13th c is one of the three oldest tower houses in Scotland, and has connections with Robert the Bruce; snacks, shop, limited disabled access; cl am, wkdys Apr and Oct, all Nov-Mar; £3.30. The Lairhillock Inn at Netherley a few miles south is good for lunch.

Pitlochry NN9458 has the comfortable feel of a place that's been an inland resort town for a good long time, and is beautifully set in fine countryside; a happy sort of place. EDRADOUR is Scotland's smallest distillery, founded in 1825 and virtually unchanged since Victorian times; shop, disabled access; cl Sun, and all Nov-Mar, exc for the shop. The POWER STATION has exhibitions on the production of electricity, with access to the turbine viewing gallery. You can see the salmon as they pass upstream to their spawning grounds from the salmon ladder viewing chamber; shop; cl Nov-Mar; *£1.50. Lovely woodland on the banks of man-made Loch Faskally with walks and nature trails.

Pitmedden NJ8927 PITMEDDEN GARDEN was originally planted in the 17th c and hasn't really changed since, with sundials, fountains and pavilions among the elaborate formal gardens; also a museum of farming life. Snacks; shop; disabled access; visitor centre and museum cl Oct-Apr; *£2.80.

Port of Menteith NN5801 INCHMAHOME PRIORY Famous as the refuge of the infant Mary, Queen of Scots in 1543 (or, depending on your allegiances, as the burial-place of Robert Cunningham Grahame), this Augustinian priory was founded in 1238 on an island in the middle of the lake, and in spring and summer you can get a boat across. Robert the Bruce prayed here before the Battle of Bannockburn; shop; cl all winter; £2 inc ferry.

Rothes NJ2749 GLEN GRANT DISTILLERY The whisky distilled here is used in many first-class blended whiskies as well as being sold as a single malt; shop; disabled access; cl wknds, cl Oct-Mar.

St Andrews NO5116 is a civilised university town as well as a rather dignified seaside resort, and outstanding for golfers. Despite its atmosphere today it's had a rather turbulent past, its two grandest buildings, the castle and the cathedral, both damaged in waves of anti-Catholic feeling. The 13th-c CASTLE was the scene of Bishop Beaton's murder during one of these periods in 1546 – his mistake had been to burn a Protestant leader to death. Before this he had managed to refortify the castle, but it was demolished in the 17th c to provide stone for the harbour, though some substantial ruins remain; shop, disabled access; cl am Sun; £1.20. The twin-towered remains of the Norman CATHEDRAL are impressive, and in its time this was the largest cathedral in Scotland; angry locals sacked it in the 16th c; shop, disabled access; £1.50. Beside it the Romanesque ST RULE'S TOWER is part of the older church the cathedral was built to replace (perhaps pre-Conquest), and if you can face over

150 steps it gives wonderful views from the top. Important Celtic and medieval artefacts are housed in the MUSEUM in a nearby 14th-c building. John Knox had a chequered career in St Andrews: he preached his first sermon in Holy Trinity Church (South St) in 1547, but when the French came to relieve the castle from the Protestants soon afterwards he was packed off to the galleys for 18 months. The GOLF MUSEUM (Bruce Embankment) should fascinate anyone really keen on the game, with audio-visual displays going through the game's 500-year history and memorable moments, and lots of memorabilia, documents and relevant artefacts – inc the most unlikely-looking old cleeks and so forth. Lots of the exhibitions use incredibly up-to-date technology, with some of the most advanced features you're likely to come across in any museum; shop, disabled access; cl Tues and Weds Nov-Apr, 25 Dec-1 Jan; *£3. SEA LIFE CENTRE (The Scores) Similarly comprehensive coverage of British native marine life, with all the species of fish you'd expect to find off the coastline, lively touch displays and three resident seals, now displayed in a pool in an expanded viewing area; meals, snacks, shop, disabled access; cl 25 Dec; £3.95. Besides the Vine Leaf (see Where to eat), Ma Bell's (pleasant seafront views outside) and the St Andrews Wine Bar are useful for lunch, and the Grange just outside the town does good food.

Scone NO1126 SCONE PALACE was the seat of government in Scotland from Pictish times, though the current building is largely 16th c behind an 18th-c castellated façade. It was the site of the Stone of Destiny – the famous coronation stone – until it was seized by the English in 1296, and indeed Scottish kings were crowned at Scone until 1651. Now there are good displays of porcelain, furniture, clocks and needlework and the grounds are pleasant; meals, snacks, shop, some disabled access; cl Sun am exc July and Aug, mid-Oct-Good Fri; £4.

Spey Bay NJ3565 TUGNET ICE HOUSE This early 19th-c structure is the largest ice house in Scotland, now housing displays on the history and techniques of commercial salmon fishing; exhibitions cl Oct-Apr.

Stonehaven NO8786 An old fishing town, with its more seasidey but discreet Victorian streets in the upper part; the harbourside Marine is a pleasant pub. TOLBOOTH Now a fishing and local-history museum, but before that the 16th-c storehouse of the Earls of Marischal; cl 12-2 pm, Weds am, all day Thurs and Sun, all Oct-May. Just south on its precipitous sea-girt crag is the bleak and battered but still extensive and well-preserved ruin of 14th-c DUNNOTTAR CASTLE. It sheltered the Scottish crown jewels during the Civil War, but has seen much darker episodes in its time; shop, limited disabled access; cl winter wknds, 25-26 Dec, 1 Jan; *£1.50.

Stirling NS7993 Strategically placed on the Firth of Forth, this is a very unstuffy place, with the university students putting quite a bit of buzz into the atmosphere, and all sorts of lively events through the summer – virtually all of them with at least a touch of history about them. STIRLING CASTLE provides magnificent views from its lofty hilltop site. It became very popular with the royal family in the 15th and 16th c, and most of the buildings date from that period. The finest features are the Chapel Royal built by James VI (and I of England), and the Renaissance palace built by James V. There's also a museum devoted to the Argyll and Sutherland Highlanders; snacks, shop; cl am Sun in winter, 25 Dec and 1-2 Jan; *£2.50. In a restored building next door the STIRLING CASTLE VISITOR CENTRE adds a lot to one's enjoyment and understanding of the background of both the castle itself and the surroundings; shop, disabled access; cl 25-26 Dec; *60p for audio-visual display. Dropping down the steep hill on which the castle stands is an attractive and interesting network of old streets, with a lot of character in their old-to-ancient buildings; MARY'S WALK is an interesting ruined Renaissance-style mansion. The Settle Inn (St Marys Wynd) is a useful and atmospheric pub, and the SMITH ART GALLERY AND MUSEUM presents a variety of exhibitions throughout the year; snacks, shop, disabled access; cl Mon, winter cl am exc Sat, summer cl Sun am.

Tarves NJ8631 HADDO HOUSE is renowned for its Choral Society and the concerts they hold here. It was designed by William Adam, and refurbished in the 1880s in the 'Adam Revival' style; the surrounding parkland is lovely. Meals, snacks, shop, disabled access; open pm wknds only Apr and Oct, daily May-Sept, am too Jun-Aug; *£3.30.

Tomintoul NJ1619 MUSEUM Good re-creations of a blacksmith's shop and a farm kitchen, as well as displays on local geology, folklife and wildlife, geology, climate and landscape; disabled access; cl Sun am exc July/ Aug, cl Nov-Mar. The Glenavon Arms is useful.

Turriff NJ7250 FYVIE CASTLE Each of the five towers was built in a different c by the family that lived here throughout – the oldest parts date back to the 13th c, and the whole thing is one of the most fantastic examples of Scottish baronial architecture. The wheel stair is one of the best in the country, and there are collections of armour, tapestry and notable paintings, inc works by Romney and Gainsborough; snacks, shop, some disabled access; cl am (exc Jun, July and Aug), Oct-Apr; £3.30. The Towie Tavern does good food.

Of the area's abundance of **lochs, Loch Rannoch** NN6580 is among the quieter and more beautiful ones. **Loch Tay** NN6535 seems to change moment by moment as the clouds flit across the sky, and has a quiet road along its southern side; **Ben Lawers** NN6340 is an interesting spot, with alpine wild flowers not found elsewhere in Britain and a quite different feel from other Highland mountains; a steep road leads up the side. **Loch Ericht** NN5574 is very peaceful but does involve foot-slogging to make the most of it. **Loch Katrine** NN4510 is a lovely stretch of water that inspired Scott's *Lady of the Lake*, and has a Victorian steamer in summer. **Loch Voil** NN5020 further N is, like Loch Katrine, served by just a narrow back road, so fairly peaceful even in summer; it's famous for having Rob Roy's grave at Balquhidder NN5320. **Loch Earn** NN6523 with a trunk road alongside is largely given over to water-skiing and that sort of thing. Loch Ness is of course the grand-daddy of them all, and a place of great beauty; the calmest drive along it is the B862, though it leaves the loch shore more than the trunk road on the other side.

Besides those we've mentioned as places to eat at or stay in, inns where you can get a decent bite to eat and which are particularly well placed for walkers, drivers or just strollers in these parts include the Fife Arms at Braemar NO1491, Ship at Broughty Ferry NO4630, Loch Ericht Hotel at Dalwhinnie NN6384, Dores Hotel at Dores by Loch Ness NH5930, Anchor at Dunipace NS8083, Ship on the shore at Elie NO4900, Hungry Monk at Gartocharn NS4286, Old Mill at Killearn NS5285, Trossachs Hotel near Loch Achray NN5106, Corriegour Lodge near Altrua on Loch Lochy NN2390, Loch Tummel Hotel above Loch Tummel NN8460, Potarch Hotel at Potarch NO6097 and Sheriffmuir Inn on Sheriff Muir NN8202.

Walks

For general remarks about walking in the Highlands, see the Walks section of the **West, Argyll and Loch Lomond.**

This area is not quite so rewarding to the walker as the west coast, or the borders, but does have plenty of well-above-average walking. Some enjoyable strolls and easier walks include the **Knock of Crieff** NN8622, a wooded hill with a good viewpoint above Crieff; the **Lomond Hills** NO2206, a level walk from the car park by the road above Falkland NO2507 – not to be confused with Loch Lomond, this Fife upland gives views over most of south-east Scotland; forest tracks and paths over **Kinnoull Hill** NO1322 above the River Tay just outside Perth NO1123; or the signposted circular walk from **Comrie** NH4155 into **Glen Lednock** NN7327.

The **Trossachs** NN5007 are ever popular, with dense conifer forests, steep glens, and beautifully framed lochs. They are not brilliant for low-level walks unless you like forests (the route on to Callander Crags NN6308 from Callander NN6307 is one of the best). However, they allow some good mountain walks comparable in difficulty to some of the fells of the English Lake District: Ben Venue NN4706 and Ben Vorlich NN2912 are among the best.

Glen Roy NN2985 and its curious Parallel Roads (not actually roads but the tubmarks of a former glacier) can be seen from an easy track along its bottom, a spectacular 4-mile route from Brae Roy Lodge NN3392 (return the same way).

Loch Tay NN6838 is dominated by the towering bulk of Ben Lawers NN6341, nearly 4,000 ft but with a good track up. There are easier walks at the east end of the loch, from the attractive estate village of Kenmore NN7745 along the banks of the River Tay, or into the adjacent forest to a viewpoint over the loch.

The **Ochil Hills** NO0409 are a range of green mountains which rise without preamble from the lowland plain – a striking textbook example of the Highland Fault. A path from Tillicoultry NS9197 up Mill Glen NS9198 takes you to Ben Cleuch NN9000, the highest point of the range. Don't miss the amazing short path around the base of Castle Campbell NS9699 above Dollar NS9698 – catwalks, rock overhangs, jungle-thick vegetation, and a swirling stream below.

On the **Fife coast**, you can walk along the sand and rock shore from St Andrews NO5116 to the picturesque East Neuk fishing village of Crail NO6108, where a clear path continues past Anstruther Easter NO5703 and Pittenweem NO5402 to St Monance NO5201, all of them attractive.

A ski-lift from Glen More NH9807 above Aviemore is the easy way up to the summits of the **Cairngorms**, and there are manageable paths down. Loch an Eilean nestles beneath Cairn Gorm NJ0004, on the Aviemore side; a forest track encircles this delightful little loch, with its castle romantically placed on an isle.

From the **Linn of Dee** NO0689 not far from Braemar are long glen walks into the Cairngorms along Glen Dee and the Lairig Ghru. From Braemar itself NO1491 you can follow a steep path up **Morrone** NO1388, along a route used for a race in the Highland games. **Bennachie** NJ6522 on the E edge of the Grampians, nr Inverurie NJ7721, rises to only a modest height but has tremendous views over lowland Grampian; the gently rolling moorland top has several colour-coded Forestry Commission trails (the lower slopes are forested).

The **coast** around Banff NJ6864 can be followed for some stretches (a bus service along the main road is a useful method of return), for instance from **Portsoy** NJ5866 to **Findlater Castle** NJ5467, a windswept ruin on the cliff-edge.

Driving

In and approaching the Highlands, the network of roads thins out, so you have to drive quite long distances to make satisfactory round tours: but this is the part where the drives are really memorable. Among a wealth of handsome roads, one fine route N, with exhilarating views much of the way, is the A823 through Glen Devon and Glen Eagles to join the A822 through Crieff and on up through the very pretty Sma' Glen, and then over the heather moors to fork left on the A826 to Aberfeldy. Around Aberfeldy many good drives include the run along Loch Tay (the very slow back road along the S side of the loch gives much better views of mighty Ben Lawers than the main road, though you don't then have the option of the very steep alpine detour up the gated road to Bridge of Balgie). The B846 N from Aberfeldy starts mildly though with good views of the lower slopes of volcano-looking Schiehallion, but after the turn left along Strath Tummel becomes a memorable drive along Loch Rannoch, before coming to a dead end above the trees among sweeping heather moors.

The A93 from Blairgowrie through Glenshee to Braemar and the Dee Valley is a glorious road with some tremendous mountain views, before you reach the richly wooded valley – also impressive, particularly in autumn. Right down to Banchory you can pick almost any spot to start a walk in lovely scenery, and part of the beauty of it is the way that majestic open moors are within such easy reach of the sheltered valley itself. It's a popular route, though, with quite a stream of slow summer traffic – particularly along the hook of back road forking off at Braemar to Mar Lodge and the long rapids of the Linn of Dee, spectacularly furious after heavy rain.

The steep A939 N of Ballater is one of the roads built by the Hanoverians after the 1745 rising, to tame the Highlands – and forges up over what still seems an untameably wild area, to Grantown-on-Spey. Between here and Kingussie the scenery is very grand, though with a lot of tourist development; the B970 is the quieter road down the valley, and has the side road up into Glen More, ancient Scots pine forest below the defiantly beautiful Cairngorms.

An alternative route between Deeside and Speyside is further E, the A97 to Rhynie and then the A941 to Dufftown: less travelled, more circuitous and through rather less awesomely magnificent high country, but still giving some fine views.

As we've taken the Great Glen itself as our divide from the North, this area includes the B862 which runs down its SE side – the quieter of the two roads, unpocked by Nessie attractions, with places to stop by Loch Ness.

Cutting across the heart of the area, the A86 from Newtonmore to Spean Bridge is quite a pleasant drive.

Off the B957 and A94 between Kirriemuir and Stonehaven little-travelled roads run up the Angus glens: not so dramatic as the better-known Highland glens, but very secluded, with a succession of pleasing views, attractive rivers, and occasional castle ruins. Glen Esk is perhaps the most rewarding, with an empty road running for miles alongside the North Esk up to black Loch Lee with its ancient church; but Glen Isla and Glen Clova run it close.

In what's known as the Central Region, around Stirling, there's a lot of potential for driving through attractive countryside without having to embark on such long runs as the Highlands often entail. The quiet road over Sheriff Muir is a surprisingly sudden foray into wild high moorland right on the edge of quite a busy conglomeration of urban areas, while to the west of the M9 the countryside is largely open and pleasant, with the B roads giving good, changing hill views. The A821 through the Trossachs carries a lot of coach traffic in summer, as does the A81 and even the narrower B829 up Loch Ard to Loch Katrine, drawn by this area's very picturesque scenery.

There are no really memorable roads down in Fife, though the busy A92 along the coast between Inverkeithing and Kinghorn has some pleasant views across to Edinburgh, the B925 through Auchtertool is quite pleasant, the A909 climbing steeply out of Burntisland has an attractive passage as it passes the haunted Stenhouse Reservoir, and the A823 N from Dunfermline into the Cleish Hills is a good drive.

The M90 and A9 are strong spinal roads giving fast runs right up to Inverness; 3½ hours is a comfortable estimate from Edinburgh, though the A9 still has some single-carriageway stretches which are tiresome.

Where to eat

Anstruther NO5603 CELLAR 24 East Green (0333) 310378 Characterful restaurant off little courtyard with beams, stone walls, open fires, wonderful fresh fish, and good wines; cl Fri/Sat am, Tues-Sat pm, disabled access. **£35.70**|£5.25.

Aberfoyle NN5200 BRAEVAL MILL (087 72) 711 Converted mill with stone walls and flagstones, careful and extremely good food inc fine French cheeses, and helpful friendly staff; cl Sun pm, Mon, Tues-Sat am. **£35.**

Cupar NO3714 OSTLERS CLOSE 25 Bonnygate (0334) 55574 Cosy, unpretentious restaurant with lovely food using local fresh produce, game and fish; good puddings and decent wines; cl Sun, Mon, 1 wk Jun, 25-26 Dec, 1-2 Jan; disabled access. **£28 dinner, £16 lunch**|£8.

Kingussie NH7500 THE CROSS (0540) 661166 Fine food based on local fish and game in old tweed mill beside a stream; very good wines; cl Tues, Weds am, Dec-Feb; children over 6 in evening. **£25 dinner, £15 lunch.**

St Andrews NO5116 VINE LEAF 131 South St (0334) 77497 Though perhaps the alleyway and first impressions of the restaurant itself are slightly off-putting, the warmth of the welcome, attractively laid-out tables, very good food, unobtrusive service and decent wines soon dispel any doubts; evenings only; cl Sun, Mon, 2 wks Jan, 2 wks Jun. **£20.**

Turriff NJ7250 TOWIE (0888) 4201 Good friendly atmosphere, stylish comfort, well-presented, generous bar food, beautifully prepared food in no-smoking restaurant, good choice of wines, and quietly efficient service; handy for Fyvie Castle and Delgatie Castle; cl 1-2 Jan, disabled access. **£19.50**|£1.95/£5.

Drybridge NJ4362 OLD MONASTERY (0542) 32660 Lovely views from this former monastery as well as very good fish and game (fresh local produce) and friendly service, cl Sun, Mon, 1st 2 wks Nov, last 3 wks Jan, no under-8s. **£17.50**|£5.25.

Weem NN8449 AILEAN CHRAGGAN (0887) 820346 Emphasis on well-presented fish dishes in comfortable, friendly inn with lovely views; cl 1-2 Jan. **£16**|£2.85/£5.75.

Perth NO1123 TIMOTHYS 24 St John St (0738) 26641 Owned by the same people for 24 years, this dimly lit restaurant serves consistently good food using home-grown and fresh local produce garnished with home-picked flowers, particularly good, often unusual home-made soups, a daily pudding and excellent for morning coffee (yummy warm-from-oven home-made biscuits or freshly made doughnuts); carefully chosen wine list; cl Sun, Mon, Christmas; disabled access. £13|£2.50/£3.85.

Glamis NO3846 STRATHMORE ARMS (0307) 840248 Picturesque, unspoilt village with simply decorated old inn, well-presented delicious food inc wonderful puddings, roaring log fire in lounge, and good caring service; cl Mon pm, 16 Feb-14 Mar; disabled access. £3.50/£4.95.

Callander NN6208 MYRTLE (A84 just outside) (0877) 30919 Attractive old dining pub with two cosy, pretty restaurant rooms serving reasonably priced, well-cooked and presented food and outstanding puddings; cl last 2 wks Nov; disabled access. £2.75/£5.

NORTH OF SCOTLAND

The west coast scenery is sensational, and there are very comfortable places to stay.

The plum of this area is the west coast with its glorious sea, mountain and island scenery. Skye in particular is wonderful in good weather (the island really is a place where the success of a short stay depends on a spell of settled weather). The north coast is relatively wild and empty: addictive to some people, harsh and inhospitable to others. The east coast has good golf courses and long empty sandy beaches – perhaps more suitable for a quiet summer holiday than a weekend break, though Cromarty is a very attractive small town (its courthouse has an extraordinarily convincing reconstructed trial scene).

The few places to visit are best seen as an accompaniment to a holiday spent mainly enjoying the scenery. The highlights are Dunvegan Castle on Skye, Inverewe Gardens near Poolewe and Dunrobin Castle at Golspie; the Loch Ness Monster centre at Drumnadrochit is fun.

There are some excellent places to stay – many of them so embracingly comfortable that when the weather does turn bad you might even be glad of an excuse not to go out.

The area is usually at its best between late May and early July, while the days are very long and before the midges have really got into their stride. The big snag is sheer distance: for most people, it takes too long to get up here for a short break.

We welcome reports from readers . . .

Readers who help us with reports for the GUIDE are offered a discount on the next edition: so please do help if you can!

Where to stay

Ullapool NH1294 ALTNAHARRIE Ross-shire IV26 2SS (085 483) 230 **£200 inc dinner**; 8 rms. On the shores of Loch Broom and reached by a ten-minute boat journey, this carefully restored house was originally built for drovers; two lounges with lots of books, open fire, a mix of Scandinavian and English furnishings, marvellously quiet, relaxing atmosphere, room service (they think tea-making facilities in rooms are a sign of neglect), magnificent food – five set courses with much of the food home-grown or caught locally – and very good wine list; no smoking; cl Nov-just before Easter; children over 10.

Glenborrodale NM6060 GLENBORRODALE CASTLE Acharacle Argyll PH36 4JP (097 24) 266 **£160**; 16 lovely rms. Overlooking Loch Sunart and across to the Isle of Mull, this marvellously relaxed castle has antiques, pictures, flowers, books and games and lots of outdoor pursuits such as fishing, riding, clay-pigeon shooting, croquet and tennis – and hotel boat; keep-fit equipment, beauty salon, sauna; cl Nov-Easter.

Arisaig NM6586 ARISAIG HOUSE Inverness-shire PH39 4NR (068 75) 622 **£130**; 11 most attractive rms with wonderful views, and 2 suites. Beautifully furnished and extremely comfortable hotel in attractive wooded and terraced grounds close to the shore; elegant drawing room, cosy morning room, lovely flowers, and very good, imaginative food using fresh local produce; billiard room, croquet; cl end Oct-Easter; children over 10.

Lochinver NC0923 INVER LODGE Lairg Sutherland IV27 4LU (057 14) 496 **£112**; 20 spacious rms. Very comfortable modern hotel in wonderful position overlooking Loch Inver and surrounded by wild dramatic hills; big lounge with open fire and fine views, good food (esp locally caught fish and oysters) in airy dining room, billiard room, sauna and solarium; marvellous for fishing, bird-watching and walking; cl mid-Oct-mid-Apr.

Glenelg NG8119 GLENELG Kyle Ross-shire IV40 8JR (059 982) 273 **£110 inc dinner**; 6 individually decorated and comfortable rms, all with fine views. Overlooking Skye across its own beach and sea loch, this carefully refurbished homely hotel has a friendly bar, comfortable sofas and open fires, friendly staff and locals, good food using local venison, local hill-bred lamb and lots of wonderfully fresh fish and seafood, and quite a few whiskies; the drive to the inn involves spectacular views from the steep road of Loch Duich; cl Oct-Easter (though open for house parties by arrangement); disabled access.

Drumnadrochit NH5029 POLMAILY HOUSE Inverness IV3 6XT (045 62) 343 **£100**; 9 rms, most with own bthrm. Very relaxing and homely hotel in 18 acres of grounds with comfortable lounge and library, and excellent food in the no-smoking restaurant (wonderful packed lunches too); a good base for exploring the nearby glens; cl Oct-Mar.

Ullapool NH1294 CEILIDH PLACE Ross-shire IV26 2TY (0854) 612103 **£99**; 13 rms, plus 10 in annexe across the road. White-painted hotel in quiet side street with attractive conservatory dining room, stylish café-bar with attractive modern prints and plants, good food, decent wines and cognacs, and a relaxed, friendly atmosphere; cl 2 wks Jan.

Skeabost NG4148 SKEABOST HOUSE Isle of Skye IV51 9NP (047 032) 202 ***£92**; 26 rms. Smart, friendly little hotel overlooking lawn that runs down to Loch Snizort (good salmon fishing), bog-and-water garden, 9-hole golf course; spacious no-smoking lounge with good buffet table, lovely afternoon tea, log fires, high-ceilinged bar off stately hall, and billiards room; cl end Oct-1 Apr.

Harlosh NG2842 HARLOSH HOUSE Dunvegan Isle of Skye IV44 8ZG (047 022) 367 **£90**; 6 rms, 5 with own bthrm, and most with lovely views. One of the oldest buildings in north-west Skye, this 18th-c house is on a small peninsula of land jutting out into Loch Bracadale; wonderfully quiet, lochside gardens, lots of wildlife, a homely atmosphere, lounge, and home-made breads and good, fresh food in evening restaurant; cl Oct-Easter.

Isle Ornsay NG6912 KINLOCH LODGE Isle of Skye IV43 8QY (047 13) 214 ***£90**; 10 rms. Surrounded by rugged mountain scenery and close to the shore, this charming little hotel has a relaxed atmosphere in its attractive drawing rooms, antiques, log fires, and portraits, and good, imaginative food; cl 1 Dec-28 Feb; children by arrangement.

Achiltibuie NC0208 SUMMER ISLES Ullapool Ross-shire IV26 2YG (085 482) 282 **£85**; 12 comfortable rms. Beautifully situated above the sea towards the end of a very long and lonely road, this warm, friendly and well-furnished hotel has delicious set menus using fresh ingredients (in which it's largely self-sufficient), a choice of superb puddings and excellent array of uncommon cheeses; pretty watercolours and flowers; cl mid-Oct-Easter; children over 8.

Scarista NG0996 SCARISTA HOUSE Isle of Harris PA85 3HX (085 985) 238 **£82**; 8 rms, some in annexe. Marvellously wild countryside and empty beaches surround this isolated small hotel with its homely rooms and warm, friendly atmosphere; excellent for wildlife, walks and fishing; cl mid-Oct-Easter; children over 8.

Altnaharra NC5635 ALTNAHARRA Lairg Sutherland IV27 4UE (054 981) 222 ***£80**; 20 rms. Isolated 19th-c inn in fine countryside and very popular with keen fishermen with lots of facilities for them inc ghillies; cl mid-Oct-1 Mar; disabled access.

Scourie NC1544 EDDRACHILLES Lairg Sutherland IV27 4TH (0971) 502080 ***£74**; 11 rms. Well-run hotel in 320 acres overlooking Badcall Bay with wonderful views; popular with nature-lovers – bird sanctuary nearby, seals, fishing and walking; cl Nov-Feb; children over 4.

Portree NG4843 ROSEDALE Isle of Skye IV51 9DB (0478) 613131 ***£74**; 24 rms, many with harbour views. Built from three fishermen's cottages with lots of passages and stairs, two traditional lounges, small first-floor restaurant, lots of whiskies, helpful staff, harbourside garden and marvellous views; cl Oct-Apr.

Isle Ornsay NG6912 TIGH OSDA EILEAN IARMAIN Isle of Skye IV43 8QR (047 13) 332 **£72**; 12 individual rms, some in cottage opposite, and all with fine views. Sparkling white hotel with Gaelic-speaking staff and locals, big, cheerfully busy bar, pretty dining room with lovely sea views, and very good food; disabled access.

Shiel Bridge NG9318 KINTAIL LODGE Kyle Ross-shire IV40 8HL (0599) 81275 ***£70**; 12 good-value big rms. Pleasantly informal and fairly simple hotel with good well-prepared food inc wild salmon, fine collection of malt whiskies, and magnificent loch views; cl 23 Dec-3 Jan, 2 wks Nov.

Glen Shiel NH0711 CLUANIE Kyle Ross-shire IV3 6YW (0320) 40238 **£69**; 11 large, clean, modern rms in newish extension. In marvellous countryside miles from anywhere, with good-value bar food and decent breakfasts; disabled access.

Raasay NG5641 (off Skye) ISLE OF RAASAY Kyle Ross-shire IV40 8PB (0478) 660222 **£64**; 12 rms. Victorian hotel with marvellous views over the Sound of Raasay to Skye and popular with walkers and birdwatchers; no petrol on the island; cl Oct-mid-Mar, disabled access.

Invermoriston NH4117 GLENMORISTON ARMS Inverness IV3 6YA (0320) 51206 ***£62**; 8 good rms. Warmly friendly family-run hotel with cosy lounge, cheery stables bar, good restaurant (book ahead), decent bar food, lots of malt whiskies, quick, friendly staff, and fishing and stalking by arrangement; not far from Loch Ness; cl 25 Dec.

Kilchoan NM4863 MEALL MO CHRIDHE Acharacle Argyll PH36 4LH (097 23) 238 **£59**; 3 warmly comfortable rms. Attractive 18th-c former manse in 45 acres with really lovely views over the Sound of Mull; log fire and sea views in homely lounge, very good food eaten at polished, candlelit dining table using fresh local and home-grown produce, their own free-range eggs, and home-made bread, scones and preserves (which they also sell in their small farm shop), and very friendly owners; take your own wine; cl Nov-Jan/Feb; children over 12.

Mey ND2873 CASTLE ARMS Thurso Caithness KW14 8XH (084 785) 244 ***£58**; 8 good-value rms. Warm, friendly village inn in wide open countryside with magnificent restaurant food, wide range of good bar food, interesting whiskies, and welcoming staff; cl am Oct-Easter, 1-3 Jan, disabled access.

Ardvasar NG6203 ARDVASAR Isle of Skye IV45 8RT (047 14) 223 **£56**; 10 rms. Comfortably modernised 18th-c inn run by obliging, friendly owners with spectacular views, nice residents' lounge and cocktail bar, popular locals' bar, open fire, good, fresh food inc local fish and shellfish and very good breakfasts; no accomm 23 Dec-1 Mar.

Garve NH3969 INCHBAE LODGE Ross-shire IV23 2PH (099 75) 269 ***£56**; 12 rms. Friendly, family-run, former hunting lodge in lovely Highland setting with comfortable, homely lounge, log fire, small bar, and good, imaginative restaurant food using fresh local produce; lots of wildlife, marvellous walks; cl 25-26 Dec; disabled access.

Lybster ND2436 PORTLAND ARMS Caithness KW3 6BS (059 32) 208 **£55**; 20 rms. Staunch old granite hotel with really friendly staff, attractive dining room, generous helpings of decent food, small, cosy panelled lounge bar, and plain locals' bar; shooting/fishing can be arranged.

Melvich NC8765 MELVICH HOTEL Thurso Caithness KW14 7YJ (064 13) 206 ***£55**; 14 rms, 4 with shared bthrms. Small, traditional hotel in lovely spot with homely furniture and peat fires in the civilised lounge, bar, very relaxing atmosphere, friendly owners and staff, good food (esp local seafood and wild salmon), fine views over Melvich Bay; cl 25 Dec, 1-2 Jan.

Tongue NC5957 BEN LOYAL HOTEL Lairg Sutherland IV27 4XE (0847) 55216 ***£53**; 18 rms, 6 in annexe, most with own bthrm. Recently carefully refurbished family hotel with lovely views over the bay (fine sunsets Jun/July), friendly staff, and fine food using fresh seasonal produce; fishing can be arranged for sea trout, salmon and brown trout; cl Jan, 1st 10 days Feb; disabled access.

Kylesku NC2234 KYLESKU Lairg Sutherland IV27 4HW (0971) 502231 ***£50**; 7 peaceful rms. Glorious coastal surroundings with bird-watching, walking or fishing, short choice of particularly good bar food (esp local seafood), friendly staff, and happy mix of locals and visitors; disabled access.

Strontian NM8161 LOCH SUNART HOTEL Acharacle Argyll PH36 4HZ (0967) 2471 ***£50**; 11 rms. 18th-c family-run country house with wonderful views over Loch Sunart, excellent birdwatching, wildlife and walking, homely rooms, friendly staff, and good food; cl Nov-Mar; partial disabled access.

Drumnadrochit NH5029 BORLUM FARMHOUSE Inverness IV3 6XN (0456) 450358 **£49**; 5 rms. Traditional stone farmhouse with marvellous views over

Loch Ness, warm, comfortably furnished sitting room with log fire, summer sitting room in glass conservatory, friendly atmosphere, and good Scottish breakfasts; BHS approved riding centre and can help with animals on farm; good provision for families; self-catering and caravan/camping also; cl part Nov, 18-27 Dec.

Thurso ND1168 PENTLAND HOTEL Caithness KW14 7AA (0847) 63202 **£46**; 53 rms. Well-run rambling hotel with consistently good food, unobtrusive, efficient service, and a good mix of visitors.

Strontian NM8161 KILCAMB LODGE Acharacle Argyll PH36 4HY (0967) 2257 **£40**; 9 rms. Friendly little hotel in 30 acres by Loch Sunart with log fires in two lounges, good, fresh home-made food, fine choice of malt whiskies, and relaxed atmosphere; cl 1 Nov-31 Mar.

Shieldaig NG8154 TIGH AN EILEAN Strathcarron Ross-shire IV54 8XN (052 05) 251 **£39.70**; 11 rms. Attractive hotel in outstanding position, private fishing and sea fishing arranged, within easy reach of NTS Torridon Estate and Beinn Eighe nature reserve; pretty, comfortable residents' lounge with well-stocked help-yourself bar and modern dining room with good value local fish and game; cl Nov-Easter.

Portree NG4843 CRAIGLOCKHART Beaumont Crescent Portree Isle of Skye IB51 9DF (0478) 2233 **£36**; 3 rms. Small family-run guesthouse overlooking harbour with fine views through picture windows in lounge and dining room and good breakfasts; cl mid-Jan-mid-Feb.

To see and do

Balmacara NG8127 This huge estate surrounding the Kyle of Lochalsh has beautiful walks in breathtaking scenery. There are fantastic coastal views, and the stunning landscape is interspersed with lochs and impressive landmarks like the Five Sisters of Kintail and Beinn Fhada. LOCHALSH HOUSE has wonderful gardens with woodland walks, and lovely views towards Skye; £1. NTS. Guided walks are available from Balmacara on the Kyle to Plockton Peninsula; Plockton itself is an idyllic waterside village, with palm trees along the village street, and the Plockton Hotel is good for lunch.

Bettyhill NC7062 STRATHNAVER MUSEUM Good exploration of the notorious Clearances of the Highlands which allowed market forces in the shape of sheep farming to eradicate the traditional crofters; also Gaelic books and furnishings. Shop, some disabled access; cl Sun, may be closed 1-2 pm; *£1.50. The village is named after Elizabeth, Countess of Sutherland, who built it for her evicted tenants. The museum is in the former village church, which has a pulpit dating from the late 12th c. In the churchyard is a carved stone, a fine example of Celtic art, dating from the 10th c. The beach nearby is attractive.

Cape Wrath NC2575 The stormy tip of coast is guarded by a lonely lighthouse. From Durness NC4067 near the beautiful sea loch Loch Eriboll you can make an adventurous summer expedition to here, by boat across the Kyle of Durness and then along a very long rough track to the lighthouse.

Dornie NG8826 EILEAN DONAN CASTLE, connected to the mainland by a causeway, is unforgettably beautiful. It was first built in 1220, destroyed in 1719 after being held by Jacobite troops, and restored at the beginning of this century. It's perfectly positioned at the meeting point of Lochs Long, Duich and Alsh; shop; cl winter; *£1.50.

! Drumnadrochit NH5029 URQUHART CASTLE Once Scotland's

biggest castle, this dates mainly from the 14th c and overlooks Loch Ness; shop; £2. No visit to Loch Ness would really be complete without a look at the OFFICIAL LOCH NESS MONSTER EXHIBITION, the centrepiece of which is a lively 40-minute audio-visual display looking at the development of the monstrous myth from its beginnings in Highland folklore to the present controversy. Also a kilt-maker and glassblowing on the site; meals, snacks, shop, disabled access; cl 25 Dec; *£4.

Dunbeath ND1630 LAIDHAY CROFT MUSEUM A 200-year-old thatched Caithness long house, with the living quarters, byre and stable furnished as they would have looked 100 years ago, and a collection of early farm tools and early farm machinery; snacks, disabled access; cl Nov-Feb; *50p.

Duncansby Head ND4073 is an attractive spot on a fine day, with cliff walks giving a good view of the spectacular Duncansby Stacks offshore. It's near John o' Groats ND3872, which gets its share of visitors under the mistaken impression that it's the most northerly point on mainland Britain – see next entry.

Dunnet Head ND2076 really is the furthest point north, with views to Orkney. A lovely spot on a clear early summer's day, with spring flowers in the close turf, and puffins pottering around – but wild and unforgiving when the weather changes.

Falls of Shin NC5806 (B864 S of Lairg) There's a good chance of seeing SALMON LEAPING here in June or early July, especially if there's been a dry spell followed by rain so that the river is in spate.

Gairloch NU8077 GAIRLOCH HERITAGE MUSEUM is perhaps the best of the several Heritage museums in the Highlands, giving a good indication of life in the area. As well as the reconstructed rooms, boats and houses, look out for the secret portrait of Bonnie Prince Charlie which at first looks like the meaningless daubings of a child, but when revolved at speed in a metal cylinder reveals a portrait; meals and snacks; cl Sun, Oct-Easter; *£1. The Old Inn here is useful for lunch.

Glenfinnan NM8980 JACOBITE MONUMENT Built in 1815 to commemorate the Highlanders who fought and died for Bonnie Prince Charlie, in a commanding position at the head of Loch Shiel; good snacks, shop, limited disabled access; cl 1-2 pm, Oct-Mar; £1.

Golspie NC8300 DUNROBIN CASTLE Splendid castle – a gleaming turreted structure with views out to sea and gardens modelled on those at Versailles. The site has been the family home of the Earls and Dukes of Sutherland longer than anyone can remember, but was named after Earl Robin in the 13th c: he was responsible for the original square keep. It was drastically renovated in the 19th c and now has fine collections of furnishings and art inc several Canalettos; snacks, shop; cl Sun am, and all mid-Oct-May; *£3.20.

Helmsdale ND0315 TIMESPAN VISITOR CENTRE Another good display devoted to the Clearances; cl Sun am, all Nov-Easter.

Kirkhill NH4455 MONIACK CASTLE The Highland Winery here is quite an unusual enterprise, for two reasons: it's rare to find a winery producing country wines in Scotland, and especially at an old castle like this, the former fortress of the Lovat chiefs; meals and snacks; shop; disabled access; cl Sun.

Poolewe NG8580 INVEREWE Unmissable beautiful gardens full of rare and subtropical plants, with a magnificent background of mountain scenery. The Atlantic Drift is responsible for the special microclimate which lets these unusual plants flourish even though this is further N than Moscow; meals and snacks, shop, disabled access; visitor centre cl Sun

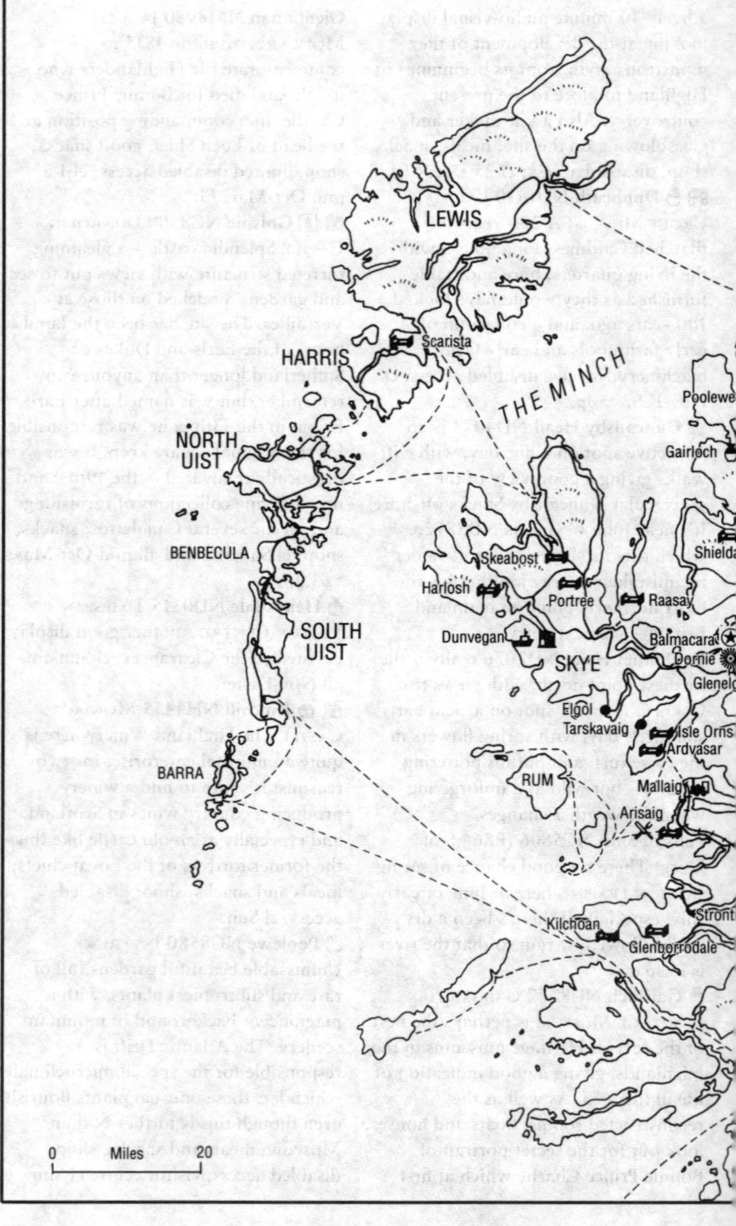
North of Scotland
LEWIS
Scarista
HARRIS
THE MINCH
Poolewe
Gairloch
NORTH
UIST
BENBECULA
Shielda
Skeabost
Harlosh
Portree
Raasay
SOUTH
UIST
Dunvegan
Balmacara
Dornie
SKYE
Glenelg
Elgol
Tarskavaig
Isle Orns
Ardvasar
BARRA
RUM
Mallaig
Arisaig
Kilchoan
Stront
Glenborrodale
0
Miles
20

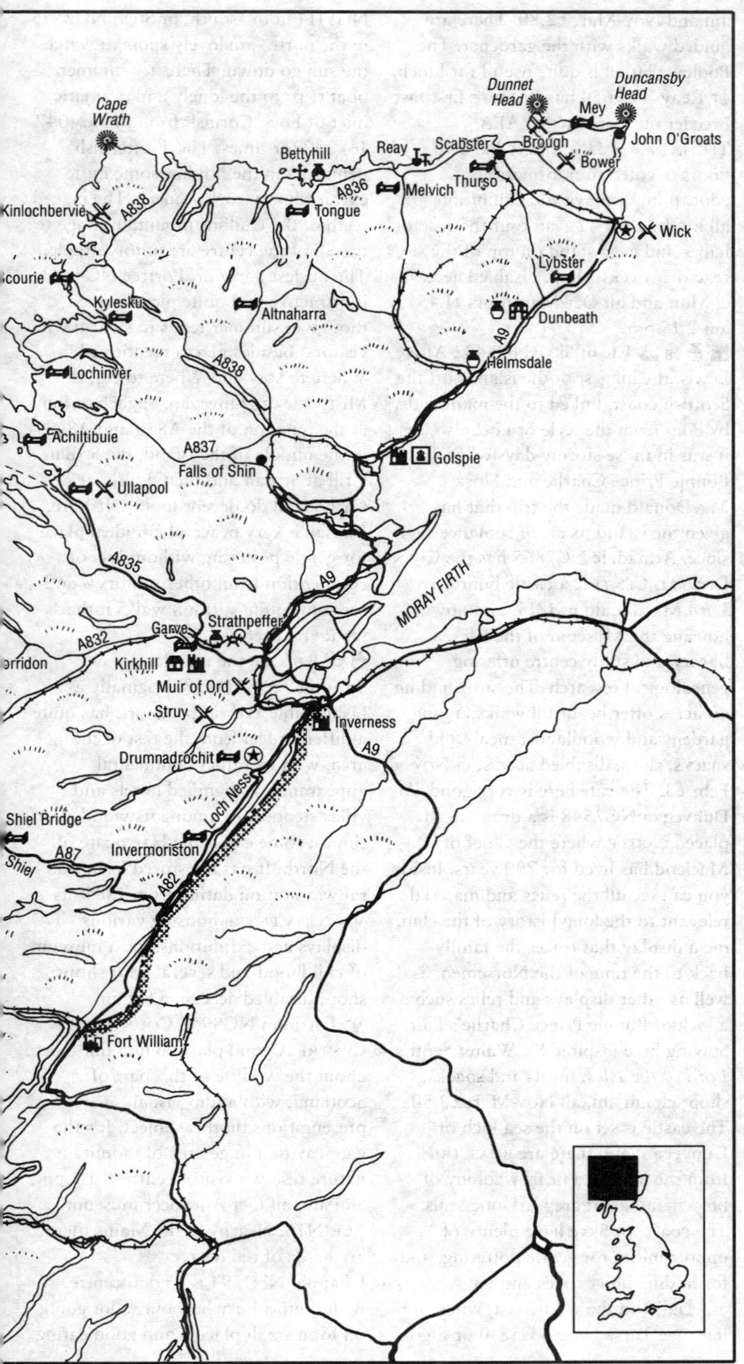

Cape Wrath
Dunnet Head
Duncansby Head
Mey
John O'Groats
Brough
Bower
Scabster
Reay
Thurso
Bettyhill
Melvich
A836
Tongue
Kinlochbervie
A838
Wick
Lybster
Scourie
Kylesku
Altnaharra
Dunbeath
A9
Helmsdale
A838
Lochinver
Achiltibuie
A837
Golspie
Falls of Shin
Ullapool
A835
A9
MORAY FIRTH
Strathpeffer
Garve
A832
Torridon
Kirkhill
Muir of Ord
Struy
Inverness
A9
Drumnadrochit
Loch Ness
Shiel Bridge
Invermoriston
A87
Shiel
A82
Fort William

am and Nov-Mar; £2.80. There are guided walks with the gardener. The Poolewe Hotel is quite useful for lunch.

Reay NC9654 has Britain's first fast breeder nuclear reactor; AEA TECHNOLOGY DOUNREAY has two floors devoted to information, education, displays and exhibitions of all kinds. Over-12s can tour the reactor hall – and even stand on top of the reactor; snacks, shop, disabled access; cl Mon and all Oct-Mar, tours 11.45 am-2.15 pm.

Isle of Skye NG4432 After Lewis, the biggest of the islands off the Scottish coast, linked to the mainland by boat from the Kyle of Lochalsh, as it was in those stormy days when Bonnie Prince Charlie and Flora MacDonald made the trip that has given the island its air of romance ever since. **Armadale** NC7865 has the CLAN DONALD CENTRE, a castle built for Lord Macdonald in 1815, and now housing the Museum of the Isles, a library and study centre offering genealogical research. The surrounding 40 acres offer beautiful walks among gardens and woodlands; meals and snacks, shop, disabled access; cl Nov-Feb; £3. The café here is very good. At **Dunvegan** NG2548 is a dramatically placed CASTLE where the Chief of Macleod has lived for 790 years. Inside you can see all the relics and material relevant to the long history of the clan, inc a display that traces the family back to the time of the Norsemen, as well as other displays and relics such as a lock of Bonnie Prince Charlie's hair. Staying here inspired Sir Walter Scott's *Lord of the Isles*; meals and snacks, shop; cl Sun am, all Nov-Mar; £3.80. The castle is set on the sea loch of Dunvegan, and there are BOAT TRIPS from the jetty to a nearby colony of brown and great grey Atlantic seals. The coasts of Skye have plenty of opportunities for gentle pottering, and for finding quiet coves and bays, especially on the west coast, where for instance Tarskavaig NG5810 or Elgol NG5114 in the south, or Stein NG2556 in the north, are lovely spots to watch the sun go down. There are summer boat trips to the lonely and dramatic inlet of Loch Coruisk from Elgol: (047 16) 230 for times. The Trotternish peninsula in the NE has some quite extraordinary rock scenery. The jagged teeth of the Cuillins mountain range to the SE of the centre are unforgettable. The busiest harbour, **Portree** NG4843, is attractive and quite picturesque, though in summer tends to swarm with visitors. Besides places mentioned in Where to stay and Where to eat, the Misty Isle at Dunvegan, Sligachan Inn at the junction of the A850 and A863 in the middle of the island, the Struan Grill at Struan and the Old Inn at Carbost all do decent food. Offshore, Raasay is very peaceful, an ideal place for gentle pottering without lots of competition from other visitors – and for some quite stiff hill walks if that's what you prefer.

Back on the mainland **Strathpeffer** NH4858, originally a fashionable 19th-c spa resort, has quite a different feel from the rest of the area, with its rather continental appearance of dignified hotels and villas stepped up among its wooded slopes; some call it the Harrogate of the North. It has a restored Victorian railway station dating from 1885, its VISITOR CENTRE housing various displays and exhibitions, inc a museum of childhood and several craft shops; shop; disabled access; cl Sat am.

Torridon NG8956 COUNTRYSIDE CENTRE A good place to find out more about the wildlife of this part of Scotland, with audio-visual presentations on this subject. It's the gateway to a huge area of mountain nature reserve; visitor centre cl 1-2 pm, Sun am, all Oct-Apr; deer museum *£1. NTS. Nearby at the Mains there are herds of red deer.

Ullapool NH1294 is a good centre, with quite a busy harbour, a lot going on for a small place – and good eating (besides the places we've mentioned, the fish and chip restaurant is very good, with surprisingly presentable white wines, and the Ferry Boat is useful).

Wick ND3551 CASTLE OF OLD WICK A ruined four-storey square tower just S of town, probably dating from the 12th c. The history of the town is well presented at the WICK HERITAGE CENTRE, in eight buildings by the harbour. Displays include a working reconstruction of a 19th-c lighthouse and an interesting exhibition on the herring fishing industry; cl Sun and Oct-May; *£1.50. You can buy factory seconds at the CAITHNESS GLASS FACTORY after following through the glassmaking process from start to finish; meals and snacks; shop; disabled access; no glassmaking at wknds; may be cl Sun winter.

A good way of seeing the scenery of the Highlands is by train: the WEST HIGHLAND LINE runs **steam trains** in summer between Fort William and Mallaig, and year-round normal trains. The views are terrific. One way of turning this into a round trip is to drive to Armadale on Skye, catch the 11.30 am ferry to Mallaig, the 12.30 (summer only) train to Fort William, sitting on the right-hand side facing the engine for the best views, then catch the 2.05 (summer only) train back for the 4.30 crossing to Armadale.

Another good train service is the cross-Highland line from Inverness to Kyle of Lochalsh, in 2½ hours – the last minutes of which are much the best.

This is a part of the world where inns doing a decent bite to eat are very much at a premium, and a welcome sight indeed after miles of empty road. Besides those listed elsewhere, ones we can recommend for their positions include the Applecross Inn at Applecross NG7144, Aultbea Inn at Aultbea NG8689, Badachro Inn at Badachro NG7773, Royal Hotel at Cromarty NH7867, Northern Sands at Dunnet ND2170, Lock at Fort Augustus NH3709, Old Inn at Gairloch NG8077, Kinlochewe Hotel at Kinlochewe NH0262, Lewiston Arms at Lewiston NH5029, Loch Carron Hotel on Loch Carron NG9039, Glenuig Hotel at Lochailort NM7682, and Scrabster Inn at Scrabster ND0970.

Walks

The Highlands offer **ultra-tough mountain walking**, but relatively few easier routes on defined paths (see general remarks in the Walks section of West Scotland); shorter circular walks are few and far between. Given good weather, full equipment and strong legs, the roadless country of **Knoydart** NG8000 on the W coast beckons: a real Highland wilderness. The areas of **Torridon** NG8956 and **Kintail** NG9917 on this coast are also wonderful for challenging walks, but there are also a few outstanding easier ones, based, for example on Loch Torridon's shores. The **Falls of Glomach** NH0125 (Kintail) are a tremendous waterfall in a wilderness setting.

Inland, **Glen Affric** NH1922, one of the most majestic glens, has a walking route along its floor. The easier mountain ascents include **Ben Eighe** NG9660 (the Mountain Trail is well marked; it makes a circular route above Loch Maree) and **Stac Pollaidh** NC1010.

Skye has lovely shoreside walks, such as from **Elgol** NG5213 to **Loch na Creitheach** NG5120 at the heart of the formidable Cuillins, a mecca for rock-climbers. The **Quiraing** NG4569 in the NE is a fascinating tumbled mass, with a surprisingly manageable path through it.

The **east coast** lacks the Highland drama but is blessed with a much drier climate: it's often nice to escape here from the W when the rain gets you down. **Duncansby Head** ND4073, the NE tip of Britain, offers an absorbing coastal walk S to see the 200-ft-high Stacks of Duncansby, rock pinnacles now detached from the land. There's also a pleasant stroll along the little road from the car park to the lighthouse on **Strathy Point** NC8269 (W of Thurso), at the end of a narrow peninsula. **Tarbat Ness** NH9487 juts out from the S side of Dornoch Firth; rather isolated, but worth the journey. You can walk around the peninsula here, from **Portmahomack** NH9184, past the lighthouse, and then along the S coast past a ruined castle to reach **Rockfield** NH9283.

Driving

On the W coast the roads give a glorious succession of intoxicating sea views, and as they often dip across country inland for short cuts, they alternate moorland and mountain scenery (the stretch between Loch Assynt and Ullapool is particularly wild), so you never get sated with the ocean and the rugged-shored sea lochs. There are so many beautiful views all along the coast road that it's difficult to rate any one stretch as finer than the rest; but two particularly memorable views are that of Plockton nestling along its sheltered inlet, from the side road just S of Stromeferry; and the famous view of Eilean Donan castle nr Dornie, E of the Kyle of Lochalsh. The A861 along the foot of the mountains on the N shore of Loch Sunart, and B8007 beyond it, is very attractive though very twisty.

When the main road leaves the coast for a cross-country short cut, there's usually a longer seaward detour. Such side roads are generally very slow – well worth taking, in a slightly pioneering spirit, if you're in no hurry whatsoever. One of the easiest and most rewarding of these detours is the A837 to the beautifully placed village of Lochinver. From here you can do an arduous circuit N to rejoin the main road, or head S into the unspoilt beauty of the Inverpolly nature reserve (again looping round to join the main road), or follow the dead-end road to Achiltibuie for an idyllic view of the Summer Isles. Another worthwhile coastal detour is the little road over to Loch Moidart from just N of Acharacle, for the views of the loch itself and of ruined Castle Tioram. For the more adventurous, there's a long, narrow road round the coast from Shieldaig to Applecross, which steely-nerved souls can turn into a loop back to the main road by taking the staggeringly high and sharp-twisting 'Pass of the Cattle' – Britain's highest pass.

The N coast, tracked by the A836 and the A838, is very severe country indeed, particularly up around Durness (the little villages are so unexpected they seem like flowers growing out of a boulder). There's the same stern, dark feel about the country the A838 crosses on its way down to the W coast at Laxford Bridge.

Inland, the roads heading N through the centre, after leaving the healthy-feeling former spa valley of Strathpeffer, all strike through increasingly wild countryside. The A832 is fairly level to Achnasheen, then climbs through more mountainous scenery, with some sensational views; it meets the W coast road at Kinlochewe. The A835 is quite a good fast road up to Ullapool, the most civilised of all these routes, yet still with a good mix of forest, loch, river, moor and mountain. The A836 up to Bonar Bridge gives you a choice of three routes through highland wastes of moor, peat, lochs and lochans (little lochs), and bog – great if you want solitude. Once past the conifer plantations oozing out from Bonar Bridge and Lairg, the A837 climbs into a wild world with terrific mountain views. The A838 is the road for loch-lovers, scarcely leaving the side of one loch or another, twisting among the fine desolate peaks that tower over it (and sometimes making you wish you'd taken a gentler road) before it reaches the lumpier country of the NW coast. The A836 crosses vast bleak peat bogs, shimmering here and there with lochs or smaller stretches of water (almost the only people you're likely to see here are fishermen or naturalists); the right fork down the B873 to Strathnaver gives perhaps the best acquaintance with this type of lonely country if it appeals to you.

The A831 looping NW of Drumnadrochit on Loch Ness is a good drive despite some rather gloomy stretches of conifer plantation; its main joy for drivers in search of great scenery is that at Cannich it gives access to a narrow road up Glen Cannich to Loch Mullardoch, a beautiful peaceful mountain valley; and to the one up Glen Affric, if anything even more beautiful. There's also a private gated track up Glen Strathfarrar which you may be able to get permission to use (ask at the Struy Inn about this).

To reach anywhere N of Kinlochewe by car from the south, incidentally, it's much quicker to go by Inverness than to make your way all the way up the W coast.

Where to eat

Muir of Ord NH5250 DOWER HOUSE (0463) 870096 Very good modern cooking in attractive hotel restaurant, fine wines, and friendly service; cl 25 Dec, disabled access; bedrooms. **£31**|£2/£13.

Bower ND2363 BOWER Half mile S of B876 (0955) 86292 Small, fairly simple country inn with good-value food, dining room, low ceilings, open fires, warship and submarine memorabilia, and friendly, informal service; cl Mon-Thurs between Nov and Apr; **£20**|£2.50/£7

Ullapool NH1294 MOREFIELD MOTEL (0854) 612161 Large helpings of exceptionally fresh fish and seafood (owners are ex-fishermen and divers), cooked enterprisingly, Aberdeen Angus steaks, daily roast beef, and vegetarian dishes in modern lounge and smart restaurant of basic hotel; cl Nov-Feb; disabled access. **£18**|£4.75/£5.95.

Kinlochbervie NC2156 OLD SCHOOL HOUSE (0971) 521383 Very good food in old school building with school-related items like photographs, maps, notebooks on tables; home-grown vegetables, local fish and venison, and good puddings; very good service; bedrooms in newish building; cl 25 Dec, 1 Jan; disabled access. **£15**|£1.65/£2.40.

Struy NH3939 STRUY INN (046 376) 219 Clean, pleasant and friendly small pub with very good, fairly priced food, and good range of malt whiskies; cl Mon, Tues, only open Thurs-Sun in winter; disabled access. **£13.50**|£1.50/£5.

Wick ND3652 LAMPLIGHTER 43 High St (0955) 3287 Extremely good food using local produce in small, cosy lunchtime restaurant (evening meals only summer Fri/Sat); friendly service; cl pm except Thurs-Sat in summer, cl Oct; **£10.50**|£2.10/£4.20.

Brough ND2274 DUNNET HEAD TEAROOM/RESTAURANT (084 785) 774 Small traditional, unpretentious cottage with good, reasonably priced food and snacks served all day by friendly owners; good choice of vegetarian dishes, fresh salmon, local seafood, and local beef; take your own wine; cl Sept-Easter; children must be well behaved. 69p/£5.

Help this year from: *Mrs R C F Martin, Richard Chew, John Townsend, G D and M D Craigen, Dilys Unsworth, Alan Wilcock, Christine Davidson, Mrs S Gillotti, Janet Brown, Colin Steer, Brian Murphy, Nick Haslewood, Ilona Pocsik, David Mervin, Peter Gannon, Howard Bateman, Brian Skelcher, Andrew and Ruth Triggs, J Goodwill, Capt F A Bland, Keith Stevens, Dave and Jules Tuckett, John and Joan Wyatt, Michael Sandy, J Goodwill, Janet and Gary Amos, A and M Jones, Duncan and Vi Glennig, D S Jay, H M C Quick, Emma and Dennis Dickinson, Ross Lockley, I A McCaskey, E Evans, Graham and Belinda Staplehurst, Julian Holland, Les Mackay, Robin and Anne Denness, J E Tong, Ian Phillips, JW, CW, Mr and Mrs R Stewart, R C Wiles, Keith Stevens, Julie Clarke, Paul and Ursula Randall, Sara Price, TBB, R M Macnaughton, P Corris, J D Maplethorpe, J R and H Soulsby, Basil Minson, John Fazakerley, Ron Corbett, Nigel Pritchard, John Whitehead, Jim Cowell, Mrs Pat Crabb, Iain Grant, R J Herd, Neale Davies, Mark Walker, Ian and Sue Brocklebank, Dave Braisted, Bob Smith, Michael and Harriet Robinson, Owen and Helen McGhee, Duncan Glennie, Nigel and Helen Aplin.*

Scotland Calendar

Some of these dates were provisional as we went to press.

JANUARY

1st **Comrie** New Year's Day Run; **Kirkwall** *(Orkney)* New Year's Day Ba' Games – *mass street football played for 200 years, goals for the 'uppies' and 'doonies' are the site of an old castle and the harbour, over 100 men lurch in a massive scrum through the narrow streets*

8th **Dundee** Wildlife Photographer of the Year Exhibition – *till 12 Feb*

11th **Burghead** Burning of the Clavie – *trad ceremony totally unaltered, half barrel on stake filled with burning wood and tar carried through old part followed by villagers, embers considered good luck and sent to exiles throughout the world – 6 pm*

25th **Lerwick** (Shetland) Up-Helly-Aa Traditional Viking Fire Festival, *inc burning a longship*

29th **Glenmore** Siberian Husky Club Rally – *till Sun 30*

FEBRUARY

1st **Aberdeen** Swan Lake, *Vienna Festival Ballet*

5th **Edinburgh** Rugby Union Scotland v England *at Murrayfield*

7th **Dundee** Swan Lake, *Vienna Festival Ballet – till Weds 9*

22nd **Inverurie** Aberdeen Agricultural Show *at Thainstone Agricultural Centre;* **Isle of Arran** One-act Drama Festival – *till Sat 26*

26th **Aberdeen** Europeans in Caricature *at Art Gallery – till 19 March*

MARCH

6th **Aviemore** International Curling Week – *till Sat 12*

7th **Largs** Women's Week – *till Sat 12*

14th **Kingussie** Badenoch and Strathspey Music Festival, *inc gaelic, country dancing and piping – till Fri 18*

18th **Aviemore** Euro-curl Curling – *till Sun 20*

SCOTLAND CALENDAR

MARCH cont.

19th **Edinburgh** Rugby Union Scotland v France *at Murrayfield*

25th **Edinburgh** Folk Festival – *till 3 Apr*

27th **Gatehouse of Fleet** Festival of Music, Arts and Crafts – *till Tues 29*

30th **Edinburgh** International Puppet and Animation Festival – *till Sat 9*

APRIL

1st **Inverness** Folk Festival – *till Sun 3*

2nd **Dundee** Spring Flower Show *at Caird Hall – till Sun 3;* **Girvan** Cycle Race – *till Mon 4*

3rd **New Lanark** Easter Fun – *till Mon 4*

7th **Edinburgh** International Festival of Science and Technology – *till Sat 23*

10th **Oban** Fiddlers Rally

13th **Kirkcaldy** Fair *at Links Market – till Mon 18*

16th **New Lanark** Food and Gift Fair – *till Sun 17;* **St Andrews** Kate Kennedy Procession

17th **St Andrews** Golf Week – *till Sat 23*

23rd **Inverurie** Garioch Fiddlers Rally; **Isle of Mull** Music Festival – *till Mon 25*

25th **Machrihanish** Golf Festival

29th **Girvan** Folk Festival – *till 1 May*; **Glasgow** Mayfest – *till 21 May*

30th **Edinburgh** Calton Hill Beltane Fire – *grand Mayday ceilidh, re-enactment of pagan festival – till 1 May*; **Coatbridge** Spring Fling – *till 2 May*; **Machrihanish** Pro-Am Golf Tournament

MAY

1st **Aberdeen** May Day Celebrations *at Westburn Park*; **New Lanark** Antique Fair

7th **Oban** Music and Dance Festival – *till Mon 9*

16th **Largs** Environment Week – *till Sun 22*

18th **Perth** Festival of the Arts – *till Sun 29*

19th **Aberdeen** Royal Scottish National Orchestra Proms – *till Sat 21*

21st **Isle of Arran** Goat Fell Race; **Oban to Troon** Scottish Islands Peak Race, *sailing and fell running competition – till Tues 24*

23rd **Edinburgh** International Children's Festival – *till Sun 29*

26th **Stromness** Orkney Traditional Folk Festival – *till Sun 29*

27th **Bute** Jazz festival – *till Mon 30*; **Dumfries** Arts Festival; *also* Drumlanrig Castle Cycle rally, *sociable cycling in superb scenery*; **Tarbert** Sailing Week – *till 2 Jun*; **Thornhill** Drumlanrig Castle Cycle Rally

28th **Bathgate** Highland Games; **Blackford** Highland Games; **Blair Atholl** Highland Gathering *at Blair Castle – annual parade and inspection of the Duke of Atholl's unique private army*; **Bowmore** Isle of Islay Festival – *till 12 Jun;* **Kilburnie** Garnock International Highland Games *at Lakeside Park*; **Monklands** Festival – till 11 Jun; **Thornhill** Field Sports Fair *at Drumlanrig Castle – till Sun 29*

Scotland Calendar

May cont.

29th **Atholl** Highland Gathering; **Oban** Raft Race

30th **Nairn** British Amateur Golf Championships – *till 4 Jun*

June

4th **Inverness** Shinty Cup Final; **Stonehaven** Feein' Market

6th **Kilmarnock** and Loudon Burns Day; **Isle of Arran** Folk Festival – *till Sun 12*

10th **Hawick** Common Riding, *inc ride-outs, proclaiming of the Burgh officer, Cornets walk, snuffing ceremony and procession – till Fri 11*

11th **Dumfries** Guid Nychburris Festival – *till Sun 19*; **Golspie** Sutherland Triathlon; **Lesmahagow** Highland Games; **Millport** Jazz Day; **Monymusk** Sheepdog Trials

12th **Aberdeen** Kildrummy to Queens Links Vintage Vehicle Rally; **Keith** Grange Highland Games; **Oban** Kilmore and Kilbride Highland Games; **Turriff** Pipe Band Contest

14th **Linlithgow** Palace Jazz Festival; *also* Riding of the Marches, *annual celebration to check the burgh's boundary*

17th **Campbeltown** Kintyre Music Festival – *till Sun 19*; **Selkirk** Common Riding – till Sat 18

18th **Alyth** Show; **Kirkconnel and Kelloholm** Gala; **Newburgh** Highland Games

19th **Aberdeen** Highland Games; **Girvan** Civic Week – *till Sun 26*; **Melrose** Summer Festival – *till Sun 26*; **Peebles** Riding of the Marches and Beltane Festival – *till Sat 25*

20th **Aberdeen** Highland Games *at Hazlehead Park – till Sat 25*; **Collin** Gala – *till Sat 25*

23rd **Edinburgh** Royal Highland Show *at Ingliston – till Sun 26*

25th **Aberdeen** Steam Engine Rally *at Hazlehead Park – till Sun 26*; **Armadale** Sheepdog trials *at Clan Donald Centre (Isle of Skye)*; **Jedburgh** Jetharts Callants Festival – *till 8 July*

26th **Cairngorm** Hill Race; **Coatbridge** Historic Vehicle Rally, *Summerlee Heritage Trust*; **Garmouth** Maggie Fair; **Leven** Veteran and Vintage Car Rally; **Perth** Scone Palace Coronation Pageant – *re-enactment of James IV coronation with period stalls*; **Seil** Highland Games; **South Knapdale** Sheepdog Trials

27th **Galashiels** Braw Lads Gathering – *till 2 July*

July

1st **Glasgow** International Jazz Festival – *till Sun 10*; **Kincraig** Summer Fête

2nd **Annan** Riding of the Marches

3rd **Isle of Barra** Festival of Gaelic, *song, dance and drama – till Fri 15*

6th **Kenmore** Highland Games

7th **Castle Douglas** Galloway Craft Guild Summer Exhibition – *till Sun 31*; **Mull** Children's Highland Games *at Tobermory*

9th **Boat of Garten** Gala; **Dingwall** Highland Games *at Jubilee Park*; **Jedburgh** Border Games *at Riverside Park*

SCOTLAND CALENDAR

JULY cont.

10th **Keith** Festival of Traditional Music and Song – *till Tues 12*; **Poltalloch** Mid-Argyll Sheepdog Trials

11th **Moffat and district** Gala Week – *till Sat 16*

14th **Turnberry** British Open Golf Championships – *till Sun 17*

15th **Irvine** Harbour Festival – *till Sun 17*

16th **Lamlash** Isle of Arran Laughabout Week – *till Sat 23*; **Lochcarron** Highland Games

17th **Kelso** Civic Week – *till Sat 23*

20th **Inveraray** Highland Games *at Winterton Park*

22nd **Inverness** Country and Western Festival – *till Mon 25*; **Isle of Mull** Highland Games

23rd **Dornoch** Sutherland Agricultural Show; **New Luce** Gala; **Nairn** Gala Week – *till Fri 29*

24th **Aberdeen** Massed Pipe Band Display *at Duthie Park*; **Islay** Bridgend Sheepdog Trials; **Rothiemurchus** Highland Games; **Taynuilt** Highland Games

25th **Inverness** Tattoo – *till Sat 30*; **Newton Stewart** Galloway Pageant – *till Sat 30*

27th **Stranraer** Agricultural Show

29th **Langholm** Common Riding, *inc processions, cornet's chase, Highland games and open-air evening dance*

30th **Palnackie** Flounder Tramping Championships; **Golspie** Gala Week – *till 6 Aug*; **Lauder** Common Riding – *till 6 Aug*

31st **Coldstream** Civic Week – *till 6 Aug*; **New Lanark** Antique Fair – *till 1 Aug*

AUGUST

1st **Clyde to Mull** West Highland Yachting Week

2nd **Loch Morlich** Sailing Club Regatta

3rd **Aberdeen** International Youth Festival – *till Sat 13*; **Isle of Skye** Highland Games *at Portree*; **Wigtown** Agricultural Show

4th **Castle Douglas** Stewartry Agricultural Show; **Kelso** National Sheepdog Trials *at Floors Castle – till Sat 6*; **Muir of Ord** Black Isle Show

5th **Dornoch** Highland Gathering; **Edinburgh** Military Tattoo – *till Sat 27*; *also* International Jazz Festival – *till Sat 13*; **Perth** Agricultural Show – *till Sat 6*

6th **Campbeltown** Agricultural Show; **Dornoch** Festival Week – *till Sat 13*; **Innerleithen** Traquair House Fair – *till Sun 7*; **Isle of Arran** Highland Games; *also* Corrie Capers – *till Sat 13*; **Linlithgow** Palace Celebration of Mary, Queen of Scots – *till Sun 7, also on 13, 14, 20, 21, 27, 28 Aug*

7th **Lorn** Show; **Parton** 13th Scottish Alternative Games

11th **Fortrose** St Boniface Fair; **Irvine** Marymass Festival, *inc Scotland's largest horse-drawn parade on Sat 20 – till Mon 22*

Scotland Calendar

August cont.

12th **Islay** Agricultural Show *at Bridgend*; **Mull** Salen Show *at Glenaros*

13th **Aberfeldy** Atholl and Breadalbane Games and Show; **Edinburgh** International Film Festival – *till Sun 28*; **Glasgow** Bellahoustan Park World Pipe Band Championships

14th **Edinburgh** International Festival and Fringe – *till 3 Sept*; **Roslin** Rosslyn Chapel Events – *till 3 Sept*

20th **Campbeltown** Sheepdog Trials; **Canonbie** Flower Show; **Coatbridge** Grand Steam Fair – *till Sun 21*; **Crieff** Highland Gathering; **Lairg** Crofters Show; **Rothesay** Bute Highland Games

21st **Golspie** Vintage Motor Rally *at Dunrobin Castle*; **Skipness** Sheepdog Trials

25th **Blair Atholl** International Horse Trials *at Blair Castle – till Sun 28*; **Oban** Argyllshire Highland Gathering – *till Fri 26*

26th **Dunoon** Cowal Highland Gathering – *till Sat 27*

27th **Aberdeen** Royal Horticultural Show *at Duthie Park – till Sun 28*; **Drumnadrochit** Highland Games; **Largs** Viking Festival, *inc opera and battle re-enactments – till 4 Sept*; **Moffat** Agricultural Show *at Holm Road Parks*

28th **Dunbar** Vintage Vehicle Rally; **Kincraig** Balnespick Farm Carriage Driving Event – *till Sun 28*

September

2nd **Dundee** Caird Hall Flower Show – *till Sun 4*

3rd **Annan** Flower Show; **Braemar** Royal Highland Gathering

4th **Blairgowrie** Highland Games

8th **Monymusk** International Sheepdog Trials – *till Sat 10*

10th **Loch Insch** Model Seaplanes Splash – *till Sun 11*

23rd **Girvan** Jazz Festival – *till Sun 25*

October

13th **Aberdeen** Alternative Festival – *till Sat 22*

15th **Mull** 2300 Club Car Rally *at Tobermory – till Mon 17*

21st **Dunoon** Jazz Festival – *till Sun 23*

25th **Edinburgh** Scottish Story-telling Festival *at Netherbow Arts Centre – till 5 Nov*

29th **Blair Atholl** Piping Championships *at Blair Castle*

November

5th **Aberdeen** Fireworks; **Kingussie** Bonfire Festival

30th **St Andrews** Day Celebrations

December

11th **Kingussie** Light-up Ceremony

23rd **Grantown-on-Spey** Torchlight Procession

25th **Kirkwall** Isle of Orkney Christmas Day Ba' Games – *the ba' is thrown up from the Mercat Cross at 1 pm (see 1 Jan)*

31st **Aberdeen** Bonfire Night Celebrations; **Comrie** Flambeaux Torchlight Procession; **Biggar** Ne'erday Bonfire, *ancient Druid custom – torchlight procession led by pipe band*; **Edinburgh** Tron Kirk; **Stonehaven** Fireball Ceremony.

Wales

Wales combines in its relatively small area an abundance of natural beauty with a good range of interesting places to visit. These vary from romantic ruined abbeys and a profusion of medieval castles to lively mining museums – mainly slate in North Wales, coal in South Wales. This is not an area for grand houses and gardens (though there are exceptions), nor for pretty villages with fine churches. North Wales has the best mix of glorious scenery with plenty of other things to do, is excellent for walking, and gets the lion's share of summer visitors. West Wales has the most attractive coastline, with some lovely walks along it; once you've got there, the far west is a civilised place for a relaxing break. Mid Wales has fewer touristy things for visitors to do – and for many that is a special attraction – but it does have grand scenery, some very pleasant small towns, certainly plenty to fill a weekend or longer stay, and a really unspoilt feel. South Wales might appeal if you want to delve into the industrial past (or if you find castles irresistible). Weather is a problem here: there tends to be a lot of it, and though the Welsh coast preserves a gloomy magnificence in poor weather, the upland areas are more or less a write-off then.

We have mentioned a handful of the Roman and prehistoric sites in which the area abounds. More information may be had from CADW, or the Welsh Historic Monuments Commission, (0222) 465511, which is also responsible for the care of the great majority of the historic castles and other monuments here.

North Wales

With richly diverse scenery culminating in Snowdonia, there is lots to do, and some excellent places to stay in this region.

Besides the dramatic mountain scenery of Snowdonia itself, this area has great expanses of hill and mountain, such as the Berwyn Mountains in the centre, which (unlike Snowdon) stay lonely year-round. It also has countryside which charms in a quite different way: the intricate and rather intimate landscapes of Clwyd, the rich Vale of Conwy, the deserted sandy shores of the Lleyn Peninsula.

A wide choice of places to visit and things to do includes a surprising abundance of picturesque railway lines, with a couple of very scenic BR routes as well as the rack-and-pinion mountain railway up Snowdon from Llanberis, the splendid Ffestiniog Railway from Porthmadog and half a dozen other former industrial lines running through pretty countryside. Among other places to visit, highlights include

Erddig at Wrexham, Caernarfon and Conwy castles, the interesting and lively slate-mining activities, particularly around Blaenau Ffestiniog, the great garden of Bodnant at Tal y Cafn, the fantasy-village of Portmeirion, and, for families, the zoo in its lovely setting at Colwyn Bay and the 'sea zoo' at Brynsiencyn on Anglesey. Betws-y-Coed is always a popular spot, and Llandudno, Beaumaris on Anglesey and Llangollen are all attractive towns with plenty to see.

There are long beaches on many of the coasts, with the traditional resorts of Prestatyn, Rhyl, Colwyn Bay and the more stylish Llandudno on the north coast, and places like Barmouth on the west coast.

One drawback is that people in North Wales do strike some visitors as unfriendly. Another is that in poor weather the views do close in; there is more likelihood of cloud and rain here than in, say, the Yorkshire Dales.

There's a good choice of places to stay, and quite a good choice of places to eat out at.

Where to stay

Llandudno SH7883 BODYSGALLEN HALL Gwynedd LL30 1RS (0492) 584466 **£162.90**; 28 deeply comfortable rms, 19 in hotel. Fine 17th-c house in its own parkland with mullioned windows, oak panelling, lovely entrance hall and first-floor drawing room, open fires, very good, imaginative food, and 18th-c walled rose garden and knot garden; children over 8; disabled access.

Portmeirion SH5937 PORTMEIRION Gwynedd LL48 6ER (0766) 770228 **£152 inc dinner** in hotel (14 rms), **£124** in village (17 rms). On the edge of an estuary and surrounded by beaches and woods (and traffic-free), this is a remarkable place. The hotel down by the water is quite luxurious – elegant rooms with marble, gilt, and rich, colourful fabrics. Behind and in the steeply landscaped grounds above it is a well-dispersed, very colourful Italianate village, luscious to look at, including all sorts of characterful cottage bedrooms tucked into the hillside. Very romantic when the day visitors have left; lots to do; cl 3 wks Jan. See description in To see and do.

Talsarnau SH6236 MAES-Y-NEUADD Gwynedd LL47 6YA (0766) 780200 **£145 inc dinner**; 16 luxurious rms. Looking out across Snowdonia National Park, this extended 14th-c attractive mansion is full of flowers and plants, antiques, and open fires, there's a peaceful atmosphere, very good food, and charming staff; children over 7 in evening restaurant; disabled access.

Llandrillo SJ0337 TYDDYN LLAN Corwen Clwyd LL21 0ST (049 084) 264 **£126 inc dinner**; 10 pretty rms. Restful Georgian house with elegantly furnished and comfortable public rooms, charming staff, very good inventive food and 3 acres of lovely gardens; fishing on 4 miles of River Dee (ghillies available) and fine forest walks (guides are available); cl 1st wk Feb; no children.

Capel Coch SH4682 TRE-YSGAWEN HALL Llangefni Isle of Anglesey LL77 7UR **£109.50**; 20 luxurious rms. Handsome Victorian stone mansion with landscaped gardens, plushly comfortable bar, carefully decorated lounge, friendly staff and fine food in conservatory-style restaurant; clay pigeon shooting; disabled access.

Abersoch SH3128 PORTH TOCYN Pwllheli Gwynedd LL53 7BU (075 881) 3303 **£88**; 17 attractive rms. On a headland with fine views, this is a lovely place to stay – especially for families (children's own sitting room with games, toys, books, video and lots of space in gardens and fields); cosy, interconnecting sitting rooms with antiques, comfortable sofas and chairs and fresh flowers, enjoyable food (children over 7 at dinner), and charming service; heated swimming pool in summer, hard tennis court; cl 8 Nov-wk before Easter; disabled access.

Penmaenpool SH6918 GEORGE III Dolgellau Gwynedd LL40 1YD (0341) 422525 **£88**; 12 rms, some in award-winning converted railway station. Cosy 17th-c inn on Mawddach estuary with good lunchtime food, imaginative evening restaurant, cosy lounge with log fire, beamed and partly panelled bar, fine nearby walks, and free salmon and trout fishing permits for residents; disabled access.

Conwy SH7381 CASTLE High St Gwynedd LL32 8DB (0492) 592324 ***£86**; 29 rms. Historic town with early 16th-c inn, one of the most characterful in the Forte chain; good food in pretty restaurant, proper pubby bar (popular with locals), friendly, helpful staff, decent breakfast, and car parking.

Llanarmon D C SJ1633 WEST ARMS Llangollen Clwyd LL20 7LD (069 176) 665 **£78**; 14 rms. Very clean, tidy and civilised, lounge bar interestingly furnished with antique settles, sofas in old-fashioned entrance hall, comfortable locals' bar, log fire, good food, friendly, quiet atmosphere, and lawn running down to River Ceiriog (fishing for residents); disabled access.

Capel Garmon SH8255 TAN-Y-FOEL COUNTRY HOUSE Betws-y-Coed Gwynedd LL26 0RE (0690) 710507 ***£76**; 9 spotlessly clean rms. Charming, partly 16th-c, no-smoking manor house in almost traffic-free area with mature gardens and marvellous surrounding countryside of Conwy Valley and Snowdonia; lounge with log fire in winter, conservatory in summer, warmly friendly, relaxing atmosphere and good food using the freshest produce inc local lamb and home-made bread; swimming pool (Jun-Oct); children over 9; no pets.

Betws-y-Coed SH7956 ROYAL OAK Gwynedd LL24 0AY (0690) 710219 **£74**; 27 rms. Pleasant hotel with grill room and wonderfully fresh fish and seasonal game.

Beaumaris SH6076 OLDE BULLS HEAD Castle St Anglesey LL58 8AP (0248) 810329 ***£72**; 11 rms with antiques and brass bedsteads. Partly 15th-c pub near castle with snug alcoves, low beams and open fire in quaint, rambling bar, interesting decorations, popular bar food, very good restaurant food (esp fish), fine wines, and cheery service; the entrance to pretty courtyard is closed by biggest single-hinged door in Britain; cl 25-26 Dec, 1 Jan; children over 7 in dining room.

Llanwddyn SJ0219 LAKE VYRNWY Oswestry Powys SY10 0LY (069 173) 692 **£69.50**; 38 rms, the ones overlooking the lake are the nicest. With particularly helpful, courteous staff, this large Tudor-style mansion has lots of sporting activities (esp fishing) and is set in 24,000 acres of woodland; log fires and sporting prints in the comfortable and elegant public rooms, a relaxed atmosphere, fine views from its hillside high over the lake, and good food using home-made preserves, chutneys, mustards and vinegars and home-grown produce from own kitchen garden.

Llanfyllin SJ1419 BODFACH HALL Powys SY22 5HS (0691) 648272 **£62**; 9 quiet rms. Elegant house in parkland with relaxed atmosphere, simple food in oak-panelled dining room, and very good local service; cl Dec-Feb.

Conwy SH7878 Old Rectory Llansantffraid Glan Conwy Gwynedd LL28 5LF (0429) 580611 **£59.50**; 6 deeply comfortable rms. Georgian house in pleasant gardens with views over Conwy estuary, Conwy Castle and Snowdonia; after introductions over cocktails the delicious food can either be eaten together around a long table or at separate tables, good breakfasts, warmly friendly staff, and lovely flowers; cl 20 Dec-1 Feb; children over 5.

Llanarmon D C SJ1633 Hand Llangollen Clwyd LL20 7LD (069 176) 666 **£58**; 14 rms. Very civilised country inn surrounded by outstanding scenery, with comfortably furnished lounge, log fire, fine restaurant food, good value bar food, and quick, friendly service; hard tennis court; disabled access.

Betws-y-Coed SH7956 Ty Gwyn Gwynedd LL24 0SG (0690) 710383 **£54**; 13 rms, shared bthrms. Welcoming 17th-c coaching inn with interesting old prints, furniture and bric-a-brac (owners own the antique shop next door), good food, and friendly service; nice setting overlooking river and a very good base for the area.

Maentwrog SH6741 Grapes Blaenau Ffestiniog Gwynedd LL41 4HN (076 685) 208 **£50**; 6 rms. Busy old coaching inn with hearty, wholesome bar food, big breakfasts, good views from terrace and garden, and interesting lamps and furnishings salvaged from chapels.

Llanrwst SH8061 Maenan Abbey Gwynedd LL26 0UL (0492) 660247 **£49**; 12 rms. Stately Victorian hotel with battlemented tower, elegant lounge, welcoming bar, good restaurant, Welsh singing Sat evenings, and lovely gardens; 11 acres of woodland across road, and close to fishing and Bodnant Gardens.

Llandudno SH7883 Dunoon Gwynedd LL30 2DW (0492) 860787 **£48**; 56 rms. Run by the same family for over 40 years, with generous helpings of food, attractive lounges, open fire, a relaxed atmosphere, and very good service; cl Nov-mid-Mar, disabled access.

Llannefydd SH9770 Hawk and Buckle Denbigh Clwyd LL16 5ED (074 579) 249 **£48**; 10 rms. Pleasant 17th-c stone inn with good choice food using local produce; a good base for exploring the area – by horse, car or on foot; cl 25-26 Dec, no under-8s.

Beddgelert SH5948 Sygun Fawr Country House Caernarfon Gwynedd LL55 4NE (0766 86) 258 **£46**; 7 rms. Marvellous views of Gwynant Valley and Snowdon range from secluded 17th-c hotel with comfortable sitting room, home-cooking in candlelit, traditionally furnished dining room; lots of walks; cl 1st 3wks Nov, 27 Dec-mid-Feb.

Llanfair D C SJ1455 Eyarth Station Ruthin Clwyd LL15 2EE (0824) 703543 ***£44**; 6 rms. Carefully converted old railway station with lovely views of the Vale of Clwyd, comfortable beamed sitting room with open log fire, good breakfasts in dining room which was once the station platform, helpful, friendly owners, and garden, sun terrace and outdoor heated swimming pool.

Beaumaris SH6076 Liverpool Arms Anglesey LL78 8BA (0248) 810362 **£44**; 8 comfortable rms, sea views. Decent food, friendly staff, lots of nautical decoration; cl 25 Dec.

Llanrwst SH8061 Cae'r Berllan Betws Rd Betws-y-Coed Gwynedd LL26 0PP **£44**; 2 rms with antique beds and fine views. Listed 16th-c manor house in 2 acres of lovely gardens surrounded by the Conwy Valley, with lots of atmosphere, massive old beams and oak partitioning, and good, imaginative food using home-grown and local produce (they think of themselves as a restaurant with rooms); cl Nov-Feb.

Maentwrog SH6741 Plas Tan y Bwlch Blaenau Ffestiniog Gwynedd LL41 3YU (0766) 85324 **£42**; 35 rms, 12 with own bthrm. Converted Victorian mansion (now the Snowdonia National Park Study Centre) with lovely valley views, satisfying, sturdy, self-service food, and lovely walks in own grounds; cl 2 wks over Christmas and New Year.

Capel Garmon SH8155 WHITE HORSE Llanrwst Gwynedd LL26 0RW (0690) 710271 **£40.50**; 5 small but clean rms. Comfortable, homely inn with friendly atmosphere, very good home-made food, marvellous breakfasts, magnificent views and delightful countryside; children at owners' discretion.

Llanerchymedd SH4284 LLWYDIARTH FAWR FARM Gwynedd LL71 8DF (0248) 470321 **£40**; 3 rms in main house, 6 cottage suites in grounds. Handsome Georgian farmhouse on 850-acre cattle and sheep farm with particularly warm, homely atmosphere and welcome, comfortable lounge with antiques, log fire, books and lovely views, second room for guests with another log fire, very good home-made food using farm and other fresh local produce, and terrace, lake for private fishing, nature walks, and birdwatching; cl Christmas.

Llangollen SJ2142 ABBEY GRANGE Clwyd LL20 8NN (0978) 860753 **£40**; 8 comfortable rms. Cosily converted, former quarrymaster's house in beautiful spot with superb views nr Valle Crucis Abbey; decent food, good wine list, efficient courteous service.

Llangollen SJ2142 BRITANNIA (Horseshoe Pass; A542 N) Clwyd LL20 8DW (0978) 860144 **£40**; 5 clean and pretty rms, all with 4-posters. Picturesque inn based on 15th-c core, though much extended and comfortably modernised, with traditional 17th-c Welsh elm furniture, generous helpings of decent food in dining area and two bars, pleasant staff, lovely views and attractive garden; cl 24-25 Dec.

Erbistock SJ3542 BOAT Wrexham Clwyd LL13 0DL (0978) 780143 **£39.50**; 1 rm with small lounge and breakfast area and river views. Popular dining pub, busy in summer, with decent food, pleasant small flagstoned bar, beamed dining room and big eating annexe, and pretty, partly terraced garden by the River Dee – enchanting on a quiet summer's day; cl 25-26 Dec, 1 Jan.

Brynsiencyn SH4867 PLAS TREFARTHEN Llanfairpwllgwyngyll Gwynedd LL61 6SZ (0248) 430379 **£36**; 8 rms. Happy and comfortable family house with panoramic views of Caernarfon Castle and Snowdonia mountain range with guest lounge, full-size snooker table, table tennis, and home-cooked food using produce grown on the farm; Mrs Roberts is a well-known soprano soloist for Welsh choirs.

Llanerchymedd SH4284 TRE'R DDOL FARM Isle of Anglesey Gwynedd LL71 7AR (0248) 470278 **£36**; 3 rms with original features. Neatly kept 400-year-old farmhouse on working mixed farm of 200 acres, with original staircase, log fire in cosy lounge, homely, relaxed atmosphere and proper farmhouse cooking; can help with day-to-day farm work, free riding for children, nature trails and bird watching; cl Dec.

Tudweiliog SH2437 LION Pwllheli Gwynedd LL53 8ND (075 887) 244 ***£36**; 5 rms, 2 with own bthrm. Extended village pub with excellent value home-made food in bar and dining rooms, a welcome for families, garden with play area, lovely views, and 10 mins walk to beaches; cl 22-28 Dec.

Hanmer SJ4639 BUCK FARM Whitchurch Shropshire SY14 7LX (094 874) 339 **£34**; 4 rms, shared bthrm. 16th-c half-timbered farmhouse in rolling dairy country with well-stocked library and very good, imaginative food using only fresh produce, often organic; lots to do in the area.

Tremeirchion SJ0873 BACH-Y-GRAIG St Asaph Clwyd LL17 0UH (0745) 730627 **£34**; 3 rms, 2 with brass beds. Wales's first brick-built house with a date-stone of 1567, this is set in a 200-acre dairy farm at the foot of the Clydian

Range; inglenook fireplace in big lounge, home-cooking using home-produced beef and lamb and own free-range eggs, and warm welcome; can join in farm activities or walk along their woodland trail; cl Christmas/New Year.

Gellilydan SH6839 TYDDYN DU Ffestiniog Gwynedd LL41 4RB (0766) 85281 **£32**; 4 rms with views of hills and mountains, 1 in private cottage suite. 400-year-old farmhouse on working farm in heart of Snowdonia National Park with beams and exposed stonework, big inglenook fireplaces in residents' lounge, and wholesome, home-made food using own free-range eggs; can help with the lambs, goats, ducks, sheep and pony; fine walks; cl Christmas.

Pwllheli SH3835 YOKE HOUSE FARM Gwynedd LL53 5TY (0758) 612621 **£31**; 3 rms, shared bthrm. Warmly welcoming Georgian farmhouse on 290-acre working farm; can watch milking, calf-feeding and there's a nature trail; cl Oct-Apr; children over 11.

Fron-goch SH9139 FFERM FRON-GOCH Bala Gwynedd LL23 7NT (0678) 520483 **£26**; 3 rms. Traditional stone farmhouse with a history going back to 14th c on 600 acres of working farm in lovely unspoilt countryside of the Snowdonia National Park; beams, log fire, antiques and old paintings, friendly atmosphere and good breakfasts; children over 9.

To see and do

Aberffraw SH3270 BARCLODIAD Y GAWRES Some 5,000 years old, this 20-ft underground passage tomb at the top of the cliff is notable for the patterns carved by the entrance and in the side chambers, which you make out with a good torch; it's sealed, but you can ask for a key at Beaumaris Castle, or at the Wayside Café in Llanfaelog. Hard to believe now, but Aberffraw was once the Welsh capital, and the native Gwynedd princes held court here from the 9th to the 13th c. There are some lovely unspoilt coves and beaches nearby.

Bangor SH5771 A quiet university town with a pleasant pedestrianised high street, some Georgian buildings, and a yacht harbour that adds a lively touch in summer; Euro-sceptics may be surprised to discover the pier was restored with an EEC grant. A cathedral was founded here 70 years before the one at Canterbury; the present building is restored 13th to 15th c, and has an interesting 16th-c carving of Christ bound and seated on a rock, as well as some fine Victorian stained glass. The Bible Garden outside contains only plants which are mentioned in the Scriptures. Opposite is a little museum of rural Welsh life.

PENRHYN CASTLE This splendid

We welcome reports from readers . . .

This GUIDE depends on readers' reports. Do help us if you can – in return, we offer a discount on the next edition to people who've helped us with reports for it. Tell us what you think about places already in it, and anything extra you think we should say about them. And send us your ideas for inclusion in the next edition: places to visit, eat at or stay in, attractive drives or walks, maybe even unusual interesting shops you know of. Use the card in the middle, the report forms at the end, or just write – no stamp needed: THE GOOD WEEKEND GUIDE, FREEPOST TN1569, Wadhurst, E Sussex TN5 7BR.

'Norman' castle was built in the 19th c: the interior – its panelling, decoration and furnishings – are all in a suitably grand style.The great hall is heated by the Roman method of hot air under the floor and one of the beds weighs over a ton – it's made out of slate. In the stableyard is a museum devoted to the industrial railways which have left Wales with such a legacy of quaint narrow-gauge lines; the exhibits include very early locomotives. Also a walled garden, adventure playground, orienteering course and pleasant walks with good views; snacks, shop, disabled access; cl am (exc July and Aug), all day Tues, all Nov-Mar; £4.20. NT.

Beaumaris SH6076 The most attractive town on Anglesey, with a good deal of character, several old buildings, a busy waterfront, and a 15th-c church. CASTLE One of the most impressive and complete of the castles built by Edward I, despite the struggle over it with Owain Glyndwr in the early 1400s, and the plundering of its lead, timber and stone in later ages. Beautifully symmetrical, it took from 1295 to 1312 to build (though the money ran out before it could be totally finished) and was the last of the great fortifications erected by that king around the coast of North Wales; shop, disabled access; cl 24-26 Dec, 1 Jan, winter am Sun; *£1.50. GAOL AND COURTHOUSE The courthouse is a unique Victorian survival – though the original building dates from the 17th c, it was renovated in the 19th. The gaol with its treadmill, the dank, poky cells and the route for condemned prisoners all provide a vivid picture of the harshness of the 19th-c prison system: you can stand in the dock and imagine you're just about to be sentenced; shop, limited disabled access; gaol cl Oct-Apr exc Easter, wkdys in May, court cl when in session; joint £2.80, jail £2.30, court £1.35. MUSEUM OF CHILDHOOD Galleries of pictures of children, early needlework produced by children, toys and dolls, and objects from nursery chairs to primitive audio-visual gadgets which were actually used by children. The exhibits are from a period covering about 150 years – it's one of the best nostalgia museums in the country; shop, some ground floor disabled access; cl am Sun and all Nov-Mar; *£2.50. THE CHURCH OF ST MARY AND ST NICHOLAS, which has a robust square tower, houses the stone coffin of Joan, daughter of King John and wife of the Welsh leader Llewellyn the Great. The Olde Bulls Head is excellent for lunch.

Beddgelert SH5948 A quiet village, which dreamed up the myth that it was the resting place of Llewelyn's faithful mastiff over a hundred years ago and has been living on it ever since. SYGUN COPPER MINE Interesting tours through underground workings of old mine, with magnificent stalactites and stalagmites and traces of gold and silver in the copper ore veins. When you come up at the end you're greeted by a wonderful view of the mountains. Also a good audio-visual presentation, and display of artefacts found during excavations; snacks, shop, some disabled access; cl 25 Dec; £3.80. Both the Prince Llewelyn and the Tanronen are good for lunch.

Betws-y-Coed SH7956 Strategically placed in a beautiful wooded gorge at the head of the Vale of Conwy, on the road to Bangor (and thence Ireland) as well as to Snowdon, this village is surrounded by picturesque woodland and river walks – so has over a century of catering to visitors behind it. The raging Swallow Falls and Fairy Glen just west of the village itself are deservedly regarded as some of the area's finest beauty spots. There are also a number of interesting bridges nearby, as well as the bizarre-looking Ugly House, which looks like a series of boulders thrown haphazardly together. CONWY VALLEY RAILWAY MUSEUM The narrow and standard gauge railways of North Wales feature

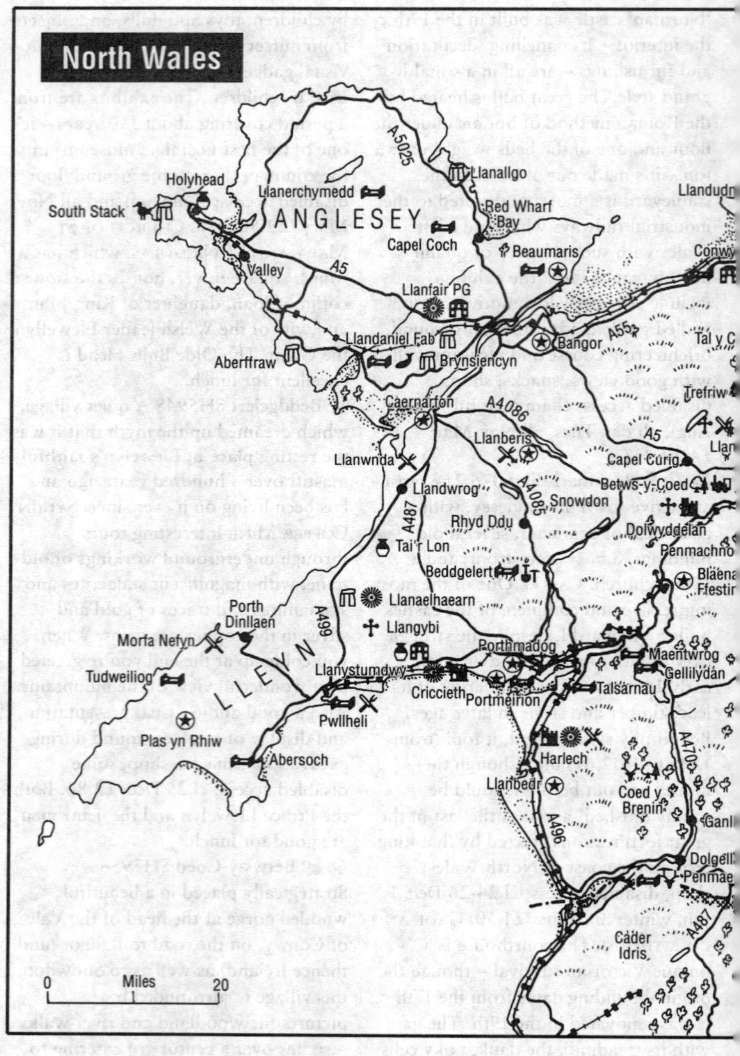

in these museums, alongside railway stock and other memorabilia. Also model railway layouts, a steam-hauled model railway in the 4-acre grounds, and a 15-in-gauge tramway to take visitors to the woods; snacks, shop, disabled access; cl winter wkdys to Christmas; *£1. The Ty Gwyn is good for lunch, and the Royal Oak Hotel is useful too. The next entry is just a short drive along the A470.

Blaenau Ffestiniog SH7045 is a straggle of village completely dwarfed by the vast spoil slopes from the slate mines all around it – once the slate capital of Wales, now with the passing of the industry like a living museum. PUMPED STORAGE POWER STATION Guided tours of the first hydro-electric pumped storage scheme

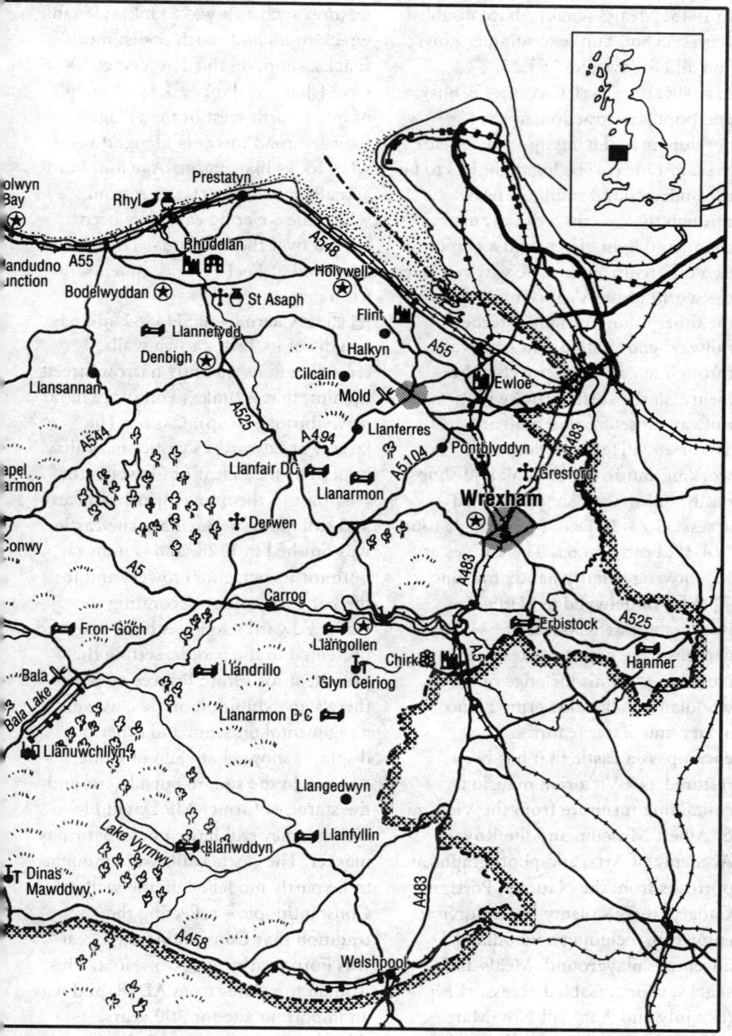

in the country, with dramatic views towards the peaks of Snowdonia; meals, snacks, shop, limited disabled access; cl Nov-Easter; *£2. From the information centre there's an attractive drive up into the mountains to Stwlan Dam, which also gives super views.

Gloddfa Ganol Slate Mine The largest slate mine in the world, with guided tours by Land-Rover. The mine has been reopened, and as well as demonstrations of the art of slate splitting and displays of the machinery, you can watch the blasting operations from the safety of the museum. You can go right down into the workings as well, and there's a little narrow-gauge railway. Above ground are three quarrymen's cottages, furnished to show changing styles from the 1880s to 1945. Meals, snacks, shop, disabled access; cl Sat, Sun (exc summer hols) and all Nov-Easter; *£3.25. LLECHWEDD SLATE CAVERNS A busy and popular attraction, always developing and bang up-to-date with the latest ideas. The highlight has to be the underground train journeys through the caverns, with dramatic sound and light effects and a choice of two different routes. One way recreates the world of the Victorian miner, while the other (along Britain's steepest railway) ends with a fantastic walk through ten atmospheric chambers. Plenty on the surface too, with a railway museum, slate mill and Victorian village complete with working smithy, pub, bank and shops; meals and snacks, shop, disabled access; cl 25-26 Dec, 1 Jan; single tour *£4.35, both *£6.65. The Grapes at Maentwrog is fairly handy for lunch.

Bodelwyddan SH9974 BODELWYDDAN CASTLE The walled gardens have been fully restored and include a glorious mélange of woodland walks, flowering plants, aviary and water features. They encompass a castle that has been restored as a Victorian mansion, containing furniture from the Victoria & Albert Museum and the Royal Academy of Arts, and photographs and portraits from the National Portrait Gallery; there's plenty for children to enjoy too, including a woodland adventure playground. Meals and snacks, shop, disabled access; cl Fri (exc July and Aug), all Nov-Mar; *£3.50. In the village itself the 19th-c 'Marble Church', built entirely of locally quarried limestone, is an unusual and quite splendid sight worth stopping to see.

Brynsiencyn SH4867 ANGLESEY SEA ZOO Housed in tanks specially designed to provide as unrestricted and natural an environment as possible, the marine creatures displayed here are all found around Anglesey and the North Wales coast. Various interesting features such as a wave tank, tide tank, wreck room and touch pools; meals, snacks, shop, disabled access; cl 20-26 Dec, 1 Jan, 3-5 Jan; *£3.95. A couple of miles north-west of the village by the back road towards Llangaffo is what looks like a Stone-Age hut, but is actually a BURIAL CHAMBER from which the covering earth has been eroded over the millennia. The Mermaid at Foel Ferry is quite useful for lunch.

Caernarfon SH4862 still has lengths of its 13th-c town walls, crowding in its quaintly narrow streets (quaint, that is, unless you're trying to drive through them). CASTLE The largest of Edward I's castles in Wales, built after the defeat of Llewelyn the Last (last of the native British princes) and still quite spectacular. The castle was finished in 1328, and is unusual both for its octagonal towers and for the bands of colour decorating the walls. Edward's son was born here and presented to the people, setting the precedent for future Princes of Wales – there's an exhibition on this, as well as a regimental museum and other displays; shop; cl am Sun in winter; *£3.50. In the square outside, around the statue of former MP David Lloyd George, they still have a busy Saturday market. The castle walls were thought to be partly modelled on the walls of Constantinople – reflecting the tradition that Constantine the Great was born nearby at SEGONTIUM. This Roman fort dates from AD78, and was an important site for 300 years. Excavations have exposed the remains of various rebuildings during that period, and there's a museum with excavated finds; shop, disabled access; cl Sun am, 24-26 Dec, 1 Jan, Good Fri. The harbour is busy with yachts in summer, and you can go over a restored steam-powered dredger moored here. AIR WORLD (Airport) has lively displays of helicopters, aeroplanes and a trainer, encouraging people to climb aboard. There are also a great many model aeroplanes, as well as pleasure SKY TRIPS – (0286) 830800 for times of these; meals and snacks, shop, disabled access; cl 24 Dec-4 Jan; £3. The Black Boy, though very local, is useful for a cheap lunch.

Chirk SJ2638 The quiet little town, important as a staging post on the 'road to Ireland', has something of a bypassed-by-time feel now. A little to the west, right by a well-preserved stretch of the earthworks of Offa's Dyke, is CHIRK CASTLE. The exterior of this late 13th-c castle remains much as it was, with its high walls and drum towers, but the inside has had many alterations over the 700 years of its occupation: many of the medieval-looking decorations were by Pugin in the 19th c, the elegant stone staircase dates from the 18th c, and the Long Gallery is 17th c; snacks, limited disabled access; cl am, all day Sat and Mon and all Nov-Mar; £3.80. The formal gardens are magnificent. The Hand and Bridge are quite useful for lunch.

Coed y Brenin SH7326 FOREST PARK AND VISITOR CENTRE Excellent introduction to this area with its wildlife conservation hides and over 50 miles of walks. The name means King's Forest, and it was so called to commemorate the Silver Jubilee of King George V; meals and snacks, shop, disabled access; cl Nov-Easter.

Colwyn Bay SH8678 This busy summer seaside resort has all that's wanted for a family beach holiday, though it's not as nice as Llandudno just along the coast (see below). The quieter end at Rhos-on-Sea has a puppet theatre. WELSH MOUNTAIN ZOO AND FLAGSTAFF GARDENS Lots of exotic animals to be seen here, all housed in natural habitats – what really distinguishes this zoo from any other is the setting overlooking Colwyn Bay. The views are quite magnificent, and the 37 acres of gardens and woodland in which the zoo is set attract plenty of local wildlife; meals and snacks, shop, disabled access; cl 25 Dec; £4.25.

Conwy SH7777 CONWY CASTLE One of the best-known castles in Wales, partly because it's so well preserved, but also because it looks exactly as a medieval fortress should. Built for Edward I in 1283-9, it's the key part of the town's elaborate defensive system – 21 (originally 22) towers linked by walls some 30 ft high, the most complete town wall in Wales. The best and most dramatic view of it is from the other side of the river, and from the castle itself there are fine panoramic views from the top of the turrets. The bridges spanning the river are also worth a second glance – the suspension bridge was built by Telford in 1826, and the tubular bridge by Stephenson in 1848. The shop has an exhibition on Edward I and the other castles he built; cl am Sun in winter, 24-26 Dec; *£2.90. ABERCONWY HOUSE The only house in the town which dates from the 14th c, surviving the turbulence of events in the frontier town (though even the newer buildings in the town still follow the grid of very narrow early medieval streets). Rooms are furnished in period style and there's an interesting audio-visual presentation; shop; cl Tues, and all Nov-Mar; £1.80. PLAS MAWR An elaborate Tudor mansion currently undergoing extensive restoration; the downstairs rooms are now open again, but it will probably be a couple of years before the whole house is ready. It's got splendid plasterwork, stone-flagged floors and huge fireplaces; *£1. SMALLEST HOUSE This building is 6 ft wide and its front wall is only 10 ft high; it's furnished in the style of a mid-Victorian Welsh cottage, and is listed in the *Guinness Book of Records* as the smallest house in the country; shop, disabled access; cl Good Fri and all Nov-Apr; *50p. There's a little aquarium on the quayside nearby. The Castle Hotel is a civilised place for lunch. New roadways nearby have eased what was an appalling traffic jam through Conwy – you may still be held up, particularly going through one of the old town gates.

Criccieth SH5038 A restrained resort with a good sheltered sandy beach. CRICCIETH CASTLE The remains of this 13th-c castle stand on a rocky, mounded peninsula above the little town, affording superb views over Tremadog Bay. Parts of the inner walls are well preserved, and there is an impressive gatehouse. Look out for the traces of a great fire, evidence of the struggle in which Owain Glyndwr took the castle in 1404. An exhibition covers Gerald of Wales and other Welsh castles, with a cartoon video; cl wkdys and am Sun in winter; *£1.80. The Prince of Wales is useful for lunch.

Denbigh SJ0566 CASTLE The gatehouse of this ruined castle is still impressive, with its trio of towers and a superb archway; the figure on the summit is believed to represent Edward I. The castle was started in 1282, as were the TOWN WALLS which describe almost a complete circuit. Among the remains are one of the gateways and LEICESTER'S CHURCH, the remains of an ambitious church built by the Earl of Leicester, favourite of Elizabeth I. A MUSEUM on the High St has interesting finds from nearby Bronze-Age sites. The Cerrigllwydion Arms at nearby Llanynys, to the south-east, is good for lunch.

Derwen SJ0751 The medieval CHURCH here has an elaborately carved rood screen and loft, with some old wall paintings and an excellent Celtic cross in the churchyard.

Dinas Mawddwy SH8514 MEIRION MILL The village, among riverside woods below the mountains on the south fringes of Snowdonia, provides a charming setting for this working woollen mill, in the grounds of the old Mawddwy railway station; snacks, shop, disabled access; cl Nov-Mar. Nearby is a picturesque packhorse bridge. The Llew Coch is useful for lunch.

Dolwyddelan SH7352 DOLWYDDELAN CASTLE You can see a restored keep of around 1200 and a 13th-c curtain wall at this castle – reputedly the birthplace of Llywelyn the Great – captured in 1283 by Edward I. It's picturesquely set on a lightly wooded crag; cl Sun am; £1.25. The village CHURCH is attractive.

Ewloe SJ2966 CASTLE The Welsh Tower in the upper ward still partially stands to its original height in this native Welsh castle. Other ruins include walls, another tower and a well in the lower ward.

Flint SJ2472 CASTLE Parts of the walls and corner towers survive, but the most impressive remnant of this castle is the great tower or donjon, which is separated by the moat. The building dates from the late 13th c and overlooks the River Dee – it was the first of those built by Edward I to subdue the natives, and has a role in Shakespeare's *Richard II*; cl am Sun in winter; 75p. The Britannia in nearby Halkyn is good for lunch.

Glan Conwy SH8352 FELIN ISAF WATERMILL 17th-c watermill with working water wheel and, in its grounds, mini golf course, fishing and craft shops; snacks, shop, limited disabled access; cl Nov-Mar; *£2.

Glyn Ceiriog SJ2038 CHWAREL WYNNE MINE Beautiful surroundings for this mine in a 12-acre site with nature trail; the education centre provides a video on the history of the slate industry, and there is a half-hour conducted tour of the underground workings; snacks, shop; cl Nov-Mar; £2. The Woolpack right by the slate tramway in the attractively unspoilt village is good for lunch, and the valley's remote landscape is popular with walkers.

Gresford SJ3555 The village CHURCH has some wonderful medieval stained glass, and its bells are often described as one of the 'Seven Wonders of Wales'. A yew tree outside is reputed to be 1,400 years old.

Harlech SH5831 CASTLE Built in 1283-90 by Edward I, this fine castle was starved into capitulation by Owain Glyndwr in 1404. The song *Men of Harlech* was written with reference to its defence not then, but in the War of the Roses. Before the sea retreated there was a sheer drop into the water on one side, but it now stands above dunes, with wonderful views of Snowdonia; shop; cl Sun am in winter, 24-26 Dec, 1 Jan; £2.90. The village around it has all that the crowds of summer visitors to the castle and the good beach could want.

Holyhead SH2582 is a long-established fishing town on a little island, now an unassuming resort with some burial chambers and ancient sites not far away (see also South Stacks below). The Victorian breakwater protecting the harbour is Britain's longest; a MARITIME MUSEUM explores its seafaring heritage.

✝ **Holywell** SJ1876 ST WINEFRIDE'S WELL has the holy spring that turned the spot into a centre of pilgrimage – it's supposed to have healing powers. The neighbouring GREENFIELD VALLEY HERITAGE PARK has the story in its little museum, as well as the remains of a Cistercian abbey.

Llanaelhaearn SH3744 Off the B4417, just up the hill from here, a signed path leads to the TRE'R CEIRI hill fort, occupied from the Bronze Age through to the Dark Ages; a massive stone wall, lots of hut foundations, and fine views. The Bryncynan and the Ship at Morfa Nefyn nearby are useful for lunch.

Llanallgo SH4985 DIN LLUGWY ANCIENT VILLAGE The remains of a 4th-c village: pentagonal stone wall surrounds two circular and seven rectangular buildings. The Parciau Arms at Marianglas is good for lunch.

Llanbedr SH5826 MAES ARTRO VILLAGE Imaginatively converted wartime RAF camp with lots to do: an original air raid shelter complete with light and sound effects, a 'Village of Yesteryear', a log fort playground, marine aquarium, and nature trails through the woodland; meals and snacks, shop, disabled access; cl Oct-Easter; £2.50. The Victoria here is useful for lunch.

Llanberis SH5760 is full of B & Bs, small hotels, and shops and cafés for the summer visitors here for Snowdon. LAKE RAILWAY The railway used to carry slate, now it carries passengers the 4-mile return journey from Gilfach Ddu along the shore of Llyn Padarn, using steam locomotives dating from 1889 to 1948; meals and snacks, shop, disabled access but no wheelchairs on the train; cl Nov-Feb, tel for timetable (0286) 870549; £3.60. SNOWDON MOUNTAIN RAILWAY This is Britain's only public rack-and-pinion railway, operated by vintage Swiss steam and modern diesel locomotives. It follows the route of an old pony track and takes passengers up over 3,000 ft to the summit of Snowdon – glorious, breathtaking views which, on a good day, might include the Isle of Man and the Wicklow Mountains. Trains leave when there are more than a couple of dozen people on board – so if there aren't many people about you may have to wait for it to start, and if there are you may have to queue (there is a sort of booking service). When trains are running to the summit, you can visit the highest postbox in Britain. Meals and snacks, shop, disabled access (check first); cl Nov-14 Mar – always best to ring first, tel (0286) 870223; £12.50 return. See Walks section for other ways to enjoy the splendid scenery of Snowdon. POWER OF WALES Interesting centre built to explore the relationship between man and these fantastic surroundings, using hi-tech audio-visual displays (which present the Dinorwig pumped storage generating station as a highlight in the story of Wales); snacks, shop, disabled access (24 hours' notice for wheelchairs in the power station); cl wknds Dec-Jan; *£5. Dolbadarn Castle Overlooking Llyn Padarn at the foot of the Llanberis Pass (A4086), this castle was built in the early 13th c by Llywelyn the Great – it has a fine round keep; cl am Sun and all Oct-Mar; 75p. Welsh Slate Museum Until it closed in 1969 this was one of the biggest quarries in the country, and this museum explains what life here was like. The quarry workshop has largely been preserved in its original state – complete with working craftsmen and machinery, including the foundry and the Dinorwic water wheel, one of the largest in the world; shop, disabled access; cl Oct-Easter; £1.50. Another good spot for Snowdon walks is the Pen-y-Gwryd at Nant Gwynant to the east; also a good place for lunch.

Llandaniel Fab SH5070 Bryn Celli Ddu A restored neolithic passage burial chamber built over a previous stone circle, at the end of a long tunnel, with a carved stone over a burial pit; locked, but key at nearby farmhouse. Take a torch.

Llandudno SH7881 is the main holiday town in the area, and though it does have a well-sheltered, long curve of good pebbly beach, a prom and a good range of resort entertainments, it doesn't feel too brash. This is largely because from the beginning it was laid out to follow a careful 19th-c design which has preserved a unified character and a sense of style and spaciousness ever since. There are charming little shops and boutiques, a well-restored pier (from where you can fish, though they no longer have sailings), and cable-cars as well as the famous tramway up the massive Great Orme headland which protects the main beach – there's a quieter but more exposed beach on the far side. Climbing up to the summit yourself is much more fun (a couple of cafés en route have views to justify stopping), and when you get there there's a 12th-c church and a visitor centre with local geology. The Great Orme Mines go back 4,000 years – they're the only prehistoric mine workings open to the public, and the biggest such site so far discovered. Displays of finds, an audio-visual exhibition and underground walks through the cavernous former copper workings themselves; teas, shop, disabled access (not underground); cl Nov-Mar; £3.50. Back in town, the The Rabbit Hole is a rather jolly exhibition devoted to *Alice in Wonderland*; the real Alice holidayed in Llandudno as a child; £2.30. They had to close for much of the summer last year after the disastrous floods that wreaked havoc in the town. The real Conwy Valley Railway, a BR line to Blaenau Ffestiniog, runs through magnificent scenery and has several useful stops en route. The Kings Head near the Great Orme tramway station is pleasant for lunch, and nearby the Queens Head at Glanwydden, off the Colwyn Bay road, does very good food; snacks, shop, disabled access; cl Nov-Easter exc wknds up to Christmas; *£1.

Llanfairpwllgwyngyllgocherychwyrndrobwllllantysiliogogogoch SH5372 Excellent views of Snowdonia and the Menai Strait from the top of the Marquess of Anglesey's column, built in 1816 to commemorate the military achievements of Wellington's second in command at the Battle of Waterloo. Fine mountain views, too, from his former home Plas Newydd, a couple of miles from the village. It's an elegant 18th-c mansion with a collection of pictures by Rex Whistler and a military museum with relics from Waterloo. Also a good spring garden with rhododendrons; snacks, shop, some disabled access; cl am, all day Sat, all Oct-Mar (exc pm Fri and Sun in Oct), garden open July and Aug only; £3.50. NT. Locals generally shorten their village's remarkable name to Llanfair PG, or Llanfairpwll. The nearby village of Penmynydd was the ancient home of the Tudor family.

Llangollen SJ2141 has a good few solid and gracious Georgian and Victorian villas built to take advantage of this charming valley above the River Dee, and among them the discreet hotels that cater for the generally older people to whom the area most appeals. VALLE CRUCIS ABBEY (A542 N) Substantial remains of the church that belonged to this early 13th-c Cistercian abbey can be seen, and also some beautifully carved grave slabs; shop, limited disabled access; cl 24-26 Dec, 1 Jan; £1.25. The ruins stand at the bottom of the HORSESHOE PASS, a nerve-wrackingly steep mountain drive offering superb views. PLAS NEWYDD Lady Eleanor Butler and Sarah Ponsonby, 'the ladies of Llangollen', lived here from 1780 to 1831. The beautiful half-timbered house has stained glass, leather wall coverings and the domestic paraphernalia of the period; shop; cl Nov-Mar; £1.50. LLANGOLLEN RAILWAY Until it closed in 1968 this 5-mile stretch was part of the Great Western Railway; it's now been restored and steam and diesel trains run from the pleasantly preserved station to the village of Glyndyfrdwy in the Dee valley. There's a special coach for the disabled (you have to book); snacks, shop; cl 25 Dec – trains don't usually run Jan-Mar, (0978) 860951 for timetable; from £2.40, 50p for just the old station. CANAL EXHIBITION CENTRE Interesting and imaginative displays illustrating the history of canals in Wales; snacks, shop, disabled access; cl Nov-Mar; *£1. They organise horse-drawn BOAT TRIPS along the Vale of Llangollen; *£2. The Abbey Grange Hotel, and the Sun Trevor at nearby Trevor Uchaf, are good for lunch, as is the attractively set Britannia up the Horseshoe Pass.

Llangybi SH4241 ST CYBI'S WELL Known to the Welsh as Fynnon Gybi, this well has been claimed to have healing properties for over a thousand years. St Cybi was a 6th-c Cornish saint known as a healer of the sick. Look out for the corbelled beehive vaulting inside the roofless stone structure, which is Irish in style.

Llanrwst SH8061 Pretty little town with old stone bridge over the Conwy river, said to be the work of Inigo Jones. GWYDIR CHAPEL, added by the influential Wynn family to the parish church in the 17th c, has a stone coffin reputedly that of Llewelyn the Great, as well as a magnificent rood screen from the ruins of Maenan Abbey. The Wynns also constructed the nearby GWYDIR UCHAF CHAPEL, with intriguing ceiling paintings. The Maenan Abbey Hotel is useful for lunch.

Llanuwchllyn SH8730 BALA LAKE RAILWAY Some of the carriages on trains using this delightful 4½-mile route are open to the elements, which seems to make the views of the lake and mountains more vivid. The locomotives were once used to haul slate in the North Wales quarries; meals and snacks, shop, disabled access (but no facilities); cl occasionally Mon and Fri in Apr and Sept, all Nov-Mar; *£4.50. The Olde Bulls Head in Bala is quite useful for lunch.

Llanystumdwy SH4738 LLOYD GEORGE MEMORIAL MUSEUM Memorabilia from the life of Lloyd George displayed in the house in which he died, in the village in which he spent his childhood; shop, disabled access to museum; cl Nov-Easter, restricted opening Oct – tel (0766) 522071; £2.

Mold SJ2464 has a richly decorated parish CHURCH built to commemorate the victory of Henry Tudor at Bosworth Field in 1485. The We Three Loggerheads out on the Ruthin road is useful for lunch.

Penmachno SH7950 PENMACHNO WOOLLEN MILL Timeless watermill powered by the River Machno, with displays and weaving demonstrations explaining the history and craft of the cottage weaving industry; snacks, shop. TY MAWR

Wybrnant (on forest rd W of village) Picturesque, lonely thick-walled medieval cottage, birthplace of Bishop William Morgan who first translated the Bible into Welsh (see St Asaph). The National Trust are restoring the site so it may not be open – check first (069 03) 213 (it has been open pm Weds, Thurs, Fri and Sun – just Fri and Sun in winter).

Penmaenpool SH6918 There is a small NATURE RESERVE here, and a very useful nature INFORMATION CENTRE which will direct you to promising places throughout this whole area, which has good walks. The George III is useful for lunch.

Plas yn Rhiw SH2532 PLAS YN RHIW Small manor house, originally medieval with Tudor and Georgian additions. The gardens and woodlands include a waterfall, snowdrop wood and subtropical specimens; shop, limited disabled access; cl am, Sat and all Nov-Apr; £2.20. The Glyn-y-Weddw at Llanbedrog is quite useful for lunch.

Porthmadog SH5638 is quite a busy shopping town of low, slate-roofed houses, with a spacious harbour. The famous narrow-gauge FESTINIOG RAILWAY opened in 1836 to carry slate from Blaenau Ffestiniog to Porthmadog by gravity. The first passengers were carried in 1865, and the line shut down in 1946; it was reopened in 1955 and has gradually been extended to climb the 13¼ miles to Blaenau Ffestiniog; meals and snacks, shop, disabled access; cl weekdays Nov-Feb (exc school hols), all Mar; fares vary up to £11.40. The adjacent FESTINIOG RAILWAY MUSEUM tells the story of the railway, with exhibits inc a four-wheeled hearse converted from an old quarryman's coach, a slate wagon, and one of the original steam locos from 1863, as well as maps, documents and drawings; open as railway. The railway links with the British Rail CAMBRIAN COAST LINE, hugging the coast from Pwllheli to Machynlleth, with many stops along the way. POTTERY You can watch pottery being made here and even make a piece yourself, with special activities organised for the disabled. Displays on the history of pottery and a mural illustrating the town's history, in the engine rooms of a 19th-c flour mill; shop, disabled access; cl wknds exc July, Aug and bank hols, all Nov-Easter; 50p, £2.25 for activities. The Ship is useful for lunch, as is the Golden Fleece in nearby Tremadog.

Portmeirion SH5937 On the shores of an inlet from Tremadog Bay, this fairy-tale holiday village, designed by Welsh architect Sir Clough Williams Ellis, is set in 175 acres of lush coastal cliff and woodland gardens. Very picturesque, it's one big folly – pastel-washed cottages interlaced with grottoes, cobbled squares, also a bell tower, castle, lighthouse, and long picturesque flights of steps zigzagging down to the water, which at low tide dries to miles of sand. Some of the buildings were painstakingly brought here to save them from destruction, and the central hotel building has a library which was originally in the Great Exhibition of 1851 in London. Enveloping the village are Gwyllt gardens which cover 60 acres with wild woodlands, famous for fine displays of rhododendrons, azaleas, hydrangeas and sub-tropical flora. You have to pay a toll to enter the village, but once in you can see the house where Noel Coward wrote *Blithe Spirit* and the locations for the cult TV series *The Prisoner*, while children can play in the playground, on a make-believe schooner apparently moored by the hotel, or, tide permitting, on the beach. A lovely relaxing place, quite unlike anywhere else; meals and snacks, shop; cl 9 Jan-5 Feb; £2.90, half price Nov-Mar.

Prestatyn SJ0783 Bustling seaside resort standing at one end of the 168-mile route of Offa's Dyke, marked by a stone pillar above the main beach.

Rhuddlan SJ0878 Once a busy port, now a sleepy little town with a fine old CASTLE adapted by Edward I from an earlier Norman structure. It was from here that the King organised the ministration of Wales. Overlooking the river, it's a pretty spot. Nearby Dyserth has BOODRRYDDAN HALL, the home of the Constable of Rhuddlan Castle (with an interesting well-house built by Inigo Jones), a good, partly 13th-c parish church and a plunging waterfall.

Rhyl SJ0181 is an often rather brash seaside resort, but if you're passing with children, the KNIGHT'S CAVERN, a lively interpretation of Welsh history, should amuse them, and there's another of the SEA LIFE CENTRES that we've described elsewhere; cl 25 Dec; £3.95.

St Asaph SJ0475 Tiny little city with the smallest CATHEDRAL in Britain, founded in 537. A column in the grounds commemorates its most famous cleric Bishop Morgan (see Penmachno) and his work translating the Bible into Welsh. There's also a little museum with finds from the site.

South Stack SH2082 The cliffs near the LIGHTHOUSE are full of seabird breeding colonies, and there's an RSPB reserve. Nearby is a large group of the foundations of HUT CIRCLES, probably around 2,000 years old, still with some visible traces of stone sleeping slabs.

Tai'r Lon SH4450 MUSEUM OF OLD WELSH COUNTRY LIFE Wide range of exhibits from Wales in past times housed in an old watermill in the hills by the River Desach; meals and snacks, shop, limited disabled access; cl Sat, and all Oct-Easter; £1. The Goat at Llanwnda a bit further north is good for lunch.

Tal y Cafn SH7971 BODNANT GARDEN Started in 1875 but improved in 1900 (and indeed ever since, in the hands of the green-fingered family which has owned them), these gardens are among Britain's greatest. Part of the grounds have a beautiful woodland garden in a sheltered valley, notable for its rhododendrons and azaleas, while below the house are five terraces in the Italian style, with a canal pool, reconstructed Pin Mill and an open-air stage on the lowest. There are many fine rare plants including unusual trees and shrubs; meals and snacks, shop, disabled access (but it is steep in places); cl Nov-mid-Mar; *£3.30. The Ferry and Tal y Cafn Inn are useful for lunch, and also in this lovely valley are the good Groes Inn at Tyn y Groes, and the Olde Bull up on the hillside opposite at Llanbedr y Cennin.

Trefriw SH7863 TREFRIW WOOLLEN MILL The same family have run this woollen mill for 135 years, using the same water to power the machinery (if in a slightly more modern way) as when they first bought it. Two hydro-electric turbines are driven by the fast-flowing Afon Crafnant, and there's a weaver's garden growing plants traditionally used by textile craft-workers. The products of the mill – tapestries and tweeds – are on sale; snacks, shop, disabled access; mill cl wknds and all Nov-Easter but turbine house is open Sat (and pm summer Suns) all year, often with weaving demonstrations. Trefriw used to be a spa, and you can still see the wells on the outskirts of the village. There's a 14th-c church, and the Maenan Abbey Hotel at Llanwrst is good for lunch.

Wrexham SJ3350 ERDDIG Superb late 17th-c house, especially interesting for the way you can explore the life of those 'upstairs' and 'downstairs' just as thoroughly; the gallery of servants' portraits is especially touching. Enlarged and improved in the early 18th c, the house is filled with splendid original furnishings, inc a magnificent state bed in Chinese silk. The restored outbuildings have a laundry, bakehouse, estate smithy and sawmill – some still in working order, and the surrounding parkland is very pleasant to stroll through. It's one of the most attractive places to visit in all of Wales; meals and snacks, shop, disabled access with prior notice; cl Thurs and Fri, and all Oct-Mar; £5 all incl, below-stairs tour £3. NT. BERSHAM INDUSTRIAL HERITAGE CENTRE A Victorian schoolhouse with a good overview of medieval and modern industry in the area, particularly the local ironworks. The area is famous for its ironworking, and the centre is the focus of an industrial history trail covering 8 miles. Various relevant temporary exhibitions, with workshops and demonstrations of various traditional skills; shop, disabled access (limited to ironworks); cl Nov-Easter, ironworks cl am and all winter; *£1. Wrexham's 15th-c CHURCH is worth a look, with its magnificent steeple. The Boat at Erbistock on the Dee, a few miles south of Erddig, is good for lunch.

★ **Attractive villages** in the area, all with decent pubs but in general tending to appeal for their surroundings more than for the beauty of their buildings, include Capel Curig SH7258, Cilcain SJ1865, Erbistock SJ3542, Halkyn SJ2172, Hanmer SJ4639, Llanarmon DC SJ1633, Llandwrog SH4456, Llangedwyn SJ1924, Llansannan SH9466, Pontblyddyn SJ2761 and Porth Dinllaen SH2741 (an idyllic seaside spot, but you have to walk to it); other pubs and inns in attractive areas or with notable views include the Porth Tocyn Hotel at Abersoch SH3226, White Horse at Capel Garmon SH8255, Grouse at Carrog SJ1144, T'yn y Groes at Ganllwyd SH7224, Druid at Llanferres SJ1961, Ship on Red Wharf Bay SH5281, Cwellyn Arms at Rhyd Ddu SH5753, White Eagle at Roscolyn near Valley SH2979 and Caerffynon Hall at Talsarnau SH6236.

Walks

This area has plenty of fine walking, both gentle and taxing – somewhere to justify a walking holiday.

Snowdonia's main mountain group soars dramatically, many of its peaks having easily identifiable shapes (if you can see them at all through the mist). **Snowdon** SH6054 itself, the highest mountain in England and Wales, has a number of ways up, ranging from the easy path alongside the mountain railway, to the enthralling Horseshoe Route, which makes its way along knife-edge ridges; the Pyg Track and Watkin Path are among the favourites. For a taster of the mountain without actually going up it, follow the start of the Miner's Track (from the Pen-y-pass car park on the A4086), which really is a track as far as Glaslyn, the last of four lakes passed. Recommended lower-level rambles include the **reservoirs** N of Capel Curig SH4682, the nature trail around **Llyn Idwal** SH6459 (a superbly sited lake beneath Glyder Fach), the **Aberglaslyn Pass** SH5947 S of Beddgelert, the **riverside walk** along the old railway track by the Afon Llugwy W from Betws-y-Coed SH7596, Bala Lake SH9134, and the signposted **Precipice Walk** SH7321 N of Dolgellau SH7318.

Much of the coast is built up or ribboned by roads. Notable exceptions giving good walks are **Great Orme Head** SH7683 (quaintly reachable by a steep 'tram' from Llandudno), **Conwy Mountain** SH7577 (not a real mountain but with views of Anglesey worthy of mountain status), **Lavan Sands** SH6376 near Aber SH6573, and the old railway track beside the **Mawddach Estuary** between Penmaenpool SH6918 and Fairbourne SH6114. The very unspoilt **Lleyn Peninsula** has an 1,849-ft mountain, Yr Eifl SH3644 (the Rivals) close to the coast. The peninsula's extremity has some good coastal walks starting W from Aberdaron SH1726, and E of here is the spectacular bay of Hells Mouth SH2626 (decent pub food at the Sun in Llanengan).

In Clwyd, **Castell Dinas Bran** SJ2243 is the place to head for from Llangollen SJ2142. The hill-fort site commands views over the vale and is close by the Panorama Walk (actually a surfaced minor road). The highest point of the Clwydian Range, a bulging massif with clearly marked paths, is **Moel Fammau** SJ1663 (walk up from the car park through colour-coded forest trails or over open land), from where you can see much of Snowdonia, the edge of the Peak district and the Wirral.

Anglesey is too flat to offer much interest inland, but its lovely beaches, as at Newborough Warren SH4263, are satisfying enough. Paths intermittently follow the indented coastline around Amlwch SH4493. **Holyhead Mountain** SH2182 is a dramatic hill at the W tip of Holy Island.

Driving

This area, criss-crossed with roads that are excellent for country drives, has superb possibilities for a touring holiday or for day and half-day outings. The main routes attract a great many touring visitors, by car, coach and caravan, so in high season you will find quite a lot of traffic on these main roads, and quite a lot of touristy things by the roadside. But it's easy to forge off into lovely areas which get less attention, and outside high summer even the trunk roads through the area settle down into an altogether more relaxed pace of life. In poor weather the higher routes do get quickly swathed in mist.

Around Snowdon the A4086, A498 and A4805 are all very splendid. The roads through the rich Vale of Conwy are not to be missed, with broad hill views all around. The A5 across the area must rank as the most scenic of all 'single-figure' trunk roads, though the scenery, combining mountains with rivers and grand fir forests, is even better on the A470 trunk road (not too busy except in high summer) S from Betws-y-Coed to Dolgellau. (On this road, if you're heading S, as you come to the end of the Trawsfynydd lake on your right and cross the river bridge, the second left turn takes you along a lane which in about 2½ miles gives access to an enormously tall standing stone out on the moor quite near the road.)

The A499 down into the quiet landscapes of the Lleyn Peninsula, and the B4417 continuing along its N coast, is a more scenic route than the A497 on its S side.

The A494 up to Bala is a striking valley road, with high mountains above it. Lake Vrnwy has more character than Bala Lake, even though it's a reservoir and the pine-forested landscape around it is largely an artificial creation of the 1880s; good B roads lead to it, and there's a fiercely steep back road through dramatic passes between its W end and Dinas Mawddwy – a rewarding adventurous drive for the steely-nerved.

The A487 between Dolgellau and Machynlleth has some attractive scenery, particularly around Corris; the dead-end side road up past Corris itself takes you into a charming peaceful valley.

Though it's a there-and-back drive, when the high mountain snows are melting in spring or after heavy rain it's worth taking the back road from Llanrhaeadr ym Mochnant up to Tan y Pistyll to see the remarkably high waterfall of Pistyll Rhaeadr. Another road into equally quiet but higher country is the B4501 up around Llyn Brenig.

The area around Llangollen has some fine drives; the A542 N has some memorable mountain views, and to the S the B4500 from Chirk to Llanarmon DC and beyond takes you into extremely tranquil countryside, a beautifully secluded valley. The roads around the Clwydian Hills, including the B5429 and even the trunk A494 between Mold and Ruthin, are filled with pleasant views.

The A496/A493 coast roads are for the most part undramatic; the best parts are around the Mawddach Estuary, and along the tidal flats of the Dovey estuary around Aberdovey. Above here, the back road cutting off the Aberdovey 'corner' of the A493 runs prettily through the so-called Happy Valley, below high hills.

Driving on Anglesey is not memorable in its own right.

Reasonably good roads mean that from Llandudno in the N, say, one can get to almost any part of even this large area in little more than 1½ hours. The A55 across the N coast has improved dramatically in the last few years, and is now largely dual carriageway all the way to Bangor.

Where to eat

Pwllheli SH3735 PLAS BODEGROES (0758) 612363 Lovely Georgian manor house surrounded by tree-filled grounds with comfortably restful rooms, good food using superb fresh local produce and very good wine list; bedrooms; cl Mon, Nov-Feb; disabled access in restaurant only. **£30** for 5 courses.

Llanberis SH5760 Y BISTRO 43-35 High St (0286) 871278 Friendly, no-smoking restaurant with good local produce used in the Welsh cooking – fine fish; cl Sun, Mon in winter. **£27.**

Llanwrst SH8061 MEADOWSWEET Station Rd (0492) 640732 Good, imaginative cooking in nice little hotel; best to book for lunch. **£24|£11.**

Harlech SH5831 CEMLYN High St (0766) 780425 Very popular unassuming little restaurant with warmly relaxed atmosphere and very good imaginative food – especially the fresh seafood; cl Sun at end of season, Nov-Easter; children over 8; disabled access. **£20.50 for 4 courses.**

Llandudno Junction SH8180 QUEENS HEAD (0492) 546570 Busy but comfortable pub, lots of very good seafood, excellent home-made puddings, good daily specials, interesting evening extras, and decent wines; cl 25 Dec; children over 7. **£17.50|£2.95/£4.95.**

Mold SJ1962 WE THREE LOGGERHEADS (035 285) 337 Carefully refurbished old pub on two levels, good bar food with interesting daily specials; cl 25 Dec pm. **£16|£2.95/£4.95.**

Morfa Nefyn SH2840 BRYNCYNAN Gwynedd (0758) 720879 Comfortable country pub which is buzzing in summer, quiet in winter, with quickly served bar food from soup through fish pie and summer seafood to steaks and good restaurant food; cl Sun, 25 Dec. **£15.75|£15/£6.30.**

Bala SH9236 NEUADD-Y-CYFNOD (OLD SCHOOL RESTAURANT) Trwyddedig Gwynedd (0678) 521269 Relaxed and informal restaurant with huge helpings of good-value food (morning coffee, lunch, tea and dinner), pleasant service, and attractive furnishings; cl Nov-Mar (open from Easter); disabled access. **£9|£1.75/£3.95.**

Llanwnda SH4758 GOAT (0286) 830256 Old-fashioned genuinely Welsh pub with excellent help-yourself cold lunchtime buffet Easter-Sept – **£5** eat as much as you like.

West Wales

This area has quiet appeal, with fine unspoilt coast and interesting places to potter around.

The best of the scenery here is on the coast, which has many extremely attractive stretches and plenty of first-class walking. The most appealing parts are between St David's and Strumble Head near Fishguard (largely unspoilt, full of rocky coves and exhilarating cliff walks), St Bride's Bay (low cliffs flanking surfing beaches), the attractive fishing villages of Solva and Little Haven, the wild places around Marloes, and the civilised small resort of Tenby – formerly a well-fortified medieval town.

St David's is the most interesting place to visit, with its cathedral a real surprise in such rural surroundings, and a good few things to look at nearby. Elsewhere, of the many castles Kidwelly, Carew and Pembroke are particularly impressive. Though there is not a large number of other places to visit, and virtually no 'bright lights' attractions, there's plenty to fill a short stay, with highlights including boat trips to the offshore islands (seabirds and seals), the ancient gold mines at Pumsaint and the woodland garden at Amroth. It's quite a good area for families, with particular attractions at Narberth and St Florence.

On the whole, the inland scenery here, though unspoilt, is less interesting than the coast – mainly pastoral farmland – so there aren't the dramatic scenic drives of North and Mid Wales, but there is a decent amount of pleasant gentle motoring. The best parts are around Brechfa and Abergorlech.

We've nearly doubled our list of recommended places to stay here: prices in this area represent good value for money, and readers have helped us find some very attractive and individual places.

Where to stay

Crugybar SN6537 Glanrannell Park Llanwrda Dyfed SA19 8SA (0558) £56; 8 rms. Surrounded by lawns and overlooking a small private lake in 23 acres of parkland, this peaceful hotel has two comfortable lounges, bar, good food using fresh local produce where possible, and friendly, helpful staff; lots of wildlife, pony-trekking, and fishing; cl Nov-Mar.

Saundersfoot SN1304 Glen Beach Swallow Tree Woods Dyfed SA69 9DE (0834) 813430 £50; 13 rms. Holiday hotel just 3 mins walk through woods to sandy beach, with comfortable lounge bar, log fire, good choice of food using local produce, and garden where you can watch badgers and foxes feeding at night.

Newport SN0539 Cnapan East St Dyfed SA42 0WF (0239) 820575 *£48; 5 rms. Attractively furnished and homely little family-run hotel with very friendly owners, decent food (lots of vegetarian dishes), and relaxed atmosphere; lovely countryside and coastal walks nearby; cl 24-26 Dec, Feb; in winter, except for residents, the restaurant's open only at wknds.

Broad Haven SM8614 DRUIDSTONE Haverfordwest SA62 3NE (0437) 781221 **£46**; 9 rms sharing bthrms (and 4 holiday cottages, 2 with wheelchair access). Alone on coast above effectively private beach with exhilarating cliff walks, this roomy and very informally friendly hotel with something of a folk-club and Outward Bound feel at times, is extremely winning and relaxing if you take to its unique combination of good wholesome and often memorably inventive food, slightly fend-for-yourself approach amid elderly furniture and plumbing, and glorious seaside surroundings. All sorts of unusual sporting activities inc sand-yachting. Restaurant cl Sun (but bar food available then); cl Mon-Weds nights for 6 wks from 1 Nov and 6 wks from 5 Jan; don't go on spec – strongly advised to book for accommodation and meals.

Carew SN0403 OLD STABLE COTTAGE Tenby Dyfed SA70 8SL (0646) 651889 **£45**; 3 rms. Originally a stable and carthouse for the castle, this attractive place has an inglenook fireplace and original bread oven, games room, conservatory overlooking the garden, and good Aga-cooked food; cl Dec-Feb.

Mynydd-y-Garreg SN4308 GWENLLIAN COURT Kidwelly Dyfed SA17 4LW (0554) 890217 ***£45**; 12 rms, most with own bthrm. Family-run hotel in Gwendraeth valley by old tin-working museum with salmon-fishing in river at end of garden, superbly furnished restaurant, big bar with polished floorboards and lots of sofas and cane furniture; good choice of food, and friendly service.

Nevern SN0840 TREWERN ARMS Newport Dyfed SA42 0NB (0239) 820395 **£45**; 9 rms. Welcoming creeper-clad old inn in pleasant riverside hamlet near interesting pilgrims' church, with good, generously served food, and atmospheric slate-floored bar.

Pontfaen SN0134 TREGYNON COUNTRY FARMHOUSE Gwaun Valley Fishguard Dyfed SA65 9TU (0239) 820531 **£45**; 8 rms. Peacefully set 16th-c farmhouse on valley edge in lovely unspoilt countryside with lots of wildlife and walks, big inglenook fireplace in beamed lounge, friendly welcome, and very good, imaginative additive-free food using own and produce from neighbouring farms, home-smoked meats, and home-made preserves.

Fishguard SM9537 MANOR HOUSE Dyfed SA65 9HG (0348) 873260 **£42**; 7 comfortable rms. Georgian house with fine views of harbour, well-planned basement restaurant with good choice of home-made food; cl 24-28 Dec.

Brechfa SN5230 FOREST ARMS Carmarthen Dyfed SA32 7RA (0267) 202339 **£40**; 4 comfortable, good-value rms, shared bthrm. Simply renovated and spotless stonebuilt village inn with generous home cooking, unusually big inglenook fireplace in its flagstoned bar, quick, cheerful family service, lovely walking and wildlife around.

Pen-y-Cwm SM8423 LOCHMEYLER FARM Llandeloy Haverfordwest Dyfed SA62 6LL (0348) 837724 **£40**; 10 rms. Attractive 16th-c farmhouse on 220-acre working dairy farm, two lounges (one is no smoking), log fires, traditional farmhouse cooking in pleasant dining room, and mature garden; can walk around the farm trails; children over 10; disabled access.

Rhydlewis SN3447 BRONIWAN Llandysul Dyfed SA44 5PF (0239) 851261 **£32**; 2 pretty rms, 1 with own bthrm. Grey stone house with pine-panelled windows on small farm surrounded by beech and pine trees, fine views of the Preseli Hills in the distance; lots of wildlife, sandy coast 10 mins drive, can help with calves, hens, and cows, and stone barn with games, table tennis and books; woodburning stove in comfortable sitting room, separate dining room, and good, naturally produced food from garden and farm; no smoking; children over 5.

St David's SM7525 TY OLAF Mount Gdns Dyfed SA62 6BS (0437) 720885 *£27; 3 rms. Pleasant, well-run modern bungalow that takes guests who enjoy being part of the owners' home; good service; cl Nov-Easter; disabled access.

To see and do

❀ **Amroth** SN1607 COLBY WOODLAND GARDEN Beautiful woodland gardens in sheltered valley – very pleasant and colourful; snacks, shop, limited disabled access; cl Nov-Mar; £2.50. The New Inn down on the seafront is good for family lunch.

✝ **Bosherston** SR9694 ST GOVAN'S CHAPEL Simple, recently reroofed 14th-c ruin, included for its exciting position halfway down the sea cliffs, down rough rock steps; the former holy well just below has now dried up. The St Govan's pub up at the village is useful for lunch.

Carew SN0403 CAREW CASTLE AND TIDAL MILL This magnificent Norman castle was the setting for the Great Tournament of 1507. The mill is one of just three restored tidal mills in Britain, with records dating back to 1558; there's a new exhibition on the story of milling. Shop, limited disabled access; cl Nov-Easter; £2 both, £1.40 each. It's a very nice spot, and by the friendly Carew Inn nearby is the Carew Cross, an impressive 13-ft Celtic cross dating from the 11th c.

Carmarthen SN4120 Busy regional market town, according to legend the birthplace of Merlin: an old tree once stood in the centre and the saying was 'When Merlin's Oak shall tumble down, then shall fall Carmarthen town'. Nothing gets in the way of modern road planners and down came the tree – it's preserved in a glass case but some still say modern additions to the town have fulfilled the prophecy. There are the remains of a 13th-c castle, and just out of town at Abergwili SN4321 the CARMARTHEN MUSEUM. Housed in the old palace of the Bishop of St David's, very good displays on local history from the Romans, and crafts such as butter-making or pottery. Surrounded by 7 acres of attractive grounds; shop, disabled access to ground floor only; cl Sun, 24 Dec-1 Jan, Good Fri. The Salutation and Crescelly Arms along the A40 E at Pont ar Gothi are good for lunch.

Castell Henllys SN1139 (signed off A487 E of Newport) Iron-Age hill fort in beautiful countryside overlooking River Gwaun, with interesting reconstruction of three big conical roundhouses along lines suggested by excavations here, also a forge, smithy, primitive looms and a herb garden; snacks, shop; cl Nov-Mar; £1.60.

Cilgerran SN1943 CASTLE Picturesquely placed on a crag above the River Teifi, this twin-towered Plantagenet fortress has good views from its towers and high walls, though, as usual, you have to go up a spiral staircase to see them; shop; cl am Sun in winter; £1.25. The CARDIGAN WILDLIFE PARK was closed as we went to press, but hopes to reopen in some form in 1994. The ancient Pendre is useful for lunch.

Dre-Fach Felindre SN6416 MUSEUM OF THE WELSH WOOLLEN INDUSTRY Part of the National Museum of Wales, a fascinating museum with a collection of textile machinery and tools dating back to the 18th c. There are also displays on the industry from the Middle Ages, factory trails and demonstrations of fabric-making; snacks, shop, disabled access; cl Sun and Sat too in winter; *£1. Not far from Llandybie, and the Red Lion.

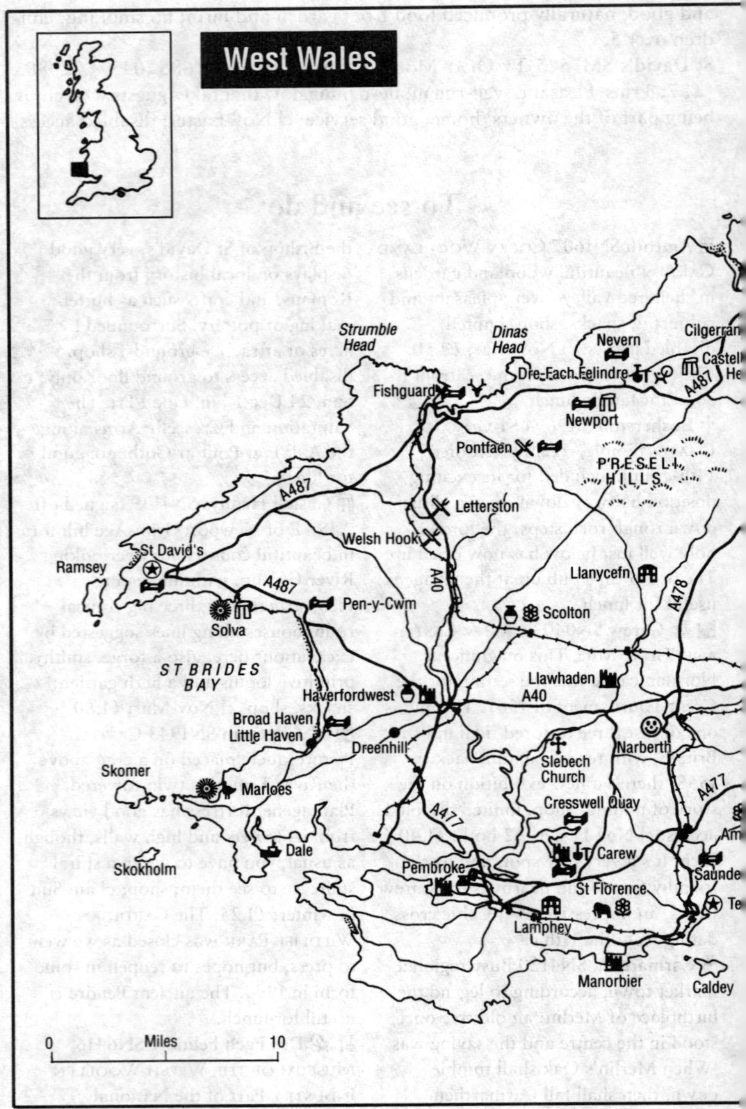

Fishguard SM9537 is a dual-character town, with an old fishing harbour surrounded by appropriately small streets of terraced cottages, and an entirely separate big commercial harbour used by the Irish ferries. In between, the upper town has some attractive old buildings, and is pleasant to saunter through. You can drive or walk up on to the high headland which protects the harbour; its cliffs are quite grand, particularly where the seas boil through the narrow neck cutting off the rock on which Strumble Head lighthouse stands – down on the rocks there you quite often see seals, even in

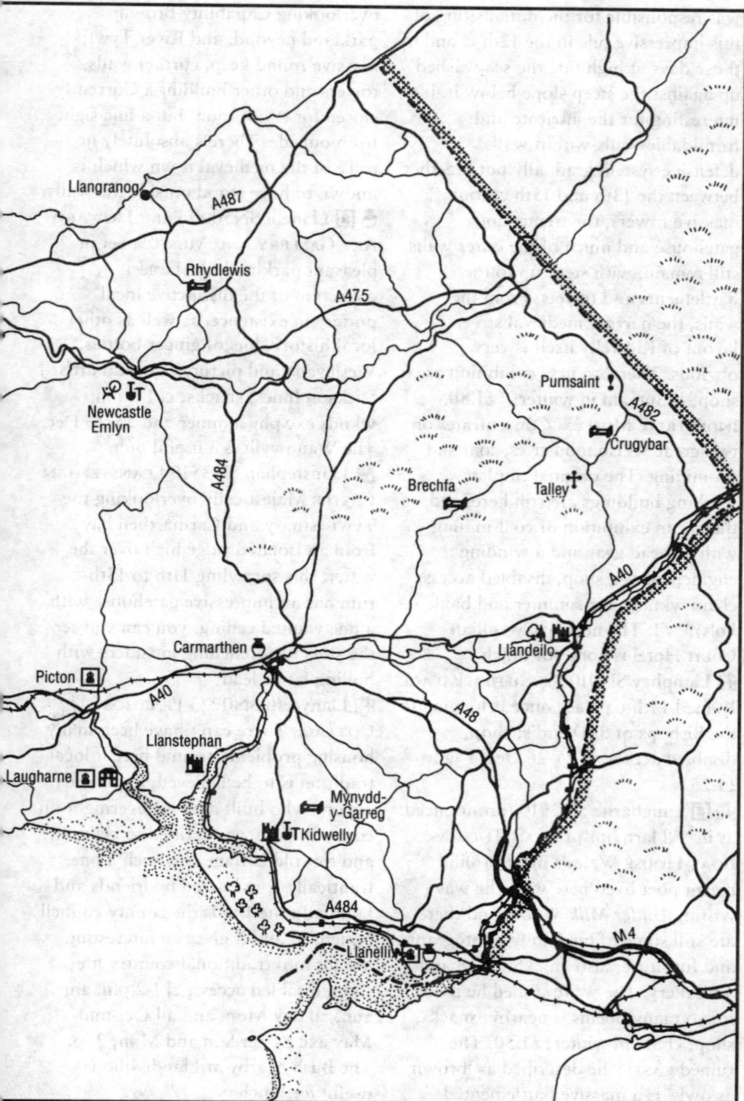

the spring, though they're more common in late summer.

Haverfordwest SM9515 HAVERFORDWEST CASTLE, MUSEUM, ART GALLERY AND RECORD OFFICE As the name suggests, quite a busy complex, and that's much as it's always been; the 12th-c ruins were used as a jail and police headquarters before becoming a museum. Shop, disabled access; cl Sun, 24 Dec-New Year, Good Fri; 50p. The George in Market St and Market Trader down by the water are useful for lunch.

Kidwelly SN4006 KIDWELLY CASTLE Roger, Bishop of Salisbury, was responsible for the initial siting of this impressive pile in the 12th c, and in those days at high tide the sea washed up against the steep slope below it. It's interesting for the intricate and formidable walls-within-walls defensive system gradually put together between the 13th and 15th c: four massive towers, the tremendous gatehouse and much of the outer walls still remain, with steps up to the battlements and turrets. From the walls, the narrow medieval street layout of Kidwelly itself is very obvious. There's a new exhibition area; shop; cl Sun am in winter; *£1.80. INDUSTRIAL MUSEUM Concentrates on two great Welsh industries, coal and tin-mining. The original tinplate working buildings are still here, and there's an exhibition of coal-mining with pithead gear and a winding engine; snacks, shop, disabled access; cl am wknds (exc summer and bank hols); *£1. The nearby Gwenllian Court Hotel is good for lunch.

Lamphey SN0100 LAMPHEY PALACE Ruined 13th-c palace once belonging to the Bishops of St David's; shop, disabled access; cl 25-26 Dec, 1 Jan; £1.25.

Laugharne SN2910 (pronounced as in 'I'll larn 'im') DYLAN THOMAS' BOAT HOUSE Wales's most prolific recent poet lived here while he was writing *Under Milk Wood*, and there are still some of his family photographs and furniture; also an exhibition and art gallery. The writing shed he used for so many poems is nearby; snacks, shop; cl Sat in winter; £1.50. The ruined CASTLE he described as 'brown as owls' is a massive battlemented compilation of styles from the 12th to 16th c, giving views of the estuary; it's currently closed for restoration, but you can see the outside.

Llandeilo SN6200 DINEFWR CASTLE (20 mins' walk from riverside lodge at S edge of town; follow Dyfed Wildlife Trust path) Isolated, largely 13th-c castle on wooded hill overlooking Capability Brown parkland beyond, and River Tywi; massive round keep, curtain walls, towers and other buildings. Currently closed for restoration, but a fine sight from outside. There's absolutely no trace of the medieval town which is known to have stood outside the walls.

Llanelli SN5000 PARC HOWARD ART GALLERY AND MUSEUM Set in pleasant parkland, the largest collection of the distinctive local pottery in existence, as well as other local history, lots of ginger bottles, Wesleyana and pictures by local artist J Dickson Innes; snacks; cl 1-2 pm, wknds exc pm summer and 25-26 Dec. The Waunwyllt is a useful pub.

Llanstephan SN3510 LLANSTEPHAN CASTLE Majestically overlooking the Tywi estuary and Carmarthen bay from an isolated ridge high over the water, this sprawling 11th to 13th-c ruin has an impressive gatehouse with a fine vaulted ceiling; you can still see the slots for drenching intruders with boiling fat or lead.

Llanycefn SN0923 PENRHOS COTTAGE There can't have been many housing problems around here if local tradition is to be believed; apparently anyone who built a house overnight on common land was entitled to claim it, and this old cottage was such a one, frantically constructed by friends and family. In the 1960s the county council bought it, and it gives an interesting insight into traditional country life; shop, disabled access; cl 1-2 pm, am Sun, all day Mon, and all Oct-mid-May exc Easter Sun and Mon; 20p. The Bush nearby at Llandissilio is useful for lunch.

Llawhaden SN0617 LLAWHADEN CASTLE 12th-c castle surrounded by deep moat, with the remains of the 13th and 14th-c bishop's hall, kitchen and bakehouse. The Post Office nearby sells guides and postcards.

Manorbier SS0697 MANORBIER CASTLE Unusual for a Welsh castle in that it's still in the hands of the family who have owned it for over 300 years, this impressive partly 12th-c castle looking down to the beach has massive medieval outer walls and an early round tower, with a 13th-c chapel and other buildings, and more modern buildings within the walls; shop; cl Oct-Apr; *£1.40. The quiet village is attractive, and there's a striking view of the castle from the church. The Castle Inn is useful for lunch.

Marloes SM7908 DEER PARK Not actually a deer park, but a wild cliffy headland a couple of miles west, joined to the mainland by quite a narrow isthmus showing steep Iron-Age defences; a place to watch birds (choughs breed here) and maybe seals on the offshore rocks. The Lobster Pot in Marloes is a useful and informal family pub.

Narberth SN1114 OAKWOOD ADVENTURE AND LEISURE PARK Lively theme park in 80 acres of landscaped countryside, with lots of rides and attractions, boats on the lake and a theatre; meals and snacks, shop, disabled access; cl wkdys in Oct (exc half-term), all Nov-Easter; £6.95. The Coach & Horses does good cheap snacks.

Newcastle Emlyn SN3040 FELIN GERI MILL One of the last cornmills in the UK to use completely traditional methods of production; visitors can see them all, and there's also a sawmill and museum, craft shops and trout ponds; meals and snacks, shop, some disabled access; cl Nov-Easter; £2.

Newport SN0937 PENTRE IFAN BURIAL CHAMBER (N of Brynberian off B4329) Ancient long barrow with the old capstone, three uprights and a circular forecourt. The Trewern Arms in the interesting old village of Nevern to the north is good for lunch.

Pembroke SM9801 PEMBROKE CASTLE The birthplace of Henry VII and thus the Tudor dynasty, this impressive 13th-c castle is largely intact, and its endless passages, tunnels and stairways are great fun to explore. There's a good visitor centre too; snacks, shop, disabled access; cl 25-26 Dec, 1 Jan; £2. MUSEUM OF THE HOME All sorts of everyday objects from the past three hundred years in a pleasant domestic setting; cl wknds and all Oct-Apr; *£1.20. The Pembroke Ferry by the water at the foot of the bridge over the estuary is good for lunch, inc imaginative fish dishes, and the Watermans Arms, also nicely sited with lovely castle views, is good value.

Picton Castle SN2717 GRAHAM SUTHERLAND GALLERY A large collection of Sutherland's incredible paintings, many reflecting his self-declared obsession with Wales. Part of the National Museum of Wales, with regular special events and exhibitions; meals, snacks, shop, disabled access; cl 12.30-1.30 pm, all day Mon, all Oct-Mar; *£1.

! **Pumsaint** SN6540 DOLAUCOTHI GOLD MINES 2,000 years of gold-mining are the focus of this unique mine, used since Roman times; tours of both the Roman adits and the deeper 1930s workings complete with miners' lamps and helmets. There's a good visitor centre; snacks, shop; cl Nov-Mar, underground tours late May-late Sept; £4.50 for full tours. Out of season you can still get to much of the site.

St David's SM7525 The cathedral here can boast a longer continuous settlement than any other in Britain, but thanks to the relative inaccessibility of the place, St David's hasn't developed in the way one might have expected, and today it seems little more than a village. CATHEDRAL The Norman building on the site of an earlier Celtic monastery had largely collapsed by the 15th c and elaborate repairs had to be made; the new roof is an impressive lace-like oak affair, and oak features in most of the rest of the church. There's a fine collection of Celtic sculptured crosses. Shop, disabled access. Lots of colourful flowers in spring. BISHOPS PALACE

Impressive ruins of what was clearly the very grand main residence of the bishops. Lots of quadrangles, stairways and splendid arcaded walls, with all sorts of intricate and often entertaining details (like the carvings below the arcaded parapets); there's a good exhibition of the history of the site. It's a very atmospheric and tranquil place, particularly out of season when you may have it largely to yourself; shop, limited disabled access; cl 25-26 Dec, 1 Jan; £1.50. OCEANARIUM A very good insight into sea and shore life; highlights include the shark tank and the rock pool, where you can see a variety of marine creatures; meals and snacks, shop, limited disabled access; *£2.25. In summer there are boat trips to rocky RAMSEY ISLAND, where seabirds nest in great numbers. About ½ mile away is the reputed birthplace of St Non, the mother of St David; there are lovely sea views from the very scant ruins of the CHAPEL here, signed down a track from the useful St Non's Hotel, with a holy well nearby. The area is extremely rich in ancient sites, such as the neolithic burial chambers up by St David's Head or over towards Solva, and the ramparts of the coastal hill forts right on the point of St David's Head and overlooking Caerfai Bay just south of the town. It's a good place for coastal walks – always something interesting to see, whether it's a prehistoric monument or a bird you can't quite make out. The Old Cross Hotel near the cathedral is a civilised place for lunch, and the Farmers Arms is cheap and cheerful; recently we've also had quite promising reports on the Sea Breeze (good sea views) and Grove.

St Florence SM0801 MANOR HOUSE WILDLIFE AND LEISURE PARK Over 25 acres of wooded grounds and gardens with exotic birds, reptiles and fish, a pets' corner, playground, model railway and twice-daily falconry displays (not Sat); meals, snacks, shop, disabled access; cl Oct-Easter; *£3.50.

Scolton SM9822 SCOLTON MANOR MUSEUM Early Victorian mansion showing the history and natural history of the Pembrokeshire area, with newly opened period rooms. The 60 acres of grounds have fine trees and shrubs; snacks, shop, disabled access; cl Mon (exc bank hols), all Oct-Apr; *50p.

✝ **Slebech Church** SN0313 (off A40 5 miles E of Haverfordwest; though there is a track from the main road, it's best to turn down the A4075, take the next right turn and park by the mill, walk over the bridge and down the track through the woods above the river). Gloriously isolated ruined 12th-c church, formerly a temple of the Knights Hospitaller, by the tidal waters of the East Cleddau.

Solva SM8024 One of the prettiest villages on the coast, with a great deal of character. On the opposite bank from the harbour a high crag (enclosed by the ramparts of an Iron-Age fort) gives pretty views of the attractive little fishing village and the coast. The Cambrian Arms does good food – a mix of Italian and Welsh – and the Ship near the harbour is a good cosy fishermen's pub; the Harbour House on the harbour is also worth knowing for food.

✝ **Talley** SN6332 TALLEY ABBEY Ruins of once-magnificent 12th-c abbey, still looking good, especially the two pointed archways.

Tenby SN1300 is a pleasantly restrained family seaside resort, with sheltered beaches, rock coves, and little tat. It's a walled town, the splendidly preserved 13th-c wall still having many of its towers left, and a magnificent 14th-c arched barbican gateway; a moat used to run the whole length of what is now a tree-lined street. There are some 13th-c remains of the CASTLE on the headland above the yachting harbour – sections of wall, watch-towers, and gateway. Within the castle site is a good local-history and geology MUSEUM, with changing exhibitions on local themes such as the town's development as a seaside resort or the local lifeboat, and interesting finds from several of the West Wales prehistoric sites. Also an art gallery with a collection of Augustus and Gwen John; shop; cl 12-2 pm and winter wknds; *£1. TUDOR MERCHANT'S HOUSE Fine example of gabled 15th-c architecture, good Flemish chimney and the remains of frescoes on three walls; shop; cl Sat and all Nov-Mar; £1.60. St Mary's is an interesting 13th-c CHURCH with a huge steeple and a plaque commemorating a local invention that many of us use every day – the equals sign. There are summer boat trips to CALDY ISLAND, still a monastic island, where the Cistercian monks have good cream and honey for sale, as well as more durable crafts. Besides the modern abbey, there is a 13th-c church with a simple cobbled floor, still in use, on one side of the small cloister of the original priory; these ancient priory buildings (which you can see from outside but not enter) give a better sense of the past than almost anywhere else in West Wales. In the church is a stone with Ogam writing dating back to the Dark Ages, as well as a later Latin inscription, supporting the belief that there has been some sort of holy place here for 1,500 years. Much older, back on the mainland, is HOYLES MOUTH CAVE (off A4139 just SW, Trefloyne Lane towards St Florence; short path through wood on left after 500 yds). Running more than 100 ft back into the hillside, this spooky place has yielded Ice-Age mammoth bones, as well as human tools dating back over 10,000 years. Take a torch; don't go in winter, which would disturb the hibernating bats. The Lamb is useful for lunch.

Particularly worth a visit are the three islands of **Skomer** SM7209, **Skokholm** SM7305 and, much further out to sea, **Grassholme** SM5909, all of which can be reached by boats run by the National Parks. Skomer has 720 acres of spectacular wild scenery with countless birds and flowers, as well as seals playing on the shore – maybe common seals briefly in Jun or July, more likely grey seals and their pups in Sept and Oct; it's also remarkable for the easily traced remains of the Iron-Age settlement here – there's a well-laid-out trail. It's currently popular with birdwatchers thanks to the presence of several breeding pairs of short-eared owls. Grassholm is notable for its 30,000 pairs of gannets. Skokholm has Britain's first bird observatory. Sailing times from Dale Sailing Co, (0646) 601636. In Dale SM8005, where the boats usually leave from, the Griffin overlooking the anchorage is useful for lunch.

Two other delightful **seaside villages**, both with decent pubs right by the sea, are Little Haven SM8512 and Llangranog SN3054. Pubs and inns doing food elsewhere that are noteworthy for their fine positions include the Forest Arms at Brechfa SN5230, Cresselly Arms at Cresswell Quay SN0406, Denant Mill at Dreenhill SM9214 and Sailors Safety at Pwllgwaelod at the foot of Dinas Head SN0139.

Walks

The best of the area's walks are along sections of the **Pembrokeshire Coast Path**, which snakes around the intricate Pembrokeshire seaboard. In the S, the lily ponds at **Bosherston** SR9694 merit a diversion off the path. Just W of here is the oddly sited hermit's chapel beneath the cliff by St Govan's Head SR9792. At the entrance to the huge natural harbour of Milford Haven, the **Dale penin-**

sula SM8103, with gentle level-topped terrain, gives views of the shipping activities, reducing the giant oil tankers to a pleasantly toy-like scale. With the **Marloes peninsula** SM7708 to the W, similarly gentle above its cliffs, it supplies memorable walkers' routes that need only minimal inland walking to complete the circuit – from Marloes' peninsula, Skomer Island is in sight.

There are some attractive sandy-floored rock coves to explore around **Little Haven** SM8512 and the Druidstone Hotel SM8616 to the N; with, N of that, the long sweep of sand and surf at Newgale Sands SM8421. The fishing village of **Solva** SM8024 occupies a narrow, precipitous creek – very picturesque: there's a good, interesting, shortish path E from here to **Dinas Fawr** SM8022, the opposite headland.

From the cathedral city of **St David's** SM7525, paths lead S to St Non's chapel on the coast; W, **St Justinian** SM7225 (there is yet another chapel here) looks over Ramsey Island. **St David's Head** SM7227 is noticeably more rugged; from the top of Carn Ledi, the moorland hill close by the coast path, you can often see Ireland.

Strumble Head SM8941 (where there is a car park near the lighthouse) typifies the rocky, big-dipper coastline of northern Pembrokeshire. **Dinas Head** SN0041 is a nice miniature headland which takes about an hour to tour.

In Cardigan Bay, **Cemaes Head** SN1350 gives good views over the mouth of the Teifi estuary and out over the Irish Sea. Cardiganshire lacks a coast path for much of the way, but the fishing village of **Llangranog** SN3054 offers a pleasant stroll to a headland to the N.

Inland, the **Mynydd Preseli** or Prescelly Hills SN1032 give pleasant walks with some interesting views on largely unspoilt moors capped by ancient cairns and other antiquities. The lusher **Gwaun Valley** offers pretty walks along the wooded river either upstream or downstream of Pontfaen SN0234.

Driving

The most memorable scenery for drivers in this area is well inland, along the attractive B4310 through Brechfa and Abergorlech; particularly between these two villages, the countryside is reminiscent of alpine or Pyrenean foothills, with a good mix of forest, valley, river and mountain views. Meeting this road at Llansawel is another good varied hill road, the B4337, which links with the B4302 along the Dulais Valley from Llandeilo. More or less along the boundary of what we've described as West Wales is the A482 from Llanwrda to Lampeter (not quick, but a good hill road), and on to Aberaeron.

On the coast between St David's and Fishguard, the slow road through Llanrhian, Trevine and Abercastle gives some good sea views. Inland from Fishguard, the B4313 runs up into the lonely Prescelly Hills with some far views, and the left turn on to the B4329 down to Eglyswrw is an attractive little-travelled road, also with some good views. The little back road off the B4313 running through the Cwm Gwaun valley is quite delightful: intricate, rather lush pastoral scenery with lots of ancient woodland, a marked contrast to the rest of the area. If you're travelling from Newport to Cardigan, the B4582 is a good short cut.

Near Cardigan, an attractive drive off the A478 S takes you through Cilgerran then bears left towards Llechryd: turn right just before the Llechryd bridge to follow the River Teifi, then cross the B4332 at Penrhiw to run almost due S on very narrow country roads to the B4299 at Trelech. A very different sort of road in much the same area is the surprisingly fast one all the way from the E end of Whitland on the A40 following the ridge route up to Tegryn (the highest village in the former county of Pembrokeshire), and on through Boncath on the B4332 to meet the A478 a little S of Cardigan.

Along the southern coast to the SW corner there's little memorable driving, as the country's either too flat or too hedged to give many views; this stretch of coast is altogether better for walkers. However, the little back roads twisting around the complex estuary inland from Pembroke are pleasant for pottering (especially around Carew and Cresswell Quay). At the mouth of Milford Haven, the roads down to Dale Point and St Ann's Head off the B4327 are worth taking if you're in the area, as are the coastal lanes around Little Haven and Broad Haven, running up above the surfing beaches from Nolton Haven to Newgale on the A487.

Where to eat

Pontfaen SN0134 GELLI FAWR COUNTRY HOUSE Dyfed (0239) 820343 Outstanding food served in very generous helpings; must book and best to phone for winter closing dates; comfortable bedrooms too; disabled access. **£22.50|£2.95/£4.65.**

Welsh Hook SM9327 STONE HALL Dyfed (0348) 840212 Imaginative French food and fine wines in 14th-c house; bedrooms too; cl Mon, Tues-Sun am, 3 wks Nov-Dec, 26 Dec. **£20.50.**

Letterston SM9429 SOMETHING COOKING Dyfed (A40 5 miles S of Fishguard) (0348) 840621 Outstanding fish restaurant and very reasonable prices; cl Sun, 24 Dec for one wk. **£11.40|£3.50.**

MID WALES

Excellent for a really quiet break, this region has splendid unspoilt scenery, with a limited but interesting choice of places to visit.

If not quite up to the very best that Snowdonia and the West Wales coast can offer, this area does have spectacular scenery and well-above-average walking, with plenty of it. Its advantage over those other two areas is that in summer it's much less visited: it's one of the best parts of Britain for a really quiet break. There is no proliferation of off-the-shelf amusements, but the area does have a handful of particularly interesting places to visit: Powis Castle at Welshpool; the unique Centre for Alternative Technology near Machynlleth; Hay-on-Wye, with its millions of secondhand and antiquarian books; the showcaves at Abercraf; and the lively silver-lead mine museum near Ponterwyd, close to the beauty spot of Devils Bridge. The castles which dominate the other parts of Wales peter out here – this part of Wales was simply too wild for the invaders to reckon with, but there are a couple of good scenic steam railways, from Aberystwyth and from Llanfair Caerinion.

For drivers as well as for walkers, there's lots to discover here. Little-used mountain roads gingerly penetrate the huge tracts of forest and moorland around the Llyn Briane reservoir, and the reservoirs above the Elan Valley, giving access both to the hardier walkers and to those who stay firmly in their cars. Other kinder ranges of hills tempt out more people, most notably the western Black Mountain, the Brecon Beacons and the eastern Black Mountains, as well as the range stretching all the way up the borders from Brecon to the Kerry hills and beyond.

A change of mood down in the valleys centres on a string of inland spas or former spa towns surrounded by hills, dignified and slightly old-fashioned in the style of many such places on the Continent. Llandrindod Wells is the most prominent, but Builth Wells and the much smaller Llanwrtyd Wells share the same character; Llanidloes (with its Elizabethan timbered market hall, unique for Wales) and Presteigne are also attractive small towns with some interesting buildings. The area's river valleys are among the finest in Wales: the friendly Usk, the rather more imposing Upper Wye, and above Aberystwyth, the beautiful Vale of Rheidol.

A good choice of places to stay spans a wide range of prices: you can be sure of comfort indoors, even if part of your reason for being here is to enjoy all the discomfort of the great outdoors.

Where to stay

Llyswen SO1337 LLANGOED HALL Brecon Powys LD3 0YP (0874) 754525 ***£135**; 23 very pretty rms with luxurious touches. Fine, partly 16th-c house, beautifully converted into a first-class hotel with lovely house-party atmosphere, handsome hall, elegant and spacious public rooms with antiques, fresh flowers and views over the grounds, imaginative food, and very good Welsh breakfasts; marvellous surrounding countryside; children over 8.

Eglwysfach SN6996 YNYSHIR HALL Machynlleth Powys SY20 8TA (0654) 781209 **£95**; 9 rms. Carefully run old manor house in landscaped gardens adjoining the Ynyshir bird reserve, with antiques, log fires and paintings in the light and airy public rooms, extremely good food using home-grown vegetables, and thoughtful service; children over 9; partial disabled access.

Presteigne SO3265 RADNORSHIRE ARMS Powys LD8 2BE (0544) 267406 **£92**; 16 rms. Rambling, handsomely timbered 17th-c Forte hotel with elegantly moulded beams and fine dark panelling in the lounge bar; polite, attentive service, and decent food and wines.

Llandrindod Wells SO0561 METROPOLE Temple St Powys LD1 5DY (0597) 823700 **£77**; 122 rms. Run by the same family for over a c, this big hotel has spacious public rooms and good food in bar and restaurant; disabled access.

Aberdovey SN6296 PENHELIG ARMS Gwynedd LL35 0LT (0654) 767215 ***£68**; 10 comfortable rms. Carefully refurbished building in fine position overlooking sea with cosy bar, pleasant dining room, popular food, and good wine list; lovely views of Dyfy Estuary; no accom 25-26 Dec.

Montgomery SO2296 DRAGON Market Square Powys SY15 6AA (0686) 668359 **£67**; 15 rms. Attractive, welcoming small hotel with pleasant grey-stone tiled hall, comfortable bar, good bar and restaurant food, and welcoming licensees; swimming pool.

Crickhowell SO2118 GLIFFAES COUNTRY HOUSE Powys NP8 1RH (0874) 730371 ***£65**; 22 rms. Run by the same family for over 40 years with an enjoyably informal and relaxed atmosphere, comfortable, homely public rooms, good food and cheerful staff; wonderfully quiet, peaceful surroundings; cl 5 Jan-25 Feb.

Llangurig SN8482 GLANSEVERN ARMS Llanidloes Powys SY18 6SY (055 15) 240 **£55**; 8 rms. Welcoming inn 1,050 ft up among hills and forests of upper Wye valley, with good restaurant, log fires, cosy bar, and lots of books in lounge; cl 1 wk over Christmas; 1 mile of private fishing on River Wye.

Cwmystwyth SN7974 HAFOD LODGE Aberystwyth Dyfed (0974) 282247 ***£50**; 3 rms. Comfortable and spacious late 18th-c house in lovely scenery with log fires, generous helpings of good food (lovely home-made bread, unusual picnics and candlelit dinners), and fine, friendly service; from the terrace you may be able to watch the rare red kite.

Llyswen SO1337 GRIFFIN Brecon Powys LD3 0UR (0874) 754241 ***£50**; 8 rms. Old-fashioned and warmly welcoming inn with very good food in no-smoking restaurant (brook trout and salmon caught by the family, local game in season), interesting, comfortable bar, and helpful service; cl 25-26 Dec.

Newbridge-on-Wye SO0158 NEW INN Powys LD1 6HY (059 789) 211 ***£50**; 7 rms. Friendly, well-modernised old village inn nicely set in upper Wye Valley; generous lunchtime hot dishes, good evening restaurant, spacious carpeted back lounge, public bar, and welcoming licensees; cl 25 Dec pm.

Llanwrtyd Wells SN8746 CWMIRFON LODGE Powys LD5 4TN (059 13) 217 ***£48**; 2 comfortable rms. Former sporting lodge in 3 acres of grounds adjoining Forestry Commission land, with woodburning stove in the sitting room, attractive dining room with open fire, very good food, and extremely friendly atmosphere; cl Christmas; no children; also do self-catering.

Aberdovey SN6296 BODFOR Sea Front Gwynedd LL36 0EA (0654) 767475 **£46**; 16 rms with showers. Small, family-run hotel on sea front with bar, good restaurant food, and very good service; cl 22 Dec-3 Jan.

Crickhowell SO2118 BEAR Powys NP8 1BW (0873) 810408 **£40**; 33 rms, the back ones are the best. Particularly friendly coaching inn with good civilised atmosphere, excellent food (Welsh specialities as well), some fine wines and ports, and lots of antiques, deeply comfortable seats, and a roaring log fire in the heavily beamed lounge; disabled access; dogs welcome.

Hay-on-Wye SO2342 OLD BLACK LION Hereford Powys HR3 5AD (0497) 820841 **£39.90**; 10 rms. Ancient town inn with good food in restaurant and bar (inc vegetarian), low beams and black panelling, and close to fishing (private salmon and trout fishing) and riding; children over 5; limited disabled access.

Carno SN9697 ALEPPO MERCHANT Caersws Powys SY17 5LL (0686) 420210 ***£35**; 6 rms, shared bthrm. Welcoming and reliable 17th-c inn with decent food inc vegetarian and Indian dishes, and comfortably modernised rooms; no children.

Cwmdu SO1823 FARMERS ARMS Crickhowell Powys NP8 1RU (0874) 730464 ***£35**; 2 rms. Welcoming cottagey pub with decent bar food, pleasant staff, tables in big garden, and handy for Black Mountains; cl 24-26 Dec.

Felinfach SO0833 TREHENRY FARM Brecon LD3 0LN (0874) 754312 **£34**; 3 rms. 18th-c farmhouse on 200-acre farm with lovely views of Black Mountains and Brecon Beacons; inglenook fireplaces, beams, TV lounge, good food, and large garden.

Church Stoke SO2794 Drewin Farm Montgomery Powys SY15 6TW (0588) 620325 £32; 2 rms, 1 with own bthrm. Attractive 17th-c farmhouse with lovely views, warm welcome, comfortable lounge, dining room and games room with snooker table in converted granary; Offa's Dyke footpath runs through the mixed farm of sheep, cattle and crops; cl Dec-Feb.

Newtown SO1191 Lower Gwestydd Powys SY16 3AY (0686) 626718 £32; 3 rms. Traditional 17th-c black-and-white half-timbered house in lovely countryside and on 200 acres of mainly sheep and arable land; comfortable lounge and dining room, and good food using their own chicken, home-grown fruit and veg, and Welsh lamb; can wander around farm; cl Christmas.

Pennal SH7000 Gogarth Hall Farm Machynlleth Powys SY20 9LB (0654) 7911235 £32; 2 rms, shared bthrm. Mid-18th-c house on working farm of suckler cows and sheep with marvellous views of Dovey Estuary, dining room and lounge, and guests welcome to walk around farm; babysitting available; self-catering also.

Rhayader SN9768 Beili Neuadd Powys LD6 5NS (0597) 810211 £32; 3 rms. Charming, partly 16th-c stone-built farmhouse in quiet position with log fires in renovated rooms; fishing, pony-trekking and guided walks all nearby; cl Christmas/New Year; children over 10.

Gladestry SO2355 Royal Oak Kington Powys HR5 3NR (054 422) 669 £30; 3 spotless, well-equipped rms, shared bthrm. Unpretentious, welcoming beamed and flagstoned inn on Offa's Dyke, quiet and relaxing, with welcoming licensees, good home-cooked bar food, refurbished lounge, separate bar, picnic-table sets in lovely secluded garden behind; good breakfasts; cl 25 Dec.

To see and do

Aberdovey SN6296 Attractive, restrained resort with very pleasant sheltered beaches but none of the crowds or tat they usually bring. Legend has it that there's a lost city beneath the sea, inundated by the crashing waves in a great storm 1,500 years ago. Sometimes at night imaginative people can hear the mournful tolling of its bells. Besides the Penhelig Arms Hotel, the Britannia does good food.

Aberystwyth SN5881 Low-key resort with long shingle beaches and sedate cliff railway to large camera obscura high above town. Also a university town, with the National Library of Wales. This specialises in Welsh and Celtic literature, with exhibitions of fine early manuscripts; also art exhibitions, and reserve collections of pictures, music, prints and drawings; snacks, shop, disabled access; cl Sun, bank hols and first full wk Oct. There is a good museum, and one of the very few of Edward I's castles in this part of Wales. Its main attraction for families is the Vale of Rheidol Railway, with steam trains (surprisingly not private, but run by BR) for several miles along the picturesque twists of the Rheidol Valley, with some fine hill views, to the dramatic beauty-spot gorge of Devils Bridge; snacks, disabled access; cl Oct-Easter; £9.80.

Borth SN6090 Animalarium There's a play area for children here but the exhibits should keep them enthralled – all sorts of mammals, birds, reptiles and invertebrates from mice to monkeys; shop, disabled access; cl Nov-mid-Mar; £2.

Brecon SO0428 Brecknock Museum Local history and archaeology, with sections on folk life, decorative arts and natural history; shop, disabled access (prior notice preferred); cl 1-2, Sun Oct-Mar, Christmas-New Year, Good Fri. SOUTH WALES BORDERERS (24TH REGIMENT) MUSEUM This regiment has been awarded 23 Victoria Crosses since it was raised in 1689. An interesting Zulu War Room; shop, disabled access; cl 1-2, all day Sun and Sat too in winter; *70p. The striking Norman priory became a CATHEDRAL in 1923.

Carreg Cennen Castle SN6619 (nr Trapp, SE of Llandeilo) Few castles can boast such an excellent setting as this old place, dramatically dominating its limestone crag high above the river, and overlooking the unspoilt countryside towards the Black Mountains as it has for centuries. Rebuilt in the 13th c (and again in the 19th – you can easily distinguish the new stonework), it has a mysterious passage in the side of the cliff, and there's a rare-breeds farm; snacks, shop; cl 25 Dec; £1.80. The Red Lion over in Llandybie is good for lunch.

Dan-yr-Ogof Showcaves SN8316 (A4067 NE of Abercraf) Lots to do here – for a start, the caves themselves are fascinating, and well lit to bring out the extraordinary rock formations. They include Cathedral showcave which is the largest single chamber in any British showcave, while 3,000 years ago Bone Cave was lived in by humans. But there's also a dinosaur park, artificial ski-slope, museum and audio-visual displays; snacks, shop; cl Nov-Mar; £4.95. The Lion at Defynnog 10 miles or so over the Brecon Beacons is good for lunch.

Devils Bridge SN7477 Pretty bridges and dramatic waterfall, tucked away in an atmospheric wooded gorge. The oldest bridge gave this beauty spot its name, when it was built by the Devil in order to trap an old woman into giving him her soul; she outwitted him. Wordsworth was inspired to write a sonnet after a visit here (see also Driving section below). The entertaining Halfway Inn at Pisgah on the A4120 to Aberystwyth is good for lunch.

Fairbourne SH6114 FAIRBOURNE AND BARMOUTH STEAM RAILWAY Running the 2½ miles to the end of the peninsula and the ferry for Barmouth, this started life in 1890 as a horse-drawn railway used to carry building materials for the seaside resort of Fairbourne; meals, snacks, shop; cl Oct-Easter, (0341) 250362 for timetable; £3.35. The Fairbourne Hotel is quite useful for lunch, as is the attractively set George III along the estuary at Penmaenpool.

Hay-on-Wye SO2342 is a pleasant small town which has become a world centre for secondhand and antiquarian books, with a growing number of antique shops too. The Old Black Lion and Wheatsheaf are useful for lunch. Hay Bluff nearby has lovely walks, and it's within easy reach of the Black Mountains, the Golden Valley over the English border, and the attractive unspoilt countryside just over the Gwent border that we've mentioned in the South Wales section. Besides the fine Old Black Lion, the Kilvert Court (0497) 821042 can be recommended both for food and as a place to stay.

✝ **Llanbister** SO1173 The CHURCH here is interesting, with a chimney instead of the usual tower, and there's an even better one a mile away at Llananno, with an astonishingly elaborate rood screen that wouldn't be out of place in a cathedral.

Llandrindod Wells SO0561 is a civilised inland resort, formerly a spa town: an array of imposing white-rendered buildings on broad avenues and terraces, with elegant flower displays, that comes as a surprise after the empty forested hills around; the pump room has been reopened, and there's a very old-fashioned boating lake. LLANDRINDOD WELLS MUSEUM Displays in this charming little town museum include a good collection of dolls, archaeological finds from the area and a Victoria spa gallery with costumes and 19th-c chemist's equipment; shop,

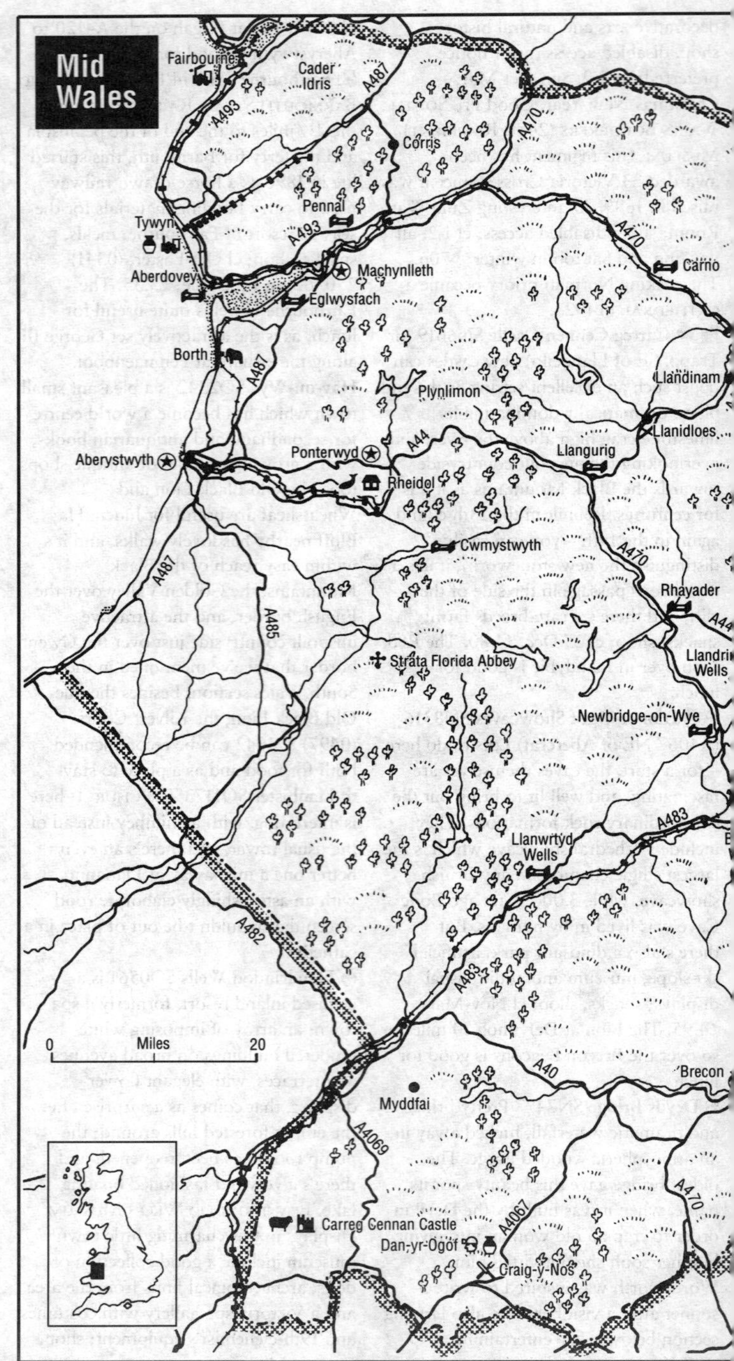
Mid
Wales
Fairbourne
Cader
Idris
A493
A487
Corris
A470
Pennal
Tywyn
A493
Aberdovey
Machynlleth
Eglwysfach
A470
Carno
Borth
A487
Llandinam
Plynlimon
Llanidloes
Llangurig
A44
Aberystwyth
Ponterwyd
Rheidol
Cwmystwyth
A470
Rhayader
A44
A487
A485
Strata Florida Abbey
Llandri
Wells
Newbridge-on-Wye
A483
Llanwrtyd
Wells
A482
A483
0
Miles
20
A40
Brecon
Myddfai
A4069
A470
A4067
Carreg Cennan Castle
Dan-yr-Ogof
Craig-y-Nos

disabled access; cl 12.30-2 pm, winter Sat pm and Sun all day. The Llanerch is good for lunch, and the altogether smarter Metropole Hotel generally does some food all day.

Llanfair Caereinion SJ1006 WELSHPOOL & LLANFAIR LIGHT RAILWAY The track between Welshpool and Llanfair Caerinion is 8 miles long; there are colonial and Austrian steam locomotives among the wide variety of engines operating on this line, and the Welshpool end has an award-winning station reconstruction. Snacks, shop, disabled access; cl Oct-Mar exc Santa Specials, (0938) 810441 for timetable; £6. The Goat is useful for lunch.

Machynlleth SH7400 CENTRE FOR ALTERNATIVE TECHNOLOGY (just outside) Technologies for the improvement of the environment have been researched and displayed here for some 20 years, with demonstrations of windpower, organic gardening and solar energy – you can even ride a water-powered cliff railway. The site, an old slate quarry, overlooks the Snowdonia National Park, and they look after children well; wholesome restaurant, good bookshop, disabled access; cl 24-30 Dec, limited opening in winter; £4.20 inc cliff railway, £3.20 without. The 16th-c PARLIAMENT HOUSE has a display of photographs, relics, models and books depicting Welsh history in the middle ages, with particular emphasis on the rebellion of Owain Glyndwr (it's built on the spot where he held parliament). Also brass-rubbing centre; shop, disabled access; cl 12.30-1.30 pm, all Oct-Easter. The wide main street has a handsome 78-ft 19th-c clock tower, and the White Lion is useful for lunch.

Newtown SO1191 Pleasant rural market town dating back to the 14th c, despite its fringes of light industry and new housing. Museum devoted to Robert Owen, who encouraged the co-operative movement after moving to Scotland, and another devoted to high-street stalwart W H Smith, above their timbered shop which has been restored to the style of the late 1920s. There's also a Textile Museum which concentrates on all aspects of the woollen industry – you need to ask at 7 Commercial St for the key.

Ponterwyd SN7581 LLYWERNOG SILVER-LEAD MINE (A434 just W) Set against a beautiful sweeping mountainside backdrop, regular displays of silver panning, museum, a mine trail, underground tunnel and working water-wheels. This is a busy, lively place: they're constantly improving and expanding the mine workings, with sound and light tableaux now installed underground. You can try panning for Fool's Gold or dowsing for mineral veins; snacks, shop, disabled access (exc underground); cl Nov-Easter; £2.95 museum and site, £3.95 inc underground. BWLCH NANT-YR-ARIAN FOREST VISITOR CENTRE (Llanafan) Forest walks in the vicinity – this centre interprets all aspects of the forest; shop, disabled access; cl Oct-Easter. The Dyffryn Castell in the spectacular valley to the east is good for lunch.

Rheidol SN7178 HYDRO-ELECTRIC SCHEME Guided tours of power station with its unexpected fish farm, also good nature trails, scenic lakes and reservoirs, trout fishing; shop, limited disabled access; cl Oct-Apr; £1.70.

Strata Florida Abbey SN7566 This Cistercian abbey was an important centre of learning in the Middle Ages, but now little remains except the ruined church and cloister. It's thought that the 14th-c poet Dafyd ap Gwilym is buried here; snacks, shop, disabled access; cl am Sun and all Oct-Mar; £1.50. The surroundings are lovely, and the road plunges on up through the pine forests into the mountains, eventually reaching the Llyn Brianne reservoir.

Tretower SO1821 TRETOWER COURT AND CASTLE vividly illustrate the change from castle to less fortified accommodation over the ages. The medieval manor house dates from the 14th c, though it has been developed over the centuries; beside it is the substantial ruin of an 11th-c motte and bailey, with 9-ft-thick walls and a three-storey tower; shop, limited disabled access; cl Sun am, 24-26 Dec, 1 Jan; *£1.80. The Nantyffin Cider Mill is handy for lunch. Crickhowell further down the road is a pleasant village-sized 'town', with an excellent inn in the Bear, and a fine ancient bridge over the Usk (which the good Bridge End Inn overlooks).

Tywyn SH5800 TALYLLYN RAILWAY This railway journey affords glorious views, climbing from the little seaside resort up the steep sides of the Fathew Valley and stopping for passengers to admire Dolgoch Falls and visit the Nant Gwernol Forest (there's a waterfall two minutes away from the platform at this end). The 27-in-gauge railway, the oldest of this gauge in the world, was built in 1865 to serve the slate mine at Abergynolwyn, and was one of the earliest to be rescued by a preservation society; snacks, shop, disabled access with prior notice; cl Nov-14 Feb (exc up to Christmas), (0654) 710472 for timetable; £6.50. A MUSEUM shows locomotives, wagons and signalling equipment whenever the railway is running.

Welshpool SJ2207 POWIS CASTLE Set in magnificent gardens with splendid 18th-c terraces, this dramatic-looking castle was built in the 13th c, but far from falling into decay like so many others, has developed into a grand house over the centuries, its finer improvements including the 16th-c plasterwork and panelling and a 17th-c staircase. The house has been constantly occupied since its construction, once by the son of Clive of India – there are displays about his father's life; meals, snacks, shop; cl Mon (exc bank hols) and Tues (exc

July and Aug) and all Nov-Mar; £5.80, Clive museum and garden only £3.60. The Raven in the town is useful for lunch, and the town's main BR station is rather unusual.

★ **Attractive villages** and small towns in the area, all with decent pubs, include Corris SH7608, Llandinam SO0388, Llangenny SO2417, Llanidloes SN9584, Montgomery SO2296, Myddfai SN7730, Newbridge-on-Wye SO0158, Presteigne SO3265 and Talybont-on-Usk SO1122. Pubs doing food that are particularly worth noting for their positions include the Farmers Arms at Cwmdu SO1823, Coach & Horses above the canal at Llangynidr SO1519 and Royal Oak at Pencelli SO0925 (another canalside pub).

Walks

The **Brecon Beacons** proper are a pair of graceful pointed summits connected by a short ridge that seems to be visible from most of South Wales, and that gives a magnificent high-level walk along the crest, which has massive drops on the northern side. **Pen y Fan** SO0121 (2,906 ft) is the highest Welsh summit outside Snowdonia, and the main E-W upland spine effectively stretches about 5 miles. The most popular route up from Pont ar Daf SN9819, from the A470 to the W, is straightforward enough although there has been some serious footpath erosion, but the N approaches are more exciting and surprisingly little walked.

The **Black Mountains,** making up the E part of the Brecon Beacons National Park, are a range of finger-shaped ridges bordering on to Herefordshire (and shared with South Wales), with steep-sided valleys in between. Most of the best views are from the **Offa's Dyke Path** along the E flanks: the land eastwards slopes abruptly down to low-lying agricultural Herefordshire, and views far into England give you a feeling of true border country. Circular walks here tend to be long and hefty, often with two major ascents to get you up on to the different ridges, but the scenic Gospel Pass road from Hay-on-Wye SO2342 lets you drive up to within reasonable striking distance of **Hay Bluff** SO2436 (2,200 ft). Twmpa SO2234 (2,263 ft) is better known by its intriguing English name of **Lord Hereford's Knob**; though it's not itself on the Offa's Dyke Path, it is nearby, and you can combine it with Hay Bluff in a longer walk. **Llanthony Abbey** (described in South Wales section), with a pub, makes a beautiful objective in the valley below, where diligent map-reading is needed for a cross-fields route from Cwmyoy SO2923, with extensions on to the Offa's Dyke Path on the ridge to complete a satisfying circuit.

Confusingly, the westernmost range in the national park is called **Black Mountain** SN7417. Distances from the road to much of the high terrain are quite substantial, so this part is more the preserve of the committed long-distance walker. The craggy ridge known as Carmarthen Fan protrudes dramatically above the moors and provides the high point of a long but rewarding walk from the N.

The southern parts of the National Park, within easy reach of South Wales, have gentler walking, in the form of **forest walks** in the large conifer plantations there, where waterfalls and a series of attractive reservoirs are the main features. The lusher swathes of the **Usk Valley** can be enjoyed by walks along the towpath of the 33-mile Monmouthshire & Brecon canal. **Cader Idris** SH7113, a great peak in the S of the National Park, offers various ways up its friendly slopes.

Just inside the southern park boundary and also good objectives from South

Wales, the deep, wooded gorges of the Nedd, Hepste and Mellte are graced with a series of mighty **waterfalls** that have few rivals in Britain. An easy path from Pontneddfechan SN9007 nr Glyn Neath leads along the River Nedd, while Porth yr Ogof car park SN9212 nr Ystradfellte is convenient for the Mellte. Dire warning notices ward you off getting too close to the edge (it is certainly hazardously slippery), but you can accompany the river most of the way to its junction with the Hepste. Here, a path actually crosses the river by going behind the curtain of Sgwd yr Eira waterfall – a rock ledge holds you in safely, but it's an excitingly damp experience.

Further west, the **Fforest Fawr** is, despite its name, largely treeless apart from a few patches of commercial forestry, for example around Usk Reservoir SN8228; the uplands are large-scale and empty, and rather too bleak for some tastes.

The Offa's Dyke Path again provides the major walkers' attraction further N, in the former county of **Radnorshire.** On its coast-to-coast route over the Welsh Marches it takes in some very attractive hill-farm country between Hay-on-Wye and Knighton SO2872, including Hergest Ridge (see Herefordshire chapter) and some well-preserved stretches of Offa's 9th-c boundary marker between Knighton and Kington SO2956. Away from Offa's Dyke, Radnorshire is less well known than it deserves to be, with old drovers' tracks providing some enjoyable escapist walking and a reasonable network of field paths. There are few major objectives, but it is all very pleasant: the best bets include the **River Wye** around Aberedw SO0847 and Boughrood SO1339, the **hills** between Aberedw, Glascwm SO1553 and Gladestry SO2355, and the upland massif of **Radnor Forest** (open country for the most part, with conifers on the northern slopes), where walks include New Radnor SO2160 to the modest summit of the quaintly named Whimble SO2062, and from the A44 between Llanfihangel-nant-Melan SO1858 and New Radnor to Water-break-its-neck waterfall SO1860 (don't miss the path at the top of the fall).

From Llandrindod Wells SO0561, a sedate walk around the town's lake can extend into an expedition E of **Cefnllys Castle** SO0861, an impressively sited hill fort with a lonely church below, close to Shaky Bridge (no longer shaky); a nature trail here takes you along the banks of the River Ithon.

West of Rhayader, some high-level trackways afford magnificent views over the Cambrian Mountains and adjacent **Elan Valley** SN9768; lower-level options start from the Elan Valley visitor centre and neighbouring reservoirs, and include forest walks and strolls along the old railway track by the water's edge – very attractive, as the lakes built at the turn of the century have weathered in well now, and there's quite a bit of wildlife.

The former county of Montgomeryshire consists of the quintessential sheep-grazed lands of rural Wales. Much of it lacks major objectives for walkers, with few major peaks and fair distances between villages, but **Montgomery** SO2296 itself, with its castle perched above, is rewarding for a short exploration on foot, and the windswept (often boggy) uplands of **Plynlimon** and the **Cambrian Mountains**, though not endowed with the friendliest of climates, can be magnificently exhilarating.

On the **coast**, you can do a one-way walk along the straight stretch between Aberystwyth SN5882 and Borth SN6189, using the train service between the two for the other half of the round trip. Similarly, walks in or above the pretty **Vale of Rheidol** between Aberystwyth and the Devils Bridge SN7376 can be aided by the private railway between the two. The most dramatic parts here are around Devils Bridge.

Driving

One of the most scenic roads in the area is the main A44 across to Aberystwyth, particularly where it climbs high beside the Upper Wye past Rhayader, around Pant Mawr, and then over the watershed into the gauntly swooping valley around Dyffryn Castell. Just past here at Ponterwyd a left turn on to the A4120 passing the Devils Bridge beauty spot gives the best views of the Vale of Rheidol as you approach Aberystwyth.

The B4574 from Devils Bridge takes you through conifer plantations to a quiet road up a very narrow river gorge past Cwmystwyth. This broadens out into the Elan Valley, with a series of attractively landcaped reservoirs. This is one of the nicest parts of Wales for country drives, and can also be reached by the B4518 up past buzzard crags from Rhayader.

From Llanwrtyd Wells a slow back road follows the Irfon Valley into the hills, hemmed in by conifer plantations for part of the way, and rarely free from their presence brooding over the landscape; but it does take you into a huge area of otherwise untracked mountainous country deep in central Wales, and eventually right over to Tregaron, with a worthwhile southerly detour to see the Llyn Brianne reservoir among its dark pinewoods. There are some very steep and twisty sections on this road, for instance the Devils Staircase when you leave the first valley to climb over the watershed into the next. For the fainter-hearted, the altogether easier but busier A483 between Llanwrtyd Wells and Llandovery passes through some fine scenery.

Along the Usk between Crickhowell and Brecon, the B4558 on the S side of the river is a pleasant, quiet road through this lovely scenery. From Talybont a narrow road goes steeply up into the Brecon Beacons with its outcrops of rock beckoning you over the empty moorlands; the main roads over the Beacons from Brecon and from Sennybridge give a good feel of this expansive area too.

A good stretch of coast road is the main A487 between Aberaeron and Aberystwyth, which runs on high enough ground to show Ireland as a shadow on the horizon; as does the B4572 just N of Aberystwyth.

Right over in the E, pleasant roads into good scenery include the B4560 from the South Wales valleys up through Bwlch and Llangorse to Talgarth, and the B4594 up over the hills through Painscastle, Newcastle and Gladestry, forking left up to Old Radnor with its lovely views over the Radnor Forest, and then on by the B4362 to Presteigne, or perhaps the B4357 on to Knighton.

Where to eat

Llowes SO1941 Radnor Arms Powys (0497) 847460 Small, modest and very old, with log fire in bar, neat little cottagey dining room, and tables in imaginatively planted garden; very wide choice of notably good food (tempting puddings), congenial atmosphere, and friendly staff; cl Sun pm, Mon (exc bank hols). **£21.50**|£3/£6.

Craig-y-Nos SN8315 Coach House Powys (0639) 730767 Originally the stables to the castle, this is a carefully converted restaurant with Victorian features, attractive pine furniture, decent food inc Welsh teas, friendly, and efficient service; also a craft shop where you can watch potters, saddlers and textile artists at work; cl Tues, and in winter it's best to phone beforehand. **£10**|£1.30/£5.20.

Many of the places listed in the Where to Stay section serve very good food, too.

SOUTH WALES

This is the best part of Wales for sightseeing; also some attractive countryside, though it can't score over other parts of Wales for that.

There are more sights to see and interesting places to visit in this part of Wales than in any other – particularly industrial heritage attractions at Porth, Blaenavon and Cardiff, the opulent Castell Coch at Tongwynlais, the scenic Brecon Mountain Railway out of Merthyr Tydfil (which itself is well worth exploring), the gardens at St Nicholas, a good number of spectacular medieval castles (with the one at Caerphilly prime among them), the idyllic ruined priory at Llanthony and the better-known abbey at Tintern, the Roman remains at Caerleon, showy Tredegar House in Newport and the hawking centre in Barry. Cardiff, though not a desirable town to stay in, has lots to see on a day visit, including a first-class museum and art gallery, and an enjoyable hands-on science centre too lively to be called a museum. Monmouth and Chepstow are small towns of great character. The zoo at Cilfrew is attractive.

Though the area has no really outstanding scenery, it has some very attractive and unspoilt countryside, for example around the further edges of the Gower peninsula, in the hills on the edge of the Brecon Beacons above the former mining valleys, along the Wye Valley and on the edge of the Black Mountains (which are discussed in the Mid-Wales section).

Overall, a short stay here will appeal most to people – including children – who will enjoy finding out at least a little about the area's remarkable past. Coupling some of the interesting memorials of that past with the quieter delights of some of its better countryside could make for a memorable stay.

Where to stay

Whitebrook SO5306 CROWN AT WHITEBROOK Monmouth Gwent NP5 4TX (0600) 860254 **£120 inc dinner**; 12 rms. Small hotel in beautiful Wye Valley with friendly, caring service, relaxed atmosphere, comfortable lounge and bar, and excellent, original food and fine wines in small cosy restaurant; cl 25-26 Dec.

Govilon SO2613 LLANWENARTH HOUSE Abergavenny Gwent NP7 9SF (0873) 830289 *£70; 4 spacious, comfortable rms. Fine family-run 16th-c manor house in quiet grounds within Brecon Beacons National Park, with gracious sitting room, log fires, antiques and fresh flowers, fine food using local game and fish and home-produced meat, poultry and garden veg in elegant candlelit dining room, and friendly, helpful staff; lots to do nearby; croquet; cl mid-

Jan-1st wknd Mar; children over 10; disabled access.
Monmouth SO5113 RIVERSIDE Gwent NP5 3EY (0600) 715577 **£66**; 17 rms. Comfortable, recently refurbished hotel near River Monnow; disabled access.
Monmouth SO5113 KINGS HEAD Agincourt Sq Gwent NP5 3DY (0600) 712177 ***£65**; 28 rms. 17th-c coaching inn with friendly staff, little bar with log fire, decent food, and private car park; disabled access; cl 24-25 Dec.
Abergavenny SO3014 LLANWENARTH ARMS Brecon Rd Gwent NP8 1EP (0873) 810550 **£59**; 18 rms with lovely views. Extended hotel with 16th-c heart in marvellous position on the bank of the River Usk with its salmon and trout fishing; two bars, Victorian conservatory, warm welcome, wide choice of home-made food in bar and restaurant, and terrace; disabled access.
Tintern Parva SO5301 PARVA FARMHOUSE Chepstow Gwent NP6 6SQ (0291) 689411 **£58**; 9 comfortable rms, 7 with own bthrm. Friendly stone farmhouse, rebuilt in mid-17th-c, with leather chesterfields, woodburning stove and honesty bar in large beamed lounge, books (no TV downstairs), and very good food and wine (inc wine using home-grown grapes) in cosy restaurant; 50 yds from River Wye and lovely surrounding countryside.
Oxwich SS5286 OXWICH BAY Swansea SA3 1LS (0792) 390329 ***£40**; 13 rms. Refurbished hotel on edge of beach with hardworking staff, food served all day, restaurant/coffee shop with panoramic views, and popular with locals; lovely area; cl 24-25 Dec.
Little Mill SO3203 PENTWYN FARM Pontypool Gwent NP4 0HQ (0495) 785249 **£34**; 4 rms. Most attractive pink-washed 16th-c longhouse on mixed farm of 120 acres; open fire in big sitting room, lots of books and games, good country cooking around large table in beamed dining room, large garden with swimming pool, table tennis in barn, and rough shooting in woods; cl Christmas; children over 4.

To see and do

Aberdulais SS7799 ABERDULAIS FALLS Since the 16th c these falls have been used to power a range of industries from copper-smelting to tinplate. Renovations on the turbine house are now complete, and the water wheel is once again generating electricity; shop, disabled access; cl wk at Christmas; £2.50. NT.

Abergavenny SO2914 has some attractive ancient buildings in Nevill St and particularly Market St. There's a busy Tues and Fri market. The CHURCH has a remarkable collection of memorials. The remains of the 12th- and 14th-c CASTLE include the walls, towers and rebuilt gatehouse; the early 19th-c keep and an adjoining house now contain a museum with craft tools, a Welsh kitchen, saddler's shop and carriage rooms; shop; cl 1-2 pm, Sun (exc pm in summer), 24-26 Dec, 1 Jan; *£1. The Hen & Chickens is useful for lunch, while just outside the King of Prussia (B4598 SE), Horse & Jockey (old Raglan rd) and Llanwenarth Arms (Brecon rd) also do decent food.

Barry ST1268 Lively seaside resort which, along with its jutting-out peninsula Barry Island, grew as a centre for the coal industry. Remains of 13th-c castle, and usual fairground attractions for children. WELSH HAWKING CENTRE (Weycock Rd) Over 200 birds of prey, flying demonstrations at regular intervals, and you can see and photograph them in the mews and breeding aviaries as well. Also a variety of tame and friendly animals; snacks, shop; cl 25 Dec; *£3. Nearby, the Star and Three

Horseshoes in Dinas Powis are good for lunch.

Blaenavon SO2508 BIG PIT MINING MUSEUM Sample the life of a miner by donning a safety helmet and descending 300 ft in the cage into the Big Pit, which closed as a working coal mine in 1980. Also a reconstructed miner's cottage, and an exhibition in the old pithead baths. Good fun – but make sure you dress sensibly; meals and snacks, shop, disabled access with prior warning; cl most of Dec-Feb; *£4.95.

Bridgend SS9079 NEWCASTLE Ruined 12th-c castle with surviving rectangular tower, richly carved Norman gateway and massive curtain walls; key-keeping arrangement. The prosperous industrial town isn't much of a place for visitors, but nearby Merthyr Mawr SS8877 (with its interesting warren of high sandhills), Ogmore SS8674 and Southerndown SS8873 are attractive.

Caerleon ST3490 FORTRESS BATHS, AMPHITHEATRE AND BARRACKS One of the best examples of an amphitheatre in the country, alongside one of the most complete examples of a Roman legionary bath building, now under cover. Also the foundations of barrack lines and parts of the ramparts, and the remains of the cookhouse and latrines. This fort was an important military base housing thousands of men, and the site gives some idea of how they lived; shop, disabled access; cl am winter Sun, 25-26 Dec, 1 Jan; *£1.25. More remains at the nearby ROMAN LEGIONARY MUSEUM, which illustrates the daily life of a Roman garrison, with displays of armour and equipment, gemstones and other relics; shop, disabled access; cl am Sun, 24-26 Dec, 1 Jan; £1.25. A joint ticket for both the Museum and the Baths is *£2.

Caerphilly ST1587 An oddly strung-out small town, dominated by the CASTLE, the largest in Wales, with extensive land and water defences. Rising sheer from its broad outer moat, it's a proper picture-book castle, pleasing for this reason to the most casual visitor. It also enthrals serious students of castle architecture, as it's a remarkably complex design of concentric defences. Look out for the leaning tower of Caerphilly which outdoes even Pisa; cl am winter Suns; *£2. The ancient Courthouse overlooking the castle is quite good for lunch, and the thatched Travellers Rest is good value.

Caerwent ST4791 ROMAN WALLS These walls enclose the large site of Venta Silurum – over 40 acres, enough for a sizeable town, though all that's left now is sections of the massive outer wall, still standing to some 15 ft high in places.

Caldicot ST4888 The 12th-14th-c CASTLE was restored as a family home in the 1880s, and lived in until 20 years ago – since when it's been a local museum. It's now surrounded by a country park; snacks, shop, limited disabled access; cl 1-2 pm, Nov-Feb; *£1.20.

Cardiff ST1876 The civic centre has a range of grand 20th-c white stone civic or governmental buildings around a formal park. The old city centre is closer to Cardiff Castle (see below), which has Capability Brown's 18th-c landscaped park between it and the river. In the centre, parts are pedestrianised (for example around the fine CHURCH of St John the Baptist, and there are many covered shopping arcades, Victorian and modern. CARDIFF CASTLE Despite its fairy-tale medieval appearance, the present building is largely from the 19th c, when the Marquess of Bute employed William Burges to rebuild and restore it, adding richly romantic wall paintings, tapestries and carvings. In fact, the castle does date from Norman times, and there's even a piece of a 10-ft-thick wall which formed part of a previous Roman fort here. The Norman keep survives, and there's a

13th-c tower – it looks right too, perched on a little mound; snacks, shop; cl 25-26 Dec, 1 Jan; *£3.15, grounds only *£2.10. Inside the tower are two REGIMENTAL MUSEUMS, of the Welch Regiment and the Queen's Dragoon Guards. NATIONAL MUSEUM OF WALES (Cathays Park) Considerably enlivened recently and now truly of national interest, with interactive displays and exhibitions on subjects as diverse as ceramics, coins and prehistoric sea monsters. The East Wing has an impressive collection of paintings, with notable French Impressionists; meals, snacks, shop, disabled access; cl Mon exc bank hols, 25 Dec; *£2. WELSH INDUSTRIAL AND MARITIME MUSEUM (Bute St) Set at the heart of the Cardiff Bay Development Area, this large and ambitious museum tells the story of the industrial and maritime development of Wales, using five buildings that were once part of Cardiff's docklands. One gallery houses ancient trams, cars and so forth, another various industrial engines (many of which may clank, whirr, thud or grind noisily into life), another locomotives, full size or model, yet another ships and shipping, and there's more outside. Also a miniature railway; shop, disabled access; cl Mon exc 1 May, 24-28 Dec, 1 Jan; £1. TECHNIQUEST (Bute St) Fun as well as interest at this hands-on high-tech science centre, with some fascinating displays – even a realistic dragon conjured up by laser. They also have frequent special events ranging from one-day demos to longer-term fixtures like Starlab which provides a guided tour of the night sky inside an inflatable planetarium. All exceptionally well done, and an excellent family excursion; snacks, shop, disabled access; cl Mon during term-time, and 25-26 Dec; £3. LLANDAFF is a mile or two out from the centre, where the CATHEDRAL has been rebuilt several times; it includes some delightful medieval masonry, Pre-Raphaelite works, a marvellous modern timber roof, and a central concrete arch that you may think a mistake. The nearby green has an attractive collection of buildings around it. Further west at St Fagans the WELSH FOLK MUSEUM is an excellent 100-acre open-air museum representing the life and culture of Wales, with a variety of reconstructed buildings from castles to cottages illustrating styles and living conditions throughout the ages. Buildings have come from all over Wales, and there are some remarkable exhibits in the museum. The latest addition is a celtic village showing life 2,000 years ago. With crafts and lots of seasonal events too, there's a lot to fascinate here; meals, snacks, shop, disabled access; cl Sun Nov-Mar, 25-26 Dec, 1 Jan; *£3.50. In Cardiff centre the Cottage and Philharmonic both in St Mary's St and Golden Cross in Custom House St are quite useful for lunch, as is the newish Wharf down by the docks.

Chepstow ST5393 is a steep but civilised small town, still with its battlemented 13th-c town gate. CHEPSTOW CASTLE is the first recorded Norman stone castle, proudly standing on an easily defended spot above the Wye, overlooking the harbour. It was used as a base for advances into Wales, and you can still look out through the variety of slots for weapons cut into the massive walls and towers. The huge gatehouse with its portcullis grooves and ancient gates is splendid, while the remains of the domestic rooms are evidence of the wealth and magnificence of its past. A new exhibition looks at siege warfare and the English Civil War, when the castle was besieged twice – you can even try on a period helmet; shop, disabled access; cl am Sun in winter, 24-26 Dec, 1 Jan; £2.90. CHEPSTOW MUSEUM Good comprehensive local-history museum, with period reconstructions, displays of pictures and prints and temporary exhibitions on subjects as

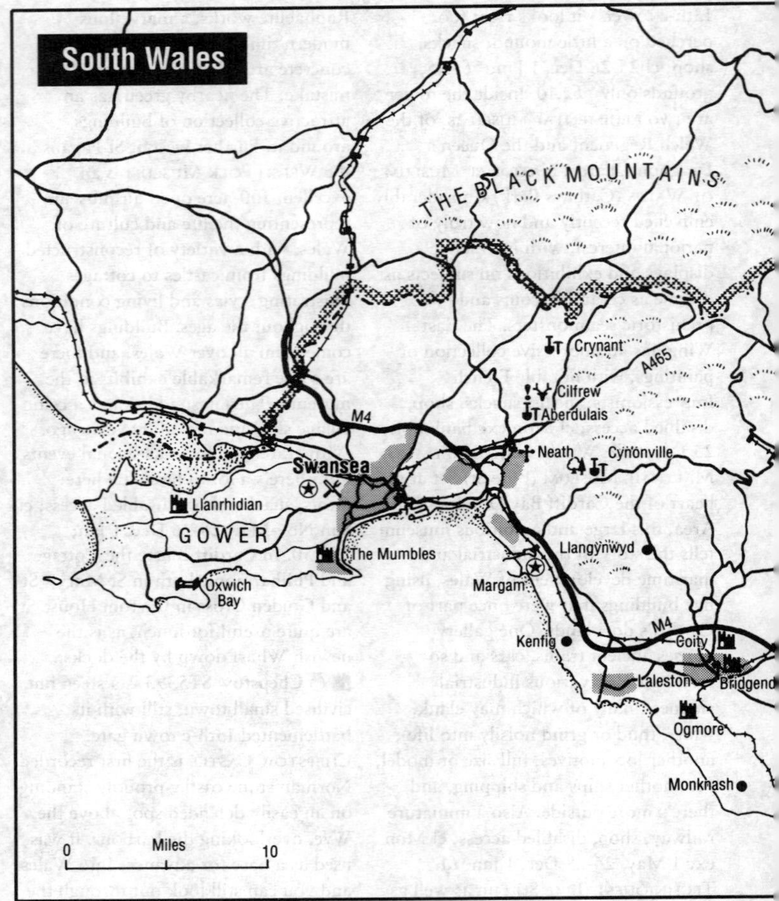

diverse as William Morris, local quilts and Panama indians; shop, disabled access to ground floor only; cl 1-2 pm, am Sun; *£1. The Bridge and Castle View are both good for lunch.

! Cilfrew SN7700 Penscynor Wildlife Park Lots of animals in a charming setting, including sea lions, parrots and tropical birds. You can feed rainbow trout or take a ride to the clifftop for an exciting bobsleigh ride; meals, snacks, shop, disabled access; cl 25 Dec; *£4.

Coity SS9281 Coity Castle Hall, chapel and remains of a square keep are preserved on this site, which was used as a stronghold from the 12th to the 16th c; key-keeping arrangement. The Six Bells opposite is useful for lunch.

Crynant SN7904 Cefn Coed Colliery Museum The story of mining in the Dulais Valley on the site of a former colliery. It still has a steam winding-engine, though the winding gear is now run by electricity. Also a simulated underground mining gallery, boilerhouse and compressor house; summer snacks, shop, disabled access; cl 25 Dec-1 Jan; *£1.25.

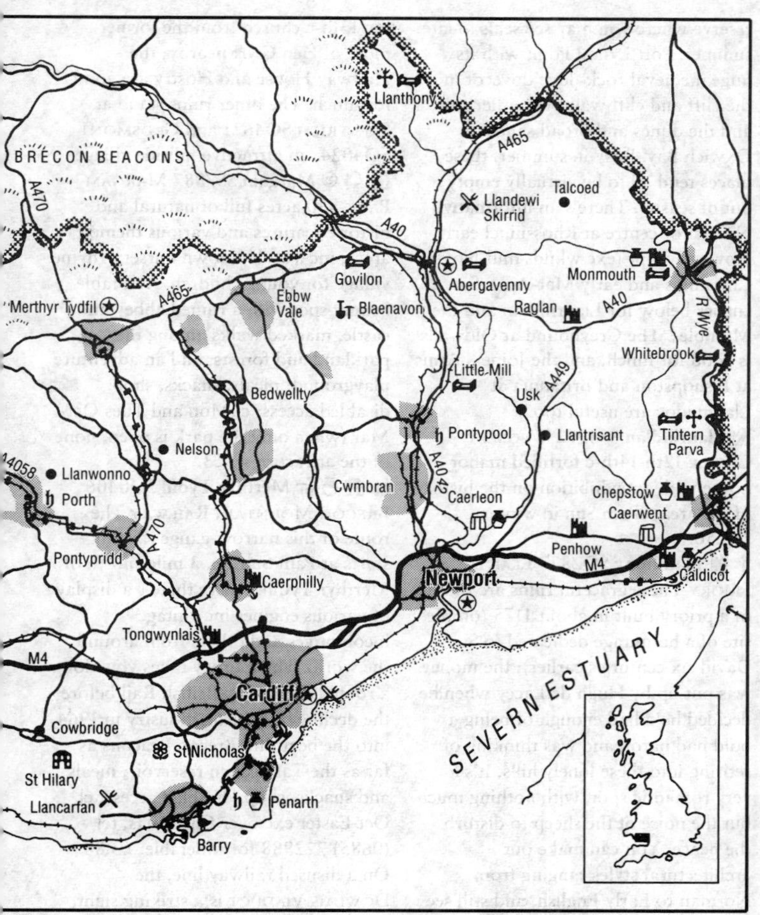

Cynonville SS8395 WELSH MINERS MUSEUM In Afan Argoed Country Park with forest walks and a visitor centre, this museum gives a vivid picture of life as a miner with coal faces, pit gear and mining equipment among the displays. It's been closed recently, but should be open again now; meals and snacks, shop, disabled access; cl wkdys Nov-May; admission charge not yet known at time of going to press.

The Gower Too big to give a map reference for, this peninsula stretching west of Swansea has quite a bit of off-putting ribbon development along the roads entering it, but it's well worth persevering as the further parts are full of interest around the coast: the long glistening cockle sands below Llanrhidian, the dunes and marshy slacks of the Whiteford Burrows nature reserve, the islet of Burry Holms with its ruined chapel and Iron-Age fort (you can walk out at low tide), the long surfers' sands of Rhossili Bay below rough-cropped windswept open moorland that seems a million miles from Swansea yet as the crow flies is only about ten from the outskirts, the tidal rocks of Worms Head nature reserve where you may see seals in late summer, Port Eynon Point with its huge medieval rock-dove dovecot in the cliff and cliff walks on either side, and the dunes and broad sands of Oxwich Bay. Busy in summer, these places tend all to be virtually empty out of season. There's an informative NT visitor centre at Rhossili, cl early Nov-early Apr (exc wknds mid-Nov-Christmas and early Mar-Apr). See entries below for Llanrhidian and the Mumbles. The Greyhound at Oldwalls is good for lunch, and the Joiners Arms at Bishopston and Britannia at Llanmadoc are useful too.

Llanrhidian SS4992 WEOBLEY CASTLE 12th-14th-c fortified manor house with an exhibition on the history of the area; cl am Sun in winter; *£1.50.

Llanthony SO2827 LLANTHONY PRIORY These graceful ruins are those of a priory built in about 1175 (on the site of a hermitage dedicated to St David six centuries earlier); the money was put up by Hugh de Lacey when he decided he'd had enough of being a bold bad baron and was thinking of retiring into these lonely hills. It's a very romantic spot, with nothing much but the noise of the sheep to disturb the peace. You can make out architectural styles ranging from Norman to Early English, and still see the west towers, north nave arcade and south transept. The very ancient crypt bar below the Abbey Hotel, right among the priory buildings, is useful for a snack lunch. On the way up the valley, turn off to see medieval CWMYOY CHURCH SO2923: repeated landslips have left the whole church twisted, and its tower leans at an angle that makes the Tower of Pisa look positively sober.

Llantilio Crosseny SO3915 To defend the Welsh Marches, Hubert de Burgh built a trio of moated castles. The remains are most substantial here, in his White Castle. The village is attractive, and there's a lovely view of the 13th-c church from the former moat of Hen Cwrt nearby; the Halfway House and Hostry are good for lunch. The other ruins stand at SKENFRITH SO4621 and GROSMONT SO4024, an attractive hillside village.

Margam SS7887 MARGAM PARK 850 acres full of natural and historic features and various themed areas, inc a scaled-down nursery-rhyme village for young children. A notable beauty spot with a ruined abbey and castle, marked walks among the parkland and forests, and an adventure playground; meals, snacks, shop, disabled access; cl Mon and Tues Oct-Mar (when only the park is open, none of the attractions); £3.

Merthyr Tydfil SO0406 BRECON MOUNTAIN RAILWAY The route of this narrow-gauge railway starts at Pant Station, 3 miles north of Merthyr Tydfil, where there's a display of various engines inc vintage locomotives and others from around the world. The journey takes you along a route last used by British Rail before the decline of the iron industry in 1964, into the beautiful Brecon Beacons as far as the Taf Fechan reservoir; meals and snacks, shop, disabled access; cl Oct-Easter exc over Christmas, tel (0685) 722988 for timetable; £3.80. On a disused railway line, the DOWLAIS VIADUCT is a striking sight, well worth a detour. CYFARTHFA CASTLE Impressive early 19th-c castellated Gothic mansion, set in beautiful gardens dating from the same period. It's another remnant of the past prosperity of this area's iron industry, built for the owner of what were then the largest ironworks in Britain, and looking down on them. The state rooms contain a museum covering the social and industrial life of the area, and displays on Egyptology and archaeology; a recent refurbishment has restored the rooms to their full Regency glory. There are extensive grounds; snacks, shop, disabled access; cl am Sun, and Sat too in winter, when also cl 1-2 pm; *65p. GARWNANT FOREST CENTRE Looking out over the Llwyn-On reservoir on the S edge of the National Park, these carefully restored old farm buildings have displays on forestry, wildlife and conservation, with information on nature trails through the local landscape and cycle routes through the forest; snacks, shop, disabled access; cl Oct-Easter. JOSEPH PARRY'S COTTAGE (Chapel Row) The composer of *Myfanwy* was born here, and the ground floor has been restored and decorated in the style of the 1840s. Also displays about the industrial and social history of the area in those prosperous 19th-c days; shop, limited disabled access; cl am and all Nov-Mar; 30p. YNYSFACH ENGINE HOUSE Models, photographs and an excellent audio-visual programme recount the history of this area's iron industry. The displays are housed where once stood the beam-engine of the Ynysfach Iron Works; snacks, shop; cl am wknds, 25 Dec; *£1. The interesting Red Lion up at Penderyn is useful for lunch and not that far off, and the Glan Taff down the road in Treharris (off the road and over the bridge) is useful too.

Monmouth SO5102 is an attractive market town of considerable character; below the remains of the 12th-c CASTLE where Henry V was born, and the 17th-c Great Castle House (built with enormous blocks of masonry in its precincts), the main Agincourt Square is surrounded by handsome buildings, inc the imposing central Shire Hall with its arcaded market floor. The town nestles in the crook formed by the River Wye and the River Monnow, with a splendid 13th-c gatehouse bridge over the Monnow. The NELSON MUSEUM (Priory St) has a tremendous collection relating to Nelson – china, books, prints, letters, glass, medals and best of all his fighting sword. Nelson has nothing to do with Monmouth, but the collection was originally put together by Lady Llangattock who lived nearby. Also displays on local history including a display on Charles Stewart Rolls who co-founded Rolls-Royce, as well as being a pioneer balloonist and aviator; shop, disabled access but no facilities; cl 1-2 pm, all day Sun and bank hols; *£1. The Punch House is the most enjoyable place here for lunch, and the Kings Head Hotel and Riverside Hotel are also good.

Mumbles SS6188 OYSTERMOUTH CASTLE Ruins of the de Breose family castle, in a small park. The gatehouse, chapel and great hall date from the 13th-14th c; cl Oct-Mar; *80p. Mumbles is a pleasantly unspoilt resort, and the White Rose is cheap for lunch.

✝ **Neath** SS7597 NEATH ABBEY The remains of a Cistercian abbey founded in 1130 by Richard de Grainville; disabled access; cl am Sun, 25-26 Dec.

Newport SO1408 TREDEGAR HOUSE Magnificent 17th-c house and gardens set in 90-acre landscaped park. The Morgans, later Lords Tredegar, lived here for five centuries, and the activities of the household, below and above stairs, are well illustrated. In the grounds are carriage rides, self-guided trails and craft workshops, as well as boating and an adventure playfarm; meals and snacks, shop, disabled access; cl Mon and Tues, and all Oct-Mar exc wknds in Oct; £3.40. MUSEUM AND ART GALLERY Collections ranging from Roman finds, through the Chartist movement of 1838-40, to the John Wait teapot collection; shop, mostly disabled access; cl Suns and bank hols. The Greenhouse at Llantarnam on the A4042 N is useful for lunch.

Ogmore SS8876 OGMORE CASTLE Three-storeyed 12th-c keep with a preserved hooded fireplace, a dry moat surrounding the inner ward and a surviving 40-ft west wall. The setting of this ruin on the River Ogmore is attractive: odd to think that what this impressive fortress was built to defend was the row of stepping stones which still cross the river; key-keeping arrangement. The Pelican is useful for lunch, and the cheery Three Golden Cups along the road at Southerndown gives sea views to Devon on a clear day. Just past it there's a car park by the interestingly preserved remains of the seaside gardens of entirely demolished Dunraven Castle SS8873, with walks by the cliffs over the sands and rock pools, and around to the fragmentary remains of an Iron-Age promontory hill fort above the sea.

Penarth ST1871 COSMESTON MEDIEVAL VILLAGE Set in the Cosmeston Lakes Country Park, this living museum of medieval life is reconstructed on the site of an actual village which was deserted during the 14th c; snacks, shop; cl Dec; £1.20. TURNER HOUSE Small gallery with temporary exhibitions from the National Museum of Wales; shop, disabled access to ground floor only; cl 12.45-2 pm, Sun am, all day Mon (exc bank hols), Christmas; *50p. Down by the sea south of the town at Swanbridge the Captains Wife is fun for lunch.

Penhow ST4290 PENHOW CASTLE The oldest lived-in castle in Wales, with tours of the restored rooms taking you from the 12th-c ramparts and Norman bedchamber through the 15th-c Great Hall with its minstrels' gallery to the Victorian housekeeper's room. By arrangement ((0633) 400800) they do candlelit tours in the evening, and you can stay here; snacks, shop, limited disabled access; cl Mon (exc bank hols) and Tues Easter-Sept, all Aug, and all winter exc pm Weds and some Suns; £2.95.

Pontypool SO2800 VALLEY INHERITANCE The story of a South Wales valley, with exhibitions, displays and films housed in this Georgian stable block of Pontypool Park House; snacks, shop, disabled access; cl Sun am, all Jan; *£1.20. The Open Hearth just below the canal at Griffithstown is good for lunch.

Porth ST0491 RHONDDA HERITAGE PARK Based in the last colliery buildings in the area, this is devoted to the social and industrial history of the Rhondda and South Wales Valleys. Realistic recreations of the life and work of the miners, and the pithead buildings are brought to life with the sights, smells and sounds of the days when coal was king. Also concerts and art gallery expressing the cultural life of the district, an authentic Valley chapel, and a new themed play area for children; meals, snacks, shop, disabled access; cl 25-26 Dec; *£3.50.

Raglan SO4107 RAGLAN CASTLE Quite magnificent ruins of 15th-c castle, particularly notable for its Yellow Tower of Gwent. Its intricate history is displayed in the closet tower and two rooms of the gatehouse; cl winter Sun; £1.75.

St Hilary ST0173 BEAUPRÉ CASTLE Well-preserved ruined Elizabethan courtyard mansion with an extraordinarily elaborate three-storey Italianate porch; disabled access through owner's land with prior notice (write to the castle); cl Sun. The Bush is good for lunch.

St Nicholas ST0974 DYFFRYN GARDENS Small themed gardens and seasonal bedding displays help break up the 50 acres of rare plants and shrubs which make up these lovely gardens. There are also extensive plant houses, including a large temperate house and a succulent house, and an arboretum; meals, snacks, shop, disabled access; information centre cl Nov-Mar; *£2.

Swansea SS6592 has few buildings of any age or great appeal to visitors. Among some high spots is the 1934 Guildhall, containing the Brangwyn Hall with its 16 huge British Empire murals painted by Sir Frank Brangwyn for the House of Lords – Wales's gain, as they were judged too controversial. There are some castle ruins (which one is not allowed into but can see from outside), inc a striking 14th-c first-floor arcade. It's primarily a commercial and post-industrial town; its long sandy beaches have also made it something of a family summer resort. MARITIME AND INDUSTRIAL MUSEUM Set in the Swansea docks, the displays in this museum deal with the history and development of the Port of Swansea and include a selection of floating boats (Apr-Oct) and a complete working woollen mill; shop, disabled access; cl Mon (exc bank hols), 25-26 Dec, 1 Jan. SWANSEA MUSEUM (Victoria Rd) Displays of archaeology and natural and local history, inc a recreated 19th-c Welsh kitchen; shop; cl Mon exc bank hols, 25-26 Dec, 1 Jan; may be small charge. GLYNN VIVIAN ART GALLERY AND MUSEUM (Alexandra Rd) Good changing exhibitions, with permanent displays of porcelain from Swansea's all-too-brief but brilliant period of production between 1814 and 1824, local, European and oriental pottery, and paintings, drawings and sculptures by British, French and, above all, Welsh artists – especially the locally born Ceri Richards; shop, disabled access; cl Mon exc bank hols, 25-26 Dec, 1 Jan. PLANTASIA (Parc Tawe) Tropical and desert plants in big futuristic landscaped glasshouse, also aviary; snacks, shop, disabled access; cl Mon, 25-26 Dec; *£1. The Hanbury in Kingsway is popular for lunch.

Tongwynlais ST1382 CASTELL COCH This spectacular hillside landmark, designed in 1875 by William Burges for the Marquis of Bute, is actually based on a 13th-c castle in spite of its improbable appearance, something by Disney out of Wagner – red sandstone, conical towers, drawbridge and portcullis. It's a very successful pastiche, and inside is just as impressive: an idyll of gilt, statues, murals and carvings – especially spectacular is the bedroom of Lady Bute, decorated on the theme of Sleeping Beauty; shop, disabled access to ground floor only; cl am winter Suns, 24-26 Dec, 1 Jan; *£2.

✝ **Tintern** SO5200 TINTERN ABBEY Established in 1131 and rebuilt in the late 13th c, this monastery prospered until the 16th c when the Dissolution led to the decline which produced the ruins we see today. Remarkably well preserved, these were considered an essential spot for 18th-c artists and poets to visit, lying as they do in a lovely part of the steeply wooded Wye Valley; shop, disabled access; cl 24-26 Dec, 1 Jan; *£2.

★ **Attractive villages** or small towns, all with decent pubs, include Bedwellty SO1600, Cowbridge SS9974, Laleston SS8879, St Hilary ST0173 and Usk SO3801. Pubs or inns elsewhere which are particularly useful for their attractive surroundings or views include the Lamb & Flag out on the Brecon road from Abergavenny SO2515, Prince of Wales at Kenfig SS8383, Old House at Llangynwyd SS8588, Greyhound at Llantrisant ST3997, Brynfynnon at Llanwonno ST0295, Plough & Harrow at Monknash SS9270, Rowan Tree at Nelson ST1195 and Halfway House at Talycoed SO4115.

We welcome reports from readers . . .

Do send us reports on places in the GUIDE, or ones you think should be in. Use the card in the middle, the report forms at the end, or just write – no stamp needed: THE GOOD WEEKEND GUIDE, FREEPOST TN1569, Wadhurst, E Sussex TN5 7BR.

Walks

In Gwent some of the best walks are up into the Black Mountains, described under Mid Wales. Part of its boundary with England is made up of the picturesque **Lower Wye** gorge. The Wye Valley Walk connects Chepstow ST5394 with Tintern SO5301 – there are only occasional views down to the river, but the short detour up steps to the Wynd Cliff viewpoint ST5297 gets an extensive panorama. Further good sections of the gorge can be walked from Monmouth SO5113 to Fairview Rock SO5514, a lofty crag near the Biblins suspension bridge; a level track supplies an easy riverside route.

The **industrial valleys** have rather scrappy moorland and patches of conifer plantations rising high above the towns; it's not a pretty scene, but its gruff sense of place appeals to some. There are some interesting examples of post-mining land reclamation, including Parc Cwm Darran in the Rhymney Valley near Bargoed ST1499, which now provides a wide variety of natural habitats for wildlife and plants, with scenery ranging from the valley floor through forest areas to upland moors with superb views of the Brecon Beacons; and the Afon Lwyd Valley between Cwmbran New Town ST2995 and Blaenavon SO2509.

The abrupt transition from here into the empty wildness of the **Brecon Beacons National Park** (described under Mid Wales but very easily reached from here) is startling. The **Black Mountains**, too, are discussed under Mid Wales, though the valleys stretching up into them from Gwent, for instance past Llanthony SO2827, offer some of the best approaches.

The **Gower Peninsula** encapsulates on a small scale many different types of Welsh landscape, once beyond the creeping urbanisation W of Swansea. It rises to rounded moorland hills such as Cefn Bryn SS4989 and Rhossili Down SS4190, which offer breathtaking views of both – or all three – coasts. From Rhossili you can also take in Mewslade Bay SS4187, where the sands are enclosed by limestone cliffs. As good a walk can be had from Penmaen SS5388 (NT car park near the church), following the lane to Threecliff Bay, then heading W along the coast as far as Nicholaston Farm to end with the mild ascent of Cefn Bryn ridge. Whiteford Burrows SS4495 (pine trees and sand dunes), Oxwich Bay SS5196 (more dunes, presided over by Oxwich Point on its W side), and tiny Brandy Cove SS5887 (walk down the wooded Bishopston Valley to get there) are among other highlights. The N coast is attractive only at its western extreme.

Closer to Cardiff, the curious striped cliffs of the Glamorgan coast look over the Bristol Channel to Exmoor. **Nash Point** SS9168 is the best access point, as it is worth getting to shore level to see the cliffs in their full glory.

Driving

The NW corner of Gwent has some of this area's most attractive drives, through lonely and unspoilt hill country. A delightful run is from Llanfihangel Crucorney a few miles N of Abergavenny up the Vale of Ewyas into these sheep-dotted hills, passing Llanthony Priory and on to Hay-on Wye in Mid Wales. Near the bottom of this charming valley, the side road to Crickhowell (also in Mid Wales) is another pleasant drive. Gwent also has a fine stretch of the Wye Valley, and the slow A466 following the river between Chepstow and Monmouth, passing Tintern and dodging across into Gloucestershire, has lovely scenery, particularly in autumn; this is the most dramatic if not the most lonely of the Gwent valleys, twisting through high hills.

Other parts of Gwent are less striking, though still pleasant for country drives. N of Monmouth, the B4347 up to Grosmont is a pleasant drive through quiet rolling farmland with a succession of gentle views, typical of this area between Abergavenny, Usk, Monmouth and Grosmont itself; the views are generally more interesting in the N, where the hills add a touch of grandeur, than in the S. The B4521 and B4233 across the heart of the area, and the B4598 from Abergavenny to Usk, share this pastoral mood, and the many side roads which straggle off into this farmland bring you into very rustic territory. The B4235 from Chepstow to Usk has some good views over this Gwent countryside, framed by distant hills. Almost paralleling it is a road between Usk and Caerwent through the high country of Caerwent, for the most part pretty, though a mile or two winds through dense conifer plantations.

The roads up the narrow former mining valleys of Glamorgan are interesting for the way the brick houses are so steeply terraced along the sides, and also for the way that side roads take you so quickly into higher untouched mountain pastures – and even hamlets that over the last two centuries seem to have paid no attention to the coming and going of the coal and iron industries in the valleys below them. An example is the back road up through Mynyddislwyn and on back down into Abercarn, off the A4048 above Wattsville. In the same area there's a well-laid-out hill-and-forest drive signposted above Cwmcarn, which has good views in between the conifers.

In this part the hills between the valleys are increasingly blanketed with conifer plantations. One pleasant road that winds around the edges of the forest, with good valley views, as well as taking you into it is the hill road off the A4233 above Ferndale, zigzagging very steeply up towards the remote-feeling St Gwynno Forest around Llanwonno. Another busier road with a good mix of forest and valley views is the A4061/A4107 between Rhondda and Cwmafan. Up the Rhondda Valley, once past Treherbert the A4061 linking at Hirwaun with the A4059 is an attractive road to Brecon in Mid Wales, as is the quite busy A470 from Merthyr Tydfil.

On the coast, the B4524 from Ewenny past Ogmore gives a good view of ruined Ogmore castle, the extensive Merthyr Mawr sand dunes, and then past Ogmore-by-Sea some brief but fine sea and coast views – best from the side road in Southerndown down to the beachside Dunraven car park. From the W exit roundabout at junction 46 of the M4 (first left off the A48 back towards Neath), the back road to Ammanford is quite good, up over high lonely sheep pastures.

Around the Gower, the B4295 and then the coast road through Oldwalls to Cheriton give good views out over the Loughor cockle flats.

Besides the M4 itself, the M50 to Ross-on-Wye gives a good connection with the M5, and from Ross the A40 is a good dual carriageway, through attractive scenery, to Abergavenny. Three good N/S dual carriageways which also help to open up the area are the A449 between Newport and Raglan, the A4042 from Newport up past Pontypool, and the A470 from Cardiff up towards Merthyr Tydfil. These good communications put most parts of the area within an hour or so of the Severn Bridge, and if the traffic's flowing freely you can, for example, get to Abergavenny from Birmingham in about an hour and a half.

Where to eat

Llandewi Skirrid SO3416 WALNUT TREE Gwent (0873) 852797 Comfortable, stylish dining pub run by the same licensees for over 25 years, with outstanding, imaginative – though not cheap – food (wonderful puddings and fine cheeses), attractive choice of wines (particularly strong on Italian ones), and efficient, friendly service; cl Sun, Mon, 2 wks Feb; disabled access. **£32|£5.50/£11.50.**

Cardiff ST1877 HAPPY GATHERING (0222) 397531 Very good Chinese food; cl 24-26 Dec. **£18.75|£8.**

Swansea SS6187 ROOTS W Glamorgan (0792) 366006 Fresh, home-made vegetarian food in simple restaurant/café (most choice in evening), relaxed atmosphere, friendly staff, and bring your own wine; Fridays are reserved for non-smokers, other days there is a no-smoking area; cl Sun, Mon, 25 Dec. **£17.50|£1.60/£4.75.**

Cardiff ST1877 LUCIANOS Park Lane (0222) 382367 Good Italian food warmly recommended by contributors; cl Sun, bank hols. **£3.50.**

Llancarfan ST0570 FOX & HOUNDS S Glamorgan (0446) 781297 Comfortably modernised, friendly old pub in lovely village with rambling bar, open fire, popular restaurant, tasty food, good coffee, and helpful service; no food winter Sun pm. **£1.50/£4.50.**

Help this year from: *Dilys Unsworth, Martyn and Mary Mullins, Haydn Roberts, M and J Back, Joan and Michel Hooper-Immins, P W Knatchbull-Hugessen, Colin Martin, Janet and Gary Amos, Jed and Virginia Brown, Barbara Graham, Mike and Trew Mehaffy, Carol and Phil Byng, A Kilpatrick, P D Putwain, Mrs D Nisbet, John and Beryl Knight, John Coatsworth, J N Howe, Mrs J S England, David Thompson, Margaret Mason, Christopher Kilburn, Ann Marie Stephenson, Gwyneth and Salvo Spadaro-Dutturi, Ken and Monica Charlton, Iris and Eddie Brixton, Jed and Virginia Brown, H K Dyson, Michael Stroud, JT, J E Rycroft, Joan and Jim Griffiths, Mr and Mrs N Sanders, S and E Timerick, B Haywood, Mr and Mrs T J Anslow, Hugh Spottiswoode, M A Cameron, C Roberts, Simon Reynolds, Neville Kenyon, Steve Thomas, Ian Jones, George Atkinson, K R Harris, M Barrell, Canon Michael Bourdeaux, Mr and Mrs A E McCully, Mrs J E Hilditch, Paul and John Gibbon, D J Underwood, Andrew and Barbara Sykes, Peter Rees, Brian and Gill Hopkins, KC, Klaus and Elizabeth Leist, Roy Cove, K F Glasby, Gill Owen, David Green, Mr and Mrs P B Dowsett, J Boylan, Michael Sandy, Gordon Theaker, Jason Caulkin, E H and R F Warner, Mrs J Oakes, Nicholas Wright, J E and A G Jones, John Nash, Bryan Hicks, Prof J R Leigh, H Saddington, P Boot, Jeff Davies, Dr and Mrs Marchington, Martyn and Mary Mullins.*

We welcome reports from readers . . .

This GUIDE depends on readers' reports. Do help us if you can – in return, we offer a discount on the next edition to people who've helped us with reports for it. Tell us what you think about places already in it, and anything extra you think we should say about them. And send us your ideas for inclusion in the next edition: places to visit, eat at or stay in, attractive drives or walks, maybe even unusual interesting shops you know of. Use the card in the middle, the report forms at the end, or just write – no stamp needed: THE GOOD WEEKEND GUIDE, FREEPOST TN1569, Wadhurst, E Sussex TN5 7BR.

Wales Calendar

Some of these dates were provisional as we went to press.

JANUARY

1st **Cardiff** The Snow Queen, *a play for children at the Sherman Theatre – till Fri 7*

2nd **Swansea** New Year's Gala Concert *at Brangwyn Hall, 3.30 and 7.30*

14th **Llanwrtyd Wells** The Second Saturnalia *at the Nevadd Arms – a Roman feast, fun and festivities – till Sun 16*

15th **Cardiff** Rugby Union Wales v Scotland *at Cardiff Arms Park*

19th **Cardiff** Rugby Union Wales v France *at Cardiff Arms Park*

FEBRUARY

1st **Cardiff** Prehistoric Sea Monsters *at National Museum of Wales – till Sun 27*

MARCH

1st **Cwm-felin-fach** St David's Day Celebrations *at Ynys Hywel Countryside Centre – evening*

11th **Llanwrtyd Wells** Folk Weekend *at the Neuadd Arms – till Sun 13*

25th **Port Talbot** Welsh Beautiful Homes and Gardens Exhibition *at the Orangery, Margam Park – till Sun 27*

26th **Swansea** Bach Choir, St Matthew Passion *in St Mary's Church*

APRIL

1st **Cardiff** International Rugby Festival *at Cardiff Arms Park – till Mon 4*

3rd **St Nicholas** Craft Fair *at Dyffryn House – till Mon 4*

4th **Botachowyn** Lyn and District Agricultural Show

7th **Cardiff** South Asian Arts Festival *at St David's Hall – till Sun 10*

30th **Llandudno** Extravaganza – *town centre closed to traffic; Victorian parades and vintage car rally – till 2 May*

MAY

1st **Holyhead** Arts Festival – *till Tues 10*

2nd **Holywell** Carnival

5th **Bridgend** Drama Festival *at Recreation Centre – till Sat 7*

7th **Cardiff** Rugby Cup Final *at Cardiff Arms Park*

8th **Porthcawl** Open Shore Fishing Festival

12th **Bridgend** Drama Festival – *till Sat 14*

13th **Newport** Folk Music and Dance Festival *at Tredegar House – till Sun 15*

14th **Haverfordwest** Pembrokeshire Young Farmers County Rally *at County Showground*

16th **Cardiff** International Animation Festival *at St David's Hall – till Sun 22*

20th **Llangollen** International Jazz Festival – *till Sun 22*; **Hay-on-Wye** Literature Festival – *till Mon 30*

Wales Calendar

May cont.

28th **Conwy** and District Goat Weekend, *inc milking competition at Bolondeb Fields (Bangor Road) – till Sun 29*

29th **Abergavenny** Steam and Vintage Rally *at Bailey Park – till Mon 30*; **Beaumaris** Festival, *orchestral concerts, jazz, street events and regatta – till 5 Jun*; **Newport** Festival of Musical Theatre, *competitive platform for the best amateur musical societies at Dolman Theatre – till 4 Jun*; **Swansea** Show and Country Fair *at Singleton Park – till Mon 30*

30th **Caldicot** Carnival *at Castle*; **Dolgellau** Eisteddfod, *largest youth festival in Europe at Eisteddfod ground – till 4 Jun*; **Tregaron** May Festival

June

4th **Welshpool** Montgomeryshire County Show *at Powis Castle Showground*

9th **Llantilio Crossenny** Festival of Music and Drama *at St Teilo's Church – till Sun 12*

11th **Cardiff** World Harp Festival *at St David's Hall – till Sat 18*; **Llanwrtyd Wells** Man v Horse v Mountain Bike 22-mile Marathon, *£15,000 prize if a runner wins, currently 4 mins gap*

16th **Mumbles** Victorian Festival *– till Sun 19*

17th **Monmouth** Flower and Music Festival *at St Mary's Church – till Sun 19*

18th **Criccieth** Music and Art Festival *at Memorial Hall and other venues – till Mon 27*; **Llandeilo** Welsh Game Fair *at Gelli Aur – till Sun 19*; **Llanwrtyd Wells** Drovers Walk *– 10, 15 or 25-mile challenge*

24th **Trellech** Festival of Music and Flowers *at St Nicholas Church – till Sun 26*

25th **Chirk** Country Fair *at Chirk Castle Park*; **Tregynon** Gregynog Festival *at Gregynog Hall – till 3 July*

July

1st **Trefriw** Bluegrass Festival *– till Sun 3*

5th **Llangollen** International Music Eisteddfod *at Eisteddfod ground – till Sun 10*

8th **Llandysul** Welsh Celtic Festival, *performances from various Celtic countries – till Sat 9*

10th **Llanfyllin** Festival *at St Myllin's Church – till Sun 17*

15th **Cardiff** Welsh Proms *at St David's Hall – till Sat 23*

16th **Abergavenny** Medieval Market

18th **Llanelwedd** Royal Welsh Show *– till Thurs 21*

24th **Barry** Carnival Week *– till Sat 30*; **Haverfordwest** Vintage Car Club Show *at Scolton Manor*

25th **Conwy** Festival *in the streets – till Sun 31*

27th **Cardiff** International Festival of Street Entertainment *– till 7 Aug*

WALES CALENDAR

JULY cont.

30th **Glynneath** National Eisteddfod of Wales, *inc concerts, fringe, ceremonial pageantry – till 6 Aug*; **Scolton** Model Aircraft Weekend *at Country Park – till Sun 31*

31st **Llanwrtyd Wells** Festival and Canal Day *– till 7 Aug*

AUGUST

6th **Cardiff** Lord Mayor's Parade

11th **Llanwrtyd Wells** Mountain Bike Festival, *inc night rides, skills courses, mountain bike polo and football at The Square and surrounding venues – till Sun 14*

12th **Brecon** Jazz Festival *– till Sun 14*

14th **Begelly** Vintage Car Show *at Folly Farm*

17th **nr Aberporth** Air Day *at Blaenannerch Airfield*

18th **Denbigh** Denbighshire and Flintshire Agricultural Show *at The Green*; **Llandeilo** National Sheepdog Trials *– till Sat 20*

19th **Pontardawe** International Music Festival, *linked to Swansea Canal bicentenary celebrations – till Sun 21*

20th **Llandrindod Wells** Victorian Festival *– till Sun 28*

21st **Machynlleth** Festival *– till Sun 28*

25th **Monmouth** Monmouthshire Show *at Vauxhall*

26th **Pontrhydfendigaid** Tregaron Trotting Club Races *at Dolyrychain Farm – till Sat 27*

28th **Harlech** Merioneth County Show

SEPTEMBER

17th **Cardiff** Festival, *women in the arts – till 18 Oct; also* Festival of Music *at St David's Hall – till 9 Oct*

OCTOBER

3rd **Laugharne** Big Court Night *at Town Hall; probably the last place in Britain where the Portreeve, Corporation and Grand Jury still function – new Portreeve elected in trad ceremony*

22nd **Llandudno** International Festival of the Voice, *inc music, drama and poetry at New North Wales Theatre and other venues – till Sun 30*

30th **Nant Peris** *nr Llanberis* Snowdonia Marathon

NOVEMBER

14th **Llanwrtyd Wells** Mid-Wales Beer Festival *– till Sun 20*

DECEMBER

2nd **Caldicot** Christmas Spectacular

National Calendar

This Calendar combines events of national importance with our selection of those more local events which might interest you enough to influence your choice of area, if you're planning to go away when they're on. Fuller details of some events can be found in the regional calendars at the end of each chapter. A few of these dates were provisional as we went to press.

January

1st **Winton Fell, Cumbria** Nine Standards Fell Race; **Westminster Abbey, London** Lord Mayor of Westminster's Parade; **Kirkwall, Scotland** (Orkney) New Year's Day Ba' Games

6th **Haxey, Humber** Ancient Hood Game; **Earls Court Exhibition Centre, London** International Boat Show – *till Sun 16*; **Guildford, Surrey** Wassailing, *Twelfth Night pub tour by Morris men who act out the old tiptearers' or mummers' play*

7th **Whittlesey, Cambs** Straw Bear Festival; **Sheffield, Yorks** British Ice Dance Championships *at the Arena – till Sun 9*

11th **Burghead, Scotland** Burning of the Clavie – *6 pm*

17th **Carhampton, Somerset** Wassailing the Apple Trees, *ancient ceremony*

22nd **Nantwich, Cheshire** Holly Holy Day, *celebration of the Battle of Namptwyche*

25th **Lerwick, Scotland** (Shetland) Up-Helly-Aa Traditional Viking Fire Festival *inc burning a longship*

February

4th **York** Jorvik Viking Festival – *till Fri 19*

6th **Grasmere, Cumbria** Wordsworth Winter School *at Dove Cottage – till Fri 11*

7th **St Ives, Cornwall** Feast Monday, *with hurling and throwing of the silver ball*

13th **Soho, London** Chinese New Year Celebrations

15th **Olney, Bucks** Pancake Race, *the oldest in the country*; **Ashbourne, Derbys** Shrovetide Football Game; **Atherstone, Midlands** Shrovetide Football; **Scarborough, Yorks** Shrovetide Skipping Festival

22nd **Inverurie, Scotland** Aberdeen Agricultural Show

25th **Grasmere, Cumbria** Book Collectors Weekend *at Dove Cottage – till Sun 27*

March

5th **Truro, Cornwall** Cornwall Brass Band Assoc Annual Contest *at City Hall*

10th **Birmingham, Midlands** NEC Crufts Dog Show; **Norwich, Norfolk** Blues Festival, *performers from the US – till Sat 12*

MARCH cont.

11th **Kings Lynn, Norfolk** Fiction Festival – *till Sun 13*; **Sheffield, Yorks** Industrial Hamlet Working Days *at Abbeydale – till Sun 13*

14th **Kingussie, Scotland** Badenoch and Strathspey Music Festival *inc gaelic, country dancing and piping – till Fri 18*

17th **Kiplingcotes, Humber** Derby: *oldest flat race in the country, the only race where winner gets less money than runner-up*; **Earls Court Exhibition Centre, London** Ideal Home Exhibition – *till 10 Apr*

19th **Peterborough, Cambs** National Shire Horse Show *at East of England Showground, with over 300 entries*

20th **Olympia, London** International Book Fair – *till Tues 22*

25th **Edinburgh** Folk Festival – *till 3 Apr*

26th **Putney to Mortlake, London** Oxford v Cambridge University Boat Race; **Swansea, Wales** Bach Choir, St Matthew Passion *in St Mary's Church*

27th **Lynton, Devon** Jazz Festival – *till Tues 29*

30th **Edinburgh** International Puppet and Animation Festival – *till Sat 9*

31st **Olympia, London** International Spring Gardening Fair – *till 4 Apr*

APRIL

1st **Long Melford, Suffolk** Re-creation of Tudor Life *at Kentwell Hall – till Mon 4*; **Harrogate, Yorks** International Festival of Country Music – *till Mon 4*

2nd **Ellesmere Port, Cheshire** Boaters' Gathering, Maritime Festival – *till Mon 4*; **Bacup, Lancs** Britannia Coconutters, *elaborately costumed black-face clog dancers in the streets from 9*; **Grange de Lings** Horse Trials *at Lincs Showground with crafts and flower show – till Sun 3*

3rd **Knebworth, Herts** Jousting Tournament – *till Mon 4*; **West Stow, Suffolk** Saxon Market *at Anglo-Saxon Village – and Saxon traders on Mon 4*; **Singleton, Sussex** Traditional Food Fair *at Weald and Downland Open Air Museum – till Mon 4*

4th **Hallaton, Leics** Hare Pie Scrambling *at Hare Pie Bank*; **Regent's Park, London** London Harness Horse Parade

8th **Morpeth, Northumbria** Northumbrian Gathering, *festival of Northumbrian traditions – till Sun 10*

9th **Colliers End, Herts** Game and Countryman Fair *at St Edmund's College – till Sun 10*

16th **Derby** Festival, *outdoor and indoor music and dance – till 1 May*; **Sulgrave, Midlands** Living History 1643, *Sulgrave Manor run as it was – till Sun 24*

21st **Harrogate, Yorks** RHS Spring Flower Show – *till Sun 24*

22nd **Newton Abbot, Devon** Tuckers Maltings Real Ale Festival, *over 80 ales to sample in Britain's only traditional working malt house*; **Sutton Bonington, Notts** National Folk Festival – *till Sun 24*

23rd **Gloucester** St George's Day Celebrations *with mummers and Morris dancers*; **Stratford-upon-Avon, Midlands** Shakespeare Birthday Celebrations; **Haywards Heath, Sussex** Festival of Gardening *at Borde Hill Garden – till Sun 24*

APRIL cont.

29th **Glasgow, Scotland** Mayfest – *till 21 May*; **Barnard Castle, Northumbria** Teesdale Thrash – *till 2 May*

30th **Minehead, Somerset** Hobby Horse Parade – *till 2 May*; **Bath, Somerset** Spring Flower Show – *till 2 May*; **Long Melford, Suffolk** Re-creation of Tudor Life *at Kentwell Hall – till 2 May*; **Hastings, Sussex** Jack-in-the-Green Festival of Morris Dancing – *till 2 May*; **Edinburgh** Calton Hill Beltane Fire – *grand May-Day ceilidh, re-enactment of pagan festival – till 1 May*; **Llandudno, Wales** Extravaganza – *town centre closed to traffic*; Victorian Parades and Vintage Car Rally – *till 2 May*

MAY

1st **Padstow, Cornwall** 'Obby 'Oss Celebrations, *trad May-Day custom*; **Randwick, Glos** Cheese Rolling; **Southsea, Hants** Heavy Horse Parade and Obstacle Driving Championships *at Castle Field Arena*; **Leicester** Leics County Show *at Braunstone Park*; **Berwick-upon-Tweed, Northumbria** Riding the Bounds, *ancient and colourful ceremony*; **Oxford** May Morning: *medieval celebration, college choristers sing from Magdalen college tower at 6 am, Morris dancers in Radcliffe Sq and Broad St, pubs and restaurants open early for breakfast*; **Horsington, Somerset** Jack-in-the-Green Festival; **Guildford, Surrey** May Celebrations, *at 5.30 Morris dancing to greet sunrise on St Martha's Hill*

2nd **Stilton, Cambs** Cheese Rolling; *also* **Reach, Cambs** Fair, *held here for over 700 years*; **Norton, Cheshire** Priory May-Day Celebrations; **Sandbach, Cheshire** Elizabethan Market, *costumed market with jugglers, jesters, fire-eaters*; **Newborough, Staffs** Well Dressing; **Blackawton, Devon** International Worm-Charming; **Marsh Mill Village, Lancs** May-Day Clog Dancing *in Town Sq*

5th **Hatfield, Herts**, Crafts Fair *at Hatfield House: 300 stands, maypole dancing, Morris men, Punch & Judy – till Sun 8*; **Badminton, Somerset** Horse Trials – *till Sun 8*

6th **Winthorpe** Notts County Show *at Newark Showground – till Sat 7*; **Brighton, Sussex** Horse Driving Trials *at Stanmer Park – till Sun 8*; *also* International Arts Festival – *till Sun 29*

7th **Knutsford, Cheshire** Royal May Day, *processions on pavements carpeted with sands of different colours in elaborate patterns*; **Helston, Cornwall** Furry Dance, *spring festival*

8th **Mytholmroyd, Yorks** World Dock Pudding Championships

11th **Windsor, Berks** Royal Windsor Horse Show – *till Fri 15*; **Whitby, Yorks** Upper Harbour Planting of the Penny Hedge

12th **Tissington, Derbys** Best-known Well Dressing, *since 1349*; **Bisley, Glos** Well Blessing; **Beverley, Humber** Early Music Festival – *till Sun 15*

14th **Chester, Cheshire** Lord Mayor's Show & Festival of Transport, *procession, Morris dancing and over 400 veteran cars*; **Stratton, Cornwall** Re-enactment of the Civil War Battle of Stamford Hill – *till Sun 15*; **Randwick, Glos** Wap – *fair and procession with cheese, mayor carried shoulder high and dipped in the pond*; **Leeds, Kent** Festival of English Wines *at Leeds Castle – till Sun 15*

15th **Stafford** Staffs International Tattoo, *at Wolseley Garden Park*

MAY cont.

16th **Cardiff, Wales** International Animation Festival *at St David's Hall – till Sun 22*

19th **Chester, Cheshire** Beating the Retreat, *trad military ceremony in Castle Sq*

21st **Nottingham** Lord Mayor's Show

22nd **St Briavels, Glos** Bread and Cheese Ceremony, *in which they are thrown from a wall near the castle to be scrambled for in the lane below*

23rd **Corby, Midlands** Pole Fair, *starts with sunrise charter reading, ox roast, climbing a greasy pole*

24th **Chelsea, London** Flower Show – *till Fri 27*

26th **Stromness, Scotland** Orkney Traditional Folk Festival – *till Sun 29*

27th **Netley, Hants** D-Day Celebrations, *at Royal Victoria Country Park, international veterans parade, sailpast, Royal Yacht Britannica – till Sat 28*; **Bath, Somerset** International Festival of Classical Music, Jazz and the Visual Arts – *till 12 Jun*

28th **Ashford-in-the-Water, Derbys** Flower Festival and Well Dressing, *sheep washed in the river Wye at Sheepwash Bridge – till 4 Jun*; **Endon, Staffs** 150th Well Dressing Festival – *till Mon 30*; **RAF Mildenhall, Suffolk** Air Fête at HQ of US 3rd Air Force – *till Weds 29*; **Bathgate, Scotland** Highland Games; **Blackford, Scotland** Highland Games; **Garnock, Scotland** International Highland Games; **Thornhill, Scotland** Field Sports Fair *at Drumlanrig Castle – till Sun 29*; **Blair Atholl, Scotland** Gathering *at Blair Castle, annual parade and inspection of the Duke of Atholl's unique private army*; **Conwy, Wales** Goat Weekend *inc milking competition – till Sun 29*

29th **Calder Bridge, Cumbria** Country Field Day: *trad pursuits*; **Castleton, Derbys** Garland Ceremony *on Oak Apple Day (anniversary of Charles II restoration in 1660)*; **Rockbourne, Hants** Roman Weekend *at Roman Villa – till Mon 30*; **Atholl, Scotland** Highland Gathering; **Swansea, Wales** Show and Country Fair *at Singleton Park – till Mon 30*

30th **Combe Martin, Devon** Hunting of the Earl of Rone Ceremony; **Blandford, Dorset** South of England Town Crier Competition; **Brockworth, Glos** Cheese Rolling *at Coopers Hill, 400-year-old ritual*; **Tetbury, Glos** Woolsack Races and Medieval Fayre; **Sandringham, Norfolk** Horse Trials; **Oxford** Lord Mayor's Parade

---

JUNE

1st **Ipswich** Suffolk County Agricultural Show – *till Thurs 2*; **Arundel, Sussex** Corpus Christi Carpet of Flowers and Floral Display *at Cathedral – till Thurs 2*; **Horse Guards Parade, London** Beating Retreat – *till Thurs 2*

2nd **Appleby, Cumbria** Horse Fair; *gypsies gather from all over Europe on Fair Hill for this 300-year-old event – till Weds 8*; **Weymouth, Dorset** D-Day, Military and Veteran Parade *inc military bands, WWII military vehicles, Royal Navy warship exercises*; **Rochester, Kent** Dickens Festival – *till Sun 5*; **Olympia, London** Fine Art and Antiques Fair – *till Sun 12*

JUNE cont.

3rd **Chipping Campden, Glos** Dover's Games and Scuttlebrook Wake, *17th-c 'Olympicks' of rural sports – till Sat 4*

4th **Liverpool** Lord Mayor's Parade; **Lincoln** Water Festival, *inc Mayor's parade*; **Warminster, Wilts** Horse Trials *at Longleat House – till Sun 5*; **Welshpool, Wales** Montgomeryshire County Show

9th **Wadebridge** Royal Cornwall Show *– till Sat 11*; **Ardingly, Sussex** South of England Show *– till Sat 11*; **Wetherby** Bramham International Horse Trials and Yorks Country Fair *– till Sun 12*

10th **Binstead, IOW** Heavy Horse Festival *– till Sun 12*; **Hawick, Scotland** Common Riding *inc ride-outs, proclaiming of the Burgh Officer, Cornets walk, snuffing ceremony and procession – till Fri 11*

11th **Worcester** Re-enactment of the visit of King Charles I *at The Commandery inc fair and procession – till Sun 12*; **Hull, Humber** Lord Mayor's Parade; **Ventor, IOW** Smuggling Pageant *– till Fri 17*; **Long Melford, Suffolk** Country Fair *at Melford Hall*; **Eastbourne, Sussex** International Ladies Tennis Championships *– till Sat 18*; **Fountains Abbey and Studley Royal, Yorks** Music *ending with fireworks – till Sun 12*; **Lesmahagow, Scotland** Highland Games; **Llanwrtyd Wells, Wales** Man v Horse v Mountain Bike 22-mile Marathon, *£15,000 prize if a runner wins*; **Horse Guards Parade, London** Trooping the Colour

12th **Singleton, Sussex** Heavy Horse Day at Weald and Downland Open Air Museum; **Keith, Scotland** Grange Highland Games; **Oban, Scotland** Kilmore and Kilbride Highland Games; **Turriff, Scotland** Pipe Band Contest

14th **Ascot, Berks** Royal Ascot, *Ascot Racecourse – till Fri*; **Malvern, Hereford & Worcs** Three Counties Agricultural Show *– till Thurs 16*

17th **Beverley, Humber** Folk Festival *– till Sun 19*; **Campbeltown, Scotland** Kintyre Music Festival *– till Sun 19*

18th **Ovingham, Northumbria** Goose Fair, *trad fair with proclamation, Morris men and pipers*; **Newburgh, Scotland** Highland Games; **Llandeilo** Welsh Game Fair *– till Sun 19*

19th **Kirkby Lonsdale, Cumbria** Brass Band Contest; **Stocksfield, Northumbria** British Field Sports Country Fair *at Bywell Hall*; **Long Melford, Suffolk** Re-creation of Tudor Life *at Kentwell Hall, 200 participants dress, speak and live like Tudors – till 17 July*; **Farnham, Surrey** Blues Festival *at the Maltings, 12 hours' non-stop blues*; **Aberdeen, Scotland** Highland Games; **Peebles, Scotland** Riding of the Marches and Beltane Festival *– till Sat 25*

20th **Aberdeen** Highland Games *– till Sat 25*; **Wimbledon, London** Lawn Tennis Championships *– till 3 July*

21st **Tabley, nr Knutsford,** Cheshire Agricultural Show *– also Sun 26*; **Stonehenge, Wilts** Druid Summer Solstice Ceremony *at midnight, vigil till dawn, Presider crowned at noon*

22nd **Grange de Lings** County Show *at Lincs Showground*

23rd **Edinburgh** Royal Highland Show *at Ingliston – till Sun 26*

25th **Willaston, Cheshire** 15th World Worm Charming Championships; **Ottery St Mary, Devon** Pixie Day; **Leeds, Kent** Open Air Concert *at Leeds Castle*; **Thirsk** North Yorks County Show

JUNE cont.

26th **Bakewell, Derbys** Well Dressing and Carnival – *till 2 July*; **Perth, Scotland** Scone Palace Coronation Pageant – *re-enactment of James IV coronation*; **Seil, Scotland** Highland Games

28th **Henley, Oxon** Regatta – *till 3 July*

29th **Norwich** Royal Norfolk Show *at Royal Norfolk Showground – till Thurs 30*

JULY

1st **Warrington, Cheshire** Walking Day, *northern trad*; **Exeter, Devon** Festival – *till Sun 17*; **Lyme Regis, Dorset** Jazz Festival; **Glasgow, Scotland** International Jazz Festival – *till Sun 10*

2nd **Musgrave, Cumbria** Rushbearing; **Lake Windermere, Cumbria** Festival – *till Sun 10*; **Ambleside, Cumbria** Rush-bearing; **Cheltenham, Glos** 50th International Festival of Music, *extensive fringe – till Sun 17*; **Leeds, Kent** Open Air Concert *at Leeds Castle*; **Sulgrave, Midlands** Living history 1746, *Georgian times at Sulgrave Manor – till Sun 10*; **Long Marston, Yorks** Re-enactment of the Battle of Marston Moor – *till Sun 3*

3rd **Newquay, Cornwall** 1900 Victorian Week *with carnival, torchlight procession and fireworks – till Sun 10*; **Alport, Derbys** Lovefeast, *Alport Barn, 1 mile W of Woodlands Chapel up Snake Pass, dates back to 18th-c religious revival*; **Isle of Barra, Scotland** Festival of Gaelic – *till Fri 15*; **City of London** Festival – *till Weds 20*

4th **Stoneleigh, Midlands** Royal Agricultural Show *at Stoneleigh Park – till Thurs 7*

6th Tour de France from **Dover** through Kent to **Tunbridge Wells** through Sussex to **Brighton**; **Kenmore, Scotland** Highland Games; **Hampton Court Palace, London** Flower Show – *till Sun 10*

7th Tour de France **Hants** leg, starts and ends **Portsmouth**

8th **Windsor, Berks** Royal Windsor Rose & Horticultural Show, Windsor Castle Grounds – *till Sat 9*; **Ryton, Midlands** National Organic Food and Wine Fair *at Ryton Organic Gardens – till Sat 9*; **Norwich, Norfolk** Lord Mayor's Procession, *celebration of 800 years of Norwich – till Sun 10*; **Fountains Abbey and Studley Royal, Yorks** Music by Moonlight – *till Sat 9*; **York** Early Music Festival – *till Sun 17*; **Llandysul** Welsh Celtic Festival – *till Sat 9*

9th **Witcham, Cambs** World Pea Shooting Championships; **Charmouth, Dorset** Challenge and Fun Run *over NT land along cliffs*; **Winchester, Hants** 20th Hat Festival, *celebration of street theatre – till Sun 10*; **Durham, Northumbria** Miners Gala, *orig 1871; miners march behind colliery band and banner, trade union rally, gala and dancing*; **Dingwall, Scotland** Highland Games; **Jedburgh, Scotland** Border Games

10th **Keith, Scotland** Festival of Traditional Music and Song – *till Tues 12*

12th **Harrogate** Great Yorks Show – *till Thurs 14*

13th **Esher, Surrey** Claremont Landscape Garden Fête Champêtre – *till Sun 17*

14th **Detling, Kent** County Show – *till Sat 16*

JULY cont.

16th **Stratford-upon-Avon, Midlands** Festival – *till Sun 31*; **Chester-le-Street, Northumbria** County Agricultural Show *at Lambton Park – till Sun 17*; **RNAS Yeovilton, Somerset** International Air Day; **Lamberhurst, Sussex** Firework and Laser Symphony Concert *at Bewl Water*; **Lochcarron, Scotland** Highland Games; **Royal Festival Hall, London** Jazz Parade – *till Sun 24*

17th **Tolpuddle, Dorset** Martyrs Rally, *national march of unions; speakers, possibly from South Africa*; **Weymouth, Dorset** Cutty Sark Tall Ships Race *with over 100 ships – till Weds 20 when the ships parade*

18th **Grasmere, Cumbria** Sports, *trad inc Lakeland wrestling*; **Llanelwedd** Royal Welsh Show – *till Thurs 21*

19th **Peterborough, Cambs** East of England Show *at East of England Showground – till Thurs 21*; **Earls Court Exhibition Centre, London** Royal Tournament

20th **Stourton, Wilts** Stourhead Fête Champêtre, *firework finale – till Sat 23*; **Inveraray, Scotland** Highland Games

21st **Newport, IOW** County Agricultural Show *at Northwood Showground*

22nd **Chester, Cheshire** Summer Music Festival – *till Sat 30*; **Petworth, Sussex** NT Craft Festival *at Petworth House and Park*; **Isle of Mull, Scotland** Highland Games

23rd **Whitstable, Kent** Oyster Festival – *till Sun 31*; **Nottingham** Rock and Reggae Festival – *till Sun 24*; **Middlesbrough, Northumbria** Cleveland County Show; **Weston-super-Mare, Somerset** Carnival and Fun Day at Beach Lawns, *helicopter fly-in – till Sun 24*; **Dornoch, Scotland** Sutherland Agricultural Show

24th **Chatham, Kent** Heavy-Horse Day *at the Historic Dockyard*; **Aberdeen, Scotland** Massed Pipe Band Display *at Duthie Park*; **Rothiemurchus, Scotland** Highland Games; **Taynuilt, Scotland** Highland Games

25th **Inverness, Scotland** Tattoo – *till Sat 30*; **Newton Stewart, Scotland** Galloway Pageant – *till Sat 30*

27th **Barnstaple, Devon** Royal Air Force Chivenor Air Day; **West Witton, Yorks** Burning of Bartle, *the effigy of a legendary outlaw*; **Cardiff, Wales** International Festival of Street Entertainment – *till 7 Aug*

28th **Lancaster, Lancs** Georgian Legacy Festival *inc re-enactments – till Sun 31*

29th **Stowe, Bucks** Music and Fireworks – *till Sun 31*; **Northampton** Town Show – *till Sun 31*; **Worthing, Sussex** Seafront Fair, *gaslight market, torchlight procession, fireworks, vintage cars – till Sun 31*; **Langholm, Scotland** Common Riding, *processions, cornets' chase, highland games and open-air evening dance*

30th **Lake District, Cumbria** Summer Music Festival – *till 13 Aug*; **Grasmere, Cumbria** Wordsworth Summer Conference *at Dove Cottage*; **Cowes, IOW** Yacht Racing – *till 7 Aug*; **Glynneath** National Eisteddfod of Wales – *till 6 Aug*

AUGUST

1st **Edwinstowe, Notts** Robin Hood Festival – *till Sun 7*

AUGUST cont.

2nd **Egton Bridge, Yorks** Old Gooseberry Show

3rd **Land's End, Cornwall** Air Day *with Red Arrows and Falcon display*; **St Mawgan, Cornwall** International Air Day; **Malvern, Hereford & Worcs** National Pony Society Show *at Three Counties Showground – till Thurs 4*; **Isle of Skye, Scotland** Highland Games

4th **Ings, Cumbria** Lake District Sheepdog Trials; **Honiton, Devon** Show

5th **Penrith, Cumbria** Lowther Horse Driving Trials and Country Fair *– till Sun 7*; **South Zeal, Devon** Dartmoor Folk Festival, *ceilidh, workshops, Dartmoor step-dance and broom-dance championships, pub music sessions – till Sun 7*; **Portsmouth, Hants** Southsea Show *– till Sun 7*; **Broadstairs** Kent Folk Week *– till Fri 12*; **Warwick, Midlands** Folk Festival *– till Sat 6*; **Dornoch, Scotland** Highland Gathering; **Edinburgh** Military Tattoo *– till Sat 27*; *also* International Jazz Festival *– till Sat 13*; **Perth, Scotland** Agricultural Show *– till Sat 6*

6th **South Perrott, Dorset** Open Weekend; **Southend-on-Sea, Essex** Jazz Festival *– till Sun 7*; **Garstang, Lancs** Agricultural Show; **Nottingham** Riverside Festival *at Victoria Embankment – till Sun 7*; **Ryton, Midlands** Organic Gardening Weekend *at Ryton Organic Gardens – till Sun 7*; **Bristol, Somerset** Harbour Regatta and Fireworks *– till Sun 7*; **Isle of Arran, Scotland** Highland Games; *also* Corrie Capers *– till Sat 13*; **Linlithgow, Scotland** Palace Celebration of Mary, Queen of Scots *– till Sun 7, also on 13, 14, 20, 21, 27, 28 Aug*; **Cardiff, Wales** Lord Mayor's Parade

7th **Derby** Military Tattoo, *at Moorways Stadium*; **Stafford** Highland Gathering *in Wolseley Garden Park hosts all the England Pipe Band Championships*; **Alnwick Castle, Northumbria** Tournament Day; **Parton, Scotland** 13th Scottish Alternative Games; **Hyde Park,** *Rotten Row*, London Riding Horse Parade

8th **Derby** Summer Extravaganza *– evening events in the week leading up to the weekend which inc the Royal Navy, shire horses and parade – till Sun 14*; **Arreton, IOW** Manor Pageant

10th **Holkham, Norfolk** Pageant and Son-et-lumière *– till Sat 13*

11th **Northleach, Glos** National Sheepdog Trials *– till Sat 13*; **Irvine, Scotland** Marymass Festival *inc Scotland's largest horse-drawn parade on Sat 20 – till Mon 22*

13th **Fleetwood, Lancs** Fireworks and Birdman Competition *on the Pier*; **Rochdale, Lancs** Rush-bearing Ceremony; **Billingham, Northumbria** International Folklore Festival *– till Sat 20*; **nr Chichester, Sussex** Sussex Game and Country Fair *at St Michael's School (Burton Park) – till Sun 14*; **Aberfeldy, Scotland** Atholl and Breadalbane Games and Show; **Edinburgh** International Film Festival *– till Sun 28*; **Glasgow** World Pipe Band Championships *at Bellahoustan Park*; **Worcester** Tudor Festival *at The Commandery to celebrate the visit of Queen Elizabeth in 1575 – till Sun 14*

14th **Macclesfield Forest (Forest Chapel), Cheshire** Rush-bearing Ceremony; **Bridport, Dorset** Carnival Week *ending with torchlight procession – till Sun 21*; **Edinburgh** International Festival and Fringe *– till 3 Sept*; **Roslin, Scotland** Rosslyn Chapel Events *– till 3 Sept*

AUGUST cont.

16th **Wadebridge, Cornwall** Cornwall Folk Festival – *till Mon 29*; **RHS Halls, London,** *Greycoat St*, RHS Summer Flower Show – *till Weds 17*

17th **Weymouth, Dorset** Carnival, *inc air, sea and firework displays*

18th **Denbigh, Wales** Denbighshire and Flintshire Agricultural Show; **Llandeilo, Wales** National Sheepdog Trials – *till Sat 20*

19th **Pontardawe, Wales** International Music Festival *linked to Swansea Canal bicentenary celebrations – till Sun 21*; **South Bank Centre, London,** *Purcell Room*, Folk Week – *till Fri 26*

20th RAF **Alconbury, Cambs** Air Display – *till Sun 21*; **Allendale, Northumbria** Agricultural Show; **Falstone, Northumbria** Border Shepherds Show; **Leyburn, Yorks** Wensleydale International Brass Festival – *till Mon 29*; **Crieff, Scotland** Highland Gathering; **Lairg, Scotland** Crofters Show; **Rothesay, Scotland** Bute Highland Games

21st **Maidenhead, Berks** Vintage Day *at Courage Shire Horse Centre*; **Edington, Wilts** Music Festival, *music within the liturgy – till Sun 28*; **Salisbury** and South Wilts Agricultural Show

25th Port of **Dartmouth, Devon** 150th Royal Regatta – *till Sat 27*; **Newport, IOW** Carnival; **Blair Atholl, Scotland** International Horse Trials *at Blair Castle – till Sun 28*; **Oban, Scotland** Argyllshire Highland Gathering – *till Fri 26*; **Monmouth, Wales** Monmouthshire Show

26th **Reading, Berks** Rock Festival, *Richfield Avenue – till Sun 28*; **Chelmsford, Essex** Spectacular, *fireworks concert at Hylands Park – till Mon 29*; **Havenstreet, IOW** Steam Extravaganza – *till Mon 29*; **Liverpool** International Beatles Convention – *till Tues 30*; **Glastonbury, Somerset** Children's Festival – *till Mon 29*; **Long Melford, Suffolk** Re-creation of Tudor Life *at Kentwell Hall – till Mon 29*; **Arundel, Sussex** Festival – *till 4 Sept*; **Dunoon, Scotland** Cowal Highland Gathering – *till Sat 27*

27th **Eyam, Derbys** Well Dressing – *till 3 Sept*; **Matlock Bath, Derbys** Illuminations Switch-on, *inc illuminated boats every weekend evening – till end Oct*; **Yealmpton, Devon** Medieval Combat *at National Shire Horse Centre*; **Southend-on-sea, Essex** Thames Sailing Barge Race; **Portsmouth, Hants** International Kite Festival – *till Sun 28*; **Hartham** Hertford Horse Show *on the Common*; **Stoneleigh, Midlands** Town and Country Festival *at Stonleigh Park – till Mon 29*; **Sulgrave, Midlands** Re-enactment of 1644 Civil War Siege of Sulgrave Manor – *till Mon 29*; **Mildenhall, Suffolk** Cycling Rally, *largest in the south of England – till Mon 29*; **Ravenscar, Yorks** Bonfire, Barbecue and Music *at National Trust Centre*; **Leyburn, Yorks** Wensleydale Agricultural Show; **Ripley, Yorks** Crafts Show *at Ripley Castle – till Mon 29*; **Aberdeen** Royal Horticultural Show *at Duthie Park – till Sun 28*; **Drumnadrochit, Scotland** Highland Games; **Largs, Scotland** Viking Festival *inc opera and battle re-enactments – till 4 Sept*

28th **West Stow, Suffolk** Saxon Market *at Anglo-Saxon Village – Saxon traders on Mon 29*; **Neston, Wilts** Vintage Rally – *till Mon 29*; **Wroughton, Wilts** Great Warbirds Air Display *at Science Museum inc massed formation flypasts*; **Ladbroke Grove, London** Notting Hill Carnival, *Europe's largest street festival – till Mon 29*

AUGUST cont.

29th **Bourton-on-the-Water, Glos** Football in the River Windrush; **Ledbury, Hereford & Worcs** Street Carnival; **Leominster, Hereford & Worcs** Agricultural Show; **Ross-on-Wye, Hereford & Worcs** Regatta; **Brigg, Humber** Folklore Fayre and Dance Festival *at Elsham Hall Country Park*; **Epworth, Humber** Show; **Ramsbottom, Lancs** World Black-pudding-throwing Championships; **Aylsham, Norfolk** Agricultural Show; **Newcastle** Free Festival, *open air events, circus, concerts, comedy – till 3 Sept*; **Hovingham, Yorks** 18th-c Street Fair; *also* Gardens Open *at Hovingham Hall*

31st **Tarrant Hinton, Dorset** Great Dorset Steam Fair *at Showground inc exhibits from abroad – till 4 Sept*

SEPTEMBER

1st **Weedon** Bucks County Show; **Stamford, Cambs** Burghley Horse Trials, *at Burghley House – till Sun 4*

2nd **Glossop, Derbys** Victorian Weekend – *till Sun 4*; **Faversham, Kent** Hop Festival – *till Sun 4*; **Goudhurst, Kent** Finchcocks Music Festival, *every Fri and Sat – till Sat 25*; **Woodstock, Oxon** Autumn Flower Show *at Blenheim Palace – till Sun 4*

3rd **Dorchester, Dorset** Agricultural Show; **Shepton Mallet, Somerset** Countryside Cavalcade – *till Sun 4*; **Alfriston, Sussex** English Wine and Regional Food Festival *at English Wine Centre – till Sun 4*; **Hastings, Sussex** National Town Criers Championships; **Pewsey, Wilts** Carnival *inc race of 100 decorated wheelbarrows from pub to pub, procession Sat 17*; **Warley to Sowerby Bridge** *on Sat and* **Sowerby to Ripponden, Yorks** *on Sun 4*, Rushbearing, *markets and entertainments*; **Braemar, Scotland** Royal Highland Gathering

4th **Spencers Wood, Berks** Wokingham & Reading Agricultural Show, *at White House Farm*; **Derby** Darley Park Concert *with fireworks*; **Woodchurch, Kent** Rare Breeds Show *at Rare Breeds Centre*; **Blairgowrie, Scotland** Highland Games

5th **Abbots Bromley, Staffs** Ancient Annual Horn Dance *in the village streets*; **Farnborough, Hants** International Aerospace Exhibition and Flying Display – *till Sun 11*

6th **Newquay, Cornwall** Festival *ending with Chinese dragon dance – till Sat 10*; **City of London** Flower Show, *rare opportunity to see the Guildhall interior*

8th **Worcester** Jolly Small Brewers Beer Festival *at Faithful City Brewery – till Sun 11*; **Monymusk, Scotland** International Sheepdog Trials – *till Sat 10*

9th **Long Ashton, Somerset** International Balloon Fiesta – *till Sun 11*

10th **Lichfield, Staffs** Sherriff's Ride; **Weston** Staffs Great Autumn Show, *at County Showground – till Sun 11*; **Westbury, Wilts** Medieval Fayre

11th **Norwich, Norfolk** Town and Country Show

13th **Westminster, London** RHS Halls Great Autumn Flower Show – *till Weds 14*

15th **Royal Albert Hall, London** BBC Henry Wood Promenade Concerts – *till 10 Sept*

SEPTEMBER cont.

16th **Harrogate, Yorks** RHS Great Autumn Show – *till Sat 17*

17th **Newbury, Berks** Berks Show; **Winsford, Cheshire** Vale Royal Show; **Egremont, Cumbria** Crab Fair *inc world gurning (pulling a face) championships*; **Finningley, Yorks** RAF Air Show; **Cardiff, Wales** Festival, *women in the arts – till 18 Oct*; *also* Festival of Music *at St David's Hall – till 9 Oct*

18th **Painswick, Glos** Clypping of the Church Ceremony; **Epworth, Humber** Festival of the Plough; **Worsbrough, Yorks** Festival of the Horse *at Country Park*

23rd **Eastbourne, Sussex** Orchestra Festival *for amateur musicians at Sandhurst Hotel, book in advance – till Sun 25*

24th **Dronfield** NE Derbys Brass Band Festival; **Cirencester, Glos** Cotswold Country Fair – *till Sun 25*; **Hopton, Shrops** British Isles Horse and Tractor Ploughing Championships; **Frome, Somerset** Illuminated Carnival

25th **Urswick, Cumbria** Rushbearing

OCTOBER

1st **Maidenhead, Berks** Heavy Horse Show, *Courage Shire Horse Centre – till Sun 2*; **Ilminster, Somerset** Carnival, *illuminated floats*; **Masham, Yorks** Sheep Fair *inc Bishop Blaise procession*

2nd **Trafalgar Square, London** Pearly Harvest Festival Service *at St Martin-in-the-Fields, best occasion to see Pearly Kings and Queens*; **Covent Garden Piazza, London** Punch and Judy Fellowship

4th **Wembley, London** Horse of the Year Show *at Arena – till Sun 9*

5th **Nottingham** 700th Goose Fair – *till Sat 8*

6th **Norfolk and Norwich** Festival – *till Sun 16*

7th **Goudhurst, Kent** Finchcocks Fair – *till Sun 9*

8th **Exeter, Devon** Carnival, *grand illuminated procession*; **Sulgrave, Midlands** Tudor Living History *at Sulgrave Manor – till Sun 16*; **Alwinton, Northumbria** Border Shepherds Show

9th **Ashton, nr Oundle, Cambs** World Conker Championships

12th **Perranporth, Cornwall** Lowender Perran; *festival of Celtic culture*; **Tavistock, Devon** Traditional Goosey Fair

13th **Aberdeen** Alternative Festival – *till Sat 22*

15th **Taunton, Somerset** Illuminated Carnival and Cider-barrel Rolling Race; **Albert Hall, London** National Brass Band Championships

17th **Windermere, Cumbria** Power Boat Record Attempts – *till Fri 21*

21st **Faversham, Kent** Brogdale Trust Apple Day, *also Mon 24*

22nd **Birmingham** International Motor Show and Ideal Homes Show *at the NEC – till Sun 30*; **Wincanton, Somerset** Illuminated Carnival; **Singleton, Sussex** Steam Threshing and Ploughing *at Weald and Downland Open Air Museum with heavy horses and vintage tractors – till Sun 23*; **Llandudno, Wales** International Festival of the Voice, *inc music, drama and poetry – till Sun 30*

25th **Edinburgh** Scottish Story-telling Festival *at Netherbow Arts Centre – till 5 Nov*

OCTOBER cont.

27th **Nottingham** Robin Hood Pageant – *till Sun 30*

28th **Castle Donington, Leics** Wakes – *till Mon 31 (not Sun)*

29th **Blair Atholl, Scotland** Piping Championships *at Blair Castle*

30th **Bolsover, Derbys** Castle Fireworks and Laser Spectacular

31st **Newton Abbot, Devon** Halloween Hauntings *at Tuckers Maltings (ghost said to be very friendly)*

NOVEMBER

3rd **Bridgwater, Somerset** Guy Fawkes Carnival, *over 80 brilliantly lit floats; 10 pm hand-held fire-fountain poles*

4th **Kendal, Cumbria** Festival of Jazz and Blues; **Bishop Auckland, Northumbria** Fireworks and Funfair

5th **Lewes, Sussex** Torchlight Procession; *best of Britain's bonfire celebrations, town closed to traffic at 5.30, bands, effigies, burning tar barrel race*; **Ottery St Mary, Devon** Tar-barrel Rolling and Carnival; **Weymouth, Dorset** Guy Fawkes Night *inc beach bonfire, fireworks, fair and barbecue*; **Leeds, Kent** Fireworks Display *at Leeds Castle*; **Fleetwood, Lancs** Fireworks and Birdman Competition *on the pier*; **Kenilworth, Midlands** Bonfire *at Kenilworth Castle*; **Sulgrave, Midlands** Chamber Concert and Fireworks *at Sulgrave Manor*; **Alnwick** Northumbrian Gathering, *small pipes, fiddles, concert and ceilidh*; **Ironbridge, Shrops** Traditional Gaslight Night *at Blists Hill Open Air Museum culminating in firework display*; **North Petherton, Somerset** Guy Fawkes Illuminated Procession; **Embsay, Yorks** Steam Railway Bonfire, *fireworks and night steam trains*; **Liverpool** River Mersey Fireworks

7th **Burnham-on-Sea, Somerset** Illuminated Procession

9th **Shepton Mallet, Somerset** Illuminated Procession

11th **Wells, Somerset** Illuminated Procession

12th **The City, London** Lord Mayor's Procession and Show; **Glastonbury, Somerset** Illuminated Procession

14th **Weston-super-Mare, Somerset** Illuminated Procession, *bands*

17th **Wasdale Head, Cumbria** Biggest Liar in the World Competition; **Huddersfield, Yorks** Contemporary Music Festival – *till Sun 27*

20th **Cleethorpes, Humber** Victorian Christmas Fair; **Farnham, Surrey** Blues Festival *at the Maltings, 12 hours' non-stop blues*

24th **Birmingham** BBC Good Food Cooking and Kitchen Show *at the NEC – till Sun 27*

25th **Hornsea, Humber** Lights Night *inc craft stalls, mince pies and sherry*

DECEMBER

1st **Warwick, Midlands** Victorian Street Fair; **York** St Nicholas Fayre *– till Sun 4*

DECEMBER cont.

3rd **Chalfont St Giles, Bucks** Victorian Christmas Weekend *at Chiltern Open Air Museum – till Sun 4*; **Kirkby Lonsdale, Cumbria** Christmas Fair; *lights-on celebration*; **Allington, Kent** Snow Queen Carnival and Old English Fayre; **Rochester, Kent** Dickensian Christmas – *till Sun 4*; **Grassington, Yorks** Dickensian Christmas *also on Sat 10 and Sat 17*

4th **Keswick, Cumbria** Victorian Fayre

13th **Looe, Cornwall** Torchlight Procession

15th **Hull, Humber** Christmas Fair; **Olympia, London** International Showjumping Championships – *till Mon 19*

18th **Haworth, Yorks** Father Christmas, *torchlight procession and carol service*

23rd **Salisbury, Wilts** Carol Service *at Cathedral*; **Grantown-on-Spey, Scotland** Torchlight Procession

25th **Eastbourne, Sussex** Band Concert *at Grand Parade*; **Kirkwall, Scotland** Isle of Orkney Christmas Day Ba' Games *at 1 pm*; **Hunstanton, Norfolk** Christmas Day Swim; **Hyde Park, London** Serpentine Peter Pan Cup Swimming Race *at 8 am*

26th **Winslow, Bucks** Boxing Day Hunt Meet, *Market Sq*; **Gloucester** St Stephen's Day Morris Dance – *12 noon at Gloucester Cathedral and 1 pm at New Inn*; **Sunderland, Northumbria** Boxing Day Dip *at Coastal Road, over 1,000 dippers in fancy dress*; **Eastbourne, Sussex** Open Air Dancing *at Grand Parade*; **Ripon, Yorks** *Pilgrimage from Cathedral to Fountains Abbey*

31st **Allendale, Northumbria** Baal Festival, *tar barrels lit 11.45 pm*; **Ripon, Yorks** Cathedral Watchnight Service and Torchlight Procession; **Aberdeen, Scotland** Bonfire Night Celebrations; **Biggar, Scotland** Ne'erday Bonfire, *ancient Druid custom – torchlight procession led by pipe band*; **Comrie, Scotland** Flambeaux Torchlight Procession; **Edinburgh** Tron Kirk; **Stonehaven, Scotland** Fireball Ceremony

We welcome reports from readers . . .

This GUIDE depends on readers' reports. Do help us if you can – in return, we offer a discount on the next edition to people who've helped us with reports for it. Tell us what you think about places already in it, and anything extra you think we should say about them. And send us your ideas for inclusion in the next edition: places to visit, eat at or stay in, attractive drives or walks, maybe even unusual interesting shops you know of. Use the card in the middle, the report forms at the end, or just write – no stamp needed: THE GOOD WEEKEND GUIDE, FREEPOST TN1569, Wadhurst, E Sussex TN5 7BR.

Special interest lists

Self-sufficient hotels

The hotels, inns and other places listed here have plenty to do on the premises or in their grounds – enough for most people to be happy to stay put there all day.

BERKSHIRE
Streatley, Swan Diplomat
Windsor, Oakley Court

BUCKINGHAMSHIRE
Aylesbury, Hartwell House
Marlow, Compleat Angler
Taplow, Cliveden

CAMBRIDGESHIRE
Flitwick, Flitwick Manor
Needingwath, Pike and Eel
Six Mile Bottom, Swynford Paddocks
Wansford, Haycock

CHESHIRE
Macclesfield, Sutton Hall Hotel
Nantwick, Rookery Hall
Sandiway, Nunsmere Hall

CORNWALL
Carne Beach, Nare
Gerrans Bay, Pendower Beach House
Looe, Talland Bay
Mawnan Smith, Meudan
Mawnan Smith, Nansidwell Country House
Mullion, Polurrian
Newlyn, Higher Faugan
St Keyne, Old Rectory
Isles of Scilly
Tresco, Island

CUMBRIA
Brampton, Farlam Hall
Crook, Gilpin Lodge
Derwent Water, Lodore Swiss
Grasmere, Michael's Nook
Grasmere, White Moss House
Grasmere, Wordsworth
Pooley Bridge, Sharrow Bay
Rydal, Glen Rothay
Seatoller, Seatoller House
Watermillock, Old Church
Windermere, Langdale Chase

DERBYSHIRE
Ashbourne, Callow Hall
Bakewell, Hassop Hall
Barslow, Cavendish
Matlock, Riber Hall

DEVON
Burgh Island, Burgh Island
Chagford, Gidleigh Park
Chittlehamholt, Highbullen
Clawton, Court Barn
Dulverton, Ashwick Country House
Dulverton, Tarr Steps
East Portlemouth, Gara Rock
Gittisham, Combe House
Goveton, Buckland-tout-Saints
Higher Bulstone, Bulstone
Lewdown, Lewtrenchard Manor
Marlborough, Soar Mill Cove
Salcombe, Tides Reach
South Molton, Whitechapel Manor
Torquay, Imperial
Whimple, Woodhayes

GLOUCESTER
Buckland, Buckland Manor
Charingworth, Charingworth Manor
Cheltenham, Greenway
Clearwell, Clearwell Castle
Lower Slaughter, Lower Slaughter Manor
Tetbury, Calcot Manor
Upper Slaughter, Lords of the Manor
Westonbirt, Hare and Hounds

HAMPSHIRE
Hurstbourne Tarrant, Essebourne Manor
Lymington, Passford House
New Milton, Chewton Glen
Rotherwick, Tylney Hall

HEREFORD AND WORCESTER
Bromsgrove, Grafton Manor
Ledbury, Hope End Country House
Pontrilas, Howton Court

LANCASHIRE
Whitewell, Inn at Whitewell

LEICESTERSHIRE, LINCOLNSHIRE AND NOTTINGHAMSHIRE
Leics
Oakham, Hambleton Hall
Packington, Springs Hydro
Stapleford, Stapleford Park
Lincs
Stamford, George
Notts
Bestwood Country Park, Bestwood Lodge

THE MIDLANDS
Ansty, Ansty Hall
Leamington Spa, Mallory Court
Stratford-upon-Avon, Welcombe
Sutton Coldfield, New Hall
Wishaw, Belfry

NORFOLK
Grimston, Congham Hall
Hethersett, Park Farm

NORTHUMBRIA
Allendale, Bishopsfield Country House
Cornhill-on-Tweed, Tillmouth Park
Easington, Grinkle Park
Longframlington, Embleton Hall

OXFORDSHIRE
Great Milton, Manoir aux Quat' Saisons
Horton-cum-Studley, Studley Priory
Wallingford, Shillingford Bridge
Weston-on-the-Green, Weston Manor

SOMERSET AND AVON
Freshford, Homewood Park
Hunstrete, Hunstrete House
Kilve, Meadow House
Ston Easton, Ston Easton Park
Thornbury, Thornbury Castle

SUFFOLK
Hintlesham, Hintlesham Hall
Woodbridge, Seckford Hall

SURREY
Bagshot, Pennyhill Park

SUSSEX
Alfriston, Deans Place
Amberley, Amberley Castle
Climping, Bailiffscourt
East Grinstead, Gravetye Manor
Rusper, Ghyll Manor
Uckfield, Horsted Place

WILTSHIRE
Colerne, Lucknam Park
Easton Grey, Whatley Manor
Ford, White Hart
Warminster, Bishopstow House

YORKSHIRE
Bilbrough, Bilbrough Manor
Bolton Abbey, Devonshire Arms
Dunsley, Dunsley Hall
Hackness, Hackness Grange
Otley, Chevin Lodge
Sedbusk, Stone House
York, Middlethorpe Hall

SCOTLAND
South
Edinburgh, Balmoral
Gatehouse of Fleet, Cally Palace
Gullane, Greywalls
Kelso, Sunlaws House
Kilwinning, Mountgreenan Mansion House
West
Kilfinan, Kilfinan Hotel
Port Appin, The Airds
Strachur, Creggans
North of the Forth
Advie, Tulchan Lodge
Auchterarder, Gleneagles
Auchterhouse, Old Mansion House
Ballater, Craigendarroch Hotel
Balquhidder, Monachyle Mhor
Banchory, Invery House
Blairgowrie, Kinloch House
Dunblane, Cromlix House
Dunkeld, Kinnaird House
East Haugh, East Haugh House
Kenmore, Kenmore
Killiecrankie, Pitlochry
Monymusk, Grant Arms
Scone, Murryshall House

North
Altnaharra, Altnaharra
Glenborrodale, Glenborrodale Castle
Isle Ornsay, Kinloch Ledge
Skeabost, Skeabost House

WALES
North
Llandrillo, Tyddyn Llan
Llandudno, Bodysgallen Hall
Llanwddyn, Lake Vyrnwy
Portmeirion, Portmeirion
Talsarneau, Maes-y-Neuadd
Mid
Eglwysfach, Ynyshir Hall
West
Broad Haven, Druidstone
Crugybar, Glanrannell Park

Waterside hotels

The hotels and other places to stay listed here are right beside the sea, a sizeable river, canal, lake or loch that contributes significantly to their attraction.

BERKSHIRE
Hungerford, Marshgate Cottage
Kintbury, Dundas Arms
Streatley, Swan Diplomat
Windsor, Oakley Court

BUCKINGHAMSHIRE
Marlow, Compleat Angler
Taplow, Cliveden

CAMBRIDGESHIRE AND BEDFORDSHIRE
Huntingdon, George
Needingworth, Pike & Eel

CHESHIRE
Sandiway, Nunsmere Hall

CORNWALL
Bodinnick, Old Ferry
Calstock, Danescombe Valley
Carne Beach, Nare
Constantine Bay, Treglos
Crafthole, Finnygook
Fowey, Fowey Hotel
Fowey, Marina
Gerrans Bay, Pendower Beach House
Gillan, Tregildry
Golant, Cormorant
Lamorna Cove, Lamorna Cove
Looe, Talland Bay
Mawnan Smith, Meudon
Mawnan Smith, Nansidwell Country House
Mullion, Polurrian
Padstow, Old Custom House
Port Isaac, Port Gaverne
Portloe, Lugger
Portloe, Seal Cottage
Portscatho, Roseland House
Sennen, Old Success
Sennen, State House
St Ives, Garrack
St Mawes, Rising Sun
Trelights, Long Cross
Isles of Scilly
Pelistry Bay, Carnwethers
St Mary's, Tregarthens
Tresco, Island

CUMBRIA
Alston, Lovelady Shield
Ambleside, Wateredge
Dent, Sportsmans
Grasmere, Oak Bank
Grasmere, White Moss House
Mungrisdale, Mill Hotel
Pooley Bridge, Sharrow Bay
Silloth, Skinburness
Thirlmere, Dale Head Hall
Watermillock, Leeming House
Watermillock, Old Church
Windermere, Holbeck Ghyll Country House
Windermere, Langdale Chase

DERBYSHIRE AND STAFFORDSHIRE
Ashford-in-the-Water, Riverside Country House

DEVON
Ashprington, Watermans Arms

Burgh Island, Burgh Island
Chagford, Mill End
Dartmouth, Royal Castle
East Portlemouth, Gara Rock
Exebridge, Anchor
Ilfracombe, Altro
Lifton, Arundell Arms
Lynmouth, Rising Sun
Malborough, Soar Mill Cove
Salcombe, Tides Reach
Torquay, Imperial

DORSET
Swanage, Pines
Wareham, Priory

ESSEX
Burnham-on-Crouch, White Harte
Dedham, Maison Talbooth
West Mersea, Victory

HAMPSHIRE
Lee-on-the-Solent, Belle Vue

GLOUCESTERSHIRE
Bibury, Swan

HEREFORD AND WORCESTER
Symonds Yat, Saracens Head

ISLE OF WIGHT
Yarmouth, Bugle
Yarmouth, George

HUMBERSIDE
Hull, Forte Crest

LANCASHIRE
Bilsborrow, Guy's Thatched Hamlet
Blackpool, Imperial
Whitewell, Inn at Whitewell

LEICESTERSHIRE, LINCOLNSHIRE, NOTTINGHAMSHIRE
Leics
Empingham, White Horse
Oakham, Hambleton Hall

NORFOLK
Blakeney, Blakeney Hotel

NORTHUMBERLAND
Chollerford, George
Seahouses, Olde Ship

OXFORDSHIRE
Abingdon, Upper Reaches
Henley, Red Lion
Moulsford, Beetle & Wedge
Newbridge, Rose Revived
Wallingford, Shillingford Bridge

SHROPSHIRE
Llanfair Waterdine, Red Lion

SOMERSET AND AVON
Exebridge, Anchor
Somerton, Lynch Country House

SUFFOLK
Aldeburgh, White Lion
Beccles, Waveney House
Needham Market, Pipps Ford

SUSSEX
Bognor Regis, Royal Norfolk
Eastbourne, Grand
Eastbourne, Hydro
Eastbourne, Seacroft
Wisborough Green, Old Wharf

WILTSHIRE
Rowde, Lower Foxhangers Farm
Salisbury, Old Mill
Salisbury, Rose & Crown
Warminster, Bishopstrow House

YORKSHIRE
Burnsall, Red Lion
Egton Bridge, Horse Shoe
Richmond, Howe Villa

LONDON
Conrad, SW10
Tower Thistle, E1

SCOTLAND
South
Auchencairn, Balcary Bay
Ettrick Valley, Tushielaw
Kelso, Ednam House
Portpatrick, Crown
Portpatrick, Knockinaam Lodge

West
Arduaine, Loch Melfort
Crinan, Crinan Hotel
Duror, Stewart
Eriska, Isle of Eriska Hotel
Kilchrenan, Ardanaiseig
Kilchrenan, Taychreggan
Kilmore, Glenfeochan House
Onich, Allt-Nan-Ros
Port Appin, The Airds
Strachur, Creggans
Tiroran, Tiroran House
Tobermory, Tobermory
North of the Forth
Carronbridge, Lochend Farm
Inverness, Bunchrew House
Kenmore, Kenmore
Lower Largo, Crusoe
Spean Bridge, Letterfinlay Lodge
North
Achiltibuie, Summer Isles
Arisaig, Arisaig House
Dornie Loch, Duich
Glenborrodale, Glenborrodale Castle
Glenelg, Glenelg
Kylesku, Kylesku
Melvich, Melvich Hotel
Scourie, Eddrachilles
Shieldaig, Tigh an Eilean
Strontian, Kilcamb Lodge
Strontian, Loch Sunart Hotel
Tongue, Ben Loyal Hotel
Ullapool, Altnaharrie
Skye
Isle Ornsay, Kinloch Lodge
Skeabost, Skeabost House
Sleat, Ord House

WALES
North
Aberdovey, Bodfor
Aberdovey, Penhelig Arms
Betwys-y-Coed, Ty Gwyn
Erbistock, Boat
Llanwddyn, Lake Vyrnwy
Portmeirion, Portmeirion
Mid
Penmaenpool, George III
West
Broad Haven, Druidstone
Mynydd-y-Garreg, Gwenllian Court
South
Abergavenny, Llanwenarth Arms
Monmouth, Riverside
Oxwich Bay, Oxwich Bay

Hotels well placed for walks

The hotels, inns and other places we list here are placed where you can go for a good longish walk, straight from the door.

BUCKINGHAMSHIRE
Aylesbury, Hartwell House
Fawley, Walnut Tree
Hambleden, Stag & Huntsman
Ibstone, Fox
Taplow, Cliveden

CHESHIRE
Higher Burwardsley, Pheasant

CORNWALL
Botallack, Manor Farm
Buryas Bridge, Rose Farm
Carne Beach, Nare
Constantine Bay, Treglos
Gerrans Bay, Pendower Beach House
Lamorna Cove, Lamorna Cove
Mawnan Smith, Meudon
Mawnan Smith, Nansidwell Country House
Mullion, Polurrian
Pendeen, Trewellard Manor Farm
Port Isaac, Port Gaverne
Portloe, Lugger
Portloe, Seal Cottage
Portscatho, Roseland House
Sennen, Old Success
Sennen, State House
Trelights, Longcross
Isles of Scilly
Pelistry Bay, Carnwethers
Tresco, Island

CUMBRIA
Alston, Middle Bayles Farm
Barbon, Barbon Inn

East Haugh, East Haugh House
Kenmore, Kenmore
Killiecrankie, Pitlochry
Monymusk, Grant Arms
Scone, Murryshall House
Crook, Gilpin Lodge
Crook, Wild Boar
Dent, Sportsmans
Derwent Water, Lodore Swiss
Dockray, Royal
Elterwater, Britannia Inn
Eskdale Green, Bower House
Far Sawrey, Sawrey
Garrigill, George & Dragon
Grasmere, Michael's Nook
Grasmere, Swan
Grasmere, White Moss House
Grasmere, Wordsworth
Grizedale, Grizedale Lodge
Hawkshead, Highfield House
Hawkshead, Summer Hill
Ireby, Overwater Hall
Langdale, Langdale
Langdale, Old Dungeon Ghyll
Little Langdale, Three Shires
Lorton, New House Farm
Mungrisdale, Mill Hotel
Pooley Bridge, Sharrow Bay
Ravenstonedale, Fat Lamb
Seatoller, Seatoller House
Spark Bridge, Bridgefield House
Torver, Church House
Torver, Old Rectory
Troutbeck, Mortal Man
Wasdale Head, Wasdale Head
Winton, Bay Horse
Witherslack, Old Vicarage

DERBYSHIRE AND STAFFORDSHIRE

Butterton, Black Lion
Castleton, Castle
Castleton, Olde Nags Head
Dovedale, Peveril of the Peak
Great Longstone, Barn
Greendale, Old Furnace Farm
Hathersage, George
Hathersage, Highlow Hall
Hope, Poachers Arms
Monsal Head, Monsal Head Hotel
Rowland, Holly Cottage

DEVON

Bossington, Orchard Guest House
Chagford, Gidleigh Park
Chittlehamholt, Highbullen
Countisbury, Exmoor Sandpiper
Croyde, Whiteleaf
Dulverton, Highercombe
Dulverton, Tarr Steps
East Portlemouth, Gara Rock
Exford, White Horse
Haytor Vale, Rock
Holne, Church House
Knowstone, Masons Arms
Lydford, Castle
Lynmouth, Rising Sun
Lynton, Hewitt's
Lynton, Lynton Cottage
Malborough, Soar Mill Cove
Moretonhampstead, Great Sloncombe Farm
Oakford, Newhouse Farm West Buckland, Huxtable Farm
Porlock, Ship
Porlock, West Porlock House
Salcombe, Tides Reach
Slapton, Tower
Topsham Bridge, Yeo Farm

GLOUCESTERSHIRE

Buckland, Buckland Manor
Clearwell, Clearwell Castle
Clearwell, Wyndham Arms
Great Rissington, Lamb
North Nibley, New Inn
St Briavels, George
Viney Hill, Lower Viney Country Guest House

HAMPSHIRE

Beaulieu, Montagu Arms
Eastleigh, Park Farm
Emery Down, New Forest
Rotherwick, Tylney Hall

HEREFORD AND WORCESTER

Chaddesley Corbett, Brockencote Hall
Frith Common, Hunt House Farm
Kinnersley, Upper Newton Farmhouse
Leysters, Hills Farm
Pontrilas, Howton Court
Ruckhall Common, Ancient Camp
Stretton Grandison, Moor Court Farm

Symonds Yat, Saracens Head
Vowchurch, Croft Country House
Whitney-on-Wye, Rhydspence
Woolhope, Butchers Arms

KENT
Ashford, Eastwell Manor
Chartham, Thruxted Oast
Groombridge, Crown
Headcorn, Bletchenden Manor Farm
Pluckley, Elvey Farm
Sissinghurst, Sissinghurst Castle Farm
St Margaret's-at-Cliffe, Cliffe Tavern Hotel
Teston, Court Lodge
Warren Street, Harrow

LANCASHIRE
Ashworth Valley, Leaches Farm
Chipping, Carr Side Farm
Darwen, Old Rosins
Gibbon Bridge, Gibbon Bridge Country House
Newton, Parkers Arms
Slaidburn, Hark to Bounty
Slaidburn, Parrock Head Farm
Waddington, Backford Cottage
Waddington, Peter Barn
Whitewell, Inn at Whitewell

LEICESTERSHIRE, LINCOLNSHIRE, NOTTINGHAMSHIRE
Leics
Empingham, White Horse
Oakham, Hambleton Hall
Stapleford, Stapleford Park
Notts
Bestwood Country Park, Bestwood Lodge

NORFOLK
Grimston, Congham Hall
South Lopham, Malting Farm
Thornham, Lifeboat
Titchwell, Manor Hotel
Winterton-on-Sea, Fishermans Return

NORTHUMBERLAND AND DURHAM
Allendale, Bishopsfield Country House
Bamburgh, Lord Crewe Arms
Cornhill-on-Tweed, Tillmouth Park
Cotherstone, Fox & Hounds
High Force, High Force Hotel
Middleton-in-Teesdale, Teesdale
Newton-by-the-Sea, Joiners Arms
Romaldkirk, Rose & Crown
Tarset, Earls Lodge

OXFORDSHIRE
Asthall, Maytime
Checkenden, Highwayman
Minster Lovell, Hill Grove Farm
Minster Lovell, Old Swan
Woodstock, Feathers

SHROPSHIRE
Church Stretton, Long Mynd
Church Stretton, Mynd House
Clun, New House Farm
Hopesay, Old Rectory
Llanfair Waterdine, Red Lion
Strefford, Strefford Hall Farm
Wenlock Edge, Wenlock Edge Inn
Woolstaston, Rectory

SOMERSET AND AVON
Dulverton, Ashwick House
Dulverton, Tarr Steps
Dunster, Luttrell Arms
Emborough, Redhill Farm
Exford, White Horse
Hunstrete, Hunstrete House
Isle Brewers, Bushfurlong Farm
Kilve, Meadow House
Lower Vellow, Curdon Mill
Middlecombe, Periton Park
Pinksmoor, Pinksmoor Millhouse
Roadwater, Wood Advent Farm
West Bagborough, Rising Sun
Wiveliscombe, Deepleigh

SUFFOLK
Aldeburgh, White Lion
Hintlesham, College Farm
Southwold, Crown
Southwold, Swan
Westleton, Crown

SURREY
Albury, Drummond Arms
Bagshot, Pennyhill Park

SUSSEX
Alfriston, Deans Place

Alfriston, Star
Amberley, Amberley Castle
Battle, Netherfield Place
Bosham, Kenwood
Bosham, Millstream
Ditchling, Bull
Fittleworth, Swan
Fletching, Griffin
Poynings, Manor Farm
Shipley, Goffsland Farm
Storrington, Abingworth Hall
Telham, Little Hemingfold Farmhouse
Turners Hill, Alexander House
Winchelsea, New Inn

WILTSHIRE

Alderton, Manor Farm
Ebbesbourne Wake, Horseshoes
Gastard, Boyds Farm
Rowde, Lower Foxhangers Farm
West Grafton, Rose Garth

YORKSHIRE

Ainthorpe, Fox & Hounds
Ampleforth, Carr House Farm
Arncliffe, Falcon
Askrigg, Kings Arms
Austwick, Game Cock
Bainbridge, Rose & Crown
Blakey Ridge, Lion
Bolton Abbey, Devonshire Arms
Buckden, Buck
Burnsall, Red Lion
Chapel-le-Dale, Old Hill
Cloughton, Hayburn Wyke
Cray, White Lion
Danby Wiske, White Swan
Egton Bridge, Horse Shoe
Egton Bridge, Postgate
Fadmoor, Plough
Feizor, Scar Close Farm
Goathland, Mallyan Spout
Grassington, Black Horse
Hackness, Hackness Grange
Hawes, Cocketts
Kilnsey, Tennant Arms
Lastingham, Blacksmiths Arms
Lastingham, Lastingham Grange
Malham, Buck
Markington, Hob Green
Middlesmoor, Crown
Otley, Chevin Lodge
Ramsgill, Yorke Arms
Richmond, Whashton Springs Farm
Robin Hood's Bay, Coble
Rosedale Abbey, Blacksmiths Arms
Rosedale Abbey, Milburn Arms
Rosedale Abbey, White Horse
Sedbusk, Stone House
Settle, Falcon Manor
Simonstone, Simonstone Hall
Stainforth, Craven Heifer
Starbotton, Fox & Hounds
Wath-in-Nidderdale, Sportsmans Arms
West Burton, Fox & Hounds
Wigglesworth, Plough

SCOTLAND

South

Annanwater, Corehead Farm
Auchencairn, Balcary Bay
Beattock, Auchen Castle
Ettrick Valley, Tushielaw
Lockerbie, Dryfesdale Hotel
Minnigaff, Creebridge House
Nenthorn, Whitehill Farm
Portpatrick, Knockinaam Lodge
Quothquan, Shieldhill
Rockcliffe, Barons Craig
Selkirk, Philipburn House
Tweedsmuir, Crook Inn

West

Arduaine, Loch Melfort
Eriska, Isle of Eriska Hotel
Kilberry, Kilberry Inn
Kilchrenan, Ardanaiseig
Kilchrenan, Taychreggan
Kilfinan, Kilfinan Hotel
Kilmore, Glenfeochan House
Onich, Allt-Nan-Ros
Port Appin, The Airds
Strachur, Creggans
Tarbert, Stonefield Castle

North of the Forth

Advie, Tulchan Lodge
Ardeonaig, Ardeonaig
Auchterarder, Gleneagles
Ballater, Craigendarroch Hotel
Ballater, Tullich Lodge
Balquhidder, Monachyle Mhor
Banchory, Invery House
Carronbridge, Lochend Farm
Crianlarich, Allt-Chaorain Country House
Dalcross, Easter Dalziel Farm

Dulnain Bridge, Muckrach Lodge
Dunblane, Cromlix House
Dunkeld, Kinnaird House
East Haugh, East Haugh House
Fintry, Culcreuch Castle
Glendevon, Tormaukin
Kenmore, Kenmore
Kirkton of Glenisla, Glenisla
Pitlochry, Killiecrankie
Scone, Murrayshall House
Spean Bridge, Letterfinlay Lodge
Whitebridge, Knockie Lodge

North

Achiltibuie, Summer Isles
Altnaharra, Altnaharra
Ardvasar, Ardvasar
Arisaig, Arisaig House
Culnaknock, Glenview
Dornie Loch, Duich
Drumnadrochit, Borlum Farmhouse
Drumnadrochit, Polmaily House
Garve, Inchbae Lodge
Glen Shiel, Cluanie
Glenborrodale, Glenborrodale Castle
Glenelg, Glenelg
Invermoriston, Glenmoriston Arms
Isle Ornsay, Kinloch Lodge
Isle Ornsay, Tigh Osda Eilean Iarmain
Kilchoan, Meall Mo Chridhe
Kylesku, Kylesku
Lochinver, Inver Lodge
Melvich, Melvich Hotel
Mey, Castle Arms
Portree, Rosedale
Raasay, Isle of Raasay
Scourie, Eddrachilles
Shiel Bridge, Kintail Lodge
Shieldaig, Tigh an Eilean
Skeabost, Skeabost House
Sleat, Ord House
Strontian, Loch Sunart Hotel
Tongue, Ben Loyal Hotel
Ullapool, Altnaharrie

WALES

North

Abersoch, Porth Tocyn
Beddgelert, Sygun Fawr Country House
Betws-y-Coed, Royal Oak
Betws-y-Coed, Ty Gwyn
Brynsienecyn, Plas Trefarthen
Capel Garmon, Tan-y-Foel Country House
Capel Garmon, White Horse
Frongoch, Fferm Fron-Goch
Gellilydan, Tyddyn Du
Hanmer, Buck Farm
Llanarmon D C, Hand
Llanarmon D C, West Arms
Llandrillo, Tyddyn Llan
Llanerchymedd, Llwydiarth Fawr Farm
Llanerchymedd, Tre'r Ddol Farm
Llanfyllin, Bodfach Hall
Llangollen, Abbey Grange
Llangollen, Britannia
Llanwddyn, Lake Vyrnwy
Maentwrog, Plas Tan y Bwlch
Portmeirion, Portmeirion
Pwllheli, Yoke House Farm
Tremeirchion, Bach-y-Graig

Mid

Cwmdu, Farmers Arms
Cwmystwyth, Hafod Lodge
Eglwysfach, Ynyshir Hall
Gladestry, Royal Oak
Llangurig, Glansevern Arms
Llanwrtyd Wells, Cwmirfon Lodge
Llyswen, Llangoed Hall
Newport, Cnapan
Newtown, Lower Gwestydd
Old Radnor, Harp
Penmaenpool, George III
Pennal, Gogarth Hall Farm
Pontfaen, Tregynon Country Farmhouse
Rhayader, Beili Neuadd
Rhydlewis, Broniwan

West

Brechfa, Forest Arms
Broad Haven, Druidstone
Mynydd-y-Garreg, Gwenllian Court
Newport, Cnapan

South

Llanthony, Half Moon

Well-placed hotels

The hotels, inns and other places listed below are placed very conveniently for sightseeing – there are interesting things nearby which you can get to on foot.

CHESHIRE
Chester, Chester Grosvenor

DEVON
Dartmouth, Royal Castle
Exeter, White Hart
Plymouth, Mayflower Post House

DORSET
Bournemouth, Langtry Manor
Dorchester, Kings Arms
Poole, Mansion House

HAMPSHIRE
Winchester, Royal
Winchester, Wykeham Arms
Portsmouth, Sally Port

HEREFORD AND WORCESTER
Worcester, Fownes

HERTFORDSHIRE
St Albans, White Hart

HUMBERSIDE
Hull, Forte Crest

KENT
Canterbury, Thanington

LANCASHIRE
Blackpool, Imperial
Lancaster, Post House

LEICS, LINCS AND NOTTS
Lincoln, D'Isney Place
Lincoln, Edward King House
Lincoln, White Hart
Stamford, George
Nottingham, Royal Moat House

THE MIDLANDS
Stratford-upon-Avon, Arden Thistle
Stratford-upon-Avon, Coach House
Stratford-upon-Avon, Melita
Stratford-upon-Avon, Shakespeare
Stratford-upon-Avon, Stratford House
Stratford-upon-Avon, Welcombe

NORTHUMBRIA
Durham, Royal County

OXFORDSHIRE
Oxford, Old Parsonage
Oxford, Randolph

SOMERSET AND AVON
Bath, Brocks
Bath, Dorian House
Bath, Haydon House
Bath, Priory
Bath, Queensberry
Bath, Royal Crescent

SUSSEX
Brighton, Topps
Chichester, Bedford
Chichester, Suffolk House
Rye, George
Rye, Jeakes House

WILTSHIRE
Salisbury, Old Mill
Salisbury, Red Lion
Salisbury, Rose and Crown

YORKSHIRE
Harrogate, Old Swan
Harrogate, Russell
York, 4 South Parade
York, Grange
York, Holmwood House
York, Middlethorpe Hall
York, Mount Royale
York, Viking

SCOTLAND
Edinburgh, Balmoral
Edinburgh, Caledonian
Edinburgh, Howard
Edinburgh, Roxburghe
Glasgow, Babbity Bowster
Glasgow, One Devonshire Gardens
Glasgow, Rab Ha's

Hotels with good food

In the hotels, inns and other places listed below, the quality of the food is high enough to make it a significant part of the pleasure of staying there.

BERKSHIRE
Hampstead Marshall, White Hart
Kintbury, Dundas Arms
Pangbourne, Copper
Windsor, Oakley Court
Yattendon, Royal Oak

BUCKINGHAMSHIRE
Aston Clinton, Bell
Aylesbury, Hartwell House
Fawley, Walnut Tree
Marlow, Compleat Angler
Taplow, Cliveden
Winslow, Bell

CAMBRIDGESHIRE
Cambridge, Cambridge Lodge
Eltisley, Leeds Arms
Flitwick, Flitwick Manor
Huntingdon, Old Bridge
Stilton, Bell
Wansford, Haycock

CHESHIRE
Bickley Moss, Cholmondely Arms
Brereton Green, Bears Head
Chester, Crabwell Manor
Chester, Grosvenor
Knutsford, Long View
Nantwich, Rookery Hall

CORNWALL
Calstock, Danescombe Valley
Carne Beach, Nare
Fowey, Marina
Gerrans Bay, Pendover Beach House
Golant, Cormorant
Mawnan Smith, Nansidwell Country House
Padstow, Old Custom House
Pelynt, Jubilee
Port Isaac, Port Gaverne
Portloe, Lugger
Sennen, Old Success
St Ives, Garrack
Tregadillet, Eliot Arms
Treleigh, Inn For All Seasons
Isles of Scilly
Tresco, Island

CUMBRIA
Alston, Lovelady Shield
Ambleside, Rothay Manor
Barbon, Barbon Inn
Brackenthwaite, Pickett Howe
Cartmel, Uplands
Crosby-on-Eden, Crosby Lodge
Eskdale Green, Bower House
Grasmere, Michael's Nook
Grizedale, Grizedale Lodge
Ireby, Overwater Hall
Kirkby Lonsdale, Snooty Fox
Lorton, New House Farm
Lupton, Lupton Tower
Mungrisdale, Mill
Pooley Bridge, Sharrow Bay
Seatoller, Seatoller House
Spark Bridge, Bridgefield House
Watermillock, Leeming House
Watermillock, Old Church
Windermere, Miller House
Witherslack, Old Vicarage

DERBYSHIRE
Ashbourne, Callow Hall
Ashford in the Water, Ashford Hotel
Ashford in the Water, Riverside Country House
Baslow, Cavendish
Baslow, Fischer's Baslow Hall
Biggin-by-Hartington, Biggin Hall
Buxton, Westminster Hotel
Grindleford, Maynard Arms
Hope, Poachers Arms
Matlock, Riber Hall
Monsal Head, Monsal Head
Rowland, Holly Cottage
Rowsley, Peacock
Shottle, Dannah Farm
Staffordshire
Alrewas, Claymar

DEVON
Bishops Tawton, Halmpstone
Chagford, Gidleigh Park
Chittlehamholt, Highbullen
Croyde, Whiteleaf
Dartmouth, Royal Castle
Dulverton, Ashwick Country House

Exeter, White Hart
Gittisham, Combe House
Goveton, Buckland-tout-saints
Gulworthy, Horn of Plenty
Haytor Vale, Rock
Haytor, Bel Alp House
Knowstone, Knowstone Court
Lewdown, Lewtrenchard Manor
Marlborough, Soar Mill Cove
Porlock, West Porlock House
Rousdon, Dower House
Salcombe, Tides Reach
South Molton, Whitechapel Manor
Stockland, Kings Arms
West Buckland, Huxtable Farm
Whimple, Woodhayes

ESSEX
Dedham, Maison Tollbooth
West Mersea, Blackwater

GLOUCESTERSHIRE
Bibury, Swan
Bledington, Kings Head
Charingworth, Charingworth Manor
Cheltenham, Greenway
Cirencester, Fleece
Clearwell, Wyndham Arms
Corse Lawn, Corse Lawn House
Lower Slaughter, Lower Slaughter House
Moreton-in-Marsh, Manor House
Tetbury, Calcot Manor
Tetbury, Close
Upper Slaughter, Lords of the Manor

HAMPSHIRE
Copythorne, Old Well
Emery Down, New Forest
Hayling Island, Cockle Warren Cottage
Hurstbourne Tarrant, Esseborne Manor
Lymington, Stanwell House
Middle Wallop, Fifehead Manor
New Milton, Chewton Glen
Rotherwick, Tylney Hall
Winchester, Wickham Arms

HEREFORD AND WORCESTER
Abberley, Elms
Brimfield, Roebuck
Broadway, Collin House
Broadway, Dormy House
Broadway, Lygon Arms
Bromsgrove, Grafton Manor
Chaddesley Corbett, Brockencote Hall
Evesham, Evesham
Ledbury, Evesham
Ledbury, Hope End Country House
Symonds Yat, Saracens Head
Ullingswick, The Steppes
Vowchurch, Croft Country House

ISLE OF WIGHT
Seaview, Seaview

KENT
Ashford, Eastwell Manor
Pluckley, Dering Arms
Shipbourne, Chaser
Snorden, Chequers
St Margaret's-at-Cliffe, Walletts Court
Tunbridge Wells, Mount Edgecombe

LANCASHIRE
Bury, Normandie
Cowan Bridge, Hipping Hall
Gibbon Bridge, Gibbon Bridge Country House
Slaidburn, Hark to Bounty
Slaidburn, Parrock Head Farm
Waddington, Peter Barn

LEICESTERSHIRE, LINCOLNSHIRE AND NOTTINGHAMSHIRE
Leics
Empingham, White Horse
Market Harborough, Three Swans
Medbourne, Nevill Arms
Oakham, Hambleton Hall
Stapleford, Stapleford Park
Stretton, Ram Jam Inn
Lincs
Barkston, Barkston House
Dyke, Wishing Well
Stamford, George
Notts
Drakholes, Griffin

THE MIDLANDS
Culworth, Fulford House
Hockley Heath, Nuthurst Grange
Leamington Spa, Mallory Court
Stratford-upon-Avon, Stratford House
Sutton Coldfield, New Hall

NORFOLK
Erpingham, Saracens Head
Great Snoring, Old Rectory
Grimston, Congham Hall
South Lopham, Malting Farm
Swaffham, Strattons

NORTHUMBRIA
Chatton, Percy Arms
Easington, Grinkle Park
Longframlington, Embleton Hall
Middleton-in-Teesdale, Teesdale
Romaldkirk, Rose and Crown
Tow Law, Greenwell Farm
Wall, Hadrian
Warkworth, Warkworth Country House
Wylam, Laburnam House

OXFORD
Burford, Angel
Charlbury, Bell
Chedlington, Manor
Clanfield, Plough
Great Milton, Manoir aux Quat' Saisons
Henley, Red Lion
Kingham, Mill House
Moulsford, Beetle & Wedge
Shipton-under-Wychwood, Lamb
Stonor, Stonor Arms
Woodstock, Feathers

SHROPSHIRE
Church Stretton, Mynd House
Hodnet, Bear
Hopesay, Old Rectory
Ludlow, Dinham Hall
Much Wenlock, Talbot
Norton, Hundred House
Wenlock Edge, Wenlock Edge Inn
Worfield, Old Vicarage

SOMERSET AND AVON
Ansford, Bonds Hotel
Bath, Haydon House
Bath, Royal Crescent
Croscombe, Bull Terrier
Freshford, Homewood Park
Hunstrete, Hunstrete House
Kilve, Hood Arms
Langley Marsh, Langley House
Lower Vellow, Curdon Mill
Stoke St Gregory, Rose & Crown
Ston Easton, Ston Easton Park
Thornbury, Thornbury Castle
Vellow, Curdon Mill

SUFFOLK
Campsea Ashe, Old Rectory
Ipswich, Marlborough
Lavenham, Angel
Lavenham, Swan
Needham Market, Pipps Ford
Southwold, Crown

SURREY
Bagshot, Pennyhill Park

SUSSEX
Amberley, Amberley Castle
Battle, Netherfield Place
Chichester, Suffolk House
East Grinstead, Gravetye Manor
Eastbourne, Grand
Hartfield, Bolebroke Mill
Seddlescombe, Brickwall
Telham, Little Hemingfold Farmhouse
Turners Hill, Alexander House
Uckfield, Horsted Place

WILTSHIRE
Bradford-on-Avon, Woolley Grange
Burbage, Old Vicarage
Castle Combe, Manor House
Colerne, Lucknam Park
Corsley, Lane End Cottage
Ford, White Hart
Heytesbury, Angel
Hindon, Lamb
Horningsham, Bath Arms
Nettleton, Fosse Farmhouse
Warminster, Bishopstrow House

YORKSHIRE
Askrigg, Kings Arms
Elslack, Tempest Arms
Pickhill, Nags Head
Richmond, Howe Villa
Richmond, Whashton Springs Farm
Sedbusk, Stone House
Sheffield, Charnwood
Shipton-by-Beningbrough, Sidings
Thornton Watlass, Buck
Wath-in-Nidderdale, Sportsmans Arms

York, 4 South Parade
York, Grange
York, Holmwood House
York, Middlethorpe Hall

SCOTLAND

South

Annanwater, Corehead Farm
Auchencairn, Balcony Bay
Auchencairn, Collin House
Beattock, Auchen Castle
Canonbie, Riverside
Edinburgh, Balmoral
Edinburgh, Caledonian
Ettrick Valley, Tushielaw
Glasgow, One Devonshire Gardens
Gullane, Greywalls
Innerleithen, Caddon View
Kirkcowan, Craighlaw Arms
Melrose, Burts Hotel
Newton Stewart, Kirroughtree
Peebles, Cringletie House
Portpatrick, Crown
Portpatrick, Knockinaam Lodge
Quothquan, Shieldhill
Selkirk, Philipburn House
Swinton, Wheatsheaf
Tweedsmuir, Crook Inn

West

Arduaine, Loch Melfort
Eriska, Isle of Eriska
Kilberry, Kilberry
Kilchrenan, Ardanaiseig
Kilfinan, Kilfinan Hotel
Kilmore, Glenfeochan House
Port Appin, The Airds
Tiroran, Tiroran House

North of Forth

Aberfeldy, Farleyer House
Advie, Tulchan Lodge
Alyth, Lands of Loyal
Auchterarder, Auchterarder House
Ballater, Tullich Lodge
Banchory, Invery House
Blairgowrie, Kinloch House
Dunblane, Cromlix House
Dunkeld, Kinnaird House
East Haugh, East Haugh House
Elgin, Mansion House
Findhorn, Strathiolaire
Fintry, Culcreuch Castle
Glendevan, Tormaukin
Kinclaven-by-Stanley, Ballathie House
Nairn, Clifton House
Newtonmore, Ard-na-Coille
Peat Inn, Peat Inn
Pitlochry, Killiecrankie
Scone, Murrayshall House
Whitebridge, Knockie Lodge

North

Achiltibuie, Summer Isles
Arisaig, Arisaig House
Culnaknock, Glenview
Drumnadrochit, Polmaily House
Garve, Inchbae Lodge
Glenelg, Glenelg
Harlosh, Harlosh House
Isle Ornsay, Kinloch Lodge
Kilchoan, Meall Mo Chridhe
Mey, Castle Arms
Skeabost, Skeabost House
Sleat, Ord House
Thurso, Pentland Hotel
Ullapool, Altnaharrie

WALES

North

Abersoch, Porth Tocyn
Betws-y-Coed, Royal Oak
Capel Garmon, Tan-y-Foel Country House
Capel Garmon, White Horse
Conwy, Old Rectory
Hanmer, Buck Farm
Llanarmon D C, Hand
Llandrillo, Tuddyn Llan
Llandudno, Bodysgallen Hall
Llanerchymedd, Llwydiarth Fawr Farm
Llanrwst, Cae'r Berllan
Llansantffraid Glan Conwy, Old Rectory
Llanwddyn, Lake Vyrnwy
Talsarneau, Maes-y-Neuadd

South

Govilon, Llanwenarth House
Oxwich Bay, Oxwich Bay
Tintern Parva, Parva Farmhouse
Whitebrook, Crown at Whitebrook

Mid

Crickhowell, Bear
Cwmystwyth, Hafod Lodge
Eglwysfach, Ynyshir Hall
Llyswen, Griffin
Llyswen, Llangoed Hall

Newtown, Lower Gwestydd
Penmaenpool, George III
West
Broad Haven, Druidstone
Pontfaen, Tregynon Country Farmhouse
Rhydlewis, Broniwan

Hotels in secluded places

These hotels, inns and other places to stay are either secluded in their own grounds or in a very quiet spot, with attractive surroundings.

BUCKINGHAMSHIRE
Taplow, Cliveden

CAMBRIDGESHIRE
Needingworth, Pike & Eel

CHESHIRE
Higher Burwardsley, Pheasant

CORNWALL
Botallack, Manor Farm
Buryas Bridge, Rose Farm
Carne Beach, Nare
Constantine Bay, Treglos
Gerrans Bay, Pendower Beach House
Looe, Talland Bay
Mawnan Smith, Meudon
Mawnan Smith, Nansidwell Country House
Mullion, Polurrian
Port Isaac, Port Gaverne
Isles of Scilly
Tresco, Island

CUMBRIA
Alston, Lovelady Shield
Alston, Middle Bayles Farm
Brackenthwaite, Pickett Howe
Brandlingill, Low Hall
Cockermouth, High Stanger Farm
Dockray, Royal Ullswater
Garrigill, George & Dragon
Grasmere, Michael's Nook
Grasmere, White Moss House
Grizedale, Grizedale Lodge
Hawkshead, Highfield House
Ireby, Overwater Hall
Langdale, Old Dungeon Ghyll
Mungrisdale, Mill Inn
Pooley Bridge, Sharrow Bay
Seatoller, Seatoller House
Spark Bridge, Bridgefield House
Talkin, Hullerbank
Torver, Old Rectory
Wasdale Head, Wasdale Head
Windermere, Miller Howe
Witherslack, Old Vicarage

DERBYSHIRE AND STAFFORDSHIRE
Ashbourne, Callow Hall
Bakewell, Hassop Hall
Monsal Head, Monsal Head Hotel
Rosland, Holly Cottage
Rowland, Holly Cottage
Shottle, Dannah Farm
Staffs
Greendale, Old Furnace Farm

DEVON
Aveton Gifford, Court Barton Farmhouse
Bossington, Orchard Guest House
Branscombe, Look Out
Burgh Island, Burgh Island
Chagford, Gidleigh Park
Chagford, Mill End
Chittlehamholt, Highbullen
Dulverton, Ashwick Country House
Dulverton, Tarr Steps
East Portlemouth, Gara Rock
Gittisham, Combe House
Lewdown, Lewtrenchard Manor
Lynton, Hewitt's
Malborough, Soar Mill Cove
Morchard Bishop, Wigham
Moretonhampstead, Great Sloncombe Farm
Oakford, Newhouse Farm
Salcombe, Tides Reach
Sidmouth, Higher Weston Farm
Topsham Bridge, Yeo Farm
West Buckland, Huxtable Farm

DORSET
Chedington, Chedington Court
Evershot, Summer Lodge
Halstock, Halstock Mill

GLOUCESTERSHIRE
Buckland, Buckland Manor

HEREFORD AND WORCESTER
Chaddesley Corbett, Brockencote Hall
Frith Common, Hunt House Farm
Ledbury, Hope End Country House
Leysters, Hills Farm
Malvern Wells, Cottage in the Wood
Ruckhall Common, Ancient Camp

LANCASHIRE
Chipping, Carr Side Farm
Slaidburn, Parrock Head Farm
Whitewell, Inn at Whitewell

LEICESTERSHIRE
Oakham, Hambleton Hall
Stapleford, Stapleford Park

NORTHUMBRIA
Allendale, Bishopsfield Country House
Cornhill-on-Tweed, Tillmouth Park
Easington, Grinkle Park
Edlingham, Lumbylaw Farm
High Force, High Force Hotel
Longframlington, Embleton Hall
Tarset, Earls Lodge
Tow Law, Greenwell Farm

SHROPSHIRE
Clun, New House Farm
Gretton, Court Farm
Hampton Loade, Old Forge House
Hopesay, Old Rectory
Strefford, Strefford Hall Farm

SOMERSET
Dulverton, Tarr Steps
Emborough, Redhill Farm
Hunstrete, Hunstrete House
Lower Vellow, Curdon Mill
Middlecombe, Periton Park
Roadwater, Wood Advent Farm

SURREY
Bagshot, Pennyhill Park
Haslemere, Lythe Hill

SUSSEX
Battle, Netherfield Place
East Grinstead, Gravetye Manor
Poynings, Manor Farm
Rusper, Ghyll Manor
Rusper, Rusper House
Shipley, Goffsland Farm
Telham, Little Hemingfold Farmhouse
Turners Hill, Alexander House

WILTSHIRE
Castle Combe, Manor House
Rowde, Lower Foxhangers Farm
Stourton, Spread Eagle

YORKSHIRE
Ampleforth, Carr House Farm
Arncliffe, Falcon
Bolton Abbey, Devonshire Arms
Country House
Chop Gate, Hill End Farm
Cloughton, Hayburn Wyke
Feizor, Scar Close Farm
Hackness, Hackness Grange
Lastingham, Lastingham Grange
Markington, Hob Green
Middlesmoor, Crown
Otley, Chevin Lodge
Richmond, Howe Villa
Richmond, Whashton Springs Farm
Rosedale Abbey, White Horse
Sedbusk, Stone House
Wath-in-Nidderdale, Sportsmans Arms

SCOTLAND
South
Annanwater, Corehead Farm
Auchencairn, Balcary Bay
Auchencairn, Collin House
Beattock, Auchen Castle
Gatehouse-of-Fleet, Cally Palace
Kelso, Sunlaws House
Peebles, Cringletie House
Portpatrick, Knockinaam Lodge
Quothquan, Shieldhill
Rockcliffe, Barons Craig
West
Arduaine, Loch Melfort
Duror, Stewart
Eriska, Isle of Eriska Hotel
Kilchrenan, Ardanaiseig
Kilchrenan, Taychreggan
Kilmore, Glenfeochan House
Onich, Allt-Nan-Ros
Port Appin, The Airds
Strachur, Creggans

Tarbert, Stonefield Castle
Tiroran, Tiroran House

North of the Forth

Aberfeldy, Farleyer House
Advie, Tulchan Lodge
Ardeonaig, Ardeonaig
Auchterarder, Gleneagles
Ballater, Craigendarroch Hotel
Balquhidder, Monachyle Mhor
Banchory, Invery House
Blairgowrie, Kinloch House
Callander, Roman Camp
Carronbridge, Lochend Farm
Cleish, Nivingston House
Dalcross, Easter Dalziel Farm
Dulnain Bridge, Muckrach Lodge
Dunblane, Cromlix House
Dunkeld, Kinnaird House
Fintry, Culcreuch Castle
Inverness, Bunchrew House
Kinclaven by Stanely, Ballathie House
Kirkton of Glenisla, Glenisla
Pitlochry, Killiecrankie
Scone, Murrayshall House
Spean Bridge, Letterfinlay Lodge
Whitebridge, Knockie Lodge

North

Achiltibuie, Summer Isles
Arisaig, Arisaig House
Dornie Loch, Duich
Drumnadrochit, Borlum Farmhouse
Garve, Inchbae Lodge
Glen Shiel, Cluanie
Glenborrodale, Glenborrodale Castle
Glenelg, Glenelg
Kilchoan, Meall Mo Chridhe
Kylesku, Kylesku
Lochinver, Inver Lodge
Melvich, Melvich Hotel
Scarista, Scarista House
Scourie, Eddrachilles
Shieldaig, Tigh an Eilean
Strontian, Loch Sunart Hotel
Ullapool, Altnaharrie

Skye

Culnaknock, Glenview
Harlosh, Harlosh House
Isle Ornsay, Kinloch Lodge
Isle Ornsay, Tigh Osda Eilean Iarmain
Raasay, Isle of Raasay
Skeabost, Skeabost House
Sleat, Ord House

WALES

North

Beddgelert, Sygun Fawr Country House
Capel Garmon, Tan-y-Foel Country House
Conwy, Old Rectory
Gellilydan, Tyddyn Du
Hanmer, Buck Farm
Llanarmon D C, Hand
Llanarmon D C, West Arms
Llandrillo, Tyddyn Llan
Llanerchymedd, Llwydiarth Fawr Farm
Llanwddyn, Lake Vyrnwy
Maentwrog, Plas Tan y Bwlch
Portmeirion, Portmeirion
Pwllheli, Yoke House Farm
Tremeirchion, Bach-y-Graig

Mid

Crickhowell, Gliffaes Country House
Cwmystwyth, Hafod Lodge
Eglwysfach, Ynyshir Hall
Llangurig, Glansevern Arms
Llanwrtyd Wells, Cwmirfon Lodge
Llyswen, Llangoed Hall
Newtown, Lower Gwestydd
Old Radnor, Harp
Pennal, Gogarth Hall Farm
Rhayader, Beili Neuadd
Church Stoke, Drewin Farm

West

Broad Haven, Druidstone
Crugybar, Glanrannell Park
Pen-y-Cwm, Lochmeyler Farm
Pontfaen, Tregynon Country Farmhouse
Rhydlewis, Broniwan

South

Govilon, Llanwenarth House
Little Mill, Pentwyn Farm
Llanthony, Half Moon
Tintern Parva, Parva Farmhouse

Report forms

Please report to us: you can use the card in the middle of the book, the forms on the following pages, or just plain paper – whichever's easiest for you. We need to know what you think of the places mentioned in this edition – especially if you think we should add to or change our descriptions of them. We also need to know about other places worthy of inclusion and about ones that should be omitted.

If you are recommending a new entry, the more detail you can put into your description, the better. This will help not only us but also your fellow-readers gauge its appeal. A description of a place's character and even its furnishings is a tremendous boon. Imagine you're writing about it for the *Guide* itself, and put in the sorts of things you'd want to know yourself before deciding whether to visit it.

The atmosphere and character of a holiday hotel or simpler place to stay, or of a restaurant, are very important to us – why it would, or would not, appeal to people who don't know it. And, of course, the quality and type of its food matter a lot, too, so please tell us about that as well. It's even more helpful if you can provide a full address and telephone number.

We'd also very much like you to let us know of places you've enjoyed visiting – anything from a little village to a stately home, from a shop selling unusual things to a factory visit, from an outstanding plant nursery to a hot-air balloon festival, from a hidden-away country church to a cathedral, from a peaceful wood or a nature reserve or a stretch of unspoilt coastal cliff to a theme park or a zoo or a pleasure beach. We're also particularly interested in hearing about walks and drives you've discovered. Whatever it is, if you've enjoyed it, please tell us about it.

When you go to a hotel, restaurant, or anywhere else, don't tell them you're a reporter for the *The Good Weekend Guide*; we do make clear that all inspections are anonymous, and if you declare yourself as a reporter you risk getting special treatment – for better or for worse!

When you write to *The Good Weekend Guide*, FREEPOST TN1569, WADHURST, E Sussex TN5 7BR, you don't need a stamp in the UK and we'll gladly send you more forms (free) if you wish. The information you send us will be stored in our computer files.

Though we try to answer letters, we do have other work to do, besides producing this *Guide*. So please understand if there's a delay. And from June till at least the end of summer, when we are fully extended getting the next edition to the printers, we put all letters and reports aside, not answering them until the rush is over. The end of May is pretty much the cut-off date for reasoned consideration of reports for the next edition - and the earlier the better, if they're suggestions for new entries.

We'll assume we can print your name or initials as a recommender unless you tell us otherwise.

I have been to the following hotels/restaurants/attractions/places in *The 1994 Good Weekend Guide* in the last few months, found them as described, and confirm that they deserve continued inclusion:

PLEASE GIVE YOUR NAME AND ADDRESS ON THE BACK OF THIS FORM

Your own name and address (BLOCK CAPITALS PLEASE)

Please return to:
The Good Weekend Guide, FREEPOST TN1569, WADHURST, E Sussex TN5 7BR

The Good Weekend Guide: Your Top Nominations

Please list for us your personal choices as special recommendations, in each or any of the following categories. In each category you can give UP TO THREE CHOICES, in order – starting with your first choice.

BEST AREA ALL ROUND, FOR A WEEKEND OR SHORT BREAK

BEST TOWN OR CITY, FOR A SHORT BREAK

AREA WITH MOST FRIENDLY PEOPLE

NICEST PLACE TO STAY (hotel, inn, B&B, farmhouse, etc)

BEST MEAL OUT

ATTRACTION OR PLACE YOU'VE MOST ENJOYED VISITING

EVENT / FESTIVAL YOU'VE MOST ENJOYED

PRETTIEST VILLAGE YOU'VE SEEN

Your own name and address (BLOCK CAPITALS PLEASE)

Please return to:
The Good Weekend Guide, FREEPOST TN1569, WADHURST, E Sussex TN5 7BR

Place to visit / Event

Its name:

Address:

Postcode: Telephone:

Description/why it appeals

Special tips

PLEASE GIVE YOUR NAME AND ADDRESS ON THE BACK OF THIS FORM

Your own name and address (BLOCK CAPITALS PLEASE)

Please tick this box if you would like more forms ☐

Please return to:
The Good Weekend Guide, FREEPOST TN1569, WADHURST, E Sussex TN5 7BR

Place to eat at or stay in

Its name:

Address:

Postcode: Telephone:

What is this? (eg hotel, restaurant, B&B, inn, farmhouse)

Description/why it appeals *NB please describe character, food, service, and if relevant mention views, surroundings, walks direct from establishment, nearby attractions etc*

PLEASE GIVE YOUR NAME AND ADDRESS ON THE BACK OF THIS FORM

Your own name and address (BLOCK CAPITALS PLEASE)

Please tick this box if you would like more forms ☐

Please return to:
The Good Weekend Guide, FREEPOST TN1569, WADHURST, E Sussex TN5 7BR

Place to visit / Event

Its name:

Address:

Postcode: Telephone:

Description/why it appeals

Special tips

PLEASE GIVE YOUR NAME AND ADDRESS ON THE BACK OF THIS FORM

Your own name and address (BLOCK CAPITALS PLEASE)

Please tick this box if you would like more forms ☐

Please return to:
The Good Weekend Guide, FREEPOST TN1569, WADHURST, E Sussex TN5 7BR